USA

FODOR'S TRAVEL GUIDES

are compiled, researched and edited by an international team of travel writers, field correspondents, and editors. The series, which now almost covers the globe, was founded by Eugene Fodor in 1936.

OFFICES
New York & London

FODOR'S USA:

Area Editors: Stephen Allen, Jeanie Blake, Victor Block, Curtis W. Casewit, Toni Chapman, Edgar Cheatham, Patricia Cheatham, Joyce Eisenberg, Alma Eshenfelder, Patsy Fretwell, Ralph Friedman, Harry E. Fuller, Jr., Johanna Guzik, Phil Halpern, Shirley Rose Higgins, Tony Hillerman, Iris Sanderson Jones, Robert Karolevitz, Bern Keating, Candace L. Kumerfield, Carolyn R. Langdon, Jane E. Lasky, Fred LeBrun, Karen Lingo, Bette McNear, John Maxymuk, Ira Mayer, Lyle Nelson, Monique Panaggio, John D. Phillips, Paul Robbins, Archie Satterfield, William G. Scheller, William Schemmel, Norma Spring, Richard G. Stahl, Barc Wade, Katharine D. Walker, Ed Wojtas, Jane Zarem, Pat Zimmerman

Drawings: Sandra Lang

Maps: Pictograph

FODOR'S
USA

The material in this guide is based on
the 1986 edition of *Fodor's USA* and
may not be up-to-date.

FODOR'S TRAVEL GUIDES
New York

MANUFACTURED IN THE UNITED STATES OF AMERICA
20 19 18 17 16 15 14 13 12

CONTENTS

THE SOUTH

THE MIDWEST

CONTENTS

THE SOUTHWEST

THE ROCKIES AND THE PLAINS

THE FAR WEST

CONTENTS

FOREWORD

Fifty-four years is a long time for a love affair, but that is how long I have been an ardent suitor of the United States. Now, at the beginning of this country's third century, it gives me enormous pleasure to present to travelers what was but a gleam in my eye in 1930, this guide to the U.S.A.

When I first visited here, America still was the pot of gold at the end of the rainbow—so big, so far away, so desirable, so worth pursuing. And so expensive. Only the very rich could contemplate a trip to the United States, so I counted myself lucky beyond my dreams when I was able to set foot on the shores of New York harbor nearly half a century ago.

What a unique opportunity had been presented to a young man, European-born and bred, just out of college and serving as an interpreter aboard the old *SS France*. (At a later time my ship put in at the most exotic ports of the world, and the articles I sent back to a French newspaper syndicate launched my career as a travel writer and editor.) Back in 1930 America was my first major port of call.

You can imagine my excitement. I was eager to see as much as I could, to devour all the sights and sounds and smells of the New World. I took a three-month leave of absence and set out on a tour of adventure and exploration that took me all across this great land.

By bus and train I went to the shores of the Great Lakes, crossed the Great Plains, saw my first real cowboys and Indians in Wyoming, marveled at the Rockies in Colorado, the canyons of Utah, and enjoyed the agreeable lifestyle of San Francisco. The cascade of overflowing impressions was more than just an eye-opener, it was truly hypnotic.

I now live in a pre-Revolutionary saltbox in a lovely New England village, a tiny corner of America, but in my mind's eye I still recall my astonishment at the immense size of the United States on that first trip.

The sweeping variety of scenery, the awesome timelessness of the wilderness area, the futuristic shape and rhythm of the cities, and, above all, the simple and direct warmth of the people made an indelible impact on me.

Like everyone else in the world, I had my conceptions of America, but no amount of reading or movies or stories told by returning travelers could have prepared me for so much that was unexpected.

Somehow the idea germinated then, barely on the threshold of what was to become a lifetime career, that I wanted to produce a book on the United States. It has been an elusive dream, sometimes just a will-o'-the-wisp, and I often despaired that it would ever come to fruition. Interruptions were legion: other places, other books, World Was II, financial problems. . . .

No matter where I traveled, however, I always managed to carry with me this love that was proving to be so elusive.

My series of articles for the French new syndicate in 1930 showed what a monumental task it would be to condense the torrent of information, impressions, and emotions I had about America. These impressions continued to pile up between the years of 1934 and 1942, when I became an American citizen. While in the Army, I made a number of other cross-country trips along with many regional excursions. I lived on the east coast and in California, Missouri and Pennsylvania.

"Organizing" the United States

Now, some explanations are in order concerning the manner in which this book was constructed.

Obviously, within the covers of one manageable guide on so vast a subject, it was impossible to cover the country in painstaking detail from A to Z. There had to be a process of selection.

We have therefore striven to include only those places that have the widest possible touristic appeal nationally and internationally. Given the time and the interest, the traveler around the United States can easily check out other places and events of lesser interest, with the willing help of official state and city tourist bureaus. And, quite often, the people you meet will be eager to show you their very special places.

Naturally, we do not claim to be infallible, and it is possible that we are guilty of some important omissions. We depend on you, our readers, to notify us so we can make additions in subsequent revisions. Send your letters to the editors at **Fodor's Travel Guides, 2 Park Avenue, New York, N.Y., 10016.** Continental or British Commonwealth readers may prefer to write to **Fodor's Travel Guides, 9–10 Market Place, London W1N 7AG, England.**

Geographical and practical information for the country has been divided into 50 states and the District of Columbia, organized in nine regional sections.

We remind those of our readers who are interested in regional, local and special interest information in even greater depth that we have a number of other U.S. guidebooks in print. They are listed on the copyright page.

In this tenth year of our third century as a nation, and my Fiftieth as a travel editor, I join my fellow Americans throughout this extraordinary land in extending a hand of welcome to people everywhere, from one region or state to another, from one continent or nation to another.

Eugene Fodor

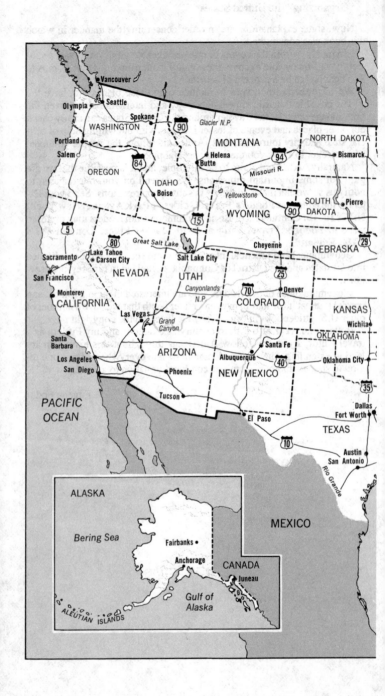

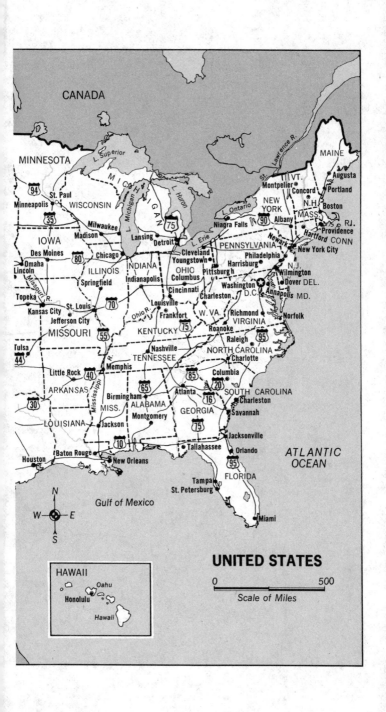

CANADA

MINNESOTA

MAINE

L. Superior

St. Lawrence R.

Montpelier VT. Augusta
St. Paul Concord Portland
Minneapolis Albany N.H. Boston
WISCONSIN L. Ontario NEW MASS. R.I.
Milwaukee YORK Providence
Madison Niagra Falls 90 Hartford CONN
IOWA Lansing Detroit L. Erie Newark New York City
Des Moines Chicago Cleveland PENNSYLVANIA Philadelphia
Omaha Youngstown N.J. Wilmington
Lincoln ILLINOIS INDIANA OHIO Pittsburgh Harrisburg Dover DEL.
Springfield Indianapolis Columbus Washington Annapolis MD.
Topeka Cincinnati Charleston D.C.
Kansas City St. Louis Louisville W. VA. Richmond Norfolk
Jefferson City Frankfort VIRGINIA
MISSOURI KENTUCKY Roanoke Raleigh
Tulsa Nashville NORTH CAROLINA
Little Rock Memphis TENNESSEE Charlotte
ARKANSAS Columbia
Birmingham Atlanta SOUTH CAROLINA
MISS. ALABAMA Charleston
LOUISIANA GEORGIA Savannah
Jackson Montgomery
Jacksonville
Houston Baton Rouge Tallahassee Orlando
New Orleans ATLANTIC OCEAN
Tampa FLORIDA
Gulf of Mexico St. Petersburg
Miami

MINNESOTA 94 35
MICHIGAN 75
80 70 55 75 95
44 40 65 85 20 16 75
30 10 95

N
W E
S

HAWAII
Oahu
Honolulu
Hawaii

UNITED STATES

0   500

Scale of Miles

FACTS AT YOUR FINGERTIPS

13.06
5.34
2400
$2.30

WHAT WILL IT COST? The United States is not one of the world's cheaper countries for tourists, and many kinds of inexpensive accommodation that are helpful in other countries (such as pensions, Youth Hostels, and government-run inns) either do not exist or are underdeveloped here. Costs will vary somewhat by region (New York City is more expensive than rural Maine, for example), but the rise of nation-wide, standardized hotel, motel and restaurant chains with their standardized facilities and prices has been a mixed blessing. Obviously, it is convenient to be able to reserve a room anywhere in the country, to have it ready even if you arrive late, and to know exactly what you may expect when you enter it. On the other hand, you may have removed yourself from a range of cheaper, local accommodations which may offer more personal service and regional atmosphere.

There has been a growing spread of budget motel chains which make a special effort to cut frills and prices both. There are now a number of these, and they are discussed in detail below in the section on *Hotels and Motels.*

A result of this spread is that the downtown areas of most cities now have older hotels, formerly elegant, that have had to lower their prices to meet the competition of the newer places on the outskirts. Most guidebooks do not list these older and cheaper hotels (although we have tried to indicate some of them in this one), and you may have to spend a little more time hunting them out and checking their conditions. Often, however, they will prove quite adequate and may compare favorably with European, if not American, standards.

Two people can travel in the United States on a basic budget of about $125 a day (not counting gasoline or other transportation costs), as shown in the table below. This is an average; New York is the most expensive area, at about $160 a day; while in the Plains, Rockies, and Southwest, expenses can be kept closer to about $100 a day.

You can often cut expenses by traveling off-season when hotel rates may be lower; and in dealing out-of-season with smaller, locally-owned motels you may be able to arrange reduced prices that the fixed policies of chain and franchise places do not permit. On the New England coast, for example, off-season prices are generally in effect from mid-October to mid-May, with peak season July 4 to Labor Day and the times in between as transitional. (However, many of the resort hotels in this area close completely during the off season, so your choice will be more limited.) New England is also a region where, traditionally, rooms are available in many fine old private houses, some of them offering meals and run as inns, others providing breakfast only and usually called Guest Houses or Bed and Breakfast. In other parts of the country the term "Tourist Home" is often used. These places can be appreciably less expensive than the more modern and lavishly equipped motels. Larger towns and cities may have YMCA's and YWCA's with family accommodations, and there are government-supervised hotels, usually run by concessionaires, in some state and federal parks.

Another possibility, still not too well known, is college campuses. About 180 colleges and universities in the United States and Canada open their dormitories, cafeterias, and cultural and recreational facilities to vacationers outside of term time. Although requirements vary, usually reservations are required, pets are not allowed, eligibility is: "students, alumni, adults, families and prospective matriculants," baths are shared, prices per person per day are in the $5 to $15 range, weekly rates are available, and cafeteria meals are from $1–$5. A directory of these opportunities is *Mort's Guide to Low-Cost Vacations and Lodgings on College Campuses,* US & Canada edition, available from Mort Barish Associates Inc., Research Park, 218 Wall St., Princeton, N.J. 08540.

Youth Hostels here are much less developed than in Europe or Japan. There are some 200 hostels in the U.S., most of them in the compact areas that are New England and the Mid-Atlantic area, few in cities. Of equal interest with their possibilities as inexpensive lodgings are the conducted group hiking and bicycle tours that the American Youth Hostel Association offers. These vary

3

from year to year, of course. See below under "Roughing It" for further details; and for complete up-to-date information write to: *American Youth Hostels,* Inc., 1332 I St., N.W., 8th Floor, Wash., D.C. 20005; or, 132 Spring Street, New York, New York 10012. The Association's Directory is now sold in regular bookshops, too.

YMCA's and YWCA's vary considerably from one city to another in age, equipment, lodgings, prices and policies. For complete listings write to: *YMCA of the U.S.A.,* 101 N. Wacker Dr., Chicago, Illinois 60606.

Another point to bear in mind is that the Interstate Highway System and the various State thruways are designed to speed you from city to city, not necessarily to show you a region's best scenery or local color and certainly not to take you to out-of-the-way resorts and quiet small towns where you may often find facilities that are older—but more typical of the area—clean and attractive, run by local people, and definitely less expensive than more crowded places. When you look at your road map, ask yourself where people went before the Interstates were built. Route 1 up the coast of Maine is a good example, or the Boston Post Road through southern New England.

In planning your budget don't forget to allow a realistic amount for recreation and entertainment expenses such as sports equipment rental (boats, canoes, skis and boots, golf clubs, etc.); entrance fees to amusement parks, museums, galleries and historical sites; and tickets to movies, concerts, plays and exhibitions. You'll also need to include tolls for bridges and highways (this can add up to more than you think), souvenirs, extra camera film and perhaps some developing, and incidental medical fees that might not be covered by your insurance. Tipping will be another big extra; see below for a special section on where, when, whom and how much, and remember that in some situations this can raise your costs by up to 15–20%.

Typical Daily Budget for Two People

Room at a moderate hotel or motel	$50.00
Light breakfast for two at coffee shop (incl. tip)	6.00
Lunch for two at an inexpensive restaurant (incl. tip)	12.00
Dinner for two at a moderate restaurant (incl. tip)	28.00
One sightseeing bus tour (two fares)	15.00
One evening cocktail for each of two persons (incl. tip)	6.00
Admission for two to one museum or historic site	6.00
	$123.00

These figures are a rough average for the entire country. Region by region, we suggest the following adjustments: *New England*—up 5%; *New York-New Jersey*—up 30%; *mid-Atlantic states*—down 5%; *South*—down 5%; *Midwest*—down 5%; *Rockies and Plains*—down 10%; *Southwest*—down 10%; *Far West*—no change. The figure for New York-New Jersey is skewed somewhat by including prices for its chief tourist area, New York City, and for several expensive resorts. Likewise, within a given region, conditions will vary somewhat. In the South, for example, Miami Beach between South Beach and Bal Harbor has a wide range of prices both in and out of season; and small towns on the Gulf Coast of North Florida's panhandle may be notably cheaper than the gaudier Atlantic Coast resorts. Generally, both hotels and motels are cheaper in the South and the West than in the rest of the country.

After lodging, your biggest expense will be food. To trim expenses, you might try picnicking. This will save you time and money, and it will help you to enjoy the scenery more as you travel toward your next destination. Most scenic highways and thruways now have well-maintained state picnic and rest areas equipped with tables, benches and trash cans, and often fireplaces, running water, and toilets.

Before you leave home put together a picnic kit. Sturdy plastic plates and cups will be cheaper in the long run than throw-away paper ones; and the same goes for metal flatware rather than the throw-away plastic kind. Pack a small electric pot and two thermoses, one for water and one for beverages—or, one hot and one cold. If you go by car take along a small cooler. Bread, milk, cold cereal, jam, tea or instant coffee, bouillon cubes and instant soup packets, fruit, fresh vegetables that need no cooking, cold cuts, cheese, nuts, raisins, eggs (hard boil them in the electric pot in your room the night before)—with only things like this you can eat conveniently, cheaply, and well.

Even in restaurants there are ways to cut costs. 1) Always stop at the cash register and look over the menu *before* you sit down. 2) Order a complete dinner; à la carte *always* adds up to more, unless you see someone with an enormous Chef's Salad and figure that's all you need. 3) If there is a salad bar or any kind of smorgasbord arrangement, fill up there and save on desserts and extras. 4) Ask about smaller portions, at reduced prices, for children. Some places are providing them now. 5) Go to a Chinese restaurant and order *one less* main dish than the number of people in your group. You'll still come away pleasantly full. 6) Ask for the Day's Special, House Special, Chef's Special, or whatever it's called. Chances are that it will be better, and more abundant, than the other things on the menu. 7) Remember that in many restaurants lunch may be a better bargain than dinner. 8) Below, in the section on restaurants, we suggest some chains that offer good value for your money.

If you like a drink before dinner or bed, bring your own bottle. Most hotels and motels will supply ice free or for very little, but the markup on alcoholic beverages in restaurants, bars, lounges, and dining rooms is enormous, and in some states peculiar laws apply anyway.

Roadside diners often provide food that is cheap, unpretentious and solid, however look carefully before you leap in.

Camping, a mode of travel already very popular and highly developed in Europe, provides one of the cheapest and best ways of seeing some of the best parts of the entire country—its state and national parks. There are well over 4,000 campsites in America's National Parks, National Forests, and State Parks. Fees vary but are low; in the last several years advance reservations have become increasingly necessary for nearly all the parks, so write ahead as early as possible, and make your plans with alternative choices in mind. For fuller information, write to: *National Parks Service,* U.S. Department of the Interior, Washington, D.C. 20240; or *National Forest Service,* U.S. Department of Agriculture, P.O. Box 2417, Washington, D.C. 20013.

SPECIAL TRAVEL RATES. All transportation companies (motor, rail, plane) offer a variety of special rates, seasonal and year-round. For example: car rental companies have special rates for inexpensive, intermediate, and expensive cars, for daily hops, weekend jaunts, or extended trips. The major companies will let you rent a car in one city and drop it off in another for a modest service charge. Some also offer a 10% discount to holders of foreign passports. Car rental rates vary greatly. When comparing, take into account whether the fees are a flat rate or subject to a per-mile charge, and what will be the charge for insurance.

Buses are already the least expensive way to go; and here there are two possibilities. The first is that the country's two nationwide bus networks, Greyhound and Trailways, offer both sightseeing packages of their own and also various types of reduced fares. For example, there may be a 10% reduction on round-trip tickets. Special round-trip excursion fares are available between many cities if you agree to a pre-set time period. Children under 5 ride free; children 5–11 years old go for half fare. Special rates also available for friends and relatives, groups, and the handicapped (see below), for clergy and members of the Armed Forces. Hotel rooms may be available at special prices tied in with your bus ticket, too. *Greyhound's Ameripass* is available for 7 days, 15 days and 30 days at any time of the year, and will give you unlimited travel on any of its lines anywhere in the country. Rates, in 1985, were 7 days for $189, 15 days for $289, and 30 days for $349. Children under 5 go free, from 5 through 11 for half fare. There are no Senior Citizen discounts. In addition, Ameripass entitles you to other discounts—on car rentals, some hotel accommodations, special sightseeing excursions, and a number of museums, theme parks, and other "attractions."

Trailways' Eagle Pass gives unlimited mileage anywhere in the country; rates in 1985 were: 7 days for $189, 15 days for $249, and 30 days for $349. Each of these tickets may be extended for $10 a day up to a total of 30 extra days of travel. Children under 5 go free, from 5 through 11 for half fare. Either of these passes may be used on buses of the other line, on a space-available basis; and the basic fares quoted above are subject to surcharges as the price of fuel varies.

The second is that the sightseeing packages offered by the many regional motor tour companies using their own buses on special-interest itineraries are so numerous and so diverse that surely you can find one that will be a bargain, dollar for dollar, over what you might see or do on your own. New England—7 days; Washington and Colonial Virginia—5 days; the Smoky Mountains—8 days; the Black Hills—7 days; the Pacific Coast—11 days; these are only a few examples. Packages generally include: transportation, lodging, baggage handling, some meals, some sightseeing and excursions, guide-escort service, and range in length from 4 to 31 days.

Amtrak, the major American rail system, serves about 500 communities in 44 states, and offers connecting motor coach service and car-rental programs to many others. It also has special rates, seasonally for some areas of the country, and year-round for other areas, as well as family rates, group rates and a number of attractive package tours and excursions. Tickets may be bought not only at railway stations but also at downtown ticket offices in larger cities and from over 7,000 appointed travel agents throughout the country.

In many large cities and notable tourist areas such as Boston, Niagara, Washington, D.C., central Florida and others Amtrak offers combinations of lodging, meals, local sightseeing, side trips, shopping discounts, and car rental. For example, from Oakland and San Francisco, California, you can board a train for a Reno weekend, January through April. The all-inclusive rate covers round trip rail transportation, dance car and band, two nights first class accommodations, three breakfasts, one luncheon buffet, and a Reno hospitality coupon book.

Check with your travel agent for similar offerings in other parts of the country, such as autumn foliage trips and ski specials.

Amtrak's family plan ticket is good for unlimited rail travel on its routes. The ticket is for coach or first class trains where regular fare is $20.00 or more. The head of the family pays full fare, spouse and children from 12 through 21 go for half fare, children 2 through 11 go for ¼ fare, children under 2 go free. Family-plan travel may not be combined with other discounts, such as round-trip excursion fares. Amtrak gives a 25% reduction on ordinary round-trip fares of $40 or more to riders over 65. Proof of age must be shown.

Since 1978 the deregulation of *airline carriers* has produced a rash of competitive fare reductions with new ones coming out every month. There is no way to predict what will be current when you read this, except to say that the lower the fare the more limiting conditions there will be. Read the small print carefully. The main categories of special airline fare are the same as those for train and bus fares: unlimited mileage, family plan, tour package, and discounts for the elderly. In addition there are various "super-saver" schemes that change from airline to airline, from season to season, and between day and night fares. There are also "supplemental" airlines which fly between the two coasts for less than the usual fares. *Capitol International Airways, World Airways,* and *Trans International Airlines* are three of these.

 TIPPING. This can be one of the biggest problems confronting travelers anywhere. Customs vary from one country to another. Theoretically, tipping is supposed to be personal, your way of expressing your appreciation of someone who has taken pleasure and pride in giving you attentive, efficient and understanding personal service. By and large, however, tipping has become a largely impersonal formula, and frequently an automatic demand. Standards of personal service are highly uneven, so when you do in fact get genuinely good service feel secure in rewarding it, and when you feel that the service you receive is slovenly, indifferent or surly, don't hesitate to show this by the size of your tip. Remember that in many places the help are paid very little and depend on tips for the better part of their income. This is supposed to give them the incentive to serve you well.

Although you will want to suit your tipping to the service you do in fact receive, here are some guidelines to follow. When in doubt, remember that the minimum tip for any service is 25¢, that 25¢ is the usual tip for miscellaneous small services, and that larger tips are rounded off to the nearest 5¢. In restaurants in this country the tips are not usually included in the bill (as they are in France, for example) but are decided by the guest and left on the table separately. Recently, in major resorts, tipping has become standardized to the point where guests receive printed lists of "suggestions" on how much to give. The "suggestions" are rarely, if ever, too little. If you consider this impertinent, do not hesitate to say so.

Many service people who may be tipped in other countries are *not* tipped here. These include: government employees, mailmen, airline personnel, store clerks, receptionists, bus drivers, elevator operators, gas station attendants, hotel clerks and managers, theater and movie ushers (although ushers at sports events may expect tips), and sightseeing guides at historical and artistic sites.

Restaurants: Waiters expect 15%; if the service is exceptional, leave 20%. Tip on the amount *before* taxes. Good captain service merits a dollar or two. In higher-priced places, the beverage waiter gets 15% of his separate bill. Coat checkers expect 25¢ per item in addition to the fixed house charge. Restroom attendants get 25¢. Tipping the maitre d' to get you a good table in a crowded place is officially discouraged, but it does happen, of course. Tipping at counters is not a universal practice, however many people do leave 25¢ on anything up to one dollar and 10% on bills over that.

Hotels and motels: For one-night stays in most hotels and motels you leave nothing. But if you stay longer, at the end of your stay leave the maid $1.25 to $1.50 per day or $7 per person per week for double occupancy or more. If the place is American Plan (meals included), leave your waiter or waitress either 15% of the bill or $1.50 per guest per day. If there have been various extra attendants (one for relishes, one for rolls, etc.) add a few extra dollars and give them to the captain or maitre d' when you leave, asking him to allocate the money.

For the many other services that you may encounter in a big hotel or resort, figure roughly as follows: doorman—25¢ to $1 for taxi handling, 50¢ to $1 for help with baggage; bellhop—50¢ per bag (or $1 per person or couple), more if you load him down with extras; parking attendant—50¢ to $1; bartender— 15%; room service—10–15% of that bill; laundry or valet service—15%; pool attendant—50¢ per day; snackbar waiter at pool, beach or golf club—15% of the check; locker attendant—50¢ per person per day, or $2.50 per week; golf caddies $2 to 3 per bag, or 15% of the greens fee for an 18-hole course, or $3 on a free course; barbers—15%; shoeshine attendants—50¢ to $1; hairdressers —15%; manicurists—$1; masseurs and masseuses—20%.

Transportation: 15% is standard for taxi fares, plus something additional if extra bags or waiting time is involved, however, drivers in New York, Las Vegas and other major resort areas *expect* 20%. Limousine service—10%. Car rental agencies—nothing. Bus porters are tipped 50¢ per suitcase, drivers nothing. On charters and package tours, conductors and drivers usually get $5–$10 per day from the group as a whole (but be sure to ask whether this has already been figured into the package cost). On short local sightseeing runs, the driver-guide may get 25¢ per person, more if you think he has been especially helpful or personable. Airport bus drivers—nothing. Redcaps, 50¢ per suitcase. Tipping at curbside check-in is unofficial, but same as above. On the plane, no tipping.

Railroads suggest you leave 15% per meal for dining car waiters, but the steward who seats you is not tipped. Sleeping-car porters get about $1 per person per night. For a railway station baggage porter, 50¢ per bag or more depending on how heavy your luggage is.

CREDIT CARD TRAVEL. There are three main types of credit cards in this country. The general, or travel and entertainment cards are issued by: *American Express Card Division,* 770 Broadway, New York, N.Y. 10003; and *Carte Blanche,* 183 Inverness Dr. W., Englewood, Colorado 80112. For one of these you pay a flat rate, usually about $45 a year; and interest charges, which may run 21% a year, apply only to certain types of purchase such as airline tickets and escorted tours, if bills are not paid upon receipt. The principal bank cards are: *Visa* and *MasterCard;* these are issued through banks all over the country; inquire locally to see where they are available in your area. For these you pay a membership fee of about $15 to $20 in addition to which there may be a system of minimum monthly payments and of carrying charges or interest that again comes to 18–21% a year. They are affiliated with many foreign banks, whose customers can use, for example, *Barclaycard* or *Sumitomo* card here. These are properly *credit* cards whereas the first kind is rather a *charge* card, although some brands do offer bank credit possibilities. In addition, there are cards issued for more limited use, such as: *Macy's* and *National Car Rental.*

To get either type of credit card you will need to have a dependable job, a salary of at least $12,500 a year, and to furnish personal, family and financial information as well as personal references in order to establish your creditworthiness.

These cards have various advantages. Obviously they spare you the danger of carrying large amounts of cash, or even of Traveler's Checks, which can occasionally be awkward to cash without full identification. Cards can be used to draw extra funds in case of emergencies, or to take advantage of sales and special opportunities. For foreigners here, as for Americans abroad, charge cards can help to avoid losses due to unfavorable rates of exchange and commissions in hotels, restaurants and resorts. For people traveling on expense accounts, or seeking tax deductions for business and professional expenses, they provide the records needed. They can make it easier to return unwanted merchandise to stores because the store simply makes out a credit slip to your card's account.

Despite these conveniences, there are various special restrictions and charges that apply in particular cases and which can raise your actual, final cost. Before you apply for a credit or a charge card, it is wise to talk with someone you know who has used one extensively and to obtain fully detailed information and examples of what your actual costs will turn out to be in every situation you can foresee.

Another disadvantage is the losses you can incur if your credit card gets lost or stolen. Report this *immediately* to the company that issued it. *Credit Card Service Bureau* (Courthouse Sq., 510 King St. Alexandria, Va. 22314) offers insurance coverage to all cards registered by its members and will notify all appropriate credit card companies for you if you report your cards stolen or missing.

 WHEN TO GO. About 3,300 miles in length from Alaska to Texas and 2,900 in breadth from Maine to California, the United States covers over three and one-half million square miles and includes deserts, rivers, mountains, plains, forests, perpetual glaciers and tropical swamps, five inland seas and a great variety of climate, landscapes and resources. When you prefer to go will depend on what you like in the way of weather, sports, sightseeing, cultural events and local color. In this section we describe the advantages of the various seasons in each of the eight major regions. Be sure also to consult the sections on *Seasonal Events,* because America's pageants, fairs and festivals of every kind, from symphony and opera to corn-husking and pie-eating, should be an important part of your planning and enjoyment of this vast and varied country.

Every one of the 50 states maintains a tourist information agency that provides free leaflets, brochures, directories and maps to help you plan your vacation. Because the amount of material is so great you will get the most efficient service if you observe four simple rules in making your request. First, be as specific as possible about your interests, season, and area. Second, inquire well in advance, and allow about one month for processing and mailing (third class) your reply. Third, make your request on a simple, time-saving post card. Fourth, be sure to supply your return address.

Calendars of special events are usually published four times a year, by the seasons, so specify which one you want. Information on state-operated facilities such as parks and rest areas will usually be precise, objective, and reliable. Information on privately operated facilities such as hotels, motels, restaurants, camps, shops, theme parks, marinas, and "attractions" is usually promotional material put out by trade associations, and is of little help in judging quality.

If you call a toll-free 800 number, remember that outside of usual business hours you will probably get a general-information-type recorded announcement. Allow for differences in time zones, too, when calling.

New England

New England attracts visitors all year round, with both downhill and cross-country skiing the lure in winter; a plethora of internationally acclaimed music, theater, and dance festivals in summer; spectacularly colorful fall foliage and a concurrent hunting season; and springs that are perfect for exploring the Appalachian Trail or other hiking and climbing paths. In recent years, the country-side of New England has come to be dotted with lovely, European-style country inns—some decorated with genuine European and American antiques and featuring *haute cuisine,* and others that are closer to what the English refer to as bed-and-breakfasts. The latter, generally called "guest houses," can usually be counted on for simple, clean accommodations even at the last minute on holiday weekends; the popularity of inns during high season (regardless of the time of year), however, makes advance reservations for weekends mandatory. The official summer season runs from July 4 to Labor Day when the coastal areas from Mystic, Connecticut, to Newport, Rhode Island, to Kennebunkport, Maine, are favorites for sunbathers, swimmers, sailers, fishers, and the like, while inlanders take part in the numerous cultural festivals that are to be found. Summer courses in the region's many excellent colleges and universities have also become a popular way to combine vacation, education, and local color with cutting expenses. For further information, write:

Connecticut: *Connecticut Department of Economic Development, Travel Director,* 210 Washington Street, Hartford, Conn. 06106. 800–243–1685.

Maine: *Maine Publicity Bureau,* 97 Winthrop St., Hallowell, Me. 04347. (207) 289–2423.

Massachusetts: *Massachusetts Department of Commerce and Development,* (Division of Tourism), 100 Cambridge St., Boston, Mass. 02202. (617) 727–3201.

New Hampshire: *NH Office of Vacation Travel,* Box 856, State House Annex, Concord, N.H. 03301. (603) 271–2343.

Rhode Island: *Rhode Island Department of Economic Development,* 7 Jackson Walkway, Providence, R.I. 02903. (401) 277–2601.

Vermont: *Vermont Travel Division,* 134 State St., Montpelier, Vt. 05602. (802) 828–3236.

New York—New Jersey

The unbelievably rich cultural life of New York City is probably unequaled anywhere else in the world, no matter the season. If time allows, though, you will want to keep in mind that the state of New York also has much to offer, and that while the Long Island beaches—from the Hamptons to Coney Island—represent a getaway on hot, muggy summer days, other alternatives include resort areas such as Lake George (popular in winter for skiing, as well) and Saratoga Springs. The latter remains popular among horse-racing enthusiasts but has increasingly drawn attention and crowds for its summer season of New York Philharmonic, City Ballet, and popular music concert series. Still other possibilities for peaceful retreat throughout the year are the Lake Placid–Saranac Lake part of the Adirondacks (scene of a recent winter Olympics), the Catskill mountain region in the central part of the state, and the Woodstock/New Paltz area (inhabited largely by artists, musicians, and writers) about 100 miles north of the city. Of course its natives insist that even the most humid of summer days on Manhattan Island are tolerable when visiting Central or Riverside Parks! Popular for hiking are New Jersey's Ramapo Hills and for gambling, Atlantic City, New Jersey, also lays claim to pleasant south shore beaches. For detailed information write to:

New Jersey: *New Jersey Division of Travel & Tourism,* CN 826, Trenton, N.J. 08625. (609) 292–2470.

New York: *New York Division of Tourism,* 1 Commerce Plaza, Albany, N.Y. 12245. 800–342–3810, or (212) 225–5697

New York City only: *New York City Convention and Visitors Bureau,* 2 Columbus Circle, New York, N.Y. 10019. (212) 397–8222.

The Mid-Atlantic States

In this region temperatures range from just below freezing, in the deep of winter, to the upper 80's in mid-summer. Humidity may be high in the river valleys and in the low-lying areas along the coast; Washington, the capital, is notorious for combining the disadvantages of both. Spring is spectacular in the mid-Atlantic region, with millions of blossoms bursting forth everywhere. Washington, in April, is as famous for its cherry trees as Tokyo or Kyoto. Azaleas, dogwood, camellias and apple blossoms follow each other through April and May. Summer can be enjoyable if you do as the local people do and slow down. It is in this region that you will first notice a very different pace to life from what you found in the North. The South really begins in Virginia, and you will begin to sense its different rhythm and flavor from Washington onward. Virginia has some good beaches and the scenic drives along the crests of the Appalachian mountains in the western part of the state are magnificent. In early spring and late fall county fairs attract visitors. Tourists and locals alike take advantage of the Farmers' Markets in Lancaster and Lebanon, Pennsylvania year round. The Christmas festivities in colonial Williamsburg, Va., and Bethlehem, Pa. are outstanding. There are winter sports in the Alleghenies and their foothills; and the region's colorful tobacco auctions go on year round everywhere, especially in Virginia. For more precise information write to:

Delaware: *Delaware State Travel Service,* 99 Kings Highway, Box 1401, Dover, Del. 19903. (302) 736–4254.

Maryland: *Maryland Office of Tourist Development,* 45 Calvert St., Annapolis, Md. 21401. (301) 269–2686; (800) 331–1750 for brochures only.

Pennsylvania: *Pennsylvania Bureau of Travel Development,* Pennsylvania Department of Commerce, 416 Forum Building, Harrisburg, Penn. 17120. 800–233–7366.

Virginia: *Virginia State Travel Service,* 202 N. 9th St., Suite 500, Richmond, Va. 23219. (804) 786–4484

District of Columbia: *Washington Area Convention and Visitors Association,* Suite 250, 1575 I St. NW, Washington, D.C. 20005. (202) 789–7000

West Virginia: *West Virginia Travel Development Division,* 1900 Washington St. Bldg. 6, Room 564, State Capitol, Charleston, W. Va. 25305

The South

Winter temperatures here average in the low 40's inland and in the 60's along the coast. Summer temperatures, modified by mountains in some places, by sea breezes in others, range from the high 70's to the mid 80's, with occasional low 90's; but because of the tempering effect of the Atlantic and Gulf breezes and the prevalence of air conditioning, summer is becoming increasingly popular with tourists who formerly thought of the South only as a winter resort. This is especially true of Florida. The inland heart of the region is the hills and mountains of the southern Appalachians; and in addition to their lakes and rivers, seven Southern states share a total of over 10,000 miles of salt water coastline, much of it in fine sandy beaches. The climate makes for lush, brilliant vegetation: Spanish moss, magnolia, roses, dogwood, iris, camellias, azalea, poinciana, poinsettia, orange blossoms and orchids in Florida, peach blossoms in Georgia. Fairs and festivals, art shows, parades and fiestas are mostly January to May and mid-September through October. For further information write to:

Alabama: *Alabama Bureau of Publicity and Information,* 532 South Perry St., Montgomery, Ala. 36104. 800–252–2262

Arkansas: Arkansas Department of Parks and Tourism, 1 Capitol Mall, Little Rock, Ark. 72201. 800–643–8383

Florida: *Florida Division of Tourism,* 107 W. Gaines St., Room 410, Collins Bldg., Tallahassee, Fla. 32301. 904–488–8185

Georgia: *Georgia Tourist Division,* Georgia Bureau of Industry and Trade, Box 1776, Atlanta, Ga. 30301. (404) 656–3590.

Kentucky: *Kentucky Department of Tourism,* Capital Tower Plaza, 22nd floor, Frankfort, Ky. 40601. (502) 564–4930.

Louisiana: *Louisiana Office of Tourism, Inquiry Department,* Box 94291, Baton Rouge, La. 70804–9291. (504) 925–3860.

Mississippi: *Mississippi Division of Tourism,* Box 849, Jackson, Miss. 39205. (601) 359–3414.

North Carolina: *North Carolina Travel & Tourism Division,* 430 North Salisbury Street, Box 25249, Raleigh, N.C. 27611. (919) 733–4171.

South Carolina: *South Carolina Tourism,* Box 71, Columbia, S.C. 29202. (803) 758–8735.

Tennessee: *Tennessee Tourist Development,* Box 23170, Nashville, Tenn. 37202. 615–741–2158.

The Midwest

Late spring, summer and early fall are the best seasons in the Midwest, although winter provides ice skating, ice fishing, and more skiing than you might expect. In the north, mid-winter temperatures average in the 10–20 degree range, mid-20's in the central areas, and low to mid-30's in southern Illinois, Indiana and Ohio. Summer temperatures usually average in the mid-to-upper 70's, sometimes mid-to-upper 80's. However, every state in the Midwest (except Iowa) borders on at least one of the Great Lakes, and these waters do much to moderate summer heat and winter cold.

This is an agricultural region with a green-thumb population. In every city and town are gardens and parks that are proudly shown to visitors, and from mid-May through mid-July are flower festivals (tulip, lilac, rose, carnation, cherry, dogwood, magnolia, etc.), music, summer theater, showboats and colorful celebrations of the region's twenty or more ethnic groups. From mid-July to mid-September the calendar is solidly booked to state and county fairs, and then, in fall come the harvest and the foliage. Other festivals celebrate glass, pumpkins, turkey racing, bluegrass music and canal boats, to name only a few. The life of the Midwest is a panorama of genuine Americana that will delight foreigners and may well astonish Americans themselves who come from other parts of this country. For more specific information write to:

Illinois: *Illinois Office of Tourism,* Travel Information, 310 S. Michigan Ave., Chicago, Ill. 60604.

Indiana: *Indiana Tourism Development Division,* 1 N. Capitol, Suite 700, Indianapolis, Ind. 46204–2243.

Iowa: *Iowa Development Commission, Tourist Development Division,* 600 E. Court Ave., Des Moines, Iowa 50309. (515) 281–3100.

Michigan: *Michigan Travel Bureau,* 333 S. Capitol, Suite F. Lansing, Mich. 48933. 800–248–5703 (out of state), 800–292–2570 (Mich. only).

Minnesota: *Minnesota Tourist Information Center,* 240 Bremer Bldg., 419 N. Robert, St. Paul, Minn. 55101. 800–652–9747 (Minnesota only) or 800–328–1461 (from out-of-state).

Ohio: *Travel Ohio,* 175 S. 3rd St., Suite 250, Columbus, Ohio 43215. 800–BUCKEYE.

Wisconsin: *Wisconsin Division of Tourism,* Box 7970, Madison, Wisc. 53707. 800–372–2737 (from Wisc., Minn., Mich., Iowa, and Ill.). 608–266–2161.

The Southwest

This region, which runs from northern Missouri, with about the same latitude as Pittsburgh, to the southern tip of Texas, which is nearly parallel to Miami, has wide variations of temperature in all seasons. In general there is plenty of sunshine and low humidity except along the Gulf Coast. Arizona and New Mexico, though hot (up to 110–115°), are very dry, so 85° in St. Louis can seem worse than 105° in Tucson. Air conditioning is almost universal throughout the hotter parts of the region, especially in newer cities such as Houston and Phoenix. The biggest tourist season is late December through April, with February and March the peak months. Average temperatures in the winter months range from the mid-50's in the south to the 40's in the north. Summer highs are around 90 in the north to around 100 in the south (in June, July, August). However, anywhere away from the coastal plains, the summer nights can be chilly. For information write to:

Arizona: *Arizona Office of Tourism,* 1480 E. Bethany Home Road, Suite 180, Phoenix, Ariz. 85014. 602–255–3618.

Kansas: *Kansas Department of Economic Development,* 503 Kansas Avenue, Topeka, Kans. 66603.

Missouri: *Missouri Division of Tourism,* Box 1055, Jefferson City, Mo. 65102.

New Mexico: *New Mexico Travel Division,* Bataan Memorial Building, Santa Fe, N.M. 87503. 800–545–2040.

Oklahoma: *Oklahoma Division of Tourism Promotion,* 500 Will Rogers Building, Oklahoma City, Okla. 73105. 405–521–2464.

Texas: *Texas Tourist Development Agency,* Box 12008 Capital Station, Austin, Texas 78711. 512–475–4326.

The Rockies and The Plains

Running from Canada to New Mexico, this region naturally shows great variations in topography and temperature in all seasons. It can be 110° in the desert within clear sight of snow-covered mountains; but humidity is low and sunshine plentiful everywhere. Summer brings clear, hot days with temperatures ranging from the mid-80's in the north to around 100 in the south, with cool, often cold, nights. Winters average in the low 20's; spring and fall can go up to the high 80's. From Thanksgiving to mid-April there is some of the best skiing in the country in places like Aspen and Vail in Colorado and Alta and Snowbird in Utah. January and February are the best months for winter festivals, and June-July for rodeos and historical pageants. County and state fairs run from mid-July to early September; Kansas, from early July through mid-September, has about 90; and Nebraska has 61 in the single month of August. The region's cultural life in the sense of music, drama and the arts is largely concentrated in Kansas City, Denver, and the various university towns, and certain resorts in Colorado. For more specific information, write to:

Colorado: *Tourism Board,* 5500 S. Syracuse, Englewood, CO 80111. 303–779–1067.

Montana: *Montana Travel Promotion Unit,* Department of Commerce, 1424 Ninth Ave., Helena, Mont. 59620. 800–548–3390.

Nebraska: *Nebraska Travel and Tourism Division,* Box 94666, 301 Centennial Mall South, Lincoln, Neb. 68509. 402–471–3796.

North Dakota: *North Dakota Travel Division,* State Capitol Ground, Bismarck, N.D. 58505. 800–472–2100 (in state only), 800–437–2077 (out of state).

South Dakota: *South Dakota Division of Tourism,* Box 6000, Pierre, S.D. 57501. 605–773–3301.

Utah: *Utah Travel Council,* Council Hall, Capitol Hill, Salt Lake City, Utah 84114. 801–533–5681.

Wyoming: *Wyoming Travel Commission,* Frank Norris Jr. Travel Center, Cheyenne, Wyo. 82002. 307–777–7777.

The Far West

With the cold Humboldt Current along its south coast and the warm Japan Current to the north, with America's highest, coldest mountains, thickest, wettest forests, and deepest, hottest, driest valleys, this region, stretching over 2,500 miles from north to south, has almost every natural and climatic condition you could ask for. In some places sea breezes can cause temperatures to vary up to 15 degrees in a single city. Southern California is in season all year round as far as weather and tourism are concerned. January through March can be cold, windy and damp along the coast, so that is the season for skiing or hunting inland. California north of Sacramento is best in summer when temperatures range between 45 and 60 degrees. The state's mountains are always cool but its deserts, in the south, are usually too hot for even brief stays.

Oregon, Washington, Idaho and Alaska are best in late spring, through summer and into early fall, though skiing is becoming more popular there, especially in Idaho. Nevada, largely desert, is best October through April. Southern Alaska and the coastal regions average 50 to 60 degrees in summer while inland valleys are cooler. The arctic north is hardly a tourist area yet. For more precise information write to:

Alaska: *Alaska Division of Tourism,* Pouch E, Juneau, Alaska 99811. 907–465–2010.

California: *California Office of Tourism,* 1121 L. St., Suite 103, Sacramento, Calif. 95814. 916–322–2881.

Idaho: *Idaho Division of Tourism and Industrial Development,* Room 108, State Capitol Building, Boise, Idaho 83720. 208–334–2470.

Nevada: *State of Nevada Commission on Tourism,* Capitol Complex, Carson City, Nev. 89710. 702–885–4322.

Oregon: *Oregon Travel Information Office,* 595 Cottage, N.E., Salem, Ore. 97310. 800–547–7842.

Washington: *Washington Travel Information,* General Administration Building, Room 101, Olympia, Wash. 98504. 206–753–5600.

Hawaii

Hawaii is a land of perpetual spring, where the mean temperature fluctuates between 71 and 78 degrees from "winter" to "summer." Waikiki is the best known area on the most popular island of Oahu, and it is the place for sunbathing among fellow travelers. The other islands offer a more tranquil vacation—on some you may never see other tourists—and can be reached via boat or helicopter.

Hawaii: *Hawaii Visitors Bureau,* 2270 Kalakaua Avenue, Suite 801, Honolulu, Hawaii, 96815. 808–923–1811.

TIME ZONES. The continental United States is about 3,000 miles from east to west and stretches across four complete Time Zones: Eastern, Central, Mountain and Pacific (see map). Alaska and Hawaii are separate cases, of course. Normally, this will cause no trouble. If you are driving, you will be able to adjust easily enough, an hour at a time, to local rhythms and conditions as you encounter them, and be annoyed only when a time zone cuts *through* a state, as in Kentucky, Tennessee, the Dakotas, Nebraska, Idaho, and bits of Kansas, Oregon and Texas. On long train trips you will have plenty of time to reset your watch and your mealtimes. Real inconvenience is likely only with plane schedules and long-distance phone calls.

In planning plane flights remember three factors: local time, flying time and elapsed time. For example, Anchorage, in the Alaska Standard Time Zone, is 5 hours behind New York; 11 A.M. in New York is 6 A.M. in Anchorage. If you fly, you will be in the air for about six hours of flying time, but with stopovers your elapsed time will total about seven hours. Thus, if you leave New York at 10 A.M., you will arrive in Anchorage at 5 P.M. according to your original New York time—but high noon local (Alaska) time.

In telephoning, you will need to think what people are likely to be doing at the other end. Eight A.M. in New York is 7:00 in Chicago, 6:00 in Denver, and 5:00 in San Francisco. You may feel like a nice chat as you have your breakfast coffee in New York, but your friends on the West Coast probably won't be in the same sunny mood. There is a map showing states, area codes and time zones for the entire country in the front of your telephone directory, along with information on how to save money by calling at night or during off hours. Economy rates take effect at the point of origin of the call, of course; if you call San Francisco from New York, you will be charged according to New York time.

For overseas calls, 11:00 A.M. in New York is 10 A.M. in Mexico City, 4 P.M. in London and Paris, 6 P.M. in Athens, Istanbul and Tel Aviv, and 1:00 A.M. the next day in Tokyo. (All comparative times subject to change when summer, or daylight, time is in effect.)

SEASONAL EVENTS. Even Americans themselves are likely to be astonished by the number, variety and exuberance of their festivals, fairs, contests, commemorations, parades and pageants, games, jubilees, days, weeks, week-ends, celebrations, tournaments, tours, fiestas, shows, expositions, carnivals, frolics, races, derbies, rodeos, roundups, jamborees, "world" championships, sings, birthdays, bakes and homecomings. Surely there is much to be said for a country that can celebrate, among other things, cranberries, corn pone, swamp cabbage, chicken plucking, egg striking, dragon boats, Mozart, and the Holy Ghost.

There is no day in the year that does not have something going on, and hardly any inhabited place however small that has not found something to celebrate, exalt or commemorate, from favorite sons like *Jonathan Hager* (Hagerstown, Md. in mid-July) to local products like *apple butter* (Burton, Ohio in mid-October), to remarkable attainments like *Watermelon Seed Spitting* (Paul's Valley, Okla. in late June). Apart from the major and legitimate holidays, there is a vast range of politically and commercially motivated non-events of the National-Eat-More-Kumquats-Week variety that can be largely ignored except when they reach such heights of inspired inadvertance as the simultaneous proclamation of National Music Week and National Noise Abatement Week.

"**Culture**" in the usual sense of music, dance, drama, painting, sculpture and literature is generally more abundant in the larger cities, and the opera, ballet, concert and gallery "seasons" in the major American cities are Fall, Winter and Spring just as they are in London, Paris, Stockholm or Tokyo. However, there is no American city of any size that has not by now a summer season as well, from the world-famous Boston Pops concerts, and Shakespeare in New York's Central Park, through al fresco symphony, opera, recitals, dance, light opera, musicals and "shows" in St. Louis, Cleveland, Miami, Chicago, Jacobs Pillow (Massachusetts), Marlboro (Vermont), Center Harbor (New Hampshire), Glens Falls (New York), and Lake Maxinkuckee (Indiana), to name only a few.

Much of this decentralized activity tends to center around resorts and college towns, but the fact that there are over 2,000 colleges and universities in the United States simply serves to indicate the vigor, abundance, and healthy distribution of the country's cultural and artistic life. Thus, New Hampshire's *Music Festival* (July-August) takes place in the heart of the state's Lakes Region with its many summer resort towns. Elsewhere, in late August and early September, the members of the *Society for Creative Anachronism* gather at the Snoqualmie Falls Forest Theater in Bellevue, Washington to perform music, dances and sports of the 15th and 16th centuries in their *Renaissance Faire*. Some of the world's finest and most innovative *opera* is found in Santa Fe, New Mexico, some of America's best *theater* in Minneapolis, Minnesota. At this point, distinctions of amateur and professional erode completely, for most of the country's local performing arts groups combine people from all walks of life, local and imported, to produce remarkably sophisticated activity in quite unexpected places.

Festivals based on local and indigenous culture range all the way from painstaking preservations of artistocratic historical traditions like the *fox hunts, candlelight concerts* and *Madrigal singing* of Virginia, through the various authentic *American Indian ceremonials,* to *historical pageants* like North Carolina's *Lost Colony of Roanoke.* There are expositions of rare and *historic handicrafts* and *traditional skills* like carding, dyeing, spinning, weaving and quiltmaking; *popular arts* like ballad singing, fiddling and folk dancing; *work skills* like log-rolling, steer roping, cabinet making, glass blowing and bread baking.

Many festivals celebrate very directly the local economy—*corn and rhubarb* in South Dakota, *maple syrup* in Vermont and Michigan, *tobacco* in Kentucky, *chicken* in Delaware, *oysters, cotton and rice* in Louisiana.

Sports. The range of events available includes not only football, skiing, yachting and other such familiar sights but also: wild cow milking (Colorado), chicken plucking (Florida), greased pig wrestling (Maryland, South Carolina), baseball on snowshoes (Minnesota), soccer played with firehoses (Washington), husband-calling (Tennessee), and fox-horn blowing (Virginia). There is *horse racing,* of course, but Americans also race king crabs in Alaska, terrapins in Arizona, shrimp boats in Florida, tricycles and bathtubs in Washington, wash tubs in South Carolina, sled dogs in New Hampshire, and lawn mowers in Indiana. As well as turkeys and canal boats. Frog jumping contests are held in Louisiana, Ohio, South Carolina and California. Ohio accepts contestants from foreign countries, and South Carolina's winning frog gets a free trip to California to compete for the national championship. The *National Cow Chip Throwing Contest* is held at Beaver, Oklahoma in April, and politicians are given a special welcome. Other contests include hollerin', Easter egg fights, rolling pin throwing, luring worms with fiddle music, and banjo playing (national championship in Virginia in July).

Fairs. Seriously, however, one of the finest ways to see a basic America that has held fast through all the changes of recent years is to attend some of the innumerable town, county and state fairs. Some of them, like the one in Reno, Nevada, with everyone wearing silk cowboy shirts on pain of paying a fine, are transparently commercial gimmicks; others, like the one in the little town of Lee, New Hampshire, in September, are unpretentious, totally genuine, and totally enjoyable. These fairs take place mostly in summer and fall, beginning, in the South and West, in July with rodeos and going on as late as November (in Arizona). The *Iowa State Fair* in mid-August, the *Eastern States Exposition* in Massachusetts in mid-September, and the *Texas State Fair* in mid-October are among the most notable. There are at least a few in every state in the country, and they are particularly numerous in the mid-West.

Flower and foliage festivals are particularly popular through the mid-Atlantic and mid-West regions and include: tulip, rose, lilac, carnation, cherry, dogwood, magnolia, rhododendron, apple, daffodil and golden raintree, among others. Foliage viewing is, of course, for autumn, and is outstanding in New England and the Adirondacks.

Ethnic festivals. Still another kind of festival celebrates the many ethnic strains that have contributed to this country's development, beginning with the American Indians and going on to Blacks, Asians and almost every country of Europe. In New York City, the Italian, Irish, Jewish, Puerto Rican and Chinese festivals are important. Through the mid-West are celebrations for Germans, Swedes, Swiss, Danes, Norwegians, Italians, Czechs, Poles, Slovaks, Ukrainians, Scots, Irish, and even Arabs (in Detroit). These festivals invariably feature local and ethnic cooking and sometimes the proportions of this can become awe-inspiring. Louisiana's late-October *Gumbo Festival* features a 4,000-gallon gumbo pot, and Ohio's mid-October *Circleville Pumpkin Show* features the Largest Pumpkin Pie Ever Baked—over 260 lbs.

It is, in the last analysis, almost impossible to find any generalizations that can cover such variety and ingenuity. Every region, every season, every occasion, every product or activity imaginable—and then some—is likely to have its own festival somewhere in this country. Almost the only thing you can do is decide when you can travel, where you want to go, and then begin to check into what will be going on there then. In addition to the events listed state-by-state and interest-by-interest throughout this book, the various state tourist offices and local chambers of commerce are goldmines of information not only fascinating but sometimes overwhelming. For the months of June, July and August alone, Vermont, 43rd in size and 48th in population among the 50 states, lists over 450 events and attractions in a 32-page booklet that opens with the modest disclaimer, "Many Vermont events are not listed because information was not final at our printing deadline." (sic!) And a nationwide directory listing several thousand events is *Mort's Guide to Festivals, Feasts, Fairs and Fiestas,* published by Mort Barish Associates Inc., Research Park, 218 Wall St., Princeton, N.J. 08540.

 HOLIDAYS AND BANK CLOSINGS. There are five major national holidays that are observed in all the 50 states. They are: *New Year's Day*—January 1; *Independence Day*—July 4; *Labor Day*—the first Monday in September; *Thanksgiving Day*—the fourth Thursday in November; and *Christmas Day*—December 25. The Congress, in the Uniform National Holiday legislation of 1971, arranged that other national holidays falling on a Sunday should be observed on the following day, and that various others should in any case be observed on Mondays in order to provide the country with a number of three-day weekends.

Thus, in addition to the above, there are: *Washington's Birthday*—the third Monday in February; *Memorial Day*—the last Monday in May (not observed in Alabama and South Carolina); *Columbus Day*—the second Monday in October (not observed in Alaska, Iowa, Maine, Mississippi, Nevada, Oregon and South Carolina); and *Veteran's Day*—the fourth Monday in October (observed as Armistice Day on November 11 in 16 states).

Lincoln's Birthday is celebrated on February 12 in 23 states, on February 3 in Delaware and Oregon, and is not observed in the remaining 25 states. *Robert E. Lee's Birthday* is observed on January 19 or 20 in 11 Southern states; and *Confederate Memorial Day* comes in late April or early May in seven Southern states.

There are also various holidays that have a particular impact in certain areas. The *Jewish High Holy Days* of Rosh Hashanah and Yom Kippur, which usually fall in September, are important in New York City. Similarly, *Saint Patrick's Day,* March 17, is enthusiastically celebrated in Boston, and in New York City as well. New Orleans is world-famous for its *Mardi Gras* in February or March, and Louisiana celebrates *All Saints Day* on November 1. In Suffolk County, Massachusetts, March 17 is *Evacuation Day.* And so on.

Bank hours are usually 9 A.M. to 2 or 3 P.M., Monday through Friday. Some banks stay open until 9 P.M. one evening each week and a few are open on Saturdays. Many have also installed automated 24-hour "tellers"—computers able to accept deposits or give cash provided you have an account with that bank or one subscribing to a system of "ATMs" (Automated Teller Machines) that is national and/or linked to a charge card. Banks in particular regions close for local or regional holidays; and *all* banks close on: *New Year's Day, Lincoln's Birthday, Memorial Day, Independence Day, Labor Day, Columbus Day, Election Day* (which falls in the first week of November in even-numbered years), *Armistice Day, Thanksgiving Day,* and *Christmas Day,* though the ATMs operate even on these occasions.

PLANNING YOUR TRIP. If you would rather not bother making reservations on your own, a travel agent can be of help in suggesting vacation possibilities you hadn't thought of, for finding package tours that can save you time, money and planning, and for deciphering the increasingly volatile and complex fare structures of the nation's carriers.

"Package tours" usually touch upon a variety of important places, point out selected restaurants, offer tour guides, and present the possibility of meeting other people in the group, for an all-inclusive rate. Tours of the fly/drive variety also are quite popular since they offer the "do-it-yourself" opportunity.

If you don't belong to an auto club, now is the time to join one. They can be very helpful about routings and offering emergency service on the road. The *American Automobile Association* (AAA), in addition to its information services, has a nation-wide network of some 26,000 service stations which provide emergency repair service. Its offices are at 8111 Gatehouse Rd., Falls Church, Va. 22047. The *Exxon Travel Club,* 4550 Decoma, Houston, Texas 77092, provides information, low cost insurance, and some legal service. The *National Travel Club,* 51 Atlantic Ave.,Travel Building, Floral Park, N.Y. 11001, offers informational services, insurance, and tours. If you plan the route yourself, make certain the map you get is dated for the current year. Some of the major oil companies will send maps and mark preferred routes on them if you tell them what you have in mind. Try: *Exxon Touring Service,* 4550 Decoma, Houston, Texas 77092; *Texaco Travel Service,* P.O. Box 538, Comfort, Texas 78013; or AMOCO Motor Club, Box 9049, Des Moines, Iowa 50369–0010. In addition, most states have their own maps, which pinpoint attractions, list historical sites, parks, etc. The addresses of the various state tourist information services have already been given above. City chambers of commerce and the convention and visitors bureaus also are good sources. Their addresses are given under *Tourist Information* in the individual state chapters.

The tradition of free road maps at gasoline stations has almost totally disappeared. Only Exxon provides them to any extent. When you do find them there is usually a charge of at least 75¢. The alternative is, of course, a road atlas, purchased at a bookstore, and costing anywhere from $1.50 to $4. Three major ones are published in this country, by Rand McNally, Grossett, and Hammond.

Plan to board your pets, discontinue paper and milk deliveries, and tell your local police and fire departments when you'll be leaving, when you expect to return. Ask a kindly neighbor to keep an eye on your house or apartment; fully protect your swimming pool against intruders. Have a neighbor keep your mail, or have it held at the post office. Consider having your telephone temporarily disconnected if you plan to be away more than a few weeks. Empty your refrigerator and turn it off, turn off the hot water, and turn the thermostat down according to the weather. Look into the purchase of trip insurance (including baggage), and make certain your auto, fire, and other policies are up to date. Convert the greater portion of your trip money into travelers' checks. Arrange to have your lawn mowed at the usual times, and leave that kindly neighbor your itinerary (insofar as possible), car license number, and a key to your home (and tell police and firemen he has it).

TRAVEL AGENTS. The *American Society of Travel Agents, Inc.* (*ASTA*) is the world's largest professional travel trade association, composed of all elements of the travel business. ASTA was established in New York in 1931 to promote travel, to prevent unethical practices, and to provide a public forum for travel agents. It is the duty of every ASTA member agency to protect the public against any fraud, misrepresentation, or unethical practices. To avoid being victimized by fly-by-night operators who might claim better bargains, look for the ASTA member shield—the hallmark of dependable travel service. You'll find the shield on entrance doors, windows, and all office forms of the member agency you select.

ASTA membership indicates that the agent has been in business for at least three years and is officially approved by the Society to sell tickets on behalf of airlines and cruise ships. ASTA agents also will arrange bookings for trains, buses, or car rentals. For further information write ASTA, 4400 MacArthur Blvd., N.W., Washington, D.C. 20007.

The volatility of the travel field in the last several years has led to the failure of some tour operators and to losses on the part of their clients. To avoid this, a number of leading tour operators have formed a bonding association. For a list of these agencies whose stability is protected, write to: *United States Tour Operators Association,* 211 E. 51st Street, Suite 4B, New York, NY 10022.

The best feature of the travel agent's role is that he does all your arranging, leaving you free to use your precious time elsewhere. But what should not be overlooked is his value in suggesting tailor-made vacations. Experienced agents have seen many tourist attractions firsthand and can suggest the best places for you—your purse, your age, your needs, and your desires. It is in the agent's best interest to help you avoid the problems or complexities of traveling.

For all this service, the travel agent does not charge you a fee. His fee is collected from the transportation carriers and hotels as a commission for promoting and making the sale. Your only charge might be for extra phone calls, cables, or other special services. On package tours and groups, the agent's and organizer's services are included in the total price. If an agent has to arrange a complex itinerary and perform myriad services, he may charge you, and you should discuss his charges in advance.

PACKING. Don't try to pack at the last moment. Instead, begin in advance and make a list of things each member of the family will need; then check off the items as you pack them. It saves time and reduces confusion.

Be wise about packing. Regardless of how you plan to travel, it is less confusing to travel light—and less expensive, too, considering less weight and fewer bags for you to carry yourself, thus avoiding baggage assistance and tipping. Check the climate and dress standards along your route and select clothes accordingly, sticking to the basic styles and colors which can be interchanged to create different outfits.

If you wear prescription glasses or contacts always take an extra pair or set; at the very least have a copy of your prescription. This is true of prescription sunglasses, too. A travel iron often comes in handy as do plastic bags (large and small) for wet suits, socks, etc. They are also excellent for packing shoes, spillable cosmetics, and other easily damaged items. Extra photo film (plenty), suntan lotion, insect repellent, enough toothpaste, soap, and so forth, if purchased before you go, will help reduce those nuisance stops to pick up things you forgot. Fun extras include binoculars, a compass, a magnifying glass (for reading those fine-print maps). If you fly, remember that, despite claims to the contrary, airport security X-rays do in fact damage your films in about 17% of the cases. Have them inspected separately, or pack them in special protective bags.

All members of the family should have sturdy shoes with nonslip soles. Keep them handy in the back of the car. You never know when you may want to stop and clamber along a rocky trail. Carry rain gear in a separate bag in the back of the car (so no one will have to get out and hunt for it in the middle of a downpour).

If you're stopping on route, you'll find it's convenient to pack separately those few things you'll need for just an overnight stay. It saves unloading the entire car, only to reload it the next morning.

Women will probably want to stick to one or two basic colors for their wardrobes so that they can manage with one set of accessories. If possible, include one knit or jersey dress or pants suit. The general consensus among well-traveled women is that a full-skirted traveling dress will show less wear and wrinkling. For dress-up, take along a couple of "basic" dresses you can vary with a simple change of accessories. That way you can dress up or down to suit the occasion. Remember that nowadays pants are acceptable almost everywhere.

Men will probably want a jacket along for dining out, and include a dress shirt and tie for the most formal occasions. Many restaurants in large cities, most hotels and resorts, and many motels require skirts for women and jackets and ties for men, especially for dinner. Don't forget extra slacks.

Apart from these general considerations, when you put together your traveling wardrobe you need to take the temperature and weather of the region you're traveling to into account. Light, loose-fitting clothing is best for really hot areas. And if you're planning a lot of time in the sun, don't forget something sufficiently cover-up to wear over swimsuits en route to the pool, beach, or lakefront, and for those few days when you're getting reacquainted with sun on tender skin. For the cold and snow, you'll want a very warm coat, gloves, hat, scarf or muffler, and even galoshes. A slicker or an umbrella is a must.

INSURANCE. In planning your trip, think about three kinds of insurance: *property, medical,* and *automobile.* The best person to consult about insuring your household furnishings and personal property while you are away is your insurance agent. For Americans, he is also the person to consult about whatever special adjustments might be advisable in your medical coverage while traveling. Foreigners visiting the United States should bear in mind that medical expenses in this country may seem astronomical by comparison with those they are accustomed to at home, and that the kind of protection that some countries (Britain, for example) extend to their own nationals and foreigners alike does not exist here.

Every state has some sort of Financial Responsibility law establishing the minimum and maximum amounts for which you can be held liable in auto accidents. Most states require insurance to be offered, and 17 states require you to have it in order to register a car or get a license within their jurisdictions. In any case, it is almost essential to have at least third party coverage, or "liability insurance," as claims can run very high both for car repairs and medical treatment. Insurance premiums vary according to place and person; they are generally highest for males under 25, and for drivers who live in large urban areas.

One possiblity is the *American Automobile Association* (AAA), which offers both group personal accident insurance (from $2,500 to $3,750) and bail bond protection up to $5,000 as part of its annual membership (fee $35). The AAA can also arrange the validation of foreign driving permits for use in the United States. Foreigners should consider getting their insurance before leaving their own countries since short-term tourists will find it difficult and expensive to buy here. For the AAA, write to *AAA,* 8111 Gatehouse Rd., Falls Church, Va. 22047. Travel insurance is also offered by the *Exxon Travel Club,* 4550 Decoma, Houston, Texas 77092; and by the *National Travel Club,* 51 Atlantic Ave., Travel Building, Floral Park, N.Y. 11001. Persons over 50 who are members of NRTA/AARP may join that organization's motoring plan which offers, among other things, reimbursement for legal fees, hospital emergency room bonding, arrest bonding, and emergency breakdown service. Write to: *NRTA/ AARP Motoring Plan,* 215 Long Beach Blvd., Long Beach, Calif. 90801.

Trip cancellation insurance is also available (usually from travel agents) to protect you against losing any advance payments should you have to cancel your trip at the last moment.

AMERICA BY CAR. The first precaution you should take is to have your car thoroughly checked by your regular dealer or service station to make sure that everything is in good shape. The *National Institute for Automotive Service Excellence,* Suite 515, 1825 K Street, NW, Washington, D.C. 20006, tests and certifies the competence of auto mechanics.

If you don't have a car of your own, there are a number of companies from which you can rent one. Perhaps it would be wise to first check the data of major companies individually, such as *Hertz,* 800–654–3131; *Avis,* 800–331–1212; *National,* 800–227–7368; *Dollar,* 800–421–6868; *Thrifty,* 800–331–4200; or *Budget,* 800–527–0700. Those telephone numbers are toll free for 24-hour information and rental service.

Most companies require a minimum age of 25, but under certain conditions will rent to a lower age group, usually not lower than 21.

Most companies also will honor certain major charge cards in lieu of a cash deposit. If cash is the means of deposit and payment, an advance cash deposit computed on the basis of the estimated rental charge is payable at the time of the rental. In addition, it is usually required for cash transactions that you fill out an application for verification by the rental company, which can be difficult after regular business hours and during weekends.

Be sure to check into the rent-it-here/leave-it-there information which allows you to rent the car in one place and drop it off at any other company location in the United States for a modest drop-off charge. Also check into special rates offered for different categories of cars, for weekends, holidays and extended trips. Rates and conditions can vary enormously; this is one area in which comparison shopping will pay off.

Car rental companies generally charge substantial per-day fees for insurance coverage. You should check the company of your choice for specifics. Here again, the services of a travel agent can save you time, money, and trouble, as he will have on file the relevant data for the major rental firms so that you will not have to check them all one by one yourself.

In most cases, a valid driver's license issued by any state or possession of the United States; by any province of Canada; or by any country which ratified the 1949 Geneva Motoring Convention, is valid and is required to rent a car.

By Federal law, 55 mph is now the maximum speed limit. If the wide open spaces of the nation's highways tempt you to go faster—don't. Not only will you save gas by observing the speed limit, you also may save your life. Government studies have shown a substantial drop in the number of highway deaths, directly attributable to the lowered speed limit. All the states use sophisticated speed detection devices, including radar and aircraft. So watch your speedometer!

Beware of the danger of highway hypnosis, especially prevalent on roads which stretch for miles without a break. Highway hypnosis results from steady driving over long distances at set speeds. Principal symptoms are drowsiness and the inability to concentrate on what you're doing. The cure: vary your speed occasionally, stop to stretch your legs, have a cup of coffee or tea, take a little exercise, take a brief nap.

Superhighways, known as *Interstates,* turnpikes, expressways, or toll roads, have at least two lanes of traffic in each direction with a dividing strip between the opposing lanes. There are no traffic lights or cross traffic on some roads, Interstates especially, and service plazas, with gas stations, repair shops, and restaurants, are limited. Access is limited, so plan your exit points and rest stops well in advance.

There are four cross-country Interstate routes—all now almost complete coast to coast—that bear the same number for their entire length: I–10 from Jacksonville, Florida to Santa Monica, California; I–40 from Greensboro, North Carolina to Barstow, California; I–80 from the George Washington Bridge, New Jersey, to San Francisco, California; and I–90 from Boston, Massachusetts to Seattle, Washington.

When you enter a limited-access highway, be sure to allow plenty of space between you and the onrushing cars before you merge into the right lane. Once on the highway, keep your speed in tune with traffic. Keep an eye on cars in front and behind. If someone crowds your rear, slow down gradually, and let him pass; he's in a bigger hurry than you. Don't follow the car ahead too closely; tailgating is a major cause of highway accidents. And keep an eye on the signs, so you won't miss your exit. If you pass your exit, don't back up to try again; go on to the next exit and live to try the highways once more.

Except for terrain differences on the east coast, west coast, and mid-section of the country, driving conditions are basically the same. The major highways in the northeast section of the country are well-designed with frequent rest stops and gas stations. You occasionally will encounter a desolate stretch of highway, such as those in central and upper Maine, and begin to wonder where you're going to find the next service station. You'll soon learn that driving in the east can offer the same wide variety—albeit of a different kind—as driving in the west. You will encounter more than double the number of postings for speed limits for special conditions that you find elsewhere. Unmarked side roads should be inquired about or explored on foot if at all; they may be private or long out of use, hence unfit for modern autos.

In the South you will find, along with somewhat different scenery, the same sort of long, lonely stretches of straightaway as those in the central, west and southwest sections. There will be considerably more variety, however, to keep you alert, with gradual curves, for example, stretching for half a mile or more.

The area around Canyonlands National Park in southern Utah is wild, rugged country where you follow routes, not roads, through shifting sand, up trickling stream beds which can turn into raging torrents during a sudden storm, where the wheels of even four-wheel drive vehicles can sink hopelessly into the sand if they don't move along briskly, and where you climb a 27-degree face of sheer rock as part of getting over Elephant Hill.

The Rockies and Plains provide a wide variety of scenery: the country of the Badlands of North and South Dakota, the mule-riding country of the Grand Canyon, the country of towering mountains interspersed with the broad flat spaces of the Plains—an area where the motorist can have virtually any driving experience he cares to meet.

Unless you venture onto exotic mountain roads, you should have little trouble with mountain driving. Today's mountain roads are engineered for the ordinary driver. They are normally wide, well graded, and safe. Be especially wary of exceeding the speed limits posted for curves. Keep to the right. If your normal driving is at low altitudes, have a garage mechanic check your carburetor. It may need adjusting for mountain driving. Use your motor for downhill runs—second or low gear—to save your brakes. If your car stalls, and your temperature gauge is high, it could mean a vapor lock. Bathe the fuel pump with a damp cloth for a few minutes.

California, with a motor vehicle registration of almost 16 million, easily outranks its two closest contenders, New York with 8 million and Texas, with 10 million license plates. This may explain why in California running out of gas is punishable by fine. If you enter a California freeway, be sure to have a full tank of gas.

Whenever you park on a hill, turn your wheels to the curb. If you park downhill, turn your steering wheel to the right to put your tires into the curb. If you park uphill, do the opposite. Turning your wheels to the curb in hilly San Francisco is the law, even on level stretches, because runaway automobiles have been a problem, and it's hard to tell where the hills end and the level stretches begin.

California's Death Valley is a pleasant place in winter. However, if you must cross it in summer, carry plenty of water, don't stop too often, keep to the main routes, and get out as fast as you can. In summer, daytime temperatures can reach 120 degrees for days on end.

You will encounter other stretches of desert driving in the Pacific states. Service industries across the desert have grown in number during the past decade, to the point that the hazards of desert driving have been minimized. The desert won't resemble the sands of the Sahara, but will have considerable vegetation and rock outcroppings. The principal check before crossing the hot desert should be your tires. Put them at normal driving pressure or slightly below. Heat builds pressure. If your car seems to be bouncing too readily, stop to let your tires cool. If you have a good radiator, don't bother about extra water—except for Death Valley—but keep an eye on the water gauge. Be alert for sudden sandstorms and rainstorms. If you have a car radio, keep it tuned to local stations for information about unusual weather conditions. In spite of its dryness, there are occasionally deadly flash floods in the desert.

If you get stuck on any kind of road, pull off the highway onto the shoulder, raise the hood, attach something white (a handkerchief, scarf, or some other white cloth) to the door handle on the driver's side of the car, and sit inside and wait for help. This is especially effective on limited-access highways, diligently patrolled by state highway officers. A special warning to women stalled at night: Remain inside the car with doors locked, and make sure the Good Samaritan who approaches you is indeed a Good Samaritan. If you are a member of an automobile club and have access to a telephone, call the nearest garage listed in your service directory—or ask the operator for help. But by all means don't get out of your car and start walking along the highway looking for help. This is (a) dangerous and (b) illegal in some states.

TRAFFIC SIGNS AND ROAD MARKINGS. Since 1970, the United States has been moving more and more toward internationally accepted markings on road signs. This applies especially to the signs you most need to watch out for—those that get you in trouble when you miss them.

So, for "no left turn," or "no trucks," and other such prohibitions, you'll see the internationally familiar shapes and colors—the white background, black symbol, and the red circle with the diagonal slash. Usually, the prohibition symbolized on the sign will be repeated in words on a small sign just beneath it. You will sometimes find them as the only sign, without the accompanying international signal, in parts of the country that haven't caught up to the most modern standards yet.

America has adopted two other international regulatory signs, those for "yield" and "do not enter." The first is the inverted triangle with the red border. The second is a red circle with a white bar in the middle. America puts the words "do not enter" on the latter, unlike most other countries. One other regulatory sign is a yellow pennant, or sideways triangle, with the words "no passing zone." It marks the beginning of an area where you are not allowed to pass, and is located on the left hand side of the road.

American road signs are color-coded. Briefly: warnings are yellow; directions are green; recreational features are often brown; services are blue; construction sites are orange. Now, in more detail, warning signs—upcoming pedestrian crossings and traffic lights, slippery spots, low bridges etc—are yellow diamonds with black markings or symbols. Below these signs, the message is given in words, on a smaller, rectangular sign. Again, learn to read them, and look out for the old-fashioned yellow triangles with just words, no symbols. There are still quite a few around.

The only warning sign that departs from the shape mentioned above is that for a school crossing. The new sign is yellow, but instead of diamond-shaped, it is a pentagon with the point up—sort of the shape of a small house. Inside the sign are stick figures symbolizing children with school books.

Many of the symbolic shapes used in warning signs will be familar to the international traveler. A rear view of a car with wiggly lines means "slippery when wet." A black triangle with a vehicle, usually a truck, going down one side means "hill." The pedestrian crossing is a stick figure walking between parallel lines.

When you begin to wonder if you are going in the right direction, or where you should turn to get someplace, start looking for a sign with a green background. They give directions. Green signs with exit numbers will help you off the highway by telling you the main towns and routes served by the upcoming exit, and how far away they are. Mileage markers alongside the road are green, too. Knowing that you are at mile 44 may help you in trip-planning. There are also green directional signs pointing to biking and hiking trails.

One special sign falls in this group. It has a brown background and gives information about routes to public parks and recreation areas. So, if you're looking for one of those, look for brown signs.

Signs telling you where to find services such as hospitals, restaurants, motels, telephones, and camping areas are blue. They have recognizable symbols for the service indicated, plus directional arrows, and often a word sign as well.

The color which tells you of road construction is orange. That includes detour signs, and orange striped barriers, and often the words "road construction 1500 feet."

As for pavement markings, the main thing to remember is never cross a solid line on your side of the road. If you see a dotted line on your side and a solid line beyond it, you may pass.

Here's a word of warning: In some foreign countries, it is the practice to pay the policeman the fine on the spot. *In America that is not done.* An attempt to do so can be misinterpreted as an attempt to bribe the police officer, and that can mean big trouble. In order to know what is the right thing to do, ask the policeman. Another source of information is the ticket itself. They almost always have instructions on the back.

 FLY/DRIVE VACATIONS. Among the many ways you can travel, the fly/drive package offers a bit more, or perhaps a different way, to satisfy a deeper curiosity. Most airlines, in conjunction with car rental companies, offer these combination opportunities to most parts of the country all year round. Fly/drive package rates and flexibilities vary considerably from one to another. Generally, they cover one or more cities plus the use of a rented car for the specified number of days.

Car usage also varies from one to another. For example, with some you can drive an unlimited number of miles, free. On others you get a specified amount of mileage free, and then must pay an additional charge per mile for the overage. Gas, generally, is not included.

Some packages offer plans for small groups and a choice of hotel accommodations. Some even offer motor homes, if you're interested in roughing it. Check into special children's rates.

Before booking, though, you should check with your agent about where you pick up the car (at airport or other station), and about the time it will take you to arrive at your hotel to meet your reservation. If you are not going to pick up the car at the airport, you should check ahead on airport limousines and bus and taxi service to your hotel. These are important details that should be included or provided for by any good package-tour combination. It should also be noted that it is frequently cheaper to rent at airports rather than in downtown areas, even when there are two locations run by the same company.

If you decide to fly to the destination and not drive while there, check into the substitutions some companies make with bus tours, rail tours, local sightseeing excursions, admissions to theme parks, museums, zoos, amusement parks, sports events, curiosities and "attractions," etc. There may be a number of such substitutions and fringe benefits in your package.

AMERICA BY PLANE. A network of thousands of airline flights a day makes America only five and a half hours wide and two hours from top to bottom. Even with the limited time most vacations allow, you can see a lot of this country by flying from place to place.

Here are some typical distances and times to help you plan your travel in the United States: The distance from Boston, Massachusetts in the northeast of the country to Los Angeles, California on the West Coast is 2,600 miles. Flying time is about five and a half hours. From Chicago, Illinois in the north to New Orleans, Louisiana in the south is 837 miles. Flying time is two hours. Miami, Florida is a long way from Seattle, Washington—2,934 miles, but it takes only eight hours to fly. From the West Coast to Honolulu takes about five and a half hours, to Anchorage, Alaska, about four and a half. To Puerto Rico from Washington, D.C., expect to fly for three and a half hours.

Ten airlines link the major United States cities. These are called *trunk lines*. They are *American, Continental* (only from Chicago west), *Delta, Eastern, National, Northwest Orient, Trans World (TWA), United* and *Western* (from Minnesota west). However, deregulation has opened the airways to literally dozens of other lines, many of which had formerly been limited to regional runs. Among the latter are *People Express,* primarily in the northeast but also serving some Midwest points and California; *USAir,* in the Northeast; *Ozark,* mostly the central section, plus New York and Washington, D.C.; *Frontier,* midwest and west except the west coast; *Piedmont,* middle east, north to New York; *Republic,* Ohio to Kansas and points north, as well as the southeast: *Texas International,* the southwest and Mexico.

Once you get to Alaska, *Alaska Airlines, Wien Air Alaska,* a dozen commuter airlines, and a hundred "air taxis" help you get around—to almost anywhere in the state. Look at a map and see how big Alaska is, and you'll really appreciate the need for these flights.

Information on connecting flights between trunk and regional airlines is available from any of the airlines or your travel agent.

You don't have to stay on the American Continent to stay in America. Try Hawaii, Puerto Rico, or the Virgin Islands.

To get to Hawaii from the mainland there are 7 airlines: *American, Canadian Pacific, Continental, Northwest Orient, Pan American, United* and *Western.* Within the island state, two carriers give reguarly scheduled service: *Aloha Airlines* and *Hawaiian Airlines.* In addition, there are commuter/air-taxi services, such as *Royal Hawaiian Air Service, Mid-Pacific Airlines,* and others.

Pan American will get you to Hawaii (among other carriers), as well as to Guam and American Samoa. *Eastern Airlines* Caribbean service out of Miami, Florida will take you to the Virgin Islands.

Three major cities have time-saving helicopter flights to beat the heavy road traffic when you're in a rush. However, because there are many different reasons why a flight may be delayed in arriving, you will usually be very unwise to schedule tight connections anyway.

In New York, *New York Airways* ties together LaGuardia and Kennedy Airports with Newark and two smaller airports in New Jersey, Morristown and Teterboro. *Chicago Helicopter Airways* links downtown to Midway and O'Hare International Airport weekdays, and provides a charter service. *SFO Helicopter Airlines* serves San Francisco International Airport, Oakland International Airport, Berkeley and Marin County.

Helicopter flights may be the fastest way to get around, but aren't the cheapest—unless they can be included as a connecting flight on your regular ticket. This is often the case. Check with your ticket agent. You may even fly free.

There also are nine charter airlines whose business is mostly international tours booked overseas.

For getting to even more out-of-the-way places quickly, you can choose from more than 200 commuter airlines. They fly scheduled flights, mostly in two engine planes carrying four to 19 passengers. The more than 2,500 air taxi firms in America do not have regular schedules, but will fly you between any two points on a charter, contract, or demand basis. They'll even get you to hidden lakes in the woods you can't reach any other way.

Two classes of service, first class and coach, are the most commonly found. As in the rest of the world, first class is more spacious, meals more elaborate, drinks are free. Coach is the standard service. Meals are served at appropriate times. You pay for your drinks. This is comparable to the economy class on international flights.

A third type of fare seen recently on some airlines to some destinations is economy class. You sit in the same cabin as coach passengers, but you don't get food or beverages. So, bring your lunch. Still others offer business class (usually under a trade name) in which services and price fall somewhere between first and coach.

Baggage allowances are now computed by size rather than weight. You may carry with you one piece of baggage no more than 9" high (so that it can fit underneath the seat ahead of you) and you may check through free one large piece where height, length, and width together total no more than 65", and one medium piece where dimensions total no more than 55".

Remember, also, to identify all your bags by firmly affixing your name to the outside and inside. The airlines will not accept them for checking otherwise. Name tags ensure a faster tracing of misdirected luggage. They also avoid the possibility of picking up someone else's bag.

 AMERICA BY TRAIN. *Amtrak* is the semi-governmental corporation that has taken over passenger service on most of the nation's railroads. At present the system has some 26,000 miles of track linking over 500 cities and towns in 44 states (except Maine, New Hampshire, South Dakota, Oklahoma, Alaska and Hawaii) and since mid-1979, under the pressure of soaring gasoline prices the number of passengers carried has risen sharply. Equipment, at best, is among the most modern and comfortable anywhere in the world. However, not all equipment is at best, and the auxiliary services (stations, meals, punctuality) are uneven. In general, the system seems to work best in the Northeast, the Boston-New York-Philadelphia-Baltimore-Washington megalopolis, and in southern California, where distances are short and getting to and from airports is inconvenient and expensive. On medium and longer runs the advantages of rail travel are the spaciousness of the cars (against the cramped immobility of bus and plane) and the chance to enjoy the scenery.

Once again you can ride in relative comfort on trains with magic names—the *Broadway Limited* from New York to Chicago; the *Silver Meteor* from New York to Miami; *Merchants Limited* between Boston and New York; the *Crescent* from New York via Washington and Atlanta to New Orleans, the *Southwest Limited* (formerly the *Super Chief*) and the *San Francisco Zephyr*. You can ride *Turbo Trains* out of Chicago, the all-electric, high-speed *Metroliner* from New York to Washington, or take a trip clear across the continental United States without ever changing cars.

Some sample times are: New York to Washington, four hours; Chicago to San Francisco, 23½ hours; San Francisco to Los Angeles, 10 hours. New York to New Orleans, 29 hours. On some popular runs there is a high speed Metroliner service that cuts travel time by about a third. Still, it must be admitted that due to the deteriorated condition of many roadbeds even the best trains may often run late.

The simplest is, of course, day coach. There you ride in reclining seats, which may be reserved, with ample leg room, never more than two abreast. Next up is the leg-rest coach with (of course) leg rests, head rests and deeper cushioning for the simplest kind of long distance nighttime accommodation. Slumbercoaches have lounge seats that convert into either a single bed or upper and lower berths at night. For more space and privacy, a roomette gives a sitting room by day and at night a sleeping room with a full-length bed and private toilet facilities. Bedrooms have two separate sleeping berths and private washing and toilet facilities. Superliner cars, operating between Chicago and the West Coast, also have family bedrooms that can sleep up to two adults and two children. Other types of special cars include dining cars, of course, and tavern lounges—an informal setting for a quiet drink, a game of cards, or just conversation. Some trains, especially where the scenery is best, have dome lounge cars, which give a view of the countryside through high glass domes.

First class tickets are valid for parlor and club cars, and sleeping cars—the roomettes and bedrooms. Coach class tickets are for reserved and unreserved coaches, either day coach or leg-rest coaches. The reservation system is computerized and operates nationwide.

Amtrak has about 75 different package tours to choose from, too, ranging from a weekend package in New York or Washington to a 24-day, coast-to-coast circle tour, plus 16 different Broadway show tours in New York City. A sample is the *Bonanza Americana*, out of Chicago stopping at Yosemite National Park, San Francisco, Big Sur, Los Angeles, Las Vegas, the Grand Canyon among other places and returning to Chicago after 16 days.

Because the Boston-Washington corridor is so heavily traveled, various special discounts of up to 25 percent obtain on round-trip tickets, *with stopovers*, in this area. And in addition, an entirely different system of discounts applies to round trip fares anywhere *outside* the Boston-Washington corridor. A number of connecting rail and motor coach services are available locally out of the major cities along the Northeast Corridor—Boston, the south shore of Connecticut, Long Island from New York, New Jersey out of Newark or Philadelphia, and suburban Philadelphia and Washington.

Senior Citizens and the *Handicapped* receive 25% off all regular round-trip fares of $40 or more except on Metroliners. Proof of age (65 and above), or of Handicapped status must be shown. Groups of 15 or more may get reductions of 15% on regular one-way coach fares and 25% on round trips, except on Metroliners between New York and Washington.

Some sample one-way coach fares are (in 1985): Chicago-San Francisco $242; New York–Chicago $127; San Francisco-Los Angeles $57. Be sure to check current fares before you book.

In Montreal, Boston, New York, Philadelphia, and Washington, *Amtrak* packages include rail fare, hotel reservations, and various combinations of meals, sightseeing, and theater tickets.

Not all American trains have been updated. Some have been back-dated. Romantic old steam trains that have been restored and put back into special service now dot the country. Many feature events of local history on their runs. You can be chased by Indians, stop in colonial villages, or probe deep into the heart of a redwood forest on an old logging train. There are some very special trips into the past, to an era full of the romance of trains.

 AMERICA BY BUS. The most extensive and one of the less expensive means of travel in America is the motor coach—the bus; 1,050 inter-city and suburban bus companies operate to about 15,000 cities, towns and villages in the United States, 14,000 of which have no other kind of intercity public transportation. The network totals over 277,000 miles of routes, carrying 10,000 buses. Two of these are major national lines, *Greyhound Lines* and *Trailways*, operating 6,700 buses between them, and covering the entire country with regularly scheduled routes. America's intercity buses carry over 350,000,000 passengers a year, more than Amtrak and all the airlines combined.

Reservation and ticketing procedures are basically the same for both. With more than 8,000 coaches on the road daily, you can go almost anywhere with little delay at connecting points. Reservations can be made for only a few trips. "Open date" tickets, good for travel any day, any time, are the rule. So, you just get your ticket, choose the time you want to travel, and show up early enough to get your bags checked in (15 minutes ahead in small towns, 45 minutes in cities).

Both companies offer bargain-rate passes for unlimited travel on any regularly scheduled route in the United States and Canada. These passes are available to both residents and visitors, so there are no restrictions about when and where you can buy them. If they are bought abroad, the period of validity begins on the first day of use in this country; if they are bought here, it begins on the day of purchase.

As of 1985, Greyhound's *Ameripass* is priced at $189 for 7 days, $289 for 15 days, and $349 for 30 days. Children 5 to 11½ travel for half fare, and those under 5 go free. Trailways' *EaglePass* has almost identical rates. Both passes may be extended indefinitely at a fixed rate of $10 per day. Furthermore, although the two companies do not stress the fact, either pass can be used on buses of the other company provided space is available. Greyhound also offers regional unlimited-mileage passes within California, Florida, and New England (including New York City and the New York-Albany-Montreal route).

Both companies offer discounts to travelers over 65; the rates change, however; in 1985 both companies offered 10% discounts. Two other special situations are: unlimited one-way travel with unlimited stopovers; and promotional discounts between particular points. These change frequently, so enquire specifically for the area and time that you are planning for.

The main U.S. office of Trailways is at 1500 Jackson St., Dallas, Texas 75201; that of Greyhound is Greyhound Tower, Phoenix, Ariz. 85077.

Long-distance buses carry about 45 passengers. They are air-conditioned in summer, heated in winter. Baggage goes underneath, so the passenger compartment is up high, providing a better view through the big, tinted windows. Seats are the lounge chair type, with reclining backs and adjustable head rests. Reading lamps are individually controlled. Almost all long-distance buses have rest rooms.

Some sample, point-to-point times are: New York City to Washington, D.C. —four and a half hours; Los Angeles to San Francisco—nine hours; Chicago to New Orleans—24 hours. Buses must adhere to the recently imposed national speed limit of 55 mph.

A wide variety of tours is offered by the two national lines and many others. They are of three main types. First is the "city package," which includes hotel and sightseeing in one city or the immediate surroundings. Second is the "independent package," which combines inter-city travel on regular schedules with hotel and sightseeing in several cities or places of interest. Third is the "escorted tour," which is a scheduled departure for groups only during certain seasons of the year, leaving from major cities. These range from 4 to 31 and are led by an escort, usually only English-speaking.

Some representative one-way bus fares: New York City-Chicago $90, Boston-Philadelphia $39, Seattle-San Francisco $96. On major city runs, however, commuter airlines often offer comparable rates—albeit with no views of the countryside.

Sightseeing is often an important part of the traveler's vacation. Even "independent types," who usually go it alone, find sightseeing bus tours one of the best ways to get oriented to a new city or area. The most familiar of the sightseeing bus companies is the *Gray Line*, actually an association of independent companies that coöperate with each other to make more than 11,000 motor coaches available all over the country for tours, circuits, and excursions of from 2 to 10 hours duration every day of the week. Gray Line and *American Sightseeing International* offer tours in virtually every major city and tourist area in the country. You may even get to ride on something else when you take your bus jaunt. Here are some examples from Gray Line: take a five-hour trip in New Mexico, and ride on the longest tramway in the western hemisphere at Sandia Crest; tour the Redwood Forest aboard California's Roaring Camp narrow gauge railroad; ride the giant log flume at Busch Gardens, Los Angeles.

 TRAVELING WITH CHILDREN. If the children are very young or the trip is a long one, you may want to have medical and dental checkups before your departure. The doctor may also want to advise special prescriptions or feeding formulas that should be taken along.

Minor medical problems can easily be handled with a good first-aid kit. Include the standard contents as recommended by the Red Cross, any special prescriptions required, spare glasses, a cough syrup, a stomachache remedy, a laxative, children's aspirin, an opthalmic ointment, and antidiarrheal tablets (they travel more safely than the liquid). One of the greatest triumphs of medical science, as far as traveling is concerned, is the individually packaged gauze pad pretreated with antiseptic and a mild local anesthetic (such as Clean and Treat, made by Pharmaco, Inc.). These are ideal for cleaning up the scrapes and scratches children are prone to. A tube of zinc oxide is a versatile aid for sun and wind burn, diaper rash, and minor abrasions. The dosage and directions for all medicines should be checked with the physician before departure. Pack the kit in a small shoulder bag so it can easily be kept handy.

The itinerary itself should take the youngsters into consideration. Because children's "biological clocks" are more finely tuned than adults', long trips should be divided into short segments to allow the children to adjust to time-zone changes. This also decreases the period of time in which children can repeat the age-old question "Are we there yet?"

In your sightseeing, try to include something of interest to children. Public parks, zoos, amusement parks are perfect child-pleasers and often have special attractions for the kids. Beaches, circuses, forts, and aquariums also make big hits with tiny tourists. Many hotels and motels have baby-sitting services, day-care centers, playrooms, cribs and baby carriages to make things easier for the traveling family.

Tours and excursions for children should allow as much freedom as possible. Probably the ideal (though certainly not the only) way for a family with young children to travel would be in their own auto on their own schedule. Conveniently located camping sites offer children the space and freedom not found in hotels. Whenever possible, children should be able to set their own pace. A tightly scheduled and confined tour of more than a half-day's length is generally too restrictive.

Packing for children requires a little extra effort. Clothing should be as simple, comfortable, and versatile as possible. Wash-and-wear and stain-resistant fabrics will make life easier. One of the handiest items is a box of small premoistened towelettes for impromptu clean-ups of hands and face. If a child is not yet a good walker, it is a good idea to pack him too—in one of the back carriers that allows a parent to carry the child while keeping his own hands free or take along a collapsible stroller.

The times which try parents' and progenies' souls alike usually occur at the scores of times each day when the family is waiting for a plane, waiting for a meal to be served, waiting for everyone else to get ready to leave for an outing. The solution is deceptively simple: toys. A few small cars, a mini-doll, small notebooks and pencils, small puzzles and games could be kept on reserve in pocket or purse ready to be produced if boredom rears its ugly head. Easily portable collections of stamps, coins, jacket emblems, seashells, or minerals can also serve this purpose.

Hunger pangs have a way of striking children at the exact moment when food is not available. An offering of small snacks can help keep sunny dispositions from clouding.

In the end, of course, it is impossible to plan for every situation which may arise; indeed, the unpredictability of children is part of the charm of traveling with them. A little imagination on your part can turn an otherwise trying situation into a game. And however inconvenient and ill-timed their demands can be, children bring to traveling a freshness and sense of discovery that can make even the most hardened traveler alive to the places they visit.

HINTS TO HANDICAPPED TRAVELERS. One of the newest, and largest, groups to enter the travel scene is the handicapped, literally millions of people who are in fact physically able to travel and who do so enthusiastically when they know that they can move about in safety and comfort. Generally their tours parallel those of the non-handicapped traveler, but at a more leisurely pace, and with all the logistics carefully checked out in advance. Four important sources of information in this field are: 1) the book, *Access to the World: A Travel Guide for the Handicapped,* by Louise Weiss, available from Facts on File, 460 Park Ave. S., New York, N.Y. 10016; 2) the *Travel Information Center,* Moss Rehabilitation Hospital, 12th Street and Tabor Road, Philadelphia, Pa. 19141; 3) *Easter Seal Society for Crippled Children and Adults,* Director of Information and Education Service, 2023 West Ogden Ave., Chicago, Ill. 60612; 4) *Rehabili-*

tation International USA, 1123 Broadway, New York, N.Y. 10010. In Britain, there are *Mobility International,* 62 Union St., London SE1 (tel. 403–5688); and *The Royal Association for Disability and Rehabilitation,* 25 Mortimer St., London W1. (tel. 637–5400).

The President's Commission on Employment of the Handicapped, along with the Easter Seal Society, has put together a series of guide books for every major city in the United States and a special book called *Guide to the National Parks and Monuments.* Each book lists only those places that are reasonably accessible to the handicapped or are so well known that information is frequently requested. The Commission has also issued a guide to over 330 roadside rest area facilities considered "barrier free" for the disabled. Write to the Commission at Washington, D.C. 20210.

Lists of commercial tour operators who arrange or conduct tours for the handicapped are available from the *Society for the Advancement of Travel for the Handicapped,* 26 Court St., Brooklyn, New York 11242. For more information and a catalog of the books available write to the Easter Seal Society. The Greyhound Bus system has special assistance for handicapped travelers; International Air Transport Association (IATA) publishes a free pamphlet entitled *Incapacitated Passengers' Air Travel Guide.* Write IATA, 2000 Teel Street, Montreal, Quebec H3A 2R4. For rail travel, see *Access Amtrak,* a 16-page booklet published by the national railway passenger corporation.

 HOTELS AND MOTELS. *General hints.* Don't take potluck for lodgings. You'll waste a lot of time hunting for a place, and often you won't be happy with what you finally get. If you don't have reservations, begin looking early in the afternoon. If you do have reservations (but expect to arrive later than five or six P.M.), advise the hotel or motel in advance and/or "guarantee" your night's stay by charging it to a major credit card in advance. Some places will not otherwise hold reservations after six P.M. and if you hope to get a room at the hotel's *minimum* rates, be sure to reserve ahead or arrive early.

If you are planning to stay in a popular resort in season, reserve well in advance. Include a deposit. Most chains or associated motels and hotels publish directories of their memberships and will make advance reservations for you at affiliated hostelries along your route.

A number of hotels and motels have one-day laundry and dry-cleaning services, and many motels have coin laundries. Most motels, but not all, have telephones in the rooms. If you want to be sure of room service, however, better stay at a hotel. Many motels, even some in the heart of large cities, have swimming pools, as do many beachfront hotels.

Free parking is assumed at motels, motor hotels, country and resort hotels; you must pay for parking at most city hotels, though certain establishments have free parking, frequently for occupants of higher-than-minimum-rate rooms.

Baby sitter lists are always available in good hotels and motels, and cribs for the children are always on hand, usually at minimal cost. Cots to supplement the beds in your room also will involve a minimal cost. Better hotels and motels generally add a moderate charge for moving an extra single bed into a room.

Hotel and Motel Chains. In addition to the hundreds of independent hotels and motels throughout the country, there also are many that belong to national or regional chains. A major advantage of these chains is the ease of making reservations en route, or at one fell swoop in advance. If you are a guest at a member hotel or motel, the management will be delighted to secure you a sure booking at one of its affiliated hotels at no costs to you. Chains also usually have toll-free WATS (800) lines to assist you in making reservations on your own, saving you time, worry and money. In addition, the chains publish directories giving detailed information on all their members so that you can, if you prefer this style of travel, plan your entire trip ahead with great precision, albeit less flexibility. Request free copies either through your nearest member motel or by the chain's WATS line. The insistence on uniform standards of comfort, cleanliness and amenities is more common in motel than in hotel chains. (Easy to understand when you realize that most hotel chains are formed by buying up older, established hotels while most motel chains have control of their units from start to finish). However, individuality can be one of the great charms of a hotel.

Some travelers prefer independent motels and hotels because they are more likely to reflect the genuine character of the surrounding area. There are several aids to planning available in this sphere. The *Hotel and Motel Redbook,* published annually by the American Hotel and Motel Association, 888 Seventh Ave., New York, N.Y. 10019, covers the entire world; *Hotel and Travel Index* is published quarterly by Ziff-Davis, 1 Park Ave., New York, N.Y. 10016. Both are expensive, so best consulted at your travel agent's office. On a more modest scale, the AAA supplies, *to its members only,* regional *Tour Books* that list those establishments recommended by the Association. The *Travel Guides* published by Rand McNally & Co. with the Mobil Oil Corporation list independent local accommodations, some of them inexpensive. Members of the *NRTA/AARP Motoring Plan* can get a certain amount of local information through this organization. For the traveler interested in the best in individualized service and in local color and tradition, we recommend the books *Country Inns and Back Roads, North America* and *Bed and Breakfast, American Style,* both by Norman T. Simpson, published by Harper and Row, 10 E. 53rd St., New York, NY 10022, under the Berkshire Traveler Press imprint.

Since the single biggest expense of your whole trip will be lodging, you may well be discouraged at the prices of some hotel and motel rooms, particularly when you know that you are paying for things that you neither need nor want, such as a heated swimming pool, wall-to-wall carpeting, a huge color TV set, two huge double beds for only two people, meeting rooms, a cocktail lounge, maybe even a putting green. Nationwide, motel prices for two people now average $40 a night; hotel prices run from $60–$90 with the average around $70. This explains the recent rapid spread of a number of chains of budget motels whose rates average $20 for a single and $25 for a double, an advantage that needs no further comment. These are listed in detail below.

Hotel and Motel Categories

Hotels and motels in this guidebook are divided into five categories, arranged primarily by price, but also take into consideration the degree of comfort you can expect to enjoy, the amount of service you can anticipate, and the atmosphere which will surround you in the establishment of your choice. Failure to include certain establishments in our lists does not mean they are not worthwhile—they were omitted only for lack of space.

Although the names of the various hotel and motel categories are standard, *the prices listed under each category will vary widely. Regionally* speaking, the Northeast is the most expensive part of the country, followed by the Mid-Atlantic states, the Midwest, the South Central states, the Plains and Far West, and the Southeast, in that order. Within a region prices vary: Mississippi is cheaper than Florida; Maine is cheaper than New York. Prices vary within a state: Syracuse will be cheaper than New York City. Average prices vary between chains; among the national (non-budget) motel chains, the upper price range is occupied by Hilton, Marriott and Sheraton; the middle range includes Holiday Inns, Howard Johnson, Quality Inns, and TraveLodge; and the least expensive are generally Best Western, Ramada, and Rodeway (mostly in the South). Even within a given chain prices may vary startlingly: a Ramada Inn in one city may charge $24 for a double while one in another city in the same region asks $40. A Holiday Inn in one city may ask $28 for what is $90 in one elsewhere. Thus, as you travel you will have to apply any system of classifications on an ad hoc basis wherever you stop. *In every case, however, the dollar ranges for each category used in this book are clearly stated before each listing of establishments.*

Note: In some instances, prices reflect a certain number of meals. *Full American Plan* (FAP) includes three meals daily. *Modified American Plan* (MAP) automatically means breakfast and dinner. *Continental Plan* (CP) offers European style breakfast (roll or croissant and tea or coffee). *European Plan* (EP) means no meals are included in the price quoted.

Super Deluxe: In addition to offering all the amenities discussed under the deluxe category (below), the super deluxe hotel has a special atmosphere of glamor, good taste, and dignity. It will probably be a favored meeting spot of local society, as well as world-famed personalities. In short, super deluxe means the tops in services and expense.

Deluxe: Minimum facilities must include bath and shower in all rooms, valet and laundry service, available suites, a well-appointed restaurant and a bar (local law permitting), room service, TV and telephone in room, air conditioning and/or heat, pleasing decor, and an atmosphere of luxury, calm and elegance.

There should be ample and personalized service. In a deluxe motel, there may be less service rendered by employees and more by machine or automation (such as refrigerators and ice-making machines in your room), but there should be a minimum of do-it-yourself in a truly deluxe establishment.

Expensive: All rooms must have bath or shower, valet and laundry service, restaurant and bar (local law permitting), limited room service, TV and telephone in room, heat and/or air conditioning, and a pleasing decor. Hotels and motels in this category are frequently designed for commercial travelers or for families in a hurry and are somewhat impersonal in terms of service. Valet and laundry service will probably be lacking; the units will be outstanding primarily for their convenient location and functional character, not for their attractive or comfortable qualities.

Moderate: Each room should have an attached bath or shower, TV available, telephone in room, heat and/or air conditioning, relatively convenient location, clean and comfortable rooms. Motels in this category may not have attached bath or shower, may not have a restaurant or coffee shop (though one is usually nearby), and may have no public rooms to speak of.

Inexpensive: Nearby bath or shower, telephone available, and clean rooms are the minimum.

In the last few years, the soaring prices of hotel and motel accommodations have given rise to a number of chains of budget motels. A few of these are nationwide, most of them are still regional. However, as their prices, in 1985, average $25–30 for a double, their advantage over ordinary hotels and motels is obvious. Grouped by region, they are as follows. (The addresses and phone numbers of the central offices which supply free directories are given with the first listings.)

Nationwide: *Budget Host Inns,* Box 10656, Fort Worth, Texas 76114, (817) 626–7064; *Friendship Inns International,* 739 South 4th W., Salt Lake City, Utah 84101, (800) 453–4511 (out of state), (800) 438–5400 (in Utah). *Western 6 Motels,* 2020 Delavina, P.O. Box 3070, Santa Barbara, Calif. 93130–3070; (805) 687–3383. *Scottish Inns of America,* 1152 Spring St., Atlanta, Ga. 30309, (800) 251–1962.

New England: *Suisse Chalet International,* Chalet Drive, Rt. 101, Wilton, N.H. 03086, (800) 258–1980; *Econo-Travel Motor Hotel Corp.,* 6135 Park Road, Suite 200, Charlotte, N.C. 28210–9981, (800) 368–7283.

Mid-Atlantic (incl. N.Y. and N.J.): *Econo-Travel; Imperial 400 National, Inc.,* 1000 Wilson Blvd., Suite 820, Arlington, Va. 22209, (800) 368–4400; *Thr-rift Inns, Ltd.,* P.O. Box 2699, Newport News, Va. 23602, (800) 446–1066.

Southeast: *Coachlight Inns,* Route 5, Box 208, Tyler, Texas 75706, (214) 882–6145; *Days Inns of America,* 2751 Buford Highway NE, Atlanta, Ga. 30324, (800) 325–2525; *Econo-Travel; Family Inns of America,* Box 10, Pigeon Forge, Tenn. 37863, (615) 522–7373, (800) 251–9752 (out of Tenn.), (800) 332–9909 (in Tenn.). *Imperial 400; La Quinta Motor Inns,* P.O. Box 32064, San Antonio, Texas 78216, (800) 531–5900.

Midwest: *Days Inns; Econo-Travel; Exel Inns of America,* 4706 East Washington Ave., Madison, Wisc. 53704, (608) 241–5271; (800) 362–5478 (in Wisc.), (800) 356–8013 (out of state); *Family Inns of America; Friendship Inns,* 739 South 4th West, Salt Lake City, Utah 84101, (800) 453–4511; *Imperial 400; Interstate Inns,* Box 760, Kimball, Neb. 69145, (308) 235–4616; *La Quinta; L-K Restaurants & Motels, Inc.,* 1125 Ellen Kay Drive, Marion, Ohio 43302, (614) 387–0300, (800) 282–5711 (in Ohio), (800) 848–5767 (out of Ohio). *Red Roof Inns,* 4355 Davidson Rd., Hillard, Ohio 43026–9699, (614) 876–3200, (800) 848–7878. *Regal 8 Inns,* Box 1268, Mount Vernon, Ill. 62864, (618) 242–7240; (800) 851–8888; *Super 8 Motels,* Box 4090, Aberdeen SD 57401, (800) 843–1991.

Southwest: *Coachlight Inns; Days Inns; Friendship Inns; Imperial 400; Interstate; La Quinta, Mission Valley West Travel Lodge,* 1631 Hotel Circle S, San Diego, Calif. 92108, (619) 293–7792, (800) 255–3050; *Regal 8.*

Rockies and Plains: *Econ-O-Tel of America,* I29 and 13 Ave. S., Fargo, N. D. 58103, (701) 282–6300, (800) 641–1000 (out of N.D.), (800) 472–1000 (in N.D.) *Friendship Inns; Imperial 400; Interstate; La Quinta; Magic Key; Regal 8;* and *Super 8.*

Far West: *California 6; Imperial 400; Magic Key; Penny Lodge; Regal 8;* and *Super 8.*

Senior Citizens may in some cases receive special discounts on lodgings. *The Days Inn* chain offers various discounts to anyone 55 or older. *Holiday Inns* give a discount to members of the NRTA (write to National Retired Teachers Association, Membership Division, 215 Long Beach Blvd, Long Beach, Ca. 90801) and the AARP (write to American Association of Retired Persons, Membership Division, 215 Long Beach Blvd., Long Beach, Calif. 90801). *Howard Johnson's Motor Lodges, Marriott, Quality Inns, Ramada Inns, Rodeway Inns, Sheraton,* and *Treadway Inns* (a New England chain) are chains which have offered varying discounts to members of AARP and other Senior Citizens' organizations; however, the amounts and availability of these discounts change so it is wise to check their latest status. The *National Council of Senior Citizens,* 925 15th St. NW, Washington, D.C. 20005, works especially to develop low-cost travel possibilities for its members.

Increasingly popular throughout the country but especially in New England and the Northwest since the mid-1970s are European-style country inns. Reliable sources are Norman T. Simpson's *Country Inns and Back Roads, North America,* and *Bed and Breakfast, American Style* (Harper & Row, 10 E. 53 St., New York, N.Y. 10022). In popular tourist areas, state or local tourist information offices or chambers of commerce usually have lists of homes that let out spare rooms to paying guests, and such a listing usually means that the places on it have been inspected and meet some reliable standard of cleanliness, comfort, and reasonable pricing. Their rates are generally under $20 per night for two persons. One of the most reliable listings is *Bed and Breakfast U.S.A.: A Guide to Guest Houses and Tourist Homes,* published by Tourist House Associates of America, Inc., RD2, Box 355A, Greentown, Pa. 18426 ($7.85 plus 63¢ postage). Also helpful: *Bed & Breakfast Registry,* Box 8174, St. Paul, MN 55108, (612) 646-4238, is a nationwide bed-and-breakfast reservation service. Nightly charges vary greatly, running $20–$150/night. *INNter Lodging,* Box 7044, Tacoma, WA 94807, 206–756–0343, is a cooperative in which members offer rooms in their own homes but are thereby entitled to the same from other members. Nightly charges are $4 to $5 per adult per night; breakfast is extra.

In larger towns and cities a good bet for clean, plain, reliable lodging is a YMCA or YWCA. These buildings are usually centrally located, and their rates tend to run to less than half of those of hotels. Non-members are welcome, but may pay slightly more than members. A few very large Ys may have accommodations for couples, but usually the sexes are segregated. Decor is spartan and the cafeteria fare plain and wholesome, but a definite advantage is the use of the building's pool, gym, reading room, information services, and other facilities. For a directory, write to: *YMCA of the U.S.A.,* 101 N. Wacker Dr., Chicago, IL 60606.

ROUGHING IT. More, and improved, **camping** facilities are springing up each year across the country, in national parks, national forests, state parks, in private camping areas, and trailer parks, which by now have become national institutions.

Farm vacations continue to gain adherents, especially among families with children. Some are quite deluxe, some extremely simple. For a directory of farms which take vacationers (including details of rates, accommodations, dates, etc.) write to *Adventure Guides, Inc.,* 36 East 57 St., New York, N.Y. 10022 for their book *Farm, Ranch & Country Vacations.* Their other directory, *Adventure Travel,* gives details on guided wilderness trips, backpacking, canoeing, rock climbing, covered wagon treks, scuba diving, and more. The directories are available for $10.50 each, postpaid, fourth class mail, or $12 each, first class. Around the country, 22 local offices of the Department of Agriculture supply information on farms in their areas. For the list itself, write to: Special Reports Division, Office of Governmental and Public Affairs, Room 460-A, United States Department of Agriculture, Washington, D.C. 20250.

Because of the great size of the United States, the distances involved, and the consequent dominance of private automobiles, **Youth Hostels** have not developed in this country the way they have in Europe and Japan. In the entire 3½ million square miles of the U.S. there are upwards of 200 Youth Hostels, most of them in the compact areas that are New England and the Mid-Atlantic states. Other groupings are in Michigan, Ohio, central Colorado, and around Puget Sound in Washington. Elsewhere, not much. As they are, in any case, designed primarily for people who are traveling under their own power, usually hiking or bicycling, rather than by car or commercial transportation, they tend to be away from towns and cities and in rural areas, near scenic spots. Of equal interest with their possibilities as inexpensive lodgings are the conducted group hiking and bicycle tours that the American Youth Hostel Association offers. These vary from year to year, of course. For up-to-date information write to: *American Youth Hostels, Inc.,* 1332 I St., N.W., 8th Floor, Wash., D.C. 20005; or, 132 Spring St., New York, N.Y. 10012. Although the membership is mainly younger people, there is no age limit. Membership fees: under 18—$10; 18 and over—$20. You must be a member to use Youth Hostels; a copy of the Hostel Guide and Handbook will be included in your membership. (Since 1979, the *Handbook* for the U.S. has been commercially available in bookstores as well.) Accommodations are simple, dormitories are segregated for men and women, common rooms and kitchen are shared, and everyone helps with the cleanup. Lights out 11 P.M. to 7 A.M., no alcohol or other drugs allowed. In season, it is wise to reserve ahead; write or phone directly to the particular hostel you plan to stay in. Rates vary from one hostel to another, but a rough national average is now about $5.00.

The excellent topographical **maps** published by the Federal Government are available in some bookstores and usually in stores handling hiking, camping and backpacking equipment. Failing that, however, for states east of the Mississippi and including Minnesota, write to: Branch of Distribution, United States Geological Survey, 1200 South Eads St., Arlington, Va. 22202. For states west of the Mississippi and including Louisiana, the same agency at P.O. Box 25286, Federal Center, Denver, Colo. 80225.

Useful Addresses: *National Parks Service,* U.S. Dept. of the Interior, Washington, D.C. 20240; *National Forest Service,* P.O. Box 2417, U.S. Dept of Agriculture, Washington, D.C. 20013. For information on state parks, write *State Parks Dept., State Office Building* in the capital of the state in which you are interested.

The National Campers & Hikers Assoc., 7172 Transit Rd., Buffalo, N. Y. 14221. Commercial camping organizations include: *American Camping Assoc., Inc.,* Bradford Woods, Martinsville, Ind. 46151. Also *Kampgrounds of America, Inc.,* P.O. Box 30558, Billings, Mont. 59114. The great popularity of recreational vehicles in the past few years has led to the development of a kind of intermediate level of "camping" which provides an exposure to the great outdoors that is well moderated by Americans' love of comforts and gadgetry. Great numbers of commercial "campgrounds" have appeared to cater to this market, and various directories have appeared to guide campers to them. Here are two, each running to well over 600 pages. *Woodall's Campground Directory,* Woodall Publishing Co., 500 Hyacinth Place, Highland Park, Ill. 60035, distributed by Grosset and Dunlap. Eastern edition and Western edition; *Rand McNally Campground and Trailer Park Guide,* published annually by Rand McNally Co., 10 East 53 St., New York, N.Y. 10022.

 DINING OUT. *General hints.* For large cities, make reservations in advance whenever possible for mid-day and evening meals. In other areas remember that at dinner time most travelers have settled in a particular place for the evening and will quickly fill up the nearby restaurants. Most hotels and farm vacation places have set dining hours. For motel-stayers, life is simpler if the motel has a restaurant, as their hours are more accommodating to early and late traffic.

Although dress standards have become more casual, some restaurants are fussy, especially in the evening. For women, pants and pants suits are now almost universally acceptable. For men, tie and jacket remains the standard, although no longer in the guise of the more formal "suit." Shorts are almost always frowned on for both men and women with the exception of resort establishments, some of which might allow very casual dress at breakfast or lunch meals. If you have any doubt about accepted dress at a particular restaurant, call ahead. At fast-service places, turnpike restaurants, cafeterias, and roadside stands there are no fixed standards of dress. If you're traveling with children, you may want to find out if a restaurant has a children's menu and commensurate prices, as many do.

When figuring the tip on your check, base it *only* on the total charges for the meal, including cocktails and wine, if any. Do *not* tip on any taxes there may be.

Restaurant Categories

Restaurants located in large metropolitan areas are categorized in this volume by type of cuisine: French, Chinese, Armenian, etc., with restaurants of a general nature listed as American-International. Restaurants in less populous areas are divided into price categories as follows: *super deluxe, deluxe, expensive, moderate,* and *inexpensive.* As a general rule, expect restaurants in metropolitan areas to be higher in price, although many restaurants that feature foreign cuisine are often surprisingly inexpensive. Our price categories, unless otherwise stated, are for a complete dinner (appetizer or soup, entrée and dessert) but do not include drinks, tax, or tips.

We should also point out that limitations of space make it impossible to include every establishment. We have, therefore, included those which we consider the best within each price range. Also consider that new places are established constantly, and our omission of a worthy one would only indicate an early publication date precluding mention.

Although the names of the various restaurant categories are standard in this volume, *the prices listed under each category may vary from area to area.* This is meant to reflect local price standards, and take into account the fact that what might be considered a moderate price in a large urban area might be quite expensive in a rural region. *In every case, however, the dollar ranges for each category are clearly stated before each listing of establishments.*

Super deluxe: This category indicates lavish decoration, glamorous atmosphere, comfort, excellent service, immaculate kitchens, and a large, well-trained staff. (Such places sometimes turn out to be overpriced and overrated, unfortunately). Perhaps a *nationwide average price per person,* excluding the above-mentioned extras, for a typical roast beef (prime ribs) dinner at a restaurant in this category *will run around $30*—maybe lower, and maybe even higher.

Deluxe: Many a fine restaurant around the country falls into this category. It will have its own well-deserved reputation for excellence, perhaps a house specialty or two for which it is famous, and an atmosphere of comfort, elegance, attentive service, perhaps unique decor. It will have a good wine list where the law permits, and will be considered the best in town by the inhabitants.
Nationwide average price: $20 up.

Expensive: Restaurants in this category will have a general reputation for very good food, and in addition to the expected dishes, will offer one or two house specialties. They will have wine lists and serve cocktails (where the law permits). They also will have an adequate staff, air conditioning (when needed), elegant decor, and attract appropriately dressed clientele.
Nationwide average price: $15 up.

Moderate: This category is indicative of a general reputation for good, wholesome food. Restaurants will have clean kitchens, adequate staff, better-than-average service, and air conditioning (when needed). They also will serve cocktails and/or beer where the law permits.
Nationwide average price: $10 up.

Inexpensive: This is the bargain place in town. It will be clean, even if plain. It will have, when necessary, air conditioning, tables (not a counter), a clean kitchen, and will make an attempt to provide adequate service.
Nationwide average price: under $10.

Budget Chains: *Inexpensive* to *Moderate.* There are now a number of restaurant chains, some nationwide, others regional, some of the crudest and most minimal fast-food type, others offering restaurant service and amenities, most of them having fixed and fairly limited menus, but all at budget prices. Often for the same, or less, money you can do much better in a grocery or delicatessen by buying the makings for a picnic (where, after all, you save 15% on the tip!). This much said, here are some suggestions for restaurants, and cafeterias, that can save you money. When you arrive in a place, look in the phone book under the names given below.

Nationwide: *Far West Services* (individual restaurants are usually named *Moonraker* or *Plankhouse;* most numerous in California; lunch is a better bargain than dinner); *Holiday Inns* (for their all-you-can-eat buffets); *Mr. Steak* (children's rates, Senior Citizens discounts, various specials); *Red Barn Restaurants; Red Lobster Inns; Sambo's Restaurants; Sheraton Hotels* (for their all-you-can-eat buffets); *Village Inn Pancake Houses* (try their other dishes, too).
Southeast: *Admiral Benbow's; Morrison's Cafeterias;*

Midwest: *Bishop's Buffets and Cafeterias; Bob Evans Farm Restaurants;*
Southwest and West: *Luby's and Romano's Cafeterias; Pancho's Mexican Buffets; Wyatt Cafeterias.*

NIGHTLIFE. In the large cities the problem is never what to do in the evening but how to choose. Whether you like theater, music, dance or the cinema, famous performers or undiscovered talent, ornate and multi-tiered opera houses, or the bare walls and wooden seats of a tiny cabaret, the city inevitably offers something to suit your taste. To find out what's going on in a city consult the local papers or entertainment magazines.

Outside the big cities, abundant entertainment is still available, at least in the on-season, in those regions that cater to tourists. Big-name shows and performers are often scheduled for the summer months. But in a small town or during the off-season, the problem of finding something to do may be more acute. You'll certainly not have a wide range of choices. Local festivals, larger rodeos, state fairs, and the like, may have entertainment associated with them; but most often nightlife in a small town, if it exists at all, is confined to the weekends and consists of the motel lounge or roadhouse-with-a-bandstand-in-the-corner variety. Your desk clerk or local residents are probably the best sources of information about what's going on.

DRINKING LAWS. These vary from state to state, and there are sometimes differences between the individual counties of the same state. In general, however, you must be at least 18 years of age to buy or drink alcohol, although some states require that you be at least 21. Wine and hard liquor are rarely sold in package stores on Sundays, holidays, or after midnight any day; Nevada is a notable exception.

Some states prohibit the sale of mixed drinks; you may, however, bring your own bottle to a restaurant or club and they will supply glasses, ice, and mix. Some states which prohibit the sale of mixed drinks in public bars permit private clubs to do so. Often you can join these clubs on the spot for the price of your first drink, which you then get free. Unfortunately, these clubs can be difficult to locate without the benefit of an informed local guide. Sometimes liquor is not for sale at all—in locales known as "dry" areas—and sometimes only beer and/or wine are available.

Most bars close at the hours set by state law; there are, however, after-hours clubs where you can drink when the regular bars have closed, that is, in states which permit after-hours clubs. On the whole, then, drinking laws are complex and sometimes confusing, so your best bet is to consult the rules which apply to each state separately. Also, penalties for drunk driving are becoming increasingly severe and more strictly enforced; random checks of drivers on major thoroughfares have been instituted in many states.

SUMMER SPORTS. *New England's* 500-mile-long ragged coast provides abundant opportunity for many kinds of boating and excellent, if sometimes chilly, swimming. For the fisherman, there is everything from surf-casting to deep-sea fishing. The inland waters offer boating, canoeing, swimming, water skiing, and, of course, freshwater fishing. Hiking, mountain climbing, and horseback riding are popular ways to take in the region's beauty. And there are golf courses throughout.

In *New York and New Jersey,* you'll find yachting in Long Island Sound and body surfing along the Atlantic Coast, golf, especially at Great Gorge, and hiking in the hills and mountains. Fishermen take to the lakes, rivers, and streams or go out to sea. And hunters track down big and small game. For spectators there is New York's favorite baseball team, the Yankees, and thoroughbred and harness racing.

The lakes and golden beaches found in much of the *South* invite the swimmer, waterskier, skin- and scuba diver. Tennis and golf are played virtually everywhere. All forms of boating are popular including sailing. Freshwater fishermen take to lakes, rivers, and streams, while sailwater enthusiasts cast in the surf or fish the deep seas. For the spectator there is plenty of thoroughbred and harness racing, greyhound or stockcar races. And in Florida there is the excitement of *jai alai,* the lethally fast Basque version of handball, played nowhere else in the country (except Bridgeport, Conn.).

Lake Erie's beaches, the Atlantic coast, and the lakes, rivers, and streams throughout the *mid-Atlantic* states provide ample opportunity for the water sport enthusiast and fisherman. Crabbing and clamming are popular in some areas. Hikers take the famous Appalachian Trail, a strenuous footpath which runs from Maine to Florida, or less demanding walks through the lush hills. Golf courses and tennis courts are everywhere. Spectators have thoroughbred races, horse shows, and major league baseball.

The Great Lakes and the Missouri and Mississippi rivers make boating of all types, including sailing, a popular pastime of the *Midwest.* And where there is water, there are sure to be swimmers and water-skiers. In gentle streams and quiet ponds anglers look to take a variety of freshwater fish, and there are several fisherman's dude ranches. Others take to the outdoors on golf courses, tennis courts, or the backs of horses.

In the *Rockies and Plains,* the water sport enthusiast takes to the lakes and reservoirs, the swimmer to the hot springs, the fisherman to the rivers and streams, and the canoer, kayaker, and rafter to the white-water rapids. The rugged mountains offer plenty of opportunity for hiking, backpacking, climbing, or horseback riding. Recalling the frontier heritage, rodeo is the most pervasive of spectator sports, attracting national champions. Golf and tennis are available in nearly every major city and resort.

The *Southwest's* lakes and the Gulf of Mexico offer excellent swimming, water-skiing, boating, and even sailing. Freshwater fishing lures literally millions to rivers and giant lakes, and sailfish and tarpon swim the deep seas of the Gulf. Sportscar racing, bullfighting (just over the border in Mexico), horse shows, and, of course, rodeos draw crowds of cheering spectators.

All along the coast of the *Far West* you'll find every variety of water sport and, in the north, clam digging. Inland there is golfing, swimming, boating, tennis, backpacking, rock-hounding, freshwater fishing, rafting down turbulent rivers, and panning for gold. You can even ski year-round on Mt. Hood in Oregon and into July in some areas of Washington. For the spectator there is thoroughbred and greyhound racing.

WINTER SPORTS. To many, *New England* has almost become synonymous with skiing. Facilities for both downhill and cross-country are excellent and widespread. With skiing has come the resurgence of ice-skating, particularly in well-lighted rinks at night. Snowmobiling, ice-fishing, even sled dog-racing are included in the region's winter activities. In the late fall, hunters come to stalk big and small game with rifle or bow and arrow.

New York and New Jersey have many ski areas, not the least of which is Lake Placid in upstate New York. There are seasons for big and small game, and archery certificates are available if you want to give the animals a better chance. *New York Jets & Giants* football and *Knickerbockers* basketball attract thousands of devoted fans.

Skiers in the *mid-Atlantic* states head for the Pocono and Allegheny mountains of Pennsylvania, though even Virginia and West Virginia are not without slopes. Frozen lakes invite ice-boating and ice-fishing. Large and small game, waterfowl, even exotic birds await the hunter. And the spectator can thrill to professional football and basketball, and horse and auto racing.

In the *South,* where winters are less cold, fishermen are still out for both freshwater and saltwater varieties, and hunters bag big and small game. Even midwinter swimming, water-skiing, and skin-diving are possible. Spectators can choose from among rodeos, stockcar races (including Daytona and Sebring), greyhound and thoroughbred racing, horse shows, and even jai alai and polo. Football, especially the New Year's Day Bowl games, captures the attention of many.

Except in Iowa, skiing is available in the *Midwest,* and ice-skating and tobogganing are popular wherever there is a frozen pond or snow-covered hill. The hunter can go after large and small game; along the Mississippi Flyway duck hunting is exceptional. Basketball, college and professional football, and winter carnivals entertain spectators throughout the season.

The spectator in the *Southwest* can enjoy basketball, football, bowl games, thoroughbred racing, and polo matches and horse shows. Hunters look to bag small game and birds. Swimming in heated pools runs later than usual, and deep-sea fishermen go after record catches in the temperate Gulf. Taos, New Mexico, is one of the finest and most challenging ski areas in the country, and there is good skiing near Albuquerque and Santa Fe.

Skiing is without a doubt the major winter sport of the *Rocky Mountain* area. New facilities continue to be developed. Ski touring or cross-country skiing has become increasingly popular, and more and more people take up the sport of snowmobiling. Ice-skating, on frozen ponds or lakes or in year-'round rinks, has its share of enthusiasts. Hunters in this region go out for large and small game and a variety of fowl.

The mountains that run throughout the *Far West* ensure an abundance of skiing, and there are hundreds of well-developed facilities. Ice-skating is popular and more readily available as you go farther north. For something unusual, you might look into the old Scottish favorite curling, now practiced in Alaska.

In Southern California even the primarily summer sports of golf, tennis, water-skiing, swimming, and surfing are practiced year-round.

Entertainment for the spectator includes professional football, basketball, and ice hockey, as well as rodeos and horse shows.

CHURCHES AND OTHER PLACES OF WORSHIP. For information about the location of the church, synagogue, or other place of worship of your choice and the hours of services, masses, or prayer, consult either the local newspaper, or the desk clerk at your hotel. He should also be able to tell you what is available in the immediate neighborhood and throughout the city.

Although you may not be interested in the religious services themselves, there are hundreds of churches throughout the United States that are of historical or architectural interest. Temple Square in Salt Lake City, the Vatican of the Mormons, is one such example. The Temple itself is closed to all but Mormons in good standing, but the Tabernacle is open, and the famous choir performs during Sunday services. Throughout California and the Southwest the Spanish left a trail of missions as evidence of their influence upon the religion and architecture of the region. Similarly, the Puritans left their mark on New England in the form of white, often austere meetinghouses and churches. Many of these remain and are outstanding examples of early American architecture. In smaller towns, particularly in the Midwest, different Protestant sects have competed on occasion to build the grandest church, frequently on opposite sides of the same street, or on opposite corners of an intersection. Their positions often tell you much about their sects' standings in the community.

MAIL. Stamps can be purchased at any post office in the United States, often from your hotel desk, or from coin-operated vending machines located in transportation terminals, banks, and some shops (stationers and drugstores, for example). They cost a little more if you get them from a machine—you pay for packaging and convenience—so for the sake of economy you may wish to buy as many as you think you will need when you find a handy post office. Postal rates are listed in the table below.

Post offices are usually open from 9 A.M. (0900 hours) to 5 P.M. (1700 hours), Monday through Friday, and until noon on Saturday. They are closed on national holidays. Substations and branch offices in the bigger cities observe the same hours, but the main central post office is often open 24 hours a day.

Stamped mail can be posted in the letter drops at the post office, in the letter chutes of some hotels and office buildings, in the red-white-and-blue mailboxes on many street corners, or you may leave it with your hotel desk, which will take care of posting it for you.

If you expect to receive mail while traveling, you can have it addressed to you in care of your hotel(s). If you don't know where you'll be staying, you can have mail from home sent to you at the main post office, in care of General Delivery, as, for example: Your Name, c/o General Delivery, Main Post Office, Miami, Florida, USA. All General Delivery mail must be collected in person, and you will be asked to show identification.

POSTAGE. There is no separate Air Mail rate for letters or postcards posted in the United States for delivery within the country or to Canada. Mail for distant points is automatically airlifted. The following are the postal rates in effect as of early 1985:

	Letters	Postcards
United States and Canada	22¢ 1st oz.	14¢
Mexico		
Air Mail	22¢ 1st oz.	14¢
Surface Mail	22¢ 1st oz.	14¢
*Overseas		
Air to Europe	40¢ 1st ½ oz.	28¢
Air to Central America and Caribbean	35¢ 1st ½ oz.	19¢
Air to most other countries	40¢ 1st ½ oz.	28¢
Surface to Europe	30¢ 1st oz.	19¢
Surface to Central and South America	30¢ 1st oz.	19¢
Surface to most other countries	30¢ 1st oz.	19¢
Air Letter Forms to all countries	30¢	

*All are subject to change.

TELEPHONE. Coin-operated public telephones are available almost everywhere: in hotel lobbies, transportation terminals, drugstores, department stores, restaurants, gasoline filling stations, in sidewalk booths, and along the highway. To use the coin telephone, just follow the instructions on the phone box. Local calls usually cost 10 to 25 cents and can be dialed directly. If you don't reach your party, your money is refunded to you automatically when you hang up.

For long-distance calls, dial "0" (zero) and have plenty of coins available, or ask to have the call charged to your home telephone (U.S.A. only; someone must be home to accept the charges.) The operator may ask for enough change to cover the initial time period before she connects you. Often a "1" must be dialed before the area code; check the directions on the phone. To place a call outside the United States, dial "0" and ask for the overseas operator.

In hotels, your switchboard operator will either place your outside call for you, or tell you how to dial directly from your room. The telephone charges will be added to your hotel bill (although many times local calls are free) and you will pay for them when you check out.

TELEGRAPH. To send a telegram to a destination anywhere within the United States, ask for assistance at your hotel, or go to the nearest *Western Union* telegraph office. You'll find it listed in the classified section (yellow pages) of the telephone directory under "Telegraph." Overseas cablegrams can also be dispatched by Western Union, or by any cable company (also listed under "Telegraph"). You can phone Western Union and have a telegram charged to your home telephone (U.S.A. only). Mailgrams are similar to telegrams only they are delivered with the following day's mail and cost less than half what is charged for regular telegrams.

NATIONAL PARKS. A vacation unequaled elsewhere in the world is a week or two in one of the 40 national parks that preserve in beauty and naturalness the variety of landscapes and climates that make the United States so fascinating both to lovers of free space and clear air and to all kinds of students of the outdoors. There are glaciers and tropical swamps; volcanic mountains and parched, endless deserts; pounding seacoasts and tranquil rivers; Cliff Dwellers' ruins and geysers and medicinal springs. There are crashing mountain brooks alive with trout and rain forests where herds of elk brush silently through the luminescent yellow-green of heavy foliage. In the parks you can find nearly every kind of physical geography that the world provides—the mysterious sculptures in glowing red and orange and yellow stone of the Utah highlands, the endless vistas of flat grass in the prairies, the giant sequoias and redwoods.

With some 26½ million acres, the National Park Service has within the last half century managed to preserve about one percent of the total American land as it was before the coming of civilization so that future generations will forever have access to some parts of their country that are unfenced, unworked, unsullied by man's incessant urges to profit from his ground, change it, force his will upon it. The goal of the parks, according to former Director Newton B. Drury, is "to conserve them, not for commercial use of their resources, but because of their value in ministering to the human mind and spirit."

In spite of this goal of naturalness—the parks are like living museums that may forever show man how the world was before he and his machines took charge—there is plenty of space in the parks for people and much for them to do without so much as leaving a mark behind them. They hike, and camp out, and cook out, and take pictures, and fish, and study the trees and the flowers. They can study in fossils the passage of earlier living creatures and in some of the parks there are petroglyphs and ceremonial mounds that give intriguing clues to earlier civilizations of man. There is much to be learned on the nature trails—every park has these, clearly marked, sometimes even in braille (blind persons can touch and feel nearby trees and plants as they follow a rope strung along posts beside the path). Visitors centers provide museums displaying what is helpful in understanding the peculiarities of that particular park land; slides and movies do the same thing. You can learn as much or as little as you like.

Or you can just walk out into these open spaces and breathe and open your eyes to the original world taken straight, and then often return to a comfortable rustic lodge with a log fire glowing in a fieldstone fireplace—if it's the season for it. Many parks have bridle trails or pack trips (you can ride a mile down into the Grand Canyon on muleback), and several parks provide river float trips. In summertime, the busy season in most parks, rangers put on frequent programs of informal talks or guided tours. Some of the talks are given at dusk around a communal campfire and provide for many visitors the most memorable moments of their park vacations. Almost all the parks have towns near them that offer accommodations and other tourist needs, but within the borders of the parks you feel as if you could be a thousand miles away from the nearest outpost of that life you've left behind.

NATIONAL MONUMENTS AND OTHER PARK PROPERTY. Although the *national parks* are unquestionably the most important parts of our national trust of scenic wild lands, there is much more territory under the National Park Service administration that is designated as *national monuments, historic parks, national seashores,* and *national recreation areas.* The official distinction between a national park and the other properties is that the former have all been created by Acts of Congress, while the latter were either purchased by the government or deeded to it.

Many of the features of the national parks—visitor centers, campgrounds, ranger-led tours and campfire talks, nature trails and hiking and bridle paths—can also be found in the national monuments and other Federal lands, and many of them, in the opinion of some travelers, equal the national parks in magnificence of natural surroundings or in areas of specific interest.

Almost as impressive in value to the future of the country are the *national forests,* many of which also offer a variety of recreational opportunities. The woodlands cover almost 189 million acres of the country from Puerto Rico to Alaska to Hawaii in 154 national forests, among which a score have visitors centers similar to those of the park service.

For information on national parks, battlefields and recreation areas, write to National Parks Service, Dept. of the Interior, Washington, D.C. 20240. For information on national forests and recreation areas, write to National Forest Service, P.O. Box 2417, U.S. Dept. of Agriculture, Washington, D.C. 20013.

INFORMATION FOR FOREIGN VISITORS

HOW TO GET TO THE UNITED STATES FROM ABROAD. Although **air travel** is considerably quicker than other means, and often less expensive, it's not always easy to arrange these days. Air fares are changing constantly, and the airlines' unceasing efforts to better each other's bargains can turn the simple task of buying an airplane ticket into something difficult, confusing, and ultimately frustrating. To save yourself headaches, it's best to consult a travel agent. They are well-equipped to keep up with the latest offerings, and they charge no fee, their commission paid by the airlines themselves.

However you arrange your flight, here are some things worth keeping in mind. You'll pay the highest fares if you travel during peak summer months, but often less if you go during the off-season. Most airlines offer two basic fares: first class and economy. First class, of course, is the most expensive, often well over three times the cost of others. In return for your investment you get all the on-board amenities the airlines can dole out, including shortened flight time on the Concorde, which sells only first-class tickets. Moreover, first-class tickets are without restrictions; you may book, travel, and change flight plans at any time, and stopover as you wish. Economy cuts back a bit on the luxuries and is less expensive than first class, but still not cheap. Again, there are no restrictions on your travel, though stopovers may cost extra. APEX (Advance Booking Excursion) fares are just about the best bargains available. They offer enormous reductions on the price of a first-class or economy ticket, though there are a number of conditions imposed on you in exchange for the savings. In general, APEX seats are round-trip only, must be booked and paid for 21 days in advance, require a minimum seven-day stay, and once booked cannot be changed.

Other possibilities include package tours, straight charters, and standby. A package tour usually includes an airfare (at a charter price) plus various land arrangements. There are hundreds of different ones offered each year, so the most we can do here is advise you to consult your travel agent for the current offerings. Straight charters give you airfare only and leave you to make your own land arrangements. An excellent guide to these is the book, *How to Fly for Less,* published annually by Travel Information Bureau, 44 County Line Road, Farmingdale, N.Y. 11735, a concise, lucid, and complete survey, analysis and directory of the charter flight business and how to use it to your advantage. At time of writing, the least expensive fares on major carriers must be booked either 21 days in advance, or 2–3 days prior to departure—the latter requiring considerable flexibility on the part of the traveler. One can fly standby, but there is no monetary advantage to doing so. Finally, in the spirit of Freddie Laker, People Express and Virgin Atlantic have inexpensive, regularly scheduled flights between New York and London. People Express also flies between many major U.S. cities.

At international airports you will find exchange facilities and special visitor information booths. We suggest, however, that you try to have about $50 in U.S. currency in small denominations, already on hand when you arrive, as exchange facilities in this country are still far from what they are in Europe and some other parts of the world.

Arrangements for getting from airports into the cities they serve vary; in some cases there is train service, but the choices are usually bus, limousine, and taxi, in that rising order of expense. Unless you have cumbersome baggage, the bus will be cheapest. *Inquire carefully at the airport as to what is available and what it should cost, especially in regard to taxis.* Most drivers are honest, but every so often there is a flagrant abuse; and taxis are expensive in this country anyway. Major car rental companies also maintain services at all international airports. If you want to be assured that there will be a car waiting for you, and if you want to be assured the best rates, particularly on weekends or holidays, you should reserve in advance of your arrival.

By sea. The opportunities to travel by ship across the Atlantic grow fewer and fewer each year. In the past, sea lovers had a choice between ocean liners and freighters. Now, however, the number of ocean liners in service on trans-

Atlantic routes has diminished to one, Cunard's *Queen Elizabeth II,* and the possibilities of freighter travel have dwindled almost as drastically. Nonetheless, the persistent can be rewarded with passage on the rare freighter offering relatively comfortable one-class accommodations for a maximum of 12 people. What they lack in entertainment and refinement these ships make up for by being informal, relaxing, and relatively inexpensive (though flying is almost always cheaper). For details, and current updates on the lines operating, consult either of the following specialists: Air Marine Travel Service, 501 Madison Avenue, New York, N.Y. 10022, publisher of the *Trip Log Quick Reference Freighter Guide;* or *Pearl's Freighter Tips,* 175 Great Neck Road, Great Neck, N.Y. 11021. In England, Pitt and Scott Travel puts out a booklet entitled *Freighter Voyages,* which lists current cruises. Write to Pitt and Scott Travel, Shipping Dept., 3 Cathedral Place, London EC4M 7DT.

Cunard has had ships on the North Atlantic route since 1839. The company's flagship *QEII* now maintains regular service from April to October between Cherbourg (France), Southampton (England), and New York. Fares are subject to change, but are always cheaper off-season than during the peak summer months. Among special promotions are air-sea combination tickets, with Cunard providing service in one direction on the *QEII* and in the other by jet. For more information on other tour programs and special land arrangements contact Cunard, 555 Fifth Avenue, New York, N.Y. 10017 or South Western House, Canute Rd., Southampton S09 1ZA. Royal Viking also has 8–10 day one-way trips to New York or Fort Lauderdale, Florida, departing from Malaga (Spain) and Funchal (Portugal); round-trip passage can be arranged. Deluxe two-bedroom accommodations begin at about $2,200 per person/double occupancy.

By rail. Visitors coming from Canada and Mexico may also enter the United States by rail, bus, or automobile. The National Railroad Passenger Corporation *(Amtrak)* is the principal rail carrier in the United States, operating passenger service to some 500 towns and cities in 44 states. Trains operate on frequent schedules and most are temperature controlled and equipped with dining cars or snack bars. Hand luggage is carried free, as are trunks in the baggage car. Rail terminals in the bigger cities house a wide variety of services, including waiting rooms, information and Travelers Aid centers, restaurants and snack bars, baggage lockers, barber shops, drugstores, newsstands, and public telephones.

From Mexico, the best rail connection is at Nuevo Laredo. Another good one is the Ciudad Juarez/El Paso gateway, where direct connections can be made between *Mexico National Railways* and *Amtrak* trains. For information in the U.S. contact Mexican National Railways, 489 Fifth Ave., New York, NY 10017.

From Canada, you can board *Amtrak* trains directly at Montreal or Vancouver, but connecting services are provided through most major cities along the United States-Canada border.

By bus. Both *Greyhound* and *Continental Trailways,* the two largest motorcoach carriers, offer varied tours and passes including unlimited-travel, fixed-price tickets, and discounts on circle tours. For more details see *America by Bus,* earlier in this chapter, as well as the section on bus travel below.

As with train travel, the best places for visitors *from Mexico* to make direct connections with major domestic bus services are Laredo and El Paso, although connecting service is also available out of Tijuana, Mexicali, Nogales, Ojinaga, Piedras Negras, and Matamoros.

Canadian Visitors will have no difficulty making connections out of Vancouver, Winnipeg, Sault Ste. Marie, Toronto, Ottawa, Montreal, and other border cities.

By car. Arrival by private automobile affords the greatest personal flexibility in entering the United States at your own convenience and offers the additional opportunity to stop wherever, whenever, and however long you wish. Highways are excellent. You may bring your automobile into the United States free of duty for your own personal use. Citizens of most countries may tour in the United States with their own national license plates (registration tags). See *America by Car* section for details.

You may also choose to enter the United States by *private boat* or *plane.* Local air and marine authorities can advise you about the necessary documentation.

PHYSICAL FEATURES. The United States, excluding Alaska, lies between 25° and 50° latitude, or roughly from the northern border of France farther south even than the Pyramids in Egypt. Alaska is as far north as Sweden, Norway, and Finland. Europeans may find it helpful to bear in mind that from New York to Washington, D.C. is about the same distance as from London to Paris, New York to Chicago as from London to Berlin, and New York to Los Angeles farther than from London to Baghdad or from Lisbon to Moscow.

The continent itself is unequally divided by the chain of Rocky Mountains. Often rising over 14,000 feet, these form what is known as the Continental Divide, so called because the waters on one side of the chain flow eastward, those on the other westward. Between these peaks and the Pacific Ocean is a region made up largely of mountains and high plateaus, but the landscape is remarkably varied. In the states bordering the coast, there are rain forests, giant redwoods, glaciers, fiords, active volcanoes, scorching deserts, craggy mountain peaks, deep gorges, and turbulent rivers. In the Southwest, mountains forested with ponderosa pine and aspen overlook the mile-deep Grand Canyon. Much of it is desert, and mesquite cactus is as probable a backyard tree as any other; yet the Colorado and Rio Grande rivers flow here. The Rocky Mountain states themselves, composed generally of majestic peaks, forests, placid valleys, blue lakes, and deep canyons, contain such contrasting scenery as sand dunes, arctic tundra, waterfalls, curious rock formations, glaciers, hot springs, geysers, salt flats, and the Great Salt Lake.

East of the Rockies the land descends imperceptibly across the Great Plains. Beyond these lies mid-America, known more commonly as the Midwest. The land here is broad and flat with clusters of rolling hills but no mountains and, in the north, dense forests. The Mississippi River system, with such major branches as the Missouri, Ohio, and Arkansas, spreads like an enormous tree throughout this region.

Between the plains and the Atlantic Coast lies another range of mountains, the Appalachian and Blue Ridge. Older than the Rockies, these seldom rise above 5,000 feet. For the most part heavily wooded, they are shot through with lakes, valleys, and rolling farmlands. To the south of this range along the Gulf of Mexico is a subtropical region of palm-shaded beaches and trees thick with Spanish moss.

Along the Atlantic itself stretches a wide coastal plain. From Delaware to New York, the area bordering the ocean is largely populated, but inland is some of the world's richest farmland. Finally, in the northeast the plain gives way to New England's rocky coast and rugged mountains.

IMMIGRATION AND CUSTOMS. There are a few simple travel formalities you will be asked to complete before you enter the United States. You will need a passport, usually a visitor's visa and, depending on where you come from, some kind of health record.

First you must have a current passport, which authorizes you to travel outside your own country. You will be asked to present it when you apply for a visitor's visa from the United States Embassy or Consulate nearest you, which you may do either in person or by mail. In some countries visa applications can also be obtained from the leading transportation companies and travel specialists.

Along with your application you will be required to supply one passport-size photograph of yourself, and some kind of evidence that you intend to return home after your visit. There is no special form for providing such evidence and the United States Embassy or Consulate will consider whatever you wish to submit. It might be a letter from your employer stating that you will be returning to your job, or from a community leader, such as a government, bank, school official, or a clergyman, describing ties in your community that would give you good reason to return.

As soon as your credentials are found to be in good order you will be issued a visitor's visa. The period of time it covers and the number of entries permitted will be specified on the visa.

WARNING! When you arrive in the U.S.A., the immigration officer may grant you less time here than your visa specifies. He may do this *without telling* you, simply by writing down an arbitrary date on your I-94 form, the white piece of paper which he will attach to your passport. This form shows the visa classification under which you have arrived, the date of your arrival, the purpose of your visit, and the departure date which the Immigration Service assigns to you. Be sure to make clear to him before he writes this in how long you want to stay and ask him to grant you that period of time or to explain why he has not. As the inflow of illegal immigrants seeking jobs in the USA has been increasing in recent years, Immigration authorities are getting tougher toward everyone, bona fide tourists included. Be sure to get this point settled before accepting your passport back at point of entry.

Later on, if you want to extend your stay, you must apply for an extension *at least one month* before your assigned departure date. Also, if you are 21 or over and happen to be in the United States over a January 1st, you must fill out a short Alien Registration card which you can get at any post office.

Exceptions: There are certain persons who are exempted from passport and/ or visa requirements. The following, among others, are not required to present either passports or visas:

Canadian citizens, if arriving in the United States after a visit only in the Western Hemisphere. (Border-crossing cards are issued by the United States Immigration Service at Canadian border offices to facilitate admission.)

British subjects residing in Bermuda or Canada, if arriving after a visit only in the Western Hemisphere.

Citizens of Mexico holding valid United States border-crossing cards, if arriving from Mexico or Canada.

Certain government and military travelers.

Holders of *Belgian* identity cards issued in lieu of passports are exempt from the passport requirement, but must have a valid visa.

Among those who need a passport, but who are excused from the visa requirement are:

British subjects residing in and coming directly from the Cayman Islands, and who are in possession of a political affiliation certificate and a clerk of court certificate.

Bahamian nationals residing in the Bahamas and coming directly to the United States on a precleared flight from Nassau.

Citizens of any country admitted to the United States on a single entry visa may visit Canada or Mexico for not more than 30 days and reenter the United States without a new visa, provided the reentry falls within the specifications of the original admission.

If you have a work visa and you remain in the United States more than 90 days in any one year, or if you have worked and earned over $3,000 in one year, you should check with the U.S. Government Internal Revenue Service to see if you have to pay any taxes in this country. Your own country's Embassy or consulates can advise you on this too, as well as on whether or not your country has a treaty with the United States so that you do not get taxed by both countries at the same time. Lists of cities having foreign consulates are given at the end of this section.

HEALTH REQUIREMENTS. On May 8, 1980, the World Health Organization officially declared smallpox to have been eradicated from the earth, the first time in history that a naturally transmitted disease has been totally stopped. Hence, smallpox vaccinations are no longer even available! Other vaccinations, for cholera or yellow fever, for example, might be required, depending on the areas in which you have traveled. These vary all the time, according to local conditions, so check carefully when you get your visa.

CUSTOMS. When you get to the United States, you will be processed through Customs, even if you have nothing to declare. United States citizens go through the same procedure. The Customs inspector will probably ask you to open your luggage, so it will save time if you have your keys handy.

All items intended for your own personal use (not including gifts or anything you plan to sell) can be brought into the United States duty and tax free. This includes anything from wearing apparel, jewelry, toilet articles, cameras, sports equipment, and other personal effects to baby carriages, bicycles, boats, and automobiles. Household effects and professional equipment or instruments may also come in duty-free if you have had them for more than one year. There is no limit on the amount of money you may bring with you, but if it's more than $5,000 you'll be asked to file a report with Customs.

You may also bring with you up to $400 worth of gifts, tax and duty free, provided you remain in the United States not less than 72 hours and have not claimed the exemption within the prior six months. Within this allowance, adults may bring one quart of liquor (0.946 liters).

Adults are also permitted 100 cigars as gifts, plus 50 cigars, or 300 cigarettes, or 3 pounds (1.359 kilograms) of tobacco for personal use. You may choose instead to bring a combination of cigars, cigarettes, and tobacco for personal use. Children are also allowed 100 cigars as gifts. Importation in any form of tobacco orginating in Cuba is prohibited.

You may, of course, bring more than $400 worth of gifts with you, but you will have to pay duty and any applicable taxes: 10% on the next $1000 and a variable rate based on value above that.

If you're thinking about bringing the family dog along on your trip to the United States, probably the best advice you'll get is "don't." No matter how well behaved, it can seriously limit your choice of transportation, lodgings, and itinerary. But, if you decide to, a certificate of rabies vaccination is required for dogs, signed by a licensed veterinarian and stating that the dog has been vaccinated at least 30 days prior to entry. Dogs without certificates must be vaccinated at the port of entry and quarantined for 30 days.

No vaccination is required for dogs coming from countries designated as rabies-free by the United States Public Health Service. These are currently listed as Australia, the Bahamas, Bermuda, Fiji, Great Britain, Iceland, Northern Ireland, Republic of Ireland, Jamaica, New Zealand, Norway, and Sweden. This list is subject to change as conditions warrant.

Cats are not required to have a rabies vaccination, but are subject to inspection on arrival and must be free of communicable diseases. All animals entering the United States are examined at the port of entry for evidence of disease, even if they have been certified. If an animal is not in apparent good health it may be subject to examination by a veterinarian at the owner's expense. If, as a result, the pet or other animal is excluded from entry, it must either be deported or destroyed.

Exception: Hawaii requires that all dogs and cats entering the state be quarantined at the owner's expense for 120 days, unless they are coming from Australia or New Zealand. This requirement applies even to guide dogs for the blind.

Dogs and cats entering the United States are subject to a Customs duty of 3 and one-half percent of their value, but the amount may be included in your $400 exemption.

Your travel agent or the United States Consulate can give you more detailed information about traveling with your pet. They can also advise about state and local regulations, which sometimes, as in the case of Hawaii, are more stringent than the federal regulations. Ask the consulate for the brochure entitled, *So You Want to Import a Pet,* or write to the: Foreign Quarantine Program, U.S. Public Health Service, National Communicable Disease Center, Atlanta, Ga. 30333.

Also consult the Consulate if you plan to bring along any fruits, vegetables, plants, seeds, meats, or any plant or animal products. Many are admitted without restriction other than inspection, some are prohibited entry, and a few are generally prohibited but may, under certain conditions, be admitted.

The following indicates some of the things you are—and are *not*—permitted to bring into the United States.

Admitted: Bakery goods, candies, fully cured cheeses, medicinal cotton, fresh cut or dried flowers, canned or processed fruits, jams and jellies, Mexican jumping beans, rocks and minerals, dried spices, truffles.

Permit required: Fresh berries, corn, eggs, fresh fruit and vegetables (some kinds prohibited).

Prohibited: Pine branches, citrus peel, fresh dairy products, fresh meat, plants in soil, items stuffed with straw, sugarcane, packing materials made from plant and animal fibers.

As with all Immigration and Customs regulations, the above are subject to revision and modification. For latest details on this, ask your nearest U.S. Consulate for Program Aid No. 1083, *Traveler's Tips on Bringing Food, Plant and Animal Products into the United States,* or write to: Quarantines, Department of Agriculture, Federal Center Building, Hyattsville, Md. 20782.

SPECIAL FARES AND SERVICES FOR INTERNATIONAL VISITORS. Private and public agencies offer a number of special courtesies to international visitors, not least valuable of which are the bargain rates on transportation. Outlined below are some that are currently available, but modifications are frequent, new discounts are introduced as others are retired, so check with your travel agent for latest information.

Airlines. Many domestic airlines offer special "Visit USA" discounts of up to 40 percent off regular coach fares on travel within the continental United States. In order to qualify, you must live at least 100 miles (161 kilometers) outside the border of any state in the United States. Usually you must also stop at a minimum of two cities on each Visit USA trip, not counting the cities of arrival and departure (except on Western and Continental Airlines, which have minimal stopover requirements). A stopover counts if the layover is at least eight hours. These discounted tickets cannot be used in combination with other special airfares or excursions. Visit USA tickets are valid for up to one year. Reservations must be made before you arrive in the U.S.A. and tickets must be confirmed within seven days of arrival, travel must begin no later than the 15th day after arrival.

Bus Services. Discount-priced international rates on point-to-point travel are available from either of the two giant American motorcoach companies, *Greyhound Lines* and *Continental Trailways*. International rates are listed on a separate schedule, but discounts amount to around 10 percent off regular fares. Tickets must be purchased overseas from authorized agents or representatives. *Trailways* has "Visit USA" offices in: Luxembourg, Mexico City, Johannesburg, Taipei, Tokyo, Seoul, Sydney, Brussels, Frankfurt, Guatemala City, and London.

Both companies also offer bargain-rate passes for unlimited travel on any regularly scheduled route in the United States and Canada. Passes are available to residents as well as visitors, so there are no restrictions about when or where you can purchase them. If you buy it after you arrive, its period of validity begins on the date of purchase. If you buy it at home, validity begins on the first day of use.

For rates and other conditions, see *America By Bus* earlier in this section.

Automobiles. You can rent a car almost anywhere in the United States, including the major airports. Many times it is possible to pick up a car in one city and leave it in another.

Accommodations. Many hotels and motels, both independent and chain-affiliated, offer special Visit USA reductions that can amount to as much as 35 percent off the average double room-rate. Some of the same facilities specialize in accommodating non-English-speaking travelers and will provide language and other helpful services. Hospitality packages providing for prepurchase of specified meals and accommodations at reduced rates are also available. Your travel agent can tell you which facilities offer discounts to international visitors.

Tour Packages. Tour operators, because of the volume of business they generate, are entitled to quantity discounts on travel services and accommodations and can offer a prepackaged itinerary at often far lower cost than you could if you tried to assemble it yourself. Such package tours are available in seemingly endless variety, and you're almost certain to find one going wherever you are. There are also special interest tours in abundance, and whether your own penchant is for horses or health, skiing or snorkeling, art, antiques, theater, music, cowboys and Indians, sports, the outdoors or whatever, you can probably find one that suits you—and perhaps meet some congenial traveling companions along the way. Again, your travel agent is the man to see.

Hospitality Programs. *The National Council of International Visitors* (NCIV), Meridian House, 1623 Belmont St., N.W., Washington, D.C. 20009, (202) 332–1028, publishes a free pamphlet with information regarding maps, guides, language services, American hosts and other pertinent facts for those wishing to spend time in private homes around the U.S. Included also is a state-by-state listing of local NCIV chapters. Bed-and-breakfasts, increasingly popular in the U.S., are another way of gaining a glimpse at non-tourist life in America. Contact *Bed & Breakfast Registry*, Box 8174, St. Paul, MN 55108, 612–646–4238, a nationwide bed-and-breakfast reservation service, or consult *Bed and Breakfast American Style* by Norman T. Simpson, Harper & Row, 10 E. 53 St., N.Y., N.Y. 10022.

Many cities also have other public and privately sponsored hospitality programs, some for specific nationals, some for all. They offer information, assistance, numerous small advisory services and sometimes operate a hospitality center where you can go and meet other travelers. They will also seek or supply language services for visitors who need them. You can find out about such programs from the Visitors and Convention Bureau in any major city. Some are also listed in the telephone book.

See "Interpreter Services" for other courtesies extended to foreign visitors.

 INTERPRETER SERVICES. There was a time when you couldn't hope to travel comfortably in the United States without a passable acquaintance with English. A little bit still helps, especially outside the gateway cities, but recent efforts on the part of both public and private agencies have made language services far more readily accessible to international visitors who need them, or who just feel more comfortable communicating in their own language.

French, German, Spanish, and Japanese are the services most widely available, but in the major cities you should have little difficulty finding someone to interpret for you in any language.

Look for the *multilingual Golden Girls* who are now stationed at a number of international airports to assist you through Immigration and Customs. They will also help you to make transportation connections. At many ports of entry you will also find an information desk staffed by multilingual agents who will help you with local transportation or in locating various services. The *Travelers Aid Society* desk at city bus and railroad terminals can assist you in several languages.

You will find a plaque at the registration desk of many hotels, issued by the United States Travel Service, which indicates that French, Spanish, German and/or Japanese are spoken at the front desk, at the telephone switchboard and in the hotel dining room. Even if you don't see the plaque, you can ask to speak to someone in your own language. If the hotel has such a person on its staff, it will ask him to interpret for you.

Many sightseeing services offer conducted tours with multilingual tour guides, both day trips and longer excursions of two or three days to a week or more. Some provide each passenger with a tape recorded commentary in his own language. Many major tourist attractions will also provide interpreter services on request.

Large city department stores have multilingual employees who will be glad to assist you with your shopping, either by appointment or by request at the store. You will also often find smaller shops with signs in the window indicating what languages are spoken there.

A good source of information about local interpreter services is the city's *Visitors and Convention Bureau,* usually itself staffed by multilingual personnel. Ask your hotel desk where they are, or look them up in the telephone book. They will also advise you about where to go, what to see and do in the city.

In large metropolitan areas, the publishing offices of foreign language newspapers and magazines can frequently advise about interpreter services, too. For information about where to find them, or about foreign language radio programs, ethnic groups and organizations in the United States, you can contact the *American Council for Nationalities Service* at 20 W. 40th St., New York, N.Y. 10018. Tel. (212) 398–9142. The Council has member agencies in more than 30 cities which serve as centers of service and fellowship for all nationalities.

Many cities also maintain their own local service agencies, such as the *International Visitors Information Service,* 801 19th St. N.W., Washington, D.C. 20006, (202) 872–8747, which offer language assistance as well as information and hospitality services to international visitors.

A multilingual telephone service for foreign tourists is *Hotel, Auto, Tour, Air (HATA),* based in Madison, Wisconsin. Its number is 800–356–8392. HATA provides general information, emergency road service for users of Hertz rental cars (call 800–654–3131), and makes travel reservations.

International symbol signs, which circumvent any potential language problems, are more and more being used at international airports, along the highways, in hotels and restaurants.

If you want the reassurance of full-time interpreter service, you might want to consider a conducted tour package that includes your transportation, accommodations, and guide service on a prearranged itinerary—many times the choice of first-time visitors to the United States. Your travel agent can make all the necessary arrangements.

Interpreters are available at all major gateway cities. Some in-land cities have this service, too. Akron, Ohio; Buffalo, New York; Charleston, West Virginia; Cleveland, Ohio; Pittsburgh, Pennsylvania; Rochester, New York; and Youngstown, Ohio are examples. Languages covered are: Arabic, Chinese, Croatian, Czech, Dutch, Filipino, French, German, Hungarian, Italian, Japanese, Lithuanian, Polish, Rumanian, Russian, Serbian, Serbo-Croatian, Slovak, Turkish, Ukrainian.

 CURRENCY. The United States puts no limit on the amount of money you may bring into the country. For your own convenience, however, come with a supply of smaller bills, credit cards, and travelers cheques (preferably in US dollars).

Denominations. The basic United States monetary unit is the dollar ($), which is equivalent to 100 cents (¢). Coins are minted in 1¢ (penny), 5¢ (nickel), 10¢ (dime), 25¢ (quarter), 50¢ (half dollar), and $1 denominations. Half dollars are rare and inconvenient; silver dollars are very rare; and the recent $1 coins are rather unpopular. Coin-operated telephones and vending machines accept nickels, dimes, and quarters. Try to keep a fair supply of coins on hand while you are in the United States. Shops usually dislike to make change unless you make a small purchase; and in many cities bus drivers are not allowed to make change so you must pay the exact fare.

Paper currency is printed in $1, $2, $5, $10, $20, $50, $100, and $1,000 denominations. While the amount is clearly indicated on each bill, all are the same size and the same green color. To avoid mistakes, keep the different denominations separated in your purse or billfold; and when you pay for a small purchase with a large bill, state the amount of your bill. For example: "Two seventy-nine out of ten" (meaning, that you have paid for a $2.79 purchase with a $10 bill and expect $7.21 in change). Two-dollar bills are not common, and in some parts of the country they are actively disliked. You will have trouble changing any bills greater than $20s.

Currency Exchange. Visitors who arrive by air can usually exchange their currency at the gateway airport. Not all exchange facilities offer 24-hour service, however, and we suggest that you have with you when you arrive about $50 in bills of various sizes to cover tips and your transportation into the city.

Some hotels in the United States, particularly in major gateway cities, will exchange or accept foreign currency, but many more will not. Unless you have been assured in advance that your hotel(s) will change your money for you, don't count on it. You will in any event get a more favorable rate of exchange at the bank. Outside of large gateway cities you will probably have trouble exchanging any foreign currency other than the half dozen major ones. (Visitors from Central and South America would do well to establish some kind of bank relationship in Miami before going on to other parts of the U.S.)

Outside the downtown areas of larger towns and cities, most American banks do not handle foreign exchange, especially of the (in America) less common currencies, so plan accordingly. Banks are open Monday through Friday from 9 A.M. to 3 P.M. (0900 to 1500 hours), and *sometimes* later, except on national holidays.

When you do change your money, you can ask for the denominations you want. For day-to-day expenses, small bills are more convenient than large, preferably nothing larger than a ten. Many small shops and other small businesses, such as filling stations and fast-food establishments, may well refuse a fifty, and, if your purchase is small, be grudging about accepting a twenty. Banks sometimes refuse to break a large bill unless you carry an account with them.

Travelers Checks. The best alternative to carrying currency and the enduring hazards of exchanging it is travelers checks in United States dollar denominations, which are accepted as cash by many but not all shops, restaurants, and other commercial establishments. You will receive your change in dollars. Almost any bank will cash them for you, as will your hotel cashier. You local bank can advise you about how to purchase and use travelers checks.

Letters of Credit. If you wish to have extra money available to you in case of emergency, or for some expensive serendipity, a letter of credit will do it for you. Your local bank can arrange for such a letter with its corresponding bank in the United States.

Credit Cards. Charge cards are accepted in many shops and restaurants and at all major hotels (and most smaller ones). You will be charged in your own currency when you return home. The most common cards are the bank-linked *Visa* and *Mastercard*—their non–U.S. equivalents are recognizeable because they share the same colors and designs—and *American Express.*

MEASUREMENTS. The United States, out of step with most of the rest of the world, does not widely use metric measures—at least not yet. The table below indicates the metric equivalents for the measures you will most likely encounter as a traveler. For table of equivalent garment sizes, see "Shopping."

United States Measure	Metric Equivalent
Weight	
Ounce	28.349 grams
Pound	0.453 kilograms
Capacity	
Pint	0.473 liters
Quart	0.946 liters
Gallon	3.785 liters
Length	
Inch	2.540 centimeters
Foot	30.480 centimeters
Yard	0.914 meters
Mile	1.609 kilometers

BUSINESS HOURS. With few exceptions, American business offices are open from 9 A.M. to 5 P.M. (0900 to 1700 hours) Monday through Friday. There is an hour's break for lunch anywhere between 12 noon and 2 P.M. (1200 and 1400 hours), but the schedule is staggered so that everyone doesn't leave at the same time. Business is often conducted over lunch among executives and salespersons and such working luncheons may extend to two or even three hours.

Hawaii is one exception to the general 9-to-5 rule. Business hours in the Islands tend to begin and end earlier than they do on the Mainland: 7:30 or 8 A.M. to 4 P.M. (0730 or 0800 to 1600 hours), an arrangement that permits residents to enjoy some of the outdoor activities that tourists find so attractive. The practice is also followed by some companies in California and other fair-weather areas.

Retail stores operate on a somewhat different time schedule than business offices do. Most department stores and specialty shops in downtown areas are open Monday through Saturday from 9:30 or 10 A.M. until 5:30 or 6 P.M. (0930 or 1000 hours to 1730 or 1800 hours). Major department stores are also open unil 9:30 P.M. (2130 hours) at least one night a week for the convenience of shoppers who can't get there during regular business hours. Late nights vary from city to city, but are often Monday/Thursday or Tuesday/Friday.

In tourist and resort areas, shops may be open seven days a week to accommodate visitors and vacationers, though hours may be shorter on Sundays.

If you're looking for snacks or sundries, city and suburban supermarkets, groceries, and delicatessens are usually open Monday through Saturday from 9 A.M. to about 9 P.M. (0900 to 2100 hours). Some are also open on Sundays, depending on the area, but often close earlier than on weekdays. Some are open 24 hours.

Drugstores usually operate Monday through Saturday from 8 or 9 A.M. (0800 or 0900 hours) often until late in the evening. In almost any big city neighborhood there is sure to be least one open until midnight and all day on Sunday, but most of them aren't.

Usual banking hours are from (at least) 9 A.M. to 3 P.M. (0900 to 1500 hours), Monday through Friday. Museums are open from around 10 A.M. to 5 P.M. (1000 to 1700 hours), with local variations. Many are open on Sunday afternoons and some are closed on Mondays.

All banks, government and business offices in the United States are closed on national holidays, as are many retail outlets and services. Restaurants, motion picture theaters, and other entertainments are open, more often than not. Big downtown department stores are always closed on Thanksgiving, Christmas, and New Year's Day, but are often open on such other holidays as Columbus Day, Veteran's Day, and George Washington's Birthday—now traditionally sale days on which the stores offer particularly attractive bargains.

Reminder: Most of the United States observes Daylight Saving Time from April through October, during which period the clocks are set forward by one hour. Thus 12 noon Standard Time becomes 1 P.M. (1300 hours) Daylight Saving Time. It might be later than you think!

ELECTRICITY. The current in electric outlets in the United States is 110–115-volt, 60-cycle AC, as compared with the 220–240-volt DC or 220–240-volt, 50-cycle AC that is standard in some other parts of the world. Most small electric appliances—razors, electric hair curlers, dryers, and the like—will operate efficiently on the lower voltage. However, if your razor (or other electrically operated device) has a round-prong plug, you will need to bring along an adapter in order to connect it to American outlets, which accept only flat-prong plugs. In any case you won't have to carry a travel iron. One-day cleaning and even while-you-wait pressing service is available in all major cities.

SHOPPING. The word "souvenir" is French for "memory," and the best souvenirs are those you carry inside you. Take along a notebook and keep a diary of your trip; it will fix your impressions and experiences much more clearly and firmly in your mind. If, however, you do want to buy things, choose those that you can really use in your daily life back home.

If you're looking for inexpensive novelties, color transparencies, or postcards, you'll find them in the souvenir shop at any self-respecting tourist attraction. For something a little more unusual, look for such locally crafted products as Rocky Mountain jade jewelry, buckskin jackets from Colorado, hand-stitched quilts from the mountains of West Virginia, leather cowboy boots from New Mexico, Indian basketry, jewelry and handwoven rugs from Arizona, miniature totem poles from the Northwest, red clay Indian pipes from Minnesota, Eskimo walrus ivory carvings from Alaska, leis from Hawaii, saddles, cowboy clothes, pottery, toys, and much more.

Products such as these are most generally available in the areas where they are crafted: at local shops and specialty stores, at crafts centers, and at state and county fairs. If your hotel is a large one, you might also find one or more boutiques in the shopping arcades that specialize in local handicrafts.

Museums are another source for unusual gifts and souvenirs. Museum shops often offer excellent reproductions of some of their art objects at prices from reasonable to moderate.

Foreign visitors find that very practical everyday items are often cheaper and of better quality in the U.S. than at home. Favorite purchases are: cotton goods (towels, shirts, bedding), low-priced watches, cosmetics, sporting goods, phonograph records and tapes, clothing, luggage, pens, and sunglasses. Big cities, rather than small towns and rural areas, are the best place to shop for practicalities—both because of the variety of merchandise they offer and because they are most accessible to international visitors. The following is a guide to the shopping facilities in a typical American city. Most are easy to recognize, but if you want advice you can consult the desk at your hotel.

Specialty Shops. Many shops in the United States have very narrow specialties. They stock only one kind of merchandise, but in a complete range and assortment of models, sizes, colors, design, manufacture, etc. In any major city there are shops that specialize in books, records, sporting goods, radios and television sets, cameras, antiques, stationery, jewelry, clocks and watches, men's clothing, women's clothing, children's clothing, linens, shoes, toys, china, housewares, needlecraft, or you name it. You might sometimes have to venture off main thoroughfares to find the specialty shops you're looking for, but the effort can be worth it because of the large selection they offer—often unusual items that you can't easily find anywhere else.

Chain Stores. Somewhere in size between the specialty shops and the giant department stores are the chain stores, which operate under the same name throughout the country—names such as *J. C. Penney, Sears Roebuck,* and *Montgomery Ward.* They tend to specialize in ready-to-wear clothing, accessories, household goods, home appliances, hardware, and gadgets. They don't offer the range of choice in brand names that either the specialty shops or department stores do, but they generally offer very good value at a moderate price.

There are also low-cost chain stores, properly called variety stores, but locally known as "dime stores" or "five-and-tens." (At one time much of their merchandise did sell for 5 or 10 cents). Today the prices are up, but they still carry an inexpensive line of products that includes cosmetics, accessory items for men and women, stationery supplies, notions, hardware, toys, and games. Names by which you will recognize them include *K Mart, Kress, Lamston,* and *Woolworth.*

Department Stores. A department store in any major city in the United States tends to be very large and may have as much as 3 million square feet (more than 900,000 square meters) of selling space and carry up to 160,000 items in 150 or more separate departments. The enormous variety of its goods also covers a broad range of price and quality. Often the budget department is located in the basement, where merchandise is low-cost, but can be of very good quality. Some stores also offer higher-cost merchandise that hasn't sold in its regular department upstairs at reduced prices in the basement, a practice that spawned the descriptive terms "bargain basement" and "bargain-basement prices."

Clearance sales are also conducted periodically throughout the store, often on national holidays when most government and commercial offices are closed. General sales are advertised in the newspapers, but you might find a clearance rack or counter or corner in many departments at any time during the year. It's worth looking over the merchandise, which often sells for one-fourth to one-third off, sometimes even at half the regular price.

Department stores also offer many small services for customers, such as shopping advice services, child care, rest rooms, wrapping and mailing, gift wrapping, etc. Often there is a restaurant where you can have lunch without leaving the building.

Discount Stores. Big discount stores offer substantial savings—20 to 25 percent—over what the same merchandise would cost at a department store or specialty shop. Most houses started as discount dealers in appliances, but many have expanded to clothing, sporting goods, records, photo equipment, and many other lines. They are often located outside the main shopping area, their décor is functional and they offer few amenities. By doing so they can reduce their operating costs and pass the savings along to customers. If you know what you want, you can often realize a substantial saving by purchasing it at a discount store. It is unlikely that they will be able to pack for export, or handle the shipping for you, so be prepared to carry your purchase with you. The repair services offered by discount houses are often much more limited than those given by regular dealers, however, so you may wind up losing money in spite of the lower initial cost, particularly if you do not get well-established brand-name merchandise. The atmosphere of large discount houses can be noisy and frantic in a way that interferes with calm judgment, too.

Factory Outlets. Run by the manufacturers themselves, these retail outlets sell their own products at prices below those charged by competing retail stores. Merchandise you can expect to find includes clothing, shoes, linens, furniture, pottery, china, and cigarettes. Like discount stores, factory outlets are frequently outside the shopping district and you'll probably have to go a bit out of your way to find them—a sightseeing opportunity in itself. If you have time, order a copy of *Factory Outlet Shopping Guide,* by Jean Bird, from P.O. Box 256–N, Oradell, N.J. 07649. Volumes run about 100 pages, large size softbound, and are available for: New England, New York and New Jersey; Pennsylvania; Washington, Maryland, Delaware and Virginia; North and South Carolina. Bear in mind that to pursue this kind of shopping seriously you'll need a car.

Shopping Centers. Enormous shopping centers are part of the suburban landscape all across the United States. Usually located a few miles outside the city, they house branch outlets of the big downtown department stores, at least one supermarket, fast food stands and ice cream parlors, and as many as 50 or more specialty shops offering perhaps as many kinds of merchandise. Surrounded by acres of parking space, the newer shopping centers are fully enclosed, heated in winter and air-conditioned in summer, with fountains, ponds, plants, and flowers in the walkways between the stores. If you have the opportunity you might want to sample what has become, in the suburbs, a way of life. Even smaller towns have their own modified versions of the suburban shopping center. Prices are comparable to those at the downtown stores. Here, too, a car is essential.

Food and Drug Stores. You can buy food and beverages for between-meal snacks or picnics either at supermarkets or from neighborhood grocery stores. Supermarkets, which may carry anywhere from 6,000 to 8,000 items, are usually plentiful in and around the downtown area. The smaller neighborhood stores, fresh produce stands, bakeries, delicatessens, health food, cheese, and ethnic specialty stores are more often out of the way for visitors, but do sometimes offer unusual or gourmet items that are difficult to find elsewhere.

Sales Taxes. There are no federal sales taxes in the United States, but many states and a few cities do impose their own taxes on the retail price of merchandise. The combined state-city rate runs anywhere from 2 percent to as high as 8¼ percent of the purchase price. In most places if the merchandise is sent outside the state, the tax is not charged. On any substantial purchase, you might save money by having it shipped home. You'll want to weigh the shipping charge versus the amount of tax you will save in making your decision. You might not always get a remission of the tax charge, since laws do vary from state to state, but it's worth asking.

You can also avoid sales taxes by shopping at the tax-free stores located at most international airports. Merchandise here is not subject to customs duties or sales or excise taxes, and you can save 25 to 50 percent or more compared to what you would pay in the city. Heavily taxed items such as liquor and cigarettes are especially favorable buys. Whatever you buy, you'll have to take it with you. Most tax-free shops are accessible only to those who can show a boarding pass for a flight whose destination is outside the United States.

SIZES*. If you're shopping for shoes or clothing, the table below will help you find your way to the right size. Even so, it's best to try the item on since sizes do vary slightly from one manufacturer to another.

		Men									
Suits	United States	34	36	38	40	42	44	46	48		
	Metric	44	46	48	50	52	54	56	58		
Shirts	United States	14	14½	15	15½	16	16½	17	17½		
	Metric	36	37	38	39	40	41	42	43		
Shoes	United States	7	7½	8	8½	9	9½	10	10½	11	11½
	Metric	39	40	41	42	43	43	44	44	45	45

		Women						
Suits Coats/ Dresses	United States	8	10	12	14	16	18	20
	Metric	36	38	40	42	44	46	48
Blouses/ Sweaters	United States	32	34	36	38	40	42	44
	Metric	40	42	44	46	48	50	52
Stockings	United States	8	8½	9	9½	10	10½	11
	Metric	0	1	2	3	4	5	6
Shoes	United States	5	5½	6	6½	7	7½	8	8 ½	9
	Metric	35	35	36	37	38	38	39	39	40

Gloves   Same designations

* *All size equivalents are approximate*

TOBACCO. You are permitted to bring a limited amount of tobacco into the United States with you (see *Immigration and Customs*), and if you're a smoker you'll probably want to do so. If your visit lasts longer than your cigarette supply, you'll probably be looking for your own brand. You may even find it, especially in gateway city tobacco shops or ethnic neighborhood stores. One shop in New York City's Times Square sells cigarettes from 30 different countries.

If you can't find the brand you're accustomed to, very good American tobacco products are available in wide variety. You might want to sample some of them in any event. The tobacconist can tell you which are strong, mild, menthol, low-tar, etc. Tobacco or smoke shops offer the greatest assortment of both domestic and imported brands, but you can also buy cigarettes at drugstores and supermarkets and from vending machines in restaurants, bars, gasoline filling stations, and elsewhere.

Tobacco is heavily taxed in the United States, as are alcoholic beverages. In addition to government excise taxes there are state and local sales taxes. The rates vary from one area to another, so a pack of cigarettes you pay 45 cents for in one city might cost you 90 cents somewhere else. As a rule, though, cigarettes are less costly if you buy them by the carton (ten packs per carton) than by the pack, and more costly if you buy them from vending machines.

COSMETICS. Cosmetics are not subject to the same limitations as tobacco and you may bring with you whatever you think you'll need for your stay in the United States, tax- and duty-free. If you do need to make a purchase—lipstick, cleansing cream, face or eye makeup—the bigger metropolitan drug and department stores carry some imported cosmetic lines. Among them are *Eve of Roma, Lancome, Myurgia, Orlane, Mary Quant, Kanebo* and *Shiseido*. Outlets in ethnic neighborhoods are also good bets if you're looking for familiar labels.

If you want to venture into American-made cosmetics, the domestic brands are excellent. You can find them in the cosmetics section of any department store, or at the cosmetics counter of most drugstores, though the latter will usually offer a smaller selection. Well-known labels include *Max Factor, Estée Lauder, Revlon, Helena Rubinstein, Ultima II,* and the hypo-allergenic lines *Almay* and *Clinique*.

Cosmetics can also more purchased in variety stores (such as the Woolworth chain), which carry such lower-priced lines as *Cutex, Flame-Glo, Maybelline, Helen Neushaefer,* and *Westmore*. They are also very good products, but are sometimes less expensively packaged than the higher-priced lines.

TELEPHONE. Post offices in the United States provide only postal services. They don't have the telephone and telegraph facilities that they do in some other countries. On the other hand, this country has more telephones per capita than any other country in the world, and the system functions superbly. Americans take this for granted and make full use of their phones—to an extent that foreigners may find disconcerting at first. The telephone is far and away the chief means of communication in the United States, and life in a city like New York would be physically impossible without it. Public telephones are everywhere, in every kind of public facility and private commercial establishment—bus and train stations, air terminals, gas stations, the lobbies of office buildings and hotels, every hotel room, bars and restaurants, many shops, and in small booths along streets and highways. Each phone has a small plaque with operating instructions on it; the usual basic charge is $10¢$ to $25¢$ for three minutes.

Telegraph service in the United States has been in decline for many years now, and for domestic communications the telephone is much faster and more reliable. For overseas communications you can go through Western Union, the telegraph company, to either R.C.A. (Radio Corporation of America) or I.T.T. (International Telephone and Telegraph Company), both of which handle cables to other countries.

THE MEDIA. You can learn much about a country from its mass media; they are often inadvertently very revealing.

Newspapers. *USA Today* and the finance-oriented *Wall Street Journal* constitute the national newspapers in the United States. Every city also publishes its own daily newspapers covering local, national, and international events, which are distributed throughout the metropolitan area. A degree of "national" quality, or of standardization, is provided by the national feature and wire services which distribute news, feature articles, comic strips, and editorial columnists' comments from a central source to local newspapers all over the country. You can find the local papers at news agencies, at newsstands on street corners or in office building and hotel lobbies, in many cities in coin-operated vending boxes outside supermarkets, drugstores, restaurants, and elsewhere.

Small towns also publish their own newspapers, though often on a weekly rather than a daily basis, and usually confine themselves to news of local events.

In the major gateway cities, there are usually one or more news agencies or distributors who specialize in foreign and foreign-language publications. Your hotel desk or the local Visitors Bureau can tell you where to find them. In cities with large ethnic populations, such as New York City, there are also many local foreign-language newspapers, published for foreign-born residents. The languages used and the number of different newspapers available depend on the size and composition of resident populations. Often these newspapers are not distributed city-wide, but you can find them listed in the classified telephone directory under "Newspapers."

Books and Magazines. Book stores, numerous in any American city, offer the largest selection of hard-cover and paperback books, although paperback editions of currently popular titles can also be purchased in some drugstores, supermarkets, at news and tobacco stands, and in the book departments of chain and department stores (which also carry hard cover editions, but usually have a smaller selection than book stores do). Foreign language books are also available in larger cities from dealers who specialize in one (often) or more languages. Again, ask your hotel desk or the local Visitors Bureau about where to find them, or look in the classified telephone directory under "Book Dealers—Retail."

Magazines in the United States cater increasingly to special interest groups, as, for example, sports, fashion, news digest, motion pictures, travel, home decoration, gardening, skiing, cycling, photography, camping, boating, stamp collecting, antiques, architecture, and many others. Most major cities even have their own magazines, with current entertainment listings & features. Magazines are sold by the same vendors who sell newspapers. Some of the foreign language news agencies also carry major foreign-language magazines.

Radio and Television. Most United States hotel and motel accommodations are equipped with radios and television sets, with color TV likely in deluxe and first-class facilities. There are three major national television networks and more than 1,000 local stations. Some broadcast 24 hours a day, others may shut down from around midnight until 6 A.M. (0600 hours).

The number of channels you can receive depends on where in the country you are, but in New York City, for example, there are seven regular channels. Additional programming is carried on cable television and on the UHF channels, but most sets in public facilities are not equipped to receive it.

Almost all television in the United States is commercially sponsored and consists mostly of entertainment combined with periodic newscasts, all frequently interrupted for delivery of the sponsor's advertising message. There is no government-sponsored radio or television. There is, however, a national network of educational television stations, supported by public contributions and grants from corporations and philanthropic foundations. These stations carry no advertising and their programs are designed to interest as well as educate. They are public service oriented and cover a broad spectrum that includes science, health, sociology, classical drama, dance, music (from rock to opera), historical perspective, special programs for children, and interviews with prominent persons from many different fields.

Radio stations tend to specialize mostly in music, with newscasts every hour or half hour, although some interrupt regular programming to cover such sporting events as football, baseball, basketball, hockey, and boxing. All programming is locally originated. Some stations broadcast only news, repeating and updating as necessary throughout the day and evening. Some specialize in rock or folk or classical or semiclassical music, so if at first you don't hear what you want, switch.

There are more than 4,000 AM stations in the United States and nearly 3,000 FM stations, almost all commercially sponsored, so commercial interruptions are frequent. Exceptions are listener-sponsored radio stations, with no commercials, and their programs are designed to serve the public interest.

Foreign-language programming is carried by certain stations to serve the local ethnic population, but often not on a 24-hour basis.

 MEDICAL ASSISTANCE. Medical care in the United States is very good—and very expensive. A visit to the doctor's office can cost you $20 and up, more if laboratory tests, injections, drugs, or surgical supplies are required. If the doctor comes to treat or examine you in your hotel room, his fee will be not less than $35, usually more. If you must be hospitalized, your room and board alone can run well over $100 a day (over $200 in New York), with extra charges for lab tests, medication, doctors, special nurses, use of operating room, anesthetist, etc. The cost of even a short stay is substantial.

With all this in mind you will probably want to take the precaution of purchasing insurance to cover your medical expenses in case of accident or illness during your trip. Many package tour and charter operators now offer insurance as part of their overall packages. By way of example, some may offer an inclusive policy covering medical expenses, personal accident, baggage, and certain cancellations, with provision for extra coverage if needed, and the premium is payable with your deposit on any of its Self-Catering Vacations in the U.S. If your travel arrangements don't include such insurance, or if your present policy doesn't cover you outside your own country, then your best investment is the low-cost holiday coverage available from certain of the big international insurance companies.

One such is *American International Underwriters*, which issues International Holiday Travel Insurance with accident and sickness coverage for about as little as $32.30 for a 15-day visit. This buys you approx. $5,000 worth of medical insurance and will also pay about $15.00 per day on your hotel room if you are confined there by illness or injury.

You may elect to purchase greater coverage at proportionately greater cost. Plans are available for periods from seven to 180 days, with coverage from approx. $5,000 to $50,000, at premiums ranging from about $4.75 to $144. The company will also provide personal effects and baggage coverage (only in combination with its accident and sickness policy) at modest extra cost. American International Underwriters offices in more than 130 countries can issue a policy for you, or write to: American International Underwriters Inc., 1225 Connecticut Ave., N.W., Washington, D.C. 20036.

The only domestic private company still to offer short-term (30 to 60-day) insurance to foreign travelers is Mutual of Omaha, whose Foreign Visitors Plan may be bought through travel agents abroad and at some airports in the U.S.

Railway, bus, and air terminals in the United States also sell accident insurance policies on individual trips, available at insurance counters or from coin-operated vending machines.

More recently companies such as *MediCall* (c/o The Siesel Company, Inc., 845 Third Ave., New York, N.Y. 10022); *Assist-Card* (347 Fifth Ave., New York, NY 10016); and *International Underwriters* (8027 Leesburg Pike, Vienna, Va. 22180) have begun to offer actual medical assistance to the traveler through networks of affiliated doctors. Rates vary but are relatively inexpensive ($25 for a single trip, $75 for a year, with family rates often available). Some though not all of these programs cover the often neglected but frequently considerable cost of emergency transportation; avoid unpleasant surprises by asking if this is included in your policy.

If you do need a doctor or an ambulance while you are traveling in the United States, notify your hotel desk or, if you are outside the hotel, dial *Operator* from any telephone. The telephone operator can summon an ambulance, direct you to the nearest hospital, help locate a doctor, or refer you to a medical emergency service. Several cities also have an *emergency telephone number*— 911—to call for an ambulance or the fire and police departments.

For people with a chronic illness, such as diabetes, or those taking a drug that might interfere with emergency treatment, or who are allergic to penicillin or other drugs sometimes given in emergencies—even for those who wear contact lenses—there are internationally recognized tags that can be worn on a bracelet or around the neck, specifying the condition. If any of them are yours, you should wear this little bit of jewelry, which can help avoid mistakes in case of emergency.

If you are under medication, you should bring along any pills or compounds that you are required to take, plus any necessary doctor's prescriptions. Your prescription will probably have to be rewritten by a United States doctor before a pharmacist can fill it in any event, but if you have it with you, it will often not be necessary for the doctor to reexamine you. Most towns have at least one drugstore that stays open evenings and on Sunday where you can have a prescription filled, or purchase emergency nonprescription drugs.

It's also a good idea, if you wear glasses or contact lenses, to carry an extra pair as a safeguard against the inconvenience of loss or breakage. You might also want a written copy of your lens prescription.

LEGAL AID. Unless you are deliberately engaged in illegal activity, it is unlikely that you will run afoul of the law in the United States. Traffic violations are always a possibility, of course, especially if you aren't thoroughly familiar with local regulations. For minor infractions, however, you often don't have to appear in court at all. You will simply be fined a set sum, depending on the nature of the violation (speeding, illegal turn, or whatever). Do *not* attempt to pay it to the officer who tickets you. He will suspect that you are offering a bribe—another, more serious offense. All fines must be paid, in person or by mail, to a clerk of the court.

If you do have to appear in traffic court, no legal representation is usually necessary, although if you are not fluent in English, you might want to have an interpreter with you.

You will need a lawyer if you run into more serious difficulty and find yourself accused of a criminal offense. If you are arrested, you will be permitted to make one telephone call to whomever you choose. You will probably choose to call your nearest consulate (or someone who can contact them for you) for assistance and advice about obtaining legal counsel or arranging for bail. If you are unable to pay a lawyer to defend you, you may ask to be assigned a public defender, whose services are free of charge.

EMBASSIES AND CONSULATES. In the unlikely event that you run into any difficult or unusual problem during your travels in the United States, your embassy in Washington, D.C., or your consulates in the other major cities, can help or advise you. The following lists a few of the embassy addresses. For consular office locations, check with your Foreign Affairs Department at home, your embassy in Washington, or the local telephone directory.

Australia
1601 Massachusetts Ave., N.W.
Washington, D.C. 20036
Tel. (202) 797–3000

The Bahamas
600 New Hampshire Ave., N.W.
Washington, D.C. 20037
Tel. (202) 338–3940

Barbados
2144 Wyoming Ave., N.W.
Washington, D.C. 20008
Tel. (202) 939–9200

Belgium
3330 Garfield St., N.W.
Washington, D.C. 20008
Tel. (202) 333–6900

Canada
1746 Massachusetts Ave., N.W.
Washington, D.C. 20036
Tel. (202) 785–1400

Denmark
3200 Whitehaven St., N.W.
Washington, D.C. 20008
Tel. (202) 234–4300

France
4101 Reservoir Rd., N.W.
Washington, D.C. 20007
Tel. (202) 944–6000

Germany
4645 Reservoir Rd., N.W.
Washington, D.C. 20007
Tel. (202) 298–4000

Great Britain
3100 Massachusetts Ave., N.W.
Washington, D.C. 20008
Tel. (202) 462–1340

Greece
2221 Massachusetts Ave., N.W.
Washington, D.C. 20008
Tel. (202) 667–3168

India
2107 Massachusetts Ave., N.W.
Washington, D.C. 20008
Tel. (202) 939–7000

Ireland
2234 Massachusetts Ave., N.W.
Washington, D.C. 20008
Tel. (202) 462–3939

Israel
3514 International Drive, N.W.
Washington, D.C. 20008
Tel. (202) 364–5500

Italy
1601 Fuller St., N.W.
Washington, D.C. 20009
Tel. (202) 328–5500

Jamaica
   1850 K Street, N.W.
   Washington, D.C. 20006
   Tel. (202) 452–0660

Japan
   2520 Massachusetts Ave., N.W.
   Washington, D.C. 20008
   Tel. (202) 234-2266

Luxembourg
   2200 Massachusetts Ave., N.W.
   Washington, D.C. 20008
   Tel. (202) 265–4171

The Netherlands
   4200 Linnean Ave., N.W.
   Washington, D.C. 20008
   Tel. (202) 244–5300

New Zealand
   37 Observatory Circle, N.W.
   Washington, D.C. 20008
   Tel. (202) 328–4800

Norway
   2720 34 St., N.W.
   Washington, D.C. 20008
   Tel. (202) 333–6000

Portugal
   2125 Kalorama Rd., N.W.
   Washington, D.C. 20008
   Tel. (202) 328–8610

South Africa
   3051 Massachusetts Ave., N.W.
   Washington, D.C. 20008
   Tel. (202) 232–4400

Spain
   2700 Fifteenth St., N.W.
   Washington, D.C. 20009
   Tel. (202) 265–0190

Sweden
   600 New Hampshire Ave., N.W.
   Washington, D.C. 20037
   Tel. (202) 298–3500

Switzerland
   2900 Cathedral Ave., N.W.
   Washington, D.C. 20008
   Tel. (202) 745–7900

Trinidad and Tobago
   1708 Massachusetts Ave., N.W.
   Washington, D.C. 20036
   Tel. (202) 467–6490

THE AMERICAN SCENE

THE ARTS IN AMERICA

Film, Music, Theater, and Fine Arts

by
ROY BONGARTZ

(*Roy Bongartz, a travel writer with an eye for the offbeat, is a frequent contributor to newspapers and national magazines.*)

This brief survey of the state of the arts today begins with film, an art form the world associates instinctively with the USA, then continues with rock, jazz, and folk music, also prime products of our own culture. The older arts, learned largely from Europe, are then considered in their adapted, and often improved, conditions.

THE FILM SCENE

One word sums up the main aims of the American film industry at the moment: entertainment. Although the term covers a good deal of subject matter, American films have been getting away from the once-fashionable auteuristic personal statements of screenwriter-directors who used film in somewhat the way they might use a novel or a poem. In spite of the fact that foreign imports had lost their place as eminent source of social message or artistic experiment, Hollywood has not gone far to fill that vacuum. As it has always been in American filmmaking, money comes first—but there are nevertheless some recent changes.

The overriding control of the industry by half a dozen major studios has loosened somewhat, allowing many younger writers, directors, and producers to make notable inroads. Four-walling is a recent innovation whereby a film producer rents a theater for a flat fee, takes his own chances on a flop, but wins all the rewards with a hit. The system is risky to the producer, but it encourages the production of films that major studios would not have financed because the studios find them difficult to pigeonhole into their often rigid marketing systems.

Another important development in the American movie scene is the rise of home video cassettes and pay-television networks as significant markets for films. Major Hollywood movies typically appear on video cassette six months after their original theatrical release and on pay-television six to nine months after that. Prerecorded video cassettes can be rented in almost any town or city for three or four dollars a night and watched on a television set if played back through a video-cassette recorder (VCR). Almost 30 percent of American homes owned at least one VCR by the end of 1985, and VCRs are becoming popular accoutrements in many hotel and motel rooms. Many hotel rooms also come equipped with cable television, offering at least one pay service predominantly showing movies.

The insatiable appetite for product demonstrated by these two "new" media has led companies involved in each to lend significant financial support to producers of theatrical films in exchange for the home-video or pay-television rights to those movies. Many hungry producers have found these sources of capital to be welcome sustenance after having had their projects turned down by the studios. The net effect is that more films are being made, including more modest, quirky, and frequently interesting films that found no home in Hollywood. Examples include such critically lauded films as *Amadeus* and *A Soldier's Story,* along with *Repo Man, The Brother from Another Planet,* and *Blood Simple.*

As for Hollywood itself, fads change, but the pattern stays the same. Each year the average cost of producing a major film rises, increasing the financial risk to the producers. Consequently, most Hollywood big shots would be just as happy making the same proven hit over and over again. That being impractical, they do the next best thing—imitate each others' hits until the consumer cries "enough."

The current fad seems to be live-action cartoons—films of exaggerated imagination and escapism based on comic book heroes or premises. Examples are *Superman I–III, Supergirl, Star Wars, Raiders of the Lost Ark, Dune, Romancing the Stone,* and *2010*—the somewhat comic-like follow-up to Stanley Kubrick's *2001.* Use of the term "escapism," by the way, should not be interpreted in an exclusively pejorative sense. Escapism may be what Hollywood does best, in the thirties, forties, and fifties and again in the eighties.

Providing a running counterpoint to these flights of escapism is Hollywood's never-ending struggle to remain topical. Hence the exclusively male buddy-buddy movies of the seventies (Hollywood's initial response to feminism) have given way in the eighties to films which at least acknowledge the changing role of women in the workplace and at home. Early attempts at this, such as *Tootsie* and *Mr. Mom* were both commercially successful but also exhibited Hollywood's rearguard resistance to altering the status quo. Both films dealt with role reversals between men and women and both ended up glorifying "women's work" or a woman's triumph over sexism by placing men in the roles traditionally thought of as belonging to women. The message seemed to be that the best women were really men, or that women still need men, albeit in disguise, to fight their battles for them.

Subsequent attempts have been more encouraging, in part because of the rise of several certified leading ladies, including Meryl Streep, Jane Fonda, Sally Field, and Goldie Hawn. The professional careers of these women in many ways parallel the characters they often play.

Having established their appeal at the box office, all of these stars have used their stature to become quasi-moguls, often getting producer or executive producer credits for the films in which they appear. The rise of powerful women able to put together their own deals and mix it up with the big boys is a change in Hollywood, the effects of which will be felt for years to come. The initial few steps taken by these women have been halting ones for sure, since most are not yet secure enough to risk alienating the audience that made them stars in the first place. But the ability of box-office appeal to confer power on women in Hollywood, as it has done for men for years, bodes well for the future.

Straight pornography without restriction is shown nearly everywhere in the U.S. in spite of a 1973 court decision that community standards had to be followed in determining what could be permitted in any given locality. After a jury in Georgia banned a Mike Nichols film, *Carnal Knowledge,* in 1974, it was thought that the recent freedom to show pornography was ending. But a Supreme Court reversing of that decision now allows anything except "sexual conduct in a patently offensive way," a definition so vague that there have since been no landmark cases involving pornography based on it, and filmmakers continue free to do as they like and show what they please. All that remains are restraints on the public advertising of these pictures.

New Places, New Types

Although Hollywood still remains the movie capital, where much of the traditional commercial film-making energy now goes into materials for television, among the younger newcomers there is a scattering geographically, with films being made in many places far from southern California. The center of this breakaway may be New York City. In the opinion of critic Charles Hingham, "The wheel has swung full circle, and we are presently almost back to the situation at the dawn of silent films. Motion pictures are again being shot by young people in the landscapes and city streets of the real America, in wind, rain, snow, and fog. New directors prefer to shoot in real houses, real huts, so that audiences can look through a window to see a real sky. Once again, New York, instead of Hollywood, has become the focus for film-makers. That city, with all its abrasions, is still enormously more potent a source of drama and pictorial interest than Los Angeles. Its very tensions and stresses are the essential matter of film-makers who must come to grips with the realities of our time."

With the scattering of movie makers, there is a parallel splitting-up of audiences, so that we have dozens of types of films: black films, karate films, pornography, cop, and many others all searching out a special segment of the moviegoing population which is—like the reading public—diminished by the pervading force of television. Specialization is the film-maker's answer, yet he hopes to come up with something—like *The Exorcist, Star Wars* and, *Raiders of the Lost Ark* —that will bring in everybody. Instead of the monolithic film corporation, it is now the independent who makes most American films, yet says critic Kaufman, the word independent "is one of the funniest words in the film lexicon; it means independent only of the old assembly line. In some ways it is more harried, less self-confident, than the old studio procedure where picture people know precisely what they were doing, or thought they did, and for whom they were doing it. Now independent production means that, for each project, a producer not only needs to acquire script and director and actors and studio facilities and distribution, he also has to acquire an audience—possibly a different audience for each film, or at least not a relatively dependent general audience as in the past. No longer is there any resemblance to a keeper throwing fish to trained seals."

Thus the so-called "independents" have not brought in an era of artistic excellence, although there has been some furthering of film experiment. The only notable attempt in widening the audience for serious film is the recent establishment of the American Film Theater that is making filmed versions of classical and contemporary plays. On a very restricted subscription circuit, they are criticized as "canned theater" and have not been much of a success as yet. Interestingly, the proliferation of cable television and home video devices such as video-cassettes and videodiscs have accelerated the growth in sophistication of filmed and videotaped theater, opera and dance. As for avant garde and experimental film and video, samples can be viewed on college campuses and at specialized "festivals" in major cities.

For travelers interested in having a first-hand look at the traditional old-style Hollywood, a Universal Studios Tour is highly recommended —over a million and a half visitors show up every year to see what is claimed to be the world's largest movie and television center. The tour, with attendance at five live shows in an elaborate visitors center, *can take up a whole day.* The high point is an hour-and-a-half tramway tour of the back lots. The 420 acres of outdoor sets might include a full-scale European street, a western town, a colonial American street, a Mexican street, a jungle, a lake in a real (man-made) storm, and a burning building that never burns down. There are stunt shows by movie daredevils, marionettes, animal acts, and a makeup show. Another highlight is a 90-minute movie filming in which visitors are given scripted parts. After shooting, sound is added and the film is shown. Regular movies and television shows in the process of being filmed or taped can also be seen at certain times. The studios are in Universal City, part of Los Angeles; for information on rates and special programs, telephone 213-980-9343.

THE FOLK-ROCK-JAZZ SCENE

The various strains of pop music in the U.S. constitute the nation's biggest moneymaking attractions, outdrawing movies, or all sports combined, to an estimated total of *four billion dollars* annually in record sales alone. The fast-changing styles of pop music have never been more widely played and appreciated live than at present, and everywhere we find all forms of music and their latest refinements being played, side by side, in the same communities. There is no American city, or even large town today, where you cannot frequently hear folk, rock, jazz, country and western, and usually the latest stylistic offshoots of each.

As the teenagers of the post-World War II "baby boom" mature into adulthood, their musical tastes are veering away from the loud, hard sounds of late sixties and seventies rock and roll. Instead, these young adults are listening to more "middle of the road" artists—country and pop singers, balladeers, people who might have been termed "crooners" a few generations ago but who have assimilated something of the rock experience and sound into their own music. Younger fans, however, still embrace the chainsaw-like wailing of "heavy metal" bands, and are dancing to heavily synthesizer-based rock sometimes aptly termed "techno-pop." Yet, if there was one development at the turn of the decade that symbolized such growth and change, it was the "localization" of popular music: The mammoth stadium and festival concerts, which continue to be given only by the biggest of superstars, gave way to hundreds of small clubs and concert halls across the nation; these feature famous as well as local talent playing everything from rock to jazz to folk to country—much of it for dancing.

Country and Western

Country music may only be "as 'country' as rapid urbanization and commercial pressures will allow," as historian Bill C. Malone notes, but the rural attitudes and values, and the traditional folk-culture origins of the form undeniably endure. The themes of contemporary country music are the concerns of blue collar America—the dreams and disappointments, the yearnings and unfulfilled desires of factory workers, truck drivers, salesmen, industrial laborers. Yet, where country music was once the exclusive domain of the rural South and West, today its sound and influence extend to every region and every walk of life.

The capital of what has come to be known as "commercial" country music continues to be Nashville, Tennessee, home of the 50-year old Grand Ole Opry and of literally hundreds of record companies, music publishers, studios and entrepreneurs bent on keeping up the flow of new country recordings and artists. Additionally, through movies such as *Urban Cowboy* and *Honeysuckle Rose,* and through nationally televised country music series and specials, performers such as Willie Nelson, Kenny Rogers, Dolly Parton, and Mickey Gilley are now national and international celebrities of the first rank—a far cry from the "hillbilly" tag once derisively applied to them.

The Opry, newly ensconced in its own "opera house," has, since its inception, been the scene of a weekly country music extravaganza that is broadcast live throughout the U.S. But, as is the case with other forms of popular music, country music has branched out, with major new outposts located in Austin, Texas (Willie Nelson's hometown and the center for the "outlaw" country musicians and singers who strayed from the formulas Nashville tried to impose on them); Muscle Shoals, Alabama; and Bakersfield, California. Today, too, country music can be heard in local bars from New York to Seattle and on radio stations just about 24-hours a day in almost every city.

Many country stars have been singing and playing for decades and have legions of their own dedicated fans, but in spite of big money and adulation, most of them have not lost their informal ways or rural roots. Some big names in addition to those already mentioned, and who perform regularly in nightclubs, on record, and in concert, are Johnny Cash, Waylon Jennings, Ronnie Milsap, Merle Haggard, Dottie West, Barbara Mandrell, the Oak Ridge Boys, Crystal Gayle, Loretta Lynn, Eddy Arnold, Charlie Rich, Glen Campbell, Tanya Tucker, Tom T. Hall, Roy Clark, Alabama, and Statler Brothers.

Two of the more lasting off-shoots of country music have been bluegrass and country-rock. Bluegrass is a virtuoso stringband music also characterized by "high lonesome" vocals—high lonesome translating into a kind of pinched, nasal sound often sung in multi-part harmony. It is foot-stomping, good-for-dancing music first developed by Bill Monroe in the 1940s and still played by such well-known artists as the Stanley Brothers, Jimmy Martin, Jim and Jesse, the Country Gentlemen, the Oak Ridge Boys, and others. Country-rock is an electrified hybrid favored by many of the younger country-based artists including Willie Nelson and Waylon Jennings, along with Emmylou Harris, Hank Williams, Jr. (son of one of the most beloved early country singers and writers), Kris Kristofferson, the Eagles, Bobby Bare, and Eddie Rabbitt.

Rock

The youth culture, seen as a separate society from that of the mainstream, reached its apex in 1969 at the *Woodstock Music and Art Fair,* near Monticello, New York, where a rock festival drew some 400,000 young music fans and would-be revolutionaries. In the opinion of many observers of the rock scene, its apogee was also the start of its decline. From the bitter social consciousness of Bob Dylan's poetic songs of 1966, there gradually came the introspective love songs of the country rock singers. The Beatles disbanded and when there was a killing at the Rolling Stones' concert in California, the temper of rock changed; its anger waned, as if its promise, like the promise many young people had seen in their country, had failed them. Today, however, rock is in the ascendancy again, fueled, on the one hand, by the inevitable superstars and, on the other, by a profusion of new young bands (many of them from Great Britain) playing a brand of rock and roll based upon and reminiscent of early sixties pop.

The superstars themselves fall into two categories: artists such as the Rolling Stones, Michael Jackson, and Elton John who have been making hits more less regularly for 15 years and more, and "newcomers" such as Bruce Springsteen, Billy Joel, and the Police, who have been crisscrossing the country playing every theater and club they could for a decade or more, but who have only relatively recently graduated to playing sporting arenas and baseball stadiums. Of the newer bands, the Pretenders, Cyndi Lauper, and Pat Benatar appear to have the wherewithal to sustain what have been quick rises to superstardom, coming as they did from the undisciplined foment that was known as "punk" and "new wave." In actuality, this "new" wave was really but a renewed expression of rock's original anger and contempt for authority. By the time the music made it to mass appeal, however, it had been filtered through eminently danceable rhythms and a heightened sense of theatricality, while the musicianship was considerably more sophisticated than that of far more flamboyant bands.

A decade ago, rock stars were mainly the property of the very young, but today they hobnob with chic society and make more money than the fabulous movie stars of the thirties and forties. Says Rolling Stones mainstay Mick Jagger, "Me and Nureyev have flaming rows about whether it takes more talent and discipline to be a ballet dancer or a pop singer." Rock critic Mike Jahn described what the former teenage-craze scene has turned into these days, by picturing a Rolling Stones concert at Madison Square Garden:

"Jagger throwing rose petals taken from a silver bowl held by a middle-aged black porter; Truman Capote exercising his adenoids behind 16,000 watts of rock 'n' roll; *Atlantic Records* spending a small fortune renting the *Four Seasons* restaurant for a midnight reception for which Jagger showed up late; the cream of world chic and half the radical movement turning out in honor of a singer who writes about whipping slaves ('Brown Sugar') as though it were a nice funky way to kill a couple of hours. . . . "

For the youngest rock fans, it often seems as though nothing can be too loud or garrish enough. The success of groups such as Foreigner, Van Halen, AC/DC, Iron Maiden, and Rush attest to the continuing appeal of "heavy metal"—a simplistic, visceral style of playing that places its highest values on volume and intensity. At the other end of the spectrum is the pop styling of the likes of Barbra Streisand and Neil Diamond, and groups such as ABBA and the Bee Gees—all of whom transcend categorization in one sense, but whose music concentrates on strong, hummable melodies and emotionally intense performances.

But, the scope of popular music, even as distinct from country and jazz, is hardly restricted to such extremes. There is an enormous middle territory that can best be sampled by turning a radio dial in any major city and stopping at each of several stations. Thus, one might come into contact with the "soul" music of Stevie Wonder, Stephanie Mills, or Teddy Pendergrass, the classic rock of everyone from Elvis Presley to James Taylor, the different kinds of dance music that are made by Kool & the Gang and Manhattan Transfer, or the jazzy pop of Chuck Mangione and George Benson, to name but a few.

A tightened economy and the lack of the kind of social issues that mobilized folk and rock musicians in the sixties and seventies have interestingly led to a more decentralized performance situation than has existed here in some years. People who don't want to travel far or spend much, or people for whom music is a part of, rather than the focal point of, their entertainment needs, are paying more attention to local attractions. Meanwhile, performers who once sold out multiple-night engagements at 20,000-seat arenas now often play small theaters and dance clubs (or a combination of both) when they hit major cities. New York is perhaps the perfect illustration, where a group might come in and play Madison Square Garden, with 19,000 seats, one night, the 1,500-capacity Ritz Ballroom the next, and the 500-seat Bottom Line the third. The rock scene is a healthy one indeed.

Jazz

Jazz, too, as noted, is in the middle of a great revival. Jazz spots are a shade more centered geographically: New York and Los Angeles, although there has never been more jazz in the smaller cities than now. Many old-timers are coming out of retirement while youngsters are arriving on the music scene with what seem miraculous talents out of the past. For jazz in New York check the following: *Blue Note, Bradley's, Fat Tuesday's, Greene Street, Gregory's, Hanratty's, Knickerbockker Saloon, Lush Life, Michael's Pub, Rainbow Room, Seventh Ave. South, Sweet Basil, Village Vanguard, West Boondock,* and *West End Cafe.* There are dozens of others in virtually every city. Also of great importance in jazz are annual festivals which feature everything from traditional *Dixieland* to *jazz-rock,* or *"fusion,"* (which combines the improvisational base of traditional jazz with the electronic impulses of rock). Among the most prestigious of these are the *New Orleans Mardi Gras* in January, the *New Orleans Jazz and Heritage Festival* early in May, the *Memphis Cotton Carnival, Jazz and Blues Festival* in May, the *Kool Jazz Festival* New York for ten days around July 4, and *California's Monterey Jazz Festival* in August.

As for the birthplace of jazz, New Orleans, much good and some bad can be heard here. In the French Quarter, drop in one of the bars, sit at the counter surrounding the stage, and call out your requests. If you can stand the crush, go to *Preservation Hall,* where some of the older musicians can still be seen.

Wherever you travel you'll find music, usually any kind you want. For folk, ask the first college student you meet. For rock, ask a teenager. And for jazz, play it safe and call the amusements department of any local newspaper.

THE FINE ARTS

As the United States has become the center of the world of modern art it has become a progressively more fascinating land for the art lover and the art explorer. Alongside the considerable treasures of traditional art schools that have come out of the long histories of art in Europe and the Orient, collected originally by American "robber barons" a century ago and now being greatly expanded by our major art institutions, there are two special American areas, native art and the avant-garde. Both of these strongly color the American art scene today.

An art lover, if he is able to travel about the land, should acquaint himself with the major museums, galleries, and centers of art that form the landmarks of the American art world. Some of these hold world-famous collections in some specialized period or style, many so extensive they form a necessary part of any definitive study of that particular art. As the country has become a world leader in art—both in collecting and in producing it—it has lost much of an earlier provincialism. Although American artists form an important part of any imaginable grouping of modern makers of art today, there has developed no chauvinistic spirit to insist on calling the avant-garde "American." The modern world of art is almost completely international in feeling—you simply cannot sense any narrow nationality consciousness in current works—but there is no question that a great many of the leading practitioners live, work and display in the U.S. The native art, on the other hand, comes by its "Americanness" purely, originating as it does before colonists disturbed the civilizations of the Indians and Eskimos. Primitive, or "naive", art done by unschooled painters—Grandma Moses is our most famous example—makes another category, with much delightful work to be seen.

New England

To begin in the East and move West, the first major art center is Boston and Cambridge. In the Harvard University complex are found the *Fogg Art Museum,* with special shows as well as a permanent collection of European and ancient art, and the modern, Le Corbusier-designed *Center for the Visual Arts.* Boston has one of the country's most important museums, the *Museum of Fine Arts,* noted for Impressionist, Colonial, Greek, Roman, and Egyptian art collections. The *Yale Art Gallery,* New Haven, displays notable modern art and recently acquired a reworked Claes Oldenburg sculpture called *Lipstick*—a giant lipstick tube mounted on the body of an army tank—that travelers will understand to be typical of many monumental sculptures he has done, and others have done, that are finding acceptance in commercial and academic outdoor sites. *The Clark Museum* in the popular Berkshire Mountain resort Williamstown, Mass., has an outstanding collection of Impressionist and modern art.

New York and Conceptual Art

New York City is of course the heart of the American art world. For a modern artist or sculptor, acceptance in one of the contemporary-art museums here means to have become an established success: the *Museum of Modern Art,* the *Solomon R. Guggenheim Museum,* the *Jewish Museum,* and the *Whitney Museum of American Art.* The first, the world's most outstanding museum of the modern movement, has undergone considerable renovation; it can be counted on for excellent permanent as well as visiting shows. The Guggenheim, all 20th-century works, displays its treasures in a famous spiraled structure; the Jewish Museum shows Jewish art back into history as well as outstanding current works. The Whitney is said to have the most comprehensive 20th-century collection in the world. Fabulous treasures of art of other eras and lands are seen at the *Frick,* the *Metropolitan,* the *Pierpont Morgan Library,* the *New York Historical Society,* and the *Brooklyn Museum.* Definitive art collections in special areas include the *Museum* of American Folk Art, the Museum of the American Indian, the Museum of Primitive Art, the Studio Museum in Harlem, and the Store Front Museum (Jamaica, Queens)—the last two showing the work of black artists, and even a Museum of Holography, in SoHo.

But New York is also the center of art business—the site of the country's major galleries and of many important art auctions (notably (Sotheby-Parke Bernet and Christie's). Traditionally art has for generations been sold in the well-established dealers' room of 57th Street and Madison Avenue, many of them specializing in "stables" of their own contemporary artists. A decade ago a breakaway group of painters and sculptors working in avant-garde forms moved to new, more unrestricted showrooms on West Broadway south of Houston Street (thus the nickname SoHo), where today such galleries as Castelli, Circle, Emmerich, Weber and scores of others represent artists, many of whom are trying to find ways to make art with no intermediaries at all because of generalized resentment in seeing their works become mediums of exchange rather than objects of pleasure. This movement has resulted in what are called body artists, conceptual artists, or head artists, whose work is performed on the artist's own body or merely thought of in his mind. Yet the dealer-artist relationship continues, even if it is only where a dealer introduces a patron to underwrite such a "work" as Ian Wilson simply talking (on philosophy for example) for an hour. The artist gets paid and the art lover gets a receipt, which he may frame if he likes.

Washington

Another fabulous trove of modern art is the Hirshhorn Museum and Sculpture Garden—dubbed the "doughnut" for its cylindrical form—in Washington, which has some 2,000 sculptures and 4,000 paintings, the gift of Joseph Hirshhorn to the Smithsonian Institution. A good deal of the country's heritage of art is shown in various publicly-owned museums here: the National Collection of Fine Arts, the National Portrait Gallery (including the famous Indian Gallery of George Catlin, with 445 paintings), and the National Gallery of Art, holder of such European masters as Rembrandt's Self Portrait, Raphael's Alba Madonna, and Renoir's Girl With a Watering Can. The townhouse of Frederick Douglass, called "the father of the Civil Rights movement," houses the Museum of African Art. The Corcoran Gallery traces American art from the early colonists' work to the present.

Midwest

Chicago is the home of another of the world's great art collections at the Art Institute of Chicago, which has a vast assemblage of Impressionist works. The Museum of Contemporary Art welcomes experimenters in the avant-garde art movements. Chicago also has intriguing, excellent, and rarely seen works in a number of ethnic museums and galleries, particularly in the Ukrainian Institute of Modern Art, the Polish Museum of America, and the Balzekas Museum of Lithuanian Culture. Minneapolis displays modern works the equal of those anywhere in the country at the Walker Art Center, and the influence of immigrants is again seen here in the American Swedish Institute. Chicago is also the center for a new group calling themselves the "Favoritistes, recalling old favorites in watercolors, with a twist."

Southwest

Down in Houston is a $4-million wing which is part of the city's excellent *Museum of Fine Arts;* called the Brown Pavilion, it houses recent works and was designed by Mies van der Rohe. Farther West, in Santa Fe, those interested in American Indian arts should visit the *Fine Arts Museum,* part of a five-unit museum complex dealing with the lore of the Southwest. The *Arts Museum,* in the form of six ancient Spanish missions, has shows by local artists, many Indians among them.

Far West and Far Out

But for mainstream up-to-the-minute art, you must keep on all the way to Los Angeles, where a couple of years ago Chris Burden created a "sculpture" consisting of having himself crucified, with real nails pounded through his palms, to the back of a Volkswagen. This late conceptual art comes after the work of a group of so-called earth artists, whose diggings, made in the early 1970s, still exist in the Nevada desert and in principle can still be seen, if you can find them. One of the works, for example—*Double Negative,* by Michael Heizer, consisting of 40,000 tons of cliffside cut out of a mesa top to form two huge notches—is a favorite spot for a Sunday drive for the residents of the nearby town of Overton. The exact location of other works by Heizer, Walter de Maria and others remains a secret, in keeping with the continuing attempts to wrest art works from the control of museum curators and gallery owners.

La Cienega Boulevard in Los Angeles is the site of a number of modern galleries, and considerable respect and encouragement for avant-garde experimenters is given by the *Los Angeles County Museum of Art* and by the *Pasadena Art Museum.*

Smaller Collections

Besides the major collections, there are more modest displays, often easier for the traveler to deal with, in every important city, and some of them, like the Worcester (Mass.) *Art Museum,* take on a cameolike quality in their perfection and balance. Likewise, American university art departments often build up impressive galleries of their own: the *Finch College Museum of Art* in New York City, and the *Rhode Island School of Design Museum* in Providence, are examples taken at random.

A characteristic of the American art world is that a variety of styles and levels of excellence go on side by side, so that where representational art, and even the abstract art that seemed bent on displacing it, were both consigned by some critics to oblivion in the early Seventies, they are both still thriving alongside the conceptual forms that presently seem so much more difficult for many to understand. But in a land with the physical variety and the great distances of the U.S. it may be a good idea to be cautious about using labels on any style of art. One reason is that the artist may well not agree with the label you put on him, and another reason is that labelling may prejudice you against enjoying works you might really appreciate seeing. There may, also, be excellences in native art or folk art that simply ought not to be compared with other forms.

Perhaps quite special to the U.S., too, is the proliferation of amateur and semi-professional artists' shows all across the land, especially in summer. Well mixed with stands selling leather belts, turquoise jewelry (rarely real), and organically-grown apricot juice, much of this art work, displayed in a brief carnival atmosphere for a day or two before being moved away to the next outdoor show, is banal: sad clowns, watery-eyed children, flamingo cutouts on backgrounds of black felt. Usually the crowd is more rewarding to study than are the art works, but some good finds occur, especially in the area of the primitive painting—which means simply works done by untaught people who felt like painting something. One in, maybe, a thousand has some innate feeling for form and color that might repay your effort in searching it out. Among locations of outdoor shows, chosen here as examples at random, are Provincetown, Mass.; Wickford, R.I.; Greenwich Village in New York City; Cedar Key, Fla.; and Park City, Utah—there are literally hundreds, in every part of the country.

Meanwhile American museums are making purchases of single paintings by old masters for more than one million dollars apiece: the *Detroit Museum of Art* paid as much for a Caravaggio, and the *National Gallery* about the same price for a Georges de la Tour. American influence goes out into the world; the world's paintings come to America. An exhibit opened in 1975 in the Louvre in Paris reflected this spirit perfectly. For some 4,000 years a neo-Sumerian statue has been broken, its head separated from its body. Then the *Metropolitan* in New York lent the head, which it owns, to the *Louvre,* which had the body, so the work could be put back together again. After a three-year stand in Paris, it was shown in New York for a like period of time.

THE THEATER SCENE

There is a no more volatile art in the United States than its theater, with its many factions reacting to one another, rejecting one influence to follow another, sprouting and blooming in benighted prairie and desert cities, attacking the traditional forts of Broadway or merely spurning them. At any given moment there are always critics proclaiming that the American theater is dead, but while Broadway—the most visible symbol of American theater—may rarely be the seat of theatrical invention, its overwhelming success during economically hard times is also a sign of the theater's national well-being.

The U.S. has no tradition of theater that can be compared with that of Europe. There was a time when the melodramas and musicals of Broadway became the staple fare of popular entertainment—half a century or so, beginning in the Gay Nineties—but already, by the late twenties, it was the motion picture that reached the mass of the people, not theater. Today it's the movies and television, not the theater, and yet the theater still carries a spiritual significance no other medium can equal.

New York

Where *Broadway* used to put on 100 plays and musicals in a single season, it's a good year now that brings us 30, and yet the bubbling turmoil of stage productions has never been more steamy than it is in New York City today—on a good night at the height of the season there will be as many as 250 theaters (some with as few as 50 seats) with footlights on and curtains ready to part.

So the place to start tasting American theater is New York. For every Broadway theater that has been ignominiously turned into a television studio or torn down for a hotel, half a dozen new theaters have sprung up *off-Broadway* and *off-off-Broadway* in lofts, churches, garages, and storefronts on Second Avenue or the Upper West Side or even in Brooklyn. Yet Broadway itself, in terms of attendance, continues to be the main theatrical drawing card. Stephen Sondheim's work during the last decade (*Sunday in the Park with George, Sweeney Todd, A Little Night Music*) is the exception that makes the rule as far as the general lack of innovation most critics find on Broadway. Yet, a late '70s boom in revivals of classic musicals led to the creation of a number of new old-fashioned revue-like entertainments such as *My One and Only,* starring Twiggy and Tommy Tune in a wonderfully silly but musically enchanting retrospective of Gershwin favorites; and *42nd Street* (a live remake of the film). Many of these have gone on as touring companies even after their Broadway runs have expired. The surprise hit of recent seasons has been *La Cage Aux Folles,* based on the movie of the same name about a gay couple and their cabaret, while *Dreamgirls* is a none-too-camouflaged re-enactment of the rise and fall of the classic Motown singing group the Supremes—one of whose members was the now internationally acclaimed singing and film star Diana Ross.

Our serious theater is producing a number of significant young playwrights, including Pulitzer Prize-winning David Mamet (*Glengarry Glen Ross, American Buffalo*), Tony Award-winning Harvey Fierstein (*Torch Song Trilogy*), and David Rabe (*Hurlyburly*), among others. Imports have yielded long-running Broadway hits such as *The Real Thing.* But, there has also been a resurgence of successful American-originated drama developed and nurtured at such regional theaters as the *Long Wharf* in New Haven, Connecticut and the *Arena Stage* in Washington D.C. The most sterling examples are *'Night, Mother,* the brilliantly harrowing play depicting the relationship between a suicidal woman and her mother.

It is not that excellent theater *cannot* be created on Broadway, but the expense of producing a play there first—while it is still undergoing rewriting and polishing—is prohibitive. Thus most original work mostly comes from outside, from Off-Broadway theaters that were originally centered in Greenwich Village but spread into other parts of the city, from Off-Off-Broadway theaters that started out as amateur, free-admission shows that wanted to experiment more freely than even the Off-Broadway theaters could do, from regional theater everywhere in the country. As the Broadway theaters close up, one by one, and the Off-Broadway shows charge more and more for tickets and put on increasingly elaborate productions, the meaning of "Broadway theater" does become blurred. Yet a couple of dozen midtown theaters still qualify for the old tag, drawing as they do on huge advance out-of-town sales of tickets for entertainment guaranteed to be comic, or cute, or sentimental, or sprightly-musical, or otherwise somehow entertaining without ever troubling the mind.

A study of the listings on Broadway will uncover some rare good theater, seriously intended whatever its tone, but for an earlier meeting with good works a visitor is advised to note what the group theaters are doing. These are not "repertory" groups in the strict sense because they usually put on new plays rather than repeating their productions. Joseph Papp's *New York Shakespeare Festival Public Theater* (which originated two Broadway blockbusters with *A Chorus Line* and *Pirates of Penzance* in order to finance its more experimental endeavors) is probably the most active and best-known of these. Others include the *LaMama Experimental Theater Club,* the *Negro Ensemble Company, Equity Library Theater, Circle Rep,* and the *American Place* company.

After explosive activity in experimentation, much of it spurred by the now exiled *Living Theater* in the sixties, innovation is presently at a somewhat static stage. Audiences have been surrounded by actors; they now loom overhead on perches or leap about through the spectators without causing much surprise anymore. Performers appear nude in many shows and sex onstage has lost its shock value. In such ways the radical experimenters, although mainly gone from sight right now, have made sharply felt their influences, and not only in superficial ways. Sweet "wholesome" views of life are replaced with realistic and coldly bitter views; compare World War Two hero plays with David Rabe's blind Vietnam veteran who on returning home can no longer "see" his family. A great leaping clattering loudmouthed production from Italy, *Orlando Furioso,* involved audiences in the middle of the action itself—there was no longer a space between performer and spectator, and this, too, portends theatrical usages to come: the audience will no longer be safe in its seats to observe, unaffected, invulnerable. One critic defines this as "theater as 'contact' sport," describing it further as "like walking into your most heroic dream awake."

"Regional" Theater

If the U.S. has a thin theatrical tradition compared with older lands, then the regional theaters are even more like children beginning to learn—yet today much of their work is first-rate, serious without being pompous, and, more important to the future of American theater, not interested in leaving town and making it to the "big time." In the past few years the regional groups have become so well grounded and so much a part of the cultural fabric of their home cities that they have no interest in moving to anything supposedly higher up on the cultural scale. Officials of Lincoln Center in New York were dismayed to discover that their lordly invitations to a number of small-city group theaters to perform in New York were simply turned down cold—producers, directors, and actors were far too busy at home to travel.

Nevertheless, there is a recently developed sense of brotherhood and co-operation among many regional groups. Called the "spirit of Providence," it had its impetus in a plan by Adrian Hall, director of the *Trinity Square Company* in Providence, to exchange productions with the *Cincinnati Playhouse* company; now many local theaters enjoy one run they don't have to worry about, while their people get a refreshing trip to another part of the country. There is nothing regional, incidentally, about American regional theater—as might, for example, be said of the theater of French Canada or of Ireland, where a provincial or narrowly national preoccupation colors almost every work of expression. American actors move about freely, working in this city or that in plays that may be written by Chekhov or Jerzy Grotowski or a local high school English teacher. Among the major American companies outside New York there are the *Yale Repertory* and *Long Wharf Theater,* New Haven; *Stage,* Hartford; *Stage West,* Springfield, Mass.; *Play House,* Cleveland; *Playhouse,* Cincinnati; *Goodman* and *Organic* theaters, Chicago; *Repertory Theater,* Milwaukee; *Arena Stage,* Washington; *Guthrie Theater,* Minneapolis; *Dallas Theater Company,* Dallas; *Alley Theater,* Houston; *Mark Taper Forum,* Los Angeles; *American Conservatory Theater,* San Francisco; and the *Repertory Theater,* Seattle.

In spite of the predictions of some critics, such as John Lahr, who writes that "Broadway comedy, like the society it reflects, is fulfilling a death wish," it is more likely that fresh ideas will someday again brighten the Times Square stages, if indeed any are left standing. It is to the country at large that we must look for this adrenalin. Says Joseph Zeigler, who has directed half a dozen regional theaters, "For the first time in American history, the contextual power of Broadway and the creative quality of the institutional theater (inside and outside New York) can combine to create a truly superior expression of the art. It is a matter not of overthrowing Broadway's power, but of using it. Coexistence is now possible."

Travelers in the U.S. will discover a good deal of other types of theater, too—more or less pale imitations of Broadway shows in *"dinner theaters,"* where the musicals compete with the rattle of dishes, and the *summer theater circuit,* that began (and still thrives mostly) in New England, employing Equity, or union, actors. Established traditionally in barns outside small towns, the latter usually present works a decade or so out of Broadway, but a rare few still give new works a chance on the boards. Their limited season makes it impossible to establish full-time, year-round organizations that could have the cultural impact of the regional companies.

In a similar position is the so-called *outdoor theater,* flourishing mainly in the South and West, where huge casts, mostly amateurs (but with a minimum of three Equity players in each show) put on cheerful, simple-minded historical musicals on subjects connected with local lore: *The Lost Colony* (North Carolina), *Hatfields and McCoys* (West Virginia), *The Stephen Foster Story* (Kentucky), etc. One of these, *Ramona,* in Hemet, California, is America's longest-running play—over 50 years, several times each weekend in the Spring, and going strong. (By contrast, *The Fantasticks,* in New York, has played year-round performances for more than 24 years.) Since audiences are numerous and many of them far from the outdoor stage, actors, according to one outdoor director, "should look as if they felt tall . . . and stick to the bigger gestures." Some 40 of these dramas draw millions of playgoers every season.

Akin to these are the *Shakespeare Festivals* around the country, the best being Joe Papp's in Central Park. Others flourish in Stratford, Conn. (and another is famous in Stratford, Ontario); Cleveland; Boulder, Colo.; San Rafael, California; and Ashland, Oregon—all of them in the summer season.

As in all the arts, many levels of theater exist at the same time in the U.S., from the audience assaults of some experimental stages to the cotton candy of Broadway farce or under-the-stars melodrama. For those with a real theatrical interest, it will be the successful experiments —and they arise out of many, many miserable flops—that capture the imagination. An English director who has had much influence on American experimental stagings, Peter Brook, tells us: "Whatever is defined as theater misses the point. Whatever has been handed down to us has been cheapened out of recognition. Whoever claims to know what theater was or could be, doesn't. We are now before a long period of perpetual revolution, in which we must search, attempt to build, pull down and search again."

THE MUSIC SCENE

In spite of a faltering economy that has reduced some of the classical music programs in American cities the overall situation is that opportunities for concertgoing are becoming more and more widespread. It is not only because of national tours by musical groups from the likes of the Metropolitan Opera in New York or the major symphony orchestras, but also, and more importantly, that regions far from New York, Chicago, Washington or Los Angeles now have their own professional groups.

The Opera

The state of the opera is lively and growing throughout the U.S., although there remains a curious unsureness in the American mind about just what the opera in this country ought to become. One composer of modern American opera, Ned Rorem, says there is "confusion about American opera: outwardly we react as though it were European, inwardly we wish it to conform to our indigenous musical comedy. The sole difference today between American opera and musical comedy (which can be tragedy, too, as *Show Boat* showed 30 years before *West Side Story*) is that one uses conservatory-trained voices while the other uses microphone-trained voices."

New York's *Metropolitan Opera* celebrated its centennial in 1984; under the direction of conductor James Levine, the premiere American opera company has for the first time taken serious strides forward in embracing 20th-century repertory. There is much exchanging and cross-fertilization in the world of music; a production of the *Cincinnati Summer Opera,* for example, of *Manon Lescaut,* by Puccini, was directed by Italian film director Luchino Visconti, who was brought in for the assignment from the Spoleto Festival. It is clear that performers and directors of international caliber no longer restrict appearances to traditional capitals of music.

Of course the major American cities, with their larger music audiences, still do draw the star performers more regularly; the excellent *New York City Opera* owes much of its excitement to Beverly Sills, soprano-turned-company president who turned heads in the critical world with a first-rate production of Janáček's *Cunning Little Vixens.* In Washington, the Kennedy Center is the scene of productions of the *Opera Society of Washington,* which presents such works as a Monteverdi opera in a realization by the English musicologist Raymond Leppard, whose work is also seen in the *Santa Fe Opera's* summer season in the Cavalli opera *L'Egisto.*

New works in opera, like those in other arts, meet resistance in finding a production, and it is here that some of the regional companies are more open to innovation than the older-established ones. An example is the world premiere of *Willie Stark,* with music and libretto by Carlisle Floyd in a production directed by Broadway's Harold Prince at the *Grand Opera of Houston.* The *Boston Opera Company* produced a mammoth 4½-hour version of the Prokofiev *War and Peace,* taken from the Tolstoy work. Another groundbreaking organization is the *St. Louis Opera,* which gave the American premiere of *Fennimore and Gerda* by Frederick Delius. And the Brooklyn Academy of Music housed the New York première of Philip Glass's *Satyagraha,* a striking minimalist interpretation of Gandhi's life.

The *Chicago Lyric Opera* enters its 30th year in 1984. In nearby Evanston, *Northwestern University* is the scene of new opera productions, such as a 1970 work of Michael Tippett, *The Knot Garden.* The fine *San Francisco Opera* underwent its first change in general directors in 25 years as Terry McEwen took the helm from Kurt Herbert Adler. Experimental opera is welcomed at the *Minnesota Opera,* which has put on an improvisational work entitled *The Newest Opera in the World.* The Reno-based *Nevada Opera* is now is now a decade old and it, too, likes to break new ground, as, for example, with the first American production of a Busoni work. In even such a small town as Indianola, Iowa, the annual *summer opera festival* plays to full houses every night. Other *summer operas* worth the trip are in Des Moines, Iowa; Vienna, Virginia (*Wolf Trap Farm*); Central City, Colorado; Lake George, New York; and Lake Placid, New York. San Antonio, Texas, has a *festival* in March. The sparkling new Heinz Hall is the home of productions of the *Pittsburgh Opera.* And for a fascinating experience of opera, go to Jackson, Mississippi for a production of *Opera/South,* the country's only all-black company.

Orchestras Galore

In spite of the fact that an old reputation dies hard—in this case it is the redneck whose musical boundary extends no farther than Bob Wills and his Texas Cowboys—nearly every American city has a symphony or philharmonic orchestra and their audiences are growing steadily. It is worth looking at the state of Texas. Besides orchestras in Dallas, Houston, and San Antonio that have annual budgets of over half a million dollars each, there are permanent orchestras with regular seasons in Amarillo, Austin, Corpus Christi, El Paso, Fort Worth, Irving, Laredo, Lubbock, Midland, Richardson, San Angelo, and Tyler, as well as teaching orchestras at half a dozen universities within the state. New York City of course numbers a good portion of its population among music lovers and is the music center of the country, if there is one, yet there is no part of the land where the people must do without serious music.

The musical heart of New York is Lincoln Center, which includes Avery Fisher Hall, home of the *New York Philharmonic;* the Metropolitan Opera House; the New York State Theater, home of the *New York City Opera* and *City Ballet;* Alice Tully Hall, used primarily for chamber and other small-scale recitals; and the outdoor Guggenheim Bandshell. Carnegie Hall, saved from the wreckers a few years back, remains the goal of many concert performers—an appearance here can still give a sort of old-fashioned stamp of fame, of permanent status in the music world. A $200,000 Rodgers electronic organ installed in Carnegie Hall is used for concerts by such virtuosi as Virgil Fox. Free concerts by the *New York Philharmonic* (as well as by the *Metropolitan Opera*) are given in various city parks in all boroughs in summertime. From October to June there are free Sunday evening sacred music programs at *St. Bartholomew's Church.*

Among the country's great orchestras are the *Boston Symphony,* the *Chicago Symphony,* the *Philadelphia Orchestra* (where Richard Muti has taken the conductor's baton from Eugene Ormandy), the *Cleveland Orchestra,* the *Pittsburgh Symphony,* and the *National Symphony* in Washington. Other fine orchestras are based in Cincinnati, Detroit, Rochester (Minnesota), Des Moines, Atlanta, Shreveport, Rochester (New York), Newark, Phoenix, Oklahoma City, St. Louis, Baltimore, San Francisco, Miami, Seattle, Portland (Oregon), and Los Angeles. Although there is a good deal of exchange done from one city to another among conductors and featured soloists, and each city's organization is free to make up its own musical programs, there are nevertheless criticisms that American directors stick too closely to the tried and safe and ignore the obscure or difficult works. A conductor who is also a music critic, Robert Craft, complains that certain areas of the world of music are simply never played in this country. The music of the Renaissance is rarely heard, he says—partially because of a lack of the old instruments to play it, and lack of musicians who know how to use them, but also, he feels, because of a lack of adventurousness. The same situation holds for much of the so-called "new music," atonal works by such relatively modern composers as Schoenberg, Stravinsky, Varèse, and Ives, which are perhaps considered too far from the more popular works in style to be able to draw large audiences. The recent Ives and Stravinsky centennials, however, did provide a nationwide spate of concerts of their works.

Craft has appeared at some of the outdoor *summer concert festivals* that bloom in many parts of the land beginning every June, and they provide some excellent listening in pretty settings even though what may at first sound like applause is really the sound of hands slapping hungry mosquitoes. In Colorado there is the *Aspen Music Festival,* in a delightful mountain resort that's a ski center in winter, as well as stately concerts in the imposing Broadmoor Hotel in Colorado Springs. *Wolftrap Farm Park,* less than a half hour into Virginia from Washington, D.C., will be operating from temporary housing for a few years following a devastating fire; it offers visiting orchestras, ballet companies, opera, jazz, pop, and folk concerts. Watermelon Concerts of the *Grand Teton Music Festival,* Jackson Hole, Wyoming, are so named for the audience-performer discussions that follow concerts, accompanied by servings of watermelon to everyone. Some festivals involve music camps where music students practice together for several weeks at a time and give regular concerts. One of these, the *International Music Camp,* is given in the lovely surroundings of the International Peace Garden on the U.S.-Canadian border in North Dakota. Another, called the *National Music Camp,* takes place in Interlochen, Michigan, in a lakeside setting.

The *Berkshire Festival,* at Tanglewood, near Lenox, Massachusetts, takes the Boston Symphony into the highlands under the skies, and there are other outdoor music celebrations in Marlboro, Vermont; Hanover, New Hampshire; Oakland, Michigan; Door County, Wisconsin; Brevard, North Carolina; Saratoga Springs, New York; Ojai and Saratoga, in California; and even in Anchorage, Alaska. There has recently been opened the country's first state park dedicated to the arts, in Lewiston, N.Y., where the *Buffalo Philharmonic* is in residence.

THE DANCE SCENE

"Dance is the mother of all the art forms," says Arthur Mitchell, director of the Dance Theater of Harlem. "Before a child is even out of the womb it kicks—and kicking is dancing." Mitchell's black dancers are part of the reason that New York City has become the world center for every kind of modern dance and ballet. The combination of enthusiasm and professionalism in New York dance companies, whose members come from all ethnic sources (or in some cases as defectors from the U.S.S.R.), has built up a solid audience for dance that is gradually reaching out to include people in every part of the land.

Already rich in choreographic and dancing skills, the American companies have been further gifted by former members of the Soviet ballet: Rudolf Nureyev, Natalia Makarova, Ivan Nagy, the Panovs, Mikhail Baryshnikov, the last of whom recently took over as artistic director (along with continuing as a principal dancer) of *American Ballet Theater.* Despite growing American interest in dance, public financing has diminished—the *National Ballet* in the nation's capital had to close down permanently for lack of support—which means that the Russians face a less secure future here than they did at home. Explaining his action in coming to the U.S., Baryshnikov says, "While there are many great schools in other countries, which produce great dancers, all the great choreographers are in the West. In America alone you have three of the very few living geniuses of classical choreography: George Balanchine, Antony Tudor, and Jerome Robbins." All three work mainly in New York.

One of the great companies is the late George Balanchine's *New York City Ballet.* Born in 1904, Balanchine was a Russian who left for Paris half a century ago and built a strong company by the force of his commanding personality as well as his skills in ballet. His dancers have been made into a sort of family, and the women are not supposed to marry, though he married five of them (one at a time). He has been criticized for making standardized dancers—all tall and rangy—and he replied, "If somebody doesn't like it, he doesn't have to come and look at it." Among the company's dancers, Patricia McBride might qualify as America's prima ballerina, while Edward Villella and new company director Peter Martins are likely the best-known American male dancers.

Villella has described the dancer's enthusiasm that characterizes the great American companies: "I sense dance. I simply like to *do* it—to experience it. When I'm throwing myself around the stage with complete abandon, yet complete control, I feel totally honest. I cannot lie. When you talk, you can't be totally honest. Where you're there just dancing—that's *you.*" A modern spirit of youthful experimentation pervades the work of some troupes, notably the *City Center Joffrey Ballet,* some 40 dancers directed by Robert Joffrey in ballets described by critic John Gruen as "drenched in multimedia razzmatazz. The company loves to jive, rock, swing, bump, and grind. Lights flash, music blares, scenery moves, wind machines blow, and both stage and dancers vibrate and gyrate to electronic devices and music."

Other noted New York-based companies include the *Eliot Feld Ballet,* Feld having been called "the most important artist we have in dance, along with Balanchine and Robbins"; the *Paul Taylor Company,* which consistently wins unanimous raves and national press attention for its annual New York season; and the *Alvin Ailey Dance Theater,* an integrated company originally influenced by the great black dancer and choreographer of modern dance, Katherine Dunham. It is only recently that black dancers have found places regularly in ballet companies; there had been strange prejudices that blacks had special rhythms or that their bodies could not accomplish the demands of ballet. There are in fact some all-black modern dance companies (*Arthur Mitchell's* is the outstanding one), but they are not the only ones to draw on the black American experience. Alvin Ailey has been criticized by militant blacks for using nonblack dancers. He replies, "It's a question of everybody being human. I think that we have to get together—and dance together. I'm very happy when I see an audience in Houston, Texas, applauding my mixed company when they walk down the stage hand in hand."

"The woman who invented modern dance," as the *New York Times* calls her, is Martha Graham (born 1894), who has come out of retirement to go back to her startlingly original works of the thirties and forties in revivals by her great company of women dancers. (One alumna is Betty Ford, wife of former President Ford.) Of her 150 works, only a few have been annotated, and without performances by those who remember them, they would be lost forever. She plans to revive half a dozen of her early works every year. Comparing dancers of half a century ago with those today, Graham told dance writer Elizabeth Kendall that the current dancers are not as strong as the women of her own dancing youth but are "slimmer, very much slimmer, with longer legs. They're not built aggressively. They're built more for air, swiftness, not for argument."

From the same era as Graham was Ted Shawn, whose more conventional choreography predated Graham's revolutionary works. Though Shawn died in 1972, the dance school he founded is still active, and the Jacob's Pillow festival he began in 1942 still appears every summer at his farm near Lee, Massachusetts. The growth in public interest since the thirties is amazing; in 1933 there was but one major ballet company in the whole country; today there are over 100 of them, many performing year-round seasons. A dozen companies from various cities had a recent New York season together in New York's Roundabout Stage One, in a program called *Dance Umbrella,* while the American Place, also in New York, gave programs of the *Contemporary Dance System.*

Ballet or Modern Dance?

The line between ballet and modern dance is hardly a sharp one, but ballet involves the more classical movements, yet keeps changing over the years. After the more literary, dramatic works of the pre-war years, ballet has now become more abstract, in what is called pure-dance ballet. This is sometimes faulted for leaving out the more popular "story" dances that usually draw a larger public. One critic, Katherine Sorley Walker, says of modern ballet, "It is hard to realize how little it has to say to the world outside. Little? Almost nothing. The ballet scene these days, viewed from outside, looks at times like a blur of young male and female bodies mixing themselves up in complicated physical patterns with heavy sexual connotations, to a series of sometimes rather horrible accompaniments of electronic music, *musique concrète,* or half-intelligible speech."

Yet a small town the size of Cheyenne, Wyoming, was recently host to the *Murray Louis Dance Company* and to a Canadian ballet troupe. Of the latter's performance, a rancher in the audience commented, "Those little twinkle-toes are mighty cute, and the men—they're real athletes." The regional ballets take part in one of four regional ballet associations, and are nonprofit and nonprofessional, although there is the possibility of becoming professional. This has been the case with the *Boston Civic Ballet* and the *Pennsylvania Ballet.* Philadelphia, Chicago, and San Francisco are the main centers of ballet outside New York, but traditional ballet may now be seen in almost every state. There will likely be a Christmas performance of *Nutcracker,* and parts of *Swan Lake* or *Sleeping Beauty* will be staples in many regional companies, yet there is a notable strain of originality and regional subject matter in much of the work of the lesser known ensembles. The *Houston Ballet,* for example, is producing a *Texas Trilogy* of full-length ballets, one on the founding of the city, another about a famous Texas coastal storm, and one about the moon landing (of course, Houstonites consider this a Texas event!). Joe Frantz, who provided money for the dance from the state's Bicentennial Commission, says, "People don't have to understand the language to know what's going on."

There is also a jazz ballet in Houston, while the *Austin Ballet* prides itself on having "a good slice of music hall" in its repertoire. Ballet in the small cities covers a lot of ground; in Witchita Falls, Texas, the czarda and mazurka are danced as part of the local ethnic heritage. The *Iowa Dance Theater of the Hemispheres,* in Cedar Rapids, presents works on farm and prairie themes. Although their aims are sometimes conventional and their dancing skills imperfect, the regional companies have become an important force in the American cultural world. The respected dance critic Walter Terry says, "Regional ballets have brought acceptance of ballet, enthusiasm for ballet, and even profound respect for ballet to the major communities of the United States."

A sign of the rising quality of ballet outside the East is the appointment of Ben Stevenson, who had been with the National Ballet, as artistic director of Ruth Page's excellent *Chicago Ballet.* Perhaps even more significant, however, was an invitation, which has been accepted, that was made to the *Phoenix Metropolitan Dance Theater* by the Bureau of Indian Affairs. This company will be presenting special programs on tours to native Indians of the Hopi and Navajo reservations—a sort of payment in kind for all those rain dances, rabbit dances, and corn dances the Indians have let us enjoy for so many years.

FOOD AND DRINK IN AMERICA

Native, Imported and Glorious Mixture

by
WILLIAM CLIFFORD

(*William Clifford writes a weekly newspaper column,* Wine on the Table, *as well as articles for various magazines. Among his books are* The Insiders' Guide to Chinese Restaurants in New York *and* Dagmar Freuchen's Cookbook of the Seven Seas.)

"Tell me what you eat: I will tell you what you are," said Jean-Anthelme Brillat-Savarin, jurist and philosopher of gastronomy who fled the Terror of the Revolution and supported himself in New York City from 1794 to 1796 by teaching French and playing his violin.

The people of a nation as large as ours are many different things, and inevitably we eat many different foods. In fact, despite our ever-increasing mass production and standardization, we continue to enjoy great diversity. For example, consider the fruits of the sea. We can hardly be called a fish-loving people, certainly not to be compared with the Sicilians and Portuguese, the Bengalis and Japanese. We do not even approach the consumption of the British (largely neutralized in packets of fish and chips). Yet what a quantity of fish finds a place in our diet, all but surreptitiously, as tuna salad and sandwiches, canned salmon and sardines, clam chowder, and the quick food service of fillets or fish sticks. And note how many of our regional specialties come from the sea: Maine lobsters, codfish balls, oyster stew, clambakes, Maryland crab cakes, Florida pompano, stone crabs, New Orleans oysters Rockefeller, California abalone, cioppino, Dungeness crabs, Olympia oysters,

76

Columbia River salmon. All natural enough in a land washed by two of the world's great oceans.

Acting as a brake on our profusion and diversity has been our strong Puritan tradition of frugality. Even our extraordinary agrarian-epicure, Thomas Jefferson, spoke simply of the primary needs of "bread and covering"—though he himself lived far better than that. Most Americans would be shocked by the lavish Lucullan indulgence of European travelers, who frequently spend more money on their dinner than on their lodging for the night. We still budget less than 25% of our earnings on food, while many nations allow 50% or more.

Amber Waves of Grain

A separate reason for this economy is our capacity for surplus agricultural production. We are the granary of the modern world, the only nation with the resources to confront crop failures and population growth on a global scale. Until the recent global energy crisis, our farmers were paid to limit production. Then when demand suddenly depleted long-standing surpluses and markets were assured, they set to work and brought in record crops seemingly overnight. Obviously our nation is blessed with a favorable climate, and we have developed the essential technology. But plain hard work has much to do with it—the work ethic goes hand in hand with Puritan frugality.

Production of food in vast quantities, both for a nation of 213 million generally-well-fed citizens and for export, leads to standardization. First it requires pesticides and preservatives and processing, some of which have been overdone. But far more food processing is beneficial both to health and pocketbook than otherwise. What it does not benefit, alas, is individuality, the infinite variety that many of us treasure as the spice of life.

Travelers complain of this standardization. Between the score of major American cities, they say, there stretch wastelands of hamburgers and Coke, of the inevitable fried chicken and steak. Admittedly the fare in roadside diners is bleak. One is tempted to recall the pioneers, more of whom were killed by the frying pan, it is said, than by the Indians. But you can usually find something of interest by leaving the highway and searching in local markets. I have put together a picnic of cold meat and local cheese, good bread, inexpensive fruit, and even local wine, in New York, New Jersey, Pennsylvania, Maryland, Ohio, and, of course, California. With prudent planning or inquiry and a bit of luck, you may even find a farmers' market. Always worth asking for, these markets sometimes exist in quite unexpected places, e.g. Chevy Chase, Maryland, where plain farm ladies of Montgomery County still sell the home produce of their country kitchens and smokehouses to fat bureaucrats. Except for a few special restaurants, most of the regional cooking in America, like most of the best cooking of every sort—the most exact, imaginative, time consuming, sensitive, and honest—is home cooking. Unfortunately visitors are not always invited to the homes of our hundreds of thousands of passionate gourmet cooks, but a farmers' market can serve as a window.

Vinland

The Vikings found such a profusion of wild grapes growing along the northeastern coast of America that they named the country Vinland. Where grapes grew, they thought, wine could be made. Unfortunately, these hopes were dashed. For the grapes of New England turned out not to be members of the European Vitis vinifera or wine-bearer family, but of several other families of vines native to America. Making wine from them was somewhat like trying to squeeze orange juice from lemons.

Perhaps, then, European grapes would flourish in their place? A colonial Governor of Virginia went so far as to report that his colony would soon be supplying all of Britain's vinous needs. But three centuries of effort were doomed to failure, the vinifera plantings in Eastern America invariably succumbing to our unfamiliar climate and pests. Not until the 1950s was the problem solved, when an immigrant viticultural genius named Dr. Konstantin Frank grafted Rieslings and Chardonnays onto hardy rootstocks from Quebec and made New York's first European-tasting wines for connoisseurs.

Meanwhile an important wine industry grew up around the native American grapes (actually around their hybrids), and many easterners came to like the grapey tastes of Concords and Catawbas. The problem never arose in California, where the climate—the many variations of climate—suited the viniferas to perfection. Here the obstacles were ignorance (of several sorts), greed, legal restrictions, and time. Only once each year does a wine grower have a chance to try something new, and many experiments take five or ten years to prove out. Founded after the Gold Rush, the California industry was stopped in its tracks some 60 or 70 vintages later by Prohibition. Hardly more than 40 years have brought the wines of California from that sad period of oblivion to their remarkable place in the world today. Improvements in each of the past few years have been so great that it would be foolhardy to try to predict the future.

Despite the recent upsurge of interest in gourmet food and wine, we are still a beer-and-whiskey drinking nation. Perhaps the current "Pepsi generation," and each succeeding Pepsi generation, will take en masse to wine. (Or perhaps they will just take to *Diet Pepsi*, or branch water.) But as things stand today, we drink roughly as many gallons of distilled spirits as we do wine, and many times this quantity of beer. If you are a serious beer drinker, local beers are worth trying when you travel. While many of them are distinguished primarily for their inoffensive mildness, occasionally you can find one with real character. Spirits are, of course, the same wherever they are sold, but you will be offered a wider selection of bourbons in Louisville, while straight rye may be easier to come by in Baltimore. If the present trend continues, no one will be drinking anything but vodka or white wine by the year 2001.

Indians and American Immigrants

The eastern seaboard Indians ate oysters and other mollusks in such abundance that their heaps of discarded shells have not yet worn away. Like other primitive peoples, they evolved some highly sophisticated means of ensuring their nourishment. Without their skill and generosity the Pilgrims might not have survived. Still, we all prefer what we already know. Corn and fish and wild turkeys may serve to keep body and soul together, but "give me a good loaf of bread and a piece of fat pork," wrote one of the settlers. "We are so fed up with lobsters that the thought of one more almost makes me sick. Oysters are worse—whatever do the Indians see in them?"

A similar question might have been asked about the diamondback salt-marsh turtle by the early settlers of Chesapeake Bay. Later to become an obligatory course at every opulent banquet in the era of Diamond Jim Brady, terrapin was so common and cheap in colonial times that the Maryland Assembly passed a law limiting the victualing of slaves on it to once a week. The reasoning was that, being free for the taking, it could not be so good as food which cost money, and valuable property had to be protected from abuse by its miserly masters.

Not every religious group of colonists was so severe toward pleasures of the table as the Puritans. The Shaker communities stretching from Maine to Ohio enjoyed great simmering stockpots, capacious communal ovens for baking bread, cakes, cookies and pies, and lavish use of herbs. They invented excellent recipes for such native foods as corn, sweet potatoes, lima beans, pumpkins and cranberries. They improved crops and marketed the first commercial canned goods, made beautiful furniture, practiced celibacy and danced for joy—or at least for exercise, "to drive away wrong desires."

The current flowering of ethnic restaurants in all of our large cities—in the opinion of some critics they are the restaurants most worth going to, and the only ones where fine food is reasonably priced—indicates that we continue to be, as we always have been, a cosmopolitan, polyglot, polyculinary nation of immigrants. One cannot ignore more than 1,000 Chinese restaurants in the greater New York area alone as a factor on the American culinary scene. "Show me a typical American restaurant," a foreign visitor requests, and New Yorkers fumble for something skyscraper-chic, pseudo-colonial, southern or soul. Each will do, but so will a *Café des Artistes* or a *Shun Lee Dynasty*. In fact an ordinary Chinese-American restaurant symbolizes a good part of our unique history and virtues. Chop Suey is not a Chinese dish but a Chinese-American invention, an improvisation on leftovers or whatever materials happen to be at hand. It represents a commitment to making do, adapting to local conditions, and practicing strict economy. (Perhaps today we have changed, but "waste not, want not" was long as central to American life as it still is to Chinese.) It demonstrates the fact that anything, no matter how exotic, can be assimilated. We can do it the American way. Then, once the door is opened, a part of real Chinese cooking can come into our lives, be known and found everywhere, belong to all of us.

New England

In October 1794 Brillat-Savarin went hunting for partridge, squirrel and wild turkey on a farm five leagues from Hartford, Connecticut, surrounded by virgin forest with undergrowth "so dense and prickly it would have stopped a snake." Today few patches of virgin forest and even fewer wild turkeys are left in Connecticut. Nevertheless, on the land where I live, not many more leagues from Hartford, I have this year seen numerous deer, a red fox, various small and edible animals of the underbrush, and many ducks and geese overhead. The Connecticut state seal shows three grapevines bearing purple fruit. So far as I know, the state has never had a wine industry, but the time may come. Amateurs are growing wine grapes for their own use, and the shores of Long Island Sound, both north and south, have begun to prove as hospitable to wine producing as they have long been to the cultivation of oysters (this is the home of the bluepoint) and the seasonal visitation of various fine fish. (Long Island has produced one fine label, *Hargrave*.)

Rhode Island has given its name to a chicken, Cape Cod is named after a major food fish, Maine supplies us with excellent potatoes as well as those incomparable lobsters, and Vermont calls to mind maple syrup and Cheddar cheese—even if more of both are made in neighboring New York. Country stores often keep two wheels of Cheddar, "this year's" and "last year's," or mild and sharp. A dish to savor in local restaurants is Cheddar cheese soup.

In and around Boston one eats codfish cakes and broiled scrod (young cod or haddock), Cotuit oysters and steamer clams, Cape Cod cranberries and Indian pudding (corn meal flavored with molasses and ginger—well no, the Indians didn't have ginger), steamed brown bread and baked beans. Usually small navy or pea beans (probably grown in Michigan, Idaho or California) seasoned with salt pork and mustard but not tomato sauce. Everyone eats oyster stew and lobster, as much as he can afford. (European visitors are not disturbed by the cost, for they customarily pay twice as much at home.) Massachusetts is the mother of Yankee cooking. Once a year the entire nation sits down to a Massachusetts colonial dinner. We call it Thanksgiving. Happily a similar full-course roast turkey dinner appears frequently on restaurant menus at all seasons. It's usually an acceptable choice, even where foods come frozen from central kitchens and local cooking skills are minimal.

Mid-Atlantic States

New York City can provide anything and everything. Not always the best of everything, and not without a struggle. But at a price, the Baghdad of the modern world can supply whatever you wish, more than anywhere else on earth. I once offered to make good on this boast to a Japanese guest who replied thank you very much, he would like to visit an African restaurant. Central African, for big game, perhaps a ragout of elephant foot or giraffe neck. (I also made the mistake of asking him if he ate persimmons in Japan—the fruit was then in season in New York—and he replied yes, he believed they had 200 varieties.) I failed him on the restaurant but subsequently discovered that such African curiosities are imported, frozen, by at least one New York meat market, and they have been served at the Explorers Club.

While the city is a microcosm of the whole world, the rest of New York State is surprisingly rural, traditional, and spiritually as well as geographically attached to neighboring New England. Dutch settlers brought a predilection for pancakes, and since buckwheat grew in New York, buckwheat cakes with buckwheat honey got a start that has never stopped. The Dutch also contributed *koolslaa,* or cabbage salad. Where would any American delicatessen be without *koolslaa*/coleslaw? *Koekje*/cookie is another Dutch word.

Potato chips were a New York State invention, so we believe, known first as Saratoga chips. The Hudson River Valley has made more so-phisticated contributions than this—shad and their delicious roe, for example. Sturgeon swam here a century ago, and their caviar was shipped down from Poughkeepsie to fetch higher prices at *Delmonico's* and *Rector's* than the stale import from Imperial Russia. Latest intelligence suggests that the sturgeon may be coming back. Early Hudson Valley vineyards died out after supplying the first vines to the upstate Finger Lakes, but several new ones now receive visitors. In the much more important wine country of western New York, visitors to Hammondsport may tour three of the giant wine companies, plus a wine museum on Bully Hill and, by appointment, the *Vinifera Wine Cellars* of the legendary Dr. Frank. Neighboring Penn Yan, Naples and Canandaigua complete the tour, in beautiful countryside well worth two or three days of your time on the way to Niagara Falls. Wines can be tasted on the house and bottles bought to take away. Dr. Frank's wines and one or two from *Gold Seal* are made from viniferas, *Bully Hill* and *Boordy* stress French-American hybrids, and the big companies still feature native flavors.

New Jersey, our fifth smallest state, ranks sixth largest in growing vegetables, perhaps overshadowed by the fact that it is seventh in manufacturing. Indigenous foods include very fine blueberries (a vast improvement on European huckleberries) and strawberries, virtually every vegetable for the commercial freezer, and various fruits of the sea. Since the southern tip of the state reaches to the center of Maryland (with its first Mason-Dixon marker), we should not be too surprised to find snapping turtles, for soup.

George Washington was so taken with Pennsylvania Dutch food when he wintered at Valley Forge that he persuaded his Pennsylvania cook to migrate to Virginia. "Better die eating than fighting," runs a maxim of these food-loving Rhinelanders ("Dutch" meaning *Deutsch,* or German), whose diet features meat three times a day (with heavy reliance on the smokehouse), a strong emphasis on baking, vegetables stewed from sunrise to noon, and four or five desserts at a go. As for pickles—the sours to balance the many sweets, though not necessarily a mystical seven of each—possibly the Mennonites couldn't survive without them. "You shouldn't eat so many pickles," a kindly matron once advised her servant girl, "because the vinegar will drain the color from your cheeks."

"Who wants pink cheeks if they're at the expense of pickles?" the girl replied.

Of course that's not all. Scrapple and Philadelphia Pepper Pot (tripe soup with red pepper) are also Pennsylvania Dutch, together with Snits and Knep (dried apples and dumplings) and Shoofly Pie (molasses and brown sugar). Henry J. Heinz of Sharpsburg extended his wife's repertory of ketchup, horseradish and pickles, not to seven, but to 57, varieties.

Maryland must be included as one of the handful of states central to American gastronomy. Diamondback, canvasback, razorback—the turtle, duck and hog are three of the prime ingredients. Once ensconced in every high-society chafing dish, terrapin is rarely served today except by private clubs and a few hotels. (If you want to eat turtle, go to Indonesia or the Philippines.) Wild ducks are plentiful overhead, but they have to be brought down, cleaned, and then carefully roasted for only 20 or 25 minutes, an operation more likely to be carried out successfully by devoted amateurs than in modern restaurant kitchens. Country hams are free of such complexities, although Marylanders sometimes complicate their service by stuffing them smartly with finely chopped greens. The Atlantic Ocean and great inland sea of Chesapeake Bay provide a profusion of other fine fare, beginning with the rockfish or striped bass that decorates the state seal. Connoisseurs particularly treasure the bay's sweet and tender crabs, both in their crunchy softshell stage (which occurs some 20 times during their first year of growth) and with mature hard shells patriotically colored red, white and blue. Crab cakes and crabmeat salads are the most popular in restaurants, although crab boil with hot spices and crabs at clambakes win the prize if you are willing to roll up your shirtsleeves. Also delicious sautéed with country ham, deviled, and souffléed. And not wasted in soup. Clams both soft and hard shell, steamer and surf, abound. The competition being what it is, oyster lovers may have difficulty with their feelings toward clams. The oysters are in trouble, they have long been in trouble, and clams are only a small part of it. But for all their fragility, they survive. Perfection on the half shell, they also make a lovely thick creamy soup or stew. An inspired Maryland combination is a plate of hot fried oysters with cold chicken salad. Maryland fried chicken requires cream gravy and cornbread (or corn pone, spoon bread, hoecake or johnnycake) or beaten biscuits. You put your gravy only on the bread if you like crisp chicken.

Maryland hams are first cousins of the world-famous hams from Smithfield, Virginia. For many years of Queen Victoria's reign the

Buckingham Palace Household kept a standing order for six Smithfield hams a week. That's a lot of ham considering its strength, which is such as to suggest eating in small slivers, say as a condiment on butter-drenched biscuits. Virginia cooking was English until Thomas Jefferson brought in French influence: stews, soufflés, ices, sauces, cooking with wine. He tried to grow everything at Monticello including wine grapes, lavishing the finest food and drink on his many guests both there and in the White House (where his steward noted that the Presidential salary did not cover his costs of entertaining).

The South

Fried chicken and country ham with cornbread and gravy are southern cooking. So is soul food—cheap cuts of meat and bones, offal, rejects from the kitchen of the big house, cooked with collard greens and other edibles picked free from the fields and woods. Chitterlings (pig tripe) seasoned with pepper, Kentucky Burgoo (including squirrel) with pepper, Carolina barbecue (shredded pork) with pepper, pickled Jerusalem artichokes (sunflower roots) with pepper, Louisiana's ubiquitous Tabasco sauce—one senses the same attachment to hot food, and for the same reasons, that East Indians have for their curries.

Brunswick stew, roast possum, country sausages with fried apples, shrimp, hominy grits, red rice, black-eyed peas, okra, gumbo, barbecued ribs, catfish stewed or fried, sweet preserves made from every fruit, baked sweet potatoes, candied sweet potatoes, sweet potato pudding, sweet potato custard, sweet potato cookies, sweet potato pie, chess pie (that's cheese pie, often made without the cheese), pecan pie, scripture cake, Tennessee wedding stack cake, watermelons, iced tea, mint juleps, Scuppernong grape wine—all of these foods proclaim The South. Florida contributes more fruits of the sea—stone crab claws, spiny lobsters, conch, pompano, green turtles—together with fruits of the tropical orchard ranging from Key limes and mangoes to the never-never world of akees, sweequassas, cherimoyas and carambolas. Cuban cooking brings additional dimensions.

Louisiana means Creole—French, Spanish and African—superimposed on southern: shrimp gumbo, jambalaya, crawfish, oysters, crabs, pompano, frog's legs, duck, rabbit, squirrel, opossum, coffee with chicory, Tabasco with everything, sauces, wine. Whether for Oysters Rockefeller or Poor-Boy Sandwiches, New Orleans is the favorite eating place between the coasts. There must be something to it.

The Midwest

No one expects any gastronomical earthquakes from the middle west, but it is worth remembering that Irma Rombauer, whose *Joy of Cooking* tells all there is to know on the subject, came from here. America's heartland, "that ocean of good grass," turns its hand to a little of everything and does much of it well. Michigan and Ohio make wine—*Meier's* is the leading producer, with a whole company island (surely that beats a company town) growing Catawbas, the Isle St. George in western Lake Erie. Meier's headquarters is down near Cincinnati, where an enterprising young lawyer named Nicholas Longworth began to make wines nearly a century and a half ago. He produced 150,000 bottles a year of Ohio Sparkling Catawba, selling it in the best New York hotels (which, he was showman enough to proclaim, sometimes dared to pass off French Champagne as his superior product), and even in London, years before there was any wine industry in either New York or California.

Ohio also makes Liederkranz cheese, America's first and foremost candidate in milk's leap toward immortality. Liederkranz was invented in Monroe, New York in 1882. When they moved the factory to Van Wert, Ohio, the cheese refused to go along. To reproduce authentic Liederkranz they had to smear some of the old Monroe mold on the new Ohio walls—so important are airborne yeasts to cheese-making. Of course Wisconsin is our primary cheese state, with American Muenster (unrelated to the pungent Muenster of Alsace), Cheddar (closely related), Swiss (in the middle distance), and blue cheeses all commanding respectable followings. German and Scandinavian foods are popular here in the dairyland, as in neighboring Minnesota and Illinois.

When you visit Michigan, go late in the Spring, to join the search for morels, those most treasured of wild mushrooms. Like Wisconsin, Michigan has lakes teeming with fish. And woods choked with game. (Minnesota lakes teem with wild rice.) Chicago enjoys city sophistication buttressed by plenty of meat—"hog butcher to the world." It was Cincinnati they called Porkopolis in Longworth's time. Indiana grows excellent tomatoes, the whole middle west grows corn. Iowa grows tall corn—for fattening pigs, not men.

The Southwest, Rockies and Plains

A guidebook to Colorado recommends "local specialties, such as fine Mexican food." Cuisines as powerful as the Mexican speak with voices that are heard, smelled, tasted, totally sensed, far north of the border. Nobody right on the border has even a ghost of a chance: witness the food of Texas, New Mexico, Arizona and southern California. Each state also harbors other influences and preferences. Besides Tex-Mex chili con carne, our colossus of the southwest has its own Gulf Coast decked with seafood, the same that reaches all the way here from Florida; its cattle, steak on the hoof for outdoor barbecue; and its beans. Beans, sourdough bread, and coffee are the essential trio to accompany Texas meat. But how far are we from Mexico, when the beans and the barbecue sauce are both hot with chili powder?

Indians, who hunted for meat, picked wild fruits and vegetables and grew corn. Oklahoma, New Mexico and Arizona offer opportunities for research, primarily in dried corn, summer squash, and prairie dogs baked in clay. In Tulsa you can eat blackbird pie. Missouri cookery takes in bullhead (catfish) soup and prime Kansas City sirloin. The St. Louis World's Fair of 1904 invented the ice cream cone and iced tea—it must have been a hot summer. Kansas eats sunflower roots and seeds, together with sweet corn and fried rabbit.

Colorado provides superb mountain brook trout plus the problems of high altitude cookery. Either boil your Rocky Mountain goat an extra 24 hours at the camp on Pike's Peak or use a pressure cooker. Mormon elders of arid Utah must be chagrined to think that their state supplies fragrant juniper berries to flavor the world's gin. Carrots from soup to nuts (actually to pie) are a particularity of Montana. Heavyweight game, cattle, all sorts of meat, beans, wheat and corn—these are the essential foods of the mountains and plains. Good they can be. Gourmet they are not, where sparse populations still wrestle with strong forces of nature. There's no time for culinary chic.

The Far West

The West Coast is a world apart. Agriculturally, California has everything. (Well—perhaps it does not have Florida's variety of oranges, but it has everything else.) It has beautiful wines to taste and stunning wineries to visit, in such profusion that a full book is needed to guide you to them. Fortunately, several such books can be found, and many wineries are listed in this volume. One memorable day and the taste of one great wine can make a visit to the Napa Valley memorable for a lifetime. But a month is not too long to begin to know the valley well.

The California cornucopia of fruits and vegetables, seafood and all the rest defy naming, not to mention describing. On my last visit I ate abalone at eight different restaurants in San Francisco, trying to find the best. I rarely eat eggs but never pass up an opportunity for Hangtown Fry, the omelet that shows Olympia oysters to perfection. Nor do I overlook Dungeness crab at Fisherman's Wharf. Where else can one eat like this? I stood on a street corner waiting for the light to change, glanced around, and found nine different species of plums on sale in a sidewalk market at my back. Living here might be almost too rich.

Oregon shares the smallest Olympia oysters with her northern neighbor, Washington, but harbors the largest Empire clams. More familiar than either is the superb salmon, eaten fresh, smoked or kippered. Washington has razor clams and geoducks, ten-pound clams nearly rivaling the man-eaters of the South Seas. The crabs are Dungeness and their mayonnaise dressing is often Louis. Huckleberries, loganberries and filberts are local treats. Washington grows superb apples. Alaska has bigger king crab than anywhere else, also great quality salmon, and reindeer.

We can say *au revoir* to the West with a reverential bow to the Idaho potato, which is plainly the greatest potato on earth. Peru may grow 200 varieties, but Idaho has found *the* one. This natural masterpiece should be baked, brushed with butter, and sprinkled with coarsely-ground pepper. For gastronomical indulgence, drench it with sweet butter and cover with caviar. Like the Swiss gourmet society which honors this blessed union annually, you will groan with delight at such delectable détente.

Many regional foods have withstood processing and homogenization. We must take heart, search for the individual who cares, and look for variety even within mass production. The *National Biscuit Company* actually makes saltines by different formulae for different parts of the country. And fortunately the ongoing thrust of nature is difficult to abort. Every Spring the shad swim up the rivers of the eastern seaboard, between March and May or June. As with the appearance of morels, one can date the end of winter at each latitude by their return. Recently sturgeon have reappeared in the Hudson and Connecticut Rivers, after one hundred years. Springtime indeed!

DISTINCTIVE AMERICAN VACATIONS

National Parks, Space Projects, Dude Ranches and More

Many vacation opportunities are basically similar throughout the world. But there are some holidays which are distinctively American—things you can't do anywhere else, or perhaps, can't do *easily* in some other land. This chapter discusses just such uniquely American travel destinations. You will of course want to consult the individual state chapters for more detailed information on the places mentioned here, as well as for additional vacation ideas, but use this section as a means of making your travels in this very large country more focused, more manageable, more enjoyable.

National Parks

A vacation unequaled elsewhere in the world is a week or two in one of the 35 national parks that preserve in beauty and naturalness the variety of landscapes and climates that make the United States so fascinating both to lovers of free space and clear air and to all kinds of students of the outdoors. There are glaciers and tropical swamps; volcanic mountains and parched, endless deserts; pounding seacoasts and tranquil rivers; Cliff Dwellers' ruins and geysers and medicinal springs. There are crashing mountain brooks alive with trout and rain forests where herds of elk brush silently through the luminescent yellow-green of heavy foliage. In the parks you can find nearly every kind of physical geography that the world provides—the mysterious sculptures in glowing red and orange and yellow stone of the Utah highlands, the endless vistas of flat grass in the prairies, the giant sequoias and redwoods.

The following is a listing of national parks by area and by state.

NEW ENGLAND

Maine

Acadia National Park. Here is a combination of mountain and seashore, with a paved road leading to the bald summit of smooth rockface atop Cadillac Mountain. From this vantage you look out over the Atlantic islands off the rocky Maine coast and down upon the green fir forests and ponds of Mt. Desert Island below, most of which is park land. The lively summer resort town of Bar Harbor also lies at your feet.

Campsites along the waterfront of broad craggy rocks are close enough to the sea to be within constant earshot of the sound of the surf. Some 120 miles of trails lead hikers along quiet beaches, atop sea cliffs, and through the woods to fresh-water ponds inland. Northeast Harbor is the starting point for a car tour along Sargent Drive leading to a fjord at Somes Sound. Horseback riding is popular on the trails, and there is excellent surf casting and, for those with patience, beachcombing. Bird watchers can count on spotting ospreys, bald eagles, and many species of duck, and on ledges along the shoreline many harbor seals disport themselves.

Campgrounds are open from May 10 to October 15, but the park is open all year. All services at Bar Harbor. Information from Superintendent, Acadia National Park, Bar Harbor, Me. 04609. (207) 288–3338.

MID-ATLANTIC

Virginia

Shenandoah National Park. The long, narrow 105-mile stretch of this wooded Blue Ridge Mountain sanctuary is, on certain fall weekends when the leaves are at their height of color, known as "traffic jam national park" when thousands of motorists stream along the Skyline Drive here. But you can pull off the road anywhere, or stop at the entrances to any of the many marked trails, and hike up into the wilderness and leave the noise behind within just a few minutes. A gift to the nation from the Commonwealth of Virginia, Shenandoah still has ruins of old farms abandoned a generation or more back. Forgotten orchards can be found where gnarled old apple trees are still producing fruit free for the taking. An excellent lodge, open year around, draws visitors at all seasons—this is the nearest wilderness park to the nation's capital—and there are camp sites, many picnic areas, nature trails, and bridle trails. Within the 300 square miles of highland are the spiny ridges of many steep hills that shoot out from the sides of the Blue Ridge, so that a map of the park roughly resembles the spine of a fish.

All kinds of tourist services and accommodations at Front Royal, near the north entrance, and at Rockfish Gap, near the south entrance.

THE SOUTH

Florida

Everglades National Park. The beauty of Everglades National Park escapes some people, but it wouldn't if they'd slow down enough to really look at it. At first, there seems a sameness, a monotony to the landscape. But there are subtle blendings of plant and animal life in cycles that began, ended, and began again thousands of years ago. At the Royal Palm Hammock visitors' center, park rangers can tell you what to look for and can show it to you through exhibits and color movies. But the vastness, the variety, the shadings do not appear in miniature representations. You can only see them in their larger-than-life actuality.

Branching off from the main road are various viewing areas and trails which sample the complexity of the Everglades. Pa-hay-okee overlook is elevated to give you perspective on a sea of grass stretching endless miles. Gumbo Limbo Trail leads you through a tropical density where you can see only a few feet through the dark foliage. At Taylor Slough, alligators, water birds, ducks, turtles, otter, deer, panthers, black bears, and bobcats congregate. You will see some of them. The Anhinga Trail is a boardwalk which reaches out over a slough, in which the visitor can observe the everyday life and death drama of the glades.

About the time you have become convinced that you are near the outer limits of civilization, that only you, the road, and your strange vehicle remain as outcroppings of the man-made universe, you will reach Flamingo and the familiar world of martinis and steaks and air conditioning. Flamingo has a lodge, a dining room for 200 guests, a drugstore, a marina, rental boats, groceries, gas, tires, oil, and all the accoutrements you suspected were far behind you. From here you can go on to see more of the park—and there is much more to see—but from here you go by boat, and with a guide, of necessity. Morning and evening excursion boat tours can accommodate the mildly curious; those with their own or rented craft may join the Saturday ranger-conducted boat-a-cades, which ramble along sixty-five-mile tours, or houseboat solo by the week.

There are picnic and camping areas at Flamingo and Long Pine Key. The Flamingo campsites hold 60 mobile homes and 171 tents or trailers; a small store sells groceries, fishing supplies, and sundries. Long Pine Key has 108 camp units, each including a picnic table, cookout grill, and a paved strip for trailer or tent, with drinking fountains and comfort stations close by. You can fish all year here and do pretty well. You won't even need a license for saltwater fishing. But no hunting of any kind at any time is allowed. (You may, of course, defend yourself against the mosquitoes, but they are the hunters in this case.)

For information write Everglades National Park, Box 279, Homestead 33030. (305) 247-6211.

Kentucky

Mammoth Cave National Park. A river of blind fish is one of the fascinations of the dark cavernous underground world here in Kentucky that can lead explorers no less than 294 miles along natural corridors on five different levels. The lowest level, at 360 feet under the ground, carries the slow movement of the waters of Echo River—visitors can take boats along this dark waterway. A great onyx formation, Frozen Niagara, has been intriguing visitors for a century, since the days when Edwin Booth recited Shakespeare from a rocky stage now called Booth's Amphitheater. The park includes over 50,000 acres of woodland up on the land side, and there are seven nature trails and guided walking tours. Scenic boat trips on the Miss Green River wind past natural parklands. Open all year are a hotel, lodge and dining room, and there are also a museum and a gift shop. Hiking trails, tennis courts, and fishing in the river, as well as campsites and picnic grounds, are all available year round. Housekeeping cottages are available only on a seasonal basis at Mammoth Cave. The park is on Rte. 70, a few miles from the Cave City interchange of I-65.

North Carolina-Tennessee

Great Smoky Mountains National Park. At the North Carolina entrance to this 800-square-mile park there is an excellent pioneer farmstead maintained by the rangers. Just outside this entrance the town of Cherokee, the capital of the Cherokee Indian reservation, has a street lined with shops purveying Indian-made crafts. The park has some 150 miles of roads, half of them paved, and 700 miles of horseback and hiking trails. At the highest point in the park, Clingman's Dome, an evergreen rain forest can be explored with the help of a self-guiding trail. Trout streams are open to fishing from May through August. Some roads are closed because of snow in the 5,000- and 6,000-foot-high ridges but otherwise the park is open all year—it gets over 8-million visitors annually.

The main North Carolina entrance is on US 441 near Cherokee and the southern terminus of Blue Ridge Parkway. Oconaluftee Ranger Station, with Pioneer Exhibits and Farmstead, at the Park entrance, is open daily. Tent and trailer camping allowed at developed campgrounds; rough camping by permit from rangers. Pets must be kept leashed or restricted at all times. Marked hiking trails include 70 mi. of Appalachian Trailway along the crest of Great Smokies Divide. Livery stable concessionaires rent horses from June through Aug. Trout fishing mid-May to Sept. US 441 is the transmountain highway through the Park. At Newfound Gap on the North Carolina-Tennessee line, it intersects with a paved Park road to Clingman's Dome, highest peak in the Great Smokies. Tourist accommodations at Waynesville, North Carolina, and at Gatlinburg, Tennessee, among other places. For further information write to Headquarters for National Forests in North Carolina, 50 S. French Broad Ave., Box 2750, Asheville, N.C. 28801.

MIDWEST

Michigan

Isle Royale National Park. This magnificent park, a 45-mile-long island in Lake Superior, and a part of Michigan, is the most completely wild of any of the park service's wilderness areas—it has no roads or cars or villages of any kind. Campsites can be reached by boat only, and the park itself is accessible from Houghton, Michigan (50 miles), or Grand Portage, Minnesota (20 miles), by power launch or seaplane. The area actually includes some 200 small islands, once the destination of fur trappers, fishermen, and miners. Abandoned copper mines are still to be seen along some of the 100 miles of hiking trails. The sight of moose swimming out from a harbor shore is fairly common, and fishing in the lake and in some of the inland streams is good. Information from Park Superintendent, Isle Royale National Park, 87 North Ripley St., Houghton.

There is a lodge at Rock Harbor reached from both Houghton, Mich., and Grand Portage, Minn. The Park is open from late June through Labor Day.

SOUTHWEST

Arizona

Grand Canyon National Park. The arrival at Grand Canyon, north via State 64 from Williams or US 180 from Flagstaff, is breathtaking since thick pine forests give little hint of the awesome gorge until you are on its southern edge. Although only a small part of the 277-mile-long canyon is seen by visitors from the South and North Rims, it is the most spectacular part, with widths varying from four to fourteen miles between rims and with depths of up to 5,750 feet from North Rim points. The climate within the canyon—it has six of the Northern Hemisphere's seven botanical life zones—is, from top to bottom, the same as one would encounter traveling from Canada to Mexico. However, without doubt, the most striking feature of Grand Canyon is its geological story and scenery. There is nothing like the canyon anywhere else on earth. Its saga is estimated to be one and one-half billion years old; some of the multicolored strata, for instance, took more than 170 million years to be formed, and each layer was built upon the top of a lower one that took about as long for its creation. Parts of the canyon even formed the bed of an ancient sea, and one can see marine fossils along Bright Angel Trail as it snakes from Grand Canyon Village down to the Colorado River.

If the mighty gorge seems unbelievable, like a two-dimensional stage back-drop, don't be surprised. Only through repeated meetings can one begin to appreciate its vastness. A trip into its heart—via foot or mule—helps to create a greater sense of reality. Even so, one can leave wondering if all the scenes were not part of a dream. If you can, go in autumn—after the summer crowds are gone and before the first snow falls. It's then that the crisp air and the chance for solitude can heighten the canyon's grandeur so that you can get a better feeling for the scope of this wonder.

The majority of travelers view Grand Canyon only from the South Rim, since it is open year-round and is most accessible from the major northern Arizona tourist centers. To reach the North Rim, only 14 miles away, means a 200-mile drive, unless one wants to hike or ride a mule on a jaunt of at least two days to canyon bottom, across the river, and up the other side. But, assuming it is not the season (from October to April) when heavy snows prevent a visit, try to include it. For the North Rim vistas—from high points like Point Imperial, Cape Royal, Point Sublime, and others—lend an entirely different interpretation to Grand Canyon's depths and citadel-like formations.

South Rim sightseeing, other than excursions to Phantom Ranch or to Plateau Point, halfway down, is chiefly confined to the so-called East and West Rim drives, the former being part of State 64 to Cameron. Focal point is Grand Canyon Village, where, in addition to nature walks and forest bridle trails, there are several attractions. One, near El Tovar Hotel, is Hopi House, a curio shop built somewhat like the Hopi pueblo homes. The eight-mile West Rim Drive goes by several panoramic view-points and ends at Hermits Rest with its curio-snack shop.

The 25-mile East Rim Driver from Grand Canyon Village to Desert View is the real motoring gem. There are about a half dozen major lookout points, the best of which—for its expansive vistas up and down the canyon-cutting Colorado far below—is Yavapai Point. It has binoculars aimed at important gorge features, a small museum dealing with fauna and flora, a relief map of the canyon, and ranger-naturalist talks on the creation of the canyon. This point is about a half-mile east of the Visitor Center, where there is another, larger museum describing all aspects of the region. About three miles before reaching Desert View, the Tusayan Ruin and Museum, near the south side of the road, gives an insight into how early man lived in the area and how he built his small stone pueblos. At Desert View, the Watchtower overlooks canyon views as well as part of the western section of the Painted Desert. A cafe and curio shop are nearby.

Tourists seeking remote, off-the-beaten-path locales should try Havasu Canyon just below the south-central part of the national park. Access, via a good-to-rough 62-mile road, is best from US 66 about five miles east of Peach Springs. Entrance to this isolated canyon—where Havasupai Indians live amid dashing streams, waterfalls, green fields, and ruby walls—is Hualapai Hilltop. From here you can hike or take a horse down the twisting, eight-mile trail to Supai, the main village, where the white man's civilization has only recently begun to make an impression. Some people have called this canyon America's Shangri-la; certainly there's no better place to completely get away from the sometimes frantic tempo of today—if you don't mind plain accommodations or, more likely, camping out.

Petrified Forest National Park. A part of the brilliant and somber fantasy of the Painted Desert, the six forests of great fallen logs, now turned to jasper and agate, are the petrified remains of trees that grew here 160-million years ago. Flooding waters covered the trees with mud and volcanic ash, and various minerals—silica, iron, manganese, and carbon—filled the wood cells and changed the logs to stone. The broken pieces of log visible have been cleared of their cover by the elements over the millenia, but a vast treasure of unseen logs is thought to lie below the surface all the way down as deep as 300 feet. A 28-mile road leads past the main forests and points of interest between the north and south entrances. Newspaper Rock is a mysterious slab covered with the untranslated picture-writings of prehistoric Indians—there is a nearby ruin of a village that was lived in up to 600 years ago. This is the only national park where you might pass something like a customs inspection on leaving; *Rangers strictly enforce the rule against taking out samples of petrified wood.* But at souvenir shops just outside both entrances you can buy bits of this ancient wood from sites outside the park.

Accommodations and tourist services at Holbrook, on Interstate 40, 27 miles from the north entrance, 15 miles from the south entrance.

Arkansas

Hot Springs National Park. These 4,700 acres in the Ouachita Mountains of central Arkansas have 47 thermal springs flowing at temperatures of an average of 143 degrees F. Famous bathhouses on "Bath House Row" attract visitors from all over the world who come for the "cure." A number of fine old hotels with broad porches accommodate guests who often come for a complete rest, confining their activity to their baths, to visiting the gift shops in the surrounding town of Hot Springs in many areas reminiscent of a turn-of-the-century European spa. For the more energetic there are miles of trails and bridle paths along the slopes of the park. The park officials advise visitors to get the advice of a physician—a number of federally licensed doctors reside here—before taking water from the hot springs, because the waters are not beneficial in all ailments.

Any season of the year is a good time to visit this city of spas and thermal baths, that virtually surrounds the national park. The sixty-five-day horse racing season at Oaklawn Park, usually held from early February until early April, draws a great number of visitors; but tourists congregate here at all seasons.

Other diversions are boating, fishing, swimming, and water-skiing on the surrounding chain of lakes, and hiking or auto tours to the lookout tower atop Hot Springs Mountain. From there a panoramic view of lakes and pine-covered hills stretches before you.

While in Hot Springs you can try your luck and dig for quartz at Coleman's Crystal Mines. Wildwood, a handsome Victorian-era mansion restored in period, is open to visitors during summer. Each room on the first floor is highlighted by a different native wood.

For lovers of the arts, the *Fine Arts Center* houses the gallery of the local Southern Artists Association. Productions of the *Community Players* are staged at the Center.

Children will find much to amuse them: *Animal Wonderland,* on US 270; the *Arkansas Alligator Farm; Magic Springs Family Fun Park; I.Q. Zoo,* with performances by trained small animals; *Tiny Town* and the *Tussaud Wax Museum.*

Many special events are held here during the year, including an inspiring *Easter* Sunrise Service; the Arkansas Fun Festival in early *June;* the Arts & Crafts Fair in *October;* and the Christmas Pageant, held in the Convention Auditorium in early *December.*

New Mexico

Carlsbad Caverns National Park. There are caves here big enough to contain the whole of the Capitol in Washington. Guided tours take you through many of the caverns on a 3½-mile exploration—the full extent of the caverns has never been completely discovered. A jacket or sweater is comfortable down here, where the temperature is always exactly 56 degrees F. If you don't feel like so much walking, a 750-foot-deep elevator will drop you down into one of the caverns, where you can patronize one of the world's strangest lunchrooms if you like. Besides thousands of visitors, the caverns contain millions of bats whose ancestors have lived in here for 15 centuries—at least 100,000 tons of guano had been hauled out of the caves before the National Park Service took possession here. A very early visitor was identified by a sandal he left behind 4,000 years ago—a prehistoric Basketmaker Indian. For the patient traveler, one of the strangest sights in the world is that of the midnight flight of the millions of these bats who flap and clatter their way into the sky and then return at dawn. Fifteen miles southwest of Carlsbad. Accommodations and tourist services at Carlsbad.

Oklahoma

Platt National Park. This smallest of all National Parks has many bromide and sulphur springs, all running cold, that should be taken on a doctor's advice only. Saddle horses are available in the town of Sulphur for use on the park's bridle trails, and there is an eight-mile circuit drive that links three modern campgrounds. The park was once part of the holdings of the Chickasaw Indians, who traditionally drank these waters for therapeutic reasons. Thousands of redwoods budding in April make a delightful sight for springtime travelers here, and there are several streams with waterfalls and cascades easily reached in short walks on trails. There is a nature trail, as well, and in summer a naturalist leads guided tours. Accommodations and tourist services at nearby Sulphur.

Texas

Big Bend National Park. This vast sloping desert reaching up into the Chisos Mountains along the Rio Grande in southwest Texas gives the traveler a marvelous sense of isolation in stark arid beauty. There are the fantastic shapes and colors of the cactuses and other desert plants, and the sweeping shadowy changing colors of the mountain faces; and then, when you get well into the park and find your way along the paved roads through passageways down to the river, you come to one of the two wondrous canyons reachable by car—Santa Elena, to the east or Boquillas, to the west. Except at flood time you can walk along the sandy edge of the riverbed alongside the looming canyon walls, and take a rowboat across to a Mexican village—this is the international border, of course

—where quartz prisms are sold for a dollar (and you can buy a welcome cold beer, Mexican from Monterrey, as well). Back up in the Chisos basin there is a restaurant, gas station, and some furnished cabins, as well as a campground, and there's a stable of good horses for mountain treks far up into the high reaches from where you can see for many many miles down in the Sonoran desert of Mexico. A shorter trip, to a fine scenic hole in the mountain wall, called the "window," leaves every morning and gets you home before lunch.

The 708,000-plus acres of scenic delights are reached from Marathon by US 385, from Alpine over State 118 and from Marfa traveling US 67 and FM 170.

Information and reservations are obtainable through *National Park Concessions, Inc.,* Big Bend National Park, Texas 79834.

Boquillas Warm Springs adds to Big Bend with mineralized waters where temperatures vary from 95 to 105 degrees. And some twenty miles west and on the north edge of Big Bend is the ghost town of Terlingua. Here a national chili cooking contest is held in the fall of each year.

Chisos Mountain Lodge has dining rooms and snack service as well as lodging facilities for over 150 guests. Reservations are prudent. Trailer sites are available at Rio Grande Village.

Other activities may include a horseback ride up South Rim for the awe-inspiring view at 7,200 feet, visits to the Sierra del Carmen and Fronteriza ranges. Camera buffs may simply want to take advantage of the spectacular scenery.

Accommodations and other tourist services also at Marathon, Texas, about 100 miles from the park entrance.

Guadalupe Mountains National Park. Guadalupe Peak here in west Texas is the highest in the state, at 8,751 feet, towering over a region of primary geological importance—the world's most famous area of fossil organic reefs, remains of an era when the sea covered this desert. The park has the further interest of having four distinct climatic zones within its borders, from that of northern Mexico to that of southern Canada. First there are cactuses, then highlands of pine and aspen. Trees native to Canadian climate are found at the higher reaches. The 75,000 acres of the park were until recent years used partly for raising angora goats, but now the land has been returned to aboriginal species, elk and wild turkey. The ranch buildings have been restored to recreate the pioneer era. Accommodations and tourist services at Carlsbad, New Mexico.

In the Guadalupe Mountains National Park, there are daily bus trips to McKittrick Canyon, and hiking in back country or up Guadalupe Peak. A historic ranch site recreates the spirit of the frontier era.

ROCKIES AND PLAINS

Colorado

Mesa Verde National Park. Some 800 years ago the prehistoric Indians who lived and farmed this "green tabletop" were forced to abandon it after a long drought, and they left behind their stone cities built into cliffs here that fascinate archeologists, both professional and amateur. Although some of the dwellings were modest—the pithouses had tiny rooms and housed a single family—there are the remains of great structures as well. The Cliff Palace was built into the cliffside 200 feet up the wall and had 200 rooms; the Spruce Tree House, with 114, is like a modern apartment building in many ways. An excellent museum at park headquarters helps to bring alive this old civilization, and besides evening campfire talks by rangers and archeologists, neighboring Navahos give regular demonstrations of their chants and dances. As for the original Mesa Verdeans, nobody knows when they may have gone after having lived here for 1,300 years. They left unfinished a temple to the sun, and may simply have gradually mingled with other tribes to the south. The fascination here is to trace the development of their architecture from the simple pit house to the sophisticated palaces.

The museum at Park Headquarters will add to the visitor's understanding of Mesa Verde and her people of long ago. Mesa Verde may be reached by car on US 160, thirty-eight miles west of Durango, then on twenty-one miles on park roads from the park entrance. Bus service from Spruce Tree Lodge is available for those who do not wish to drive their cars into the park; *Continental Trailways* has daily buses to Spruce Tree Lodge from Durango. *Frontier Airlines* serves Durango and Cortez ten miles west of Mesa Verde. A limited number of overnight accommodations are available at the park entrance, as are improved facilities for house trailers. A restaurant, service station, AAA road service, and tire agency are available. Evening campfire talks are given by park rangers and archeologists, and visiting Navahos from the neighboring reservation frequently demonstrate tribal dances and chants. Horseback trips through the area can be arranged at headquarters. Lodge is open May 15th to Oct. 15th. Accommodations and tourist services at Cortez, 10 miles west, and at Durango, 38 miles east.

Rocky Mountain National Park. Rocky Mountain National Park is a 405-square-mile reserve of towering peaks and untouched forests first set aside for public enjoyment and as a national treasure back in 1915. The wilds of the park can be explored afoot at leisure, or one can drive through it over the nation's renowned Trail Ridge Rd., skirting chasms a thousand feet deep, and winding over the wind-swept tundra above the timberline. Near the top of Milner Pass, 10,758 feet high (where you cross the Continental Divide), is a museum of tundra ecology that displays wonderfully diverse flora and fauna of this climatically inhospitable land. Summer comes late to the high country, but brings with it a profusion of exquisite, tiny wildflowers. Trail Ridge Rd. is usually closed by snow in late October or early November and not reopened until Memorial Day, when young athletes celebrate the event by skiing on the snow which blankets the top. In midsummer, however, the country above the timberline is refreshingly cool after the heat of the plains. Grand Lake (8,380 feet) is reputed to be the world's loftiest yacht anchorage.

The gateway town of Estes Park has a year-around population of only about 1,600, but in summer tens of thousands of visitors flock to the resort hotels, dude ranches, motels, and campgrounds in the area. Estes Park is not really a park—park is an old western term for a mountain valley, and this was Joel Estes' domain in 1860. When two other families moved in to share this huge rugged hollow in the Rockies, Estes moved out, complaining about the "crowds." An aerial tramway to the top of 8,896-foot Prospect Mountain offers a sweeping view of the peaks and valleys. Boating and fishing on Lake Estes, scores of miles of riding and hiking trails, and hundreds of miles of trout streams are other attractions in this area. The summit of Long's Peak (14,256 feet) can be scaled via trail by most persons in reasonably good health, but its sheer East Face is one of the nation's most challenging climbs.

Montana

Glacier National Park. There are still some 40 glaciers among the peaks and ridges of the 1,600 square miles of this great scenic area that adjoins a Canadian section to make up the Waterton-Glacier International Peace Park.

The park season runs from June 15 to September 10, when most hotels and cabin camps are open. The main roads, however, may stay clear until mid-October depending on the weather.

Most of Glacier Park is accessible only by its one thousand miles of foot and horse trails; on-the-spot inquiry and attention to park regulations is essential—this is rugged country. When the park itself is closed, US 2 may be used to the south from Browning to West Glacier. Local inquiry is advisable if the weather looks bad. And, don't feed the bears.

Starting from Browning, you'll visit the Glacier Park Lodge at East Glacier on US 2. This hotel, like its sisters, Many Glacier Hotel and Lake McDonald Lodge, offers a variety of riding, hiking, golf, and fishing (no license needed in the park). Be sure to inquire about guided tours and lectures offered by the National Park Service naturalists. They will increase your enjoyment of this alpine beauty spot.

From St. Mary you can also swing north to Waterton-Glacier International Peace Park in Canada, an extension of the same kind of mountain terrain as you find on the American side, but perhaps less crowded in the peak months. Also note on the north route the access road to Many Glacier Hotel on Swiftcurrent Lake; you leave the highway at Babb and drive a few miles west to what many consider the park's most varied center of activity. All of the recreation activities are developed here, with trails to Grinnell Lake and Glacier. George Bird Grinnell, the naturalist, was instrumental in the establishment of the park.

On a quick tour, you'll want to see Two Medicine Valley and Lake. Turn west about four miles north of East Glacier on State 49. A seven-mile road leads to a lake (launch trips during the season) ringed by high peaks. There is a self-guiding, well-marked nature trail at Trick Falls, a safe, quick introduction to Glacier.

There's a good campground at St. Mary Lake and another at Rising Sun on the north shore highway. Four miles west of the latter at Sun Point there are an information station and self-guiding trails. The frontal range of the Rockies at this point is known as Lewis Range.

The most spectacular drive through Glacier is over the Continental Divide via the Going-to-the-Sun highway. From Browning and East Glacier, drive north on State 49 and 287 to St. Mary, and then turn westward for the 50-mile drive over Logan Pass to the west end of the park. If you are hauling a camper, and your rig is over thirty feet in length—including your car—you had better make arrangements to leave your camper and pick it up later. Park rules forbid vehicles over thirty feet long on this highway and you will realize why when you begin your climb.

From St. Mary Lake in the east to Lake McDonald in the west the highway crosses 6,664-ft. Logan Pass. It is the great spot to stop and view the park for from here you have 100-mile vistas. Ask about the trail to Granite Park Chalet.

After Logan Pass, descend west along the Garden Wall, one of America's greatest mountain highways. Below at Avalanche Campground, there is an easy two-mile trail to Avalanche Basin, a natural amphitheater with walls two thousand feet high and waterfalls for a backdrop. The red cedars and the rushing streams give you a sense of what the park must be like deep in the interior if you haven't the time for longer hikes or rides.

Lake McDonald is ten miles long and a mile wide. Lake McDonald Lodge near the head of the lake on our highway is the center. There are public campgrounds here and at the foot of the lake at Apgar, as well as several classes of accommodations at both spots. The hike to Sperry Glacier and Chalet is popular.

Accommodations and tourist services at Hungry Horse and Whitefish.

North Dakota

Theodore Roosevelt National Park. The stark shadowy badlands loom over the plains where Teddy Roosevelt set up as a ranchman in 1883, branding his stock with the sign of the Maltese Cross. For 15 years he stuck with the difficulties and disasters of raising cattle through the killing winters of this land that only the doughty bison could survive with any certainty. Finally, before going to Cuba with his famed Rough Riders, he ended his operation here, but he always kept a strong affection for this bleak country. Today a visitors' center recalls TR's life, and hiking and motor trails lead through the isolated grasslands where a herd of bison again has possession of the prairie.

There are two major units to the Park: the Soutl. unit whose attractions include prairie dog towns, nature trails, burning coal veins, columnar junipers and a variety of wildlife; and the North Unit, 65 mi. N on US 85, which offers a majestic view of a more rugged section of the badlands. A third unit, Teddy Roosevelt's Elkhorn Ranch site on the Little Missouri River north of Medora, is accessible only over rough dirt roads. Consult Park Headquarters in Medora before setting out.

The rebuilt *Old West cowtown of Medora* is located at the entrance to the South Unit. The park headquarters has a visitor center and museum, open 8 to 8 in the summer and 8 to 5 in winter. Theodore Roosevelt's original Maltese Cross cabin stands nearby.

South Dakota

Wind Cave National Park. The special peace of the prairie surrounds the visitor to the Black Hills of South Dakota, where in this park a herd of buffalo follows ancient pathways, and there are prairie dog "towns" and fast-running pronghorn antelopes. According to the air pressure outside, wind whistles in or out of this cave, giving it its name. Rare crystal formations make this cave different from those with usual stalagmites and stalactites—honeycombed crystals called "boxwork" and "frostwork" clusters decorate the seven miles of caverns that have been explored—most of the cave remains to be discovered by man. Conducted tours are provided by rangers, except in the winter; on hot summer days a walk down into the 47-degree F. air can be a welcome experience. Elk and deer are easily observed at sunrise and at sunset, and naturalist talks around a fire are a daily summer attraction. Buffalo steaks and hamburgers are served at a nearby lodge during summer. The cave is open year round, except

on Thanksgiving, Christmas and New Year's Day. Accommodations and tourist
services at Hot Springs and at Custer.

Utah

Bryce Canyon National Park. The painted canyon country of Utah can be
dazzling in the yellow light after dawn, the Pink Cliffs here looking like fairyland. A drive of 34 miles takes motorists along the high rim parkway, where
overlooks are starting points for hiking trails into this land of fantasy. As the
altitude of the drive is around 9,000 feet, hikers should take it easy to keep from
getting out of breath. Horses can be hired to make things simpler.

There are roads in the park, but some sections are accessible only on a mule
or horse. For those without cars, the park provides transportation at a nominal
charge. In addition to a hotel and lodge the park has improved camp sites.
Camping is limited to 14 days. Bryce Canyon also has a well-organized museum
with lectures and illustrations explaining the origins of its outstanding features.
Accommodations and tourist services at Panguitch, 26 miles away.

Canyonlands National Park. The wild, colorful, rocky scenery of this wilderness has not been invaded by paved roads or tourist facilities. Travel is on foot
or horseback, or by four-wheel-drive vehicle. The Green and Colorado Rivers,
in their natural gorges, meet within the park in settings of excitingly stark
isolation. The town of Green River has boat trips into the park. There are
primitive campsites.

Many Jeep camp tours are available for a good, close look at Utah's newest
National Park. They can be engaged at Moab, Blanding or Monticello. This
park is divided roughly into the Needles Section at the southern end and the
Island in the Sky at the northern end. Between the two are fascinating formations in The Maze, Land of Standing Rocks, Doll House, Salt Creek, Horseshoe
Canyon and White Rim. In the south lies Chesler Park, a secluded valley
completely ringed by fingers of rock jutting skyward.

Autos are advised to proceed with advance knowledge about conditions
ahead. Local pilots have offered sightseeing flights over the area and information
on such possibilities is available at the Arches Visitor Center.

For a less expensive bird's-eye view of the Canyonlands region, a black-
topped county road leads west from US 163, north of Moab, to Dead Horse
Point State Park, a magnificent overlook on the Colorado gorge. Accommodations and tourist services in Moab and Monticello.

Zion National Park. The lavish colorations of rockface everywhere in the
Southwest is at its best here in a wonderland of canyons, mesas, and spindly
stone towers. Hanging gardens of columbine, shooting star, and cardinal flowers
are at their height of color in springtime. A specialty is the famous Zion
moonflower that grows two feet high or taller on the floor of the canyon, with
white horn-shaped flowers opening at night and closing in the morning sun.
Early Basketmakers were followed by Cliff Dwellers, in turn displaced by the
Paiute Indians still here when the Spaniards finally arrived in the 1780s. Later
the Mormons arrived and named the area Dixie Land, hoping, without any
success, to attract cotton planters from the South. The park has many trails, and
is open all year, with lodge rooms and cabins available in summer only. There
is a dining room and campground.

Zion National Park is located directly south of Cedar City, off I–15 and then
along state routes that take motorists through small prim Mormon settlements
named Toquerville, LaVerkin and Virgin. A tranquil, wooded camping site east
of Cedar City off State 14 is Navajo Lake. The lake is cold enough for good trout
fishing and big enough for boating. Accommodations and tourist services at
Springdale.

Wyoming

Grand Teton National Park. The magnificent scenery of the Grand Teton
National Park extends continuously from the lakes and valleys skyward to
13,000-foot mountain peaks. Snowcapped and glacier covered, the towering
mountains are a backdrop to the placid, emerald lakes, to craggy canyons and
pristine forests.

The 485-square-mile park is quite a compact area with possibilities for you
to spend several weeks, with each day revealing something new.

Scattered throughout Teton National Park are a variety of facilities and campgrounds. In fact one of the most interesting ways of touring the park is to hedgehop from one accommodation to another. First stop could be Colter Bay Cabins and Signal Mountain Lodge, set in the natural wooded area on the shores of Jackson Lake. Facilities include well-appointed cabins (some with kitchens), opportunities for fishing outings or horseback riding, and a fully equipped marina. By way of contrast, the Jackson Lake Lodge has 385 luxurious rooms, and features a floor-to-ceiling picture window in the lodge that frames the lake and the Grand Teton Range. Down the road toward Jackson is the Jenny Lake Lodge where the peak of Grand Teton Mountain rises almost from the front porch. Most of these areas also have ample campgrounds. However, both the indoor and outdoor vacationer is advised to reserve in advance if possible.

The other major way to experience the Tetons is to reach the back country by hiking or by horseback. The Park Service maintains a wide assortment of routes—some designed for a few hour's hike, some for both horse and foot trips, and some for hikers with only good hiking shoes and strong legs. One famous trail reaches the 11,000-foot summit of Static Peak Divide. Another climbs to the contemplative, glacier-formed Lake Solitude. The lowland regions can be traversed via the Lakes Trail or paths through Death Canyon, Cascade Canyon, or Indian Paintbrush Canyon.

If water is your element, full- and half-day float trips down the Snake River are available at the Lake or from Jackson. Along the route the majestic bald eagle may be seen high in the trees in one of its few remaining natural habitats.

Gateway to the Tetons and the National Parks is Jackson. Located at the southern entrance to the parks, Jackson is headquarters for the Teton National Forest, an area of 1,701,000 acres of wilderness bordering on both Grand Teton and Yellowstone National Parks. This resort community offers year-round recreational opportunities, abounding in dude ranches, motels and entertainment centers, good fishing and hunting, and three exceptional ski slopes—Snow King, Teton, and Grand Targhee. There is a modern airport with transportation to hotels and motels in Jackson, Teton Village, and Jackson Lake Lodge. The culture and historic sides of Jackson on one hand remain entirely western and on the other boast 20 art galleries, a summer fine arts festival, a summer symphony, and summer stock theater. The Silver Dollar Bar in the Wort Hotel is world famous, and the Pink Garter Theater is home of the performing arts. For sheer natural beauty, don't miss seeing the huge elk herd which winters right on the edge of town. Beginning in November, as many as 10,000 elk come into the refuge and remain into early May.

Nearby Pinedale offers a slightly slower pace than the well-trafficked Jackson area. Pinedale is a true western cowtown and is surrounded by working cattle ranches, but also offers modern motels, dude ranch accommodations, and restaurants. Pinedale is also gateway to the Bridger National Forest and some beautiful relatively undervisited camping and hiking areas.

Another major attraction in the Jackson region is the Dubois area, located on the upper Big Wind River and surrounded on three sides by Shoshone National Forest, and one of the richest places in the nation to prospect and search for rocks. Found in the region are gem-quality agatized opalized wood, cast material, pine and fir cone replacements, amethyst-lined trees and limb casts, and many types of high-quality agate.

Shoshone and Arapahoe Indian Reservations can be found near Riverton and Lander. In July, first the Shoshone and then the Arapahoe Indians hold their sun dances. Dressed in full costumes, they dance continuously for three days and nights without taking food or water. Nearby is Crowheart Butte, a state monument, commemorating the scene of the great battle between the Shoshone and Crow Indians. In Riverton, located in the center of the Reservation, the Riverton Museum has Indian displays. Three Indian missions are in the vicinity: St. Stephen's on State 789; St. Michael's mission at Ethete; and Ft. Washakie, the Indian headquarters in Ft. Washakie. Sacajawea, the Indian guide of the Lewis and Clark expedition from the Missouri River to the Pacific Coast and back during 1805–06, is buried in the Indian cemetery at Wind River.

For information write Wyoming Travel Commission, Cheyenne, WY 82002. Phone, 1–800–443–2784.

John D. Rockefeller, Jr. Parkway. Linking Grand Teton and Yellowstone National Parks is a short stretch of highway along the Snake River that with its adjoining forest land makes up another National Park Service property. The area has hot springs, bridle trails, and a number of campgrounds.

Yellowstone National Park. So vast is Yellowstone National Park—3,472 square miles—that weeks on end are needed to explore all of its scenic and varied attractions. Most outstanding among attractions in America's first national park are the world's largest geyser basins and the thundering falls and canyon of the Yellowstone River. The park may also be the world's most varied wildlife sanctuary—with binoculars still the safest way to observe the bear, elk, buffalo, moose, deer, antelope and birds prevalent in the region.

Starting out from Fishing Bridge, a loop road leads to Canyon Village at Canyon Junction and one of the park's most spectacular sights, the Grand Canyon of Yellowstone. This twenty-four mile long, 1,200 foot deep gorge is aglitter with shades of red and yellow rocks and is surrounded by emerald green forests. Inspiration Point, on the north rim, is the best place for viewers and photographers to see the two largest waterfalls.

The road to Tower Junction passes Mt. Washburn (10,317 ft.) and slips through Dunraven Pass and to the rustic accommodations of Roosevelt Lodge at Tower Falls. Mammoth Hot Springs, at the North entrance, has the impressive travertine terraces of the geological domes—some vividly colored, some snow white.

South past Norris and Madison Junctions is geyser turf. Some erupt in rage and fury spewing thousands of gallons of water over one hundred feet in the air, others merely splash up a few inches. Most beloved is Old Faithful. It "blows" every hour on the hour and has not missed a performance in over eighty years. The visitor center here describes the unique geological wonders. Those wishing to see more geysers should go to Shoshone Geyser Basin or Heart Lake Geyser Basin, near West Thumb Junction.

Yellowstone may be visited year-round. Different ways to see the park are by hiking the Howard Eaton or smaller trails, horseback riding on the 700 miles of trails, or by snowmobiling or snowshoeing in during the winter. Accommodations, although of excellent quality, are far from adequate especially in peak season. Early reservations are advised at lodges and inns.

Yellowstone's five entrances are: from the north, via Livingston and Gardiner, Montana, and I-90; from Billings and Silver Gate, Montana, on the northeast; on the east, from Cody, Wyoming; from Jackson on the south; and via West Yellowstone on the west.

FAR WEST

Alaska

Denali National Park. There is a no more powerful sight in North America than the double peaks of Mt. McKinley, the highest one rising to 20,320 feet in the Alaska Range southwest of Fairbanks. The 2-million-acre park is traversed by a 90-mile highway that is like a giant natural history museum of mountain, tundra, and wildlife.

From Anchorage and Fairbanks, the park can be reached by plane (a 3,000-foot airstrip is maintained for light aircraft); by Alaska Railroad; by car and motorcoach via the paved George Parks Highway, Alaska 3; and by the Denali Highway, Alaska 8, a 135-mile road, of which some 20 miles leading from Paxson are paved. The road extends from Paxson, on Milepost 185.5 on the Richardson Highway, Alaska 4, to the village of Cantwell, located 1.8 miles beyond the junction of the Denali Highway with the Anchorage-Fairbanks Highway. Charter flights are available from Anchorage or Fairbanks. Besides passengers, the railroad transports freight, including vehicles.

When the historic hotel inside the park burned, it was rebuilt with a railroad theme and renamed Mt. McKinley Station Hotel, now Denali Park Hotel. Also near the park entrance are the McKinley Chalets and Mt. McKinley Village, a motel.

Tundra Wildlife Tours leave daily in summer in early morning and in mid-afternoon. Led by knowledgeable driver-guides, they penetrate deep into the park. Frequent stops during the 6–7-hour tours enable you to photograph flowers, birds, mountains, and animals (particularly grizzlies), caribou, Dall's sheep and moose.

On clear days, the north summit of Mt. McKinley, 19,470 feet, is visible 31 miles off, to the southwest. In the foreground is Muldrow Glacier, which drops from the mountain and spreads out over the valley floor.

There are several campgrounds within the park. Since firewood is scarce, the motorist should bring a kerosene- or gas-burning camp stove with plenty of fuel, as well as all the supplies he thinks he will need, the nearest store being many miles away.

Camp Denali, 2 mi. N. of Wonder Lake and about 90 mi. from park headquarters, is smack in the middle of the wilderness. Rustic, it is primarily for vacationists, not overnighters.

California

Lassen Volcanic National Park. Bumpass Hell, stinking of sulphur and bubbling and fuming, is a reminder of the volcanic explosions that blasted out of the top of Lassen Peaks for some three years, between 1914 and 1917 here in the Cascade Range of northern California. Hot lava poured down upon the snowpack, melted it, and caused an avalanche and a landslide. There are several hot springs, and in the clear, cold lakes, good catches of rainbow, eastern brook, and German brown trout are to be had. There are four campgrounds, and, at Manzanita Lake, cabins for rent. Accommodations at Mineral and nearby Red Bluff, Redding, and Chester.

Park snowed in most of the year, highway impassable. Best time to visit is summer or early fall.

Redwood National Park. This rare combination of sea and forest is 46 miles long and up to seven miles wide, and besides its magnificent redwood forests it has 30 miles of Pacific coastline here in northern California, with its own cliffs and sand and pebble beaches. The redwoods creep down some of the steep slopes overlooking the seashore, where mounds and scatterings of driftwood attract beachcombers. There are campgrounds in the park and in the adjoining Six Rivers National Forest. Accommodations and tourist services at Eureka.

Sequoia National Park and Kings Canyon National Park. Sequoia and Kings Canyon National Parks are a pair of natural beauties running wild from the gentle foothills of the San Joaquin Valley to the splintered crest of the Sierra Nevada. Although the parks were established 50 years apart, they adjoin and are referred to as a team. Their combined area covers 1,347 square miles.

The trees for which Sequoia Park was named *(Sequoia gigantea)* began reaching for the California heavens about the time Troy fell to the Greeks. Largest of the park's sequoias is the General Sherman Tree in the Giant Forest, over 36 feet wide and 101 feet around at the base. It soars to just over 272 feet—higher than a 20-story office building—and is estimated to be 3,500 years old. A man could lie crosswise on some of its massive branches. The tree's weight has been estimated at 2,145 tons (as heavy as a small ocean-going steamship), and it also has been estimated that the General Sherman Tree could produce 600,000 board feet of lumber—enough to build a small town.

Kings Canyon Park also has giant sequoias. The General Grant Tree is only five feet shorter than the Sherman and exceeds the Sherman's base circumference by six feet. In 1965, Kings Canyon Park, already noted for its lakes, canyons, waterfalls and rushing rivers, was greatly enhanced when President Lyndon B. Johnson signed into reality the dream of naturalist John Muir, adding the Cedar Grove tract and the Tehipite Valley to the national park area.

Other notable sights in these parks include Tharps Log (where the road goes through, rather than around, the trunk of a tree), the Fluted Column and Chimney Tree. Moro Rock, which you can climb on a safe, 300-foot stairway for a view over the Great Western Divide, and Crystal Cave, a marble cave with elaborate limestone formations, may also prove fascinating. Crystal Cave is open during the summer, with guide service available.

There is a museum at the ranger station. Stop by the Lodgepole and Grant Grove Visitor Centers for expert advice on organizing your sightseeing, park data and campfire information. Highways to the parks are kept open year-round, and accommodations are available year-round.

Yosemite National Park. Yosemite National Park is a meadowlike valley threaded by mountain streams, noble groves of trees, and waterfalls; it is surrounded by almost vertical walls taking the shapes of great domes and pinnacles.

You can approach the park through either the Merced route, State 140, or by the slightly longer State 41, which passes through such small towns as Kismet, Coarsegold and Ben Hur. Following the latter, you enter the park through a magnificent stand of big trees, the Mariposa Grove. This "slow" route has the advantage of showing you the highlights of the park en route to Yosemite Village. If you come this way, be sure to stop at Wawona (the entrance) and visit the log cabin Pioneer Yosemite History Center.

When you reach Yosemite Village itself, you're suddenly in a land where giant forests clothe the mountains' flanks and waterfalls leap off craggy cliffs. Recommended point for a breathtaking vista is Glacier Point, with a 180° view; majestic El Capitan, the world's largest mass of visible granite; Half Dome, rising 4,800 feet above the Valley floor; and Yosemite Falls, best viewed in spring.

Although the valley gorge is seven miles in extent, it is now too small for the over 2½ million yearly visitors. You can get away from the people by hiking or driving into the higher mountains, especially in the area called Tuolumne Meadows, accessible by car. Other high-country places in Yosemite require horseback or hiking. Trips in the saddle in the High Sierras go up Tuolumne Meadows and usually do only 10 miles per day. You ride through alpine meadows, vast stands of pine, along trails sprayed by waterfalls. Lakes abound, large and small, hidden away in the mountains. Accommodations are adequate and well-arranged. At night you bunk down at park campsites in the tents. Meals are served under canvas too, family-style.

If you want to do the Yosemite High Sierras on foot, you can join one of the guided hiking expeditions. Seven-day treks are offered weekly in summer. Buses take hikers to May Lake, and the walking starts from there.

Cycling rentals and trail information are available at Yosemite Lodge and Curry Village bike stands. Rental horses are available in Yosemite Valley, as well as at sites at Wawona, Tuolumne Meadows and White Wolf.

Best season to visit the park? Autumn or spring. Next best, winter. Beginning skiers find the Badger Pass slopes superb. Winter also brings the Christmas banquet pageant, very Old English, at Ahwahnee Hotel. This event is so popular that one has to make reservations a year ahead. Although Yosemite is beautiful in summer, the crowds of tourists make it the least enjoyable visiting season.

Oregon

Crater Lake National Park. Crater Lake, a 2-square-mile circle of an unforgettable blue that is nearly 2,000 feet deep, is fed only by melting snows, and has no outlet. Sometimes visitors have to wait for an hour or two until a cloud settling close down over the surface of the water decides to move away and let them have a look. Every morning a ranger leads a "caravan" of visitors in their cars around the lake, stopping frequently. Launches also make tours of the lake and stop at the strangely formed volcanic islands.

The lake was created thousands of years ago when Mt. Mazama, a 15,000-foot volcano, erupted and formed a crater now filled by the lake. First seen by white men in 1853. Drives through the 250-square-mile park, especially the 35-mile route around the rim, bring a succession of spectacular views: Wizard Island, a symmetrical cone rising 760 feet above the surface of the lake; Phantom Ship, a mass of lava resembling a ship under sail; Llao Rock, a lava flow on the north rim that fills an ancient glacial valley. The view from Cloudcap, on the east rim, is considered the best of many excellent views. There are many fine mountain viewpoints, but even the athletic are liable to be short of breath after climbing to the cap of 8,060-foot Garfield Peak or to the 8,926-foot lookout station atop Mt. Scott.

The northern entrance drive, off Oregon 138, opens about June 14, and Rim Drive about July 4. Overnight accommodations, meals, garage and gasoline services are available from about June 15 to September 15. In addition to the 75-room lodge there are sleeping cottages. (Sites in the campground, if available, are included in the daily vehicle fee.) There are daily lectures by park naturalists, guided drives and hikes, and geological exhibits. During the off-season the coffee shop serves skiers. Reached by Oregon 62 from Medford, Oregon 138 from Roseburg, or off US 97 onto Oregon 138 or Oregon 232.

Washington

Mt. Rainier National Park. Mighty Mt. Rainier, the state's best known and highest mountain, is the great pillar of that "Arctic island in a temperate zone," Mt. Rainier National Park. An ice-clad, dormant volcano, Mt. Rainier rises 14,410 feet a few miles west of the Cascade Range. Its gleaming mantle of ice is composed of more glaciers than there are on any other single mountain in the United States south of Alaska.

The park is the best known tourist attraction in Washington. It symbolizes the region's wealth of natural wonders—glaciers, waterfalls, forests, wildflowers, lakes, abundant wildlife, and stunning vistas. For hikers and climbers, the park offers a variety of trails, some for experts only. Motorists can get a close look at Emmons Glacier, on the east slope of the mountain, by taking the winding road that twists west to Sunrise, off US 410. Emmons is the largest glacier in the United States. For extended visits to the park, there are campgrounds, an inn, and varied eating facilities.

North Cascades National Park. This park, lying along the northern boundary of Washington, has the most outstanding alpine scenery in the U.S. within its 1,053 square miles. There are hundreds of icefalls, hanging valleys, waterfalls, jagged peaks, and lakes caught within glacial cirques. Three dams that provide power for Seattle form lakes of considerable size, one 24 miles long. This is a winter aerie of the bald eagle, who preys on salmon in the Skagit River here. There are 350 miles of trails open to hikers and horsebackers.

The park is divided into tour units—North and South Units of the Park and Ross Lake and Lake Chelan National Recreation Areas. Outdoor recreation can be enjoyed from early April to mid-October at lower elevations and on the big lakes. At higher elevations, the season is from mid-June to mid-September. The western side of the North Cascades gets more rain, has more lakes and streams, and more abundant vegetation, including rain forests. It has less sunshine and cooler days than the eastern side of the mountains, where more sunshine and dry climates produce warm rock surfaces, dry shrublands, warm days, and cool nights.

There is no motel or lodge inside the North and South Units of North Cascade National Park. The larger towns and cities near the North Cascades group have the usual tourist accommodations, but are 2- to 3-hour drives from area boundaries. Smaller communities within Ross Lake NRA and Lake Chelan NRA or adjacent to the areas have limited guest accommodations. Chambers of commerce for each of the towns surrounding the North Cascades group (Sedro Woolley, Chelan, Wenatchee, Okanogan, Bellingham, Mount Vernon) have information on packers, guides, and other outdoor services.

Access to the North Cascades area from the west follows Wash. 20 from Burlington to Colonial Creek Campground and branch routes to Baker River and Cascade River. Hiking access and roadside views of the northwest corner are offered from Wash. 542 from Bellingham. Access from the east is via Wash. 20 from Winthrop, 40 miles northwest of Okanogan. A good chunk of the North Cascades area can be seen by car, along the recently completed Wash. 20—but there are no facilities for 75 miles. A picturesque way to enter the area is from Stehekin, reached by boat from Chelan, 55 miles to the south. (Daily boat services; 2 lodges at Stehekin.) There is scheduled boat service on Diablo Lake as well. Chartered local plane flights are available, and private planes are for hire. There are independent, charter-flight companies at Bellingham, Anacortes, Seattle, Tacoma, Omak, Chelan, and Yakima. Next to climbing a mountain whose peak affords immense vistas, the best overlooks, of course, are from a plane. About 350 miles of hiking and horse trails spindle the wilderness. Permits, required for all backcountry camping, are obtainable at any Park Service office or ranger station. Horsemen may bring their own animals or rent horses and mules at rural communities on the west, east, and south approaches to the park and recreation units. Camping is not of the luxury type. Colonial Grounds and Goodell are developed, drive-in campgrounds off Wash. 20 in Ross Lake NRA, but apart from these, campsites are pretty primitive. There are no campgrounds in the North Unit of the national park, and only 2 in the South Unit. Ross Lake NRA has about 15 campgrounds, Lake Chelan NRA has about 5. Fishing for sport has become popular. In addition to the named lakes, there are many small mountain and valley lakes, and so many streams that no count has been made of them. The principal game fish are rainbow, Eastern brook, Dolly Varden, and cutthroat trout. Swimming is not suggested—the waters of the lakes and rivers are quite chilly. Even in August, water activities are mainly confined to boating and fishing. For further information, write: Superintendent, *North Cascades National Park,* Sedro Woolley, WA. 98284.

Olympic National Park. It is said that the average rainfall decreases at the rate of an annual inch for every mile as you move inland from the Pacific Coast through Olympic National Park. The rain forest near the sea is a remarkable dripping jungle of lush ferns and dense foliage of many kinds. Up higher in this 1,400-square-mile expanse of meadowland and mountain run herds of Roosevelt elk and black-tailed deer. There are 140 species of birds in the park. Besides many lovely, hidden lakes, the park has 50 miles of primitive, log-strewn Pacific coastline: cliffs, bluffs, rocks, and sand. A magnificent view of the Strait of Juan de Fuca is had from Hurricane Ridge, accessible by car.

Probably no other national park offers such contrasts in hiking—from glaciers and blizzard-ridden mountain peaks to dense, tangled valleys of rain forest where the light of day is dim even at high noon. Mountain climbers must check in with the rangers; only the experienced should attempt the peaks. Points of special interest include the rain forests and their rivers, trails leading to beach adventure above Kalaloch, and the spectacular view from Hurricane Ridge, reached by a fine highway off US 101, near Port Angeles.

There are concession-operated cabins, lodges, and trailer parks at Sol Duc Hot Springs, Lake Crescent, La Push, and Kalaloch. For rates and other information, write: Superintendent, Olympic National Park, 600 E. Park Ave., Port Angeles, WA. 98362. (The season usually runs from Memorial Day through Labor Day).

Meals are available at Lake Crescent lodge and Hurricane Ridge. There are within the park 17 campgrounds, only a few of which will accommodate trailers of 21 feet or longer. None of the campgrounds has shower, laundries, or utility connections. Most consist of individual campsites, with tables and fireplaces; piped water and toilet facilities are usually near a cluster of campsites. All campsites are on a first come, first served basis. Some campgrounds at lower elevations are open all year, but high-elevation areas are covered by snow from early November to early July.

The park has 3 visitor centers—Pioneer Memorial Museum, near Port Angeles (open all year); Storm King Visitor Center, at Lake Crescent; and Hoh Rain Forest Visitor Center, southeast of Forks. Lectures, campfire talks, exhibits, and tours are provided by the National Park Service. Check visitor centers for details, interpretive publications, and maps.

Natural Wonders

There are other natural spectacles to be found outside the national parks.

NEW YORK

Niagara Falls. Native Americans regarded the Falls as a sacred shrine, and heard in the waters' roar the voices of their gods. In 1678, Father Louis Hennepin, a French missionary, became the first European to visit them, and now the Falls are international, with the State of New York and the Province of Ontario cooperating to preserve the surroundings of this natural wonder.

In its thirty-six-mile run from Lake Erie to Lake Ontario, the Niagara River drops 326 feet, more than half of it in this single plunge. Actually, there are three falls: the American Falls, 182 feet high and 1,075 feet wide; the Canadian (Horseshoe) Falls, 176 feet high and 2,100 feet wide; and the Bridal Veil Falls. They move upstream about a foot each year. What makes Niagara unique is that you can stand next to it, descend to the bottom, and even ride almost into it. Start on the U.S. side. The three crests are all visible from Prospect Point, where an observation tower gives a panoramic view of the entire scene. Goat Island, in the middle of the river, is a seventy-acre park where you can stroll along the very edge of the Falls. "Viewmobile" sightseeing cars circulate around the principal points of interest, and you can get on and off anywhere. From Goat Island you may take a helicopter to survey the Falls from above. And try to see them after dark, when they are colorfully lighted up—it is an entirely different spectacle.

A magnificent way to view them is from the bottom looking up. The Prospect Point Observation Tower elevators descend into the gorge, where you board the *Maid of the Mist* and approach to within yards of the Falls. From here also, giant rafts depart on a White Water Tour of downriver rapids. An elevator on Goat Island takes visitors to the Gorge Walkway, which ends under Terrapin Point below Horseshoe Falls, or to the Cave of the Winds, where you trek across the base of Bridal Veil Falls.

U.S. and Canadian citizens may cross the river and pass customs and immigration with few formalities. While you are on American soil, you may visit Devil's Hole, Whirlpool, and other state parks in the area offering bathing, camping, colorful foliage, winter sports, hiking, and picnicking. The Canadian side offers the highest panoramic towers: the Seagram Tower, 525 feet above Horseshoe Falls; the Oneida Tower, 450 feet; and the Niagara International Center, which features exhibits of science, industry, and government, 775 feet. There is also a Canadian landing at which you may board the *Maid of the Mist.*

FAR WEST

California

The Mojave Desert and Death Valley. Known as the "High Desert" because of its elevation, ranging up to more than 6,000 feet, the Mojave Desert is a vast expanse of natural desert beauty, with traces of century-old ghost towns, wildlife and softly hued plants. The flashy color of the California golden poppies, which bloom in the spring of a rainy year, can be seen 10 miles away. Much of the Mojave Desert is mining country. Near the town of Mojave, once the terminus of the 20-mule-team-borax wagons out of Death Valley, is the lonesome hump of Soledad Mountain. The mountain is pocked by mine shafts that were closed after giving up millions in gold. Tropico Mine is behind the mountain and now a visitors attraction. A Gold Town and museum of relics are interesting to explore. The gold town of Randsburg is what a movie set of an old mining town should look like. Some of the walls of buildings are made of old dynamite boxes. The Old Time Mining Celebration is held in late August. At Boron, visitors can observe borax mining operations. Calico, an old silver town, restored by Walter Knott of Knott's Berry Farm, is now a San Bernardino County regional park, with numerous attractions and festivals.

Death Valley, north of the Mojave Desert, is the lowest and, in summer, one of the hottest and driest spots in the United States. At more comfortable times of the year, many regard the valley as one of the more geologically fascinating places on earth. Third largest of the national monuments, Death Valley is a trough in the northern reaches of the Mojave Desert, 140 miles long and 6 to 20 miles wide. The annual rainfall averages about 2 inches, and the National Park Service has recorded the hottest summertime temperature at 134 degrees, July 10, 1913.

The sun-blasted valley was called Tomesha, which means "ground afire," by the Paniment Indians. Its present name is supposed to have originated in 1849 when a party of gold rushers, the Bennetts and Arcanes, were rescued after wandering the sea of salt for 80 days. One of the emaciated members of the group is supposed to have looked back and said, "Goodbye, Death Valley!" Today the valley is a well supervised monument, with excellent highways, plenty of water and a wide range of accommodations.

Among the interesting features to be seen in Death Valley are brilliantly colored canyons and mountains, freakish natural formations, and authentic artifacts of the Old West. There are hourly guided tours of Scotty's Castle, an eccentric's desert showplace. The Devil's Golf Course is a bed of rugged salt crystals rising to pinnacles as high as four feet and still growing. Ubehebe Crater is an 800-foot pit formed by a volcanic eruption about 3,000 years ago. The National Park Service maintains the Death Valley Museum at Death Valley National Monument. Natural-history exhibits, charcoal kilns and Harmony Borax Works are featured.

Oregon

The Oregon Coast. Of all sections of Oregon, the coast is the most famous and the most visited. It has often been termed the most scenic marine border drive in the world, and for good reason; none who sees it is disappointed.

Take hundreds of miles of shore fronting the Pacific, fill with rolling sand dunes, mouths of swift rivers, freshwater lakes, craggy cliffs, toppled mountainside, battered headlands, hills bursting with greenery, secret coves, deep inlets, picturesque lighthouses, broad beaches, herds of sea lions, grassy state parks, millions of wildflowers, leaping waterfalls—and you have the Oregon coast. To the purple-shadowed range skirting the shores and the virgin stands of giant firs, add the unsurpassed vistas of surf and sea—and you have one of the nation's grandest terrains. Add to all of this a salubrious climate, fabulous fishing, the taste of world-famous cheese in the valley where it is produced, colorful seashore towns, and a wealth of recreational opportunities—and the pleasure is double.

Almost all of the tideland of the coast belongs to the people; only a few miles are privately owned. More than thirty state parks, including the choicest scenic spots, are reserved for public use. In addition, there are many national forest camps.

It is a bit ironic, perhaps, that the most scenic and historical route linking Portland to the coast should be the longest and most time consuming; nevertheless, US 30, which skirts the Columbia River, is a storybook way to reach Astoria (the northern terminal of the littoral). On the other hand, US 26, the most popular route, is also the most crowded.

Astoria sits at the mouth of the Columbia River—its northern shore is the southern border of Washington. In 1966 a spectacular 4.1-mile-long toll bridge was completed, crossing to Megler. Astoria calls itself the "Oldest American City West of the Missouri." It possesses, in this respect, many firsts, including the first post office west of the "Big Muddy." Local historians claim that there has been "more history made within twenty miles of Astoria than all the rest of Oregon put together." This claim is disputed by others, but Astoria is so steeped in history that some citizens would like to turn the city into a "Williamsburg of the West."

Seaside, farther down the coast, has the finest beach in the state, boasting in addition a two-mile-long concrete promenade. More people swim in the ocean here than anywhere else on the Oregon coast. There are also more tourist facilities—and their variety is legion—than in any town twice its size. The "Miss Oregon" pageant is staged here, which seems appropriate since many people in the state think of Seaside as the Coney Island of the coast because of its main street, hurdy-gurdy atmosphere. For years Seaside was the chief resort community in Oregon, but in the past few years it has lost much of its luster.

Not lacking the least in luster is Salishan Lodge at Gleneden Beach, the innkeeper's Taj Mahal of the Oregon coast. The swankiest resort in the state and the prime convention center of the coast these days, Salishan contains a fine collection of coastal art and spells the finest in taste and the highest in price to most Oregonians.

In the five miles between Salishan and Depoe Bay, there are three excellent state parks: Gleneden, Fogarty Creek, and Boiler Bay. Depoe Bay, long-settled but incorporated only in 1973, is geographically the most exciting town on the coast. It overlooks a rockbound bay, usually jammed with fishing boats.

Two miles south of Depoe Bay, US 101 encounters the north junction of the Otter Crest Scenic Loop, which rejoins the highway at Otter Rock after winding along the rugged shore to Otter Crest View Point.

Otter Crest Wayside, 1.6 miles south of the junction, is a must stop for anyone who wants to appreciate the glory of the Oregon coast and imbibe a heady draught of beauty. From the 50-car parking area on the promontory, miles of scalloped, battered, gossamer coastline are visible. The Lookout, 500 feet above the sea on Cape Foulweather, faces Oregon's most photographed seascape. Large observatory telescopes are available. Sometimes, focusing on offshore rocks, one sees more than the riled or rhythmic ocean; namely, sea lions, Oregon penguins, and sea turkeys.

The area between the coast towns of Yachats and Florence is a camper's paradise—no fewer than seven state parks and forest camps. There are also in this stretch several freshwater lakes for boating, swimming, and fishing. Florence, on the Siuslaw River, is the shopping center of a beautiful lake and sand-dunes area. In spring and early summer, rhododendrons run riot over hills and lowlands.

Little more than three miles south of Florence is what is probably Oregon's most-used state park, Jessie M. Honeyman. It has 313 campsites and 66 trailer spaces, electric stoves, showers, laundry, boat ramp, and many other facilities including an outdoor theater. Day-use facilities include picnic tables, toilets, and bathhouses. The 522-acre tract includes a dense forest, swarms of rhododendrons and Cleawox Lake. Trails lead from the park into the cool forest or up to the undulating sand dunes. The dunes area, extending south about 50 miles to the Coos Bay country, is now the Oregon Sand Dunes National Recreational Area, Oregon's only one of this kind.

The dunes, mutable and mysterious, rise to heights of more than 250 feet. Commercial sand buggies—motorized vehicles that range in size from jeep to bus—grind across the dunes with absolute safety. Drivers halt frequently to permit passengers to take pictures.

Mile-long McCullough Bridge, 11 miles down from Lakeside Junction, spans the channel of Coos Bay and leads into North Bend, a virile lumber town. This is myrtlewood country, and by taking drives off the main road to the southeast you will see the groves of myrtle, which grow nowhere else in the nation. The hub of the myrtle area is Coquille, 17 miles south of Coos Bay, reached via US 101 and 42.

The prime scenic package in the Coos Bay-North Bend area is the Empire-Cape Arago excursion. Empire, three miles from either Coos Bay or North Bend, boasts a sports-fishing fleet, crabbing, and clamming. Charleston, five miles below Empire, is a busy fishing village. Within six miles south of Charleston are clustered three of Oregon's grandest state parks: Sunset Bay, Shore Acres, and Cape Arago.

On the last 15 miles to Brookings, six miles above the California state line, is some of the grandest scenery along the entire coast—including Whaleshead Beach, where at incoming tide the rock formation resembles a whale spouting. Spectacular indeed is the seaward view from 350-foot-high Thomas Creek Bridge, higher than San Francisco's Golden Gate Bridge.

Headquarters for travel and tourist information is the Economic Development, Tourism Division, 595 Cottage St., N.E., Salem, OR 97310. The Oregon coast is supplied by the Oregon Coast Association, P.O. Box 670, Newport, OR 97365.

A visit to the United States could focus entirely on the outdoors, on experiencing all that the country naturally has to offer: the diversity of the geography, the plant and the animal life.

Wilderness Vacations

Note: For vacations that are truly in the wilds, we recommend strongly that you use professional guides or seek qualified local advice before setting out. People have been lost, some for months, or injured.

In spite of the rapidly growing population of the United States, the land provides incredibly vast stretches of wilderness for people who want to get away from every trace of civilization—even that of a jet trail overhead. While metropolitan areas grow, the great deserts, forests, and mountain chains remain unpopulated and provide terrain for hiking, horseback riding, and canoeing vacations that can be personally fulfilling as well as providing spectacular scenery. Although there are many areas where it is easy to get off by yourself and run little risk even of meeting somebody else on the trail, access to the trails and to the canoeable streams is usually easily reached by car.

Throughout the land there are wilderness areas, from the great stretches of forest owned by paper corporations in northern Maine to the infrequently seen valleys and slopes of Alaska. The national parks and forests have designated great areas of every type of land to remain untouched except for foot trails or bridle paths. The land is not marked by man and after you have traveled through it, and camped in it, and departed, there should be no mark of your passage either. Isolation is certainly one of the attractions of these vacations, but there is often the fun of companionship on some of the hikes and pack-trips regularly organized in these havens of unmarred beauty among lakes, mountain peaks, fast running streams, towering desert rock formations, and lost, flowering meadowland.

Up in northern Minnesota there are canoe trips that can go on for weeks—one along the international boundary with Canada is 235 miles long, departing from near the town of Howland. The Appalachian Mountain Club in Boston publishes books of wilderness trail maps, including the famous 2,000-mile-long Appalachian Trail that pretty successfully skirts the civilized world in a twisty route, mostly along mountain crests, all the way from Maine to Georgia. The Sierra Club organizes hiking vacations not only in California but also in Wisconsin. The Federal government has furthered the wilderness concept in specially designated wild rivers that are supposed to remain uninhabited and uncluttered for posterity, and all of these make first-rate wilderness trips; a good example is the Rio Grande Gorge, where a navigable stream runs for 70 miles.

Some of the country's best trout fishing is had in streams rarely reached by fishermen. Around the base of the Trinity Alps in California you can combine the wilderness treks with the luxury of resort-ranches, some 15 of which arrange pack trips and will welcome you back to comparative luxury on your return. Mountain climbers can easily find expert advice and, if desired, guides to accompany them at the points of access to many western and Alaskan wilderness areas, and in Alaska there are such special experiences as a two-week tundra trek. Such a vacation is the best way to discover that the wilderness is indeed still as wild as it was before man ever arrived on earth.

See our other books on the U.S.A. for more details.

White-Water Adventures

Note: We recommend strongly that you go on this kind of vacation with well-qualified professional boatmen, and not on your own. Accidents have happened; the powerful force of these waters is unbelievable.

The American white-water adventure, crashing down steep rocky sluiceways on barely enough water to keep a flimsy craft afloat as the foamy water shoots and splashes all around, used to be restricted to those skilled sportsmen who could handle a canoe or kayak without capsizing over long series of rapids. But today the bumps and twists and turns can be negotiated more safely by rubber raft, and, *with experienced raftsmen at the helm,* even inexperienced outdoor lovers can join in the fun without much danger.

Some of the most lovely and imposing natural scenery in the country is to be had in the distant, isolated valleys where the almost inaccessible white-water rivers run, whether in the lost woodlands of northern Maine, in the shadowed brooks of the Appalachians, or the rough, spectacular slopes of the Rockies. For those skilled at handling a canoe, organized white-water trips can be joined at many famous waterways, such as the wilderness of the Allagash in Maine, or the rapids of the Rifle River in Michigan. But the unsinkable rubber rafts have become more popular with people whose idea of fun is not so much risking broken bones or drowning. The rafts bounce off rocks, and since they are inflated by separate compartments, are unsinkable. Some can take as many as 30 passengers, but the smaller ones are the choice of those who want to feel the thrill of shooting the rapids on their own or with one or two companions—it may be safer than a canoe, but it still takes some courage to streak down the Snake River through Hells Canyon or slip through the "Double Hydraulic" boulders of the Youghiogheny River in Pennsylvania. Some excursions last a week or more—there is a 300-mile stretch on the Colorado that takes rafters all the way through Grand Canyon, with placid stretches alternating with rapids.

See our other titles on the U.S.A. for more details.

Flowerlands

A feature of American life often overlooked is the love of flower gardens in every part of the land that has created scores of elaborately laid-out floral parks, some as delicately formal as any in France, England, or the spas of Czechoslovakia. Many of these gardens were started back in Victorian days as private delights for rich families, and today have been maintained for the enjoyment of the public. Municipalities also provide displays of growing flowers in botanical gardens, arboretums, and city parks. Some localities specialize in a single kind of flower and surround it with festivals and other annual hoopla.

There are azalea festivals in Oklahoma, Texas, Louisiana, and Georgia, while Tyler, Texas, arranges over a million roses in displays for its Rose Festival. Lubbock, Texas, is the Chrysanthemum Capital of the World (80,000 plants). Worth special trips are Middleton Place Gardens, in Charleston, South Carolina; Avery Island, Louisiana—for the McIlhenny gardens; Callaway Gardens in Georgia; and the Holden Arboretum, Mentor, Ohio. The foothills and meadowland of the Rockies, and of the eastern mountains too, come alive with wildflowers in the spring. Public gardens in cities and towns may be missed on the main routes, so it is well worth asking locally about nearby displays, nurseries, and flower shows.

Wildlife Sanctuaries

(See also *Wilderness Vacations.*) There is a strange emotional experience in the sight of what may be as many as a quarter of a million Canada geese all squatting and bobbing around and honking and flapping away on short flights—the twice-yearly scene at the Horicon National Wildlife Refuge in Wisconsin as the birds stop for feeding for a few weeks on their trips north and south. All over the country there are quiet backwaters, deserted stretches of grassland or swamp or isolated upland where birds and beasts are free to live unmolested by man. Visitors are nevertheless welcome to these sanctuaries, whether operated privately, by states, or by the Federal government; and there is no wildlife experience that can equal seeing animals living in their own environment, in their own place, without fear of man, who is generally restricted to limited pathways or to the peripheries of the refuges, but can still see plenty of live action.

Almost every state has refuges for birds, but there are a number of special areas for wild animals, such as the intriguing Nunivak National Wildlife Refuge in Alaska with its herds of reindeer and musk oxen. Herds of elk roam free just outside Jackson, Wyoming, where visitors can ride feed sleds into their midst. An annual buffalo roundup at the National Bison Range in Montana makes as exciting a scene as anything out of the Old West. In its refuges, the U.S. has a wealth and variety of wildlife that compare with that of Africa, but since the refuges are there for the animals' protection they are often not much publicized, so it may take some hunting to find them, and then some patience when you get there. It is all well worth the effort, however.

Bird Watching

Bird watchers (and bird listeners, too; there are specialists among bird lovers who collect birdsongs) are a growing legion in the United States. Armed only with a notebook and a pair of binoculars, bird watchers silently invade every quiet place in the land to spot and record the wide variety of birds that reside in or visit the many climates of America. The Audubon Society has branches in most states that organize bird watching tours such as the fall visit to Block Island, Rhode Island, where thousands of birds make a regular stopover of but a few days' duration. You can watch birds in Central Park in New York City, or on mountaintops or in swampland or in a trim-lawned suburb. The experienced bird watcher soon becomes proud of his "lifetime list" of birds seen and noted, and whatever a person's reasons for traveling may be, a little extra time, and some patience, will reward him well when he explores the quiet thrills of this special pastime.

Spelunking

Note: Many lives are lost when amateurs venture into unexplored caves for the first time; we recommend strongly that you go into places unknown to you with local, *experienced* spelunkers.

Many of the hundreds of caves and labyrinths to be found in all parts of the country have traditions of being old hideouts for bandits or for being holy places of Indians. Two famous caves are part of National Parks—Carlsbad Caverns and Wind Cave—and many others are in state parks. Almost all visiting is done in group tours, and *special permission must be had before setting off on private spelunking expeditions.* Besides rainbows of colors in the rocks and crystals, the caves provide endless fascination in the fancifully sculptured forms in floors, ceilings, and walls. One of the oddest is a clear map of the state of Texas outlined in alabaster—in an Oklahoma cavern. Caverns exist in all parts of the country, particularly in mountains, and in riverside country in Missouri and Kentucky. Besides being a good way to tire out the kids during a summer trip, a cave tour makes a great way to cool off on hot days; temperatures are steady year round, and some caves are as cool as 46 degrees F.

See our other titles on the U.S.A. for more details.

Lakeside Vacations

The countless small and medium sized resorts on the shores of American lakes go nearly unnoticed by the country as a whole, in comparison with salt-water destinations; but many of the lakes, especially the Great Lakes and other sizable bodies of fresh water, provide all the wide beaches, lighthouses, rocky cliffs, and picturesque ports that the ocean shore does—everything but the salt. And of course Great Salt Lake, in Utah, makes up for that, by being five times saltier—it is true that a bather will bob up and down in this water unsinkably like a cork.

The world's second-highest lake, Tahoe, on the California-Nevada line, has the country's coldest water, and the Finger Lakes of western New York have the best vineyards—and maybe the prettiest green-covered ridges between them as well. A lake vacation in the U.S. is a localized, family-oriented holiday with the usual domestic pleasures of swimming, boating, fishing—and maybe scuba diving or water-skiing. At lovely Flathead Lake in Montana you can look for a lake monster, and on the shores of Moosehead Lake in Maine you can expect to see a live moose grazing. High mountain lakes in Colorado—Grand Lake and Echo Lake are two accessible by car—have snow around them in August. Lake Pend d'Oreille in Idaho has vast stocks of the largest American trout, kamloops. There are resorts to compete with Atlantic City rarely heard of far from home—Michigan City, Indiana, on Lake Michigan, or Cedar Point, Ohio, on Lake Erie. Door County, an arm of Wisconsin poking out into Lake Michigan, makes a lakeside world of its own with a great cherry-tree culture, fish boils, and ethnic festivals. Mackinac Island, between the lower and upper peninsulas of Michigan, sits quietly in its blue water without a single motor-car to mar its peaceful carriage roads. Every sort of recreation can be found along the shores of American lakes, but the special attraction is that they bring a visitor into localized scenes unheard of in the next state or the next county. He will be a welcome explorer.

Down by the Seashore

There is enough shoreline in the U.S. to give every man, woman, and child in the country two feet all his own, but in spite of that a single mile stretch of Jones Beach, on Long Island, will have 6-million visitors over an average summer. What is unique about some of the American shoreline is the considerable part of it being kept unchanged for the future in the national seashores, where in Cape Code, Massachusetts, and Fire Island, New York; in Maryland, Virginia, and North Carolina, and along the Gulf Coast of Texas, vast reaches of sandy beach are both protected and made accessible at certain points.

Beachgoing is, in principle, the same the world over, but American beaches have some special attractions as well—first-rate surfing all along the Southern California coast, mussel-gathering in Maine, clamming in Cape Cod and Rhode Island, and shipwreck diving off North Carolina's Outer Banks. Lighthouse visiting is a magnet to certain travel buffs, and there are those who love to drive dune buggies over dunes or their regular cars down hard beaches (Daytona, in Florida, or Long Beach out in Washington). San Diego offers whale watching as these animals swim past on their way south in January, and there are sea lions to look at off Point Lobos, California. Canyon Beach, Oregon, and Hampton Beach, New Hampshire, still qualify as summer hotspots for young people, but there are of course all kinds of resorts from the Victorian primness of Ogunquit, Maine, to the flat white motels of Miami. Where public access is guaranteed all along the West Coast and in parts of the Texas Gulf Coast, private ways still persist in the East, but a new Federal law to open up eastern beaches is now before the Congress. Meanwhile, even in the East, all the shore up to high tide lines is in the public domain.

CITIES

The natural beauty of the United States may leave visitors awestruck, feeling that man is nearly insignificant compared to the world surrounding him. But to see man's own awesome achievements, visit the cities. As magnificent and diverse as the country's geography, the cities must be seen by everyone desiring insight into life in the United States. We mention some of the largest cities here to whet visitors' interests; turn to the sections on the cities themselves for more details.

New York City

This Gateway to the New World, mecca for many Americans and foreigners and City of the Damned for domestic critics, will not fail to make some kind of impression upon the visitor. Whether you love it or hate it, or just want to visit it and get out when you're finished, it has to be seen to be believed (or to be disbelieved).

Washington, D.C.

A favorite with Americans and foreign visitors alike, Washington attracts many young visitors, especially at Easter, when busloads of school children come from around the nation to see the capital at its most beautiful. Having lost some of its small-town reputation in the last two decades, it now offers visitors much more than imposing vistas, magnificent public buildings and patriotic pomp.

New Orleans

City of Mardi Gras and good restaurants, this capital of former French North America has an ambience unlike that of any other city in the U.S.A. Its detractors say it isn't a southern U.S. city, but a northern South American city.

Chicago

Chicago, long renowned as America's crossroads of transportation and industry, is more recently acclaimed for its new corporate buildings—tall, modernistic and very striking. While you're there don't ignore the exceptional restaurants and sports facilities.

Los Angeles

Few visitors to Southern California will want to miss Los Angeles and its glamorous suburb, Hollywood. Los Angeles is unlike any other American city, yet it may be the most American of cities; and Hollywood still retains that old tinsel magic.

San Francisco

America's Pacific Gateway was also a destination for thousands of pioneers, beginning the rush with the discovery of gold and continuing with the realization that the pursuit of happiness seemed most attainable in California. Many consider this to be the most civilized city in the United States.

Las Vegas

The ultimate in plastic, tinsel, and artificial entertainment, Las Vegas is one of those places that is so awful, and yet so enjoyable, that it ranks as a genuine American Travel Wonder. If you don't dig beneath the surface (and there's little chance you'll have the time or desire to do so), you'll have a lot of fun . . . for pure pleasure, good food, stimulation (and even quiet relaxation if you really look hard enough for it), Las Vegas can't be bested.

PEOPLE

Time spent in any American city obviously will mean constant contact with the American people. And certainly there is no way to generalize about the people a visitor may meet in the country's major metropolitan areas—except perhaps to say that they will differ from each other in every way imaginable. Trips beyond the cities will lead visitors to other facets of the American people and their culture.

The American Indian

There was a long time when it didn't look as if it would turn out that way, but the fact is that while American cowboys are rapidly diminishing in number, Indians are rising fast in population. The Indians in New Mexico, for example, have doubled in number since World War II. They and their fellow Indians have made a sort of separate world just below the surface of American life. The Indian has held to more of his identity than might be supposed by the strength of pressures of the modern society around him. Even in the East the Indian has kept much of his traditions, and regularly forsakes his conventional dress and his workaday job in the larger economy in order to meet with members of his tribe and other tribes, to visit, to renew the sparks of old languages and old chants, to dance, or even to join in a demonstration for Indians' rights.

Penobscots in Maine, Narragansetts in Rhode Island, and Wampanoags in Connecticut still present irregular programs of Indian lore in the summer, as do the Six Nations of the Iroquois at their reservations in upstate New York. Where the Indians are gone they have often left behind fascinating traces of their civilizations. The Mound Builders, as they are now called, have left burial mounds in Ohio that are preserved by the Ohio Historical Society, including the largest in America, Serpent Mound, that twists along a length of 1,335 feet. Many sites are marked for grim scenes of Indian massacres; a museum at Gnaddenhutten, Ohio, commemorates the place where drunken soldiers shot and killed 96 Indians.

Indian crafts are demonstrated and sold at Indian villages of the Chippewas in northern Michigan and in Minnesota, and Wisconsin has five large reservations and another that a decade ago became a self-operating county (Menominee County). In many midwestern reservations guests are welcomed at tent and trailer sites on a lakeside, or even in cabins and motels. Pageants are part of the pow-wow festivities at some reservations in the summer, notably at Lac de Flambeau, Wisconsin, a summer meeting place for scores of midwestern tribes, and at Black Hawk State Park at Rock Island, Illinois, the Labor Day site of an important annual meeting of the Fox and Sauk tribes. Wherever you travel in the Midwest you will see markers of Indian battles, such as one at a gas station in Mankato, Minnesota, that reads: "Here were hanged 38 Sioux Indians—Dec. 26, 1862."

It is of course the western Indians who have more fully kept their Indian customs, language, and way of life, and it is also in the West where the Indian population is greatest. Many colorful events celebrate certain crops or are otherwise scheduled without regard to the calendar, sometimes spontaneously. Although most celebrations take place in summer, a visitor to Arizona or New Mexico can expect to find some sort of festival or ritual program taking place at almost any time of the year. In Arizona the Hopi and the Navajo Indians put on many arts and crafts exhibitions, rodeos, trade fairs, pow-wows, and dances. The Southern Utes are renowned for their Bear Dance at their Colorado reservations. In Idaho the Nez Perce tribe has a Spring Root Festival in May, while the Coeur d'Alene tribe displays Indian games in Whaa-Laa Days in July. A reenactment of the Custer battle takes place at Crow Agency, Montana, every July—with local cowboys taking the roles of the Federal troops and local Crow Indians playing Indians. There is also a Crow Fair there in August. In September there are hand games and a barbecue at the Indian Nevada Day celebration in Nixon, Nevada, and so it goes throughout the Far West—pow-wows, homecomings, foot races, rabbit hunts, and unforgettable tribal dances dating back into prehistory. A visit with the Indians is a rare and irreplaceable experience, and anyone willing to listen to the Indian will quickly discover that he has much to say about his present-day identity and his place in the scheme of life in the U.S. But most impressive of any visit to the western scene is a visit to what is probably the oldest continuously inhabited town in the country, Acoma, New Mexico, sitting atop a 370-foot-high mesa in a grand and unsullied isolation. A walk through the quiet streets of this ancient place will make any visitor feel he is a newcomer to this land.

Cowboys and Pioneers

The cowboys of tradition, of the western movie, live mainly in ree-nactments of old derring-do adventures, or in museums or other hallowed sites holding mementoes of famous shootouts or standoffs—although there are of course working cowboys still who round up the cattle in the trackless prairie, or who make their living mainly from rodeo competition (dealt with in another section in this book). Annie Oakley, the famous sharpshooter, is also part of the American cowboy-and-Indian tradition; a star of Buffalo Bill's Wild West Show, her medals are displayed in a museum in Greenville, Ohio.

Even though modern cowboys are more often found aboard a pickup truck than a mustang, cowboy lore abounds in the West in such towns as Tombstone, Arizona, where such landmarks as the OK Corral, the Wells Fargo office, and Boot Hill have been restored. There are reenactments of famous deeds, such as the James Brothers' bank robbery, in Northfield, Minnesota, every July.

Dude Ranches and Guest Farms

Watching people work is becoming an American pastime, especially when the workers are farmers living a life that seems totally alien to city dwellers today. Out on the farms of Pennsylvania and the Midwest vacationers are having the times of their lives just breathing sweet air and strolling through cornfields, and looking at placid cows. These special holidays are available at working farms, and, out West, on working ranches, and they give a particular flavor of American life that can be had in no other way. Although farming methods are hardly all that different from those now in use in other parts of the world, there is a unique flavor about the spirit of an American farm—part stolid, part businesslike efficiency, part innovative and joyful—that makes a farm holiday special.

The dude ranch is of course a famous institution but it can still hold its intrigue and even surprises. Some will take you out on a real round-up where you can sleep in your own bedroll out on the prairie and follow the cowboys in their work. All the great variety of adventure and sightseeing and sporting activity of the West is available from the dude ranch—horseback riding first of all, and canoeing, river raft trips, mountain climbing, and such unforgettable events as the campfire steak cookout or the hunt breakfast. One ranch has what it calls "optional herding," while another lets you help in "moving cows." Kids feed the animals while in many of the same ranches the parents meet in a stylish cocktail lounge, or around a swimming pool, or in a small dance hall supplied with a brand-new jukebox and the latest records. From the Pacific Northwest, where cabins with fireplaces can be rented in the middle of a redwood forest, to the desert moonscapes of Utah, ranch vacations make a great approach to living and feeling the life of the West both as it used to be and as it remains today.

The farms in the Midwest have their own unique peacefulness and many of them provide boating, archery, pistol ranges, hot dog roasts, hay rides, picnics, and the old swimming hole. Some farms will gladly keep the children occupied while the parents are off to some nearby town for shopping or a show, and there are ranches and farms that specialize in children's vacations of several weeks, where the kids join the farmers in real work. Food is hearty and of the "all-you-can-eat" variety, and many are open in winter, when guests often go in for the winter sports locally available. Some of the western ranches seem a thousand miles from nowhere, but even among the most isolated there are those for every taste—rambling desert resorts with every facility from swimming pool to air-conditioned dining room, and rustic layouts where you sleep in your own bedroll in a bunkhouse and sweep out in the morning. In nearly all of them, eastern and midwestern farmstead, or western ranch, you get an unmistakably fresh taste of American life.

Religious Settlements

Nowhere does the famed variety of American life show itself more obviously than in the proliferation of its religious denominations that originated in every part of the world. Many religious groups formed their own communities—in fact the process continues even today— some of which keep old customs, building styles, foods, dress, and rules for living. Some groups have had their presence used by their neighbors for commercial purposes; the Amish of Pennsylvania have brought on a huge influx of tourists around the city of Lancaster, even though the so-called Amish homesteads and restaurants are never visited by a real Amish man or woman. But many settlements do give a strong taste of the individuality and perseverance that characterized the building of the U.S.

Descendants of Zoarites, a German communal group, still occupy the community, in eastern Ohio, called Zoar Village, their great-grand-fathers founded over a century ago. Harmonists founded New Harmony, Indiana, and today welcome visitors to their old homesteads. Of special interest is the headquarters of the Spiritualists, in Chesterfield, Indiana, where mediums give demonstrations of their powers. In Iowa there are six thriving villages of the Amana Colony founded 120 years ago by the Inspirationalists and now manufacturers of electric appliances distributed nationally. Monasteries dot secluded country areas in many parts of the country and often welcome visitors to enjoy the calm atmosphere; many of these produce crafts and wines for sale as well. Temple Square of Salt Lake City is the sacred ground of an original American sect, Mormonism. A number of the old Spanish missions of California are still occupied by monks who conduct tours of their ancient premises. A vegetarian-religious group called the House of David, in Benton Harbor, Michigan, serves visitors in its own restaurant. One who approaches these communities with a certain respect is almost always sure of a warm welcome and some new insight into the many ways of American life.

Industrial Sightseeing

The flavor of America comes across strongly in her mills and factories, and a feature of traveling in this country is that industrialists generally welcome visitors on free guided tours that can be extremely absorbing and instructive. From a brewery in Massachusetts to a winery in California or a king crab packing plant in Alaska, workers and administration people will welcome your visit if—as is usually the case—you give advance notice of your visit. Every large city has tours of local plants, and details can easily be had from the local chamber of commerce office. Many tours are unique in the U.S., for no other country has such vast auto factories, tire plants, or even musical instrument makers as Detroit, Akron, and Elkhart, Indiana.

A tour of the *Chicago Tribune* lets visitors watch reporters and editors at work from a glassed-in gallery, while wineries in upstate New York, Ohio, Michigan, and especially in California welcome tasters as well as sightseers. Breweries, too, offer samples to their guests, while television and radio stations are glad to take you behind the scenes to inspect their electronic marvels before you become part of the audience for a broadcast show. No city on earth makes as much breakfast cereal as Battle Creek, Michigan, and the makers are happy to have you watch them at work there; the special American spirit of pride in the nation's tremedous variety of industry is obvious in the welcoming attitudes of both management and workers. Outdoor spectaculars include visits to such open-pit mines as Iron Mountain, in the Mesabi Range of Minnesota, whereas in Hershey, Pennsylvania, you will be mesmerized by a sea of swirling chocolate. Industrial tours can quickly draw you into a world that perhaps you know nothing of—a macaroni factory in Dallas, a soap factory in Cincinnati, a tobacco warehouse in North Carolina where the babbling chant of the auctioneer sounds like a new language. If you happen to have a special interest in a particular manufacturing field, these tours can provide you with an entire education in your chosen subject. A whole vacation could be mapped out with stops from factory to factory, but wherever you may be visiting, ask locally about what unique work may be going on that you can see.

CULTURAL LIFE

To investigate the wide range of cultural activities with which Americans surround themselves is to learn a great deal about the people that live in this country.

Outstanding Museums

There are over 7,000 museums in the United States, and it would take you over 18 years to visit them all if you could tour one every day of the year. But by the time you had finished you'd have a new crop ahead of you that would take another 13 years, because five new ones are opening every week, almost as fast as McDonald's hamburger stands.

The variety of American museums boggles the mind: a Sun Museum in Alcova, Wyoming; a Cobblestone Museum in Albion, New York; a Ham Museum in Dubuque, Iowa. A Collar Museum is in Troy, New York; and the A. D. Babcock Open Door Museum is in Goodland, Indiana. There is a Dish Museum in Kissimmee, Florida; a Paper Museum in Appleton, Wisconsin; a Museum of Quackery in St. Louis. There are oil museums, coal museums, glass museums, beer museums, whiskey museums. There is the World's Smallest Museum, in Weslaco, Texas.

Besides these museums celebrating unique or unlikely subjects there are of course hundreds of general historical museums and a constantly growing and improving national community of fine art museums. Much of the flavor of the United States can be felt in museums run by local historical societies and in the countless collections of Americana —both paintings and artifacts—in general-interest and art museums. Every city and town is proud of its own local treasures and its own artists, both early and contemporary. Since most art museums have regularly changing shows, local inquiry is the best way to find out what is going on that will interest you.

As the United States becomes the center of the modern art world, many art museums across the country are building up important collections of current work by American and foreign artists. The art lover may begin with New York City, the acknowledged art capital, by touring private galleries on Madison Avenue and the avant-garde ones on West Broadway (SoHo). Besides the Metropolitan, the Museum of Modern Art, the Whitney, the Guggenheim, the Jewish Museum, the Frick, and the Brooklyn Museum, all in New York City, many other first-rate collections exist. To name only a few: the Art Institute of

Chicago and the Museum of Contemporary Art of Chicago; the Cleveland Museum of Art; Philadelphia Museum of Art; and the National Gallery of Art and National Collection of Fine Arts in Washington. The Winterthur Museum in Delaware has the country's largest collection of decorative arts; other fine arts museums of outstanding quality can be found in Worcester, Massachusetts; Boston (the Museum of Fine Arts and Cambridge's Fogg Art Museum), Denver, Phoenix, Los Angeles, Houston, Atlanta, New Haven (the Yale Art Gallery), Hartford (the Wadsworth Atheneum), Minneapolis, Toledo, and Pittsburgh. Exceptional collections of western art can be seen in many western cities. There is an endless feast in store for the art lover.

Architectural Highlights

Nowhere is the history and character of the various eras and spirits that made America more evident than in the architecture of her homes and public buildings, her forts, theaters, inns, and factories. A very large number of older structures of historical and architectural importance are open to the public, and many old privately owned homes are made available for inspection by the public for a few days each year in many lovely old communities that organize visiting tours. From the early houses of the Pilgrims to the forts of the pioneers' West, from the adobe hut of the Southwest to the modern grain elevators of the plains, from the staunch brownstone houses of Manhattan to the pristinely white farmsteads of Maine, the way things were built seems to reflect the mind and the eye of the people.

Every region has its special attractions—St. Augustine, the oldest city, with its old cathedral and its St. Francis Inn; Savannah with its old brick and wrought iron grillwork; New Orleans with its shaded balconies; Litchfield, Connecticut, Bristol, Rhode Island, Manchester, Vermont—among 100 other New England towns—with their stately Colonial frame houses. There are the outrageously ornate "cottages" of Newport and the old churches of Boston and the restored town houses of Portsmouth, New Hampshire, and of Providence. Mansions reflect the aristocracy of Virginia in Mt. Vernon and Monticello, and the soft glow of red brick in the modestly pleasant row houses of Annapolis recalls the sailing-ship era. Our oldest public building predates the Pilgrims—the Palace of Governors, in Santa Fe, with its Spanish-Colonial design. In every city and town a hint of the hopes and pretensions of the place can often come if you look closely at the city or town hall, at the library building, at the older schools, even at the old mills and warehouses. It is not only the historically important structure that has strong architectural value, no matter what age it comes from, so the visitor is best served by a curious eye. He will, for instance, find examples of innovative modern architecture by hazard rather than on any organized tour—a tip is to look for new churches, university structures, and suburban corporate office structures.

Surprising to many is the fact that Chicago has been, and remains, in the forefront of modern architectural development. Not only Sullivan, "father of the skyscrapers," and Frank Lloyd Wright, but many others have labored here to erect one of the finest skylines in the nation (not to mention the tallest building in the world).

Regional Theater

The health of the American theater seems to be in a variety of states all at once—from robust, vigorous, and thriving to perfunctory or even dormant—but among all the theater going on there is always a good deal worth seeing. Summer is the big season, of course, for it is then that the professional summer theaters operate, putting on a different play every few weeks. Having originated in Maine, they are most numerous and best-run in the New England states, but there are good ones elsewhere too.

Summer is also the time for the unique American concept of outdoor theater where amphitheaters fill up with fans who like their history with a dose of melodrama, sentimentality, or comedy. "The Stephen Foster Story," or "The Lost Colony" (about the Virginia colonists) packs them in, and in a similar, but lighter vein, are the little theater productions of villain-and-victim shows especially popular out West.

Serious theater is produced year-round by a number of excellent repertory companies whose fates are often in doubt from year to year even though Americans are supporting more theater than ever before. Such cities as New Orleans, Houston, San Francisco, Hartford, and Providence have repertories; the best may well be the Guthrie Theater in Minneapolis. The American Players Theater performs classical works in an idyllic outdoor setting in Spring Green, Wisconsin. Alongside these professional theaters, the amateur Little Theater, which began in Columbia, South Carolina, in 1919, continues in many communities, sometimes aiming at serious theater. The best place to look for original work, however, is on the college campuses.

American theater has some oddities: there are Passion Plays put on every year in Arkansas, Illinois, and South Dakota, and the list of Shakespeare Festivals grows longer—besides the free Shakespeare in Central Park, New York City, there are festivals in Cleveland; Stratford, Connecticut (and a sister festival in Stratford, Ontario); San Diego; Ashland, Oregon; and Boulder, Colorado. Showboats and dinner theaters abound, and the lover of good theater has to pick his way among programs of pretty commercialism, but if he searches out the local theater listings carefully he will be amazed by the good theater going on in many of our cities.

Concerts and Music Festivals

Every major American city, and most middle-sized cities, have symphonies and philharmonic orchestras that provide year-'round programs, but summertime brings a vast selection of concerts and festivals, most of them held outdoors, that can make an American tour unforgettable. There are music camps where students give free concerts and ethnic festivals where songs and melodies from everywhere in the world are brought to life.

Standard operatic and symphonic works, chamber music and choral singing are presented in every major population center. Some special events are worth noting, however, that evade easy categories. The Grand Ole Opry, in Nashville, broadcasts a weekly country-and-western show before a devoted audience, while dulcimers and lutes are heard at the Ohio Hills Folk Festival in Ohio. Wolf Trap Farm, near Washington, D.C., is a federally run national park for performing arts. Polka festivals, a Heidi festival, a Swedish Day are all midwestern gala affairs. Berryville, Virginia boasts a National Bluegrass Championship, while the towns of Athens and Crockett, in Texas, join to produce the World's Champion Fiddlers Contest.

Festivals that draw lovers of serious music outdoors include the Monadnock Concerts in New Hampshire, the Tanglewood Festival in Lenox, Massachusetts, and summer-long symphonies in Saratoga Springs, New York. Jazz is blown at the Memphis Cotton Carnival Jazz and Blues Festival, at the Burlington Dixieland Jazz Festival in Iowa, at the Newport Jazz Festival (now in New York City), and at the Monterey Jazz Festival in California. The Mormon Tabernacle

Choir merits a special esteem for many lovers of religious music, while hundreds of southern churches still welcome visitors to hear the remarkably moving strength of spirituals sung by black choristers. The Santa Fe Opera presents many of its works outdoors under the clear dry skies of the Southwest. There is Chinese opera in New York City and Seattle. There is music of every kind in the air everywhere, and a glance at the cultural events section of any Sunday newspaper will clue you in on where to start.

Art Colonies

The typical American art colony was a modest seaport or mountain village that drew a few serious artists to take up residence both for the visual surroundings and for the peacefulness and inexpensiveness of life there. Later crafts and gift shops sprouted, and tourist accommodations proliferated, and the original artists moved on. But even in some of the most commercialized "colonies," as they are called even when the artists migrate seasonally, the beauty of the place is still a strong attraction. Some of the centers hold annual art festivals that go on for several days or a week, and although you are in danger of being swamped by amateur paintings of clowns, bullfighters, and children with big wet eyes, a persevering search will often turn up works of real interest, and those usually at modest cost.

Among the many scores of more or less self-styled colonies, important ones include Boothbay Harbor, Maine; Provincetown, Massachusetts; Wickford, Rhode Island; New Hope, Pennsylvania; Cedar Key, Florida; New Orleans (the Vieux Carré); Taos, New Mexico; Aspen, Colorado; and Monterey-Carmel, California.

On Campus

Some of the most valuable and extensive libraries, art collections, museums, and special collections are to be found on university campuses across the U.S., where year-round cultural programs welcome the visitor and often give him a chance to enjoy some of the loveliest environments in the land. From the stately old halls of Yale and Harvard to the sparkling modernity of new campuses in Texas and the Far West, travelers discover a world quite apart from the workaday scene of town and city. Many American campuses make up the living centers of the college towns they occupy, and to spend a few days in one or another of these is to taste the special American flavor of academe that is not quite equaled anywhere else.

The Ivy League universities of the East actually do have ivy on many of their old buildings. These institutions pride themselves on their history, and on their particular contributions to the world's knowledge, and are pleased to show visitors around, usually in guided tours, or else by a point-by-point printed guidebook and map. A stop at the administration offices of almost any university will start you off on an informed walking tour to be followed by many pleasing options: a student-produced play, a film festival, a musical concert, an art show, a dance recital, a football or basketball game.

Much of the cultural treasure of the U.S. is kept in the universities, from the shrinelike Olin Library of Wesleyan University in Connecticut, holder of the original manuscripts of Albert Einstein's theory of relativity, to the brand-new Popular Culture Center of Bowling Green University in Ohio, originator of this new branch of study. World War II memorabilia fills the George C. Marshall Museum of Virginia Military Institute. A twelfth-century English church, removed to the U.S. stone by stone in 1966, forms a part of the Winston Churchill Memorial and Library of Westminster College, in Missouri. Every university may hold one surprise or another; for example the University of Wyoming displays a collection of over 270,000 plant specimens. Universities and colleges often lead a life apart from the surrounding community, so it is best to query the administration directly to find out what is going on currently that may interest you.

HISTORY

A traveler in the United States can spend just about as much time visiting America's past as seeing what the country is like today.

Historic Trails

Another unique facet of American traveling is the historic trail, which can be either the actual path of an oldtime right-of-way, such as the Oregon Trail, or a more recent route set up and marked to take you past sites of historic interest in some particular area that can include parts of several different states: the Hiawatha Pioneer Trail, which leads you through Illinois, Iowa, Minnesota, and Wisconsin for 2,400 miles, is a good example.

These trails not only provide the enthusiast of American history with an easy route to important sites, but also give the average tourist a varied series of destinations that can include everything from a towering bluff that was the scene of a great Indian battle to a well-preserved or restored old mansion or public building that played some major role in the making of the country. Although there are a few trails intended for walking, most of them extend for many miles and are designed primarily for the motorist; the Freedom Trail in Boston, which leads you to many sites of the Revolutionary era, is an example of the former. Then there are trails not traversible by car, but reachable at many intersections with regular highways along their way, such as the old Overland Trail used by the pioneers out West, preserved by markers near Laramie, Wyoming. Where highways follow the old routes—the Oregon Trail, the Mormon Trail, the old pony express routes—historic markers help you to envision the scenes of struggle and endurance when the early covered wagons moved West. In Nebraska, an interstate highway follows alongside the Oregon Trail, but at highway speeds it is hard to get your imagination to work back to the last century. More satisfying are such trails as the Iroquois War Trail in northern Ohio and the Gunflint Trail, an old route of the *voyageurs* that leads through northern Minnesota to the Canadian line. A cattle path, the Chisholm Trail, is marked by a museum in Oklahoma, whereas the Heritage Trail of New England was set up in modern times to lead the tourist to the most important sites of the Colonial days. Another old trail, the Natchez Trace, in Mississippi, is now paved but retains an oldtime peacefulness. Many of these trails can be a key to considerable enjoyment along your way even if you pick them up for only part of their whole way.

Reconstructed Villages and Ghost Towns

The comparative newness of the United States may account for the mania of its citizens to revere everything they can dig up out of their past, and, if they can't find the real thing, to build something old anyhow. Thus we have a bewildering proliferation of "old" towns, "old" villages, "old" buildings that may or may not be really old. As you visit the many restorations, some excellently done, with extreme attention to authenticity, the distinction between "old" old and "new" old may soon blur for you. At any rate wherever you go among restorations and ghost towns you will get plenty of American history, much of it in very palpable and memorable form.

Among the most real of restorations is Strawbery Banke, the old center of Portsmouth, New Hampshire, that was saved from the wrecker's ball in the nick of time. It not only has real houses, mostly dating back 250 years or so, but also has real people living in them. Old Sturbridge Village, in Massachusetts, also has real houses and other structures, and the craftsmen who display their arts do so convincingly. Williamsburg, Virginia, the country's largest restoration, has built many of its houses from scratch but only after painstaking research into period architecture. Mystic Seaport, in Connecticut, is a mixture of old and new, the aim always being to preserve what would otherwise be lost in the onrush of mass-produced modern construction.

Some of the restorations are openly commercial. Helen, Georgia, a small whistle stop, has incredibly disguised itself as a Bavarian village for no better reason than to get tourists to stop, look, and maybe buy something. Holland, Michigan, pretends in a like way to be a Dutch town—although it does have some residents of Dutch ancestry as justification. But whatever the degree of historical veracity there is plenty to learn in most of the restorations—many cities have set aside part of their centers as memorials to the past, with early stores and businesses remade: Old Fort Wayne, Old Abilene, Old San Diego.

A recent history—that of the miners of the 1850s—is to be seen first-hand, *without* restoration, in many of the ghost towns of the West. Jerome, Arizona, for example, once had 15,000 people living in it—now there are a handful. You can visit some 150 ghost towns in Utah alone. Tombstone, Arizona, has been rediscovered as a site for movies, and Virginia City, Nevada, now has more restauranteurs than it ever had sourdoughs. Wherever you go you'll find ample opportunity to go back in history, and it's even easy to choose your century.

SPACE PROJECTS

A visitor moves rapidly out of the past when visiting one of the U.S. space projects. There is nowhere else in the world where the casual tourist can get a closeup look at space-vehicle design and launching sites.

Cape Canaveral

Cape Canaveral (named Cape Kennedy after the assassination of the late president, then renamed Cape Canaveral once again a decade later), the Kennedy Space Center, the Merritt Island moon-launch site, Patrick Air Force Base Missile Test Center—together the jumping-off place for our epochal strides into space—are aligned along a forty-mile strip of erstwhile deserted sandpits. With luck and an adjustable schedule, you can watch. Major space ventures are advertised days in advance, so if you hope to see the blast-off, you may wish to visit other nearby attractions until it appears the attempt is "go," and then join the caravan enroute to Cocoa Beach, several miles south of Cape Canaveral for the best view.

There will be experts aplenty around you, so make sure you're looking at the right launching pad. Neophytes have been known to keep their binoculars trained on a 165-foot tall object, painted with black and white stripes, throughout a countdown only to stand befuddled as it sits there motionless while everyone is screaming at the liftoff. What they've observed with such dedication is the Cape Canaveral Lighthouse, which hasn't moved an inch in almost a hundred years.

If there's no blast-off scheduled, you can tour the main launching area for the Atlantic Missile Range and the pad from which astronauts are shot into space, and/or NASA's moon-launch area on Merritt Island. The only authorized guided bus tours of the area are Kennedy Space Center Tours, operated by TWA and conducted regularly throughout the day from the Visitors Information Center. Operational activity at the space center makes the tours subject to change. While it won't really put you very close to things, the moon-launch tour will certainly give you something to look at. This is the Vehicle Assembly Building, the world's largest building in terms of enclosed space—129 million cubic feet. The VAB will permit assembly of four space vehicles as large as the Apollo moonshot rocket and is fifty-two stories high, covering eight acres. Nearby stand the giant mobile launchers, in which the missiles are transported to the launching pad three miles away. You will also see the launch complexes and a small space museum.

On Sundays you can drive your own car around the Cape Canaveral Air Force Station at no charge. Be sure to stop at the recently expanded Visitors Center, located at the space center, six miles east of US 1, south of Titusville. It has splendid free exhibits, movies and detailed lectures on the space program, including the Shuttle. For those who can't take the weekend tours, there's a display of missiles at nearby Patrick Air Force Base.

In other parts of the country, the unique U.S. space program can be seen in some of its many aspects of Redstone Arsenal, Alabama, which has a great array of rocket models, and at the Space Orientation Center at Marshall, Alabama, which features an exhibit on the history of rocketry from its earliest origins in China. The Mercury capsule that carried the third U.S. manned flight in 1962 is also shown here.

In Pasadena, California, the NASA Jet Propulsion Laboratory shows visitors the work of designing satellites that go to the moon and the distant planets, while in the lava beds near McKenzie Pass, in the Cascades Mountains of Oregon, those curious about what the moon feels like can walk over the astronauts' training ground here, chosen for its resemblance to the lunar surface.

THEME PARKS

Walt Disney World

Walt Disney World, in the Orlando area, is the world's single most popular tourist attraction. You can spend a day or a week and still not see everything the Magic Kingdom has to offer, but since it opened the average visitor has spent nearly nine hours there. Located on US 192, just west of I–4, Walt Disney World offers golf, boating, swimming, camping, hiking, waterskiing, horseback riding, canoeing, and night life as well as the theme park. The park is divided into sections: Fantasyland, with Cinderella's Castle, Mickey Mouse revue, and Captain Nemo subs; Main St. USA, a study in nostalgia; Tomorrowland, a preview of the future; Adventureland, with jungle cruises, luau, tree house; Frontierland, a re-creation of the Old West; Liberty Square, with colonial shops, Hall of Presidents; and a haunted house. Two years old, the Experimental Community of Tomorrow (Epcot), is a world of the future, a high-tech adult playground of programmed fantasy.

Disneyland

Disneyland, the "Magic Kingdom," 1313 Harbor Blvd., Anaheim, CA., 27 miles southeast of the Los Angeles Civic Center, celebrated its

25th anniversary in 1980. From the entrance into Main Street, a typical thoroughfare in the United States, circa 1900, one journeys through six other "theme" lands—Adventureland, Bear Country, Fantasyland, Frontierland, New Orleans Square, and Tomorrowland.

Tomorrowland is typified by the great gleaming monorail that whisks passengers around the park. There is a miniature reproduction of the freeways of the future with scale automobiles that can be driven, as well as Space Mountain, with its rocket flight.

Fantasyland is highlighted by Sleeping Beauty's Castle, the most photographed site in all the park. This is the realm of storybook characters—Alice in Wonderland, King Arthur's Carrousel, and the happy land of It's a Small World.

Frontierland recaptures yesterday. A train ride takes you back into Gold Rush days, past a drowsy little mining camp, into the desert and through a mine lit with myriad-colored waterfalls. There are rivers of America on which two boats, the stern-wheeler *Mark Twain* and the sailing vessel *Columbia,* take visitors on a tour around Tom Sawyer Island.

Bear Country, a four-acre Pacific Northwest wilderness, features Davy Crockett's Explorer Canoeing on your own, plus a Nashville-styled country western jamboree starring 18 bruin Brandos.

In Adventureland the most popular rides are the Jungle River Cruise and the Pirates of the Caribbean. Another favorite adventure is a climb into a tremendous tree, like the one in Disney's *Swiss Family Robinson* movie. This one has three tree-houses to poke through.

The late Walt Disney's promise that "Disneyland will continue to grow, to add things, as long as there is imagination left in the world" is still the theme.

When you want to take a break or a rest, you can head for one of the 50 shops and 30 restaurants. Merchandise ranges from inexpensive gifts to exquisite, expensive items. And you can take your choice of dining—there are many refreshment stands and fancy restaurants.

No matter when you visit Disneyland—winter or summer, early morning or late evening, you'll be impressed by its freshness and cleanliness, as well as the friendliness and courtesy of its staff. The park is open year-round. Plan on a good six hours to see everything—there's well over $200 million worth of magic. And do inquire about special prices on ticket books. A special attraction all summer is Disneyland's Big Band Festival at Main Street's Plaza Garden Stage.

SPORTS

No experience of the United States could really be complete without touching on sports—a passion, often an obsession, of American life.

Rodeos

Of the seven traditional main events in a rodeo, it is the bull riding that is the toughest and most dangerous. Rodeos, which began a century ago as a diversion for cowboys to prove their bravery, strength, and stamina, have now become so widespread a western sport that nearly 100 colleges offer rodeo scholarships, and many cowboys do nothing but follow the rodeo trail from town to town, state to state, through the year. There is nothing quite like a rodeo anywhere outside North America, although there is, in the defiance of dangerous animals, some resemblance to the Spanish bullfight. Both must produce occasional injury to contestants and participants, for without that they would be little more than a sort of stock roundup. Ropers and steer wrestlers can have fingers burned off by rope yanked through a hand, or be trampled or gored in their specialized events, but it is the rider who gets hurt more frequently.

The rodeo reflects the western belief that to stand up to pain shows a man's mettle, and to show this in the presence of 7,000 spectators at the National Finals Rodeo in Oklahoma City, in December, is to reach the height of this strange profession, which is what it is becoming. There are, for example, over 3,500 members of the Rodeo Cowboys Association, which sanctions officially scored rodeos all over the West (and even one in Madison Square Garden in New York City), and many of these contestants do nothing else but ride, rope, and wrestle animals for a living. But in over 500 official RCA rodeos (there are of course hundreds of other, smaller contests that do not get recorded in the record books) in one year, only 67 cowboys earned over $10,000 each.

Cowboys show a practiced stoicism in the face of injury. This is their pride. They never wear any protective gear at all, and thus look down on such padded gladiators as football players. A Fort Worth cowboy, Del Heiliger, will tell you enthusiatically how he had a hole opened in his skull by the hammering flip of a horse's head in a rodeo fall—"I could put two fingers right into my brain," he says proudly. He also broke his neck ten years ago in another rodeo. By the end of a Finals—a week of rodeos—in Oklahoma City, there are scores of broken ribs, torn ligaments, sprains, and wrenched joints that cowboys try to ignore for just that eight-second trip on a bronco, or nine seconds aboard an angry bull. They claim they do it for the money, not to show off their bravery, and it is true that nobody but the winners get anything at all; expenses are not paid. But there is also this belittling of pain that you can detect in the announcer's drawl as he brings on a steer wrestler, telling of a horn that had recently caught the man under the chin, piercing upward into his mouth: "Walt Linderman here still ain't chewin' his tobacco too well."

Oklahoma is the center of the rodeo world but there are meets all over the West, small and large, starting with the Fat Stock Show and Rodeo in Fort Worth, Texas, in January, and continuing with Salinas Big Week, in California, in July, and Cheyenne Frontier Days, in Wyoming, later the same month. Prison rodeos are a tradition, too, in which originally inmates would earn time off their sentences for exceptional bravery. (The McAlester, Oklahoma, prison rodeo also features music by the prison band, the Oklahoma Outlaws.) In September the Pendleton Round-Up, in Oregon, draws all the famous rodeo contestants. The rodeo at Beaver, Oklahoma, includes the World Championship Cow Chip Throwing Contest each year. Bucking broncos are not raised mean but are simply chosen when they prove untrainable for any other purpose; a good one can bring as much as $5,000. They have an automatic aim of sending an unwelcome cowboy flying off their backs into the dirt, where he may, with luck, be stomped, gored, kicked, or even bitten. Thrills abound at even the smallest rodeos, and every western town has one, but the big one is the Finals in Oklahoma City.

The Races

Wherever you travel in the U.S. you will find people watching and often betting on races. Lovers of horseflesh are especially welcome at several places around the country, most notably around Lexington, Kentucky, where a score of world-renowned thoroughbred farms accept visitors daily. Among the most famous are Spendthrift, Darby Dan, Dixiana, Main Chance, and Crown Crest. You can see the horses grazing and romping in their handsome fields of bluegrass. An unforgettable scene is the annual yearling sales at Keeneland race track in mid-July; these youngsters sometimes sell for half a million dollars or more.

A newer region of grassy land given over to thoroughbred raising that also welcomes visitors is in the vicinity of Ocala, Florida, a sort of neo-Kentucky with a milder climate. Oklahoma, around the town of Sayre, is the home breeding grounds of the American quarterhorse, most of the breed descending from a single champion named Peter McCue. A show in May is the best time to visit Sayre. And every August, down in Shelbyville, Tennessee, the world champion walking horse is chosen at the finish of the Walking Horse Celebration.

Besides the thoroughbred races and trotting races, there are greyhound tracks in many parts of the country. Americans love a race, and will back favorites of almost every kind—a crab race in Maryland, a jumping frog contest in California. Most famous is of course the Kentucky Derby in Louisville, the only individual race to have its own museum. But the richest race in the country is held at Ruidoso Downs, a track situated over a mile high on a plateau of New Mexico.

The world's biggest sport event, the Indianapolis 500, draws 300,000 people to watch racing cars (both the qualifying heats and final races on Memorial Day). Bonneville Speedway out on the Utah salt flats is the scene of speed-record attempts of all kinds. A major 500-mile motorcycle race takes place in Ontario, California. The world's fastest car track, Daytona, has a 400-mile annual run. Stock-car races roar and crash every weekend in nearly every part of the country. Whether you are an expert with the racing form or just a lover of crowds and excitement, there will be racing attractions for you in nearly every state.

Baseball Training Camps

Late vacationers can see some early baseball at the Florida training camp cities, where major leaguers repair their rusty throwing arms. The *Washington Senators* tried Florida in 1888, and most teams since have followed suit. Two hundred exhibition games start mid-March and continue for a month. Seventeen of twenty major league teams train on the lower coast—Winter Haven built a $300,000 stadium to catch a defector, the *Boston Red Sox.* The *Houston Astros* have a super, five-diamonds, $800,000 training complex at Cocoa. Bradenton's million-dollar stadium (for the *Pittsburgh Pirates*) has a winged canopy roof extending far out over the center seating section. Ticket costs vary, but about $3.50 is tops, and often it's $1.

Home bases: *Atlanta Braves* at West Palm Beach; *Chicago White Sox* at Sarasota; *Cincinnati Reds* at Tampa; *Detroit Tigers* at Lakeland; *Kansas City Royals* at Fort Myers; *L.A. Dodgers* at Vero Beach; *Minnesota Twins* at Orlando; *St. Louis Cardinals* and *New York Mets* at St. Petersburg; *New York Yankees* at Fort Lauderdale; *Phillies* at Clearwater; *Twins Farm Teams* at Melbourne; *Texas Rangers* at Pompano Beach.

Ski Trails

Except for the South and Midwest, few areas of the U.S. lack some sort of ski slopes, from the frostbitten heights of Vermont and New Hampshire to lowland intermediate runs in Rhode Island and Connecticut; from towering peaks two miles high in the Rockies to milder forest overland trails in Georgia and the Appalachian states. There are skiers in New Mexico and Arizona, in Alaska and Minnesota, in Pennsylvania and upstate New York.

Among the noted resort centers is the Reno-Lake Tahoe area of Nevada and adjoining California; the super-Austria of Vail, Colorado;

Aspen, Colorado, which doubles as a cultural center; and Sun Valley, Idaho, a world to itself lost in the high snows. Washington State claims the longest skiing season outside Alaska, from early November to late May. Big Mountain Resort is served by the Great Northern Railway in Montana and is a favorite for those who like an extended stay in uncrowded facilities. Back East Tuckerman's Ravine on Mt. Washington in New Hampshire is the roughest trail, also boasting the country's worst weather (130-mile-an-hour winds). The heated pool at Mt. Snow, Vermont, quickly dissipates the tingle of frostbite for skiers fresh off the slopes. A great majority of the American population is now within an easy day's drive of skiing of some kind, while many areas in flatlands are being used more for the increasingly popular sport of cross-country skiing.

American Oddities

Travel in the U.S. is often spiced by unexpectedly strange sights: an entire mountain being sculpted into the form of an Indian on horseback by dynamite blasts over a period of a quarter-century, an entire town built up around a vast, rambling drugstore, and the famous old London Bridge itself sitting incredibly out on the Arizona desert. The first is the Crazy Horse monument in South Dakota, the second is Wall Drug, also in South Dakota, and the last is in Lake Havasu City, Arizona. Americans have a failing for the superlative, and the world's largest, smallest, widest, or tallest of almost anything suffices to bolster civic pride. Zanesville, Ohio, has the world's only bridge in the form of a Y, while a North Carolina town has the world's largest chest of drawers—a three-story building in the form of a dresser. Greatest oddities of all, however, are the myriad of festivals described in the *Facts at Your Fingertips* section earlier in this book, under "Seasonal Events." We won't attempt to top that list by describing more oddities here. Wherever you travel you can add a lot to the fun of touristing by keeping an eye out for this specially American flair for the unexpected.

AMERICA'S VACATIONLANDS

CONNECTICUT

The Constitution State

Connecticut's four seasons offer year-round pleasure. Spells of rain, fog, or snow are usually short-lived, and the climate is never extreme.

Connecticut is home to a cosmopolitan population. All branches of the military are represented here. Industrial employment is varied and includes shipbuilding, aeronautics, electronics, pharmaceuticals, tool-making, and diverse manufacturing. The insurance business, centered in Hartford, employs many of the state's residents. Farming, both poultry and dairy, as well as truck gardening, continues to be important here, even as an avocation, perhaps due to the greater emphasis on good nutrition programs and home-grown products.

Numerous colleges and universities attract students from around the world—followed by parents, friends, and peers—all acknowledging the stimuli to be found in this state.

Access to Connecticut is easy from almost anywhere. Amtrak has regular daily schedules in and out of the state. Local transportation is available between New Haven and New York via Fairfield County. Bradley International airport, just north of Hartford (in Windsor Locks), has regular domestic and international arrivals and departures. Commuter planes serve airports within the state as well as LaGuardia and Kennedy airports in New York.

From Long Island and Fishers Island, New York, and from Block Island, Rhode Island, ferries accommodate both people and cars en route to Connecticut.

Connecticut has an area of 5,000 square miles, 75 percent of which is forest or woodland. There are picturesque villages and towns throughout the state, both on Long Island Sound and in the hills to the north.

With 96 boat or canoe launching sites (10 with access to saltwater), bow and arrow as well as muzzle-loader and shotgun hunting seasons, six downhill and eight cross-country ski areas, more than 100 recreational areas (state parks and forests), and with more than 1500 campsites in 20 of the 100 state-operated recreational areas and 57 private campgrounds, Connecticut not only welcomes visitors—it caters to them.

EXPLORING HARTFORD

The state's capital is one of Connecticut's largest and, perhaps, its most interesting city.

The first building one passes approaching the city from the south on I–91 is easily identified by its onion-shaped dome, topped by a gilded horse. The building is owned by the Colt Patent Firearms Company, which manufactured the famous Colt revolvers that "won the West."

Proceeding north along the Connecticut River, the highway turns into a maze of intersections. Urban renewal projects have resulted in tall buildings that have changed the skyline of downtown.

Entering the city via State Street, Constitution Plaza—a complex of office buildings, a hotel, TV studio, and a tree-dotted mall lined with shops and investment offices—is on the right. Across the street is the Phoenix Mutual Insurance Company's unique headquarters, which resembles a green glass boat.

Directly facing you as you proceed on State Street is the lovely Old State House (1796), a Colonial red brick masterpiece with a white dome designed by Charles Bulfinch. It is now open to the public as a museum. Of special interest in the building is the beautiful Senate Chamber and a graceful unsupported spiral staircase.

South on Main Street is the Travelers Insurance Company building. The 527-foot-high tower may be visited on weekdays, by advance reservation. A plaque on the front of the tower building marks the spot of the old Zachary Sanford Tavern.

Past the Travelers on Main Street is the Wadsworth Atheneum (America's oldest public art museum), the Avery Art Memorial, and the adjoining Morgan Memorial, a museum with a fascinating gun room, an excellent collection of Middle Eastern and Oriental archeological relics and one of the largest exhibits anywhere of Meissen china. The gun room displays muskets, rifles, and Colt revolvers. The Avery boasts paintings by Rembrandt, Wyeth, Daumier, Gilbert Stuart, Picasso, Goya, Giordano, Cézanne, Whistler, and Sargent. The statue on the lawn in front of the Morgan Memorial honors the young Connecticut schoolteacher, Nathan Hale, who was caught by the British while spying on Long Island for Washington's forces and was hanged in New York City.

Beautiful Capitol Hill

The present state capital sits dramatically atop the highest point in Bushnell Park, the central park of Hartford. While the governor and top officials have their offices in the gold-domed capitol, most state workers are housed in the State Office Building at the edge of the park.

Across the street, in the imposing building shared by the State Library and the Supreme Court, there is an interesting collection of early rifles and revolvers and the table upon which President Abraham Lin-

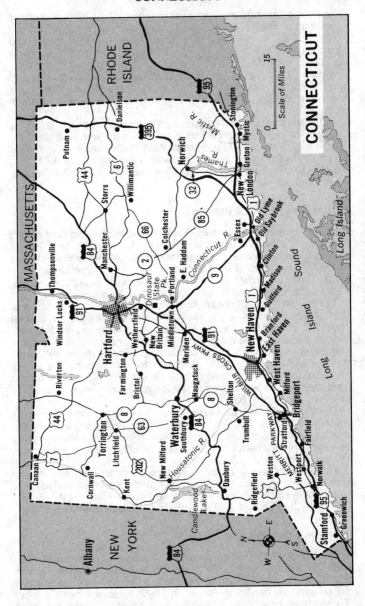

coln signed the Emancipation Proclamation that freed all slaves during the Civil War.

Two other buildings of note stand in the Capitol complex: the State Armory and the Bushnell Memorial. The Armory, to the west of the Capitol, is headquarters for the Connecticut National Guard and the military Reserve units. The Bushnell Memorial, on the east flank of the

Capitol, is a beautiful auditorium that serves as the cultural heart of a community that places a high premium on theater and music.

Hartford's Civic Center offers major shows, entertainments, and sports events, shops, meeting rooms, boutiques, restaurants, and parking garage for 4,000 cars. The Civic Center is headquarters for Connecticut's NHL hockey team, the Hartford Whalers. The Hartford Stage Company, renowned for new productions and standard plays, has a new theater, the John W. Huntington Theater, at 50 Church Street.

In the south end of the city, high on a ridge of traprock, is Trinity College. The college chapel is a masterpiece of neo-Gothic architecture. The Trinity Watkinson Library owns Audubon's masterwork, *Birds of America,* the folio considered the second most valuable in the United States. The collection also includes fine examples of medieval manuscripts and books.

Tom Sawyer's "Birthplace"

At 351 Farmington Avenue, on the few remaining acres of a tract once known as Nook Farm, is the grand old Victorian home of Samuel Clemens (Mark Twain). Today the venerable old house is much as it was when the Clemens family lived here. The neighboring house, in which Harriet Beecher Stowe lived and worked, is filled with Mrs. Stowe's furnishings and is open to the public as a museum.

The modest little saltbox house in which Noah Webster, compiler of the first American dictionary, was born is on South Main Street in West Hartford. The saltbox, an architectural form unique to New England, evolved because of the tax policies of the first colonies. Any building with more than one floor paid higher taxes. The Colonists solved the problem and avoided taxes by building what was essentially a lean-to on top of the first floor, masked by a slanted roof. The name derived from the structure's similarity to the design of a box housewives of the day used for storing salt.

The Children's Museum of Hartford, one of the most complete in the country, is in West Hartford. Youngsters are fascinated with the numerous exhibits, ranging from Colonial artifacts to natural history displays to planetarium shows to a "Hands On" room with signs saying "Please touch."

The 200-acre campus of the nonsectarian, independent University of Hartford is also located in West Hartford. Chartered in 1957, the university was the result of a merger among the Hartford Art School (1877), Hillyer College (1879), and Hartt College of Music (1920).

Touring the Suburbs

Metropolian Hartford encompasses a number of interesting attractions. Immediately south of the city you can tour the Webb House, close to Wethersfield Green, one of the most beautiful village greens in the country. In the Webb House (1752), Washington and Count de Rochambeau, head of the French forces in America, plotted the strategy that led to the allied victory at Yorktown over the British. As the Webb House reflects the life of a wealthy Connecticut family during the Revolution, the nearby Buttolph-Williams House, built in 1692, shows how the Colonists lived under much sterner conditions nearly a century earlier. Additions were made in keeping with the original building, a common practice in Colonial times. Most interesting in this house are the numerous artifacts in the large kitchen.

Other interesting buildings in Wethersfield are: Silas Deane House (1766), home of one of the special envoys sent to Europe by the Continental Congress, and the Old Academy Museum (1801), where household tools, utensils, and a loom are on display. North of Hartford is Windsor, a town which probably has more well-preserved pre-Revolutionary War houses than any other in the state. Only a few buildings are open to the public, but in them you can see examples of early architecture and early furnishings. The New England Air Museum at Bradley International Airport has one of the largest collections of aeronautical memorabilia in the world, and is open from 10 A.M. to 6 P.M. daily.

Farmington, on State 4 west of Hartford, is a lovely old community with many Colonial homes set on quiet, elm-lined streets. It's the home of Miss Porter's School, an exclusive preparatory school for girls. The Stanley-Whitman House (1660), now a museum, is one of the oldest frame houses in Connecticut. The Hill-Stead Museum, was built in 1901 for Alfred Atmore Pope, whose daughter, Mrs. John Wallace Riddle, willed the property in 1946 to be a museum. The furnishings and extensive collection of French Impressionist paintings are in place as they were when the house was occupied by the Riddles.

PRACTICAL INFORMATION
FOR THE HARTFORD AREA

HOW TO GET AROUND: *By air:* Commuter air carriers operate between Hartford, New Haven, New London and Bridgeport. *By car:* There are several intra-state roads. I-91 runs from New Haven north through Hartford and to the Massachusetts border. I-84 will take you from Hartford to the Massachusetts border. Other good roads are US 2, 44, 7, 25, and 84. *By bus:* Interstate bus lines make stops in Hartford, and there are several inter-city buses operating between many Connecticut cities and Hartford.

Car rental: Avis, Hertz, Budget, and *Dollar* and several other rental agencies have offices in downtown Hartford and at Bradley International Airport.

By train: Both *Amtrak*'s inland and shoreline routes from New York to Boston have regular stops at stations in Connecticut. *Conrail* has commuter service from New York to New Haven.

MUSEUMS AND GALLERIES. *Wadsworth Atheneum,* 600 Main St., 36 galleries, a special gallery for the sight- and hearing-impaired, a 300-seat theater, art library, shops and restaurant. *Connecticut Historical Society Museum,* 1 Elizabeth St. *Austin Arts Center,* Trinity College. *Joseloff Art Gallery,* University of Hartford. *Old State House* (1796), 50 State St. Bulfinch-designed brick and brownstone museum of state's legislative, governmental and judicial history, the oldest State House in the country. *Real Art Ways,* 40 State St., an alternative arts center. Gallery exhibits, poetry, films, video, music events weekly.

Old Newgate Prison Museum, Rte. 20, East Granby. *Farmington Museum* (Stanley-Whitman House, c. 1660), High St., Farmington. *Hill-Stead Museum,* 671 Farmington Ave., Farmington. *Old Academy Museum,* 150 Main St., Wethersfield.

The *Children's Museum,* 950 Trout Brook Drive, West Hartford, has a planetarium with daily shows and an aquarium. Also, historical, natural history and doll exhibits.

TOURS. Visit *Constitution Plaza,* where the modern high-rise buildings look down on the *Old State House* (1796), an outstanding landmark-museum. *Trinity College Campus Tours* (free) can be arranged. The *Hartford Civic Center,* with many shops, boutiques, and restaurants, is in downtown Hartford. Bushnell Park (surrounding the State Capitol), where children enjoy the nostalgic carousel.

Special Interest Tours: Elizabeth Park, 915 Prospect Rd., has 99 acres of outstanding gardens, considered the most beautiful municipal rose gardens in this country. For best blooms plan to vist mid-June to July 4. *Heritage Trails Tours* (Box 138, Farmington, CT 06034, 677–8867) offers a wide variety of long and short tours.

Bus Tours: Gray Line has a 1½-hour tour of the city.

MUSIC. *Bushnell Symphony Series,* distinguished orchestras, Bushnell Memorial, Lafayette Circle (Oct.-Mar.); *Conn. Opera Assn. Series* (four operas with famous artists), Bushnell Memorial (Nov.-Apr.). *Symphony band concerts* at Elizabeth Park during outdoor season. *Trinity College Campus Carillon concerts,* June and July. *Hartford Symphony* presents an annual series of concerts.

STAGE & REVUE. *Hartford State Company,* a professional repertory company, provides classics, modern works, and occasional tryouts in the John W. Huntington Theater. *Hartford Ballet Co.* performs at Bushnell in fall and winter.

HOTELS AND MOTELS. Hartford has added many modern accommodations in recent years. Rates are based on double occupancy in season: *Deluxe,* $70 and up; *Expensive,* $50–70; *Moderate,* $30–50; *Inexpensive,* under $30. Hotel-motel chains are represented in the Hartford area as follows: Ramada Inns, 6; Howard Johnson's, 5; Holiday Inns, 2. For toll-free numbers, call 1 (800) 555–1212. Rates vary. Senior Citizen rates and handicapped access at most.

HARTFORD *Deluxe:* **Sheraton-Hartford,** at Civic Center. Pool, sauna, entertainment. All the best this excellent chain can provide. Pets. Airport limo service.

Expensive: **Holiday Inn,** Civic Center, 50 Morgan St. Heated pool, pets, restaurant, bar.

Moderate: **Ramada Inn.** 440 Asylum St. Convenient, a block from the railroad station and bus terminal. Restaurant.

EAST HARTFORD. *Moderate:* **Ramada Hotel.** 100 E. River Dr. Heated pool, restaurant, bar. Convenient location.

Inexpensive: **Imperial "400" Motel.** 927 Main St. Nearby restaurant. Pool. 10 min. from downtown Hartford.

AVON. *Moderate:* **Avon Old Farms Hotel.** Junc. Rtes. 44 and 10. Health club and children's playground. Restaurant and lounge at Inn across street.

FARMINGTON. *Deluxe:* **Hartford Marriott Hotel.** 15 Farm Springs Road. 10 minutes from Hartford. A full-service hotel with conference facilities.

Moderate: **Farmington Motor Inn.** Farmington Ave. Restaurant and coffee shop. Lounge entertainment.

DINING OUT in the Hartford area includes everything from steak houses to a variety of ethnic restaurants. Price ranges: *Expensive,* $25–and up; *Moderate,* $15–$25; *Inexpensive,* under $15. Price ranges are based on a full meal, without alcoholic beverages.

Expensive: **Brownstone.** *Expensive* or *inexpensive*—depends on where you eat in this large restored Victorian house. Corner of Asylum St. and Trumbull St. Varied menu.

Cloister Restaurant. In the Sheraton-Hartford Hotel. Featuring continental specialties.

Moderate: **Benihana of Tokyo.** 270 Farmington Ave., Farmington. Japanese food prepared on a tepinyaki (Oriental griddle) at tableside.

Carbone's Ristorante. 588 Franklin Ave. A fine Italian menu and worth the ten-minute drive from midtown.

Gaetano's. A varied, seasonal menu served in an atmosphere of elegance. One of the highlights of a visit to the Civic Center.

Inexpensive: **Brown, Thomson & Co. Food & Drink Emporium.** 942 Main St. Something for everyone, price included.

The Goodwin. 219 Asylum St. An international pub with interesting atmosphere. Imported wines and beers. Open late.

Jonathon's at the Wadsworth Atheneum. 600 Main St. Overlooking the museum's courtyard. A 21-foot long buffet lunch; international specialties at dinner.

EXPLORING CONNECTICUT

A tour of Connecticut will traverse both superhighways and country roads. Out exploration will take us into the southwest corner of the state to New Haven, after which we will circumscribe a loop of the western, hilly half of the state, and thence swing eastward to the popular seacoast areas around New London, Groton, Mystic and Stonington.

Although Connecticut has its share of excellent art galleries and museums, the prime sightseeing attractions are the many carefully preserved old Colonial houses that dot medium-sized towns or frame a central village green. A good number are open to the public, but it's wise to keep in mind that many of these are closed during the winter months.

Entering the state from New York, one passes through a series of well-manicured towns. Nature lovers may want to pause in the Audubon Center, Greenwich, the Stamford Museum and Nature Center, or the New Canaan Bird Sanctuary and Wildlife Preserve. Or you may wish to visit the first of Connecticut's 100 state parks, the Bartlett Arboretum in Stamford. By the time you've reached the creative, lively community of Westport, you may want to stop at the Nature Center for Environmental Activities or the Westport Country Playhouse (firstrate theater, end of June–Labor Day).

Bridgeport, second major city in the state (topping Hartford's population), is principally a manufacturing center. Space-age-minded visitors may be interested in the city's Museum of Art, Science and Industry, circus fans will enjoy the P.T. Barnum Museum, and animal fanciers will want to stop at the Beardsley Park Zoo, "the biggest little zoo in New England." Carry on from Bridgeport to one of the loveliest theatrical settings in Connecticut, the American Shakespeare Theatre/Connecticut Center for the Performing Arts at Stratford. The building, modeled after the Globe Theater in Stratford-upon-Avon, England, has been the site of plays (Shakespearean and other), opera, ballet, concerts, and other cultural performances.

New Haven

New Haven has a treasure trove of things to see, many of them connected with Yale University. A guided tour or an individual walking tour provides an overall view of the university. Next, visit the Art Gallery, the Peabody Museum of Natural History, or perhaps the Yale Center for British Art, the Rare Book and Manuscript Library and the Yale University Library, which stages regular exhibits. The Long Wharf Theatre, which offers one of the finest theatrical series in the East, and the Yale Repertory Theater, have outstanding winter seasons.

The historic Shubert Theatre, now the Shubert Performing Arts Center, in downtown New Haven, where many Broadway hit shows were first presented, has been completely renovated and refurbished. The Palace, formerly the Roger Sherman Theater, has been refurbished and reopened.

Riverton, Litchfield, and Other Northwestern Towns

Northwest of Hartford, via Rte. 44, lies Riverton on State 20 at the far side of the People's State Forest. Here the Hitchcock Chair Factory, founded in 1818, is still making chairs modeled after the original design. Visitors can watch the "rushing" operation on chair seats through glass windows or visit the John T. Kenney Hitchcock Museum specializing in nineteenth-century furnishings and artifacts. State 8 south through Winsted and Torrington is picturesque as it winds along through state forest areas on the way to the city of Waterbury, an industrial city known especially for its brass factories.

The historic town of Litchfield should not be passed by en route south. State 118 will lead from State 8 right to the village green, which is dominsted by a beautiful (reconstructed) white-steepled Congregational Church. The area has been declared an historic district by the state, so the white clapboard homes with their black or green shutters must remain unchanged. Harriet Beecher Stowe, Henry Ward Beecher, and Ethan Allen were born on North Street.

Nearby Litchfield is Bantam Lake, largest natural lake in the state and a popular summer playground. While there is much private property on the lakeside, there's public swimming at Sandy Beach; and at least half the lake is bordered by the 4,000-acre White Memorial Foundation, a bird and animal sanctuary. Lake Waramaug, in the town of New Preston, has several country inns on or overlooking the lakefront. Year-round activities include cross-country skiing, swimming, boating, tennis, and golf. Washington is a short distance from Litchfield and is a remarkable example of a colonial village—exquisite white houses around a small green, flanked with old elms. The American Indian Archaeological Institute and Museum, just off I-84, displays Indian artifacts and offers a natural habitat trail and a weekend film series.

Sharon, Kent, Cornwall (with its one-lane covered bridge) and Canaan are lovely towns to explore in the northwest corner of the state; and farther south (toward Danbury) Roxbury, Bridgewater, Brookfield and New Milford are charming as well. Nearby are Candlweood Lake and Squantz Pond State Park, popular public swimming and boating areas.

One aspect of the more technical side of Connecticut history is reflected in the area of Thomaston, Terryville, Bristol. This is clock country, with two of the towns taking their names from pioneer clockmakers. Seth Thomas started his clock works in Thomaston in 1812, after learning the trade with Eli Terry, who patented a clock with wooden works that became hugely successful. In Bristol, more than 1,600 clocks, some dating back to 1680, are on display at the American Clock and Watch Museum. Terryville has a Lock Museum of America where over 18,000 locks and keys manufactured in Connecticut over a century ago are housed.

Cutting east across the middle of the state on I-84 from the Danbury-Waterbury area, Rte. 66 from Bristol leads through Meriden back to Middletown. The space-age oriented may want to make a pilgrimage to the Wesleyan Olin Library, where the original manuscripts of Albert Einstein's theory of relativity are kept. The Davidson Art Center exhibits excellent examples of European and American art.

Across the Connecticut River through Portland and East Hampton is the Salmon River State Forest, providing a scenic drive along the river with a view of the Comstock Covered Bridge, one of the few remaining in Connecticut, but closed to traffic.

Connecticut's Southeastern Corner

Continuing on Rte. 66 and then on Rte. 2, you arrive in Norwich, "the rose of New England" and one of the earliest settlements in the state. The Leffingwell Inn (1675), where Washington and his officers were frequent guests, is now a museum of Colonial times. The Slater Memorial Museum, particularly noted for its Indian and Japanese collections, is located on the grounds of the Norwich Free Academy, a private school. The Rose Arts Festival in June is a week-long celebration in Norwich, attracting thousands of visitors to its variety of programs.

Those who follow American Indian lore will want to stop in Montville, rich in the history of Uncas, chief of the Mohegans but born a Pequot. Reminders of Uncas are everywhere. Near the Mohegan Congregational Church is a small museum of Indian relics, the Tantaquidgeon Indian Museum. The frames of both a long house and a round house, types of dwelling common to eastern Indians, who didn't live in teepees as did their western counterparts, are on display in the yard.

South of the Connecticut Turnpike, then on State 32, lies New London, one of Connecticut's earliest towns and one integrally connected with the sea. Like Nantucket and New Bedford in Massachusetts, New London was home for whaling ships. Whaling provided the fortunes that built the mansions of Yankee sea captains and ship owners, some of which still stand today. New London is the site of the U.S. Coast Guard Academy. Visitors may tour the grounds, stopping first at the fine Visitors' Center, then visiting some buildings and the beautiful sailing vessel used in cadet training, *Eagle,* when she's in port. The Shaw Mansion (1756), now the New London County Historical Society, the Joshua and Nathaniel Hempsted Houses (17th century), the Old Town Mill (1650, rebuilt in 1712), and the Lyman Allen Museum are only a handful of the places to see here. Charter fishing and pleasure boating out of New London marinas attract sports fisherman from considerable distances.

Just across the Thames River is the headquarters of the North Atlantic submarine fleet. The vast U.S. Naval Submarine Base is open to visitors by appointment only. The USS *Nautilus,* world's first nuclear-powered submarine, is berthed here. A Submarine Memorial Museum is located on the banks of the Thames River in Groton, and a decommissioned submarine, USS *Croaker,* may be boarded.

Just east of Groton, in Mystic, the "Age of Sail" is recalled at Mystic Seaport Museum. The Seaport is a re-creation of an early 19th-century New England coastal village. The featured exhibit is the *Charles W. Morgan,* a venerable old whaleship which spent an incredible 80 years in pursuit of whales. The *Joseph Conrad,* a former Danish maritime training ship, is also permanently berthed at the Seaport and is headquarters for the Seaport Youth Training program. *Sabino,* one of the last passenger-carrying steamboats, operates seasonal daily tours on the Mystic River. A planetarium is an interesting complement to the tiny village scene, and several galleries house seafaring treasures. A library of maritime books and manuscripts is part of the complex.

The Mystic Marinelife Aquarium, just north of the Seaport at Exit 90, I-95 (on the edge of Old Mystick Village, a unique shopping center), has natural displays of known and less-known varieties of sea animals. An hourly dolphin, whale and seal show in the 1,400-seat marine theater is a bonus held daily for visitors.

The Borough of Stonington is east of Mystic and reached via Rte. 1. There are interesting landmarks, elegantly restored homes once owned by sea captains, and the less pretentious cottages of the fishermen. A visit to this elm-shaded community leaves lasting memories.

All tourist attractions, historic sites, state parks, or points of interest in general have not been included in this tour due to space limitations. There is much of interest in Connecticut awaiting the curious explorer.

PRACTICAL INFORMATION FOR CONNECTICUT

HOW TO GET THERE. Connecticut is accessible via: 27 airports, of which Bradley International (Windsor Locks) is the largest; *Amtrak* has regular schedules from New York and Boston, inland and shore routes, with stops throughout Connecticut. *Greyhound, Trailways* and *Bonanza* buses; private car on about 4,039 miles of state-maintained highways and roads; ferry or private boat landings along the 253 miles of Long Island Sound shoreline.

HOW TO GET AROUND. *By air:* Commuter carriers operate between Bradley International and New Haven, Bridgeport, Waterbury and Groton/New London. *By car:* The Merritt Pkwy. is most scenic; I-95 follows the Long Island Sound shoreline; I-91 cuts the state roughly in half vertically and I-84 does the same horizontally; smaller roads abound. *Car rental: Avis, Hertz, National* and *Budget* are available in most locations. *On foot:* The Appalachian Trail enters Connecticut from N.Y. west of Kent, and leaves the state north of Salisbury, into Massachusetts.

TOURIST INFORMATION SERVICES. Connecticut Department of Economic Development, Hartford 06106, has free Vacation Guide. *Parks & Recreation Division*, State Dept. of Environmental Protection, Hartford, 06106, has lists of parks, forests, campsites. The Old State House in Hartford has a state information center. *Connecticut Commission on the Arts,* Hartford, 06106, gives information on creative events. Hiking trail lists come from *Connecticut Forest and Parks Association,* P.O. Box 389, East Hartford 06108; *New England Tourist Information Center* in Old Mystick Village, Mystic 06355; *Greater Hartford Convention & Visitors Bureau,* One Civic Center Plaza, Hartford 06103; *New Haven Convention & Visitors' Bureau,* 155 Church St., New Haven, 06510. Tel. 787–8367; and an information center at Bradley International Airport, Windsor Locks.

State-operated information centers are located along I-95, I-84, I-86, I-91 and the Merritt Parkway, but are open only during the summer.

MUSEUMS AND GALLERIES. Since the mid-1600's Yankee foresight has preserved much of historical interest. Yale University has a most comprehensive treasure house of arts and culture in its museums, including *Yale Art Gallery, Peabody Museum of Natural History.* In Bridgeport, visit the *Museum of Art, Science, Industry* with its Planetarium, and the *P.T. Barnum Museum.* Also, *Stamford Museum and Nature Center; Bruce Museum of Natural History,* Greenwich; *Silvermine Art Guild,* Norwalk; *Litchfield Historical Society,* Litchfield; *Davidson Art Center,* Middletown; *Lyman Allyn Museum* in New London. Almost every city and town boasts a museum or gallery.

HISTORIC SITES. Note: Most historic buildings have limited hours; check first. *Lockwood-Mathews Mansion,* Norwalk. *Keeler Tavern,* Ridgefield. *Thomas Lee House,* Niantic. *Nathan Hale Homestead,* Coventry, near Storrs. *Hyland House, Thomas Griswold House, Henry Whitfield House,* Guilford. *Judson House,* Stratford. *New Milford Historical Society Museum,* New Milford. *Denison Homestead,* Mystic. *Shaw Mansion, Hempsted House, Nathan Hale Schoolhouse, Old Town Mill,* New London. *Leffingwell Inn,* Norwich. *Groton Monument* and *Fort Griswold,* Groton. *Lighthouse Museum,* Stonington. *Fort Nathan Hale,* New Haven.

TOURS. *Yale University* has daily tours. *River cruises,* Mystic, Essex and Haddam; *harbor cruise,* New Haven; *Valley Railroad,* Essex. Also nature tours at *West Rock Nature Center,* New Haven, *Pequotsepos Nature Center,* Mystic, *The Audubon Center,* Greenwich, or the *Thames Science Center,* New London. *Gray Line* offers bus tours in most major cities. *Heritage Trails Tours* (Box 138, Farmington, CT 06034, 677–8867) has a wide variety of special interest tours.

DRINKING LAWS. Local option in towns; a few, therefore, are "dry" while others permit beer only. Packaged liquor, beer, and wine are sold at licensed liquor and drug stores. Beer by the carton is sold in supermarkets and grocery stores by permit. No packaged liquor sales on Sunday, Good Friday, Christmas. Liquor by the drink available in licensed bars and restaurants.

SPORTS. *Golf:* There are 75 public and 9 semi-public courses in the state, some of them among America's greatest. Details and lists from Tourism Division, Connecticut Economic Development Commission, 210 Washington St., Hartford, CT 06106. *Tennis:* Tennis courts are open to the public in many city parks and schools. Indoor tennis courts have been popular additions in many communities, and racquetball courts are on the increase.

Boating: Boats are easily rented in many state parks and along Long Island Sound. Charter fishing boats go out from most shoreline communities. Launching ramps are provided throughout the state for visitors transporting their own boats.

Although Conn. doesn't have the high slopes of other New England states, *skiing* is increasingly popular at the state's six downhill ski areas. There are eight cross-country ski areas and all state parks and forests are open to skiers.

Jai alai frontons in Bridgeport, Milford, and Hartford have brought pari-mutuel betting to Connecticut (year-round). Dog racing in Plainfield has seasonal meets.

SHOPPING. Connecticut abounds in antique shops and factory outlets as well as fine stores and shopping villages. Glen Lochen in Glastonbury and West Farms Mall in West Hartford are attractive shopping centers. Unique shops include: *Old Avon Village,* 35 shops featuring unusual gifts; urban shopping areas in New Haven, Bridgeport, Norwalk, and Stamford; handcrafts at *Bittersweet Farm* in Branford. In southeastern Connecticut, *Old Mystick Village* in Mystic and *Crystal Mall* in Waterford, an 80-acre retail center with more than 150 shops and four major department stores.

WHAT TO DO WITH THE CHILDREN. Many of the parks in Hartford and New Haven have swimming pools, tennis, and often golf. In Hartford the *Old State House* and *Mark Twain Memorial* interest children. Best *amusement parks* are at Lake Quassapaug, Middlebury, and Lake Compounce, Bristol. Both lakes have swimming, boating, rides, and picnic groves. *Ocean Beach Park* in New London has a boardwalk, a wide white sand beach on Long Island Sound, amusements and refreshments of various kinds. *The American Indian Archaeological Institute,* Washington, has Indian displays. *Mystic Seaport Museum,* and the *Mystic Marinelife Aquarium,* Mystic, are of interest to all ages. *Bates Woods* and the *Moran Zoo* in New London attract children's groups.

HOTELS AND MOTELS. Accommodations are listed by price range for double occupancy, at peak season: *Deluxe:* $70 and up; *Expensive:* $50–70; *Moderate:* $30–50; *Inexpensive:* under $30. Many hotel chains are represented in Connecticut, including Ramada, Sheraton, Holiday Inn, Howard Johnson, Quality Inn, Days Inn, and Susse Chalet, and most have toll-free reservation numbers. Family plans and rates for senior citizens. For state-wide information and reservations for *bed and breakfast* accommodations, contact Nutmeg Bed and Breakfast, 222 Girard Ave., Hartford 06105, (203) 236–6698; Bed and Breakfast, PO Box 216, New Haven 06513, (203) 469–3260; Covered Bridge Bed & Breakfast, West Cornwall 06796, (203) 672–6052; and Pineapple Hospitality, 384 Rodney French Blvd., New Bedford, MA 02744, (617) 990–1696.

BRIDGEPORT. *Expensive.* **Sheraton-Bridgeport Hotel.** Midtown location. Indoor pool, restaurant. Shopping plaza close by.

CHESTER. *Expensive:* **The Inn at Chester.** A restored 18th-century home with modern facilities. Health center, jogging trails, conference center, and fine restaurant.

DANBURY. *Inexpensive:* **Super 8 Motel.** I-84 Exit 4. New in late 1983. Half-mile from airport, near theaters and restaurants.

DARIEN. *Expensive:* **Holiday Inn.** Restaurant, cocktail lounge with weekend entertainment. Room service, babysitting.

ENFIELD. *Deluxe:* **Harley Hotel.** Indoor and outdoor pools, coffee shop, restaurant and lounge. Airport limo.

GREENWICH. *Deluxe:* **Homestead.** Restored 1799 farmhouse in residential area near Sound. Excellent restaurant.
Expensive: **Showboat Inn.** Large, modern motel on waterfront. Docking available. Good restaurant, entertainment. Pool. Pets. Airport limo service.

GROTON. *Expensive:* **Groton Motor Inn.** Well-furnished motel. Restaurant, bar. Pool. Overlooks Thames River.
Quality Inn. *Moderate:* Restaurant, coffee shop, pool.
On the Thames Motel/Boatel. Dock, beach rights. Pets. Party fishing boat *Hel-cat* based here.

MYSTIC. *Deluxe:* **The Inn at Mystic.** A restored Victorian mansion with luxury accommodations; moderate rates available in motel rooms on premises.
Expensive: **Howard Johnson's Motor Lodge.** Restaurant, bar. Indoor pool. Senior citizen and family rates.
Seaport Motor Inn. Restaurant, bar, pool. Family plan.
Moderate: **Ramada Inn.** Restaurant and lounge. Cable TV. Pool, suana.
Inexpensive: **Days Inn.** Budget rates, 122 rooms and a swimming pool, restaurant.

NEW CANNAN. *Moderate.* **The Maples Inn.** Rte. 124. Breakfast for guests. Walking distance to train, restaurants and shopping.

NEW HAVEN. *Expensive:* **Colony Inn.** Restaurant, lounge. Continental breakfast. Near Yale art gallery and repertory theater.
Park Plaza. 155 Temple Street. Rooftop restaurant, bar, pool, garage.

NEW LONDON. *Moderate:* **Holiday Inn.** Restaurant, bar, pool; pets.

NORWALK. *Moderate:* **Silvermine Tavern.** 200-yr.-old New England inn, furnished with antiques. Rural locale. Fine restaurant. Country store adjacent. Easy access to historical sites and shopping centers.

NORWICH. *Expensive:* **Norwich Inn.** A country inn with elegant furnishings, fine restaurant and health spa. 18-hole golf course adjacent, cross-country skiing.

RIDGEFIELD. *Moderate:* **Ridgefield Motor Inn.** Airport limo and rental cars. Restaurant, waterbeds. Antique shops nearby.

OLD SAYBROOK. *Expensive:* **Howard Johnson's Motor lodge.** One I-95. 24-hour restaurant. Bar, indoor pool.

STAMFORD. *Deluxe:* **Marriott Motor Hotel.** Restaurant, coffee shop, indoor and outdoor pools, all services, convention center.

STRATFORD. *Moderate:* **Stratford Motor Inn.** Attractive motel overlooking Housatonic river. Good restaurant and lounge with entertainment. Pool. Balcony.

WALLINGFORD. *Expensive:* **Yale Motor Inn.** Plesant, convenient accommodation between New Haven and Hartford. Fine restaurant and health spa.

 DINING OUT. Many old houses in Connecticut have been converted into "inns" which serve meals. Get off the superhighways and seek out some of the more rural establishments. Price range is for full dinners without wine or drinks, as follows: *Deluxe:* $30 and up; *Expensive:* $25–30; *Moderate:* $15–25; *Inexpensive:* under $15. Fast-food chains for snacks and meals dot the state and are inexpensive.

BRIDGEPORT. *Moderate:* **Ocean Sea Grill.** Fine seafood. Lobster a specialty. Closed Sundays.

CHESTER. *Moderate:* **The Inn at Chester.** American cuisine served in early American barnboard and antiques atmosphere.
Restaurant du Village. Country French, simple but elegant. Charcuterie next door with kitchen specialties from restaurant. Closed Sunday and Monday.

ESSEX. *Moderate:* **Griswold Inn.** Catering to travelers for 200 years, featuring seafood and New England fare. Music in bar nightly.

GREENWICH. *Deluxe:* **Homestead Inn.** A magnificently restored 1799 building. French cuisine. Reservations.
Expensive: **Showboat Inn.** Seafood specialties on the former riverboat *Mark Twain.* Breakfast available.

MIDDLETOWN. *Moderate:* **Town Farms Inn.** Restored building on the river. Under new management.

MYSTIC. *Expensive:* **Seamen's Inne.** Typical local fare. Bar. Oyster bar.

NEW CANAAN. *Moderate:* **Roger Sherman Inn.** Country inn with superb continental cuisine. Lounge. Summer dining alfresco.

NEW HAVEN. *Expensive:* **Leon's.** Long-famous, award-winning Italian restaurant.
Sherman's Taverne. Near Yale and the Green. French menu served in elegant atmosphere. Homesite of Roger Sherman.
Inexpensive: **Picnic on the Green.** A food court with 25 restaurants for take-out or eating in, overlooking the historic New Haven Green.

NEW LONDON. *Expensive:* **Ye Olde Tavern.** Pub-like atmosphere. Seafood and char-broiled specialties. Closed Sundays.
Moderate: **Bulkeley House.** A restored 18th-century home for drinks or dinner.
Lighthouse Inn. A refurbished Victorian mansion overlooking L.I. Sound. Renowned for fresh seafood. Dancing, live music weekends.

NEW PRESTON. *Moderate:* **The Inn at Lake Waramaug.** Candlight dining, antique furnishings.

NORWICH. *Moderate:* **Norwich Inn.** Two charming dining rooms with designer decor, and terrace overlooking golf course. American cuisine.

OLD LYME. *Expensive:* **Old Lyme Inn.** French-inspired menu changes with seasons. Sunday brunch.

RIDGEFIELD. *Deluxe:* **Stonehenge.** Continental cuisine in renowned country inn.
The Inn. Continental cuisine. Game, venison, wild boar in winter; fresh fish and squab in summer. Piano in lounge.

STAMFORD. *Deluxe:* **Le Parisien.** Classic French menu specializing in seafood. Reservations necessary on weekends.

STONINGTON. *Expensive:* **Harbor View.** Restaurant; cocktail lounge for lighter menu. Overlooking Stonington Harbor and typical New England waterside boating activity. Seafood a specialty.

TORRINGTON. *Expensive:* **Yankee Pedlar Inn.** Traditional 19th-century inn serving American menu. Piano, Thursday–Saturday.

WESTPORT. *Deluxe:* **Le Chambord.** Haute cuisine and excellent service.
Moderate: **Chez Pierre.** Downtown Westport. Quaint upstairs rooms and a superior French menu. Nice for a luncheon rendezvous.
Rocco's. Authentic northern Italian cuisine. Closed Sundays.
The Three Bears. American menu served in several rooms of historic tavern.
Inexpensive: **Tanglewoods.** Wicker and plants give a California-style ambience. Open daily, serving fresh seafood, pasta, omelets and very good salads.

WILLIMANTIC. *Moderate:* **The Clark's.** Leading restaurant in area since 1949. Variety menu. Special homemade desserts.

MAINE

The Pine Tree State

To a lover of sea and scenery, the drive along the Maine coast on US 1 from Kittery all the way "down east" (northeast) to Eastport is a feast for the senses: crisp air, sparkling water, dark pines, the Atlantic crashing on rocky promontories, and quiet secluded harbor towns that hardly feel the impact of the 20th century. On a straight line the coast of Maine is about 250 miles long, but if you follow the shoreline around the bays and harbors, capes and peninsulas, it would be some 3,500 miles.

Your introduction to Maine generally begins across the Piscataqua River from Portsmouth, New Hampshire in the shipbuilding town of Kittery. Here, along US 1, you will encounter the large Maine Information Center and several factory outlets characteristic of those found throughout this manufacturing state.

Northward, along the coast, lies historic York and a string of other resort colonies. Kennebunkport is one of the most colorful of these communities. The entire area from York Beach to Scarborough, just south of Portland, is very popular for summer vacations—with quiet coves, long stretches of sandy beach, and a variety of entertainment possibilities.

To many, Portland is the gateway to Down East Maine. It is here that the coast changes from beach and marshy lowland to rocky coast, bays, and peninsulas, and myriad offshore islands.

Portland, on Casco Bay, is the largest city in Maine and the state's cultural and commercial center. The old buildings and warehouses in the Old Port Exchange district (adjacent to the bustling waterfront) have been painstakingly restored and converted into an endless variety of shops, boutiques and restaurants. The Portland Museum of Art is

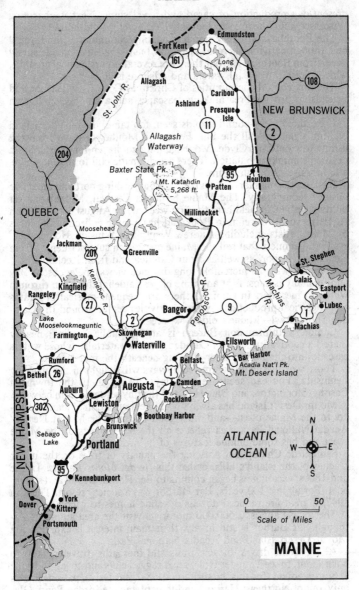

a fascinating building with beautifully displayed American art exhibits that feature Maine artists.

If you drive up the coast on US 1 north of Portland, you'll pass through several of Maine's charming and interesting towns. Freeport (home of the expert outfitter, L.L. Bean) is first, then on to Brunswick (home of Bowdoin College). Farther on, you'll come to Bath, the "City of Ships," with a reputation dating from its first ship built in 1607 to present-day production of cargo and naval ships. Next is charming Wiscasset; tour the area to look at the marvelous old houses.

The Boothbays are very popular boating communities, and you'll find enough activities here to keep you busy—but at a nice leisurely pace. From Boothbay Harbor there are several excursion boats to take, which cruise the coastal waters and offshore islands.

The tiny coastal communities of Christmas Cove, New Harbor and Friendship provide breathtaking seascapes and a glimpse of "Down East" village life.

If Portland's bay-bound islands seem too tame, the offshore island of Monhegan will fill the bill. Ferries to Monhegan leave from the fishing town of Port Clyde. Monhegan, long a haven for artists, has a devoted summer population. There are dramatic cliff formations here, a lighthouse, and a museum.

Back on the mainland, Rockland is a busy fishing port and an active business community. The Maine Seafoods Festival, Maine's largest outdoor festival, is held here the first weekend in August. The William A. Farnsworth Museum in Rockland has a large collection of works by Maine artists, including Andrew Wyeth and Winslow Homer. Several windjammers that sail the Maine coast each summer depart from Rockland Harbor, as well as from Camden and from Rockport.

Camden, with its incredible long-distance views of Penobscot Bay and its many islands, is at any time of year a delightful town through which to meander. In summer, there are frequent musical programs and theatrical productions. Winter activities center around the Camden Snow Bowl—Maine's oldest ski area.

Camden's Information Bureau is at the public landing; nearby there's a captivating view of Camden River's waterfalls, whose waters cascade into the harbor after running beneath the main street.

Those seeking the untrammeled byways will delight in the Naskeag Peninsula. You can spend several days poking about the towns of Castine, Stonington, and Blue Hill, and the tiny settlements in between.

Mount Desert Island has always been the destination of many travelers to the Maine coast—and with good reason. The Mount Desert/ Acadia National Park area reflects all the best aspects of the Maine coast and has some unique features of its own.

Samuel de Champlain, noticing the paucity of trees on the upper reaches of the island's hills, called this *Île des Monts Deserts.* In the mid-1800s, vacationers began coming to Bar Harbor by rail and steamboat. For almost 100 years, Bar Harbor was a society resort. Then, in 1947, a great fire reduced dozens of estate homes to rubble.

These days almost 2,500,000 motorists visit the area annually. Although Bar Harbor is still lovely, their main interest is experiencing Mount Desert Island and Acadia National Park.

Along scenic drives, bicycle trails and footpaths, travelers stop to poke about, to see Thunder Hole, great ragged cliffs and coves, the fjord at Somes Sound (for this, be sure to take Sargent Drive, passenger cars only, out of Northeast Harbor) and to contemplate Jordan Pond. Glaciers, winds and sea have worked marvels here. Cadillac Mountain rises 1,530 feet and commands an unmatched view of both coastal and inland Maine. The summit is easily reached by car from Bar Harbor.

While in the area, take one of the numerous cruises from Bar Harbor. See the seawall that nature has built at Seawall and the Bass Harbor Head Lighthouse. The visitor who wants to read more about this area will find a rich literature. Recommended is *The Story of Mount Desert Island,* by distinguished historian Samuel Eliot Morison.

Washington County, way down east, has a definite frontier feeling about it—blueberry barrens and a rugged coast which marks the highest tides in the country (20–28 feet); it is the easternmost point in the United States.

And in enormous Aroostook County, the eastern portion is mainly potato farms, but the far northern and western regions are vast unspoiled wilderness: a sportsman's paradise for hunting, fishing, canoeing, and snowmobiling—and the center of Maine's logging industry.

Other areas of interest in Maine are: Augusta, the state capital and home of the State Museum, and nearby Hallowell, an antiques center; the spectacular mountains and crystal-clear lakes in the Rangeley and Bethel areas, without parallel for four-season vacationing; and the Sebago-Long Lakes region, a popular recreation area just 25 miles northwest of Portland.

PRACTICAL INFORMATION FOR MAINE

HOW TO GET THERE. *By air:* There are scheduled flights from Boston to Augusta, Bar Harbor, Bangor, Portland, Rockland, Waterville, Auburn/Lewiston, and Presque Isle and from New York to Portland. In addition, light aircraft are accommodated at the many airfields throughout the state.

By car: I-95 (which links up with four-lane Maine Tpke.) cuts the state nearly in half diagonally. US 1 meanders "Down East" along the coast and then northward along the Canadian border. Primary access from Canada is through the province of Quebec via US 201.

By car ferries: Passenger-auto service between Bar Harbor or Portland and Yarmouth, Nova Scotia.

By bus: Daily service from Boston, Mass., to Portland and along Rte. 1 to Caribou; Canadian service available from Montreal to Bangor and to Portland, between Quebec and Augusta, and from the Maritime Provinces along Rte. 1 to Bangor.

HOW TO GET AROUND. *By air:* Flights are available between cities. Float planes from Greenville, Jackman, Brewer, Millinocket, Patten, Rangeley and Portage carry fishermen and hunters to remote areas.

By car: I-95 is the major through-route. US 1 follows the coast. Other roads you may wish to travel are US 201 and 202, State 2, 3, 9, 11, 26, and 27.

Car rental: Major car rental companies are represented in Augusta, Bangor, Bar Harbor, Brunswick, Camden, Portland, Presque Isle, Rockland and York Beach.

By car ferries: Maine leads the New England states in the number of ferries. Service at Rockland, Lincolnville, Bass Harbor, Bar Harbor, and Portland. Passengers only between Rockland and Matinicus, Port Clyde and Monhegan, and on the mailboat between Stonington and Isle au Haut.

By boat: Primary canoeing region is Allagash Wilderness Waterway; pleasure and fishing boats are available for rent or charter at most coastal towns.

TOURIST INFORMATION SERVICES. Consult the Maine Publicity Bureau, 97 Winthrop St., Hallowell, Me. 04347; New England Vacation Center, Shop #2, Concourse Level, 630 Fifth Ave., New York, N. Y. 10020; and InfoRoute USA, Centre Capitol, 1200 McGill College Ave., Montreal, Quebec, Can. H3B 4G7.

There are regional *Tourist Information Centers* located in Kittery, Portland, Bangor, Fryeburg, Bethel, Calais, and Houlton.

STATE PARKS. In addition to Acadia National Park, 29 state parks provide excellent facilities and outdoor experiences. The season generally runs May 15-Oct. 15. Best know is *Baxter State Park,* with Mt. Katahdin, in Millinocket. Other major parks are: *Aroostook,* Presque Isle; *Bradbury Mountain,* Pownal; *Cobscook Bay,* Dennysville; *Lake St. George,* Liberty; *Lamoine,* Lamoine; *Lily Bay* (Moosehead Lake), Greenville; *Mount Blue,* Weld; *Quoddy Head,* Lubec; *Sebago Lake,* Naples; *Rangeley Lake,* Rangeley; *Warren Island,* Islesboro; *Grafton Notch,* Newry; *Camden Hills,* Camden; and the *Allagash Wilderness Waterway.*

 MUSEUMS AND GALLERIES. Historical: *The Robert Abbe Museum of Stone Age Antiquities,* Acadia National Park; *Willowbrook-at-Newfield,* Newfield; *Maine State Museum,* Augusta; *Univ. of Maine Anthropology Museum,* Orono; *Acadian Village,* Van Buren.

Art: *Portland Museum of Art,* Portland; *Colby College Art Museum,* Waterville, *Walker Museum of Art* (Bowdoin College), Brunswick; *Wm. A Farnsworth Museum,* Rockland.

Special Interest Museums: *Lumberman's Museum,* Patten; *Penobscot Marine Museum,* Searsport; *Boothbay Railway Village,* Boothbay; *Seashore Trolley Museum,* Kennebunkport; *The Jackson Laboratory,* Bar Harbor; *Peary-MacMillan Arctic Museum,* Brunswick; *Maine Maritime Museum,* Bath.

 HISTORIC SITES. *York Village,* York, includes Emerson-Wilcox House (1740), Old Gaol Museum (1720), Jefferd's Tavern (1750), Old School House (1745), Eliz. Perkins House (1730), Marshall Store Museum (1867), and John Hancock Warehouse. The *Wadsworth-Longfellow House,* Portland, was the poet's home. In Bristol, the *Colonial Pemaquid Restoration* is adjacent to Fort Wm. Henry, site of the 16th and 17th-century Indian settlements. *Eagle Island,* Harpswell, is the home of Adm. Peary, Arctic explorer. *Fort Western,* Augusta, was built to defend the Kennebec River during the French & Indian War.

 TOURS. *By boat:* Casco Bay lines, Portland, has daylight, sunset, and moonlight cruises to Casco Bay Islands. For a week's tour of the Maine coast on a large windjammer, contact the Maine Windjammer Association, Box 317, Rockport, Me. 04856. Out of Boothbay Harbor, excursion boats cruise the coastal waters and offshore islands. Boats leave Bar Harbor and Northeast Harbor for sightseeing trips around Mt. Desert Island.

By bus: A variety of bus tours are available in popular touring areas around the state: Rockland area, Portland, Boothbay Harbor, and Bar Harbor/Mt. Desert Island.

Walking tours are outlined for the capital city of Augusta, the Old Port section of Portland, the Marginal Way in Ogunquit, and the historic districts of Bath, Bethel, Wiscasset and Camden.

Sightseeing flights are available from Bar Harbor Airport over Acadia National Park and Cadillac Mt. Seaplane trips can be arranged at Rangeley.

Fall foliage: The western and northern mountain areas offer the most colorful panorama from mid-Sept. to early Oct.

 WILDLIFE. *Acadia National Park,* the most important point for the Atlantic Flyway, has nature walks scheduled daily during the summer months; *Moosehorn National Wildlife Refuge,* Calais area; *Rachel Carson National Wildlife Refuge,* Wells (4,000 acres of coastal marsh area—habitat for a wide variety of birds, mammals and plants); *Baxter State Park,* Millinocket.

SPORTS. For the *fisherman,* this is the only state where Atlantic salmon may be caught. Saltwater fisherman go after cod, pollock, haddock, striped bass, mackerel, flounder, halibut, and tuna. Charter boats are available at many coastal towns. Licenses are required for freshwater fishing, best of which are trout and bass. (Write: Dept. of Inland Fisheries & Wildlife, State House, Augusta, Me. 04333).

Boating: The endless coastline and hundreds of miles of inland waterways offer opportunities for all types of boating. The coast is dotted with towns where boats are for hire and excursion boats embark. Rentals and guides are available at lakeside towns as well.

Flat-water and *white-water canoeing* are popular on the many lakes and rivers. Best-known region is the Allagash Wilderness Waterway. *White-water rafting* has become popular, especially on northern reaches of the Kennebec and Penobscot Rivers.

Hunting: In Oct., Maine's woods open for bow-and-arrow deer hunting; deer hunting with firearms opens generally for two weeks in Nov. Contact the *Dept. of Inland Fisheries and Wildlife,* Augusta, for licensing and for information on bear, bobcat, duck, geese, woodcock, pheasant and snowshoe rabbit hunting.

Skiing extends through Easter. Major ski areas are: Camden Snow Bowl, Camden; Squaw Mountain, Greenville; Sunday River, Bethel; Mount Abram, Locke Mills; Pleasant Mountain, Bridgton; Saddleback, Rangeley; and Sugar-loaf USA, Carrabassett Valley, with Maine's only gondola. Major cross-country ski-touring centers are located in Acadia National Park, Sunday River (Bethel), Carrabassett Valley, and Squaw Mtn. (Greenville). Other winter sports are *snowmobiling,* especially in the Allagash Wilderness Waterway area, *icefishing, snowshoeing* and *sled dog races.*

WHAT TO DO WITH THE CHILDREN. York Beach, Wells, and Old Orchard Beach all have amusement parks. *Seashore Trolley Museum* in Kennebunkport features open trolley rides. *Boothbay Railway Museum* offers rides on a narrow-gauge railroad. *Schooner Museum,* Boothbay Harbor, is a fishing dory to tour from stem to stern. *Andre the Seal,* Rockport, performs daily at 4 P.M. in the summer.

HOTELS AND MOTELS. Accommodations in Maine range from the expensive and sometimes spectacular resorts to the plain and simple hotels and motels in the small towns. Cottages, guest houses, delightful tourist homes and "bed and breakfast" inns abound and are often the most charming and least expensive alternative. Rates are based on double occupancy, in season: *Deluxe Rates,* $70 and up; *Expensive,* $55–70; *Moderate,* $40–$55; and *Inexpensive,* under $40. There is a 5% room tax throughout the state. On the coast, many hotels and motels are open from May to Sept. or Oct. only, so it's best to check ahead.

BAR HARBOR. *Deluxe:* **Bar Harbor Motor Inn.** Luxurious, old (1887) motor hotel, on the shore of Frenchmen's Bay. Pool, sundeck, restaurant, lounge.

Expensive–Deluxe: **Manor House Inn.** Guest house. Turn-of-the-century décor in restored Bar Harbor "cottage"; intown location. Privileges at Bar Harbor Club across street—pool, tennis.

Expensive: **Park Entrance Motel.** Pleasant rooms with patios and balconies overlooking the ocean. Pool, beach, putting green.

Moderate–Expensive: **Cleftstone Manor Motor Inn.** Historic English–style mansion at foot of Cadillac Mtn. Gracious rooms, library and game room.

Inexpensive: **McKay Cottages.** Guest house and attractively furnished cottages. Walk to restaurants, shopping, and waterfront.

BETHEL. *Expensive:* **Bethel Inn & Country Club.** Classic country resort. Large, comfortable rooms, elegant dining, and friendly, personal service. Golf, pool, lake swimming and boating.

BOOTHBAY. *Deluxe:* **Spruce Point Inn.** Picturesque location on peninsula. Tennis, boating, fishing, pools. Lobster bakes, lounge.

Expensive: **Fisherman's Wharf Inn.** Large motel on pier overlooking the bay. Located in center of shopping activity. Seafood restaurant.

Moderate: **Captain Sawyer's Place.** The "yellow house" in the heart of town. An old sea captain's home remodeled into a charming guest house.

BRIDGTON. *Moderate–Expensive:* **Tarry-a-While Resort.** Hospitable lakeside resort—Alpine theme. All watersports available. Fine Swiss cuisine in dining room.

BRUNSWICK. *Moderate-Expensive:* **Stowe House.** Historic, Federal–style house with modern accommodations. Excellent restaurant, tap room. Bowdoin College, theater, and sports activities nearby.

CALAIS. *Moderate:* **Heslin's Motel and Cottages.** Informal family resort overlooking St. Croix River. Canoeing, fishing and wilderness expeditions available. Pool, play area, dining room and lounge.

CAMDEN. *Deluxe* **Whitehall Inn.** Historic colonial inn. Gracious dining. Tennis, sailing, cruises.

Expensive–Deluxe: **Camden Harbor Inn.** Spectacular harbor view. Old-fashioned charm; quiet and comfortable. Dining room, lounge, entertainment.

Moderate–Expensive: **Aubergine.** Cozy rooms available in restored Victorian inn. Small, quiet, and classy. Excellent French restaurant.

CASTINE. *Inexpensive-Moderate:* **Pentagöet Inn.** Small Victorian inn right on the coast; informal; comfortable. Full dinner service.

GREENVILLE. *Moderate:* **Greenville Inn.** Former lumber baron's home (1895). Ten cozy guestrooms. Snowmobile trails, skiing, golf, and tennis nearby.

KENNEBUNKPORT/KENNEBUNK. *Deluxe:* **The Colony.** Massive white clapboard resort hotel on the water. Pool, fishing, boating, golf, good restaurant.

Expensive–Deluxe: **The Captain Lord Mansion.** An intimate Maine coast inn, vintage 1812. Quiet elegance, fireplaces. Walk to shops and restaurants. Sports nearby. Open year-round.

Expensive: **Cape Arundel Inn.** A small, intimate inn directly on the ocean. Excellent dining.

Moderate: **The Kennebunk Inn** (Kennebunk). Fine lodging and meals in restored historic inn. Cocktail lounge. Centrally located in village.

MONHEGAN. *Moderate:* **The Island Inn.** Rather plain food and furnishings. Peace and quiet. No smoking. Appeals to birdwatchers, artists, and fishermen.

MOOSE RIVER/JACKMAN. *Expensive:* **Sky Lodge and Motel.** "Luxury in the rough" in remote back country. Mountain and lake views. Excellent food. Pool, archery, rifle range. Rustic.

NORTHEAST HARBOR. *Deluxe:* **The Asticou Inn.** Rambling, formal, turn-of-the-century resort inn and modern housekeeping cottages. Bar, pool, pets.

OGUNQUIT. *Deluxe:* **Sparhawk.** Fine accommodations, with ocean views from the balconies. Tennis, play area, golf nearby, good restaurant.

Expensive: **The Colonial Inn.** Comfortable, gracious and informal Victorian inn. Continental breakfast, heated pool. Short walk to beach, harbor, and town.

PORTLAND. *Deluxe:* **Black Point Inn.** Prout's Neck (Scarborough). Luxury oceanfront resort inn. Elegant and impressive, with fine service. All sports, including PGA golf course.

Sonesta Hotel. Luxurious in-town hotel. Pool, two restaurants, and rooftop lounge.

Expensive: **Holiday Inn** (two locations). Convenient to airport, ocean and sightseeing.

RANGELEY. *Expensive:* **Country Club Inn.** A delightful resort overlooking Rangeley Lake. Good restaurant, golf, pool.

Moderate. **Rangeley Inn.** A graceful restored inn, dating from the 1870s, on crystal-clear Rangeley Lake. All sports available nearby. Pleasant dining.

ROCKPORT. *Moderate:* **Windjammer Motor Inn.** Pleasant, comfortable units. Conveniently located. Breakfast available.

STONINGTON. *Moderate:* **The Captain's Quarters Inn & Motel.** Harborside location offers a panoramic view of the bay. Rooms, suites, efficiencies, or apartments.

YORK HARBOR. *Deluxe:* **Stage Neck Inn.** An inviting resort on the ocean. Modern, attractive rooms with balconies. Saltwater pool, beach, golf, tennis and fishing.

 DINING OUT. Seafood and Maine are virtually synonymous. No visit is complete without a meal or meals of lobster, clams, salmon and/or trout. Dinner price ranges are for complete dinners per person, exclusive of cocktails and wine, as follows: *Deluxe,* $25 and up; *Expensive,* $20–$25; *Moderate,* $15–$20; *Inexpensive,* under $15.

BAILEY ISLAND. *Moderate:* **Dockside Steak & Lobster House.** Dine or have cocktails overlooking the water.

BANGOR. *Moderate:* **Pilot's Grill.** Home-style family owned and operated. Delectable lobster; well-rounded bill of fare. Children's menu.

BAR HARBOR. *Expensive:* **Lorenzo Creamer's Lobster Pound.** Very good food and view. Lobsters, of course; shore dinners, seafood, and charbroiled steaks.

Moderate–Expensive: **Jordan Pond House.** In Acadia National Park. Homemade soups, steak, poultry, seafood. Afternoon tea on the lawn—homemade ice cream and popovers. Magnificent view.

Moderate: **Testa's.** Grill Room and Garden Room. Steaks, shellfish, Italian specialties; fresh fruit pies; inspired green salads.

BETHEL. *Moderate–Expensive:* **Bethel Inn.** Superb cuisine served in elegant dining room, tap room, or on the veranda. Sunday brunch.

The Sudbury Inn. Bright, airy dining room in lovely restored inn. Inspired New England fare; delicious homemade soups and desserts.

Moderate: **The Boiler Room** (Bryant Pond). Nineteenth-century powerhouse of a clothespin mill converted into a striking restaurant. Excellent German-American food.

BLUE HILL. *Expensive:* **Firepond.** Gourmet dining in this historic building. Continental cuisine, with fresh seafood daily.

BOOTHBAY. *Expensive:* **Brown Bros. Wharf.** Complete menu, including lobster from the tank and native seafood.

Moderate: **The Blue Ship.** Seafood, steak, sandwiches, and chowder. Homemade breads and pastries. Wonderful cinnamon buns for breakfast. Harbor view.

Inexpensive: **Robinson's Wharf** (Southport). Lobster, clams, and sandwiches to eat on the wharf or take out. Homemade pies. Beer and wine.

CAMDEN. *Expensive:* **Aubergine.** Intimate French restaurant in old, renovated inn—or light supper and snacks in the bar. **Whitehall Inn.** Gracious dining; memorable meals. Fresh fish.

GREENVILLE. *Moderate:* **Greenville Inn.** A former lumber baron's home on Moosehead Lake. Changing menu includes Continental-style entrees.

KENNEBUNKPORT. *Expensive:* **The Lobster Claw.** Very pleasant, rather quaint seafood restaurant facing the water. Specialties include lobster and shore dinners, but meat and poultry dishes are also well prepared.
Olde Grist Mill. Dine in an historic (1749) tide-water mill. Traditional menu. Country store and gift shop adjacent.

KINGFIELD. *Expensive:* **The Winter's Inn.** Lovely inn with panoramic mountain views. French cuisine, prepared with care.

LINCOLNVILLE. *Moderate–Expensive:* **Lobster Pound.** Lobsters are caught, cooked, and eaten here. Open-air or indoor dining. Complete menu available for landlubbers.

OGUNQUIT. *Expensive:* **Whistling Oyster.** On Perkins Cove since 1907. Comfortably elegant dining. Seafood and continental dishes.
Inexpensive: **Barnacle Billy's.** Perkins Cove. Dining outside by the cove or inside by the hearth. Chicken and stews, sandwiches and seafood salad plates. Scenic cruises from the wharf.

PORTLAND. *Expensive–Deluxe:* **The Vineyard.** Intimate French restaurant with limited menu. Exquisite meal preparation and service. Extensive wine list.
Expensive: **Boone's.** On the waterfront at Custom House Wharf. Ocean-fresh seafood specialties—lobster, fish, chowders and stews—as well as steaks.
DeMillo's Floating Restaurant. Very popular seafood restaurant in a former ferryboat. Fresh fish, lobster, shore dinners, steamers.

RANGELEY. *Expensive:* **Country Club Inn.** Fine dining, pleasant service, magnificent view of lake and surrounding mountains. Traditional American fare. Nightly specials.
Moderate: **The Oquossoc House** (Oquossoc). Family restaurant, rustic décor. Charcoal-broiled steaks, seafood, salad bar, and daily specials.

ROCKPORT. *Moderate–Expensive:* **The Helm.** French and American specialties individually prepared. Steaks, seafood, and homemade pies. Good service and pleasant atmosphere.

SEBAGO LAKE. *Moderate:* **Barnhouse Tavern** (N. Windham). Rustic barn (1872) carefully restored, with lots of exposed wood and windows. Dine in the main dining room or in the loft. Steaks and seafood (lobster in summer), with daily luncheon and dinner specials.

SOUTHWEST HARBOR. *Moderate:* **Long's Downeast Clambakes.** Lobster, clams and corn—steamed in rockweed and served outdoors.

YORK. *Expensive:* **Nubble Light** (York Beach). Choose your own lobster from the tank. Home baking.
Moderate: **Bill Foster's Down East Lobster & Clambake** (York Harbor). Clams, lobster and all the "fixins" (or steak or chicken). Features an old-fashioned sing-along. Reserve ahead. Summer only.

MASSACHUSETTS

Boston, the Berkshires, and the Cape

A tour of Massachusetts properly starts in Boston—and on foot. The most historic sites are located along the Freedom Trail, a well-planned walk of only one and one-half miles. The tour leads through the heart of the historic old city, linking sixteen famous colonial, revolutionary, and other historic sites. As you follow the trail, which is marked by a red line, you will walk not only into the past of Boston, but into some of the most exciting chapters in the early history of the United States. Visit the Freedom Trail Information Center on the Tremont St. mall adjacent to the Boston Common for brochures and maps.

First stop is the Park Street Church, built in 1809. Henry James called it "the most interesting mass of brick and mortar in America." It was here that William Lloyd Garrison gave his first anti-slavery address (1828) and that *America* was first sung (1831), both on July 4th. The corner on which the church stands was once known as Brimstone Corner because at the time of the War of 1812 brimstone, a component of gunpowder, was stored in the church.

After leaving the church, walk up Park Street towards the gold-domed brick structure which faces Boston Common. This is the "new" State House, built on what was John Hancock's cow pasture and completed in 1798. It is an excellent example of the work of Charles Bulfinch, our first important native-born architect. Among the rooms open to visitors are the Archives Museum (annals of American history) and the Hall of Flags, a memorial to those who died in the Civil War and later conflicts. One of the more interesting artifacts housed in the State House is the "Sacred Cod," which hangs in the portal of the visitors' gallery. The 200-year-old carving pays homage to the fish on which Massachusetts built its colonial economy.

149

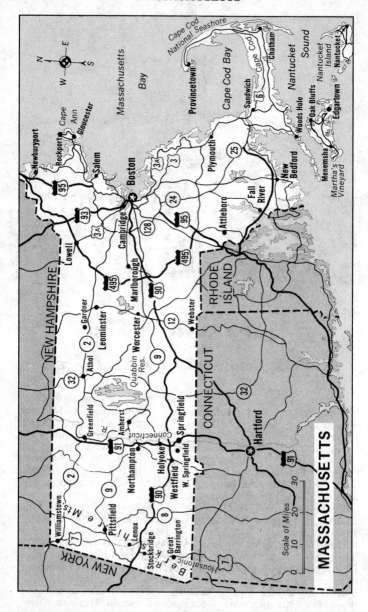

Return to the Park Street Church and follow the Freedom Trail north along Tremont St. On the left is the Granary Burying Ground, once the site of Boston's granary which gave its name to the cemetery. The graves of John Hancock, Robert Treat Paine, and Samuel Adams, signers of the Declaration of Independence, are here, as are those of Paul Revere, Peter Faneuil, James Otis, many governors, Benjamin

Franklin's parents, and victims of the Boston Massacre.

At the corner of Tremont and School Sts., turn right down the hill to King's Chapel, Boston's first Episcopalian church. The present building was completed in 1754, although the congregation was organized in 1686. In Colonial days the church was a royal favorite. Queen Anne donated the red cushions and George III supplied the communion plate. The burying ground beside the church was the colony's only cemetery for many years and contains the graves of Governor Winthrop and William Dawes, Jr. On the opposite corner is the Parker House Hotel, which gave its name to Parker House rolls.

On the left as you head down School St. is Boston's old City Hall. A schoolhouse built near the hall in 1635 became Public Latin School, the first public school in the country. The Rev. Cotton Mather, Emerson, Hancock, and Samuel Adams are a few who studied there and went on to make their mark on American history. On the lawn of City Hall is a statue of Benjamin Franklin which was erected in 1856. One side of Franklin's face is smiling while the other is sober; sculptor Richard S. Greenough seems to have presaged Picasso in his ability to convey two sides of his subject's personality at once.

On the left, where School St. meets Washington St., is the Old Corner Bookstore. Built in 1712–1715, the building was a meeting place for such writers as Emerson, Hawthorne, Longfellow, Oliver Wendell Holmes, and Harriet Beecher Stowe. It now houses the Globe Corner Bookstore, specializing in New England authors and subjects.

The Tea Went Overboard

Across Washington St. is the Old South Meeting House. Here, the colonists held many mass meetings that culminated in the Revolutionary War. The plot for the Boston Tea Party took shape here and during the war the building was used by the British for practicing equestrian maneuvers. Returning along Washington St. to the north, turn right on State St. and enter the Old State House, once the seat of the British colonial government. From its balcony, citizens of Boston heard the news that King George III had been crowned. Here, too, the Declaration of Independence was first read in Boston on July 18, 1776. Below the balcony, mobs burned symbols of the hated British. Generals Gage, Clinton, and Howe planned the strategy for the battle of Bunker Hill in the building. Across State St. from the Old State House is a circle of cobblestones marking the site of the Boston Massacre when, on March 5, 1770, British soldiers fired into a taunting mob of colonists, killing five men. One was Crispus Attucks, the first black person to die in America's battle for liberty. In a rare show of cooperation, the British agreed to a trial of their soldiers involved in the massacre. Eager to prove their fair-mindedness, the colonists provided John Adams and Josiah Quincy, Jr. to conduct the defense. All but two were acquitted, and those convicted of manslaughter were branded on the hand and discharged from the army. That might have been the end of it, but Sam Adams got Paul Revere to do an engraving of the Redcoats shooting down the peaceful citizens of Boston. Widely circulated, it inflamed the populace against the British.

The Old State House, now carefully restored, once again displays the lion and the unicorn at the corners of its east gable. These ancient symbols of British imperial power flanked the current monarch, George III's descendant, Queen Elizabeth, when she spoke from the building's balcony during her bicentennial good-will visit to Boston.

Continue down State St. and turn left at New Congress St. Dock Square and Faneuil Hall will be in front of you. The hall, originally built by Peter Faneuil as a market, is called the "Cradle of Liberty"

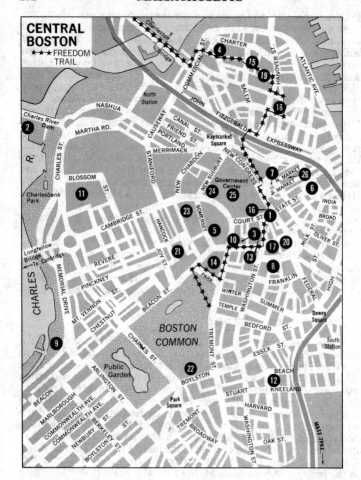

CENTRAL BOSTON
★★★ FREEDOM TRAIL

Points of Interest

1) Boston Massacre Site
2) Boston Museum of Science
3) Old City Hall
4) Copp's Hill Burying Ground
5) Court House
6) Custom House
7) Faneuil Hall
8) Franklin's Birthplace Site
9) Hatch Memorial Concert Shell
10) King's Chapel
11) Massachusetts General Hospital
12) Tufts New England Medical Center
13) Old Corner Book Store
14) Park Street Church and Old Granary Burying Ground
15) Old North Church (originally Christ Church)
16) Old State House
17) Old South Meeting House
18) Paul Revere's House
19) Paul Revere Statue
20) Post Office
21) State House
22) Central Burying Ground
23) State Office Building
24) John F. Kennedy Federal Building
25) New City Hall
26) Quincy Market

because so many meetings were held here by advocates of American freedom. The building later was presented to the city and now houses a museum of flags, photographs, and weapons of the Ancient and Honorable Artillery Company of Boston. The great balconied hall on the upper floor is still used as a forum for public discussion and debate.

The ground floor of Faneuil Hall has been renovated as a part of one of the most talked-about urban "recycling" projects of recent years. Restaurants, food, and specialty shops dominate the three stately granite-and-brick arcades of the old Quincy Market, which stand behind Faneuil Hall; beyond this chic bazaar stretches the new waterfront park and the handsomely restored wharf buildings.

The next point on the Freedom Trail is the Paul Revere House, where Revere lived from 1770 to 1780, and from where he set out on his historic ride to Lexington in April, 1775. The house, probably the oldest wooden structure in Boston, was built in the 1670s and is furnished with seventeenth- and eighteenth-century antiques, a few of which belonged to Revere.

From the Revere House it is a short walk (via Prince, Hanover, Bennett, and Salem Sts.) to Old North Church (1723), the oldest church in Boston. The two lanterns hung from its steeple on the night of April 18, 1775, signaled that the Redcoats were leaving for Lexington and Concord and started Paul Revere on his ride. In 1781, the old bells in the steeple rang out the good news that Cornwallis had surrendered at Yorktown. The Cyrus Dallin equestrian statue of Paul Revere graces the small park at the rear of the Church.

You are now in the middle of Boston's North End. As you will no doubt gather from the narrow, winding streets, this is the oldest part of the city. Since its heyday as an eighteenth-century residential neighborhood, this compact area has been home to waves of foreign immigrants. The last great influx, around the turn of the present century, was Italian, and it is an Italian flavor which continues to prevail here. Plan to arrive in the North End hungry—and if you are traveling in summer, try to take in one of the many street festivals with which saints' days are still celebrated.

Charlestown, the Bunker Hill Monument, and the *Constitution* (*Old Ironsides*) are on a Freedom Path across the Charlestown Bridge. Follow local signs to the Bunker Hill Monument. You can climb the spiral staircase of this 221-foot granite obelisk commemorating the first major battle of the Revolution and enjoy a grand view of historic Boston. Built in the early nineteenth century to commemorate the famous battle of June 17, 1775, the monument actually stands on Breed's Hill, where the misnamed battle was fought; Bunker Hill is just north of it. At the bottom of the hill can be seen the docks of the Charlestown Navy Yard and the tall masts of the *Constitution*. There are adequate parking facilities at the ship if you are driving. Walk up the gangplank onto the wonderfully preserved ship that never lost a fight. The 44-gun frigate first put to sea in 1798 and is the oldest commissioned ship of the U.S. Navy. The navy yard, now decommissioned, is being restored as a part of Boston National Historic Park.

Beacon Hill

No visit to Boston would be complete without at least a brief walk through the beautiful, gas-lit, tree-lined streets of Beacon Hill, past the shuttered brick townhouses where many of Boston's wealthy, socially prominent families lived throughout the nineteenth century.

A good place to start is on Beacon St. opposite the New State House. From here continue west along the edge of the Common so that you can view the townhouses that line the side of Beacon St. The twin mansions at numbers 39 and 40, mirror images of each other, belong to the Women's City Club of Boston. Beacon Hill began to be a fashionable residential area after the completion of the State House in 1798. Around 1814 or 1815, Nathan Appleton, a textile manufacturer, and Daniel Parker, a shipping merchant, engaged the architect of the State

House, Charles Bulfinch, to design homes for them. After completing plans for their Federal exteriors he was called to Washington to design the Capitol. His associate, Alexander Parris, finished the designs and is responsible for most of the interiors, with their Greek Revival touches. Parris later achieved renown for his design of Quincy Market.

The graceful bow fronts of the two houses both contain original panes of the fashionable purple glass of Beacon Hill. Its mauve tint was produced accidentally by the action of strong sunlight on a batch of defective glass purchased abroad for these early homes. The distinctive shade was coveted by others but, owing to its accidental origins, it could not be duplicated exactly. In its rarity, the glass became a sign of age, wealth, and distinction. If you'd like to see what Boston Common looks like when viewed from the other side of these purple panes, inquire at the Women's City Club for guided tour schedules.

Back Bay

The most ambitious of Boston's 19th-century land reclamation projects was the filling of a stagnant backwater of the Charles River called the Back Bay. The brick and brownstone mansions with which the new streets were lined still stand, although most have long since been renovated into apartments. The Back Bay today is not only an architectural treasure but the cultural center of Boston as well. It houses schools, colleges, and galleries, the Museum of Fine Arts, and the Boston Symphony Orchestra. Here also, built over the Massachusetts Turnpike Extension, is the thirty-one-acre Prudential Center, the northeastern home office of the Prudential Insurance Company. Around the central 52-story office tower are clustered apartments, a shopping mall, and department stores. The Prudential Center also includes the 5,800-seat Hynes Auditorium and the Sheraton-Boston Hotel. Nearby is an even larger development, the recently opened Copley Place. This complex includes two hotels, dozens of shops, and apartments. Beyond the Prudential Center to the west stands the domed Mother Church and modern headquarters buildings of the Christian Science faith.

Adjacent to Copley Place, at Boylston and Dartmouth Sts., is Copley Square, one of the most attractive public places in the nation. On the left as you enter the square is Trinity Church, designed by H.H. Richardson and built in 1877. Across the square is the Public Library, designed in the style of the Italian Renaissance. An interior courtyard and many artworks by Puvis de Chavannes, John Singer Sargent, Daniel Chester French, and others give it uncommon interest. The library has been expanded with a large addition designed by Philip Johnson. Copley Square is bounded on the south by the elegant old Copley Plaza Hotel. Behind the hotel rises the sixty-story John Hancock Tower, a thin rhomboid covered with reflective glass, designed by I. M. Pei. On clear days, the shapes and colors of surrounding buildings, especially Trinity Church, are visually echoed in the walls of the Hancock. From the John Hancock Observatory on the 60th floor of the Tower, the highest man-made observation point in New England, you'll have a panoramic view of eastern Massachusetts from New Hampshire to Cape Cod. Also worth your time are four observatory exhibits: "Boston 1775," "Uncommonly Boston," "Skyline Boston," and "Photorama." The Prudential Tower also has an observation deck.

On your return walk from Back Bay to downtown, relax as Bostonians do in the Public Garden. This earliest of American botanical gardens features colorful, seasonally changing plantings and a lovely lagoon, home of the famous swan boats that have charmed generations of Boston children and adults.

Cambridge

Across the Charles River from Boston is Cambridge, an industrial city world-famed for its educational institutions. Harvard University, oldest in America, was founded in 1636. Center of collegiate life is the original campus, Harvard Yard, mellow with age and teeming with youth. The architecture of Harvard ranges from the red brick Georgian of Massachusetts Hall, the oldest building on the campus (1720), to the Visual Arts Center, designed two and a half centuries later by Le Corbusier. In mid-course of Harvard's architectural evolution is University Hall, a handsome granite edifice designed in 1813 by Charles Bulfinch. Among Harvard attractions that should not be missed are the Fogg Art Museum and the University Museums. The latter include the Peabody Museum of Archeology and Ethnology, as well as separate collections devoted to comparative zoology, minerals and geology, and botany (be sure to see the famous glass flowers). The Busch-Reisinger Museum houses German and northern European art.

Sharing the Charles River waterfront with Harvard is the Massachusetts Institute of Technology, founded in 1861 and now considered the world's leading school of science and engineering. M.I.T.'s architecture ranges from neo-classical to ultra-modern (see the Saarinen chapel and the auditorium).

Two of Cambridge's traditional landmarks are Christ Church (facing Cambridge Common), a beautiful Georgian edifice designed by Peter Harrison in 1761 and used during the Revolution as a barracks for Colonial soldiers, and Longfellow House at 105 Brattle St., about half a mile from Harvard. George Washington used this house as headquarters in 1775. A young Harvard instructor, Henry Wadsworth Longfellow, bought the house in 1843 and lived here until his death in 1882. Open to the public, the house is furnished with the poet's furniture and books.

Lexington and Concord

Northwest of Boston by way of Arlington is the attractive suburb of Lexington. In the center of town is Lexington Green. Here, on April 19, 1775, 77 Minutemen stood up to 700 British soldiers and lost eight of their number in the opening skirmish of the Revolutionary War. Buckman Tavern, still standing on the Green, was the mustering place of the Colonials. Nearby is the Hancock-Clarke House where John Hancock and Samuel Adams were awakened on the 18th of April in '75 by Paul Revere's announcement that the British were coming. British headquarters were in the Munroe Tavern at 1332 Massachusetts Ave. All these buildings, open to visitors and furnished as they were, will help you re-create the events of that day, which made Lexington "The Birthplace of American Liberty."

Having dispersed the rebels, the Redcoats marched west to Concord in search of a cache of colonial gunpowder. They found it in unexpected form from the muskets of the local farmers. No British blood had flowed at Lexington, but at Concord it was a different story. By Emerson's "rude bridge that arched the flood," the Colonials fired for the first time on His Majesty's troops. This was the "shot heard round the world." Twelve British soldiers fell. The rest began their retreat to Boston. All afternoon the yeomen of Middlesex County sniped at them from behind the stone walls of the countryside. By the time the British reached Boston they counted 73 killed, 174 wounded, 26 missing. There was no doubt now that they had a full-scale revolution on their hands.

At Minuteman National Historical Park you will see the famous Old North Bridge across the Concord River, with Daniel Chester French's equally famous statue of the Minuteman standing guard. Visit the Concord Museum on Lexington Road to see Paul Revere's signal lantern, relics of the battle, and a diorama of the Battle of Concord. And if you are here on Patriot's Day (the Monday closest to April 18th), see the battle re-enactment at Lexington and the parade over the North Bridge in Concord.

PRACTICAL INFORMATION
FOR BOSTON AND CAMBRIDGE

HOW TO GET THERE. *By air: Logan International Airport,* about 3 miles from Boston, is served by all major airlines. Facilities have been designed with handicapped travelers in mind. There is adequate taxi service to downtown Boston, as well as private bus service and Massachusetts Bay Transit Authority (MBTA) public transportation (bus and subway).

By train: Boston is the northern terminus of *Amtrak's* northeast corridor, and is served several times daily by trains from Washington and New York. *South Station* is the point of arrival and departure for these trains. The *Lake Shore Limited,* serving Boston, Chicago, and points between, arrives and departs daily at South Station. Worcester, Springfield, and Pittsfield are other Massachusetts stops. *North Station* is the terminal for rail service to the north shore and western suburbs.

By boat: Se^rvice from Boston to Provincetown, daily in summer from *Rowe's Wharf.*

By bus: Greyhound terminal is at Park Square; *Trailways* is near South Station. The MBTA operates local and suburban bus, subway, and trolley lines. Maps available at Park St. station.

TOURS. *Gray Line of Boston,* departing from Park Plaza, Sheraton-Boston, and Copley Plaza hotels, has a number of good tours covering historical and business sections; also other sites of interest.

SPECIAL INTEREST TOURS. *Harbor: Bay State Spray Cruises,* 20 Long Wharf, and *Massachusetts Bay Lines,* 344 Atlantic Ave., offer tours of the inner and outer harbors, some with stops on Georges Island. Mass Bay Lines runs lunch, dinner and sunset cruises with live music.

Bicycle Tour: Planned and frequently ridden by famed heart specialist Dr. Paul Dudley White, marked 11-mi. path begins and ends at Eliot Bridge across Charles River.

Walking Tours: Self-guided *Harborwalk;* maps avail. info. kiosk on Boston Common. Also *Black Heritage Trail,* Beacon Hill, by appt.; call 445–7400. *Boston by Foot* tours, varied itineraries; write 77 North Washington St. for information. The City of Cambridge publishes *Old Cambridge Walking Guide,* available free at information center in Holyoke Center, Harvard Sq., or at Cambridge City Hall, Central Square.

The Harvard Information Center at Holyoke Center offers university maps and information on guided tours, which leave twice each day and once on Saturdays from the Admissions Office, 8 Garden St. Saturday tours leave from Holyoke Center. Free guided tours of the M.I.T. campus depart weekdays from the Information Center, Building 7, on the Institute's Mass. Ave. campus. Call for details.

MUSEUMS. *Museum of Fine Arts,* 465 Huntington Ave. American, European., Oriental collections; period rooms, musical instruments, silver. Lectures, films, special children's programs. The MFA's spectacular new West Wing should not be missed. *Institute of Contemporary Art,* 955 Boylston St., Boston. *Isabella Stewart Gardner Museum,* 280 The Fenway. Home of Mrs. Gardner, patron of arts. Paintings, sculpture. Both the Museum of Fine Arts and the Gardner Museum are the site of frequent concerts of classical music given by local chamber ensembles. *Fogg Art Museum,* Harvard Univ., 32 Quincy St., Cambridge. Paintings, drawings, sculpture, photography. *Peabody Museum,* 11 Divinity Street, Cambridge: Mayan and other ancient artifacts. *Busch-Reisinger Museum,* Kirkland Ave., Cambridge. On Harvard campus; specializing in art of Germanic countries from medieval through modern periods. Free concert programs weekly during school year. *Museum of Science,* Science Park. Natural history, physical science demonstrations, astronomy, medical science displays. *Charles Hayden Planetarium,* part of Museum of Science. 45-min. shows. *Children's Museum,* Museum Wharf, 300 Congress St., downtown Boston. Hands-on, "do-it-yourself" exhibits. *New England Aquarium,* Central Wharf, over 2,000 species; dolphin exhibit. *John F. Kennedy Library,* Columbia Point, houses late President's papers and effects; film on JFK's life shown daily. *Museum of Transportation,* 15 Newton St., Brookline. Old cars, public transportation.

HISTORIC SITES. *Freedom Trail:* Booklet outlining walking tour is available at Tremont St. Information Center, the Greater Boston Chamber of Commerce, 900 Boylston St., and at points along the way.

John F. Kennedy National Historic Site, 83 Beals St., Brookline. Birthplace of Pres. Kennedy. *Bunker Hill Monument,* Monument Sq., Lexington & High St., Charlestown. Spiral staircase to top of 221-ft. obelisk. Headquarters of *Boston National Historic Park,* 15 State St., across from Old State House, has information on all local historic sites.

MUSIC. *Boston Symphony Orchestra.* Winter season begins the end of Sept. with concerts in Symphony Hall, Massachusetts & Huntington Aves., Fri. afternoon, Sat. evening and occasionally on Sun., Mon., or Tues. Several rehearsals are open. *Pops Concerts* in Symphony Hall, May, June, and holiday season. Outdoor *Esplanade Concerts* in Hatch Memorial Shell, along Charles River, in July. Oldest U.S. active choral group, Boston's *Handel and Haydn Society,* performs in Boston and Philharmonic Hall, New York. New York's *Metropolitan Opera* visits Boston each spring, performing at the Wang Center, 268 Tremont St. The *Boston Opera Company,* under the direction of Sarah Caldwell, performs during the winter season at the Company's new home, the Savoy Theater, 539 Washington St. in downtown Boston. *Berklee College* and the *New England Conservatory of Music* have concert series. The *Boston Globe* Calendar section, published Thursdays, announces upcoming musical events.

STAGE AND REVUES. Boston has three downtown theaters famous for pre-Broadway premieres. The *Wilbur Theatre, Shubert,* and *Colonial* begin their season soon after the first week in Sept. The *Wang Center* occasionally features theatrical as well as musical events. Engagements, with top stars, last two or three weeks. *Charles Playhouse,* 74 Warrenton St., *Boston Shakespeare Company,* 300 Mass. Ave., and *Next Move Theater,* 1 Boylston Place, offer more experimental fare. *Shear Madness* at the Charles Stage II is a comedy whodunit in its sixth year. Tufts and Boston University have good student drama groups, and Harvard is now the home of Robert Brustein's *American Repertory Theater.* Emerson College also stages theatrical productions.

GARDENS. *Public Garden,* next to Boston Common, has formal gardens, rare trees, swan boats, and gorgeous plantings which change with the season. *The Arnold Arboretum,* Jamaica Plain, offers a non-stop, year-round show of flowers, shrubs, trees. Don't miss *Lilac Sunday,* held there each May.

BARS. *Ritz Bar,* a local institution. Quiet, intimate, reserved. Impeccable service. *The Last Hurrah,* at the Parker House, Tremont St., Boston, serves lunch and dinner, and has a resident swing band. *Hampshire House,* 84 Beacon St., Boston, has a cellar pub and a paneled lounge overlooking the Public Garden. The *Copley Plaza Hotel* houses two of the city's most beautifully appointed drinking salons. *Satin Doll,* at the Back Bay Hilton, is a popular new spot for 30s and 40s jazz and swing. In *Cambridge,* the *Wursthaus* in Harvard Square offers a selection of international beers. Bars near Central and Inman Squares in Cambridge, such as *Springfield's, Inn Square Men's Bar,* and *Ryle's,* offer jazz, rock, and bluegrass. And if you don't mind swirling your ice cubes while being swirled yourself, visit the revolving *Spinnaker* lounge atop the Hyatt Regency hotel on Memorial Drive. Views of the Charles and the Boston skyline are magnificent. The *Regatta Bar* at the new Charles Hotel, Harvard Sq., features top-drawer local jazz acts in plush surroundings.

COFFEE HOUSES AND CAFÉS. *Café Florian,* 85 Newbury St., runs a good sidewalk café in season. *Il Dolce Momento* on Charles St., Beacon Hill, for Italian gelato. In Cambridge: *Passim,* 47 Palmer St., Harvard Square, featuring folk music, jazz, and occasional poetry readings; and *Café Pamplona,* Bow St. Also *Coffee Connection* in the Garage Complex, JFK Street.

SPECTATOR SPORTS. *Racing:* Suffolk Downs Racetrack has thoroughbred racing Mar. to mid-July and from mid-Oct. to early Dec. *Dog Racing* at Wonderland Dog Track in Revere.

The Red Sox play *baseball* at Fenway Park; the Celtics, *basketball,* and Bruins, *hockey,* at Boston Garden; and the Patriots, *football,* at Sullivan Stadium, Foxboro.

SPORTS. *Boating* and *fishing* (on Charles and Mystic rivers, harbor bay, and inland lakes); *golf, tennis, horseback riding* in Franklin Park; *ice skating* in winter.

SHOPPING. *Filene's,* 426 Washington St., Boston's most famous store, includes *Filene's Basement,* a bargain-hunter's paradise. *Jordan-Marsh Co.,* 450 Washington St., has everything from records to designer dresses. Haute couture shops are located on Newbury St. *Quincy Market* houses innumerable shops, from European boutiques to chocolate chip cookie emporia. Prudential Center has *Saks, Lord and Taylor. Nieman-Marcus, Gucci, Tiffany's,* and other luxury shops in Copley Place. Charles St., Beacon Hill, has many antique shops. Outdoor supplies at *Eastern Mountain Sports,* 1041 Commonwealth Ave. In Cambridge, visit Harvard Square bookstores and clothing shops; also, *Crate & Barrel* with its colorful housewares showing through a striking glass façade, on Brattle Square.

WHAT TO DO WITH THE CHILDREN. Young people will enjoy the *Freedom Trail Walking Tour* or a sightseeing bus trip to *Paul Revere's House,* the site of the Boston Massacre, *Old Ironsides* (in the U.S. Naval Shipyard), and other highlights of the country's history. Other points of interest include: *Franklin Park Zoo* (Dorchester), *New England Aquarium, Children's Museum, Museum of Science* and the *Charles Hayden Planetarium,* as well as the *Public Gardens.* For children 6–12, contact *Boston by Little Feet* tours at 77 North Washington St., Boston.

HOTELS AND MOTELS. Boston has just undergone an unprecedented hotel-building boom. The famous Ritz-Carlton, Copley Plaza, and Parker House have been joined by a half-dozen new hostelries. Although truly inexpensive lodgings are best found a half hour's drive or more into the suburbs, the downtown hotels offer convenience and freedom from traffic once your car is garaged. Even expensive hotels have reasonable weekend packages; call for details.

The following ranges pertain to double occupancy in both Boston and Cambridge hotels and motels: *Deluxe,* $125 and up; *Expensive,* $95–$125; *Moderate,* $75–$95; *Inexpensive,* $45–$75; *Rock Bottom,* under $45.

BOSTON. *Deluxe:* **Ritz-Carlton.** Arlington and Newbury Sts. Understated elegance, superb service. Some rooms with garden views, fireplace suites. New tower now open. Fine restaurants and famous bar.

Copley Plaza. 138 St. James Ave., Copley Square. Showier than the Ritz, though still very proper. Set amidst architectural jewels of Back Bay. Several restaurants and bars.

Parker House. 60 School St. Boston's oldest grand hotel, in heart of downtown. Excellent restaurants; entertainment in lounge.

Meridien. 1 Post Office Sq. Member of respected French chain, in renovated Federal Reserve Bldg., financial district. Airy, well-lit rooms; some loft suites. French restaurant; bar with N.C. Wyeth murals.

Westin. Copley Place. Boston's tallest (36 floors) hotel, with big, handsome rooms and great views. Indoor pool, health club, three restaurants.

Bostonian. At Quincy Market, Dock Sq. A new, intimate, European-style hotel. Some rooms have fireplaces. Fine restaurant.

Expensive: **Holiday Inn-Government Center.** 5 Blossom St. Adjacent to Beacon Hill, Govt. Center, Mass. Gen. Hospital. Pool. Restaurant, bar, dancing.

Moderate: **Lenox.** 710 Boylston St. A small hotel in the Back Bay, nr. Copley Place and Prudential Center. Restaurant, bar.

Ramada Inn-Airport. 225 McClellan Hwy., E. Boston. Convenient to Logan. Pool, play area. Restaurant, bar.

Eliot. 370 Commonwealth Ave., cor. Mass. Ave. Small Back Bay hotel is home of Eliot Lounge, famous watering hole of runners in Boston Marathon.

Inexpensive. **Terrace Motel.** 1650 Commonwealth Ave. Near Boston University; 15-minute drive downtown. Restaurants nearby.

Rock Bottom: **Susse Chalet.** 800 Morrissey Blvd., Dorchester. Basic accommodations; restaurants near. Pool. Area's lowest prices.

CAMBRIDGE. *Deluxe:* **Charles.** Eliot and Bennett Sts. Brand-new 300–room Harvard Square hotel features luxury touches such as TVs and phones in all bathrooms, custom-made bed quilts. Restaurant; live jazz in Regatta Bar.

Hyatt Regency. 575 Memorial Dr. Modern luxury. Glass elevators, terraced patios, revolving rooftop lounge. Three restaurants. Nr. Harvard, MIT.

Expensive: **Sheraton Commander.** 16 Garden St. opp. Common. Just renovated. Quiet location, yet 5 min. walk to Harvard Sq. Good restaurant, bar.

Sonesta. 5 Cambridge Pkwy. Near Museum of Science. Views of Boston and the Charles. Pool. Restaurant, bar, entertainment.

Moderate: **Howard Johnson's.** 777 Memorial Dr. Rooftop pool; outdoor platform tennis. Japanese steak house. Near MIT campus.

Harvard Motor House. 110 Mt. Auburn St. Adjacent to Harvard Sq. and bus, subway terminal. Dozens of restaurants near.

Rock Bottom: **Susse Chalet.** 211 Concord Tpke. (Rte. 2). Member of chain. Basic lodging at low price. Short drive into Cambridge.

DINING OUT. Boston is one of America's best restaurant towns. The basis for our price range is an à la carte dinner of three courses, not including tax, tip, or drinks. *Deluxe,* $30 and up; *Expensive,* $22–$30; *Moderate,* $16–$22; *Inexpensive,* under $16.

Deluxe: **Julien.** Hotel Meridien, Post Office Sq. The French *nouvelle cuisine* is given a splendid interpretation here, in one of Boston's newest hotels. Recent offerings have included salmon and sole mousse, veal kidneys with red wine butter, and medallions of duck. Fine desserts.

L'Espalier. 30 Gloucester St. A small, austere yet gracious dining spot. Dinners are prix fixe, and may include quail salad, venison sauté, or loin of lamb. A "tasting menu" offers a sampling of entrees.

Locke-Ober. 3 Winter Place. A landmark of Victorian Boston. The menu, too, is traditional—solid and good. Stop in at lunch for a bowl of rich oyster stew in the magnificent downstairs bar.

Ritz-Carlton. Arlington and Newbury Sts. One of America's best hotel dining rooms. Impeccable French service. Known for *lobster etuvée au whiskey* and a legendary wine cellar.

Bay Tower Room. 60 State St. Thirty-odd stories above Boston, with harbor views. French and American cuisine, with seafood, steak, and veal Orloff. Open at lunch for members only.

Parker's 60 School St. Still serving Parker House rolls. Also red snapper *en croûte*, châteaubriand, Dover sole, crêpes Suzette. Elaborate Sunday brunch.

Grill 23. 161 Berkeley St. A fine steak house in New York style. Steaks and roasts first-rate; so are the veal chops and a la carte vegetables.

Polonaise. 384 Boylston St. Classic Polish cuisine: veal with gooseberry sauce; game dishes. Good desserts and Polish after-dinner wines.

Expensive: **29 Newbury St.** Small new restaurant with an ambitiously eclectic yet successful menu, from homemade pasta to sashimi. Open till 12:30 A.M.

Moderate: **Fedele's.** 30 Fleet St. One of Boston's favorite Italian spots. A seemingly endless repertory of veal dishes; ask about the nightly specials.

Tiger Lilies. 23 Joy St. French country ambience in a Beacon Hill townhouse. Fireplaces, patio dining in season. "American nouvelle" menu changes weekly; strictly fresh ingredients. Sunday brunch.

Kai-Seki. 132 Newbury St. Japanese Sushi bar. Also full dinner menu featuring authentic Japanese dishes.

BROOKLINE. *Inexpensive:* **Chef Chang's House.** 1004–1006 Beacon Street. Peking duck; also a broad repertory from the Mandarin, Szechuan, and Shanghai cuisines. Luncheon specialties weekdays.

CAMBRIDGE. *Expensive:* **Ferdinand's.** 121 Mt. Auburn St. French dishes, plus simple things done well, like filet mignon with béarnaise sauce. Good, moderate-priced wine list, plus vintage rarities.

Moderate: **Athenian Taverna.** 567 Massachusetts Ave. Souvlaki, kebabs, steaks, lamb and *baklava*. Greek ensemble entertains evenings.

Cajun Yankee. 1193 Cambridge Street. The real thing. Blackened redfish, jambalaya, crayfish etouffée. Very small—reservations a must.

Peasant Stock. 421 Washington St., Somerville (out Kirkland St. and just over the Cambridge line). Off the beaten track, and with a limited menu, but featuring hearty, well-prepared meals, wines, and frequent after-dinner chamber music.

Inexpensive: **Lucky Gardens.** 282 Concord Ave. A Chinese restaurant with a following. Szechuan, Hunan, you name it. Wonderful dumplings. Peking Duck. Bring own beer or wine.

Oh Calcutta. 468 Massachusetts Ave. Lamb, chicken, and other curries; Indian breads and condiments.

EXPLORING CAPE COD

Although fishing, lobstering, and boatbuilding industries are alive and the Cape is an important source of cranberries, tourism is by far the biggest industry on the Cape today. With its miles of varied beaches, charming New England villages of white clapboard mansions and silver-shingled cottages, pine woods, grassy marshes and rolling dunes, and its mild ocean climate, Cape Cod has been one of the country's most loved vacation spots for years. True, the new prosperity brought by the tourists who flock there in ever-increasing droves has significantly altered the appearance and the ecological balance of the Cape. The great dangers are that the primitive natural beauty that draws travelers to the Cape will be destroyed by the growth of tourism or that the Cape may be transformed into a southern suburb of Boston, a process which has already begun. At any rate, the Cape is not what it was twenty years ago and will undoubtedly continue to change.

Although you can make a complete circuit of the Cape in 2 ½ hours, it's really a place for relaxing. You can find all sorts of accommodations from guest houses to resort motels or housekeeping cottages. Reservations are a good idea, especially in summer, but the off-season traveler will likely turn up accommodations without much trouble.

An interesting side trip along Route 3 includes Plymouth. The first permanent colonial settlement in the United States, Plymouth has become a national shrine visited annually by thousands. Since that historic day in December 1620 when the weary, weakened Pilgrims landed there on the *Mayflower*, Plymouth has grown and thrived and is now a busy city. But, thanks to the many restorations and museums, the imaginative visitor to Plymouth will find that sense of the past he seeks. Plymouth Rock now rests under a canopy of granite to protect it from souvenir hunters. A few yards from the hallowed boulder is the *Mayflower II*, a replica of the original ship. Built in England, it sailed across the Atlantic in 1957. Visitors are welcome aboard. From the Rock, climb the stairway leading to Cole's Hill. This is where the Pilgrims buried their dead by night, so that the Indians could not calculate the number of survivors. If it had not been for the friendship of Massasoit, the great chief of the Wampanoags, all would have perished. His statue stands near the sepulcher. Nearby is the First Parish Church, home of a congregation begun by the Pilgrims. The original building was erected in 1683 and the present church is the fifth on this site. Walk up the stone steps beside the church to Burial Hill, which overlooks the square. The fort was built in 1622 and contained five cannons. It was also used as a meeting house and burial ground. You can pick out the graves of such early settlers as Governor Bradford, Edward Gray, Thomas Clark, and John Cotton. Also of interest is the town brook, which furnished water to the Pilgrims. The town established Brewster Gardens nearby, on the site of the settlers' original gardens.

Another worthwhile spot to visit, the Pilgrim Hall Museum, has an interesting collection of Pilgrim relics and paintings. Next, travel to Plimoth Plantation, a re-creation of the original Pilgrim colony as it looked in 1627. Costumed men and women enact the day-to-day life of the Pilgrims there.

The Cape Cod Canal, which separates the Cape from the mainland, is crossed on the eastern side by the Sagamore Bridge and from Route 28 by the Bourne Bridge. The canal was dug between 1909 and 1914 by the U.S. Army Corps of Engineers, 300 years after Myles Standish first proposed it to eliminate the dangerous trip around the shallows off Provincetown.

From the canal to the elbow (Cape Cod resembles a crooked arm), the Cape is traversed by three major roads: Rte. 6A on the north; Rte. 6, a two-lane highway down the middle; and Rte. 28 to the south. They all join at Orleans, and Rte. 6 continues to Truro and Provincetown. The three main highways traverse contrasting regions. Rte. 6 passes through the relatively unpopulated center of the Cape, which is characterized by an undulating landscape of scrub pine and scrub oak. It is generally the fastest route east and the most direct to the National Seashore.

The Southern Shore

The southern side of the Cape, reached by Rte. 28, is the most heavily populated and the major center for tourism. Its growth as a resort area has been abetted by its abundance of scenic harbors overlooking Nantucket Sound and its fine beaches. At the extreme southwestern corner is Woods Hole, where the car ferries depart for Martha's Vineyard and Nantucket. It is also the location of the Woods Hole Oceanographic Institute, the *Marine Biology Laboratory,* and the aquarium of the U.S. Bureau of Commercial Fisheries. Falmouth and the surrounding villages comprise one of the Cape's main commercial and resort areas. It was settled in 1660 by a group of Quakers and was an active center of trade and shipping. The bell in the Congregational Church was cast by Paul Revere. Mashpee, where Otis Air Force Base is now located, is the home of many descendants of the original Wampanoag Indians. Wampanoag crafts are for sale at the *Indian Craft Shop* on Rte. 28 in Mashpee. There are also some cranberry bogs as well as beautiful Mashpee Pond and two nature reserves. Hyannis, with its fashionable satellite resort towns, is the commercial hub of tourism on the Cape. The late President Kennedy's family compound is located behind a high fence in Hyannisport. There are some fine sea captains' mansions in South Yarmouth.

Chatham is a typical Cape village, but is free of the commercialism that mars many towns and villages on the south shore of the Cape. Rigid zoning laws have helped to keep Chatham the way it was at the turn of the century. You can watch the boats unloading their catch around noon at the Fish Pier. The view of the ocean from the Chatham Lighthouse is spectacular. South of Chatham, trailing off from the "elbow" of the Cape, lies Monomoy, accessible only by boat. This fragile spit of land now enjoys protection as a federally designated wilderness area—although this political distinction did nothing to mitigate the ravages of the freak tides which accompanied the blizzard of '78. In the words of an Audubon Society official, there are now "two Monomoys." From Chatham, Rte. 28 curves north and joins 6 and 6A at Orleans on the northern part of the Cape. In Orleans you can follow Rock Harbor Road to the town landing where in 1814 the militia of Orleans routed a British landing party. Many citizens of Massachusetts, though, were opposed to the War of 1812 because of its adverse effect on trade. From Orleans go east on Nauset Beach Road to Nauset Beach. From here, federally protected beaches stretch for 40 miles to Provincetown.

National Seashore

Three miles north on US 6 is the town of Eastham; just beyond the village is the headquarters of the Cape Cod National Seashore, established in 1961 to preserve the Cape's natural and historic resources. At Nauset, Marconi Station, Pilgrim Heights, and Province Lands, there are visitor centers and parking areas. Starting out on foot from these points, you can find superb ocean beaches, great rolling, lonely dunes, various types of swamps, marshes and wetlands, and all kinds of wildlife. The headquarters building in Eastham has displays, literature, and an auditorium for nature lectures. Rte. 6 continues on through Wellfleet, once the location of a large oyster industry, and, along with Truro, a colonial whaling and codfishing port.

For an excellent account of how the beachlands which make up the National Seashore looked 130 years ago, read Thoreau's *Cape Cod.* The author walked the beach from Orleans to Provincetown, encountering characters whose lives and spirit he set down in his narrative. "It is a wild rank place," said Thoreau, "and there is no flattery in it."

Historically, Provincetown, or P-Town as Cape Codders abbreviate it, has an ancient quarrel with Plymouth. The Pilgrims' first landfall in the New World was at the tip of Cape Cod. The Mayflower remained offshore for four or five weeks. P-Towners wonder why Plymouth, a Pilgrim afterthought, should get all the glory and fame, so the town has done everything possible to encourage the association of the Pilgrims with Provincetown. They erected a 252-foot stone tower to mark the place the Pilgrims landed, and built an historical museum to house an excellent collection of early relics. In summer, Provincetown attracts a considerable population of artists and writers, along with a sizable gay population. And there are tourists. Souvenir shops, art galleries, craft shops, and restaurants are jammed together along the narrow main street. The summer theatre in which Eugene O'Neill presented his first plays is still active.

The northern shore or Bay side of the Cape is different from the south shore and tends to be marshy. The water is far calmer than that of Nantucket Sound and the Atlantic, and the area is less developed. The towns have retained more of their original quality; main streets are lined with fine old shade trees and stately white clapboard mansions built by sea captains. Brewster has several such mansions as well as saltbox Cape Cod cottages. In West Brewster you can visit a working corn mill, a museum of natural history, and Sealand of Cape Cod, which features a marine aquarium, seal pool, and trained dolphins. At Dennis's Scargo Hill, the highest spot in the mid-Cape, the view of the Bay is spectacular. Yarmouth and Yarmouth Port are particularly lovely old seafaring towns and some of the captains' homes are open to the public.

As you continue west on 6A, you will come to Barnstable, a lovely town of large old homes, many built when the town had a brisk trade in codfish, rum, and molasses. Great salt marshes extend into the bay. Sturgis Library, dating from 1644, is the country's oldest public library building.

Sandwich is the oldest town on the Cape and one of the most interesting and charming. It remains famous for the beautifully colored glass which bears its name. The glass was produced there from 1825 until 1888, when labor-management disputes closed the factory. The *Sandwich Glass Museum*, Rte. 130, contains relics of the early history of the town as well as an outstanding collection of pressed and lace glass. You may visit the nearby Hoxie House, a 17th-century shingled saltbox cottage, and see Dexter's Gristmill in operation. Heritage Plantation is a complex of various museums and craft exhibits housed in a collection of old buildings, some real and some reproductions.

PRACTICAL INFORMATION FOR CAPE COD

HOW TO GET THERE. *By air: Provincetown-Boston Airline* flies from Boston and from New York City to Provincetown Airport. *Will's Air* flies from Boston to Nantucket and between Nantucket and Hyannis. *Gull Air* connects Hyannis with the islands.

By car: The Southeast Expwy. and State 3 travel from Boston to Cape Cod's Sagamore Bridge; then US 6 and State 132 continue to Hyannis. US 6 continues to Provincetown.

By ferry: The *Provincetown* sails daily in summer for P-Town from Rowe's Wharf, Boston. Foot passengers only; no cars.

By rail: Cape Cod and Hyannis Railroad runs from Buzzards Bay to Hyannis, Falmouth, and Sandwich. Mid-Apr.–Oct. 31.

By bus: Plymouth & Brockton Bus Company connects Boston with Cape points as far as Chatham.

MUSEUMS AND GALLERIES. Cotuit: *Crocker House,* Main St. Americana. June-Oct. Barnstable: *Donald G. Traser Memorial Museum,* Main St. Historical documents, marine exhibits.

Brewster: *Drummer Boy Museum.* Rte. 6A. Guided tours. *New England Fire and History Museum.* Rte. 6A. An adventure into America's past. *Cape Cod Museum of Nat'l. History,* Main St. Animal, marine exhibits, nature trails.

Centerville: *Centerville Historical Society Museum,* Jct. of West Bay Rd., Parker Rd. Sea captain's home. Doll collection, ship models. Late June to mid-Sept.

Chatham: *Old Windmille* (1797), Shattuck Rd. Working mill with meal for sale, July-Labor Day. *Railroad Museum,* Depot Rd., off Rte. 28. Thousands of models, photos. Late June to early Sept.

Eastham: *Old Grist Mill* (1793), Grist Mill Park. Late June to mid-Sept. *Schoolhouse Museum,* off Rte. 6. Early schoolhouse, Indian artifacts, farming tools. Also *Swift-Daley House.* July to Sept.

Falmouth: *Historical Society Museum.* Whaling, period furniture, tools, costumes. Garden. Mid-June to mid-Sept. *Saconesset Homestead Museum,* Rte. 28A, W. Falmouth. Restoration of 1678 house, 15 acres. Mid-June-Oct.

Provincetown: *Pilgrim Memorial Monument,* Town Hill. Commemorates Pilgrims' first landing. Historical Museum has marine relics. *Mayflower* diorama. Open year-round.

Sandwich: *Historical Society, Sandwich Glass Museum,* Town Hall Sq. Examples of renowned Sandwich glass. April-Nov. *Hoxie House & Dexter's Grist Mill.* Restoration of 17th-century home and mill. Mid-June-Oct. *Heritage Plantation,* Grove & Pine Sts. Round barn houses Barney Oldfield diorama, historic cars. *Military Museum* contains Lilly collection of miniature soldiers, antique firearms; Arts & Crafts Bldg. exhibits colonial tools, paintings. May to mid-Oct. *Yesteryears Museum,* Main & Rivers Sts. Dolls, doll houses, furnishings, June to mid-Oct.; May, wknds.; by appt. rest of year.

Truro: *Truro Historical Society Museum,* South Highland Road. Also visit nearby Highland Light; tours in season to top of lighthouse.

Yarmouth: *Winslow Crocker House,* Rte. 6, Yarmouth Port. Period furnishings in restored late-18th-century house. June-Sept. *Captain Bangs Hallet House,* Strawberry Lane, Yarmouth Port. Sea captain's home with original furnishings. Mid-June to early Sept. Closed wknds.

TOURIST INFORMATION SERVICE. Free folders, brochures, and maps may be obtained from *Cape Cod Chamber of Commerce,* Hyannis, Mass. 02601; resort directories can be obtained at Chamber of Commerce booths in Bourne and Sagamore. For information about Cape Cod National Seashore, write Superintendent, Cape Cod National Seashore, South Wellfleet, MA 02663.

SPECIAL INTEREST TOURS. The Mass. Audubon Society and National Seashore sponsor *birdwatching and wildflower tours;* contact the Society at Box 236, S. Wellfleet, MA 02663. *Whale watching* out of Provincetown harbor on Capt. Al Avellar's *Dolphin IV* and *Dolphin V.* Also out of Provincetown: *dune buggy tours; sailboat cruises.*

STAGE & REVUES. Cape Cod offers excellent summer theater, usually Broadway favorites with professional casts. Chatham: *Monomoy Theatre,* Rte. 28. Ohio Univ. Players. July-Aug. Dennis: *Cape Playhouse,* Rte. 6A. July-Aug. Falmouth: *Falmouth Playhouse,* off Rte. 151. Early July to early Sept.; West Harwich: *Harwich Junior Theatre,* Willow & Davidson Sts. Drama, musicals for children. July-Aug. Hyannis: *Cape Cod Melody Tent.* W. Main St.

Late June-Labor Day. Orleans: *Academy Playhouse.* Late July to early Sept. Provincetown: *Provincetown Playhouse,* July-Labor Day.

SPORTS. *Fishing:* Surf casting and deep-sea fishing are deservedly popular. Charter party boats can be hired for the day at Falmouth, Hyannis, Provincetown, Wellfleet, Oak Bluffs, and Nantucket. No license needed. *Surfing:* Nauset Beach, East Orleans, and White Crest Beach, and Wellfleet have special areas for the surfer. Special sections of Coast Guard Beach and Nauset Light Beach, Eastham, are also set aside.

HOTELS AND MOTELS. The Cape offers a wide range of accommodations, from luxurious seaside resorts to the most basic motel. Many close down completely during the off-season; others offer much lower prices. Policies regarding season length change frequently; always check well ahead of time. Our price rating is based on double occupancy, European plan, in season. *Deluxe,* $80 and up; *Expensive,* $65–$80; *Moderate,* $50–$65; *Inexpensive,* $35–$50. For information on low-cost bed and breakfast accommodations, contact Bed and Breakfast Cape Cod, Box 341, W. Hyannis Port, 02672.

BASS RIVER. *Deluxe:* **Blue Water.** S. Shore Dr. Resort hotel with private beach, pool, tennis. Restaurant, bar, dancing wknds. No pets or children under 12.

Expensive: **Beach House Motor Lodge.** 73 S. Shore Drive. Beach. Children over 10. No pets. Complimentary continental breakfast.

Red Jacket Beach Motor Lodge. S. Shore Drive. Restaurant, bar, pools, beach, water sports, tennis.

Riviera Beach. S. Shore Drive. Private beach. Some efficiencies. Indoor pool, restaurant, bar.

Surf and Sand Beach Motel. S. Shore Dr. 36 efficiency studios, patios or balconies. Beach. No children under 12; no pets.

Yarmouth Seaside Village. S. Shore Dr. On private beach. Motel and cottage accommodations. Kit. units avail, some with fireplace.

Moderate: **Village Green.** S. Shore Dr. Pleasant motel opp. beach. Pool, play area. Restaurant nr. Pets off-season.

Inexpensive: **Pine Knot Motel,** Rt. 28. Some kitchens. Pool. Nr. golf, beach, restaurants.

BOURNE. *Moderate:* **Mashnee Village.** Mashnee Village Rd., 5 mi. W of Bridge, off Rte. 28. Pool, tennis, play area. Beach dock. Cottages with kits. Bar. Pets.

Panorama Motor Lodge. South Bourne Bridge Rotary, Rte. 28. Bar, pool.

BREWSTER. *Expensive:* **Bramble Inn.** Main St. Pleasant village setting. Restaurant; free continental breakfast. Half-mile to beach.

Old Manse Inn. Rte. 6A. An attractive country inn, open all year and with modest off-season rates.

BUZZARDS BAY. *Inexpensive:* **Quintal's Motor Lodge.** Rte. 28 at Bourne Bridge. Indoor pool, sauna. Refrigerators in rooms. Open all year.

Buzzards Bay Motor Lodge. Sawyer Road, Wrentham. On private beach with dock. Some cottages with kitchens. No pets.

CHATHAM. *Deluxe:* **Chatham Bars Inn & Cottages.** Shore Rd. All resort pleasures: beach, boating, tennis, lawn games, Dining rm., bar. Dancing, entertainment. Roomy cottages. AP.

Wequassett Inn. Beautiful resort complex on Pleasant Bay. Rooms and suites in cottages overlooking water. Tennis, sailing, pool, nightclub. Golf nearby. Fine food served in 18th-century mansion. EP, AP, or MAP avail.

Moderate: **Hawthorne.** 202 Shore Rd. Private beach. Breakfast avail. Children over 8. No pets.

Dolphin of Chatham. 352 Main St. Spacious grounds off hwy. Kit. units and cottages avail. Heated pool, play area.

Seafarer. Rte. 28. Spacious rooms, quiet location ½ mile from beach. Some 2-room efficiencies.

CRAIGVILLE. *Deluxe:* **Trade Winds Inn.** Craigville Beach Rd. Luxurious inn with private beach, lovely gardens. Dining rm. Bar. Entertainment. No pets.
Moderate: **Craig Village by the Sea.** Craigville Beach Rd. Cottages with fireplaces opp. beach. Pets off-season only. Play area.

DENNIS. *Deluxe:* **Lighthouse Inn.** W. Dennis, 1 mi. S off Rte. 28. Resort hotel designed for family. On beach. Pool, play area, tennis, boating, fishing. Special rec. program for the kids. Dining rm., bar, entertainment. **MAP.**
Expensive: **Cross Rip.** 33 Chase Ave., Dennis Port. 2-story motel built around pool. Private beach. Restaurant nr. Children over 5. No pets.
Spouter Whale Motor Inn. 405 Old Wharf Road., Dennis Port. On ocean with private beach. Children over 5. No pets.
Moderate: **Lamplighter Motor Lodge.** Rte. 28, Dennis Port. Family motel with picnic and play areas. Pool. Restaurant nr. Pets.
Ocean View Lodge and Cottages. Depot St. Motel and efficiency accommodations. TV lounge. Weekly rates avail. Near beach.

EASTHAM. *Moderate:* **Now Voyager.** Rte. 6, 3 mi. N of Nat'l. Seashore entrance. Comfortable quarters on wooded grounds. Pool, play area. Restaurant, bar.
Cranberry Cottages. Rte. 6, north of Orleans rotary. Pleasant Cape Cod cottages set in a shady grove. Kitchen facilities. A nice, old-fashioned setup.

FALMOUTH. *Expensive:* **Coonamesset Inn.** Jones Rd. & Gifford St. Beautiful gardens, Cape Cod-style buildings. Excellent restaurant, bar, entertainment, dancing.
Falmouth Marina. Robbins Rd. In attractive grounds overlooking harbor. Pool. No pets.
Green Harbor. Acapesket Rd., E. Falmouth. Pools. Private beach. Boats avail.
Holiday Inn. 824 Main St. Pool, restaurant, bar, entertainment.
Sheraton Inn-Falmouth. 291 Jones Rd. Spacious rms. Pool, restaurant, bar. Entertainment.
Moderate: **Ox Bow Motel.** Nicely kept, nicely furnished. Pool.
Inexpensive: **Elm Arch Inn.** Off Main St. Pool. Charming family-owned colonial inn.
Mostly Hall. 27 Main St. Cozy family inn nr. ferries and beaches. Big breakfasts. Children over 16; no pets.

HARWICH. *Expensive:* **Seadar Inn.** Bank St. & Braddock Lane, Harwich Port. Opposite beach. Includes buffet breakfast. Mid-May–Oct.
Moderate: **Moby Dick.** Main St., S. Harwich. Pool, play area. Pets.
Stone Horse. Rte. 28, S. Harwich. Beautiful gardens. Pool, play area. Nr. beach, marina, golf.

HYANNIS. *Deluxe:* **Dunfey-Hyannis.** West End Circle. Resort hotel, golf, tennis, pools, play area. Restaurant, bar, dancing, entertainment.
Expensive. **Heritage House.** 259 Main St. Pools, private balconies. Saunas. Restaurant, lounge. Package rates avail.
Moderate: **Country Lake Lodge.** Rte. 132. On lake, with fishing, boating avail. Pool, play area. Restaurant nr.
Hyannis Harborview. 213 Ocean St. Opp. pier. Pools. Sauna. Cocktail lounge. Nr. island ferries.
Hyannis Star. Rte. 132 & Pine Needle Lane. Pool, play area. Full kitchen cottages avail. Pets. Wkly. rates avail.
Hyannis Town House Motor Inn. 33 Ocean St. Restaurant nr.
Hyannis Travel Inn. 16 North St. Pool. Restaurant nr. No pets.
Park Square Village. 156 Main St. Comfortable rooms in two main houses, built 1710 and 1855; cottages and efficiencies.
Presidential Motor Lodge. On lake; water sports; convenient.

NORTH TRURO. *Moderate:* **Crow's Nest.** Rte. 6A. Motel set in dunes on opp. side of road from beach, but with private beach. Close to Provincetown.

Whitman House. Great Hollow Rd. Family-oriented inn. Pool, play area. Restaurant, bar. Weekly rates.

Inexpensive: **Anchorage.** Rte. 6A, Beach Point. Motel units or efficiencies. Private beach, sundeck. Apr.–Nov.

ORLEANS. *Expensive:* **Nauset Knoll Motor Lodge.** Nauset Beach. Attractive rms. have ocean view. No pets.

Orleans Holiday. Jct. Rtes. 6A & 28. Pool. Restaurant. Color cable TV. Year round.

Skaket Beach. Exit 12, Rte. 6. Pleasant rooms with refrigerators. Continental breakfast. Heated pool, play area.

Moderate: **Cove House and Cottages.** Rte. 6A. Inn rooms or efficiency cottages with decks and fireplaces. Open all year.

Inexpensive: **Ridgewood Motel & Cottages.** Jct. Rtes. 28 & 39. Play area. Comfortable rooms and housekeeping cottages. Pets.

PROVINCETOWN. *Expensive:* **Provincetown Inn.** 1 Commercial St. Fine location near tip of Cape. Restaurant. Dune tours and bike rentals avail.

The Moors. Beach Rd. and Bradford St. Ext. Restaurant. Free coffee and rolls. Pool.

Bradford House & Motel. 41 Bradford St. Pleasant, centrally located. Restaurant nr. No pets.

Moderate: **Tides Motor Inn.** Beach Point Road. Pool; most rooms on private beach.

SAGAMORE. *Inexpensive:* **Windmill Motel.** Mid-Cape Hwy. Pool; rest.

SANDWICH. *Expensive:* **Daniel Webster Inn.** Main St. Pool, restaurant, bar, entertainment. No pets.

Moderate: **Earl of Sandwich Motor Manor.** Rte. 6A. Charming small motel with Tudor décor. Free cont. breakfast.

WELLFLEET. *Moderate:* **Southfleet Motor Inn.** Rte. 6. Pools, rest., bar, entertainment. No pets.

Wellfleet Motel. Rte. 6. Play area. Heated pool. Bar. In-room coffee and refrigerators. No pets.

WOODS HOLE. *Expensive:* **Nautilus.** Woods Hole Rd. Pool, bar, restaurant, tennis. Island ferries nearby.

YARMOUTH. *Expensive:* **Colonial Acres.** 114 Standish Way, W. Yarmouth. Pool, play area. Restaurant.

Blue Rock Motor Inn. Off High Bank Rd. Pool, shuffleboard, tennis. Affiliated with par 3 golf course. Apr.–Nov.

Green Harbor Village. 182 Baxter Ave., W. Yarmouth, Pool, private beach. Very attractive. Cottages with sundecks.

Moderate: **Jolly Captain.** Rte. 28 at Bass River Bridge. Pool, boat ramp on river.

Irish Village Motel. Rte. 28. Pool, sauna. Irish gift shop. Irish bar.

 DINING OUT. Cape Cod is liberally dotted with interesting restaurants and inns. Although some restaurants are closed after the summer season, many are open the year round for those interested in seeing the Cape after the sun worshippers have all gone.

Our ratings are based on the price of an à la carte dinner without drinks, tax and tip: *Expensive,* $18 and up; *Moderate,* $12–$18; *Inexpensive,* under $12.

BARNSTABLE. *Moderate:* **Mattakesse Wharf.** Seafood. Outdoor dining. Bar. On Barnstable Harbor.

BREWSTER. *Expensive:* **Chillingsworth.** Rte. 6A, E. Brewster. Classic and *nouvelle cuisine* French dining in lovely Colonial inn. Own baking. Dinner served by reservation only. Two seatings nightly.

Moderate: **Bramble Inn.** Main St. A cheery spot serving soups, salads, sandwiches. Art gallery. Closed winter.

BUZZARDS BAY. *Moderate:* **The Windjammer.** 3131 Cranberry Hwy. Seafood. Own baking: popovers, breads, pastries. Bar.

CHATHAM. *Moderate:* **Captain's Table.** 580 Main St. Yankee cooking: chicken pie, fish.

Cranberry Inn. 359 Main St. Down-home New England cooking; seafood a specialty.

DENNIS. *Expensive:* **Columns.** Main St., W. Dennis. Lovely old mansion. Tournedos Rossini, frogs' legs, fettucini Alfredo. Entertainment under tent.

FALMOUTH. *Expensive:* **Flying Bridge.** Scranton Ave. at Marina. Open-hearth cooking. Overlooks harbor. Bar, dancing.

Moderate: **Coonamessett Inn.** Jones Rd. & Gifford St. Lovely traditional dining room. Open for breakfast, lunch, dinner. Bar with pianist, trio, dancing.

HARWICH. *Expensive:* **Bishop's Terrace.** Main St., W. Harwich. New England specialties: lobster, roast beef, steak. Terrace dining. Dinner only.

HYANNIS. *Moderate:* **Alberto's.** 337 Main St. A small, unpretentious Italian spot with a loyal summertime following (formerly Dom's).

NORTH TRURO. *Expensive:* **Méditerranée.** Pond Rd., off Rte. 6. One of the Cape's best. Mostly French menu; excellent wine list. Summers only. Reservations advised.

PROVINCETOWN. *Expensive:* **Ciro and Sal's.** 4 Kiley Ct. A 30-year tradition in P-town. Northern Italian specialties; good veal, innovative sauces.

Café at the Mews. 359 Commercial St. Seafood, duckling, châteaubriand. Bar with fireplace. Sunday brunch.

Moderate: **Napi's.** 7 Freeman St. Good food and atmosphere; local art on display. Breakfast off-season.

Tip for Tops'n. 31 Bradford St. Seafood and Portuguese specialties, marinated pork chops, homemade puddings.

Inexpensive: **Cookie's.** 133 Commercial St. A local favorite. Portuguese cooking—squid stew, kale soup, marinated fish. Order a side of fava beans.

WELLFLEET. *Expensive:* **Sweet Seasons.** Chilled poached lobster, homemade caviar mayonnaise. Good place for Sunday brunch.

YARMOUTH. *Moderate:* **Cranberry Moose.** 43 Main St. International cuisine in 200-yr.-old building. Paella, roasts, duckling.

Old Yarmouth Inn Restaurant. Rte. 6A. In historic inn. Curries as well as local specialties. Bar, dancing.

EXPLORING MARTHA'S VINEYARD AND NANTUCKET

Martha's Vineyard

Most of the island's visitors, who come via passenger ferry, land at Vineyard Haven, the main port, shopping center, and winter community. Its busy harbor and a varied shopping district make it a pleasant place to visit. You may want to visit the Liberty Pole Museum on Main Street, housed in the town's oldest building, which was originally a church. Oak Bluffs, where the rest of the ferries dock, was settled in the 17th century, but its fascinating architecture dates from the 19th century, when it became the center for Methodist camp meetings. These began as tent revivals, but eventually permanent buildings were erected. A conical ironwork tabernacle was built in the center of the campgrounds surrounded by Victorian gingerbread cottages, each striving to outdo its neighbors with the ornateness of its patterned shingles and colorful decorative moldings. The predominance of these whimsical pastel-colored dwellings gives the whole community the look of a seaside toyshop. Oak Bluffs is one of the oldest black resort communities in the United States, in addition to being a Methodist center.

The oldest town on Martha's Vineyard and a famous whaling port in the 18th and 19th centuries, Edgartown is now characterized by the beautiful old houses and tree-lined streets of its past and the elegant stores, fine hotels, and restaurants that make it the most fashionable summer resort on the island. It's a perfect place for walking and windowshopping. You might stroll to the Thomas Cooke House, headquarters of the Dukes County Historical Society. Built in 1765 by shipbuilders, the house is a whaling and historical museum. At the end of Cooke, the island's oldest street, is the Edgartown Cemetery. North and South Water Streets are lined with captains' houses, some with widow's walks on the roofs. When the first colonists came to Martha's Vineyard in the mid-17th century, they found the island's earliest settlers, the Wampanoag Indians, living at the western tip, now called Gay Head. The Indians taught the colonists how to kill whales and plant corn, and where to fish. Later on, the Indians were hired by whalers and today many descendants of the Wampanoags still live and work in the area.

Gay Head also offers the Vineyard's finest views. The cliffs themselves are an extravaganza of yellow and russet hues at sunset, and you can see the Elizabeth Islands across Vineyard Sound. Gay Head is "Up Island," as are the settlements of Tisbury, Menemsha and Chilmark; Edgartown, Oak Bluffs, and Vineyard Haven are "Down Island." The terms "up" and "down" refer to longitude, not latitude, and are a remnant of seafaring days. There are good beaches at Menemsha, and also at Katama, near Edgartown.

Nantucket

There are a number of summer colonies on the island, but Nantucket is the only real town. The marvelous Whaling Museum on Broad St. has fascinating exhibits on whales and the various operations involved in catching and processing them. Main St., lined with white captains' mansions and shaded by elm trees, reflects the affluence of the town at the peak of its whaling trade. The elegant Hadwen-Satler Memorial House at 96 Main St. is open to the public. The Historical Museum at 8 Fair St. consists of a collection of primitive portraits and period furniture and a wing of the Friends Meeting House. The Jethro Coffin House was built in 1686 and is the oldest house on Nantucket. The 1800 House on Mill St. is a restored early-American dwelling dating from Nantucket's early whaling days. Many buildings are restorations, and the museum quality of the town stems from firm regulations prohibiting exterior changes of buildings in Nantucket. One welcome new addition to Nantucket's town waterfront, however, is the fine new boat basin, which easily accommodates sailing and motor yachts. The new buildings clustered around the basin, though, are all in the island's correct period style.

Like Martha's Vineyard, Nantucket has beaches for all tastes. The south shore looks out on the Atlantic, which crashes on the wide sandy beaches in powerful breakers. The ocean is wildest on the Madaket side. The water on Nantucket Sound is calmer and the harbor's beaches are the most placid of all. Great Point, the northern peninsula's tip, is a good area for fishing.

PRACTICAL INFORMATION

FOR MARTHA'S VINEYARD AND NANTUCKET

HOW TO GET THERE. *By air: Provincetown–Boston Airlines* serves Martha's Vineyard from New York and Boston; *Will's Air* flies to Nantucket from Boston and Hyannis. *Gull Air* connects Hyannis with the Vineyard. *By ferry:* Car ferries are regularly scheduled to Martha's Vineyard and Nantucket from Woods Hole. Reservations well in advance required. Write Woods Hole Steamship Authority, Box 284, Woods Hole, Mass. 02543. Pier parking is available for ferry passengers. Ferries operate from Hyannis to Martha's Vineyard and Nantucket (passengers only in off-season) and between West Falmouth and Oak Bluffs. Passenger-only ferry service between New Bedford and Martha's Vineyard is provided from mid-May through mid-October by *Cape and Islands Express Lines,* Box J–4095, Leonard's Wharf, New Bedford, Mass.

MUSEUMS AND GALLERIES. Martha's Vineyard: Dukes County Historical Society, Cooke & School Sts. Edgartown. Restored Thomas Cooke House (1765) with furnishings, scrimshaw, whaling relics, library, is open mid-June to mid-Sept.

Nantucket Island: Jethro Coffin House (1686). Beautiful restoration of island's oldest house. June-Sept. Whaling Museum, Broad St. Late May to mid-Oct. Peter Foulger Museum, Broad St. Historical museum with reference library. Old Mill (1746), Mill Hill. June to early Sept. Maria Mitchell Assoc. (1790), 1 Vestal St. Birthplace of famous astronomer; observatory, library, natural science museum. Mid-June to mid-Sept. Hadwen House-Satler Memorial, Main & Pleasant Sts. Early 19th-century furnishings. 1800 House, Mill St. 19th-century home. Mid-June to mid-Oct. Old Gaol, Vestal St. Used from 1805 to 1933. June to early Sept.

TOURIST INFORMATION SERVICES. Nantucket Chamber of Commerce, Nantucket, Mass. 02554. Martha's Vineyard Chamber of Commerce, Box 1698, Vineyard Haven, Mass. 02568.

TOURS. *Casser Tours,* 46 W. 43 St., New York, N.Y. 10036, has a 4-day tour to Cape Cod (Falmouth, Hyannis), Nantucket, and Martha's Vineyard (Edgartown, Gay Head). Nantucket has several sightseeing services, including *Island Tours, Inc.* Martha's Vineyard is the destination of a 9-hour round-trip tour from Boston offered by the *Gray Line,* 420 Maple St., Marlboro, MA 01752.

SPORTS: *Swimming, fishing, sailing, tennis, bicycling,* and *golf.*

HOTELS AND MOTELS. Our price rating is based on double occupancy in peak season. *Deluxe,* $80 and up; *Expensive,* $65–$80; *Moderate,* $50–$65; *Inexpensive,* $35–$50.

MARTHA'S VINEYARD. *Deluxe:* **Harborside Inn.** S. Water St., Edgartown. Boating. Pool, play area, restaurant. Over 6 only. Bar, dancing, entertainment. Open Apr.-Oct.

Expensive: **Charlotte Inn.** S. Summer St. Very elegant. On quiet side street. Chez Pierre restaurant on premises.

Daggett House. N. Water St., Edgartown. Lovely traditional inn, gardens. Free breakfast served in antique-furnished room.

Governor Bradford Inn. 128 Main St. Restored inn with gracious period details. Lounge, continental breakfast.

Moderate: **Oak House.** Oak Bluffs. Oak paneling, leaded glass windows, ocean views. Very cozy.

Edgartown Inn. N. Water St., Edgartown. Traditional inn. Breakfast avail.

Tisbury Inn. Main St., Vineyard Haven. Big comfortable inn with pool and health club.

NANTUCKET. *Deluxe:* **Jared Coffin House.** Broad & Center Sts. Charming restored mansion with many antiques, handwoven fabric. Restaurant, bar, entertainment.

Expensive: **Gordon Folger Hotel & Cottages.** Easton St. Restaurant. MAP, EP avail. Bar. A grand hotel, with a broad veranda and old-fashioned elegance.

House of Orange. Orange St. A tidy, comfortable inn in an old sea captain's house. Lots of antiques, plants, and atmosphere.

Moderate: **India House.** India St. Fireplaces and four-poster beds. Huge, tasty breakfasts.

EXPLORING THE BERKSHIRES

On the outer edge of the northeast urban corridor, yet easily accessible from Boston, New York, and the north, stand the Berkshire hills. This is a region that combines a gentle, pastoral landscape with some of the finest cultural attractions in New England. The Berkshires have long been settled but, as in the quiet shires of old England, the terms between man and nature are relaxed.

Near Pittsfield is Mt. Greylock, occupying an 8,660-acre state reservation with bridle paths, picnic facilities, hunting, and camping. At 3,491 feet, Greylock is the state's highest peak, overlooking magnificent panoramas of western Massachusetts, the Hudson Valley of New York, and the Green Mountains of southern Vermont. Many foot trails, including the Appalachian Trail, cross the summit. After driving down the mountain, continue to State 2, driving west to Williamstown, one of the loveliest towns in New England and the site of Williams College (1793), which evolved from a free school. The attractive campus is well worth a walking tour. On South St. is the Sterling and Francine Clark Art Institute, one of the finest small museums in America. It boasts great paintings, including a memorable collection of Renoirs, rare silver, furniture, and china. The college's Thompson Memorial Chapel, a Gothic structure built in 1904, is on the north side of Main St. Its stained-glass windows are seen to best advantage from inside. Diagonally across the street is the Lawrence Art Museum, identifiable by its octagonal form and Grecian rotunda. It houses fine collections of glass, pottery, bronzes, paintings, and sculpture.

Williamstown, with good restaurants, motels, and inns, is a delightful place to pause, with excellent skiing nearby as well as areas for hiking, riding, golfing, and foliage-watching. Another local feature is Adams Memorial Theater, regarded as one of the leading summer theaters in the nation.

Should you decide to turn east on Rte. 2, you will be traveling on the Mohawk Trail, once an Indian path which stretched to New York's Finger Lakes. The modern highway will take you past the town of Shelburne Falls, with its famous Bridge of Flowers, to Whitcomb Summit, overlooking the Deerfield River valley and the entrance of the Hoosac Railroad tunnel, and through the Mohawk Trail State Forest.

If traveling from Williamstown to Pittsfield in summer, plan to stop at the Hancock Shaker Village. Each year, as more buildings are restored and opened to the public, more fascinating objects attesting to the genius of these spiritually motivated people for coping with the material world are revealed. The Round Stone Barn, scrupulously restored, is an architectural treasure.

The easterly road south, Route 8, goes through Adams and Cheshire. Vistas in these towns sometimes resemble the English Lake District and sometimes the factories and row houses of a Dickens setting. The environs are lovely to drive through at foliage time. South of Savoy, about a half mile to the left of Route 9, is Cummington Road and the William Cullen Bryant homestead, open to the public for a small fee.

Continuing west on Route 9, the ride down from the hills approaching the town of Dalton offers excellent views, particularly during foliage season. Pause here to visit the Crane Museum of paper-making, housed in the Old Stone Mill on the banks of the Housatonic. At the foot of the hills, a well-marked road on the left leads to Wahconah Falls, a state park created around a waterfall in a clear, cold mountain stream. Continue west on Route 9, through Dalton to Pittsfield.

Pittsfield, the Berkshire County seat, is at the county's geographic center. It is also a center of commerce and industry in a most inviting setting surrounded by mountains. Visit the Berkshire Atheneum, with its splendid Melville collection; if you are especially interested in this one-time Berkshires resident, you may wish to take a short side trip to Arrowhead, the recently restored farmhouse where he wrote *Moby Dick*. At the southern edge of Pittsfield, toward the great Berkshire cultural centers of Lenox, Lee, and Stockbridge, is South Mountain with its fine vistas and seasonal programs offered by the South Mountain Chamber Music Concerts. Lenox, of course, is the home of the Tanglewood summer concerts. Here every summer, on a 200-acre estate, students and famous performers, the Boston Symphony, and just plain music lovers gather to learn, enjoy, and perform. The main shed seats 6,000, but many prefer to listen outside on the great lawn, relaxing on blankets or their own folding chairs. Near Lenox is the Pleasant Valley Wildlife Sanctuary, a Massachusetts Audubon Society facility sheltering many living specimens of regional plant and animal life. In West Becket, take in the Jacob's Pillow Dance Festival and visit the school founded by the late Ted Shawn and continued by Walter Terry. Top dancers from all over the world give regular performances to packed houses. Also in Lee is the 14,000-acre October Mountain State Forest. The Appalachian Trail runs through it and there are facilities for fishing, camping, and other outdoor activities.

Stockbridge

Return via US 20 to Stockbridge. Stockbridge, to many the archetype of the small New England town, has a long history of attracting creative people. Here is where Jonathan Edwards spent the last eight years of his life writing theological treatises and serving as missionary to the Indians. The late playwright Robert Sherwood summered here, and the town provided inspiration for its most famous recent resident, Norman Rockwell, who died in 1978. Many Rockwell paintings are on exhibit in the Corner House's permanent collection. There's an inviting inn here (the Red Lion) and one of the nation's top summer theaters, the Berkshire Playhouse. Other places worth visiting are the Mission House, Naumkeag Gardens, the library, and Chesterwood, a 150-acre estate containing the studio of Daniel Chester French, sculptor of the famed Lincoln Memorial Statue and of Concord's Minuteman. Chesterwood, now a national trust, is located off Rte. 183, two miles west of Stockbridge.

A short scenic drive south from Stockbridge on US 7 takes you to Great Barrington, largest town and economic center of the south Berkshires. The townspeople seized the courthouse from the British in August 1774; it has been claimed that this was the first act of open resistance to the Crown in America.

Take Route 23 a few miles southwest to South Egremont and then left to Highway 41. At the intersection, follow the Mt. Washington Road to Bash Bish Falls Reservation. A large parking area is provided and a short, pleasant footpath leads to the falls and a picnic area. Following a gorge cut deep into solid rock, the Bash Bish Brook plunges 50 feet into a deep, clear, rock-bottomed pool. According to a legend told, it seems, at every waterfall in North America, an Indian maiden, unhappy in love, jumped to her death from the rocks above. Her tortured spirit, of course, haunts the falls.

Streams, falls, and historic houses are easy to find in this lovely south Berkshire farm country, with its gentle mountains, inviting woods, and towns like Mt. Washington, Sheffield, New Marlborough, Sandisfield, Monterey, Otis, and Ashley Falls. Just to the west of Ashley Falls is nature's own rock garden, Bartholomew's Cobble, a protected public reservation noted for wildflowers and an extraordinary variety of ferns. Sheffield has the double falls of Sage's Ravine as well as Glen Falls, Bear Rock Falls, and Race Brook Falls. The first Berkshire town to be chartered, Sheffield is the only one left in the state with two covered bridges. These hill towns, along with the rolling pastures and woodlands that separate them, make up an entirely different Massachusetts —one that balances well against the man-made charms of Boston and the seascapes of the islands and Cape.

PRACTICAL INFORMATION

FOR THE BERKSHIRES

HOW TO GET THERE. *By car:* The Berkshires can be approached from several directions; from Conn. on US 7 and Mass. 8, along feeder roads off New York's Taconic Parkway, through Columbia and Rensselaer counties, or from Vermont on Routes 7 and 8. The Mohawk Trail (part of Route 2) is the most spectacular. The most direct route from Boston is via the Massachusetts Turnpike (toll); the Turnpike also links with the New York State Thruway to accommodate travelers from Albany and New York City.

By air: Bradley International, Windsor Locks, Conn., would be nearest, necessitating a drive from that point. *By train:* Amtrak offers service to Springfield and Pittsfield via Boston and Albany and also to Springfield from New York; bus connections and car rentals are available at those points.

 MUSEUMS AND GALLERIES. Stockbridge: *Chesterwood,* studio of Daniel Chester French, sculptor of Lincoln Memorial statue, Washington, D.C., and Minuteman, Concord. *Old Corner House.* Major collection of Norman Rockwell's work, including many of the artist's magazine paintings. Williamstown: *Sterling and Francine Clark Institute.* Renoirs, Corots, Sargents, and many other masterpieces. Free. Closed Mondays. Pittsfield: *The Berkshire Museum.* Art, science and local history. Lee: *Tyringham Art Galleries.* Primitive art.

 STATE PARKS. Beartown State Forest, access from State 23 or 102 near Great Barrington. Camp and swim at Benedict Pond. Ski in winter. More than 8,000 acres. Mohawk Trail State Forest, State 2, near Charlemont. Fish for trout, take scenic photographs. Mt. Greylock State Reservation, near N. Adams. Mt. Greylock is highest mountain in the state. Hunt, ride, camp, ski on more than 8,000 acres. October Mountain State Forest, near Lee. Good camping, fishing. Largest Mass. forest of nearly 15,000 acres. Pittsfield State Forest, near Pittsfield. Sports galore, including skiing.

GARDENS. Stockbridge. Naumkeag Gardens. Exotic, with Chinese motif, moongate. Mansion belonged to Joseph Choate, Ambassador to England. Open July—Labor Day.

 MUSIC. Lenox: Berkshire Festival, Tanglewood. Summer festival begins early July. Performances in Music Shed, Fridays, Saturdays, Sundays. Pittsfield: South Mountain Concerts. Chamber music, opera, young people's concerts Sun., July, Aug.; Sat., Sept., Oct. Lee: Jacob's Pillow Dance Festival. Ballet and modern dance. July, Aug.

The Berkshire towns in the Tanglewood vicinity are lately becoming known for jazz in summer. Check listings in *Berkshire Eagle* for places and schedules.

STAGE. Among many excellent summer theaters throughout the state, the Berkshire Playhouse, Stockbridge, and the Williamstown Theatre, Williamstown, present plays and revues.

 **HOTELS AND MOTELS IN BERKSHIRES.** Our price rating is based on double occupancy in summer. Rates are much higher during Tanglewood season, lower rest of year. *Expensive,* $80 and up; *Moderate,* $50–$80; *Inexpensive,* under $50.

GREAT BARRINGTON. *Expensive:* **Windflower Inn.** Rte. 23. Pleasant, rambling, antique-filled inn. Some rooms with fireplace. MAP; excellent cuisine.

Moderate: **Briarcliffe Motor Lodge.** Rte. 7. Play area. Free morning coffee.

LEE. *Expensive:* **Oak n' Spruce Resort.** Nightclub, full outdoor sports, skiing in season. Wknd. packages.

Moderate: **Morgan House.** A 100-year-old inn. Restaurant and lounge. Antique shop on premises.

Inexpensive: **Gaslight Motor Lodge.** On Greatwater Pond; full water sports.

LENOX. *Expensive:* **Eastover.** East St. Huge old mansion in resort, with cottages, etc. Pool, sauna, riding, archery, tennis, entertainment from skiing to hayrides on huge acreage.

Tanglewood Motor Inn. Pittsfield Rd. Pool, play area.

Moderate: **Lenox Motel.** Pittsfield Rd. 2 miles from ski area. Pool. In-room coffee.

PITTSFIELD. *Moderate:* **Heart of the Berkshires.** 970 W. Housatonic St. Pool, play area.

Inexpensive: **Town & Country Motor Lodge.** 1350 W. Housatonic St. Efficiencies avail.

SOUTH EGREMONT. *Moderate:* **Egremont Inn.** Old Sheffield Rd., S. Egremont. 200-yr.-old inn furnished with antiques. Pool, tennis. MAP.

STOCKBRIDGE. *Expensive:* **Williamsville Inn.** Rte. 41, W. Stockbridge. 18th-century farmhouse. Quiet, secluded. Pool and tennis courts. Good French restaurant.

Moderate: **Pleasant Valley.** Mass. Tpke., Exit 1. Pets.

Red Lion Inn. Rte. 7. Pool. Pets. Traditional colonial inn. Excellent restaurant, bar.

WILLIAMSTOWN. *Expensive:* **Williams Inn.** Pool, saunas, restaurant, bar, entertainment; on college campus.

Moderate: **Carriage House.** Rte. 7, New Ashford. Restaurant, bar.

1896 Motel. Quiet, secluded. Restaurant, bar.

 DINING OUT IN THE BERKSHIRES. Our ratings are based on the price of an à la carte dinner but do not include drinks, tax and tip. *Expensive,* $20 and up; *Moderate,* $14–$20; *Inexpensive,* under $14.

LEE. *Moderate:* **Cork 'n Hearth.** Rte. 20. Steak, seafood, Italian dishes. Closed Tues.

LENOX. *Expensive:* **Candlelight Inn.** Walker St. Steak and kidney pie, coquilles St. Jacques, veal Marengo.

Moderate: **The Restaurant.** 15 Franklin St. Cantonese duckling, marinated beef, shrimp.

PITTSFIELD. *Moderate:* **Latshaw's.** Lovely old house. Continental specialties.

SOUTH EGREMONT. *Expensive:* **Egremont Inn.** Roast beef, baked salmon. Entertainment wknds. Lunch and brkfst. on verandah in season.

STOCKBRIDGE. *Expensive:* **Red Lion Inn.** Continental menu, elegant atmosphere.

Williamsville Inn. 18th-century farmhouse. Scampi provençale, breast of chicken stuffed with artichokes, mushrooms, and gruyère. Fine desserts and wines.

WILLIAMSTOWN. *Moderate:* **Country Restaurant.** Escaloppe de veau Oscar.

Williams Inn. Pleasant restaurant; bar.

Inexpensive: **British Maid.** Crêpes, omelettes, quiche. Fine homemade desserts. Full license. Entertainment wknds.

PRACTICAL INFORMATION
FOR THE REST OF MASSACHUSETTS

HOW TO GET THERE. *By car:* Mass. Tpke. (I–90) runs east to west from Boston to the New York border at W. Stockbridge, connecting with New York Thruway. Route 128 circles Boston from Gloucester to Braintree. Route 15 links Wilbur Cross with Mass. Pike at Sturbridge. I–91 runs north-south along the Connecticut River. *Car rental: Avis, Hertz, National,* and *Budget* have offices in key localities. *By bus: Trailways* and *Greyhound* serve the state. *By air:* Boston's Logan International is served by major airlines. Springfield is served by Bradley International, Windsor Locks, Conn. *By train:* Amtrak service from Washington, D.C., Philadelphia, Newark, New York, New Haven, and Providence to Boston; also trains to Springfield and Boston from Chicago.

HOW TO GET AROUND. *By car:* The Mass. Tpke., a toll expressway, from downtown Boston to New York state. State 128 circles Boston. State 15 links Wilbur Cross with Mass. Tpke. Route 9 connects Boston with Worcester. State 2 is scenic Mohawk Trail. *By bus: Trailways* and *Greyhound* travel statewide. Local bus lines serve larger cities. Local *taxi* companies are listed in telephone directories. *By air: Delta* flies to New Bedford and Worcester from Boston. Air-taxi, New England Flyer's Air Service operates from Beverly Airport. *By train: Amtrak's Lake Shore Limited* provides service from Boston to Worcester, Springfield, Pittsfield, and points west.

TOURIST INFORMATION SERVICES. Free folders, brochures, and maps can be obtained from Mass. Department of Commerce, Division of Tourism, 100 Cambridge St., Boston 02202. There is a Visitor's Information Center at Tremont St., Boston Common.

MUSEUMS AND GALLERIES. Andover: *Addison Gallery of American Art,* Phillips Academy, Chapel Ave. Works of artists, glassware, sculpture, ship models. Framingham: *Danforth Museum.* Local art and history.

Lexington: *Museum of Our National Heritage.* Exhibits cover U.S. history and social development; also history of freemasonry. Free. Milton: *Museum of the American China Trade.* Oriental artifacts imported in days of clipper ships. Closed Sun., Mon., holidays. North Andover: *Merrimack Valley Textile Museum.* Old tools, photos trace growth of important New England textile industry. Special demonstrations Sun.

Salem: *Salem Witch Museum,* 19 ½ Washington Sq., N. Salem. Re-creations of witch trials. Witch House (1642), Essex St., is where witches were interrogated. *Peabody Museum.* Marine history, ethnology, and natural history. *House of the Seven Gables,* made famous in Hawthorne's novel, is restored 17th-century home.

Springfield: *Springfield Armory Museum.* American military arms were made here for 174 years. Now houses world's largest small-arms collection. *George Walter Vincent Smith Museum.* Oriental art; excellent collection of carpets.

Sturbridge: *Old Sturbridge Village.* 36 restored 18th-century homes surround green on 200-acre site. Costumed guides explain exhibits, crafts.

Williamstown: *Sterling and Francine Clark Art Institute.* Renoirs, Sargents, Corots, other masterpieces in impressive marble building.

HISTORIC SITES. There are several national historic sites in Massachusetts. In Concord the *National Minuteman Historical Park* commemorates the first skirmish of the Revolution. Visitor's Center has audio-visual program. *The Longfellow National Historic Site,* 105 Brattle St., Cambridge, is a Georgian house (1759) which served as Gen. Washington's headquarters in 1775 and was Henry Wadsworth Longfellow's home. *Adams National Historic Site,* Quincy, was given to nation by the descendants of John Adams. Original furnishings. *The Salem Maritime National Historic Site,* Salem, includes visitor center in the Custom House, Derby St., and Derby House, which has been restored and furnished as a Salem merchant's home. *Saugus Iron Works* on Central St., Saugus, includes restorations of an ironmonger's house, blast furnace, forge slitting mill, and a museum. *The John F. Kennedy National Historic Site,* 83 Beals St., Brookline, is birthplace of president, with original furnishings, memorabilia. In Brookline, *Frederick Law Olmsted National Historic Site,* Warren St., commemorates life and work of great landscape architect. In South Boston, *Dorchester Heights National Historic Site* marks spot where Washington placed guns for siege of Boston. Also, visit *Deerfield,* site of Indian Massacres, 1675, 1704. Six Colonial homes are open. In Salem is the *Essex Institute,* displaying 300 years of history, including 5 period houses: Pingree House (1804), John Ward House (1684), Pierce-Nichols House (1782), Crowninshield-Bentley House (1727), Assembly House (1782). *Pioneer Village,* Forest River Pk., has reproductions of 1630 village. (Open summers.) In Plymouth, *Plymouth Rock* and the exact replica of the *Mayflower.* Ship closed in winter. Also *Plimouth Plantation,* recreated Pilgrim village. Guides demonstrate 17th-century crafts and farming methods. Closed winter. In Lowell, *Lowell National Historical Park,* with its 19th-century mill buildings, interprets early U.S. industrial history. Trolley and canal boat rides, museums. *Old Sturbridge Village,* Sturbridge, offers a unique view of 18th- and early 19th-century life through restorations of period buildings and working craft exhibits.

TOURS. *Gray Line,* 420 Maple St., Marlboro, MA 01752. Wide variety of tours. Recent offerings include *Plymouth Pilgrimage;* tours of villages on Cape Cod; circuit of north shore, including Marblehead and Salem; Martha's Vineyard ferry-bus tours; also tours of Cambridge, Lexington, and Concord, 1-day excursions along the Massachusetts seacoast to New Hampshire and Maine, and 3-day fall foliage tours. *Peter Pan Lines,* 1776 Main St., Springfield, Mass. 01103, offers a bus-and-boat summer tour to Provincetown, via Boston; also excursions from Boston to the Eastern States Exposition, held late Sept. in Springfield. Peter Pan also operates bus service to Old Sturbridge Village from Springfield and Boston. From New York, *Tauck Tours,* 475 Fifth Avenue. Vacations from Manhattan to Concord-Lexington-Sturbridge.

DRINKING LAWS: Drinks available until 1 A.M. daily, midnight on Saturdays, if over 20. No package sales Sundays. Stringent drunk-driving laws.

SUMMER SPORTS. *Golf:* Massachusetts has many fine courses, including the Kittansett Club, Marion; Salem Country Club, Peabody; Trull Brook Golf Club, Tewksbury; and Taconic Golf Club, Williamstown. *Boating:* Charter party boats available at all major ports. Larger lakes, ponds have ramps. Boats may be rented. *Fishing:* Excellent freshwater fishing in many lakes and streams stocked by Division of Fish and Game. When the bluefish and striped bass are running (May-Oct.; varies from season to season) Massachusetts beaches offer some the the East Coast's most challenging surfcasting. *Water skiing:* Chaubunagungamaug Lake, 1,400-acre lake in Webster, is best. *Swimming:* There are pools, lakes, and beaches throughout state.

WINTER SPORTS. *Skiing:* Novice-Expert trails include Brodie Mt., New Ashford, with 1,250-ft. drop, 12 trails; Berkshire East, Charlemont, with 1,150-ft. drop, 12 trails; Jiminy Peak, Hancock, with 1,130-ft. drop, 20 trails; Catamount, S. Egremont, with 1,000-ft. drop, 7 trails. Areas with shorter drops are: Butternut Basin, Gt. Barrington, with 975-ft. drop, 10 trails; Mt.

Tom, S. Holyoke, with 840-ft. drop, 3 trails; and Bousquet, Pittsfield, with 750-ft. drop and 10 trails. Cross-country skiing is popular throughout the state, with trails near most towns and cities.

WHAT TO DO WITH THE CHILDREN. For the young set, there are summer *amusement parks* at Salisbury Beach; Mountain Park, Holyoke; and Riverside Park, Agawam. *Zoos:* Franklin Park Zoo, Blue Hill Ave, Dorchester. Hundreds of animals and excellent aviary on 50-plus acres with picnic grounds. Also Stoneham Zoo, Stoneham. Forest Park, Springfield, has zoo, picnic grounds. *Old Sturbridge Village* re-creates an 18th-century farming village. *Dinosaur Land,* S. Hadley, exhibits assorted dinosaur prints. Children will also enjoy *Storrowton Village,* a collection of 18th- and 19th-century homes and shops in West Springfield.

HOTELS AND MOTELS. Rates are based on double occupancy. *Deluxe,* $80 and up; *Expensive,* $65–$80; *Moderate,* $50–$65.

LEXINGTON. *Expensive:* **Sheraton-Lexington Motor Inn.** Attractive rooms. Pool. Restaurant, bar.
Moderate: **Battle Green Motor Inn.** 1720 Mass. Ave. Restaurant.

SALEM. *Expensive:* **Hawthorne Inn.** 18 Washington Sq. Homey. Many antiques. Restaurant, bar, entertainment.

STURBRIDGE. *Expensive:* **Sheraton Sturbridge Inn.** Rte. 20. Pool, restaurant, bar.
Moderate: **Publick House.** I–86, exit 3. Charming late-18th-century inn. Restaurant, bar, entertainment.

WORCESTER. *Moderate:* **Holiday Inn.** 70 S. Sturbridge St. Pool. Restaurant, bar, entertainment, dancing.

DINING OUT. The restaurants listed below are only a small sample of what's available in these areas. Price range for dinner: *Moderate,* $11–17.

CONCORD. *Moderate:* **Colonial Inn.** Concord Green. Traditional New England fare. Tap room. Antiques.

SALEM. *Moderate:* **Folsom's.** 7 Dodge St. Seafood.

WORCESTER. *Moderate:* **Leo's.** 56 Shrewsbury St. Italian home cooking.

NEW HAMPSHIRE

The White Mountains and the Lakes

New Hampshire's highlights lie in three regions—the seacoast, the White Mountains, and the lakes region—each with historic sites, scenic beauty and well-developed tourist facilities.

First, and most compact, is the seacoast region, 18 miles of coast and an extensive system of rivers and inland saltwater bays. Its gateway, historic Portsmouth (pop. about 30,000), was settled in 1630; 350 years of prosperity from fishing, shipbuilding and manufacturing endowed it with some of America's finest colonial mansions. Oldest of all is the Jackson House (1664) with its sweeping saltbox roof and somber siding. The Warner House (1716) is the earliest Georgian building in New England. Equally stately and graceful houses are the Moffat-Ladd (1763), Wentworth Gardner (1760) and Governor John Langdon (1784), among others. The more modest lives of ordinary people—craftsmen, artisans, mariners, shopkeepers—are preserved in Strawbery Banke, a 10-acre restoration around Puddle Dock, the original port; some traditional crafts are still practiced here.

The beaches are all along shoreline Route 1A. Well-equipped state parks are at Wallis Sands and at 2-mile Hampton Beach. Less commercialized public beaches are found also at Rye and Seabrook. Elegant summer estates line the rocky bluffs at Great and Little Boars Heads.

Inland, Exeter (pop. 10,000) has a famous boys' prep school, Phillips Exeter, and many lovely houses along its elm-shaded streets. In Durham, the University of New Hampshire's Paul Creative Arts Center is particularly interesting for visitors; and in Dover, the Woodman Institute preserves an original garrison farmhouse from 1675.

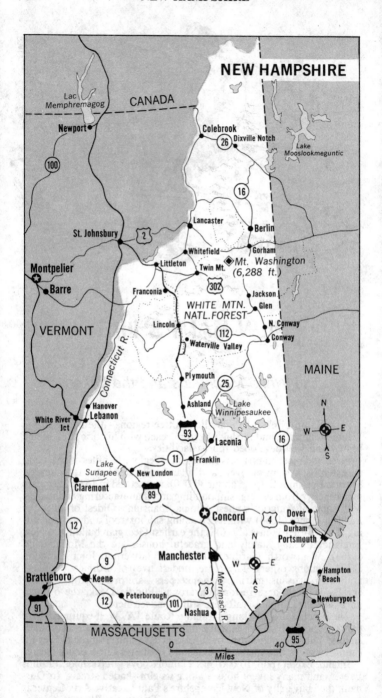

NEW HAMPSHIRE

Lac Memphremagog

CANADA

Newport

100

Colebrook

26 Dixville Notch

Lake Mooslookmeguntic

16

Lancaster

Berlin

St. Johnsbury

2

Whitefield

Gorham

Littleton

Twin Mt.

◆ Mt. Washington
(6,288 ft.)

Montpelier

Franconia

302

Jackson

Barre

Glen

WHITE MTN. NATL. FOREST

VERMONT

Lincoln

112

N. Conway

Conway

Waterville Valley

Plymouth

25

MAINE

Ashland

Lake Winnipesaukee

N

Hanover

W   E

White River Jct

Lebanon

S

93

Laconia

11

Franklin

16

Lake Sunapee

New London

Claremont

89

12

Concord

4

Dover

Durham

Portsmouth

9

Manchester

N

Brattleboro

Keene

W   E

Hampton Beach

S

12

Peterborough

101

3

91

Nashua

Newburyport

Merrimack R.

MASSACHUSETTS

0   40

95

Miles

The White Mountains

The 724,000-square-acre White Mountain National Forest covers most of north-central New Hampshire. Beyond lies the relatively undeveloped "North Country," some of the finest still-unspoiled areas in New England.Three main passes cut through the mountains: Pinkham Notch in the east, Crawford Notch in the center, Franconia Notch in the west; and the scenic Kancamagus Highway crosses the entire range east-west.

There are four ways up 6,288-ft. Mt. Washington, tallest peak in the Northeastern US: hike, drive the 8-mile toll road, ride in specially engineered "stage" vans, or ride the 3½-mile Cog Railroad from Crawford Notch. On top are tourist facilities and superb views. In North Conway you can ride the Skimobile up Mt. Cranmore; and in Franconia Notch the Cannon Mountain aerial tramway takes you up above the state's most famous landmark, the Old Man of the Mountains, Hawthorne's "Great Stone Face." Here too is the Flume, a lovely river gorge 70 feet deep by 800 feet long with waterfalls and deep clear pools. Lost River offers chances to clamber over, under ¾ mile of toppled boulders. North Conway is gateway to Mt. Washington Valley's ski areas and X-C trails (125 miles in Jackson alone) as well as forests, parks, rivers, campgrounds, family attractions.

The Lakes Region

Lake Winnipesaukee (72 square miles) dominates central New Hampshire. Laconia is the chief town. Steamer cruises on the lake leave from Weirs Beach, Wolfeboro, Center Harbor and Alton Bay. Summers, the New Hampshire Music Festival gives chamber and orchestral concerts at Center Harbor, Meredith, Plymouth and Gilford. Northeast of the lake, near Moultonborough, the Castle in the Clouds is a 6,000-acre area of great natural beauty, with hiking trails and views of both the lake and the White Mountains. Weirs Beach has water slide and its Boardwalk is a-hum all summer. Alpine Slide at Alpine Ridge Ski Area.

Currier and Ives Country

Southwest New Hampshire is a land of lovely old villages with white churches and graceful homes grouped around village commons. Amherst, Antrim, Peterborough, Hillsboro, Henniker, Candia are but a few of the many. If you are here in August or September, inquire locally for the town and county fairs; they are superb for local color.

Two Cities

In Concord, the State Capitol is architecturally and historically interesting, and the New Hampshire Historical Society shows traditional domestic interiors, 1680–1720. Here too is the main showroom of the League of New Hampshire Craftsmen, at 36 North Main Street. Manchester, the state's largest city (pop. about 100,000), has an outstanding collection of American work in its Currier Gallery of Art, 192 Orange St. The Amoskeag Manufacturing Company was once the world's largest textile mill; in the Depression they went bankrupt. Now diversified, the area holds over 100 manufacturing and service companies.

PRACTICAL INFORMATION
FOR NEW HAMPSHIRE

 HOW TO GET THERE. *By air:* New Hampshire is the end of the pipeline for flights. *Precision* and *Command* fly into/out of Manchester, Laconia, Keene and Lebanon from Boston and New York City.

By car: From Boston take I–95 for Portsmouth and the seacoast, I–93 for Manchester, Concord, the Lakes and the White Mountains. From New York take I–95 to New Haven, Conn., then I–91 north along the Vermont–New Hampshire border to reach White River Junction. From New York 222 miles, 5 hours; from Chicago 903 miles, 21 hours; from Montreal 112 miles, 2½ hours.

By bus: Greyhound and *Trailways* have year-round service, with extra buses in summer, foliage and ski seasons.

By train: Amtrak indirect route only: New York (or Boston via Springfield, Mass.) to White River Jct., Vt.; it's faster, cheaper, and easier to take the bus.

 HOW TO GET AROUND. Car rentals in Concord, Hanover, Keene, Laconia, Lebanon, Manchester, Nashua, North Conway and Portsmouth. There are good roads to all points of interest in New Hampshire, and sections of I–93 and I–89 are among America's most scenic highways. Availability of gasoline at 603-224-2525.

 TOURIST INFORMATION SERVICES. Maps, recreational calendars and pamphlets on special facilities and activities from *New Hampshire Office of Vacation Travel,* Box 856, Concord, NH 03301. Turnpike information booths at Dover, Hooksett, Hampton, Merrimack and Rochester toll plazas; tourist booths on various highways in summer. White Mountains News Bureau staffs Information Center daily, all year, at the jct. of Rtes. I–93 and I–3 in North Woodstock. In New York, the New England Vacation Center, 630 Fifth Ave., NYC 10020. The N.E. Innkeepers Assn. is headquartered at Box 4977, Hampton, NH 03842.

 SEASONAL EVENTS. *Antiques Shows:* Lebanon, early April, Amherst, Apr.-Oct.; New London, July; Wolfeboro, Aug.

Arts and Crafts: Annual Craftsmen's Fair, Mt. Sunapee State Park, early Aug.

Fairs: Belknap County 4-H Fair, Laconia, Aug.; *Plymouth State Fair,* late Aug.; *Rochester Fair,* Sept.; *Sandwich Fair,* Columbus Day.

Fall Foliage Festival, Warner, Oct.

Dartmouth Winter Carnival, Hanover, Feb. Ski jumping, hockey, ice sculpture, invitational Alpine and Nordic ski races.

Sports Events: Mud football in North Conway, early Sept.

 MUSEUMS AND GALLERIES. There are at least 25 in New Hampshire, ranging from antique autos to modern art. Portsmouth's *Strawberry Banke* is the most ambitious; other valuable historical collections are in Concord, Dover, Durham, Candia, Canaan, Manchester, Peterborough and Hampton. Art collections reward visitors in Hanover, Durham, Manchester, Sharon, Cornish, Keene, and Belmont-Laconia.

HISTORIC SITES. Write to the State Historical Commission in Concord for details on the state's 29 historic sites, including Daniel Webster's birthplace, near *Franklin;* the State Capital in *Concord;* the Franklin Pierce Homestead in *Hillsboro;* Shaker Village in *Canterbury;* Stonehenge in *North Salem; St. Gaudens* estate in Curnish; *Maxfield Parrish Museum and Estate* in Plainfield; and the colonial mansions of *Portsmouth*.

 TOURS. On Lake Winnipesaukee boat excursions may be boarded in season from Weirs Beach, Center Harbor, Wolfeboro, Alton Bay, Meredith, and Glendale. On Lake Sunapee there are cruises from Sunapee Harbor. From Portsmouth, July through September, cruises around the Isles of Shoals (reservations required). Saltwater fishing from Rye Harbor.

 DRINKING LAWS. State liquor stores are open Monday through Saturday; beer and wine are sold by grocers. Minimum age 20. Hotels, clubs and restaurants serve liquor by the drink in some towns, depending on local laws; minimum age 20.

 SUMMER SPORTS. New Hampshire has 18 miles of *seacoast,* over 1300 lakes and ponds for *boating* and 1500 miles of streams for *fishing*. Public beaches, piers, launching areas and boat rentals available on all major lakes. Marked *hiking* trails cover the state, especially in the White Mountains; the Appalachian Mountain Club sells a White Mountain Guide (AMC, 5 Joy St., Boston 02108) and issues a free pamphlet, AMC Huts System, giving details.

 WINTER SPORTS. Alpine ski season runs mid-Dec. to Easter, although big areas like Waterville Valley and Loon Mountain may open on Thanksgiving with snowmaking. Jackson has model cross-country system looping eastern side of Mt. Washington and environs; runs for 125 miles. Bretton Woods hosts 50km ski marathon late Jan., offers 50-plus miles of X-C trails, while Waterville Valley has been an annual stop on the alpine World Cup ski schedule in recent years.

 SPECTATOR SPORTS. These include *ski events, sled dog racing,* winter carnivals, *greyhound racing* at Seabrook, *bicycle racing* at Gunstock, *tennis* in early August in North Conway, *yacht racing* off New Castle, and *football* in the college towns of Durham, Hanover, Plymouth and Keene.

 WHAT TO DO WITH THE CHILDREN. Museums, playlands and theme parks are particularly abundant in the Lakes Region, at Weirs Beach. White Mountains region (Jefferson, No. Woodstock, Glen). The Mt. Washington Cog Railway is for *all* ages.

 SHOPPING. For the best in modern and traditional work, the shops of the League of New Hampshire Craftsmen are open all year in Concord, Exeter, Hanover, Nashua, and North Conway—in season elsewhere. Typical New Hampshire products available everywhere include maple syrup and sugar, colonial furniture, hand weaving, ceramics, herbs and spices, and specialty foods. Also check the factory outlets in North Conway, Lanconia and Manchester.

HOTELS AND MOTELS. Some New Hampshire hotels rival the scenery for magnificence. Some are very reasonable, including even housekeeping facilities. If you can, stay awhile; many resorts offer less expensive rates for longer stays. Others offer options that include some or all meals. Rates based on double occupancy, in season: *Deluxe,* $65 and up *Expensive,* $50–65; *Moderate,* $30–50; *Inexpensive,* $30 and under.

BEDFORD. (See also Manchester.) *Expensive:* **Sheraton-Wayfarer Motor Inn.** Handsome grounds, including waterfall, covered bridge. Fine dining and lounge. Indoor, outdoor pools, sauna.

BRETTON WOODS. *Deluxe:* **Mount Washington Hotel.** Large, renowned year-round resort in heart of White Mountain National Forest. Hotel, built in 1902, open only in warm weather.
   Moderate: **Lodge at BW.** Fancy name for nice motel, across the highway and open all year. Skiing in winter with summer fun including dancing, pools, tennis, riding, 18-hole golf course.

CONCORD. *Moderate–Expensive:* **Brick Tower Motor Inn.** Exit 12S off I–93. Restaurant, pool, sauna, cable TV (color).
   New Hampshire Highway Hotel. A few blocks from downtown. Colonial atmosphere. Restaurant, pool, bar, on-premises shops.

DIXVILLE NOTCH. *Deluxe:* **The Balsams.** Century-old resort with Moorish architecture in the woods, elegant accommodations, continental cuisine. Lounge entertainment. Outdoor sports all year.

EXETER. *Expensive:* **Exeter Inn.** Georgian setting, excellent dining.

FRANCONIA. *Moderate–Expensive:* **Lovett's by Lafayette Brook.** Restored 190-year-old inn, 2 cottages, motel. Comfortable family-owned resort with trout streams, pond, heated pool. Near ski areas. Open late June-mid-Oct.; late Dec.-Mar.
   The Homestead on Sugar Hill. Like going to visit grandmother. Comfortable, homelike inn with superb, hearty meals.

GLEN. *Moderate–Expensive:* **Storybook-Best Western Motor Inn.** Colonial inn main building & motel units. Restaurant, bar. Tennis, pool, sauna, cable TV (color).

HAMPTON AND HAMPTON BEACH. *Moderate–Expensive:* **Sheraton Motor Inn.** Early American furnishings, traditional New England food. Bar. Five minutes to Hampton Beach. Seasonal rates.
   Moderate **Town and Beach.** Some kitchen units. Restaurant near. Outdoor pool (heated). B & W TV.

HANOVER. *Deluxe:* **Hanover Inn.** A delightful blend of old and new, on Dartmouth Quadrangle, restaurant with children's menu. Coffee shop, lounge. Pets.
   Moderate: **Chieftain.** A small facility near Dartmouth College. Family rates and units. Continental breakfast.

INTERVALE. *Deluxe:* **The New England Inn.** Authentic 1809 colonial inn. Cottages. Outstanding Yankee cooking.

JACKSON. *Expensive:* **Christmas Farm Inn.** A small Colonial inn with recreation barn, swimming pool, putting green, on town's touring trail system in winter. See if you can get the Sugarhouse room.
   Moderate: **Eagle Mountain House.** An older, comfortable hotel on 400 acres overlooking Wildcat Valley. Sports, dancing, movies.

LACONIA. *Expensive:* **Christmas Island Resort Motel.** Medium-sized Lake Winnipesaukee motel with scenic view. Restaurant, bar, beach, pool, color cable TV.

Moderate: **The Anchorage.** Housekeeping units. Beaches, boating, canoeing, sailing. Open mid-may to mid-Oct.

LINCOLN-NORTH WOODSTOCK. *Deluxe:* **Jack O'Lantern Resort.** Motel and cottages. Pool, playground, restaurant, bar. Golf. Entertainment, dancing. Free transportation from bus station. Open mid-May–mid-Oct.

Moderate–Expensive: **Beacon Motel.** Motel and cottages. Three pools (2 heated outdoor, 1 indoor). Tasty family fare for dinner in 2 restaurants. Cable TV (color).

Moderate: **Parker's Motel.** Nestled in woods at the entrance to Franconia Notch, halfway between Loon and Cannon Mountain ski areas.

MANCHESTER. (See also Bedford.) *Expensive:* **Howard Johnson's.** Queen City Ave. Pool, sauna, entertainment. 24-hr. restaurant; bar.

NORTH CONWAY. *Expensive–Deluxe:* **Red Jacket Motor Inn.** Main St. Modern resort on 22-acre hilltop setting. Air-conditioned, indoor and outdoor swimming and tennis, 2 lounges, 2 dining rooms. Game room, saunas.

Stonehurst. Restored mansion that oozes class and elegance. Excellent dining, plus tennis, pool, color cable TV, and marvelous wooded grounds.

Expensive: **Eastern Slope Inn.** Recently refurbished with restaurant and lounge. Sports packages for summer, winter.

Forest Glen Inn. Country inn in beautiful setting. Excellent sports.

Moderate: **Scottish Lion.** One of the early bed-and-breakfasts. Homey touch. Pint-size pub, imports shop.

White Trellis Motel. Nothing fancy, just clean, cozy, and close to everything. Cable TV.

PORTSMOUTH. *Expensive:* **Anchorage.** Pool, sauna. Restaurant near.

Moderate: **Inn at Christian Shore.** Federal-era home with plenty of period pieces. Breakfast included.

Hoyt's Lodges. Beachfront kitchenettes. Open late May to mid-Oct.

RYE AND RYE BEACH. *Moderate–Expensive:* **Orwood Lodge.** Small motel and cottages, nr. restaurants and shops.

Seafarer. Modern, small motel and housekeeping cottages overlooking ocean. Continental breakfast.

WATERVILLE VALLEY. *Expensive:* **Snowy Owl Inn.** No restaurant, but it's got everything else, including sauna, pool, game room, whirlpool and handsome fieldstone fireplace.

WEIRS BEACH. *Moderate:* **Lakeside Hotel and Motel.** Large family hotel, with cottages and kitchenettes, private beach at Lake Winnipesaukee.

St. Moritz Terrace Motel & Chalets. Rooms and efficiency family units with lovely view of lake. Beach.

Inexpesnive: **Hi Spot Motor Court.** Small, with private beach. Housekeeping cottages.

WHITEFIELD. *Deluxe:* **Mountain View House.** Distinguished resort on 300 acres. Superb cuisine. Heated pool. Golf, tennis. Pets.

WOLFEBORO: *Moderate:* **Clearwater Lodges.** Housekeeping cottages on lake. Beach, water sports. Game room.

DINING OUT. The clear mountain air or a visit to the coast stirs a hunger in most visitors. Fortunately, New Hampshire can dish up tasty food aplenty. Not just seafood and New England fare, though; there's plenty of international cuisine to go with the lobster, steak, turkey, ducklings, and home-made baked goods. The price ranges used are: *Expensive:* $25 (and up); *Moderate:* $10–25; *Inexpensive:* under $10. Of course, meals ordered à la carte will cost more. Listings are in order of price ranges.

ALTON BAY. *Moderate-Expensive:* **William Tell Restaurant.** Rte. 11—West Alton. Excellent Swiss cuisine.

BARTLETT. *Moderate:* **W.W. Doolittle's.** Lively scene, fine meals of steak, seafood, fowl.

BETHLEHEM. *Moderate:* **Wayside Inn.** Continental cuisine.

CLAREMONT. *Moderate-Expensive:* **Annie McCassar's.** Relaxed, leafy atmosphere; macramé shades. Menu is just as enjoyable—recommended: veal.

CONCORD. *Moderate:* **Brick Tower.** Open for breakfast, lunch, and dinner; Sat. night buffet. Seafood and steaks specialties, but nice selection of other dishes.

EXETER. *Moderate:* **Exeter Inn.** Popular restaurant open from breakfast daily. No lunch served. Specialties are seafood and steak. Bar.

FRANCONIA. *Moderate–Expensive:* **Lovett's by Lafayette Brook.** Gracious and delectable dining in delightful Colonial atmosphere. Desserts especially worth noting. Jacket and tie requested for the gents at dinner. Reservations suggested.
     Horse and Hound Inn. Tranquil surroundings; award-winning cuisine. Suggested: beef bourguignonne. Wide, wide wine selection, too.

GLEN. *Expensive-Moderate:* **Bernerhof Inn.** European cuisine with cheese and wine on top of tasty veal, great schnitzel.
     Moderate: **Red Parka Pub.** Heavy on the steaks and seafood. Very active apres-ski scene.

HANOVER. *Expensive:* **Jesse's.** Oversized log cabin with big-city prices for tasty steaks and seafood; worth a try; steak teriyaki and Alaskan king crab.
     Moderate: **Peter Christian's.** Wooden decor. Terrific soups, sandwiches, stews—but leave room for dessert.

INTERVALE. *Moderate:* **Anna Martin's at N.E. Inn.** Continental flare in Yankee country. Fine fish dinners.

JACKSON. *Expensive:* **Christmas Farm Inn.** Heavy on the homemade goodies (soups, breads, etc.). First-rate beef, especially prime ribs.
     Moderate: **Wildcat Tavern.** Across from the golf course. Excellent spot. Scampi is worth noting.

LACONIA. *Moderate:* **Hickory Stick Farm.** Country-style roast duckling and beef are specialties of this converted farmhouse. Open Memorial Day–Columbus Day.
     Mr. Turnip's Steakhouse. Sandwiches at lunchtime, dinner is heavy on the beef and haddock dishes.

LITTLETON. *Moderate:* **Clam Shell.** Seafood and more seafood, from shrimp to sole scallops.

MANCHESTER. *Moderate.* **The Millyard.** Steak and seafood in an old woolen mill building.

MEREDITH. *Moderate:* **Hart's Turkey Farm.** Specializes in family-style turkey dinners with home-grown birds, but has varied menu & take-out orders.

NASHUA. *Moderate-Expensive:* **Chart House.** Nashua Dr. Housed in a 1919 hydroelectric plant overlooking a waterfall on Nashua River. Seafood and prime rib. Bar, lounge.
Green Ridge Turkey Farm. Besides turkey raised on local farm, you will find chops, roast beef, seafood. Entertainment, dancing.

NEW LONDON. *Moderate:* **Peter Christian's.** "Brother" to same-name restaurant in Hanover. Same good sandwiches, atmosphere, and desserts.
Millstone Restaurant. Far–reaching menu but seafood coquille rates a mention.

NORTH CONWAY. *Expensive:* **Stonehurst.** One of the finest restaurants in the state. Elegance of the restoration carries over to excellent cuisine. 3 dining rooms and, among other things, 11 different veal dishes.
Moderate: **Barnaby's.** Reputation as a steakhouse, but veal and seafood are good too.
Horsefeathers. Good "Yuppies" place. Spinach and lamb salad is unrivaled. Ditto for Back Bar Mixed Grille.
Snug Harbor. Nautical corner in the middle of the mountains. Seafood galore with a couple of steak dishes, too. Closed Tues.

NORTH WOODSTOCK. *Inexpensive:* **Truants Taverne.** Academic environs (circa 1850). Superb sandwiches. Get there early before pie disappears.

PLYMOUTH. *Moderate:* **Tobey's.** Specializing in New England dishes such as chicken pie, Yankee pot roast, and homemade pastries. Wine list.

PORTSMOUTH. *Expensive:* **Blue Strawberry.** Reservations a must for this gourmet's dream. So good it has its own cookbook.
Moderate-Expensive: **Flagstone's.** Early American decor. Seafood, prime rib.
The Oar House. Former warehouse converted into first-rate eatery. Seafood, of course, and good veal.
Moderate: **Clarence's Chowder House.** You can fill up on a different chowder each day but Sun.

WATERVILLE VALLEY. *Expensive:* **William Tell Restaurant.** Rte. 49, Thornton. Superb Swiss cuisine. Schnitzel and veal are top dishes.
Moderate–Expensive: **O'Keefe's.** Village center. Relaxing fireside dining, with the emphasis on steak and seafood dishes.
Inexpensive: **Finish Line.** At tennis courts. Fine lunch stop. Big burgers, bigger fries. Italian dinners.
Valley Inn & Tavern. Village center. Focus on prime rib. Fine seafood, too.

WOLFEBORO. *Expensive:* **Wolfeboro Inn.** A Colonial atmosphere and regional menu. Baking on the premises. Bar. Children's portions.
Moderate: **Lakeview Inn & Motor Lodge.** Distinctive food served in Early American dining room. Salad and relish buffet. Bar.

RHODE ISLAND

Newport, Block Island, and Providence

Colonial Newport, founded in 1639, is one of New England's most fascinating towns. The first Quakers in America settled here in 1657. Sephardic Jews came in the following year, establishing a center of Jewish culture which has endured for three centuries. With its salubrious climate and splendid bluffs overlooking the sea, Newport became the first American resort. Wealthy merchants came here for the summer as early as 1720. The resort reached its apogee at the end of the 19th century, in the extravagant and tax-free "Gilded Age," when such wealthy families as the Vanderbilts, Astors, Belmonts, Berwinds and Fishes built a series of "cottages" along Bellevue Avenue. The cottages were often full-size, 70-room imitations of Italian palaces and French châteaux, aglitter with imported crystal chandeliers, mirrored walls, rose-colored marble, mosaic floors, gilded woodwork, and every conceivable sign of conspicuous consumption. Many of these opulent residences are now open to the public as "museum mansions." Considered the most stunning is "The Breakers," originally designed for Cornelius Vanderbilt. First among the Bellevue Avenue estates is "The Elms," built for the late E.J. Berwind, Philadelphia coal magnate, by Horace Trumbauer, and known for its French garden and arboretum. William K. Vanderbilt's "Marble House," also known as the "Sumptuous Palace by the Sea" and the "Chateau-sur-Mer," are two other Bellevue Avenue museum cottages to ogle. Oliver Hazard Perry Belmont's [a descendant of Commodore Perry] "Belcourt Castle" contains possibly the world's largest private collection of stained glass. Finally, there's Rosecliff, a mansion designed by Stanford White that was the setting for the motion picture "The Great Gatsby," and in 1978, "The Betsy," and Kingscote, a charming Victorian cottage.

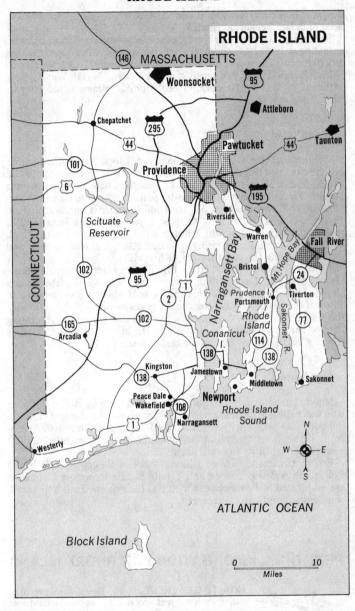

RHODE ISLAND

MASSACHUSETTS

Woonsocket

Attleboro

Chepachet

Pawtucket

Taunton

Providence

CONNECTICUT

Scituate Reservoir

Riverside

Warren

Fall River

Bristol

Mt. Hope Bay

Prudence I.
Portsmouth

Tiverton

Rhode Island

Arcadia

Conanicut

Sakonnet R.

Kingston

Jamestown

Middletown

Sakonnet

Peace Dale
Wakefield

Newport

Narragansett

Rhode Island Sound

Westerly

N
W — E
S

ATLANTIC OCEAN

Block Island

0 — 10
Miles

Even with the seeming worship of opulence, the town is not without religious landmarks. Trinity Church, built in 1726, with its three-tier, wine-glass pulpit and well-preserved wooden structure has been called a supreme and matchless wonder of Colonial America. Newport also has America's oldest Seventh Day Baptist Church, built in 1729, and America's oldest synagogue, constructed in 1763. Touro Synagogue, designed by Peter Harrison, is done in Georgian style but modified to accommodate Sephardic ritual.

Returning to the secular world, other must-sees are: Hunter House, a National Historic Landmark; the Newport Casino, home of the International Lawn Tennis Hall of Fame; the Old Colony House; White Horse Tavern, America's oldest tavern; Naval War College Museum; and, in Portsmouth, Green Animals, a famous topiary garden.

Block Island

About nine miles south of the mainland, Block Island is a summer beach resort and fishing center. Visitors spend many pleasant hours on Block Island State Beach or at the resorts where privately owned beaches are at the disposal of guests. Some deep-sea fishing for tuna, bluefish, cod, swordfish, striped bass and flounder is another interest. At the southeastern corner of the island, you can see Mohegan Bluffs, spectacular cliffs of clay, which bear a strong resemblance to the chalk cliffs of Dover, England, rising to about 180 feet above sea level and stretching along the coast for about five miles.

Whittier's poem "The Palatine Light" commemorates the Palatine Graves area near Dickens Point, where the crew of an ill-fated Dutch ship lie buried. A man-made harbor, New Harbor, graces the western shore of the island. It was constructed by connecting the Atlantic with the Great Salt Pond by means of a channel dug across the separating narrow barrier of land. Old Harbor, on the other side of the island, is where a small fishing fleet and pleasure boats dock.

Providence

Rhode Island's capital city was founded in 1636 by Roger Williams who was banished from Massachusetts for his non-conformist views on religion. Two years later he founded the First Baptist Church in America. It is the oldest church of any denomination in the state, and has been preserved in its Colonial form.

Brown University, Rhode Island School of Design, Rhode Island College, Providence College, and Trinity Square Repertory Company, are all located in Providence, which has become the State's financial, commercial, and cultural center.

PRACTICAL INFORMATION FOR RHODE ISLAND

HOW TO GET THERE. *By air:* Providence is served by major carriers, with connecting limousine service to major destinations. *By car:* New York to Providence via the New England Thruway (I–95). For the Narragansett seashore, exit at Connecticut Rte. 2 to R.I. Rte. 78 and follow U.S.1 to R.I. Rte. 108. Signs mark routes to Jamestown and Newport bridges.

By rail: Providence is served by *Amtrak.* From New York, 4 hrs; Boston, 1 hr.

By bus: Greyhound and *Bonanza.*

By ferry: To Block Island from New London, Conn., Providence and Newport R.I., mid-June to about Labor Day. From Galilee (Point Judith), year-round.

HOW TO GET AROUND. *By air:* Scheduled shuttle and charter service from Providence, Westerly, Newport and Block Island. *By car:* I–95 goes diagonally from southwest Conn. line through Providence to the Mass. border. U.S. Rte. 6 runs east-west. State 1A is the scenic highway. U.S. 1 from Westerly to Providence is on the Americana Trail and part of the New England Heritage Trail. *Car rentals:* Available at Providence airport, Newport, Warwick, Woonsocket, Block Island, Watch Hill and Westerly. *By bus:* Local service throughout the state. *By ferry:* Daily from Galilee to Block Island, and to Prudence Island from Portsmouth (Melville) and Bristol.

TOURIST INFORMATION SERVICES. The Rhode Island Department of Economic Development, 7 Jackson Walkway, Providence, R.I. 02903, supplies reams of tourist information. Information, licenses and permits for state parks and fishing streams from Division of Parks and Recreation, Dept. of Environmental Management, 83 Park St., Providence. Almost every town has its own chamber of commerce, some with visitor centers. The state maintains a visitor information center year-round at the Theodore Francis Green State Airport.

SEASONAL EVENTS. One of the most important is Rhode Island Heritage Month, the annual May celebration commemorating the state's declaration of independence from Britain. Galilee is the base of several deep-sea sportsfishing tournaments for sword, shark and giant bluefin tuna, with other major tournaments being held at Pawtuxet, Newport, and Block Island. The Newport Motor Car Festival is held in the middle of June, and the Narragansett Auto Fair at the end of July. Newport has a steady stream of yachting events. Block Island Week Sailing Regatta is held in late June on odd-numbered years—the East Coast's largest yachting event. In even-numbered years a cruising class week is held in late June. The month-long "Christmas in Newport" is now an annual event.

MUSEUMS AND GALLERIES. In Bristol, Haffenreffer Museum of Anthropology. In East Greenwich, the Varnum Military & Naval Museum. The Fire Museum, in Jamestown. In Newport, The International Lawn Tennis Hall of Fame and Tennis Museum. In Peace Dale, the Museum of Primitive Culture. Slater Mill Historic Site, Pawtucket. Tomaquag Valley Indian Memorial Museum, in Arcadia, includes a trading post, a nature trail and ceremonial programs. For Newport mansions and castles, consult The Preservation Society of Newport County, 118 Mill St. Reduced combination tickets are available at their mansions.

HISTORIC SITES. History, Providence and Roger Williams have been synonymous since he stepped ashore in 1636. The Roger Williams Rock at Power, Williams and Gano Sts., the Roger Williams Spring at N. Main St. (now included in the currently developing Roger Williams National Memorial), the First Baptist Meeting House in America, and the Roger Williams Memorial all commemorate the founder. Historic homes in Providence include that of Stephen Hopkins, a signer of the Declaration of Independence, and the John Brown House, once visited by George Washington. The State House, which boasts the second-largest unsupported marble dome in the world, houses Gilbert Stuart's full-length portrait of George Washington. Newport has its share of historic landmarks, including the Brick Market, in Washington Square; the Newport Historical Society and Marine Museum; the Redwood Library, the oldest library room in continuous use in the United States; and the Naval War College Museum. The nation's oldest Quaker Great Meeting House (1699) has recently been restored. The Babcock-Smith House, Westerly, was often visited by Benjamin Franklin.

TOURS. Viking Tours of Newport highlights at least 150 points of interest, including the 10-mile Ocean Drive and a visit to a mansion. Arrangements are made for groups and parties. Viking also conducts walking tours of Newport. Viking and Newport Harbor Tours give tours of the historic waterfront and United Tours feature Newport and vicinity.

GARDENS. Formal *Sunken Garden* at The Elms in Newport, with labeled trees and shrubs, is modeled after the Chateau d'Asnieres near Paris. The famous "Green Animals," Portsmouth, is considered one of the best topiary gardens in the country. *Roger Williams Park,* Providence, is noted for its Japanese garden. *Blithewold Gardens & Arboretum,* Bristol.

DRINKING LAWS. Minimum age is 21. Package stores closed Sun.

SUMMER SPORTS. *Swimming:* Good beaches are always nearby in Rhode Island. Recommended state beaches are Scarborough State Beach, Roger W. Wheeler State Beach, at Narragansett; Misquamicut, at Westerly; and Block Island State Beach. *Fishing:* Fishing tournaments are sponsored by some sea-coast towns. Charter boats available for big game fish, the biggest fleets found at Galilee and Jerusalem. Skiff rentals also obtainable. License required only for fresh water.

HOTELS. Accommodations range from family-style cottages to luxurious seaside resorts. Price ranges are based on double occupancy, peak season, EP. Listings for price ranges: *Deluxe:* $100 and up; *Expensive:* $75–$100; *Moderate:* $50–75; *Inexpensive:* under $50. There are not many places that charge less than $50 in summer season.

BLOCK ISLAND. *Expensive:* **1661 House.** Near Old Harbor, overlooks the Ocean.
    Moderate: **Ballard's Inn.** Popular. Dining room and bar.
    Surf Hotel. Home-like atmosphere, cooking.
    Inexpensive: **Narragansett Inn,** Airy, pleasant hotel and annex overlooking New Harbor.

NEWPORT. *Deluxe:* **The Inn at Castle Hill.** On Ocean Drive. A former mansion.
    Treadway Inn. In center of historic wharf district.
    Sheraton-Islander Inn. On Goat Island. A resort facility.
    Expensive: **Howard Johnson's Motor Lodge.** Well-known chain.
    The Inn on the Harbor. Time-sharing facility.
    Moderate: **Guest House Association of Newport County.** Near Newport, in Jamestown, **Bay Voyage Inn.**
    SeaView Motel. Aquidneck Ave.
    Inexpensive: **Budget Motor Inn, Pine Motel, Gateway Motel,** all on Route 114.

PROVIDENCE. *Deluxe:* **Biltmore Plaza Hotel.** Dorrance St. Landmark hotel, reopened in 1979 after $14-million renovation. Outside elevator.
    Marriott Inn Providence. Charles & Orms Sts. All the amenities associated with this fine chain, including an indoor pool connecting to an outdoor pool.
    Expensive: **Holiday Inn Downtown.** 21 Atwells Ave. Heated pool, restaurant, bar. Center of city. Adjoins Providence Civic Center.
    Moderate: **Wayland Manor.** 500 Angell St. Bar, dining room. Near to shopping.

RESTAURANTS. *Expensive:* $20 and up; *Moderate:* $10–20; *Inexpensive:* under $10. Prices are for a complete meal but do not include drinks, tax or tip.

BLOCK ISLAND. *Inexpensive:* **Finn's.** Water Street. Cozy atmosphere, good chowders.

Barone's Restaurant. Water Street. Featuring Italian dishes.

Cat 'n' Fiddle. Beach Street. Rustic decor, serves dinners year round.

NEWPORT. *Expensive:* **Clarke Cooke House.** Exceptional seafood, excellent French cuisine in lovely restaurant on Bowen's Wharf.

La Petite Auberge. 19 Charles St., excellent French cuisine, very good frogs legs and Chateaubriand for two.

The Pier, Christie's, Black Pearl, and **Frick's,** which features excellent continental cuisine, all on or off Thames St.

White Horse Tavern. Farewell & Marlborough St., oldest tavern in America (1673). Seafood, steak.

Moderate: **The Chart House.** Bowen's Wharf. Steak, lobster and terrific prime rib.

La Gourmandise. 136 Thames St., and **Cappuccino's,** 92 William Street. Tea and expresso with very good French pastry.

The Mooring. Sayer's Wharf on Newport harbor, off America's Cup Ave. Former New York Yacht Club Station No. 6; steak, seafood, sandwiches, salads, nautical theme, patio and deck on the water.

Inexpensive: **Mack's.** 117 Long Wharf. Ideal for families.

PROVIDENCE. *Expensive:* **Capriccio.** 2 Pine St. European cuisine, elegant decor.

L'Apogee. atop Biltmore Plaza Hotel. Continental cuisine combined with spectacular view of Providence.

Pot au Feu. 44 Custom House St. Serves good French cuisine.

Moderate: **Camille's Roman Gardens.** 71 Bradford St. The best Italian restaurant in town.

City Lights. 4 Davol Square. A shopping arcade converted from a rubber factory.

Near Providence, in Bristol, try the **Lobster Pot** for a Rhode Island Shore Dinner, specialty of the state, or **Rocky Point,** Warwick, where clambakes have been served since the 1840s.

VERMONT

Green Mountains, Ski Heaven

Vermont is primarily rural; its man-made attractions are small in scale, graceful, and scattered. Only Burlington has a population over 25,000, and the charm of this state for the tourist will lie in the way its historical and cultural heritage, its natural setting and recreational facilities, and the life of its people today all interpenetrate to form an inseparable whole, something unique in America. In 1970 the state enacted this country's most comprehensive and stringent development control law, to save the harmony and balance that make Vermont a handsome mix of mountains and valleys, woodlands and open spaces.

Anywhere you drive in Vermont you will find rewarding scenery, but some of the best is in the 40 state parks and 34 state forests (information, maps, reservations, etc., from the Department of Forests, Parks and Recreation, Montpelier, 05602). Mt. Mansfield State Forest, near Burlington, surrounds Vermont's highest mountain (4,393 feet). Allis State Park, south of Montpelier, is well equipped for recreation; Monroe State Park is a bird, plant, and game sanctuary; and Emerald Lake State Park in Dorset has swimming and boating on a lake of unusual beauty. The department operates 35 public campgrounds with 2,200 campsites, 33 State Recreation Areas, and 13 major state beaches. There are also 73 private campgrounds.

The Green Mountain National Forest, in central and southern Vermont, comprises 293,376 acres and is served by US 4, US 7, Rtes. 11 and 100. Twelve of Vermont's leading ski areas are within it, including famous names like Mt. Snow, Bromley, Sugarbush Valley, Sugarbush North, and Stratton Mountain. Summer camping, hunting, hiking on the 263-mile Long Trail and fishing in 3,233 acres of ponds and 349 miles of streams add to the attractions of the landscape.

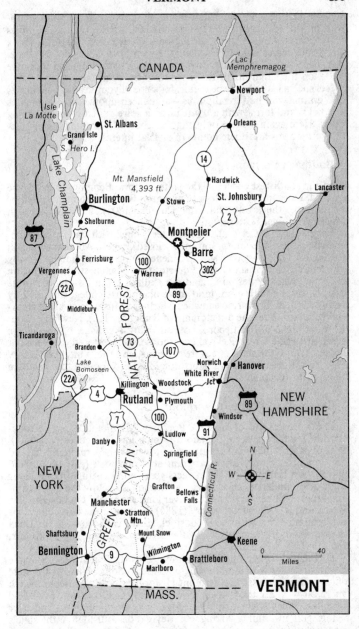

Particularly scenic sights are: the Mt. Equinox Skyline Toll Road near Manchester in the Southwest; Brandon Gap, a 2,170-foot-high mountain pass north of Rutland; the 163-foot-deep Quechee Gorge near White River Junction; the toll road to the top of Mt. Mansfield;

Lincoln Gap, a 2,424-foot-high mountain pass about 30 miles south-west of Montpelier and nearby Granville Gulf Reservation, "six miles of wilderness forever"; the Burlington–Port Kent or Charlotte–Essex ferry rides across Lake Champlain; the view from 3,861-foot Jay Peak, just south of the Canadian border (aerial tram to the top); and McIndoe Falls, on the Connecticut River south of St. Johnsbury.

Yet such a list can only be unfair, for some of your loveliest memories of Vermont will be serendipitous—a chanced-upon harmony of hills and fields and forest with a white church spire or red barn set among them. Here again we can only suggest a few of Vermont's many pic-turesque towns and their points of special interest.

Southern Vermont

In the southwest corner of the state, historic Bennington has a fine regional museum, the 306-foot Bennington Battle Monument (elevator to the top), the lovely Old First Church (1805), Park-McCullough House (National Historic Site).

Farther north, Rte. 7 into Manchester is lined with stately old homes and the large old Equinox Inn (now closed), where Abraham Lincoln stayed; his son's 24-room estate, Hildene, is open to the public. Nearby Dorset's elegance is simpler and quieter than Manchester's, and its inn is at the town's center on a handsome village green. Marlboro, to the east, is the site both of an innovative liberal arts college and, in July and August, of the world-renowned Marlboro Music Festival (15 week-end concerts under the directorship of Rudolf Serkin). Newfane, about 12 miles north of Brattleboro, is another lovely village; on the village green are a fine Greek Revival courthouse, well-restored old Vermont homes, two of the state's finest restaurants, and the Windham County Historical Society Museum. North on Rte. 35, Grafton, too, has been restored to its colonial elegance.

Central and Northern Vermont

In the central part of the state, Poultney, Middleton Springs, Castle-ton (on Lake Bomoseen), Pittsford (which has four covered bridges), Weston, and Windsor all are attractive towns with Vermont flavor; and the community restoration program at Woodstock (east of Rutland and toward Hanover, N. H.) attracts year-round visitors from all over the world. Galleries, antique shops, boutiques occupy the eighteenth- and nineteenth-century houses. Power lines are buried out of sight. The Romanesque-style public library (1885) has one of the best collections in Vermont, along with the Woodstock Historical Society, in the Dana House. Four of Vermont's eight Paul Revere bells are in Woodstock, too.

Farther north, Montpelier is dominated by the State House, a simple Doric structure with an imposing gold-leafed dome. Nearby, the state office building houses the Vermont Historical Society Museum. North and a bit west are the two ski mountains of the Stowe–Mt. Mansfield complex. Most of the area's 65 lodges stay open summers and offer tennis, golf, swimming, hiking, etc. Beyond lies Burlington, the state's largest city (population about 40,000). In 1842 Charles Dickens called it "an exquisite achievement of neatness, elegance and order." Parts of it still are. The Fleming Museum of the University of Vermont has a fine collection of American, ancient, and Oriental art; the city has fine views over Lake Champlain, and in July and August there is the Champlain Shakespeare Festival. There are a number of historic site markers throughout the city.

Don't miss the Shelburne Museum, a 100-acre park containing 35 historic buildings brought here from all parts of the state to house an enormous and top-quality collection of American art, folk art, folk craft, and technology—samples of architecture, furniture, household articles, toys, quilts, carriages, farm implements, smithing and wood-working tools, country stores, a locomotive, a 220-ft. sidewheel steamer —and even an old lighthouse—tens of thousands of articles beautifully displayed. A full visit is at least a two-day project; if your time is short, go directly to your special interest.

Main points of interest in the Northeast Kingdom (Essex, Orange, Caledonia counties) are St. Johnsbury; Danville, site of a dowsers' convention in mid-September; the Jay Peak winter and summer sports area; the scenic valley of the Connecticut River; and the largely un-spoiled quality of the entire region.

PRACTICAL INFORMATION FOR VERMONT

HOW TO GET THERE. *By air:* The major airport is at Burlington, served by *United* (from Chicago), *Air North, USAir* and *Command Airways. Precision Airlines* serves Rutland, Springfield and two border airports in New Hampshire, Keene (near Brattleboro) and Lebanon (near White River Junction).

By car: From New York take the Thruway to Exit 24 to Rte. 7. Out of Troy, Rte. 7 to the Vermont border, at which point it becomes Rte. 9. I–91 from New Haven, Connecticut, through Massachusetts to southeastern Vermont.

By bus: Greyhound buses operate to Vermont out of other states.

By train: Amtrak has two daily trains from Montreal and Washington. For further information contact any Amtrak office.

HOW TO GET AROUND. There are general aviation facilities at Bennington, Stowe, Mt. Snow, Basin Harbor-Champlain, Middlebury, Springfield, Lyndonville, Newport, and Highgate Springs. *Air taxi* service available at Barre-Montpelier, Bennington, Springfield, Rutland, Middlebury, and Burlington. For information on weather conditions, contact the National Weather Service at Burlington International Airport, Burlington, Vt. 05401, tel: 802-862-2475.

By car: I–89 and I–91 allow swift traffic through much of the state. I–91 enters Vermont in the southeastern-most corner and exits to Canada at Derby, Vt. I–89 picks up at White River Junction (where it connects to I–91) and proceeds northwest, through Randolph, Montpelier, Burlington, and St. Albans. Both highways are surrounded by luxurious landscapes and startling mountains. For information on road conditions, contact the Vermont Agency of Transportation, Montpelier, Vt. 05602, tel: 802-828-2585.

Car rental: At the Burlington, Rutland, and Springfield airports, Bennington, Brattleboro, Middlebury, White River Junction, and Montpelier.

By bus: Vermont Transit Lines has extensive bus routes throughout the state, connecting with *Greyhound* in other states.

By bicycle: The roads of Vermont are well traveled by hostelers and those just out for a day trip; 10-speed bikes easily negotiate the steep grades of Vermont's roads. Send $1 to the Vermont Department of Forests, Parks and Recreation, Montpelier, 05602, for their complete guide to bicycle touring.

TOURIST INFORMATION SERVICES. Travel suggestions mailed free by the *Vermont Travel Division,* 134 State St., Montpelier, 05602. Literature is also available from Vermont Attractions, Box 1284, Montpelier, 05602; Northeastern Vermont Development Association, Box 640, St. Johnsbury, 05819; Stowe Area Association, Stowe, 05672. Vermont Transit Co., Inc., 135 St. Paul St., Burlington, 05401, has information on bus service. Lake Champlain Transportation Co., King St. Dock, Burlington, 05401, will send information on Lake Champlain ferry service. Write the Dept. of Forests, Parks, and Recreation, Montpelier, 05602, for information on forests. Vermont Association of Private Campground Owners & Operators, Box 214, Middlebury, 05753, has information about private campgrounds. Long-trail hiking information can be obtained from the Green Mountain Club, Inc., P.O. Box 889, 43 State St., Montpelier, Vt. 05602. For information about the Appalachian Trail write the Appalachian Trail Conference, Box 236, Harpers Ferry, W. Va. 25425. In New York City, the New England Vacation Center is at 630 Fifth Ave., New York, N.Y. 10020. In Montreal the Vermont Information Center is at 2051 Peel St.

Within Vermont there are official information stations on I–91 at Guilford, Putney, Westminster, White River Junction, Bradford, Lyndonville and Coventry. On I–89 they are at Fairfax, Georgia, Williston, Randolph, Sharon and Highgate Springs. On Rte. 4 at Fair Haven, and at Waterford on I–93.

For a complete listing of lodgings, restaurants and attractions, write to the Vermont State Chamber of Commerce, Box 37, Montpelier, Vt. 05602 and ask for *Vermont's Gazetteer.*

SEASONAL EVENTS. In general, for schedules and details of any of the following events, write to the *Vermont Travel Division,* 134 State St., Montpelier, Vermont 05602.

During the winter months, *skiing* is the most popular pursuit. Until recently, alpine skiing was the heavy favorite; however, cross-country skiing, or ski touring, is fast catching up. The ski season usually begins in November and ends in early April. Ski races, demonstrations, and cross-country meets take place through the winter, as do winter carnivals held at Stowe and Ludlow (both mid-Jan.), Brattleboro (mid-Feb.), St. Albans, Mt. Snow, and Middlebury College. The state and various localities have set aside clearly marked areas for *snowmobiling.*

The *Vermont Symphony Orchestra* tours the state during the winter. The *Vermont Farm Show* is held in Barre in late January.

In the spring, the major event is *sugaring off;* and the Vermont Maple Festival at St. Albans is the main celebration, with folk music and dancing, parades, a flea market, art and craft shows, an ice review, and much more, early April; for details write to the Director, Vermont Maple Festival, Chamber of Commerce, Box 109, St. Albans, Vermont 05478. There is also a festival at Fairfax the first weekend of April. And in late March, in Burlington, there is an Annual Maple Sugar Square Dance Festival.

Summer brings antiques, art and craft shows and demonstrations around the state. Participating artists are both native and out-of-state people. In July, Newbury has a *Cracker Barrel Bazaar,* and Barre holds its annual *Ethnic Festival.* Castleton celebrates *Colonial Day* and has open house in midsummer. The *Fleming Art Museum* and the *Southern Vermont Art Center,* in Burlington and Manchester respectively, host impressive exhibits. A Mozart Festival is held in Burlington in July and August. The *Annual Antique and Classic Car Show* in Stowe in mid-August and in Bennington on the second weekend in September.

One of the most exciting events is the series of concerts given by the *Marlboro Music Festival* at Marlboro College during July and August. The *Champlain Shakespeare Festival,* staged by professionals, begins in August and runs through October in the *University of Vermont's Royall Tyler Theatre,* Burlington. Summer stock is presented at several theaters, notably the *Dorset Playhouse* and the *Weston Playhouse.*

Aquatic competitions are held during the summer on Lake Champlain and on many of the state's 400 lakes. Outing and canoe clubs sponsor *slalom championships* on West River, Jamaica, in May. There are numerous horse shows throughout the state. A favorite event of those staged by the *Green Mountain*

Horse Association of South Woodstock is the *100-Mile Trail Ride,* which originates at South Woodstock during the last weekend in August.

For golf enthusiasts, the *Vermont State Open Golf Tournament* is held at Lake Morey Inn, Fairlee, in June. Stratton Mtn. hosts the *Volvo International Tennis Tourney* in early August.

Fall harvest and the turning of the leaves inspire festivals in all parts of Vermont. The beginning of the Fall country fair season is the *Connecticut Valley Fair* at Bradford in late July. Some fairs are held in August before vacationers leave the state. For example, the *Addison County Field Days* are held in New Haven in August and feature horse shows and cattle judging. Others are held in September and October to celebrate the bountiful harvest. A week-long *State Fair* is held in Rutland in September. Danville holds its annual *Dowsing Convention* in September. Montpelier has a *Square Dance Festival* in October and a *Statewide Crafts Fair* on Columbus Day weekend. Community programs are planned around the brilliant foliage displays, and bus tours around the state visit these. An outstanding regional festival is the *Fall Foliage Festival of the Northeast Kingdom,* involving the villages of Walden, Cabot, Plainfield, Peacham, Barnet and Groton, held in early October. There is one full day of activities in each of the participating towns: auctions, square dances and country music, hikes, bazaars, craft demonstrations, hymn sings, tours, local cooking, and more. For details, and reservations (advisable), write to the Fall Festival Committee, Box 38, Danville, Vermont 05873.

An Oktoberfest is held in Stowe in early October. The *Stratton Mountain Arts Festival* continues from mid-September to mid-October, with fine arts, crafts and performing arts all represented. For schedules, write to the Director, Stratton Arts Festival Office, Stratton Mt., Vermont 05155.

 MUSEUMS AND GALLERIES. Vermont's historic, cultural, and artistic memorabilia are preserved in 25 museums: the *Bennington Museum,* on West Main St. Weston, on the common, the *Farrar-Mansur House;* the *Shelburne Museum,* US 7, in Shelburne, 4100 acres of Americana; *Peter Matteson Tavern Museum,* East Rd., Shaftsbury; *Brattleboro Museum and Art Center; Sheldon Museum,* Middlebury; *Walker Museum,* US 5, Fairlee; *Bixby Library Museum,* 258 Main St., Vergennes; *Wilson Castle,* off Rte. 4, Proctor; *Vermont Wildflower Farm,* Rte. 7, Charlotte.

 HISTORICAL SOCIETIES. *Vermont Historical Society Museum,* Pavilion Office Bldg., Montpelier, Vt. 05602; *Grafton Historical Museum; E. Poultney Historical Society Museum; Dana House,* 26 Elm St., Woodstock; *Barre Historical Society Museum,* Washington St.; *Brookfield Historical Society Museum; Rokeby,* US 7, Ferrisburg; *Windham County Historical Society,* Newfane; *Peacham Historical Society Museum; Bennington Museum,* West Main Street, Old Bennington.

  ART MUSEUMS. *Wood Art Gallery,* 135 Main St., Montpelier; *Fleming Museum,* University of Vermont, Colchester Ave., Burlington; *Athenaeum Art Gallery & Library,* St. Johnsbury; *Southern Vermont Art Center,* Manchester; *Bundy Museum,* Waitsfield; *Chaffee Art Center,* Rutland; *Springfield Art & Historical Society; Bennington Gallery,* 125 North St., Bennington; *Brattleboro Museum and Art Center,* Old Union Railroad Station, Brattleboro.

 HISTORIC SITES. In 1961, the *Vermont Board for Historic Sites* was established by people eager to preserve the state's heritage. For a complete guide to Vermont's official state historic sites write to: Vermont Division of Historic Preservation, Montpelier, 05602.

TOURS. *Fall Foliage Tours:* Vermont is ideal for self-conducted tours. The most popular are held during the foliage period, usually September 25 to about October 15; color changes begin in the upper reaches of the Green Mountains, usually by mid-September, and radiate southward. Most newspapers throughout New England, especially the major Boston ones, carry regular reports on the progress of the foliage; and the bus companies offer special tours during this period.

The *Vermont Travel Division,* Montpelier 05602, publishes a brochure with 13 proposed scenic tours which take the motorist along marked paved roads lined with flaming colors in fall. Adequate housing accommodations are available in these areas.

DRINKING LAWS. Drinking in restaurants and hotels is legal; and alcohol is sold by the drink Mon.–Fri. from 8 A.M. to 2 A.M., Sat. until 1 A.M., and Sun. from noon to 2 A.M. Minimum age is 19. Bottled beer and light wine to take out are sold at grocery stores with second-class licenses, open Mon.–Sat. 6 A.M. to midnight, Sun. 8 A.M. to 10 P.M. Bottled liquor is sold at state liquor stores and agencies.

Along Rte. 100, north from Wilmington to Stowe, restaurants, lounges, and nightclubs are too numerous to list.

SUMMER SPORTS. *Golf:* There are over 40 public golf courses in Vermont, as well as a number of private ones open on a limited basis. The following are among the best in Vermont: *Mount Snow C.C.,* West Dover, a rolling course at 2,000-ft. *Haystack,* Wilmington. *New Desmond Muirhead course* with spectacular mountain scenery. *Lake Morey Inn & C.,* Fairlee, lakeside, rolling; site of annual *Vermont Open. Crown Point C.C.,* Springfield, flat, pretty. *Equinox Hotel & C.C.,* Manchester, superbly groomed, rolling course. *Manchester C.C.,* Manchester, attractive layout. *Stratton Mountain C.C.,* Stratton Mt., designed by Geoffrey Cornish. *Sugarbush C.C.,* Warren, Robert Trent Jones course. *Stowe C.C.,* also Cornish-designed, with large, well-trapped green; open to guests of Stowe member lodges. *Woodstock C.C.,* Woodstock, Robert Trent Jones course in beautiful valley with brook. *Basin Harbor C.,* Vergennes, bordered by woodland and Lake Champlain; broad, rolling fairways.

In addition, there are 11 18-hole courses and 26 9-hole courses, some of which are open only to guests of acceptable lodges. Inquire locally. Free list of public courses from Vermont Travel Division. The *Vermont State Open Golf Tournament* is held at Lake Morey Inn, Fairlee, in late June; and the *Stratton Mountain Golf Academy* is located in Stratton.

Tennis: Many of Vermont's hotels, inns and lodges have their own courts, of course, but there are in addition several "big name" tennis resorts, among them *John Newcombe's Tennis Center* at Stratton, the *Killington School for Tennis,* the *Topnotch* resort at Stowe, John Gardiner's tennis camp at the *Sugarbush Inn* in Warren, *Bolton Valley* resort with Ian Fletcher as teaching pro, and the *Lake Morey Inn* at Fairlee. Stratton Mtn. is home to the *Volvo International Tennis Tourney* early in August.

Riding: From late May to late Sept., there are more than 30 riding events in Vermont. *Arlington, Brookfield, Proctorsville, Woodstock, Killington,* and *Windsor* are some of the villages in which horse shows and riding events take place. Most stables offer trail rides, instruction, and boarding. For a complete listing of Vermont riding stables, write the Travel Division, Montpelier, 05602. Dog racing has replaced harness racing at Green Mountain Track in Pownal and the greyhounds run from March to November. Minimum betting age is 18.

Boating: Canoe, sailboat, rowboat, and motorboat rentals are available throughout the state. In most state parks, rowboats and canoes are for rent. Canoeing is best in the spring, when the waters are high.

Lake Champlain is a favorite area for summer boating; multi-day cruises on a two-masted schooner or paddlewheel-ship daylong excursions also are available on Champlain. Other good spots are: *St. Catherine, Seymour, Bomoseen, Memphremagog, Dunmore, Fairlee, Caspian.* For a complete listing of boat rental areas write: Vermont Travel Division, Montpelier, 05602.

Mountain rides: Alpine Slide made its North American debut at Bromley Ski Area outside Manchester; the world's longest (4,600 ft.) and only triple track layout is at Bromley. Double terrain-tailored tracks are at Stowe and Pico, near Rutland. Gondola rides at Killington, Stowe, and Jay Peak.

Hunting and fishing: The hunting season begins in October and ends in November. Fishing starts in the early part of April and extends through September. All licenses are available from local town or city clerks. Nonresidents must prove that they have licenses in its home states, or that they have previously held licenses in Vermont, or that they have passed a hunting safety course. For full information contact the Vermont Fish & Game Dept., Montpelier, 05602.

Hiking: The Long Trail is a 263-mile hiking path extending the length of the state. Some 80 miles of the trail pass through the Green Mountain National Forest. For information on the trail write to the Green Mountain Club, P.O. Box 889, 43 State St., Montpelier, Vermont 05602, for its *Long Trail Guidebook*. For information on the forest, write to Supervisor, Green Mountain National Forest, Box 519, Rutland, Vt., 05701. For information on hiking in other parts of the state, ask for the Green Mountain Club's brochure, "Day Hiking in Vermont."

WINTER SPORTS. Alpine and cross-country skiing, skating, snowshoeing, ice fishing are things to do during the winter. Vermont has 20-plus major ski resorts, fully equipped; for details, write to the Vermont Travel Division or Vermont Ski Areas Association, 26 High St., Montpelier 05602, for the annual ski directory.

Cross-country skiing is available at more than 60 touring centers; among the best: Woodstock, Blueberry Hill in Goshen, Stowe's Trapp Family Lodge, Craftsbury Common, Stratton Mountain, Mtn. Meadows at Killington, Tucker Hill Lodge in Waitsfield, and Living Memorial Park in Brattleboro. A 60-kilometer race is held in early February from Ripton to Brandon.

Ice skating: There are rinks at *Killington, Middlebury Snow Bowl, Mount Snow,* and *Sugarbush Valley* ski areas.

WHAT TO DO WITH THE CHILDREN. *Santa's Land, U.S.A.,* north of Putney (I–91 and US 5), includes *Santa's Alpine Railroad;* open May to Christmas, daily. The *Shelburne Museum* (US 7), south of Burlington, comprises 35 early American buildings on 45 acres; open daily, May 15 to Oct. 15. The *Springfield Library,* 43 Main St., has a special children's room. *The Discovery Museum,* 51 Park St., Essex Junction, is terrific for kids of all ages.

SHOPPING. Although Vermont is limited in large shopping centers, there are many unique and interesting shops featuring pottery, leather, and other crafts that are designed and made by local artists. Among the best-known shops are: In Putney: *Carol Brown,* for fabrics, especially Irish wool and linen. In White River Junction: *North Country Shop,* for exclusively Vermont crafts. In Middlebury: *Frog Hollow State Craft Center,* for exceptional pottery and other crafts. In Windsor: *Windsor House,* also a State Craft Center. In Bennington: The *Bennington Gallery,* fine array of art; *Potters Yard,* contemporary stoneware. In Arlington: *Griffin's* for early American furniture. In East Arlington: the *Candle Mill* for candles made in colonial molds by the dipping method. In Manchester and Putney: *Basketville,* bursting with baskets and wicker items. In Manchester: *The Enchanted Doll House,* dolls, authentic old doll houses, stuffed animals, toys; *Gooseberry* sells quality cookware and accoutrements; the *Tree House* has Lilly Pulitzer fabrics. In Wilmington: *Quaigh Design Centre,* local crafts, imports. In Jacksonville: *Stone Soldier Pottery.* In Burlington: *The Sundance,* for leathers, pottery, woods, and other crafts. In Rutland: *The Tuttle Publishing Co.,* rare old books. In Quechee Gorge: *Dewey's.* In Thetford Center: *Ronald Voake* makes large wooden toys. In Healdville-Ludlow: the *Crowley Cheese Factory* and shop, handmade cheese daily. In Weston: *Vermont Country Store* and restaurant, everything from calico, to coffee, to churns; Weston Priory, sculptures, books, cards, musical recordings, produced by the Benedictine monks. In Wilmington: *Cooms Beaver Brook Sugar House,* maple syrup and gift items. In Londonderry and South Londonderry: *Toni Totes,* makers of popular carryalls. In Dorset: *J. K. Adams Co.,* wooden items—from tape measures to furniture. On Rte. 30, heading towards Bondville and Stratton Mt.: *Ann Taylor,* branching out from stores in Connecticut. In Brattleboro: the *Book Cellar,* a popular, well-stocked store. In Woodstock: *The Looking Glass* for children's wear and items; *Present Perfect* for fine glassware, jewelry, gifts.

Antiquing: Antique shops are common along Vermont's roads and highways.

 HOTELS AND MOTELS. Generally speaking, the accommodations in Vermont are excellent, with many of the establishments gearing their entire range of services to the winter sportsman and the summer loafer. Recreation facilities, broad vistas of lakes and mountains, and strategically sited locations make these hotels, lodges, and motels perfect bases for vacation activities. Price ranges are based on double occupancy, peak season, European plan, unless otherwise indicated. In Vermont particularly, off-season rates can offer a considerable saving; think about a stay-put vacation at a ski resort out-of-season.

Listings are based on the following price ranges: *Deluxe:* $75 and up; *Expensive:* $50–75; *Moderate:* $30–50; *Inexpensive:* under $30. We have listed, generally under *Inexpensive,* a few of the many excellent guest houses and tourist homes to be found in Vermont, a state where this type of lodging flourishes. There are many more of these than we have had space for here; and as they are both characteristic of New England and generally *Inexpensive* or, at most, *Moderate,* we refer you to the several guides and directories listed in the section on Hotels and Motels in the beginning of this volume, under Planning Your Trip.

BENNINGTON. *Moderate–Expensive:* **New Englander Best Western.** 220 Northside Dr., near Bennington College. Museum, shopping. Golf nearby. Pool, playground. Pets allowed. Free airport pickup.

Moderate: **Catamount Motel.** 500 South St. Charming Colonial decor. Pleasant, spacious rooms. Restaurant near. Outdoor pool.

Hillbrook Motel. US 7–A, Shaftsbury, off from the hwy., with nice view. Restaurant near. Pool, play area. Pets allowed.

Inexpensive: **Friendship Inn.** South Gate Road and US 7, near Green Mountain Racetrack. Heated pool. Near restaurants.

BRANDON. *Expensive:* **Brandon Inn.** 20 Park St., on US 7. Historic inn off village green. Near antique shops, library, sports. Good restaurant. Pool.

BRATTLEBORO. *Moderate:* **Colonial Motel.** Rte. 5. Tavern. Pool.
Inexpensive: **Susse Chalet.** At I–91, Exit 3. Outdoor pool. Valet and sewing service, secretarial service, baby-sitters. Restaurant, bar.

BURLINGTON. *Expensive:* **Radisson Burlington Hotel.** Downtown, with view of Lake Champlain. 200 rooms, indoor pool, restaurant, coffee house, ballroom, convention or meeting facilities. Largest hotel in Vermont. Good chain-run property.

Moderate-Expensive: **Redwood Master Hosts Inn,** Rte. 7. Well known for restaurant. Steam baths, kitchenettes.

Moderate: **Bel Aire Motel.** Rte. 7. Small motel but neat rooms.

Colonial Motor Inn. US 7. Attractive rooms. In-room coffee. Pool.

Inexpensive: **Econo Lodge.** South Burlington, near Shelburne Museum, airport, university. Pool on premises. Member of a nationwide budget chain.

Hayes' Guest House. 236 Shelburne St., 9 rooms, 3 shared baths, a private home, open year round, very inexpensive.

Trinity College (contact Faculty Coordinator, Mann Hall, Trinity College, Burlington 05401) has rooms available July 1–August 15 on a limited basis. Daily and weekly rates, cafeteria available. *Very inexpensive.*

CHESTER. *Moderate–Expensive:* **Chester Inn.** Rte. 11, on Town Green. Country inn with fine dining. Tennis, pool.

DORSET. *Deluxe:* **Barrows House.** Pleasant accommodations in a renovated inn which dates to 1775. Fine seafood, steaks in dining room; bar, library. Tennis courts, heated pool, sauna. Notable cuisine.

Moderate: **Dorset Inn.** Medium-size, with bath or combination bath, restaurant, bar. Terrace for steak cookouts. Pool, horseback riding, boating.

GRAFTON. *Expensive-Deluxe:* **The Old Tavern.** An 1801 stagecoach inn, small; 34 rooms in 3 buildings; canopy beds; semiprivate baths, 3 pleasant dining rooms. Previous guests include Theodore Roosevelt, Woodrow Wilson, Ulysses S. Grant, Rudyard Kipling, Joanne Woodward and Paul Newman, and Henry David Thoreau.

KILLINGTON. *Deluxe:* **Summit Lodge.** Access Rd. Vest-pocket resort with racquetball, saunas, skating and then Killington just up the block.
Expensive: **Grey Bonnet Inn.** Rte. 100. Saunas, whirlpool. Continental cuisine in restaurant. Game rms. Color TV. In-rm. movies.
 Cortina Inn. Rte. 4. Hefty breakfasts, topnotch Sunday brunch. Continental cuisine at night. Health & fitness center, sauna, whirlpool. Indoor pool, game rm. Tennis. Color TV.
The Cascades. Access Rd. Short walk to ski slopes. Indoor pool, sauna, whirlpool. Cafe, lounge.
Moderate: **Val Roc Motel.** Rte. 4. In-rm. coffee. Pool, tennis. Color TV (cable).

LUDLOW. *Moderate–Expensive:* **The Winchester Inn.** Rooms in 1813 inn or motel section. Restaurant (excellent steaks) and pint-size bar. Tennis.

MANCHESTER. *Deluxe:* **Wilburton Inn.** Triple-story Georgian inn superbly furnished. Lovely view of the Green Mts. Restaurant, bar.
Expensive: **Four Winds Motel.** Beautiful view. Private patios, tennis. Restaurant, shops, galleries, golf nearby. Convenient to skiing. Summer rates moderate.
Moderate: **Toll Road Motor Inn.** Convenient to all outdoor sports. Pool. Restaurant nearby.
Weathervane Motel. Beautiful setting just south of Manchester Village, large rooms, pool. Many extras, including free bicycles, antique shop.
Inexpensive: **Brook-n-Hearth.** Rte. 11. Bed and breakfast. Game room. BYOB. Color cable TV.
Skylight Lodge. Rte. 11. Throwback to early days of skiing after WW II. Family feeling. Dorm bunks or cozy rms. Family-style meals. Warm.

MARLBORO. *Moderate:* **Whetstone Inn.** Small, 170-year-old country inn with pleasant rms. Friendly atmosphere, fine period furniture.

MIDDLEBURY. *Moderate:* **Middlebury Inn and Motel.** Year-round colonial inn in an elegant 1827 home, with a modern motel annex on the Green. Comfortable rooms, most with bath; dining room. Near Middlebury College.

MONTPELIER. *Moderate:* **Brown Derby.** Rte. 12, away from downtown. Restaurant, bar. Cable TV (color). Pets.

NORWICH. *Expensive:* **Norwich Inn and Motel.** Medium-sized country inn, Vermont cooking featured. Year-round. Across river from Dartmouth College.

RUTLAND. *Moderate–Expensive:* **Holiday Inn.** Offers transportation to ski slopes in winter. Pool, play area, restaurant, dancing. Pets allowed in kennel.
Howard Johnson's. Large rooms, pool (enclosed), saunas, restaurant.
Moderate: **Rutland Travelodge.** Well-appointed rooms. Indoor pool, saunas. No pets.
Inexpensive: **Friendship Inn Tyrol Motel,** on US 4, 5 mi. east of Rte. 7. Member of a national budget chain. **Country Squire,** 4 m. south in N. Clarendon; **Green-Mont,** 138 N. Main St.

SPRINGFIELD. *Moderate:* **Howard Johnson's.** Indoor pool, saunas, playground.

Inexpensive: **The Hartness House.** A former residence of a governor, now a small, tastefully decorated inn, plus modern motel units. Unusual underground lounge. Restaurant. Pool (heated), play area. Open year-round.

STOWE. *Deluxe:* **Topnotch at Stowe.** Conversion of the Lodge at Smugglers' Notch to condos leaves Topnotch as the lone, true luxury resort in Stowe. Intimate atmosphere, individually decorated rooms, superb cuisine plus extensive sports facilities: indoor or outdoor tennis, cross-country skiing, horses, heated pool and saunas.

Trapp Family Lodge. New section, replacing photogenic main lodge destroyed by fire in 1980, and older motel annex. Great views, even better food. Superb cross-country skiing in winter, walking trails in summer, and even a chapel in the woods.

Expensive-Deluxe: **Notch Brook Resort.** View of Mt. Mansfield. Pool, saunas, tennis. Townhouses with fireplaces also available.

Stowehof Inn. Pool, sauna, many other amenities. Open year-round. 3 miles from town toward Mt. Mansfield. 20 rooms.

Expensive: **Golden Eagle Motel.** Pool, color TV, steambath, tennis, nicely furnished complex with main motel plus nearby apartments. Restaurant across the street from motel, coffee shop. Open all year.

Moderate-Expensive: **Alpine Motor Lodge.** Panoramic view. Pool, putting green, patios. Close to sports and village.

Green Mountain Inn & Motel. 61 rooms in the motel, with cozy old inn alongside, from 1833. Traditional New England cooking. Million-dollar facelift revived sagging property.

WATERBURY. *Moderate-Expensive:* **Holiday Inn.** Pool, saunas, steambaths, restaurant, tennis. Golf nearby, Stowe 10 mi. up Rte. 100.

WHITE RIVER JUNCTION. *Moderate:* **Howard Johnson's.** Indoor pool, sauna, playground, restaurant, dancing.

Inexpensive: **Suisse Chalet.** At I–89—I–91 interchange. Pool. Restaurant nearby. Valet, sewing and secretarial services, baby-sitters. Handy to bus station. Health club next door.

WOODSTOCK. *Deluxe:* **Woodstock Inn.** Historic landmark on the town's Green, with excellent restaurant, coffee shop, small piano bar, outdoor pool, summer barbecues and guest privileges at tennis and paddleball facilities as well as Robert Trent Jones golf course. Alpine or cross-country ski packages available.

Moderate: **Ottauquechee Motel.** Small motel situated in appealing country area. Rooms are neat, tastefully furnished. Library.

Village Inn at Woodstock. Converted Victorian era home with fine dining and just nine guest rooms.

Kedron Valley Inn. South Woodstock. Two dozen rooms spread over main building (1828), Tavern Building (1822), and log cabin-style "annex" (1969). Rustic and relaxing.

 DINING OUT. Restaurants in Vermont take pride in several local specialties, such as roast turkey, clam chowder, griddle cakes with maple syrup, maple-cured ham, maple butternut pie, rum pie, and country-style sausage. In addition, however, the increasing sophistication of both taste and transportation in this country plus Vermont's growing tourism industry means you are very likely to find crêpes suzette, lobster thermidor, beef stroganoff, and every other kind of imported and exotic cuisine you could wish for somewhere in Vermont. Price ranges are based on a full dinner, but remember that many restaurants serve à la carte meals, which will boost your tab.

Listings are based on the following price ranges: *Expensive:* $25 per person; *Moderate:* $10–25; *Inexpensive:* under $10.

ARLINGTON. *Inexpensive:* **West Mountain Farm.** A cozy inn on a 145-acre estate. Roast beef and steak dinners are specialties. Bar. Children's portions. Open year-round, but closed Tues.

BENNINGTON. *Expensive:* **Four Chimneys.** In a former mansion. Continental cooking, featuring lobster. Lounge and wine cellar. Open late May to Nov. 1. Reservations.

Moderate: **Heritage House.** Small family restaurant, proud of its Vermont dishes, especially the roast turkey, steak. Clam chowder on Fri. Open all year.

Publyk House. Rte. 7A. Remodeled barn, great views. Steak and seafood. Fresh baked goods.

BRATTLEBORO. *Moderate:* **Country Kitchen.** Dark paneled rooms. Small bar. Steaks, seafood. Children's portions. Reservations.

BURLINGTON. *Moderate-Expensive:* **The Ice House.** As the name implies, converted ice house on Lake Champlain. Excellent fresh fish with seafood from Boston.

The Sirloin Saloon. Rte. 7. Plenty of beef dishes but don't overlook the seafood. Good salad bar.

Inexpensive–Moderate: **Carbur's.** Mod-Victorian decor. Dazzling array of sandwiches on 26-page menu. Good for families.

CHITTENDEN. *Expensive:* **MountainTop Inn.** A favorite of the late Dwight Eisenhower. Charming dining area in colonial decor featuring prime ribs of beef. Bar. Dancing Wed. and Sat. nights in season. Children's portions. Open for breakfast, lunch, and dinner. Closed in late spring and late fall.

DORSET. *Expensive:* **Barrows House.** A 1775 home used as an inn since 1900. Specializing in roast beef, cream baked chicken, bisque and seafood. Bar.

Village Auberge. Rte. 30. Quiet luxury. Chef-owned. Superb French cuisine. Where the locals go when they want something special.

Moderate: **Dorset Inn.** New England meals. Wed. steak cookouts. Sun. buffet. Children's portions. Bar. Open mid-June–mid-Oct.

GRAFTON. *Expensive:* **The Old Tavern.** A delightful old country inn in 1801 homestead. Year-round dining with New England beef and chicken specialties. Liquor privileges. Jackets preferred for men.

KILLINGTON–PICO. (See also Rutland.) *Moderate:* **Back Behind Saloon.** Jct. of Rtes. 4 & 100. The traditional resort fare of steak and seafood, but the burgers are extraordinary. Ex-caboose forms one section of the building.

Charity's. Access Rd. Rustic décor with a Victorian twist. Excellent lunch or dinner stop. Can't go wrong with soup & burger at lunch, beef at dinner.

LUDLOW. *Moderate:* **Nikki's.** Rte. 100 & Okemo Access Rd. Lunches and dinners. Fine soups. Seafood suggested at dinner.

The Winchester. Rte. 103 Across-the-board excellence, from beef and chicken to almost any fish dish.

MANCHESTER. *Expensive:* **Reluctant Panther.** Charming place, dinner only. Baking on premises. Excellent menu and results.

Toll Gate Lodge. Dining by a brook in a forest setting. Specializes in continental and French alpine cuisine. Wine list. Open late May–mid-Oct. Reservations.

Moderate: **Colburn House.** Yankee foods. Bar. Open for breakfast, lunch, and dinner. Small inn, centrally located.

Harvest Inn Restaurant. Continental fare, with own baking.

MARLBORO. *Moderate:* **Marlboro Inn.** Small country inn commanding scenic view. Varied New England meals. By reservation only. Closed Mon. in winter, two weeks in Apr. and Nov.

Skyline Restaurant. At summit of Hogback Mtn. with 100-mile view, opposite *Marlboro Inn.* Vermont specialties. Try waffles or griddle cakes with homemade sausage. Children's portions.

MIDDLEBURY. *Moderate:* **The Dog Team Tavern.** Charming country inn atmosphere, home-baked bread, New England cooking. Popular spot. Menu posted on a blackboard. Children's portions. Bar. Closed Mon.

Middlebury Inn. Situated on the Green, this Colonial inn has been a longtime favorite with Middlebury College families. Children's portions. Cocktails in *Snow Bowl* and *Pine Room.*

MONTGOMERY CENTER. *Expensive:* **Zack's On The Rocks.** An out-of-the-way but excellent small restaurant. Exciting view of Jay Peak. Specialties are onion soup, lobster thermidor, frogs' legs, and sirloin steak. Wine list. Bar. Reservations.

MONTIPELIER. *Moderate:* **Brown Derby.** Steak, seafood. Children's portions. Entertainment, dancing.

The Stockyard. Your basic steak house just far enough away from the downtown bustle.

NEWFANE. *Expensive:* **Four Columns Inn.** Dine on the terrace at this colonial inn featuring continental cuisine. Bar. Reservations.

Old Newfane Inn. Distinguished 1787 inn with superb French cuisine. Attractive dining room with brick fireplace. Reservations.

NEWPORT. *Moderate:* **The Landing.** Only restaurant on Lake Memphremagog. Fresh fish—what else?—a specialty. Steaks good, too. Popular lunch spot.

NORWICH. *Moderate:* **Norwich Inn.** 1 mi. from Dartmouth College. This country inn serves Vermont foods such as maple-cured ham, country sausage, and pancakes in *Four Seasons Dining Terrace.* Bar.

RUTLAND. *Moderate–Expensive:* **Royal's Hearthside Restaurant.** Restored colonial inn. Specializing in lobster, charcoal broiled steak, baked stuffed shrimp, roast prime ribs beef, chowders. Lunch and dinner. Bar. Children's portions. Gift shop. Closed Wed. Reservations.

Moderate: **Vermont Inn.** Charming farm house with cozy fireplaces. American and continental cuisine. Bar. Children's portions. Closed Tues. and May.

Countryman's Pleasure Restaurant. On the Mendon town line. Different specialty nightly. Plenty of sauces.

ST. JOHNSBURY. *Moderate:* **Aime's Restaurant.** Distinguished restaurant in the area for over 30 years. Friendly atmosphere. Seafood, roast beef the specialties. Homemade pastry. Children's portions. Bar.

Rabbit Hill Motor Inn & Motel. Attractive dining room overlooks the Connecticut River and White Mts. Menu features veal parmigiana, baked stuffed shrimp. Homemade pastries. Bar. Closed Tues. in winter.

SOUTH LONDONDERRY. *Expensive:* **Three Clock Inn.** European cuisine. Excellent veal, if you have to pick just one thing.

SPRINGFIELD. *Moderate:* **Hartness House.** Country inn on former residence of Gov. James Hartness. New England meals are served daily. Bar. Buffet on Tues. and Wed. Look for *Underground Lounge.* Open for breakfast, lunch, and dinner.

Penelope's. Soup and sandwich at lunch. Dinner menu features fish entrées, Cordon bleu. Carrot cake terrific, as is homemade cheesecake.

The Paddock. Rte. 11. Piles of superb food. Home baking at its best; in a remodeled horse barn.

STOCKBRIDGE. *Moderate–Expensive:* **Annabelle's.** Rte 100. Excellent for lunch or dinner. Soups are a must, especially the pumpkin. At dinner, you'll have no beef about the Tournedos Rossini or roast duckling.

STOWE. *Expensive:* **Topnotch at Stowe.** Unrivaled for elegance (and expense). Varied cuisine in keeping with the hushed, luxurious settings. Candlelight and comfort.

Trapp Family Lodge. New lodge opened in 1983, after a fire in 1980, but the coffee shop was untouched. It's like dining in Vienna, thanks to wide variety of calorie-costly pastries.

Moderate: **Green Mountain Inn.** Dine in a charming colonial inn with friendly atmosphere. Menu features crabmeat au gratin. Homemade pastries. Bar. Limited wine list. Children's portions.

Spruce Pond Inn. Renovated farmhouse. Specializes in brook trout. Homemade soups, pastries. Bar. Children's portions. Closed mid-Apr.–late May; late Oct.–mid-Dec.

Inexpensive: **Food for Thought.** Tiny, casual natural-foods restaurant with homemade soups, shop and bookstore. Lunch, single-entrée dinner.

STRATTON MOUNTAIN. *Expensive:* **Birkenhaus.** Small, intimate place to go. Continental cuisine extraordinaire.

VERGENNES. *Expensive:* **Basin Harbor Club.** Wide range of dishes served in this 700-acre lakeside resort's spacious dining room and cocktail area. Open late spring to mid-fall. Jackets and ties for dinner.

WARREN–WAITSFIELD (Sugarbush Valley). *Deluxe:* **Sugarbush Inn.** Large colonial-style dining room and terrace, two lounges. Features roast duckling, lobster, and beef dishes. Bar. Closed Oct. 16–Dec. 14, Apr. 16–June 14.

The Common Man. European dishes in a 100-year-old former hay barn, complete with crystal chandeliers, huge fireplace and classical music. Recommended: pork chops.

Moderate: **Phoenix.** Sugarbush Village. Exposed beams, wooden decor. Skip dinner and go straight to desserts.

China Barn. Rte. 17, Waitsfield. Szechuan and Mandarin cuisine. Closed Tues.

WEST DOVER–WILMINGTON (Mount Snow). *Expensive:* **Inn at Sawmill Farm.** Dine in a converted sawmill. Charming, colonial decor. Continental-French cuisine.

The Hermitage Inn. Off Rte. 105. Amazing mix of first-rate dining, several thousand game birds and fowl to feed the menu, plus maple sugar operation. Deep wine cellar, too. No credit cards.

The White House. Rte. 9, Wilmington. Mansion converted to country inn. Continental menu. Try the veal.

WESTON. *Moderate:* **The Inn at Weston.** This small country inn offers imaginative meals, with everything fresh and homemade. Reservations for dinner.

Inexpensive: **Vermont Country Store Restaurant.** Old-fashioned dining rooms, specializing in Vermont foods (chicken, sausage, ham, and griddle cakes).

WOODSTOCK. *Expensive:* **Woodstock Inn.** This charming historic landmark replaces the original, which was destroyed by fire. New England dinners served to music in dignified surroundings. Terrace dining in summer. Eye-popping Saturday night buffet. Own baking. Background music. Jackets preferred.

Bentley's. Candlelight dining or crowded lunchtime scene. Excellent eats at either time, however. Monte Carlo sandwich at lunch is tops.

Moderate: **Rumble Seat.** Restaurant in Woodstock East. Another popular lunch spot which is too often overlooked at night. Suggested: sirloin steak.

Kedron Valley Inn. South Woodstock. Service can be erratic and summertime can mean plenty of folks from nearby Green Mountain Horse Association stables. Food is good enough to attract even the locals. Fine Saturday-night buffet.

Spooner's. Rte. 4. Newest eatery in town and already one of the best. You can get steak and seafood anywhere but Spooner's is the only restaurant in the region with terrific stir-fried (i.e., wok) dishes. Mmmm.

DELAWARE

America's First State

Too often travelers know Delaware only as a state to pass through on the way to somewhere else. They know the impressive twin-span Delaware Memorial Bridge, and they've heard of the Du Pont Company which was born here. They may not know, however, that Delaware was the first state to ratify the Constitution; hence its nickname.

But the visitor who takes the time to wander through Delaware, to visit the historic sites, to see the lovely little towns, to spend some time at Rehoboth Beach, to enjoy the excellent food of the area, will come away with a new concept of this small but interesting state. (Only Rhode Island is smaller.)

From the north, whether it's over the Memorial Bridge from the New Jersey Turnpike or down I–95 from Philadelphia, all roads lead to Wilmington, largest city in the state. Settled by Swedes who landed in 1638, Wilmington has not forgotten its heritage; in fact, it maintains a strong tie with Sweden through its sister city, Kalmar.

Willingtown Square, in the heart of the city, is a conclave of six 18th-century houses which have been moved to this site beside the Market Street Mall and are being used as a series of museum displays, workshops, and offices. Modern inside, these small buildings have been completely restored to their original appearance on the outside.

Across the Mall is Old Town Hall (1798), restored even to the basement cells which made up the jail. The Mall itself, after years of planning and construction, is a charming place to stroll, shop, or stop at a sidewalk cafe for a bite to eat. Dominating the Mall, the Grand Opera House, one of the finest in America, has been renovated with funds donated by Delaware citizens. It's the scene of year-round cultural events.

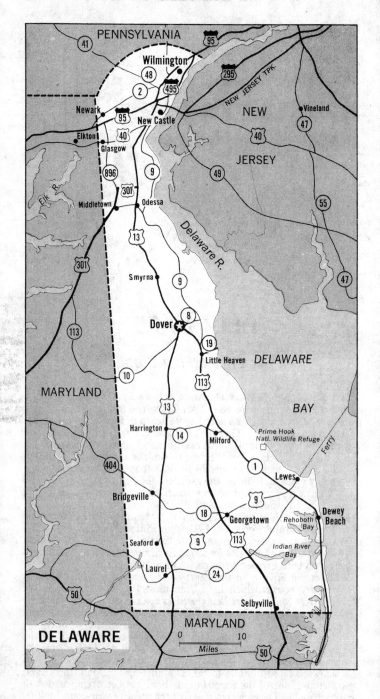

DELAWARE

Six miles northwest of Wilmington on Del. 52 (Kennett Pike) is the world-famous Henry Francis du Pont Winterthur Museum, with fourteen rooms open for a nominal fee. The remaining 100-odd rooms may be seen by appointment.

Traveling south from Wilmington on US 13, follow the signs to New Castle, a delightful town designed by Peter Stuyvesant and preserved, house by house, by individuals who live in them. On occasion these private homes are open to the public, but any time of year the visitor may tour the Amstel House, the Old Dutch House, the elegant George Read II House, and the Old Court House of 1732. The historic Immanuel Episcopal Church on the Green, destroyed by fire in early 1980, has been beautifully restored.

Driving west from New Castle on Del. 273, take a left on Old Baltimore Pike and continue to Cooches Bridge, scene of the only Revolutionary War battle fought in Delaware, and where the first American flag made by Betsy Ross was flown in land battle.

Continuing on Old Baltimore Pike, you'll soon come to Del. 896. A right turn will take you into Newark (pronounced New Ark, please) and the University of Delaware campus. Newark is a typical college town with some nice shops; the campus is charming with its ivy-covered colonial brick buildings.

Take Del. 72 southeast to U.S. 13 and head south to Odessa, with its three historic buildings maintained by the Winterthur Museum and worth a stop. Continue south and you'll find Dover, the capital of Delaware, which grew around the site of a county courthouse and prison laid out by William Penn in 1683. The green, center of this complex, still remains, and Delaware's capitol buildings are quite beautiful, arranged like a college campus. Stop by the Visitor Center in the State House annex on Federal Street for information, or join a tour there.

About 10 miles south of Dover on Rte. 113, watch for signs pointing to the Island Field Museum, a left on Del. 19 at a place called (honestly!) Little Heaven. There you can see archeologists at work, unraveling the story of the Webb Phase People who lived here long before Columbus arrived. It's a fascinating place, one of five in the world of its type; the museum was actually built over the excavation site.

Follow Del. 113 to Georgetown and go around The Circle, with its imposing, beautifully restored buildings, and pick up Del. 9 to Lewes, site of Delaware's first white settlement in 1631. There are several interesting places to see here, including the Zwaanendael Museum, a replica of the Hoorn Town Hall in Holland, built to commemorate the 300th anniversary of the landing of Dutch colonists.

A relaxing, enjoyable ride aboard one of three sleek bay liners comprising the Cape May–Lewes Ferry will take you across the Delaware Bay to Cape May, N. J., and a world of gingerbread and Victoriana. It's a 70-minute ride, and you

Back in Lewes, pick up Del. 14 south to Rehoboth Beach, a favorite playground for Washingtonians. Here you'll find all kinds of hotels, motels, guest houses, and inns; there's a boardwalk, ocean swimming, and the fishin's good. A few miles farther south are Indian River Inlet and Bethany Beach. Just below Bethany is Assawoman Wildlife Area.

Delaware's parks are open for public use on a year-round basis with limited facilities available from November 1 through March 31. The parks are open from sunrise to sunset.

PRACTICAL INFORMATION FOR DELAWARE

HOW TO GET THERE. *By car:* Wilmington is 30 miles south of Philadelphia and 50 miles north of Baltimore via I-95. From New York, take the New Jersey Turnpike to the Delaware Memorial Bridge. Wilmington is just beyond. Dover, the capital, is about 50 miles south of Wilmington on U.S. 13.

By train: The *Amtrak* station in downtown Wilmington has recently been restored. Service is frequent in and out of the city. There is no passenger service south of Wilmington.

By bus: Trailways and *Greyhound.*

By air: United Airlines has service to and from Chicago at the Greater Wilmington Airport, south of the city on US 13. Delawareans use the Philadelphia International and Baltimore–Washington Airports.

TOURIST INFORMATION: *Delaware State Travel Service,* 99 Kings Highway, Box 1401, Dover, DE 19903. Toll-free 1–800–441–8846.

HISTORIC SITES. *Lewes Historic Complex.* At 3rd and Shipcarpenter streets, Lewes. *Thompson Country Store; Rabbit's Ferry House,* a small 18th-century farmhouse. Open June 30 through Labor Day, Mondays through Saturdays, 11 A.M.–4 P.M. Individual buildings, 50¢.

Old Swedes Church, Wilmington. Believed to be the oldest Protestant church still in use in America. Guide service. *Fort Christina,* Wilmington. Built by Swedes after landing in Delaware in 1638. *Caesar Rodney* statue, Rodney Square, Wilmington. Depicts horse and rider making famous trip from Dover to Philadelphia to break the tie vote on Independence, July 2, 1776. *Fort Delaware* State Park, Pea Patch Island. Fort Delaware was a Union prison camp during the Civil War. Reached by launch from Delaware City.

Great Cypress Swamp. Trussum Pond, near Laurel. Northernmost natural stand of cypress in U.S. Follow signs from Trap Pond State Park (Del. 24 west of Laurel) for best view.

Mason-Dixon Monument. West of Delmar via Del. 54. Double crownstone erected in 1768 by Charles Mason and Jeremiah Dixon as the southern end of the north-south portion of the Mason-Dixon Line, which resolved boundary disputes between Calvert and Penn families.

Bombay Hook National Wildlife Refuge. Off Del. 9, north of Leipsic. 15,110-acre haven for migrating and wintering waterfowl. Open daily sunrise to sunset.

MUSEUMS AND GALLERIES. *Henry Francis du Pont Winterthur Museum.* Fourteen rooms in South Wing open Tues.–Sun., holiday Mons. To see the Main Museum (some 100 rooms) write Reservations Office, Winterthur Museum, Winterthur, Del. 19735. 6 miles northwest of Wilmington on Kennett Pike (Del. 52). *Delaware Art Museum.* 2301 Kentmere Pkwy., Wilmington. Open Tues.–Sat. *Old Town Hall* and *Willingtown Square,* downtown Wilmington on the Market St. Mall. Guide service. *Rockwood Museum.* Off Washington St. Extension, Wilmington. Fine Victorian home built by one of founders of city, maintained by New Castle County. Open year-round. Guided tours Tues.–Sat, 11–3. Adults, $2, seniors $1, and children, 50¢.

Hagley Museum, near Wilmington. Preserved and restored site of the original powder works of the Du Pont Company. *Eleutherian Mills,* home of É. I. duPont de Nemours (1803), on hill overlooking Hagley, open Tues.–Sun.

Old Court House, New Castle. Delaware's colonial capital and the county seat for many years, now a state museum. *Old Dutch House Museum,* New Castle. Said to be oldest house in state, *Amstel House,* New Castle. Fine examples of early Delaware furnishings. *George Read II House,* The Strand, New Castle. Outstanding example of Georgian architecture, formal gardens. Built by son of a signer of the Declaration of Independence. *Corbit-Sharp House, Wilson Warner. Houses, Brick Hotel Gallery of American Art,* Odessa. Open Tues.–Sat. 10–4:30, Sun 1–4:30. $3 per building or $7 for all three. Maintained by Winterthur Museum.

Delaware State Museum, Dover. Housed in four separate buildings with exhibits on many phases of Delaware life. Especially interesting is the Eldridge Reeves Johnson collection of old talking machines and records. *Woodburn,* the governor's mansion, Dover. Open Saturdays, 2:30–4:30, except Jan., Feb. *Agricultural Museum.* On U.S. 13 just south of Del. State College. Open Tues.–Sat. 10–4, Sun. 1–4.

Island Field Archeological Museum. South Bowers Beach. Site of prehistoric cemetery, still being excavated (open March–Nov. 30). *John Dickinson Mansion,* Kitts Hummock Road near Dover. Dickinson has been called the Penman of the Revolution. House was built in 1740 by his father, Samuel. Fine restoration. *Barratts Chapel,* near Frederica, is known as the Cradle of Methodism in America.

Historic complex, Lewes. Includes *Marine Museum, Lightship Overfalls,* several other buildings. *Zwaanendael Museum,* Lewes. Charming example of Dutch architecture housing Dutch artifacts.

HOTELS AND MOTELS in Delaware range from plain, comfortable roadside establishments in the country to the luxury (and high prices) of some Rehoboth Beach hotels.

The price categories in this section are for double occupancy: *Deluxe,* $75 and up; *Expensive,* $50–75; *Moderate,* $35–50; and *Inexpensive,* under $35.

DOVER. *Expensive:* **Holiday Inn.** On lake with pool and restaurant.

Sheraton Inn. N. duPont Highway. Pool, restaurant, entertainment, tennis.

Moderate: **Capitol City.** A Best Western. Pool, snack room, washer, dryer.

Quality Court South. Heated pool, restaurant.

TravelLodge. Pool, restaurant adjacent.

Inexpensive: **Caravan.** Pool, restaurant adjacent.

Towne Point. Color TV, pool, adjacent restaurant. ½ mile sout of Dover Downs Raceway.

LEWES. *Expensive:* **Angler's.** Rooms overlooking canal. Open all year with reduced winter rates.

NEW CASTLE. *Expensive:* **Howard Johnson's Motor Lodge.** At Del. Memorial Bridge. Pool, restaurant.

Ramada Inn. Pool, color TV. Restaurant, lounge, live entertainment Tuesday through Saturday.

Moderate: **Dutch Village.** 3 miles south of Del. Mem. Bridge. Pool, Howard Johnson's on premises.

Gateway Motor Inn. 2 miles south of bridge. Pool, some waterbeds, efficiencies.

Park Plaza. U.S. 13–40 and 301. Pets OK. Restaurant adjacent.

Skyways Motor Lodge. At Greater Wilmington Airport. Two heated pools, Dutch Pantry Restaurant. A Quality Inn.

NEWARK. *Expensive.* **Howard Johnson's Motor Lodge.** At I–95 and 896. Pool, restaurant, *Chart Room Lounge.*

REHOBOTH BEACH. *Deluxe:* **Atlantic Sands.** Open all year, seasonal rates. On beach. Restaurant, pool.

The Henlopen Hotel. A Best Western Hotel on beach. Closed Nov. 1 to April 1. Fine restaurant on top floor, two lounges, live entertainment in season. Ocean swimming. Condominiums.

Expensive: **Frances Anne.** West of Rehoboth, 1 mile from ocean. Closed mid-October to mid-March. Seasonal rates. Restaurants nearby.

Hobo Beach. Open Easter to early October, seasonal rates. Efficiencies. Pool, restaurant, baby-sitter list. (Most Rehoboth hotels and motels have a three-day minimum for reservations in season. There are also guest houses, small inns open during summer.)

The Breakers. New, convenient to Convention Center. No food service, but close to restaurants.

Moderate: **Shirl-Ann Motel.** 2 Olive Ave. at Boardwalk. Seasonal rates, some apartments. Restaurants nearby.

WILMINGTON. *Deluxe:* **Hotel du Pont.** Market St. at 11th. Top-drawer. Excellent service, rooms furnished in antiques, original paintings. Two fine dining rooms, coffee shop, lounge. Close to Market St. Mall. Limousine service to Phila. International Airport.

Deluxe: **Wilmington Hilton.** I–95 at Naamans Rd. Whispers Lounge, Evergreens Res. VIP floor has lounges, concierge service.

Radisson Wilmington. Customs Plaza, 700 King St. Two restaurants, indoor pool, whirlpool. Limousine service to Philadelphia airport.

Expensive: **Holiday Inn.** 400 Concord Pike. Pool, restaurant, pets O.K. Free kennel on premises.

Holiday Inn. I-95 at 273. Restaurant on premises, pool, pets O.K. Weekend entertainment.

Sheraton Brandywine Inn. 4727 Concord Pike. Pool, restaurant, car rental, limousine service to Phila. International Airport.

 DINING OUT in Delaware often means chicken, since the state raises a great deal of poultry; it can also mean crabmeat, often in some interesting form—Crab Imperial, crab cakes or deviled crabs. You might also want to sample stuffed crab, or sauteed or deep-fried soft shell crabs. Delawareans delight in attacking great mounds of steamed crabs with mallets, extracting every last morsel. You might want to take a whack at it.

Restaurant price categories are as follows: *Deluxe,* $15 and up; *Expensive,* $10–15; *Moderate,* $5–10; and *Inexpensive,* below $5. Not included are drinks and tips. There is no sales tax in Delaware.

DOVER. *Expensive:* **Blue Coat Inn.** Seafood, beef, chicken. Overlooking Silver Lake.

Dinner Bell. 121 S. State St. Seafood the specialty here. Excellent luncheon buffet.

The Nuts. More elegant than it sounds. 1068 S. State St. Lunch Mon.–Fri., dinner daily. Excellent cuisine.

Inexpensive: **Orient Express.** Rte. 113 south end of town. Open 7 days. Good Chinese food.

Kirby & Holloway Family Restaurant. Rt. 13, just north of Dover. Homestyle meals, popular with locals. Famous for sausage.

GLASGOW. *Expensive:* **Glasgow Arms.** Favorite of locals.
Moderate: **The Glass Kitchen.** Good family-style meals.

GREENVILLE. *Expensive:* **Greenery Too.** 3801 Kennett Pike. Excellent food. Lunch, dinner, Mon.–Sat.

LEWES. *Expensive:* **Angler's Restaurant.** Good seafood.
Schoonover's. Powder Mill Square. Excellent food, service.

LITTLE CREEK. *Expensive:* **Coral Reef.** On Rt. 8 east of Dover. Fine seafood menu.
Village Inn. On Rt. 9. Seafood, excellent cuisine. Early American decor.

NEWARK: *Expensive:* **Goodfellow's.** 177 E. Main St. International cuisine, fresh seafood specialties.

Moderate: **Dragon's Den.** Excellent Chinese food. On Cleveland Ave.

Iron Hill Inn. German specialties. Open 7 days. On College Ave., just off I–95, 896 exit.

Inexpensive: **Ivystone II.** Family fare, children's menu, 32 kinds of pie. In Newark Shopping Center.

Klondike Kate. On Main St. Old mining-town atmosphere. Dinners, omelets, soup, glorified hamburgers.

NEW CASTLE. *Expensive:* **New Castle Inn** (formerly Arsenal on the Green). In center of historic town. Excellent food, atmosphere.

Moderate: **The Arsenal.** In old armory. Rebel Cork Irish Pub, below, has entertainment weekends. Lunch, dinner.

REHOBOTH BEACH. *Expensive:* **Dinner Bell.** Specialties are chicken, crab, and steak.

Horizon Room, Henlopen Hotel. Lobster thermidor a specialty. Popular place for Sunday brunch, with great variety of dishes.

Sea Horse. On Rehoboth Avenue. Excellent seafood, especially oysters, served several ways.

Sir Boyce's Pub. Nice atmosphere, good seafood, super prime ribs. On main highway near Dewey Beach.

Moderate: **Avenue.** Homemade rolls and pastries.

Crab Pot. Seafood, take-out menu.

Rusty Rudder. In Dewey Beach on Dickinson Street. Eat, drink, and be merry with locals, vacationers. Boatmen.

ST. GEORGES. *Inexpensive:* **Ches Del.** Just south of St. Georges Bridge. Homemade soups, desserts. Children half-price. Open daily at 6 A.M.

SMYRNA. *Expensive:* **Thomas England House.** On US 13 below Smyrna. Excellent seafood, chicken, beef. Try their deviled crab cakes.

Moderate: **Wayside Inn.** DuPont Highway and Mt. Vernon St. Good homemade pies.

WILMINGTON. *Deluxe:* **Hotel du Pont** (*Brandywine Room* or *Green Room*). Considered best in the area by the most critics. Special Sunday buffet in *Green Room.* Great collection of Wyeth paintings in *Brandywine Room.*

Timothy's. In Hercules Plaza, downtown. Continental cuisine in Victorian setting. Lunch, dinner Mon.–Sat.

Expensive: **Columbus Inn.** Old established restaurant. Fine original paintings, candlelight, friendly bar, fireplaces. Closed Sun.

Constantinou's House of Beef. 1616 Delaware Ave. Very popular.

Sal's Place. 603 N. Lincoln. Classical French and Northern Italian cuisine.

The Waterworks Café. 103 E. 16th St. Was just that; now a pretty restaurant overlooking the Brandywine River.

Moderate: **Oscar's.** On Market St. Mall. Featuring Sunday brunch. Once an elegant candy company, the décor has been preserved.

Haberdashery. In the Radisson Hotel. Informal. Excellent soups and sandwiches.

Hearn's. 2008 Market St. Open Sundays. Good, old-fashioned cooking, friendly atmosphere. Lunch, dinner, cocktails.

Jack Lundy's. 3604 Miller Rd. New York style delicatessen and restaurant. Open 7 days.

Inexpensive: **Charcoal Pit.** 2600 Concord Pike. Specialty is steak sandwich.

H. A. Winston & Co. In Independence Mall, Concord Pike. Great variety of gourmet hamburgers, fun décor. (Also in Newark and Dover.)

MARYLAND

Baltimore, the Bay and the West

You can drive from Washington to Baltimore over US 1, I-95 or the Baltimore-Washington Parkway. You may be surprised to find yourself in one of the most vibrant of U.S. cities. Center of much activity in Baltimore is the redeveloped Inner Harbor, a 95-acre recreational park and plaza, site of a continuing series of ethnic festivals, concerts, art shows and other activities during much of the year. Serving as a reminder that Baltimore has been a seaport since Colonial days, the Inner Harbor setting includes the U.S. Frigate *Constellation,* which was built in 1797 and is the oldest United States Navy ship afloat as well as a National Historic Landmark. There are also a World War II submarine, a public marina, tour boats, and rental sail and paddleboats.

HarborPlace is a two-story, glass-enclosed collection of restaurants, shops, boutiques and food markets that jumps with activity day and night. The National Aquarium in Baltimore is two piers away.

Be sure to see Ft. McHenry, a national monument and historic shrine where the original Star-Spangled Banner flew—visited by over half a million people a year.

The Star-Spangled Banner Flag House, home of Mary Pickersgill, who made the Star-Spangled Banner (all 1,260 square feet of it), is also open to the public. Mt. Vernon Place is the site of the first completed architectural monument to George Washington, begun in 1815 and completed in 1829. Mt. Vernon Place is known as one of the most beautiful city squares in America.

The Walters Art Gallery, which has a brilliant collection of modern and classic works, can be visited with no inconvenience, and the Peale Museum, founded in 1814 and devoted to Baltimore life, is also extremely interesting. The Baltimore Museum of Art, which has a huge

216

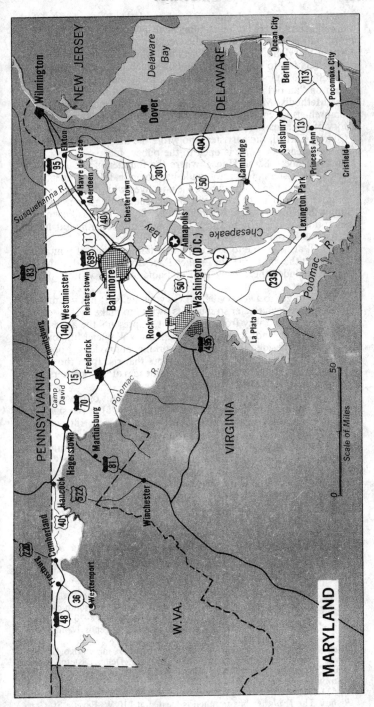

MARYLAND

collection of classic and modern work, and the Baltimore & Ohio Railroad Museum are both intriguing. The latter is the greatest collection of railroad memorabilia in the world.

At the Maryland Historical Society you will find a vast collection of exhibits relating to state history, among which is the original manuscript of the "Star-Spangled Banner," which, incidentally, was not written on "an old envelope," as a popular legend has it.

The Methodist Museum of the Lovely Lane Methodist Church has a comprehensive collection of records and exhibits pertaining to the history of American Methodism. Mount Clare, the magnificent home of Charles Carroll, the barrister who wrote the Maryland Declaration of Independence in 1776, is open to the public, too.

Saint Elizabeth Seton House, where the founder of the American Order of the Sisters of Charity made her home in 1806, is open, as is the Edgar Allan Poe House, where the poet lived while he was courting his future wife. The Lloyd Street Synagogue, dating from 1845, is distinguished for its architectural beauty. So is the Basilica of the Assumption of the Virgin Mary, the first Catholic cathedral in the United States (1806).

You will also be able to see racing at a famous track, if you are in Baltimore at the right time, for Pimlico Race Course lies within the city limits. It includes the Jockey Hall of Fame, open to visitors during racing seasons.

Try also to get to Dickeyville, on Gwynns Falls. It lies within Baltimore, but has a character so much its own as to make the visitor feel he has gone quite a way from the present. It presents the appearance of an 18th-century industrial village. The Dickey Woolen Mill, founded in 1772, stands beside the stream, still working, but no longer operated by water power. On both sides of the slopes that rise from the stream bed are graceful stone houses, once the residences of mill workers, now of professional people with gardening interests.

Hampton House makes an interesting side trip out of the city. It is reached by turning off the Baltimore Beltway (I–695) at the sign near Towson. Hampton House, a National Monument, is an 18th-century mansion once owned by the Ridgely family of Maryland. Now, with all its original furnishings and works of art unchanged, it is a museum.

National Social Security Headquarters, located on Security Blvd. (Baltimore Beltway, I–695, Exit 17), offers an interesting educational tour featuring its vast complex of sophisticated electronic data-processing equipment.

PRACTICAL INFORMATION FOR BALTIMORE

HOW TO GET THERE. *By car:* Baltimore is on I–95, 40 mi. north of Washington and 90 mi. south of Philadelphia. From Hagerstown in the west I–70 runs to the city, as does I–83 from Harrisburg, Pennsylvania, to the north.

By air: Baltimore-Washington International Airport, 10 mi. south of the city, is served by numerous airlines, including American, Delta, Eastern, Ozark, Piedmont, Republic, TWA, United, USAir and World.

By train: Baltimore is on the *Amtrak* line. The station is 1500 N. Charles St. (800) 523-8720.

By bus: The *Trailways* bus terminal is located at 210 W. Fayette St. *Greyhound* is at Howard and Centre Sts.

HOW TO GET AROUND *By car:* The Baltimore Beltway, also known as I–695, circles the city limits. I–95, coming from the northeast, is called the John Kennedy Memorial Thruway outside the city, and the Harbor Tunnel Thruway in the city. Similarly, I–83 from the north is known as the Jones Falls Expressway. US Routes 1 and 40 are major east-west streets. US 1 is Belair Rd. at its eastern end, and North Ave. downtown. From the east, US 40 is Orleans St., Franklin St., Edmonson Ave., and the Baltimore National Pike. From the north, State 45 is York Rd. and Greenmount Ave.

By subway: The 8-mile Metro line runs from downtown northwest to Reistertown, and is more useful to resident commuters than to visitors. Basic fares are $.75–$1.50.

By bus: The bus fare is 75 cents and exact change is required.

By taxi: Within the city the taxi rate is $1.40 when you get in and 10 cents for each 1/7 mile. If you go out of the city there is an additional charge of 30 cents per mile. Diamond Cab Co.'s number is 947-3333.

From the airport: Limouisines leave the Baltimore-Washington International Airport twice hourly for major downtown hotels. Fare is $5.00. A taxi will cost about $13.00 to the downtown area.

TOURIST INFORMATION. The Baltimore Office of Promotion & Tourism, 110 W. Baltimore St., Baltimore 21201, will be glad to answer any questions. Their phone number is (301) 752–8632. Call (301) 873–INFO for 24-hour visitor information tape. At the end of Pier 4 off Pratt St. is an information center where visitors may obtain literature, and the Baltimore Box Office—a one-stop ticket shop for cultural, sporting, and other events.

MUSIC. The Baltimore Symphony Orchestra season runs from September to May on Thursday and Friday nights with solo guest artists. All concerts at the Joseph Meyerhoff Symphony Hall, 1212 Cathedral St. (at Park Ave.) Very popular also are the Saturday-evening pop concerts.

STAGE AND REVUES. The *Morris A. Mechanic Theater* presents Broadway dramas, comedies, and musicals. *Baltimore Civic Center,* 201 W. Baltimore St., presents everything from rock shows to the Ice Follies and the Ringling Bros. and Barnum and Bailey Circus. *Lyric,* Baltimore's oldest music hall and home of the symphony, also is host to the Baltimore Civic Opera Co., touring concert performers and orchestras, and Broadway musicals. *Center Stage,* the city's famous repertory company, features productions ranging from classic to contemporary.

TOURS. Guided historic tours of Baltimore, including Fort McHenry, Mt. Vernon Place, Star-Spangled Banner Flag House, and other attractions are offered by *Alexander Tours* (301) 664–5577.

GARDENS. Spring begins in Baltimore when the *Sherwood Gardens* bloom, usually in mid-May. Follow the crowd to hundreds of thousands of flowers at 204 E. Highfield Rd., just east of 4100 block N. Charles St.

HISTORIC SITES. *Edgar Allan Poe House,* 203 Amity St. In this tiny house, the melancholy poet lived and courted his cousin, who later became his wife. His grave is in nearby Westminster Churchyard. *First Unitarian Church,* North Charles St. at Franklin St. Built in 1819, it is considered the birthplace of the Unitarian Church.

Fell's Point. This historic community served as a shipbuiling center from the 18th into the 20th century. Some of the oldest houses in Baltimore still stand here.

Ft. McHenry, foot of Fort Ave. Overlooking Baltimore harbor, this star-shaped fort with brick walls 20 feet thick withstood the might of the British fleet

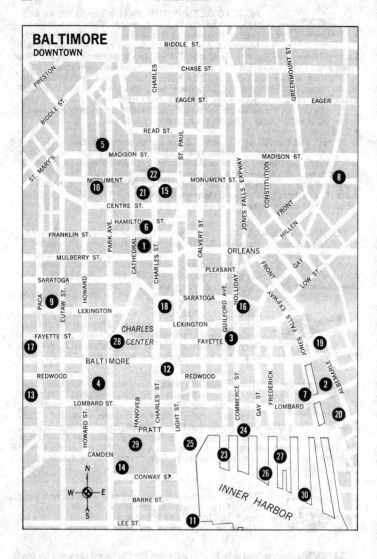

BALTIMORE
DOWNTOWN

Points of Interest

1) Basilica of the Assumption
2) Carroll Mansion
3) City Hall
4) Civic Center
5) First Presbyterian Church
6) First Unitarian Church
7) Fish Market
8) Johns Hopkins Medical Center
9) Lexington Market
10) Maryland Historical Society
11) Maryland Science Center
12) Morris Mechanic Theater
13) Medical College (Univ. of Maryland)
14) Otterbein Church
15) Peabody Institute
16) Peale Museum
17) Edgar Allan Poe's Grave
18) Saint Paul's Rectory
19) Shot Tower
20) Star-Spangled Banner Flag House
21) Walters Art Gallery
22) Washington Monument
23) U.S. Frigate Constellation
24) World Trade Center
25) HarborPlace
26) National Aquarium in Baltimore
27) U.S.S. Torsk and Light Ship Chesapeake
28) Baltimore Office of Promotion and Tourism
29) Convention Center
30) Pier Six Concert Pavilion

on Sept. 13–14, 1814. Francis Scott Key, witnessing the bombardment and the flag at dawn, was inspired to write what became the National Anthem.

Lexington Market, Lexington and Eutaw Sts. One of the oldest markets in the nation (1782), it has now been modernized but still has stallkeepers whose fathers and grandfathers had stalls there before them. *Lloyd St. Synagogue,* Lloyd St. off 1100 E. Baltimore St. Third-oldest synagogue in the United States is now a museum.

Mount Clare Station, Pratt and Poppleton Sts. The first passenger and freight station in the United States, it was here that Samuel F. B. Morse's first telegraph message, "What hath God wrought," was received. The station serves as entrance to the B&O Railroad Museum.

Washington Monument, Charles and Monument Sts. The Monument is in a gracious square. Laid out in 1830, the square itself is known for more than the Monument: fountains, mini-parks, and surrounding architecture, including elegant townhouses, Walters Art Gallery, and Peabody Conservatory of Music.

MUSEUMS AND GALLERIES. *Baltimore Museum of Art.* This popular institution has achieved national stature for its collection of Picasso, Matisse, and Cézanne. *Walters Art Gallery,* Charles and Centre sts. Ranks among the most comprehensive American art museums.

Star-Spangled Banner Flag House, 844 E. Pratt St. In this tiny brick house, Mrs. Mary Pickersgill made the flag which Francis Scott Key saw "by the dawn's early light."

SPORTS. A favorite way to spend a Saturday afternoon or a weekday evening out is to eat peanuts and hot dogs while watching the Orioles play nine innings of *baseball* or a twilight doubleheader at Memorial Stadium. The old Indian game of *lacrosse* is the national sport of Canada, but Baltimore is the game's unofficial capital. A rough sport, games are played at most high schools and colleges. Landscaped with dogwoods and pines, Pine Ridge is generally rated as the best of the *golf courses* owned by the city. It's on Dulaney Valley Rd. near Loch Raven. With nearly 50 *yacht clubs* around the Chesapeake Bay area, there is hardly a weekend that does not feature a sailboat race. They continue right up through the "frostbite season." A good vantage point is along the seawall inside the U.S. Naval Academy grounds in Annapolis. In winter, the Baltimore Blast indoor *soccer* team and Skipjacks *ice hockey* team, attract large crowds to the Civic Center.

With spring meets starting in January and fall meets ending in December, there is almost continuous *horse racing* at one of the following tracks: Laurel (Rte. 198 off I–95 about midway between Baltimore and Washington, D.C.); Bowie (Rte. 197 from the Baltimore-Washington Expy.); Pimlico, in Baltimore; and Timonium (I–83 just north of Baltimore). Transportation is provided daily by Baltimore Motor Coach buses from the Civic Center. No reservations needed.

WHAT TO DO WITH THE CHILDREN. *Baltimore and Ohio Railroad Museum,* Poppleton and Pratt Sts. A collection of replicas and original "iron horses" from America's first railroad. Especially fun is climbing into cabooses and coaches that once were the last word in luxurious travel.

Children's Zoo in Druid Hill Park. Besides the usual zoological attractions, there are farm animals and various playground apparatus.

Maryland Science Center and Planetarium, 601 Light St. Scores of fascinating displays and learning experiences.

Cloisters Children's Museum, 10440 Falls Rd. Demonstrations and entertainment at a "castle."

Children's Creative Center, 608 Water St. This unusual recycling center features an ever-changing stock of "affordable" goodies, such as paper and fabrics, buttons, spools, foam scraps and industrial surplus.

The National Aquarium in Baltimore, largest in the U.S., rises seven stories above the Inner Harbor. Of special interest to children are the shark tank and playful dolphins.

Six Flags Power Plant, Pier 4, Inner Harbor. This turn-of-the-century power plant reopened in 1985 as an indoor fantasy land with a "sensory environment" trip through the past, robot theater show, Gay Nineties musical presentation, and other attractions.

 HOTELS AND MOTELS in Baltimore are characterized, with few exceptions, by the ultramodern atmosphere. Almost all of the old-line establishments, with traditional plush accommodations, have closed in the last few years. It is wise, therefore, to check these listings carefully and to make advanced reservations always. Price categories are *Deluxe,* above $80; *Expensive:* $70–80; *Moderate,* $50–70; and *Inexpensive,* under $50.

Deluxe: **Brookshire.** 120 E. Lombard St. European-style luxury with 91 suites facing the harbor.

Holiday Inn–Downtown. 301 W. Lombard St. Across from Civic Center.

Hyatt Regency. 300 Light St. Overlooks the Inner Harbor. Indoor atrium, waterfall and other Hyatt touches.

Omni International. 101 W. Fayette St. Centrally located.

Tremont. 8 E. Pleasant St. Small, luxurious all-suite hotel.

Expensive: **Days Inn.** 100 Hopkins Place. A 10-story hotel with pool, 1 block from Convention Center.

Moderate: **Comfort Inn.** 24 West Franklin St. Waterbed, Jacuzzi suites. Pub, restaurant.

Harbor City Inn (Best Western). 1701 Russell St., exit 7 from Baltimore–Washington Expwy. Modern, handsome.

 DINING OUT in Baltimore can involve some serious exploring. Though one hears a lot about Maryland's traditional dishes—spoon bread, beaten biscuits, terrapin soup, oyster stew—the truth is that it's not so easy to find them on menus. However, those whose business it is to know say that the equal of Baltimore's Maryland roast turkey, Maryland fried chicken, crab cakes, or fried oysters is nowhere to be found. Oyster crackers are hard to find these days, but you can still stand in Lexington Market and eat succulent bivalves raw as the stallkeeper shucks them, along with a seemingly endless variety of other regional and ethnic specialties.

Restaurant price categories are as follows: *Deluxe,* $25 and up; *Expensive,* $20–25; *Moderate,* $10–20; *Inexpensive,* below $10. These prices are for hors d'oeuvres or soup, entrée, and dessert. Not included are drinks, tax, and tips.

Deluxe: **Danny's.** Charles and Biddle Sts. Sumptuous service, but expensive.

Haussner's. 3244 Eastern Ave. Impressive variety, with a German touch.

John Eager Howard Room. In the Belvedere Hotel. Fine continental dining in a formal setting.

Peerce's Downtown. 225 N. Liberty St. Features Louisiana gourmet specialties.

Prime Rib. 1101 N. Calvert St. Beautifully decorated.

Tio Pepe. 10 E. Franklin St. Excellent Spanish cuisine.

Expensive: **Marconi's.** 106 W. Saratoga St. An old standby, popular with city residents.

Moderate: **American Café.** HarborPlace. Wide selection of American dishes.

Chart House. Pier 4, E. Pratt St. Prime ribs, seafood.

Rusty Scupper. 402 Key Highway. Good seafood, best view of the harbor.

Sabatino's. 901 Fawn St. One of the best in Little Italy.

Inexpensive: **Pub Down Under.** 201 N. Charles St. Soups and sandwiches.

Food stalls at HarborPlace. Over three dozen eateries, from inexpensive ethnic carryouts to expensive French and seafood restaurants.

EXPLORING MARYLAND

In the tiny village of Wye Mills, you will find a water mill dating from the late 17th century, a Colonial schoolhouse with original furnishings, an 18th-century church, and Maryland's official State Tree, the Wye Oak, more than 400 years old and sometimes called a "one-tree forest."

Oxford was originally an important port of entry and is still devoted to boats; in fact, it is a well-known center for sailing enthusiasts. In it you may visit shipyards and a sail loft. And you will certainly want to stop at the Robert Morris Inn, a well-run hotel occupying the early 18th-century home of the father of the famous financier of the American Revolution. Its dining room is excellent, its decor charming.

The oldest ferry in the United States, the *Oxford–Bellevue,* will carry you across the Tred Avon River. Take State 33 to St. Michaels. For 250 years it was a shipbuilding community. Today, it has the Chesapeake Bay Maritime Museum, where relics of that work may be seen, while tied up at the museum wharf are some of the old vessels themselves. Also, there is an original 19th-century Bay lighthouse on display. See St. Mary's Square, where they still ring the bell that used to call the carpenters to work. Take a look at the Log House, an example of pioneer building with its skin peeled back, as it were, to display the workmanship. Visit the Cannonball House, a reminder of a joke the townspeople are said to have played on the British in the War of 1812. With St. Michaels targeted for night bombardment, the people hung lanterns in the treetops and English gunners, taking these for the town lights, aimed high. Only one shot hit a house, still named for the missile intended to destroy it.

Annapolis

Your first stop on the Western Shore will be Annapolis, founded in 1649, the capital since 1695. Its historic area (a National Historic Landmark District) contains the State House (1772), William Paca House and Garden (1765), Hammond-Harwood House (1774), Chase-Lloyd House (1773), Brice House (1773)—all Registered National Historic Landmarks. The United States Naval Academy is open daily for visiting. Harbor Cruise Boats operates from the city dock, late spring through fall.

Then go south on US 301. If your trip is made between March and May, you will be able to see the world's greatest loose-leaf-tobacco sales and auctions along your way, weekday mornings at Upper Marlboro, Waldorf and La Plata, and at nearby Hughesville on State 5. Visitors are welcome at the warehouses and there is no charge.

Take 301 and State 6 west to Port Tobacco, one of the oldest inhabited sites in the country. Today located half a mile from the river, this quiet town was once the port through which southern Maryland's vast tobacco crop was shipped abroad. In spite of changes, Port Tobacco retains its historical attractiveness. The central square still contains an 18th-century courthouse, tavern, and many of the original homes.

St. Mary's County Highlights

Go first to St. Mary's City, on State 5, where the first Maryland colony was established in 1634. See the replica of the 1676 State House, and foundations of buildings uncovered in restoration work. Nearby, north of Hollywood on State 245, is Sotterley, a magnificent Colonial working plantation dating to 1717.

Go on to Point Lookout, still on 5. Here the 10-mile-wide Potomac rolls into the 20-mile-wide bay, the nearby state park offering excellent camping facilities. In the Civil War, there was a Confederate prison camp there. Two monuments have been erected to the prisoners who died, one by the Federal government, another by Maryland. Nearby is Ft. Lincoln, where Union soldiers kept guard.

Maryland's Not-So-Wild West

In the town of Frederick, the National Historic District includes the beautiful Court House Square; the tomb of Francis Scott Key in Mt. Olivet Cemetery; plus numerous other historic homes and attractions. The Visitor's Center at 19 E. Church St. is open daily year round and May–October offers guided walking tours.

A few miles east of Frederick just off I–70 is New Market, called the "Antiques Capital of Maryland." It is a tiny village that is entirely supported by the sale of antiques. More than four dozen high-quality shops line its brief streets. Any antiques fancier should see this place.

South of Frederick is Stronghold, a private estate, the grounds of which are open to the public, and well worth seeing. They include Sugarloaf Mountain on the slopes of which are overlooks and picnic grounds along a well-planned drive. One reaches Stronghold by going south on I–270 to State 109 via Comus.

Go by US 40 or Interstate 70 to Hagerstown. In the City Park there, see the Hager House, built by the founder of the city in 1739. This building combines the aspects of a mansion and a fort, reminding the modern traveler that in 1739 this area was the American "West.".

On the field of Antietam on September 17, 1862, the Union Army repulsed the first Confederate attempt to invade the North. The field, a National Monument and Historic Battlefield Site, can be reached by State 65 out of Hagerstown. There is a Visitors' Center and Museum, a good place to begin your tour. The Burnside Bridge over Antietam Creek is an impressive stone structure.

Leave Hagerstown and proceed west via I–70. A highway sign will direct you to Ft. Frederick State Park. Here, there is a huge stone fort of the French and Indian War period (1756). The structure and recon-structed barracks remind you vividly of the dangers of frontier exis-tence.

The above is an outline of one possible tour. It is not the full list of what there is to see in the Old Line State, but it will give you an idea of how much is waiting for you should you go there.

PRACTICAL INFORMATION FOR MARYLAND

HOW TO GET THERE. *By car:* I-95 enters the state near Wilmington, Del., passing through Aberdeen and Baltimore and leaving the state at Washington, D.C. I-70 connects central Pennsylvania and Baltimore, en-tering Maryland at Hancock. US 301 is the primary north-south route on the Eastern Shore, entering the state from Middletown, Del. The Chesapeake Bay Bridge-Tunnel connects Cape Charles, Va. (near Salisbury, Md.) and Cape Henry, Va. (Bayside).

By air: There is scheduled air service to Baltimore (Baltimore-Washington International Airport), Hagerstown, Salisbury, and Washington, D.C. Number-ous airlines fly to Baltimore and Washington, D.C. *Piedmont* has commuter flights to Hagerstown and Salisbury.

By bus: Greyhound and *Trailways* are the major carriers to Maryland, and Baltimore is the major terminal.

By train: Amtrak has service to Wilmington, Delaware, Baltimore, BWI Airport, Washington, D.C., and western Maryland.

TOURIST INFORMATION. Maps, brochures, and information of all kinds are available from the Division of Tourist Development, Maryland Department of Economic & Community Development, 45 Calvert St., Annapolis 21401 (301) 269–3517. Toll-free (800) 331–1750.

 NATIONAL PARKS AND FORESTS. *Chesapeake and Ohio Canal.* Stretching from the Georgetown section of Washington, D.C. to Cumberland, along the Maryland bank of the twisting Potomac River, this is the longest of all national parks, 185 miles. An idea of George Washington's, the canal was started by President John Quincy Adams on July 4, 1828—the same day the Baltimore and Ohio Railroad was begun.

Catoctin Mountain Park, just three miles west of Thurmont, includes the site of Camp David, the Presidential retreat. For the public there are a seven-mile scenic drive, twelve miles of well-marked hiking trails, two picnic areas, and a modern camp for five-day family camping from mid-April to October.

 MUSEUMS AND GALLERIES. *Calvert Marine Museum,* Solomons. A museum dedicated to preservation of local marine history, featuring a lighthouse, boat models, bay boats, paintings, and other exhibits.

Washington County Museum of Fine Arts, in City Park, Hagerstown. The only real art museum in the state outside Baltimore. Features a new exhibit every month and Sunday afternoon concerts year-round.

Chesapeake Bay Maritime Museum, on State 33 off US 50, in St. Michael's. Established in 1965 to keep alive the memories, adventures, romance, and artifacts of America's great inland sea, the museum has always had an impressive collection of boat models, name boards, and figureheads, but it also now has a lighthouse and several sailing craft which can be boarded.

 HISTORIC SITES. *Central Maryland,* all within less than an hour's drive from Baltimore. *Clara Barton House.* MacArthur Blvd. in Glen Echo, three mi. north of District of Columbia line. Home of the Civil War nurse who founded the American Red Cross, built for her by grateful survivors of the 1889 Johnstown flood who used lumber from emergency barracks erected while she was director. Served as Red Cross Headquarters from 1897 to 1904.

Great Falls of the Potomac, on State 189 near Potomac, Md. A spectacular sight the year round. The *Chesapeake and Ohio Canal,* which skirted the falls in 1828, is restored at this point. The canal begins in the Georgetown area of Washington, D.C. and reaches 185 miles to Cumberland along the Maryland shore of the Potomac River.

Southern Maryland, Annapolis. The capital of the Old Line State offers much for the visitor to see and all of it within easy walking distance. Included are the State House, oldest in America in continuous legislative use; many 18th-century mansions which are Registered National Historic Landmarks; the colonial waterfront; and the United States Naval Academy. *Old State House,* St. Mary's City, Rte. 5. A replica of the original built in 1676, was erected in 1934 as part of tercentenary celebration. *Sotterley,* three mi. east of Hollywood, State 235. Many Marylanders say this is their favorite house. Overlooking the Patuxent River, the long, low structure, built 1711–27, has a notable Chinese Chippendale stairway and other fine woodwork. Since it never deteriorated, it never had to be restored. It's still surrounded by a plantation-size farm. *London Town* on the South River, off State 2, the site of a once-thriving seaport, consists of a mid-18th century Publik House inn, reconstructed colonial log tobacco barn, visitors' center, and 10-acre woodland gardens.

Eastern Shore. The Eastern Shore of Maryland, nine counties on the Delmarva Peninsula, is the area most often associated with Maryland by out-of-staters.

Wye Mills, on State 404 off US 50. Here is the location of the Wye Oak, Maryland's official tree, said to be over 400 years old. Nearby is a restored 18th-century grist mill which ground flour for George Washington's army, a one-room schoolhouse, and restored Old Wye Chapel (1721).

Oxford-Bellevue Ferry is the oldest continuous ferry in the nation, having made its first crossing of the Tred Avon River in 1760. The present diesel-driven barge carries six cars. Reached from Easton via St. Michaels Rd. to Royal Oak or from Easton via Oxford Rd. Oxford is a charming waterside village, where log canoe and sailboat races are held many summer weekends.

Ocean City, eastern terminus of US 50, is Maryland's only oceanside resort. White clapboard hotels and boarding houses face the Atlantic on one side and Sinepuxent Bay on the other in the oldest section, but its northern end now has all the glitter of Atlantic City. Beautiful wide beach. Three amusement parks. Deep sea and bay fishing available.

TOURS. *Historic Annapolis,* Inc., Old Treasury, State Circle, Annapolis 21401, conducts several walking tours. So does *Three Centuries Tours of Annapolis,* P.O. Box 29, Annapolis 21404, tel. (301) 263–5357. Sightseeing water cruises are offered by *Chesapeake Marine Tours,* P.O. Box 3350, City Dock, Annapolis 21403.

GARDENS. *Lilypons,* a 300-acre tract of exotic water plants and ponds, 8 miles south of Frederick, off State 85, features water lilies named after such famous personalities as Colonel Lindbergh and Dorothy Lamour.

DRINKING LAWS. The minimum age is 21 for beer and wine, 21 for hard liquor. It is best to inquire locally about drinking restrictions, but most bars, restaurants, and hotels are open from 6 A.M. to 2 A.M., except Sundays (when hours are shorter) and election days.

HOTELS AND MOTELS in Maryland range from deluxe to inexpensive, and include resorts over a century old and the latest in up-to-the-minute motels. Price categories for double-occupancy rooms in Maryland are divided into the following ranges: *Deluxe,* $50 and higher; *Expensive,* $40–50; *Moderate,* $25–40; and *Inexpensive,* under $25.

ANNAPOLIS. *Deluxe:* **Annapolis Hilton Inn.** On the water.
Governor Calvert House. Part of structure dates from early 18th century.
Maryland Inn. Gracious inn, built in 1770.

BETHESDA. *Deluxe:* **Marriott.** Pool, tennis, two outstanding restaurants.

EASTON. *Expensive:* **Tidewater.** Golf and tennis.

GAITHERSBURG. *Deluxe:* **Marriott Hotel.** Two dining rooms, year-round swimming.

GRANTSVILLE. *Moderate:* **Casselman Inn.** Main St. (US 40). Inn built in 1824, plus model units.

OCEAN CITY. *Deluxe:* **Carousel.** Oceanfront. Indoor ice rink, spa, exercise room.
Castle in the Sand. Includes 56 new oceanfront efficiencies.
Phillips Beach Plaza. Oceanfront. An air of elegance graces this pleasant hotel. Open year-round.
  Sheraton Fontainebleau. Indoor pool, tennis, sauna, gourmet dining.
Expensive: **Misty Harbor.** Reasonable rates, 2 blocks from beach.

SALISBURY. *Deluxe:* **Sheraton Inn.** Restaurant, lounge.

SILVER SPRING. *Deluxe:* **Sheraton-Silver Spring.** Class accommodations. Also indoor pool, fitness center, sauna.

YOUTH HOSTELS. Betterton. Ye Lantern Inn. Country inn, 20 beds.

Cambrdige Home Hostel. Friendly atmosphere. **Knoxville Kiwanis Hostel.** 16 mi. W of Frederick. Small, open summers only.

 DINING OUT. In Maryland this can involve not only fine local dishes, but also the pleasure of a country drive; if you have the time you should definitely try to sample some of the more out-of-the-way places. Restaurant price categories are as follows: *Deluxe,* $20 and up; *Expensive,* $15–20; *Moderate,* $10–15; *Inexpensive,* below $10. These prices are for hors d'oeuvres or soup, entrée, and dessert. Not included are drinks, tax, and tips.

ANNAPOLIS. *Deluxe:* **Annapolis Hilton Inn.** At the city dock.
Treaty of Paris Room, at Maryland Inn. Sophisticated seafood and Continental cuisine.
Expensive: **Harbour House.** Inviting atmosphere overlooking the harbor.

BETHESDA. *Deluxe:* **Bello Mondo** and **Kona Kai.** In Marriott Hotel. The first serves sophisticated Italian cuisine, the latter specializes in Polynesian food and drink in an exotic setting.
La Miche. Outstanding French cuisine, pleasant atmosphere.

COLUMBIA. *Deluxe:* **King's Contrivance.** Old Southern hospitality.

CUMBERLAND. *Deluxe:* **Bistro.** Elegant setting, food worth a detour.

GRANTSVILLE. *Moderate:* **Penn Alps.** Pennsylvania Dutch cuisine. Craft demonstrations in summer.

HAGERSTOWN. *Expensive:* **Nick's Airport Inn.** Seafood specialties.
Red Horse. Homey atmosphere; steak and seafood.
Tortuga. Old establishment. Popular with area residents.

OCEAN CITY. *Deluxe:* **Bonfire.** An old favorite. Steaks and seafood; lounge.
Embers. Steaks and seafood.
Philip's Crab House. Crab delicacies, seafood.
Reflections. Flambé entrées, intimate atmosphere.
Moderate: **Bayside Skillet.** Good crepes and omelettes, fresh fruit.

OXFORD. *Expensive:* Robert Morris Inn. Sophisticated dining room.
Moderate: Pier Street Marina and Restaurant. Historic site.

ST. MICHAELS. *Expensive:* **Longfellow's.** Fresh seafood. Overlooks the water.

URBANA. *Moderate:* **Peter Pan Inn.** Family recipes.

NEW JERSEY

Lakes and Seashore

Known as the "Garden State," New Jersey offers a winning combination for vacationers from near and far. Because it is convenient to other metropolitan areas, the state is experiencing a tourism boom. All of New Jersey's many attractions may be reached via economical, energy-saving public transportation, or a network of super highways.

The Atlantic Ocean hasn't changed any. The "wonderful sea" still washes 127 miles of New Jersey shore from Sandy Hook to Cape May. But things have changed at the seaside, particularly in Atlantic City, the queen of the state's vacationland. There's renewed vitality in this changing resort, with its broad beaches and rolling waves. Casino gambling has arrived.

Resorts International and Caesar's Boardwalk Regency were the first casinos to open. They were followed by Bally's Park Place, the Sands (formerly the Brighton), Harrah's, the Golden Nugget, Atlantis (formerly, Playboy), the Claridge, and the Tropicana. The second wave of casinos was ushered in with the opening of Trump Plaza in 1984.

But fear not. Boardwalk life, as well as deep-sea fishing, bathing, and the Miss America Pageant the week after Labor Day—all those famous Atlantic City ingredients—will continue as usual.

Visitors pouring into the state from all points are discovering that New Jersey is not just a part of the megalopolis running from Boston to Washington, D.C. The visitor who shuns this crowded area finds a reason for the nickname "The Garden State." To the south are the ocean, farmlands, pine barrens; to the north are mountains and lakes where recreation and the rustic life are fostered.

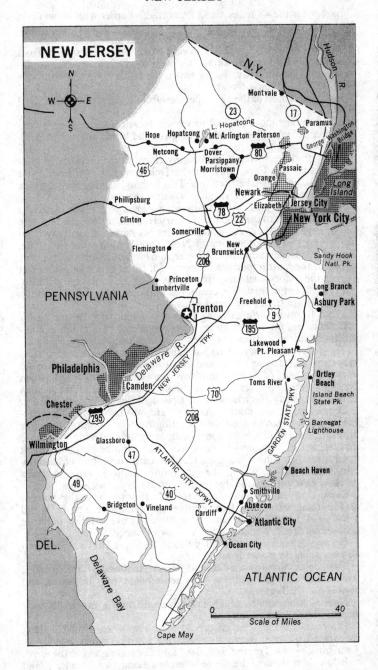

Except for the 48 miles along its northern border with New York, New Jersey is washed on all sides by water. Other than the Hawaiian islands, it is the most completely water-locked state in the union.

The western border is the Delaware River, flowing 280 miles from New York (with Pennsylvania to the west and Delaware to the southwest) into Delaware Bay. To the east is the Hudson River, New York Bay, and the Atlantic Ocean.

Just behind most of the 127-mile oceanfront is the gentle Intercoastal Waterway.

Whether they move by boat or wheels, travelers—fishermen, swimmers, boatsmen, or just vacationers—will find beach and water facilities to meet any taste.

Along the ocean stretch from Sandy Hook, at the entrance to New York Harbor, to Cape May on the Delaware Bay, the beachfront provides some unusual attractions. This bathing, fishing, relaxing area alone attracts millions of vacationers each year.

Sandy Hook is part of the Gateway National Recreation Area. Its history goes back to the time when Henry Hudson, in 1609, tied up here before exploring the river which carries his name. It has played an historic part in the protection of New York Harbor since that time, through the Revolution, the Civil War, and the development of the port as one of the most important in the world. National Parks guides can explain the history, including that surrounding the Twin Light Houses, built in 1828. For strictly recreational purposes there are swimming, fishing, nature trails, and picnicking.

From Rumson through Long Branch to Deal, once the mecca for presidents and the rich, is an area now populated by families of commuters from the metropolitan New York region.

Then there is Asbury Park, which still maintains its boardwalk, miniature golf courses, rides and concessions, and its beach. It is no longer the resort of distinction it was more than a century ago, when New York manufacturer James A. Bradley bought a considerable area of beach property and named it for Episcopal Bishop Francis Asbury.

Ocean Grove, next door to Asbury Park, was another Bradley contribution. Operated by the Camp Meeting Association since 1871, it is now in a state of flux, with some factions fighting to bring it into the modern world. Liquor is banned, as is any form of business except hotels and their dining facilities. Until recently, operation of automobiles was forbidden within the city limits on the Sabbath. A court decision now permits the distribution of Sunday newspapers.

Ocean Grove appeals not just to the elderly or the very religious, but also to young people, who find a simpler way of life here. You can spend a few days, a week, or a summer at Ocean Grove; address inquiries concerning accommodations to the Town Council, 07756.

Beyond Ocean Grove is Bradley Beach, featuring mostly sophisticated homes on the ocean front.

Then come Avon-by-the-Sea and Belmar, followed by Spring Lake, once a haven for the wealthy. Now some homes may be rented, and motels dot the highway.

Next is Manasquan, which has developed into a minor "Muscle Beach" for the young set.

Short-stay facilities outside any of these resorts are available along the main highways. Write to either the town's visitors' agency or Tourism, CN 384, Trenton, N.J. 08625, for listings on any of the areas.

Below Manasquan, the shore stretches along two islands, Island Beach and Long Beach Island, where accommodations are mostly homes and cottages, which families both use and rent.

Then comes Atlantic City. Farther south are: teetotaling Ocean City, founded by Methodist ministers and still with no public bars or liquor stores; Stone Harbor, summer home of bird-watchers, yachtsmen, and regular seasonal boarders; the Wildwoods, a booming series of three seaside towns claiming 10,000 motel accommodations; and finally, elegant old Cape May, the earliest and most aristocratic shore resort in America, with many historic homes on view.

Alongside all of this seascape runs the Garden State Parkway, which starts at the New York state line, where it connects with the New York Thruway, and runs to the Delaware Bay at Cape May. There you can take a ferry to Lewes, Delaware.

To the east of the parkway, on its way south, is the Garden State Arts Center, a summer showcase for theatre, ballet, music, and drama; west is Great Adventure, a combination theme park and jungle safari; and, in the southern extremities, the Pine Barrens. Here is an incredibly varied mass of plant life, with 60 miles of wilderness canoe trails.

Out of New York City, I–80 has blazed a six- to eight-lane highway across the state to the Delaware Water Gap. What was formerly a time-consuming trip is now an hour's drive and leads to one of the state's most delightful mountain settings, the Delaware Water Gap National Recreation Area. And, of course, I–80 goes from there on across the nation to San Francisco.

Trenton and Princeton

Farther south on the Delaware River is the state capital, Trenton. Much of the town can be seen on a walking tour from the state capitol, including Trent House and Watson House.

Princeton, the home of Princeton University, has more residents in *Who's Who* per capita than any other U.S. municipality. The university offers excellent tours. Princeton also is home of the Educational Testing Service, the Gallup Poll and the Institute for Advanced Study, where scholars like Albert Einstein have done research.

The middle of the state has several towns of historical interest. New Brunswick is the home of Rutgers, the state university. Menlo Park is the site of Edison's laboratory, which is now a museum.

Newark and the North

Newark is the third-oldest of the major American cities, and New Jersey's largest. A tour should include the Newark Museum, with working scientific models, natural history items, the Victorian Ballentine House, and the Symphony Hall, formerly the Mosque Theater.

Before heading west, go a bit farther north for a drive along the Hudson River and the Palisades—cliffs climbing straight up on the Jersey side of the river.

The northwestern corner of New Jersey looks much like New England, with rolling hills, lakes and forests. Among the high points are the Franklin mines, where you may scavenge for minerals and keep what you find, and the 10,000-acre Wawayanda State Forest in Sussex County. If you're rock hounding, bring a hammer, chisel and gunny sack for treasures. The 5,830 treetopped acres of Worthington Forest, just above the Delaware Water Gap, intersects the Appalachian Trail and is nestled in the Kittatinny Range. In McAfee is the Great Gorge/Vernon Valley ski area and a developing year-round resort.

PRACTICAL INFORMATION FOR NEW JERSEY

HOW TO GET AROUND. *By air:* Newark Airport is a major international airport, served by many major airlines. Other New Jersey airfields: Teterboro, Caldwell, Monmouth County, Morris County, Princeton, Trenton, Atlantic City and Pomona.

By bus: Transport of New Jersey and other locally operated lines, plus major transcontinental services running primarily from bus terminals in New York and servicing towns on major New Jersey highways in all directions. Consult bus companies at the New York City Port Authority Terminal, 8th Avenue at 41st St., NY 10018, for schedules.

By car: Toll highways and interstate highways cross New Jersey in every direction. Tolls: New Jersey Turnpike bisects state diagonally from northeast to southwest (with connections with I–80 and the Pennsylvania Turnpike); Garden State Parkway runs from New York state line southward past all shore areas to Cape May (with connections with New York State Thruway in north, I–80 in Saddle Brook, the New Jersey Turnpike, and the Atlantic City Expressway). Atlantic City Expressway runs from Philadelphia to the resort city. Interstates: I–80 enters New Jersey via the George Washington Bridge from New York City and is complete to the Pennsylvania border at Delaware Water Gap. Other interstate highways connect these thoroughfares or cross the state from north to south.

By train: Amtrak has frequent daily service on Penn Central lines from Boston, New England, and New York, through Newark, Elizabeth, and Trenton to points from coast to coast. Its Metroliner service to Washington is considered one of the finest rail accommodations in this country.

TOURIST INFORMATION: N.J. Division of Travel and Tourism, CN 384, Trenton, N.J. 08625, (609) 292–2470.

SEASONAL EVENTS for which the Garden State is famed include the annual Easter parades on the Boardwalks at Atlantic City and Asbury Park, spring floral attractions in many different areas, with cherry blossoms, dogwood, and even hydrangeas as the main attraction, and the ethnic Liberty State Park Festival each September.

In May, the ocean is "unlocked" to ceremoniously open the summer season at Atlantic City. In August, nearby Ocean City sponsors "A Night in Venice," a colorful bayside boating parade.

Summer theater at its best is found at the Garden State Arts Center at Holmdel, off Exit 116 of the Garden State Parkway. It offers a parade of top talent, plus rousing ethnic festivals. Other theaters are the Gateway Playhouse in Somers Point, near Atlantic City; the Playhouse on the Mall at Paramus in the Bergen County Shopping Mall; the N. J. Shakespeare Festival at Madison, Morris County; and the McCarter Theater at Historic Princeton.

MUSEUMS AND GALLERIES. The *New Jersey State Museum* in the Cultural Center, Trenton, adjacent to the state capitol, has a varied and changing series of exhibitions featuring Jerseyana; also a planetarium and an auditorium where lectures, slides, films and live shows are presented. Write the museum in advance for programs and for tickets—205 West State Street, Trenton, N.J. 08625. The *Newark Museum* has a Junior Museum. *Paterson Museum* has John P. Holland's original submarine from 1878. The SS *Ling,* a World War II submarine, has been reactivated and is docked as a museum in a special berth at Borg Park, 140 River Street, Hackensack.

Historical sites include the *Morristown National Historic Park,* in and around Morristown, where George Washington and the Colonial army spent the winters of 1777 and 1779–80; three unique ironmaking villages, situated in state parks: the 78-room *Ringwood Manor* in Ringwood State Park, the *Batsto Village* in the Southern Pine Barrens, where cannons were made during the Revolutionary period, and *Allaire State Park,* site of the historic Howell's Ironworks.

Thomas Edison's laboratory—for 44 years—is in West Orange. *Washington Crossing State Park,* on the Delaware River above Trenton, marks the spot where Colonial troops, under Gen. Washington, crossed the ice-clogged river on Christmas night, 1776, and proceeded on to defeat the British at Trenton.

Major libraries are the *Harvey Firestone Library* at Princeton University, with over 2 million volumes, including the writings of Woodrow Wilson, William Faulkner, and F. Scott Fitzgerald, and *Rutgers University Library,* with its Walt Whitman papers. The *Walt Whitman House* is in Camden.

Both *Liberty Village* in Flemington and the *Historic Towne of Smithville* near Atlantic City are re-created Colonial towns with shops, businesses, and restaurants serviced by participants in costumes.

DRINKING LAWS. Legal drinking age is 21.

SUMMER SPORTS. *Fishing:* New Jersey's coastal waters have most species of saltwater fish known in North America: tuna, striped bass, marlin, kingfish, swordfish, flounder, albacore, and bluefish. Charter fishing boats are available along the entire coast, with the principal headquarters at Asbury Park, Atlantic City, Briele, Long Beach Island, the Wildwoods, and Cape May. No license is required for deep-sea and surf fishing. Inland fishing offers trout, pickerel, bass, and sunfish. A license is required.

Freshwater fishing is also great, with many rivers and well-stocked streams. For information, check the local sporting goods store or write the Division of Fish, Game and Shell Fisheries, CN400, Trenton, NJ 06825.

And, of course, the miles of coastline are wonderful for swimming and boating.

HUNTING. Over a quarter of a million acres are available for hunters, with waterfowl hunting particularly good. There is deer hunting, including a bow-and-arrow month. Other game are quail, pheasant, woodcock, grouse, raccoon, and opposum. All have special seasons. Write the Division of Fish, Game and Shell Fisheries, CN400, Trenton, N.J. 06825.

WINTER SPORTS. Major ski areas are Great Gorge and Vernon Valley in the northern hilly area. Stokes State Forest, in the high northwest corner of the state, offers cross-country skiing and snow-shoe trails. The Appalachian Trail runs across the high section of the state, providing excellent back-packing tours, and the Palisades, along the Hudson River, offer some fine hiking. There is a Ski Touring Center at Blairstown, Sussex. You will find all of the ice sports—even ice boating—on the many highland lakes and on rivers off the Jersey Shore.

SPECTATOR SPORTS are a major attraction throughout the state, starting with the Meadowlands Sport Complex in the Hackensack Meadowlands, just minutes from mid-town New York City. It is described as the "greatest sports center in the U.S." Its football stadium is the home of the Giants and Jets, as well as the Cosmos soccer team. The indoor arena houses Nets basketball. The complex also offers top thoroughbred and harness racing, and all of the other top sports events.

There's also top thoroughbred racing at Monmouth Park, Eatontown—the "resort of racing" which is just minutes from the Golden State Parkway—and at the Atlantic City Race Course. In addition, Cherry Hill's Garden State Race Track is slated to reopen in 1985. Harness racing may also be enjoyed at historic Freehold, the oldest track in the country, and at Atlantic City.

WHAT TO DO WITH THE CHILDREN. *Turtle Back Zoo,* West Orange, offers miniature train rides, seal pool and many animals. *Wild West City,* Netcong, is a real life western reproduction, with live-action shows. *Raggedy Ann Doll Museum,* Flemington, is open Apr.–Nov.

For the young—and the young at heart—there's *Six Flags Great Adventure* in Jackson Township, just off the N. J. Turnpike. You can drive through to see an outstanding collection of wild animals in naturalized habitats or spend the day exploring a spectacular theme/amusement park.

The *Land of Make Believe,* just off I–80 in Hope, is an amusement park with rides, shows, and various theme attractions.

The *Space Wild Animal Farm* on Route 519, Beemerville, Sussex County, has wild animals, a mink farm, a museum of early American farm tools, Indian relics, and antique cars.

There's a children's storyland at *Fairy Tale Forest* in Oak Ridge, with the Candy Rock Line Train Ride. In Cardiff, *Storybook Land* is a similar attraction.

HOTELS AND MOTELS. *Deluxe:* $100 and up; *Expensive:* $80–100; *Moderate:* $60–80; *Inexpensive:* under $60. All based on double occupancy. *Note:* accommodations in Atlantic City are generally more expensive.

ATLANTIC CITY. By far, the nicest and most expensive places to stay are the casinos such as *Resorts International, Caesar's Boardwalk Regency, Bally's, The Sands, Golden Nugget, Harrah's, Atlantis, The Claridge, The Tropicana,* and *Trump Plaza.*

Also try: *Deluxe:* **Best Western Inn.** Sauna, heated rooftop pool.

BEACH HAVEN. *Expensive:* **The Engleside.** Oceanfront, efficiencies.

CAMDEN. *Expensive:* **Hyatt Cherry Hill.** Rt. 70. Pool, tennis courts, suites. **Sheraton-Poste Inn.** Rt. 70 and I–295. Pool, tennis courts, suites.

CAPE MAY. *Expensive:* **Atlas Motor Inn,** Madison Ave. & Beach Drive. Also write to the Cape May County Department of Public Affairs, Box 365, Old Court House, Cape May, NJ 08204, for a list of Victorian-style guesthouses.

LAMBERTVILLE. *Inexpensive:* **Lambertville House.** Historic Inn.

NEWARK. *Expensive:* At the airport: **Holiday Inn** and **Howard Johnson's. Hilton Gateway.** Opposite railroad station. Pool, suites.

OCEAN CITY. *Expensive:* **The Sting Ray.** Seasonal, oceanfront. **Port-of-Call** Open all year. Rates range from *inexpensive* to *expensive,* depending on season.

SADDLE BROOK. *Deluxe:* **Marriot,** I–80 and Parkway Exit 159. Pools, health club.
Expensive: **Howard Johnson.** I–80 and Parkway Exit 159. Pools.

WILDWOOD. *Expensive:* **El Coronado.** Oceanfront, efficiencies.

DINING OUT. *Deluxe,* $17.50 and up; *Expensive,* $12.50–17.50; *Moderate,* $7.50–12.50; *Inexpensive,* under $7.50. Prices are for a complete meal but do not include drinks, tax or tip.

ABSECON. *Deluxe:* **Ram's Head Inn.** Beef, seafood. Jacket required.

ATLANTIC CITY. *Deluxe:* **The Knife and Fork Inn.** Seafood and steaks. **Johan's.** Prix–fixe dinners. Intimate settings. Reservations.

Peking Duck House. Lovely setting for Chinese cuisine. Duck, of course, the specialty.
Inexpensive: **The White House Sub Shop.** Local landmark.

CAMDEN. *Expensive:* **Cinelli's Country House.** In Cherry Hill. Varied menu. Consult Philadelphia guide.

CAPE MAY. *Expensive:* **Top of the Marq.** 6 stories up, overlooks Atlantic.
Moderate–Expensive: **Lobster House.** On Fisherman's Wharf. Seafood.

COLLINGSWOOD. *Moderate:* **Sagami Japanese Restaurant.** Fine Japanese food.

HAMMONTON-BATSTO. *Moderate:* **Sweetwater Casino.** Specialties with seafood and river fish. Lovely backwoods setting.

HOHOKUS. *Moderate–Expensive:* **Hohokus Inn.** Historic landmark.

MORRISTOWN. *Deluxe:* **The Grand Café.** French food in a relaxed atmosphere.

NEW BRUNSWICK. *Deluxe:* **The Frog and the Peach.** State-of-the-art food in a state-of-the-art building.
Expensive: **McAteer's.** Southern ambience.

OCEAN CITY. *Expensive:* **The Pearl.** Italian cuisine in an Art Deco setting.
Moderate: **Watson's.** In large old house. Seafood. Open seasonally.

PRINCETON. *Moderate:* **Nassau Inn.** Menu reflects cosmopolitan university.

SMITHVILLE. *Expensive:* **Smithville Inn.** Stuffed pork chops, roast duck. A restored Colonial Inn.

TRENTON. *Moderate:* **Glendale Inn.** Outside city. Homemade Italian food.
Landwehrs. Fireplaces, paneled rooms. Steaks.

WANAQUE. *Expensive:* **Berta's.** Family-style Italian restaurant in old house, barn. Hearty meal. Home-grown vegetables.

WILDWOOD-WILDWOOD CREST. *Moderate–Expensive:* **Ed Zaberer's.** Steaks and seafood. Try the lobster. Open seasonally.

NEW YORK

City, Island, and Fabulous Upstate

New York City is made up of five separate boroughs—Manhattan, Queens, Brooklyn, the Bronx, and Staten Island. The great majority of tourist sights and facilities are on Manhattan Island, and when people say, "We're going to the City," they mean Manhattan. While the other boroughs offer a few attractions, they are primarily residential areas.

New York City is easy to explore with the aid of a city map which you can pick up at the New York Convention and Visitors' Bureau at the bureau's new offices at Columbus Circle. The bus systems and the more than 500 miles of subways will take you to almost any sight you want to see; for in-town touring, a car is an expensive handicap. You will find walking the most rewarding way to come to know the city and its people, to savor its flavor, and to make little discoveries of your own.

The Battery Park area, where the city's history began, is an excellent starting point for lower Manhattan. Bus and subway systems converge here at Bowling Green, the little "Green before the fort" where early burghers bowled on summer evenings. Within a small radius are some of the city's most historic sites.

The Statue of Liberty

The Statue of Liberty was a gift from the people of France to the people of the United States commemorating the long friendship between the two nations—a friendship which dated from the American Revolution, when French aid to General George Washington helped turn the tide of victory to the side of the Colonies. The Statue of Liberty Enlightening the World was dedicated October 28, 1886, with these words by President Grover Cleveland: "We will not forget that Liberty has here made her home; nor shall her chosen altar be neglected."

The 151-foot statue is a monument to the genius of its sculptor. To achieve the correct proportions, Frederic Auguste Bartholdi made a four-foot study model, then cast and recast it until it was 36 feet high. The statue was then divided into dozens of sections and each section enlarged four times. Liberty's eyes became two feet wide, her nose four feet long, her waist an ample 35 feet. On the mold of each section, copper sheets 3/32 inch thick were pressed and hammered into shape. Bartholdi had chosen copper for several reasons. It was light, easily worked, strong enough to withstand the stress of shipment, and largely impervious to New York's salty air. Its pedestal, one of the heaviest pieces of masonry in the world, towers 89 feet above its foundation, the 11-pointed star-shaped old Fort Wood.

After a 10-minute ferry ride from Battery Park to Liberty Island, you will find National Park Service guides on hand to answer questions and provide a free souvenir pamphlet detailing the statue's history. An elevator will take you up 10 floors to the balcony which runs around the top of the pedestal. For the stout of heart and strong of limb there is a staircase spiraling up twelve more stories to Liberty's crown for a stratospheric view. Rest platforms are located every third of the way up, where you also can cross over and climb back down if you have a change of heart about making it all the way to the crown. When you come down, be sure to see the Museum of Immigration, which highlights the history of the settling of the U.S. Allow yourself at least two-and-a-half hours for the ferry ride and tour of Liberty Island. (Note: The statue is currently being restored and is encased in scaffolding—an interesting sight in itself. The museum and base are open; the inside of the statue, however, will be closed until the planned completion date, July 4, 1986.)

Battery Park

On your return to Battery Park, you might find a circular stroll rewarding; the handsome Marine Memorial is especially worthy of a few moments. Stand behind the memorial—an eagle on a black marble pedestal facing a corridor of huge granite slabs engraved with names of those who gave their lives to the sea—and you will see the Statue of Liberty dramatically framed.

The gray Victorian building, with its gay red window frames and bright green roof (near the park's exit), is the home of the city's fireboats; and the round brownstone building near the entrance to the park is Castle Clinton, built in 1811 to defend New York against British attack. In 1823 the fort was ceded to New York City and transformed into Castle Garden, which served as a theater and public center. From 1855 to 1890 the castle was used as the nation's principal immigrant depot, more than 7,000,000 "tempest-tost" souls passing through its gate into a bright new world until Ellis Island became the new depot. After years of being closed, Ellis Island is now open to the public once more. From 1890 till 1924, this served as the processing center for new arrivals. Opposite Bowling Green is the Customs House, an ornate Maine granite edififice studded with statuary by Daniel Chester French, which reflects the sprawling, rococo period of building at the turn of the century. The streets here are narrow, cut up, and squeezed awry by the confluence of the Hudson and East rivers. If there is one place you'll need a street map to guide you, it is here. Tucked in among them are a few historic buildings which have managed to escape destruction or have been cleverly reconstructed.

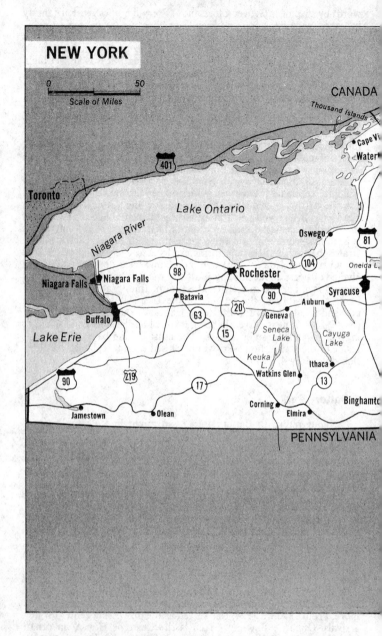

One is Fraunces Tavern on Pearl Street, a block east of the Customs House. Erroneously called "the oldest building in Manhatton," it is in fact an excellent reconstruction dating from 1907. Its square proportions, hipped roof edged with a light balustrade, regular window spacing, and white portico are perfect examples of the Georgian Colonial style favored in the early 18th century. Built of brick—which likely

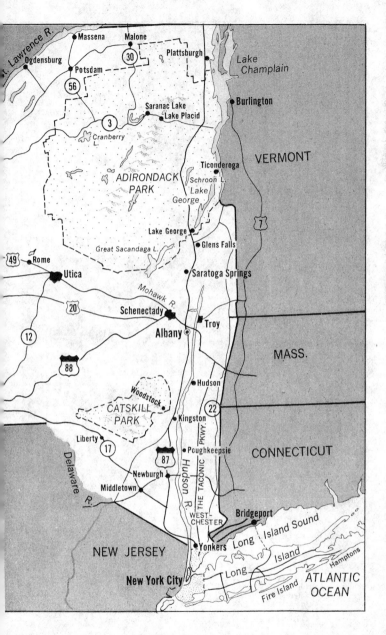

saved it from going up in flames during the disastrous fires of the Revolution—and turned from a residence into a successful business building (which staved off demolition), it has had a long, colorful history. The building was erected in 1719 as a residence for Etienne de Lancy, a wealthy Huguenot. His grandson turned it into a store and warehouse in 1757, and in 1762 it was sold to Samuel Fraunces, a West

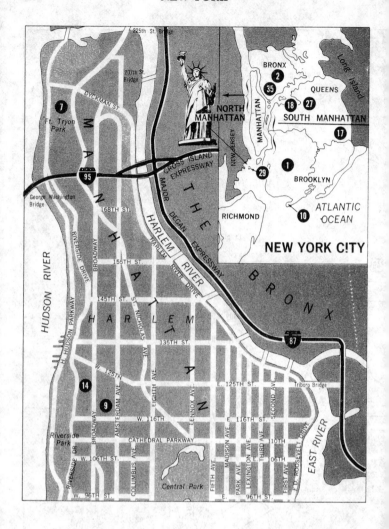

Points of Interest

1) Brooklyn Museum
2) Bronx Zoo
3) Carnegie Hall
4) Central Park Zoo
5) Chinatown
6) City Hall
7) Cloisters
8) Coliseum
9) Columbia University
10) Coney Island
11) Empire State Building
12) Gracie Mansion
13) Grand Central Station
14) Grant's Tomb
15) Guggenheim Museum
16) Hayden Planetarium
17) Kennedy International Airport
18) La Guardia Airport

Indian, who renovated it, making it the Queen's Head Tavern. Taverns in those days were often used as meetings halls, and it was at Fraunces Tavern that the Chamber of Commerce of the State of New York was founded in 1768 to help press the fight against the Stamp Act and the

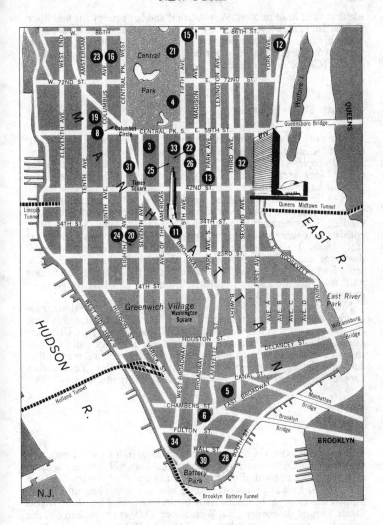

tax on tea. Here, too, George Washington called his officers together in the tavern's Long Room to bid them farewell.

The Sons of the Revolution in the State of New York purchased the property in 1904, faithfully recreated the original building, and today use it as their headquarters. A restaurant and bar occupy the first floor. On the floors above you can view the Long Room, where Washington made his adieus, and wander through a small museum of relics from the Revolutionary period, paintings and prints depicting historical events. (Closed on weekends.)

South Street Seaport

New York City gained much of its prominence and wealth as a major seaport. A non-profit organization with a membership of more than 25,000 people established the South Street Seaport Museum, covering a four-block area around the former Fulton Fish Market in lower Manhattan, in remembrance of the city's early seafaring days. At the heart of the renovation is a giant shopping and restaurant mall housing some 70 different enterprises along with the Seaport Museum and Gallery. Schermerhorn Row, which opened to the public in mid-1983, consists of a series of Georgian/Federal-style warehouses built in the early 1800s. Today they sport fancy shops downstairs and private loft dwellings above. The area's Visitor's Center is in this complex. Museum Block houses the Seaport Museum itself (207 Front Street) along with the Museum's shops, and a multi-media film that provides an overview of the Seaport and its history.

Not to be missed on a Seaport visit are the square-rigged sailing ships on view at Pier 16 at the foot of Fulton Street: the four-masted *Peking,* the *Ambrose* lightship and the schooner *Lettie G. Howard.* These are open to the public for a fee ($3.50 for adults, $1.50 for children, free to senior citizens). During the summer there are free concerts and other activities throughout the area, and daily sails into New York harbor aboard the 1885 schooner *Pioneer.* General information: 669–9400.

Wall Street

Wall Street, which is only seven blocks long, follows what once was the walled northern boundary of the original Dutch colony and became a financial center soon after the Revolutionary War. Today the New York Stock Exchange has over 1,500 member firms, and up to sixty million shares might be traded daily behind the ornate façade on Broad Street, around the corner from Wall Street. Visitors are welcome to the second-floor gallery (weekdays until about 3:30) where you can look down on the Exchange floor and listen to a recording describe what all the frantic business is about. Guides take you on a tour and demonstrate how a sale is recorded on ticker tape.

Around the corner from the Exchange is a handsome Greek Revival building, on the corner of Wall and Nassau Streets. It is Federal Hall National Memorial built in 1842 on the site of New York's first City Hall. Here, freedom of the press and freedom of speech were won by John Peter Zenger in 1735, the first Congress convened, and on April 30, 1789, General Washington was inaugurated president. It was here that the Congress adopted the Bill of Rights. Administered by the National Park Service, Federal Hall is filled with permanent exhibits.

At the head of Wall Street, fronting on Broadway, is one of New York's richest landlords, Trinity Church. The present church building, erected in 1846, is the third to occupy this site. Its graveyard dates from even before 1697; if the gate is open you can seek out the final resting places of Alexander Hamilton, Robert Fulton, and others who figured in the city's early history.

North of Trinity Church on Broadway and Fulton Streets is one of the city's few remaining examples of Colonial architecture, St. Paul's Chapel, one of many Trinity built throughout the city. When it was erected in 1766, it stood in a field outside the city. Townspeople complained that it was much too far to go to church; yet it is only a five-block walk from Trinity. On either outer aisle you will find a handsome box pew. One was the special preserve of the governors who worshipped here in the comfort of upholstered chairs and draft-deflecting canopies. The pew on the left was also used by George Washington. Original William and Mary chairs in bright red satin brocade give the pew an air of elegance seldom seen in churches. The altar, its railing, and a great deal of ornamentation in the church is the work of Major Pierre L'Enfant, the designer who later planned the city of Washington, D.C.

Directly behind St. Paul's is the gigantic World Trade Center, operated by the Port Authority of New York and New Jersey. The Center takes up sixteen acres of lower Manhattan and nine million square feet of office space is included in two 110-story tower buildings surrounding a landscaped five-acre plaza. The Center is so large, in fact, that each tower has its own postal ZIP code.

City Hall

Return to Broadway and stroll up to City Hall. It is both a museum and a municipal capitol. Architecturally it is considered one of the finest public buildings in America. During the period between 1803 and 1811 when it was being built, construction costs rose to $538,000—a shocking amount in those days. The Common Council members, pinching pennies wherever they could, decided considerable money could be saved by using marble on the front and sides only. Brownstone would be used to face the back. Most of the city's population lived south of the park and it would be a waste to use marble where it seldom would be seen. In 1956, the outside was faced in limestone on all four sides.

A handsome, curving double staircase leads to the Governor's Room on the second floor of City Hall. The elegant quarters, "appropriated as an office to His Excellency the Governor of this State," have been the scene of many gala, historic receptions and are now a showcase of antique furnishings and priceless portraits of early American heroes. One of the most notable items in the museum is George Washington's desk.

Chinatown

On leaving City Hall, walk around to its rear and over to the tall-towered Municipal Building. A passageway through its arch will bring you out on Park Row, near the approach to the Brooklyn Bridge, the city's oldest span. From here, it is but a five-minute walk north to Chinatown. It is tiny, encompassing something like nine square blocks. Thousands of Chinese are crowded into tenements lining the narrow, crooked streets. Pseudo-pagodas crowning their roofs, bright banners garlanding the streets, and temple bells help create an aura of China's civilization all around. Emporiums have modern adding machines but prefer to do their bookkeeping with the beaded abacus; apothecary and herb shops still compound family medicinal formulas. Stalls and shop windows are piled high with exotic displays of condiments and herbs, snow peas, bean curd, shark fins, duck eggs, dried fungi, squid, and other ingredients used in delectable Chinese dishes. In keeping with the Oriental theme, even the sidewalk telephone booths have been designed as tiny pagodas. The juncture of Worth and Mott Streets, across from Chatham Square, is the gateway to Chinatown. A Chinese Museum is located at 7 Mott Street, and for a small admission fee, you can view exhibits of Chinese coins, costumes, deities, and dragons. There are displays of flowers, fruits, chopsticks, and incense with explanations of their history and the symbolism attached to each. The museum also supplies you with a walking-tour map which is most helpful in identifying the Buddhist Temple, Christian churches, Chinese theaters, and other local attractions. Chinese symbols and English appear on most signs. There are dozens of shops to browse through. Jade and ivory carvings, good luck charms, slitted brocade dresses, tea sets, and sweets are to be had for generally lower prices than those uptown.

When the Chinese New Year comes in, the whole town joins in colorful parades of fire-breathing monsters which mark the start of the lunar New Year sometime in February. Firecrackers explode everywhere. Huge dragons, unicorns, and lions prowl through the streets to scare away evil spirits. Old and young dance along behind, shouting "Kung hay fat choy!" (Happy New Year with prosperity). Merchants offer gifts to the dragon and heads of lettuce sprouting dozens of dollars to be dispensed to the poor, for the dragon is an emblem of guardianship and generosity. It is a time when Chinatown is at its gayest, most colorful best.

The Bouwerie, The Bowery

Just north of Chinatown, in the shadow of the Williamsburg Bridge, is the Bowery. Once an Indian trail used by Peter Stuyvesant to ride to his *bouwerie* ("farm"), the thoroughfare grew into a fashionable amusement and theater center in the early 19th century, then went into a decline as people moved uptown to new neighborhoods. For almost a century the Bowery has been the "street of forgotten men." You'll see them curled up in doorways or sprawled on the street, a newspaper or hat cushioning their heads, sleeping off an ever-present hangover. There are beds in flophouses above gin mills and pawnshops, but the bed that used to cost 25¢ a night now goes for $1.45 or even more. The men here live by panhandling and on the charity of such groups as the Salvation Army.

The Lower East Side

Between the Bowery and the East Village is probably New York's most integrated area; the mile-square area (bounded roughly on the south by Canal Street and on the north by 7th Street) is the most dramatic example of the blending of many races, religions, and cultures in the world. Here, immigrants were crammed into ghettos and English was treated as a foreign language. Only those with the greatest stamina survived and those with the greatest will succeeded in escaping from it. From here came Alfred E. Smith, a son of Irish immigrants, who became governor of New York State. Several sons of Jewish immigrants made the climb to success, too. Among them were Senator Jacob Javits, composer George Gershwin, comedian Eddie Cantor. A little Italian boy made it also—Jimmy Durante. The Lower East Side was, and in a way still is, an enclave which is sufficient unto itself.

"The Village"

Greenwich Village is not an entity but rather a collection of little villages. Its heart is Washington Square, at the end of Fifth Avenue, and its extremities reach out farther each year. Roughly, it is bounded by Houston Street on the south, 13th Street on the north, Hudson Street on the west—although much of the area between Hudson (the street) and Hudson (the river) has been restored and has taken on a "village" look. Its eastern boundary now extends to Lafayette Street and the beginnings of the East Village, where some of the Bohemians have migrated. Today's Village residents are largely career people—business executives, lawyers, doctors, teachers, successful writers and artists—who have been drawn by its small town neighborliness and convenient location to the city's business centers, and live in old houses they have renovated. You'll see little clusters of these tidy row houses on tree-shaded side streets, their tiny rear gardens bright with blooms and redolent of steak and chicken barbecuing over charcoal grills.

The Village also is home to a large segment of New York's Italian population. Their province, usually called Little Italy south of Washington Square, is a tangle of shops strung with tangy cheeses, breads, red peppers, garlic, bunches of oregano and rosemary. Hordes of housewives stream in from all parts of the Village to thump the melons, poke through the endive, and argue a bit about prices before making their selections.

In the early '20s the Village was a lively and bawdy place, a Montmartre in the midst of Manhattan. Since the turn of the century, it has been a center of creativity and intellectual curiosity which nurtured some of America's greatest writers and artists: Henry James, Edith Wharton, O. Henry, e. e. cummings, Maxwell Bodenheim, Rockwell Kent, and many others. To explore the area, a detailed map is mandatory. Even then, it is difficult to find your way without asking directions. You'll find the Villagers friendly and willing to help you out of the maze.

South of Houston

SoHo has fast become one of New York's most exciting and desirable neighborhoods. The area's century-old cast-iron buildings that housed the notorious "sweat shops" in the late 1800s have been converted into fashionable and functional lofts and studios for many of the city's art community. Floor space is at a premium in New York, and SoHo's buildings offer the kind of room many artists, photographers, and sculptors need for their work.

Dozens of fine art galleries crowd SoHo's streets, and new restaurants and shops seem to pop up almost weekly. The area is still busy with light industry on weekdays, but on weekends, SoHo becomes a very busy cultural center. You'll see artists in their paint-splattered work clothes walking side-by-side with beautifully dressed patrons or buyers. SoHo has become so overrun with visitors, in fact, that many of the early residents (the artists) are leaving in search of quieter quarters. But for the visitor to New York, whether art lover or not, SoHo is a must.

Focal Point of the Village

Washington Arch, at the foot of Fifth Avenue, is the best point to start a stroll through the most colorful and historic Village areas.

Choose a Sunday in spring, summer, or fall for one of the town's best known free entertainments. The fountain in the square is a meeting place for jazz musicians, guitar players, and pluckers of home-made instruments. Sunday strollers are apt to include young parents with toddlers, a multitude of dog-walkers and arms-around-each-other couples of all ages, in all manner of dress.

The fountain is a good vantage point for viewing the red-brick, white-trimmed houses which line the square's north side. Built around 1830, they remained a fashionable center of New York for a generation, sheltering members of old New York's aristocracy and a long-gone way of life so vividly described in Henry James's *Washington Square*. Edith Wharton lived in the old Boorman house on the northeast corner of the square, a setting which inspired her novel *The Age of Innocence*. At No. 3, John Dos Passos wrote *Manhattan Transfer* and artist Norman Rockwell painted his own brand of "primitives." Rose Franken, author of *Claudia*, lived at No. 6 before this, while other lovely patrician homes began to vanish.

New York University, which has been here since the 1830s, owns and leases about four-fifths of the land around the square. In its original building, which stood at 100 Washington Square East, Professor Samuel F. B. Morse developed the telegraph and Samuel Colt invented the single-shot pistol. When its student body began bursting the seams of the campus buildings on and around the square, the university reluctantly gave notice to artists and writers along "Genius Row," and the row of garrets has been replaced with the Georgian-style Law School at the southwest end of the square and modern Roman Catholic Holy Trinity Chapel. Other N.Y.U. additions are the Hagop Kevorkian Center for Near Eastern Studies and Bobst Library. Up the street, the tall brick and glass Loeb Student Center covers the site of Madame Blanchard's boarding house, whose boarders included Theodore Dreiser, Eugene O'Neill, Zona Gale, Frank Norris, O. Henry, and many other literary greats.

MacDougal Street Promenade

From here it's a short walk to MacDougal Street, which is called Washington Square West at this point. A few steps up MacDougal Street brings you to MacDougal Alley, one of the most charming back streets in the Village. Most of the little homes here were former stables and carriage houses of the elegant old homes on Washington Square North. Brightly painted, with doorways lit by gas lamps, they are among the most prized studios and apartments in all New York City. At the rear of the old homes on the east side of Fifth Avenue is a similar cobbled street lined with converted carriage houses, called Washington Mews.

Returning to the west side of Washington Square, passing the Law School, and walking on into the lower part of MacDougal Street, you will see the rebuilt Provincetown Playhouse, a pioneer off-Broadway theater made famous by the early works of Eugene O'Neill. There are boutiques where you'll find witty, trendy, and ethnic clothes and jewelry; leather goods shops and fortune-telling ateliers; a few good restaurants; coffee houses (the latter now, alas, a Village rarity); and pizza and souvlaki eateries. The young types who flock here, with their casual clothes and lifestyles, completely confound the Italian families who have lived here all their lives—although recently there have been signs that the two groups are "adapting" to each other.

MacDougal Street leaves this mood behind as it crosses Bleecker Street, downtown home of the Circle-in-the-Square Theater, which produced the early works of Tennessee Williams. Between Bleecker and Houston (New Yorkers pronounce it Howstun, a Dutch term meaning "house garden") is a row of well-kept, old brick houses where well-to-do professional people live. A similar row on Sullivan Street backs onto them, and the private park between is shared by householders on both sides.

Turn back to Bleecker Street, head west across Sixth Avenue ("Ave. of the Americas") and you'll come to Father Demo Square and the Renaissance-style Church of Our Lady of Pompeii; its lovely stained-glass windows and religious paintings are well worth your time. You are now at the beginning of the Italian shopping mart, which stretches from Sixth to Seventh Avenues. Pushcarts have vanished from this colorful neighborhood, as have all but a very few produce stores. But the aromatic fish stores, bakeries with mouth-watering Neapolitan cakes and pastries, meat and cheese and grocery shops make this one of New York's unique streets, with a character and flavor all its own.

The Village's meandering streets can really defeat you at this point, but find Leroy Street and follow its bend to St. Luke's Place. Here you'll come upon a poplar-lined street of handsome Anglo-Italian houses, almost as elegant as those of Washington Square. Built in 1880, they have housed many a New York celebrity. At the end of the street, turn right on Hudson and explore the streets which twist and turn off it: Morton Street, with its attractive but seedy houses, and Bedford Street, where Edna St. Vincent Millay and John Barrymore lived (at different times) in New York's narrowest house. It is numbered 75½ and is only nine feet broad, having been built in the driveway of the old Cardoza farmhouse.

Three of the most contradictory houses in the Village are found at the corner of Grove and Bedford Streets. The house on the corner, a faded historic mansion, is backed up against a little dollhouse which is said to have been used for slave quarters a century ago. Next door, at 100 Bedford, is a gingerbread house known as "Twin Peaks." Local legend claims it was designed as a "dream house" by a Village artist and that the sketches of his fairy-tale domicile caught the eye of financier Otto Kahn, who financed the dream. To many it is a nightmare.

Follow Grove Street to the point where it bends, and you will see the gate to Grove Court, a fenced-off cluster of small brick houses circling a shady garden. Grove Court was the home of O. Henry when he became affluent and it is the setting of his story, *The Last Leaf.* Today, it is home to well-to-do career people and business executives.

While you're following these winding streets, look for Commerce Street and the Cherry Lane Theater, the famous playhouse (converted from a box factory) which has given many a struggling playwright an opportunity to display his works. Follow Grove Street to St. Luke's Chapel on Hudson Street. St. Luke's was built by Trinity Church in 1822, and still maintains many of its old traditions. Wings of little brick houses jut out from St. Luke's. These old row houses also date from the 1820s and one was the boyhood home of Bret Harte.

Now, follow Grove in its eastward course, and before long you'll emerge into a nine-way intersection at Sheridan Square. The area around the square is studded with restaurants, shops, theaters, and cafes.

Meandering Mood

If you still are in the mood for meandering, pick up Waverly Place, and don't be startled when you find it meeting itself after awhile. Richard Harding Davis, who lived at No. 108, often walked in circles, too. Nearby is Gay Street, a crooked little path punctuated here and there with Greek Revival houses built in the 1820s. Ruth McKenney lived in the basement apartment of No. 14 with *My Sister Eileen*. A worthwhile detour, before you reach the square, is a walk along Bleecker Street, turning left from Grove and following it to where it comes to an end, at Bank Street and Eighth Avenue. This stretch of Bleecker, like much of the Village, is a designated landmark district, and most of the buildings along it date from the early 19th century. Some of the most attractive antique and gift shops in the city are along here, and, in company with the good eating places and well-kept (for the most part) apartment houses, they have made this one of New York's most charming areas.

Follow Gay to Christopher, and then walk westward on Christopher for a few blocks' worth of good window-shopping and browsing. This route will take you across the Sheridan Square intersection again.

Village Square

Back at the Gay-Christopher intersection, turn right into the intersection that takes in Greenwich Avenue, Eighth Street, and Avenue of the Americas. This is Village Square, one of the crossroads of the Village. The open-fronted vegetable stand to the right was once Luke O'Connor's Columbian Gardens, where back in 1896 young John Masefield, the late Poet Laureate of England, hauled beer kegs and mopped floors. Across the Square to the north is Jefferson Market Courthouse, a cherished landmark since 1878. Its unusual Italian Gothic architecture is the work of Calvert de Vaux, one of the architects of Central Park, and Frederick Withers, who designed the picturesque gate of the Little Church Around the Corner. Its clock tower once served as the neighborhood fire lookout. Long unused, the Courthouse was refurbished inside and out and is now a branch of the New York Public Library. Diagonally northwest between this intersection and Eighth Avenue is Greenwich Avenue, one of the more interesting promenades in the Village. Cafes, some good restaurants, eye-catching clothing shops (both trendy and classic), and interesting Villagers to ogle make it a fun strolling route, and most of the neighborhood is out every weekend, bound on errands or the pursuit of pleasure. The farther northwest you go, the more conservative the shops and people seem. Greenwich Avenue is the Village in microcosm!

The East Village

The East Village, which was the new Bohemia of the late sixties and early seventies, is more or less bounded by 14th Street on the north, Houston Street on the south, and the East River. (Its western boundary is a subject for argument, but could be said to be Broadway.) The area has inherited many of Greenwich Village's ways of the '20s. St. Mark's Place is the main promenade for the East Village. It is a stretch between Third and First Avenues, the extension of East Eighth Street, and along it you'll see one or two emporiums that frankly proclaim themselves "head shops," a reminder that just a few years ago the East Village was one of New York's major outposts of the drug culture. Some remainder of this sub-culture still exists, and this is another area of the city where old-time, immigrant-family citizens and the young, free-living newcomers are learning to co-exist without antagonism.

On St. Mark's Place, there are also several clothing shops, mostly of the "funky" variety; boutiques with jewelry and leather goods; record stores; and a popular movie house. Between Second and First Avenues, the architecture is considerably more attractive, and do note the really charming edifice that is the First German Methodist Episcopal Church.

What was the East Village before the invasion of hippies? The square, named for one of New York's governors, Daniel B. Tompkins, was a quiet neighborhood of mixed cultures: Ukrainian, Czech, German, Polish, Russian, Italian, Jewish, and, lately, Puerto Rican. Russian and Turkish baths, delicatessen, meat, and produce stores reflect the heterogeneous ways of the neighborhood. Handsome churches of all faiths—among them, St. Nicholas Russo-Carpathian and St. Brigid's-on-the-Square—have served generation after generation. St. Mark's-in-the-Bouwerie, built in 1795, on the site of the Stuyvesant family's chapel, was partially destroyed by fire in 1977. The floor of the church creaks, the entrance is sooty, and yet it is one of New York's most charming churches. Two of its stained glass windows are especially noteworthy. One is a portrait of Peter Stuyvesant, the other a colorful version of the symbolic Tree of Life.

The City Moves North

Fortunately there were enough parade grounds scattered around the city to break up the forward march of square block upon square block of brownstone houses. The city was lucky, too, in having a few imaginative builders. One was Samuel Ruggles, who had bought a large tract of land between what are now 20th and 21st Streets, extending east of Park Avenue South and west of Third Avenue. It is now known as Gramercy Park, center of one of the most exclusive residential areas in the city. The elite of New York were attracted with the promise that only those who built houses around the square would have use of its park. Two golden keys to unlock the gate of the fenced-in park were given to each homeowner. Snob appeal made the venture an instant success. The Social Register tenants are gone and the homes have been broken up into apartments occupied by decorators, writers, business executives, and wealthy widows. You'll see lucky key-holders sitting in the park on a sunny afternoon, reading or watching youngsters play quiet games. It is an oasis of peace and solitude, for no dogs, bikes, or swings are permitted. Theodore Roosevelt's birthplace (28 East 20th Street) is now a National Historic Site. It is a fine example of a typical well-to-do Victorian home. The home, and the adjacent museum of relics Roosevelt collected during his years of adventuring, are open weekdays.

New York's Own Chelsea

The Chelsea area, on the west side across town from Gramercy Park, has let many historic landmarks slip through its fingers. Yet many writers find the remnants of its past gentility and the unfrenetic pace of Chelsea to their liking. The Chelsea Hotel, at 222 West 23rd Street, has been home to many celebrated writers. Thomas Wolfe and Dylan Thomas lived here and Brendan Behan wrote his book on New York in one of its apartments. The Victorian Gothic edifice with wrought iron balconies, turrets, and chimney stacks has been designated by the Municipal Art Society as one of New York's architectural monuments which should be preserved at all costs. In 1978 it was designated a National Landmark by the federal government.

The oldest building in Chelsea, which dates from 1785, is a two-and-one-half-story house with a steeply pitched roof and dormer windows at 183 Ninth Avenue, corner of 21st Street. Its ground floor now is occupied by a dairy store. If you wander through 20th, 21st, and 22nd Streets between Eighth and Ninth Avenues, you will see evidence of Chelsea's struggle to maintain its gentility. Many of the old brownstones have been tinted a lively pink, yellow, or blue. Their intricate wrought-iron balustrades gleam and their tiny front gardens are well tended.

Midtown

Midtown Manhattan, which ranges roughly from 34th Street to 59th Street and river to river, is a center of superlatives. The biggest buildings, best restaurants, most art galleries, brightest lights, greatest concentration of big business, largest complex of theater, concert, and opera houses, best bargain basements, most exclusive couture houses, and the most specialized services are all here.

Midtown does not readily lend itself to cut-and-dried walking tours. It is an area to be explored according to one's whims and particular interests. There are museums which specialize in collections of modern art, contemporary crafts, folk art, primitive art, costumes of all nations, reruns of old silent movies, and lecture programs. There are scores of foreign-tourist information centers and airline ticket offices with information and advice to inspire your next vacation. There are awesome views to be seen from observatories atop midtown's tallest buildings, a world to explore underground, a hundred little personal discoveries to be made, world-renowned stores, and countless small specialty shops. The most famous shops are located between 34th and 57th Streets on the showcase avenues, Fifth and Madison. Three of the city's greatest attractions are in this midtown area: Times Square, Rockefeller Center, and the United Nations.

The Great White Way starts at Times Square, a point where meandering Broadway crosses 42nd Street and Seventh Avenue. It is a monument to the vision and the gambling spirit of three men: Oscar Hammerstein I, an impresario who in 1894 sank a two-million-dollar fortune, and then some, into building the first theaters here; August Belmont, a financier who more than matched Hammerstein's gamble by extending the subway to bring the crowds uptown to the new theater district; and publisher Adolph S. Ochs, who built the Times Tower in 1904 as the headquarters for his newspaper, *The New York Times.*

The theater district has tarnished since the glamorous pre-Depression days; Times Square has taken on a midway bazaar-like look, with its soft-drink and pizza stands, pinball and shooting galleries, racy lingerie and fake "fire sale" shops. Many of the old prestige theaters now feature X-rated movies, and ladies of the evening roam the streets along with a hodge-podge of derelicts and eccentrics. Within the radius of a few blocks in the 40s, however, there still remains surely the greatest concentration of dramatic and musical productions you will find anywhere in the world. This tight little center of entertainment offers a rare opportunity for last-minute shopping. If you've neglected to order theater tickets in advance, check with the Times Square Ticket Service ("Tkts") office at 47th Street and Broadway, where tickets for theater are usually available for half-price for on-, off-, and even off-off-Broadway performances. A separate booth selling tickets for concerts, opera, and ballet is at 42nd Street between Fifth and Sixth Avenues.

The aircraft carrier *Intrepid* is a museum at Pier 86 on the Hudson River at 46th Street.

The Avenue of the Americas

Sixth Avenue, also known as the Avenue of the Americas, is changing as glittering new skyscrapers take the place of older edifices. Bryant Park, located between 40th and 42nd Streets behind the New York Public Library, is a green and relaxing spot to visit and rest. Named in 1884 for William Cullen Bryant, poet and journalist, it is a gathering place for impromptu public speeches and their eclectic sort of audience. The park is also an excellent vantage point from which to view one of the city's more unusual new skyscrapers. Located between the Avenue of the Americas and Fifth Avenue, with entrances on 42nd and 43rd Streets and adjacent to the Graduate Center of CUNY, the Monsanto Building slopes gently upward, narrowing from its base to its towering roof, producing the rather uneasy effect of a hill carved from glass and stone. A similar one curves inward from both 57th and 58th Streets, also between Fifth Avenue and the Avenue of the Americas.

Walk north from 42nd Street and you'll see many other recently-constructed buildings. At 1133, corner of 43rd Street, is the Kodak Exhibition Center where you might stop in to see the exhibits in its downstairs gallery. Now a short detour east on 44th towards Fifth Avenue to the Algonquin Hotel and restaurant still operating at No. 59. Behind its rather unimposing Renaissance façade many noted literary figures have wined, dined, and talked the hours away: Dorothy Parker, Harold Ross, and Robert Benchley, among others. At 47th Street, you just might be tempted to take another detour east for a look at the block-long area known as the city's diamond center—it's obvious why when you see the countless glittering shop windows.

For the next three blocks on the Avenue, west side, you'll be passing three of the newer skyscraper members of the Rockefeller Center community: the 45-story Celanese Building; the 51-story McGraw-Hill building (featuring *The New York Experience* film daily); and the 54-story home of Exxon.

Radio City Music Hall, on the east side of the avenue at 50th Street, is a wondrous Art Deco attraction. It is the largest indoor theater in the world, with a seating capacity of six thousand. Two major television and radio network headquarters are located a couple of blocks beyond —CBS between 52nd and 53rd Streets and designed by Eero Saarinen, and ABC at 54th Street. Both are on the east side of the avenue. On 55th Street, almost to Seventh Avenue, is the New York City Center, 131 West 55th Street; and two blocks north along Seventh Avenue, around the corner of 57th Street, is Carnegie Hall.

If you have an artistic bent, backtrack to 53rd Street and turn east towards Fifth Avenue. On this one block you'll find the handsome sculpture garden and avant garde works of the Museum of Modern Art at 11 West 53rd Street, the Museum of American Folk Art at 49, and the Museum of Contemporary Crafts at 44.

On Columbus Circle at Central Park is architect H. Van Buren Magonigle's "Maine Memorial" with figures by sculptor Attilio Piccirilli. That massive building over to the northwest is the New York Coliseum, where exhibitions of varying interests and degrees of interest are held. On the south side of the circle, in a building which closely resembles a huge refrigerator, the New York Convention & Visitors' Bureau has an information office.

Rockefeller Center

Rockefeller Center is a city-within-a-city; you could easily spend a whole day within its complex of twenty-one buildings. Many of its residents—it has a daytime population of 240,000—never leave from their arrival in the morning until they go home. There is no need to, for the center has just about everything one could ask for. There are almost thirty restaurants, several shoe repair shops, drugstores, chiropodists, dentists, oculists, gift and clothing shops, bookstores, hairdressers, barbers, banks, a post office, movie theaters, schools, and subway transportation to all parts of the metropolis. Consulates of twenty foreign nations have offices in the center, as do twenty airlines, railroad and steamship lines, and fifty-eight state and other travel information bureaus. A shop-lined concourse, an underground passageway almost two miles long, ties together all its buildings.

The Channel Gardens—six formal beds running from Fifth Avenue to the Lower Plaza—with their ever-changing seasonal plantings, draw millions of visitors. Artists, designers, and sculptors work year-round to devise new and dramatic floral patterns for the ten seasonal displays. The showings run consecutively, starting with thousands of lilies at Easter and ending with the greatest Christmas tree of all. The Lower Plaza, where you can ice skate from the end of September through April and dine alfresco in warm weather, is a kind of ceremonial town square where distinguished visitors are greeted, occasional concerts given, and special events commemorated with colorful ceremonies. From the Observation Roof of the 70-story RCA building, at 30 Rockefeller Plaza, you'll be treated to a spectacular view. A visit to the observatory is included in the guided tour of Rockefeller Center's highlights, an hour-long educational stroll which takes you to a landscaped roof garden, the interior of the Music Hall, the famous murals and art works scattered throughout the center, and along the concourse of shops of all nations. When in doubt about what to see and where it is, visit the center's information booth in the main lobby at 30 Rockefeller Plaza, just behind the statue of Atlas at the Fifth Avenue entrance.

Fifth Avenue

New York's most famous thoroughfare, Fifth Avenue, was originally Millionaire's Row. The Astors, Vanderbilts, and numerous others built five mansions here after the Civil War. Fifth Ave, which is the dividing line between East Side and West Side, is still the most fashionable in the city. With dozens of high-quality shops and department stores lining the avenue from 34th to 59th Street, a stroll along here is very pleasureable. The Empire State Building stands at 34th St.; walk north from there (after visiting the observation tower 102 floors up), and you'll take in the best of New York. At 51st Street is the Gothic-styled St. Patrick's Cathedral, framed by Saks Fifth Avenue to the south and Olympic Towers to the north. At 59th Street and Central Park South you'll see Grand Army Plaza and F. Scott Fitzgerald's old haunt, the venerable Plaza Hotel.

The United Nations

New York City grew from a metropolis to a cosmopolis in 1952, when the United Nations moved into its elegant new home overlooking the East River between 42nd and 48th Streets.

Acres of parkland make the U.N. grounds a pleasant place to stroll and watch the busy river traffic of freighters, tankers, and pleasure boats plying the rolling Hell Gate waters.

The visitors' entrance to the United Nations Headquarters is at the north end of the marble and limestone General Assembly Building, at 45th Street and First Avenue. There is a museum-like quality to the vast lobby with its free-form multiple galleries, soaring ceiling, and collection of art treasures contributed by member nations.

Visitors are welcome to attend most official meetings and admission is free. Tickets to the meetings are issued in the lobby fifteen minutes before meetings are scheduled to start. Because there is no advance schedule of meetings for any given day, and since they may be cancelled or changed at the last minute, the majority of tickets available to individual visitors are issued on a first-come, first-served basis.

At most meetings, speeches are simultaneously interpreted in Chinese, English, French, Russian, and Spanish and there are earphones at each visitor's seat with a dial system to tune in the language of your choice.

Taking the hour-long guided tour through the headquarters buildings is the most satisfactory way to see all the meeting rooms, to learn the aims, structure, and activities of this world body, and to appreciate fully the art works and exhibits displayed. To lunch with the delegates, stop by the information desk in the main lobby and ask about making a table reservation in the Delegates' Dining Room. Tables for visitors are in short supply and are assigned on a first-come basis. The earlier you make the reservation, the better.

On the lower concourse there is a coffee shop for a quick snack and lounges to rest. Here, too, are several shops which offer books, art, and handicraft products of the U.N.'s member nations.

Up in Central Park

Central Park, an 840-acre oasis of rural beauty in the midst of a concrete jungle of midtown spires, runs from 59th to 110th Street and from Fifth Avenue to Central Park West (an extension of Eighth Avenue). Masterfully designed by Frederick Law Olmstead and Calvert de Vaux, the park was designated a National Historic Landmark in 1965. A stroll through the park will reveal the woodland terrain of New York as it might have been in the days of the Dutch settlers, before dredges and bulldozers leveled the hills and rocky outcroppings to erect a fence of apartment houses. If you take a drive down through the park from the north end at dusk, just as lights begin to sparkle in windows and the last rays of the sun silhouette the spires at the south end, you will be rewarded with a strikingly beautiful sight. Or hire a carriage—they park across the street from the Plaza Hotel—and take a leisurely turn around the ponds, lakes, and woodlands.

The park is a many-splendored melange of fountains and ponds, statues and monuments, promenades and wooded paths. On warm weekdays, office workers find a favorite rock by the pond, spread out their lunches, and share them with the water birds. In the winter, they skate at Wollman Memorial Rink. On Sundays, families come to picnic, play softball, pitch horseshoes, ride the merry-go-round, fly kites, row boats, ride bicycles on the curling, car-free drives, and absorb enough sun and fresh air to last them through another week of molelike living. Off the 64th Street entrance on Fifth Avenue is a small zoo with a splendid collection of birds, wild animals, and a seal pond. (Both the Wollman Rink and the zoo were under renovation at press time.)

Lincoln Center

Lincoln Center for the Performing Arts is an elegant four-block cultural world, located between 62nd and 66th Streets west of Broadway, on the West Side. Get acquainted with the buildings by taking one of the guided tours, or wander around the open plazas and parks on your own. Standing on Broadway, the building you see to the left of the large central fountain plaza is the New York State Theater, home of the New York City Opera and the New York City Ballet. On the right is Avery Fisher Hall, home of the New York Philharmonic. Between the two stands the Metropolitan Opera House, with its two colorful Marc Chagall windows depicting motifs and themes relating to music. It houses The Metropolitan Opera Company and has the Center's largest seating capacity: for over 3,700 people in its main auditorium. Tucked behind Philharmonic Hall is the charming Eero

Saarinen-designed Vivian Beaumont Theater. And in back, with an entrance on Amsterdam Avenue, is the Library and Museum of the Performing Arts, a branch of the New York Public Library. Also on these grounds is the Guggenheim Bandshell for alfresco concerts. Across 65th Street is the Juilliard School campus, which includes Alice Tully Hall, a Lincoln Center facility noted especially for its chamber music presentations.

The American Museum of Natural History

If you are interested in tracing the history and growth of New York, visit the New York Historical Society's headquarters at 77th Street and Central Park West. A block or so north is the American Museum of Natural History, founded in 1869 "for the purpose of encouraging and developing the study of natural science, advancing the general knowledge of kindred subjects, and of furnishing popular instruction." It has been operating for over a century and houses tens of millions of zoological, geological, anthropological, and botanical specimens that are studied by scientists, students, and scholars from all over the world.

To make the most of your visit, pick up a guide book and check off the exhibits you want to see first. Two of the museum's greatest attractions are the 94-foot life-size model of a blue whale on the first floor and the two huge halls' worth of dinosaur fossils on the fourth floor. Other highlights include the 64-foot long Haida Canoe, made from the trunk of a single cedar tree; the Hall of the Biology of Man, which is devoted to the evolution, structure, and function of man as an organism; reconstruction of the extinct dodo; the recently completed exhibition of the Courtship of Birds; the collection of mammals; the Northwest Coast Indian Hall; the Hall of Man in Africa; and the demonstration-participation lectures in the new People Center where onlookers are invited to try on costumes or play instruments, for example, of various cultures.

A connecting passageway takes you to the Hayden Planetarium, at 81st Street and Central Park West, the department of astronomy of the American Museum of Natural History. The planetarium has numerous exhibits: murals of lunar landscapes, eclipses, and the aurora borealis; collections of meteorites (some weighing up to thirty-four tons); ancient Chinese, French, and German astronomical instruments.

East Side Museums and Galleries

On the Fifth Avenue side of Central Park and on the side streets of Madison Avenue in the 70s is the city's greatest concentration of art galleries and museums. You might work your way up Fifth Avenue to 92nd Street, then over to Madison Avenue and down to the 60s. A good starting point is the Frick Collection on Fifth Avenue at 70th Street, a splendid example of French Classic architecture (formerly the home of Henry Clay Frick), enclosing a peaceful glass-roofed courtyard; the private collection of fine paintings, ornaments, and furnishings will give you an idea of the scale of living enjoyed by New York society before the income tax.

Across the way, facing Fifth Avenue between 80th and 84th Streets, is the Metropolitan Museum of Art. The neo-Renaissance design of this imposing structure infringing on the reaches of Central Park was taken from the Columbian Exposition (Chicago World's Fair) of 1893. The museum houses one of the most comprehensive collections in the world, more than a million art treasures representing the work of fifty centuries. The whole of it cannot be enjoyed in one visit, so it would be best to ask for a floor plan at the information booth and choose the galleries which hold the most interest for you. There are also Acousti-guides for rent here; the recorded tour takes approximately forty-five minutes. Its departments include Egyptian Art, Near Eastern Art, American painting, sculpture, furniture, armor, and arms.

Frank Lloyd Wright's Spiral

One of the most extraordinary buildings in New York is the Solomon R. Guggenheim Museum at 88th Street, a six-story spiral staircase designed by the late Frank Lloyd Wright, which provides a quarter-mile of ramp, its walls hung with an ascending collection of contemporary art. It's best to take the elevator to the top and meander down. At 91st Street the former home of steel tycoon Andrew Carnegie is now the Cooper-Hewitt Museum of Design. One block north is the luxurious former home of banker Felix N. Warburg, whose widow presented it to the Jewish Theological Seminary to be used as a museum. The Jewish Museum has become the repository of the most extensive collection of Jewish ceremonial objects in the United States and also is one of the three most important in the world, the other two being in Jerusalem and Prague.

Now head east to Madison Avenue and down to the Seventies where New York's art gallery district is centered. Many of the galleries which once clustered around 57th Street have moved up to these quieter surroundings. Here you will find the Christie Galleries; the Danenberg Galleries; the Graham Galleries, established in 1857; Perls Galleries; and the elegant Wildenstein Gallery. There are dozens of noted galleries, smaller and more intimate, besides these.

In the midst of all this art is yet another great museum, the Whitney Museum of American Art at Madison Avenue and 75th Street. The building itself is at first startling. Given slightly less than one-third of an acre on which to build, architect Marcel Breuer's solution was to turn the traditional ziggurat (or "wedding cake") design upside down, with the second, third and fourth floors each projecting fourteen feet farther out over the street than the one below.

The International Center for Photography at 94th and Fifth offers excellent photo shows year-round.

From here, go to the fine Museum of the City of New York at 103rd Street. The museum's collections are extensive and cover a wide variety of fields, reflecting both the city of today and yesteryear. Its decorative arts collection includes fine examples of costumes, furniture, and silver.

West Side

The rocky ridge that begins in Central Park rises gradually as it travels uptown through Harlem and Morningside Heights to the precipitous lookout at Washington Heights. One of the most scenic drives in the city is along Riverside Drive, which follows the Hudson River shoreline from 72nd Street up to Inwood, at the northern tip of Manhattan. Along the route you will pass the boat basin, at 79th Street, where large yachts anchor. Next, the Soldiers and Sailors Monument comes into view, a handsome Italian Carrara marble "silo" circled by twelve Corinthian columns. The 392-foot Gothic tower of Riverside Church can be seen a mile to the north. Its 72-bell carillon is the largest in the United States and its range of tonal quality is superb. The largest bell, the *Bourdon,* weighs more than 20 tons, while the smallest weighs 10 pounds.

World's Largest Church

Directly east, if you want to make a detour at this time, is the Church of St. John the Divine, on Morningside Heights (Amsterdam Avenue and 112th Street). Started in 1892, it will be the largest Gothic cathedral in the world when it is finally completed. The campus of Columbia University fills the center of the Heights and just north of it are those of Union Theological Seminary and the Jewish Theological Seminary.

General Grant's Tomb is at 123rd Street, and at about this point Riverside Drive begins to skirt Fort Washington Park. At 155th Street you might want to make another short detour east to Broadway to visit a unique cultural center which houses five special-interest museums. Here you'll find the Museum of the American Indian-Heye Foundation, which has an outstanding collection of Indian art and relics of North and South America. The Hispanic Society of America has a museum of ancient and modern Spanish culture. At the American Numismatic Society, you can see a vast collection of coins and medals, and the country's most comprehensive library on the subject. A large collection of historic maps is displayed at the American Geographical Society, and at the American Academy of Arts and Letters, you can view the memorabilia of many famous artists, writers, and musicians.

At 160th Street and Edgecombe Avenue, you'll come to the Morris-Jumel Mansion, one of the city's few remaining examples of pre-Revolutionary Georgian architecture. Built in 1765 by Roger Morris and later occupied by Madame Jumel, a wealthy widow who married Aaron Burr in his old age, the home has many exquisite architectural details. It has been turned into a museum devoted to the Revolutionary War period.

Heading north and west, pick up Fort Washington Avenue and follow it to Fort Tryon Park. This is the brow of Manhattan; from this vantage point, you have an uninterrupted view of the magnificent sweep of the Hudson River up to the Tappan Zee, the precipitous Palisades shoreline of New Jersey, the graceful arc of George Washington Bridge, and the far reaches of the Bronx beyond Spuyten Duyvil.

Set in the midst of this woodland park is The Cloisters; sections of medieval European monasteries have been connected by a charming colonnaded walk and merged with a French Romanesque chapel, a chapter house of the 12th century, and a Romanesque apse which is on loan from the Spanish Government. Among the museum's most notable treasures are the *Hunt of the Unicorn* tapestries, which are considered to be among the world's greatest.

Sailing Around Manhattan

The Circle Line lecture trip leaves from Pier 83 on the Hudson River, at 43rd Street and 12th Avenue. Heading south you pass Manhattan's lower West Side. The ferry rounds the island's southern tip, giving a superb view of the Statue of Liberty and of the Wall Street skyline. Heading up the East River, you'll pass under three very different spans to Brooklyn: the Brooklyn, Manhattan, and Williamsburg bridges. A glimpse of fashionable Brooklyn Heights is available and you may see, a mile or so upriver, a huge U.S. Navy cruiser or carrier in dry dock at the Brooklyn Navy Yard. Looking back to the Manhattan side, you'll have passed Chinatown and the lower East Side and now be closing in on the United Nations Building at 44th Street and 1st Avenue. On your right will be the Delacorte Geyser and Roosevelt Island with its new housing developments. The bridge overhead is the stolid Queensborough or "59th Street."

Then it's upstream under the Triborough Bridge (linking Manhattan to Queens and the Bronx). After several smaller spans, you'll see refurbished Yankee Stadium on the right. Rounding the northern tip of Manhattan through the Spuyten Duyvil cut, the cruise slips past Columbia University's boathouse, Inwood Hill Park, and the Henry Hudson Bridge. Once again, you're on the Hudson River flanked on the west by the towering Palisades of New Jersey. On the east you'll see The Cloisters and the heights of Fort Washington Park as you approach the George Washington Bridge, Grant's Tomb, Riverside Church, and the Soldiers and Sailors Monument. Midtown towers come into view as you head back to the dock past rebuilt luxury-liner piers between 54th and 45th Streets. It's a cruise you'll long remember. It lasts about three hours, and a guide narrates the scenes along the way.

Brooklyn

Shortly after the West India Company settled Manhattan, they sailed over to the "broken lands" southeast of the Battery to negotiate with the Indians for the purchase of the whole western end of Long Island. Their first parcel in Brooklyn (Breuckelen—broken land) was acquired in 1636. On Ilpetonga ("high sandy bank"), where the Canarsie Indians had lived in community houses, some of which were a quarter of a mile long, wealthy merchants built elegant homes. From the heights they could watch their clipper ships round Red Hook and berth at the waterside warehouses. They called the area Clover Hill. Today it is known as Brooklyn Heights. Their homes have been partitioned into studios and apartments which are handsomely restored by artists, writers, and people who enjoy the Victorian atmosphere and one of the most exciting views in the world. This view alone makes a trip to Brooklyn worthwhile.

You'll find remains of Old World gentility in these streets. New Orleans-type wrought-iron balconies, stately pillared entrances, delicate scrollwork embellishments, ivy-covered brownstones, hidden mews of converted carriage houses similar to those of Washington Square make the 20th-century skyline across the river seem a mirage of the future. Along Willow Street you'll pass a few of the Federal-style row houses of the Heights. At 70 Willow Street is the Van Sinderen House, built in the Greek Revival style in the late 1830s. The three best examples of the Federal-style row houses of the early 19th century are found at 155–157–159. An esplanade which extends from Remsen Street to Orange Street offers what photographic experts consider the most spectacular panoramic view of Manhattan.

Walking east from the esplanade you will come to the Plymouth Church of the Pilgrims on Orange Street, a severe, dark brick example of early Classic Revival architecture, with a series of memorial windows which trace the interesting history of Puritanism.

Flatbush Avenue, a few blocks from Brooklyn Heights, will lead you southeastward to the monumental Grand Army Plaza with its 80-foot-high memorial arch. A little beyond the Plaza to your left are the huge Brooklyn Museum and the beautiful Botanic Garden. The Museum's collections of primitive and prehistoric art are world renowned: North and South American Indian handicrafts; works from Oceania, Indonesia, and Africa. There is a notable collection of American painting and sculpture from Colonial times to today. Its collection of Egyptian antiquities on the third floor is considered outstanding. One floor below is a fine collection of bronzes and porcelains from China, as well as changing exhibitions from the museum's wealth of over thirty thousand prints and drawings. Up on the fourth floor the costume galleries and the series of American interiors from the 17th century to the present are also of special interest.

The 50-acre Botanic Garden behind the museum, with more than ten thousand trees and plants, is especially noted for its Garden of Fragrance, one of the few gardens in the world planted and maintained for the blind. The plants were selected primarily for their fragrance and shape so that the blind might enjoy nature's beauty by the sense of smell and touch. Signs in Braille are posted at the edge of each bed to aid the blind in identifying the flowers and plants. It is noted too for its Japanese garden, and there are acres devoted to wild flowers, herbs, roses, tropical plants, and groves of flowering shrubs.

To the south of the Botanic Garden is Prospect Park, a 500-acre expanse of woods, meadows, footpaths, bridle trails, and tree-shaded drives designed by the same men who did Central Park, Olmstead and de Vaux. Here you can visit the Lefferts Homestead, a Dutch Colonial farmhouse which was built in 1776 and originally stood at 563 Flatbush Avenue. When the Lefferts family bequeathed it to the city, the home was moved to the park as a museum.

The Bronx

The New York Botanical Garden's flower displays spread over 230 rolling acres of the northern half of Bronx Park. In its center is a forest primeval of hemlocks, one of the very few virgin tracts to have survived the axe in the East. West of Hemlock Forest is a turn-of-the-century museum building which houses an herbarium, library, auditorium, and exhibition halls. Across from the museum are a four-acre garden with hundreds of rock-loving plants, and the Conservatory, an elaborate complex of greenhouses with orchids, poinsettia, and other brilliant tropical plants. Behind the Conservatory, you'll come upon the vast Rose Garden, several thousand plantings of more than 160 rose varieties.

The Bronx Zoo—the southern half of Bronx Park—is built with moats rather than iron bars to give the illusion of a walk through the African Veldt while elephants, deer, lions, ostriches, peacocks, and other wild life roam around at will. The 252-acre zoo is one of America's largest and, for the foot-weary, there's an aerial tramway that passes directly over the African Plains, the Great Apes House, and Goat Hill.

PRACTICAL INFORMATION

FOR NEW YORK CITY

HOW TO GET THERE. *By air:* New York City is served by virtually every major (and most minor) airlines at the following airports: John F. Kennedy, in southeastern Queens; LaGuardia, in northern Queens; and Newark, in nearby New Jersey.

By bus: The Port Authority Building (Eighth Ave. and 40th St., Manhattan) is the central terminal for buses serving parts of New Jersey, the Hudson Valley area, Putnam and Dutchess Counties, the Berkshires, and the Poconos, as well as for the *Greyhound* and *Trailway* giants which serve every region of the United States. The central number for passenger information is (212) 564-8484.

By car: The Lincoln Tunnel from New Jersey, and the Midtown Tunnel and Queensboro Bridge from Long Island, are the most direct arteries to mid-Manhattan. The Holland Tunnel from New Jersey, and the Battery Tunnel from Brooklyn, reach lower Manhattan. The George Washington Bridge from New

Jersey, and the Triborough Bridge from Queens and the Bronx, give access to upper Manhattan.

The Verrazano-Narrows Bridge from Staten Island, and the Brooklyn-Queens Expressway from Queens, will get you to Brooklyn.

From New England, the New England Thruway leads to the Bruckner Expressway in the east Bronx, which you may use to get to Queens (Bronx-Whitestone or Throgs Neck bridges), Manhattan (Bruckner Expressway and Triborough Bridge), or the west Bronx (Cross-Bronx Expressway). From upstate New York the New York (Thomas E. Dewey) Thruway extends via the Major Deegan Expressway (both I–87) to the south Bronx and the Triborough Bridge. The bridge gives access to both Queens (Grand Central Parkway) and Manhattan (Franklin D. Roosevelt Drive). Most bridges and tunnels require tolls.

By train: Long-distance *Amtrak* routes reach New York from Chicago and the West, Washington, Florida and the South, plus Boston, Montreal and Toronto, and all terminate in the city at either Grand Central Station (42nd to 46th Sts. on Park Ave.) or Penn Station (31st to 33rd Sts., Seventh to Eighth Aves.). Suburban lines stretch about 75 to 100 miles north and east.

HOW TO GET AROUND. *By subway:* During daytime hours the subways are best for speed, thrift, and convenience. A pocket atlas, obtainable at book stores and some magazine kiosks, superimposes subway routes onto the street maps. Once you've targeted the proper stop, check a map of the subway system which you can get at any token booth or at the *New York Visitors' Bureau,* Columbus Circle. Subways are not recommended for late-night travel, especially for women traveling alone. Fare: 90 cents (you must buy a token).

By car: Parkways. Manhattan's West Side Highway is undergoing repairs south of 59th St. and is closed. North of there, it parallels the Hudson and meets I–95 at the George Washington Bridge. The West Side Highway continues north into the West Bronx, where it is called the Henry Hudson Parkway, and leaves the city above Van Cortlandt Park.

On the east side of Manhattan, with access to the Brooklyn Bridge, the Franklin D. Roosevelt Drive runs from the Battery to 125th St. and to the Triborough and the Willis Ave. Bridges. The road continues north beyond 125th St. under the name Harlem River Drive. On it, you can get to upper Manhattan or cut off to I–95 (George Washington Bridge west, Cross-Bronx Expressway east).

The Bronx has three major roads. The Cross-Bronx Expressway (I–95) passes through the Bronx at about 172nd St. and has exits onto almost every major north-south avenue. From west to east, it also gives access to the Major Deegan Expressway (I–87, the southern extension of the Thruway), the Bronx River Parkway, and terminates at the Bruckner Traffic Circle, where you can go to New England via I–95 or eastern Queens via the Whitestone or Throgs Neck bridges. The Bruckner Circle also leads to the Bruckner Expressway, which runs southwest to the Triborough Bridge leading to Manhattan or Queens.

Queens is accessible from the west by two highways. From the Triborough Bridge, the Grand Central Parkway runs through the northwestern edge, passing LaGuardia Airport and Shea Stadium. After an interchange with the Long Island Expressway (I–495), it crosses the Van Wyck Expressway and continues northeast to the county line. The Long Island Expressway runs straight east from the Queens Midtown Tunnel (E. 36th St., Manhattan) and continues on through Nassau and Suffolk Counties.

The main north-south highways in Queens are the Brooklyn-Queens Expressway, Van Wyck Expressway, and Cross Island Parkway. The first begins just east of the Triborough Bridge and has interchanges with most major Queens thoroughfares.

The Van Wyck is important as the road to Kennedy Airport and connects with Southern Parkway (which becomes Southern State Parkway in Nassau County). It intersects the Grand Central Parkway (which you must take to get onto the Long Island Expressway) and then becomes the Whitestone Expressway (I–678) on its way to the Bronx-Whitestone Bridge.

The Cross Island starts in the north at the Whitestone Bridge and roughly parallels the north shore of Queens until it crosses Union Turnpike. Then it angles south past the Belmont Racetrack and traces the borough's eastern border until it changes to the Southern State Parkway just east of Kennedy Airport.

Southern State Parkway continues into Brooklyn and is known as the Belt Parkway or Shore Parkway as it girdles the entire borough from the southeast boundary to the west shore. Along the way you'll see signs for the Verrazano-Narrows Bridge to Staten Island. The Belt Parkway, after passing under that huge span, continues up the west shore. Having now changed its name to the Brooklyn-Queens Expressway, it continues north to the Battery Tunnel, and the Brooklyn Manhattan and Triborough Bridges.

City Streets. Manhattan has a regular and grid-like pattern of city streets, except for the Lower East Side and Greenwich Village. Almost all the east-west streets and most of the north-south avenues are one-way. All the north-south avenues are parallel except Broadway, whose traffic winds from northwest (the 225th street bridge to the Bronx) to southeast (South Ferry). Traffic on Broadway is one-way southbound below 59th St.

The major north-south roads of the Bronx are the Grand Concourse and Jerome Ave. White Plains Ave. starts at Clason Pt. and continues north to Westchester. Webster Ave. starts in the Melrose section and travels north also to the Westchester line.

Running west to east is Tremont Ave. Fordham Rd. (U.S. 1) becomes Boston Rd. (also called the Boston Post Road on U.S. 1) at the Bronx Zoo and continues northeast to Westchester. Just past the Bronx Zoo it connects with Pelham Parkway which leads east to Pelham Bay Park. Gun Hill Rd. starts at the southeastern tip of Van Cortlandt Park and travels east to connect with the Hutchinson River Parkway and the New England Thruway. E. 233rd St. (State 22) stretches from Jerome Ave. to So. Columbus Ave., just south of the Westchester line.

In Queens the major east-west roads are Northern Blvd. in the northern section. Queens Blvd. in the central section terminates at Hillside Ave. Hillside Ave. continues east to Nassau County and at Queens Blvd. it joins Metropolitan Ave. going west to Bushwick Ave. Jamaica Ave. starts at Bushwick and Pennsylvania Aves. and travels east to Jericho Turnpike in Nassau County. Linden Blvd. starts at Aqueduct Racetrack and crosses the southern section to Nassau County. Rockaway Blvd. starts west in the Woodhaven section and travels east and south past J.F.K. Airport.

Woodhaven Blvd. starts at Queens Blvd. and on its way south becomes Cross Bay Blvd. continuing to the beach strip. Francis Lewis Blvd. starts at the northern tip of the Cross Island Parkway and terminates at the Southern Parkway.

Brooklyn is accessible from the streets of lower Manhattan via three bridges. The most northerly is the Williamsburg from Delancey St., followed by the Manhattan (Canal St.), and the Brooklyn (Chambers St.). Broadway will take you to Canal St. or Chambers St., and the Bowery, a continuation of Third Ave. below Ninth St., will take you to Delancey.

Brooklyn's most famous street, Flatbush Ave., runs diagonally from northwest (at the Manhattan Bridge) to southeast (the Belt Parkway). From the Prospect Park area and east several roads run south toward the Atlantic: Ocean Parkway, Ocean Ave., Coney Island Ave., Bedford, Rockaway and Pennsylvania Aves., and Utica and Ralph Aves.

Atlantic Ave. travels east to west, as does Ft. Hamilton Parkway, which becomes Linden Blvd. Avenue U covers the southern area in sort of a U shape.

The Staten Island Expressway crosses the northern part of Staten Island, directly off the Verrazano-Narrows Bridge from Brooklyn to the Goethals Bridge for New Jersey. Hylan Blvd. is the most reliable route to the more rural sections in Staten Island.

By bus: Free route maps are available at the *Convention and Visitors' Bureau,* Columbus Circle. The ordinary bus fare is 90¢ and you must have exact change when boarding; you can also use a subway token to pay the bus fare.

By ferry: The famous ride from the Battery to Staten Island carries cars as well as people on a glorious voyage through the New York harbor.

From the airports: Some hotels serve the airport terminals with their own limousines. The Carey Bus Co. will bring you into Manhattan near the Grand Central Terminal.

By taxi: There are well over 30,000 yellow (licensed) cabs in New York. The driver, by law, may not refuse to take any "orderly" passenger anywhere in the five boroughs, Nassau, Westchester or to Newark Airport (the last three destinations entitle him to a fare beyond that on the meter—$10 extra for Newark, double to Nassau and Westchester). Neither may he charge each passenger separately when there is more than one passenger. These rules, along with the phone number (212–869–4237) of the city's *Taxi and Limousine Commission,* are posted inside each cab. On the back of the roof-light, you'll find the vehicle's medallion (identification) number.

TOURIST INFORMATION SERVICES. The *New York Convention and Visitors' Bureau* at the south side of Columbus Circle (59th St. and Broadway, the southwest corner of Central Park), has multilingual aides to assist you in making your sightseeing plans. They offer free subway and bus maps, and information about hotels, motels, and restaurants, as well as seasonal listings of the city's special entertainment attractions.

A *Guided Tour and Information Desk* at 30 Rockefeller Plaza (212–489-2947) is open daily, except Christmas Day, and offers multilingual guided tours of Rockefeller Center, including a backstage tour of Radio City Music Hall.

New York, The Village Voice, and the *New Yorker* are weekly publications featuring a wealth of information on current entertainment and cultural happenings.

The city's daily papers, *The New York Times, The New York Post,* and *The Daily News* also list current attractions, the *Sunday New York Times* being unsurpassed for useful entertainment information.

SEASONAL EVENTS. *January* brings the National Boat Show and the Greater New York Auto Show to the New York Coliseum, while one of the big Ice Shows occupies Madison Square Garden during the last three weeks of the month.

February offers the Westminster Kennel Club's annual Dog Show and the National Antiques Show at Madison Square Garden. This is also the time that the Chinese New Year celebration fills the streets of Chinatown.

The Money Show is held at the Coliseum in *March.* The parade season begins with the festive St. Patrick's Day extravaganza.

The Easter Parade centers around St. Patrick's Cathedral. All through *April* Madison Square Garden hosts the "Greatest Show on Earth," Ringling Brothers, Barnum and Bailey's Circus. The Greek Independence Day parade is the best-attended one of the month.

In *May* visit the Washington Square Outdoor Art Exhibition. The major parade honors the Armed Forces. The Circus continues.

June is the time for the Feast of St. Anthony of Padua, held on Sullivan St. between Houston and Spring Sts. The New York Philharmonic presents a program at Avery Fisher Hall, and "Shakespeare in the Park" begins its summer season at Central Park, as does the Metropolitan Opera.

July brings fireworks on the city's rivers and ballfields in honor of Independence Day. The Newport Jazz Festival fills the city with music early in the month at many local concert halls and outdoor amphitheaters. The festival also features midnight jam sessions and Hudson River dance cruises with big name swing bands. The New York Philharmonic takes to the parks.

The Yankees and Mets usually hold their annual Old Timers' Day ceremonies in *August.* Late in the month the artists of Greenwich Village bring out their wares again for the second installment of their annual show.

The San Gennaro Festival centers around Mulberry and Grand Sts. At this mid-*September* gala, Italian-Americans honor the patron saint of agnostics. Uptown German-Americans parade on Steuben Day.

In *October* the Coliseum presents a College Fair for high school students, and the International Wine and Cheese Festival. Three parades march this month: on Pulaski Day, Columbus Day, and Hispanic Day. A Halloween parade in Greenwich Village brings a touch of New Orleans Mardi Gras to the Apple.

In *November* the Coliseum helps you get a head start on winter with the International Ski and Winter Sports Show and also presents a second chance for devotees of the National Rod and Custom Car Show. Thanksgiving Day brings the fabled Macy's Parade with huge balloon representations of comic book and TV cartoon characters. It is the traditional opening of the Christmas season in New York. The National Horse Show comes to Madison Square Garden, usually before mid-month.

Christmas displays in department store windows are almost an art form in New York. Fifth Avenue is their main gallery; *December* their month. Rockefeller Center has its Christmas Tree and illuminated Channel Gardens, as well as its ice-skaters and carol-singers. Finally, New Year's Eve finds Times Square jammed with hundreds of thousands of celebrants who count out the old year and noisily ring in the new.

 PARKS. Manhattan's *Central Park* has 840 acres that include lakes for boating, trails for horseback riding, playfields, a green for lawn bowling, and a skating rink. The roads that circle through it are travelled by cars during weekday rush hours and pedaled by bicyclists the rest of the time.

On the West Side is *Riverside Park,* stretching along the Hudson River from 72nd St. up to the tip of the island.

Van Cortlandt Park is a cool retreat in the northwest Bronx. *Pelham Bay Park* in the east Bronx is almost entirely surrounded by water.

Queens' most notable parks are *Cunningham, Kissena* and *Flushing Meadow,* all in the central part of the borough.

Prospect Park's 500 acres in Brooklyn include lakes and a boathouse.

Fort Wadsworth on Staten Island is one of the quieter green spaces in New York City, situated under the Staten Island end of the Verrazano-Narrows Bridge and commanding an impressive view of the New York harbor.

The Parks Department sponsors drama, film, poetry, music, and dance at various parks throughout the summer. Call (212) 472-1003 for their current plans.

 ZOOS. The *Bronx Zoo,* located near the intersection of Pelham and Bronx River Parkways, is one of the largest in the world. The *Flushing Meadow Zoo* is near the N.Y. World's Fair's former Hall of Science and Shea Stadium. In Manhattan's Central Park you'll find a small *Children's Zoo,* and next to it, at 65th and Fifth Ave., a larger zoo for kids of all ages.

On Brooklyn's Coney Island is located the *New York Aquarium* where mammals, fish and birds from the world's water environments are displayed and fed.

Staten Island's *Barrett Park Zoo,* not far from the ferry terminal, claims a collection of snakes and reptiles which is world-famous.

 GARDENS. *New York Botanical Garden,* directly north of the Bronx Zoo, has 230 rolling acres containing some 12,000 different species of plants, some of which bloom on specialized sites such as Rhododendron Slope, Daffodil Hill, and Azalea Glen. There is also a spectacular 100-acre Hemlock Forest, virgin land unchanged since the days the Indians camped out there.

The 50-acre *Brooklyn Botanic Garden* in Prospect Park features two of the most beautiful Japanese gardens in this hemisphere. The pond-and-hill garden is a landscape of symbols with a tori, or gate, in the pond, a shrine on top of the hill and caves echoing the delicate sound of five tiny waterfalls. The second is an exact replica of the 15th-century Ryoanji (Buddhist) Temple Garden of Kyoto, one of the most famous abstract gardens of contemplation in the Far East, with a replica of the viewing wing of the ancient Ryoanji Temple. Another unique feature of the Brooklyn Botanic Garden is its Fragrance Garden for the Blind. The plants, in raised beds, are specially selected for identification by taste, touch, or smell; the plaques describing the flowers are in Braille.

 MUSEUMS AND GALLERIES. Art abounds here in all its variegated magnificence—much of it housed in buildings which are of great architectural interest themselves. In addition, there are myriad art galleries, most of the better ones clustered near Madison Avenue in the 50s, 60s, and 70s, as well as newly founded galleries in the SoHo district just below Houston St. and Greenwich Village.

The incredible vastness of the *Metropolitan Museum of Art,* Fifth Ave. at 82nd St., is actually many museums in one. It is not only impossible, but even undesirable, to see its collection of 5,000 years of art and culture all at once. Be choosey if your time is short; otherwise plan a return visit. The museum publishes a monthly calendar of events which you may write for. Floor plans, helpful staff members, a cafeteria restaurant, and numerous special services are available.

The newly enlarged *Museum of Modern Art* at 11 W. 53rd St. is the world's most outstanding museum devoted entirely to modern art in all media. There are examples of every creative movement from the gradual birth of modern art to the explosive designs of the 1960s, and an extremely pleasant sculpture garden for eating or just musing on Henry Moore. The museum's excellent film program includes documentaries, avant-garde experiments, and classics. Tickets are free with museum admission, and you must apply for them in person at the museum. There are also gallery talks three times a week, a lively schedule of lectures and events, and a bookshop. Films and talks are free once you've paid the admission charge.

The *American Museum of Natural History,* Central Pk. W. at 79th St., is probably the largest and most fascinating museum of its kind in the world. Almost everything is on view here, from giant dinosaur skeletons to the reproduction of a rain forest. There are frequent lectures and movies, as well as a bookshop and cafeteria.

The *Museum of the City of New York,* Fifth Ave. and 103rd St., covers almost every aspect of the development of a small Dutch town into a booming metropolis of skyscrapers and neon. A small scale model shows the early island of Manhattan, and the Dutch Galleries include a life-size reconstructed portion of Fort Amsterdam, from whose bastion you have a 360° view of the city skyline (painted) as it was in 1660. From April to October the museum sponsors a series of guided walking tours around New York neighborhoods on certain Sunday afternoons. From October to May there are special programs of events. Call (212) 534-1672, or write for schedules of these and the walking tours.

Note: Many more museums are listed in *Fodor's New York 1986,* one of the multi-volume series on the U.S.A.

Manhattan. *Bartow-Pell Mansion Museum and Garden* is at Pelham Bay Park. The mansion, built in 1842, is a Greek Revival restoration with sunken gardens, period furnishings, paintings, and a 200-volume library containing books on architecture, gardening and herbs. Small admission for adults.

Brooklyn. *Brooklyn Museum,* Eastern Parkway and Washington Ave., has an outstanding collection of ancient Egyptian art, and galleries devoted to the primitive arts of Africa, Japan, and Indonesia. The Hall of the Americas has exhibits of American primitive art. Also on view are the arts of India and the Orient. The museum has concerts, films, and lectures (write or call 718–638–5000 for a schedule), and there is a cafeteria and a Gallery Shop in the building.

Manhattan. *The Cloisters,* Fort Tryon Park. Parts of 5 medieval monasteries are reassembled here. Exhibits include the famed unicorn tapestries.

Flushing, Queens. The *Hall of Science* in the U.S. Space Park of the former New York World's Fair contains full-sized manned orbital space vehicles, a Planetarium, a Chick Hatchery, a children's museum, and a cafeteria.

Staten Island. *Staten Island Institute of Arts and Sciences* is at 75 Stuyvesant Place. The science and ecology exhibits show plants, animals, and insects typical of Staten Island. The arts part of the museum contains paintings, graphics, and decorative arts.

HISTORIC SITES. *The Harbor.* If you are conducting your own walking tour of sites and sights, you might want to start out where the city did. Henry Hudson, employed by the Dutch East India Company, sailed his ship, the *Half Moon,* into the harbor in 1609 and the area's inclusion in what Europeans called the "New World" dates from then.

Battery Park. On Tuesdays at noon (from the end of June to September) your treks can be accompanied by the brassy beat of a Battery Park Band Concert.

Bowling Green, many believe, is where Peter Minuit bought the island of Manhattan from the native Algonquins. The original 1771 fence around the green is intact today.

Fraunces Tavern at the corner of Broad and Pearl Sts. is one of the few remaining restored colonial buildings in the city. Built in 1719 as a handsome private house for Etienne de Lancey, it was bought in 1762 by Samuel Fraunces. He ran it as the Queen's Head Tavern, and it was there, in the second floor dining room, that General Washington gave the farewell dinner to his officers. Souvenirs of the occasion are on the third-floor *Museum of the Revolution,* open

Monday through Friday and Washington's birthday. The ground-floor restaurant is open for lunch and dinner weekdays and Washington's birthday. (Present building dates from 1907.)

While at Battery Park you will no doubt want to visit the *Statue of Liberty.* Special ferries leave from Battery Park every hour on the hour daily. Tel. (212) 269-5755 for information on schedules. Fare includes admission to the statue. (Note: The statue is being restored, and the inside will be closed until the planned completion date, July 4, 1986. The museum and base are open.)

Lower Manhattan. Trinity Church was given a grant of land by Queen Anne in 1705 covering much of lower Manhattan, much of which the church still owns. It is one of the wealthiest and most historic churches in New York. Alexander Hamilton and Robert Fulton are buried in the church's graveyard.

Greenwich Village. The Village was the city's first residential suburb, started in the late 1730s when people fled "north" to escape the plague. Washington Square was designated as a potter's field and public execution ground. By 1826, when it became a drill ground for militia, some 10,000 bodies, victims of the plague or the gallows, had been buried there.

Washington Arch was first built in 1889 when the city celebrated the centenary of Washington's inaugural. The present version was designed by the famous Stanford White, and built in 1895.

Midtown and Uptown. The *Pierpont Morgan Library,* 36th St. between Park and Lexington Aves., in the classic Italian Renaissance style, was the financier's private library, office, and personal museum. The library is one of the most opulent rooms in the world.

The *Morris-Jumel Mansion,* W. 161st St. and Edgecombe Ave., a Georgian Colonial hilltop house, was built in 1765 and was the scene of the wedding of Aaron Burr and the wealthy Mme. Jumel.

The Other Boroughs. Bronx. *Van Cortlandt House,* Van Cortlandt Park, was built in 1748 and has furnishings and household goods which reflect both its Dutch and British owners.

Queens. *Bowne House,* 37–01 Bowne St., Flushing, is known for the Flushing Remonstrance. John Bowne, advocate of religious freedom when New York was still New Amsterdam, lived in this house built in 1661. It contains 17th-century furnishings, a pewter collection and Bowne family memorabilia.

Brooklyn. *Brooklyn Heights,* a picturesque neighborhood of brownstone, brick, and old wooden houses high on a bluff overlooking New York Harbor has recently been designated New York's first "historic district." The New York Landmarks Commission calls the Heights. "by far the finest remaining microcosm of our city as it was more than 100 years ago." Wander through the streets and you can trace the evolution of the New York townhouse: wooden and brick Federal style, Greek Revival, Gothic Revival, Romanesque Revival and Renaissance Revival.

Staten Island. *Conference House* at the south end of Hylan Blvd. in Tottenville was built in 1680, and held the only peace conference during the Revolutionary War.

 MUSIC. *Lincoln Center,* Broadway and W. 65th St., is the musical heart of New York City. Within the Lincoln Center complex are: *Avery Fisher Hall,* home of the New York Philharmonic Orchestra, which performs throughout the year except August. Twice a summer they perform in the Sheep Meadow at Central Park, and at least once in a park in every borough.

The Metropolitan Opera Company performs at the Metropolitan Opera House from September through April. They perform in Central Park and other city parks at no charge in June and July.

The *Juilliard Building* features chamber music by its own Juilliard School students and visiting performers.

Carnegie Hall at Seventh Avenue and 57th Street is a much-loved city landmark that presents classical symphonic concerts and occasional pop music programs.

The *Guggenheim Bandshell* in Damrosch Park has outdoor concerts in the summer. The Goldman Band performs popular and light classical music on summer evenings.

The *New York City Opera* performs at the New York State Theater, as does the *New York City Ballet.*

The biggest non-classical event in the city is the *Newport Jazz Festival,* held for about a week and a half that usually includes the Independence Day weekend. One of its nicest features is that it spreads out from the concert halls and presents a Radio City Music Hall jam session and a Hudson River Boatride.

Pop and rock concerts are presented all over town, all year long; the biggest attractions fill *Madison Square Garden* for several nights.

DANCE. New York has, in versatile Lincoln Center and the revitalized Brooklyn Academy of Music, facilities for every variety: classical ballet to avant-garde dance theater, African to Far Eastern. Prominent regular New York performers include George Balanchine's world famous *New York City Ballet,* the *American Ballet Theater,* the *Joffrey Ballet Company,* the *Alvin Ailey Dance Company,* and the *Dance Theater of Harlem.* For performance schedules (of visiting companies as well), contact Lincoln Center, the box office at the City Center Theater, or the Brooklyn Academy of Music. A half-price ticket booth in Bryant Park at 42nd St. between Fifth and Sixth Avenues sells remaining seats to cultural events on the day of the performance.

TOURS. The traditional bus rides are still available from midtown (*Gray Line,* 212–397–2600 and *Crossroads,* 212–581–2828, are two prominent outfits in this field). A fresher perspective and less confining atmosphere are found on boat and helicopter trips. The famous *Circle Line* (212–563–3200) leaves from 43rd St. and the Hudson River and goes all the way around Manhattan. *Island Helicopters* (718–895–1626) provides flights as short as five minutes if you're interested in an aerial view.

SPECIAL INTEREST TOURS. *Adventure on a Shoestring* (212–265–2663), plans a variety of unusual and offbeat tours and behind-the-scenes visits. If you've never been in a trans-oceanic port before, the busy piers and luxury liners may prove fascinating indeed. The newspaper shipping pages list departure schedules and if you call the line for its visiting policy, you'll be ready to stroll around the decks while passengers are being taken aboard.

Two traditionally popular guided tours shouldn't be foregotten: the *United Nations,* First Ave. and 42nd St., and the *New York Stock Exchange,* 20 Broad St.

STAGE. In New York City, the theater district—as almost all the world knows—is situated around the bright lights of Broadway and the streets in the mid-40s. Elsewhere in the city, uptown and down, are scattered the other theaters whose productions are known as "off Broadway" and are more likely to give avant-garde productions. "Off-off-Broadway" are even more avant-gard productions and are often held in places not originally designed as playhouses. Most impressive is the Joseph Papp New York Shakespeare Festival Theater on Lafayette St., near Astor Place. The theater holds about 4 different stages, and most of the productions are of new or up-and-coming American playwrights.

An important new development for the benefit of playgoers is in Duffy Square, the narrow area of W. 47th St. between Broadway and Seventh Ave. Here, at a booth named "Tkts," you may buy, at half-price, any unsold or otherwise available seats for performances on the same day or night for Broadway, off-Broadway, and off-off-Broadway shows.

NIGHTCLUBS. Old-fashioned nightclub shows featuring a singer, scantily clad kick lines, comedians, jugglers, and magicians are available (not inexpensively) at *Cafe Versailles* and the *Rainbow Grill.* Some variation on classic show and movie tunes in staged revues is usually on tap at the *King Cole Room* of the St. Regis. *The Ballroom* in Chelsea will have any of two or three different shows running at different times of the night (often with a pre-dinner 6:30 set by the likes of Blossom Dearie). Tops in class are the hotel piano rooms:

the Carlyle's *Cafe Carlyle,* with Bobby Short or Marian McPartland (high society at its highest), the *Oak Room* at the Algonquin with Steve Ross (very theatrical patronage), or the Waldorf's *Peacock Alley* (the pianists/duos/trios change regularly for a stately and statesman-like crowd).

Dance—with views to match—at the *Rainbow Room* to the best of the big bands or at the World Trade Center's *Hors D'ouverie* to light cocktail music. Late night disco dancing is still alive at *Studio 54,* and a host of clubs hidden downtown in Tribeca, where what's fashionable and the "in" place change constantly.

Jazz is everywhere. Check the *New Yorker* or *Village Voice* for the best current listings. *The Village Vanguard* is the prototypical smokey, subterranean jazz club. *Michael's Pub* is good for dinner as well as music, as is *Sweet Basil,* all leaning toward the mainstream. *Lush Life* is a favorite for contemporary and avant-garde jazz in a club setting; much in this vein is also available at lofts in Soho and Tribeca. Comfortably funky: *Seventh Ave. South, Mikell's* and *Hanratty's.*

Rock and pop are the mainstays at the *Bottom Line,* where patrons sit at long narrow tables—as opposed to the *Ritz,* a classic Art Deco ballroom with no seats, a big dance floor and the latest in new wave sounds. *The Lone Star* is for country and blues. Concerts are most likely at *Madison Square Garden,* the *Beacon, Carnegie* and *Avery Fisher* halls.

SPECTATOR SPORTS. *Baseball,* April through early October, features the Mets at Shea Stadium, in Flushing, Queens, and the Yankees at the handsomely refurbished Yankee Stadium in the Bronx.

Football. The Giants, an old team that recently gave up New York for friendlier financial climes in New Jersey was joined this year by the Jets. They will share impressive Giants Stadium, just across the Hudson River in East Rutherford.

NBA's Knicks play at Madison Square Garden. The Nassau Veterans' Memorial Coliseum in Uniondale, Nassau County, L.I., is home for the Islanders *hockey team,* while their National Hockey League neighbors, the Rangers, play in the Garden. Each of these three teams has a regular season running from October to April.

Flat and harness tracks draw millions of horse racing enthusiasts each year. The thoroughbreds run at Aqueduct and Belmont, both in Queens. The Belmont Stakes, the third jewel in the Triple Crown for three-year olds, run in mid-June, highlights the flat-racing schedule. Working folks benefit from the night-time programs of standardbred harness races at Yonkers and Roosevelt Raceways, where elaborate parlay opportunities fan the hopes of busy wagerers. *Soccer* fans in the New York area journey out to East Rutherford, New Jersey, just 15 min. from Manhattan, where the aptly named New York Cosmos play professional rivals in Giants Stadium.

Madison Square Garden has long hosted the Millrose Games, one of America's great *track and field* meets, and has the equipment for putting on almost any kind of sporting event or entertainment attraction.

SPORTS. The sports most participated in by New Yorkers are probably jogging and bicycling, since they require no in-place equipment, just some park space. Central Park in Manhattan and Prospect Park in Brooklyn have automobile roadways which are reserved for walkers, runners, and pedalers during daylight hours on weekends, and you can find plenty of places to rent a bike on the nearby side streets and avenues.

For specific details about your favorite athletic pastime, be it golf, skating, fishing, or horseback riding, contact the *New York Convention and Visitors Bureau,* at Columbus Circle.

SHOPPING. It may come as no great news that huge numbers of visitors come to New York City solely to shop. There is probably no city on earth that possesses the number and diversity of shops that New York can proudly claim. If you can't find it in New York, the chances are it just doesn't exist.

Women's Clothing: Generally speaking, the largest array of merchandise, and consequently the greatest range of choices, will be found in the larger department and specialty stores. Along Fifth Ave. are *B. Altman's* (at 34th St.), *Lord & Taylor* (at 38th St.), *Saks Fifth Avenue* (at 50th St.), *Henri Bendel* (on the south side of 57th St. just off Fifth Ave)., *Berdorf Goodman* (at 58th St.). The venerable *Bloomingdale's* is at Lexington Ave. and 59th St., and a completely new *Bonwit Teller* graces 57th St. between Fifth and Madison.

Leave some time to explore the fantastic range of unique boutiques that dot the city's landscape, particularly along Madison Ave. between 57th and 78th Sts. where the coterie of shops represent both the height of European haute couture and the best of American design.

Some of the most unique boutiques are *Riding High* (1147 First Ave), featuring imports and New York designers; *Fiorucci* (125 E. 59th St); *San Francisco* (975 Lexington Ave.), top-quality goods; *Dianne B* (729 Madison Ave.), French items; *Grecophila* (132 W. 72nd St.), fine Greek imports.

Bargain Hunting: For the indescribable thrill of "real" bargain shopping at a manufacturers' outlet, *Loehmann's* (Fordham Rd. and Jerome Ave. in the Bronx) is the granddaddy of the best buys.

Resale stores carry "gently used, good things" culled from the best private wardrobes—chances are some of their offerings have never been worn. The best-known shop is *Resale Associates,* on Madison Ave. near 80th St.

Men's Clothing: The four weekdays that follow Labor Day is the time when *Barney's,* the largest men's store in the world, holds its famous warehouse sale. All department and specialty stores also have sizable men's departments catering to all sorts of tastes.

Brooks Bros. stands conservatively at Madison Ave. and 44th St. Upper Park and Madison are the avenues for the wildly expensive shops that specialize in men's "furnishings."

Most of the best discounters are on Fifth Ave. between 14th and 23rd Sts., where men's clothings manufactures have existed for many years. *Harry Rothman* at 111 Fifth Ave. is the oldest of these value-oriented retail clothier.

Uptown, at Third Ave. and 86th St., is one of the largest stores for jeans, work shirts, and western wear, known as *The Gap* (branches all over the city). But for the wildest selection of all, you've got to head way downtown. *Hudson's* is the grandfather of all the so-called Army & Navy stores, though their merchandise encompasses a far wider range than just military surplus.

For the truly adverturous, however, there is no more interesting shopping experience than a tour of Soho boutiques, unisex and otherwise.

Children's Clothing: Every one of the major department and specialty stores has a children's department that generally reflects its basic position on the adult fashion ladder. Of all these stores, however, *Macy's* rates as the top choice, if only because of its huge selection.

There are also a great many boutique-style stores along upper Madison Ave. that specialize in nothing but children's apparel, and they too run the full spectrum of prices and styles.

Other excellent children's boutiques are: *The Chocolate Soup* (946 Madison Ave.), and *Wendy's Store* (1046 Madison Ave.).

For bargains, there's no place better than *Nathan Borlam* at 157 Havemeyer St. in Brooklyn, where name brands are available at very low prices, and bargains are easily recognizable because the original labels are all left on. Open only Sunday through Thursday.

Books: *Rizzoli* (31 W. 57th St.), *Dalton's* (666 Fifth Ave.), *Scribner's* (Fifth Ave. at 49th St.) and *Barnes and Noble* (18th St. on both sides of Fifth Ave., plus an impressive discount book store on Fifth Ave. and 49th St.) have the largest general selections, although academic and privately printed works on consignment are easier to find in the many shops near the college campuses, especially Columbia (Broadway and 116th St.)

Literature lovers who are searching for hard-to-find classics should try the famous *Gotham Book Mart,* on 47th St. between Fifth and Sixth avenues.

The hub of the used-book market (these include mint-condition reviewer's copies and unsold remainders) is along Fourth Ave. between 9th and 14th Sts. The best shop of this sort, with the largest selection, is the *Strand* at Broadway and 12th St.

Toys: The magnets for the majority of young and young at heart would have to be *F.A.O. Schwarz,* Fifth Ave. and 58th St., and the equally famous toy department of *Macy's.*

Records: *Tower Records* boasts the largest record and video outlet in the world at Broadway and West 4th Street in Greenwich Village and a sister store near Lincoln Center at Broadway and 66th Street. Also of note: *J&R Music World* near City Hall, *Colony* in midtown and *Sam Goody* with a number of branches.

If you're looking for an old album that even the original issuing company doesn't have in its warehouse, try the *Record Exchange* (Seventh Ave. and 55th St.). The largest single inventory of records (of all types and descriptions) is probably the *Colony Record Center* (1619 Broadway), and their proud boast is that they can get any record ever made.

Leather & Luggage: You can find manufacturers' labels at good prices at any number of luggage shops tucked into various corners of the city. But for the "right" names, *Gucci* occupies three separate stores along Fifth Ave. between 54th and 55th Sts. *Mark Cross* at Fifth Ave. and 55th St. is in the same class, as is *T. Anthony* at 772 Madison Ave.

Also excellent are *Lederer,* at 613 Madison Ave., and *La Bagagarie,* at 727 Madison.

Crouch & Fitzgerald, 400 Madison Ave., is the local center for the much-coveted Louis Vuitton label.

Fine Foods & Gourmet Goods: New Yorker's favorite edibles are at *Zabar's* (Broadway and 80th St.), *Cheese Unlimited* (Second Ave. and 79th St.), *Maison Glass* (58th St. E. of Madison Ave.), and *Balducci's* (Sixth Ave. and 9th St.)

The gourmet shops at *Bloomingdale's* and *Macy's* are prime sources for fine and unusual spices and all sorts of delectables. Both are great places for exotic cooking aids and gourmet cookware.

Lovely Luxuries: *Royal Copenhagen* sells its famed Danish porcelain on Madison Ave. just below 57th St.

Steuben Glass occupies the ground floor of the Corning Glass Building at Fifth Ave. and 56th St., its array of crystal inside no less shimmering than the reflection of the restful fountain pool outside.

At *Hammacher Schlemmer,* 145 E. 57th St., you'll be awed by just the sheer number of gadgets and gimcracks.

Far less expensive, and perhaps more useful for the odd, inexpensive gifts that must be purchased during every trip, are the many *Azuma* shops that are scattered all around the city filled with inexpensive trinkets of both abiding interest and plain amusement value. Among their branches are shops at Fifth Ave. and 39th St., Lexington and 55th St., and 86th St. between Second and Third Aves.

Antiques: The antique trip is interesting as an opportunity to see a unique (and fading) way of New York City life as well as for the prospect of finding some under-priced treasure.

Most of the best (and most expensive) shops are along 57th St. between Fifth and Park Aves., and also on Madison Ave. in the 50s, 60s, and 70s. Smaller and less expensive shops are scattered all over, but the general concentration is on Third Ave. between 45th and 70th Sts., and in the same boundaries, though less densely laid out, on Second and First Aves. For the adventurous, a trip to Greenwich Village and to the Lower East Side can possibly prove rewarding.

Jewelry: *Tiffany's* at Fifth Ave. and 57th St. is almost as elegant as the reputation that precedes it. But they also have some affordable items that are well within the budgets of mere mortals.

Even more elegant is the fabled *Cartier's* at Fifth Ave. and 52nd St., where the mantle of wealth and privilege hangs heavy over its gilt and plush decor; but even it takes a backseat in high prices to *Harry Winston's* at 718 Fifth Ave.

Less sophisticated, but more exciting, is *"the diamond center"* on W. 47th St. between Fifth and Sixth Aves. In shops packed with merchandise where no time or expense is wasted on decor, you can bargain over gold, silver, gems and the full spectrum of semiprecious stones.

WHAT TO DO WITH THE CHILDREN. Children will enjoy much of what fills this chapter. In addition, theaters for children are rapidly growing in number. Some of the best are the *Bil Baird* (59 Barrow St.) for puppet shows; *Courtyard Playhouse* (137A W. 14th St.); *South St. Seaport* (South and Fulton Sts.); and in the *Magic Towne House,* 1026 Third Ave., featuring magicians and clowns. Other activities include the *Fire Department Museum* at 104 Duane St., downtown, for a colorful display of fire engines and exhibits, and the

Hayden Planetarium at 81st St. and Central Park West to really see the stars and planets in fascinating reproductions.

 HOTELS AND MOTELS. Manhattan is an island literally filled with hotels, or so it seems when the unsophisticated traveler is trying to make up his mind where to stay. From the chic super-deluxe establishments to the modest, more reasonably priced hotels and motels, there is an incredibly wide range of accommodations available.

Because of the unique nature and diversity of New York City hotels, we have to add a little extra detail to our price categories, and advise you to give some consideration to geographic location as well as price and appointments.

Our *super deluxe* category refers to the top hotels in Manhattan, and in fact, these few pinnacles of service and elegance rank with the finest hotels in the world. The price for this rarified atmosphere is predictably high, and the prices range from $120 (and up) per day for double rooms.

The *deluxe* hotels in our listings are only marginally less grand. Often the only difference is one of history and tradition, and is apparent only to those who cherish the nuance as much as the accommodation. These are all fine hotels, and you can expect the maximum in service and comfort. Prices range from $90–120, double.

The hotels in our *expensive* range include many of the newer establishments, and their prices reflect the economy of today's world. While the accommodations are uniformly pleasant, they will often suffer from the sterile atmosphere that is so prevalent in contemporary hotel construction. We've also included some of the fine older hotels that do not quite achieve the deluxe rank. All hotels in this category will, of course, have a full range of services available, and such amenities as room service, television, and multiple in-hotel dining facilities are uniformly available. Expect to pay $80–90, double, per day.

Hotels in the *moderate* category are a grab bag, and encompass older, dignified establishments and new center city motel-type units. You can find some very comfortable and commodious accommodations in this category, with prices ranging from $65–80, double.

In New York City, *inexpensive* is a relative term, and you should really know where you are going before you accept a cheap bed. We've tried to list a few alternatives that are acceptable hygienically, but don't expect very lavish digs. Prices will range from $65 and below, double.

Rock bottom, in pricey New York, means any place you can find to rest your head for less than $50, double!

Most of the best of the more than 100,000 hotel rooms in New York are concentrated in the area between 34th and 59th streets, but don't expect to get a room in this area if you don't reserve in advance. That's not a bad piece of advice, regardless of where you might be staying, because New York City is not a particularly good place to come to when you don't have firm plans or a confirmed bed for the night. Although they will be able to supply you with an extensive brochure listing hotels and rates, the NYCVB doesn't find or book the rooms for you.

A note on prices: do not be misled by hotels and motels who advertise "minimum rates" and quote a dramatically low figure. In most cases, there are only a few rooms available at these rates, and the great number of rooms in the establishment will be far higher. Again, the value of reserving a room well in advance cannot be over-emphasized. In addition to the category price ranges noted, there is also an occupancy tax charge of 25¢ per day for rooms under $10.00 per day; 50¢ per day on rooms from $10 to $15; 75¢ per day on rooms from $15 to $20; $1.00 per day on rooms from $20 and up. The 8% New York City sales tax is also charged on all hotel bills. Weekend bargain rates are available; check with a travel agent for current deals.

MIDTOWN (42ND TO 65TH STREETS, 8TH AVE. TO EAST RIVER).
Super Deluxe: **Berkshire Palace.** 21 East 52nd St. Its location makes it convenient to Fifth Avenue stores and most uptown business appointments. 500 rooms.

Delmonico's. 502 Park Ave. An elegant hotel, conveniently situated on Park Avenue at 58th Street. The name Delmonico's has come to signify luxury, and this hotel lives up to the standard. The atmosphere is French Provincial; the service continental. *Regine's* nightclub next door enlivens the night. The rooms are large and give a sense of sumptuous privacy. 600 rooms.

Helmsley Palace. 455 Madison Ave., behind St. Patrick's Cathedral. This property boasts an historic town house at its entrance. New, and grand, it aspires to be the ultimate in hostelries, catering to the very rich.

Marriott's Essex House. 160 Central Park South. Park Avenue has the reputation, but Central Park South has the view. The Essex House is one of the several very fine hotels along this stretch, and one of the largest. Very close to the Coliseum, Carnegie Hall, and not far from Lincoln Center. 750 rooms.

Park Lane. 36 Central Park South. The views of the park and the city's skyline are nothing short of spectacular, and the rooms are almost on a par. Rooftop dining is similarly impressive. Staff can converse in several languages, and this is a favorite stopping place for knowledgeable foreign visitors. 640 rooms.

Pierre. 61st St. & Fifth Ave., opposite Central Park. This fine hotel, which opened in 1930, is primarily a residential hotel (cooperative apartments), and many of its 700 rooms are permanently occupied. Those which are not are, of course, available to transient guests, and these guests often occupy the highest ranks of society and celebrity. Much of the hotel's staff has been around for years, and the result is highly courteous, personal service. It's a favorite for entertaining (there are 43 private dining rooms), or you can be entertained in the *Café Pierre* or the *La Forêt* grill.

Plaza. Fifth Ave. and 59th St. The grandest hotel in the city, the Plaza is still the most imposing and beautiful in New York. With Central Park on one side, and a small plaza (complete with a graceful fountain) in front, this is New York's enclave of tradition and elegance in the European manner. Inside, the elegance is immediately apparent. Although much redecorating has been done since 1907 (when the hotel opened), none of the original flavor and feeling has been lost. The 1,000 rooms are richly decorated, mainly in the French Provincial manner. The hotel service is superb. The staff is trained to the point of remembering guests' names—and using them. The Plaza's restaurants and nightclubs are famous in their own right, and include the *Oak Room,* the *Oyster Bar,* and the *Palm Court, Trader Vic's* is also an in-hotel restaurant.

Regency. Park Ave. at 61st St. The only "modern" super deluxe hotel in New York, a $13 million gamble on "a return to elegance." In the Regency's case, this statement is made a matter of simple fact. There are 500 rooms and suites, most decorated à la Louis XVI; telephones and scales in every bathroom, kitchenettes connected to many of the suites, a garage, a fine French restaurant, and cocktail lounge.

Ritz Carlton, 112 Central Park South. Recently converted from the former Navarro with every effort to live up to the name. 231 rooms.

St. Regis-Sheraton. Fifth Ave. and 55th St. The ultimate in Old World wealth and rococo elegance. Many descendants of the famous "400," that original core of New York's social elite, still inhabit the St. Regis' 550 rooms, and the social set still congregates here for posh dining and dancing. The hotel's luxury restaurants and bars are the *Oak Room,* the *King Cole Bar,* and *La Boîte.*

Sherry-Netherland. 781 Fifth Ave. Though somewhat less well known than its neighbors, the *Plaza* and the *Pierre,* the Sherry-Netherland is a distinguished hotel with an aura of grandeur all its own. The accent is continental, and the atmosphere is sedate and elegant. The rooms are lovely and the location is very chic. A short walk downtown brings you into the midst of the best Fifth Avenue shopping. Park views are spectacular. 375 rooms.

Waldorf-Astoria. 301 Park Ave. at 50th St. Some hotels seem to improve with age, and the Waldorf is a prime example. It is certainly the most renowned of American hotels. The Park Avenue entrance is imposing and the rooms are decorated in a gracious style. Each year the hotel plays host to countless distinguished visitors, and top entertainers are the lure in the lavish *Empire Room.* 1,900 rooms.

Deluxe: **Alrae.** 37 East 64th St. Located just off Madison Avenue, a few blocks north of the principal Fifth Avenue stores. Small, but gracious, and most of its guests live there on a long-term basis. *Château Henri VI Restaurant,* accessible only by a drawbridge over a small moat. 250 rooms.

Barclay Inter-Continental. 111 East 48th St. Located half a block off Park Avenue. An older, gracious hotel with very pleasant, spacious atmosphere. Live birds frolic in the aviary in the lobby, and the *King's Court* restaurant is one of the most elegant in the city. 770 rooms, garage facilities.

Dorset. 30 West 54th St. One of the least known of NYC's top stopping places, this hotel is central to just about everything, and close to most, adjacent to the Museum of Modern Art. 450 rooms.

Drake. 440 Park Ave. After complete refurbishing, one of best hotels in city. European ambiance, American chic and efficiency. *Wellington Grill* smart new dining room.

Grand Hyatt New York. 42nd St. at Lexington. On site of old Commodore, a glittering glass box with 1,400 rooms. Restaurant features nouvelle cuisine.

Harley Hotel of New York. 212 E. 42nd St. Another new Helmsley hotel, with 800 fine rooms. Close to the UN.

Lombardy. 111 E. 56th St. This ultra-smart hotel allows you a chance to stay in grand surroundings in a fine location. The rooms offer large, distinguished accommodations, and continental breakfast is included in the rates. Very chic and quite sumptuous. 325 rooms. Home of the excellent *Laurent Restaurant.*

Loew's Warwick. 65 West 54th St. The hotel attracts people in the communications, advertising, and fashion industries, but it has all that is necessary to appeal to the average appreciative visitor. The rooms are large and now handsomely furnished. The location, just off Sixth Avenue, is central. *Sir Walter's Restaurant* has long been a favorite of showpeople. 500 rooms.

New York Hilton. 1335 Avenue of the Americas. The Hilton name is becoming synonymous with large, fancy, modern hotels and this is no exception. One of the more popular hotels in the city, it is also one of the largest. Every modern convenience (including long beds and heated bathroom floors) is available, and if one goes wanting here, don't blame the planners. The location is very good, close to almost everything, and particularly Rockefeller Center, 2,130 rooms.

Sheraton Centre. Seventh Ave. between 52nd and 53rd Sts. This is more than just a towering, undulating glass slab—this is 50 stories of modern luxury hotel, among the tallest in the world, with just about all the facilities and services one could hope for. Unfortunately, the establishment lacks warmth, and you man find the accommodations less than spacious. There are four restaurants available. Just a few blocks from the Coliseum, Broadway, and the Museum of Modern Art. 1,850 rooms.

UN Plaza. 44th St. at 1st Ave., opposite the United Nations. A splendid building, inside and out. Nice *Ambassador* grill room, but beware the many-mirrored walls, which everyone (including waiters) runs into.

Vista International. 3 World Trade Center, 825 rooms. New in 1981, this attractive property has 4 restaurants, 24-hour room service, and is within walking distance of Wall Street.

Expensive: **Algonquin.** 59 West 44th St. Every modern comfort is provided in this hotel, conveniently located near Fifth Avenue shops, Rockefeller Center and Broadway theaters. The richly paneled lobby is a popular meeting place at cocktail hour for people in publishing, theater, and TV. Superb cuisine in its restaurants, once the haunt of literature's famous "Round Table."

Barbizon Plaza. 106 Central Park South. It is usually bustling with tours and conventions, but relief from these can be found in generally bright rooms. 1,000 rooms, garage facilities.

Beverly. 125 East 50th St. Just off Lexington Avenue. Transient guests are usually businessmen. Comfortable though not distinguished. *Kenny's Steak Pub* restaurant is among NYC's best. 300 rooms.

Elysée. 60 East 54th St. Some individuality is maintained by assigning you a room having a name rather than a number, and the decor of each room varies. Home of the famous *Monkey Bar.* 110 rooms.

Gramercy Park. 2 Lexington Avenue. The area is dignified and quiet. The hotel faces out on a small private park and, although not pretentious, it is inviting and good. Very comfortable bar. 500 rooms.

Holiday Inn-Coliseum. 440 West 57th St. A bit off the beaten track, but the location avoids a lot of traffic for arrivees from the western approaches to the city. Rooftop pool and kennel. 600 rooms.

Lexington. 511 Lexington Ave. This is a good hotel, with no particular attempt made to be fancy or elegant. *Château Madrid* supper club is a city favorite. 800 rooms.

Loew's Summit. Lexington Avenue and 51st St. The rooms are very commodious, and service is great. Concierge to assist you. Rooms are equipped with many extra conveniences. ESP (Extra Special People) floor for those who want super-deluxe services. The location is just a few blocks east of Fifth Avenue and north of Grand Central. Lobby cocktail lounge, *Maude's* restaurant. 770 rooms, garage facilities.

Park Central. Seventh Avenue and 56th St. A busy hotel, popular with TV and stage personalities and also with conventions. Its location is central to many features of the city, including the Coliseum, Carnegie Hall, and the theater district. Formerly the New York Sheraton; undergoing renovations. 1,600 rooms.

St. Moritz. 50 Central Park South. The rooms are on the small side, but done in taste. The hotel is also a favorite of foreign visitors. 1,000 rooms.

Moderate: **Sheraton City Squire.** 790 Seventh Avenue between 51st and 52nd Sts. One of the better motels and closer to the city's activities than most. Indoor swimming pool and sauna; open to the public for a fee. 700 rooms, free parking.

Howard Johnson's Motor Lodge. Eighth Avenue between 51st and 52nd Sts. The interior is modern and as comfortable as one would expect. 300 rooms, free parking.

Mayflower. 15 Central Park West. This hotel is unpretentious, but it offers 600 pleasant rooms and a location close to the Coliseum and Lincoln Center.

Ramada Inn-Midtown. 790 Eighth Avenue between 48th and 49th Sts. Convenient to midtown theaters and movies. Rooftop pool. 370 rooms.

Roger Smith. 501 Lexington Avenue. An unexceptional businessman's hotel near Grand Central. Its rooms are adequate and comfortable, though hardly distinguished. 200 rooms.

Shoreham. 33 West 55th St. The rooms are modest but clean and each has its own pantry. 150 rooms.

Wellington. 871 Seventh Ave. At 55th Street, convenient to Carnegie Hall, the Coliseum, and many of the Broadway theaters. Used often by airline personnel. 700 rooms.

Windsor. 100 West 58th St. The accommodations here are considered good but plain. No attempt is made to transport you to another world, but rather to give you solid comfort. 300 rooms.

Wyndham. 42 West 58th St. Modest, though undistinguished, it is close to Carnegie Hall, Fifth Avenue, and Central Park. No room service, but a favorite among theatrical and musical folk. 225 rooms.

Inexpensive: **Edison.** 228 West 47th St. Just off Times Square, this is a good, big hotel with modern facilities and a busy atmosphere. The rooms are clean and pleasant. 1,000 rooms, garage facilities.

Mansfield. 12 West 44th St. The location is good, just off Fifth Avenue and not far from Times Square. There are no pretensions and the quarters are agreeable. 200 rooms.

Times Square Motor Hotel. 255 West 43rd St. Just west of Times Square, this hotel (it's really not a motel) offers acceptable, clean, plain accommodations. 1,000 rooms, free parking.

Wentworth. 59 West 46th St. This is an older hotel near the theater district, also close to Fifth Avenue. The rooms are undistinguished, and the area is certainly not posh. 250 rooms.

DOWNTOWN AND WEST SIDE (BELOW 42ND ST. OR WEST OF 8TH AVE.). *Deluxe:* **Doral Park Avenue.** 70 Park Avenue. This hotel is a relatively recent creation, being an amalgam of a renovated hotel and a new building. Four blocks south of Grand Central. 200 rooms.

Sheraton-Russell. 45 Park Ave. This hotel is located at 37th St. on Murray Hill and is a little removed from the heart of the city, even though it is only five blocks south of Grand Central. The hotel is used mainly by businessmen, but should appeal to other visitors. The rooms are generally large, some with fireplaces. The hotel has been recently renovated. 170 rooms, free parking.

Tuscany. 120 East 39th St. This is a small luxury hotel just south of Grand Central. All of its rooms are studios, complete with service pantries and many extras, such as a telephone in the bathroom and color television. It is both residential and transient, and is particularly popular with businessmen. 270 rooms.

Expensive: **Penta,** 401 Seventh Avenue. Formerly the New York Statler, this is a huge, busy hotel, directly across from Penn Station and very popular with conventions and businessmen. It is near the fashion manufacturing center of New York. At press time, extensive renovations were expected to be completed by mid-1985. 1,700 rooms.

UPTOWN (ABOVE 65TH STREET). *Super Deluxe:* **American Stanhope.** Fifth Ave. at 81st St. Its atmosphere is particularly gracious, and above all it has classic service. The rooms are very comfortable and tastefully decorated. The location is a posh neighborhood uptown, opposite the Metropolitan Museum. Fine cuisine, elegant atmosphere in *Saratoga Room.* Unusual attraction is N.Y.'s most beautiful sidewalk café, *The Terrace,* in summer. 275 rooms.

Carlyle. 35 E. 76th St. Located in one of New York's poshest residential areas, it is also handy to two of the city's best museums—the Metropolitan and the Whitney. All rooms are air-conditioned, suites have a pantry with refrigerator, and some suites have private terraces and/or wood-burning fireplaces. The *Regency Room* offers elegant dining, and the *Bemelman's Bar* is decorated with murals by that whimsical artist himself. Bobby Short's piano often echoes in the Vertès-decorated *Café Carlyle.* 175 rooms available (the best for full-time residents), garage facilities.

Westbury. 840 Madison Ave. at 69th St. In many ways, this is one of the better hotels in the city. The neighborhood surroundings are unimpeachable, and the dignified tone of the hotel is intended to complement them. The furnishings reflect a grand style, and the rooms are tastefully comfortable. The location is near the Frick Museum, the Central Park Zoo, and the many art galleries and *haute couture* boutiques lining Madison Avenue. Some people may consider this too far uptown, but the ambiance more than makes up for any inconvenience. 325 rooms.

QUEENS. *Expensive:* **International TraveLodge.** Belt Pkwy. and Van Wyck Expwy. at Kennedy International Airport. The consummate airport hotel. A large establishment (500 rooms) graced by the *Château Terrace* restaurant, which is an oasis of calm after the hectic pace of J.F.K.

Hilton Inn at J.F.K. 150th St. exit from the Belt Parkway, Rockaway Blvd. exit from the Van Wyck Expwy.

Holiday Inn of La Guardia. 100–15 Ditmars Blvd. (La Guardia exit from Grand Central Pkwy.).

Moderate: **Howard Johnson's Kennedy Airport.** Van Wyck Expwy. and Southern Pkwy. The usual amenities of this chain plus an indoor pool that is open from June to Sept.

Pan-American Motor Inn. 79–100 Queens Blvd. (State 25). You can have a swim here; for women there's a beauty salon. Convenient to Shea Stadium, La Guardia Airport and just about 3 mi. from the Queensborough Bridge.

 DINING OUT. There is really no effective capsule comment that can completely describe the phenomenon of eating out in New York City. As the gastronomic capital of the U.S., it has by far the most restaurants of any city in the country, and the most truly *fine* and distinguished restaurants as well.

There is finely prepared fare available in New York City fit for any palate—no matter how exotic one's tastes. And the depth of the quality of even the most "off-beat" establishments is literally staggering. There may be, for example, more than a dozen superior restaurants in N.Y.C. that specialize in nothing but the delicacies from the Balkan countries.

Interestingly enough, the prospective range of prices for a meal in New York City covers just as wide a range as the spectrum of the different foods. While a fine meal at an elegant restaurant can (and often does) extract a sultan's ransom from wealthy gourmandizers, it is also possible to have nearly a duplicate meal, served in more humble surroundings (and without a platoon of liveried attendants), at literally half the tariff. In preparing the following lists of recommended restaurants, we've sought to provide a wide enough range of choices to fit every traveler's budget.

Almost all the best restaurants in New York City center in Manhattan, though we have picked a few notables in the outlying boroughs. But Manhattan stretches thirteen miles from end to end, and this distance may prove difficult to traverse in a limited stay, so *we have arranged restaurants by area, then national or ethnic cuisine and price range.*

We regret, as you do, the prices that any meal costs anywhere these days, and the toll in New York is probably higher than anywhere else in the nation. But the following categories are the facts of today's dining-out world, and we can only suggest that you mitigate each foray to some expensive temple of gastronomy with a sojourn to at least one more modest eatery.

Super Deluxe restaurants will offer à la carte meals at a cost of $40 and up. *Deluxe* establishments will generally fit into the $35 to $40 range. *Expensive* dinners will usually cost $25 to $35 and *Moderate* meals should run between $15 and $20. A tab at an *Inexpensive* restaurant will cost under $10. All prices in the above categories are *per person,* but do not include wine, drinks, tax or tips. Table d'hôte or fixed price meals should run you about 50% *less.*

MIDTOWN (42ND ST. TO 65TH ST.) *American International. Deluxe:* **Christ Cella.** 160 E. 46th St. Perhaps the largest piece of roast beef around, and everything else is similarly served in oversized portions. Simple decor on two floors. Closed Sat. and Sun. during July and Aug.

Gallagher's Steak House. 228 W. 52nd St. Serves just what the name implies, plus a few other hearty items. Near the theaters, it has a rugged, comfortable air, red-checkered tablecloths and large bar.

The Ginger Man. 51 W. 64th St. A favorite dinner locale with those attending concerts and performances at Lincoln Center. A well-decorated, pub-style establishment that is noted for its spinach salad and steaks.

Maxwell's Plum. 1181 First Ave. Really three separate emporia in one, and it's possible to eat in the front cafe for less than $10.00. You can dine elegantly in the *art nouveau,* Tiffany-lighted dining area at the rear, where the menu is ambitious and interesting and quite reasonable for a price-fixed pre-theater menu that offered three courses for $12.50 at press time. The consummate New York City scene.

Rainbow Room. 30 Rockefeller Plaza. On the 65th floor of the RCA Building, it has a spectacular view from the windowside tables. A varied menu and a unique wine cellar. *Rainbow Grill* has dinner and dancing from about 8:30.

Expensive. **Downey's Steak House.** 705 Eighth Ave. In the heart of the theater district and a choice for performers and patrons alike. Closed Sun.

Moderate: **Century Café.** 132 W. 43rd St. Perfect before or after theater spot with excellent grilled specialties cooked over charcoal and mesquite. Stop for a light, imaginatively presented salad, fresh fish, roast duck, or a done-as-ordered steak. Great desserts and a wonderful Art Deco bar. Closed Sun.

Charlie Brown's Ale & Chophouse. At 45th St. and Vanderbilt Ave. in the Pan Am Building. Steak and kidney pie, mutton chops, Dover sole. Try a yard of ale here.

Chinese. Expensive: **Shun Lee West.** 43 W. 65th St. Directly across the street from Lincoln Center, the latest branch of this family-run series of restaurants (they're too fancy and individual to constitute a "chain") has a varied menu specializing in Mandarin and Szechuan dishes, which are served in, by Chinese restaurant standards, opulent if not especially Oriental surroundings. The food is quite good, with the *dim sum* luncheons noted near and far.

Uncle Tai's Hunan Yuan. 1059 Third Ave. Adorned with hanging plants to resemble a garden (yuan), this handsome Hunan restaurant serves exciting and unusual Hunanese/Szechuan fare including venison in garlic sauce, sea bass in black bean sauce, and lamb in white sauce, all excellently prepared. Offerings here are often piquant and sometimes infernally spicy.

Moderate: **Bill Chan's Gold Coin.** 835 Second Ave. Both Mandarin and Cantonese cuisine is served. Tiny deep-fried frogs' legs are a delightful appetizer. Everything cooked to order.

Peng Teng's. 219 E. 44th St. This is the best Chinese restaurant in New York, and perhaps one of the best in the world. It features hard-to-find specialties from the cuisines of Peking, Szechuan and Hunan. Minced squab and water chestnuts steamed in a bamboo container for 6 hours is just one reason to go—the very popular "Dragon and Phoenix" (lobster and chicken) is another. On Saturday and Sunday, *dim sum* at lunch can be inexpensive as well as satisfying.

Continental. Super Deluxe: **The Four Seasons.** 99 E. 52nd St. Paul Kovi has made this one of New York's most interesting and ambitious restaurants. His series of gastronomic "events," featuring famous chefs preparing their most famous creations, have enlivened the local culinary scene. For those who cannot afford the occasionally stratospheric tariffs, there are *prix fixe* pre-theater dinners that are priced a little closer to earth. The formal dining room is famous for its changing decor (four times each year to coincide with the seasons), and its lovely reflecting pool. The outside *Grill* room is a little less fancy. The wine cellar is extremely good, and the *Chocolate Velvet* for dessert is a once-in-a-lifetime experience. Closed Sun.

Delicatessen. Inexpensive: **Nathan's.** Broadway at 43rd St. Having acquired fame and reputation on Coney Island, Nathan's now dispenses its famous and delicious hot items, including clams, scallops, oysters, pizza, barbecued beef sandwiches, and chow mein on a bun, in Manhattan. But the most famous item is the great hot dog. Eat at stand-up counters or sit down at tables.

Stage. 834 Seventh Ave. This restaurant frequently attracts a large after-theater crowd, but is nearly always bustling and noisy. Their sandwiches are packed with meat, the rye bread is superb, their appetizers tantalizing and there is a variety of hot dishes, salads, and fish platters. Tables are for four, so if you're a couple, expect company. Open 24 hours.

French. Super Deluxe: **La Caravelle.** 33 W. 55th St. At the highest rank of New York restaurants, and among the top two or three French establishments in the entire city. A favorite with the social set at luncheon. Very fashionable clientele in the evening, too. Elegant decor, top-notch wine cellar, attentive service, the latter especially so if you are known. This is one of the restaurants where the unrecognized diner can be treated rather cavalierly. Closed Sun. and all Aug.

La Côte Basque. 5 E. 55th St. Its reputation was made by the late founder, Henri Soulé of the now legendary *Le Pavillon.* Stunning Bernard Lamotte murals enhance a totally handsome dining room. The cuisine is classic and can be superb. The service is a model of perfection. Closed Sun.

La Grenouille. 3 E. 52nd St. A sublimely beautiful setting that complements a superb kitchen. The "in" place for lunch for expense account diners. Often crowded, and the impact of the large number of diners is accented by the proximity of one table to another. Just about as good French food as exists in the city. Closed Sun. and holidays.

Lutèce. 249 E. 50th St. Here is probably the most ambitious and elaborate food served in the United States. The staff is almost uniformly pleasant, and adds immeasurably to the consummate enjoyment of a unique dinner. The setting, in a former town house, is *intime* and exquisite. If you only have the time (or budget) for one foray into fine French gastronomy, we urge you to make this your choice. Closed Sun.; also Sat. during summer.

Moderate: **Crepe Suzette.** 363 W. 46th St. A simple, unpretentious spot for hearty French country fare. All comers are treated as if they were regulars, with the staff—mostly family—catering to those with a Broadway curtain looming before them. Other patrons are encouraged to linger as long as they wish.

Hungarian. Inexpensive: **The Magic Pan.** 149 E. 57th St. Both Hungarian and French crêpes are the specialty here, though soup, salad, and steak kebabs are also available.

Indian. Moderate: **Tandoor.** 40 E. 49th St. The aroma of Indian spices permeates the spacious dining room here, which offers an inexpensive luncheon buffet as well as à la carte selections afternoons and evenings. The tandoori specialties, cooked on the walls of high-heat clay ovens, should be a first choice, with curries a not-too-distant second. Remember: Indian food is excellent for sharing.

Italian. Expensive: **Isle of Capri.** 1028 Third Ave. Generally acknowledged as one of the best Italian restaurants in the city. A "trattoria"-style operation where the food's the thing. Sidewalk café. Closed Sun.

Trattoria. In the Pan Am Building, 45th St. between Vanderbilt and Lexington Aves. Informal, though strikingly decorated with Italy's colors and posters. Elaborate *antipasto* display, rich desserts, good wines. Bar. Mostly à la carte, but some complete dinners. Closed Sat. and Sun.

Japanese. Deluxe: **Hatsuhana.** 17 E. 48th St. *The* place for *sushi* and *sashimi,* the raw fish delicacies of Japan.

Expensive: **Nippon.** 155 E. 52nd St. Like a Japanese garden, complete with a stream. Tatami rooms and regular tables in an attractive setting. Unusual Japanese dishes are featured along with familiar *sukiyaki.* Cozy bar and cocktail lounge. *Tempura* and *sushi* bar for light meals. Closed Sun.

Russian. Expensive: **Russian Tea Room.** 150 W. 57th St. A landmark right next to Carnegie Hall, and a favorite with musicians and other show-biz folk. Perhaps the city's richest food. Atmosphere is kind of zany, with Christmas decorations featured all year long. *Borscht, blinis* (pancakes with caviar), *Chicken Kiev,* and (on Wednesdays only) the legendary *Siberian Pelmeny.* Russian Cream for dessert, if you can handle it. Watch out for the lethal concoctions brewed by the "Cossack" bartenders.

Seafood. Moderate: **Oyster Bar.** Grand Central Station. A city landmark. Great stews and chowders. Closed Sat. and Sun.

Steak. Deluxe: **The Palm.** 837 Second Ave. If you're looking for the best piece of sirloin in town, this is the place. You should know that it's a madhouse at the prime dinner hours, and because of a non-reservation policy, an hour's wait is not in the least unusual. The double sirloin is a total delight; the cottage fried potatoes and crisp onion rings are unequaled in the city; and the double lobster is simply splendid. A branch called *Palm Too,* directly across the street and serving the same food, tries to handle the overflow. Closed Sun.

DOWNTOWN (BELOW 42ND ST.) *American-International. Deluxe:* **The Coach House.** Ambitious men, black bean soup, steaks and lobster tails special treats. Greenwich Village low-key service. Reservations a must. 110 Waverly Place. Dinner only Sat. and Sun. Closed Mon.

Windows on the World. Is sensational because of the quintessential view from the 107th floor of the World Trade Center. Be sure the weather is clear, however. On a cloudy day or night, the incredible view is nonexistent, and the experience is seriously hampered. The food is good, the service enthusiastic and the wine list both imaginative *and* reasonable. Eat in *Restaurant, Grill* or *Cellar in the Sky.* Reservations a must, and usually well in advance. Sunday buffets a bargain.

Inexpensive: **Janice's Fish Place.** 570 Hudson St., at 11th St. Specializing in excellent fish and vegetable dishes, some American, some Oriental. Make reservations ahead.

Chinese. Moderate: **Say Eng Look.** The Peking (Mandarin) name means "4, 5, 6" and refers to a particularly fine hand in Mah Jongg. Again, the decor is unimposing, the overall space small, and the atmosphere on the noisy side. But no lack of ambience can really distract from the *Mu Shoo Pork, Tai-Chi Chicken,* or the deep-fried fish wrapped in bean curd or seaweed. Bring your own beer, or you might like to wait to purchase some imported Chinese brew available at the grocery around the corner. 5 East Broadway.

Inexpensive: **Foo Joy.** 13 Division St. off Chatham Sq. in Chinatown. Fukien Province pork chops, steam-fried flounder, lemon chicken, or garlic spareribs are savory departures from the traditional. Bring your own beer.

Hong Fat. 63 Mott St. A little hole-in-the-wall that specializes in noodles in many delicious forms. Many consider this New York's best Cantonese restaurant. Open 24 hours.

Indian. Inexpensive: Go to Sixth Street between First and Second Avenues. Almost all of the dozen or more restaurants here are run by the same family, with largely similar menus and ambience. The food seems particularly consistent at Mitali (there's a more presentable branch at Seventh Ave. South and Bleecker Street), but at the price you won't go far wrong anywhere on the block.

Italian. Expensive: **Grotta Azzurra.** 387 Broome St. You'd expect to find the best of garlic and tomato sauce in the heart of "Little Italy," and here it is. Every imaginable specialty of a Southern Italian menu is prepared with a vengeance, and though the atmosphere and service are hardly elegant, the lines outside this legendary restaurant bespeak its quality. The one negative note is the absence of any reservation system and the long queues that are the unfortunate result. Knowledgeable patrons prefer to opt for a very late (3 P.M.) lunch or an early (5 P.M.) dinner.

Moderate: **Trattoria Da Alfredo.** 90 Bank St., in the Village. Roman and Northern Italian dishes. The service is casual, friendly and efficient. The special pastas, changed daily, are the best in the city, and the salads are sumptuous. There are always new "specials" each day. Reservations must be made a few days in advance, and you must be punctual. Bring your own wine. No credit cards, and jackets and/or ties are unnecessary.

Jewish. Moderate: **Moshe Peking.** 40 W. 37th St. A restaurant that only New York could spawn, featuring Kosher Chinese cuisine including Peking duck, beef, and veal. Closed Fri. sundown to Sat. sundown.

Inexpensive: **Ratner's.** 138 Delancey St. Only one branch of this legendary restaurant remains. No meat is served but the fish, blintzes, breads, and rolls are wonderful. Sunday breakfast is an experience. A great place to take the kids. A tourist landmark.

Spanish. Moderate: **El Faro.** 823 Greenwich St., in the Village. Don't be put off by the unappetizing exterior or the small, dark interior for this is absolutely NYC's finest Spanish kitchen. Besides the obligatory *paellas,* there is a raft of other shellfish dishes called *mariscadas*. The *sangria* is the genuine article, and *natilla* is a special treat for dessert. Again, no reservations can mean a lengthy wait.

UPTOWN (ABOVE 65TH ST.). *American International. Expensive:* **Café des Artistes.** 1 West 67th St. Elegant dining in a beautiful room. Cuisine to match. Duck, seafoods, and meats superior; their sauces might top the list. French accent, but a wide range of dishes. Bar area famous for Howard Chandler Christie murals.

Tavern on the Green. Central Park West at 67th St. (just inside Central Park). This longtime New York landmark, closed for several years, has recently been given a facelift and reopened. Three beautifully appointed rooms with views of the park, outdoor dining when weather permits. Specialties: salads, veal and beef dishes. Attentive service. Live band for dancing on some summer nights. Excellent pre-theater menu perfect for those heading to Lincoln Center —three courses for $12.50! Reserve well ahead.

Chinese. Inexpensive: **Hunan Balcony.** 2596 Broadway, at 98th St. One of the best Hunan restaurants in the city. Excellent spicy sauces, and all dishes prepared with care. Seafoods especially good.

Seafood. Expensive: **Oscar's Salt of the Sea.** 1155 Third Avenue. Stuffed lobsters are a particular specialty of this exceptional restaurant, and virtually everything on the extensive menu is prepared perfectly. The only discordant note is the inevitable wait (often quite long) for a table.

FAMOUS FOR EVERYTHING BUT THE FOOD

Super Deluxe

The Sign of the Dove. 1110 Third Ave. A complete town house with terraces and a winter garden. The *Sanctum Sanctorum* is upstairs. Pretentious, and the food seldom measures up to the setting.

"21". 21 W. 52nd St. Has great social cachet among high-class fixers, celebrity-chasers of all ranks, and slightly aging "beautiful people," and therefore in a category of its own. Somewhat difficult to enter unless you have reservations. Frequented by businessmen at lunch and "society" at night. Handsomely furnished dining rooms, a well-packed convivial bar. The only good dining choice is fresh game.

Deluxe

Sardi's. 234 W. 44th St. The place to see celebrities of the theater world, sometimes. The game here is to figure out why the personnel think the restaurant is any longer a special place, entitling them to treat ordinary customers in an offhand manner. Large dining room with convivial atmosphere has caricatures of the well-known as decoration. *Cannelloni alla Sardi* is a special. *A la carte.*

Trader Vic's. 59th St. off Fifth Ave. (in Plaza Hotel). The New York branch of the famous Polynesian food chain. Décor emphasizes South Sea carvings, canoes, and lots of nets. Chinese and Polynesian menu, which seems to feature everything smothered in sugar-based sauces.

Elaine's. 1703 Second Ave. The only legitimate reason for trying this restaurant, unless you know the proprietress, is to try to catch a glimpse of the large number of publishing and journalistic notables, all of them obviously *very* insecure, who call it home. The food's only ordinary, and mere mortals are usually treated shabbily, if not worse. Primarily Italian menu with some American dishes.

Mama Leone's. 239 W. 48th St. Known far and wide for the quantity, not quality, of food served in the complete dinners. This place can be fun if you are (a) drunk, (b) with a large group of laughing friends, or (c) starving. Though the restaurant is large, the waiting line is usually larger, so make a reservation.

Top of the Sixes. 666 Fifth Ave. Provides a view of the city from its dining room and candlelit cocktail lounge. The menu is diversified with continental overtones.

Moderate

Cattleman. 5 E. 45th St. Has to be seen to be disbelieved. A jam-packed bar, one room with an 1890 dining-car interior, another looking like a very elegant Crazy Horse Saloon, and so-so steaks, prime ribs, and tenderloin brochettes. All this, and a stagecoach to take you to the theater after dinner! Miss Grimble's cheesecake.

Fraunces Tavern Restaurant. 54 Pearl St. Original building dates from Revolutionary days (the present one only to 1907). Behind the white portico, there's a restaurant for lunch and dinner and a museum filled with Early American memorabilia. It was here that George Washington feted his officers prior to assuming the first Presidency. Quite convenient to Wall St. Closed Sat. during summer.

BRONX. *Moderate:* **Stella d'Oro.** Broadway near 238th St. Family dinners Italian style, with spaghetti à la Stella d'Oro the masterpiece, are graced with homemade pastas. The aromas from their nearby bakery may entice you to try some of their well-known egg biscuits. The restaurant is very near Van Cortlandt Park, so a visit to the area could also include a mansion tour, Gaelic Football match or some horseback riding. Open Tues.–Fri., 4 P.M. Closed Mon. unless it's a holiday, in which case they're closed the following day.

BROOKLYN. *Deluxe:* **Gage and Tollner.** 374 Fulton St. The unhurried pace of Brooklyn, before it surrendered its independence to the city, is preserved here. The menu changes with the seasons and you can expect delightful specials that follow nature's calendar. Try the Crab Meat Virginia. Closed Sun. A touristic landmark.

Peter Luger. 178 Broadway, near Bedford Ave. You'll want a cab to take you there (best to call for one rather than attempting to hail one on the street), but in spite of the neighborhood Peter Luger has long earned its reputation as the finest steakhouse in New York. They'll call a cab to take you back to Manhattan —and the trip will have been well worth it.

GENERALLY SPEAKING. You can find all the familiar fast-food chains in New York, but why come to the Big Apple for McDonald's, Burger King, Kentucky Fried Chicken, and the like? If the budget is hurting, head to *Kiev,* on Second Avenue at 6th Street, where you'll find fresh, hearty fare from French toast to goulash 24 hours a day—and get change from a $10 bill after two are more than full. New York is also full of bagel bakeries, many of which serve sandwiches (a bagel is a weighty doughnut-like bread); outstanding pizzerias (*John's* on Bleecker St. just east of Seventh Avenue South; *Ray's* at 11th Street and Sixth Avenue; *Pizza Piazza*—nicest ambience—at Broadway and 9th Street); and, when weather permits, street vendors galore with Middle Eastern sandwiches (vegetarian or with meat), sausage and peppers, frankfurters, Chinese food and more. Sixth Avenue at 49th Street is a good spot for finding these.

If you want a feel for Olde New York, try one of two cafeterias: *Horn & Hardart,* 200 E. 42nd St., which features coin-operated slots from which food is drawn; and *Dubrow's,* 38th Street and Seventh Avenue. No awards for culinary originality, but in the genre they're tops.

 MOSTLY FOR DESSERTS. New York City used to be an even greater magnet to sweet tooths than it is today, but even the passing of most of the *Schrafft's* restaurants has not really dented the opportunities for candy, ice cream, and general confection consumption within the five boroughs.

Among the chain operations, there are a number of *Howard Johnson's* scattered throughout the city, but we'd be less than candid if we didn't mention that they've been completely eclipsed by the *Baskin-Robbins, Häagen-Dazs, Seduttos, Bassetts,* and *Carvel* boys.

Moving briskly from ice cream to pastry, there are three choices we'd like to mention as special. First is *Ferrara's,* the bastion of Italian sweets nestled at 195 Grand Street in the middle of "Little Italy."

For a touch of old-fashioned sweet eating, we still like *Rumpelmayer's,* at 50 Central Park South in the St. Moritz Hotel.

Then there's the indescribable *Serendipity 3* (225 E. 60th St.), which has never quite made up its mind whether it is restaurant or boutique. A banana split goes for $7.00, but is enough for two or three *hearty* eaters.

EXPLORING LONG ISLAND

Long Island, 1,723 square miles and a population of over seven million, extends 120 miles east by northeast from New York Harbor. Although its westernmost half is an increasingly crowded jumble of residential suburbs for New York City, the eastern section still has unspoiled open spaces. The history and growth of the Northeast can be traced on a tour of Long Island—the ceremonial dances at the annual Shinnecock Indian Powwow in Southampton at the end of the summer; 18th-century Dutch windmills and English saltbox houses; a pre-Civil War farm village restoration; late 19th-century mansions such as the Vanderbilts' in Centerport; and the bedroom communities, industrial complexes, and vacation colonies of today.

Excellent fishing, public golf courses, State Parks, outdoor art shows and historical museums, the sandy beaches of its South Shore and the pebble beaches of its North Shore, have made Long Island one of the Empire State's most popular vacationlands.

To get out to eastern Long Island, take the straight Long Island Expressway or the several auxiliary highways that roughly parallel it. The Expressway goes all the way to Riverhead. The Long Island Railroad conducts guided tours to various places of interest from mid-May to mid-November on weekends; on weekdays in July and August. The New York State Division of Tourism makes available a possible traveler's itinerary in a list of suggested three-day tours of the state. A good place to start might be at Great Neck, the beginning of Nassau County's well-to-do North Shore.

At Kings Point, on Little Neck Bay, the United States Merchant Marine Academy may be visited daily from 9 to 5; and although their sailing and steam vessels will intrigue mariners more than landlubbers, the Regimental Review, held on most Saturdays in May, June, September, and October, weather permitting, will interest everyone.

You might like to walk through Adelphi University in Garden City, one of the first fully planned communities. Garden City also has the Episcopal Cathedral of the Incarnation, featuring some beautiful hand-carved mahogany and rare marble. Old Westbury Gardens, on Old Westbury Road, is the former estate of the late John Phipps, sportsman and financier, and was made available to the public in 1959. Like an 18th-century English "great park" with a stately Georgian mansion, the Gardens' flowers and trees present a continually changing picture with the seasons. Be sure to wear comfortable walking shoes, as there are miles of paths winding through the 100-acre grounds. The interior of Westbury House is preserved as it was during the family's occupancy, with gilded mirrors, classical paintings, and crystal filled with fresh flowers to re-create the gracious, unhurried atmosphere of that era.

On the North Shore

Heading back up towards the Sound and 25A, you're on your way to Glen Cove, Oyster Bay, and Huntington. Oyster Bay is renowned as the summer home of Teddy Roosevelt, although his estate, Sagamore Hill, is really down the road in Cove Neck. It is today furnished as it was when TR himself lived there, stuffed with such paraphernalia as elephant tusks from the Emperor of Ethiopia, rugs from the Sultan of Turkey, and the sword and pistol that Roosevelt brandished up San Juan Hill during the Spanish–American War. Built in 1884, it served as the family home until it was opened to the public in 1950, two years after the death of the late President's widow. Down along the water between Cove Neck and Oyster Bay are other attractions for the sightseer. About a mile east of Oyster Bay is the Theodore Roosevelt Memorial Sanctuary and Trailside Museum. An environmental center, containing the sort of nature exhibits that the conservationist President would have enjoyed immensely. He is buried in nearby Young Memorial Cemetery. Before continuing east, you might like to visit the Planting Fields Arboretum State Park. This four-hundred-acre estate, formerly the home of the late William Robertson Coe, now houses one of the largest collections of labeled trees, shrubs, bulbs, and flowering plants in the country. Visitors guide themselves around the grounds at their leisure every day of the year except Christmas Day.

Leaving the Oyster Bay area and heading east again along 25A, the traveler can stop in Cold Spring Harbor for a look through the Whaling Museum of what was once one of Long Island's leading whaling ports. Huntington is famous as the birthplace of the great American poet Walt Whitman. Turning south from 25A for a mile along State 110 will bring you to his boyhood home, now a Historic Site owned and administered by New York State; manuscripts, publications, and pictures of Whitman are on display. A church dating back over 315 years will interest many, but the other major points of interest in Huntington are the Heckscher Museum, with a collection of European and American paintings and frequent special exhibits, and the Powell-Jarvis House, over three hundred years old, which features period rooms and a pottery collection in an old farmhouse.

It's a short hop east to Centerport, where the forty-three-acre estate of the late William Vanderbilt is now a museum and planetarium with beautifully kept gardens. The Vanderbilt Museum has a staggeringly complete collection of marine life, wildlife diorama, and natural habitat groups. The mansion, a 24-room structure of Spanish-Moroccan design, has a fascinating array of items from 13th-century Portuguese handiworks to 17th-century Florentine carved walnut furniture to a $90,000 organ hidden behind an enormous Aubusson tapestry.

Heading east on 25A, at the junction of State 25, stop to take a look at a most unusual monument called the Statue of the Bull. This statue commemorates the day centuries back when Richard Smythe was granted all the land he could ride around in one day—on the back of a bull. We keep to State 25 from here, eventually turning right onto Smithtown Blvd. towards Lake Ronkonkoma, a body of water of much lore and legend and a nice place to grab a swim. One legend claims that the lake's waters never freeze over twice during one season. Another has it that the lake is bottomless and connects with Long Island Sound. Neither of these charming rumors, however, is true.

From Lake Ronkonkoma, Long Hill Road takes us back to State 25A, this time at Stony Brook, a residential community which, because of carefully planned rehabilitation, looks much as it did early in the 19th century. There is a gristmill, a modern shopping area done in the spirit of the old village, and a Post Office crowned with an eagle which flaps its wings every hour on the hour. The restored and repainted figurehead of the USS Ohio, launched in 1820, the museum, with permanent and changing exhibits of antiques and natural history, and the carriage museum, with a collection of horse-drawn vehicles and a blacksmith shop, are all worth a visit.

At Riverhead the Island splits into the North and South Forks. Although rising land prices and soaring taxes have greatly reduced Long Island's farming area, there is still a lot concentrated around Riverhead and the two forks, and Suffolk is the leading agricultural county of New York State in dollar volume. Because of Suffolk County,

New York is one of the country's top potato-growing states. A thriving business is also done in greenhouse products and strawberries, cauliflower and peaches. But Long Island is really noted for the ducks served in restaurants all over the nation.

The North Fork

Taking State 25 out the North Fork, the traveler comes into the town of Cutchogue, where the 1650 Old House is considered the finest example of English architecture in this country. Greenport, a little farther on, once a major whaling port, still bustles with dockside activity. The North Fork was the center of the oyster industry on Long Island at the turn of the century. From Greenport, you can take the short ferry ride to Shelter Island, a beautiful and lush island. A drive around it takes about an hour. The North Fork is also a paradise for sportsmen. Miles of sandy beaches offer clean, calm water both in Long Island Sound and Peconic Bay, so swimming, sailing, skin diving, and fishing are also popular here. Audubon groups find this area good for bird watching, since it is along the migratory routes of many species. There are golf courses and many fine horse trails. Finally, at the end of State 25, we reach Orient Point. The town itself is a provincial village, reminiscent of New England with its Cape Cod houses. Here are an Indian burial ground, the oldest Congregational Church in the state, and Orient Point State Park, perhaps the most strangely beautiful spot on all of Long Island. It's a strange mixture of barren sand and dirt washed up onto the beach, desolate rocks, long eerie strands of seaweed, birds who don't see enough people to be frightened of them, and nothing but water beyond.

The South Fork

Sag Harbor was a great whaling port during the 19th century, and celebrates an Old Whalers Festival each summer, with activities centered around the Long Wharf, built in 1770. In 1789, President George Washington named it a port of entry for the United States. For many years, it cleared more tonnage than any other port in the nation. Sag Harbor preserves the flavor and nostalgia of the old days of the sailing ships, and there are even today a church shaped like a sailor's spyglass and a whaleboat in front of the Masonic Temple. Inside the Suffolk County Whaling Museum you'll see relics of the whaler's trade, and nearby is the Custom House, the first in New York, which houses a number of historic documents.

The Montauk peninsula, jutting forcefully out into the pounding waters of the Atlantic, has been the scene of wars, adventure, romance, and sport, and is now a haven for city dwellers intent on beating the heat of summer. The countryside is composed of thousands of acres of natural woodlands, rolling hills, stark cliffs, fabulous ocean beaches, and sand dunes. You may stand upon a hillock, with the Atlantic stretching to the horizon in one direction and Block Island Sound in the other; and the clean fresh-water lakes have become summer homes for flocks of migratory swans.

Montauk is perhaps the liveliest fishing town on Long Island; boats for hire will take deep-sea anglers out for tuna, bluefish, or a host of other varieties. Surf-casters will find Montauk a paradise, also, as do bird-watchers, hikers, bathers, and sailors. A couple of points of interest to visitors are the Montauk Lighthouse, built in 1795 (although it is not permissible to climb to the tower, a new museum in the lighthouse has an interesting display of nautical artifacts); Deep Hollow Ranch, built in 1774 when the area was an important cattle-grazing area, and at which TR and his Rough Riders stayed on their way to war; and Hither Hills State Park, which has camping, fishing, a children's area, picnic tables, a bathhouse, showers, and areas for trailers and tents.

Turning back from Montauk, heading west towards New York City, travelers may stop off at their leisure in the Hamptons, a dozen or more small communities along the South Shore, starting at Amagansett, rimming Shinnecock Bay, and subsiding at Westhampton. Easthampton is now one of the more fashionable summer vacation colonies. Old Hook Mill, built in 1806 of oak and hickory brought from Gardiners Island, is the only one of the windmills in the area still in working order. Easthampton is also the site of Clinton Academy, the first academy chartered in the state, which now houses an historical museum featuring exhibits of Indian relics, whaling gear, early farming tools, and shipwreck mementoes. The real charm of the area, however, can be found in a quiet drive along country lanes and wide sandy beaches around Southhampton, after we turn off State 27A.

On to Quogue, Hampton Bays, and Westhampton, all offshoots of Southampton, but with a more bohemian atmosphere. Many of the summer residents are writers, artists, and musicians, although in recent years an increasing number of executives have been coming in. Quogue has a 200-acre Wildlife Refuge run by the state's Department of Environmental Conservation, while Westhampton has one of the finest beaches anywhere in the world.

Fire Island

Other than a parking lot at Smith Point County Park, south of Shirley, there are no roads on this forty-mile strip of sand dunes and barrier beach. The 25,000 persons who summer here in a dozen established communities wish to keep it that way. The United States Congress established the Fire Island National Seashore in 1964. It offers excellent facilities at several spots on the island to those who do not own or rent property there. A ten-year plan was begun in the summer of 1966 to build facilities for swimming, hiking, nature tours, bicycling, and water sports, with all public areas accessible by ferry. Robert Moses State Park at the westernmost tip of Fire Island is reached by bridge from a point a few miles west of Bay Shore.

We now wind our way westward, eventually reaching Great River and the Bayard Cutting Arboretum, a 643-acre gift to the Long Island State Park Commission on which can be seen just about every variety of tree and plant imaginable, some in hothouses.

Jones Beach State Park, along the Atlantic shore south of Wantagh, is a 2,500-acre expanse of sand and woods accommodating over 100,000 bathers, with parking space for 23,000 cars in its 14 lots. It is best reached early in the day. Jones Beach, the largest state park on the Atlantic Coast, features ocean and salt-water pool swimming, fishing facilities, restaurants, a two-mile boardwalk, athletic fields, and the famous $4 million Marine Theater, where theatrical spectaculars and water shows are presented during the summer months.

North and somewhat east by the Seaford–Oyster Bay Expressway are Bethpage State Park and the town of Bethpage, where a 2½-acre farmer's market offers over 300 indoor booths, as well as a children's amusement park and a carnival atmosphere that children and adults alike will enjoy. The farmer's market is held every Friday and Saturday, and on the Fourth of July. Old Bethpage is a nice restoration village with various activities and craft demonstrations in the same area.

PRACTICAL INFORMATION FOR LONG ISLAND

HOW TO GET AROUND. *By car:* Most highways alternate between limited-access sections and double-duty stretches as the main streets of towns and villages. They usually have names as well as numbers, so asking directions may elicit a confusing, though well-intentioned answer. By all means, have a map along.

Towns on the South Shore are served directly by State 27A, called *Merrick Road* in the western half of the island; *Montauk Highway* in the eastern. It is a winding and busy thoroughfare. A bit to the north, but requiring less perseverance, is State 27, called *Sunrise Highway.* It runs as far out as Southampton, then joins State 27A for the last lap to Montauk. The *Southern State Parkway* runs from Kennedy Airport to East Islip. Down the center, take the *Long Island Expressway* from Manhattan to Riverhead. Thereafter, take State 25 to the north fork and Orient Point or State 24 southeast for a link-up in Hampton Bays with State 27 to Montauk. The northern routes out of the city: Queens Boulevard, State 25, becomes *Jericho Turnpike* in Nassau County. It takes a fairly straight inland path northeast to Orient Point. Northern Boulevard, State 25A, becomes *North Hempstead Turnpike* and serves the North Shore communities— Great Neck, Huntington, Port Jefferson and Wading River—before dissolving into State 25 ten miles west of Riverhead. The *Northern State Parkway* continues from the city's Grand Central Parkway.

By train: The *Long Island Railroad* reaches almost every town, and runs out to Montauk in less than 4 hours. From Manhattan, the line operates out of Penn Station (31st–33rd Sts. between 7th and 8th Avenues). There are also stations in Woodside, Queens and downtown Brooklyn. Most trains headed for Suffolk pass through Jamaica, Queens, and it's about even money you'll have to make a change there. The best way to get information is to go to Penn Station and consult timetables. Or try calling one of the stations on Long Island close to your destination.

MUSEUMS. Centerport: *Vanderbuilt Museum and Planetarium.* Open May–Oct., Tues.–Sat., 10 A.M.–4 P.M.; Sun., holidays, 12–5 P.M. Little Neck Rd., off State 25A. Marine and wildlife exhibits in mansion on former Vanderbilt estate.

Cold Spring Harbor: *Whaling Museum.* Main St. Exhibits and relics to show the whaling industry, including a fully equipped whaleboat from a 150-year-old brig. Open daily, except Mon., 11 A.M.–5 P.M.

East Meadow: *Museum in the Park.* Eisenhower Park, between Old Country Rd. and Hempstead Tpke. Changing exhibits trace the history of Nassau County. Open Wed.–Sun., 9 A.M.–5 P.M.

Huntington: *Hecksher Museum.* Prime Ave. Fine collection of European-American art. Open Tues.–Fri., 10 A.M.–5 P.M.; weekends, 1–5 P.M.

Port Washington: *The Polish-American Museum.* 5 Pulaski Pl. Arts and antiques from Poland, along with displays that show the important roles the Polish played in the shaping of American history. Open Tues.–Fri., 10 A.M.–5 P.M.; weekends, 1-5 P.M.

Sag Harbor: *Suffolk County Whaling Museum.* Main St. Tools, pictures, oddities of the fascinating whaling era on Long Island. May–Sept., Mon–Sat., 10 A.M.–5 P.M., Sun. 1–5 P.M.

Stony Brook: *The Museums at Stoney Brook.* Main St. off State 25A and continuing onto State 25A itself. An historic grouping of the best; an art museum, carriage museum, several period buildings, a crafts center, and museum shop.

HISTORIC SITES. Bay Shore *Sagtikos Manor.* State 27A. Built in 1692, this home was one of the centers of pre-Revolutionary War aristocracy. Period furnishings and antiques throughout its 42 rooms.

Cutchogue: *The Old House.* A mid-17th-century house filled with tools, household goods and furniture of that grand era.

East Hampton: *"Home Sweet Home."* 14 James Lane. Saltbox house, circa 1660, where John Howard Payne, the composer of "Home Sweet Home" lived. Lots of Payne mementos; windmill on the site.

Great Neck: *Saddle Rock Grist Mill.* On Bayview Ave. off State 25A. Tide-powered mill, built in 1702, which still grinds corn meal for visitors.

Huntington: *Powell-Jarvis House.* 434 Park Ave. The oldest house in the village, with grand antiques, pottery, and paintings on display. *Walt Whitman Birthplace.* On Walt Whitman Road, a by-pass off State 110, 1 mile north of Northern State Parkway. All period furniture and mementos of his day.

Oyster Bay: *Raynham Hall.* W. Main St. Built in 1738, this was the home of Robert Townsend, spy of George Washington. The unsuspecting British used it as military headquarters during the Revolution. *Sagamore Hill.* Cove Neck Rd. The very impressive Summer White House of Theodore Roosevelt.

Roslyn: *George Washington Manor.* 1305 Northern Blvd. Hessian quarters during the Revolutionary War.

Sag Harbor: *Old Custom House.* Garden St. A lovely old landmark that was the first custom house in New York State (1789) and Long Island's first post office (1794).

 TOURS. The Long Island Railroad offers day-long tours from Penn Station, Brooklyn or Long Island's Jamaica Station. Their "Around Long Island Tour" includes the train to Westhampton, a bus ride to Greenport and ferry rides to Shelter Island and Sag Harbor, a visit to Montauk Point and return. Tickets and information from the Long Island Railroad Tour Dept., Jamaica, N.Y. 11435. Tickets are also on sale during the week of the trip at Penn, Flatbush Ave. and Jamaica Stations.

 GARDENS. Albertson: *Clark Garden.* (Nassau Branch of the Brooklyn Botanic Garden.) Reflecting ponds, running streams; wildflower, herb and rock gardens; Hunnewell Rose Garden. Great River: *Bayard Cutting Arboretum.* 690 acres of trees, shrubs, and wildflowers, some growing since 887. Old Westbury: *Old Westbury Gardens.* Group of 18th-century gardens on former John S. Phipps estate. Richly furnished Georgian mansion an added attraction. Upper Brookville: *Planting Fields.* This magnificent 409-acre estate, once owned by William R. Coe, is open all year, but magnolias and bulb display are April features, with blossoming azaleas, rhododendron, and dogwood at their best in May & June.

 MUSIC. Throughout the year there are concerts, opera and ballet performances at half a dozen colleges and universities on the island. The *Westbury Music Fair,* Westbury, runs year-round, and features top performers and musicals. Summer theaters include the *Gateway Playhouse,* Bellport; *John Drew* at East Hampton; and the *Jones Beach Marine Theater.*

 SPORTS. *Swimming: Jones Beach State Park,* Wantagh Pkwy. *Hither Hills State Park,* Montauk, offers bathing, fishing and picnicking. Superb *public beaches* at East Hampton, Fire Island, Patchogue, Quogue, Sayville, Shelter Island, Southampton and Westhampton Beach, all on the Atlantic side. Most beaches on Long Island Sound are private.

Fishing, water sports and sailing: Charter boats and marina facilities available at many places in Montauk, Sag Harbor and Shelter Island. The public dock in East Hampton provides excellent fishing. Unmatched saltwater fishing and freshwater angling at the Hamptons.

Golf: Bridgehampton, *Poxabogue Course,* 9 holes. Commack, *Commack Hills Course,* 18 holes. Farmingdale, *Bethpage Color Courses,* five 18-hole courses.

Huntington, *Dix Hills Course,* 9 holes. Northport, *Crab Meadow,* 18 holes. Rocky Point, *Tall Tree,* 18 holes. Greenport, *Island's End,* 18 holes. There are more than 130 golf courses on Long Island; call *Long Island Tourism* (516) 585–6660.

SPECTATOR SPORTS. There is *harness racing* at Roosevelt Raceway in Westbury. Aug. & Sept. bring annual *Horse Shows* at Piping Rock Club, Locust Valley, and C. W. Post College show grounds, Jericho Turnpike, Old Brookville. *Sports car racing* at Bridgehampton is a weekend feature from May to Sept. From Oct. to March, there is *pro hockey* (the *NHL* New York Islanders) at the Nassau Veterans Memorial Coliseum in Uniondale.

HOTELS AND MOTELS on Long Island number about 600 altogether. Most motels have swimming pools, restaurant, cocktail lounges, and television; a few have beauty shops, massage rooms, and saunas. Most do not allow pets. At the western end of Long Island, most are open all year; at Montauk and the Hamptons, the majority close for the winter.

Prices for double-occupancy rooms in this region are: *Deluxe,* $75 and over; *Expensive,* $50–75; *Moderate,* $40–50; *Inexpensive,* under $35.

AMAGANSETT. *Expensive:* **Sea Crest.** Navaho Lane. Oceanfront setting, but on week minimum stay in summer season.

BAY SHORE. *Moderate:* **Capri Bay Shore.** Attractive, comfortable rooms. Pool.

EAST HAMPTON. *Deluxe:* **East Hampton House.** Montauk Hwy. Landscaped grounds, invididual patios, and outdoor dining. One week minimum stay in July and August, reservation deposit required.

FREEPORT. *Moderate:* **Yankee Clipper Motor Inn.** 3-story lodge with restaurant, located on the water.

Moderate; **Freeport Motor Inn.** Cabanas, marina with docking facilities, restaurant and lounge.

GARDEN CITY. *Moderate:* **Garden City Motel.** Relaxed and convenient spot near the Island's busiest hub.

HAMPTON BAYS. *Deluxe.* **Allen's Acres Resort Motel.** Year-round resort on the bay, with coffee shop, cocktail lounge, two swimming pools. Recreation facilities; golf.

Moderate: **Cedars of Tiana Bay.** On landscaped grounds along bay. Heated pool, playground, water sports. Three-day minimum summer weekends.

MONTAUK. *Deluxe:* **Gurney's Inn.** Posh resort and spa with full dining, entertainment and sports facilities.

Expensive: **Driftwood.** Private beach, surf casting, golf, tennis—this luxurious resort motel has everything. One week minimum stay during July and August, reservation deposit.

SOUTHAMPTON. *Expensive:* **Squaw Island Resort.** Well-groomed grounds, private sand beach, playground, café, tennis.

UNIONDALE. *Moderate:* **Long Island Marriott.** Across the street from the Nassau Coliseum.

WESTBURY. *Expensive:* **Island Inn.** 204-room hotel opposite Roosevelt Raceway. Pool, good restaurant, shops.

DINING OUT. The cuisine here accentuates seafood, Long Island duckling, and beefsteaks, but ethnic specialties are excellent and easy to find. Categories reflect the cost of a mid-priced meal at each establishment. Included in the mean are *hors d'oeuvre* or soup, *entree* and dessert. Not included are drinks, tax and tip. The categories are: *Deluxe,* $30 and above; *Expensive,* $25–30; *Moderate,* $20–25; *Inexpensive,* under $15.

AMAGANSETT. *Moderate:* **Gordon's.** Montauk Hwy. Veal and seafood specialties nicely served in a pleasant atmosphere.

AMITYVILLE. *Expensive:* **The Mansard.** Family-owned restaurant serves outstanding steaks and seafood. Dinner only.

BAY SHORE. *Moderate.* **Hisae at Old Gil Clark's.** A nice blend of East and West here, with seafood, fish and Oriental specialties.

EAST NORWICH. *Expensive:* **East Norwich Inn and Restaurant.** Burt Bachrach's place. Long Island duckling and German cuisine a specialty.

GARDEN CITY. *Moderate:* **The Hunt Room.** Good food served in pleasant surroundings. Their own desserts.

GLEN COVE. *Expensive:* **Villa Pierre.** Wine cellar, Continental menu, handsomely furnished 18th-century establishment. Jacket required.

GREENPORT. *Expensive:* **Mitchell's.** Delicious scallops, crab, and lobster.

JERICHO. *Expensive:* **Milleridge Inn.** Hicksville Rd. An historic old inn serving quality seafood and other fare. A local favorite.
Moderate: **Maine Maid.** Duck, lobster and cordon bleu are specialties.

LINDENHURST. *Inexpensive:* **Barnacle Bill's.** E. Montauk Hwy. Seafood and steak on the water. Informal attire.

MATTITUCK. *Moderate:* **Old Mill Inn.** Patio tables and candlelight in this early 19th-century building. Menu features fresh seafood.

NORTHPORT. *Moderate:* **Karl's Mariners Inn.** Home-baking, seafood, L.I. duckling, sauerbraten. On the waterfront.

MONTAUK. *Moderate:* **Gosman's.** West Lake Dr. Overlooking the harbor and open on all sides, magnificently situated. It has several large dining rooms where family-style dinners feature fresh seafood.

PORT WASHINGTON. *Moderate:* **Louie's Shore.** Patio dining. Own baking, seafood, L.I. duckling, steaks, etc. On Manhasset Bay.

SOUTHAMPTON. *Moderate:* **Balzarini's.** Northern Italian-American cuisine, with veal, seafood in season, pasta and desserts all homemade. Family-owned, with quiet, roomy dining area.

STONY BROOK. *Moderate:* **Three Village Inn.** Antiques displayed in an Early American setting. Well-prepared shrimp and clam dishes.

EXPLORING THE HUDSON VALLEY AND WEST-CENTRAL NEW YORK

The Hudson Valley

Three main regions conveniently divide most of the state's remaining tourist attractions. These are: the Hudson River Valley, the Capital District, and the West-Central/Finger Lakes Region.

As important rivers go, the Hudson is not long; it rises in a lonely pond in the Adirondacks and flows only 315 miles to New York Harbor and the sea. Yet without it neither the city nor the state of New York would exist as we know them today. This is the highway up which much of America's early history advanced: Henry Hudson in 1609, crucial campaigns of the Revolution in 1776, Robert Fulton's first steamboat in 1807, and the Erie Canal in 1825. The Hudson Valley is also Sleepy Hollow country, depicted last century by Washington Irving, who used Tarrytown as his setting. The river is lined with splendid mansions; some of the important ones open to the public are: the Jay Homestead in Bedford Village, the Van Cortlandt Manor in Croton-on-Hudson; Boscobel in Garrison; the Brett Homestead in Beacon; the Roosevelt and Vanderbilt estates in Hyde Park; and others in Kinderhook, Coxsackie, Kingston, New Paltz, Newburgh, North Tarrytown, Hastings and Yonkers. West Point offers the US Military Academy; and there are a number of parks and recreational areas all along the river. Bear Mt. State Park is always a popular place; it's just south of West Point. An hour to the north is Poughkeepsie, home of Vassar College. Highways are excellent, and there is train and bus service to main points. For more details, write to the Hudson River Valley Association, 150 White Plains Road, Tarrytown, N.Y. 10591.

Albany

In Albany, the principal sight is the Rockefeller Empire State Plaza, a $2 billion extravaganza, which now makes the capital one of the world's most brilliant, beautiful and efficient, complete with a $2 million permanent exhibit of New York School abstract expressionist works. Another of the newer sights is the nearby Tower Building with its 44th-floor observation deck and panoramic view. Don't forget the older attractions, most notably the Capitol, an imposing edifice resembling a French château. Albany's leading museums are the Albany Institute of History and Art and the New York State Museum (in the Empire State Plaza), both with Hudson River School regional paintings, silver, Shaker furniture, plus displays on the natural history and Indian groups of the region, and changing exhibits of art, as well as research libraries. The Schuyler Mansion, Cherry Hill, and the Ten Broeck Mansion are the most important of the capital's stately old homes.

The Capital District

Outside the capital, the village of Duanesburg, near Schenectady, contains a number of lovely 18th-century houses, some of them octagonal, and an 1807 Quaker Meeting House. Southwest are Howe Caverns, an elaborate series of limestone caves with an underground river and lake and a hundred-foot waterfall. To the north of Albany is Saratoga

Springs, noted both for its National Historical Park on the site of one of the crucial battles of the Revolution (in 1777) and for the opulent resort which grew up around its mineral springs in the second half of the 19th century. It is also famous for the Saratoga Performing Arts Center, a gorgeous amphitheater that serves as the summer home of the New York City Ballet and Philadelphia Orchestra, and the Saratoga Racetrack, oldest thoroughbred track in the country.

West-Central and Finger Lakes

Western New York State, with Rochester, Syracuse, Rome and Utica, was the creation of the Erie Canal which, in 1825, linked the Hudson River with the Great Lakes and the center of the continent. Its main geographical feature is the lovely Finger Lakes, center of a rich agricultural area (vineyards), much fine scenery and over twenty state parks. Fifty miles south of Rochester, in Letchworth State Park, the Gorge of the Genesee River is a 17-mile-long, 600-foot-deep canyon full of spectacular rapids and falls. Rochester, the state's fourth-largest city, is noted for photographic equipment, of course, and for a fine music school and several good museums. New York's famous wine region is between lakes Canandaigua and Keuka, and Naples and Geneva are the towns to work from. Ithaca, at the end of Cayuga Lake, is the home of Cornell University and of some rather extraordinary topography—hills and deep, scenic gorges. Syracuse is the site, in August–September, of the New York State Fair; and Cooperstown, on Otsego Lake, is the baseball shrine.

Don't forget about New York State's biggest tourist attraction, the fabulous Niagara Falls. There are three falls to watch—the American Falls, 182 ft. high and 1,075 ft. wide; the Canadian Horshoe Falls, 176 ft. high and 2,100 feet wide; and the smaller Bridal Veil Falls. You can watch from observation towers, or tour the falls along catwalks below. Niagara Falls offers several fine museums, too.

PRACTICAL INFORMATION FOR THE HUDSON VALLEY AND WEST-CENTRAL NEW YORK

HOW TO GET THERE. *By car:* Interstate 81 goes through New York, passing through Binghamton, Syracuse, and Watertown. Interstate 87 connects New York City, Kingston, Albany and Glens Falls, and continues north to Montreal. Interstate 95 connects New York City to East Coast cities from Bangor to Miami. Interstate 90 traverses the state from Pennsylvania to Massachusetts through Buffalo, Rochester, Syracuse, Utica, and Albany.

By air: The airports handling interstate traffic (besides New York's) are at: Binghamton, Elmira, Ithaca, Buffalo, Rochester, White Plains, Syracuse, Poughkeepsie, and Albany.

By train: Amtrak has good service to the larger cities in New York State. Buffalo, Rochester, Syracuse, Utica, Albany, Poughkeepsie are on the New York City–Toronto line. *Conrail* has service to Westchester County, Albany and towns along the Hudson from New York.

By bus: Trailways and *Greyhound* have terminals in nearly every major city.

TOURIST INFORMATION. The New York State Division of Tourism publishes the *"I Love New York State Travel Guide,"* an all-purpose, 72-page booklet in full color with just about everything the casual traveler needs to know. Other literature includes pamphlets and folders on boating, hiking trails, horseback-riding, county fairs, ski areas, historic sites, museums, suggested tours, children's attractions, lists of events by date and area, scientific exhibits, campgrounds, and dude ranches. All literature of the New York State Division of Tourism is free, from New York State Division of Tourism, 99 Washington Avenue, Albany, N.Y. 12245, 800–225–5697. There are branch offices in: Binghamton, Buffalo, Elmira, Kingston, Jericho on Long Island, New York City, Ogdensburg, Rochester, Syracuse, and Utica.

 STATE PARKS. The state of New York has over 150 state parks, forests, and recreation areas, plus numerous private and public campgrounds, many of which have excellent facilities for the camper. Usually there is a nominal fee for the use of a campsite. In most places there are toilet and cooking facilities, complete with running water.

 DRIVING LAWS. The speed limit is 55 miles per hour unless otherwise posted. Motorists must show proof that they have $10,000/$20,000/$5,000 liability insurance with a company that covers New York State. Check with your insurance agent. Out-of-state drivers may drive in New York State if they are at least 16 years old. Drivers under 18, however, may not drive at any time in New York City or Nassau County, and may not drive elsewhere in the state between the hours of 8 P.M. and 5 A.M. unless accompanied by a parent or guardian.

 SPORTS. Saratoga Springs is the scene of *thoroughbred racing* in August, *harness racing* April-November. The *Eastern States Speed Skating Championships* are held in January. Many fine public 9-hole and 18-hole *golf* courses dot the countryside including Albany, Amsterdam, Canajoharie, Cobleskill, Hoosick Falls, Saratoga Springs, Schenectady, and Troy. *Skiing* can be found at numerous resorts throught the area. Some are Royal Mountain (in Johnstown), Maple Ski Ridge (Schenectady), and Belleayre Mountain (Pine Hill). A list of ski areas is available from the New York State Division of Tourism.

Boating: Especially popular along *Lakes Erie* and *Ontario* and in the *Finger Lakes* region. Any of these lakes could be a starting point for a cruise along New York's famed barge-canal system. Splitting the state horizontally, the historic *Erie Canal* crosses to the *Hudson River* which flows southward to the Atlantic and is connected by the *Champlain Canal* to *Lake Champlain.*

Gliding and *soaring: Elmira* and *Harris Hill* are the centers of motorless flying,

Sports car racing: Watkins Glen is the home of the famed Grand Prix Race Circuit, whose season runs May through September.

Ice boating, ice fishing, ice skating: Popular on many lakes and rivers in winter.

 DRINKING LAWS. The minimum age is 19. You may purchase any type of liquor at private package stores during the week, but the stores are closed on Sundays. Bars are open six full days a week, and on Sundays after noon. A word of caution: the state's laws against driving while intoxicated are stringent, punishable by heavy fines and incarceration.

 HOTELS AND MOTELS. Categories for this region are: *Expensive,* $40 and up; *Moderate,* $30–35; *Inexpensive,* under $30. No accommodations here qualify as *Deluxe,* but many are charming, some are quietly sited, and several are worth a special trip.

CANAAN. *Moderate:* **Inn at the Shaker Mill Farm.** Route 22. A restored Shaker mill has been transformed into a wonderful inn. Modest rooms are set beside a waterfall in a woodland setting. Fine food.

Queechy Lake Motel. A beautiful setting high above the lovely lake. Large, commodious rooms.

Inexpensive: **Berkshire Spur.** In a scenic hillside location, it's convenient to Tanglewood.

CATSKILL. *Inexpensive:* **Catskill Starlight.** Rates are for late June-Labor Day; even lower during remainder of year. Close to the Rip Van Winkle Bridge.

HIGHLAND FALLS. *Moderate:* **Palisade.** State 218, 1 mi. S. Convenient to Storm King, West Point, and Bear Mountain.

HYDE PARK. *Inexpensive:* **Hyde Park.** It has well-kept rooms, café across the road. Rates are lower after Labor Day.

NEWBURGH. *Moderate:* **Howard Johnson's Motor Lodge.** 75 air-conditioned rooms in 2-story complex. Swimming pool, tennis court, restaurant.

PEEKSKILL. *Inexpensive:* **Peekskill Motor Inn.** Nicely appointed rooms. Restaurant, cocktail lounge, pool.

POUGHKEEPSIE. *Moderate:* **Best Western Red Bull Motor Inn.** This is a nicely furnished two-story inn. Pool, pets allowed, restaurant.

TARRYTOWN. *Expensive:* **Hilton Inn.** King-sized beds, tasteful décor, and gardens.

 DINING OUT. Cost categories are comparisons between medium-priced meals from all the menus listed. In this wealthy region, the categories are as follows: *Deluxe,* $30 and up; *Expensive,* $25–30; *Moderate,* $15–25; and *Inexpensive,* under $15. Included in these prices are hors d'oeuvres or soup, entree and dessert. Not included are drinks, tip, and tax.

BANKSVILLE. *Deluxe:* **La Cremaillere.** Building is classic Early American, but everything else is French, from wine cellar to service to cuisine with their own pastries.

CANAAN. *Expensive:* **Inn at the Shaker Mill Farm.** Unique dining experience inside a real old Shaker mill (built in 1824). Family-style service, but the informal atmosphere is half the charm. Hors d'oeuvres, drinks, and dessert around a cozy fire. Good food with lots of *vin ordinaire.*
Shuji's. US 20 at State 22. Japanese cuisine served in a former baronial mansion. Sukiyaki, tempura, hibachi cooking. Dinner only. Closed in winter.
Moderate: **Queechy Lake Inn.** Lots of good American food at this picturesque restaurant, hung over an arm of the lake. Stuffed shrimps are a specialty. Bar.

CENTRAL VALLEY. *Moderate:* **Gasho of Japan.** The original timbers of a 15th-century Japanese Samurai warrior hideout have been reassembled with traditional rice rope and wood pegs. Tableside hibachi cooking. Oriental gardens.

CHATHAM. *Moderate:* **Jackson's Old Chatham House.** Rustic tavern atmosphere. Excellent American fare, with emphasis on homemade soups, breads, and charcoal-broiled steaks.

DOVER PLAINS. *Expensive:* **Old Drover's Tavern.** Quaint 200-year-old building with original taproom and antique furnishings. 20% service charge. Jacket required.

HILLSDALE. *Deluxe:* **L'Hostellerie Bressane.** Antiques and 18th-century atmosphere, fine food. Cuisine is *haute,* with prices to match.

LARCHMONT. *Expensive:* **La Cote D'Argent.** French setting, superb French entrees, and delectable desserts.

MAMARONECK. *Moderate:* **Lum Yen.** Small, but well worth a visit for special Chinese dishes which are specially prepared to order.

PEEKSKILL. *Moderate:* **Monte Verde.** Former Van Cortlandt mansion features Continental specialties, overlooks Hudson.

STORMVILLE. *Deluxe:* **Harralds.** Cozy English Tudor setting featuring fine silver and crystal, haute French cuisine priced accordingly.

TARRYTOWN. *Expensive:* **Tappan Hill.** Mark Twain once owned this estate, but now it's home to fine duck and Rock Cornish hen, served lovingly.

AROUND THE CAPITAL DISTRICT AND SARATOGA AREA

HOTELS AND MOTELS. Double-occupancy rates are categorized as follows: *Deluxe:* $50 and over; *Expensive,* $45–50; *Moderate,* $30–35; *Inexpensive,* under $30. Good base for Adirondack excursions.

ALBANY. *Deluxe:* **Hilton.** First-class accommodations. Located on the corner of State and Lodge Sts.
Expensive: **Best Western Inn Towne.** Downtown place to stay, near State Capitol. Spacious rooms, patio café, lounge, coffee shop, pool.
Moderate: **Holiday Inn.** A choice of 3 locations, with all the expected H.I. facilities. You'll find them at 1614 Central Ave.; on State 32, 1 mil. S.; and on US 9. They all have facilities for handicapped travelers.

BALLSTON SPA. *Moderate:* **Westwood.** Lovely setting in a wooded area near Saratoga.

COLONIE. *Expensive:* **Americana Inn.** Excellent in-house restaurant, large glassed-in courtyard. Near Albany Airport.
Moderate: **Best Western Turf Inn.** Convenient Wolf Road location; Olympic-size heated swimming pool in huge, enclosed courtyard.

HOWES CAVE. *Inexpensive:* **Howe Caverns.** The location opens up a spectacular view. Closed mid-October to mid-May.

SARATOGA SPRINGS. *Deluxe:* **Gideon Putnam.** Especially high-priced in August. All the advantages of a resort are offered at this fine hotel where years of experience make visits memorable. Specialized service. Many sports available. Pool, mineral baths, spa facilities.
Expensive: **Hotel Adelphi.** Authentically restored Victorian-era hotel in the grand style; antiques abound.
Inexpensive: **Best Western Playmore Farms.** A very comfortable family-style lodge that includes a swimming pool and playground.

SCHENECTADY. *Inexpensive.* **Imperial "400" Motel.** Small, pleasant place, with a heated swimming pool. Continental breakfast included in the low rate.

SHARON SPRINGS. *Inexpensive:* **Horseshoe.** Small but nice motel near the beautiful spa and recreation center below Canajoharie.

DINING OUT. All the places recommended below can be categorized *Moderate,* with mid-priced full-course dinners costing between $20 and $30. Not included in the prices are drinks, tax and tips.

ALBANY. **Century House.** Route 9. Colonial décor and the service is good. Own cheesecake, duckling, and frogs' legs specialties. Lunch and dinner.
Jack's Oyster House. State Street. An extensive menu of well-prepared dishes features seafood, delicious pastries.

L'Auberge. Broadway. Excellent French dishes, intimate atmosphere. Own soups, pastries.

Yates Street Cafe. Manhattan charcuterie in Prohibition-era dining room. Mesquite charcoal grilling a specialty.

COBLESKILL. Bull's Head Inn. Beef filets or brook trout. Own baking, too, in this pleasant 1802 edifice with early American decor.

GREENWICH. Wallie's of Greenwich. Good, substantial meals are served up in a pleasant atmosphere.

JOHNSTOWN. Union Hall Inn. A landmark, this inn has been serving the public for more than 175 years. Dinner only.

SARATOGA SPRINGS. Coach House. Directly opposite the historic race-track. Comfortable, good value, and a touch of elegance.

Court Bistro. The city's most innovative dining spot. Hodge-podge menu, but never dull.

WEST SAND LAKE. Old Journey's End. American and Continental cuisine, with a touch of the nouvelle in a restored 1890's inn.

AROUND WESTERN AND CENTRAL NEW YORK

 HOTELS AND MOTELS. Cost categories for double-occupancy rooms in this region are: *Deluxe,* $50 and above; *Expensive,* $40–50; *Moderate,* $30–40; and *Inexpensive,* under $30. Somewhat higher during July and August.

BATH. *Expensive:* **Ramada Inn.** Attractive accommodations in the heart of the Finger Lakes. Swimming pool, restaurant, cocktail lounge.

BEMUS POINT. *Expensive:* **Lenhart Hotel.** Nice setting on the lake, adjacent to Bemus Point Park. Dining room, lounge, beach, tennis and water sports.

BINGHAMTON. *Moderate:* **Holiday Inn-SUNY.** Swimming pool, kennels, nice rooms. Restaurant.

CANANDAIGUA. *Expensive:* **Sunaqua.** Convenient to lake. Lawn games, boats available.

COOPERSTOWN. *Deluxe:* **Otesaga.** Outstanding hotel with many mementoes of Cooperstown's historic past. Heated pool, 18-hole championship golf course, sailing, waterskiing, outdoor games.

Expensive: **Cooper Inn.** Chestnut St. (State 80). Small inn furnished with antiques and mementoes of the 19th century. Open mid-Apr. to late Oct. Continental breakfast included; there are also a restaurant and cocktail lounge. Facilities of Otesaga Hotel available to guests.

GENEVA. *Moderate:* **Chanticleer Motor Lodge.** Relax in the heated pool and sauna bath. Restaurant, cocktail bar.

ITHACA. *Expensive:* **Sheraton Motor Inn.** Near Cornell and Ithaca College, it has a swimming pool; pets are allowed.

Rose Inn. Intimate restored early 19th-century estate turned into bed-and-breakfast inn.

Moderate: **Collegetown Motor Lodge.** Convenient location, nicely decorated.

NIAGARA FALLS. *Expensive:* **Best Western Red Jacket Inn.** 7001 Buffalo Ave. Private patios overlook river. Restaurant, cocktail lounge.

Niagara Hilton. Superior accommodations; restaurants, cocktail lounges, entertainment. Heated pool.

Ramada Inn. 401 Buffalo Ave. View of upper rapids. Outdoor dining at restaurant.

ROCHESTER. *Expensive:* **Hilton Inn on the Campus.** Over-sized rooms in a modern low-rise hotel. Dining room, lounge, indoor heated pool, and saunas.

Moderate: **Sheraton Inn-Rochester Airport.** Close to the airport and downtown. Heated pool, coffee shop, restaurant and cocktail lounge.

TraveLodge Colony East. Minutes from downtown and close to the museums. 140 well-appointed rooms.

SYRACUSE. *Expensive:* **Sheraton Motor Inn.** Very attractively furnished rooms, with free use of laundry facilities.

Expensive: **Syracuse Airport Inn.** Convenient to Hancock Airport. Restaurant, heated pool, lounge. Pets allowed.

UTICA. *Moderate:* **Sheraton Inn & Conference Center.** 200 Genesee St. in the heart of downtown. Air-conditioned rooms with TV, two restaurants, health club, shopping boutiques.

 DINING OUT. Price categories are determined by comparing costs for full-course dinners from the middle range of each menu sampled. For this region, the categories are: *Expensive,* $25 and higher; *Moderate,* $15–25; and *Inexpensive,* under $15. Included in these prices are hors d'oeuvres or soup, entree and dessert. Not included are drinks, tax and tip.

AURORA. *Moderate:* **Aurora Inn.** Dining with a view of Owasco Lake. Charming atmosphere in this old inn makes you glad you came.

BINGHAMTON. *Moderate:* **Vestal Steak House.** Generous portions of well-prepared seafood and prime ribs distinguish this locally popular establishment.

CANANDAIGUA. *Expensive:* **Caruso's.** Menu features Italian dishes and seafood specialties. Reservations advised.

EAST BLOOMFIELD. *Expensive:* **The Original Holloway House.** Early American atmosphere in a century-old home. Baked specialties.

ELMIRA. *Expensive:* **Pierce's 1894 House.** Huge, well-prepared menu, high quality. An upstate find.

Inexpensive: **Moretti's.** Friendly family atmosphere in an establishment that has been in the clan for over 55 years. Very nice selection of American and Italian dishes. Dinner only.

ITHACA. *Expensive:* **L'Auberge Du Cochon Route.** Fine dining on excellent French entrees in a restored farmhouse.

Moderate: **Turback's.** Specializing in all N.Y. State produce, including wines. Large selections, unusual preparations.

MOUNT UPTON. *Moderate.* **The Old Mill.** 18th-century mill overlooking the Unadilla River. Menu features delicious chicken, beef, shrimp. Own baking. Dinner only.

NAPLES. *Moderate:* **Vineyard.** State 245 at State 21. Locally popular outdoor restaurant. Listen to music while dining on well-prepared dishes, homemade pastries. Salad bar. Menu features stroganoff and local wines. Cocktail lounge. Dinner only, closed during winter.

NIAGARA FALLS. *Moderate:* **John's Flaming Hearth.** Steak and lobster specialities, interesting desserts. Locally popular.
The Crown Restaurant. Hearty portions of good Italian/American cuisine.

PENN YAN. *Moderate:* **The Dresden.** A charming Finger Lakes atmosphere enhances the fine steaks and seafood served here.

ROCHESTER. *Moderate:* **Cartwright Inn.** Country dining in delightful surroundings. Menu features live lobsters, special desserts.
Spring House. This well-known dining room sets out lobster thermidor and excellent baked Alaska.

SYRACUSE. *Moderate:* **Grimalkidi's.** Excellent Northern-edged Italian menu, with a fine antipasto. Cozy lounge.

UTICA. *Expensive:* **Trinkaus Manor.** Cornish game hen is the featured delicacy in this 150-year-old mansion.
Moderate: **Hart's Hill Inn.** View of valley from tables near windows. Menu features fine regional fare.

WATKINS GLEN. *Moderate:* **Town House.** Attractive establishment has nice atmosphere. Crab, ribs, duckling specialties. Dinner only.

WAVERLY. *Moderate:* **O'Brien's.** An incredible place, with its own salad dressings, sausage, cheese, baking, and desserts. Specialties are turkey, aged beef, seafood.

EXPLORING THE CATSKILLS

Grossinger's, the Concord, lox and bagels—right? No. The Borscht Belt cliché began to go out in the fifties. There are still large numbers of Italian, Irish, Greek, Polish, and Jewish guests, but sectionalism has broken down so much that this area is now attracting Americans of all origins. The famous resorts, with their all-inclusive environments, are doing better than ever. Alternatively, with horse trails, county fairs, camping areas, skiing, hiking, fishing, canoeing, historic sites, a host of state parks, and so many other fine things to do, you can have a marvelous time without ever reaching them.

Quiet country inns offer the chance to enjoy the countryside, savor good food in a myriad of styles, and haunt back roads for antiques. Any time of the year is good for a Catskills vacation, as new facilities are making this area one of the most popular ski centers in a state which has more ski areas than any in the country.

We shouldn't ignore the resorts totally, however. Luxury fiefdoms like the Concord and Grossinger's have brought the region renown. Most of the better-known Catskill hotels are self-contained city-resorts, and no guest need ever leave the premises for something to do. On the grounds are tennis courts, badminton, pitch-and-putt greens, golf courses, baseball diamonds, outdoor and indoor swimming pools, archery, horseback riding, ice-skating rinks, toboggan runs, skiing, card rooms, recreation halls, nightclubs, and hiking trails. Instructors teach arts, crafts, painting and dancing. There are children's day camps and evening watchmen.

Kingston into the Catskills

A good entrance to the Catskills is over the Thruway to Kingston. Like many other early towns, it was burned during the 17th century by the mountain Indians and rebuilt within a stockade by Peter Stuyvesant, only to be looted and set aflame by the British during the Revolution. For the third time it rose from the ashes to become a prosperous village, visited by George Washington, and the meeting place of New York's first Senate.

South of Kingston in High Falls is the Delaware & Hudson Canal Museum, an interesting and worthwhile trip for anyone interested in the history of the canals that made the Empire State great.

Five miles from Kingston, State 28 forks around the Ashokan Reservoir which provides much of the water for New York City. (Ashokan is an Indian word for "drinking water.") Circling the reservoir, we can appreciate the full grandeur of the Catskills. On the north rise The Overlook, Mount Tobias, Mount Tremper, and others. Toward the west are Mount Pleasant, Panther Mountain, The Wittenberg, and in the distance the monarch of the peaks, Slide Mountain, highest of the Catskills (4,180 feet) and an easy climb via the trail from Winnisook Lake.

The Onteora Trail

The Onteora Trail reaches from the Hudson Valley over the divide of the southern mountains to the East Branch of the Delaware River. An ancient Indian pathway for many miles, the trail runs beside streams bordering vast forests. No other road in these mountains leads to so much unspoiled natural charm. Leaving Kingston by the Plank Road, the Onteora Trail crosses the Esopus and enters the mountains a few miles on through Stony Hollow. From West Hurley, turn north on State 375 to Woodstock. It is like no other community in the Catskills. Incorporated in 1787, it remained a sleepy little village until 1902, when Ralph Radcliffe Whitehead set up a home and handicraft community. The Art Students League of New York established a summer school a few years later. Since then, it has blossomed into a sophisticated community of artists, writers, music lovers, and stage folk. There are art exhibitions, concerts, indoor and outdoor theater presentations, curio shops and bazaars in a free and easy atmosphere.

Farther along on State 28 is Phoenicia, summer resort, trout fishing capital of the eastern slope, scene of annual White Water Races on Esopus Creek in June, and, in winter, a popular ski resort. The 688,660-acre Catskill State Park, a part of the huge Catskill Forest Preserve, covers this area, with over 200 miles of marked hiking trails.

At Hunter, a few miles north, summer skiing was introduced during the 1960s. The owners of the Hunter Mountain ski area had a plastic carpet installed on one of their smaller slopes, and it is still popular.

Beginnings of Great Rivers

Slide Mountain is at about the center of the State Park; almost all of the other notable Catskill summits are within the boundaries of the State Park, too, and here also begin tributaries of three rivers: the Hudson, Delaware, and Mohawk. Of this area, John Burroughs wrote: "Of all the retreats I have found among the Catskills, there is no other that possesses quite so many charms for me as this valley. It is so wild, so quiet and has such superb mountain views."

North of the park, at Schoharie Reservoir and Gilboa Dam, contractors excavating found a fossilized prehistoric forest, the oldest known in the world. Hundreds of stumps and branches covered with fernlike foliage were unearthed. Geologists believe that this forest grew during the Devonian period of the earth's formation, some 200 million years ago. Near the dam is an interesting exhibit of these fossilized ferns, the ancestors of today's trees.

From Hunter, State 23A goes to Prattsville, named after its founder, colorful industrialist Zadock Pratt. Shortly after he came to the area, he had amassed a fortune from a general store, and soon constructed his own village, building more than one hundred houses for new settlers. At one point, he operated a grist mill and a hat factory, as well as the largest tannery in the Catskills. Mountain neighbors called him "the most wonderful man the country ever produced." The local park and museum contain bits of "Prattiana."

From here, State 23 heads east through the winter ski center of Windham until it reaches Cairo (pronounced CARE–row). North along State 32 is the Catskill Game Farm and its large collection of animals and birds, also a nearby picnic ground and children's amusement area. Hunter, just south of Cairo on State 32, is the mid-July scene of an annual German Alps Festival, with oompah bands and imported beer only two of the many attractions. West along State 23 is the attractive town of Stamford, home of a Maple Sugar Museum that displays old-time maple sugar manufacturing equipment. Above the town's maple-lined streets towers Mount Utsayantha, named for a Mohawk princess who fell in love with an Algonquin brave, but was not allowed to marry him. She leaped into a lake and was drowned, and her grave marker is on the summit of the mountain.

Roxbury, south on State 30, was the home of John Burroughs. His home, Woodchuck Lodge, is open when the family is in residence. A short distance beyond the home is his "Boyhood Rock," which now has a bronze tablet incribed with a verse from his poem "Waiting." A rectangular stone wall in front of the rock marks his grave; nearby bubbles a spring where he used to drink.

Southern Catskills

State Routes 10 and 28 come together in Delhi, site of the Delaware County Historical Museum, where early farm tools and a country schoolhouse are on display in the restored 18th-century home of one Judge Gideon Frisbee. Downsville has a covered bridge built in 1854, and from here the Bear Spring Forest Preserve is accessible. Below that is Livingston Manor, a site of four covered bridges. Located at the juncture of the Beaver Kill and Willowemoc rivers, known locally as the Trout Fishing Capital of the World, this marks the gateway to the southern Catskills. Actually, there are a number of ways to approach the southern half of this region. State 17, the Quickway, is a fast direct drive through the Catskills, but the leisurely sightseer will start at Hancock and head south along State 97, the Hawk's Nest Drive. The Drive parallels the Delaware River, running high above the gorge and permitting spectacular views for almost its entire length. Turn east at Callicoon onto State 17B for Monticello, the "Capital of the Mountains." There's a lot more besides Monticello in this area. Loch Sheldrake has a number of famous resorts, as well as the popular Big Vanilla ski slopes. A bit east, Ellenville, the center of the Ulster County resort area, has several places frequently visited by tourists. One is Ice Caves Mountain, 2,255 feet above sea level, with a view of five states and a host of scenic nature trails and rock formations.

Along the Delaware

Back along the Delaware, thirteen more miles of the Hawk's Nest Drive, mostly in sight of the river, bring you to Narrowsburg. Fort Delaware, now the Museum of the American Frontier, dramatizes life in the area between the French and Indian War and the American Revolution in its replica of a 1754 stockade. Snug Harbor is a collection of old country store furnishings and stock.

Middletown is the home of the Orange County State Fair, and the scene of an annual September Steer Roast held at the Fairgrounds. It is also the home of the Empire State Railway Museum, no collection of miniatures but the real thing. There are an old-fashioned depot and an operating steam train, rides in antique coaches, an observation car, and what is said to be the largest caboose in the U.S. Nearby Goshen is the site of the oldest race track in America, which dates back to 1838, when trotters were raced under saddle. Harness races are still held there on the afternoons of the first week in July. The Hall of Fame of the Trotter, in a famous old stable, contains records, Currier and Ives prints, paintings and statues, dioramas of famous horses, and a library. Warwick, pleasantly situated along a branch of the Wallkill River, has an interesting 1810 house with period furniture from Queen Anne to Duncan Phyfe, as well as an intriguing collection of sporting equipment, antique dolls, and flowering fruit trees. The Shingle House, a 1764 saltbox, has carriages and sleighs, plus interesting farm tools and machinery.

PRACTICAL INFORMATION FOR THE CATSKILLS

HOW TO GET THERE. *By car:* The Quickway (State 17) runs from Exit 16 on the Governor Thomas E. Dewey Thruway to Binghamton through the Catskills south of the Forest Preserve. Exits 16–21 from the Thruway will also take you into the Catskills.

By bus: Adirondack Trailways has very complete coverage of the Catskills. Their main office is at 18 Pine Grove Ave., Kingston 12401. *Greyhound Short Line* (Hudson Transit), and *Monticello Transit* also have service to the Catskills.

TOURIST INFORMATION. Catskills Resort Association, 10 Hamilton Ave., Monticello 12701. Sullivan County Office of Public Information, County Government Center, Monticello, NY 12701.

MUSEUMS. Hurleyville, *Sullivan County Museum and Cultural Center.* Middletown, *Empire State RR Museum,* picnic grounds; scenic ride, June to mid-Oct., Sat. & Sun. Narrowsburg, *Fort Delaware,* Museum of American Frontier. Prattsville, Route 23, *Zadock Pratt Museum.* Rock carvings represent life of the village founder.

HISTORIC SITES. Roxbury, Burroughs Memorials, state-owned historic sites, in Memorial Field. Grave and "Boyhood Rock" of John Burroughs, his farmhouse birthplace and summer cottage, "Woodchuck Lodge," are nearby. Open when the family is in residence. Minisink Battlefield Memorial Park, Minisink Ford. Site of a Revolutionary War battle.

MUSIC. Music festivals during the summer in Woodstock. Hunter: *German Alps Festival* in July; *National Polka Festival* in August, both at the base of the ski lodge.

TOURS. Pine Hill. Belleayre Mountain Chairlift. Late June-Labor Day, daily; Labor Day-Oct., weekends (depending on foliage). Picnic area at summit.

SUMMER SPORTS. Outdoor activities include golfing and hiking. There are beautiful courses everywhere. *Golf:* Liberty, *Grossinger's Hotel,* a private course extending privileges to guests of hotels and motels, 18 holes; *Sullivan County Course,* 9 holes; Roscoe, *Twin Village,* 9 holes; *Tennanah Lake,* 18 holes; Windham, *Windham Course,* 18 holes. *Hiking:* Slide Mountain, Catskill State Park. *Fishing:* Phoenicia, trout fishing capital of the Catskills, Schoharie Creek through Catskill State Park. *Races:* Monticello Raceway, at jct. State 17 and State 17B. Harness racing, spring, Mon.–Sat; summer, daily.

WINTER SPORTS. There are too many areas to list them all. The New York State Division of Tourism makes available lists of *ski areas* throughout the state. A few of the popular ones in the Catskills are Belleayre (in Pine Hill), Big Vanilla (Woodbridge), Holiday Mountain (Monticello), Hunter Mountain (Hunter), Scotch Valley (Stamford), and Ski Minnewaska (Lake Minnewaska), open daily; and Highmount (in Highmount). Other areas have tobogganing, sleighing, and skating.

WHAT TO DO WITH THE CHILDREN. *Catskill Game Farm* between Cairo & Palenville. *Carson City,* between Cairo & Palenville, *Old Wild West Town,* with picnic area.

HOTELS AND MOTELS are so plentiful and varied that you can stay anywhere you like in the Catskills. Price categories for double-occupancy rooms in this region are: *Super Deluxe,* over $60; *Deluxe,* $40–60; *Expensive,* $31–40; *Moderate,* $21–30; and *Inexpensive,* $20 and under. (Slightly higher during peak seasons.) Call first to be sure the place you want accepts guests other than by the week.

BARRYVILLE. *Moderate:* **Reber's.** Bavarian-style architecture has provided large, comfortable rooms overlooking the Delaware River. Heated pool, barber shop. Pets are allowed.

CAIRO. *Moderate:* **Rexcroft Resort Motel.** Comfortable rooms in cottages or in main lodge. Restaurant, pool, lawn games.

DELHI. *Inexpensive:* **Buena Vista.** Relax in attractive, well-kept rooms. Pets are allowed, cribs are free, breakfast is available.

DEPOSIT. *Expensive:* **Hanson's.** Luaus, barbecues, 9-hole golf course, pets allowed in cottages, water sports on Oquaga Lake, plenty more at this resort. Family-owned since 1919. Weekly rates.

ELLENVILLE. *Deluxe:* **Fallsview.** Accommodates 500 guests. Pools, sports, 9-hole golf course, skiing, steam rooms, yoga. Kosher dietary.
The Nevele. Accommodates 900 guests. Pools, health club, tennis, 18-hole golf course, playhouse, private lake, lawn games, sauna, ball fields. Jewish-American menu, weekly rates available.

KERHONKSON. *Expensive:* **The Granit.** Accommodations for over 800, indoor ice-skating rink, indoor tennis, indoor and outdoor pools, 9-hole golf course, health club. Social director, teen programs; nightclub seats 1,500 people. Winter skiing.

KIAMESHA LAKE. *Super Deluxe:* **The Concord.** Accommodations for over 3,000 guests. One 9-hole golf course, two 18-hole courses, tennis, horseback riding, health club, sports director, world's largest artificial outdoor skating rink, skiing, enormous outdoor pool, indoor pool, sauna, fishing. Cocktail lounges, top entertainers, dance bands, social director, weekly rates available. Kosher dietary.

LAKE MINNEWASKA. *Deluxe:* **Lake Minnewaska Mountain House.** 3,500-acre resort in the Shawangunk Mountains. Library, concerts, outdoor games, surrey rides, horseback riding, lake swimming, sailboats, putting green, woodland walks, square dancing. Winter sports, lakes, streams, and waterfalls. Reservation deposit.

LIBERTY. *Super Deluxe:* **Grossinger's.** The original, accommodates over 1,300 guests. Olympic-size pool, indoor pool, children's pool, putting green, 18-hole golf course, tennis, skiing, skating, tobogganing. Award-winning kosher cuisine, 1,200-acre grounds, social director, top entertainment, dance orchestras, children's dining room. The complete year-round resort.

LIVINGSTON MANOR. *Inexpensive:* **Willowemoc.** Hunting and fishing nearby, pets limited, coffee in rooms. Comfortable.

LOCH SHELDRAKE. *Deluxe:* **Brown's.** They can accommodate over 800 guests with indoor and outdoor swimming pools, health club, tennis, nearby golf. Kosher dietary. Social director, top entertainers, dance bands.

MIDDLETOWN. *Deluxe:* **Sheraton.** A new location with first-class accommodations.
Moderate: **Middletown Motel.** Pleasant accommodations, with restaurant, cocktail lounge and swimming pool.

MOHONK LAKE. *Deluxe:* **Mohonk Lake Mountain House.** Worth the required reservation. Enjoy riding (lessons available), tennis (lessons available), 9-hole golf course, swimming at lake beach with lifeguard, boating and fishing. Social director, hayrides, concerts, dancing, skiing. Over 7,500 wooded acres, miles of trails, lovely gardens, gazebos, many rooms have porch or balcony, fireplace. Dignified resort since 1869.

MONTICELLO. *Deluxe:* **Kutscher's Country Club.** Accommodations for 800, golf course, indoor and outdoor pools, health club, day camp for children, horseback riding. Kosher dietary. Social director, dance bands, teen program. Skiing, tobogganing, sleighing.
Moderate: **Holiday Mountain Motor Lodge.** Seasonal skiing and hunting attract many to this fine motel. Restaurant and cocktail lounge, pool, very nicely furnished rooms. Reservation deposit; three-day minimum weekend in summer.
Patio. In center of village, with pool, café, 500 acres of private hunting grounds, fishing nearby.

SOUTH FALLSBURG. *Deluxe:* **The Pines.** Accommodations for 700 guests include 9-hole golf course, indoor and outdoor pools, health club, indoor ice skating, winter tobogganing and skiing. Kosher dietary. Social director, entertainers, dance bands, teenage program.

STAMFORD. *Moderate:* **Red Carpet Motor Inn.** Large attractive rooms in two-story motel. Swimming pool, café, dancing, and entertainment.

DINING OUT in the Catskills means eating in the hotel to most travelers, but there are plenty of excellent independent restaurants, too. Many of the hotels and resort hotels in the Catskills specialize in both kosher and non-kosher cuisine, with separate menus. Prices: *Expensive,* $25 and up; *Moderate,* under $25. This does not include drinks, tax or tip.

BARRYVILLE. *Expensive:* **Eldred Preserve.** Trout, steak, duckling. Children's portions.

    Reber's. Sauerbraten, Wiener schnitzel, and goulash are some of the specialties in this fine family-owned establishment.

MIDDLETOWN. *Expensive:* **Flo-Jean.** (Port Jervis.) Lovely spot along the Delaware. Own baking tops the menu, with fine duckling and filet mignon.

WINDHAM. *Expensive:* **La Griglia.** Fine restaurant, featuring northern Italian cuisine, game, an excellent wine cellar.

WOODSTOCK. *Moderate:* **Deanie's.** Ribs, seafood, and home-baking. Locally popular. Dinner only.

EXPLORING UPSTATE NEW YORK

The Adirondacks and Thousand Islands

New York State's North Country, stretching from Lake Ontario and the St. Lawrence River to Vermont, and from Quebec to Saratoga, is a year-round vacation paradise. One of the major attractions of the Adirondacks is that they offer genuine isolation relatively near big cities; the very vastness of the region swallows up not only the year-round residents but visitors as well. The Adirondack Park, established in 1892, contains about 8,900 square miles (6,000,000 acres), considerably more than the entire state of Massachusetts. Of this, over 2,400,-000 acres—an area larger than any of our national parks—is state-owned land which must be kept forever wild. The region is an outdoor Eden: spring-fed streams and lakes stocked with trout, perch, bass, and salmon; hills and wooded mountains ideal for hunting and hiking, with over 500 miles of marked trails and scenic paths; excellent public camping grounds and plenty of motels and restaurants in the popular resorts; and dozens of skiing areas only 200 miles north of Manhattan. Actually the Adirondacks are not part of the Appalachian chain, and although 42 of them are over 4,000 feet high—topped by Mt. Marcy at 5,344 feet—many are not impressive because they take off from a 1,500-foot plateau. Access is fast and direct. The Governor Thomas E. Dewey Thruway connects with the Adirondack Northway at Albany, and that takes you to Lake George at the southern boundary of the preserve.

A Jesuit missionary was the first white man to see Lake George's blue waters, in 1646. Today, most of the islands—there are more than one hundred in the thirty-two-mile lake—are state-owned and available for camping and picnicking. Lake George Beach, a public facility with every amenity, can accommodate 6,000 bathers along its sandy half-mile; and in and around the village are accommodations for 25,000 visitors. In summer, strollers, shoppers and automobiles jockey for space, while the lake buzzes with motorboats, and even planes. Visitors have a choice of boat tours, speedboat rides, and moonlight cruises. The historically-minded will enjoy Fort William Henry, a restored fort of the French and Indian War, which stands on a 19-acre plot in the village and commands the head of the lake. Rebuilt from original plans, it is a museum of Colonial America, with mock military drills and demonstrations of musketball molding, and cannon and flintlock firing. What you will be unable to avoid is the barrage of commercial amusements (for children and adults alike) that has sprouted here in recent years. Performing dolphins, duck races and Greta Garbo's Duesenberg, among other "attractions."

Three Forts

At Ticonderoga, on Lake Champlain, is the fort made immortal to Americans in 1775, when it was taken from the British by Ethan Allen and his Green Mountain Boys "in the name of Jehovah and the Continental Congress." Today, the fort has been restored and contains a museum. A nearby blockhouse, Fort Mount Hope, has also been restored, and features the ruins of a colonial warship. At Mt. Defiance, a toll road follows a British military trail to the summit for a spectacular panoramic view of the entire area, and at Ticonderoga you can take a ferry across Lake Champlain and back for a delightful scenic ride. Nearby is the Crown Point Reservation, a National Historic Landmark, where the French built their southernmost outpost in 1731, and where the British later constructed a fort of their own.

Ausable Chasm

Opened in 1870, Ausable Chasm is one of America's oldest organized attractions. The Ausable River plunges through a cut several hundred feet deep and a mile and a half in length. There are spectacular waterfalls, rushing rapids, and massive rock formations carved into strange shapes by millions of years of erosion. The chasm can be explored on stairways, walks, and footbridges, and the trip ends with a boat ride "shooting" one of the (safer) rapids.

Plattsburgh, site of an important victory over the British in the War of 1812, is the largest city in Clinton County, and has a number of spots of interest to vacationers. The Kent–Delord House Museum is one. An 18th-century home and British headquarters during the War of 1812, today it contains historical exhibits, and is furnished as it was when occupied by the Kent and Delord families, with china, glassware, silver, and furniture of the period.

At the northernmost tip of US 9 is Rouse's Point, where the United States built Fort Montgomery just north of the town, only to discover too late that it was in Canadian territory. The kindly Canadians ceded the few feet of land necessary to bring the fort home again. It became known as Fort Blunder, and its ruins are still there today. The nearby town of Chazy, south of Rouse's Point, is graced by the Alice T. Miner Colonial Mansion and Wayside Garden, an excellent early-19th-century home tastefully furnished.

Mountain Resorts

At Wilmington, Whiteface Mountain (4,867 feet) is one of the most popular of the Adirondack peaks to visit, winter or summer. A scenic, eight-mile toll road rises almost to the summit, and from there you can continue by foot or by elevator. Whiteface is also a skiing area, with six chair lifts, two lodges, and 28 trails and slopes.

West from Wilmington is High Falls Gorge, where the Ausable River plummets seven hundred feet in a series of falls which may be seen on walks and bridges at important vantage points.

Lake Placid is a beautiful resort community sitting in a bowl surrounded by some of the Adirondacks' highest peaks. It has every imaginable facility for both winter and summer sports and one that is unique, the mile-long Olympic bobsled run on Mt. Van Hoevenberg, seven miles south of town along State 73. Heavy iron racing sleds rush down the mountainside at speeds of close to one hundred miles an hour, and climb 20 feet of glare ice on the curves. Lake Placid was chosen twice—in 1932 and in 1980—as the site for the Winter Olympic Games.

Lake Placid is a year-round resort, and there is always something going on, be it the New York State Junior Ski Jumping Championships, an annual Winter Carnival, a cross-country race, the annual Ausable River Canoe Race, a golf tournament, or a square dance festival. Near Lake Placid is the John Brown Farm, where the body of the militant abolitionist, hanged for his part in a raid to free slaves, lies a-mould'rin' in the grave. Throughout the Adirondack region are many marked sites denoting stations along the Underground Railroad, an escape route for runaway slaves.

Lake Resorts

Saranac Lake lies 10 miles west of Lake Placid and here, too, can be found an abundance of sports facilities. The Dickert Memorial Wildlife Collection is the natural-history wing of the Saranac Lake Library. It features volumes of Adirondack lore, maps and photographs, and a variety of mounted birds, game, and fish. The Stevenson Cottage, where author Robert Louis Stevenson hoped to be cured of his tuberculosis, is maintained as a literary shrine and is open to visitors. The annual Winter Carnival at Saranac Lake has been held here since before the turn of the century. There are boat races in July, an annual show and sale of antiques at the Town Hall, and an August Paint and Palette Festival. To the west is Tupper Lake, a popular resort, where a chair lift will carry you on a 3,000-foot ride to the summit of Big Tupper. Skiing, hunting and fishing, boating and swimming, hiking and camping, and looking at the scenery all have their devotees here. The Adirondack Museum, at the intersection of State Routes 30 and 28, is a superb place: It has 20 buildings and is outdoors as well as indoors. Exhibits of paintings, maple sugaring, horse-drawn transportation, and tools, along with its dioramas of life in the 19th century, tell the complete story of Americans' relationship to the Adirondacks.

The Tri-Lakes Area embraces Friends, Loon, and Schroon Lakes. Off US 9 near Pottersville is an unusual formation consisting of a natural stone bridge and caves, grottoes, potholes, waterfalls, lighted caves, and stunning nature trails. Near Friends Lake is the famous Floating Rock, surrounded by Indian mounds, an old mica mine, and lots of scenic trails.

The Thousand (and More) Islands

Thousand Islands is no exaggeration. In fact, there are more than 1,800 of them, some mere points of rock, some large enough for an entire village. Most can accommodate a home or summer camp, and there are numerous old stone houses and mansions on them. A good place to begin is at Natural Bridge. Here travelers can go on an underground boat trip along the subterranean Indian River, and see fascinating natural rock formations while a guide expounds on geology and the natural history of the area. Sackets Harbor, on the shores of Lake Ontario, was a War of 1812 battlefield and military cemetery. It has probably the only navy yard in the world at one time commanded by a woman. Regional history and artifacts are displayed at the Pickering–Beach Historical Museum. Sackets Harbor was defended during the War of 1812 by Jacob Brown, and his home, the 150-year-old stone Brown Museum in neighboring Brownville, has portraits and mementoes of this early settler. A railroad museum in the town features a restored New York Central depot, with displays and photographs. Stone Mills, also in the vicinity, has an agricultural museum housed in an 1837 stone church, which shows antique farm tools and implements, and holds an annual summer crafts fair.

Along the Seaway

At Cape Vincent the waters of Lake Ontario flow into the St. Lawrence. Here are a state-owned aquarium, the ruins of an old fort, the Tibbits Point Lighthouse, and a fisheries station of the State Department of Conservation. The stretch of the St. Lawrence between Cape Vincent and Ogdensburg is an angler's delight, with bass, pickerel, pike, and muskellunge all ready to give you a run for your money. Fishing isn't the only water activity around; there's lots of swimming, too, and scenic boat tours of the islands on the sightseeing vessels that depart frequently from many of the towns along the river. At Alexandria Bay is the Thousand Islands Bridge, from which motorists can see two hundred of the islands, part of a seven-mile span of uniquely beautiful scenery between E Pluribus Unum and Maple Leaf Country. Here also, on Heart Island, is German-style Boldt Castle, planned by a wealthy hotel owner for his wife, and left uncompleted after an expenditure of over $2 million upon her death in 1902. The grieving widower just left it there, and it stands today, eerie, vacant, and full of crates of the marble and rare woods that were to have been installed. At Ogdensburg, the Frederic Remington Art Memorial, housed in an 1809 mansion, contains the largest single collection of the noted artist's paintings, bronzes, and sketches of the Old West. There is also a re-creation of his last studio. The town itself was founded in 1748 and is northern New York's oldest settlement. Massena, the power plant and shipping center of the North Country, is the place to see the famed St. Lawrence Seaway at its most spectacular. From Barnhart Island some of the locks and other engineering marvels of the Seaway are visible. You can see the great Moses–Saunders Power Dam, one of the world's largest hydroelectric plants, and take tours in the administration building. From a grandstand, you can watch the Dwight D. Eisenhower Lock raise or lower seagoing ships 35 feet. Air-Flight tours are also available from the Massena Airport, which tour about 20 miles of the St. Lawrence River.

PRACTICAL INFORMATION FOR

UPSTATE NEW YORK

HOW TO GET THERE. *By Car:* I–87 (Adirondack Northway) through the eastern Adirondacks from Albany to Plattsburgh. State 30 (Adirondack Trail) travels north from I–90 at Amsterdam through the heart of the Forest Preserve. For the Thousand Islands take I–81 through Syracuse or State 12 from Utica and along the St. Lawrence on the American side from Wellesley Island to Morristown.

By air: Air North flies to Plattsburgh and Saranac Lake-Lake Placid. Massena, Ogdensburg, and Watertown, in the Thousand Islands area, are also served by Air North.

By bus: Greyhound and *Adirondack Trailways* have service throughout the Adirondack and Thousand Islands areas.

By train: Amtrak heads north right through the mountains, with several stops en route to Rouse's Point at the Canadian border. It does not quite reach the Thousand Islands but does service Utica and Syracuse.

TOURIST INFORMATION. Write to the Adirondack Park Association, Adirondack, N.Y. 12808, (518) 891–4050, and the St. Lawrence County Chamber of Commerce, Canton, N.Y. 13617, (315) 386–4000.

MUSEUMS AND GALLERIES. Blue Mountain Lake: *Adirondack Museum.* Indoor and outdoor exhibits relating to the history of Adirondacks. Elizabethtown: *Adirondack Center Museum and Colonial Garden.* Exhibits relating to the area. Glens Falls: *Hyde Collection.* Museum of old masters. Ogdensburg: *Frederic Remington Museum.* Collection of works by America's foremost artist of the Old West. Saranac Lake: *Dorothy Yepez Gallery without walls.* Changing exhibits. *Stevenson Cottage.* Robert Louis Stevenson literary shrine. Watertown: *Jefferson County Historical Society Museum.* Regional history.

HISTORIC SITES. Canton: *Silas Wright House and Museum.* Restored rooms depict the period of mid-1800's. Upstairs exhibit gallery. Fort Edward: *Old Fort House Museum.* Historic exhibits. Lake Placid: *John Brown Farm.* Home and grave of the abolitionist. Lake George: *Fort William Henry.* A restored fort of the French and Indian War. May–Nov. Ticonderoga: *Fort Ticonderoga.* A museum and restored fort and dungeon.

TOURS. Alexandria Bay: *Boat Trips.* Hourly May, June, Sept., less often in Oct. *Boldt Castle.* On Heart Island. Tour boats stop here. May–Oct. *Ausable Chasm.* Tour of gorge, climaxed by boat ride through the "flume." Mid-May–mid-Oct. Lake George: *Boat Trips.* Daily sightseeing trips, speedboat rides and moonlight sails. Lake Placid: *Boat Trips.* Daily from George & Bliss dock, May–Oct. *Seaway and Power Development Bus Tour.* Guided tour covers locks, Robert Moses State Park, N.Y. State Power Authority Building, power dam. Leaves Chamber of Commerce parking lot. Natural Bridge: *Natural Bridge Caverns.* ¼-mile boat trip on Indian River, which flows underground. North Creek: *Carnet Mines Tour.* Tour of open pit mine. Tupper Lake: *Big Tupper Chair Lift.* Scenic 3,000-ft. ride to summit. Picnic area, hiking trails.

MUSIC. Glens Falls: *Lake George Opera Festival,* at Opera Festival Auditorium west of Northway exit 19. Opera productions in English. mid-July–Aug. Lake Placid: *Opera Under the Stars,* in English, July–Aug.

SUMMER SPORTS. "Long Path," in the Adirondacks, challenges hikers. It begins at Lake Placid. The New York State Division of Tourism has listings of major attractions throughout the Adirondacks and Thousand Islands, as well as guides of the main hiking and horse trails through the region.

WINTER SPORTS. There are countless ski areas in the Adirondacks and Thousand Islands area. Whiteface Mountain, in Wilmington, 4,867 feet high, has a vertical drop purported to be the highest in the East, over a dozen slopes, and three chair lifts. Lake Placid has all winter sports, including the Mt. Van Hoevenberg Olympic Bobsled Run. The area is the scene of many winter carnivals, skating and skiing championships.

HOTELS AND MOTELS. Cost categories for double-occupancy rooms in this region are: *Deluxe,* $50 and over; *Expensive,* $40–50; *Moderate,* $30–40; and *Inexpensive,* under $30.

ALEXANDRIA BAY. *Expensive:* **Capt. Thomson's Motor Lodge.** Exciting views of the Thousand Islands and Boldt Castle. Reservation deposit required.

GLENS FALLS. *Moderate:* **Queensbury Hotel.** High-ceilinged, comfortable rooms in well-preserved 1930s hotel.

LAKE GEORGE. *Deluxe:* **Alpine Village.** Lakeside resort with shaded grounds, rustic atmosphere, and comfortable accommodations.
    Frontier Village. Comfortable rooms, dormitories, log cabins. Beach, water sports, lawn games.
    The Georgian. Shoreside patio, nicely furnished rooms, water sports, and evening dancing.
    Tahoe. Stunningly terraced lakefront grounds, with heated pool, private sand beach, balconies facing the lake.
    Moderate: **Deep Dene.** Well-run motel among trees, nice rooms, and lakefront with beach.

LAKE PLACID. *Deluxe:* **Mirror Lake Inn.** Large lakefront property on hillside, with fine view and large rooms, pool, tennis, health spa, beach, boating. Reservation deposit.
    Placid Manor. Resort with lakeside setting, large comfortable rooms and cottages. Golf, tennis, fishing, boating, waterskiing, lake swimming. Deposit.
    Moderate: **Art Devlin's Olympic Motor Inn.** Gorgeous mountain view, many rooms with patio or balcony. Deposit required.

PLATTSBURGH. *Moderate:* **Pioneer.** A grove of evergreens is the setting for this excellent motel. Reservation deposit.

SARANAC LAKE. *Moderate:* **Lake Side.** Continental breakfast. Reservation deposit.

TUPPER LAKE. *Moderate:* **Shaheen's.** Nice rooms, heated pool, restaurant, deposit required.
    Inexpensive: **Tupper Lake.** Friendly motel has well-kept rooms. Heated pool. Reservation deposit.

 DINING OUT. Establishments are categorized according to the price of a dinner from the middle range of their menus. For this region: *Deluxe,* $20 and above; *Expensive,* $15–20; *Moderate,* $10–15; and *Inexpensive,* below $10. Included are *hors d'oeuvres* or soup, entree and dessert. Not included are drinks, tax, and tip.

ALEXANDRIA BAY. *Expensive:* **Cavallario's Steak House.** Food served and cooked extremely well. Steaks, lobster, Italian dishes, own baking. Dinner only.
    Edgewood Restaurant. Seafood specialties here in attractive rooms that overlook the water.

CHESTERTOWN. *Expensive:* **Balsam House.** A bucolic paradise on Friends Lake. Quaint, restored rooms; excellent dining.

GLENS FALLS. *Expensive:* **Red Coach Grill.** The ambience is pleasant with soft music. Fine steaks and ribs, shrimp and lobster are served. Dinner only.

LAKE GEORGE. *Expensive:* **Montcalm South.** Continental menu, with lots of fresh fish. Just off Northway exit.
    Moderate: **Ridge Terrace.** Dine in a rustic log cabin on lovely grounds, and enjoy good German and American cooking. Salad bar, meat cooked on the open hearth.

LAKE PLACID. *Expensive:* **Steak and Stinger.** Very good food in rustic surroundings; shrimp, scallops, lobster, juicy steaks. Salad bar and their own baking. Dinner only.

PLATTSBURGH. *Expensive:* **Royal Savage Inn.** Historic items provide a charming décor, while the country store features many items of interest. Steak and seafood specialties. Own baking.

SARANAC LAKE. *Inexpensive:* **Hotel Saranac of Paul Smith's College.** The name is a mouthful, and so are the meals, which feature home baking.

WILMINGTON. *Expensive:* **The Hungry Trout.** Victorian dining room, wild game or prime ribs dinner. Scenic view of Whiteface Mountain and the Ausable River. Dinner only.

PENNSYLVANIA

Philadelphia, Pittsburgh, and the Poconos

Let every house be pitched in the middle of its plot so that there may
be ground on each side for gardens or orchards or fields, that it may
be a greene countrie towne that will . . . always be wholesome.
—*William Penn, 1681*

Whether it be the restored Independence National Historical Park,
the "most historic square mile in America," or the narrow, cobbles-
toned streets of Society Hill, or the 8,900 acres of Fairmount Park, a
visitor to Philadelphia will find an incredible number of new things to
see and do while visiting this historic city.

A good start would be to begin a walking tour at Independence Hall,
a red-brick Georgian structure built between 1732 and 1741 as the
colonial capitol of Pennsylvania. It was designed by Andrew Hamilton,
a lawyer best remembered for his defense of newspaper editor John
Peter Zenger in the colonies' first fight for freedom of the press. Nobody
dreamed at the time that representatives of a defiant Continental Congress would gather here, that they would ratify the Articles of Confed-
eration, commission George Washington Commander-in-Chief of the
American armed forces, and sign the Declaration of Independence and
the Constitution of the United States—all in this historic hall.

Perhaps the most famous historical treasure connected with Independence Hall is the cracked Liberty Bell, one of the cherished symbols
of American freedom. Made in England in 1751, the bell cracked while
it was being tested in Philadelphia. Recast, it rang when the Declaration of Independence was signed. It rang also—but cracked again—
when knelling for Chief Justice John Marshall. The bell was moved into
its own building in front of Independence Hall in 1976.

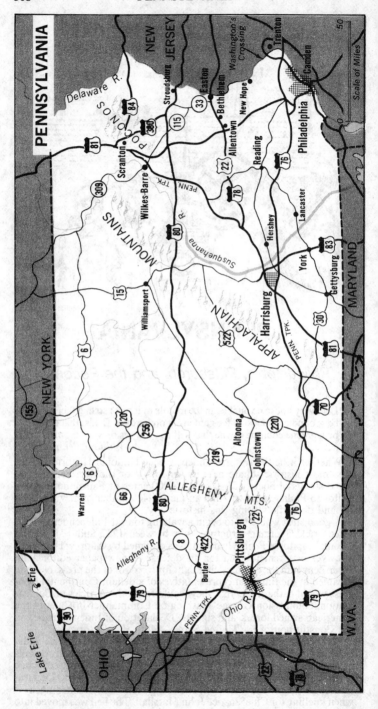

On one side of Independence Hall is Congress Hall, where Congress met from 1790 to 1800 (legislative chambers authentically restored); on the other side is the Supreme Court Building, constructed in 1789-91. Also known as the Old City Hall, it housed the nation's Supreme Court from 1791–1800. Nearby is the Second United States Bank, built between 1819 and 1824, and known as the Old Custom House.

Carpenters' Hall, at 320 Chestnut St., originally the guild hall for Philadelphia's carpenters, served as the meeting place for the First Continental Congress in 1774. The First Bank of the United States, founded by Alexander Hamilton in 1795 when he served as Secretary of the Treasury, is on S. 3rd St.

On 2nd St., between Market and Arch, stands the Georgian Christ Church. Founded in 1695, with the present structure built between 1727 and 1754, it ranks as the oldest of the city's churches. Both Franklin and Washington had family pews at Christ Church, and in its burial ground is Franklin's grave. Although it is impossible to list all of Franklin's contributions to the town, in addition to the Philosophical Society, he founded the *Saturday Evening Post,* the University of Pennsylvania, and Pennsylvania Hospital.

Philadelphia is a city of "firsts," including the first American hospital, medical college, women's medical college, bank, art school, mint, stock exchange, steamboat, lending library, fire fighting company, daily newspaper, abolition society, and public school for Negro children (1750).

Just north of Arch St., between Front and 2nd, is Elfreth's Alley, the oldest continuously occupied residential street in America. On the first Saturday in June each year Elfreth's Alley has a gala open-house Fete Day. At 239 Arch St., only a short walk from "The Alley," is the doll-like structure believed to have been Betsy Ross's house. Although many historians today question Mrs. Ross's part in the designing and making of the first flag, the house remains a leading tourist attraction with interesting memorabilia from the era.

Among other houses of note is the home of the last colonial and first post-colonial mayor, Samuel Powel, on S. 3rd St. Edgar Allan Poe, the poet and author, lived at N. 7th St. in the 1840s. During this period, "The Raven" and "The Gold Bug" were published.

Two burial grounds of historic importance are at Washington Square, where stand the Tomb of the Unknown Soldier of the Revolutionary War and the Mikveh Israel Cemetery near Pennsylvania Hospital.

In addition to Christ Church, the other churches of interest to tourists are: St. Mary's Church on S. 4th St., where the father of the American Navy, John Barry, lies buried; and Old Swedes Church, or Gloria Dei, at Christian St. and Delaware Ave.

For general strolling around, the visitor should see the old homes of Society Hill and the restored market at the foot of Pine St., Head House Square, where every summer weekend brings an outdoor craft market. Barely a block away is the revived South St. area and all its crafts shops, cafés, and charm.

New Philadelphia

The visitor who has finished his tour of old Philadelphia should not miss the attractions at the other end of town. The principal shopping streets are Walnut St. and the now closed-to-vehicles Chestnut St., with the John Wanamaker department store. The Gallery at Market East, on Market St. between 8th and 11th, has 250 shops and restaurants.

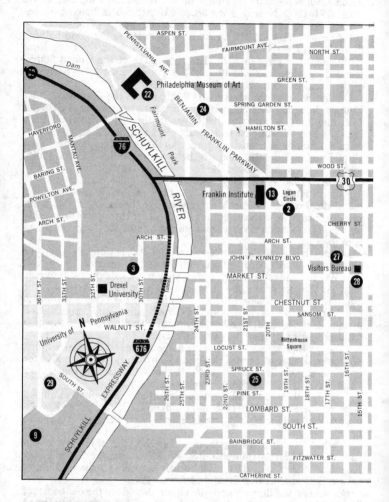

Points of Interest

1) Academy of Music
2) Academy of Natural Sciences
3) Amtrak 30th Street Station
4) Betsy Ross House
5) The Bourse
6) Chinatown
7) City Hall
8) Christ Church
9) Convention Hall/Civic Center

10) Edgar Allan Poe National Historic Site
11) Elfreth's Alley
12) Franklin Court
13) Franklin Institute Science Museum
14) Gallery at Market East/Market Street
    East Station
15) Independence Hall
16) Independence National Historical Park
    Visitor Center

For those with a penchant for markets, the Reading Terminal Market offers delicious, fresh farm cheeses, sausages, and the famous Bassetts ice cream. It's a fun spot for lunch. A popular outdoor market is the Italian Market, on 9th St., from Wharton to Christian, where neighbor-

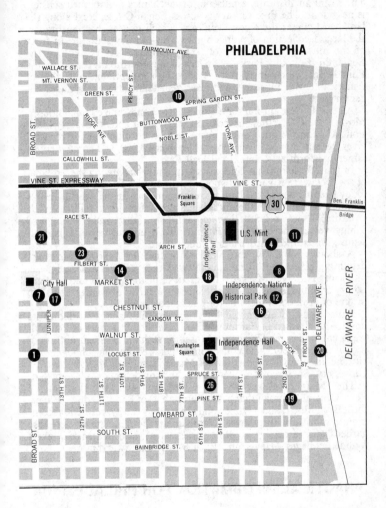

17) John Wanamaker
18) Liberty Bell
19) NewMarket
20) Penn's Landing
21) Pennsylvania Academy of the Fine Arts
22) Philadelphia Museum of Art
23) Reading Terminal Market
24) Rodin Museum
25) Rosenbach Museum and Library

26) Society Hill
27) Suburban Station
28) Convention and Visitors Bureau's Visitor Center
29) University Museum of Archeology and Anthropology
30) Zoo

hood merchants sell every variety of food. Open every day but Monday (Saturday is the day to go!) The Bourse, on 5th St. between Market and Chestnut, is a grand Victorian building with exclusive boutiques and inviting food stands.

Beyond City Hall and Penn Center, where the Tourist Center is located, Benjamin Franklin Parkway begins. Here is the oldest natural history museum in the United States, the Academy of Natural Sciences. The Franklin Institute, a museum of mechanics and applied science, is next door. The Free Library is across Logan Circle. Next along the boulevard comes the Rodin Museum, which houses, barring France, the largest collection of works by the 19th-century sculptor. In front of the museum is a casting of "The Thinker." At the end of the Benjamin Franklin Parkway, overlooking Fairmount Park, is the Philadelphia Museum of Art. It houses an exceptional collection of American crafts, furniture, and glass; renaissance treasures; and 20th-century art.

Also in Fairmount Park are a number of handsome colonial houses. Most impressive of these homes are Mt. Pleasant and Strawberry Mansion. At Mann Music Center, in the park, the Philadelphia Orchestra gives free summer open-air concerts for over 10,000, and popular entertainers perform at Robin Hood Dell East.

In 1682 William Penn landed his ship, the *Welcome,* on the left bank of the Delaware River. That spot, now known as Penn's Landing, has today become one of the largest freshwater ports in the world. Penn's Landing offers an exciting and scenic array of majestic sailing vessels (Admiral Dewey's USS *Olympia,* and the 18th-century Portuguese fishing vessel, the *Gazelo of Philadelphia*), unique restaurants, museums, landscaped gardens, and much more.

A short walk away, discover one of the most exciting, inviting, delighting places in Philadelphia: NewMarket at Head House Square, in Society Hill. NewMarket is hundreds of historic nooks and contemporary crannies. A visitor has a chance to relax, dine, wander, and shop in one of America's most historic neighborhoods.

Philadelphia is also noted for America's first zoo, and one of its finest, also situated in Fairmount Park. On the University of Pennsylvania campus is the University Museum, with an excellent anthropological and archeological collection. Other well-known schools in the city include the Curtis Institute of Music, Temple University, Drexel University, St. Joseph's College, and the Philadelphia College of Art.

The "Main Line" suburbs (so named after the Main Line of the Penn-Central Railroad that passes through it) of Paoli, Radnor, Haverford, Bryn Mawr, and Wynnewood are today wealthy, residential communities, with rolling lawns, commanding houses, spectacular rose gardens, and graceful pussy willow trees. This is also an area of Quaker-founded colleges—Haverford, Bryn Mawr, and Swarthmore.

PRACTICAL INFORMATION FOR PHILADELPHIA

HOW TO GET THERE. *By air:* Philadelphia International Airport is a major terminal for inter- and intrastate travel. *By car:* I-95 and US 1 pass through on east-west axis. The Pennsylvania Tpke. (I-76) runs eastwest; its Northeast Extension intersects I–80 north of the city.

By train: Philadelphia's 30th Street and North Philadelphia stations are on the *Amtrak* line.

By bus: Greyhound at 17th and Market. *Trailways* at 13th and Arch; *Martz, Merz,* and *Gray Line* also provide service.

HOW TO GET AROUND. *By bus:* The fare is 85 cents, exact change. Maps of the bus system are available at newsstands.

By subway: Fare is 85 cents, with exact change. Lateral transfers for 15 cents.

By taxi: United Cab and Yellow Cab are the major carriers in town.

From the airport: Bus to downtown hotels. Yellow Cab limousine and regular cab are more expensive. A train shuttle to downtown locations is scheduled to begin soon. Inquire for details.

TOURIST INFORMATION. *The Convention and Visitors Bureau's Tourist Center* is at 1525 J. F. Kennedy Blvd., downtown, (215) 568–6599. Special Events Information: Philly Fun Phone, 568–7255.

CITY PARKS. *Fairmount Park,* with 8,900 acres, is the largest city-owned park and Art Museum. Visitors may enjoy biking, hiking, tennis, picnicking, and sculling. It has more cherry blossoms than Washington, D.C., a huge azalea garden, Colonial houses, and a Japanese tea house.

MUSEUMS AND GALLERIES. The *Academy of Natural Sciences,* 19th and Franklin Parkway, is the nation's oldest museum of its kind, with a two-story-high dinosaur, fossils, and children's museum. *The Franklin Institute,* 20th and Franklin Parkway, has 6,000 exhibits including a beating heart to walk through. The *Rodin Museum* on the Franklin Parkway, contains the largest collection outside France of the sculptor's works. The *Philadelphia Museum of Art* is a major assemblage of medieval, renaissance, and modern art. It is one of the world's leading museums and offers tours in eight languages.

The *Pennsylvania Academy of the Fine Arts,* Broad and Cherry sts., is noted for its collection of American art from Revolutionary times to the present. The *University Museum,* 33rd and Spruce, has an extensive collection of ancient and primitive archeological and anthropological pieces from all over the world. Other museums are: the *American Swedish Historical Museum,* in South Philadelphia; the *Museum of American Jewish History* at 55 North 5th Street; the *Atwater Kent Museum* on S. 7th St., which tells Philadelphia's history; and the *Afro-American Historical and Cultural Museum,* 7th and Arch, with five galleries tracing black history. The *Barnes Foundation,* in nearby Merion, is open Fridays and Saturdays, 9:30 A.M. to 4:30 P.M. and Sundays from 1 to 4:30. It has a world-famous impressionist collection. *The Perelman Antique Toy Museum,* 268 S. 2nd St., has thousands of Early American cast-iron and tin toys. *The Rosenbach Museum and Library,* 2010 Delancey Place, is a 19th-century townhouse filled with antique furniture, paintings, rare books, and over 130,000 manuscripts, including James Joyce's *Ulysses.* The history and tradition of the Mummers Parade are showcased at the *Mummers Museum,* 2nd St. and Washington Ave.

Numerous galleries and antique shops are in center city on Spruce, Pine, and the lower end of South St.

HISTORIC SITES. Philadelphia contains some of the nation's most important historic treasures, many of them grouped around *Independence Mall,* between Market, Walnut, and 5th and 6th sts. Most famous is Independence Hall, where the Declaration of Independence was signed and the former home of the Liberty Bell (now moved to a more accessible location). Congress Hall, next door, is where the Continental Congress met from 1790–1800. Carpenters' Hall is where the first Continental Congress convened in 1774. The reconstructed Graff House is where Thomas Jefferson lived when he wrote the Declaration of Independence. Nearby is Franklin Court, an entire complex of reconstructed houses and unusual exhibits dedicated to the redoubtable Benjamin Franklin.

Christ Church, at 2nd and Market, is the birthplace of the Protestant Episcopal Church of America. Other churches of interest are the *Gloria Dei* at Delaware and Christian and *Old George's Methodist* on N. 4th.

The *Betsy Ross House,* on Arch St., is decorated in period furniture and has a replica of the original thirteen-star flag. The *Edgar Allan Poe House* is on N. 7th. The *Hill Physick Keith House,* on 4th St., was the home of the father of American surgery, Dr. Phillip Syng Physick. *Elfreth's Alley,* between Arch and Race, Front and 2nd., is the oldest continuously occupied residential block in America, with 33 homes dating back to the early 1700s. The *Friends Meeting House,* on 4th and Arch, is still used by the Quakers. The *Todd House,* once owned by Dolley Madison, née Todd, is at 4th and Walnut. The *Bishop White House* on 3rd and Walnut, was home of the first Episcopal bishop in the U.S. The oldest Jewish cemetery in the U.S. is the *Mikveh Israel Cemetery* on 8th and Spruce. *Pennsylvania Hospital,* at the same location, is the oldest in the country. Two other homes to see are: the *Powel House* on S. 3rd., home of Philadelphia's first post-Revolution mayor; and *Bartram's House and Garden,* 54th and Lindbergh, former home of America's first naturalist.

TOURS. The *U.S. Mint,* 5th and Arch, is the largest of the country's three mints. *City Hall,* larger than the U.S. Capitol and fashioned after the Louvre in Paris, has guided tours and an elevator ride to the top, with a view of the city. The acoustically perfect *Academy of Music* is home of the Philadelphia Orchestra and is a national landmark. *Philadelphia Stock Exchange* is the nation's oldest. *Masonic Temple* on Broad St. has rooms representing different architectural periods. Group tours (free) to the Naval Base, Nabisco, U.S. Post Office, Pennsylvania Hospital, Water Treatment Plants and Police Headquarters. Write or call the Convention and Visitors Bureau, 568–6599.

SIGHTSEEING. Visitors can see the attractions of Philadelphia in different ways. *Gray Line Tours* offers a variety of narrated sightseeing tours in air-conditioned, deluxe buses. *Philadelphia Carriage Company* takes you through Philadelphia's colonial neighborhoods in restored nineteenth century horse-drawn carriages. The *Fairmount Park Trolley Buses* use Victorian trolleys to take visitors through the Park, its museums, and a guided tour of historic mansions. *Holiday Cruises'* Spirit of Philadelphia offers luxury lunch, dinner, and moonlight party cruises on the Delaware River along with live entertainment. It takes off from Penn's Landing.

GARDENS. *Bartram's Gardens,* 54th and Lindbergh, was the nation's first botanical garden. *Morris Arboretum of the University of Pennsylvania,* Chestnut Hill, is typical of Victorian-era design. The *Schuylkill Valley Nature Center,* at 8480 Hagy's Mill Rd., has a wildlife reserve and nature museum.

MUSIC. The *Academy of Music,* home of the world-famous Philadelphia Orchestra led by Riccardo Muti, is modeled after La Scala Opera House and also hosts operas, ballets, rock concerts, and children's concerts. *Robin Hood Dell East* and *Mann Music Center* in Fairmount Park have outdoor summer concerts. The *Free Library* occasionally has free concerts. The *Philadelphia Folk Festival* hosts international performers and workshops in the folk music world in nearby Schwenksville. August.

STAGE AND REVUES. Known as a good show town, Philadelphia has many Broadway plays debut here, while others come on tour. Major theaters are the Shubert, Forrest, and Walnut St. downtown; Annenberg's Zellerbach at the University of Pennsylvania; and Valley Forge Music Fair in nearby Devon. Smaller theaters include Society Hill Playhouse and Wilma Theater downtown.

NIGHTCLUBS AND BARS. Among the most popular spots are the *Middle East* with its belly dancing; *élan,* in the Warwick Hotel; and *Horizon's,* in the Wyndham Franklin Plaza. Other popular bars include *PT's, Grendel's Lair, Downey's, Rick's Cabaret, Borgia Café, Moshulu, Not Quite Crickett* (Latham) and *Quincy's* (Adam's Mark).

SPORTS. Philadelphia has every major sport: *football* Eagles, *baseball* Phillies, at Veterans Stadium; Stanley Cup champion *hockey* Flyers and *basketball* 76ers at the Spectrum arena; and *racing* at Keystone and Liberty Bell track. Major *college basketball* games are at the Palestra. Philadelphia also hosts the U.S. Professional Indoor Tennis Championships, Jan. or Feb; the Penn Relays in March; the Dad Vail Regatta in May; and the Army-Navy football classic held at Veterans Stadium in late November or early December.

SHOPPING. Nationally known department stores are John Wanamaker, Gimbels, Strawbridge and Clothier. A specialty shop is Nan Duskin. Jeweler's Row, between 7th & 8th Streets on Sansom, offers a plethora of jewelry stores. Antique Row is along Pine St. from 9th to 18th streets. Craft market is at Head House Square. The Gallery at Market East, at 9th and Market, is an enclosed mall of 250 stores. NewMarket, at 2nd and Pine streets, is an outdoor complex of over 50 shops. The Bourse, on 5th Street, near Market Street, a stunning new indoor arcade of select shops, features haute couture and restaurants.

WHAT TO DO WITH THE CHILDREN. A good double treat is the *Academy of Natural Science* and *Franklin Institute* across the street from each other. The *Philadelphia Zoo* has a special Children's Zoo on its grounds. *Schuylkill Valley Nature Center* has trails where live animals can be fed by children. The *Philadelphia Ballet* has an annual Christmas presentation of the "Nutcracker Suite." The *Philadelphia Orchestra* has children's concerts at the Academy of Music and Mann Music Center. Temple's Theater Dept. produces children's theater on Saturdays. 1619 Walnut St., Stage Three. Children can play with exhibits on music, science, etc. at the *Please Touch Museum,* 210 N. 21st St.

HOTELS AND MOTELS. For a single room, double occupancy, rates are: *Deluxe,* $95 and higher; *Expensive,* $75–$95; *Moderate,* $55–$75; *Inexpensive,* under $55. For information on *bed and breakfasts* contact Bed & Breakfast of Philadelphia, PO Box 680, Devon 19333, (215) 688-1633.

Deluxe: **Barclay,** 237 S. 18th. On Rittenhouse Square, quiet, dignified.

Four Seasons Hotel. On the Parkway. Top-notch, exquisite.

Hershey Philadelphia Hotel. Broad and Locust Sts. New, handsome, glass-faced, convention hotel across from Academy of Music. Good family plans.

Latham Hotel. 17th and Walnut. Small, luxurious, European-style hotel.

Palace Hotel. 18th and Ben Franklin Pkwy. Overlooks Philadelphia's handsome parkway. All accommodations are lavishly furnished suites. Fine dining.

Warwick Hotel. 17th and Locust. Elegant. Popular night spot.

Westin Bellevue Stratford. Broad and Walnut. Opulent grand old hotel. Lovingly restored. Good restaurants.

Wyndham Franklin Plaza. 17th and Race. Stunning, new convention hotel.

Expensive: **Adam's Mark Hotel.** City Line and Monument Ave. Indoor and outdoor pools, health club. New. 10 minutes from downtown.

Embassy Suites. Gateway Center, near airport. Newest hotel in city.

Hilton. 34th and Civic Center Blvd. Near University of Penna.

Holiday Inn–Independence Mall. 4th and Arch. Convenient to historic areas.

Marriott Hotel. City Line and Monument Ave. Sprawling, resort-like.

Sheraton University City. 36th and Chestnut. Restaurant, dancing.

Sheraton Valley Forge. Fantasy suites, disco, dinner theater.

Moderate: **Franklin Towne Econo Lodge.** 22nd and Parkway. Comfortable, newly remodeled.

Penn Center Inn. 20th and Market. Skyscraper motel.
Philadelphia Centre Hotel. 1725 JFK Blvd. Convenient location.

DINING OUT. Restaurants are classed as: *Deluxe,* $20 and up; *Expensive,* $15–20; *Moderate,* $10–15; *Inexpensive,* under $10. This is for a complete dinner without drinks.

Deluxe: **The Fountain.** Four Seasons Hotel. Opulent setting, exceptional food.

La Truffe. 10 S. Front. Nouvelle cuisine, country French ambiance.

Le Bec-Fin. 1523 Walnut. Craig Claiborne calls it best French cuisine in U.S.

Expensive: **Dickens Inn.** At NewMarket. British specialties, English pub.

Frog. 1524 Locust. Blend of French, American, and Asian cuisine.

The Garden. 1617 Spruce. Outdoor dining in season. Continental.

Old Original Bookbinder's. 125 Walnut. Wonderful seafood. A Philadelphia tradition.

Ristorante DiLullo. 1405 Locust. Northern Italian. Seasonal specialties.

Moderate: **Arthur's Steak House.** 1512 Walnut. Old standby.

Fratelli. 1701 Spruce. Homemade Italian favorites.

Friday, Saturday, Sunday. 261 S. 21st St. Cozy spot, continental dishes.

Joe's Peking Duck House. 925 Race. Great duck dishes.

Lickety Split. 4th and South. Began the restaurant renaissance. Funky.

Mayflower. 1010 Cherry. Mandarin, Szechuan, and Cantonese.

Middle East. 126 Chestnut. Authentic food. With belly dancers.

Under the Blue Moon. 8042 Germantown Ave., Chestnut Hill. Continental cuisine with an Oriental flair.

Inexpensive: **Commissary.** 1710 Sansom. Gourmet cafeteria. Piano bar.

Jim's Steaks. 400 South St. Be sure to sample a classic cheesesteak.

Pat's King of Steaks. 1237 E. Passyunk Ave. Sidewalk steak sandwiches in Rocky's South Philly neighborhood.

Walt's King of Crabs. 804 S. 2nd. Casual bar, fresh seafood.

EXPLORING PITTSBURGH

Every city impresses people differently. Pittsburgh prevails in its own style. To most of the nation, "Pittsburgh" suggests steel, red hot from the furnace, the tense luxury of executive suites, and barges easing up the Ohio River. These images protect strength, energy, and ambition, which accurately depict Pittsburgh's atmosphere.

The last two decades have seen a dedication of Pittsburgh's best minds to the revitalization of the city. The Golden Triangle was once Iron, but now in Point State Park people enjoy the outdoors at the spot where the Monongahela and Allegheny Rivers converge to form the Ohio. At this decisive location France fought England up to and during the French and Indian War. General Forbes and his troops won a critical victory in 1758, capturing the fort they renamed in honor of their Prime Minister, William Pitt. The Blockhouse still stands and is open to the public in the recently created, beautiful Point State Park.

Pubs and gourmet restaurants surround the green mall of Market Square and you can sample some exotic produce as you move toward the central business district. Mellon Square is probably the best known of Pittsburgh's handsome inner-city open spaces, the newest of which is the plaza in PPG Place. Nearby, on Smithfield Congregational Church, is the first aluminum steeple ever raised.

On 6th St., near the Allegheny River, Heinz Hall is the home of the Pittsburgh Symphony, one of the nation's best orchestras. The hall also presents ballet, opera, and popular artists, and is named for the founder of the food-processing corporation.

The heritage of civic-minded men of wealth becomes especially apparent as we move into the Oakland section. In or near Schenley Park are two large universities, Carnegie-Mellon and the school-in-a-skyscraper, University of Pittsburgh's Cathedral of Learning. The area also includes Carnegie Institute, two museums under one roof; Phipps Conservatory, exhibiting botanical wonders; the Pittsburgh Playhouse and America's first community-supported TV station, WQED; fine art on the inside of the Frick Building and the outside of Gothic St. Paul's Cathedral. In the neighborhood are the Heinz Chapel, with its superb stained-glass windows, and the Stephen Foster Memorial, which holds a special program every January commemorating the works of the American composer.

The hills north and south of downtown are crowded with the colorful houses of Pittsburgh's more ethnic neighborhoods where German-, Italian-, and Polish-American shops and restaurants delight with unpretentious authenticity. The northside has also protected and restored residences dating back to the 1800s. Old Allegheny, as this vicinity is known, has had loving attention from the Pittsburgh History and Landmarks Foundation. Buhl Science Center and Allegheny Observatory are nearby.

The southside hills are steeper, and it's from Mt. Washington that you'll see the whole area below you. There are two railways up the slope, popularly called the Duquesne and the Monongahela Inclines. If you're wondering about the famous steel plants, most of them have moved beyond city limits.

PRACTICAL INFORMATION FOR PITTSBURGH

HOW TO GET THERE. *By car:* I-79 runs north-south through Pittsburgh; the Pennsylvania Tpke. (I-76) runs east-west just north of the city. *By air:* The Greater Pittsburgh International Airport has inter- and intrastate connection.

By rail: The station at Liberty and Grant Sts. is on the *Amtrak* line.

By bus: Greyhound at 11th and Liberty Ave. *Trailways* at 210 10th.

HOW TO GET AROUND. *By bus:* Minimum fare is $1 but varies for different zones within city. *By taxi:* Cabs are expensive, $1 to start the meter. *From the airport:* Yellow Cab limousine to downtown. Airport bus service.

TOURIST INFORMATION. *Greater Pittsburgh Convention and Visitors Bureau,* 4 Gateway Center, answers all questions. (412) 281-7711.

MUSEUMS AND GALLERIES. The city goes all out on its world-famous *Carnegie International Exhibit,* which also has a unique annual art festival. The *Frick Museum,* 7227 Reynolds Ave., Point Breeze, has an exquisite collection of French, Italian, and Flemish Renaissance paintings. *Henry Clay Frick Fine Arts Building,* in Schenley Park, houses the Lochoff Collection of fine Renaissance works and an old Italian-style cloister.

The *Pittsburgh History and Landmarks Foundation* preserves the history of Allegheny County. The *Old Post Office Museum,* 701 Allegheny Square West, is a restored Italian Renaissance building featuring changing historical exhibits of architecture, fashions, and nostalgia. Andrew Carnegie established the *Carnegie Institute* at 4400 Forbes Ave., housing a library, museums, art gallery, and music hall—the focal point of culture in the Oakland section. Its *Museum of Natural History* has over 5 million items, including a 20-foot skeleton of a tyrannosaurus dinosaur. The Sarah Scaife Gallery displays dramatic sculpture. Nearby in Oakland, the *Cathedral of Learning* has 18 international rooms, each furnished in the style of the country it represents. Most contemporary art can be seen at the *Pittsburgh Center for the Arts*, 6300 5th Ave., with exhibits changing monthly. Other art galleries include the *Art Institute of Pittsburgh*, 526 Penn Ave.; and the *Pittsburgh Plan for Art*, 407 S. Craig St. The *Stephen Foster Memorial Hall*, Forbes and Bigelow, has the songwriter's memorabilia. The *Historical Society of Western Pennsylvania*, 4338 Bigelow, has an Early America firearms collection. *Hartwood Acres*, 215 Saxonburg Blvd., a re-created English country estate, opens its mansion and gardens for tours.

HISTORIC SITES. Pittsburgh, focal point of the French and Indian War, unfortunately has only one landmark still standing, the Blockhouse of *Ft. Pitt*. Dating from 1764, it is in Point State Park, at the conflux of Pittsburgh's three great rivers. Not far from the Blockhouse is the Fort Pitt Museum, a unique reconstruction of the Monongahela bastion. A few miles north of Pittsburgh is *Old Economy*, on Ohio River Blvd., in Ambridge, site of the Harmony Society's 19th-century experiment in communal living.

TOURS. *Gateway Clipper*, Station Square Dock, operates cruises on the three rivers. Inquire for schedules, generally May–September. *Gray Line of Pittsburgh* offers tours of downtown and surrounding areas.

GARDENS. *Phipps Conservatory*, Schenley Park, is a tropical forest of exotic plants with rare blooms under glass and an orchid collection. Second-largest of its kind in the country. Spring, fall, and holiday flower shows are fabulous. The *Conservatory-Aviary*, West Park at W. Ohio and Arch Sts., displays exotic and domestic birds and plants in native habitat settings.

MUSIC. The *Pittsburgh Symphony Orchestra* is now permanently ensconced at Heinz Hall, 600 Penn Ave. The *Pittsburgh Opera*, also at Heinz Hall, combines local operatic and musical talent with guest stars. The *Pittsburgh Chamber Music Society* has an annual series of concerts. The *Civic Light Opera Association* presents a variety of shows, musicals, and light operas during the summer. The *Pittsburgh Ballet Theater* thrives under the sponsorship of Point Park College. The *Tamburitzans of Duquesne University* annually perform 100 concerts as they celebrate Southeastern Europe's heritage of music, song, and dance. The American Wind Symphony entertains from its barge, *Point Counterpoint*, moored in the Allegheny River at Point State Park.

STAGE AND REVUES. The *Syria Mosque*, Bigelow Blvd., Oakland, has Broadway road shows for limited runs. The *Pittsburgh Playhouse*, in Oakland, is a top-quality community theater with three playhouses. Summer stock nearby is at the *Little Lake, White Barn,* and *Mountain Playhouses.* Also, there is the *Little Lake Dinner Theater*, Route 19 South past South Hills Village (reservations), and *Johnny Lounders Dinner Theatre* near the airport.

SPORTS. Three Rivers Stadium provides headquarters for the Pittsburgh Pirates and the Pittsburgh Steelers. The NHL Penguins and the Pittsburgh Spirit soccer team both play in the Civic Arena. The Pitt Panthers, the number-one team in the nation in 1977, play major college-level football. Boyce Park Ski Area has beginner and intermediate slopes. Allegheny County boasts it has more golf courses than any other U.S. county.

About 1½ hours east from the city limits are a host of ski resorts that dot the Laurel Mountains—Seven Springs, Hidden Valley, White Mtn., and Bear Rock. For those more adventuresome, white-water rafting is at nearby Ohiopyle on the Youghiogheny.

SHOPPING. Gimbels, Joseph Hornes, Kaufmann's, and Saks are major department stores. Station Square, Oxford Centre, and PPG Place, the city's newest office/shopping complexes, offer a variety of boutiques and restaurants.

Monroeville Mall, South Hills Village Mall, Century III Mall, and Northway Mall offer hundreds of varied shops.

WHAT TO DO WITH THE CHILDREN. The *Carnegie Museum* and its dinosaurs are always a delight. *Buhl Science Center* has working displays. *Highland Park* has a regular and children's zoo. The *Arden Trolley Museum* in nearby Washington is open weekends. *Kennywood Park,* 4800 Kennywood Blvd. in W. Mifflin, has four roller coasters, Kiddieland, gardens, and picnic areas. *White Swan Park,* 3 mi. SE of Greater Pittsburgh Airport, has amusement rides, miniature golf, and picnic areas. *The Children's Museum,* with its handson exhibits, is housed in The Old Post Office Museum. *The Marionette Theatre Arts Council* runs year-round and the *South Park Conservatory Children's Theatre* has performances during summer months. The *Aviary-Conservatory* in Allegheny Commons houses an exotic collection of live birds.

HOTELS AND MOTELS. Rates for a single room, double occupancy, fall in these categories: *Deluxe,* $75 and up; *Expensive,* $60–75; *Moderate,* $40–60; *Inexpensive,* under $40.

Deluxe: **Hyatt Pittsburgh at Chatham Center.** Adjacent to Civic Center.

Marriott Hotel. Monroeville and Greentree. Year-round pool, sauna, tennis courts, and game room.

Pittsburgh Hilton and Towers. Gateway Center. Point State Park, scenic location.

Sheraton Station Square. The heart of downtown Pittsburgh.

Westin William Penn. On Mellon Square.

Expensive: **Airport Hilton Inn.** Greater Pittsburgh Int. Airport. Outdoor pool.

The Bigelow. Adjacent to U.S. Steel Building. Apartment units.

Holiday Inn Airport. Greater Pittsburgh Int. Airport. Indoor pool.

Moderate: **Best Western Parkway Center Inn.** Greentree. Fitness center.

Harley Hotel of Pittsburgh. Monroeville. Recreational facilities.

DINING OUT. Restaurants are classed as: *Deluxe,* $20 and up; *Expensive,* $15–20; *Moderate,* $10–15; *Inexpensive,* under $10. This is for a complete meal without drinks.

Deluxe: **Christopher's.** Atop Mt. Washington's LeGrande Apts. Beef, veal, seafood, and a view.

The Carlton. Mellon Bank Center. Classic American steak house.

Hyehold. Near airport. Elegant dining in castle-like setting.

Expensive: **Alex Tambellini's Woods Restaurant.** 213 Wood St. Italian seafood.

Anna Kao's. In O'Hara Township. Szechuan, Hunan, Peking, Cantonese, and Fukien dishes.

Brendan's. 5505 Walnut St., Shadyside. Upstairs, Continental. Downstairs, American, raw bar.

Kleins. 330 Fourth Ave. Good seafood and meat dishes.

Le Mont. Atop Mt. Washington. French, elegant surroundings.

The Samurai Japanese Steak House. 2100 Greentree Rd. Atmospheric.

Sir Loin Inns. 5841 Forbes Ave. Thick-cut steaks, seafood, giant salads.

Moderate: **1902 Tavern.** 24 Market Square. Century landmark.

Pasta Piatta. 55331/2 Walnut St., Shadyside. Italian dishes.

Poli. 2607 Murray Ave. Squirrel Hill. Varied menu of meat and seafood.

Sarah's. 52 S. 10th. Eastern European cuisine, only one in town.

Samreny's. 4808 Baum Blvd. Lebanese, in University area.

Top of the Triangle. 600 Grant St. Stouffer's atop US Steel Building. Beautiful view.

Inexpensive: **Max's Allegheny Tavern.** North Side. German cuisine.

Mick McGuires. Market Square. Old-time Irish Pub.

NIGHTLIFE. Popular are *Studebakers* and *Heaven,* downtown. The *Holiday House* is the largest supper club in Pittsburgh, big name entertainers, dancing, and shows. *Library,* in Bank Center, disco with dining. *Chauncy's* at Station Square.

EXPLORING PENNSYLVANIA

The Poconos

The Pocono Mountains resort area is a vast playland of some 2,400 square miles in northeastern Pennsylvania, and only a few hours away from New York or Philadelphia. This popular retreat for eastern city dwellers is dotted with lakes, mountains, streams (Pocono is an Indian word meaning "stream between the mountains"), and fine hotels. It offers outstanding fishing, golfing, hunting, swimming, skiing, camping, and hiking on the Appalachian trail. The Poconos offers many special honeymoon resorts that cater to newlyweds and couples as part of the area's claim to be the Honeymoon Capital of the World.

The Delaware Water Gap is a famous scenic entrance to the Poconos. This deep, tree-covered gap is especially beautiful when leaves turn in autumn, and when the mountain laurel blossoms in the spring. Just west and north of the gap are the resort areas of Stroudsburg, Big Pocono State Park, with a view atop Camelback Mountain (also a winter ski center), and Mount Pocono center. Promised Land State Park, with excellent camping facilities, is the center of the Pocono game country, and some wild deer are tame enough to wander into campsites. Nearby is Lake Wallenpaupack, Pennsylvania's largest man-made lake and regional water-sports center. Near Milford are the bluffs of Coykendall's Pool, where thousands of swallows roost from April to August. In Bushkill are the region's largest waterfalls, Bushkill Falls—the "Niagara of Pennsylvania."

Valley Forge

A necessary stop when leaving or entering the Philadelphia area is Valley Forge. Here Washington's ill-clad, poorly fed, badly supplied Continental Army suffered through the cold winter of 1977–78, after the British had occupied Philadelphia. It was at this hallowed spot, Valley Forge, that victory and defeat walked side by side and were scarcely distinguishable. Today, Valley Forge is a 2,300-acre national park, with historic displays and relics. History-minded visitors will find a host of other fascinating attractions in and around Valley Forge country. There's the birthplace of Daniel Boone, and Mill Grove, the restored first home in America of naturalist John James Audubon. Another important historic site is Washington Crossing State Park, farther north, along the Delaware River, where Washington made the historic fording in 1776 en route to battles at Trenton and Princeton. The park has an observation tower and some still standing Revolutionary period houses. Washington Crossing is also a good jumping-off point for a tour of Bucks County, one of the state's largest and loveliest, noted for rolling farmlands and artists' town of New Hope.

Northwest Pennsylvania

Presque Isle, at the northwest tip of the state, holds an important place in American history, for it was in Presque Isle Bay that Oliver

Hazard Perry, in 1813, constructed ships that met the British in combat in the Battle of Lake Erie. In nearby Erie, the commodore's flagship, the *U.S.S. Niagara,* is docked. Erie has the Perry Memorial House, also known as Dickson's Tavern, which served as Perry's quarters before the battle and later was a "station" of the Underground Railroad before the Civil War. Erie also has a replica of the blockhouse in which Revolutionary hero "Mad" Anthony Wayne died in 1806.

Between Erie and Pittsburgh is Titusville, where Edwin L. Drake drilled the first productive oil well on August 27, 1859. Replicas of the early riggings still stand. Also on the road towards Pittsburgh, in Ambridge, is the 19th-century religious community of Old Economy, with many original structures open to visit. A final site in the western end of the state is Ft. Necessity, a National Battlefield, in Uniontown. In 1754, at the age of 22, George Washington lost his first battle at the fort during the French and Indian campaign. Washington's commanding officer, General Braddock, is buried here.

Gettysburg and Central Pennsylvania

In the middle of the state is Gettysburg National Military Park, perhaps the nation's most famous Civil War monument. Here, on July 3, 1863, the continent's greatest artillery battle was fought, and General Lee was forced to retreat. Lincoln delivered his famous address on November 19, 1863. Nearby is the Eisenhower home, open for tours.

York is another central-Pennsylvania attraction. This city served as the Colonial capital between September 1777 and June 1778 and was a leading weapons producer. North is Harrisburg, the state capital. The city is abustle when the legislature sits, and also has pleasant walks and gardens on the banks of the Susquehanna River. The Italian Renaissance capitol building's dome was modeled after St. Peter's in Rome. Barely 12 miles away, following the delicious aroma, is Hershey, one of the last company towns in America. Planned and laid out by Milton Hershey in 1903, the former Lancaster caramel manufacturer decided to make chocolate here. The town now has a resort hotel, gardens with 42,000 roses and 30,000 tulips, a museum, a convention center, Hersheypark, Chocolate World, and a community center built by Hershey. Two streets in town are Chocolate and Cocoa Aves.

Pennsylvania Dutch Country

In and around Lancaster is the renowned Pennsylvania Dutch country. This is a world apart from modern America. The Amish farmers sport full beards and broad black hats; their wives don bonnets and all work is done without the use of power tools or conveniences. Lancaster itself, founded in 1718, was capital of the U.S. for one day on September 27, 1777, and is still regional center for farm produce and cpen-air markets. The religious inhabitants of the region are collectively called the "plain people" and include the Amish, the Brethren or Dunkards, and the Mennonites. All vary, to some extent, in their beliefs, conservatism, somber dress, but all are master farmers of the very rich soil. Pennsylvania Dutch cooking is unique and based on the idea of seven sweet and seven sour dishes that comprise a delicious smorgasbord— pickles, relishes, apple butter, dumplings, pretzels, molasses, and shoofly pie, to name a few. Other Dutch-country sites are James Buchanan's house in Lancaster and the Pennsylvania Farm Museum at Landis Valley.

PRACTICAL INFORMATION FOR PENNSYLVANIA

HOW TO GET THERE. *By car:* From New York and the east, I-95 runs to Philadelphia; in the northeast, I-81 passes through Binghamton, N.Y., to Scranton and Harrisburg. I-80 and Pennsylvania Tpke. bisect the state on an east-west axis. I-79 runs from Erie to Pittsburgh and Morgantown, W. Va.

By train: Amtrak serves Philadelphia, Harrisburg, Lancaster, Pittsburgh, and Erie.

By bus: Greyhound and *Trailways* serve selected cities.

By air: Philadelphia, Pittsburgh, and Harrisburg have major airports.

HOW TO GET AROUND. *By car:* Major roads noted above provide good intrastate transportation. Pennsylvania Tpke. is a toll road. *By train:* Amtrak serves Philadelphia, Lancaster, Harrisburg, Pittsburgh, and Erie. Good commuter service in Philadelphia.

By bus: Trailways and *Greyhound.*

By air: In addition to Philadelphia and Pittsburgh, airports at: Erie, Bradford, Williamsport, Scranton and Wilkes-Barre, Hazelton, Allentown, Reading, Lancaster, Harrisburg, Johnstown, Altoona, Clearfield, Dubois, and Franklin.

TOURIST INFORMATION. The Bureau of Travel Development, Pennsylvania Dept. of Commerce, 416 Forum Bldg., Harrisburg, Pa. 17120. 1–800–VISIT–PA.

MUSEUMS AND GALLERIES. In Gettysburg: *Soldier's National Museum, Battle Theatre, General Lee's Headquarters, Hall of Presidents and First Ladies, Jennie Wade House, Lincoln Room Museum, Gettysburg Address Exhibit, Lincoln Train Museum, The Conflict, National Civil War Wax Museum, National Tower,* and *A. Lincoln's Place.* In Chadds Ford, Chester County, the *Brandywine River Museum,* housing works of the famous Wyeth family. York, one-time capital of the United States, has over 300 original *Currier and Ives* lithographs. Harrisburg is home to the *State Museum of Pennsylvania.*

In Strasburg, near Lancaster, state-operated *Railroad Museum,* with Strasburg Rail Road nearby. *Pennsylvania Farm Museum,* north of Lancaster, with rural America collection. Doylestown, Bucks County, has *Fonthill Museum,* Henry Mercer's castle-like home; *Mercer Museum* of early American tools and implements; *Moravian Pottery and Tile Works Museum.* At *Reading Public Museum and Art Gallery,* find exhibitions of art, science, commerce, and Dutch folk art. A glimpse into the life of Christopher Columbus after he made his historic voyage may be had in central Penna. at the *Boat Mansion,* in Boalsburg.

HISTORIC SITES. *Washington Crossing State Park,* near Buckingham, was the General's embarkation point for battles of Trenton and Princeton. New Hope has *Parry House* from 1700s and the *New Hope–Delaware Canal Locks* and the *Barge Landing* (1890). Erie is site of *Ft. Le Boeuf* from French and Indian Wars; the *Wayne Blockhouse,* last home of "Mad" Anthony Wayne; and Oliver Hazard Perry's *U.S.S. Niagara* and *Perry Memorial House.* Near Lancaster are *Amish Village, Amish Farm and House* and *Amish Homestead. Pennsbury Manor,* in Morrisville, is a re-creation of William Penn's house of 1699–1701. Offers the largest collection of 17th-century antiques in Pennsylvania. *Mill Grove,* home of James Audubon (in Chester County), 2 miles from Valley Forge. Fallingston is a well-preserved pre-Revolutionary War village. *Gettysburg National Military Park* encompasses numerous museums, tours, monuments, and President Eisenhower's home. York has the *Golden Plough Tavern* and *General Gates House.*

TOURS. *Casser* Tours, *Parker* Tours, *Tauck* Tours, *Greyhound, Gray Line,* and *Trailways* all run out of New York to Pennsylvania Dutch country and other areas.

DRINKING LAWS. Legal age is 21. Bottled liquor only sold in state stores.

SUMMER SPORTS. Some of the best-known *golf courses* are Hershey, Shawnee-on-Delaware, Pocono Manor, Merion, Oakmont, and Ligonier. Williamsport annually hosts the World Series of *Little League Baseball.* Major league *baseball* in Philadelphia and Pittsburgh. *Flat horse racing* at: The Meadows, Meadowlands; Keystone, Philadelphia; and Penn National, near Hershey. *Harness racing* at: Liberty Bell; Pocono Downs, between Scranton and Wilkes-Barre; and the Meadows, Meadowlands. Lakes and streams throughout the state provide excellent *fishing.* Licenses required. Pennsylvania has miles of *hiking* trails including the Horse Shoe Trail and a section of the Appalachian Trail and lakes and rivers for *canoeing, sailing, boating, white-water rafting, and swimming.* There are sand beaches on Lake Erie in Presque Isle State Park, a summer vacationland. More than 100 state parks bring Pennsylvania near its goal of "a state park within 25 miles of every Pennsylvanian." For campground information, write to Bureau of Travel Development, 416 Forum Bldg., Harrisburg, Pa. 17105. For information on state parks, write: Pa. Bureau of State Parks, P.O. Box 1467, Harrisburg, Pa. 17120.

WINTER SPORTS. The Pocono Mountains have the northeast Pennsylvania centers for *skiing* at Big Boulder, Camelback, Buck Hill, Pocono Manor, Jack Frost, Shawnee, and Elk Mountain. Other winter sports; *ice-skating, tobogganing, ice-boating, ice-fishing.* In northwestern Allegheny Mountains, skiing at: Seven Springs, Laurel Mountain, Hidden Valley, and Blue Knob. Other ski areas scattered throughout the state. *Hockey* is popular in Philadelphia and Pittsburgh.

WHAT TO DO WITH THE CHILDREN. Parks featuring fairy tales and characters from children's literature: *Sesame Place,* newest cultural amusement park, in Langhorne (1 hr. from Phila.); *Storybook Forest,* Ligonier; *Dutch Wonderland,* Lancaster; *Miniature Horse Farm* and *Game Park* in Gettysburg; and *Fairyland Forest,* Conneaut Lake Park. Underground caves and caverns: *Indian Caves,* Spruce Creek; *Laurel Cavern,* Uniontown; *Crystal Cave and Onyx Cave,* Kutztown; *Indian Echo,* Hummelstown, near Hershey; *Woodward Cove,* Woodward; *Penn's Cave,* Centre Hall. Coal mines with tours: *Seldom Seen Valley Mine,* St. Boniface; and *Pioneer Coal Mine Tunnel,* Pottsville. Railroads: *East Broad Top Railroad, and Strasburg Rail Road.* Other railroads: W. K. & S., Kempton; Gettysburg Railroad, Gettysburg. Good zoos in Philadelphia and Pittsburgh. Amusement Parks include *Dorney Park* in Allentown and *Hersheypark* in Hershey. While in Hershey, visit Hershey's *Chocolate World.* Near Altoona, there is the *Forest Zoo.* The sight of rattlesnakes being milked of their venom attracts thousands to the *Pocono Snake Farm,* in Marshalls Creek. The "Grand Canyon of Pennsylvania" is upstate near Wellsboro.

HOTELS AND MOTELS. For a single room, double occupancy, rates range as follows: *Super Deluxe,* $65 and up; *Deluxe,* $55–65; *Expensive,* $45–55; *Moderate,* $34–45; *Inexpensive,* under $35.

ERIE. *Expensive:* **Bel Aire Hotel.** West of downtown. Dining, indoor, outdoor pools.
Erie Hilton. Centrally located downtown. Indoor pool, restaurants.
Holiday Inn–Downtown. 18th and Peach Sts. Restaurant, entertainment.
Holiday Inn–South. I–90 and Peach St. Dining, entertainment.
Inexpensive: **Red Roof Inn** and **Knights Inn.** Off I–90.

GETTYSBURG. *Expensive:* **Holiday Inn.** 516 Baltimore St. Ramp for wheelchairs.
 Howard Johnson's Motor Lodge. Across from Visitors' Center. Pool.
 Quality Inn–Gettysburg. Next to Visitors' Center.
 Sheraton Inn–Gettysburg. 2634 Emmitsburg Rd. Indoor pool, tennis, dining, dancing.
 Moderate: **Quality Inn Larson's.** Next to General Lee's old home.

HERSHEY. *Super Deluxe:* **Hotel Hershey.** Complete resort. Golf course, gardens. Gracious, Spanish-design hotel.
 Hershey Lodge. Resort. Superb recreation facilities.

LANCASTER. *Super Deluxe:* **Americana Host Farm.** Lavish, complete resort with tennis, pools, ice skating, and top entertainment.
 Deluxe: **Treadway Resort Inn.** Rts. 30 and 272. Children's program.
 Expensive: **Howard Johnson's.** 2100 Lincoln Hwy East. Indoor pool.

NEW HOPE. *Deluxe:* **Evermay Inn.** Outside village, overlooks river.

YORK. *Expensive:* **Holiday Inn.** Rt. 30 East. Lounge with entertainment.
 Sheraton Inn–York. US 30 at Rt. 74. Indoor pool, entertainment.
 Yorktowne Hotel. 48 E. Market St. Good restaurant.
 Inexpensive: **Modernaire.** 3311 E. Market St. Small motel with pool.

HARRISBURG. *Super deluxe:* **Americana Host Inn.** Full amenities.
 Harrisburg Marriott. 4650 Lindle Rd. Full amenities.
 Sheraton Inn East. Suites, indoor pool, health club.
 Expensive: **Penn Harris Motor Inn.** Camp Hill. Pleasant, entertainment.
 Inexpensive: **Capitol TraveLodge. Riverfront Inn, Red Roof Inn.**

 DINING OUT. Restaurants are grouped as: *Deluxe,* $20 and up; *Expensive,* $15–20; *Moderate,* $10–15; *Inexpensive,* under $10. This is for a complete meal without drinks.

ERIE. *Moderate:* **The Buoy.** By the public dock. Seafood, children's menu.

GETTYSBURG. *Moderate:* **The Dobbin House.** Colonial tavern. Homemade breads.
 Farnsworth House Dining. Civil War décor, over 100 bullet holes visible.
 Gettysburg Ad'ress. Garden-style restaurant.
 Inexpensive: **Hickey Bridge Farm.** Restored early American farmhouse.

HARRISBURG. *Expensive:* **The Gazebo Room.** Near the capitol.
 Catalano's. Just across the river. Italian and American fare.
 Moderate: **Alfred's Victorian.** 1890s atmosphere. Northern Italian, Continental.
 Caruso's. Downtown. Gourmet Italian.
 Harris Ferry. In Penn Harris Motor Inn. Continental.

HERSHEY. *Expensive:* **Hotel Hershey.** Steak. Overlooks garden.

LANCASTER. *Deluxe:* **The Restaurant at Doneckers.** Classic and country French cuisine.
 Expensive: **Groff's Farm.** Mount Joy. Famous. Pennsylvania Dutch "family style." Chicken Stoltzfus, chocolate cake appetizer. By reservation.
 The Hoar House. Victorian atmosphere. Unique Continental dining.
 Moderate: **Stock Yard Inn.** Ribs, steak, seafood.
 Two Pennsylvania Dutch "family style" restaurants are **Good n' Plenty** in Smoketown, and **Plain and Fancy** in Bird-in-Hand. Both feature family-style eating, seven sweet and seven sour courses, good home cooking.
 Inexpensive: **The Willows.** Dutch cooking, good for families.

NEW HOPE. *Deluxe:* **La Bonne Auberge.** Farmhouse. French cuisine. *Expensive:* **Chez Odette.** French country bistro. Patio dining. On river. **Karla's.** W. Mechanic St. European café.

VALLEY FORGE. *Expensive:* **Lily Langtry's.** In the Sheraton. Ornate dinner theater. Las Vegas revue. Continental cuisine.

YORK. *Deluxe:* **Chez John.** 243 W. Market St. French nouvelle and haute cuisine.
Expensive: **Archie's Place.** Italian and American.
Meadowbrook Inn. 2819 Whiteford Rd. Continental. A dining adventure.

POCONOS HOTELS AND MOTELS offer so many types of accommodations and plans at each of the large resorts that prudent vacationers will want to examine them in detail by sending for brochures. The categories used for the survey in this section are, for double occupancy: *Super Deluxe,* $75 and higher; *Deluxe:* $55–75; *Expensive,* $45–55; *Moderate,* $35–45; and *Inexpensive,* under $35. Good savings available off season.

BUCK HILL FALLS. *Super Deluxe:* **Buck Hill Falls Inn and Golf Club.** One mi. NE of State 191, off State 390. This famous resort nestles in a lovely setting. Enjoy 27 holes of golf, tennis, riding, roller skating, swimming, fishing in a nearby river, and skiing in winter. The inn has its own lifts and snow-making equipment. Restaurant, room service, bar; movies, summer entertainment.

BUSHKILL. *Super deluxe:* **Pocmont.** West off US 209 in Buskhkill. Suites with sunken tubs, king-size beds; indoor and outdoor pools, saunas. Sports program includes boating and horseback riding. A golf course is nearby. In winter, there's a ski slope. Restaurant and bar, dancing and entertainment.
Tamiment. In Tamiment, between US 6–209 and State 402. Spacious grounds include a 90-acre lake, tennis courts lighted for night-time play, winter snow-sport areas. Excellent food and top-flight entertainment.
Deluxe: **Fernwood.** On US 209 1½ mi. SW of town. Golf, tennis, private lakes, swimming pool, horses, entertainment, ski area with school and rentals, snowmobiling, and gift shops. Restaurant and bar.

CANADENSIS. *Deluxe:* **Linder's Hillside Lodge.** State 390, 1 mi. N of town. An attractive woodland setting. Motels and cottages available. Tennis courts, golf nearby; entertainment and dancing, coin laundry, rec room. There's a heated swimming pool.
Moderate: **Laurel Grove Inn and Cottages.** This establishment has a 9-hole golf course and all-weather tennis facilities. Heated pool, rec room, live music.

CRESCO. *Deluxe:* **Pocono Gardens Lodge.** Paradise Valley. Paying special attention to honeymooners, it has Roman baths, sunken tubs, log-burning fireplaces. There's an indoor pool, horseback riding, water sports, and skiing. Lounge and nightclub. "Couples-only" resort.
Crescent Lodge. State 191 at State 940. Tennis, other indoor and outdoor games. Golf, riding, and skiing nearby. Restaurant and cocktail lounge.
Expensive: **Naomi Cottages.** State 390, 1 mi. N of town. In a secluded area, this facility has fully equipped housekeeping cottages, tennis, shuffleboard, and a rec room. There's a coin laundry; early check-out time.

DELAWARE WATER GAP. *Expensive:* **Howard Johnson's Motor Lodge.** Near exit 53 from I-80. Heated pool, cocktail lounge. Fishing, hunting, golfing, skiing nearby.

EAST STROUDSBURG. *Inexpensive:* **Paramount Motel.** US 209 Business. This in-town establishment is next door to a restaurant and provides a pool and some games. Good place to locate if your interest in the Poconos is exploring rather than resort living.

GREENTOWN. *Super Deluxe:* **White Beauty View Resort.** On Lake Wallenpaupack. Has modern cottages and hotel rooms, some with fireplaces, sandy beaches, all water sports, cocktail lounge, American-European plan, skiing nearby, ice skating, and snowmobiling.

MARSHALLS CREEK. *Super Deluxe:* **Pocono Palace Resort.** US 209. Couples-only resort on Echo Lake. With sunken tubs, in-room pools, log-burning fireplaces. Full recreation facilities. Entertainment. A Caesar's Palace resort.

MOUNT POCONO. *Super Deluxe:* **Mount Airy Lodge.** Near Scotrun exit from I-80. Sports palace with indoor tennis courts, indoor ice-skating rink, indoor and outdoor heated pools, shows, dancing every night, year-round sports facilities. Family resort.
Strickland's Mountain Inn and Cottages. Honeymoon plans available. Award-winning Skytop Chalets to various suites. Three pools, free golf, tennis court, summer and winter sports. Nightclub and cocktail lounge. "Couples-only" resort.

POCONO MANOR. *Super Deluxe:* **Pocono Manor Inn.** State 314, 2 mi. W of town. Year-round 3100-acre resort "atop the Poconos." 36-hole golf course, indoor pool, skiing, with snowmakers; tennis, riding. Early American décor is charming. Dancing and entertainment.

SCOTRUN. *Super Deluxe:* **Brookdale-on-the-Lake.** NW of town, a mi. W of State 611. Brick cottages with fireplaces, rooms in the lodge with jacuzzis. Private 12–acre lake with swimming, boating, fishing, sailing. Indoor pool, tennis.

SHAWNEE ON DELAWARE. *Deluxe:* **Shawnee Inn.** Off US 209, 3 mi. NW of Delaware Water Gap. Championship golf, tennis, one indoor and one outdoor pool, boating. Dinner in Dogwood Room, followed by dancing and entertainment in Cartoon Room. Family plans. Shuttle bus to ski slopes.

STROUDSBURG. *Deluxe:* **Sheraton Pocono Inn.** 1220 W. Main St. Indoor courtyard with pool, sauna, gift shop, recreation room, indoor putting green, swimming pool, coffee shop, restaurant, new cocktail lounge.
Expensive: **Best Western Pocono Inn.** 700 Main St. 100 rooms. Restaurant, cocktail lounge, room service from the bar, coffee shop. Indoor pool, pets.
Moderate: **Antler's Lodge and Cottages.** Off State 611, E of town. A 34-acre resort, with cottages decorated in Early American style. Pool, miniature golf, fishing, boating, tennis, winter sports.

TANNERSVILLE. *Super Deluxe:* **The Summit.** At exit 45 from I-80. One of the newest resorts in the area, it has a couples-only, no-children policy and directs its format toward honeymooners. Every villa has its own enclosed sun deck, hexagonal bed, sunken bath, wood-burning fireplace. All sports, indoor and outdoor pools, sauna. Entertainment, dining room and cocktail lounge.
Birchwood. Between Tannersville and Analomink. Separate chalets with log-burning fireplaces. Indoor pool, sauna, 3 lakes, outdoor pool, bowling, skiing, sledding, tobogganing, ice skating. "Couples-only" resort.

WHITE HAVEN. *Deluxe:* **The Lodge at Split Rock.** Four mi. from Pocono exit, NE Extension of Pennsylvania Turnpike. Fifty rooms in new lodge. 50 units in cottages. All seasonal sports. Skiing on grounds, Big Boulder Ski Area 1½ mi. away, Jack Frost Ski Area 4 mi. away. Family rates available. Café, bar. Rustic atmosphere, on Lake Harmony.
Hershey Pocono Resort. (Whitehaven), just off Pa. Turnpike, Exit 35, I-80, exit 42. Indoor and outdoor pool, PGA golf course, tennis, horse and bike trails. Children's program.
For further information on accommodations in the Pocono area (including housekeeping cottages) contact the Pocono Mountains Vacation Bureau, Box K, Stroudsburg, Pa. 18360. 1–800–POCONOS.

DINING OUT in the Poconos means one thing above all else—Pocono Mountain trout, the specialty of many restaurants in this area. In addition to trout, of course, are many other foods associated with Pennsylvania, including Pennsylvania Dutch cuisine. The recent vast growth of hotels, motels and inns in the area has resulted in a similar proliferation of restaurants, and you can now get almost any kind of dish. US highways, such as 6 and 209, are dotted with truck stops and these are at their best around breakfast time.

Price categories for the region are: *Deluxe,* $20 and higher; *Expensive,* $15–20; *Moderate,* $10–15; and *Inexpensive,* under $10. These prices include first course or soup, entree and dessert. Not included are drinks, tip and the Pennsylvania 6% food tax. For a more complete explanation of price categories, see *Facts at Your Fingertips* at the beginning of this volume.

BANGOR. *Expensive:* **Selecta.** State 191. The specialty is *rijstafel,* the traditional "rice table" of Indonesia. Open weekends only, by reservation.

BUSHKILL. *Moderate:* **Fernwood Gaslight Lounge Restaurant.** On US 209. Dinner, music, dancing, and entertainment nightly.

CANADENSIS. *Deluxe:* **Pump House Inn.** State 390 at Skytop Rd. French provincial cuisine includes roast rack of lamb persille. They have their own wine list and enjoy a good reputation in the area.
Expensive: **Overlook Inn.** Cozy, quaint inn, excellent food.
Pine Knob Inn. Great service and presentation. Well-priced wines.

CRESCO. *Expensive:* **Crescent Lodge.** Over thirty entrees to choose from. Junction of Rts. 191 and 940.

EAST STROUDSBURG. *Moderate:* **Peppe's Ristorante.** A favorite with the locals, who like its Early American charm. Complete luncheon and dinner menus, cocktails from the Carriage Pub. At Eagle Valley Mall, junction of Business 209 and 477.

GREENTOWN. *Expensive:* **White Beauty View Resort.** State 507, Lake Wallenpaupack. Dining room open to public, specializes in Italian and American cooking. Spectacular, expansive view of the lake from dining rooms and cocktail bar.

HAWLEY. *Moderate:* **Perna's.** State 590, 3 mi. SW of town. Hawley is on the northern edge of the Pocono region and you'll see more nature and fewer resorts driving around here. At this locally popular, chef-owned restaurant, you'll enjoy the homemade Italian dishes.

MOUNTAINHOME. *Expensive:* **Diamond Jim's.** State 390. Reflects the splendor of the Gay Nineties, and serves lobster, lobster tails, prime sirloins, and filet mignon. One block from Pocono Playhouse, with large parking area. Closed Tues. Reservations in summer.
Moderate: **Cappuccino.** State 191 and 390. Antipasto bar. Seafood and Italian dishes. Closed Tuesdays.

MOUNT POCONO. *Expensive:* **Johnnie's Pocono Summit Inn.** Two miles west of blinker light at Mt. Pocono. Italian cuisine, steaks, chops, and seafood. Lobster tail is a house specialty.
Moderate: **Highland Inn.** State 611. Completely renovated, cocktail lounge. Features home-cooked food. Private dining room for groups. Opens at noon. Rustic fireside lounge.

STROUDSBURG. *Moderate:* **Beaver House.** 1001 N. 9th St. (State 611, 1 mi. N of town). Six dining rooms. Maine lobsters, sirloin steaks, shore dinners. Cocktails. Open at mealtimes only.

Inexpensive: **Historic Henryville House.** State 191 at 715, 6 mi. N of town. Authentically restored Victorian inn. Museum rooms open to public. All food and pastries are prepared on the premises.

VIRGINIA

Where America Began

A tour through Virginia is easily begun on the Atlantic Coast. First stops on the Eastern Shore are Assateague Island National Seashore and Chincoteague Island, home of the famous ponies whose ancestors are thought to have originally swum ashore from a shipwreck in the sixteenth century. Chincoteague National Wildlife Refuge is a sanctuary for more than 250 kinds of birds. Winter flocks include honking snow geese and whistling swans, while summer brings egrets, herons, and ibises.

Continuing south down the Delmarva Peninsula travelers must cross the unique seventeen-mile Chesapeake Bay Bridge-Tunnel to reach Norfolk, its neighboring beaches, shipyards, and water-sports centers. Norfolk has the world's largest naval base and is home port to over one hundred ships of the Atlantic and Mediterranean fleets. Boat tours of the harbor are available during the summer season. A marked tour route of this historic city includes the Chrysler Museum, the General Douglas MacArthur Memorial, the Gardens-by-the-Sea, St. Paul's Church which still has a British cannonball embedded in its wall, and the Adam Thoroughgood House, an English-style brick home dating from the 1600s. Southeast of Norfolk is Virginia Beach, a popular resort with a wide range of activities. Nearby is Seashore State Park, and historic Cape Henry.

Across the bay from Norfolk are Hampton and Newport News. Moat-encircled Fort Monroe, in Hampton, housed such "guests" as Indian chief Black Hawk and Confederate president Jefferson Davis, and would have been a great spot from which to have watched the Civil War clash of the *Monitor* and *Merrimac* ironclads. The Newport News Shipbuilding and Dry Dock Company built the passenger liner *United*

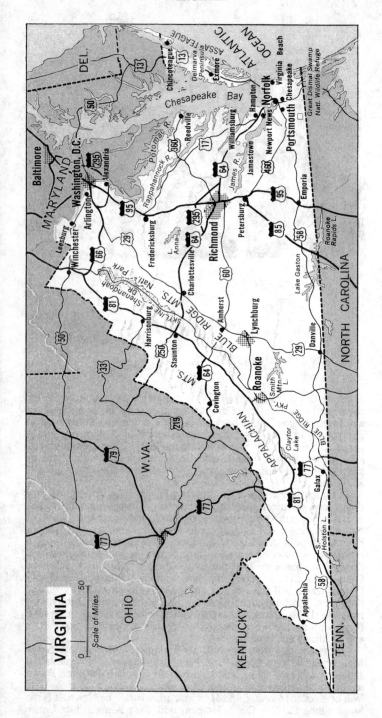

VIRGINIA

Scale of Miles

0   50

States and nuclear-powered aircraft carrier *Enterprise,* among others. Newport News also has the well-known Mariners Museum.

Jamestown—Williamsburg—Yorktown— The Historic Triangle

Three of America's most historic sites are linked by the Colonial Parkway. Jamestown, settled in 1607, was the first permanent English Settlement in the New World. Today only the old church tower and outlines of foundations remain. Adjacent to the historic site is Jamestown Festival Park with a reconstructed stockade, and full-size replicas of the three tiny ships that brought the first settlers.

A few miles away is Williamsburg, which became the Colonial capital in 1699. It is a living museum of restored and reconstructed 18th century buildings, many of which are open to the public. All visits to the area should begin at the Colonial Williamsburg Visitors' Center to see an interpretive film.

Yorktown should include a tour of the battlefields plus a visit to the National Park Service Visitor Center and the state-operated Yorktown Victory Center. In October 1781 the American and French forces defeated the British under Cornwallis, and ended British rule in the colonies.

The trip between Williamsburg and Richmond along Va. 5 passes through the historic James River plantation country. Among the great estates are: Sherwood Forest, the home of President John Tyler; Belle Air, one of America's oldest frame dwellings built in 1670; Colonel William Byrd II's plantation in Westover; Berkeley, ancestral home of Declaration of Independence signer Benjamin Harrison and his son, William Henry Harrison, the ninth U.S. President; and Shirley, the nine-generation home of the Carter family. East of Williamsburg, along US–60 E., is Carter's Grove, one of the most beautiful tidewater plantations.

Virginia's Northern Neck

Virginia's Northern Neck, lying between the Rappahannock and Potomac rivers, is noted for producing presidents, aside from its stately plantations. James Madison came from King George County and George Washington and James Monroe came from Westmoreland County, as did Robert E. Lee. Further along is Fredericksburg, a frequent target for both sides in the Civil War. In and around the area were bloody battles, including those at Chancellorsville, Wilderness, and Spotsylvania Court House. Further north is Mt. Vernon, the home of George Washington. Nearby is Gunston Hall, the home of George Mason. A visit to this area should also include historic Alexandria.

Richmond and Charlottesville

In Richmond the two most revered structures are the Capitol, designed by Thomas Jefferson, and St. John's Church, built in 1740–41, where Patrick Henry made his famous liberty-or-death speech to the Second Virginia Convention in 1775. Down the hill from St. John's is Richmond's oldest dwelling, the Old Stone House, built about 1737 and now a memorial to Edgar Allan Poe, who lived in Richmond for twenty-six years. Also see the house Chief Justice John Marshall built about 1790 and occupied until his death in 1835.

About sixty miles west of the Virginia capital is Charlottesville, which might be more appropriately named Jeffersonville. Jefferson's architectural accomplishments here include the University of Virginia campus and Monticello, his home which he spent 40 years building. Also here is Ash Lawn, the home of President James Monroe.

West of Charlottesville the character of the land changes, as perhaps does the character of the people. The Blue Ridge Mountains form the great divide in Virginia, with the Skyline Drive wriggling 105 miles along the range's backbone through Shenandoah National Park. At Rockfish Gap, near Afton, the scenic road becomes the Blue Ridge Parkway and winds 217 miles more to the North Carolina line. Beyond the Blue Ridge are the Allegheny Mountains and between the two ranges lies the Shenandoah Valley.

PRACTICAL INFORMATION FOR VIRGINIA

HOW TO GET THERE. *By car:* I–95 parallels US 1, runs north-south, passes through Washington, D.C., Richmond, and Petersburg. I–81 runs northeast-southwest in the western part of the state. I–64 and I–66 run east-west. US 13 gives direct access to the Tidewater area. Tolls at Chesapeake Bay Bridge-Tunnel.

By air: Washington, D.C., Richmond, Newport News (serving Williamsburg), Norfolk, Roanoke, Bristol, Charlottesville, Lynchburg, and Danville. Regular scheduled air service available to other cities in state.

By train: Amtrak serves Alexandria, Charlottesville, Culpeper, Danville, Fredericksburg, Lynchburg, Petersburg, Richmond. Also direct service to Williamsburg and Newport News.

By bus: Greyhound and *Trailways* throughout the state. A wide variety of motor coach tours to and through Virginia from many major cities in the Northeast. Consult your travel agent.

TOURIST INFORMATION. Virginia Division of Tourism, 202 N. Ninth St., Richmond, 23219, (804) 786–4484. Travel info is also available at 10 highway stations operated by the state along the Interstates.

MUSEUMS AND GALLERIES. In Richmond: *The Virginia Museum of Fine Arts,* the nation's first state-supported museum; *White House of the Confederacy; Edgar Allan Poe Museum;* and *Valentine Museum* for historic and costume treasures. *The Science Museum of Virginia* features a planetarium/space theater. In Newport News, the nationally known *Mariners Museum.* Norfolk has the *Hermitage Foundation Museum,* the *Chrysler Museum,* and the *Douglas MacArthur Memorial Museum.* Big Stone Gap has the *Southwest Virginia State Museum.* The *Abby Aldrich Rockefeller Folk Art Center* in Williamsburg has one of America's finest folk art collections.

HISTORIC SITES. *Alexandria:* Take a walking tour of Old Town that begins at the Ramsey House. This is George Washington's town, and many of the historic sights are associated with his life here. A short distance south via the George Washington Memorial Parkway is his estate, Mt. Vernon, overlooking the Potomac.

Appomattox: Where General Lee surrendered to General Ulysses S. Grant at McLean House on April 9, 1865.

Arlington: Arlington National Cemetery, with the Tomb of the Unknowns; the Iwo Jima Marine Corps Memorial; and the Pentagon (free tours) are military historical sights. Also see Arlington House, built by the adopted son of George Washington, and later the home of Robert E. Lee.

Charlottesville: Thomas Jefferson's Monticello; the University of Virginia; and Ash Lawn, James Monroe's country home.

Fredericksburg: Fredericksburg and Spotsylvania National Military Park encompasses four Civil War battlefields: Fredericksburg, Chancellorsville, the Wilderness, and Spotsylvania Court House.

Jamestown: A walking tour of the historic site includes an orientation at the visitor center operated by the National Park Service. Also visit Jamestown Festival Park and see the reconstructed fort, and the replicas of ships that brought the first settlers.

Norfolk: A marked tour route includes the Chrysler Museum, the General Douglas MacArthur Memorial, St. Paul's Church, and the Adam Thoroughgood House, the oldest brick house in America. Newest attraction is Waterside, a festival marketplace of over 120 shops, boutiques and eateries.

Petersburg: National Battlefield Park was the site of Lee's last stand before surrender at Appomattox where he underwent a 10-month siege in 1864–65.

Richmond: Capitol Square has the Capitol building designed by Jefferson with a life-size statue of George Washington. Nearby is Robert E. Lee's Civil War House. St. John's Church was the locale for Patrick Henry's liberty-or-death speech. Chief Justice John Marshall's house is also open for visiting.

Williamsburg: A tour of the restored and reconstructed colonial capital should begin with the movie "The Story of a Patriot" at the visitors' center. Highlights of a tour include the Capitol, the Governor's Palace, Bruton Parish Church, and the various craft shops and homes.

Yorktown: The battlegrounds where Cornwallis was defeated, ending the American Revolution. Start your tour at either of the two visitors' centers.

Historic churches dot the Virginia landscape: Trinity Church in Mathews County; St. Peter's Church in New Kent County, marriage house of George Washington and Martha Custis.

SPORTS. *Swimming* in the tidewater is superb. Atlantic coast communities such as Virginia Beach are summer resorts. Over 400 *golf* courses throughout the state. Virginia offers *riding* opportunities and horse shows and hunt club events. Licenses needed for freshwater *fishing* and *hunting*. Saltwater fishing at many towns. *Skiing* at: Mountain Run, Newmarket; Wintergreen, Massanutten near Harrisonburg; Cascade Mountain at Fancy Gap; Homestead, Hot Springs; Bryce Mountain.

DRINKING LAWS. Liquor sold through Alcoholic Beverage Commission stores unless prohibited by local option. Mixed drinks at licensed restaurants and hotels. Drinking age is 19 for beer, and 21 for all other drinks.

WHAT TO DO WITH THE CHILDREN. Jamestown, Williamsburg, and Yorktown have programs for children, with both historical and amusement value. State battlefields' features encourage climbing and touching of relics. Barter Playhouse at Abingdon schedules matinees and still swaps tickets for vittles, a custom from the Depression. There's an amusement park at Busch Gardens Old Country, Williamsburg. Kings Dominion near Ashland is a popular theme park, with rides, a scaled-down model of the Eiffel Tower, and a wild animal safari monorail. The Science Museum of Virginia in Richmond permits children to be involved with many of the exhibits.

HOTELS AND MOTELS. *Deluxe:* $40 and up; *Expensive:* $30–40; *Moderate:* $20–30; *Inexpensive:* below $20. (See also Washington, D.C., listings for suburban hotels in Northern Virginia.)

CHARLOTTESVILLE. *Deluxe:* **Boar's Head Inn.** On US 250, 296–2181. Pool, three restaurants, tennis, golf, sports club.

Expensive: **English Inn.** Junction Business 29 and US 29 and 250 Bypass, 971–9900. King suites with wet bars, exercise facility, sauna, airport limo.

Moderate: **Econo Lodge.** Two locations in town. Toll-free, 1–800–446–6900.

CHINCOTEAGUE. *Moderate:* **Mariner Motel.** Maddox Blvd. (Beach road), 336–6565. Largest in town, no pets.

FREDERICKSBURG. *Deluxe:* **Sheraton Fredericksburg Resort and Conference Center.** Va. 3 at I–95, 786–8321. Attractive rooms, balconies or patios, pool, tennis, golf, fishing pond.

NORFOLK *Deluxe:* **Omni International Hotel.** 777 Waterside Dr., 622–OMNI. On waterfront adjacent to Waterside festival marketplace.
Expensive: **Holiday Inn–Waterside Area/Downtown.** 700 Monticello Ave., 627–5555. Across street from convention center.
Quality Inn–Lake Wright. 6280 Northampton Blvd., 461–6251. Golf course, near airport, Tidewater Dinner Theater on property.
Moderate: **Econo Lodge.** Seven in area. Toll-free, 1–800–446–6900.

RICHMOND. *Deluxe:* **Commonwealth Park Hotel.** 9th and Bank Sts., 343–7300. Downtown location near the Capitol, all-suite hotel.
Hyatt Richmond. West Broad St. at I–64, 285–8666. In suburban Brookfield, two restaurants, cocktail lounge, indoor and outdoor pools.
Richmond Marriott. 5th and Broad Sts., 643–3400. Indoor pool, sun deck, saunas, accessible rooms for handicapped.
Expensive: **John Marshall Hotel.** Franklin and 5th Sts., 644–4661. Near downtown department stores and shops.
Moderate: **Econo Lodge.** Four in area. Toll-free, 1–800–446–6900.

VIRGINIA BEACH. *Deluxe:* **Hilton Inn.** 8th St. and Oceanfront, 428–8935. All rooms face ocean, indoor and outdoor pools, HBO.
Expensive: **Princess Anne Inn.** 25th St. and Oceanfront, 428–5611. Indoor heated pool, sauna, earth station satellite receiver for TV.
Moderate: **Econo Lodge.** Five in area. Toll-free, 1–800–446–6000.

WILLIAMSBURG. *Deluxe:* **Williamsburg Inn.** Francis St. in historic area. Swimming, golf, tennis.
Expensive: **Williamsburg Lodge.** South England St. near historic area.
Moderate: **King William Inn,** 824 Capitol Landing Road, 229–4933. (Toll-free, 1–800–446–1041, eastern US). Handicapped rooms available.
Motor House. Near Visitor Center. Operated by Colonial Williamsburg. Toll-free, 1–800–446–8956 (US) 1–800–582–8976 (Va.).
Inexpensive: **Motel 6.** 3030 Richmond Rd. (US 60), 565–2710. Near historic area.

CHARLOTTESVILLE. *Expensive:* **The Ivy Inn.** 2244 Old Ivy Rd. 977–1222. Steamed seafood kettle a specialty.
Moderate: **Historic Michie Tavern.** Rte. 53, Monticello Mountain 977–1234. Southern fried chicken featured. Lunch only.

NORFOLK. *Deluxe:* **Ship's Cabin.** 4110 East Ocean View Ave. 583–4659. Hampton Road's most acclaimed seafood restaurant.
Expensive: **Le Charlieu.** 112 College Pl. 623–7202. Intimate atmosphere, French cuisine.

RICHMOND. *Expensive:* **Tobacco Company Restaurant.** 12th and Cary Sts. 782–9555. Victorian décor in a restored warehouse.
Moderate: **Bill's Barbecue.** Seven locations, 353–2757. Established in 1930. Serves minced pork and beef barbecue sandwiches.
New York Delicatessen. 2929 W. Cary St. 355–6056. A Richmond tradition for 30 years. Heaping corned beef, pastrami sandwiches.

VIRGINIA BEACH. *Expensive:* **The Lighthouse.** 1st St. and Oceanfront. 428–9851. Fresh seafood specialties.
Inexpensive: **Morrison's Cafeteria.** West on US 58, two miles from ocean at 1532 Laskin Rd. 422–4755.

WILLIAMSBURG. *Deluxe:* **Regency Dining Room.** In Williamsburg Inn. Continental food and regional American specialties.
Expensive: **Cascades.** Adjacent to Motor House. American fare.

King's Arms Tavern. Duke of Gloucester St. in historic area. Virginia ham, lamb, and fried chicken featured. Waiters in period costumes.

The Trellis. In Merchant's Square. 229–8610. Regional American cuisine prepared with fresh ingredients; served in contemporary setting.

Moderate: **Christiana Campbell's Tavern.** Waller St. in historic area. Seafood specialties. George Washington's favorite eating place in Williamsburg.

Josiah Chowning's Tavern. Duke of Gloucester St. in historic area. Brunswick stew, Welsh rarebit, ribs, and roast beef. Special evening entertainment "gambols."

Inexpensive: **Motor House Cafeteria.** At visitors' center.

(Above are operated by Colonial Williamsburg. Reservations for all are highly recommended. 229–2141, or toll-free 800–446–8956 (US) or 800–582–8976 (Va.)

YORKTOWN *Moderate:* **Nick's Seafood Pavilion.** Water St. at York river. 887–5269. Seafood, steaks, and chops cooked to order.

WASHINGTON, D.C.

Favorite Tourist Target

Start a Washington walking tour—and leisurely walking is by far the best way to explore this city—from Lafayette Square directly in front of the White House. Bear in mind, however, that covering the vast distances outlined in the suggested walking tour may be practical for only the most intrepid (and fit) hiker. By all means consider riding the Tourmobile to cover at least a part of your downtown explorations. The new Metro subway route is also worthy of study. (See more details in the *Practical Information* section below.) Whatever you decide to do, obtain a good map to help you plot your route.

Named for the Marquis de Lafayette, the French nobleman who served at the side of General Washington, the square is dominated by an equestrian statue (sometimes called the "hobby horse") of Andrew Jackson, an exact duplicate of one facing St. Louis Cathedral in Jackson Square in New Orleans. Lafayette's statue, in the southeast corner, is just one of four standing on each corner of the square. Circling the square clockwise you then find the statues of three other Revolutionary War heroes who came from other lands: Rochambeau, commander of all French troops, particularly recognized for his help at the decisive last battle of Yorktown; Baron von Steuben, the Prussian drillmaster; and Thaddeus Kosciusko, the dashing Polish nobleman, who gained fame at the crucial Battle of Saratoga. The short street on the west side of the square is named Jackson Place. (That on the east is Madison Place.) Whatever the speculations about the name, it's a most pleasant little park, one on which National Capital Parks gardeners lavish much care.

At the National Geographic Society headquarters, 1145 17th St., N.W., is the society's Explorers Hall, a permanent exhibition that tells the story of 75 years of adventure and discovery by more than 200 pioneering expeditions in many fields and many lands. The society's building is the work of Edward Durell Stone, who also is the architect of the Kennedy Center for the Performing Arts. His building for the National Geographic Society is among Washington's most distinguished non-government buildings. It's only about five blocks north of Lafayette Square, a pleasant stroll up 16th St. which takes you first to St. John's Church, called the "Church of the Presidents" because every president, starting with Madison, has attended it. It's a beautiful little church, erected in 1816 from a design by Benjamin Latrobe, and now almost dwarfed by the big buildings around it. Across the street is one of Washington's more gracious small hotels, the Hay-Adams, occupying the site where once lived Henry Adams, historian son and grandson of two presidents, and John Hay, biographer of Lincoln and Secretary of State at the turn of the century.

Welcome to the White House

Probably the first of the great Washington attractions in which you will wish to spend time is the White House, just south of Lafayette Square. The line for the regular tours (10 A.M. to noon, Tuesday through Saturday, until 2 P.M. through the summer) sometimes extends for hundreds of yards. During the peak spring and summer seasons visitors must obtain an entrance ticket for a specific time, obtainable at the visible tent on the Ellipse on the south side of the White House. Should you wish to wait there, you will be provided with entertainment and a place to sit. The yearly total of visitors is more than 1.5 million. Tourists are taken through only the public ground-floor rooms. The presidential living quarters are on the second and third floors, and tourists do not see the offices, the kitchens, press room, and so on.

What you do see are the most famous rooms. The East Room, the largest of all, is a lofty, dignified salon of white and gold with touches of blue. It is associated with splendid and solemn events: weddings and funerals, receptions and small concerts or recitals. President John Adams' wife, Abigail, hung her laundry in it. Today it is mainly the public audience chamber, one of the most beautiful rooms in the world since the complete White House restoration of 1948–1952.

The Green Room, named for the wall coverings of moss-green watered silk, is done in a graceful and delicate American Federal style. It's a fashionable parlor such as Adams or Jefferson might have known. Furniture includes a particularly striking New England sofa, originally the property of Daniel Webster. Especially interesting is the portrait of Benjamin Franklin by the Scottish artist David Martin, painted in London in 1767.

The oval-shaped Blue Room was designed as the most elegant architectural feature of the President's house. The White House's first wedding took place here when President Grover Cleveland married Frances Folsom in 1886. Portraits of several of the early Presidents are on display here.

The Red Room, called the "President's Ante-Chamber" in the original plans, is hung in cerise silk with gold scroll borders and is furnished as an Empire parlor of the early nineteenth century. One touch many visitors like is a little music stand near the fireplace which holds a copy of a lively air, "Lafayette's March," dating from the room's architectural era, which was written to honor the Marquis on his triumphal tour of America in 1825.

The State Dining Room, second largest in the White House, is used for official luncheons and dinners. Much of the design is English Regency, with a mantel decorated with carved buffalo heads. One hundred and forty guests may be seated here for lunch or dinner.

As you leave the White House note the great variety of old trees. It was on the lawn in front of this entrance that the Israeli-Egyptian Peace Treaty was signed by Premier Menachem Begin and President Anwar Sadat on March 26, 1979. Across Pennsylvania Ave. you will see Blair House, the official guest house of the President. It is here that visiting heads of state stay when on a visit to Washington. President Truman and his family lived here from 1948–52 during the $5,800,000 renovation of the White House, after the discovery that the venerable mansion was "standing up purely from habit."

The Washington Monument

Waiting for the elevator at the Washington Monument is a likelihood during most of the year, but in summer tickets may be obtained from the nearby kiosk for a specific time. Winter hours are from 9 to 5; summer hours are 8 to midnight. You may no longer walk up the 898 steps, but you can walk down them, and many do so. The 555-foot shaft, believed to be the tallest masonry structure in the world, is the dominant landmark in the city. It stands straight and clean against the skyline and can be seen from almost any direction. It's almost due south of the White House and a pleasant few minutes' stroll around the Ellipse and across Constitution Ave.

The monument grounds are a particularly splendid sight on a bright, breezy day when the 50 "Star-Spangled Banners" surrounding it spank briskly in the wind. The big view is from the top of the monument—the "eye of the needle"—but there are also splendid vistas of the city from the knoll on which it stands. The elevator ride up takes only a minute, but the National Park Service takes advantage of that time to give you a capsule lecture about the monument. You are told, for instance, why there is a sharp change in the color of stone about a third of the way up the shaft: work stopped for more than 25 years when the money ran out amid religious controversy whipped up by the antipapist Know-Nothing Party.

Many of the blocks of stone in the monument were contributed by states, foreign governments, or organizations. You may read the inscriptions on the inside faces of the stones if you walk down the stairs. On summer evenings, free concerts and dramatic shows are presented in the Sylvan Theater on the south slope of the monument grounds.

The Washington Monument is the centerpiece of Washington's grandest vista, the axis of its grand design. To the east is the great, green corridor of the Mall, sweeping to the Capitol. To the west across the Reflecting Pool, bearing the shimmering image of the monument's soaring shaft, is the Doric Parthenon of the Lincoln Memorial.

In the northwest corner of Constitution Gardens—a 45-acre park bounded by Constitution Avenue and the Reflecting Pool—stands the Vietnam Veterans Memorial. Dedicated on November 13, 1982, the stunning but minimal design is that of a 21-year-old Yale architecture student, Maya Lin. The simple, V-shaped, black granite wall, descending into the ground, is etched with the names of the 57,692 Americans who died in the war. A 50-foot-high staff flying the American flag and an eight-foot high bronze statue of three U.S. infantrymen provide an "entranceway" to the Memorial.

The Lincoln and Jefferson Memorials

About the Lincoln Memorial, Roger Angell wrote of the "tired, infinitely distant eyes" of Lincoln and of the "great hands" and of "the soft light falling through the marble ceiling." The best time to visit the Lincoln Memorial, many agree, is late on a rainy night when you are likely to be alone with your thoughts, but Washingtonians urge visitors to go to the Memorial both by night, when it is floodlighted, and by sunlight. As at the Washington Monument, you have a magnificent view—in one direction back across the Reflecting Pool and the Mall; in the other, the fabled Potomac River and the Arlington Memorial Bridge. In a direct line is another memorable specimen of the Doric— Arlington House, also called the Custis-Lee Mansion, home of Robert E. Lee, high on a hill in Arlington National Cemetery. Just below the mansion, before the leaves are in full leaf, the eternal flame which marks the grave of President John F. Kennedy may be seen.

From the Lincoln Memorial it's another good hike across West Potomac Park to the Tidal Basin, famed for its flowering Japanese cherry trees, which usually bloom in early April. Just off Independence Avenue and before crossing Kutz Bridge you will see a Japanese stone lantern, which is lighted each spring by a lady from the Japanese Embassy to begin the Cherry Blossom Festival. Around the basin to the east, swan boats may be rented. On the south shore of the basin stands the Jefferson Memorial. The exterior and the setting of this John Russell Pope classic are superlative. The Memorial was built in the Pantheon form which Jefferson himself favored in designing his own Monticello and the University of Virginia rotunda. Its rounded form accents the spire of the Washington Monument to the north and the rectangular perfection of the Lincoln Memorial, which forms the other apex of the triangle of monuments to the west.

A tour for another day, again beginning at Lafayette Square, takes you down one side of the Mall to the Capitol and brings you back along the other side. Before you start out on the long walk, though, you might just take a look across Jackson Place at one of the few original private homes still facing Lafayette Square. It's Decatur House, once occupied by the naval hero who originated the toast, ". . . may she always be in the right; but our country, right or wrong." Henry Clay and Martin Van Buren, later the eighth president, also lived there. The main section of the house and a small naval museum in the rear are open to the public. A bit west of the square and facing Pennsylvania Ave. is Blair House, now the presidential guest house but not open to the public. Next door is the Renwick Gallery, the Smithsonian's showcase of American decorative arts and design. Visitors will delight in seeing the mauve Victorian gallery on the second floor, with its oriental rugs, formal furniture, potted palms, and paintings of the 19th century. This building served as the original Corcoran Gallery, which is now located a few blocks south at 17th and E streets. During the Civil War many Union Soldiers were hospitalized here.

Treasury Ruins the Plan

Heading toward the Capitol from the White House area, you come first to the Treasury building, built in 1842 and the oldest of the government department buildings. When Andrew Jackson designated its site next to the White House, he disrupted the L'Enfant plan, which provided that Pennsylvania Ave., the city's main ceremonial street, should lead directly from the Capitol to the White House. As a result of this, inaugural and other parades must dogleg around the Treasury Building. On either side of the building are statues of two famous early secretaries of the treasury: Alexander Hamilton, the first of them, on the south side; Albert Gallatin on the north. A new museum tracing the history of the Bureau of Alcohol, Tobacco, and Firearms from

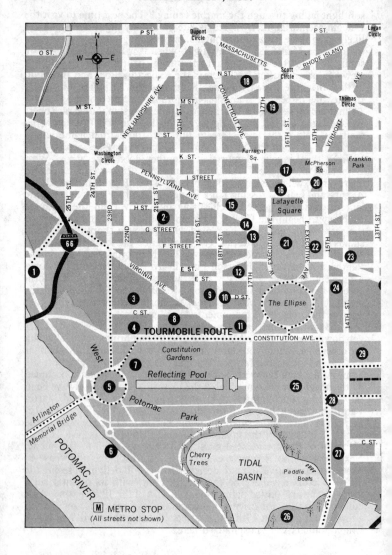

Points of Interest

1) Blair House
2) Botanical Gardens
3) Bureau of Printing & Engraving
4) Capitol
5) Constitution Hall (DAR)
6) Corcoran Art Gallery
7) Department of Energy
8) Department of Interior
9) Department of Justice
10) Department of State
11) Executive Office Building
12) FBI (J.E. Hoover Building)
13) Federal Reserve Board
14) Ford's Theater
15) Freer Gallery of Art
16) George Washington University
17) Government Printing Office
18) Hirshhorn Museum & Sculpture Garden
19) House Office Bldgs.
20) Jefferson Memorial
21) John F. Kennedy Center
22) Library of Congress
23) Lincoln Memorial
24) National Museum of American History
25) National Academy of Sciences
26) National Air & Space Museum
27) National Archives

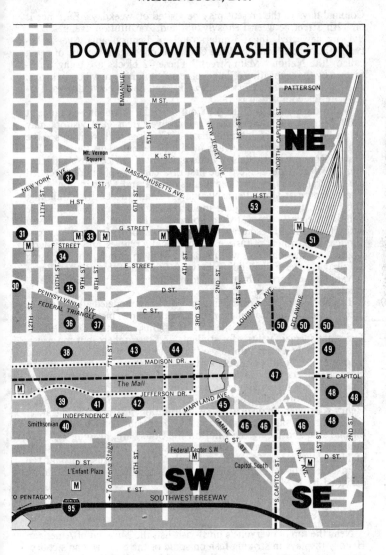

DOWNTOWN WASHINGTON

28) National Collection of American Art & National Portrait Gallery
29) National Gallery of Art
30) East Wing, National Gallery of Art
31) National Geographic Society
32) National Theater
33) National Museum of Natural History
34) Organization of American States
35) Post Office
36) Renwick Gallery
37) St. John's Church
38) St. Matthew's Cathedral
39) Senate Office Buildings
40) Smithsonian Institution
41) Supreme Court
42) Sylvan Theater
43) Treasury Department
44) Union Station
45) Veterans' Administration
46) Washington Convention & Visitors Association
47) Washington Monument
48) White House
49) Vietnam Veterans Memorial
50) Washington, D.C. Convention Center
51) Metro Center
52) Department of Commerce Visitors Center

Colonial days to the present may be visited on weekdays. Entrance is on 12th Street between Pennsylvania and Constitution avenues.

Long neglected, the 1.3-mile stretch of Pennsylvania Avenue between the White House and the Capitol is once again worthy of being called "the Nation's Main Street." These 22 blocks are being transformed by the renovation of handsome old buildings, new hotels, shops, and restaurants, kiosks, brick sidewalks, and newly planted trees. Target date for completion is 1990.

Walk south on 15th St. to the Commerce Department's entrance at 1400 Pennsylvania Ave. In the impressive Great Hall visitors may obtain helpful sightseeing information. Children will want to see the fish in the National Aquarium in the basement. The Patent Office Search Room, with models of famous patented devices, also intrigues many visitors. Commerce is the first of a complex of buildings called the Federal Triangle, between Pennsylvania and Constitution Aves. The others, east along Pennsylvania Ave., are the District Building, housing District of Columbia municipal offices; the old Post Office building, recently renovated to house The Pavilion, a tourist haven with 50 shops and restaurants; Labor Department; Internal Revenue Service; Department of Justice; the National Archives; and the Federal Trade Commission. You will probably want to stop by the imposing J. Edgar Hoover FBI Building, between 9th and 10th streets on Pennsylvania Ave., for the hour-long tour emphasizing the past achievements of the Bureau.

The National Archives, a handsome building modeled after the Pantheon, houses America's most precious documents, including the Declaration of Independence, the Bill of Rights, and the Constitution. There are special facilities for students and researchers, but most visitors make only a brief stop to see the documents, which are protected by one of the world's most elaborate burglar-alarm systems. Sealed in glass containers filled with inert gas, they also are protected against deterioration. Of special interest is a copy of former President Richard Nixon's 11-word letter of resignation addressed to Secretary of State Henry Kissinger, on display at the information desk near the entrance.

On the south side of Constitution Ave., opposite the Federal Triangle on one side and facing the Mall on the other, are, heading east, the Smithsonian's Museum of American History; the venerable Museum of Natural History, formerly called the National Museum; and the handsome National Gallery of Art with its stunning new East Building designed by I. M. Pei.

The Biggest Elephant

Near the top of everyone's must-visit list, the Museum of American History displays in striking fashion some of the Smithsonian's collections, including the famous collection of first ladies' inaugural gowns and the original American flag, which Francis Scott Key so proudly hailed flying from Port McHenry during the War of 1812. In the great rotunda of the Museum of Natural History stands the biggest elephant of record, 13 feet high, killed in Africa in 1955. This museum also houses the 44½-carat Hope Diamond, largest blue diamond in the world, and a fabled 330-carat sapphire, plus the gold nugget found by James Marshall that launched the 1848 California gold rush. The National Museum of American Art (formerly the National Collection of Fine Arts), once housed here, has been moved to the fine old Patent Office Building at 8th and G Sts. N.W., also housing the National Portrait Gallery.

The finest collection of art in Washington—and one of the very best in the world—is in the National Gallery of Art, completed in 1941, and designed by John Russell Pope. The beautiful rose-white marble building and one of the collections within it was the gift of Andrew Mellon, the Pittsburgh financier who was Secretary of the Treasury under Hoover. It also houses the collections of Dale, Kress, and Widener. Corridors from the great rotunda lead to some 100 exhibit halls. Sightseers often plan their tours so as to have lunch at the dazzling new cafeteria located between the original Gallery and the new East Building. A favorite time for Washingtonians is Sunday evening (except during the summer months), when visitors may also enjoy the free concerts of the National Gallery Orchestra under its permanent conductor, the composer-musicologist Richard Bales. Probably the most famous single painting in the gallery is Leonardo da Vinci's "Ginevra de Benci," but it also contains great works from almost all the great European schools and is strong in French Impressionists as a result of the Chester Dale bequest. Across Constitution Ave. from the Gallery splashes one of the simplest but loveliest of Washington's many fountains, a memorial to Andrew Mellon, who gave Washington its richest gift. Just east of the Gallery is the new annex designed by I. M. Pei, and constructed of the same rose-white marble as the original National Gallery. Opened in October 1978, this building has become one of the city's prime tourist attractions.

Heading on east along Constitution Ave. you'll almost have reached Capitol Hill. At the very foot of the hill, at the eastern end of the Mall is one of the biggest statuary groupings in the country, the Grant Memorial. The bronze of General Grant is said to be the second largest equestrian statue in the world, topped only by the one of Victor Emmanuel in Rome, and that by only a half an inch. Also at the western foot of the hill are statues of President Garfield and Chief Justice John Marshall. At Constitution Ave. and 1st St. stands the memorial to Senator Robert A. Taft, a 100-foot-high bell tower, with a solitary bronze figure of Taft at its base. You may hear the pleasing chimes toll the quarter hour.

Capitol Hill itself encompasses not only the 131 acres of the Capitol grounds, but in general terms also includes the two Senate Office Buildings to the north of it, the three House Office Buildings to the south, the Library of Congress and Supreme Court to the east, plus the surrounding residential and business area, which includes a half-dozen hotels. At the northernmost edge is the monumental Union Station, now being converted back to its original purpose, that of a rail terminal and gateway for passengers arriving in the nation's capital.

The Capitol—Monument on a Pedestal

L'Enfant, a French engineer who served under Washington in the Revolutionary War, selected what was then called Jenkins' Hill as the Capitol site, calling it "a pedestal waiting for a monument." Today it holds some of the country's most important buildings. The 535 members of Congress who convene in its two houses are served by more than 7,500 staff employees. The Capitol is a complicated labyrinth and few indeed are the native Washingtonians who can find their way easily about. Conducted tours through the building lasting 40 minutes are given from 9 A.M. to 5 P.M. in summer, 9 A.M. to 3:30 P.M. the rest of the year. Tours leave from the Rotunda every few minutes. There is no charge. Tight security measures are in effect here as well as other government buildings, so be prepared to open pocketbooks, briefcases, etc.

The Capitol building is 751 feet long, 350 wide, and from the base to the top of the Statue of Freedom on the dome it is 287 feet high. The 19-foot-high statue itself looks roughly like Pocahontas but the sculptor, Thomas Crawford, who did his work in Rome, said he had a freed Roman slave in mind. The cast-iron dome on which she stands weighs 4,455 tons, and engineers say it expands and contracts according to outside temperatures as much as four inches a day.

The most impressive room in the Capitol is the Rotunda under the great dome. As you stand in the Rotunda look up at Constantino Brumidi's fresco glorifying Washington. Although some of the figures are 15 feet tall, they appear life-sized from below. Directly below is the spot where most recently the flag-draped caskets of Presidents John F. Kennedy, Dwight Eisenhower, Lyndon B. Johnson, and Senator Hubert H. Humphrey lay in state as have those of other statesmen and honored servants of the republic, as a mark of the nation's esteem. The dome rises to 180 feet above the Rotunda's floor. It was in the Rotunda that President Ronald Reagan took the oath of office on January 21, 1985 for his second term.

The 10-ton bronze "Columbus Doors" leading to the Rotunda are masterworks portraying the story of Columbus' discovery. Of the eight huge oil paintings hanging on the walls by far the most important are those done by John Trumbull, aide-de-camp to General Washington. They are: The Declaration of Independence; The Surrender of Lord Cornwallis; the Surrender of General Burgoyne at Saratoga; and George Washington Resigning His Commission. "My one ambition," Brumidi wrote, "is that I may live long enough to make beautiful the Capitol of the one country on earth in which there is liberty." He was only able to complete a third of his 300-foot-long circular frieze, however, before he died after a fall from the scaffold. A pupil, Filippo Costaggini, took eight years to complete eight other sketches left by Brumidi. The final gap in the frieze wasn't completed, however, until 1953, by Allyn Cox. The frieze depicts scenes from American history. Brumidi fell as he was painting Penn's treaty with the Indians. The last scene painted was the Wright Brothers' first powered flight in 1903.

From the Rotunda the next stop is Statuary Hall; it was originally the legislative chamber of the House of Representatives. It is renowned for its reverberating acoustics. A slight whisper uttered in one part of the hall may be heard distinctly across it, a phenomenon which delights modern tourists much more than it did the legislators. When Statuary Hall was set up, each state was invited to contribute two statues of native sons or daughters they considered sufficiently worthy of the honor. Their weight, however, strained the beams supporting the floor, and now there's a limitation of one favorite son per state within the hall. The other statues have been placed in the Hall of Columns or elsewhere in the building. Just outside Statuary Hall is a statue of Will Rogers, the humorist who gained fame making jokes at Congress' expense. Below the recently renovated old Senate chamber is the original Supreme Court chamber.

The single art work which probably amuses visitors the most is in the crypt. It's an eight-ton block of marble, topped by the heads of three stern-visaged 19th-century ladies, a trio of suffragettes, Lucretia Mott, Elizabeth Cady, and Susan B. Anthony. The statuary is irreverently nicknamed "Ladies in a Bathtub."

America's Most Famous Bean Soup

Should you wish to watch Congress in session, from either the House or Senate gallery, for longer than the few minutes allowed on your escorted tour, you need a pass from a congressman or senator. While getting the passes you might also obtain permission to lunch in one of the Capitol restaurants, where the bean soup has been a popular specialty for years. It's made and served every day by special order of

Congress! A must for every young visitor to the Capitol is to ride on one of the subways connecting the Capitol with the Senate and House office buildings on either side. If you wish to watch a congressional committee meeting—and they, incidentally, are often more interesting and livelier than what transpires in the actual legislative sessions—watch the morning newspaper for a listing of the meetings, specifying which ones are public. Taxpayers who have a penchant for snorting in righteous indignation particularly like to look over the Sam Rayburn House Office Building, which cost about $75 million, as compared with a total $12 million spent for the first two.

You'll hear less indignation about another expanding institution on the Hill, the Library of Congress. It all began with a $5,000 appropriation in the early 1800s to stock one room in the Capitol. Now it's generally believed to be the largest and most important library in the world with over 75 million items on 332 miles of bookshelves covering 35 acres of floor space. It offers both permanent and special exhibitions of manuscripts and documents. An unusual feature is the Coolidge Auditorium endowed concert series. Some of these concerts are played on the library's collection of rare Stradivarius instruments. The library's musicology section also has one of the world's finest collections of folk-music recordings. The original building is of ornate Italian Renaissance design with an interesting copper dome and Neptune Fountain outside. The annex is of severe, functional modern design. The huge marble James Madison Memorial Building to the south, opened in 1980, makes room for the continuing expansion of knowledge. A handsome building just around the corner at 201 E. Capitol Street S.E. is the Folger Shakespeare Library, containing the largest Shakespearian collection in the world. It also has a model of the Globe Theater, in which many of Shakespeare's plays were first performed in 17th-century London, plus a large exhibition gallery with a wide assortment of Elizabethan-era relics. You may attend a play presented by the Folger Theatre Group, but plan ahead—tickets are hard to come by.

Just north of the Library of Congress on 1st St. is the Supreme Court Building. It is impressive in a way beyond anything else on Capitol Hill. Designed by Cass Gilbert and constructed of the whitest of white marble, its rows of Corinthian pillars and its sculptured pediment look much as the proudest temples in Rome must have appeared when those temples were gleaming new and Rome was in her glory. The Court meeting inside is equally impressive in a way even the Senate could never be. Visit here if you can when the Court is in session, arriving early enough for the opening ceremonials at 10 A.M. to hear the ancient call of the bailiff crying: "Oyez, oyez, oyez . . . ," as the black-robed figures of the Supreme Court justices file in one by one, intoning, "God save the United States and this Honorable Court." The best day of the week to visit the Supreme Court from a standpoint of excitement is Monday, which is "Decision Day." You could very well be present when an important decision is announced. Note that the court is in recess from June to October. Tours, however, are conducted during this period.

From the Supreme Court retrace your route back 1st St. S.E. to Independence Ave., turn right and stroll down past the three House Office Buildings (Cannon, Longworth, and Rayburn), and just beyond 1st St. S.W. see the U.S. Botanic Gardens, the favorite spot on the Hill for all who take their gardening seriously.

Just across Independence Ave. from the gardens is the graceful bronze Bartholdi Fountain, a creation of F. Auguste Bartholdi, sculptor of the Statue of Liberty.

Strolling west on Independence Ave., you pass the Department of Health and Human Services. It's a modern building without much character, but inside, on its second floor, is the Voice of America of the U.S. International Communication Agency. (Main office of the information agency, appropriately, is at 1776 Pennsylvania Ave., N.W.) The Voice of America broadcasts in 37 languages over a network of 114 transmitters. You can get an excellent idea of its operation in a 40-minute tour. Beyond it, heading west, are the National Aeronautics and Space Administration and the Department of Transportation. They are part of an extensive new southwest complex of buildings resulting from redevelopment.

The Smithsonian

Walk another block west, and across the street you'll see the towers and turrets of Washington's most interesting architectural curiosity—and one of its most cherished treasures—the main building of the Smithsonian Institution, built in 1852 with funds willed by Englishman James Smithson, who had never even seen America. The institution now administers numerous divisions ranging from the adjacent Freer Gallery of Art to the National Zoological Park (Washington Zoo, Connecticut Ave. at Cathedral Ave., N.W.). In the great Main Hall of the Smithsonian are exhibits showing the great scope of the Institution's work. The Smithsonian has been called "the nation's attic," and it contains, at last count, something over 70 million catalogued items. In the Smithsonian's new $41 million National Air and Space Museum are the two exhibits that most visitors wish to see: the Wright Brothers' plane, the 1903 *Flyer,* the first heavier-than-air machine to fly; and Charles Lindbergh's *Spirit of St. Louis,* the little monoplane in which he made that historic New York-to-Paris nonstop flight, which charted the way for today's commuter-like world-spanning jets. (Later Orville Wright nicknamed the first plane the "Kitty Hawk.") Allow some extra time to see the remarkable film *Living Planet* and *To Fly* shown about every 45 minutes. Charge is 50 cents for adults, 25 cents for children. A filmed flight-oriented tour of America's history is projected onto a giant screen, and six-track stereo with eleven speakers makes an indelible impression on your hearing and memory. In the Albert Einstein Spacearium, *"Cosmic Awakening"* will show how the human concept of the universe has changed over the past 200 years, and how it is likely to change in the next century.

The most talked about art collection in Washington for a while will probably be that of the Hirshhorn Museum and Sculpture Garden. Although it houses what has been called one of the world's finest collections of modern art, the round building at the east of the Smithsonian group has been dubbed "The Doughnut" by nearby office workers. Whether or not you are an aficionado of contemporary sculpture you will enjoy the works of art in the outdoor sculpture garden, with its charming reflecting pool and delightful vistas of the other Smithsonian buildings on the Mall.

On the far western side of the Smithsonian Mall complex the small but elegant Freer Gallery is famed for two quite contrasting collections. In one section are art treasures from the Near and Far East—Japanese screen paintings, sculptures in ivory, jades, and bronzes. And there are rare Greek, Aramaic, and Armenian biblical manuscripts. The other collection is of paintings by Americans, and it includes probably the world's finest collection of the works of James McNeill Whistler, who worked as a draftsman in Washington for the U.S. Coast and Geodetic Survey before moving on to London and Paris, where he achieved fame as an artist. Perhaps the most fascinating thing in the gallery is the Peacock Room, moved bodily from London, where Whistler designed it for a shipbuilder. The gallery and most of the collections in it were a gift of Charles Freer, a Detroit industrialist.

Just south of Independence Ave. at the point where 10th St. normally would be, you may make an interesting diversion via L'Enfant Promenade. Begin by walking under the Forrestal Building, a modern building on concrete stilts straddling the promenade. Cross the main line of railroads headed for their Potomac River crossing, then you're at the edge of L'Enfant Plaza, a handsome quadrangle of buildings fronting on a large square with a dancing fountain. Here are offices of such quasigovernmental outfits as Comsat, the U.S. Postal Service, and Amtrak. The bottom two floors and top three of the East Building are occupied by one of Washington's very newest hotels, Loew's L'Enfant Plaza. You can stroll on to the edge of the promenade overlooking the Potomac River and then on down to the riverfront, where a handsome array of new restaurants is finally open for business to replace the much-beloved (but smelly) waterfront markets and restaurants of an earlier era. After refreshment at one of the seafood restaurants you're strong enough to continue your stroll back up to Independence Avenue.

It's been said that only a born bureaucrat could love the Department of Agriculture Buildings, which span Independence Ave. between 12th and 14th Sts., N.W. The "Bridges of Sighs" over the avenue, however, are rather interesting to see, and there are generally agricultural exhibits in the patio of the administration building.

Making Money—by the Bushel

Of more interest is the structure just across 14th St., S.W., although the building isn't nearly so pretty. This is the Bureau of Engraving and Printing, where the government designs, engraves, and prints paper money, bonds, and stamps. It is said that the face value of money printed here averages some $40 million a day. You can actually see the money being printed from the visitors' gallery.

If you've done this tour-around-Mall in one day (and a lot of people do), you probably will want to soak your feet in hot water rather than go out on the town that night. You'll still, however, have seen only a part of Washington.

Back on your bench in Lafayette Square again, map yourself a tour to Foggy Bottom and Georgetown in the morning and wind up with a tour of "Embassy Row" in the afternoon.

From the square walk west on Pennsylvania Ave., then turn left on 17th St. past what is now called the Executive Office Building. This was originally called the War, Navy, and State Building, and all three of these important departments were housed here until the Pentagon was built. Patterned after the great Louvre Museum in Paris, it was built in 1875. Those who work in the Executive Office Building like it even more because of the high ceilings and general feeling of spaciousness. Because of security it is not open to tourists. Here are housed the offices of the Vice President, assistants to the President and commissions working on special projects for the President.

Just south and across the street is the Corcoran Gallery of Art, built by and named for a Washington banker, who endowed it in 1897 in the hopes of encouraging American artists. Its largest collection is of American sculpture, paintings, and other works from the 18th-century to the 20th. The Corcoran is best known for its Biennial Exhibition of contemporary American painting.

Continuing on south on 17th St. you'll find the headquarters of the American Red Cross in an appropriately gleaming white building. The Red Cross Museum tells the story of this humanitarian organization's worldwide activities. In the courtyard is the statue of a nurse, a memorial to the hundreds of nurses who were killed serving in World War I. There is also a Tiffany window of glowing colors on the second floor.

Another block south is the national headquarters of the Daughters of the American Revolution, whose annual convention is a Washington feature each spring. Memorial Continental Hall faces 17th St. between C and D Sts., N.W. Connected to it but facing 18th St. is Constitution Hall, seating almost 4,000, where most of Washington's major concerts were held before construction of the Kennedy Center. Continental Hall contains one of the largest genealogical libraries in the world, and you might go there to look up your own family tree—for a fee. There are also an historic museum and 28 period rooms representing various states.

Along 17th St. the Pan American Union also faces Constitution Ave. This is the headquarters of the Organization of American States, representing 21 American republics. It is the oldest international organization in the world. The building's interior patio maintains a year-round tropical atmosphere. Lush trees and plants from South and Central America grace the patio, and in the center is a lovely fountain in the Spanish-American manner. In the rear of the building is still another garden, centering around a statue of the Aztec god of flowers, Xochipilli. There is also a Hall of Heroes containing busts of the founders of the American republics and other heroes. You may also take a look at the impressive council meeting room, and don't miss the exhibitions in the Museum of Modern Art of Latin America. Entrance is at 201 18th St., N.W.

Bolivar, the Liberator

From Constitution Ave., you turn north again on 18th St. In a small triangular park on your left is a handsome statue of Simon Bolivar, liberator of many South American republics. North of this is the Interior Department Building, which covers two blocks between 18th and 19th, C and E Sts. Besides a museum, explaining the work of the entire department, the building contains a most interesting craft shop displaying and selling works of American Indians—pottery, jewelry, rugs, etc. Just north of the building is Rawlins Park, which is one of Washington's loveliest jewel-like parks, especially beautiful when its tulip-tree magnolias are in bloom, generally in late March. In the center its pool is filled with water lilies.

Facing Rawlins Park to the northeast is Octagon House, which served as the temporary White House in 1814-15 for President James Madison and his wife, Dolley, after the British burned the White House. Actually, the building has not eight sides, as its name implies, but six! It and an adjoining new building are the national headquarters of the American Institute of Architects, which offers guided tours daily except Monday and has interesting exhibits on the development of architecture.

Going east from Rawlins Square along E St., you cross Virginia Ave. and enter a section called Foggy Bottom because of the mists from the nearby Potomac River. Here, at 2201 C St., now stands the second largest building belonging to the U.S. Government, the State Department Building. A tour of the 8th floor, where the Secretary of State often entertains foreign heads of state, is available for those making reservations well in advance.

Walk north on either 21st or 23rd St. to the campus of George Washington University, where the Lisner Auditorium is a popular small concert hall. Just north of the campus is Washington Circle.

From it turn left onto Pennsylvania Ave. When you cross Rock Creek you are in Georgetown, a unique section of the city which predates Washington.

Federal Charms

Georgetown has no government buildings of note, nor any memorials, but to many it is the most charming part of the city. To your left from Pennsylvania Ave. as you enter the section is the old Chesapeake and Ohio Canal. You may walk along the Canal's towpath and two-hour trips on a mule-drawn barge are available in season. North of Pennsylvania Ave. and M St., with which Pennsylvania merges, is one of Washington's finest residential sections and seat of Georgetown University. It's a pleasure to walk along any of the brick sidewalks under the bower of trees covering its narrow streets, looking at the beautiful Federal-period homes, many of which are even more striking inside, and hide gems of gardens behind tall brick walls. Georgetown's equivalents of Main St. are M St., on which are most of the restaurants and night clubs and several galleries, and Wisconsin Ave., which intersects M at the heart of the section. Along Wisconsin Ave. are many of the fine unusual shops for which Georgetown is noted. Most of the fine Georgetown homes, of course, are closed to the public, but some are opened, as are the embassies, for special charity tours. Two fine old homes which tourists can and should visit are Dumbarton House, 2715 Q St. N.W., headquarters of the Society of Colonial Dames of America; and Dumbarton Oaks, 3101 R St. N.W., which also contains a notable museum of Byzantine art and is the property of Harvard University. (Closed Mondays.) The exquisite gardens, covering 16 acres, may be visited daily beween 2 and 4:45 P.M.; entrance is on R Street. Both the Museum and the gardens are closed on holidays and in inclement weather.

A good way to circle from Georgetown into "Embassy Row" along Massachusetts Ave. N.W. is to cross Rock Creek Park on the unique, curving Buffalo Bridge at Q St. (It's so named because of the big, life-sized buffalo sculptures at either end.) After crossing this delightful bridge, turn left on 23rd St. and you are right in the middle of the biggest concentration of Washington's embassies. On your left is that of Turkey. Across the street is Romania's. Then you're at Sheridan Circle, around which are the embassies of Ireland, Greece, Kenya, and Korea. Between Sheridan Circle and the Naval Observatory to the west are a score of embassies, the most notable being the great mansion of the British government. Just past the British Embassy, and on the same side of Massachusetts Avenue, is the towered Victorian mansion on the grounds of the Naval Observatory. It serves as the official residence of the Vice President. Heading south again toward town you will pass on your left the beautifully tiled edifice of Iran. In the center of this array, serving the embassies of the Moslem countries, is the striking Mosque and Islamic Center, with a 162-foot-high minaret. The public may attend a 45-minute service at the Mosque Fridays at 12:15 P.M.

Just off Massachusetts Ave., north a block on 21st St., is the gallery which comes to many Washington visitors as their greatest delight, their own "personal" discovery. This is the Phillips Collection in the former home of Duncan Phillips. It's a small but truly great collection, including Renoir's "The Luncheon of the Boating Party" and both an El Greco and Goya's "Repentant Peter." Other attractions worth visiting in this area are the Textile Museum and the home of Woodrow Wilson, within a few doors of one another on S Street.

Winding through this section of the city is another of Washington's greatest treasures, Rock Creek Park. This park, which snakes through the whole length of the city alongside the stream for which it is named, offers an escape from the city within minutes. Stroll along Rock Creek Park to where the stream flows into the Potomac River and you will arrive at Washington's newest major tourist attraction, the John F. Kennedy Center for the Performing Arts. Here is a building on a grand scale, 630 feet long and 300 feet wide. Guides will tell you the Washington Monument could be laid in the Grand Foyer, which runs the length of the building, with 75 feet to spare. The total area is big enough for four football fields. No athletic events are held here, however. Inside are an opera house, concert hall, two dramatic theaters, and film theater, plus three restaurants. We recommend that you take a tour between 10 and 1 P.M., Monday through Saturday. You will see rooms not open to the general public. Another way to enjoy the Kennedy Center is to go for dinner and see one of the many presentations. Between acts you'll enjoy a stroll on the riverfront terrace.

PRACTICAL INFORMATION FOR

WASHINGTON, D.C.

HOW TO GET THERE. *By car:* I-95 is the major access route from the north or south, I-270 from the northwest. From the eastern shore of the Chesapeake take US 50 over the toll bridge, through Annapolis and into Washington.

By plane: Washington National Airport handles the city's domestic traffic. Dulles International Airport, 25 miles away in Virginia, serves the larger jets and all international traffic. The Baltimore-Washington-International Airport (BWI) just west of Baltimore also serves Washington.

By train: Washington is served by *Amtrak* and the *Southern Railway System.*

By bus: Washington is a major terminal for *Trailways* and *Greyhound.*

HOW TO GET AROUND. *By car:* Never set forth without a map. Acquaint yourself with the general layout of the city, including the Virginia and Maryland suburbs. Circle your sightseeing objectives on your map. Try to avoid driving between 7:30 and 9 A.M. and between 4:30 and 6 P.M., as commuters burden the main arteries and bridges during these hours. Be prepared for many NO LEFT TURN signs in the downtown area and confusion at the traffic circles. Read with care the parking signs before leaving your car. Some meters are for 20-minute parking only, most are for an hour, and occasionally you will find one for two hours. If you leave your car parked along a main street after 3 P.M., the police will cart it off to the nearest precinct headquarters. Two-hour parking on the Mall is allowed, but finding your niche will be time-consuming. A new garage below the National Air and Space Museum (Independence Ave. between 4th and 7th Sts., S.W.) provides parking for Mall visitors. Sunday in the city provides you with relatively traffic-free avenues and easier parking. A nighttime tour of the floodlit monuments is unforgettable.

By tourmobile: We highly recommend sightseeing the Tourmobile way. You enjoy a narrated tour of all the principal monuments and points of historical interest along the way, dispense with driving and parking worries, and go at your own pace, getting on and off as often as you like at no extra charge. For information call (202) 554–7950.

By taxi: Taxis charge according to a zone plan displayed in each cab. There are no metered cabs. For trips beyond the downtown area or to suburbia, check with the driver before you board the cab.

By boat: The Washington Boat Lines, boats leave from Pier #4, 6th and Water Sts., S.W. Twice-daily trips to Mount Vernon are offered during the warm months and take about four hours. (202) 554–8000. Call for schedule and rates.

By bus: Metrobus provides bus service for Washington, Maryland, and northern Virginia areas. Fares are 65 cents (more during rush hours) within the district, and exact change or tokens are required.

By subway: Each Metro station's entrance is marked by a brown four-sided pylon with an "M" at the top. Fares vary in price according to destination and time of day. Metro Center and Gallery Place are the midtown stops where you can change from one line to the other. The fare is collected by an electronic collecting system and each passenger must have a farecard for entry and exit. Metro branches go out to National Airport, the Pentagon, Arlington Cemetery, Alexandria, Va., RFK Stadium, and to Maryland and Virginia suburbs. Buses from outlying areas feed into the rail system. Metro operates 6 A.M. to midnight weekdays, 8 A.M. to midnight Saturdays, and 10 A.M. to 6 P.M. Sundays. For information call 637–2437.

TOURIST INFORMATION SERVICES. Contact the Washington Convention and Visitors Association, 1575 Eye St., N.W., Washington, D.C. 20005 (Tel. 202-789-7000) for pamphlets and brochures on hotels, motels, restaurants and sightseeing here and in the environs. Open Mon.-Fri., 9-5.

The Washington Visitor Information Center is in the Great Hall of the Commerce Department, 1400 Pennsylvania Ave., N.W., 789–7000. Volunteers from Travelers Aid, IVIS (see below), and the National Park Service provide sightseeing information. The White House Historical Association sells its publications here.

IVIS, the International Visitors Information Service, 801 Nineteenth St., N.W. (Tel. 202-872-8747), stands ready to help foreign visitors with free maps in foreign languages and some multilingual pamphlets. IVIS also maintains a Language Bank to help visitors with a language problem and serves as the Washington coordinator of the Americans-at-Home Program.

The *Washington Post* and the new *Washington Times* carry information on movies, theater, sports and cultural events. Look for the "Day's Activities in Congress" column in the *Post* for a list of House and Senate Congressional hearings, all open to the public unless marked *Executive.* Friday's *Post* publishes "Weekend," a supplement detailing cultural activities for the week.

The monthly *Washingtonian* magazine ($1.95) covers in detail music, dance, theater, films, museums and exhibitions, lectures, sports and night life in its "Where and When" section, and readers can absorb Washington's special flavor by reading its feature articles.

MUSEUMS AND GALLERIES. *B'nai B'rith Museum.* 1640 Rhode Island Ave., N.W. Closed Jewish Holy Days and holidays. In Klutznick Hall are exhibits showing the contribution Jews have made to the development of our democracy. Open Sunday-Friday, 10 A.M.–5 P.M.

Corcoran Gallery of Art. 17th St. and New York Ave., N.W. American art from colonial days to the present, and a representative group of European works. Free. Closed Monday. Open Thursday evening until 9 P.M.

D.A.R. Memorial Continental Hall. 17th and C Sts., N.W. *Museum* at 1776 D St., N.W. Period rooms and lovely antiques. Open Monday–Friday, 10 A.M.–4 P.M.; Sunday, 1–5 P.M.

Dumbarton Oaks Collection. 1703 32nd St., N.W. (Georgetown). Collections from Early Christian and Byzantine periods and pre-Columbian art—a jewel of a museum in a perfect setting. Open daily, 2–5 P.M.; closed holidays.

Hillwood Museum, 4155 Linnean Ave., N.W. The home of the late Marjorie Meriwether Post is open for tours Monday, Wednesday, Friday, and Saturday. On display is an outstanding collection of Russian works of art. The gardens alone merit a visit. Reservations must be made well in advance; call (202–686–5807). $7 for adults; children under 12 not admitted.

Interior Department Museum. C St. between 18th and 19th Sts., N.W. Free. Indian exhibits and work of Interior Dept. The National Park Service furnishes data regarding the national parks, monuments, and other reservations under its jurisdiction. Open Monday–Friday, 8 A.M.–4 P.M.; closed holidays.

Marine Corps Museum and Historical Center. Navy Yard, 9th and M Sts., S.E. Special exhibits in an unusual setting. Open Monday–Saturday, 10 A.M.–4 P.M.; Sunday, noon–5 P.M.

National Building Museum, 440 G St., N.W. The Old Pension Building, built well before the Civil War, is undergoing a complete renovation. But don't wait for completion. Tours are given several times a week, and this great interior space should not be missed. Call 783–0690 for tour times.

National Archives. 7th St. and Pennsylvania Ave., N.W. The Declaration of Independence, the Constitution, and the Bill of Rights handsomely displayed. Open daily, 10 A.M.–5:30 P.M.

Phillips Collection. 1600 21st St., N.W. Works of the French Impressionists and post-Impressionists, including Degas, Monet, Manet, Renoir, Van Gogh, and Cézanne. Traditional and contemporary American painters are also represented. Closed Monday. Open Sunday 2–7 P.M.

Textile Museum. 2320 S St., N.W. Outstanding collection of rugs and textiles. The shop sells needlepoint and crewel original transfers taken from objects in museum collection, canvas, and wool. Open Tuesday–Saturday, 10 A.M.–5 P.M.

Truxton-Decatur Naval Museum. 1610 H St., N.W. Exhibits on naval history: prints, models, and paintings. Free. Open daily, 10 A.M.–4 P.M.; closed holidays.

Smithsonian Institution. Jefferson Dr. between 9th and 12th Sts., S.W.

Note: Smithsonian Museums on the Mall (except for the Freer Gallery) are open daily 10 A.M.–5:30 P.M. Free. The following are Smithsonian museums:

Arts and Industries Building. 9th St. and Jefferson Dr., S.W. Re-creation of The Philadelphia Exposition of 1876. Newly restored to original appearance.

Freer Gallery of Art. 12th St. and Independence Ave., S.W. Free. No tours. Paintings, ceramics, pottery, manuscripts, and sculpture from the Near and Far East are shown in this delightful small museum built around a central courtyard. The Freer houses one of the largest collections of the works of Whistler.

Hirshhorn Museum and Sculpture Garden, Independence Ave. at 8th St., S.W. Nicknamed "The Doughnut on the Mall," the Hirshhorn, opened in 1974, houses a collection of over 6,000 works of art by European and American artists dating from the late 19th century to the present. Outdoor sculpture garden with delightful vistas of the Mall. Outdoor cafeteria in summer.

National Museum of African Art. 316 A St., N.E. This townhouse was once the home of 19th-century black leader, Frederick Douglas. On display are masks, carvings, jewelry, and other art objects from African countries. Open Monday–Friday, 10 A.M.–5 P.M.; weekdays and holidays, noon–5 P.M.

National Museum of American History. Between 12th and 14th Sts., N.W., on Constitution Ave. Imposing new building containing gowns of the First Ladies, the Star-Spangled Banner, famous inventions, early automobiles, locomotives, stamps; cultural and technological development of the United States from Colonial times. Cafeteria.

National Museum of Natural History. 10th St. and Constitution Ave., N.W. Hall of Dinosaurs, Hall of Gems (see the *Hope Diamond*). Special member's dining room for Smithsonian Associates.

National Air and Space Museum, Independence Ave. and 6th St., S.W. Opened July 4, 1976. Dramatic displays of aircraft, including *The Spirit of St. Louis,* the Wright brothers' plane, and the Apollo II command module. Movie *Living Planet* and Spacearium. Cafeteria.

National Collection of American Art and the National Portrait Gallery. 8th and G Sts., N.W. Especially noteworthy are the 445 paintings of George Catlin's Indian Gallery, the "Art: U.S.A." collection of S. C. Johnson and Son, Inc., and the always outstanding special exhibits.

National Gallery of Art and the *East Building.* 6th St. and Constitution Ave., N.W. A daily schedule of events appears on bulletin boards at either entrance. If time permits, take introductory tour of the gallery. LecTour (taped lectures) may be rented for 25¢. Get free brochure of gallery with map showing the location of paintings by school and period.

Renwick Gallery. 17th St. and Pennsylvania Ave., N.W. Near White House. Victorian building filled with Americana.

 HISTORIC SITES. Some of the most interesting historic sites are little known. Open to the public is the *Woodrow Wilson House,* maintained by the National Trust, at 2430 S St., N.W. Here Wilson, 28th President of the United States, retired at the end of his second term and died three years later, Feb. 3, 1924. The house contains furnishings, portraits, books, memorabilia, and other effects belonging to the Wilsons. Open Tuesday–Friday, 10 A.M.–2 P.M. Admission $2 for adults.

A fine early Federal house is *Dumbarton House* in Georgetown, now headquarters for the National Society of Colonial Dames. Dating from 1799, this red brick mansion contains authentic period pieces and an outstanding collection of silver and china. 2715 Q St., N.W. Open Monday–Saturday, 9 A.M.–noon. Free.

Arlington House (also known as the Custis-Lee Mansion). In Arlington Cemetery. Home of Robert E. Lee, commander of the Confederate Army during the Civil War. A Tourmobile stop. Open daily, 9:30 A.M.–4:30 P.M. Free.

Arlington National Cemetery. Across Memorial Bridge from the Lincoln Memorial: the Tomb of the Unknown Soldier (change of guard every hour on the hour), the Amphitheater, Arlington House, and the graves of President John F. Kennedy and his brother, Senator Robert F. Kennedy. No cars allowed. Take Tourmobile or walk. Especially lovely in early Spring. Open daily, 8 A.M.–5 P.M.; 8 A.M.–7 P.M., April through September.

Decatur House, a block from the White House and overlooking Lafayette Square, was designed in 1818 by famed architect Benjamin Latrobe. This elegant Georgian town house is at the corner of H St. and Jackson Pl., N.W. Open Tuesday–Friday, 10 A.M.–2 P.M.; weekends, noon–4 P.M. Admission $3 for adults.

The Capitol. On Capitol Hill. Tours leave from the Rotunda every 15 minutes. Free. Explore this vast building on your own after the 45-minute tour; take a ride on the underground subway to the Senate and House Office Buildings. Should you wish to spend more time in the House or Senate gallery than the few minutes allowed on your tour, you must get a pass from the office of your Senator or Congressman. See the lighted Capitol at night, and during the summer, attend a concert at the West Front. Open daily 9 A.M.–4:30 P.M.; tours 9 A.M.–3:45 P.M. (free).

The Folger Library, 201 East Capitol St., S.E., houses the world's largest collection of Shakespeareana and an extraordinary collection of material in English dealing with the 17th and 18th centuries. The *Exhibition Hall* reproduces the great hall of an Elizabethan palace. The *Shakespearean Theater* is a full-size replica of a public playhouse of Shakespeare's day, except that it does not open to the sky. Plays are presented by the Folger Theater Group. Open Monday–Saturday, 10 A.M.–4 P.M.

Jefferson Memorial. On the south bank of the Tidal basin. Honors Thomas Jefferson, third President, the author of the Declaration of Independence and the Bill of Rights. It is particularly lovely at cherry blossom time and on a summer night. Parking at an adjacent parking lot. Gift shop. Open 24 hours a day.

The Library of Congress, (now referred to as the Thomas Jefferson Building), 1st St. and Independence Ave., S.E., ranks among the great libraries of the world, with 80 million books, periodicals, photographs, and microfilms housed in over 470 miles of shelves. Tours of this ornate, Italian Renaissance style building are conducted almost every hour, 9 A.M. to 4 P.M. Should you be exploring the Library on your own, be sure to take the elevator to the Visitors' Gallery above the second floor for a spectacular view looking down on the Main Reading Room. Open Monday–Friday, 9 A.M.–4 P.M.; tours.

Lincoln Memorial. West Potomac Park at the foot of 23rd St., N.W. The statue of Lincoln is imposing by day, unforgettable by night. Walk around the portico for fine view of the Potomac River and Arlington Memorial Bridge, Arlington House across the river, with, just below, the eternal flame marking the grave of President Kennedy. Gift shop. Parking on Ohio Drive. Open 24 hours a day.

Mount Vernon. Mount Vernon, Va. (16 miles south of Washington, D.C.—allow a half day for the trip). Washington's home on the Potomac. Outbuildings and gardens in a lovely setting. The grave of George and Martha Washington is just below the mansion. For transportation by Washington Boat Lines, see *How to Get Around—By Boat.* A Tourmobile destination in summer. Open daily March–October, 9 A.M.–5 P.M.; November–February, 9 A.M.–4 P.M. Adults, $4.

Supreme Court. 1st St. and Maryland Ave., N.E. Court is in session Oct.–June. Tours. Open Monday–Friday, 9 A.M.–5 P.M.

Vietnam Veterans Memorial, N.W. corner of Constitution Gardens. Dedicated November 13, 1982, the two long walls of polished granite contain the names of the 57,692 Americans killed in the war. May be visited day or night.

Washington Monument. On the Mall at 15th St., N.W. 555-foot obelisk; elevator ride to top for fine view. Free. Open daily, 9 A.M.–5 P.M.; longer hours in summer.

The White House. 1600 Pennsylvania Ave., N.W. Every president has lived here except Washington. Eight of 132 rooms are on display. In summer, tickets for tour distributed on Ellipse. Closed Sun. and Mon. Open 10-12 other days.

If time permits, see *Alexandria,* "The Cradle of History." Eight miles south of Washington, en route to Mount Vernon. An old tobacco port founded in 1749. See Christ Church, parish church of Washington and Robert E. Lee; Gadsby's Tavern (open for lunch and dinner); the Stabler-Leadbeater Apothecary Shop; the Old Presbyterian Meeting House with the Tomb of the Unknown Soldier of the Revolutionary War; the Carlyle House; the George Washington National Memorial; Robert E. Lee's Boyhood Home; the Lee-Fendell House, and Captain's Row, a concentration of picturesque eighteenth-century houses.

TOURS. The larger companies—*Diamond, Gray Line, White House,* and *Blue Line* amongst others—will pick you up at your hotel or motel 30 minutes before the scheduled time of your tour's departure, and return you without extra charge. *Tourmobiles* provide an efficient way to sightsee in the principal Mall-Monument area and Arlington Cemetery. Call 554-7950 for information. From June 1 to Sept. 15 a Mount Vernon tour is available. Made-to-order group tours are offered by National Fine Arts Associates. Museum-trained docents escort you. Call (202) 966–3800 for information. *Tailored Tours* will plan an insiders tour of the city. Call (301) 229–6221. *Washington a la Carte,* 1706 Surrey Lane, N.W., Washington, D.C. 20007, (202) 337–7300, offers custom-designed tours with the emphasis on the history, art and architecture of the city. Call (202) 296–0840.

NIGHTLIFE. Washington offers a wide variety of spots to sip, sup, and dance after dark. In most cases call in advance for latest information on bookings, hours, cover charges, and reservations. The area most frequented by the young crowd is "The Strip"—M St. in Georgetown. If you're over 30, however, don't despair—there's a full evening's entertainment just strolling between 28th St. and Key Bridge, and observing the street life on lower Wisconsin Ave.

A long established jazz emporium is *Blues Alley,* a converted carriage house in the alley behind 1073 Wisconsin Ave., N.W. *Clyde's,* at 3236 M St., N.W., resembles a saloon in the P. J. Clarke tradition. *Exchange Ltd.,* 1831 M St., N.W., has two singles bars and a jukebox. *Mr. Smith's,* 3104 M St., N.W., has dancing upstairs, piano bars upstairs and down. *Charlie's Georgetown* at 3223 K St., N.W. is a favorite spot for big-name musicians, including the co-owner, Charlie Byrd. *The Bayou,* 3135 K St., N.W., is perhaps the granddaddy of them all, with loud rock and two tiers of dance floor. *Desperado's,* 3350 M St., N.W. is another Georgetown favorite featuring fine rhythm-and-blues and country-rock bands.

F. Scott's, 1232 36th St., N.W., is perhaps the classiest bar in Georgetown with its unusual art deco setting. "A saloon with faded Edwardian elegance" serves oysters and hamburgers in the garden room. For the older, more sedate crowd.

The Monocle, 107 D St., N.E., just around the corner from the Senate Office Building, caters to the Hill crowd with its rather masculine decor, beef specialties, and combo for dancing in the Toby Pub.

The Astor, 1813 M St., N.W., offers the best belly dancers and bouzouki bands in town.

If it's an Irish pub you're after, try *Gallagher's,* 3319 Connecticut Ave., N.W., where you may find a folksinger on the bill of fare, and *E. J. O'Riley's,* in the alley behind 1122 18th St., N.W., with Irish folksongs upstairs. Yet another Irish bar "where the ale flows freely" is *Bit O'Ireland* (Matt Kane's), 1118 13th St., N.W. Here you will be entertained by Irish singing groups.

If you are in the Connecticut Ave. area, mount the steps of *Childe Harolde,* 1610 20th St., N.W., a turn-of-the-century converted townhouse of great charm, where you will be entertained with fine bluegrass music—and, if you're hungry, fine food. Remember tea dancing? Those who do might enjoy the ambiance at the Hyatt Regency, 400 New Jersey Ave., N.W., Thurs. from 5:30 to 8:30 P.M.

Liquor is sold in stores from 10 A.M. to 9 P.M., Mon. to Fri., until midnight on Sat., never on Sun. In restaurants it is served from 8 A.M. to 2 A.M., Mon. to Thurs.; 8 A.M. to 3 A.M., Fri. and Sat.; 10 A.M. to 2 A.M., Sun. The legal drinking age is 18 for beer, 21 for wine and cocktails. Proof of age in the form of a driver's license is usually required. Beer may be bought in grocery stores.

SUMMER SPORTS. There are three public *golf courses* open year round from sunrise to sunset—East Potomac Park, Langston Park, and Rock Creek Park, with rental bags and clubs. *Rowboats, swan boat rides, canoes,* and *pedal boats* are for hire at the north end of the Tidal Basin, 15th St. and Maine Ave., S.W. Both *Thompson's Boat Center* at Rock Creek Parkway and Virginia Ave., N.W., and *Fletcher's Boat House,* 4940 Canal Rd. on the C. and O. Canal Tow Path will rent you a canoe, rowboat, or bicycle.

WINTER SPORTS. For a list of *ice skating* rinks in and around the city, consult the Yellow Pages. Fort Dupont Indoor Ice Arena, 3779 Ely Place, S.E. (between Ridge Rd. and Minnesota Ave.), is open year round. *Pershing Park,* Pennsylvania Ave, has skating Dec.–Feb. Once every few years the C. and O. Canal freezes over, and the scene is one from an old Dutch painting. Equally picturesque are the rare occasions when the public is allowed to skate on the Reflecting Pool at the base of the Washington Monument. The finest new facility is right on the Mall. Skate at the National Sculpture Garden Ice Rink on Constitution Avenue between 7th and 9th Sts., N.W. Skates for rent. Music and great views. Open Dec.–Feb. Call 347–9041 for daily hours.

SPECTATOR SPORTS. During the fall season the *Washington Redskins* play at R.F.K. Stadium. Tickets are sometimes available at the Stadium the Monday before a home game.

Racing fans may enjoy horse racing almost year around within easy driving distance of Washington. Laurel, Maryland, tracks (18 miles), Bowie (20 miles), and Pimlico (40 miles—near Baltimore) operate in spring and fall, and a harness racing season is held at Laurel and Rosecroft. *Polo games* are played at different locations during the summer and fall, usually on Sundays. *Cricket* enthusiasts may attend games played by members of the British Commonwealth Cricket Club on the polo grounds of West Potomac Park from April to October, usually at 2 P.M. Saturdays and Sundays.

The pro ice hockey team, the *Capitals,* plays at the Capital Centre in Landover, Md., from October to early April. The pro basketball team, the *Washington Bullets,* plays at the Capital Centre from October to April. The D.C. National Bank International Tennis Tournament is held the last week in July at the tennis stadium in Rock Creek Park.

SHOPPING. To orient you to the different shopping areas, the downtown area centers at 14th and F Sts., N.W., extending northwest to about 15th and I Sts., and east to 7th St. and Pennsylvania Ave. There are three department stores of distinction: *Julius Garfinckel and Co.,* 14th and F Sts., N.W.; *The Hecht Co.,* F and 7th Sts., N.W.; and *Woodward and Lothrop,* 11th and F Sts., N.W. Just across the street from Garfinckel's is *Lewis and Thomas Saltz,* a Bond Street type of men's store. *Joseph Bank,* at 1118 19th St., N.W. is a source of fine quality menswear at remarkably reasonable prices. Another favorite for both men and women is *Raleigh's* at 1122 Connecticut Ave., N.W. (near the Mayflower Hotel). The well-known men's store, *Brooks Brothers,* is located at 1840 L St., N.W.

Georgetown is the capital's best browsing territory, and certainly the most colorful part of town. *Georgetown Park,* just west of Wisconsin Ave. on M St. in Georgetown, offers a conglomeration of luxury stores, boutiques, and restaurants. Start at the intersection of Wisconsin Ave. and M St., and work your way north to R St., stopping in at such delightful shops as the *Georgetown Coffee House,* 1330 Wisconsin Ave.; *The Phoenix,* 1514 Wisconsin Ave.; *The Little Caledonia,* 1419 Wisconsin Ave.; and *Ursell's,* 3243 Q St. Whatever your hobby, age, lifestyle—whether it's birdwatching (*Audubon Book Shop,* 1621 Wisconsin

Ave.), gourmet cooking (*The French Kitchen*, 1500 Wisconsin Ave.), fine wines and imported cheeses (*The Wine and Cheese Shop*, 1413 Wisconsin Ave.), or original needlepoint designs, canvasses and imported wool (*The American Needlework Center*, 2803 M St.)—you'll find them all here in Georgetown.

Perhaps the most important area of town for serious shoppers is the intersection of Western and Wisconsin Aves., where the Maryland and District lines join. Located within a few blocks of each other are branches of *Lord and Taylor* and *Saks Fifth Avenue*. A handsome new *Neiman-Marcus* store is one of many fine specialty stores located in the Mazza Gallerie, with underground parking via Forty-Fourth St. One of the most intriguing places to shop is *Les Champs* in the Watergate Complex, 600 New Hampshire Ave., N.W., site of more than 30 designer and specialty shops. Explore the charming shops in *The Pavilion* at the Old Post Office.

Those who live in the suburbs shop at the huge shopping malls where most of the downtown department stores have branches. Newest and most notable of these is the *White Flint Shopping Mall* on Rockville Pike, Maryland, where the famous department stores *Bloomingdale's* and *I. Magnin* have both opened branch stores. When you are tired of shopping, stop for a drink, a meal, a movie, or relax at a disco.

WHAT TO DO WITH THE CHILDREN. Washington abounds in things to do which have special appeal to children. Many of these activities, sights, or excursions will delight the parents as much as their offspring. The *National Zoo*, 3000 Connecticut Ave., N.W., has two panda bears, Ling Ling and Hsing Hsing. Also in Rock Creek Park are *Pierce Mill* at Tilden St. and Beach Drive, N.W., and the *Nature Center*, near Military and Glover Rds., where a planetarium is the stellar attraction.

In the lower lobby of the Department of Commerce Building at 14th and E Sts., N.W., the *National Aquarium* displays live specimens of food and game fishes from the inland waters of the United States.

The *Federal Bureau of Investigation* is nearby (between 9th and 10th Sts. on E Street, N.W.). Tours are free. At the *London Brass Rubbing Centre* below the Washington Cathedral, Wisconsin Ave. and Massachusetts Ave., N.W., instructions are given for doing rubbings from old British church brasses.

The *Bureau of Engraving and Printing* at 14th and C Sts., N.W., provides the opportunity to view the printing of postage stamps and paper money on a 25-minute self-guided tour, with taped commentaries explaining the steps you are observing.

The *Capital Children's Museum*, 800 3rd St, N.E. (near H St.) has wonderful "hands-on" exhibits; children learn by doing. (Closed Mondays.)

The *Smithsonian Natural History Building* at 10th St. and Constitution Ave., N.W., displays the Fenykovi elephant, estimated to have weighed 12 tons while alive, in the giant rotunda. See, too, the Hall of Dinosaurs, the Hall of Indians, and the Hall of Gems. Equally popular are the exhibits at the new *Museum of American History* at 13th St. and Constitution Ave., N.W., showing the cultural and technological development of the U.S.

Explorers Hall at the National Geographic Society, 17th and M Sts., N.W., offers a well-displayed potpourri of fascinating exhibits of National Geographic researches and explorations.

Discovery Theater in the Arts and Industries Building, 900 Jefferson Drive, offers plays for kindergartners through fourth-graders Saturday at 1 and 3 P.M. and sometimes during the week.

A trip on *The Washington Boat Lines* to Mount Vernon (see *How to Get Around—By Boat*) is especially appealing on a hot summer's day. Less time-consuming would be a *swan boat ride* at the Tidal Basin, where, at the north end, rowboats, canoes, and paddle boats may be rented.

HOTELS AND MOTELS. With more than 16 million visitors to Washington each year, tourism has become the capital's principal industry, and demand for hotel space often exceeds space available. Be sure to write or phone in advance for confirmed reservations.

Many of the downtown older, renowned hotels have undergone extensive face-lifting, resulting in a number of new luxury-class hotels. Motels have been listed at all the major approaches to the city, and none of those listed is more than 35 minutes by car from downtown Washington. Some are accessible by subway.

Double-occupancy lodgings in Washington are categorized as follows: *Deluxe,* $140 and higher; *Expensive* $110–$140; *Moderate,* $75–$110; *Inexpensive,* under $75. Special weekend bargain rates are offered at some of the finest hotels, usually for Friday and Saturday nights.

Deluxe: **The Canterbury.** 1733 N St., N.W. Small (98 units), each room a suite. Elegant hotel on quiet street off Connecticut Ave., N.W.

Embassy Row Hotel. 2015 Massachusetts Ave., N.W. Fine location near Dupont Circle. Newly decorated.

Four Seasons Hotel. 2800 Wisconsin Ave., N.W. Georgetown's newest, deluxe hotel; contender for top honors.

Georgetown Marbury House Hotel. 3000 M St., N.W. Another top-rated new hotel in the heart of Georgetown.

Hay-Adams. 16th and H Sts., N.W. Overlooking Lafayette Square, an older hotel of quiet distinction, with beautifully appointed rooms.

Hotel Bristol. 2430 Pennsylvania Ave., N.W. A brand–new 240–room hotel in a newly-developing area of Pennsylvania Ave.

Hyatt Regency Washington on Capitol Hill. 400 New Jersey Ave., N.W. Closest hotel to the Capitol. 865 rooms around a 4-story atrium.

Jefferson. 1200 16th St., N.W. Smallish older hotel, newly redecorated, with European atmosphere. Tastefully appointed.

Loew's L'Enfant Plaza. 480 L'Enfant Plaza, S.W. Luxury hotel in a dramatic location. Every amenity. Walk to Smithsonian museums on Mall.

Madison. 15th and M Sts., N.W. Top-flight hotel. Excellent restaurant.

Marriott–J.W. 1331 Pennsylvania Ave., N.W. Large (774 rooms), attractively located near the Old Post Office; the flagship hotel of Marriott Corp. Elegant public rooms.

Ritz Carlton Hotel. 2100 Massachusetts Ave., N.W. (formerly Fairfax Hotel). Furnished with antiques and located in Embassy section of town. Famous restaurant, the Jockey Club.

Sheraton Carlton. 16th and K Sts., N.W. Still the favorite among longtime visitors to the city who rate tradition and atmosphere important.

Sheraton Washington. 2660 Woodley Rd., N.W. Brand-new luxury-level hotel in park-like setting. 1500 rooms; 2 outdoor pools.

The Regent of Washington. 2350 M St., N.W. This 265-room hotel evokes European ambiance that is rich but not ostentatious. Built around manicured courtyard.

Watergate. 2650 Virginia Ave. N.W. Yes, it's that place, and you'll love the views, pool, sauna, restaurant, and proximity to Kennedy Center and the State Department.

Expensive: **Capital-Hilton.** Still among most convenient hotels in town at 16th and K Sts., N.W. Restaurants, bars, entertainment, excellent service here.

Dupont Plaza. Connecticut Ave. and Massachusetts Ave., N.W. On Dupont Circle. Pleasant, not too large. Near subway.

Georgetown Dutch Inn. 1075 Thomas Jefferson St., N.W. Rooms with kitchenettes. Just half a block from C.&O. Canal.

Georgetown Inn. 1310 Wisconsin Ave., N.W. In the heart of Georgetown, Washington's oldest section. Known for its attractively decorated rooms.

Guest Quarters. 801 New Hampshire Ave., N.W. New in 1974. Adjacent to Kennedy Center. Suites only, all with fully equipped kitchens. Continental breakfast, pool.

Henley Park Hotel. 926 Massachusetts Ave., N.W. A bit away from the downtown area; very British in feeling and amenities. Only 96 rooms.

Mayflower. 1127 Connecticut Ave., N.W. A Washington landmark for many years. Fine location; "grand" public rooms.

One Washington Circle, N.W. Lovely rooms, many with excellent kitchens. Good location near George Washington University.

Shoreham Americana. 2500 Calvert St., N.W. A very large, sprawling hotel on the edge of Rock Creek Park.

Vista International Hotel. 1400 M St., N.W. Brand new, in downtown location. Features dramatic inner courtyard.

Washington. 15th St. and Pennsylvania Ave., N.W. One of city's older, large hotels with good restaurants. Roof garden in summer with charming view of lighted monuments at night.

Washington Hilton. 1919 Connecticut Ave., N.W. Conventions meet here; within walking distance of business section. Pool and tennis courts.

Moderate: **Best Western–Mid Town.** 1201 K St., N.W. Near Greyhound and Trailway bus stations. Walk to new convention center.

General Scott Inn. 1464 Rhode Island Ave., N.W. Small (65 units), with equipped kitchens. Near White House.

Holiday Inn–Georgetown. 2101 Wisconsin Ave., N.W. At north end of Georgetown shopping and restaurant area. 220 rooms, pool, dining room.

Inexpensive: **Allen Lee Hotel.** 2224 F St., N.W. Small (90 rooms) and without frills; favorite of students.

Bellevue Hotel. 15 E St., N.W. Within walking distance of Capitol Hill area. Smallish, with "Quad" rooms for groups. Cafeteria and pub. Near subway.

Harrington Hotel. 11th & E Sts., N.W. Huge, older downtown hotel; good for families; excellent cafeteria.

 MOTELS AND HOTELS OUTSIDE CITY. ALEXANDRIA. *Moderate:* **Guest Quarters.** 100 S. Reynolds St. Suites only with kitchens. Pool, playground, coin-op laundry. Ideal for families.

Olde Colony. 1st and N. Washington Sts. Colonial Virginia architecture. Free continental breakfast.

ARLINGTON. *Deluxe:* **Crystal City Marriott.** 1999 Jefferson Davis Highway. Shuttle to National Airport. 340 rooms; indoor pool; three restaurants.

Hyatt Arlington. 1325 Wilson Blvd. Three blocks from Key Bridge and across from Metro station. 315 rooms.

Key Bridge Marriott. 1401 Lee Hwy. Just across Key Bridge from Georgetown. Great view of city from many of 561 rooms.

Moderate: **Best Western–Rosslyn Westpark Hotel.** 1900 Ft. Myer Dr. Near Key Bridge. 307 rooms; pool, 2 dining rooms.

Holiday Inn–Key Bridge. 1850 Ft. Myer Dr. In Rosslyn, just across bridge from Georgetown. Near Metro. Pool, restaurant. 177 rooms.

BETHESDA. *Expensive:* **Marriott–Bethesda.** 5151 Pooks Hill Road. Just off beltway (I-494) at Wisconsin Ave. near National Institute of Health and Bethesda Naval Hospital. Three restaurants, indoor/outdoor pool.

Moderate: **Holiday Inn.** 8120 Wisconsin Ave., N.W. 270 rooms with notable restaurant, The Peppermill.

Linden Hill. 5400 Pooks Hill Road. 1½ mi. N of I-495, exit 19. Off Wisconsin Ave. Apartment-hotel with pool, tennis courts; sauna; excellent restaurant. 150 rooms. Near N.I.H. and the Bethesda Naval Hospital.

United Inn of America. 8130 Wisconsin Ave., N.W. Near National Institutes of Health and beltway.

FAIRFAX. *Moderate:* **Quality Inn.** 11180 Main St. at Germantown Rd on Rte. 50. 118 rooms; pool.

Inexpensive: **White House.** 9700 Lee Highway. 2½ mi. E on US 29. Small, 56 rooms. Pool; a restaurant nearby.

FALLS CHURCH. *Moderate:* **Best Western Village House.** 245 N. Washington St. On US 29, 1 block N of junction State 7. Small, 65 rooms. Pool, restaurant.

Quality Inn Governor. 6650 Arlington Blvd. 1 mi. W of Seven Corners on US 50; 2½ mi. E of I-495, exit 8E. Medium size, 124 rooms. Pool and restaurant.

SILVER SPRING. *Moderate:* **Holiday Inn.** 8777 Georgia Ave. 1 mi. S of I-495, exit 21 at Silver Spring Shopping Plaza. Pool; restaurant and dancing; 231 rooms.

Howard Johnson's. 2715 University Blvd., Wheaton. 160 rooms; pool.

DINING OUT. In the past few years the number of fine restaurants has increased tremendously, with an ever-growing variety of cuisines serving authentic dishes from Europe, Asia, and Latin America.

For mid-priced dinners on each menu, the following *approximate* categories apply: *Deluxe:* $35 and up, *Expensive* $25–35; *Moderate* $15–20, and *Inexpensive* under $15. Prices are for a complete dinner for one, including soup, entrée, and dessert. Not included are drinks, tax and tip.

Always make dinner reservations and arrive on time to avoid disappointment.

AMERICAN-INTERNATIONAL. *Deluxe:* **The Prime Rib.** 2020 K St., N.W. A steak house par excellence, with fine beef, lamb chops and lobster.

Moderate: **Adam's Rib.** 2100 Pennsylvania Ave., N.W. Variety of cuisines—Greek, American, French dishes—and fish.

Billy Martin's Carriage House. 1238 Wisconsin Ave., N.W. In the heart of Georgetown. American fare, including seafood.

Evans Farm Inn. The seven-mile drive to McLean, Va., is well worth the trip. Distinctively American dishes, such as plantation chicken, roast duckling, spoon bread, and many others. 1696 Chain Bridge Rd. (McLean, Va.).

Nora. 2132 Florida Ave., N.W. Top-quality ingredients, whether seafood, meats, or vegetables. Small, crowded, but with its own special charm. Desserts a specialty.

Sir Walter Raleigh Inn, 2001 Wisconsin Ave., N.W., just north of Georgetown. Simple menu featuring steaks, salad bar, homemade bread. Attractive décor, friendly service.

Inexpensive: **Martin's.** 1264 Wisconsin Ave., N.W. Unassuming Georgetown restaurant with a down-to-earth menu.

Kennedy Center. *Encore Cafeteria (Inexpensive)* serves simple food with little variation, but if it's summertime you'll enjoy the terrace. *Curtain Call Café,* with the apprearance of a small café, offers good food at a *Moderate* price. (Same menu for lunch and dinner.) *Roof Terrace Restaurant,* as the name implies, is *Expensive,* elegant. Tel. 833–8870.

The Roundtable, 4859 Wisconsin Ave., N.W. A neighborhood family-type restaurant with few frills, but good food, reasonably priced.

BRITISH. *Moderate:* **The Piccadilly.** 5510 Connecticut Ave., N.W. Beef dishes, mutton chops in finest British tradition. Sidewalk café in summer.

CAFETERIAS. *Inexpensive:* **All States Cafeteria.** 1750 Pennsylvania Ave., N.W. Cafeteria service; summer garden.

American Café. 1211 Wisconsin Ave., N.W. Georgetown's popular cafe with good soups, salads, sandwiches and desserts. Also at 227 Massachusetts Ave., N.E., on Capitol Hill.

Au Pied du Cochon. 1335 Wisconsin Ave., N.W. Cozy and rustic with unusual French menu.

Chamberlin's Cafeteria. 819 15th St., N.W. Just plain good food, Southern-style cooking, and homemade baked goods.

Hot Shoppes. Food for the whole family at locations all over town (see Yellow Pages).

Kitcheria. 11th and E Sts., N.W. Located in Harrington Hotel; great place to feed a family.

National Gallery of Art. Constitution Ave. and 6th St., N.W. Handsome new dining room; ground floor of the Gallery. (Other good government cafeterias are also open to the public in the Smithsonian Air and Space Museum, Museum of American History, National Portrait Gallery, and in the Commerce, Health, and Human Services, Interior, State and Supreme Court Buildings.)

CHINESE. *Expensive:* **Yenching Place.** 3524 Connecticut Ave., N.W. Cuisine from all over China but Mandarin their specialty. Devoted clientele.

Moderate: **Empress.** 1018 Vermont Ave. (near 15th and K Sts., N.W.) Award-winning cuisine; Mandarin and Szechuan dishes. Peking duck available without advanced notice.

Hunan Chinatown Restaurant. 624 H St., N.W. In heart of Chinatown. Unusual dishes served by remarkably attentive waiters.

CUBAN. *Inexpensive.* **Omega.** 1858 Columbia Rd., N.W. Generous helpings; paella, cuttlefish, and cod, served with black beans and rice. Unprepossessing décor; crowded; no reservations.

FRENCH. *Deluxe:* **Dominique's.** 20th and Pennsylvania Ave., N.W. Nineteenth-century French decor, a kitchen which stays open until midnight for theatergoers, intimate dining rooms, a classic French menu, incomparable desserts, and a personable proprietaire, Dominique D'Ermo, add up to a top-notch restaurant.

Jean-Pierre. 1835 K St., N.W. Friendly and cheerful, there is the feeling that the management is genuinely interested in the diners. Fine quenelles, striped bass, and steak Diane.

La Niçoise. 1721 Wisconsin Ave., N.W. A favorite with the French community in the city. Filet de Boeuf, kidneys, and myriad dishes featuring seafood are the chief allures.

1789. 1226 36th St., N.W. This English-style cottage is nestled among the row houses of Georgetown, and divided into several distinctive dining areas. The food is beautifully prepared and elegantly served.

Le Lion d'Or. 18th and M Sts., N.W. Attractive setting and considered by many to be Washington's top French restaurant.

Expensive: **Le Bagatelle.** 2000 K St., N.W. One goes to "dine," not just eat.

Jacqueline's. 1990 M St., N.W. A most attractive restaurant with exceptionally fine French cuisine.

La Colline. 400 N. Capitol St., N.W. A fine small restaurant just down the hill from the Capitol. Seafood dishes especially noteworthy.

Moderate: **Le Gaulois.** 2133 Pennsylvania Ave., N.W. Very small and very special for lovers of fine French food at reasonable prices.

The Restaurant in Bethesda. 7820 Norfolk Ave. in Bethesda. The owners of this authentic French restaurant, Lionel Daury and Benoir Pouchelon, welcome you cordially, and serve top-flight meals at reasonable prices. Outstanding desserts.

Tout Va Bien. 1063 31st St., N.W., next to the Canal in Georgetown. Here is your opportunity to enjoy a small, attractive restaurant with a top-flight menu, without paying top dollar for your meal.

Inexpensive: **Chez Odette.** 3063 M St. in Georgetown. Small, quiet, and unassuming, with plain French food. Try the chicken Dijon.

GERMAN. *Moderate:* **Old Europe.** 2434 Wisconsin Ave., N.W. Traditional German dishes, such as weiner schnitzel and sauerbraten, are served in this time-tested gemutlich restaurant known for its superb German wines. Nightly entertainment in downstairs rathskeller.

Inexpensive: **Café Mozart.** 1331 H St., N.W. in Pennsylvania Ave. redevelopment area. Unusual combination of bar, delicatessen with carry-out, and restaurant with hearty German dishes and a delightful live pianist.

GREEK. *Moderate:* **Taverna Cretekou.** 818 King Street, Old Town, Alexandria. Delightful atmosphere and extensive Greek menu; outdoor dining in warm weather. Champagne brunch on Sunday is highly recommended.

Inexpensive: **Astor Restaurant,** 1813 M St., N.W. Authentic Greek food, reasonable prices. Booths. Deservedly crowded.

HUNGARIAN. *Moderate:* **Csikos.** 3601 Connecticut Ave., N.W. You would be unlikely to discover this restaurant on your own, but traditional dishes served with a background of gypsy music will surely please.

INDIAN. *Moderate:* **Tandoor.** 3316 M St., N.W. Contemporary, bright décor. The tandoor oven, behind a glass wall, allows diners to view chef cook specialties such as chicken, lamb, and seafood.

ITALIAN. *Expensive:* **Cantina D'Italia.** 1214-A 18th St., N.W. Many consider this to be the city's best restaurant, and we are hard pressed to disagree, First-class food and fine service.

Moderate: **Gusti's.** Lasagna al Forno, fettucine, scampi, calamari, and other Italian standards are the favorites, and the homemade spumoni is essential for dessert. Al fresco dining is available in mild weather. 19th and M Sts., N.W.

Inexpensive: **A.V. Ristorante.** 607 New York Ave., N.W. Good Southern Italian specialties served in a setting lacking in amenities and ambiance.

Floriana. 4936 Wisconsin Ave., N.W. It is worth leaving the downtown area to dine at this small, inviting restaurant with its Northern Italian cuisine. Homemade pasta and veal dishes are featured.

JAPANESE. *Moderate:* **Mikado.** 4707 Wisconsin Ave. The best Japanese menu in the city. If you really want to feast, order ahead for their 10-course dinner (about $15 per person).

Matuba. 4918 Cordell Ave., Bethesda, Md. and 2915 Columbia Pike, Arlington, Va. The finest sushi available; a small menu with delicious specialties, artistically arranged and served.

MID-EASTERN. *Inexpensive:* **Calvert.** 1967 Calvert St., N.W. Pleasing family-type restaurant with well-prepared Middle-Eastern food.

SEAFOOD. *Moderate:* **Crisfield's.** 8012 Georgia Ave., Silver Spring, Md. Out aways from town, but renowned for its excellent seafood served in an unpretentious setting. For years Crisfields has been one of the top 50 restaurants in the area. Closed Mon.

Flagship. 900 Water St., S.W. Gigantic restaurant on waterfront; all meals cooked to order.

Harvey's. 1001 18th St. N.W. An old-time favorite, known and applauded for its excellent seafood. Crowded at lunch.

Hogate's Spectacular Seafood Restaurant. 9th St. and Maine Ave., S.W. Another restaurant on waterfront.

Pier 7 Restaurant. On the waterfront at Maine Ave. and 7th St., S.W. In the Channel Inn Hotel. Fresh seafood daily served in a relaxed dockside setting.

SPANISH. *Moderate:* **El Tío Pepe.** 2809 M St., N.W. The best known; and consistently good Spanish food in attractive Georgetown townhouse.

STEAK. *Expensive:* **Blackie's House of Beef.** 22nd and M Sts., N.W. This is the original establishment in the chain that now blankets the city. Beef is king here, and there is nary a poor choice on the menu.

SWISS. *Moderate.* **The Broker.** 713 8th St., S.E. Outstanding and original Swiss cuisine; attractive décor.

THAI. *Moderate:* **Thai Room.** 527 13th St., N.W. and 5037 Connecticut Ave., N.W. Be careful to check out which dishes are extra hot, but don't hesitate to try out this excellent Oriental cuisine.

VIETNAMESE. *Moderate:* **Chez Maria.** 3338 M St., N.W. A Vietnamese/French restaurant of great simplicity serving superb dishes such as chicken soup with vermicelli and bamboo shoots.

Inexpensive: **Vietnam-Georgetown.** 2934 M St., N.W. Small and crowded, but possibly the best Vietnamese food in town. Try the grilled shrimp and the light crispy rolls.

WEST VIRGINIA

Mountains and Commerce

West Virginia was born of the Civil War. Prior to 1863, the state of Virginia stretched from the Potomac to the Ohio. The mountain people in Virginia's western area disliked being controlled by the plantation owners of eastern Virginia. At the height of the Civil War, with victories for the North piling up in their area, these mountain people formed their own state, renounced secession, and joined the union.

The green and rugged "Mountain State" has some of the most dramatically beautiful scenery east of the Rockies. You can experience a closeness to nature all too rare in the twentieth century. Raft down a wild river, the New or Gauley at Thurmond for instance. View magnificent limestone caverns, awesome Smoke Hole Scenic Gorge, and unique plant life in the Spruce Knob-Seneca Rocks National Recreation Area, part of vast Monongahela National Forest. Drive the state's "country roads" to savor its rich folkloric, musical, and handicrafts traditions. Spring through autumn, you'll find superb handicrafts statewide at many fairs and festivals. Granddaddy of them all is the famed Mountain State Art and Craft Fair each Fourth of July weekend at Ripley.

The wild mountains in the central portion are underlaid with what is probably the greatest supply of coal in the world. Here too originate mineral springs that have given rise to some notable health spas. Best known is White Sulphur Springs, still bubbling away on the grounds of the internationally renowned luxury resort, The Greenbrier.

West Virginia boasts one of the nation's best state park systems, with fine facilities for fishing, camping, tennis, golfing, swimming, hiking, boating. These include Bluestone, adjacent to 1,800-acre Bluestone Lake, and nearby Pipestone, overlooking breathtaking vistas of Blue-

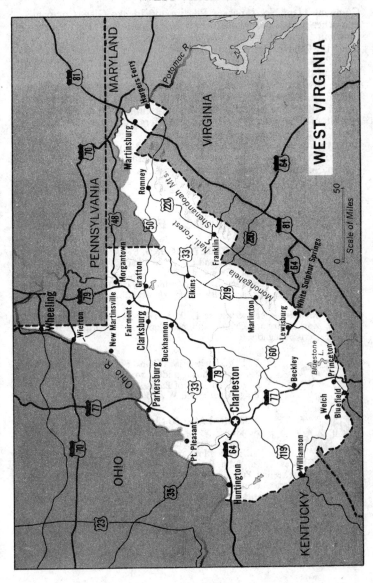

stone Gorge. There are luxurious lodges and a complete recreation center here. Hawks Nest State Park has another modern resort lodge, with spectacular views of New River Gorge.

West of Beckley, where roads twist through narrow ravines, is the home of the legendary mountaineers. Summers, the outdoor drama "Hatfields and McCoys" depicts some of their exploits.

In Charleston, the state capitol is recognized as one of the most beautiful Italian Renaissance buildings in the nation. Huntington, on the Ohio River, is a major shipping center. At this city's Viking Glass

Company Plant No. 2, nearby Pilgrim and Blenko Glass Companies, and other plants throughout the state, you can take free guided tours to see fine glass blown and shaped by hand.

Up the Ohio River, in Point Pleasant, the Point Pleasant Monument State Park commemorates a preliminary skirmish often called the first battle of the American Revolution. Northward is Moundsville, with Grave Creek, considered the world's tallest prehistoric Indian burial mound. Farther north is Wheeling, the state's first capital. Nearby Oglebay Park has beautiful Mansion Museum, with furnishings and exhibits of Ohio Valley history; the park offers golf, swimming, boating, tennis, winter sports.

Eastward, across the state, Harpers Ferry National Historical Park is site of John Brown's famed raid on the Federal arsenal in 1859. "John Brown," outdoor musical drama, is presented summer evenings.

PRACTICAL INFORMATION FOR WEST VIRGINIA

HOW TO GET AROUND. *By air.* Scheduled flights by *Piedmont* and *US Air* to Charleston, Morgantown, Elkins, Greenbrier/White Sulphur Springs/Lewisburg, Beckley, Bluefield/Princeton, Huntington, Parkersburg. *By bus. Trailways, Greyhound, Black and White,* and *Short Way* are the major carriers.

By train. Amtrak has service to Beckley, Harpers Ferry, White Sulphur Springs, Martinsburg and Cumberland, Maryland, on the border of West Virginia's eastern panhandle.

TOURIST INFORMATION. For maps, state park and accommodations guides, write *Dept. of Natural Resources,* Division of Parks and Recreation, State Office Bldg., Charleston, WV 25305.

MUSEUMS AND GALLERIES. *Exposition Coal Mine,* Beckley. Working equipment demonstrates mining techniques; miners are guides. *Pearl S. Buck Birthplace,* Hillsboro. Many original furnishings. *Jefferson County Museum,* Charles Town. John Brown memorabilia. *Mansion Museum,* in Oglebay Park, Wheeling. Period rooms, art gallery, outstanding glass collection. *Huntington Galleries,* Huntington. Paintings, ceramics, and fabrics; art and craft shop. *Sunrise,* Charleston. Restored mansion has art gallery, planetarium, live animal fair, garden center, children's museum.

DRINKING LAWS. All liquor stores in West Virginia are state-owned. Minimum legal drinking age is 18. Liquor sold by the drink in private clubs. Many hotels, motels, resorts, and restaurants offer short-term club memberships enabling guests to order mixed drinks.

SUMMER SPORTS. *Boating.* Many state parks. *Whitewater Rafting.* Between Thurmond and Fayetteville, a 15-mile stretch of the scenic New River is especially challenging, as are rapids of the Cheat, Greenbrier, Gauley and Potomac rivers. A calmer stretch from Hinton to Prince is ideal for canoeing and float trips.

Fishing. Statewide. Trout, black bass, muskie, other species year round. License required. Information and Guide Pamphlet from Div. of Wildlife Resources, Dept. of Natural Resources, Charleston 25301.

Horseback riding. Babcock, Blackwater Falls, Cacapon, Lost River, Pipestem, Watoga State Parks. Oglebay Park, Wheeling.

Mountain climbing. Seneca Rocks; Snowshoe Resort, Slatyfork.

WINTER SPORTS. *Ice-skating.* Blackwater Falls State Park, Coopers Rock State Forest, Wheeling Municipal Park, Pipestem State Park. *Skiing.* Chestnut Ridge, Morgantown; Canaan Valley State Park; Oglebay Park, Wheeling; Snowshoe Resort, Slatyfork; Alpine Lake, Terra Alta. *Tobogganing.* Blackwater Falls State Park; and Oglebay Park, Wheeling, where there is also *sleigh riding.*

SPECTATOR SPORTS. *Basketball.* West Virginia Univ., Morgantown; Marshall Univ., Huntington. *Tennis.* Snowshoe Open Tennis Tournament, Showshoe Resort, Slatyfork. August.

Football. West Virginia Univ., Morgantown.

Horseracing. Charles Town Race Course and Shenandoah Downs, Charles Town; Waterford Park, Chester.

Greyhound dog racing. Wheeling Downs, Wheeling.

West Virginia Regatta Festival, Sutton, late June; Sternwheel Regatta Race, Charleston, early Sept.; Tri–State Fair and Regatta Speed Boat Races, Huntington, mid-Sept.

WHAT TO DO WITH THE CHILDREN. Huntington. *Camden Park.* Wild animal zoo, miniature golf, amusement rides, roller skating, penny arcade, boat and train rides. Charleston. *Sunrise.* Children's museum. Exhibits, live animals, displays, class instruction, planetarium.

Bluefield. *Ridge Runner Railroad.* Miniature replica of 1863 steam locomotive and three coaches; station modeled after 1890 depot; ¾-mile run, June–Aug.

Cass. Ride old steam locomotive to top of Bald Knob for spectacular view. In Cass are a *Civil War Museum, Cass Country Store,* and horse-drawn *Cass Stagecoach Line.* In nearby Green Bank is the *National Radio Observatory,* with tours of the installation.

Wheeling. Jamboree USA. Live Saturday radio shows of country music by WWVA, Capitol Music Hall, 1015 Main St.

HOTELS AND MOTELS. The price categories in this section, for double occupancy, will average as follows: *Deluxe:* over $100; *Expensive:* $50–90; *Moderate:* $40–$50; *Inexpensive:* under $40.

BECKLEY. *Moderate to Expensive:* **Holiday Inn.** 1924 Harper Rd. Coin laundry, pool. Pets. Dining room. Private club.

Moderate: **Ramada Inn.** 1940 Harper Rd. Pool, color TV. Dining room, private club.

Inexpensive: **Days Inn.** Rte. 3 (Harper Rd.) and I–77 (WV Turnpike), 102 Harpers Pike Dr. Gasoline, handicapped facilities, restaurant. Considered one of the best in Days Inn system.

BERKELEY SPRINGS. *Expensive:* **Coolfont Recreation Center.** Rte. 9 W. Year-round resort and health spa. Art films, nature walks, square dances, classical and bluegrass concerts, dinner theater. Accommodations in cabins, chalets, lodge, deluxe mountain homes.

Moderate: **Cacapon Lodge.** Cacapon State Park. Fishing, golf, tennis, hiking, many outdoor activities.

CHARLESTON. *Expensive:* **Holiday Inn Heart-o-Town.** 1000 Washington St. E. Pool, sauna, color TV. Dining room, lounge, live entertainment.

Moderate: **Ramada Inn.** I–64 exit 56, 2nd Ave. & B St. Free in-room movies, heated pool. Dining room, cocktails, live entertainment.

Inexpensive: **Smiley's.** 6210 MacCorkle Ave. S.W., St. Albans. Color TV. Pool. Coin laundry. Café, private club with entertainment.

El Rancho Inn. 2843 MacCorkle Ave. S.W. Color TV, playground, free coffee. Restaurant adjacent.

Red Roof Inn. Two locations: 4006 MacCorkle Ave., 6305 MacCorkle Ave., SE. Color TV; restaurants nearby.

CHARLES TOWN. *Inexpensive:* **Towne House Motor Lodge.** E. Washington St. Color TV, pool, tennis, picnic tables. Café, private club. In-room steam baths. Pets.

CLARKSBURG. *Moderate to Expensive:* **Sheraton Inn.** 151 W. Main St. Coffee shop, restaurant, lounge. Heated pool. Pets.
Inexpensive: **Towne House West.** US 50, at Wilsonburg Rd. exit. Pool, restaurant adjacent.

DAVIS. *Moderate:* **Canaan Valley Lodge.** Canaan Valley State Park. Restaurant, snack bar. Golf, fishing, boating, swimming, tennis, playground, ice skating rink.
Inexpensive: **Best Western Alpine Lodge.** WV 9 at entrance to Blackwater Falls State Park. Dining room, indoor pool. Small pets. Boating, horseback riding, fishing nearby.
Blackwater Lodge. Blackwater Falls State Park. TV, restaurant, swimming lake.

HARPERS FERRY. *Moderate:* **Cliffside Inn.** 2 mi. SW on US 340. Large comfortable rooms, color TV. Two restaurants, bar–lounge, live entertainment. Indoor recreation area and large heated pool. Tennis; golfing, and hiking near. Excellent gift shop.
Inexpensive: **Hilltop House.** Restored historic hostelry overlooks Potomac, Shenandoah Rivers. Favorite retreat of Mark Twain, Woodrow Wilson.

HUNTINGTON. *Moderate:* **Holiday Inn.** 6007 US Rt. 60 E. Indoor pool, tennis, sauna. Disco, free movies.

LEWISBURG. *Moderate:* **Fort Savannah Inn.** 204 N. Jefferson St. Color TV, dining room, entertainment.
Old Colony Inn. US 219. Color TV. Free Continental breakfast.
General Lewis Inn. 301 E. Washington St. Picturesque. Old part dates from 1834.

MARTINSBURG. *Moderate* **The Woods Resort,** Mt. Lake Rd. off Rt. 9 E. Hedgesville. Restaurant, lounge with entertainment. Lodge and cabins. Swimming, tennis, nature trails, home of Eastern Fitness Institute.

MORGANTOWN. *Expensive:* **Sheraton Lakeview Resort and Conference Center.** Rt. 6, 7 mi. N. of WV 73. Attractive resort on 400 acres offers golf, tennis, lawn games, saunas, pools. Dining room, coffee shop, private club.
Moderate: **Holiday Inn.** 1400 Saratoga Ave. Racquetball, indoor tennis, pool. Pets. Dining room, lounge, live entertainment.

PIPESTEM. *Moderate:* **Pipestem Lodge.** Pipestem State Park Resort, 17 mi. SW, NW of Hinton via WV 20. Color TV, pools, playground. Fishing, social program. Restaurant, snack bar, private club.

SHEPHERDSTOWN. *Moderate to Expensive:* **Bavarian Inn.** W. end of Potomac River Bridge. Beautifully furnished rooms, all with private balconies, in four luxurious new Alpine-style chalets overlooking Potomac River. Color TV, canopied four-poster beds; some rooms with fireplaces, whirlpool baths.

SNOWSHOE. *Expensive to Deluxe:* **Quality Inn Snowshoe Mountain Ski Lodge.** Atop one of the east's finest ski mountains. Four-season recreational facilities include golf, tennis, horseback riding, fishing. Dining room, lounge, entertainment. Vacation packages.

Moderate to Deluxe: **Quality Inn at Snowshoe Base.** Snowshoe and Silver Creek ski areas just minutes away. Tennis, horseback riding, fishing, pool, sauna. Dining room, lounge, entertainment.

WEIRTON. *Moderate:* **Holiday Inn.** 350 Three Springs Dr. Dining room, lounge, live entertainment. Pool. Pets. Tennis.

WHEELING. *Moderate:* **Holiday Inn.** I–70 & Dallas Pike Triadelphia, WV. Color TV, pool. Pets. Dining room, private club, entertainment, dancing.
  Moderate to Expensive: **Quality Inn.** Exit 11, I–70, at Triadelphia, WV. Dining room, lounge, entertainment. Near Oglebay Park, Wheeling Downs, and Jamboree USA.
  Wilson Lodge. Oglebay Park. Resort lodge in 1500-acre recreational park has many outdoor activities. Accommodations in lodge, chalets, cabanas. Dining room, cocktails.

WHITE SULPHUR SPRINGS. *Deluxe:* **The Greenbrier.** US 60. Famed resort on 6,500 acres offers golf, tennis, riding, sauna, mineral baths, social program, entertainment.
  Inexpensive to Moderate: **Best Western Old White,** 865 E. Main St. Color TV, heated pool. Restaurant adjacent.

 DINING OUT. Restaurant price categories: *Expensive:* over $20; *Moderate:* $10–20; *Inexpensive:* under $10. Prices are for a complete dinner but do not include drinks, tax, or tip.

BERKELEY SPRINGS. *Moderate:* **Country Inn.** 207 S. Washington St. Roast turkey, country ham, assorted seafood specialties. Garden dining in summer. Adjoins nation's oldest health spa (1748).
  Treetop House. Rte. 9 W. Veal marsala, rainbow trout, Delmonico steak, Maryland crabcakes, fresh garden vegetables, wildflower mountain honey. All-you-can-eat buffets. Non-smokers' section.

CHARLESTON. *Moderate:* **The Corner Stone.** 3103 MacCorkle Ave., SE (Kanawha City Motor Lodge). Greek-American menu. Own baking. Moussaka, grape leaf rolls are specialties.

FAIRMONT. *Moderate:* **Tiffany's.** In the Continental Key Club, Rte. 19 N. Fine seafood, Italian specialties.

HARPERS FERRY. *Moderate:* **Cliffside Club.** Cliffside Inn. Excellent steaks, seafood; weekend buffet. Lounge, live entertainment.
  Hilltop House. Retreat of Presidents; features southern fried chicken, baked ham, stuffed flounder.

HINTON. *Moderate–Expensive:* **Riverside Inn.** WV 3, at Pence Springs. Charming colonial atmosphere. Roast goose, fruit-stuffed duckling, game are specialties. Children's plates.

HUNTINGTON. *Moderate:* **Rebels and Redcoats Tavern.** 626 Fifth St. W. One of state's finest wine selections. Lamb, quail, seafood, Bombay of beef are specialties.
  Inexpensive: **Bailey's Cafeteria.** 410 9th St. Luscious fresh vegetables, own baking. Locally popular.
  Heritage Station. Heritage Village. Vintage B & O train station has collection of railroad antiques. Features huge burgers, soups, man-sized sandwiches. Backgammon room.

LEWISBURG. *Moderate:* **General Lewis Dining Room.** General Lewis Inn. 301 E. Washington St. Grilled pork chops, fried chicken, steak, country ham.

MORGANTOWN. *Moderate to Expensive:* **Sheraton Lakeview Resort and Conference Center.** Rte. 6, 7 mi. N of WV 73. A la carte entrées, children's menu. Cocktails and entertainment in private club.

PARKERSBURG. *Moderate to Expensive:* **Point of View.** Overlooking historic Blennerhassett Island. Popular Sunday brunch, luncheon specialties, as well as food prepared at tableside.

SHEPHERDSTOWN. *Moderate:* **The Bavarian Inn.** Overlooks Potomac River. Smooth, friendly service. Elegant dining rooms decorated with antiques, deer horn chandeliers. Bavarian, continental specialties include spring lamb, veal, fresh seafood, roast pheasant, hearty game dishes, superb desserts such as apple strudel, Black Forest cake.

WHEELING. *Moderate:* **Ernie's Esquire.** 29th St. Blvd. Colorful decor, children's menu. On weekends, make advance reservations!

WHITE SULPHUR SPRINGS. *Expensive:* **The Greenbrier.** Superb Continental, American cuisine in elegant formal atmosphere. Impressive wine list.

ZELA. (Near Summersville) *Moderate to Expensive:* **Country Road Inn.** Superb Italian specialties, including homemade pasta, cakes, pies, Biscuit Tortoni. Reservations required, since everything is made from scratch.

ALABAMA

More than Cotton

Birmingham, Alabama's largest city, is a good base for touring the state. Dominating the metropolis is the 55-foot-tall cast iron figure of Vulcan surveying the city from a pedestal 124 feet high. *Vulcan,* the Roman god of fire and forge, was designed for the Louisiana Purchase Exposition in St. Louis. It was made of Birmingham iron, cast in its foundries and overlooks the city as a monument to an industry.

Arlington is Birmingham's only antebellum home and tells a story of a bygone era as it stands in quiet memory. It was built by slaves of handmade bricks and hand-hewn timbers, and later became the headquarters for Union General Wilson. On display are authentic period furniture, a plantation kitchen with authentic utensils, a 19th-century garden and a museum.

Nearby, in the wooded areas of beautiful Lane Park, are Birmingham's Zoo, Botanical and Japanese Gardens.

US 78 northwest intersects with Route 5 at Jasper. Route 5 continues north to Phil Campbell and the Mysterious Dismals Wonder Garden, then US 43 north to Tuscumbia, the birthplace and early home of Helen Keller. "Ivy Green," built by her grandfather in 1820, still stands. Helen Keller was born a normal child here in 1880, but two years later typhoid fever tragically deprived her of both sight and sound, beginning the greatest drama in Ivy Green's long history.

Much the same now as it was then, the many significant places and things—Whistle Path, the pump, her personal effects—have been kept intact for the visitor. Her story is retold each summer when William Gibson's play, "The Miracle Worker," is staged at the site.

Sheffield, north of US 43, is the principal railroad and industrial center of the Muscle Shoals area. Your chief interest, however, will be

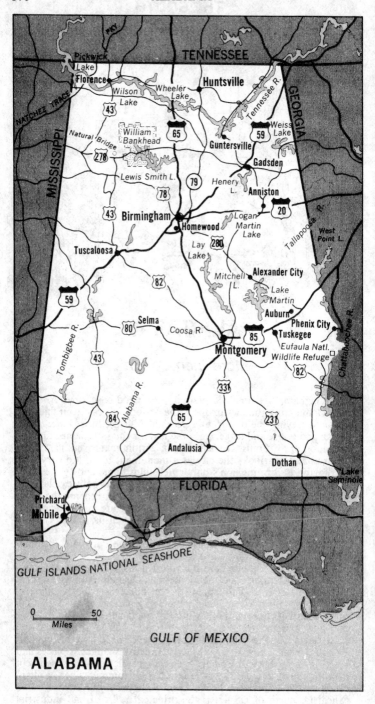

ALABAMA

the Wilson Dam, largest of the TVA dams and a National Historic Monument, 5 miles northeast on State 133. Its great bulk—4,500 feet in length, 137 feet in height and 101 feet thick at the base—creates Wilson Lake and miles of shoreline popular for aquatic vacation activities.

Florence, north of Sheffield, has the largest Indian mound in the Tennessee River Valley, rising upward 42 feet. The temple which once stood atop the mound was used for Indian ceremonials honoring the sun god. A museum traces the movement of prehistoric Indians through northern Alabama. Also in Florence is a restored stagecoach stop, now a museum, called Pope's Tavern.

US 72 continues east to Athens, still airing an antebellum atmosphere of tree-lined residential streets with noted Greek Revival houses radiating from the town square.

US 31 south takes you to Decatur, a flourishing industrial area thriving as a result of the TVA's rescue of this city literally battered to death by Civil War battles.

Decatur's Point Mallard Park provides numerous activities in its 749-acre area: two swimming pools, one with wave action; a 175-site campground; picnic facilities; biking and hiking trails; boats for use on the Tennessee River and an 18-hole championship golf course.

Huntsville

US 72 A east goes to Huntsville, once a cotton field and now the home of the Alabama Space and Rocket Center located just southwest off US 231. Here, you can ride or operate 60 do-it-yourself space-age devices, including some used to train astronauts. Bus tours available to nearby Marshall Space Flight Center, NASA's largest facility.

Huntsville's link to the past is Twickenham, a 12-block, 300-structure district on the National Register of Historic Places. In the area 159 buildings are said to have historic and architectural significance and 12 are listed in the Historic American Buildings Survey of 1935. Twickenham is the founding place of Huntsville and the cornerstone of Alabama.

US 72 continues to Scottsboro and northeast through mountainous terrain to Bridgeport, gateway to the Russel Cave National Monument, which lies about 8 miles northwest off US 72 via County 75 and 91. The cave has a possibly unparalleled continuity of cave life for some 8,000 or more years. At the Visitor Center, displays show man's use of the cave from prehistoric times, covering Archaic, Woodland, Hopewellian, Mississippian, and historic cultures.

US 72 returns south to Stevenson and Route 117 southeast past Sequoyah Caverns to the junction with US 11, which follows the Lookout Mountains south paralleling DeSoto State Park, east of Hammondville off Route 117 on County 89 which continues past rushing waterfalls and lush foliage enhancing Little River Canyon, the deepest gorge east of the Mississippi. Route 68 west meets US 11 going south past *Noculula Falls,* named for the despondent daughter of an Indian chief who leaped from the mountain to seal a broken heart. Surrounding the falls at Gadsden is a pioneer village, a collection of authentic buildings from another century.

South at Gadsden, at Broad and 1st Sts., a monument memorializes Emma Sansom, another young girl, brave in a different manner, who cunningly maneuvered the Confederate troops to safety.

I–59 south returns to Birmingham.

Montgomery

The prime point of interest in Montgomery, the state's capital, is the historic State Capitol building, one of the Southland's most beautiful. Inside, the state's rich, historical background has been caught by an artist's brush in great, colorful murals; indeed, a visual experience. Conveniently across from the Capitol is the two-story First White House of the Confederacy which contains personal furnishings of Jefferson Davis and his family. The capitol building is surrounded by other state office buildings, including the *Archives* and *History Building*.

Among the city's historic buildings are those in the Old North Hull Historic District, including a tavern, church, log cabin, grange hall, doctor's office, and 1850s townhouse.

Mobile

The busy port city of Mobile overlaps past and present on the western bank of the Mobile River at the top of Mobile Bay. Old mansions and grillwork balconies of many pre-Civil War buildings overlook boulevards fanning out from Bienville Square at the center of the city and lead through flower-gardened residential sections.

Most highly publicized of gardens in the Mobile area is Bellingrath Gardens and Home on an 800-acre spread 20 miles south of town on US 90 and then Bellingrath Rd., in the hamlet of Theodore. The Ile-aux-Oies River laces through some 65 acres of forests and gardens planted in azaleas.

State 163 leads across a bridge to Dauphin Island, a destination for vacationers seeking sun and sand. Ferry service runs from Fort Gaines on the island to Fort Morgan on the other side of Mobile Bay. From there, State 180 leads east alongside the Gulf of Mexico. Or, US 90 east from Mobile connects with either US 98 or State 59 going south to the beaches.

PRACTICAL INFORMATION FOR ALABAMA

HOW TO GET THERE. *By air:* Birmingham direct on *American, Delta, Eastern, Republic, USAir, United;* Huntsville-Decatur on *American, Delta, Republic, United;* Mobile on *Eastern, American, Delta, Air New Orleans, Scheduled Skyways, Republic;* Montgomery on *Delta, Republic, Eastern;* Dothan on *Delta* and *Republic;* Anniston on *Delta;* Tuscaloosa on *Delta.*

By car: I–59 from Chattanooga, Tenn., to Birmingham; I–20 from Atlanta, Ga., to Birmingham; both to Tuscaloosa; I–85 from Atlanta, Ga., to Montgomery; I–65 from Tenn. to Mobile; and I–10 from New Orleans, La., to Mobile.

By bus: Greyhound and *Trailways* come into the state.

By train: Amtrak into Birmingham, Anniston, and Tuscaloosa.

HOW TO GET AROUND. *By air: Republic* has local flights. *By car:* I–65 goes from the Tennessee state line to Mobile. I–20 and US 80 cross the state from the Georgia state line to the Mississippi state line. *Car rentals: Hertz, Avis, National, Econo-Car, Budget Rent-A-Car, Thrifty, Sears, American International* and *Dollar. By Bus: Greyhound, Trailways Basden Transportation, Capitol Trailways, Faith Bus Service, Gulf Transport, Ingram Transportation, Johnson Bus Service,* and *Joiner. By train: Amtrak.*

ALABAMA

TOURIST INFORMATION SERVICES. Montgomery, 36130: Alabama Bureau of Publicity and Information, 532 S. Perry St.; Alabama State Parks, State Administrative Bldg.; Alabama Travel Council, 660 Adams Ave. 36130; all local Convention & Visitors Bureaus, Tourist Information Centers or Chambers of Commerce. Toll-free information (except in-state, Alaska, Hawaii) 800–252–2262. In Alabama call 800–392–8096.

MUSEUMS AND GALLERIES. Birmingham: *Museum of Art,* 2000 8th Ave. north; *The Red Mountain Geological Museum,* 2230 15th Ave. S. Mobile: *Fine Arts Museum of the South,* Langan Park. Montgomery: *Museum of Fine Arts,* 440 S. McDonough St. *Tumbling Waters Museum of Flags,* 131 S. Perry St.

HISTORIC SITES. Dauphin Island: *Fort Gaines* stands at entrance to Mobile Bay, near scene of 1864 Battle of Mobile Bay during which Admiral Farragut defeated Confederates. Gulf Shores: *Fort Morgan,* twin fort defending entrance to Mobile Bay, captured by Union forces during Mobile Bay campaign. Alexander City: *Horseshoe Bend National Military Park,* where Andrew Jackson defeated the Creek Indians to break their strength during the War of 1812. Wetumpka: *Fort Toulouse,* erected by the French in 1717 to defend their trade with the Indians from British interlopers. Site includes a nature trail and the *William Bartram Arboretum.*

TOURS. *Gray Lines Tours* offers variety packages around Mobile. Located at 607 Dauphin Street; (205) 432–2229.

DRINKING LAWS. Liquor sold by drink in licensed places; by miniature bottles in restaurants and lounges, which also sell beer. Most metropolitan areas are "wet." Some counties are "dry." Minimun age: 19 years. No Sunday sales.

SPORTS. *Boating:* Rental boats in many state parks, and from marinas and fish camps. *Fishing:* Fresh water rivers and lakes, plus Gulf of Mexico for saltwater angling. License required at nominal cost. *Golf: Golf Digest* rates C.C. of Birmingham; Jetport G.C., Huntsville; and Langan Park G.C., Mobile, and the golf courses at the Grand Hotel at Point Clear. For other courses write Alabama Bureau of Publicity and Information, 532 S. Perry St., Montgomery 36130.

Hunting: Obtain information from Alabama Department of Conversation, Game and Fish Division, Montgomery 36130.

SPECTATOR SPORTS. *Basketball* via college teams. *Football* heavies at Birmingham's Legion Field Stadium; Senior Bowl game, Mobile in Jan.; and Blue-Gray game, Montgomery in Dec. *Horse shows:* Decatur, Montgomery, and Selma, Sept. into Nov. *Rodeo:* Montgomery and Opp in Mar.; Athens in Aug. *Greyhound racing:* year-round at Greenetrack in Eutaw, mid-Jan.–mid-Dec. Mobile.

WHAT TO DO WITH THE CHILDREN. Birmingham: *Birmingham Zoo,* 2630 Cahaba Rd., US 280. Mobile: *U.S.S. Alabama, Battleship Pkwy.,* US 90. Montgomery: *W.A. Gayle Planetarium,* 1010 Forest Ave.

HOTELS AND MOTELS. Most of the motels and hotels in Alabama, especially those along the Gulf Coast, boast various indoor and outdoor recreational facilities. Listings are in order of price category based upon double occupancy. *Expensive:* $35 and up; *Moderate:* $25–35; *Inexpensive:* under $25. For a more complete explanation of hotel and motel categories see *Facts at Your Fingertips* at the front of this volume.

ALEXANDER CITY. *Moderate.* **Horseshoe Bend.** Restaurant, pool.

BIRMINGHAM. *Expensive:* **Hyatt House,** 901 N. 21 St. 405 rooms, pool, restaurant, shops, entertainment.
Birmingham Hilton. 808 20th St. S. Complete facilities.
Sheraton Mountain Brook. Hwy 280 S. Restaurant, lounge with lively entertainment.
Holiday Inn. Four locations: Airport, 5000 10th Ave. N; South, 1548 Montgomery Hwy; East, 7941 Crestwood Blvd; Downtown Medical Center, 420 20th St S.
Ramada Inn. Three locations: 5216 Airport Hwy., 1535 Montgomery Hwy., and 951 18th St. S. All facilities.
Moderate: **Motel Birmingham.** Pleasant rooms, pool. 7905 Crestwood Blvd.
Passport Inn. 800 11th St. S. Restaurant, lounge with live entertainment. In Medical Center complex.
Tara House. 2800 20th St. S. Small, restaurant and lounge with live entertainment.

DECATUR. *Expensive:* **Decatur Inn.** Olympic pool, restaurant.
Moderate. **Holiday Inn.** Pool, restaurant, laundry.

FLORENCE. *Moderate:* **Master Host Inn.** Pool, restaurant.
Florence Tourway Inn. Some refrigerators. Restaurant, pool.

FLORENCE-MUSCLE SHOALS. *Moderate:* **Lakeview Inn.** US 72 & US 43, 5 mi. E. Restaurant, pool.

GADSDEN. *Expensive:* **Holiday Inn.** Café, laundry.

GULF SHORES. *Expensive:* **Holiday Inn.** Beachfront, pool
Lighthouse. Motel and cottages, overlooking Gulf.
Port of Call. Private beach, efficiency kitchens.

GUNTERSVILLE. *Moderate:* **Lake Guntersville State Resort Park.** Resort inn, restaurant.
Inexpensive: **Bel Air Motel.** Restaurant nearby.

HUNTSVILLE. *Expensive:* **Amberley Suite Hotel.** New, health spa, deli, coffee shop.
Huntsville Hilton. Restaurant, lounge, pool, spa. Opposite civic center.
Sheraton Inn. Specialty restaurant; entertainment.
Skycenter Hotel. At airport. Restaurant, pool, golf, tennis.
Best Western Carriage Inn. Entertainment, pool, laundry, restaurant.

MOBILE *Expensive:* **Hilton.** 3101 Airport Blvd. Restaurant, pool, shopping arcade.
Best Western Admiral Semmes. 250 Government Blvd. Restaurant, pool, in-room movies. Recently reopened following extensive renovation.
Moderate: **Riverview Plaza.** 64 Water St. Restaurant, oyster bar, pool, sauna.
Rodeway Inn. Two locations: 1500 Government St.; 1724 Michigan Ave. at I–10.

MONTGOMERY. *Expensive:* **Governor's House Motel.** Pool, specialty restaurant, entertainment, whirlpools, refrigerators.
Holiday Inn. Complete. 3 locations.
Sheraton Riverfront Station. In renovated railroad freight depot. Pool, restaurant, entertainment.

POINT CLEAR. *Expensive:* **The Grand Hotel.** Old-fashioned resort hotel with gourmet dining room. Lounge. First-class golf, tennis, and sailing facilities. Overlooks Mobile Bay.

YOUTH HOSTELS. Mobile: *YMCA,* 61 South Conception St.; *YWCA,* 1060 Government St. Montgomery: *YMCAs* at: Central Branch, 761 South Perry St.; East Montgomery Branch, 3407 Pelzer Ave.; Cleveland Ave. Branch, 1202 Cleveland Ave.

 DINING OUT in Alabama leans toward traditional Southern dishes, including Southern fried chicken, ham steak with red gravy, and chicken pan pie. The Gulf Coast is noted for creole specialties, so be sure to ask for Gulf flounder, shrimp, and other special seafoods and gumbos. In river towns try catfish caught fresh from the Tennessee River.

Restaurants are in order of price category and ranges for a complete meal, excluding drinks, are as follows: *Expensive:* $15 and up; *Moderate:* $10–15; *Inexpensive:* under $10. For a more complete explanation of restaurant categories see *Facts at Your Fingertips* at the front of this volume.

BIRMINGHAM. *Expensive:* **Hugo's Rotisserie.** French, elegant. Located in Hyatt House.
Moderate: **Michael's Sirloin Room.** Known for steaks, but seafood also available. Sports decor.
John's Restaurant. Fresh seafood, locally popular.
Fred Gang's. U.S. 280 S. Steaks, exceptionally fine salad bar.
Leo's. Fresh seafood.
Steve Leontis Smokehouse. Best barbecue in town.
Inexpensive: **Lloyd's.** Best barbecue out of town. 5301 Hwy 280 S.
Rube Burrows. 1015 20th 5. Gourmet burgers, to salads.

DECATUR. *Inexpensive:* **Gibson's.** Barbecue and Brunswick stew.

FLORENCE. *Moderate:* **Lakeview Inn Restaurant.** Regional specialties.
The Hermitage House. Varied entries. Across from Pope's Tavern Museum.

GADSDEN. *Inexpensive:* **The Embers.** Specialty is seafood.

GULF SHORES. *Moderate:* **Coconut Willie's.** Seafood, view of Gulf of Mexico.

GUNTERSVILLE. *Inexpensive:* **Reid's.** Specialties are catfish and vegetables.

HUNTSVILLE. *Expensive:* **Rib Celler.** At the Skycenter Hotel. Specialty is prime rib, also seafood and lamb dishes.
Moderate: **The Fogcutter.** Steaks, seafood, salad bar. Locally popular.

MOBILE. *Expensive:* **Bernard's.** French and Creole cuisine. Within walking distance of downtown hotels.
The Pillars. Known for steaks and seafood.
Weichmans All Seasons. Decorate with antiques. Seafood, steaks, lamb.
Moderate: **Constantine's.** Outstanding seafood. In Rodeway Inn.
Wintzell's Oyster House. Best oysters, and native seafood specialties.
Inexpensive: **Morrison's.** Chain cafeteria.

MONTGOMERY. *Moderate:* **Sahara.** Specialty is seafood; own baking, including homemade cheesecake and assorted pies.
Inexpensive: **Elite.** Steaks and seafood. Locally popular for more than 60 years.
Morrison's. Cafeteria. Two locations.

FLORIDA

Where the Sun Spends the Winter

Today's Florida is a subtropical playground, home and workplace for some ten million people, vacationland throughout the year for the seekers of something—wildlife, high life, low life; the quiet, noisy, lively, sedate, simple, luxurious, or a combination; in sum, the good life. More of them come in summer than winter. July and August are the peak months, when the school's-out family trade heads for the summer beach resorts of northern Florida from Pensacola to Apalachicola; to the Sun Coast area of Tampa and St. Petersburg, or central Florida's fun-tier, the Orlando–Disney World area.

The winter visitors stay longer, spend more, and are concentrated in the bottom half of the state, where it's warmer than anywhere else in the continental United States. Average January temperatures are 71 degrees in the Florida Keys and 69 on the mainland southern tip, compared to 54 in the northwest Panhandle.

As an alternative to the high-priced winter season, late-April through May offers dependably warm but not hot weather; many of the subtropical flowers are at their gaudiest then, and the midsummer tendency toward brief but almost daily showers has not yet begun. October and November provide low hotel rates like those of late spring, while bed and breakfast spots have mushroomed, offering even cheaper rates.

The summer average is between 80 and 83 degrees, and the undeniably high humidity is mitigated by almost constant onshore breezes. With no point in the state more than 60 miles from a seashore of some sort, the result is a mild climate, summer and winter.

Guide to Miami Beach

To get to Miami, just go south. You can't miss it—and you shouldn't. There's Miami Beach and Coral Gables, Hialeah and Miami Springs, the core city of Miami proper, and Biscayne Park, West Miami, North Miami, South Miami, Miami Shores, and others. Put them all together and they still spellMiami, the magic word.

Over five million visitors a year come to this little (7.2 square miles) island just across Biscayne Bay from mainland Miami. There is a permanent population of more than 96,000, but the island can accommodate three times this many visitors. One-fourth of all the hotels in Florida are situated here in a slender strip of architectural virtuosity. The 322 hotels have 26,761 rooms ranging from $25 to $150 a day during the winter season, about half that, or less, in summer. There are also 45,298 apartment units in 2,181 other buildings, but this isn't all, for in truth the beach and the hotels extend northward more than a hundred additional blocks: Surfside and Bal Harbour, the county's Haulover Park with a public beach and a marina, and the oceanfront motels—fancy, gaudy, pretty, monstrous, prim, ostentatious—side by side in a battle for attention all the way to the county line. The entire string, top to bottom, should be seen at least once. Start by taking A1A from Hollywood and Hallandale. The Sheraton Bal Harbour (formerly the Americana), at 97th Street and Collins Avenue, will be the first of the large, convention-oriented luxury hotels you will see, and Collins Avenue, for the next eighty-seven blocks, *is* Miami Beach, the resort, in all its variety. The block-long oceanfront parks at 71st Street, 65th Street, 46th Street, and 23rd Street; the sun-sparkled beaches along Ocean Drive and the Art Deco Historic District of South Beach, break the skein of towering hotels. The effect is a blinding, kaleidoscopic, gaudy extravagance. Most of the spectacle is new since World War II. For a number of years after the war, Miami Beach built more new hotels than all the rest of the world combined.

Getting around in Miami by automobile is fairly simple, but can run into a lot of mileage. The street numbering system is centered at Miami Avenue and Flagler Street, and is divided into quadrants surrounding that point—northeast, northwest, southeast, and southwest. Streets run north and south, as do terraces. The avenues and places run east and west. There are exceptions: Coral Gables has its own system of Spanish-named avenues. However, the basic system prevails generally, as far as 215th Street on the north, 360th Street on the south, and 217th Avenue on the west. If you want to get to Northwest South River Drive or Southwest North River Drive, however, it's perhaps best to take a cab.

The Row of Splendor

Across Collins Avenue are other hotels, but less flamboyant: they do not have oceanfront. It is a matter of supreme importance to many visitors that they stay at an oceanfront hotel, whether or not they ever go near the ocean.

The newest and most elaborate hotels and apartments stretch northward from the fabulous Fontainebleau Hilton at 44th Street and Collins Avenue, but the "older" hostelries south to Lincoln Road are aging but are still a good buy. These are the first-built, generally smaller hotels which offer good location and the same sun—plus a superior beach—at economy rates.

Once eroded almost completely away, Miami Beach has now undergone a $64 million restoration which has replaced this golden strand of sand for 10½ miles. Thanks to new engineering, with breakwaters

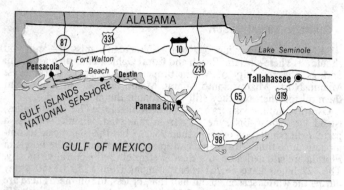

and reefs, the new beach should last for some years. For now you can beachcomb for miles along this 300-foot-wide stretch of bare feet and bikinis. A new boardwalk extends between 21st and 46th streets.

From 79th to 87th streets, North Shore Open Space Park is Miami Beach's newest attraction, a 32-acre oceanfront recreation area. Environmental restoration includes man-made sand dunes, masses of sea grapes and sea oats, and a variety of flowers, plants and trees. Along with the beachfront for water sports, the park is equipped with winding boardwalks, picnic areas, bicycle paths, and shaded pavilions.

Miami Beach is a grande dame who refuses to give up her beauty or popularity.

Downtown Miami

Biscayne Boulevard is the city's best-known thoroughfare. Since it is also US 1, it will send you to Key West or Canada if you stick with it, but, for our purposes, it is Miami's downtown "show" street. Stately royal palms line its eight traffic lanes, divided by four parking lanes, between Southeast 1st Street and Northeast 5th Street. On the west are tall, showy hotels and business buildings; on the east is Bayfront Park, sixty-two acres of tropical flora, statues, pools, shaded benches and walkways. On the north end of the park is the city's auditorium and the Port of Miami on Dodge Island access to the Dodge Island seaport, where cruise ships leave for all points of the Bahamas and Caribbean ports of call. The downtown area features $3 billion in new construction with the Miami Center/Pavillon Hotel and the James L. Knight Conference Center/Hyatt Regency Hotel the most prominent features.

Since 1961, Miami has added a whole new dimension. It is called "Little Havana," an exciting area of excellent restaurants, nightclubs, and shops which, for the English-speaking visitor, provides the flavor and feel of a foreign country. It centers around SW 8th Street and W. Flagler Street where most of Miami's more than 500,000 Cubans work and live, an area of "old Miami" two-story homes and aging commercial buildings, which was revitalized by its industrious new residents, whose per capita income was calculated at well over $10,000 a year—an amazing figure for what is supposed to be a "refugee colony." Little Havana is no hybrid; it's a completely Cuban world with hundreds of open front cafés, restaurants, oyster bars, bookstores, tobacco shops, and grocers. About all that is missing from Old Havana are the cries of lottery ticket vendors and the covered arcades. Prices in Little Havana can be ridiculously low for good Cuban dishes in some of the smaller niches to downright expensive in the fancier supper clubs.

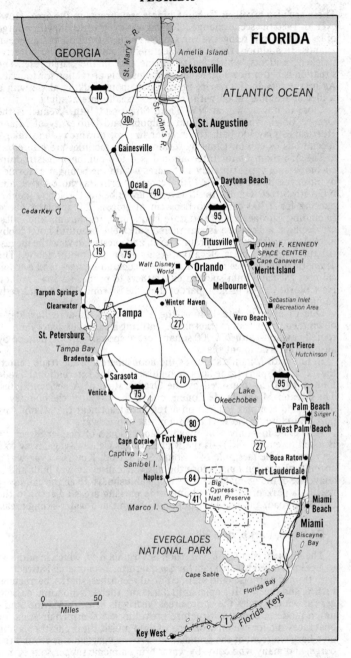

FLORIDA

GEORGIA

St. Mary's R.

Amelia Island

Jacksonville

10

ATLANTIC OCEAN

30

St. John's R.

St. Augustine

Gainesville

Ocala

40

Daytona Beach

CedarKey

95

19

75

Titusville

JOHN F. KENNEDY
SPACE CENTER
Cape Canaveral

Walt Disney
World

Orlando

Meritt Island

4

Melbourne

Tarpon Springs

Clearwater

• Winter Haven

Sebastian Inlet
Recreation Area

Tampa

27

Vero Beach

St. Petersburg

Tampa Bay

Bradenton

Fort Pierce
Hutchinson I.

• Sarasota

70

Venice

75

Lake
Okeechobee

95

1

Palm Beach
Singer I.

80

West Palm Beach

Cape Coral • **Fort Myers**

Captiva I.
Sanibel I.

27

Boca Raton

Fort Lauderdale

Naples

84

Big
Cypress
Natl. Preserve

Marco I.

41

**Miami
Beach**

Miami

Biscayne
Bay

EVERGLADES
NATIONAL PARK

Cape Sable

Florida Bay

0   50
Miles

1   Florida Keys

Key West

There are also excellent Cuban-Chinese restaurants in the area. However, in 1980 the scene changed. Miami was overburdened with a surge of less prosperous refugees from Cuba as well as from other Caribbean Islands. In addition, there was resentment from some of the poverty-stricken residents, which led to an increase in the crime rate. The situation is better now and Miami remains a big attraction for tourists. As in any city in the world, be cautious about walking alone with a wallet or handbag filled with money, especially late at night.

Close to downtown, at NW Third Street and 14th Avenue, is the Orange Bowl, where the Miami Dolphins and University of Miami Hurricanes play football. It's simpler to park downtown and take a special bus or cab on game days, for parking facilities are limited.

The 556-room Omni International is a $76-million megastructure encompassing approximately 10.5 acres within the boundaries formed by Biscayne Boulevard, NE 17th Terrace, North Bayshore Drive, and NE 15th Street. Omni's multi-layered levels below the lobby include parking for 2,700 cars, two department stores, 150 specialty shops (including European haute couture boutiques), restaurants and cafes, art displays, a Treasure Island theme park. The beautiful hotel lobby is located five floors above ground level, and guests can view the megastructure through glass elevators, rising from the motor lobby. The dramatic hotel houses restaurants, pool, cocktail lounges, and a tropical roof garden. Omni spurred city fathers to propose a $547 million New World Center project; part of that, the Bicenntial Park, is already complete.

Due to open in late 1986 is the $93 million, 20-acre Bayside, a downtown waterfront marketplace, featuring a pair of two-story metal-roofed pavilions with 200,000 square feet of specialty shops, flanked by an open entertainment plaza.

In line with Miami's status as the hemisphere's prime trade center, the city hosts many trade fairs, inaugurated by the International Trade Fair in 1978, co-sponsored by the Organization of American States. The Greater Miami Trade Zone is one of the largest in the country, a $60-million complex located on a 166-acre tract near the Miami Airport and close to the Port of Miami via expressway.

Also close in—only some twenty blocks south of Flagler Street via Brickell Avenue (US 1)—is the Rickenbacker Causeway, gateway to a very reasonable facsimile of a South Sea Island. Key Biscayne was a coconut plantation long before the postwar causeway was built and is a favorite of movie-makers for its tropical lushness. Even the causeway itself is a park of sorts, providing wide parking areas adjacent to the four-lane road, and handy swimming, boating, and water-skiing areas.

Of Keys, Parks, and Villas

The first real island you will reach is Virginia Key, which in addition to a palm-fringed beach offers the Seaquarium, a commercial attractior with trained porpoises and seals, colorful reef fishes, sharks, barracuda, turtles, and the like. It's open until dark, and there's a monorail passenger car which circles the entire area. Nearby is Miami's Marine Stadium, a modern, concrete structure providing 6,500 armchair seats for boat races and for evening concerts of light music, the orchestra playing on a barge in front of the grandstand. Private boats cluster around the barge, and many who come by water bring a picnic supper so they can arrive early and gain a good position. Special buses from downtown help escape post-concert traffic tie-ups. Concerts are usually held on Friday or Saturday nights, weather permitting.

Just past the Miami Marine Stadium on the Rickenbacker Causeway is Planet Ocean, a showcase of seven multi-media panoramic theaters,

100 dazzling exhibits—including an iceberg, many "hands on" attractions—and a real submarine for youngsters to view inside. The multimillion dollar ocean science center is world headquarters for the nonprofit International Oceanographic Foundation. Additional theme exhibits include the Ocean Reservoir of Life, The Restless Sea and Weather Engine. At present, one of the most popular exhibits, recounted on television monitors and model ships, recounts the history of the gold-laden Spanish galleons and the hurricanes that scattered these ships over the coral reefs, spewing their treasures on to the Keys and the Caribbean.

A bridge connects Virginia Key to Key Biscayne, the area's favorite recreation spot. When Nixon was president, the winter White House was here. The northern half of the 4½-mile-long island is county-owned Crandon Park, which offers a marina, 2½ miles of uncluttered beach, barbecue pits; it is also the site of the 'Superstars" TV show. The middle third of the island consists of homes, apartments, and hotels. The southern third, Cape Florida, is a state park. A good side trip is a 3-hr. boat tour of the new Biscayne National Park.

Back to the mainland, and just a few blocks south (follow the signs), is another county facility, Villa Vizcaya, the former home of James Deering of the International Harvester fortune. Deering collected art works abroad for twenty years before beginning work in 1912 on what is, in reality, an Italian Renaissance palace. With up to one thousand craftsmen at work, it took five years to complete the 69-room main palace and formal gardens, ten acres with clipped hedges, fountains, reflecting pools, and statuary in seven separate areas. As a breakwater, there is a stone version of Cleopatra's barge. Inside, architects faced the problem of accommodating a frescoed ceiling here, a sideboard from a fifteenth-century Italian church there, or the tapestry that hung in Robert Browning's villa in Asolo, Italy. What it all cost, Deering didn't say, but estimates range up to $10 million pre-World War I dollars. The fascinating story is part of the dramatic Sound and Light Show shown at certain times (check at your hotel).

Across from the Vizcaya entrance is the Museum of Science, on original Vizcaya grounds. The Space Transit Planetarium at the east end of the museum aims to make every viewer feel like an astronaut; visitors blast off and go on a reeling simulated space ride. A sixty-five-foot dome makes it the third largest planetarium in the country.

Coconut Grove is Miami's Bohemian section and at the same time the home of some of the area's oldest families, the original settlers and local aristocracy who came down before the various boom times. It is a village within the city, private, discreetly cosmopolitan, charming, with elegant shopping/dining/hotel facilities, part Greenwich, Connecticut, and part Sausalito, California, with overtones of Tahiti. To reach it, go south on Miami Ave., which becomes Bayshore Drive.

Residential Gables

Coral Gables is something else again. From US 1, look for SW 22nd St., and head west to the Spanish-towered and columned city hall where they'll give you a map and notes for a series of self-guided tour signs on the street that will hit all the high spots for 20 rambling miles of points such as the Venetian Pool, the University of Miami, the villages (little compounds of homes in Dutch, French, and Chinese architecture), the plazas, and entranceways.

Coral Gables is an example of what can be done to keep a city the way most of the residents want it. Every street was planned and plotted when it all began in the '20s. Now every new building must be approved by a board of architects and erected according to a strict zoning code.

There are no billboards, no cemeteries, no trailer parks, and industry must be clean, smokeless, and within a designated area.

PRACTICAL INFORMATION

FOR MIAMI AND MIAMI BEACH

HOW TO GET THERE. *By air:* You can reach Miami on direct flights from all major American cities via *Continental, Delta, Eastern, Northwest Orient, Ozark, Pan Am, Piedmont, Republic, US Air, American, Braniff, TWA* or *United.* Intrastate airlines serve Miami from various cities within the state. Miami is an important gateway to the Caribbean and Latin America with some 700 flights weekly.

Air Canada, Delta and *Eastern* have direct flights from Montreal; *Eastern* from Ottawa; *Air Canada* or *Eastern* from Toronto. There are connecting flights from Calgary, Edmonton, Halifax, Hamilton, and Vancouver.

Although charter airlines are not as numerous as in other cities, check them out for cheaper fares.

British Airways, Air Florida, Pan Am and others have direct flights to London; *Lufthansa* and *Pan Am* have direct service to Germany; *El Al* flies to Israel. *Pan Am* has direct service to European capitals and Mexico. *Aeromexico* has a Paris–Madrid–Miami flight. *Iberia* has service between Madrid and Miami. Both *Aeromexico* and *Mexicana* fly to Mexico.

By train: Amtrak has regular service. Even before streamlining by Amtrak, the *Seaboard Coast Line,* a Miami to New York run, was one of the last truly luxury trips by train still available in the U.S. Now it is even better. Coach fare is cheaper than by air; sleepers are much more expensive. Approximately a 24–hr. journey.

By car: From the northeast I–95 (almost fully completed) is your fastest route; I–75 from the Midwest is under construction; A1A is the beautiful, leisurely way.

By bus: Trailways or *Greyhound* will get you there.

By boat: The Intracoastal Waterway parallels the coastline and runs 349 mi. from Jacksonville to Miami.

HOW TO GET AROUND. Take the airport limousine to your hotel, if it is a major one. You will save about $4 or $5 on the trip. *Taxis* over $1 for the initial one-ninth of a mi.; 20¢ for each additional 2/9 of a mi. And the price keeps going up. Renting a car is your best bet; there's a good supply.

TOURIST INFORMATION. Metro Dade County Dept. of Tourism, 234 W. Flagler St., Miami 33130, the Miami Beach Visitor and Convention Authority, 555 Seventeenth St., Miami Beach 33139, and Surfside Tourist Board, 9301 Collins Ave., Surfside 33154.

SEASONAL EVENTS. *January:* New Year's Night, *Orange Bowl football game, International Travel Camping Show,* Miami; *Art Deco Weekend. February: Doral Open Golf Tournament,* late Feb. to early Mar., at Doral Country Club. *Miami Grand Prix auto race* on Biscayne Blvd., *Miami International Boat Show, LPGA Golf; Miami Film Festival; Coconut Grove Arts Festival; Museum of Science's Annual Around the World Fair* at Tropical Park. *Vizcaya Art Show,* 3251 S. Miami Ave., late Feb.

March: Carnaval Miami, Hispanic festival held the first two weekends in March. *Exhibition games of the Baltimore Orioles;* Dade County Youth Fair. *June: Poinciana Festival,* early June.

July: Fourth of July Parade, Key Biscayne, floats, marching units, and bicycles. *Bowling Tournament of the Americas,* Miami. Amateur bowling champions from nations of the Western hemisphere vie for top honors, July 8 to 14.

November: Jr. Tennis Championships, Coral Gables, for youngsters 8 to 12, regarded as tune-up for Jr. Orange Bowl Tennis Tournament.

December: Orange Bowl Festival, one of the nation's most celebrated festival and sporting events. King Orange Jamboree Parade highlights New Year's Eve in downtown Miami, terminating with the football classic on New Year's Night. *Junior Orange Bowl* activities in Coral Gables.

 MUSEUMS AND GALLERIES. Historical: *Cape Florida State Recreation Area,* 1200 S. Crandon Blvd., Key Biscayne. Seminole history. Restored Cape Florida Lighthouse. *Historical Museum of Southern Florida,* NW 2nd Ave. and 1st St., Miami. Maintained by nonprofit Historical Association of South Florida. Closed Mon.

Art: Bass Museum of Art, 2100 Collins Ave., Miami Beach. Paintings, sculpture, vestments and tapestries. *Bacardi Art Gallery,* 2100 Biscayne Blvd. Exhibitions by local, national, and international artists. *Dade County Center for Fine Arts,* NW 2nd Ave. and 1st St. *Lowe Art Museum,* 1301 Miller Dr., Coral Gables. Becoming one of the finer galleries in the South. *Metropolitan Museum and Art Center,* 1212 Anastasia Ave., Coral Gables. Art treasures, splendid building. *Virginia Miller Galleries,* Coconut Grove. Fine art/artifacts. *Monastery Cloister of Saint Bernard,* 16711 W. Dixie Hwy., North Miami Beach. Built in Segovia, Spain, in 1141, it was disassembled and brought to the U.S.

Special Interest: Museum of Science, 3280 S. Miami Ave., Miami. Recently upgraded; dynamic hands-on scientific exhibits and dioramas. Museum has extensive displays of Florida wildlife. Planetarium is adjacent to the Museum of Science. Afternoon and evening show daily. Weekly programs in Spanish. Programs change every 5 to 6 wks. *Planet Ocean,* just past the Marine Stadium on Rickenbacker Causeway, Key Biscayne. The mystique of the oceans is explored in seven multi-media theaters and through over 100 exhibits. The ocean showplace includes an iceberg, and a submarine for children to enter. Spectacular theme areas, including the Gulf Stream, NOAA Hurricane Center, and ship models are just a few of the fascinations here.

Others: Arch Creek Park and Museum, 1855 NE 135th St., North Miami. Eight acres of natural flora and museum/nature center. *International Design Center,* North Miami Ave. at 42nd St., Miami. A grouping of art centers that offer glimpses of interior design and the technical construction of architectural and decorating innovations. See Yellow Pages for many others.

 HISTORIC SITES. *Vizcaya,* Dade County Art Museum, 3251 S. Miami Ave., Miami. An Italian palace, created by an American millionaire with a Hollywood imagination. *Art Deco Historic District.* Ten-block concentration of Art Deco structures on South Miami Beach.

 TOURS. *Nightclub tours:* American Sightseeing, 871–4992, or see the bell captain at your hotel. *By boat: Nikko Gold Coast Cruises* offers a good variety, with special children's rates. Sails from Haulover Park Docks and Miami Beach. Phone: 945–5461. Also contact *Haulover,* 947–6105; *Show Queen,* 361–9418; *Island Queen,* 379–5119; Miami Steamboat Co., 358–4494.

By tram: Trolley Tyme Tours features "Lolly the Trolley," with passenger pickup along Miami Beach. A variety of day and night tours; children's rates. Phone: 948–8823.

By air: Cruise at fine camera height in a *helicopter* from Gold Coast Helicopters, 15101 Biscayne Blvd., Miami Helicopter, 377–0934, or try *glider-sightseeing* from the Miami Gliderport, operating from Nov. to May and located on Krome Ave. and SW 162nd St. Soaring instructions.

Everglades by airboat. Along the Tamiami Trail, on US 41 about 17 mi. W. of downtown Miami, airboat operators will whisk you off on small craft with aircraft motors and guarded propellers. These were developed for fishing and hunting forays into the remote wilderness areas. Four to twelve persons can pile aboard and the normal sightseeing tour costs only a nominal fee.

Other tours: American Sightseeing Tours offers one-day and extended tours to Disney World, shuttle service, group sightseeing, special tours, school charters and race track service, 1000 NW LeJeune Rd. *Burnside–Ott,* at the Opa

Locka Airport, offers air tours with professional pilots and late-model aircraft. The *Nikko Gold Coast Cruises* offers five sightseeing tours: Everglades, Seaquarium, Millionaires' Row, Villa Vizcaya, Gold Coast Combination.

Island and Casino Tours. Miami is the busiest U.S. cruiseport; Port Everglades, Ft. Lauderdale, is also popular. The casinos at Freeport and Paradise Island are the favored destinations. Island life lures nongamblers, also, to Nassau, Haiti, Bimini, Jamaica, and other exotic Caribbean points.

 GARDENS. *The Cloud Forest,* part of the Miami Beach Garden Center and Conservatory (a rapidly developing horticultural complex), is operated by the city without admission charge. On Washington Ave. 2 blocks N. of Lincoln Road Mall (follow in to the west). The air inside the dome is changed very frequently, but it's so hot no visitor can stay very long. The Cloud Forest plants thrive in a droopy-hot atmosphere like that in the backwaters of the Amazon. This is a compact display with many rarities. The conservatory was recently given one of the world's larger orchid collections.

Fairchild Tropical Garden, 10901 Old Cutler Rd., Miami, is always open from sunrise and the "largest tropical botanical garden in America," holds the Fairchild Ramble in early Dec. It's a benefit bargain hunt with unimaginable goods—bobcat skin, a 90-year-old baby buggy, a Japanese party set that cost the lady who gave the party $2,500. The garden itself, founded by a tax attorney, is spread out on 83 acres south of Matheson Hammock Park. Leave US 1 at SW 112th St. and take a short jog on SW 57th Ave. before turning left on Old Cutler Road. Hourly tours on a little train. Admission fee.

Other horticultural things to see: the *Miami Flower Show* is in mid-Mar. *Orchid Jungle,* 25 mi. S of Miami; *Garden of Our Lord,* St. James Lutheran Church, 110 Phoenetia, Coral Gables, displays many exotic plants mentioned in the Bible. *Japanese Garden,* Watson Park, on the MacArthur Causeway, features statutes of Hotei, arbor, teahouse, stone lanterns, pagoda, ornate main gate, rock gardens, and waterfall lagoon. *Redland Fruit and Spice Park,* 35 mi. SW of Miami, in Homestead. Intersection of Coconut Palm Dr. (SW 248th St.) & Redland Rd. (187th Ave.). A 20-acre tropical showplace featuring fruit, nut, and spice-producing plants from around the world. Guided tours Wed. at 3:30 are free.

About a 30-minute drive from Miami Beach, green-thumbers will be delighted with the *U.S. Sub-Tropical Horticultural Research Unit;* the *Ladies Garden Club* sponsors free tours Tuesdays and Thursdays from 10 A.M. to 2 P.M. Tropical fruits, such as mangos, and a splendid variety of rare plants are grown here.

 MUSIC. The *Opera Guild of Greater Miami* books important opera stars from the Continent, the Met, and elsewhere. The company keeps engagements as far off as Fort Lauderdale, but usually appears at Dade Auditorium and Miami Beach Theatre of Performing Arts (TOPA)

Miami Beach has a symphony, with a season extended into the warmer months with a *Summer Pops* series. The Miami Beach Theatre of Performing Arts box office at 1700 Washington Ave. will provide current information.

The *Youth Symphony of South Florida,* the *Chamber Music Society in Greater Miami,* the *Miami Little Orchestra,* and dozens of other groups are active in the resort area. The *Great Artists and Great Performances Series* as well as the *Prestige Series* bring blockbuster musical and dance acts to Greater Miami stages. The *Miami Herald* is a good source for information on current performances.

 STAGE AND REVUES. *TOPA,* 1700 Washington Ave., a chief outpost of the Broadway theater, plays major hits with major casts plus a variety of other types of productions.

The *Ring Theater,* Univ. of Miami, offers presentations of such high quality they could compare with Broadway performances.

The *Coconut Grove Playhouse,* 3500 Main Highway, Coconut Grove, is the most up-and-coming theater in the area, offering high quality professional productions. Aesthetically and technically, the theater itself is better than many of Broadway's more famous homes.

The *Merry-Go-Ground Playhouse and Drama Studio,* 235 Alcazar, Coral Gables, has continuous *Children's Theater;* also presents an amateur company in Shakespeare and contemporary plays.

North Miami Playhouse, at Florida International University, presents both legitimate and children's theater, Sat. matinees.

Burt Reynolds Dinner Theatre, Jupiter, presents Broadway hits.

Royal Palm Dinner Theater, 303 Golfview Dr., Boca Raton. Light, lively shows and chow. 426–2211.

Parker Playhouse, Fort Lauderdale, was created by Zev Buffman, former owner of the Coconut Grove Playhouse, and is run on the same principles. Most shows at TOPA go to the Parker for their next stop.

Sunrise Music Theater, 5555 NW 95th Ave., Sunrise, near Fort Lauderdale, with a star-studded schedule, has highlighted Frank Sinatra, Johnny Cash, Stevie Wonder, Barry Manilow, and Dolly Parton.

Check the hotel desk for free entertainment guides, as stage revues at resort hotels are subject to change. Miami has Les Violins and Flamenco, Miami Beach the Sheraton Bal Harbour for exciting shows.

 BARS. In Miami Beach, many of the cocktail lounges could swallow the nightclubs of other cities twice over and have room for more. The nightclubs, in turn, are larger than many theaters. Most bars mentioned here are swinging spots rather than tiny hideaways where a man can find room to talk to himself. One place to see and be seen is the Omni International lobby lounge bar, *The Gallery,* complete with panoramic view of downtown Miami to the sea. *Daphne's,* in the Sheraton River House, near the Miami Airport, is popular with the traveling business executive. Local execs patronize *Cye's Rivergate.* An elegant crowd passes through the *Garden Lobby Bar,* at the *Fontainebleau Hotel,* 4441 Collins Ave. Among the area top spots are: *Club Z,* 1236 Washington Ave., M. Beach; *The Place,* 6815 Biscayne Blvd.; *Rogers,* Key Biscayne Golf Course; and *Pickfords,* 395 Giralda, C. Gables. *Ginger Man, Biscayne Baby, Faces* and *Monty Trainer* are top spots in the Grove. *The Forge,* 432 Arthur Godfrey Rd., has a superb repertoire of music; contemporary music lovers are also served. Surest place to catch celebrities is the *Harbour Lounge,* located in *Place for Steak* on the 79th St. Causeway. The big moment may be at 4:30 A.M. (it's open 'til 5). Ultra-informal with casual young surfers mingling with classier folk. The *Pier 66,* in Fort Lauderdale, has a fine bar on premises. The *Sonesta Beach Hotel & Tennis Club* on Key Biscayne attracts a lively, well-dressed crowd. These are merely representative. Most of the larger hotel and motel operations have pleasant bars open to the public. Also check local papers for current happenings around town.

DRINKING LAWS. In the Miami area, service until very late (or early) in the day—see *Bars* section. The legal drinking age is 19.

 NIGHTCLUBS. Christmas Eve marks the annual opening of the great star parade. Veterans and comparatively new entries—if they bear a famous name and have whipped up what is reputed to be a headline act—are brought on here. To "fill the big room"—for the rooms can be very big—tends to be an ultimate test of personal stardom. On Miami Beach most of the important nightclubs are located in resort hotels. Most of the hotel nightclubs have developed a style; they go for revues, for smash action, or for intimacy. Prices often are in the expensive range, but the cost can be softened up by paying a very nominal fee for a nightclub tour, which can be booked at your hotel. Just about every swanky hotel has a live band for dancing.

In Miami the most lavish, and the wildest night clubs are the Cuban supper clubs. The best are *Les Violins* and *Flamenco.* They're not cheap, but money spent in a Cuban nightclub is never regretted. When the Cubans do a nightclub show, it is action-packed and the food is good.

CASINOS. Miami and Miami Beach are jumping-off spots for gambling in the Bahamas, Aruba, Puerto Rico, and Haiti. There's direct daily air service to Freeport and Nassau, also to Port-au-Prince, Dominican Republic, Aruba from Miami Also 3- and 4-day cruises are available out of Miami, the ship being the traveler's hotel during his stay (see also *Tours*).

SPORTS. Because of the semitropical climate there is no division of sports activities into summer or winter in the greater Miami area. Instead, we will list them alphabetically. *Bicycling:* There are about 100 mi. of well-marked secondary routes adjoining thoroughfares for safe, scenic cycling. Greynolds Park is a good starting point in the north part of the Miami area. Bike paths wind through picnic grounds, around a lake with boat rides and fishing. Coconut Grove has excellent bike paths, winding through the oldest and most historic section of Miami. Route maps are provided by local chambers of commerce, the Coral Gables Community Development Dept. and Miami–Metro Dept. of Publicity and Tourism. Numerous shops offer loaners; bicycles can be included in some auto rental arrangements.

Boating: Miami has berthing for over 4,000 boats and takes anything up to a 180-ft. yacht. Miamarina is the city's newest and most modern marine facility with all the downtown advantages. It offers 178 slips for pleasure craft and space for 30 commercial craft, such as charter and sightseeing boats. Circuit voyages out of Miami go through the Keys, Fort Myers and Okeechobee Waterway. As for distance on the Intracoastal Waterway, Jacksonville to Miami is a 349-mi. trip and it's 158 mi. inside the Keys from Miami to Key West. Competitive boating includes a speed classic at the Marine Stadium on Rickenbacker Causeway and, in mid-Jan., a 9-hr. endurance race. There's an 807-mi. race from Miami to Montego Bay and races from St. Petersburg to Fort Lauderdale and Miami to Cat Cay in late Feb. The Lipton Cup yacht race is considered by yachtsmen to be a warmup for the great Miami-Nassau race; both are held in Mar.

Fishing: Deep-sea fishing: You can charter boats for trolling, drift-fishing or bottom fishing. Since they carry up to six persons, you can share the costs. The deep blue of the Gulfstream is their beat for the big gamefish, marlin, sail, wahoo, dolphin and tuna. Key Largo, south of Miami in the Florida Keys, is great sport-fishing haunt. There are about 200 licensed fishing guides to take you to the Upper Keys and into the flats of Florida Bay.

Freshwater fishing: Most famous freshwater fishing in Greater Miami is the Tamiami Canal, extending from west edge of Miami along US 41. The canal is 50 ft. wide, 50 mi. long with plenty of parking and fishing spots along the banks. Skiffs and hired guides are available along the Tamiami Trail for trips into the Everglades. The *Miami Herald's* Metropolitan Miami Fishing Tournament, one of the world's largest, runs each year from mid-Dec. to mid-Apr. Despite the skill and knowledge of local anglers, a majority of the average annual 50,000 entries of fish contesting for citations and trophies are made by visitors from all parts of the world.

Golf: The greater Miami area has 45 golf courses. Greens fees begin as low as $5 on summer weekdays at most 18-hole municipal courses. Many courses offer reduced "twilight" rates, which take effect daily between 3 P.M. and 6 P.M., depending on the season.

The Doral C.C., Miami, with its five courses, ranks among the third ten of America's 100 greatest golf courses, according to "Golf Digest," which also recommends: *Melreese Lejeune G.C.,* with a gently rolling terrain; *Vizcaya G. & C.C.,* nicely landscaped with palm trees; *C.C. of Miami,* a fine resort course; *Miami Lakes Inn & C.C.,* a challenging course; *King's Bay & C.C.,* a challenging, scenic course open to members and hotel guests; *Fontainebleau C.C.,* a Mark Mahannah course with seven lakes, rolling fairways (all in Miami). Also: *Miami Shores C.C.,* Miami Shores, for members and their guests only; *Miami Springs G. & C.C.,* Miami Springs, former site of the Miami Open; *Bay Shore Municipal,* Miami Beach, a municipal course with rolling fairways, mounds and lakes; *Key Biscayne G.C.,* Key Biscayne, a unique Robert Von Hagge course, with tough tests; *Palmetto G.C.,* S. Miami, a municipal course with 13 water holes; *Biltmore C.C.,* Coral Gables, a municipal course with some tricky water holes; and *Normandy Shores G.C.* Miami Beach, on the Isle of Normany in Biscayne Bay.

Water sports: Water-skiing schools, jumps, and towing services are located along beaches and causeways. *Skiing* lessons consist of approximately three 1-hr. sessions. Boats with tow equipment and fuel can be rented. *Surfing* is practiced in Florida, although the local surfers are a frustrated lot—the waves are seldom large enough. However they do their best at Haulover Beach Park and South Miami Beach, where there are special areas reserved for surfers. There are miles of sand beaches for *swimming.* Crandon Park and Cape Florida State Park on Key Biscayne; Haulover Beach on Collins Ave., north of Bal Harbour; Lummus Park on Miami Beach; Matheson Hammock, 2 mi. south of Miami on Old Cutler Rd., Tahiti Beach in South Miami, are among the many choice spots. Another favorite swimming spot is the Venetian Municipal Pool, 2701 DeSoto Blvd., formed from the coral quarry which was mined to build the city of Coral Gables. The pool is reminiscent of a Venetian palazzo, with shady porticos, loggias and towers.

Biggest splash for water-sport enthusiasts is the new North Shore Open Space Park, a $10-million, 32-acre oceanfront recreation area, from 79th to 87th Sts., Miami Beach. There are also bicycle paths, winding boardwalks, and picnic areas.

A number of local firms specialize in scuba and skindiving instructions and excursions to sunken hulls, reefs and underwater gardens. Fowey Rock Light area, just south of Key Biscayne, is among the best for *underwater photography.* Other fine locations are Haulover, Elbow Light, Pacific Light, Carysfort Light and John Pennekamp State Park. Skindivers should observe State Conservation laws regarding crawfish (Florida lobster) and other regulations on *spearfishing.* Crawfish may not be taken by spearing. There are no special restrictions on the use of spearguns in Dade and Broward counties, but they are prohibited in Pennekamp Park and within one mile of US 1 in the lower keys. Diver flags are required.

Windsurfing is the latest "in" sport with lessons available at the Diplomat Hotel, Fontainebleau Hilton, Thunderbird and Miami Windsurfing, 7524 SW 53 Ave. *Tennis:* Larger hotels have facilities; plenty fine municipal courts.

SPECTATOR SPORTS. *Baseball:* In Miami, the Baltimore Orioles work out at the Miami Stadium, 2301 NW 10th Ave., beginning Feb. 15, with exhibition games starting Mar. 15. *Football:* The Miami Dolphins, under Coach Don Shula, won their first World Championships in 1973 and repeated in 1974—not bad for a team formed in 1966. They play in the Orange Bowl, as do the Univ. of Miami Hurricanes, the '83 national champions.

Racing: There are three horse racing tracks and one harness racing track in South Florida. *Hialeah Park,* 4 E. 25th St., is open Mar. to mid-Apr. The grounds also feature an aquarium, rare birds, flamingoes, English carriages, riding regalia, snacks and souvenirs, and a tram ride. *Gulfstream Park Race Track,* US 1, Hallandale; mid-Jan. to Mar. Miami's *Calder Race Course,* NW 27th Ave. at 210th St., has two seasons: May to Nov. and mid-Nov. to mid-Jan. All three tracks are within easy reach of Miami and Miami Beach. Special buses run from Miami Beach to Pompano Beach for harness racing at Pompano Park. mid-Dec. to early April. The races may be watched from a terraced dining room in the spectacular 7-story grandstand. Dog racing (greyhounds, of course), a Florida staple, at *Biscayne,* 320 NW 115th St.; *Flagler,* 401 NW 38 Ct.; *Hollywood,* 831 N. Federal Hwy., Hallandale. Remember, no minors admitted when there is wagering.

Jai-alai: A dangerous combination of handball, tennis and lacrosse, jai-alai requires great nerve, endurance and savvy—and lends itself to betting. The sport derives from Spain and 17th-century Basques. Players use a pelota (virgin-rubber ball covered with goatskin) and a cesta (curved basket of imported reed) which straps to the wrist. At plush *Dania Jai-Alai,* you may view the game directly or on closed circuit TV. Nightly except Sun., Apr. to Dec. The *Miami Jai Alai Fronton* is at 3500 NW 37 Ave.

SHOPPING. One of the most elaborate shopping areas in Florida is just opposite the Sheraton Bal Harbour, on the north outskirts of Miami Beach. In Miami Beach proper, *Lincoln Road Mall* has a few top stores but has lost some of its glamour. Fine browsing, but be choosy. Arthur Godfrey Rd. and 71st St. shopping areas are worth a try.

The fabulous Neiman-Marcus department store heads a group of renowned shops, such as Saks and Bonwit Teller, in Bal Harbour. The Omni Malls at the new Omni International Hotel in Miami, anchored by two department stores, J.C. Penney and Jordan Marsh (each with restaurants), have 150 distinctive shops and cafes. Among the galaxy of boutiques, the shining stars in the Plaza Versailles area are such famous ones as Givenchy, House of Hermès, House of Lanvin, Emilio Pucci, Bally's of Switzerland, etc. Just like shopping on the famous Faubourg St. Honoré in Paris! The Renaissance Place section, with at least 30 fascinating shops, is decorated European street-market style. From hand-dipped chocolates to a designer's ensemble, this is a shopping wonderland.

Miami is becoming a shoppers' paradise as suburban malls are now featuring the likes of Lord & Taylor, Macy's, and Bloomingdale's.

Here's a casual guide for those who seek better than casual shopping: some of the best shopping for all the usuals—clothes, Florida items for the home, local specialties—is in Coral Gables. Most families there are well-to-do, but not reckless spenders; the shops reflect it. *Surrey's* at 299 Miracle Mile, gives special help in selecting men's clothes that are right. For the far out, much of it beautiful (paintings, carvings, unusual housewares), try the little shops and drugstores at Coconut Grove. *Commodore Plaza* has a number of unique shops such as the *Crystal Gallery* 3197; *Copper Kettle*, 3170; and *Adam's Apple*, 3190. *Dadeland Mall,* South Miami, has half a dozen major department stores, plus dozens of specialty shops. *Saks* is a new addition here.

Surfside blends into Bal Harbour, and the area is replete with excellent shops, many better than their fairly modest facades indicate. Over 100 stores in the Miami Fashion District feature designer labels at 30 to 50 percent discount. Atmosphere is spartan (no private dressing rooms), but terrific bargains for smart shoppers in clothing for men and women, handbags, shoes. Stores border NW 20th St. from Second Ave. A group of *5–7–9 Shops* ("Specialist for Small Women of All Ages") are located at 326 Miracle Mile, Coral Gables; Westland Mall, 163rd St. and Dadeland Mall; 9517 Harding Ave. and 2426 E. Sunrise Boulevard in Fort Lauderdale. *Mayfair In The Grove,* a tri-level array of at least 50 designer-name boutiques, is becoming known as the most elegant place to shop and dine. Corner Grand Ave. and Mary St., Coconut Grove. Other ultramodern shopping centers are *The Falls, Aventura, Cutler Ridge,* and *163rd Street.*

If you come from an area where the new style in ladies' underwear has not impressed the local shops, you'll find all the free-form fashions at *Blackton's* in Fort Lauderdale along Sunrise Center. *Sunrise Center,* the *Galleria,* and *Las Olas Boulevard* give Fort Lauderdale one of the finer shopping areas in the Southland. A Florida supermarket king named George S. Jenkins has filled the territory with his *Publix Markets.* He commissioned San Francisco artist John Garth to put the mosaics on the walls. The *Jordan Marsh* and *Burdines* stores are the aristocrats of Miami area department stores.

WHAT TO DO WITH THE CHILDREN. A number of sea zoos have been created in Florida, and they are probably the most exciting of all diversions for youngsters—and perhaps parents, too. The largest and most famous is the *Miami Seaquarium* located beyond the Rickenbacker Causeway (follow US 1 to the sign with the circling shark), south of downtown. It has been there 18 years, and it is often crowded for the show in the porpoise tank. But there are also the shark show, the killer whale show, the penguin–seal–pelican show (for this you sit in an inclined grandstand), and the show down below in the great tank when the divers vacuum the bottom and feed the establishment's biggest captive. Daily 9 to 5.

Planet Ocean, just past Marine Stadium on Rickenbacker Causeway. Newest addition to Virginia Key ocean-science community, which includes The Rosensthiel School of Marine and Atmospheric Sciences of the University of Miami, and the Miami Seaquarium. A multi-million-dollar ocean-science showplace with more than 100 exhibits, including a Hurricane Center, ship models depicting Gulf Stream history, an iceberg, a submarine for children to climb into and inspect, and more. The mystery and magic of the oceans are explored in exhibits and multi-media panoramic theaters. Open seven days a week.

At the *Monkey Jungle,* about 20 mi. S. of Miami on US 1, visitors watch from an enclosure as monkeys cavort without being caged.

The new *Metrozoo* at 12400 SW 152 St., Miami, is a good place to see animals in their natural habitat. No fences or cages.

Castle Park. Potpourri of games/activities, video arcade, kiddie rides. 7775 NW 8th St. Cobra venom extraction. Daily 9 to 6. *Parrot Jungle,* 11000 SW 57th Ave. Birds perform all kinds of tricks. Winding trails through natural hammock to Flamingo Park, 9:30 to 5.

Miami Beach hotels, especially the most luxurious ones, have satisfying programs for the teenager and younger child. "Just Us Kids" is an interesting program at the Sonesta Beach Hotel and Tennis Club on Key Biscayne. All the "club" activities are supervised by special counselors. At the new Omni International Hotel, the "Treasure Island" entertainment center is fun for the entire family. Also in the mall are six first-run theaters for young film buffs.

 HOTELS AND MOTELS. To the first-time visitor, the hotels of Miami Beach will seem like one continuous city. The Flaggergast Hotels, as they have been called, are the prototypes for much of the resort architecture around the world. To the honeymooner, beautiful; to the yearning secretary, a fable; to the social reformer, a parody; but nearly all comfortable and superbly equipped.

What the hotels charge varies wildly, coming to a peak in mid-December, January, February. The labels attached here have meaning mostly as a way of establishing or another as a bit more expensive than its neighbor. Many modestly rated establishments are the equal in comfort and location of those that—usually because they are newer—have a higher standard price.

Vacationers have a choice of hundreds of hotels and motels in the Miami and Miami Beach area, ranging from the most luxurious to merely modest. Restaurants, nightclubs, shops, and stores are usually close by the hotels, while tennis courts and golf courses are within easy driving distance. The vast majority of hotels have swimming pools for guests and the larger ones maintain free recreational programs.

Rates vary according to season and quality of room. The lowest rates are in the summer, which usually begins in May and continues until Nov. 1. This is the period for bargain hunters, when you can acquire pleasing and even downright sumptuous accommodations for around $18 a day per person.

We have listed hotels and motels alphabetically in categories determined by double, in-season rates: *Deluxe:* from $85 and up; *Expensive:* from $55–85; *Moderate:* from $50–70; *Inexpensive:* From $30–50.

MIAMI: *Deluxe:* **Doral Country Club.** 4400 NW 87 Ave. Elegant resort hotel that is almost a city in itself. Pools, tennis, golf, water sports, boating.

Grand Bay. 2669 S. Bayshore. Shaped like a pyramid. Superb amenities. Regine's night club on premises.

Hyatt Regency. 400 SE 2nd Ave. Outstanding new 615-room facility. Ultramodern. 2 restaurants, 2 lounges, huge ballroom, 21 retail shops/boutiques.

Omni International Hotel. A 20-story megastructure on 10.5 acres. A self-contained world of restaurants, theaters, shops, a theme park, tennis courts, swimming pool, health club, discotheque, beautifully-appointed guestrooms.

The Pavilion. At foot of Biscayne Blvd. Part of new Miami Center, an elegant complex. Grand hotel in all respects. Unmatched facilities.

Radisson. 711 NW 72nd Ave. New, elegant. At Merchandise Mart.

Riverparc. 100 S.E. 4th St. Luxurious, all suites.

Sheraton River House. Near Miami Airport. Charming decor. Tennis courts, health club, pool. Daphne's lounge and restaurant.

Sonesta Beach Hotel & Tennis Club. 350 Ocean Dr. 20 minutes from Miami on Key Biscayne. Beautiful resort on private beach. Supervised children's programs. Award-winning Court of Two Dragons restaurant. Golf nearby. Twelve villas with indoor swimming pools part of complex.

Viscount–Miami (formerly Miami Springs Villas). Superb facilities. 500 Deer Run.

Expensive. **Airport Hilton.** 5101 Blue Lagoon. Contemporary. Full facilities.

Moderate: **Miami Lakes Inn and Country Club.** N.W. 154th St. Pool, restaurants, bar, golf, tennis, dancing.

Miami Airport Inn. 1550 LeJeune Rd. Home of Playboy Club; fine rooms.

Danker's Inn. 3-story motor inn with pools, play area, restaurant. Free airport transportation.

Holiday Inn. Many locations, each with heated pool, restaurant, bar. Foremost inns are at 495 Brickell and 950 NW LeJeune Rd.

Marriott Hotel and Racquet Club. 1201 N.W. 42nd Ave. Pool, restaurants, bars, entertainment. Another Marriott downtown, with Biscayne Bay at back door.

Inexpensive: **Arrowhead Motel.** 1050 Brickell Ave. Fam. rates avail. Some kitchen units.

MIAMI BEACH. *Deluxe:* **Doral-on-the Ocean.** 4833 Collins Ave. Stunning highrise, decorated like a Fellini set. Beautiful rooftop supper club. Golf at Doral Country Club.

Eden Roc. 4525 Collins Ave. Large, attractively furnished rooms. Penthouse suites, EP avail.

Fontainebleau Hilton. 4441 Collins Ave. Refurbished for $25 million. Outstanding restaurants and bars. A total resort with constant action and a half-acre free-form pool complete with waterfalls.

Konover Ramada Renaissance. 5445 Collins Ave. 550 guest rooms/suites. Private beach, gourmet dining, night clubs, 2 pools.

Marco Polo Resort Motel. 192nd St. & Collins Ave. Supervised program for children, teens. Casual and informal for the young at heart. New Cowboy's Corral & Wild West Lounge with western boutique.

Sheraton Bal Harbour (formerly the Americana). 9701 Collins Ave. One of the leading resort hotels in Florida. Nightclub with lavish floor shows.

Alexander. 5225 Collins Ave. Magnificent 220-suite property. Superb facilities for all tastes.

Moderate: **The Palms.** 9449 Collins Ave. Recently renovated. Near shopping. Good facilities.

Versailles. 3425 Collins Ave. Pool, private beach. Supervised children's program during holidays, summer.

Atlantic Towers/Waldman. Two hotels at 4201 Collins Ave. Cater to international guests. Central location. Friendly atmosphere.

Bancroft. 1501 Collins Ave. Pool, beach, game area.

Castaways Resort Motel. 16375 Collins Ave. Pools, beach, boating, game area. Pets. Restaurant, bar, dancing, entertainment. Lively crowd.

Newport Beach. 16701 Collins. Top notch resort. Children's program. Fine restaurant.

Pan American. 17875 Collins. Recently upgraded, good facilities. Lounge/ entertainment, tennis.

Rodney. 9365 Collins. Comfortable.

Sahara. 18335 Collins Ave. Resort motel with pool, beach, boating, game area.

Seaside Terrace Motel. 9241 Collins Ave. Small 2-story motel with beach.

Shore Club Hotel. 1901 Collins Ave. Restaurant, bar, dancing, entertainment.

Surfcomber. 1717 Collins Ave. Restaurant, bar; dancing, entertainment in season.

Inexpensive: **Beekman Towers.** 9499 Collins. Large rooms; kitchens, dishwashers.

Seville. 2901 Collins. Offers good services.

Singapore. 9601 Collins. Nice rooms; entertainment.

Fairfax. 1776 Collins Ave. Beach. Restaurant nr. Kitchen units avail.

Golden Sands Hotel and Villas. 6901 Collins Ave. Pool, pets, Restaurant, bar.

Victorian Plaza Apartment Hotel. 6917 Collins. Beach, pool. Color TV, game room, sauna. Free first-run movies. All apartments with fully-equipped kitchens.

DINING OUT. The several thousand places to dine in Miami and Miami Beach range from gourmet restaurants to sandwich shops. Some of the Cuban restaurants in Miami are among the finest anywhere. The area offers a full range of foreign restaurants, with entrées from seafoods to roast beef, turkey or steaks. Florida lobster, or crawfish, is a big favorite in these parts. You can dine on succulent Everglades froglegs, pompano or conch chowder. Stone crabs are a native south Florida delicacy, and fresh shellfish, lobsters and oysters are flown in daily.

Restaurants are listed by cuisine and price category. Dinner in a *deluxe* restaurant will run $20 and up; an *expensive* restaurant approximately $15–20; in a *moderate* restaurant $10–15; in an *inexpensive* restaurant, under $10. Drinks, tax and tip are not included. Cafeterias and hamburger houses fall into the inexpensive category, with an adequate dinner selection costing perhaps $1.50 to $3. A la carte dining will of course be more expensive.

MIAMI. *American International. Expensive:* **King Arthur's Court.** Viscount–Miami Hotel, 500 Deer Run, Miami Springs. Pleasant old English atmosphere, beef their specialty. Other good restaurants in the hotel.

Studio. 2340 SW 32nd Ave. Gourmet Dining, superb atmosphere. Delectable desserts.

Moderate: **Gulf Stream.** Jordan Marsh Dept. Stores, 1501 Biscayne Blvd. Casseroles, salads, homestyle baking.

Piccadilly Hearth. 35 NE 40th St. Glamorous pub located in Decorator's Row. Excellent continental fare.

Tony Roma's A Place For Ribs. Baby back ribs, chicken, fish and more. Inexpensive at lunch. Crowded at dinner. Five Miami locations.

Inexpensive: **Biscayne Cafeteria.** Located at 147 Miracle Mile, Coral Gables. Excellent value.

Hofbrau Bar. 172 Giralda. Tasty sandwiches, lots of atmosphere.

Sally Russell's Part I. 68 W. Flager. A varied menu of meat and fish.

French. Deluxe: **Cafe Chauveron.** New York City's loss was Miami's gain. The menu is enormous, and extraordinarily well-prepared. There is real artistry at work here, and this restaurant ranks with the finest in the entire country. 9561 East Bay Harbor Drive (Bay Harbour Island, Miami Beach).

Chez Vendome. 700 Biltmore Way. Coral Gables. Great care in food preparation. Intimate dining room. Try Sole Veronique.

Moderate: **Brasserie de Paris.** 244 Biscayne Blvd. Informal Classical French dishes. Delightful desserts.

Italian. Expensive: **Raimondo's.** 4612 S. Lejuene Rd. Good values, good wines. Splendid offerings, prepared well.

Vinton's. 116 Alhambra Circle. Coral Gables. An adventure in fine dining. Celebrated wine list.

Valenti's. 9101 S. Dixie Highway. Not to be missed if you like Italian food.

Inexpensive: **Sorrento.** 3058 S.W. 8th St. Italian food in the heart of Little Havana. Family-owned, casual. Chicken Florentine. Lunch, dinner.

Latin American. Inexpensive: **Minerva Spanish Restaurant.** 265 NE 2nd St. Convenient location downtown. Popular long before Cuban refugees arrived.

Moderate: **La Tasca.** 2741 W. Flagler St. Long time favorite. Paella valenciana and red snapper cataloman rate raves.

Oriental. Expensive: **Benihana of Tokyo.** North Bay Village, on 79th Street Causeway between Miami and Miami Beach. Showmanship in Hibachi cookery with prime steak, shrimp, and chicken. Continuous performances at every table with complete dinners from $6.95. Well-known, top-rated chain.

Court of Two Dragons. An exotic ambience overlooking a Japanese garden in the Sonesta Beach Hotel & Tennis Club. Both Chinese and Japanese cuisines are offered in two separate dining rooms, elegantly decorated. Romantic canopied wicker booths. The food is superb and served with a flourish. Fancy cocktails served in Buddha statue mugs. Highly-rated by gourmets.

Tiger Tiger Teahouse. 5716 S. Dixie Highway, Mandarin, Tsechwan, Shanghai, and Mongolian dishes. Jin jo shrimp and cashew chicken are specialties.

Polynesian. Moderate—Expensive: **Rusty Pelican.** Off Rickenbacker Causeway, nr. Key Biscayne. Open-hearth cooking. Succulent Polynesian spareribs. Beautiful water views.

Seafood. Moderate: **Port of Call.** The owners are fishermen themselves, and it is partially their own catch that graces the tables. The bouillabaisse is something special. 14411 Biscayne Blvd. (Miami).

Relections. In Miamiarina. Specialties a must. Save room for chocolate cake.

Spanish. Moderate: **El Baturro.** Interesting items dot an extensive menu, and the specialties are the paella and the sautéed red snapper. Music is live. 2322 NW 7th St. (Miami).

Steak House. Expensive: **Place for Steak.** The name says it all, and it is wise to go with the house specialty. The "house" salad dressing is also very good, and the cheesecake is truly special. 1335 79th St. Causeway (Miami Beach).

MIAMI BEACH. *American International. Expensive:* **Embers.** 245 22nd St. Duckling, stone crabs, and home-made pastries.

Joe's Stone Crab. 227 Biscayne St. The world seems to be beating a path to the door, and no one minds waiting. The stone crabs are cooked to order. Open Oct. 15 to May 15. Lunch, dinner.

The Forge. 432 Arthur Godfrey Rd. Gourmet. Porterhouse with secret seasonings a must. Excellent wines.

Moderate: **Roney Pub.** 2305 Collins Ave. Also in Newport Motel, 16701 Collins Ave. Big portions, family-style. Entrees can be shared.

French. Deluxe: **Dominique's.** 5225 Collins. Award-winning cuisine.

The Palm. 5151 Collins. Elegant. Specialty—lobster flown in daily.

Italian. Moderate: **Gatti's Restaurant.** 1427 West Ave. Continental food with Italian accent. Chicken à la tetrazzini a specialty. 5:30 to 10:30. Closed Mon. and May 1 to Nov. 1.

Jewish. Moderate: **Wolfie's,** 2038 Collins Ave. Stuffed cabbage, cheesecake, smoked whitefish.

Inexpensive: **Rascal House.** Overstuffed sandwiches and full-course meals. Deli-style founded by "Wolfie" himself. Excellent buy.

EXPLORING THE REST OF FLORIDA

Jacksonville, although surrounded by historical and recreational high spots, is not a typical Florida resort. Rather, industry and business are the city's forte, and it is a center for regional headquarters of national firms. The city makes a good base for tours to nearby beaches, natural and historic sites. A rewarding one-day adventure, including time for ocean bathing, allows a visitor to examine the area and coast northeast of Jacksonville—one that has seen French-Spanish scuffling over squatters' rights in the New World, a pirate fleet, a flamboyant slave-runner, a short-lived "Republic of Florida," and capture of the strip of land from its "Mexican" ruler by the United States Navy.

Jacksonville Beach has thousands of guest accommodations, and, along with coastal cities southward for 200 miles, is more a summer resort for inland Southerners than a winter resort for Northerners.

Oldest City

For St. Augustine, the nation's oldest city, you'll need time . . . and a separate guide book. Recommended is *St. Augustine's Historical Heritage,* a publication of the *St. Augustine Historical Society.* There are numerous illustrations, an excellent map, and a well-written text. Try the information center on Castillo Drive as you near the city gates.

Walk through the narrow streets and see 18th-century Spanish colonial houses in a restored area. From the first Spanish period, the mission of Nombre de Dios was founded on the same day as the city, its Shrine of Nuestra Señora de la Leche is a tiny jewel of a chapel. Built of coquina rock covered with ivy, it was restored in 1918, following the design of the original. The Cathedral of St. Augustine—from the second Spanish period—was completed in 1797, restored after a fire in 1887. The Llambias House reflects the English period, as does the Prince Murat House, named for Napoleon Bonaparte's nephew who lived there. Ralph Waldo Emerson was a guest in 1827. The St. Francis Inn, once known as the Dummitt House, was a headquarters for Civil War spies, before that a jail just after Florida became a U.S. territory, before that a barracks for English soldiers . . . and before that the first church of the Franciscans, in 1577.

So it is an old town. With an Old Jail, an Oldest House, Oldest Schoolhouse, Oldest Store . . . and the oldest alligator exhibition—at the St. Augustine Alligator Farm, founded in 1893. Castillo de San Marcos, the quadrangular, moated fortress just opposite the old city gates, a national monument since 1924, is being restored along with a large portion of the adjacent old colonial city. The Museum of San Agustin Antiguo, is a living history museum village which recreates daily life activities of Spanish colonialists. There's a souvenir reminder of the Old City again, 14 miles south at Matanzas Inlet. The stone fort, built in 1742 to protect the inland waterway approach to St. Augustine, is a national monument; daily from 8:30 A.M. to 5:00 P.M.

The Ormond–Daytona Complex

Only a couple of miles south is Marineland, a scientific/commercial attraction presenting displays of marine specimens, porpoise acts, a performing whale, and below-the-water ports for viewing the ocean's creatures; plus a newly added, modern playground. It's an interesting and wholesome attraction. Half an hour more on route A1A will put you in the first of the major tourist-oriented resorts on this route—the Ormond Beach–Daytona Beach Complex geared almost totally to entertainment of the fun-seeking tourists.

The Ormond Garage is virtually unchanged today from the turn of the century when Henry Ford, Louis Chevrolet, and R. E. Olds were tinkering with their machines and dreaming of records and fame. Barney Oldfield was driving there, and Glenn Curtiss did 106 miles an hour on a motorcycle. But it wasn't until 1907 that Ralph Owens managed to make the first automobile trip from New York to Daytona in the considerable time of seventeen days. Later came Sir Malcolm Campbell and his *Bluebird,* but even the beach, with risky winds and tides, wasn't suitable eventually, and in 1959 the Daytona International Speedway, world's fastest track, was opened. The $3,000,000 2.5-mile asphalt oval has seats for 100,000 people. Biggest events are the 400-mile July 4 race for stock cars, and the late February Daytona 500, "world's fastest" 500-mile race. Sports cars compete over the Labor Day weekend. Within the outer track is the sports car and motorcycle course, plus a one-mile straightaway speedboat course.

Dress is informal for almost everything—from the four-nights-a-week band concerts at the Broadway bandshell to greyhound racing and jai alai. All the popular divertissements are available: scenic boating cruises, deep-sea fishing, commercial attractions presenting colorful birds and flowers, five golf courses, tennis, square dances, beauty pageants—anything to attract and entertain people. Most are attracted during the summer months, and they are attracted most strongly by the beach, a twenty-three-mile-long, gently curved strand as much as five hundred feet wide. Driving is still allowed on the beach. Warning: beachcombers and sunbathers have been hurt by drunk drivers. Some may recall that Fred Marriott managed to goad his Stanley Steamer to a reported 197 miles an hour on the same beach in 1907, but the Steamer hit a bump and was demolished.

From Daytona Beach, it is 60 miles to Cape Canaveral directly down the coast along the US 1, or it is 60 miles to Orlando via I–4 which cuts all the way across the state to St. Petersburg.

You may wish to sample some of Florida's inland lake country. Interstate 4 skirts the towns of De Land and Sanford, and you will see some rich citrus and farm land dotted by lakes. This is the ridge section dividing the state: the watershed flows north through the St. Johns, south by the Kissimmee River to Lake Okeechobee and the Everglades.

Gold Coast Beaches

South Florida's Gold Coast begins slowly, then in a tumbling cascade as you proceed south from Melbourne along the south central coast, a 120-mile strip of oceanfront resorts, fishing villages only barely retaining their quaintness, the great millionaires' playground of Palm Beach, and a skinny megalopolis of side-by-seaside municipalities made up of motels, restaurants, shuffleboard courts and the unending beach.

Sports fishing and agriculture offer both substance and diversion in the towns of Vero Beach, Fort Pierce, and Stuart. This is Indian River citrus country, yielding some of the state's tastiest oranges and grapefruit. Citrus packing houses are open for visitors from October through May. With luck, in one of the three towns you may be able to locate a glass of fresh orange juice, rather than the frozen concentrate sort. Offshore, the sailfish is much sought after—and often found—by charter craft, while bay waters provide snook, channel bass, pompano, and sea trout. Freshwater catches are numerous and weighty in the St. Lucie River, which joins the ocean at Stuart.

Bridges and piers offer the pedestrian angler his chance, and Fort Pierce provides specially constructed balconies on either side of the bridge spanning the Indian River.

Upper Crust Palm Beach

Palm Beach is an island, with Lake Worth giving it stylish distance from the mainland. Henry Flagler saw it in 1893, some 15 years after a Spanish bark loaded with coconuts and wine went aground and broke up. The coconuts floated up on the beach, and before long the island had a new profile, with graceful coconut fronds undulating in the sea breezes. Work began on the Royal Poinciana Hotel, with the best of everything. The best was good enough for Philadelphia's Wideners, Stotesburys, and Wanamakers, who were early samplers, and spurred by such social acceptance, Palm Beach was on its way. As the winter version of Newport, Palm Beach attracted America's richest and most society-conscious families. Even the Royal Poinciana, expanded to one thousand rooms, was not elaborate enough for some, who built their own "cottages." When the huge wooden hotel burned to the ground, Flagler's heirs erected in its place an Italian masterpiece—The Breakers—which entertains guests to this day.

Flagler, in tribute to his bride, a North Carolina belle named Mary Lily Kenan, called in Carrere and Hastings again (they had done the Ponce de Leon in St. Augustine for him) and told them, simply, "Build me the finest home you can think of." To the architects of the Metropolitan Opera, the New York Public Library, and the U.S. Senate Office Building, this was a challenge indeed . . . but one they met, finishing the job in 1902. The *New York Herald* called the result, *Whitehall,* "more wonderful than any palace in Europe . . . than any other private dwelling in the world." You can judge for yourself.

After Flagler died in 1913, Mrs. Flagler lived in Whitehall until her death in 1917. The home became a part of the Whitehall Hotel when a 300-room addition was added, but Flagler's granddaughter, Jean Flagler Mook, organized a corporation in 1959 to acquire Whitehall, raze the hotel addition and restore the mansion to its original state. This has been done, magnificently, as the Henry Morrison Flagler Museum.

Addison Mizner, the prize fighter, artist-architect, and semi-conman, had the greatest impact on Palm Beach. His Everglades Club, designed in pseudo-Spanish monastery style, kicked off the great building wave during the 1920s. Many of the great mansions—for example Mrs. E. L. Stotesbury's *El Mirasol* and Mrs. Horace Dodge's *Playa Reinta*—are gone now, victims of another age and another tax scale. But the Via Mizner remains: a tiny, Old World shopping alley with some of the world's most fashionable—and expensive—goods. And the Everglades Club is still there (members only). Palm Beach is still fashionable, and it's still for those rich enough that they don't have to worry about whether it's fashionable or not. West Palm Beach, the city Flagler built for his help, now is comfortably supported by a three-way economy: tourism, agriculture, and industry.

The weather helps the resort trade in winter, for the warming Gulf Stream comes closer to shore than at any other mainland Florida point. There are diversions aplenty: greyhound racing, jai alai, fishing, a number of important boat races. West Palm Beach also has the closest thing to casino gambling—the Lucayan Beach casino at Freeport in the Bahamas is directly east and only minutes away from the West Palm airport.

The area lacks not for cultural pursuits, either. West Palm's Norton Gallery has an almost pricless collection of jades, plus current and permanent art works. In Palm Beach, the Royal Poinciana Playhouse offers direct-from-Broadway legitimate theater during the winter season, and the Society of the Four Arts with a garden entrance on Royal Palm Way has an art gallery, library, and film theater (winter only).

Strung together south of West Palm Beach, each with a mainland business section and an offshore island beachfront, the towns of Lake Worth, Lantana, Boynton Beach, and Delray Beach, have everything Palm Beach has, except the ratio of millionaires and the flossy history. Boca Raton has both, plus a Rembrandt in its Patricia Judith Art Gallery.

Addison Mizner, perhaps bored with Palm Beach, decided in 1925 to create "the golden city of the gold coast." His Cloisters Inn, a rambling, Mizner-Spanish extravaganza, drew the financial wizards of the day. Everything was fine until the boom fizzled. But the Cloisters stood, and in 1928, Clarence Geist, a Philadelphia utilities tycoon, turned it into an exclusive club. It was sold in 1956 to Arthur Vining Davis, fabulously rich ex-chairman of the board of Alcoa, who paid $22,500,000 for the property, including 1,000 acres of land. Expensive homes continue to go up on surrounding areas. The Boca Raton Hotel and Club has five golf courses and a steady convention trade.

The top-rated polo players in the United States play every Sunday, January through April, in Boca Raton. Most of the players are members of old and still very wealthy families who can afford a stable of ponies, for each player must have six ponies just to play one game. And be careful when you order two cold ones as you sit in the bleachers— the vendor sells splits of champagne as well as beer.

West Palm Beach Polo Club may be new but already it has attracted Prince Charles (in 1980) to the exciting games. It's all part of a horsey-set-resort-condominium complex.

The Lake of Plenty

From pâté and champagne to meat and potatoes, not to mention sugar, beans, corn, lettuce, celery, and 26 other vegetables, it's only about an hour's drive into the rich Lake Okeechobee area. It's worth the trip, especially during the winter growing season. More than 30,000 railroad carloads of vegetables are shipped each season from Belle Glade. In addition, there are lush grasslands by the hundreds of thousands of acres to support a growing cattle industry.

The secret of this whole area's success is the lake, which really was more of a swamp until the Herbert Hoover Dike was built along the southern edge beginning in 1930. The 66-mile-long dike, plus a network of canals and pumping stations, make possible the water control that is the key to agricultural success. It also makes possible a cross-state canal from Stuart on the East Coast to Fort Myers on the West Coast. Belle Glade, Clewiston, Pahokee, South Bay, and the other towns around the edge are actually often below the level of the lake's waters. Sports fishing is a primary diversion, and the lake, although rarely more than six or eight feet deep, is a contender for the best-fishing-in-America title. Guides and boats are available.

Sugar operations in the Lake Okeechobee region began about 1923, and today there are 11 sugar mills serving a cane-growing area of almost a quarter of a million acres. Half a million tons of sugar are produced each year. As the oldest and largest sugar firm, the U.S. Sugar Corp. laid out the town of Clewiston with an eye for spaciousness, and it also built and operates the Clewiston Inn, a good hotel and restaurant.

An oddity of the muckland, and one that has given the farmers some long-range worries, is that the land evaporates, or rather, oxidizes. It just disappears—from the top. A house the floor of which was two feet above ground 25 or 30 years ago may now have its floor five or six feet above the same ground.

The Golden Tip

Inland waterways, 165 miles of them, connect areas of subdued prosperity and manicured fingers of land spread to let the warm blue waters lick along bulkheaded back yards. Fort Lauderdale is the home of a colony of the world's wealthy who have traveled near and far and have decided that this is a congenial place for their retirement years. Fort Lauderdale's men of vision somehow saw that the city should have lots of clear, uncluttered beach and protected waters for yachts. In the case of the beach, the acquisitive city commissioners, who kept adding little chunks until there were six miles of it, were proved right when adjacent communities allowed hotels, motels, restaurants, and what-have-you directly on the oceanfront, shutting off public access, whereas here the hotels, apartments, shops, and the like are across a wide boulevard from the public's sands. In 1894 a pair of wealthy Chicago yachtsmen bought a lengthy strip of beachfront. Hugh Taylor Birch, one of them, lived well into his nineties and in 1941 gave the state 180 acres facing the ocean for a park. The gift was worth millions and preserved the length of unbroken beach.

The 17th Street Causeway on the south offers a good view of Port Everglades, a port of call for many cruise ships as well as freighters. Alongside this causeway is Pier 66, an elaborate marina-restaurant-motel complex, and, just as the beachfront is reached, there is the well-known Bahia Mar Marina. Bahia Mar can accommodate up to 425 yachts of various sizes on a 35-acre tract of bay and land. A post office, stores, swimming pool, club, and motel are included. The garden-flanked restaurant is a great favorite with many who never set foot on a boat of any kind. You can take a sightseeing boat on a three-hour trip and see most of the things you'd like to, including the fancy estates, tropical jungle areas, Port Everglades, and an Indian village. Next door to Bahia Mar is the Swimming Hall of Fame, featuring photos and memorabilia from the world of competitive swimming. Stretching north from Bahia Mar is the beach, and you can park head-in at the edge of the sand. Across from the beach are shops, hotels, restaurants, and bars.

Fort Lauderdale and its neighboring cities to the north (Pompano Beach) and south (Dania and Hollywood) draw about 2 million visitors a year. To house and feed them, the area has a wide variety of facilities and prices. There are 1,400 restaurants, rambling, torch-lit Polynesian places, huge Viking halls, early English inns, flossy Top-of-the-Mark view-givers, moon-gated Oriental spots, and Coney Island joints.

Except for the waterways, Pompano Beach, Hollywood, and Dania are much similar to and within the sphere of Fort Lauderdale. Pompano and Hollywood have excellent beaches and golf courses, and Dania helps fill out the county's supply of varied pari-mutuel plants with a well-appointed jai alai fronton. Pompano also has a horse trotting track. Hollywood has both a dog track and thoroughbred horse racing oval (Gulfstream Park).

After exploring Miami, head south to the Everglades National Park and the Florida Keys. Bus tours are conducted to both the park and Key West, and the Audubon Society conducts one- and two-day trips through parts of both, starting in Miami. If you drive, you can take old reliable US 1 south from Miami some 25 miles to Florida City and turn west on State 27 to the Everglades Park entrance and the 37-mile road which ends at Flamingo at the southern tip. Avoid US 1 congestion in Miami by taking Old Cutler Road south until it rejoins US 1. Turn east from US 1 at LeJeune Road, which is 42nd Avenue, and keep going.

To Key West

The best way to see Key West is via the Conch Tour Train or Old Trolley Train, tram affairs which ramble some fourteen miles in 1½ hr. viewings of such sites as Harry Truman's Little White House, Ernest Hemingway's home, Audubon House, the turtle kraals, the shrimp fleet, art centers, and all the attractions open to visitors. Audubon House was the Geiger House when the artist stayed there in 1831–32 sketching Keys birdlife. It's been restored and contains some of Audubon's work, plus a mixture of furnishings much like those the original owner salvaged from shipwrecks. Ernest Hemingway lived in Key West during much of his most productive writing period, working on *The Green Hills of Africa, To Have and Have Not, The Snows of Kilimanjaro* and *For Whom the Bell Tolls.* Hemingway was attracted by the old (1851) house's grillwork. He furnished it heavily with Spanish antiques and rebuilt the kitchen to put all the appliances several inches higher. A wealthy couple bought the house in 1961, intending to make it their home, but as they discovered more and more artifacts and Hemingway memorabilia they decided instead to make it a museum. The town's atmosphere seems to stimulate writers. Tennessee Williams, John Dos Passos, and Robert Frost also worked here.

If you plan to tour west across Florida on the Tamiami Trail, avoid metropolitan Miami traffic by switching to US 27 at Florida City, then turn west on US 41. The Tamiami Trail connects Miami with Tampa, sweeping through Everglades country for one hundred miles to the West Coast at Naples, then angling northward, generally inland from the "quiet coast" of Florida.

Along the Tamiami Trail

The Tamiami Canal, which parallels the road on the north, was dug to supply fill for the roadbed and automatically presented prime freshwater fishing grounds the length of the route. Most of the Miccosukee villages along the Trail are semi-tourist attractions, ranging in scope from a couple of elevated huts, called *chickees,* to an elaborate restaurant-marina-souvenir shop and filling station complex. Airboat rides are exhilarating once one gets over the shock of skimming along over an inch or two of water or perhaps only some damp sawgrass. Access to the western portion of Everglades Park is via the Shark Valley entrance. Birdwatchers will want to see this section, which includes Duck Rock, home of some 75,000 white ibises during the summer months.

Turn north on State 29 and you will reach the town of Immokalee, then Corkscrew Swamp Sanctuary, the National Audubon Society's six-thousand-acre preserve which features thousands of rare birds, elevated walkways through the heart of a jungle, and giant bald cypress trees seven hundred years old and 130 feet high. The Sanctuary also can be reached via State 846 north of Naples, if you prefer.

Gulf-central Florida yields to no other section of the state in tempting visitors. There are lovely beaches all along the generally placid Gulf Coast, centers of art and architecture such as Sarasota, metropolitan blandishments with a subtropical flavor in the Tampa–St. Petersburg area, Old World color in the Greek colony at Tarpon Springs, New World agronomy in the rolling citrus grove centers of Lakeland and Winter Haven.

Along US 41 is the turnoff point for Sanibel and Captiva Islands, which are the seashell fancier's idea of paradise because of the supply of left-handed welks, spiny periwinkles, large cockles, and coquina. Sanibel, connected to Captiva on the north end by a small bridge, was considered the ultimate in tropical splendor mixed with blessed privacy when only a ferry gave access to the mainland at Punta Rassa, but a toll causeway now makes the 3½-mile trip simple and quick. The $3 round-trip toll, a concession to islanders who didn't want so many visitors after all, keeps the traffic down. The beaches are fine, accommodations simple but comfortable to deluxe and expensive.

Culture-happy

Sarasota seems to be the place with a little something, or everything, extra. The connecting keys offer beautiful beaches and Sarasota is a cultural center, combining the best of both worlds. The John and Mabel Ringling Museum of Art, owned and operated by the state, contains one of the nation's outstanding collections of Baroque and Renaissance paintings: the Rubens collection is America's finest. Contemporary and modern art also are on display. New galleries opened early in 1967. Near the museum is the state-acquired Asolo Theater, a magnificent 18th-century interior from the castle at Asolo, Italy, which is in almost constant use for appropriate presentations: opera, concerts, and an eight-month season of plays.

The grandiloquent Ringling mansion on Sarasota Bay, and Ringling Museum of the Circus, also are part of the overall museums, which may be entered separately or with a combination ticket for all. The culture doesn't linger in the past, however. Such outstanding architects as Paul Rudolph and Victor Lundy have contributed greatly with churches, homes, shops, and schools, and I. M. Pei designed buildings for the Oxford-like New College, which had Dr. Arnold Toynbee on the faculty for the first handpicked class of 94 scholars. The intellectual life is contagious. Little theater groups, art schools, concerts, and art shows permeate all strata of the population. And everybody shares the "regular" niceties of sun, beaches, fishing, golf, tennis and patio socializing.

Bradenton has its own offshore key, Anna Maria. At the mouth of the Manatee River, five miles west of Bradenton, is De Soto National Memorial Park. Just across the river on US 41 or 301, turn east for a couple of miles to reach the Gamble Mansion, a plantation-style antebellum museum. Judah P. Benjamin, Confederate Secretary of State, hid out here briefly after the South lost the war and eventually made it to England where he became a successful barrister.

The Sunshine Skyway

Either 41 or 301 will take you to Tampa, but for a spectacular view and a quick entry into St. Petersburg switch to US 19 north or I–275, just outside Palmetto. You will cross the fifteen-mile Sunshine Skyway (toll: $1 per car) and save 45 miles. The Skyway is part causeway, part bridge spanning Tampa Bay. In 1980, the unique four-mile-long, 15-stories high section, above the entrance to Tampa Bay, was damaged by a freighter. A new span is under construction but two-way traffic between Sarasota and St. Petersburg is not affected. Cars use the causeway until the high-level bridge will be completed. When you enter St. Petersburg from the south, a "semicircle" radiates from the Municipal Pier, the yacht-clustered marina, and on to Central Avenue. The Pier, scene of most racing regattas (St. Petersburg is considered the boating capital of the U.S.A.), is also dominated by the unusual, inverted pyramid building. The five levels include a fourth-floor window-walled seafood restaurant, the Isle of Nations, with ethnic entertainment and boutiques on the main floor. Because it was named one of the healthiest cities in the good old days, retirees flocked here, but now only 25 per cent of the population is above retirement age.

At the Vinoy Basin, next to the city pier, you can (shades of Captain Bligh) crawl aboard the famed sailing ship *Bounty*. Major show business personalities star at the Bayfront Center. The beaches are easy to reach. Nearest one is via Pinellas Bayway on the left soon after you reach the mainland southern tip of St. Petersburg. This offers access to some islands to the south, such as Mullet Key. St. Pete's new cruiseport offers a Nassau trip.

Fort de Soto (1898) has become one of the Gulf Coast's most popular parks. An excellent beach, picnic sheds, barbecue pits, excellent camping areas, and prime mackerel and tarpon fishing help attract more than a million visitors a year. In 1978, the fort's cannons were dedicated as a National Historic Landmark. The gulf beaches north of Mullet Key (turn west onto State 699 if returning from Mullet Key) are known collectively as the Pinellas Suncoast and include, alphabetically, Clearwater Beach, Dunedin, the Holiday Isles, Madeira Beach, St. Pete Beach, St. Petersburg, Tarpon Springs, and Treasure Island. All told, there are twenty-eight miles of beach and beachfront accommodations range from luxury hotels and apartments to weathered frame beach houses that may be rented by the week or month.

St. Pete Beach is connected to the mainland by Corey Causeway (free) and has one of the best, wide white-sand beaches anywhere. The National Historic Landmark "pink palace" the Don CeSar Beach Resort Hotel adds a beautiful Spanish accent to the skyline. Two penthouse-topped hotels, the St. Pete Beach Hilton and Schrafft's Sandpiper Resort are among the most popular of the beachfront hotels.

Diving for Sponges

Tarpon Springs' sponge industry began in 1905, with the perfection of deep-sea diving equipment. The Greeks moved up from Key West where they had been hooking sponges with long poles from boats. Synthetic sponges and plastics have made inroads on the sponge industry now, of course, but there are still a score of boats working the offshore beds. The Sponge Exchange, where the "catch" is auctioned, is interesting, or you may prefer a sponge diving exhibition from boats at the docks.

The familiar Greek Cross Ceremony, held on Epiphany, January 6, at noon, is a gala event with a ceremonial march to the docks, where a Greek Orthodox priest releases a dove and tosses a golden cross into the water. The lucky lad who retrieves it receives a blessing with a year's guarantee. The Greek Orthodox Church of St. Nicholas is a replica of St. Sophia's in Istanbul. Its white Grecian marble interior, iconography and stained glass are should-sees. After that, try one of the many Greek restaurants—you'll very probably get an excellent meal.

US 19, a mile west of Tarpon Springs, can bring you south again, but check your map and decide which route you wish to take to Tampa. From St. Petersburg, the superhighway I-275, via the Howard Frankland Bridge, is the fastest to Tampa and the showcase Tampa International Airport, rated as one of the best in the world. Tampa is now Florida's third largest city, and it has breweries and cigar factories, plus a busy deep-water port and an excellent future. The citrus industry added shipping and canning, World War II brought shipbuilding, and the postwar years have brought a little of everything.

Man-made Africa

Busch Gardens Dark Continent, a 300-acre theme park, also has one of the world's largest aviaries. Hundreds of colorful birds and animals live among the 150,000 trees, plants, and lakes. A sleek monorail passes over a man-made African veldt, where thousands of animals roam freely in their natural habitat. There's even a Moroccan village with belly dancers, magicians, and artisans. Exciting rides include the Flume and the Python. You can tour the brewery and grounds on your own. One paid admission includes everything, and the beer is on the house.

The multimillion 1979 expansion included the new Timbuktu on seven acres, with thrilling Scorpion and Crazy Camel rides, game areas, amphitheater for the dolphin show, a German Festhaus, Carousel, etc. A highly popular addition has been the Congo River Rapids raft rides. The new 22-acre Adventure Island water park promises "the ultimate water experience" with white sand beach, waterfalls, slides, heated pools, and pools topped by three- to five-foot surf. There is an extra admission to Adventure Island. A few more blocks north on 30th Street to the Schlitz Brewery for another tour and complimentary draught. On the way a turn west onto Broadway will yield a sample of Ybor City and the Latin Quarter of Tampa, Spanish architecture and some of the nation's best Spanish restaurants. Restoration continues in the historic area, lined with fascinating boutiques and cafés.

Mr. Plant's fine hotel is now the University of Tampa. The 13 Moorish minarets on this interpretation of the original Alhambra make it hard to miss. The adjacent Fair Grounds are aswarm with people during the 11 days of Gasparilla festival in early February, a festival keyed to the "capture" of Tampa by a modern "José Gaspar" and his crew of one-day buccaneers as they cruise up Hillsborough Bay in a flag-bedecked pirate ship to accept the city's surrender. Best spot for watching is along Bayshore Blvd.

Tampa has experienced a recent energetic pace in development, especially in the realm of tourist and commercial facilities.

Lakes and Cypress Gardens

Another Florida, distinctly different from the beach—keys—ocean experience, rises into view with rolling hills and lakes east of Tampa. This is the rich citrus and farming area around Lakeland, Winter Haven, Lake Wales, and Bartow. Tourism is considerable, for many winter visitors prefer the soft inland air, redolent with orange blossoms, to the tangy salt atmosphere near the ocean. Too, there is a reassuring permanence to quiet residential streets, long-established parks, and city squares. The visitors come and go, but when they go there in no void; life goes on at a neat clip, buoyed by the citrus industry, the farms, the cattle ranches, the phosphate mines, the general prosperity of stable communities.

Take I–4 east from Tampa 35 miles to Lakeland; there are eleven lakes, large and small, within the city limits. Water-skiing, fishing, and boating are popular, but there are also fine golf courses, and major league baseball exhibitions in the spring when the Detroit Tigers train here.

On the shores of Lake Hollingsworth is Florida Southern College, said to have the largest single concentration of Frank Lloyd Wright buildings anywhere. On the same lake are held the crew races, a popular campus sport among the smaller Florida colleges that do not have football, and powerboat races. The Orange Cup Regatta, in late January or early February, attracts the fastest boats on the racing circuit, and scores of world records have been set here. In the heart of the city, along Lake Mirror, is the Civic Center with its bowling greens, shuffleboard courts, a recreation center, and tennis courts. Lakeland also is the headquarters for the Florida Citrus Commission, the state agency which oversees quality control. Polk County, of which Lakeland is the largest city, produces a third of the state's crop. Packing houses, canneries, and frozen-concentrate plants dot the area. Large trailer trucks, filled to overflowing with oranges, stream along the roads during the busiest season, from mid-September to May.

Winter Haven, where the Boston Red Sox do their spring training, can be reached quickly from either Lakeland (via US 92) or Bartow (via US 17) and from Winter Haven it is only five miles to Cypress Gardens. Perhaps as much as any place in Florida, Cypress Gardens proves what imagination, promotion, and a pliant Mother Nature can do. What was once only a swamp well off the beaten track now offers at least 164 acres of gorgeous gardens with 11,000 varieties of flowers and plants in at least a dozen themed gardens-of-the-world, plus exciting water-ski shows.

Expert professionals give the proper camera settings for every shot, and it's very hard to take a bad picture. There's even a special grandstand for the picture takers (25¢ extra to get in it) and the bronzed water-skiers put a little extra into the big smile as they glide past the camera-clickers. The water-skiers have gotten most of the publicity, but the gardens cannot be overshadowed once you're on the scene. Lagoons, moss-hung cypress, bougainvillea, banks of azaleas, and rare and exotic plants from around the world combine to present a series of "vistas" along the winding walkways (electric boats, a little extra charge). In 1979 an ambitious expansion program added even more to do and see in the "Southern Cross Roads" and "Living Forest" exhibits. In 1983, an "Island in the Sky" ride, offering a panoramic view of the Gardens, was added. Crafts shops, restaurants, a small zoo and a hotel are also part of Cypress Gardens. The Florida Sports Hall of Fame is housed here.

An Area of Sundry Attractions

Near Cypress Gardens, Lake Wales and the Bok Tower are accessible via US 27. Edward Bok, wealthy editor of the *Ladies Home Journal* and a Pulitzer Prize winner in 1920, established Mountain Lake Sanctuary on the slope of Iron Mountain. It is 324 feet above sea level, the highest point in peninsular Florida and a refuge for birds and man, as well as a proper setting for the carillon tower that now serves as his memorial. Lovely gardens surround the 205-foot tower, and there are "blinds" for visitors to observe or photograph the birdlife. A pool reflects the image of the tower, and carillon concerts are given several times weekly. There is no tourist access to the tower's top. Serenity is the attraction. Lake Wales is also the scene, from early February to mid-April, of the Black Hills Passion Play, presented four times a week in a 3,500 seat amphitheater with a stage more than one hundred yards wide.

Thirty miles south of Lake Wales—again by US 27 or Alternate 27—is Sebring, famous for its annual twelve-hour speed and endurance sports car races, held in March. The Sun 'n' Lake resort offers tennis, golf, water sports, restaurants, entertainment facilities, and spacious villas. Otherwise, Sebring is just a quiet spot for fishing, hunting, golf, and outdoor pursuits. The nearby Highlands Hammock State Park has catwalks into a cypress swamp area, as well as guided tour and small museum.

North Central Florida

North of Orlando is the outdoorsman's jackpot: Ocala National Forest. There are 31 varied recreation areas within these 362,000 acres of lakes and rolling hills; they offer swimming, camping, trailer sites, fishing, and scenery by the mile. In fact, there are 65 miles without a stoplight on State 19, which offers a north-south "vistaway" all the way from Palatka, north of the forest. Another state road, 40, is east-west and crosses 19 in the middle of the forest. Two favorite spots are Alexander Springs, near the southern entrance, and Juniper Springs, near the crossroads. Alexander Springs bubble up a torrent of 76 million gallons of 74-degree water every day of the year, and there's a white sand beach, picnic area, refreshments, a bathhouse, boats for rent, nature trails, and nearby camping and trailer sites equipped with electricity, water, and sewers. Juniper Springs offers the same, basically, plus a thirteen-mile (downstream) canoe rental trip. One can just laze along, drifting, through a subtropical forest, finally reaching a waterway park back beside State 19. The Forest Service people take the canoe back by trailer.

Southern Wild West

Ocala is in the middle of what used to be called rural Florida, but now it's pastoral. And in the pastures are some very high-class thoroughbred horses who live in $75,000 barns. Some 150 thoroughbred farms worth more than $20 million are kept parklike with white fences, green grass, and old oaks. Most of the farms welcome visitors, but the hours vary. However, the Ocala Chamber of Commerce has free maps showing the location and hours for most of the showplaces. East on State 40, Silver Springs attracts close to two million visitors a year. Glass-bottomed boats visit the wondrous sights, starting with the main spring, a cavern 12 feet high, 65 feet long, and 60 feet below the surface, from which gush 650 million gallons of beautifully clear water every day. The trip continues over fourteen other springs or groups of springs, all colorfully named, plus visits to pools where friendly or hungry fish come up to nibble for the fingers of passengers. A viewing station eight feet below the surface offers a good chance for photographers at the trip's end.

Other attractions include the Jungle Cruise, a deer ranch with more than 300 tame deer from around the world (the kids like to feed them), Ross Allen's Reptile Institute for those who are interested, and an Early American Museum. A new wild and wonderful water world, complete with flumes, pools and surf-tipped waves, was opened 1978. On State 40 just three more miles east, one can find sanctuary in the Ocala National Forest. The noncommercial springs and attractions here are noted in the tour of northeast Florida. From Ocala, the 35 miles north to Gainesville is pleasant or fast, depending on the route. Interstate 75 is quickest, but bypasses almost everything. US 441, however, threads through some Old South towns and villages that possess a genteel charm, especially in the spring, which begins in early March hereabouts. Banks of azaleas, dogwoods, the fresh green leaves of oaks, sweetgum, and camphor trees make all this seem a thousand miles from the stereotyped Florida of palms, sand, and sunglasses.

Gainesville was once just a pleasant college town; now it's a vigorous university city. The University of Florida's handsome Tudor Gothic campus and its law school have long been the breeding ground for Florida's governors, senators, and congressmen. It now is known as The Solar City because its new airport is heated by solar energy.

Back to the Old South

Just north of Lake City on US 41, at White Springs, is the Stephen Foster Memorial on the Suwannee River. Carillon recitals from the 200-foot tower feature the composer's work four times daily. Foster never even saw the Suwannee, of course, picking the name for its beauty. As it happened, he picked a good one. The rambling Suwannee, from the Georgia line to the Gulf, is a beautiful stream, and the 243-acre park at the Memorial sets it off well. The Florida Folk Festival, with two thousand or more folk dancers, singers, craftsmen, and tale tellers, is held during the first week in May each year.

West on US 90 is Tallahassee, the state's capital. Ralph Waldo Emerson noted in 1827 that the city was a "grotesque place . . . settled by public officers, land speculators, and desperadoes." Today however, Tallahassee is pleasant, though not as quiet as in earlier times. Rolling hills, giant oaks strewn with Spanish moss, and pre-Civil War mansions help Tallahassee retain its Old South look, while modern buildings climb skyward at Florida State. The Chamber of Commerce headquarters building, "The Columns," was built in 1835 and served as a financial and professional center, as well as one of the city's finest brick residences in earlier years. A skyscraper state capitol building was completed in 1975. Tallahassee (the name means Old Fields in Apalachee Indian) has one of the states's most spectacular floral extravaganzas at Maclay State Park, about five miles north of town on US 319. There are 308 acres of garden and recreation area with pools, formal arrangements of flowers bracketed by blooming trees, a walled garden, and a Camellia Walk flanked by 12-foot-high camellias. Adjacent in the recreation area are picnic shelters with grills, swimming, and a boat ramp. Near the airport is the Tallahassee Junior Museum's Pioneer Village, which presents typical farm buildings and implements of Northwest Florida farm life, circa 1880. South on highway 61 is Wakulla Springs, with its glass-bottomed boats and wildlife refuge, and St. Marks, with its state museum.

The Miracle Strip

Start southward to reach Florida's greatest expanse of beach, one hundred miles extending from Apalachicola to Pensacola and modestly termed the Miracle Strip: the sand is pure white quartz variety, and the offshore formation provides a good surf.

Panama City is a sort of Southern Atlantic City, complete with roller coaster and convention hall, but the fishing is better than Jersey's. The city claims as its share 23 miles of beach, a portion of it in St. Andrews State Park, with a 450-foot fishing pier to help pedestrian anglers get out there with the bigger ones. Sport fishing of all types is a big attraction, and the city's marina is home port for a large fleet of charter craft.

US 98 is the east-west coastal route, and in truth, the Miracle Strip extends eastward of Panama City all the way to Port St. Joe and Apalachicola. Westward from Panama City via US 98 there remain some relatively unpopulated seashore vistas, by Florida standards at least, but you will have little trouble finding accommodations almost anywhere along the route.

The last city on this tour is historic Pensacola, which has a new theme park called Lafitte's Landing, after the pirate Jean Lafitte. Pensacola Beach has been another bonanza; good causeway connections and Fort Pickens State Park on the western tip overlooking the channel entrance have added tourism to the city's economic standbys.

Gulf Islands National Seashore, stretching over 150 miles from Destin to Mississippi, is a spectacular beach. There's gulf-front camping at dozens of spots.

Driving from Fort Walton Beach on US 98, you can cross over to Santa Rosa Island on State 399 at Navarre and continue to Fort Pickens. To reach Pensacola itself, take State 399 to US 98. Buses tour the Naval Air Station, Fort San Carlos and Fort Barrancas, the Naval Aviation Museum, Sherman Field, home of the Blue Angels precision flying team, the aircraft carrier U.S.S. *Lexington* (on holidays you can go aboard), and the Old Pensacola Lighthouse, built in 1825 and still working.

PRACTICAL INFORMATION FOR FLORIDA

HOW TO GET THERE. *By air:* Major airlines serve Gainesville, Jacksonville, Ft. Lauderdale, Orlando, Panama City, Sarasota–Bradenton, Tallahassee, Tampa –St. Petersburg–Clearwater, Titusville, and West Palm Beach. There are direct flights from Canada, Mexico, Europe, and connecting flights to just about anywhere in the world. For example, *Pan Am* flies from Tampa/St. Petersburg/Clearwater International Airport to Mexico and Europe. Since deregulation, rates and routes have changed greatly, check with several airlines or a travel agent and shop around for the best deals. One of them is *People Express*, flying New York–Jacksonville, also Palm Beach–New York.

By train: Amtrak has service to Orlando, Winter Haven, Tampa, Clearwater, Jacksonville, W. Palm Beach, Ft. Lauderdale and Hollywood. The Auto Train runs between Lorton, Va. and Sanford, Fla.

By car: The speedy way to the East Coast resorts and Central Florida from the northeast is I–95. The beautiful, leisurely way is AIA. The frustrating, stoplighted way is US 1. To the west coast take I–95 to Petersburg, Virginia, then I–85 to Atlanta and I–75 as far as Tampa (currently being extended further south).

Car rentals are readily available in all major cities.

By bus: Trailways and *Greyhound* provide good service. In addition, 13 other lines operate from out of state to various cities within Florida.

HOW TO GET AROUND. *By air:* Within the state *Delta, Eastern, United, Pan Am,* and other airlines serve such major areas as Daytona Beach, Eglin Air Force Base, Fort Lauderdale, Fort Myers, Gainesville, Key West, Lakeland, Melbourne, Miami, Orlando, Pensacola, Punta Gorda, Sarasota, Tampa/St. Petersburg/Clearwater, Titusville, Vero Beach, etc.

By car: Major routes are: I–4 from Daytona Beach to St. Petersburg; I–10 from Jacksonville to the Alabama border. US 301 diverges from US 1 at Callahan, through Starke, Ocala, Wildwood, Dade City, Tampa, to Sarasota. State 60 goes cross-state from Clearwater to Vero Beach, taking Clearwater–Tampa Bay traffic. State 84 is a toll shortcut from the lower west coast to the Ft. Lauderdale area, accessible 6 mi. east of Naples and running across the Everglades to US 27 at Andytown. I-275 is the best route between St. Petersburg and Tampa (it leads right into I-4 and onward to Orlando).

By boat: The Intracoastal Waterway parallels the coastline and runs 349 mi. from Jacksonville to Miami. It is 8 ft. deep in the shallower southern portions, with many canals leading to the ocean. Write Florida Dept. of Natural Resources for *Florida Boating.*

By bus: Greyhound, *Trailways* and *Gulf Coast Motor Lines* offer service within the state.

TOURIST INFORMATION. Welcome stations dispensing information are at Pensacola (I-10), Jennings (I-75), Hilliard (US 1 and 301), Yulee (I-95), and on the Suncoast at 688, north of St. Petersburg, soon after you exit off US 275 and the Howard Frankland Bridge. Division of Tourism, 126 Van Buren St., Tallahassee 32301; Florida Dept. of Natural Resources, 3900 Commonwealth Blvd., Tallahassee 32308.

Visitor Information Center, 75 Kings St., St. Augustine 32085; Pinellas Tourist Council, 2333 Bay Dr., Clearwater 33546.

For information on specific cities, contact local Chambers of Commerce.

For information on handicapped facilities, write FCHO, PO Box 2027, Satellite Beach 32937.

STATE PARKS. Despite the often justified concern that Florida is rapidly becoming overdeveloped, there are vast areas which remain in a natural condition. Happily, many of those areas will remain so permanently, as state parks. There are 47 in all, some in the midst of crowded urban areas, others remote and relatively wild; some of historical or cultural interest, others built around outstanding scenic or natural features. For complete information write to Florida Parks and Recreation, 3900 Commonwealth Blvd., Tallahassee 32308.

MUSEUMS AND GALLERIES. There are historical collections in these cities: Pensacola, *Pensacola Historical Museum,* 405 S. Adams St.; St. Marks, *San Marcos de Apalache State Museum,* US 319S; St. Petersburg, *Haas Museum & Grace S. Turner House & Village,* 3511 2nd Ave.; Tallahassee, *Division of Archives, History & Record Management,* 401 Gaines St. (Capitol building); Tampa, *Tampa Municipal Museum,* in the south wing of the U. of Tampa's main building.

Florida's major art museums are: Daytona Beach, *Museum of Arts and Sciences,* 1040 Museum Blvd.; Fort Lauderdale, *Fort Lauderdale Museum of the Arts,* 426 E. Las Olas Blvd.; Gainesville, *University Gallery,* U. of Florida, SW 13th St. at 4th Ave.; Jacksonville, *Cummer Gallery of Art,* 829 Riverside Ave.; *Jacksonville Art Museum,* 4106 Blvd. Center Dr.; Orlando, *Loch Haven Art Center, Inc.,* 2416 North Mills Ave.; Palm Beach, *The Society of the Four Arts,* Four Arts Plaza; Pensacola, *Pensacola Art Association,* 407 S. Jefferson St.; St. Augustine, *Pan American Building,* 97 St. George St.; St. Petersburg, *Museum of Fine Arts,* 255 Beach Dr. N.; Sarasota, *John and Mable Ringling Art Museum;* Tallahassee, *Florida State University Art Gallery,* Fine Arts Bldg., *Le Moyne Gallery,* N. Gadsden St.; Tampa, *Tampa Museum,* 601 Doyle Carlton Dr. (adjacent to Curtis Hixon Convention Center); West Palm Beach, *Norton Gallery,* 1451 S. Olive Ave.; Winter Park, *Morse Gallery of Art,* Holt Ave., Rollins College. *Norton Gallery,* West Palm Beach.

Special Interest: Bradenton: *South Florida Museum and Bishop Planetarium,* 201 10th St. W., The Civil War, two World Wars, and the Seminole days are recaptured in exhibits. Tues. to Fri. 10 to 5; Sat. 10 to 5 and 7 to 9; Sun. 1 to 5. Closed Mon.

Cross Creek: *Marjorie Kinnan Rawlings State Museum,* 20 mi. SE of Gainesville on State 325. Home of the writer whose works include *The Yearling* and *Cross Creek.* Guided tours daily 9 to 5.

Fort Myers: *Edison Home,* lab, gardens just as the Wizard of Menlo Park left them. Open Mon.–Sat. 9 to 4, 12:30 to 4 on Sunday.

Fort Walton: *Temple Mounds Museum.* US 98 downtown Fort Walton Beach. Best preserved Indian mounds in Florida. Tues. through Sat. 11 to 4; Sun. 1 to 4; Thurs. 6 P.M. to 8 P.M.

Gainesville: *Florida State Museum.* Walk-through Mayan Indian exhibit with dramatic panorama and splendid palace. $1 million dollars worth of exhibits.

Key West: *Hemingway Home & Museum,* 907 Whitehead. Mementoes and mounted specimens of the Hemingway safaris. Daily 9 to 5. Adults $1; children 50¢. *Fish Museum,* Mallory Sq., Chamber of Commerce Bldg. Big game fish exhibits. Mon. to Fri. 9 to 5; Sat. 9 to 12.

Palm Beach: *Henry Morrison Flagler Museum,* 71 Whitehall Way. Tues. to Sun. 10 to 5.

Pensacola: *Naval Aviation Museum,* U.S. Naval Station. Bus tours leave the main gate daily for a 2-hr. tour of the Air Station. The Museum is open Tues. to Sat. 8:30 to 4:30.; Sun. 12:30 to 4:30. Free.

Perry: *Forest Capital State Cultural Museum,* 1 mi. S. of Perry, in largest timber producing area in state.

St. Augustine: *Museum of Yesterday's Toys,* in the Rodriquez Avero House, 52 St. George St. Collection of toys dating from the 17th century. Mon. to Sat. 9 to 5; Sun. 1 to 5. Adults 75¢; children under 8 free.

St. Petersburg: *St. Petersburg Historical Museum,* 335 2nd Ave., NE. Pioneer life, Timuca Indian artifacts. Mon. to Sat. 11 to 5; Sun., holidays 2 to 5.

Sarasota: *The Ringling Museums* include the Museum of Art, the Asolo Theater, the Museum of the Circus, and the residence itself. Mon. to Fri. 9 A.M. to 10 P.M.; Sat. 9 to 5; Sun 1 to 5.

Sarasota: *Bellum's Cars & Music of Yesterday.* US 41N. Features 150 antique, classic and race cars, and over 1,000 mechanical music machines. Blacksmith shop and country store. Mon. to Sat. 8:30 to 6.

Silver Springs: *Early American Museum,* State 40. Antique dolls, automobiles and other vehicles. Daily 9 to 9.

Stuart: *House of Refuge,* Hutchinson Island. Tues. to Sun. 1 to 5. Closed Mon. *Elliott Museum,* State 5, Hutchinson Island. Daily 1 to 5.

Tallahassee: *Tallahassee Junior Museum,* 3945 Museum Dr. Housed in 1880 farm. Pre-Columbian Indian artifacts, costumes, agriculture. Outdoor museum. Tues. to Sat. 9 to 5; Sun. 2 to 5. Closed Mon., state holidays and Christmas.

Tampa: *Museum of Science and Industry.* 4801 E. Fowler Ave. Innovative.

Others: Estero: *Koreshan State Park Museum.* Depicts the Koreshan Unity, a religious sect. Daily 8 to sunset. St. Augustine: *Zorayda Castle,* 83 King St. Modeled on the Alhambra in Spain. Daily June 15 thru Aug. 9 to 9; rest of year 9 to 6.

 HISTORIC SITES. Apalachicola: *John Gorrie State Historic Memorial,* Ave. D & 6 St. Bradenton: *DeSoto National Memorial,* 75th St. Bushnell: *Dade Battlefield State Historic Site,* on US 301. Cedar Key: *Cedar Key State Memorial,* State 24. Crystal River: *Crystal River State Archeological Site,* off US 19, 98. Ellenton: *Gamble Mansion State Museum,* US 301, 4 mi. NE of Bradenton. Fort Myers: *Edison House Museum,* 2341 McGregor Blvd. Homo-sassa Springs: *Yulee Sugar Mill State Historic Site.* 5 mi. W. of US 19 on State 490. Jacksonville: *Fort Caroline National Memorial,* 12713 Ft. Caroline Rd. Key West: *Audubon House,* Whitehead & Greene Sts. New Smyrna Beach: *New Smyrna State Historic Site,* 1 mi. W. on State 44. Olustee: *Olustee Battlefield State Historic Site,* off US 90, 2 mi. E. of Port St. Joe: *Constitution Historic Memorial.* On US 98. Rattlesnake Island: *Fort Matanzas National Monument,* 14 mi. S. of St. Augustine. St. Augustine: All of St. Augustine is, in fact, one enormous historic site, with the early days of American development written indelibly in crumbling or reconstructed stone. The Visitor Information Center has a free *Visitor's Guide* to help you decide which of dozens of historic buildings you want to inspect personally. The *Historic St. Augustine Preservation Board* has strip tickets to all the historic buildings. Be sure to see *Castillo de San Marcos,* located on site of an original Spanish fort.

St. Petersburg: *Madira Bickel Mound.* Terra Ceia Island off US 41 S. of St. Petersburg. *Heritage Park* and *Pinellas County Museum,* at 125th St. and Wal-singham Road in Largo, heading west on Ulmerton Road from St. Petersburg, and turning south on 125th St.

Tallahassee: *Natural Bridge State Historic Site; Prince & Princess Murat Home of Bellevue.*

 TOURS. *Gray Line Tours* and *American Sightseeing Tours* offer a variety of combination trips. Check local Yellow Pages for telephone numbers.

Suwanee River Bicycle Tours offers week-long and weekend guided trips from the St. Johns River in the eastern part of the state to Monticello in the west and from the Georgia border to Ocala and Yankeetown. Side trips optional for antiquing, canoeing, or tubing down the rivers. Rates include breakfasts, dinners, lodging or tent, guide and supper vehicle. Bikes can be rented. Details from Suwannee River Bicycle Tours, P.O. Box 319, White Springs 32096. Bike trail maps of other areas available, 605 Suwanee St., Tallahassee.

Pensacola offers a tour of the *Naval Aviation Museum, Sherman Air Field* (base of the Blue Angels supersonic precision team), the survival exhibit where demonstrations indicate how to live from Arctic Circle to steamiest hotlands. Also on the tour: *Fort San Carlos,* and *Fort Barrancas,* built by Spanish in the 16th century, and the old Pensacola lighthouse, built in 1825, and still operating. *By boat:* The *Captain Anderson,* sails out of Dolphin Village, St. Petersburg, for dinner cruises from October to spring. The *River Queen* sails on scenic 1½-hr. river and gulf tours three times daily from Sponge Docks, Tarpon Springs. In Sarasota there are also 2-hr. narrated boat cruises. Near Jupiter, take the narrated river trip up the wild Loxahatchee River in Johnathon Dickinson State Park. The *Steven Thomas* sails out of the Vinoy Basin, downtown St. Petersburg, on sightseeing cruises. Snacks, soft drinks aboard. The *Captain Memo* is a fun cruise from Clearwater Beach Marina. The Captain, costumed as a pirate, sails to his private island.

St. Augustine's sightseeing cruise takes 1½ hrs., leaves from Municipal Yacht Pier, Avenida Menendez. In Titusville, boat tours leave from Westlands Marina daily. Winter Park has a narrated tour of the canals and lakes to view estates, azaleas, Rollins College, etc. Cruises to nowhere, 1 day aboard a "love boat," Cocoa Beach. St. Johns River cruises out of DeLand. And at Homosassa Springs, US 19, there is a scenic boat trip to view fish and waterfowl.

Glass-bottomed boats will open a whole new world at Silver Springs and at Wakulla Springs.

Key Largo has a 2-hr. boat trip to the coral reefs daily if the weather is good and Key West a 2-hr. reef cruise on the *Fireball* from the Gulf to the ocean daily, if clear. Take a glass-bottomed boat tour of the John Pennekamp Coral Reef State Park. Skeletons of old ships lie here with tropical fish swimming among them. The remarkably visible reef has 40 kinds of coral and is 21 mi. long. The trip lasts 2½ hrs. and leaves three times daily. Those willing to take the underwater tour can hire diving equipment on the spot—tank with air, masks, fins, snorkel.

Jungle Queen cruises, leaving from Fort Lauderdale's huge and beautiful Bahia Mar Yacht Basin, has two sailings daily. The *Jungle Queen* passes Venetian Isles, winds through Fort Lauderdale, takes in exotic gardens, tropical bird grounds, Seminole villages, Dania Waterway, Intracoastal Waterway, Port Everglades and Stranahan River. Paddlewheel *Queen* also has sightseeing and dinner cruises from Fort Lauderdale. You can also cruise on the *Island Queen* from Riviera Beach and the *Bay Queen* from Sanford on St. Johns River.

 DRINKING LAWS. City and county establish their own closing times for bars and nightclubs. Package liquor stores are under control of State Beverage Commission. Supermarkets can't sell wine until past 1 o'clock on Sundays in some counties, so do check the local laws. Minimum age in Florida is 19.

SPORTS. The state's subtropical climate makes sports possible all year. For that reason, they are listed alphabetically and not by season. Florida is high on participant sports—fishing, hunting, tennis, even boccie. It is the great winter training ground for big league baseball. In addition, there are sports exotica for the tourist and the gambler—jai alai, polo, racing with dogs, horses, sulkies, sailing and powerboat events. Shuffleboard is everywhere.

Boating: There are 2,200 miles of tidal shoreline, thousands of navigable lakes and rivers. Under the out-of-state reciprocity system, Florida grants full recognition to valid registration certificates and numbers from other states for 90 days. Persons staying longer must register their vessels with the county tax collector. Write Florida Department of Natural Resources in Tallahassee for a boating directory. This gives route maps, lists marine facilities and tells where all ramps are located.

Fishing: The question isn't where—because it's everywhere. No license is needed for saltwater, but a freshwater license is necessary. You have the choice of fishing in canals, lakes, rivers, the Gulf of Mexico, piers, beaches, bridges, or from inexpensive party fishing boats that leave on half-day, full-day and weekend trips.

Freshwater equipment may be used in saltwater, but must be cleaned afterwards to prevent corrosion. If you're able, buy big gear after arrival, when you know what you want to catch. Tackle shops are everywhere.

Water sports: Florida keeps pace, with water-ski schools, skindiving shops and surfing-supply houses. Dozens of local restrictions exist on where and when water skiers may be towed, and many areas are off limits to divers (too dangerous), so inquiries should always be made.

Surfing: Florida waves are rarely conducive to first-class sport. Mobile surfers spend hours, going from Miami to Fort Pierce, and higher, seeking the best water. Cocoa Beach is a favored spot.

Windsurfing: Clearwater Beach was the scene of the 1981 International Windsurfing Competition. Windsurfing schools are located on Clearwater Beach and St. Pete Beach. The sport is hot now; rentals everywhere.

Lobster diving. Use only your hands—it's a state law. Spears and hooks aren't allowed, skindivers wear a mask, swim fins, cotton gloves, possibly a snorkel, to go after the lobsters. They're found at any depth from three feet on. In daylight, the lobster hides but can be spotted under logs or rocks by his antennae. The antennae break off easily, so the diver must get a grip on the front body shell. First he twists, then he pulls. Watch out for the moray eel, barracuda, and the black, pincushiony sea urchin.

Parasailing: Up, up and away, harnessed on a multi-color parachute towed by a speedboat: It all began in Acapulco, Mexico, and has become a favorite sport on the Pinellas Suncoast beaches.

Tennis: Popular diversion. Check local listings.

Golf: Florida is a golfer's paradise, with some of the finest courses in the U.S. According to *Golf Digest* the *Seminole G.C.*, North Palm Beach, ranks among the first ten of America's 100 greatest courses; *Pine Tree G.C.* (Florida's toughest), Delray Beach, among the second ten; *PGC National G.C.*, Palm Beach Gardens, among the third ten; *Bay Hill Club, Orlando, among the fourth ten; Innisbrook G. & C.C.*, Tarpon Springs, among the fifth ten; *Walt Disney World G.C.*, Lake Buena Vista, among the second fifty. *Mangrove Golf Course*, a public course in St. Petersburg, is rated among the nation's best.

Others recommended by *Golf Digest* are located in: Amelia Island, Ponte Vedra Beach, Tallahassee, Pensacola, St. Augustine, New Smyrna Beach, Daytona Beach, Ormond Beach, Cocoa Beach, Titusville, two in Vero Beach, Ft. Pierce, Stuart, Port St. Lucie, Tequesta, Lost Tree Village, N. Palm Beach, four in W. Palm Beach, Palm Beach, Royal Palm Beach, two in Lake Worth, Lantana, two in Boynton Beach, two in Delray Beach, six in Boca Raton. Coral Springs, four in Pompano Beach, Plantation, Lauderhill, seven in Ft. Lauderdale, six in Hollywood, Homestead, Biscayne Village, N. Key Largo, Marco Island, four in Naples, Rotondo West, four in Ft. Myers, Cape Coral, two in Lehigh Acres, Englewood, two in Punta Gorda, Port Charlotte, N. Port Charlotte, two in Venice, Captiva Island, six in Sarasota, Palma Sola, Sun City, Lake Placid, two in Sebring, three in Clearwater, five in Tampa, Leesburg, five in St. Petersburg, Dunedin, Williston Highland, two in Orlando, Sanford, Howey-in-the-Hills, Crystal River, Wildwood, Ocala and two in Panama City Beach.

SPECTATOR SPORTS. *Baseball:* Late-winter vacationers can see some early baseball at the training camp cities. *Home bases:* Atlanta Braves and Montreal at West Palm Beach; Boston Red Sox in Winter Haven; Chicago White Sox at Sarasota; Cincinnati Reds at Tampa; Detroit Tigers at

Lakeland; Kansas City Royals at Fort Myers; L.A. Dodgers at Vero Beach; Minnesota Twins at Orlando; St. Louis Cardinals and New York Mets at St. Petersburg; New York Yankees at Fort Lauderdale; Phillies at Clearwater; Pittsburgh at Bradenton; Toronto at Dunedin; Houston at Kissimmee; Texas Rangers at Pompano Beach.

Car racing: The Feb. "Daytona 500" has attracted as many as 110,000 spectators. Short and long stock car events precede the "500." Drag and sports car races are held at Lakeland International Raceway. Auto races in Tampa, Mar. to Nov. Stock car races at W. Palm Beach, Feb. to Nov. Weekly events at Sunshine Speedway, St. Petersburg, where Evel Knievel has starred.

Dog racing: Greyhound tracks are: St. Petersburg Kennel Club (Derby Lane); Sanford–Orlando Kennel Club at Winter Park; Orange Park Kennel Club at Jacksonville; The Jacksonville Kennel Club; Bonita Springs Track; Associated Outdoor Clubs at Tampa; Investment Corp. of Palm Beach in West Palm Beach; Jefferson County Kennel Club, Monticello; Keys Racing Assoc., Key West; Pensacola Greyhound Racing; Hollywood Dog Track; Ebro Dog Track, Panama City; Seminole Park in Casselberry and Daytona Beach.

Horse racing: Tampa has mid-winter racing at Tampa Bay Downs, Jan. to May., Gulfstream Park in Hallandale runs mid-Jan. to Mar. For harness horse racing, there is Pompano Beach, with races mid-Dec. to mid-Apr. There is quarter horse racing at Gator Down Racing, Pompano, June to Sept. In Hollywood, the Calder Race Course has thoroughbred racing from May to mid-Nov. and has incorporated the former Tropical Park season, mid-Nov. to early Jan.

Jai alai is played at Dania, Daytona Beach, Tampa, W. Palm Beach, Tallahassee, and Winter Park.

Soccer: The Tampa Bay Rowdies play at Tampa Stadium, where Brazilian soccer super-champion Pélé has appeared with the Cosmos for exciting games.

National *Football* League: The Bucs represent Tampa, where Super Bowl '84 was held; the Bandits are in the USFL, along with the Orlando Renegades and Jacksonville Bulls.

SHOPPING. Palm Beach: One great shopping street is *Worth Avenue. Bonwit Teller's, Elizabeth Arden's,* and *Saks* mingle with shops at least as exclusive, if not nationally known. The *Salon Français* is at 2 Via Mizner and next door is *Dita,* Naylor–Leyland's children's shop. *Lily Pulitzer* is at 11 Via Mizner. The *Congo Shop* at 333 Worth Avenue is remarkable for leather goods, while *Taylor Imported Motors, Inc.,* at 1314 S. Dixie, dealers in Rolls Royce, Bentley, Jaguar, Ferrari, have one of the country's most stunning collections of treasuries-on-wheels. Nearby *Palm Beach Mall* has 100 assorted shops.

St. Petersburg, Clearwater, and Tampa have new, stunning malls, lined with specialty shops and top department stores. Among the most interesting are *Tyrone Mall,* St. Petersburg; *Countryside, Sunshine Malls,* Clearwater; Pompano Fashion Square, *Pinellas Park Mall,* north St. Petersburg. *St. Armands Key* in Sarasota excels in European-style boutiques with elegant fashions for men and women. In the showcase Tampa International Airport, the *P. Lorence Boutique* specializes in unusually-designed young women's fashions. Orlando's many malls are headed by *Altamonte;* nearby Winter Park has quaint shops; Pensacola boasts *Seville Square.*

Elsewhere, roadside stands everywhere specialize in products from the *orange groves.* A super-deluxe box (as packers call it) may cost as much as $25. That will be over a bushel and a half of oranges, grapefruit, pecan halves, candied fruits, coconut patties. If you buy oranges, sample first. Quality varies.

WHAT TO DO WITH THE CHILDREN. *Walt Disney World,* the superstar of theme parks, has a world of activities from the Magic Kingdom to the new world-of-tomorrow EPCOT Center. Good idea to decide ahead what you want to see and do. One of the best marine shows is at *Marineland* of Florida, 18 mi. S. of St. Augustine. Six performances daily. The *Gulfarium,* E. of US 98 on Okaloosa Island, nr. *Fort Walton Beach,* has fish and scuba diving shows in reef tank; trained porpoises in the main tank. Miami's *Seaquarium* has a shark channel, killer whales, porpoise and sea lion shows. A monorail circles the 60-acre garden. Orlando's *Sea World of Florida* is a 125-acre-park with killer whale and dolphin shows, pearl diving exhibitions. It's at 7007 Sea World Dr. and continues to add facilities. The trained porpoises for many of these shows come from *Flipper's Sea School* in Key West. You can see them at their lessons daily. *Ocean World,* 1701 SE 17th St. Causeway, Ft. Lauderdale, also has performing porpoises, a seal pool and shark moat.

The *Theater of the Sea,* in Islamorada, offers hr.-long "bottomless" boat tours in addition to trained porpoise shows and the aquarium. You can also take a charter boat to visit underwater coral gardens and wreck of a Spanish galleon. Homestead's *Coral Castle* is a monument to a woman, carved by a 97-pound Latvian. He hoisted into place rocks weighing up to 30 tons; a marvel of ambition and romance.

There's lots to see at the Tarpon Springs sponge docks. *Spongeorama,* 510 Dodecanese Blvd., gives sponge-diving exhibitions, shows movies and exhibits about the sponge industry, and offers a self-guided tour of the boats. Or you can watch an auction at the Sponge Exchange on Tues. or Fri. morning, or take a sponge boat down the Anclote River for a demonstration.

On the landward side of the nature-lover's coin are animal refuges. Tiny key deer, 25 in. high, can be photographed at the *National Key Deer Refuge* off State 940 on Big Pine Key. Tame deer may be fed at *International Deer Ranch,* Silver Springs. The visitor is caged, the monkey free at *Monkey Jungle,* 3 mi. W. of US 1 in Goulds, 20 mi. S. of Coral Gables. In Tarpon Springs visit *Noell's Ark Chimpanzee Farm,* US 19. The *Jacksonville Municipal Zoo,* on Trout River off N. Main St., features animals and birds from many countries, with moated islands for bears and lions, and a miniature railroad.

Over 100 lions and other African wild animals roam at large in *Lion Country Safari,* on US 98 in West Palm Beach. You can rent an explanatory tape and tape recorder. *"Jungle Larry's African Safari"* in Naples is a 200-acre tropical garden with exotic birds, waterfowl, chimp shows, and a lion and tiger training school. *Sarasota Jungle Gardens* has an awesome number of tropical plants in wild jungle and formal gardens, exotic birds, chimp acts, and bird shows. It's at 3701 Bayshore Rd. There are a bird walk, guided boat tours, a sundown train trip to a bird rookery, and native wildlife at Myakka River State Park, 17 mi. E. of Sarasota. *St. Augustine's Alligator Farms,* on Anastasia Island, features alligator wrestling and a zoo of Florida wildlife. *Gatorland Zoo,* Kissimmee, features alligators, crocodiles, giant tortoises, zebras. Train ride.

Costumed Indians make dolls, do beadwork and make baskets at *Seminole Okalee Indian Village,* 6073 Sterling Rd., West Hollywood. Arts and crafts center, small zoo and alligator wrestling. The Seminole Indian Reservation is on State 721 W. of Brighton. Exhibits at *Temple Mound and Museum,* US 98, Fort Walton Beach, tell story of Indian culture, religion.

Circus buffs will have a heyday at the *Ringling Museums,* a complex of 4 bldgs. on 68 acres on US 41, 3 mi N. of Sarasota. The circus museum covers circus history from ancient Rome to the present day with collections of hand-bills, posters, costumes, wagons, etc. The *Ringling Residence* is a fabulous Venetian Gothic building; the *Museum of Art* has both a fine collection of contemporary work and a renowned collection of baroque art; the *Asolo Theater* is a reassembled Venetian theater. Venice is winter quarters for *Ringling Bros.– Barnum & Bailey,* with a rehearsal hall and arena on Airport Ave. *Circus World* in Haines City (near Disney World) is a big, fun place, where you can walk the tightrope, be painted up like a clown, or be a circus performer, under professional supervision, of course. Under the Big Top, there's an excellent panorama film of circus life, special shows, and all the excitement of the circus. Nearby is the *Medieval Times* featuring exciting medieval tournaments amid dinner.

Weeki Wachee Spring features underwater ballet and a special show by "mermaids" in a specially designed auditorium 16 ft. below the surface. River-boats cruise the Weeki Wachee (included in the admission), and the Rain Forest is interesting to visit. There's also an Exotic Trained Bird Show with macaws and cockatoos skating, playing cards and doing other unbirdlike tricks. The Springs are 12 mi. W. of *Brooksville* at the jct. of State 50 & US 19.

Cypress Gardens, in Winter Haven, has water skiing, aquarama shows, boat tours of the canals and exquisite gardens. Florida Sports Hall of Fame is here. New additions to park include the Living Forest, Southern Crossroads, a walk-through aquarium, and a sky ride.

Six Gun Territory, Silver Springs, is a re-creation of an Old West Frontier town. Steam train, gondolas, rides, gunfights, Indian dances add to the fun. Rides and shows are included in fee. A new water world with flumes and surf-tipped pools further enhances the accouterments at Silver Springs. *Petticoat Junction,* 10 mi. W. of Panama City at Long Beach Resort, also features cowboy

and Indian fights, steam engine rides. Mar. to Labor Day. *Atlantis,* the world's largest water theme park, now in Hollywood, offers among other rides wave pools, water slides, and rapids.

Kennedy Center–Spaceport USA tours offer views of the launch sites for the manned space program. Many exhibits and "behind the scenes" peeks.

Busch Gardens, on Busch Blvd., Tampa, is an adventure into The Dark Continent, with a 300-acre prairieland (Serengeti Plain), where 3,000 animals roam freely, including lions, zebras, rhinos, etc. The animals are observed in their natural habitat from the skyride or the monorail. In the Moroccan Village, snake-charmers, magicians, and exotic dancers are just part of the entertainment. Walk through the well-known Bird Garden, watch the famous Berosini orangutans perform, take an exciting ride on The Python, the Monstrous Mamba, Phoenix, Jungle Cruise, or Log Flume. Adults can tour the Anheuser-Busch Brewery and have some free "suds" while the youngsters enjoy, enjoy. Busch's Campgrounds are adjacent, for a stay within the sound of the lions' roars. Timbuktu with thrill rides, German Festhaus, game area, etc. draws raves as does *Adventure Island,* a fabulous water park with white sand beach, pools topped by surf, waterfalls.

The famous Goodyear Blimp is now in Pompano Beach. Rides are no longer offered, but you can see the blimp and tour the museum.

At the Clearwater Beach Marina, on the Pinellas Suncoast, a pirate-garbed captain has fun trips aboard his yacht to his private island for shelling.

Also of interest to the pirate-adventure lover is MGM's replica of *The Bounty,* the mutiny ship, in St. Petersburg, adjoining Municipal Pier. There's also a *Tahitian village,* dioramas.

Orlando's Mystery Fun House has 15 chambers of fun: laughing doors, magic floors, games galore. The *Elvis Presley Museum* is nearby.

There are many museums which will interest children. Among them: *South Florida Museum & Bishop Planetarium,* 201 10th St. W., Bradenton and the *Jacksonville Museum of Arts and Sciences* at 1025 Gulf Life Dr. Ecology, wildlife, Timaqua Indians, Planetarium shows. *John Young Museum and Planetarium,* Orlando and Ft. Lauderdale's *Discovery Center.*

The *Museum of Yesterday's Toys,* 52 St. George St., St. Augustine, displays over 4500 dolls, other toys and accessories. Guided tours of house, garden. Kids will also appreciate the *Ripley's Believe It or Not Museum,* 19 San Marco Ave. In Winter Haven, the *Museum of Old Dolls and Toys* at 1530 6th St. displays 3-century-old dolls, mechanical banks. Sarasota's *Bellum's Cars & Music of Yesterday,* 5500 N. Tamiami Trail, has antique cars, mechanical music boxes. At Crescent City, the *Pioneer Settlement* lives and works the pioneer way. Open daily. Homestead's *Pioneer Museum* is another historic spot.

Tallahassee's Junior Museum, 3945 Museum Dr., is a restoration of a pioneer farm with blacksmith shop, farm house, smokehouse, etc.; 4 museum bldgs, nature trails. The *Junior Museum* features Seminole Indian culture, and a man-in-space display.

Sunken Gardens, 1825 4th St., St. Petersburg, delights the children with more than 5,000 plants and flowers, an orchid arboretum, colorful native and exotic birds, a King of Kings exhibit, a colossal gift shop. *Tiki Gardens,* 19061 Gulf Blvd., Indian Rocks Beach, outside of St. Pete, is a veritable Polynesia, with Tiki gods, gardens, comical monkeys, and strutting peacocks outside a restaurant–gift shop complex. *London Wax Museum,* 5505 Gulf Blvd., St. Pete Beach, is a fascinating display of almost 100 of the most famous and infamous people, plus a Chamber of Horrors.

Ralph Heath's *Suncoast Seabird Sanctuary,* 18328 Gulf Blvd., Indian Shores, about a ten-minute drive from St. Pete Beach, is open 7 days a week during daylight hours. Admission is free to see how injured seabirds receive tender loving care. Or the children may want to adopt-a-bird! At least 550 birds of 40 different species are always in residence.

Waterslide sites include the *Wet 'n Wild* watersport theme park in Orlando, the *Zoom Flume* in Panama City, *Water Boggan* in Pompano Beach, *Hawaiian Slip Waterslide* in Kissimmee, *Okaloosa County Water Slide* in Fort Walton Beach, *Waterslide World* in Largo.

Miami's brand-new and growing *Metrozoo,* south of the city, rival's San Diego's pace-setting, cageless zoo; will one day be world's largest.

Alligatorland Safari Zoo, Kissimmee, is an animal jungle compound. New in Fort Myers, is *Fort Myers* (formerly Ross Allen Park) *Wildlife Park,* with exhibits, bird and wildlife shows. Adjacent to the huge *Shell Shop.*

HOTELS AND MOTELS. In Florida more than any other state, your entire schedule of activities will probably revolve around where you stay. If you want active sports, you will want one kind of hotel; if you prefer to lounge on the beach, you will prefer another. Rule of thumb on prices; the farther from the ocean, the cheaper the room. Good buys can be found up and down US 1 on the east coast. In many locations, offseason prices are as much as 50 per cent cheaper, making an expensive hotel a summer bargain.

We have listed hotels and motels alphabetically in categories determined by double-occupancy in-season rates: *Deluxe,* from $85 and up; *Expensive,* $55–85; *Moderate,* $50–70; *Inexpensive,* $30–50.

AMELIA ISLAND. *Deluxe:* **Amelia Island Plantation.** Luxurious oceanfront resort with main hotel, private villas. 4 miles of white sand beach, 90-foot pool. Beach club, tennis center, outstanding championship golf course. Observation deck atop 50-foot sand dune. Restaurants, shops, marinas. Half-hour drive from Jacksonville Airport.

BOCA RATON. *Deluxe:* **Boca Raton Hotel.** E. Camino Real. One of the most celebrated Gold Coast hotels. Polo in season. In 1981, the $20-million 212-room *Boca Beach Club* opened here with elaborate facilities. Pampered beachcombers can shuttle by boat between hotel and club. Five golf courses, 49 tennis courts. MAP avail.

Expensive: **The Bridge Hotel.** 150 rooms, Top of the Bridge gourmet restaurant and Supper Club.

Moderate: **Holiday Inn.** 2901 N. Federal Hwy. Near beach and Florida Atlantic University. Another at 1900 Glades Rd. Also 8144 Glades Rd.

University Inn. 2700 N. Federal Hwy. Fam. rates, kitchenettes avail.

BRADENTON. *Inexpensive:* **Days Inn.** US 301 & State 64. A good operation, featuring popular Tasty World restaurant. Pets.

CAPTIVA. *Deluxe:* **South Seas Plantation.** Lovely 1856 plantation with private beach. Tennis, marina, prize-winning restaurants. Delightful villas.

CLEARWATER. *Deluxe:* **Belleview Biltmore.** Belleview Blvd. Resort hotel on 625 acres. Ornate Victorian decor. Designated a National Historic Landmark. Winter season only.

Inexpensive: **Days Inn.** US 19 & State 590. Well-kept. Pool, play area.

CLEARWATER BEACH. *Deluxe.* **Sheraton Sand Key Resort Hotel.** Beautifully situated on wide, white-sand beach. Penthouse supper club.

Expensive: **Adam Mark's Caribbean Gulf.** 430 S. Gulfview Blvd. Caribbean atmosphere. Gulf-front pool, steel band entertainment. Calico Jack's restaurant.

Moderate: **Dunes.** 514 S. Gulfview. Pool. Weekly rates available.

Red Carpet Resort. 530 Gulfview Blvd. S. Heated pool, private fishing pier and boat dock. Efficiencies.

COCOA BEACH. *Moderate:* **Holiday Inn.** 1300 N. Atlantic Ave.

CRYSTAL RIVER. *Expensive:* **Plantation Inn and Golf Resort.** Just off US 19. Southern-style hotel. PGA golf course, tennis courts, marina. Restaurant open to public; cocktail lounge. Fishing, Scuba arranged. Vacation packages.

DAYTONA BEACH. *Deluxe:* **Daytona Hilton.** 2637 S. Atlantic Ave. Beachfront resort. Tennis, sauna. Rooftop dining. A fun place.

Expensive: **Beachcomber Oceanfront Inn.** 2000 N. Atlantic Ave. Kitchen units, wkly rates avail. Restaurant, cocktail lounge, pool.

Sheraton Inn. 3161 S. Atlantic Ave. Oceanfront with all amenities of this well-known chain. Part of Seven Oceans Eleven Resorts on Daytona Beach.

Moderate: **Castaway Beach Motel.** 2075 S. Atlantic Ave. Restaurant, bar, dancing, entertainment.

Hawaiian Inn. 2301 S. Atlantic Ave. Day camp for kiddies in summer & winter wknds. Barbecue areas. Kitchen units, wkly rates avail.

Holiday Inn. 2700 N. Atlantic Ave.; 400 N. Atlantic; 905 S. Atlantic, Jct. I–95 and U.S. 1; and 1790 Volusia Ave.

TraveLodge on the Beach. 3135 S. Atlantic. Restaurant, bar, lounge, entertainment. 800–255–3050.

Inexpensive: **Days Inn.** I–95 at US 92. A good buy. Pool, play area, gift shop, gas station.

DELRAY BEACH. *Deluxe:* **Talbot House.** 125 N. Ocean Blvd. Pleasant apartments. Tennis court, heated pool, putting green. Casual Brown Bag restaurant. Near boutiques and restaurants.

Expensive: **Holiday Inn.** 2809 S. Ocean Blvd. Pool (heated), beach, play area. Restaurant has bar.

Wright by the Sea. 1901 S. Ocean Blvd. Pool (heated), beach, play & barbecue area. Closed June–Sept.

Moderate: **Sea Aire Hotel.** Atlantic Ave. & Ocean Blvd. Beach, play area. Restaurant, bar.

DUNEDIN. *Moderate:* **Jamaica Inn.** Small charming European-style inn at the marina, with beautiful views of the water or pool. Spacious, well-decorated rooms and suites. Multilingual staff. Next to award-winning Bon Appetit restaurant.

EVERGLADES. *Moderate:* **Flamingo Inn.** State 27, 47 mi. SW of Homestead. Pool, play area. Bicycles avail. Great bird watching in park.

FORT LAUDERDALE. Broward City Hotel Assn., 1212 NW 4th, Ft. Lauderdale 33304, will send a free list of accommodations, and will assist in finding you a room even in peak season. Tell them your price requirements.

Deluxe: **Bahia Mar Hotel/Yacht Ctr.** 800 Seabreeze Blvd. Yachting, fishing.

Fort Lauderdale Marriott Hotel and Marina. 1881 S. E. 17th St. On Intracoastal, adjacent to Port Everglades (cruise ship harbor). Opened late 1980. Exotic landscaping, free-form pool, Jacuzzi. 4 lighted tennis courts; marina. 9 restaurants and lounges; convention facilities. Guests can arrive by car or boat.

The Hilton Inn & Conference Center at Inverrary. About 15 mi. from airport. A total resort, with 2 championship golf courses, 30 tennis courts (8 for night play), health club. Beautiful heated pool. Patio and lovely gardens. Excellent restaurant.

Pier 66. 2301 17th St. Causeway. Beautifully landscaped resort on Intracoastal Waterway. Dining room, coffee shop, revolving rooftop lounge with entertainment, restaurant. Two heated pools, wading pool, marina. Small golf course; tennis courts. Fishing, charter boats.

Sheraton Yankee Clipper and Sheraton Yankee Trader Hotels. On SR A1A. On and across from ocean beach. Excellent restaurants, lounges, entertainment. Pools, tennis courts. Some efficiencies.

Expensive: **Holiday Inn.** Nine locations, each with typical amenities of this well-known chain: Ft. Lauderdale Beach; Coral Springs; North, Airport; Plantation; North Beach; Oceanside; U.S. 1; West. 800–238–5510.

Marina Bay Resort. 2175 State Rd. 84. "Houseboat" hotel; tennis; fitness center; live entertainment nightly.

Moderate—Expensive: **Best Western Ft. Lauderdale Inn.** 5727 N. Federal. Water sports. Entertainment.

Ireland's Inn. 2220 N. Atlantic Blvd. On beach. Kitchen units, penthouse avail. Very attractive.

FORT MYERS. *Inexpensive.* **Days Inn.** 2 locations, 1099 U.S. 41 N., U.S. 41 and Beacon Manor. Pool, gas station, restaurant, near airport, mall.

Wonderland Motel. 2000 N. Tamiami Trail. Heated pool, play area. Coffee shop.

FORT MYERS BEACH. *Expensive:* **Island Towers.** 4900 Estero Blvd. Kitchen apts. Overlooking gulf. Weekly guests only.

Moderate: **Caribbean Beach.** 7600 Estero Blvd. Fishing pier, beach. Cook-out facilities. Weekly guests only.

Sandpiper Gulf Resort. 5500 Estero Blvd. Sightseeing tours. Kitchen apts. with private patios or balconies.

FORT PIERCE. *Expensive:* **Executive Inn,** 3224 US 1, South. Full facilities. 170 rooms.

Moderate: **Holiday Inn.** Pool. Restaurant, bar. Family oriented—playground. Two locations: 2600 N US A1A; 7151 Okeechobee Rd.

FORT WALTON BEACH/DESTIN. *Inexpensive—Deluxe.* **Bluewater Bay.** Niceville. 800–874–2128. Community resort, tennis golf, marina, fishing, boating.

Moderate—Deluxe. **Sandpiper Cove.** Villas, furnished kitchens. Dock, fishing, pools, private beach.

Expensive. **Sandestin Resort Inn** (formerly Sheraton). On Florida Gulf. 18 holes of championship golf, 9 tennis courts. Fishing, sailing, lawn games. Two pools. Near Indian Temple Mound Museum and other attractions.

Inexpensive. **Gulf Beach Motel.** 670 Nautilus Ct. On ocean. Apts. Family inn.

GAINESVILLE. *Moderate—Expensive:* **Gainesville Hilton.** 2900 S.W. 13th St. Mediterranean-style rooms overlooking Bivens Arm Lake. Prime Rib Room, Palm Court, Winnie's Disco.

HIALEAH. *Moderate:* **Holiday Inn.** 1950 W. 49th St. Pool. Pets. Restaurant, bar, dancing, entertainment. Free airport transportation.

HILLSBORO. *Expensive:* **Barefoot Mailman.** 1061 Hillsboro Mile, just north of Pompano Beach. Newly decorated rooms. Docking facilities on Intracoastal Waterway. 18-hole golf course. Sundeck. Private 4-mile beach. Mary Celeste dining room.

HOLLYWOOD. *Deluxe.* **Diplomat Resort,** 3515 S. Ocean Dr. One of finest anywhere. Golf, tennis, pools, restaurants, shopping; nightly entertainment, superstars in winter. Multi-million dollar refurbishment in '84.

JACKSONVILLE. *Expensive:* **Jacksonville Hilton.** 565 S. Main St. Restaurant, bars, entertainment. Overlooks city, river. Most rooms with private balcony. Own shopping mall.

Sheraton St. John's Place. 1515 Prudential Dr. at St. Johns Place, overlooking river. $. million, 350-room hotel. Pool, tennis courts. Two restaurants, lounges, entertainment.

Inexpensive: **Days Inn.** I–95 & State 102 (Airport Rd.), 5929 Ramona Blvd., and Cagle Rd. at University Blvd. Many family efficiency suites. Pool, play area, gas station and Tasty World restaurant at all addresses. Pets allowed.

Jacksonville Airport Hilton. Conveniently located at International Airport. Pool. Restaurant, lounge. Fish-stocked lake.

Rodeway Inn. 1057 Broward Rd. Pool, restaurant. Opp. shopping center.

JACKSONVILLE BEACH. *Moderate:* **Howard Johnson's on the Ocean.** 1515 N. 1st St. 800–654–2000. Beach, bar, boating, restaurant.

Sheraton Jacksonville Beach. On Atlantic Ocean beach. 10 miles from I–95. Pool, volleyball, croquet. Live entertainment in Yellow Pelican restaurant. Golf and tennis nearby.

JUPITER. *Deluxe.* **Hilton Inn.** Oceanfront. Heated pool, children's pool, two lighted tennis courts. Golf five minutes away. Half hour from Palm Beach airport. Barefoot Bar, Livingston's by the Sea restaurant, cocktail lounge. Near Burt Reynolds Dinner Theater.

KEY BISCAYNE. *Deluxe:* **Sonesta Beach.** 350 Ocean Dr. Resort hotel on private beach. Supervised children's program "Just Us Kids." Vacation period

family rates available in summer. Also 12 luxurious villas with indoor pools. Outstanding restaurants.

Expensive: **Key Biscayne Hotel & Villas.** 701 Ocean Dr. On private beach, with Sunfish available. Supervised children's program in summer & holidays.

Moderate: **Sheraton Royal Biscayne,** 555 Ocean Dr. Tropical flavor. Tennis, water sports, dining.

KEY WEST. *Deluxe:* **Marriott's Casa Marina Resort.** Spanish architecture. Private beach, pool. Restaurants, bars. 600-ft. fishing pier. Built originally by Henry Flagler for his wealthy vacationing friends. Completely refurbished and redecorated.

Pier House. 5 Duval St. Private beach. Very attractive building and rooms.

Moderate: **Southernmost Motel.** 1319 Duval St. Pleasant little place, short walk to sights. Some efficiencies.

Key Wester Inn. A1A. On ocean. Tennis, boating, restaurant.

LAKE WALES. *Deluxe:* **Chalet Suzanne Resort Inn.** US 27A. Pool (heated), play area. Fine restaurant. Kitchen units, cottages avail.

Moderate: **River Ranch Resort.** At Yeehaw Junction between Lake Wales and Okeechobee. Wild West action in Florida with horseback riding, cookouts, rodeos, square dancing, archery, hunting. Boating and fishing. Pool. Golf. Western café, Wild West saloon. Rustic, comfortable.

Inexpensive: **Emerald.** 522 S. Scenic Hwy. Pool. Pets. Restaurant nr.

LAKE WORTH. *Inexpensive:* **Midnight Sun.** 1030 S. Federal Hwy. Pool. Handy location.

Martinique. 801 S. Dixie Hwy. Free morning coffee & rolls.

MARCO ISLAND. *Deluxe:* **Marriott's Marco Island Hotel & Villas.** Beautiful resort with challenging golf course, talcum-white sand beach, watersports.

MARINELAND. *Inexpensive:* **Marineland Quality Inn.** Hwy. A1A. Scenic location. Two pools, wading pools, private marina, lighted tennis courts. Cocktails, pleasant restaurant.

NAPLES. *Deluxe:* **La Playa Beach and Racquet Inn.** 9891 Gulf Shore Dr. Pool with garden, 4 Har-Tru tennis courts. Spacious rooms. Suites. Delightful restaurants, cocktail lounges. A swanky resort.

Naples Beach Hotel and Golf Club. Famous older resort. MAP mandatory in season. Beach, lively lounge, heated pool.

Inexpensive. **Days Inn/Days Lodge.** U.S. 41 at State 84. Pool. Near shops, restaurants.

OCALA. *Inexpensive.* **Sheraton Country Inn.** 3620 S.W. Broadway. Restaurant, bar, entertainment. Pool, playground.

Days Inn. I–75 & State 40. Usual good standards. Pool, gift shop, gas station. Tasty World restaurant.

Holiday Inn. Two locations: I–75 and State Rd. 40; Silver Springs Blvd. Both near tennis and golf plus tourist attractions. Restaurant and lounge.

ORLANDO. Because of such major attractions as Walt Disney World, Sea World, Circus World, the Orlando area is replete with accommodations from the budget-priced **Days Inns** to the luxurious **Contemporary Resort Hotel** right at Disney World and **Viscount** at Disney Village. In and around Orlando, there are five **Howard Johnsons,** two **Hilton Inns,** four **Holiday Inns.** There are three **Sheraton Inns** plus the deluxe **Orlando Marriott Inn.** It would be difficult to list all the many, many good hotels and motels here. Best budget bet: request list of accommodations from Kissimmee–St. Cloud Tourist Board, 800–327–9159 (in U.S.), 800–432–9199 (Fla. only).

ORMOND BEACH. *Moderate:* **Ivanhoe Beach.** Lodge, 205 S. Atlantic Ave. All rooms with balconies. Pool, restaurant.

Maverick Motor Inn. 485 S. Atlantic Ave. Beach. Golf nr. Restaurant. Cookout facilities.

Sheraton Inn–Daytona Beach Shores. 3161 S. Atlantic Ave. Restaurant; pools, shuffleboard. Golf & tennis nr. Kitchen units, family and weekly rates available.

PALM BEACH. *Deluxe:* **Breakers.** S. County Rd. Large, posh resort hotel on private beach with cabana club. Social director, planned activities.

The Palm Beach Hilton. Beachfront at 2842 S. Ocean Blvd. Beautiful rooms. Excellent restaurant, cocktail lounge overlooking Atlantic. Director of social activities. Tennis, water sports.

PALM BEACH GARDENS. *Deluxe:* **PGA Sheraton,** 400 Ave. of the Champions. Posh, lakefront resort with pool; professional caliber golf and tennis facilities.

PENSACOLA. *Deluxe:* **Perdido Bay Inn.** 1 Doug Ford Dr. Resort hotel with 1,100 acres on bay. Free transportation to private beach, beach house 2½ mi. away.

Moderate. **Holiday Inn.** Four locations, all with pools. Call 800–555–1212 for free number in your state.

Inexpensive: **Days Inn.** I–10 & US 29N. Another branch of this dependable chain. Pool, play area, gift shop, gas station.

POMPANO BEACH. *Deluxe:* **Beachcomber Hotel & Villas.** 1200 S. Ocean Blvd. Resort motel with private beach.

World of Palm-Aire. 2501 Palm Aire Dr. Health and beauty spa is world famous. Outstanding resort on landscaped acres. Golf, tennis, private beach.

Expensive: **Holiday Inn.** 1350 S. Ocean Blvd. Pools (heated), dock, beach. Golf nearby.

Pompano Beach Motor Lodge. 1112 N. Ocean Blvd. Pool (heated), private beach, play area.

Royal Plaza. 2721 N.E. 1st. Resident-owner. Apts. Cable TV.

PONTE VEDRA BEACH (near Jacksonville). *Deluxe:* **Sawgrass.** Community resort offering villas with 2–3 bedrooms, nationally known golf, oceanfront dining. Near St. Augustine for sightseeing; Jax for nightlife.

PORT ST. LUCIE. *Deluxe:* **Sandpiper Bay Resort.** Excellent golf and tennis (4 courses; 11 courts). Luxurious junior and large suites, all with private balcony or terrace. Restaurants, cocktail lounges, dancing. Swimming, boating, fishing, too. Over 1,000 acres.

RIVIERA BEACH. *Deluxe:* **Hilton Inn.** 3800 N. Ocean Dr. Pool (heated), private beach. Tennis, sauna, play area.

Expensive: **Tahiti on the Ocean.** 3920 Ocean Dr. Pools (heated), play area, private beach. Cookout facilities.

Moderate: **Colonnades Beach.** Palm Beach Shores. Large hotel with private beach, pools, saunas.

Best Western Seaspray Inn. 123 Ocean Ave. On beach; rooms with balconies. Rooftop restaurant; entertainment.

Inexpensive: **Sand Dune Apts.** 165 Ocean Dr., Palm Beach Shores. Barbecue facilities. Kitchen units.

ST. AUGUSTINE. *Expensive:* **Ponce de Leon Lodge & Country Club.** Ponce de Leon Blvd. Resort-style motel on 350 acres. Tennis courts, 18-hole golf course, huge pool, playground.

Ramada Inn Historic Area. 116 San Marco, on A1A. Pool, lounge, tennis, near beach.

Sheraton Anastasia Inn. A1A S. at Pope Rd. Island location, beach, restaurant, pool, snorkeling, fishing.

Holiday Inn. 3 locations, all with pool, restaurant, bar, dancing, entertainment in season: I–95 at State 16; 1061 Highway A1A South (Beach); 1300 Ponce de Leon Blvd.

Inexpensive: **Days Inn.** Two branches of good chain. State 16. Pool, play area, restaurant, gift shop, gas station. Also I–95 at State 16.

Red Carpet Inn. I–95 and State Rd. 16. Pleasant 2-story motel. Restaurant.

ST. PETE BEACH. *Deluxe:* **Dolphin Beach Resort.** 4900 Gulf Blvd. Remodeled. Water sports, restaurant, and lounge.

Don CeSar Beach Resort Hotel. 3400 Gulf Blvd. National Historic Landmark "pink palace." Completely and glamorously decorated interior with everything new in guestrooms. Live entertainment, lounge, restaurant, coffee shop. Pool and Jacuzzi. Health club.

St. Pete Beach Hilton. A towering octagon with exterior elevator, and a revolving, glass-enclosed penthouse for drinks, dining, and disco. Right on the beach.

Schrafft's Sandpiper Resort Inn. 6000 Gulf Blvd. Accommodations from lanai suites to penthouse. Two pools. Family-oriented activities. Snack bar. Brown Derby restaurant in front.

Expensive: **Beachcombers Resort Motel.** 6200 Gulf Blvd. A beachfront favorite. Pool. Family oriented.

Normandy Beach Resort. 5606 Gulf Blvd. Right on beach. Efficiencies. Family-style, family-oriented activities.

Odyssey Gulf Resort and Odyssey Wilshore. 5400–5550 Gulf Blvd. Family resorts with pool, kitchens avail., pets, wide beach.

ST. PETERSBURG. *Expensive.* **Howard Johnson Motor Lodges.** 4 locations: north, south, St. Pete Beach, Treasure Island. 800–654–2000.

Sheraton St. Pete Marina/Tennis Resort. 6800 34th St. Pools, play area, beach, marina, fishing.

Moderate: **Holiday Inn.** 3 locations, each with pool, restaurant, bar, entertainment: North: 5005 34th St.; 4601 34th St, S.; 3000 34th St.

SANFORD. *Inexpensive:* **Days Inn.** I–4 & State 46. A good buy, gift shop, gas station. Pets.

SARASOTA. *Deluxe:* **Colony Beach & Tennis Club.** 1620 Gulf of Mexico Dr. Restaurant, bar, dancing, entertainment.

Hyatt House. 1000 Blvd. of Arts. 300 rooms, private lagoon, pool. 5 mi. to powdery white beaches. Excellent restaurants.

Longboat Key Hilton. Unusually designed resort on white sand beach. Caribbean atmosphere. About 13 miles from Sarasota airport. Completely renovated and newly landscaped. Delightful restaurant, cocktail lounge.

Expensive: **Azure Tides.** 1330 Franklin Dr. Pool (heated), beach, fishing, play area. Kitchen units avail.

Ramada Inn. 6545 N. Tamiami Trail. Near tourist attractions. Sports. Restaurant, bar.

Moderate: **Howard Johnson's Airport.** 6325 N. Tamiami Trail. Attractive rms. with patios or balconies.

Inexpensive: **Econo Lodge.** 5340 N. Tamiami Trail. 800–446–6900 east of Miss. R., 800–446–8134 west of Miss. R. Nr. Ringling Bros. Circus, greyhounds, golf. Efficiencies avail. Heated pool. Nr. beaches.

SANIBEL ISLAND. *Deluxe:* **Casa Ybel Resort.** On the site of the island's original resort. Villa-style accommodations. Golf, tennis, fishing, swimming. Excellent restaurant.

Moderate: **Beachview Cottages.** 306 W. Gulf Dr. On Gulf. All units have kitchens. Week minimum Christmas and Easter.

SEBRING. *Expensive:* **Harder Hall.** Golfview Dr. Golf, tennis, play area, entertainment in season. Closed May 5 to Nov. 15.

Inexpensive: **Clayton's.** Pets. Pool, beach. Restaurant, bar.

TALLAHASSEE. *Moderate:* **Hilton Hotel.** Pool, lively cocktail lounge, entertainment. Restaurant. Parking garage. Pets allowed.

Holiday Inn. 2 locations, each with pool, restaurant, bar, entertainment, dancing, airport transportation: Apalachee: 1302 Apalachee Pkwy.; Downtown: 316 W. Tennessee St.

TAMPA. *Deluxe:* **Tampa Hyatt Regency.** 2 Tampa City Center. Ultra modern in all respects. Super Bowl Hq.

Tampa Marriott. In airport. Heated pool. Special 6th-floor luxury for executives. Coffee shop. Revolving penthouse restaurant. Entertainment. Another superb Marriott; 1001 N. Westshore.

Expensive: **Bay Harbor Inn.** 7700 Courtney Campbell Causeway. Beach, heated pool, rental sailboats. Restaurant, cocktail lounge, entertainment.

Hilton Inn. 200 Ashley Dr. Balconied rooms overlook river. Lively lounge, Hearth and Embers restaurant. Near downtown, Ybor City. Another at 2225 Lois Ave.

Admiral Benbow Inn. 1200 N. Westshore Blvd. Heated pools, sauna. Restaurant, lounge, entertainment.

Inn on the Point. Campbell Causeway. (formerly the Causeway Inn). Large pool. Live entertainment, restaurant.

Moderate: **Holiday Inn.** 4 locations, all with pool, restaurant, bar: Airport: 4500 Cypress St.; Downtown: 111 W. Fortune St. I–4; East: 2708 N. 50th St.; Northeast: 2701 Fowler Ave.

Quality Inn. 2 locations, each with pool, restaurant: North: 210 E. Fowler Ave.; East: 2905 N. 50th St.

Ramada Inn. I–75 at Busch Blvd. Pool (heated). Restaurant, bar, entertainment, dancing. Another Ramada at 9331 Adamo. Also 2522 N. Dale Mabry.

Inexpensive: **Days Inn.** Three branches of popular chain. 701 E. Fletcher, Busch Blvd. & 30th St. and I–4 & State 579. Each has pool, play area, gift shop, gas station. Pets. Tasty World restaurant.

TARPON SPRINGS. *Deluxe:* **Innisbrook Golf and Tennis Resort.** 900 acres of landscaped gardens, championship golf courses, lighted tennis courts, sports pros on duty, fishing lakes, villa-style accommodations, wildlife sanctuary, three restaurants and lounges. Dancing.

TIERRA VERDE. *Deluxe:* **Tierra Verde Hotel Yacht and Tennis Club.** Elegant dining and dancing. Le Jazz Hot club for jazz aficionados. One of largest swimming pools in state. Excellent tennis courts. Yacht-fringed marina. Near 900-acre Fort DeSoto Park with beaches, fishing.

TREASURE ISLAND. *Expensive:* **Bilmar Beach Resort.** 10650 Gulf Blvd. Located on beach. Sherlock's Restaurant, popular cocktail lounge, piano bar.

Island Inn. 9980 Gulf Blvd. Colorful, small beach resort. Family-oriented activities. Snack bar. Management's cookouts.

Thunderbird. 10700 Gulf Blvd. Beachfront. Heated pool, sundeck. Some efficiencies. 24-hour coffeeshop, restaurant. Lively lounge, entertainment, dancing.

Moderate: **Sea Castle Motel.** 10750 Gulf Blvd. Efficiency apartments, perfect for longer vacations and for families. Beautiful beach.

WEEKI WACHEE. *Moderate:* **Holiday Inn.** Right on highway, across from Weeki Wachee Springs theme park and mermaid show. Pool, play area. Immaculate housekeeping has won awards.

WEST PALM BEACH. *Deluxe:* **Palm Beach Polo and Country Club.** West Palm Beach. Swanky 1,650-acre complex, about 15 mi. from Palm Beach. Riding, polo, golf, tennis. Swimming pools. Two- and 3-bedroom villas.

Hyatt Palm Beaches. 630 Clearwater Park Rd. Posh, full-service hotel with two restaurants, lounge, and swimming pool.

Ramada Inn. 1800 Palm Beach Lakes Blvd. Restaurant, bar, entertainment, dancing. Two tennis courts. Heated pool, 18-hole golf course.

Inexpensive: **Days Inn.** Neat rooms. I–95 at 45th St. State 702. Pool, play area, gift shop, gas station. Pets. Tasty World restaurant.

WINTER HAVEN. *Moderate:* **Banyan Beach.** 1630 6th St. NW. Dock, boats, fishing.

Quality Inn Town House. Cypress Gardens Rd. Restaurant nearby. Water skiing available.

Ranch House. 1911 Cypress Gardens Rd. Boating, fishing, swimming in Lake Ina. Kitchen units available.

 DINING OUT. Eating your way across Florida may not be good for the waistline—or the budget. It's hard to find a city without at least one superior eating place. Restaurant categories in the listing below reflect the cost of a medium-priced dinner at each establishment. Included are hors d'oeuvres or soup, entree and dessert. Not included are drinks, tax and tip.

Price ranges for Florida are *Expensive:* $15 and higher. *Moderate:* $10–15; and *Inexpensive:* under $10.

BRADENTON. *Moderate:* **Village Barn.** 5520 14th St. W. Primarily a night-club, but has dining room specializing in fish 'n chips.

Inexpensive: **Morrison's Cafeteria.** Fourteenth St. Fast, quiet service.

CAPE CORAL. *Expensive:* **Country Club Inn.** 4003 Palm Tree Dr. Nicely prepared continental dishes.

Inexpensive: **Carbonaro's.** 4835 Vincennes St. Italian food, beer, & wine.

CLEARWATER. *Expensive:* **Seiple's Garden Seat.** 1234 Druid Road S. Clear view of the Bay. 1920s motif. Seafood. Well known for desserts.

Kapok Tree Inn. Dazzling estate, landscaped gardens. Must be seen. Lunch, dinner, cocktails. Children's menu.

Moderate: **94th Aero Squadron.** Near St. Petersburg–Clearwater Airport. Picturesque French farmhouse on acres of land. World War I motif salutes American fliers. Super-size Margaritas. Lunch, dinner, late supper. Cocktail lounge with airport headsets.

Savoy. 924 McMullen Booth Rd. Pleasant atmosphere. Attentive service. Continental cuisine. Lounge. Reservations advised.

Tio Pepe's. 2930 Gulfview Blvd. Hacienda setting. Spanish food.

Inexpensive: **Fish House.** On US 19. Most entrees under $3. Lunch, dinner, cocktails.

CLEARWATER BEACH. *Expensive:* **Heilman's Beachcomber.** Mandalay Ave. Maine lobsters. Delicious chicken.

Pelican. Mandalay Ave. Seafood. Delicious baked goods.

Inexpensive: **Flagship.** 20 Island Way. Nice decor. Seafood.

COCOA BEACH. *Expensive:* **Bernard's Surf.** S. Atlantic Ave. Very good seafood.

CORAL GABLES. *Expensive:* **Chez Vendome.** David William Hotel, 700 Biltmore Way. Fine French cuisine in elegant surroundings.

Le Festival. 2120 Salzedo. Festive spot. Award-winning French dishes. Superb chocolate mousse.

DAYTONA BEACH. *Expensive:* **Klaus.** 144 N. Ridgewood. Sublime Continental specialties created by captain of U.S. Culinary Olympic team.

Moderate: **Chez Bruchez.** 304 Seabreeze Blvd. Delicious pastries, plus French or American food. Attentive service.

All Seasons. 1290 S. Ridgewood Ave. Italian-American cuisine in pleasant, arboreal setting.

DELAND. *Moderate:* **Hush Puppy.** West on Rte. 44. Unassuming but locally popular seafood shanty. Big selection, nicely prepared.

Moderate—Inexpensive: **Holiday House.** Buffet is good deal. Children's menu. 704 N. Woodland Ave. Open 11 A.M. to 9 P.M.

DUNEDIN. *Expensive:* **Bon Appetit.** On scenic Marina. Superbly-prepared seafood, veal, beef, and chicken specialties. Fine wines, classy service. Entertainment in cocktail lounge. Lunch, dinner. Closed Wed.

FORT LAUDERDALE. *Expensive:* **Casa Vecchia.** 209 N. Birch Rd. Italian palazzo on waterway. Each room is lovely as is food. Northern Italian, French Riviera cuisine.

Christine Lee's Northgate. 6191 Rock Island Rd. Special Oriental cuisine. Great reputation.

Le Dome of the Four Seasons. 333 Sunset Dr. View, European cuisine and service are superior. Reservations.

New River Storehouse. Part of Marina Bay hotel resort. Dinner only. Elegant dockside warehouse. Tropical Pye specialty; beef tenderloin, Florida lobster, artichoke hearts, hearts of palm.

Mai-Kai. 3599 N. Federal Highway. Good food; good surroundings; fair prices; excellent service; stunning dinner show.

Moderate: **Ernie's Booze & Barbecue.** 1843 S. Federal Hwy. Conch chowder, conch fritters, Bimini bread. Crowded during college vacations.

Patricia Murphy's Candlelight Restaurant. In Bahia Mar Yachting Center. Beautiful views. Good home-style food and popovers. Children's menu. Lunch, dinner. Cocktail lounge.

Inexpensive: **Wolfie's.** 2581 East Sunrise Blvd. Deluxe delicatessen. Own bakery. Try the strawberry cheesecake.

FERNANDINA BEACH. *Moderate:* **Palace Saloon.** Florida's oldest (100 years old '78). Antique decor. Boiled shrimp with hot tomato sauce only food served. Great drinks. Try 22-ounce Pirate's Punch, if you dare.

1878 Steak House. Unique Victorian and nautical decor; excellent steaks, seafood.

FORT MYERS. *Expensive:* **Pelican.** F.M. Beach. Great Sunday brunch with free drink. Seafood galore, steaks.

Inexpensive. **Charley Brown's Restaurant.** 6225 Estero Blvd. Along canal. Informal atmosphere. Children's menu, lounge. In Ft. Myers Beach.

JACKSONVILLE. *Expensive.* **The Admiralty.** In Sheraton, St. Johns. Superb cuisine in pre-war ocean liner décor. Great service. Dress code. Reservations.

Moderate: **The Chart House.** St. Johns Pl. at Prudential Dr. Unique design; excellent steaks and seafood.

The Homestead. Great fried chicken. Rustic setting.

Stricklands. Mayport, near Jacksonville. Fishing village atmosphere. St. Johns River views. Fresh snapper and local seafoods.

JACKSONVILLE BEACH. *Expensive:* **Le Gueridon.** French/Continental cuisine. Tops in area.

KEY WEST. *Inexpensive:* **Fourth of July.** 1110 White St. Cuban specialties, conch fritters. Take-out service.

Half Sheli Raw Bar. At foot of Margaret St. Local hot spot for real conch chowder, just-shucked oysters, draft beer. Oyster eating records made here.

Captain Bob's. Two locations. Great seafood.

LAKE BUENA VISTA. *Expensive:* **Empress Lilly Riverboat.** At Walt Disney World Shopping Village. Gourmet seven-course meals in Empress Room. Fisherman's Deck and Steerman's Quarters for seafood and steaks. Baton Rouge Lounge is good-time show bar. Disney has many other good dining spots.

LAKE WALES. *Expensive:* **Chalet Suzanne Restaurant.** Chalet Suzanne Resort Inn, US 27. Elegant dining; many furnishings are antiques.

Moderate: **Black Forest Buffet.** German recipes, 11 A.M. to 9 P.M. Alpine atmosphere.

LIGHTHOUSE POINT. *Expensive:* **Cap's Place.** Near Pompano Beach. Patronized by Churchill and Roosevelt. Delicious broiled seafood, turtle steaks, heart of palm salad. Hail boat-taxi by flicking light switch on dock at Lighthouse Point Marina. Only way to get to Cap's Place!

MADEIRA BEACH. *Expensive:* **Gene's Lobster House.** 565–150th Ave. Freshest food anywhere. Excellent preparation.
Moderate—Inexpensive: **Richard's.** 5001 Duhme Rd. Acropolis-style statuary, lavish gardens, lagoons. Ornate dining rooms. Movie set theme. Salad bar.
Paradise Pier. 196–128th Ave. Built on a pier. Informal, varied menu. Popular; expect to wait.

MARCO ISLAND. *Moderate:* **Marco Lodge.** Goodland. Delicious, freshly-prepared fish, chowders, guava jelly, coconut-banana layer cake, peanut butter cream pie. Lunch and dinner. Not fancy but terrific food. Owner-operated.

NAPLES. *Expensive:* **Pate's.** 625 Fifth Ave. South. Overlooking Naples Bay. Delicious seafood. Beef, chicken, lamb grilled over open charcoal pit. Romantic dining. Open 5 P.M. to 11 P.M.

ORLANDO. *Expensive:* **Maison & Jardin.** 430 S. Wymore Rd. Altamonte Springs, near Orlando. Garden-surrounded villa. Prize-winning dishes. Romantic.
Lili Marlene's Aviators' Pub and Restaurant. Church St. Station complex. Turn-of-century decor. Delicious wiener schnitzel, creole gumbo, stone crab.
Maggie's Plum. 743 Lee Rd. Steaks, seafood, chicken. Friendly, casual. Cocktail lounge.
Phineas Fogg's Balloon Works. Church St. Station complex. Extra-special hamburgers. Weigh in at a penny a pound for trip up in balloon. Disco.
Piccadilly. 7100 S. Orange Blossom Trail. All of the specialties of a London restaurant. Plus French pastries.
Moderate: **Rosy O'Grady's.** Church St. Station complex. Good, hearty food. Lively entertainment.

PALM BEACH. *Expensive:* **Petite Martite.** Trés chic at lunch as well as dinner; located chi-chi Worth Ave. (309). Reservations a must. Dress-up.
Moderate—Expensive: **Chez Guido.** Very special iced cucumber soup, turtle soup, excellent pastas.
Moderate: **Doherty's.** 264 S. County Rd. A popular local hangout; everyone dotes on the burgers.
Testa's. Royal Poinciana Way. Family-owned for over 50 years. Varied menu features Italian specialties, seafood. Sidewalk café, patio dining.

PALMETTO. *Expensive:* **The Sea Hut.** Pelican Point. Deliciously prepared fish and seafoods. Water views. Cocktail bar. Much less expensive at lunch. Tropical fish-house décor. Worth the trip.

PLANT CITY. *Moderate:* **Branch Ranch.** Thonotassa Rd., off I–4. Worth the drive from Tampa—or anywhere. Serves chicken, ham, chicken-ham combination. Vegetable dinner has chicken pot pie as side dish. Everything is home grown.

POMPANO BEACH *Moderate:* **Bobby Rubino's Place for Ribs.** 2501 N. Federal Hwy. Barbecued baby back ribs, chicken, steak, seafood. Four other locations in area.
The French Place. 3600 E. McNab Rd. "Undiscovered." Excellent food, served in a homey, French country atmosphere. Beef tournedos, veal.

SARASOTA. *Expensive:* **Café L'Europe.** Award-winning gourmet restaurant on St. Armands Key. Lunch and dinner features *haute cuisine.* Brandied duckling a specialty. Magnifique!
Peppercorns. In Sarasota Hyatt Hotel. A delightful dining experience. Crisply roasted duckling with unusual garnishes a specialty. Fascinating menu; excel-

lent wines. Salad bar also includes seafood. Champagne brunch Sunday. Alfresco dining at adjacent Boathouse.

Moderate: **Marina Jack.** 2 Marina Plaza. Attractive site overlooking bay. Wide variety in menu.

Inexpensive: **Main Bar.** Across from Maas Brothers. Extra-special sandwiches, salads, and beer.

ST. AUGUSTINE. *Moderate:* **The Raintree.** San Marco Ave. In renovated, turn-of-the-century home; Continental cuisine.

ST. PETERSBURG. *Expensive:* **Peter's Place.** Downtown, at Beach Drive. Very elegant. European-style *haute cuisine* dinners, impeccably served.

Rollande & Pierre. 2221 4th St. French cuisine featuring crêpe de fruit de mer.

Seaman's Cove. Maximo Moorings. Scenic view of yacht harbor. Shipshape decor. Scampi a specialty. Popular bar.

Moderate—Expensive: **PierSide Seafood House.** On fourth floor of showplace five-story inverted pyramid building on St. Petersburg's downtown Municipal Marina. Great views from window-walled dining rooms. Lunch, dinner, cocktails.

Sea Ketch (formerly the Sunbird). 8800 Bay Pines Blvd. N. Panelled wood and a garden atmosphere. Beautiful views of the bay. One of three Fish House management restaurants on Pinellas Suncoast. Cocktail lounge with music.

Moderate: **Aunt Hattie's.** 625 1st St. Chicken & dumplings, seafood. Victorian décor. *Uncle Ed's* next door is nice for sandwiches, salads and beer. No spirits served at Aunt Hattie's.

Moderate—Expensive: **Fish House.** South Pasadena Avenue. Artistically decorated with aquarium walls, antiques, greenery. Good values for seafood.

Inexpensive: **Gigi's.** Pasadena Shopping Center. Manicotti and music. Budget-priced luncheons. Attractive decor.

Ted Peters Smoked Fish. 1350 Pasadena Ave. S. Lunch or early dinner al fresco, at rustic tables. Smoked mullet, smoked mackerel, clam chowder, German potato salad. Good hamburgers, too. Beer, soft drinks. Closed Tuesdays.

ST. PETERSBURG BEACH. *Inexpensive:* **Brown Derby.** 6000 Gulf Blvd. in front of Sandpiper resort. Pleasant Tiffany-shaded decor. Help-yourself salad bar with lunch and dinner. Unbelievably priced for such good food, atmosphere.

Silas Dent's. 5501 Gulf Blvd. Multistoried, weathered wood exterior. On waterway. Great oyster bar; strolling magician.

TAMPA. *Expensive:* **Bern's Steak House.** 1208 S. Howard Ave. Serves superb steaks. 5,400 wines on hand, raises own vegetables, ages own cheeses, roasts own coffee. Dinner only. Cocktail lounge.

CK's. Atop airport Mariott. Revolving penthouse restaurant and lounge. Prize-winning menus at lunch, dinner. Impressive views. Cocktail bar.

Selena's. 1623 Snow Ave. French cuisine and excellent service. Homestyle recipes. Becoming "in" place.

Moderate—Expensive: **Columbia Restaurant.** At 7th Ave. from 21st to 22nd St. Award-winning Spanish showcase. Flamenco revue nightly. Columbia has branches in Sarasota, and Orlando.

The Verandah. 5250 W. Kennedy Blvd. Tampa's newest and most elegant dining experience. Relaxed atmosphere.

Moderate: **Mama Mia.** Fun-style Italian restaurant at 4732 North Dale Mabry, near Tampa Stadium. Dazzling array of antipasto served from flowered donkey cart. Dinner only.

Rough Riders. In Ybor City, Tampa's Latin Quarter. Teddy Roosevelt and his Rough Riders photos everywhere, antiques. Spanish-American cuisine. Sandwiches and cocktail lounge downstairs. Lunch, dinner.

TGI Friday's. Hyde Park section of Tampa. Fun and games harking back to turn of century. Looseleaf notebook menu filled with goodies from hamburgers to full-course dinners. Same menu lunch and dinner. Cocktails.

TARPON SPRINGS. *Moderate:* **Louis Pappas Riverside Restaurant.** 785 Anclote Blvd. On the sponge docks. Flavorful Greek and American foods. Chef's salads and fish delicacies. Bar.

TIERRA VERDE. *Moderate:* **The Good Times.** 1130 Pinellas Bayway. Continental specialties, rostbraten Esterhazy, veal roast florentine, roast duckling. Unique desserts. Lunch, dinner. Short drive from St. Pete en route to Fort DeSoto Park.

TITUSVILLE. *Moderate:* **Sand Point Inn.** Seafood delights in an attractive, weathered-wood building, jutting out over Indian River.

GEORGIA

Atlanta, Sea Islands, and the Hills

There's a revolving lounge atop a hotel in Atlanta from which you can *almost* see the city grow. New buildings are springing up at every compass point; old ones are being removed to make way for progress. A few years ago the Atlanta newspapers published a photograph of the skyline in the early '60s—another, of the same spot in the '70s. Two entirely different cities.

Scarlett O'Hara said: "Atlanta is full of pushy people." Pushy, ambitious, determined—whatever the word, since the early Reconstruction days following the Civil War, Atlanta has had a winning combination which is still excelling.

Much of the charm of legendary southern hospitality is tenaciously guarded, cherished. New tides of energy are surging everywhere, but the past remains as real as the present.

The Cyclorama, famous three-dimensional panoramic painting of the Battle of Atlanta, located at Grant Park, has been restored and reopened to the public. The Swan House on the grounds of the Atlanta Historical Society is an example of Italian Palladian architecture, and an interesting collection of mementos from Georgia's past are housed in contemporary McElreath Hall. Adjacent is the Tullie Smith farmhouse, which looks essentially as it did in 1840's. Nearby, Georgia's governor resides in a mansion, a show place, opened for tourists several times each week.

Six Flags Over Georgia, a family entertainment park, covers 331 acres, has over 100 attractions, rides, and live shows—all for one admission price. Rides include the Dahlonega runaway mine train, the log flume, and the Jean Ribaut riverboat adventure. The park has sections, one for each of the six flags which has flown over Georgia—

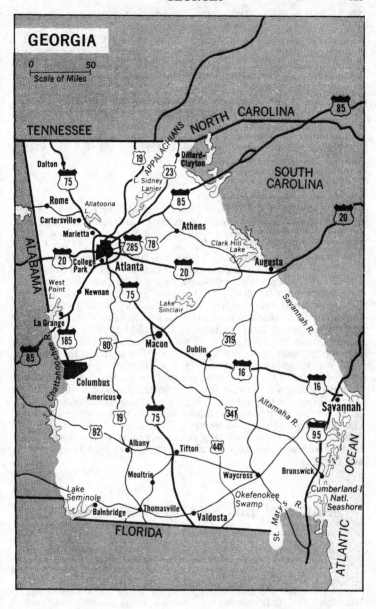

French, Spanish, English, Confederacy, United States, and Georgia. The park boasts two hair-raising roller coasters, including the triple-loop "Mind Bender." Thunder River takes guests on an exciting raft trip on a white-water river. One of the most popular rides is "The Great Gasp," a 40-foot free-fall parachute drop that ends with a slow and controlled perfect landing and a "great gasp" of relief from partakers.

Six Flags is popular with people of all ages and is kept scrupulously tidy. It's open from April through November.

Recent attractions on the Atlanta scene are the Atlanta Botanical Garden (Piedmont Park at the Prado), the Center for Puppetry Arts (1404 Spring St., NW), the Toy Museum (2800 Peachtree Road), the Bank Museum in Federal Reserve Building, and the new High Museum of Art (Peachtree and 16th Sts.).

The Metropolitan Atlanta Rapid Transit Authority (MARTA) commuter trains are a practical attraction. Trains are fast and luxurious, and stations are brightened by original artworks.

The Martin Luther King, Jr., National Historic District includes the tomb of the Civil Rights leader, his birthplace, and the church he pastored.

Stone Mountain

Stone Mountain, the world's largest mass of exposed granite, is surrounded by a 3,200-acre park. A massive Confederate carving features General Robert E. Lee with General Stonewall Jackson and Confederacy President Jefferson Davis. Lee's likeness rises 138 feet from the top of his head to his horse's hoof. His face measures twenty-one feet, his nose, five feet. The stars on his collar are bigger than dishpans and the sword, measuring fifty-eight feet in length and four feet in width, weighs one hundred tons. The giant granite dome, which rises 825 feet above the surrounding plain, stands about twenty miles east of downtown Atlanta and is visible from the top of many of the city's larger buildings. A cable car lift rises from the base of the mountain to the summit 2,600 feet distant. Two glass-enclosed cable cars, each carrying fifty passengers afford a superb view. A replica of the famous Civil War locomotive, "The General," pulls vintage coaches along a seven-mile ride that circles the base of the mountain. A Memorial Building contains a museum featuring Sherman's famous "March to the Sea," depicted in a sixty-foot relief map. Magnolia Hall, an authentic antebellum plantation, was moved from its original site at Dickey, Ga., carefully furnished and restored. There is an antique automobile museum, a steamboat operating on an adjoining lake, a marina, a carillon with concerts daily, excellent fishing, horseback riding, golf, and camping.

PRACTICAL INFORMATION FOR ATLANTA

HOW TO GET THERE. *By air: American, Bahamasair, British Caledonian, Delta, Eastern Frontier, KLM, Lufthansa, Northwest Orient, Ozark, Piedmont, Republic, Sabena, TWA,* and *United* serve Atlanta. *By car:* I–85, I–75, and I–20 will all get you to Atlanta. *By train:* Atlanta may be reached by *Amtrak's Crescent* with daily passenger service between New Orleans and Washington, D.C. *By bus: Greyhound, Trailways,* and several other companies serve Atlanta.

HOW TO GET AROUND. *By air: Delta, Eastern, Republic,* and *Atlantic Southeast* have intrastate flights. *By car:* There are four interstate highways intersecting Atlanta: I–85, I–75, I–20, and I–285. *By bus:* The Metropolitan Rapid Transit Authority operates the bus system and a partially completed subway; fares are moderate and transfers are free.

Especially for the disabled: Airports in Atlanta, Savannah, Columbus and Augusta have special accommodations for the disabled, with parking areas designated for users of wheelchairs, and ramps and special rest rooms. The Georgia Visitor Information Center has similar facilities.

 MUSEUMS AND GALLERIES. *Georgia Dept. of Archives and History,* 330 Capitol Ave. SW: history of Georgia depicted in lovely stained-glass windows. *Cyclorama:* huge canvas depicting 1864 Battle of Atlanta. *Swan House,* 3099 Andrews Dr. NW: period rms. on first floor. *Governor's Mansion,* 391 W. Paces Ferry Rd.: Federal furnishings in elegant home. *Emory Museum,* Bishop's Hall, Emory Univ., S. Oxford Rd. NE in Druid Hills: Far Eastern, African, Near Eastern, American Indian artifacts. *High Museum of Art,* Peachtree and 16th Sts.: European, American, African art in a magnificent new home. *Georgia State Museum of Science and Industry,* 4th fl. State Capitol Bldg.: displays, dioramas. *Fernbank Science Center,* 156 Heaton Park NE.: observatory, exhibit hall, forest and reference library. Third largest planetarium in the nation. Open daily.

 HISTORIC SITES. *Wren's Nest,* 1050 Gordon St. SW: home of Joel Chandler Harris, creator of Uncle Remus stories. *Martin Luther King, Jr.* is entombed beside the Ebenezer Baptist Church, 413 Auburn Ave. NE. *Kennesaw Mtn. National Battlefield Park,* off I–75, 25 miles northwest of downtown, has earthworks from the crucial Civil War battle that sealed Atlanta's fate.

 TOURS. *By bus:* Tours range from 3 to 5 hours and include downtown, Ga. Tech, Peachtree St., Lenox Sq., Emory U., Cyclorama, Druid Hills, State Capitol, Stone Mountain. Operators are *American Sightseeing: Gray Line; Arnel; Atlanta Convention Planners; Presenting Atlanta Tours; Guidelines.*

 MUSIC. The *Atlanta Symphony Orchestra* is host to many guest artists and conductors during its annual concert series from around Nov. 1 to Apr. Supplementing the symphony are top stars—popular and classical—brought to Atlanta, Columbus, Savannah, Macon, and Athens by Famous Artists, and the classical attractions booked by the civic-minded Atlanta Music Club, which formed the symphony more than 50 years ago.

 STAGE AND REVUES. *Theatre of the Stars* presents its summer season at Civic Center Auditorium, winter season at Peachtree Playhouse, 1150 Peachtree St. NE. *Academy Theatre* presents dramatic and musical productions year round. *Alliance Theatre Company,* professional productions mid-Jan. to mid-May. The Memorial Arts Center hosts some summer musical and dramatic productions.

 SHOPPING. *Rich's,* the South's largest store, has downtown stores of six stories and four stories which cover two city blocks. This full-line department store has restaurants, cafeterias, coffee shop. *Neiman Marcus* has a branch at Lenox Square. *Lord & Taylor, Saks Fifth Avenue, Tiffany's, I. Miller* and *Mark Cross* are at *Phipps Plaza,* across from Lenox Square on Peachtree and Lenox. Shopping centers are *Perimeter Mall* (I–285 and Ashford Dunwoody Rd.), *Cumberland Mall* (I–75 & US 41, Smyrna), *Southlake* (near airport), and *Northlake Mall* (I–285 and LaVista Rd.). Other fine stores are *Leon Froshin* for business, party clothing, and furs, 3393 Peachtree Rd. NE; *Muses,* moderate to higher-priced men's fashions, 52 Peachtree NW, 630 Peachtree NE, 3393 Peachtree Rd. NE; and *Spencer's Ltd,* exclusive men's store featuring British imports only, 693 Peachtree St. NE.

The *DeKalb Farmers Market,* Scott Blvd. near Decatur, is an international emporium, with cheeses, breads, sausages, herbs and spices from all over the world.

The revived *Virginia/Highland* neighborhood, three miles northeast of downtown, has many unique small shops, neighborhood cafés and bars. Likewise, the *Little Five Points* area around Moreland and Euclid Aves.

SPECIAL EVENTS: Georgia has many tours of homes and gardens; arts and crafts shows; and unique events such as: Old Time Fiddlin' at Dalton; American Cup Hang Gliding at Trenton; Pine Tree Festival, Swainsboro; Shrimp Fleet Blessings at Darien and Thunderbolt; Hawkinsville Harness Festival; Pecan Festival at Albany; Fair of 1850, Westville; Atlanta Dogwood Festival.

 **HOTELS AND MOTELS.** Atlanta's accommodations should prove pleasant for even the most discriminating traveler, and cover a wide, diverse range. Listings are in order of price category. Based on double occupancy without meals in the peak season, the ranges are as follows: *Deluxe,* $80–100; *Expensive,* $55–80; *Moderate,* $35–55; *Inexpensive,* $20–35. For a more complete explanation of hotel and motel categories see *Facts at Your Fingertips* at the front of this volume.

Deluxe: **Atlanta Hilton.** 255 Courtland St. (1250 rooms). Nice restaurants, bars, pool, health club, etc. etc.

Atlanta Marriott Hotel. Courtland at International Blvd. (763 rooms). Health club, saunas, unique pool area.

Atlanta Marriott Marquis. Courtland St., downtown: New in 1985, with 1,600 rooms in 52-story tower.

Omni International. Marietta St. 500 rooms, shops, restaurants, theaters, adjacent to Georgia World Congress Center.

Peachtree Plaza. Peachtree St. at International Blvd. World's tallest hotel (70 stories). Breathtaking, with 7-story atrium lobby containing a lake, trees, live birds, etc. Restaurants, bars, pool, health club.

Hyatt Regency Atlanta. 265 Peachtree St. NE. 1,358 rooms, spectacular inner courtyard 23 floors high. Pool. Revolving restaurant.

Ritz-Carlton. Two locations: downtown at Peachtree and Ellis Sts., and uptown at Peachtree and Lenox Rd.

Terrace Garden Inn. 3405 Lenox Rd., across from Lenox Square Shopping Center. 354 rooms.

Tower Place Hotel. 3340 Peachtree Rd. 220 rooms.

The Waverly. Glamorous Stouffer's hotel at I–75 and U.S. 41. Sumptuous rooms, elegant restaurants, health club, shops. Adjoins the Atlanta Galleria.

Expensive: **Atlanta Airport Hilton.** 1031 Virginia Ave. (350 rooms).

Atlanta Airport Marriott. 4711 Best Rd. 400 rooms.

Atlanta Central TraveLodge. 311 Courtland St. NW. Heated pool (70 rooms).

The Barclay Hotel. 89 Luckie St. Comfortable, downtown hotel.

Century Inn, Atlanta Airport. 1569 Phoenix Blvd. (160 rooms).

Colony Square. Peachtree and 14th Sts. Very stylist hotel with several restaurants. Anchors an uptown complex of shops, offices, condos.

Guest Quarters. Two locations. 7000 Roswell Rd. (US 19); I–285 at Ashford-Dunwoody Rd. All deluxe suites with complete kitchens.

Habersham Hotel. 330 Peachtree St. Tasteful, European-style hotel (94 rooms.)

Holiday Inn. 13 metro area locations.

Mark Inn. I–285, 4498 Washington Rd., East Point. Pool, restaurant, bar.

Marriott at Perimeter Center. I–285 at Ashford-Dunwoody Rd. Pool, tennis, restaurants, bars. (307 rooms.)

Northlake Hilton Inn. 4156 La Vista Rd. Pool, restaurant, bar (191 rooms).

Radisson Hotel and Conference Center. I–75 and Howell Mill Rd. Several restaurants, bars, major conference facilities.

Radisson Inn. I–285 at Chamblee Dunwoody Rd. (400 rooms).

Red Carpet Inn. Two locations: I–75 South at Locust Grove, and I–20 West near Six Flags theme park.

Sheraton. Six locations. Sheraton-Atlanta (501 rooms), 590 W. Peachtree St.; Sheraton-Cumberland (132 rooms), 1200 Winchester Pkwy., Smyrna; Sheraton-Emory (113 rooms), 1641 Clifton Rd.; Sheraton-Century Center (279 rooms), I–85 and Clairmont Rd.; Sheraton-Airport (362 rooms), 1325 Virginia Ave.; Sheraton-Northlake (164 rooms), I–285 and LaVista Rd.

Squire Inn. Three locations; 5750 Roswell Rd. NW (100 rooms); 2115 Piedmont Rd. NE (194 rooms); 2767 Windy Hill Rd. (199 rooms).

Moderate: **Admiral Benbow Inn.** 3 Locations: 1470 Spring St., NW (190 rooms); Airport, 1419 Virginia Ave. (253 rooms); I–285 & Buford Highway (250 rooms). Pool, restaurant, entertainment.

Bestway Inn. 14th St. at I–75–85 N.

Best Western Ladha Motor Hotel. 70 Houston St., downtown (219 rooms).

Downtown Motel. 330 W. Peachtree St.

Downtowner Motor Inn. 231 Ivy St. NE.

Hotel York. 683 Peachtree St. Beautifully restored old hotel. (155 rooms.)

Howard Johnson's. Six locations. Pool, restaurant. 1377 Virginia Ave., East Point; 2090 N. Druid Hills Rd.; 1701 Northside Dr. NW; 5793 Roswell Rd. NW; 759 Washington St. SW.; 100 10th St. at I–75 & I–85.

Master Hosts Inn, N.W. 2375 Delk Road (100 rooms).

Ramada Inn. Five locations. Inns at I–20 and Candler Rd. and NE Expwy Access Rd. are moderately priced. Ramada Inn Central, 1630 Peachtree St., and Ramada Hotel, Capital Plaza, near the State Capitol and Atlanta Stadium are expensive. Ramada Renaissance, near Atlanta International Airport, is one of the chain's new deluxe hotels.

Stone Mountain Inn. 1 mi. S. of 78 Stone Mountain exit. In Stone Mountain Park.

Viscount Motor Lodge. N. Druid Hills Rd. at I–85.

Inexpensive: **Bed & Breakfast Atlanta.** Referral service for accommodations in private homes. Phone 378–6026.

Days Inn. Seven motels, three lodges in Atlanta area, and a new highrise hotel adjacent to the Apparel Mart downtown.

 DINING OUT in Atlanta can mean the usual fine fare to be found in most large American cities, but it can also mean good Southern cooking—often in re-created rural surroundings. Restaurants are listed by price category as follows: A complete dinner costs $20 up in expensive category; $10–15 in moderate; and up to $10 in inexpensive. Drinks, tax and tip are not included. A la carte meals will bring the tab up. For a more complete explanation of restaurant categories see *Facts at Your Fingertips* at the front of this volume.

Expensive: **The Abbey.** 163 Piedmont Ave. French cuisine, waiters in monks' robes, in a tastefully converted church.

Hedgerose Heights Inn. 490 E. Paces Ferry Rd. Outstanding European dishes; elegant setting.

La Grotta Ristorante Italiano. 2637 Peachtree Rd. One of Atlanta's most outstanding restaurants. Exemplary Northern Italian cuisine; superior service; refined atmosphere.

Nikolai's Roof. Atlanta Hilton Hotel. Extravagant French/Czarist menu. Fine wines, service. Beautiful rooftop setting overlooking city. Reservations necessary far in advance.

Old Vinings Inn. 3020 Paces Mill Rd. Country French cuisine in charmingly converted cottage.

Petals of Jade. Waverly Hotel, I–75 and U.S. 41, NW. *Haute cuisine* from many Chinese regions, in an enchanting setting of Oriental antiques.

Red Barn Inn. 4300 Powers Ferry Rd. A strong local favorite. Steaks, seafoods in a cozy former stable. Fireplaces in equine décor.

Savannah Fish Company. Peachtree Plaza Hotel. Fresh seafood in a beautiful, sophisticated setting.

Sidney's. 4225 Roswell Rd. Eclectic French, Jewish, Hungarian menu; great wines, service.

Moderate: **Aunt Fanny's Cabin.** 375 Campbell Rd. (Smyrna). Southern-style cooking and plantation entertainment in a large, bustling place whose nucleus was a slave cabin.

Dailey's: 17 International Blvd., downtown. Excellent American/Continental dishes. Handsome brick-walled décor, friendly service.

Dante's Down the Hatch. 3380 Peachtree Rd. Fondues, wines, great jazz in a make-believe sailing ship.

Herren's. 34 Luckie St., downtown. Long-established favorite, known for seafoods and cordial staff.

Inexpensive: **The Colonnade.** 1879 Cheshire Bridge Rd. American and Southern cooking.

El Toro. Eight locations. The city's best Mexican food.

Mary Mac's. 224 Ponde de Leon Ave. Where Atlantans go for fried chicken and Southern-style vegetables.

Taste of China. 233 Peachtree St. Cheerful, downtown spot serving many styles of Chinese cuisine, full bar.

The Varsity. Enormous drive-in famous for chili dogs. North Ave. at I–75 and I–85.

Touch of India. 970 Peachtree St. Tandoori and curry dishes speak with a spicy authority.

EXPLORING GEORGIA

An awareness of history combined with an appreciation of the state's abundant natural resources is evident throughout Georgia.

Savannah preserves its past with care, and much of the downtown remains as General Oglethorpe, Georgia's founder, planned it.

Historic houses include Telfair Academy of Arts and Sciences, site of the royal governor's mansion; the Green-Meldrim Home, headquarters of General Sherman during his Savannah occupation; the birthplace of Juliette Gordon Low, founder of the Girl Scouts; Davenport House, 19th-century Georgian structure; Owens-Thomas House, designed by William Jay.

Savannah's most glorious season is spring, when millions of azaleas and dogwood bloom, and historic private homes are open to visitors. The city's St. Patrick's Day celebration is one of America's largest and most exuberant. Interesting shops, taverns and restaurants are housed in the old cotton warehouses along the Savannah River. New in 1985, the Great Savannah Exposition presents the city's long, colorful history in an entertaining blend of multimedia wizardry.

South from Savannah is Brunswick, a port town and gateway to Georgia's Golden Isles.

Sea Island is home of the world-famed Cloister hotel. It is a year-round vacation complex of luxurious private cottages, flower-bordered streets, and miles of sand beach for riding, beach walking, or bathing.

On St. Simons, largest of the Islands, the foundations of the old settlement have been re-created as they were in the 1700s at Fort Frederica.

Jekyll Island, once a favorite of millionaires, is now a state-owned, year-round vacation area. The entire ocean side is beach, and there are four noted golf courses on the island.

In sharp contrast to these islands is the primordial atmosphere of the famed Okefenokee Swamp, adjacent to Folkston and Fargo. Here visitors on boat tours may enjoy the quiet natural surroundings of the primitive wilderness area, or visit flora and fauna exhibits, as well as bird walks, nature trails, and an observation tower.

Westward is Waycross and the entrance to Okefenokee Swamp Park, which features wildlife shows and boat trips. There is also an Interpretative Center, an Ecology Center, and Pioneer Island exhibits. The swamp is the headwater of both the Suwannee River and the St. Mary's. Stephen Foster State Park, on State 177 north of Fargo, pays tribute to the famed composer.

In Columbus, often called "Fountain City" because of the many fountains, see restored homes and visit the Museum of Arts and Crafts with its Yuchi Indian exhibit and the new convention center, which once was an ironworks.

At the Fort Benning Infantry Museum follow the evolution of the infantry from the French and Indian War to the present.

South of Columbus is Georgia's peanut country, centering on Americus and Plains but best known as the land of President Jimmy Carter.

Pine Mountain is home of the famed Callaway Gardens, a 2,500-acre resort noted for its wildflowers of the Southern Appalachians. There are scenic drives, walking trails, display greenhouses, sixty-three holes of golf, a 175-acre fishing lake, horseback riding, quail hunting on a 1,000-acre preserve, and skeet and trap shooting.

Franklin D. Roosevelt chose the Pine Mountain area for his second home because of the curative qualities of the mineral waters at Warm Springs and because of the peaceful atmosphere. He came here in 1924 for treatment of his infantile paralysis. His modest white frame dwelling, the Little White House, where he died in 1945, has been operated as a shrine for over 30 years, remaining just as he left it. Nearby Franklin D. Roosevelt State Park was established in his honor.

Georgia has two national forests, the Chattahoochee and the Oconee. The Chattahoochee covers 687,000 acres in northern Georgia and the Oconee more than 100,000 in the central part of the state. Both have scenic hiking trails, mountains, stream and lake fishing, and ample camping facilities.

PRACTICAL INFORMATION FOR GEORGIA

HOW TO GET THERE. *By air:* Direct flights on most major airlines to Atlanta, Augusta, Macon, Savannah, Columbus, Albany, Athens, Moultrie, and Valdosta. *By car:* A number of interstate highways enter Georgia from South Carolina, Tennessee, Alabama, Florida, and North Carolina.

By train: Amtrak serves Atlanta from New Orleans, Washington, New York; Savannah and Brunswick have service from Florida and the East.

By bus: Trailways and *Greyhound.*

HOW TO GET AROUND. Five airlines serve cities within the state, as do three bus companies. Many interstate highways intersecting Georgia make car travel enjoyable. *Avis, Hertz, Budget,* and *National* have state-wide offices.

When motoring in Georgia it is strongly advised that you stop at the first Georgia Visitor Information Center after crossing the state line, and obtain a list of recommended service stations, historic shrines, special events and attractions, and road routing.

TOURIST INFORMATION. Twelve *Visitor Centers,* located on highways and at Atlanta Airport. Additional information: *Game & Fish,* Dept. of Natural Resources, 270 Washington St., Atlanta 30334; *State Parks,* Dept. of Natural Resources; *Tourist Division,* Georgia Department of Industry and Trade, P.O. Box 1776, Atlanta, Ga. 30301. U.S. Forest Service, P.O. Box 1437, Gainesville, Ga., for camping information.

MUSEUMS AND GALLERIES. *Thronateeska/Heritage Museum,* at Albany has Indian artifacts, science and art exhibits; *Augusta Museum* has archeological, historical, natural science exhibitions; Harris-Pearson-Walker House, Augusta, is the site of a Revolutionary War battle. In Columbus visit the *Confederate Naval Museum,* and in Fitzgerald, see the *Blue and Grey Museum.* In Washington, *Washington-Wilkes Historical Museum* displays antebellum furnishings and Civil War relics.

Art. Georgia Museum of Art, on campus of U. of Georgia, Athens, and the *Gertrude Herbert Memorial Art Institute* in Augusta, which has a small permanent collection of works from Renaissance to present. The *Macon Museum of*

Arts and Science and Planetarium exhibits regional contemporary art, as well as scientific displays.

Indian culture and history. New Echota near Calhoun is a restored 220-acre site of Cherokee Indians; at the Indian museum in *Kolomoki Mounds State Park* near Blakely, 18 exhibits interpret artifacts and culture of moundbuilders. Near Eatonton is Rock Eagle Effigy, a 10-ft.-high mound of milky quartz shaped like an outstretched bird with a 120-ft. wingspread, created approx. 6,000 years ago. 10,000 years of Indian settlements are reviewed at *Ocmulgee National Monument* near Macon.

 HISTORIC SITES. Visit the infamous Confederate prison at *Andersonville National Historical Site. Chickamauga,* site of one of the Civil War's fiercest battles, is near the Tennessee border. *Fort Pulaski,* 15 mi. E of Savannah, dates from the pre-Civil War period, and *Fort King George,* in Darien, was the first settlement in what is now Georgia. *Fort McAllister,* 17 miles south of Savannah, was site of the final victory of Gen. William T. Sherman's "March to the Sea."

Among restored houses are *Eagle Tavern,* 8 mi. S. of Athens on US 129, and *Traveler's Rest,* 6 mi. NE of Toccoa, off US 123, a restored plantation house and stagecoach inn. *Callaway Plantation,* W of Washington on US 78, has restored houses, hewn log kitchen with utensils, craft demonstrations, working farm. The *Little White House,* Warm Springs, is preserved as it was during Pres. Franklin D. Roosevelt's occupancy. *Liberty Hall,* Crawfordville, home of Alexander H. Stephens.

 TOURS. In *Columbus,* the two-hour *Heritage Tour* covers five historic houses and Springer Opera House. *Athens, Madison, Macon, Fort Gaines,* and *Sparta* offer do-it-yourself maps of historic sites. *Thomasville* Chamber of Commerce sponsors tours daily of plantations, historic homes, and gardens of the immediate area. Tours of *Okefenokee* are available at the Okefenokee Swamp Park, near Waycross, which also has wildlife displays, serpentarium, interpretive center, observation tower, and picnic areas.

A number of sightseeing companies provide several tours of Atlanta and the surrounding areas.

DRINKING LAWS. Minimum age 19. Liquor store hours: 8 A.M. to 11:30 P.M. daily except Sun. Cocktails are available seven days a week in Atlanta, Augusta, Columbus, Savannah; Mon.–Sat. in most other areas.

 SUMMER SPORTS. *Waterskiing, fishing, swimming,* and *sailing* are chief summer participant sports. See *car races* at the Atlanta International Raceway. Callaway Gardens hosts the Masters Water-Ski Tournament, and Augusta National, the *Master's Golf Tournament.* The Atlanta Braves play at the Atlanta Stadium.

Fishing: Anglers are challenged at Lake Lanier, above Atlanta, and Lake Allatoona, south of Lanier. Clark Hill, Hartwell, and Savannah Bluff reservoirs near Augusta are well-stocked. In addition, there are many mountain lakes and streams.

Golf: 131 public courses and a host of private ones. Atlanta has three excellent public courses.

Tennis: Atlanta has several excellent public tennis centers.

 WINTER SPORTS. *Skiing* is found at *Sky Valley Ski Area,* northeast from Dillard on Rte. 246; here are beginner, intermediate, and expert slopes, a lodge, and double-chair lift.

Hunting: Game is abundant on 22 public preserves. Dogs, guides, transportation, and dressing of game available at moderate fees.

SPECTATOR SPORTS. The *Atlanta Falcons* play in the Atlanta Stadium; fans also enjoy the *Yellow Jackets* from Georgia Tech and the *Bulldogs* from the U. of Georgia. The *Hawks* of the NBA play in the 16,000-seat Omni Coliseum downtown.

WHAT TO DO WITH THE CHILDREN. Pan for gold at *Old Dahlonega Gold Mining Camp* just outside Dahlonega; visit the *Toy Museum of Atlanta. Stone Mountain Park,* 16 mi. E of Atlanta on US 78, has a game ranch and antebellum plantation. *Six Flags Over Georgia,* on I–20 outside of Atlanta, is an unusual amusement park.

HOTELS AND MOTELS in Georgia run the gamut from the deluxe resort on Sea Island to the inexpensive, but attractive motels that are found along many of the state's major highways.

Accommodations are listed according to price categories, based on double occupancy in the peak season, without meals: *Expensive:* $45–80; *Moderate:* $30–45 *Inexpensive:* $18–30. For a more complete explanation of hotel and motel categories see *Facts at Your Fingertips* at the front of this volume.

ALBANY. *Moderate:* **Ramada Inn.** 2505 N. Slappey Dr. (US 19). Restaurant, lounge, pool.

Sheraton Inn. 999 E. Oglethorpe Blvd. (US 19). Restaurant, lounge, pool.

ATHENS. *Moderate:* **Best Western Colonial Motor Inn.** 170 N. Milledge Ave.

Downtowner. Pool, restaurant.

History Village. 295 East Dougherty Street, 113 rooms. 2 restaurants, 3 bars.

Holiday Inn. Broad at Hull St., 191 rooms.

Ramada Inn. 513 W. Broad St., 165 rooms.

Inexpensive: **Bulldog Inn.** U.S. 441 N. Pool. Pets.

AUGUSTA. *Expensive:* **Augusta Hilton.** 640 Broad St. Downtown. 216 rooms.

Telfair Inn. Charming colonial era inn. Restaurant, lounge. 349 Telfair St.

Moderate: **Continental Airport.** Opp. airport terminal. Pool, sauna, restaurants. 92 rooms.

Holiday Inn. 1602 Gordon HIghway. 143 rooms. Pools, restaurant.

Marriott Courtyard. 1045 Stevens Creek Rd. 130 rooms, restaurant, lounge.

Inexpensive: **Days Inn.** I–20 at Washington Rd. Chain member.

BRUNSWICK. *Moderate:* **Holiday Inn.** Two locations. 2307 Gloucester St.; I–95 US Hwy 341.

Ramada Inn. Two locations. 3241 Glynn Ave. (US 17); US 341 at I–95.

COLUMBUS. *Expensive:* **Columbus Hilton.** 800 Front Ave. New; 200 rooms; adjoining convention center.

Moderate: **Holiday Inn.** Pool, pets, restaurant. Two locations: Airport, 2800 Manchester Expwy., 173 rooms; 3170 Victory Dr., 172 rooms.

Quality Inn of Columbus. 1011 4th Ave., 180 rooms. Heated pool.

Marriott Courtyard. 3501 Courtyard Way, off Columbus–Manchester Hwy. Restaurant, lounge, 128 rooms.

FOLKSTON. *Moderate:* **Quality Inn Tahiti.** At state line on US 1, 23, 301.

HELEN. *Moderate:* **Helendorf Inn.** 305 Main St. In the heart of Georgia's "Alpine Village."

Stovall House. GA 255 between Helen and Batesville. Old farmhouse restored as a lovely country inn and restaurant.

JEKYLL ISLAND. *Expensive:* **Buccaneer Motor Lodge.** Pool. 210 rooms.
Holiday Inn. 208 rooms.
Jekyll Island Hilton. 975 Beachview Drive.
Villas-by-the-Sea. 1175 N. Beachview Dr.
Moderate: **Seafarer.** Pool. Beach opp.

MACON. *Moderate:* **Macon Hilton.** Pool, restaurant.
Ramada Inn. US 80 at I–475.
Inexpensive: **Days Inn.** 4295 Pio Niño Ave.

MARIETTA. *Expensive:* **Northwest Atlanta Hilton** and **Marriott Interstate North,** both at I–75 and Windy Hill Rd. Restaurants, lounges, pools.
Moderate: **Bon Air.** 889 Cobb Pkwy (US 41). Family and seasonal rates.

PINE MOUNTAIN. *Expensive:* **Callaway Gardens Inn,** 365 rooms. Callaway Gardens. Pools. Pets. Restaurants.
Moderate: **Callaway Cottages.** Family recreation park.

ST. SIMONS ISLAND. *Expensive:* **King & Prince Beach Hotel.** Oceanside resort hotel. 94 rooms.
Sea Gate Inn. 1014 Ocean Blvd. Pool, kitchenettes.
Sea Palms Golf & Racquet Club. Lavish resort hotel. Golf, tennis, pools, deluxe villas.
Moderate: **Queen's Court.** Comfortable, ideal for families. Pool. Restaurant.

SAVANNAH. *Expensive:* **Ballastone Inn.** Beautifully restored inn in 19th-century townhouse. 14 Oglethorpe Ave.
Hyatt Regency Savannah. Bull & Bay Sts. 350 deluxe rooms. Restaurants, lounges, sauna.
Stoddard–Cooper House. 19 W. Perry St. Charming bed-and-breakfast in historic downtown residence.
Moderate: **Best Western Riverfront Motor Inn.** 412 W. Bay St. 200 rooms.
Days Inn. 201 W. Bay St. 196 rooms. New, tastefully furnished. 24-hour restaurant.
Downtowner. 201 W. Oglethorpe Ave. 204 rooms.
Howard Johnson's. Two locations. 224 W. Boundary St. (US 17A); GA 204 at I–95.
Inexpensive: **Days Inn.** Two locations. US 17, Richmond Hill; 114 Mall Blvd. (GA 204).
Central reservations number for **historic inns, guest houses:** (912) 233–7666.

SEA ISLAND. *Deluxe:* **Cloister.** 234 rooms. Glamorous, exclusive resort.

VALDOSTA. *Moderate:* **Holiday Inn.** I–75 at GA 94. Restaurants, bars; pools, play area. Pets.

WAYCROSS. *Moderate:* **Holiday Inn.** 1725 Memorial Drive.
Quality Motel Arcade. 1800 Memorial Dr. Pool.
Inexpensive: **Pine Crest.** US 1, 23 ¼ mi. S of US 84. Pool.

 DINING OUT in Georgia usually means fine Southern-style foods in a rural atmosphere, or charming plantation house, or sophisticated French cuisine in an elegant urban dining room. Many worthwhile restaurants may be found at the hotels we have listed. Our price categories are for a complete dinner: *Expensive* means a complete dinner may run $15–20; *Moderate* will run about $15; *Inexpensive,* $10 or less. A la carte meals will, or course, bring the bill up. For a more complete explanation of restaurant categories see *Facts at Your Fingertips* at the front of this volume.

ALBANY. *Moderate:* **Villa Gargano.** 1604 N. Slappey Blvd. Pasta, pizza, steaks.

ATHENS. *Expensive:* **Martel's.** 325 N. Milledge Ave. French cuisine, wines in a refined atmosphere.

Inexpensive: **Davis Bros. Cafeteria.** 2012 Milledge Ave. Fried chicken, Southern-cooked vegetables.

AUGUSTA. *Moderate:* **Town Tavern.** 7th and Reynolds. Handsomely refurbished warehouse. Popular for steaks, seafoods, and hearth Southern breakfasts.

BAINBRIDGE. *Inexpensive:* **Jack Wingate's Lunker Lodge.** GA 310 at Lake Seminole. Excellent fresh seafood, barbecue. Locally very popular.

BRUNSWICK. *Inexpensive:* **Kody's.** 300 Gloucester St. Excellent local seafoods, Southern dishes.

COLUMBUS. *Expensive:* **Goetchius House.** 405 Broadway. Steaks, Continental dishes in beautifully restored 1839 home.

Moderate: **W.D. Crowley's.** Peachtree Mall. Casually sophisticated place for burgers, salads, steaks, potent drinks.

DILLARD. *Inexpensive:* **Dillard House.** Northeast Georgia mountain landmark, famous for family-style Southern cooking.

JASPER. *Moderate:* **Woodbridge Inn.** Imaginative Continental dishes, comfortable accommodations in beautiful mountain setting.

LAKE BURTON. *Inexpensive:* **La Prade's.** Hwy. 197 between Clayton and Clarkesville. Family-style Southern cooking at an old fishing camp on mountain lake.

MACON. *Moderate:* **Len Berg's.** Centrally located in Post Office alley. Georgia dishes.

ST. SIMONS ISLAND. *Expensive:* **Buster Crabs.** Local seafood prepared with imagination, flair.

Moderate: **Bennie's Red Barn.** Rustic atmosphere.

Blanche's Courtyard. Entertainment in evening on weekends.

Emmeline & Hessie Restaurant. Overlooks Intercoastal Waterway.

The Crab Trap. Informal spot for fresh local seafoods.

SAVANNAH. *Expensive:* **Windows.** Hyatt Regency Hotel, downtown. Continental dining with panoramic views of big river ships.

The Pirate's House. Seafoods in a delightful nautical atmosphere. 20 E. Broad St. at Bay St.

Moderate: **Elizabeth on 37th.** 105 E. 37th St. at Drayton St. Fresh seafoods in lovely old mansion.

Johnny Harris. 1651 Victory Dr. Great fried chicken, barbecue. A Savannah landmark.

Inexpensive: **The Crystal Beer Parlor.** W. Jones and Jefferson Sts. Mellow old neighborhood tavern, famous for its hamburgers and fried oyster sandwiches.

Mrs. Wilkes. 107 W. Jones St. Excellent Southern cooking served boardinghouse style.

Williams Seafood. 8010 Tybee Island Rd. Simply prepared fried and broiled seafoods. Very popular.

SOPERTON. *Inexpensive:* **Sweat's Barbecue.** GA 29, just off I–16. Excellent barbecue, Brunswick stew. Popular stop between Macon and Savannah.

VIDALIA. *Inexpensive:* **Southern Cafeteria.** Downtown. Top-notch Southern cooking in Georgia's "Sweet Onion Capital."

KENTUCKY

Horses, Caves, and Lakes

From whatever direction you enter Kentucky, you'll be able to recognize the horse country by its miles of white board fences, groves of stately trees, white-columned mansions, and legions of horse barns. The farms are elaborate developments, and many are open to visitors. At least 350 of them are scattered around Lexington. Among the most famous are Spendthrift, Calumet, Dixiana, Main Chance, and Crown Crest.

Also in Lexington, the lavish $27-million state-operated Kentucky Horse Park features a horse museum, riding concessions, horse-drawn tours, special equine events and celebrations, model working farm.

Among Lexington's most glamorous spectacles are the yearling sales. Every July the handsome animals are led into the track's flower-decked salesroom to stand in the spotlight while the bidding soars ever upwards.

Also held in Lexington is the ten-day Grand Circuit Meeting, Kentucky's most significant harness race. Big Red Mile, the world's fastest trotting track, holds more records than all other harness tracks combined.

Besides priding itself as the Horse Center of America, Lexington also lays claim to being the world's largest loose-leaf tobacco market. And, in fact, Kentucky itself ranks first among the tobacco states in Burley output, as well as growing all of the Green River dark, air-cured tobacco in the world (used mainly for chewing). Here, too, is grown over 80 percent of the entire world supply of the tobacco used for snuff.

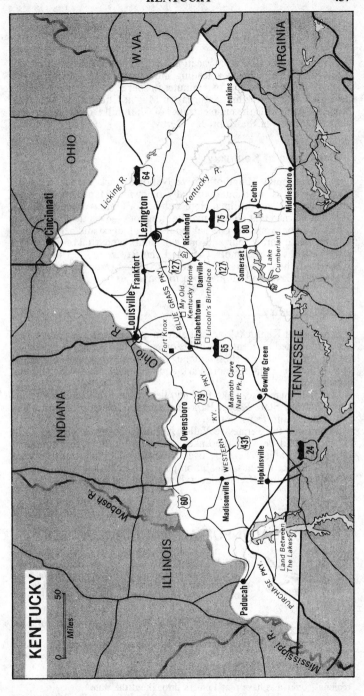

Home of the Derby

Another major Kentucky vacation center is the colorful river city of Louisville. Besides being a leading industrial city, Louisville is the home of the most exciting two minutes in sports, the Kentucky Derby, held each year on the first Saturday in May at Churchill Downs. The museum, just inside the main entrance of Churchill Downs, depicts the colorful history of the Kentucky Derby.

The Caves of Kentucky

In and around Mammoth Cave National Park are the fabulous Kentucky caves, with internationally renowned Mammoth Cave the most extensive and thrilling. Here a choice of tours is offered, and the visitor is warned that all trips may be strenuous—even the shortest one which runs only one and one-half hours. The longest and perhaps most notable excursion is four and one-half hours which takes you to the lowest depths of Mammoth Cave at Echo River, 360 feet down.

All told, there are over 235 miles of explored trails and passages in Mammoth Cave, and all are open for public use.

Lake Country

Another of Kentucky's special and unique features is its lake country, highlighted by Kentucky Lake, one of the largest man-made lakes in the world. On its shores alone, there are two major recreation spots—Kenlake State Resort Park and Kentucky Dam Village State Resort Park.

Another huge lake, Lake Barkley, lies just east of Kentucky Lake. Lake Barkley State Resort Park encompasses 3600 acres, and offers golf, tennis, and trapshooting.

Meantime, the Tennessee Valley Authority is developing the 170,-000-acre Land Between the Lakes as a major outdoor recreation and conservation area. There are over 200 miles of hiking trails. Golden Pond visitor center has orientation programs and planetarium shows. Woodlands Nature Center supervises outdoor activities.

PRACTICAL INFORMATION FOR KENTUCKY

HOW TO GET THERE. *By air:* Major airports are at Louisville and Lexington. *USAir, American, Delta, Eastern, Piedmont, Continental, Ozark, United, Southwest,* and *TWA* have daily flights to one or both cities.

HOW TO GET AROUND. *By car:* A network of interstate highways, state turnpikes, and parkways make traveling in Kentucky a pleasure. Interstate highways—I–24, I–64, I–65, I–71, and I–75—are integrated with equally modern state parkways.

Car rentals: Avis, Budget, Hertz, National, and various other national and regional companies have rental offices throughout the state.

By bus: Greyhound, Trailways, Bowling Green–Hopkinsville Bus Co., and *Tennessee Trail Blazers.*

TOURIST INFORMATION SERVICES. Kentucky Dept. of Tourism Development, Capital Plaza Tower, Frankfort, KY 40601. Dept. of Fish & Wildlife Resources, 592 E. Main, Frankfort 40601. Lexington–Fayette County Recreation, Tourist and Convention Commission, 421 N. Broadway, Lexington, KY 40508. Louisville Visitors Bureau, Founders Square, Louisville, KY 40202.

PARKS. *Cumberland Gap National Historical Park* near Middlesboro covers 20,222 acres; *Mammoth Cave National Park* has 51,354 acres of wonders both above and below ground; *Land Between the Lakes,* a 170,000-acre wooded area between Kentucky Lake and Lake Barkley, is being developed by the Tennessee Valley Authority into a national recreation and conservation education area; *Daniel Boone National Forest* covers 671,374 acres in eastern Kentucky. In the state's ruggedly beautiful eastern mountains is Breaks Interstate Park, which Kentucky shares with Virginia.

Kentucky has 40 state parks and historic state shrines in beautiful natural environments offering camping, picnicking, a wide choice of outdoor recreation. Many have attractive resort lodges and/or cottages.

MUSEUMS AND GALLERIES. Historical: *Kentucky Library and Museum,* Bowling Green. *Columbus-Belmont Battlefield State Park Museum* near Columbus, Civil War relics. Art: *St. Joseph's Proto-Cathedral,* Bardstown; *J.B. Speed Art Museum,* Louisville; *Paducah Art Guild Gallery,* in The Market House, also *Barkley Museum,* Paducah.

Special Interest: *Barton Museum of Whiskey History,* Bardstown; *Berea College* and *Appalachian Museum,* Berea; *Mammoth Cave Wildlife Museum,* Cave City; *Shaker Village of Pleasant Hill,* Harrodsburg, village museum; *John James Audubon State Park Memorial Museum,* Henderson, featuring his personal memorabilia. In Lexington: *Headley-Whitney Museum,* jewelry, bibelots; *Transylvania University Museum,* historic medical equipment. In Louisville: *Jos. Rauch Memorial Planetarium; Kentucky Railway Museum; Kentucky Derby Museum,* the *Museum of Natural History and Science, American Saddle Horse Museum, Churchill Downs Museum.*

Others: *Owensboro Museum of Fine Art,* Owensboro; *Shaker Museum,* South Union; *Ancient Buried City,* Wickliffe, an archeology museum. *National Museum,* Boy Scouts of America, Murray.

HISTORIC SITES AND HOUSES. *The Old State House* in Frankfort; *Abraham Lincoln Birthplace National Historic Site,* Hodgenville; *Federal Hill,* mansion immortalized by Stephen Foster's "My Old Kentucky Home," Bardstown; *McDowell House & Apothecary Shop,* collections: medical, herbarium, paintings, botany, Danville; *Lincoln Heritage House,* Elizabethtown.

In Frankfort: *Orlando Brown House* (1835), *Liberty Hall* dating from 1796. In Lexington: *Ashland,* home of Henry Clay; *Hunt–Morgan House; Parker Place,* site of Mrs. Lincoln's grandmother's home; *Mary Todd Lincoln House,* Mrs. Lincoln's girlhood home; *Waveland State Shrine,* 1847 Greek Revival mansion built by Boone descendants. In Louisville: *Farmington,* designed by Thomas Jefferson; *Locust Grove,* home of George Rogers Clark; *Brennan House,* elegant Victorian mansion.

SPECIAL INTEREST TOURS. *Horse breeding farms:* Many horse farms throughout the state welcome visitors. Arrangements should be made in advance. For free guide, "Kentucky—Where the Horses Are," write Kentucky Dept. of Tourism.

Mammoth Onyx Cave at Horse Cave, Ky. Tour of cave on 600-acre wildlife preserve.

Shaker Village of Pleasant Hill, 7 mi. N.E. of Harrodsburg. Authentic restoration of rural Shakertown community. Dining room open for all meals. Overnight accommodations.

MUSIC. You can hear good authentic Bluegrass bands in Lexington. For authentic *Old-Time Fiddling,* visit Renfro Valley.

In Louisville, the *Kentucky Opera Association* performs at the new $33.5 million Kentucky Center for the Arts, also home of the *Louisville Orchestra,* Sept.–May. The Orchestra's *Super Pop* series is at Louisville Gardens.

STAGE AND REVUES. Top-notch Broadway musicals can be seen at the *Pioneer Playhouse State Theatre of Kentucky,* in Danville, and there's the *Summer Music Theatre* in Prestonburg. In Louisville, there's *Shakespeare in Central Park,* produced by the Carriage House Players, Kentucky Center's *Macauley Theatre,* and the *Actors Theatre.* Lexington's *Diners Playhouse* offers Broadway plays by top professional acting talent.

For outdoor summer theater (mid-June–Labor Day) there's "The Stephen Foster Story" at My Old Kentucky Home State Park, Bardstown, and "The Legend of Daniel Boone" and "Lincoln" at Old Fort Harrod State Park, Harrodsburg.

SPORTS. *Boating:* Boat rentals are available at many of the state parks, and at cities along the Ohio River. *Fishing:* A year-round visitors' delight. There are more than 13,000 miles of fishable rivers and streams.

Hunting: For information, contact Dept. of Wildlife Resources, Frankfort.

Golf: There are 200 courses in the state, and 14 state parks have courses.

Water sports: Many of the state parks provide boating, swimming, waterskiing, and fishing.

SPECTATOR SPORTS. *The* spectator sport is horse racing. All over the world the name Kentucky has come to mean horses. From January to December there is some form of horse racing here.

HOTELS AND MOTELS. Accommodations are listed according to price categories, based on double occupancy: *Expensive:* Over $55. *Moderate:* $40–55: *Inexpensive:* under $40.

BARDSTOWN. *Inexpensive–Moderate:* **Best Western General Nelson.** 411 W. Stephen Foster Ave. Pool, restaurant.

Moderate: **Holiday Inn.** US 31E South and Bluegrass Parkway. Pool, dining room, lounge, live entertainment.

CAVE CITY. *Inexpensive:* **Quality Inn.** I–65 at KY 90, 70. Restaurant, pool, playground. Water slide and golf nearby. Family and senior citizens' plans, facilities for handicapped. Ladies' sportswear shop (factory outlet) on premises.

Interstate Inn. KY 70 and 90, S.E. of I–65. Dining room, coffeeshop, pool. Pets.

Best Western Kentucky Inn. I–65 & KY 70, 90. Dining room, pool. Pets. Handicapped facilities.

GILBERTSVILLE. *Moderate:* **Holiday Inn.** Exit 27 on I–24 at US 62. Spanish Room Restaurant. Indoor, outdoor pools, lighted par 3 golf, free tennis, game room. Home Box Office movies.

Village Inn at Kentucky Dam Village State Resort Park. US 62–641. Overlooks beautiful Kentucky Lake. Golf, tennis, horseback riding, water sports, shops, dining room, entertainment and dancing.

LEXINGTON. *Expensive:* **Hyatt Regency.** 400 W. Vine in Lexington Center. Fine dining, cocktails, shops. Tallest building in city.

Moderate: **Continental Inn.** 801 New Circle Rd., NE. Large indoor–outdoor pool in tropical setting. Barber, beauty shops, lounges, game room, dining room, entertainment. Senior citizens' discounts.

LOUISVILLE. *Expensive:* **Executive Inn and Executive West.** I–264 at Fairgrounds entrance. Elegant dining rooms and decor, beautiful landscaping, pools, lounges.

Galt House. 4th and River Streets, overlooking Ohio River. Lavish furnishings, pool, shops, rooftop dining room, lounges, entertainment.

Hyatt Regency Louisville. 320 W. Jefferson St., downtown. Indoor pool, lounges, elegant dining.

Moderate–Expensive: **Best Western Admirals Inn.** 3315 Bardstown Rd. Color TV. Pool. Free crib. Senior citizens' rates; bellhops. Restaurant, lounge, dancing, and entertainment.

Holiday Inn Shively SW. 4110 Dixie Hwy. Dining room, lounge, entertainment. Indoor pool, whirlpool, games. Near Churchill Downs.

Rodeway Inn. 101 E. Jefferson St. Pleasant restaurant, lounge, live entertainment.

Inexpensive: **Best Western Middletown Manor.** 12010 US 60, at Middletown, KY. Dining room, lounge, pool, playground. Tennis courts nearby.

Days Inns at two locations, I–71 at KY 53, and I–65 at KY 44. Pleasing rooms; pools.

Motel 6. 3304 Bardstown Rd. Color TV, pool. Café nearby.

La Quinta. 317 Warnock; N I–65, exit 133, S I–65, exit 133A. Member of excellent, fast-growing economy system. Free cable TV, lobby coffee, local phone calls. Non-smoker rooms, pool, senior citizens' discount. Kettle Restaurant adjacent.

MAMMOTH CAVE NATIONAL PARK. *Inexpensive–Moderate:* **Mammoth Cave Hotel.** 10 miles west junction KY 70 and I–65. Over 100 rooms, gift shop, dining room, tennis, boat trips aboard *Miss Green River,* April through October. Rustic cottage units (not heated) are also available.

PADUCAH. *Moderate to Expensive:* **Holiday Inn.** 727 Joe Clifton Dr. Dining room, cocktail lounge, pool, pets welcome.

Inexpensive: **Quality Inn** (formerly Red Lion Inn). 1380 S. Irvin Cobb Dr. Restaurant, pool, lounge, entertainment.

Paducah TraveLodge. 1234 Broadway. Pool. Color cable TV. Pets. Restaurant near.

Days Inn. I–24 and US 60W. Pool, restaurant, convenient to regional attractions.

SHAKER VILLAGE OF PLEASANT HILL. *Moderate* to *Expensive:* **Pleasant Hill Family Houses,** US 68 and KY 4. Lodgings in rooms furnished with historic Shaker antiques, in restored town site rich with atmosphere of interesting religious communitarians.

 DINING OUT. Kentucky cookery blends the best of "down home" Southern specialties with exciting choices of Continental and American cuisine. For full-course dinners, excluding drinks, tax and tip, restaurants are listed as: *Expensive:* $20 and up; *Moderate:* $10–20; and *Inexpensive:* $10 and under.

BARDSTOWN. *Moderate:* **Old Talbott Tavern.** 107 W. Stephen Foster Ave. Delightful fried chicken, Kentucky country ham, and live entertainment—with a chess pie dessert.

BEREA. *Moderate:* **Boone Tavern.** Dining room, a student-managed project of Berea College, features lunch and dinner specialties such as Kentucky ham, blackberry dumplings, spoon bread, in colonial atmosphere.

COVINGTON. *Moderate:* **Mike Fink's Restaurant.** Foot of Greenup St. Dining aboard an Ohio River sternwheeler—delicious lunch and dinner.

LEXINGTON. *Moderate* to *Expensive:* **Stanley Demos' Coach House.** 855 S. Broadway. Continental selections, seafood, steaks, lounge, piano.

Moderate: **The Little Inn.** 1144 Winchester Rd. Charbroiled steaks, Kentucky country ham, luncheon buffet.

Inexpensive: **Blue Boar.** Turfland Mall. Part of famous chain of fine cafeterias.

LOUISVILLE. *Expensive:* **Casa Grisanti.** 1000 E. Liberty St. Northern Italian specialties, wine list, lovely atmosphere, candlelight. National reputation.

Embassy Supper Club. 4625 Shelbyville Rd. Continental and American choices, after-theatre menu, entertainment.

The Old House. 432 S. 5 St. Good selection of French specialties, from onion soup to crêpes Suzette. Early 19th-century house. Open from lunch through dinner. Closed Sun.

Flagship Restaurant. Atop Galt House Hotel. Savor excellent beef and seafood specialties, along with dramatic views of Louisville and the Ohio River.

Moderate: **Kunz's The Dutchman.** 526 S. 4 St. Great local favorite offers hearty German and American food. Bars. Open lunch through late supper. Closed Sun.

John E's Restaurant (formerly Bill Boland's Dining Room). 3708 Bardstown Rd. Regional specialties in charming 1809 farmhouse.

Stouffer's Top of the Tower. 101 S. Fifth St. Magnificent view from 38-story First National Tower. American-Continental, some flambé.

Hasenour's. 1028 Barrett Ave., SE. Extensive menu of German, American, and regional cuisine. Continental dining in The Atrium, also on the grounds.

Inexpensive: **Blue Boar Cafeterias.** Six locations throughout the city. Nonsmoking areas, trays carried on request.

PADUCAH. *Moderate:* **The Pines Steakhouse and Lounge.** 900 N. 32nd St. Select steaks at tableside; also children's menu. Closed Sun.

Stacey's Restaurant & Lounge. 1300 Broadway. Steaks, prime ribs, smorgasbord luncheons.

PERRYVILLE. *Moderate:* **Elmwood Inn.** 205 Fourth St. Southern fried chicken, country ham, fresh vegetables, fluffy biscuits in elegant classic-columned antebellum plantation home. A favorite of the late Colonel Sanders, who liked the chicken with cream gravy here about as well as his own Kentucky Fried.

SHAKER VILLAGE OF PLEASANT HILL *Moderate:* **Trustees' House.** Just off US 68. Shaker and Kentucky specialties in a gracious atmosphere of antiques. Hearty buffet breakfasts. No tipping. Reservations requested.

LOUISIANA

New Orleans and the Bayous

New Orleans is the home of a unique attraction: the French Quarter, or *Vieux Carré* ("Old Square"), the original town laid out by the French. There is nothing quite like the atmosphere of these narrow streets, lovingly restored old buildings, flower-filled patios, antique shops, coffee bars, world-famous restaurants, and a few remaining places where authentic New Orleans jazz is still played. Within its area of about a square mile, strict legal ordinances have preserved the Quarter's special character. The façades, of French and Spanish design, are painted in their original colors. After over 200 years this harmony of graceful iron grillwork, intimate courtyards, and classic French lines remains undisturbed. Neatly bounded by Decatur St. and the Mississippi River on one side, and by the Canal, North Rampart, and Esplanade on the other three, the creation of the architects Latrobe, Galliers, De Pouillys, and Dakins—the Quarter is just the right size for a leisurely walking tour.

Starting at Canal and Royal, the tourist first notices, down Canal toward the river, the massive granite structure of the Customs House, whose cornerstone was laid in the 1840's by Henry Clay. This square-block building marks the original riverbank, now moved further off by means of landfill. The stretch of Canal between Royal and Exchange Alley was once a rendezvous where unemployed sailors ("monkeys") used to borrow money ("wrench") from friends with jobs; hence the nickname "Monkey Wrench Corner." Exchange Alley itself is lined with unusual shops. Continue down Royal St. to the Old Bank of Louisiana, now the home of the Greater New Orleans Tourist and Convention Commission (No. 334 Royal). Free tourist information can be obtained here. The Marquis de Mezières home site and reconstruc-

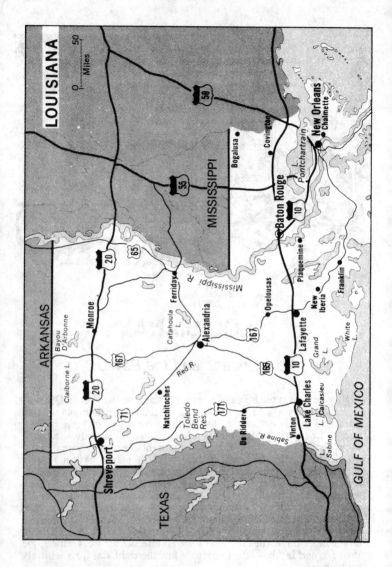

tion (No. 240) is a recent building designed in the style of the 1830s, when U.S. artist Richard Clague lived here. The balconies of the house built for Vincent Rillieux, merchant and great grandfather of artist Edgar Degas (No. 343), bear some of the Quarter's finest examples of wrought-iron work on the balconies. The Louisiana State Bank (No. 403) was built in 1821 from a design by Benjamin Latrobe. The monogram LSB is worked into the balconies' wrought iron. Similar initials decorate the balcony railing at No. 417: LB for Banque de la Louisiane, the first bank established after the Louisiana Purchase. This was also the residence of Alonzo Morphy, whose son Paul became a world's chess champion. Across the street, occupying the whole block, is the New Orleans Court Building, which houses the Louisiana Wild Life Museum.

At this point a side trip along Conti St. to the famous Conti Wax Museum might be amusing. Waxen figures in elaborate settings enact historic (and sometimes apocryphal) scenes. Nearby is Hermann-Grima House (820 St. Louis), built in the 1820's, with a beautiful courtyard. It is owned by the Christian Women's Exchange and open to the public. Around the corner, Audubon's House (509 Dauphine) is the cottage where the brilliant diarist and artist of early-19th-century American wilderness lived in 1820-21, painting birds and keeping a journal of New Orleans life. Back toward Royal St. is the Casa Hove House, 723 Toulouse St. Built in 1797, it is an excellent example of early Spanish architecture. The Hove Perfume Shop, located on the ground floor, has created perfume for men and women since 1932.

At 520 Royal St. is the particularly beautiful Brulatour House, built in 1816 by French wine merchant and furniture designer François Seignouret. His initial is carved in every piece of his furniture. The house is now occupied by WDSU radio and TV stations. The patio is open for visiting. At 533 Royal is Merieult House, now the Historic New Orleans Collection. This museum has an impressive collection of paintings, prints, documents, books, and memorabilia depicting the city's colorful past. Court of the Two Sisters (613 Royal) opens its large courtyard to visitors. At 629 Royal is the old home of singer Adelina Patti. The building at 640 Royal St., erected in 1811, is the city's first "skyscraper." It is the scene of one of George Washington Cable's many vivid stories of New Orleans life. Although Cable was a devoted observer of Creole life and of the plight of mixed-race Southerners, his antislavery views made him unpopular and finally, in about 1886, he left his native city to live in the North. Labranche House (700 Royal), built in the early 1830s, has perhaps the finest lace-iron grillwork in the Quarter. The Old Orleans Ballroom (717 Orleans, between Bourbon and Royal) was an early site for elegant Creole galas.

On St. Peter St. Between Royal and Bourbon, the first Louisiana theater and opera house, dating from 1791 and now occupied by Pat O'Brien's, opens its patio to the public at no. 718. Preservation Hall (No. 726) offers authentic New Orleans jazz nightly. The donation asked for is small, the surroundings unvarnished. But to hear what may be a vanishing breed of musicians is a special and worthwhile experience. Le Petit Salon (No. 620), a women's social club, has distinctive "bow-and-arrow" ironwork, a curved staircase, and iron-barred ground floor. Le Petit Théâtre du Vieux Carré (No. 616), formed by local actors, was the first theater of its kind in the U.S. The Arsenal (No. 615) was built in 1839 and stands on the site of the 1769 Spanish Arsenal. It houses a collection of 19th-century firefighting equipment. Jackson House (No. 619) has a collection of Louisiana Folk Art, which is considered the best single collection of this genre in the country. Facing on Chartres is the Cabildo, originally the Spanish colonial legislature, later the scene of the ceremony marking the U.S.'s Louisiana Purchase in 1803. This fine example of Hispano-Moorish architecture is now a museum displaying furnishings and portraits. Next door is St. Louis Cathedral, with wall and ceiling paintings by Canova. On the other side of the Cathedral is the Presbytere. This museum features a collection of costumes and fashions, one of the largest in the South. Behind the cathedral is St. Anthony's Garden, an attractive spot where Creole rivals once met for duels.

Returning to Royal along Dumaine affords a look at the charming house known as Madame John's Legacy (No. 632). Another Cable story, "Tite Poulette," uses this Creole building as background.

Points of Interest

1) Greater New Orleans Tourist
   Commission
2) U.S. Mint
3) Cabildo
4) City Hall
5) Civic Center
6) Theater for the Performing Arts
7) Confederate Memorial Hall
8) Louis Armstrong Park
9) Ursuline Convent
10) French Market
11) Hermann-Grima House
12) Madame John's Legacy
13) International Trade Mart
14) Municipal Auditorium
15) Lee Circle
16) Superdome

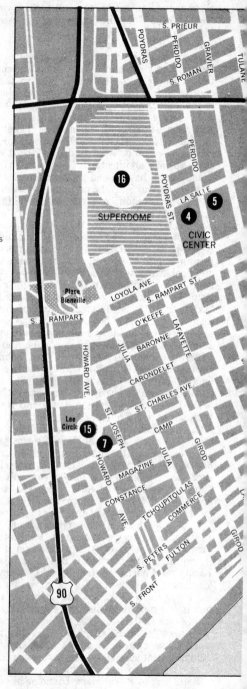

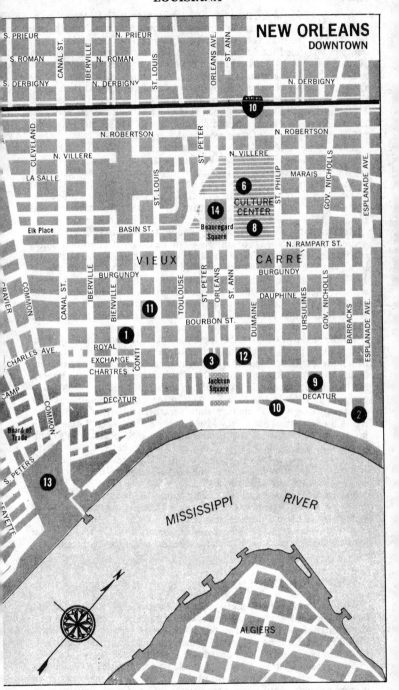

NEW ORLEANS
DOWNTOWN

At 900–10 Royal are the Miltenberger Houses, built by three brothers in 1838. At No. 915 is the famous ironwork Cornstalk Fence, made about 1850. No. 919 is the Old Courthouse, where General Andrew Jackson was fined for suspending habeas corpus during the Battle of New Orleans in 1814. No. 1132 is the home of James Gallier, Jr., the architect of many buildings in the city. The house and garden, dating from 1857, have been beautifully restored and are open to the public. Coffee and pastries are served on the iron-lace balcony. The Lalaurie House at No. 1140 has long been spoken of as haunted. After a fire, the bodies of slaves were found chained to the walls. The side street affords the best view of a portion of the original house.

Turn along Esplanade toward Chartres and walk two blocks and you'll see the U.S. Mint (No. 400). The Jazz and Carnival Museum is on the second floor. In the rear courtyard, you'll find the "Streetcar Named Desire." From here it is a short walk to the French Market; you can rest at the coffee bars with their steaming, fragrant coffee and pastries. For more than two centuries, farmers have sent food and produce to the market for wholesale.

Returning to Chartres from Esplanade, you will pass Our Lady of Victory Church (No. 1116) and the Ursuline Convent, the oldest building in the Mississippi Valley and the only authentic French structure to survive the devastating fires of 1788 and 1794. It was completed in 1734 to house the nuns who arrived from France as teachers and nurses. There are scheduled tours through the convent and gardens conducted Wednesday afternoons. Across the street is the Beauregard-Keyes House (No. 1113). This Greek Revival-style home is open to the public.

Continue down Chartres St. until you reach Jackson Square, a one-square-block park, which is the center of the French Quarter. Flanking it are the Pontalba Apartments, reputed to be the oldest apartment buildings in America, built in 1850 by the Baroness Almonester Pontalba (note the initials in the ironwork galleries) and still in use as apartments. The 1850 House, 523 St. Ann in the Lower Pontalba, is now a state museum with period furnishings and décor. Farther down Chartres is the Historical Pharmacy Museum (No. 514), where Louis Dufilho, one of the first licensed pharmacists in the U.S., practiced his craft. Admission is a mere 25 cents. The Girod House, better known as the Napoleon House, is located at the corner of Chartres and St. Louis. It is believed that this house was offered to Napoleon Bonaparte as a refuge when he was exiled in 1821.

Maspero's Exchange at 440, dating from 1788, was a popular meeting place where, legend has it, the pirate Lafitte sold smuggled goods and slaves to New Orleans merchants.

A free ferry across the river leaves frequently from the foot of Canal St. and offers a good view of the Cathedral and Jackson Square.

Beyond the French Quarter

The Louisiana Superdome, opened on August 3, 1975, is the world's largest enclosed stadium-arena, covering 52 acres and reaching 27 stories high. It seats more than 80,000 and houses major sports events, including the Sugar Bowl football games; leading entertainers, circuses, trade shows. Tours of the Superdome are conducted daily.

The Garden District, which is bounded by St. Charles Ave., Louisiana Ave., Jackson Ave. and Magazine St., is one of the city's most elegant sections, featuring old mansions, most in Greek Revival style. For exploring without a car, take the St. Charles Ave. streetcar, which runs along the edge of the Garden District, past Tulane and Loyola

Universities, to the place where the avenue meets the Mississippi River levee.

PRACTICAL INFORMATION FOR NEW ORLEANS

HOW TO GET THERE. *By air:* A number of airlines fly into New Orleans International Airport, Hwy. 61 in Kenner. *By car:* I–10 connects with Baton Rouge, Lafayette, Houston, Tex., and points west with New Orleans; I–10 also comes in from Mississippi to the east; I–55 connects New Orleans with Jackson, Miss., Memphis, Tenn., and points to the north; I–59 also comes into New Orleans from Mississippi. *By train: Amtrak* will get you to New Orleans. *By bus:* New Orleans is served primarily by *Trailways* and *Greyhound.* These lines make connections with many other bus lines.

HOW TO GET AROUND. *By car: American, Sears, Avis, Budget, Dollar, Greyhound, Hertz, National, Thrifty* all have offices at or near the airport. *By bus:* The "Streetcar Named Desire" has been replaced by a bus. *By streetcar:* Streetcars still run on St. Charles and Carrollton, starting from Canal Street. It is an economical and fun way to go from Canal St. to uptown.

SEASONAL EVENTS. *Carnival* climaxes on *Mardi Gras* (Shrove Tuesday), the forty-first day before Easter Sunday, not counting Sundays. Two-week *Spring Fiesta* is held beginning first Friday after Easter, during which tours of the French Quarter, Garden District, and plantation homes are arranged. Parade, street dancing, and outdoor art show add to fun. *Jazz and Heritage Festival* celebrates crafts, food, and music in mid-Apr. There are jazz, ragtime, gospel, blues, country, and Cajun music concerts and river cruises. Write Festival, P.O. Box 2530, New Orleans 70176. In March, the Italians celebrate St. Joseph's Day in the French Quarter, and the Irish march through the Irish Channel on St. Patrick's Day.

MUSEUMS AND GALLERIES. *The Historic New Orleans Collection,* 533 Royal St. *Louisiana State Museum,* 751 Chartres St., housed in 1791 Presbytere, is a complex of eight buildings, seven of which are open to the public: *The Cabildo, Presbytere, 1850 House, Madame John's Legacy, U.S. Mint, Jackson House* and the *Arsenal. New Orleans Museum of Art,* Lelong Ave., City Park. Closed Mon. and holidays. *Gallier House,* 1118–32 Royal St. Decorative art museum. Closed Sunday.

Special Interest: La Maritime Museum, Located in International Trade Mart. Exhibits relating to area sea events. *Pharmaceutical Museum,* 519 Chartres St. Built in 1847, the museum reflects early history of New Orleans medicine. *Confederate Museum,* 929 Camp St. Relics pertaining to military history; Civil War memorabilia. *Louisiana Wildlife Museum,* 400 Royal St. Natural history museum. *Pilot House,* 1440 Moss St., on Bayou St. John near City Park, an 18th-century plantation furnished in the Federal style. Open Wed.-Sat.

HISTORIC SITES. In New Orleans the *Vieux Carré* (Old Square) represents a concentration of historic sites, with the apex at *Jackson Square,* where the old *St. Louis Basilica* has housed the Catholic See of New Orleans continuously since 1794. It was around this square that Bienville had engineers lay out the city in 1718. Uptown, the *Garden District's* great homes are still maintained as showplaces of the antebellum period. *U.S. Custom House,* 423 Canal St., four-story 1849 building of granite, is on site once occupied by Ft. St. Louis. Used as an office by Gen. Benjamin F. Butler during the Union Army's occupation of New Orleans. *Chalmette National Historical Park,* St.

Bernard Hwy., State 39, site of the Battle of New Orleans in the War of 1812. Closed Christmas and Mardi Gras.

 TOURS. *Bus. Gray Line* offers tours covering various sections of city. Night-life tours cover the Bourbon St. area, various clubs, and cafés; make reservations. Also available are tours, including meals, to area homes, plantations, and other attractions.

Boat, MV Voyageur leaves from foot of Canal St. for cruise into Intercoastal Waterway, through Bayou Barataria, and return through Harvey Canal; five hrs. Harbor cruise to Chalmette Battlefield, 2 hrs. *Mark Twain,* diesel-powered replica of sternwheeler steamboat, leaves Canal St. Dock for bayou trip. 5 hours. Also, has 3-hr. dinner-dance cruise nightly. *S.S. President,* large sidewheel steamboat, offers daily 2½-hr. harbor cruise; Sat. night cruise with jazz band, drinks, dancing. *Natchez* (Sternwheeler) makes three daily cruises past Chalmette Battlefield. *Cotton Blossom* makes daily 5 ½-hr. trip into Bayou Country. *Creole Queen* leaves the Poydras St. wharf daily at 10 A.M. and 2 P.M. on Thurs. and Sat., 8–10 P.M. A jazz dinner is held.

Walking Tour: The Friends of the Cabildo conduct walking tours of the French Quarter at 9:30 A.M. and 1:30 P.M. Mon.-Sat.

 GARDENS. During the blooming time of camellias (late Nov.-Mar.) and azaleas (late Feb.-Apr.) New Orleans becomes a huge garden, with concentrated displays in almost all parks. Along the country roads of St. Tammany Parish, across the causeway from New Orleans, the tung trees and azaleas bloom profusely in late March. *Longue Vue House and Gardens,* 7 Bamboo Rd., is an eight-acre estate featuring a 20th-century mansion and magnificent gardens. Open to the public. Fountains, tropical fruit trees, roses, camellias, azaleas, and a wild garden with native iris. *City Park* has a conservatory featuring bromeliads and formal gardens built during the depression and now under renovation.

 STAGE REVUES AND NIGHTCLUBS. The burlesque queens and strippers of Bourbon St. are world famous, and they bring back memories and images of New Orleans' notorious Basin Street red-light district. *Le Petit Théâtre du Vieux Carré* is one of the oldest community theater groups in the country. *The Toulouse Theater,* 615 Toulouse, features "One Mo' Time," a local musical that has gained international acclaim. Along Bourbon St., at least every third door is a nightclub, with entertainment from the predominant bumps and grinds of energetic stripteasers. *Pat O'Brien's* entertainers (just off Bourbon at 718 St. Peter) rate as high as O'Brien's tall, tall glass of "Hurricane" rum punch. The Fairmont Hotel offers bands and singers who make the national circuit from Las Vegas to the east coast.

Just minutes from downtwon New Orleans, the area known as "Fat City" is headquarters for dining and nightlife entertainment in Metairie. It's bounded by Veterans Boulevard, North Causeway, West Esplanade, and Division streets. *Morning Call,* one of the French Quarter's traditional stops for café au lait and beignets, has moved to Fat City and is open 24 hours a day, seven days a week.

 SHOPPING. Royal Street in the French Quarter is filled with antique shops. Reliable firms for European and English antiques include *Waldhorn, Manheim Galleries, Rothchild's London Shop,* and *Henry Stern.* Stamps at world-famous *Raymond H. Weil. Jackson Brewery* is a six-level festival marketplace on the Mississippi River at Jackson Square. Open daily, 10 A.M. to 10 P.M. The best American antiques may be found in the Magazine St. section. Shops for both men and women, such as *Brooks Bros., Saks Fifth Ave., Gucci,* and *Laura Ashley,* can be found at Canal Place. Souvenir shops are all over the French Quarter. And don't forget the delectable Creole pecan pralines. Souvenir boxes can be mailed anywhere in the country from *Evans Creole Candy Co.,* 824 Decatur St.; *Laura's Fudge Shop,* 115 Royal St.; or *Kate Latter's,* 300–302 Royal St.

WHAT TO DO WITH THE CHILDREN. *Audubon Park and Zoological Gardens* features a special petting zoo for children and rides on the elephants. *The Louisiana Nature Center*, 11,000 Lake Forest Blvd., shows the dependence of humans on the environment. Has nature trails and exhibits.

HOTELS AND MOTELS. Minimum night stays are required at Carnival and during the Sugar Bowl football and sports events at the New Year. Listings are in order of price category. Based on double occupancy without meals, price categories and their ranges are: *Deluxe:* $95 and up; *Expensive:* $70–75; *Moderate:* $55–70; *Inexpensive:* Under $55.

Deluxe: **Fairmont.** University Pl. Restaurant, coffee shop, bar, top entertainment.

Holiday Inn-Chateau Le Moyne. 301 Rue Dauphine. In the heart of the French Quarter. Restaurant, lounge, health spa.

Hotel Maison De Ville. 727 Toulouse St. in French Quarter. Complimentary continental breakfast in a jewel of a place.

Hyatt Regency. Next to Superdome, built around 21-story atrium. Pool, patio, lanai suites, revolving restaurant, the works.

Marie Antoinette. 827 Toulouse St. in the French Quarter. Attractive rooms, suites. Dining room.

New Orleans Hilton. Located by New Orleans Cruise Terminal on the Mississippi. You can get oysters on the half-shell in the lobby. Very plush and new. Everything from atrium cafes to rooftop disco.

Pontchartrain. 2031 St. Charles Ave. Locals agree this is the finest hotel in town. Also has a superior restaurant.

Royal Orleans. Royal & St. Louis Sts. On the site of the historic old St. Louis hotel. Fine restaurant, cocktail lounge with jazz, and coffee shop.

Windsor Court Hotel. 300 Gravier St. All 330 guest quarters are suites. Afternoon tea served in the lobby from 2:30 P.M.

Expensive: **Downtown Howard Johnson's.** 330 Loyola Ave. Restaurant, pool, indoor car park.

Landmark French Quarter Motor Lodge. 920 N. Rampart. Sidewalk cafe; restaurant, bar, pool.

Lafitte Guest House. 1003 Bourbon St., has 14 rooms. Continental breakfast served.

Provincial Motel. 1024 Chartres St. in French Quarter. Pleasant rooms with antiques as part of the décor.

Sheraton Inn International Airport. 2150 Veterans Memorial Blvd. Restaurant, lounge with entertainment, pool.

Soniat House. 1133 Chartres St. in French Quarter. 25 rooms, filled with antiques, in an 1830 townhouse. Continental breakfast.

Moderate: **Bourgoyne House.** 839 Bourbon St. Three suites available with complete kitchens. This is the place to experience the French Quarter like a true native. Reservations a must.

Holiday Inn. There are seven locations in the New Orleans area. All have restaurant, lounge, pool. Some Holiday Inns are deluxe and expensive.

Howard Johnson's Motor Lodge. At two locations: **East,** 4200 Old Gentilly Rd. & I-10 at Louisa St. exit; **Airport -West,** 6401 Veterans Memorial Blvd., Metairie.

Park View Guest House. 7004 St. Charles Ave. Lovely rooms in a huge Victoria house next to Audubon Park. Continental breakfast.

Quality Inn. There are three locations. All have restaurant, cocktail lounge, pool, and color TV.

Villa Convento. 616 Ursulines St. in French Quarter. All 24 rooms decorated differently. Very friendly. Continental breakfast.

DINING OUT. Fine Creole cooking is a treat in New Orleans, but other cuisines can also be found here. Classic French fare is also a specialty. See the previous hotel listings for some other good restaurants. Price categories and ranges (for a complete dinner) are as follows: *Deluxe:* $30 and up; *Expensive:* $20–30; *Moderate:* $10–20; *Inexpensive:* under $10. Drinks, tax and tip not included. Listings are in order to price category.

Deluxe: **Antoine's.** 713 St. Louis St. This is dining in the opulent, old tradition, and regular customers even have their own personal waiters. The large wine cellar is open to the public. Specialties include oysters Rockefeller, *pompano en papillote*, and the tournedos. *Crêpes Suzette* are a favorite sweet.

Caribbean Room. 2031 St. Charles Ave. Located in the Ponchartrain Hotel, this pleasant establishment provides leisurely dining in its inviting dining rooms and patio. Specialties include shrimp saki, trout Véronique, steak Diane, and *crêpe soufflée* that must be ordered in advance.

Andrew Jackson. 221 Royal St. Elegant service and atmosphere. Tour the kitchen to see the chef prepare trout meunière, lump crabmeat, or Creole gumbo.

Le Ruth's. 636 Franklin St. (Gretna). French menu perfectly complements the intimate environment. Specialties include stuffed soft-shelled crab, frog's legs meunière, and a noisette of lamb for two.

Expensive: **Arnaud's.** 811 Bienville St., at Bourbon St. World-renowned French restaurant in the French Quarter. Specialties: oysters Bienville, shrimp Arnaud, and filet mignon Clemenceau.

Brennan's. 417 Royal St. Its bountiful breakfasts include eggs hussarde, eggs Sardou, and an appetizing omelet of eggs and crabmeat. Flaming desserts are also a specialty.

Broussards. Located 819 Conti. Most attractive interiors and the famous Bonaparte Patio. Specialties are Duck Nouvelle Orleans, Checken Ratatouille, Oysters Gresham, Trout Conti, and caramel custard.

Commander's Palace. 1403 Washington Ave. at Coliseum St. Located in the historic Garden District. Recommended are the Redfish Grieg, or Crabmeat Imperial.

Corinne Dunbar's. 1617 St. Charles Ave. Creole dishes served in a lovely Victorian dining room. No menu choice. Reservations a must.

Galatoire's. 209 Bourbon St. Excellent seafood includes trout Marguery, trout menunière amandine, and broiled pompano. Appetizers are topped by shrimp rémoulade, and the Creole gumbo is in a class by itself.

Masson's. 7200 Ponchartrain Blvd. Fine place for a leisurely suburban dinner.

Mosca's. Little atmosphere but the food is something else. Local crowd patronizes this restaurant, but it's worth asking directions for. On Highway 90, in Waggaman.

Rib Room of the Royal Orleans Hotel. Royal & St. Louis Sts. Specialties: rib roast and extensive English and American cuisine.

K. Paul's Louisiana Kitchen. 416 Chartres. Specialties include blackened redfish and Cajun popcorn, which is deep-fried crayfish claws. Expect to wait in line. Chef Paul Prudhomme is internationally known.

Moderate: **The Embers.** 700 Bourbon St. Charbroiled steaks are their specialty.

Old N'Awlins Cookery. 729 Conti St. Daily menu. Creole specialties. Local favorite. No credit cards.

Sclafani's. 1315 N. Causeway Blvd. Italian, American, and Creole dishes, served in a Louisiana plantation-style dining room.

Tujagues. 823 Decatur St. Locally popular. Well-prepared Creole and French dishes served family style. No menu choice.

Inexpensive: **Camellia Grill.** 626 So. Carrollton Ave. Pecan waffles are rich and delicious.

COFFEE HOUSES. Across the Square from St. Louis Basilica and down the street are the outdoor coffee houses of the French Market. Although the famed Morning Call coffee house has moved to Fat City, the Café Du Monde, next to the entrance to the Moon Walk (here you can watch the ships and barges make their way along the Mississippi), and the Café Maison, located a few shops over, offer the weary tourist some of that special New Orleans coffee (café au lait) and mouth-watering beignets (square, puffy doughnuts always freshly made). Open 24 hours a day year-round. The French Market has recently undergone a renovation and, in addition to the Moon Walk park area and a parking lot, there are a dozen shops and boutiques. In one shop you can watch pralines being made daily; you can purchase cookery equipment and spices; there's a candle shop, a toy store, and several snack spots, as well as a seafood house and the Farmer's Market, where shopping for fresh fruits and vegetables has been a tradition since New Orleans' earliest days. On weekends, the area next to the Farmer's Market is turned into a Flea Market. La Marquise Pastry Shop, 625 Chartres St., is a favorite spot for French pastries. The Gumbo Shop, 630 St. Peter St., is where French Quarter residents go for breakfast.

EXPLORING LOUISIANA

Travel in Louisiana was once determined by its waterways: the vast, serpentine Mississippi and the state's innumerable lakes, rivers, and bayous. Today, this watery network has been supplanted by a fine highway system, and if you drive through to New Orleans you can stop to see at as many as 40 magnificent mansions, gardens, and plantations.

Baton Rouge

The Indians called it *Istrouma*—a tall cypress marking the boundary between tribal hunting grounds. In 1699 someone in the Iberville-Bienville party pushing up to the Mississippi marked the spot on his map: *le baton rouge* ("red stick"). A good place to take a first look is from the observation platform atop the 34-story capitol building, overlooking the 27 acres of formal gardens on the capitol grounds. Main points of interest in the city are: the Old Capitol, with its hand-wrought iron fence, spiral staircase, and prism skylight, a blend of Norman, Gothic, and Moorish styles; the Louisiana State University campus; Southern University, the nation's largest predominantly black university, on bluffs overlooking the river; the Arts and Science Center, at the former Governor's Mansion (exhibits of art, natural history, and anthropology); and the zoo, a 140-acre expanse with walkways through forest settings for over 500 animals.

The Louisiana Governor's Mansion is open for tours weekdays.

Around Baton Rouge are a number of picturesque small towns and lovely plantation houses. Clinton, Jackson, East and West Feliciana, and Washington among the towns; Rosedown, the Cottage and Oakley are some of the notable plantations. Across the street from the Old Capitol is the Louisiana Arts and Science Center Riverside located in a remodeled railroad station (open daily except Mondays). Here you can find exhibits of art, natural history, anthropology, a gift shop, tea room and such, plus a marvelous viewing area of the port of Baton Rouge.

LSU Rural Life Museum depicts life in rural South in the 19th century. On Foster Road, just off Comite Drive Wide is the Cohn Memorial Arboretum, which encompasses 16 acres and features over 120 varieties of shrubs.

Acadian Lafayette

Lafayette, a fast-growing city that bills itself as the "Capital of French Louisiana," is a good base from which to explore Acadiana. Tourist information can be obtained from the city's tourist bureau at Sixteenth Street and the Evangeline Thruway.

The 800-acre campus of the University of Southwestern Louisiana has a Maison Acadienne dedicated to the perpetuation of French and Acadian traditions. Lafayette's Mardi Gras celebration is second only to New Orleans' gala festival, and draws upwards of 100,000 people.

Every September there is the Festival Acadiens, which celebrates Acadian culture, music, arts, crafts and food. From April to September, it's thoroughbred racing at Evangeline Downs.

Located just south of Lafayette is The Acadian Village and 'Round the World Tropical Gardens. The Village is an authentic Acadian Community of the 1800s. While there, you can take a horticultural walking tour of the warm weather areas of the world in the Tropical Gardens which surround the village. Southeast of Lafayette is St. Martinville, one of the oldest and most charming small places in Louisiana. Settled in the eighteenth century by Acadian and French royalist refugees, the town became an early center of culture and elegant living where richly dressed nobles attended luxurious balls and operas; often it was spoken of as "Le Petit Paris." The old church on Main St. dates from 1832, but the Evangeline Oak, on the banks of Bayou Teche at the foot of Port St., is the most popular tourist attraction in town. Across the street is the Convent of Mercy, a very old building, once a trading post, now a school run by the Sisters of Mercy. At the edge of St. Martinville is the attractive Longfellow-Evangeline State Commemorative Area. The Acadian House Museum, from about 1765, records the Acadian story of expulsion from Nova Scotia and settlement in Louisiana. Cajun crafts are displayed and sold in a reproduction of a typical small farmhouse. Camping sites, picnic shelters with tables and grills, a pool, and restaurant are also in the park.

Fourteen miles south of St. Martinville on State 182 is New Iberia. Shadows-on-the-Teche, a stately mansion in the heart of town, now the property of the National Trust for Historical Preservation, was built in 1830. Moss-draped trees and a formal garden of roses, camellias, azaleas, and other flowering shrubs adjoin a handsome lawn sloping to the banks of the Bayou Teche. The Acadian Regional Tourist Information Center is quartered in a plantation cabin built of native cypress about 1880. At 541 E. Main is the Gebert Oak, a magnificent specimen planted in 1831. Attractions in the area include the Justine Plantation (1822), the Loreauville Heritage Museum, Jefferson Island plantation house and gardens, Live Oak Gardens, Avery Island's 200-acre Jungle Gardens, and Cypremont Point seaside recreational area.

Lake Charles, Louisiana's third seaport, is the center of an important petrochemical empire.

Alexandria-Pineville

Striking north from I–10 some miles east of Lake Charles, US 165 leads toward Alexandria; the drive is about 75 miles. Alexandria marks the geographical center of the state, where the earth shades from red clay to moist black. There is a choice of side trips to be made from Alexandria before proceeding northeast to Monroe: Marksville Prehistoric Indian Park, containing a number of Indian mounds and a museum of Indian life and art; the ruins of Ft. DeRussy, a Confederate mud fort which fell to Union forces during the 1864 Red River campaign; Hot Wells Health Resort (near Boyce), mineral baths, a motel, recreation facilities, and a large swimming pool.

From Alexandria the most direct route to Monroe is US 165 north. However, if time permits, a westward swing to Natchitoches on State 1 allows more sightseeing.

Natchitoches

Natchitoches, a charming river town and farm center, is the oldest town in the Louisiana Purchase territory, established in 1714—four years before New Orleans—as a French outpost and trading center.

Front St. on Cane River provides the most charming prospect of any town in Louisiana. Many old buildings and antebellum homes remain along the river and side streets. During the Christmas season streets, buildings, riverbanks, and bridges blaze with over 140,000 lights.

Monroe on the Ouachita ("Washitaw") River is one of Louisiana's oldest settlements, established in 1785 as Ouachita Post. In the nineteenth century, Monroe was a center of cotton production and export. After the discovery that the entire parish of Ouachita rested upon a vast pool of natural gas, Monroe and West Monroe (across the river) became a thriving industrial region. Attractions in Monroe include Ft. Miro (commemorated by only a plaque), Layton Castle, Stubbs House, and Filhiol House. The Masur Museum is an attractive art gallery with educational and cultural exhibits, and there is a Little Theater housed in the new Strauss Playhouse. The Louisiana Purchase Gardens and Zoo has a 100-acre park with formal gardens, moss-laden oaks, and winding waterways.

If it is spring, you might want to take a northerly detour at Minden in order to enjoy the 18-mile Dogwood Trail Drive. Head north on State 7 about four miles west of Minden. At Springhill, the Drive winds west on State 157 to Plain Dealing. It is a drive through the state's highest hills, among flowering dogwood, redbud, and wild flowers.

Shreveport

Shreveport, founded in 1832, is one of the country's leading oil and gas centers and a natural trade center for the so-called "Ark-La-Tex" area. There are three major annual events at Shreveport. In fall, the State Fair attracts half a million visitors during its 10-day run, with music (the city considers itself a country-western capital), auto races, rodeo exhibitions, arts and crafts displays, carnival rides, band concerts, and fireworks. Adjacent to the fairgrounds, the Louisiana State Exhibit Museum contains dioramas, an art gallery, historical murals, and archeological relics. Another big event is the 10-day Holiday in Dixie each April. It is a round of flower shows, sports competitions, an air show, carnival, treasure hunt, pet show, two fancy-dress balls, and a grand finale parade. The city's brochure promises 10 days "packed with a sort of leisurely frenzy!" Then there's the Red River Revel on the riverfront, a celebration of the arts.

For entertainment while in Shreveport you might try Shreve Square, a cluster of nightclubs, restaurants, and shops in a restored part of the city.

Bossier City, just across the Red River, is the home of Louisiana Downs Thoroughbred Race Track, with its completely glass-enclosed, air-conditioned clubhouse, restaurant, and grandstand. Its season runs from late spring through the fall.

KRMD Radio once again broadcasts weekly performances of the "Louisiana Hayride," originating at Hayride U.S.A., which also has a restaurant and lounge.

The American Rose Center, with its majestic Windsound Carillon Towers, is located in Shreveport.

Some of the finest bass fishing in the country can be found on nearby Toledo Bend.

PRACTICAL INFORMATION FOR LOUISIANA

HOW TO GET THERE. *By air:* New Orleans may be reached from cities within the U.S.A. on direct flights of: *Continental, Delta, Eastern, Ozark, American, Southwest* and *United* airlines; Baton Rouge and Monroe on direct flights of: *Delta, Southern,* and *Texas International;* Shreveport on direct flights of: *Delta* and *Frontier;* Alexandria on *Delta* and *Texas International;* Lake Charles on *Texas International* and *Commuter;* Ft. Polk and Lafayette on *Commuter,* which also serves other cities. Lafayette is also served by *Texas International.*

By car: From Picayune, Miss., you can get to New Orleans via I–59; I–55 will take you from McComb, Miss., south to Kentwood and Hammond; I–20 comes in from Vicksburg, Miss., and cuts through the state west to the Texas state line. I–10 enters the state at Vidor, Texas, and goes through the state to Slidell. In the northern part of the state I–20 is complete from east to west across the state. US 71 comes in from Texarkana, Arkansas/Texas, goes south to Shreveport, and then southeast to Alexandria and New Orleans. US 61 enters the state at Woodville, Miss., goes south to Baton Rouge and then east to New Orleans.

By train: Amtrak to New Orleans from Chicago, New York and Los Angeles.

By bus: Greyhound and *Trailways* provide the most frequent service, tying in with other major lines. Several other smaller bus companies also operate around the state.

HOW TO GET AROUND. *By air: Delta, Texas International,* and *Commuter* airlines service cities within the state. Aircraft charter and rental services, including helicopter, are available. *By car:* I–55 will take you from Kentwood to Hammond. I–20, in the north, runs west from Monroe, Ruston, Minden to Shreveport. On I–10 you can go from Slidell east through New Orleans, Baton Rouge, Lafayette, Jennings to Lake Charles; I–12 leads from Baton Rouge east to Hammond and Covington. US 61 goes from New Orleans west to Baton Rouge, then US 190 west to Opelousas.

Car rental: You can rent a car in Baton Rouge, Lafayette, Lake Charles, Monroe, New Orleans, Shreveport, Alexandria, Morgan City, New Iberia, and Opelousas.

By bus: Greyhound and *Trailways,* as well as *Arrow Coach,* and other small bus companies, and *Salter Bus Lines* serve some cities within the state.

By ferry: The Mississippi River may be crossed by ferry at St. Francisville or at Lutcher.

TOURIST INFORMATION SERVICES. The *Greater New Orleans Tourist and Convention Commission* at 334 Royal St. will help you plan. The *Chamber of Commerce* at 334 Camp St. is also helpful. For the rest of the state, inquiries to specific chambers of commerce of cities and towns and to the *Louisiana Tourist Development Commission,* Box 44291, Baton Rouge 70804. *Louisiana Wildlife and Fisheries Commission,* 400 Royal St., New Orleans 70130 will supply fishing and hunting regulations. *Forest Service,* Southern Region, 50 7th St., N.E., Atlanta, Ga. 30323, offers information on national forests.

SEASONAL EVENTS. The annual *Cajun Pirogue* (Indian log canoe) *Race* is held south of New Orleans on Rte. 45 near *Lafitte* each year at varying times that the Louisiana Tourist Commission, 334 Royal St., can identify. *Spring: Mardi Gras* is the most famous seasonal event in the state, with all-out, 2-week celebration in *New Orleans,* and *Shrove Thursday* celebrations in *Houma* and *Lafayette.* In March, *Lafayette* annually observes the *Azalea Trail. Festival Acadiens* is held in Sept. *Lake Charles* has a *House and Garden*

Tour; Shreveport, a 10-day *Holiday in Dixie* festival celebrating the Louisiana Purchase. Balls, parades, water shows, art exhibits are part of the festivities. Lake Charles celebrates *Contraband Days* late May to early June with a water sports carnival.

Summer: The Morehouse rodeo takes place in *Bastrop* in June; the *KC fishing rodeo* in *Houma,* $3, is also in June, while *Ruston* celebrates its *Peach Festival* late in the month. *Many* has its *Arts and Crafts Festival* the first weekend in June. *Houma's Tarpon Rodeo* takes place in July. *Winnsboro* has a *Deep South Rodeo,* three nights in mid-Aug.

Fall: This is the time of harvest festivals: *Sugar Cane Fair and Festival* in *New Iberia,* Sept. The *International Rice Festival,* Crowley, *and Frog Derby* in *Royne, Sauce Piquante Festival* and *Pirogue Races* in *Raceland; Yambilee Festival* in *Opelousas* all take place in Oct. *Natchitoches* offers its *Historic Plantation Tour* the second weekend in Oct.

Winter: Sugar Bowl Festival begins right after Christmas, culminating in Sugar Bowl football classic on New Year's Day. *Battle of New Orleans* is celebrated in January at *Chalmette National Historical Park.*

 NATIONAL PARKS AND FORESTS. Campsites and trailer space, as well as picnicking facilities, are available throughout the nearly 600,000 acres of the Kisatchie National Forest in central and northwest Louisiana. Eleven recreation centers, open year round, with nominal charge for campsite or trailer parking. Most campsites are located on lakes or streams; and all have fireplaces and sanitary facilities. A nominal charge is made for fishing, for duck hunting, and for boats. Reservations should be made through the Forest Services, U.S.D.A., Box 471, Alexandria.

Chalmette National Historical Park, east of New Orleans on State 46, commemorates the last battle of the War of 1812.

 STATE PARKS. There are 25 state parks and commemorative areas in Louisiana; all but three permit picnicking, 10 permit camping, and four have cabins. *Audubon Memorial State Park,* near *St. Francisville* on State 965, is the site of Oakley Plantation House, a museum of Audubon memorabilia, with period furnishings. Formal garden, picnicking, hiking trails. *Bogue Falaya Wayside Park, Covington,* has a natural beach, picnicking on its 13 acres. *Ft. Jesup State Monument,* 6 mi. east of *Many* on State 6, is the site of the antebellum garrison. Replicas of two-story brick and frame building and of army field kitchen. Museum, picnicking. *Ft. Pike State Monument,* US 90, 30 mi. east of New Orleans, picnicking. *Lake D'Arbonne State Park,* off Rte. 33 west of Rte. 15 near *Farmerville,* 90-acre wooded lakeside area with picnicking, boating, water skiing. *Longfellow-Evangeline State Park* (does not allow overnight camping), 3 mi. northeast of *St. Martinville* on Rte. 31, on banks of Bayou Teche, has restored Acadian house, kitchen garden, craft shop, replica of Acadian cottage. Museum, picnicking, swimming, boating, fishing, camping.

 MUSEUMS AND GALLERIES. *Lafayette Museum,* 1122 Lafayette St., *Lafayette,* was home of Gov. Alexandre Mouton. Furniture, historical documents, portraits, Indian artifacts. Tours.

Imperial Calcasieu Museum, 204 W. Sallier St., *Lake Charles,* contains Victorian period furnishings, Gay Nineties barber shop, glass, crystal. Tour.

Louisiana State Exhibit Museum, 3015 Greenwood Rd., *Shreveport,* tells history of state through murals, dioramas, glass, china, paper money, Indian artifact collections.

In *Baton Rouge,* the *Old Arsenal Museum* houses historical exhibits in building used by federal troops during Civil War. The *Rural Life Museum,* Burden Research Center on LSU campus, is comprised of blacksmith shop, general store, overseer's cottage typical of 18th- and 19th-century plantation life.

Hanna Hall at *Monroe's* Northeast Louisiana U. campus, houses American Indian, Latin American, and African artifacts.

Loreauville Heritage Museum, 9 mi. northeast of New Iberia in *Loreauville,* is a 40-unit village and farm, telling history of territory.

Special Interest Museums. In *Baton Rouge,* LSU'S *Geoscience Museum* is open daily 8 A.M. to 5 P.M.;*Museum of Natural Science,* Foster Hall. *Louisiana Arts & Science Center & Planetarium,* 502 North Blvd., houses paintings, sculpture, cultural, historical, scientific exhibits.

Natural History Museum & Planetarium, 637 Girard Park Dr., *Lafayette,* maintains an environmental trail, changing exhibits.

Shreveport's *Meadows Museum of Art,* on Centenary Campus. A collection of paintings and drawings of Indochina by Jean Despujols.

HISTORIC SITES. Throughout Louisiana are numerous antebellum homes, many open to the public. *Oakley Plantation,* on Hwy 965, east of St. Francisville, is where Audubon became acquainted with the wildlife of the Feliciana countryside. It is now in 100-acre Audubon Memorial State Park. *Rosedown,* on State 10, east of *St. Francisville,* has antique furnishings, seventeenth-century gardens. *Cottage Plantation,* on U.S. 61, 9 mi. north of *St. Francisville,* was started in 1795. On grounds are smokehouse, school, slave cabins. In White Castle, *Nottoway Plantation,* the largest plantation house in the South, has overnight accommodations. Reservations a must. *Destrehan Manor House,* the oldest remaining plantation home on the lower Mississippi, is on River Road, 8 mi. above the New Orleans International Airport. *Derbigny Plantation* is a fine old Louisiana cottage on River Rd. (State 541) near Oak Ave., above Westwego.

St. Martinville, east of New Orleans on US 90, is center of legends surrounding Longfellow's *Evangeline.* In the churchyard of *St. Martin of Tours Catholic Church,* 133 S. Main St., is the grave of the poem's heroine, Emmeline Labiche. The *Evangeline Oak* still stands at the end of Port St. *Evangeline Museum,* 429 E. Bridge St., and *Longfellow-Evangeline State Park's Acadian House Museum,* St. Martinville, reconstruct Acadian life.

Edward Douglass White Memorial, 5 mi. north of *Thibodaux,* on State 1, includes restored homestead of Chief Justice of Supreme Court.

Oak Alley, on River Rd. near Vacherie, is a Greek Revival mansion, built in 1830's. Live oaks line a corridor from the house to the river.

Parlange Plantation, on State 1, 5 mi. south of New Roads, was built in 1750.

Houmas House, on State 942 in Burnside, is a magnificent Greek Revival mansion.

Near *Franklin* are two outstanding houses. *Oaklawn Manor,* 5 mi. off US 90, has a large grove of live oaks and lovely gardens. *Albania Mansion,* near Jeanerette, 14 mi. from Franklin on US 90, features a three-story spiral staircase.

In *Natchitoches, Rogue House,* Riverbank Dr. near Keyser Ave. Bridge, is an excellent example of pioneer Louisiana construction.

Shadows on the Teche, 117 E. Main St., *New Iberia,* is a gracious two-story, 16-room townhouse set among live oaks. *Justine,* originally built in Franklin in 1822, was added to twice and moved to New Iberia by barge. Furnished in Victorian period.

In *Reserve, San Francisco Plantation* house is 2 mi. upriver on State 44. Eighteenth-century furnishings, landscaped grounds.

TOURS. *Louisiana Lagniappe Tours* offers tours Baton Rouge and nearby plantations. *Delcambre,* 15 mi. west of New Iberia on Rte. 14, offers tours aboard paddlewheeler *Cajun Belle.*

GARDENS. Avery Island's *Jungle Gardens,* off State 329 via a toll road, is a 300-acre paradise, with camellias blooming Nov. to April, iris Mar. to July, azaleas late Feb. to late Apr. Also featured are tropical plants, sunken gardens, a Chinese garden with a centuries-old Buddha, and a bird sanctuary where egrets nest.

Hodges Gardens, 15 mi. south of *Many* on US 171, is a 4,700-acre garden in a forest. There are experimental areas, wildlife refuge, wild and cultivated gardens in bloom year-round. In Dec. there's a Christmas light tour that is free. Picnicking, boating, swimming, and fishing also available.

Rosedown Plantation and Gardens, St. Francisville, is a magnificently restored antebellum home with 17th-century-style French formal gardens.

In *Monroe, Louisiana Purchase Gardens* is a 140-acre garden and zoo with over 8,000 plants and 800 animals. Fall to spring.

In *Shreveport,* the *Barnwell Center Botanical Gardens* are open daily.

In *Shreveport, The American Rose Center* features roses from April through December. Other flowers and plants bloom year-round. *Walter Jacobs Nature Trail,* open to the public. *Around the World Tropical Gardens,* located adjacent to the Acadian Village at Lafayette, features a horticultural walking tour of the world's warm-weather area.

 MUSIC. In *Shreveport* music enthusiasts can attend a number of concerts and musical offerings ranging from classical to country. The *Community Concert Association* brings major symphony orchestras, Metropolitan Opera stars, and instrumentalists. The *Shreveport Symphony* brings guest artists, presents two performances a month during its season. The *Shreveport Civic Opera Association* also brings in guest stars for its productions. Country and western fans will want to check out the *Louisiana Hayride,* broadcast weekly by KRMD from Hayride U.S.A. *Centenary College Choir,* internationally known, regularly appears at the Convention Center, Hodges Gardens, and on local TV stations. Pop *band concerts* are held at Centenary College's Hargrove Amphitheater during summer.

 STAGE AND REVUES. In *Shreveport,* one of the best known community theater groups of the country has a year-round *Little Theater.* Summer stock is represented by the *Gas Light Players;* Centenary College's drama department regularly present plays at Marjorie Lyons Playhouse. Children's plays are regularly presented, also.

The *Monroe Civic Center* brings Broadway plays, leading entertainers, ice shows, and the circus regularly.

In *Natchitoches* an outdoor drama, *Louisiana Cavalier,* reenacts the adventures of St. Denis, the city's founder, in 1714.

DRINKING LAWS. Liquor sold by package and drink at stores or establishment with a license. Sunday sales optional in some locations. Some of northern Louisiana is dry. The minimum age is 18.

 SPORTS. *Fishing,* both fresh and saltwater, is a year-around sport. Spanish and king mackerel, jewfish, marlin, bluefish, cobia, speckled trout, pompano, red snapper, and common jack are found in the coastal areas and Gulf of Mexico. Tarpon fishing below Houma and Grand Isle is becoming increasingly popular. Many consider Louisiana a bass fisherman's dream. Crayfish are found inland. Boats, tackle, and bait are available everywhere. Nonresident fishing license costs $6; a 7-day license, $3. No license is required for saltwater fishing.

Hunting, concentrated generally during the winter months, requires a nonresident license, $10 for three days, $25 for a season, excluding bear, deer, and turkey, which require an additional $20. Visitors who are residents of Arkansas, Texas, Mississippi, Alabama and Florida must pay an even higher fee.

Licenses and information available from Wild Life and Fish Commission, 400 Royal St., New Orleans 70130.

Swimming is available at the following recreation areas: Bogue Falaya Wayside, Covington; Chemin-A-Haut, near Bastrop; D'Arbonne Lake, Farmerville; Fontainebleau, Mandeville; Grand Isle, off Rte. 1; Lake Bistineau, south of Doyline; Lake Bruin, northeast of St. Joseph; and at Cotile Reservoir, 20 mi. west of Alexandria.

Golf is popular throughout the state. *Alexandria: Bringhurst Park,* off Masonic Dr., 9 holes. *Lafayette: City Park Golf Course,* Mudd Ave. and 8th St., 18 holes, Sat., Sun., holidays. *Shreveport: Andrew Querbes Park,* Gregg and Fern Sts., 18 holes, weekends, *Lakeside,* Milam St., *Huntington,* Pines Rd., 18 holes, weekends, holidays; *New Orleans; Lakewood Country Club* sponsors Greater New Orleans Open every spring.

SPECTATOR SPORTS: New Orleans' *professional football* teams *Saints,* and *The Breakers,* and Tulane University's football team play at the Superdome. LSU's athletic teams play in Baton Rouge. *Racing:* Thoroughbred, quarter horse racing at *Evangeline Downs,* Lafayette, from Apr.–mid-Sept. Parimutuel betting. *Fair Grounds Race Track,* New Orleans, was established in 1872. Parimutuel betting. Thanksgiving–late Mar. *Jefferson Downs Race Track,* 44th St. and Williams Blvd., Kenner, has night races April to Nov. (with a short interruption during the season). Quarter-horses and thoroughbreds race at *Delta Downs* in Vinton for much of the year. Thoroughbreds at *Louisiana Downs,* Bossier City, from late spring into the fall.

WHAT TO DO WITH THE CHILDREN. *Louisiana Purchase Gardens and Zoo,* off I–20, *Monroe,* exhibit rare animals in modern buildings, some glass-fronted, some moated. Nocturnal animals are shown under red lights. The entertainment section has a Lewis & Clark Railroad, boat rides, and other amusement rides. Adults 75¢; children 4 to 12, 50¢; under 4, free. Rides, 35¢.

Hamel's Park in Shreveport is a small but good amusement park with nine outside rides, including a train and a roller coaster, with another half-dozen or so rides inside for rainy days.

HOTELS AND MOTELS. Most of the state's establishments are less expensive outside New Orleans. There are many "chain" motels along I–10 and I–12. Based on double occupancy without meals, price categories and ranges are as follows: *Deluxe:* $60 and up; *Expensive* $45–60; *Moderate* $30–45; *Inexpensive* under $30.

ALEXANDRIA. *Moderate:* **Howard Johnson's.** West of town. 24-hr. restaurant, pools, bar.
Sheraton Inn. Big beds, pool, bar, restaurant.

BATON ROUGE. *Deluxe:* **Baton Rouge Hilton.** Corporate Square. Enclosed mall, three restaurants, two cocktail lounges, nightclub.
Moderate: **Holiday Inn.** Three locations: north, south and west of town. Each has pool, restaurant, and bar.
Rodeway Inn. Pool, restaurant, bar, steambaths.
Days Inn. Pool, restaurant.

LAFAYETTE. *Expensive:* **Holiday Inn.** Two here: north and south. Each has pool, restaurant, and bar.
Howard Johnson's Motor Lodge. Attractive rooms. 24 hour restaurant. Rooms for handicapped. Airport shuttle service.
Sheraton Town House Motor Hotel. Nice rooms, cocktail lounge, live entertainment.
Inexpensive: **Imperial "400" Motel.** Downtown. Pool.

LAKE CHARLES. *Expensive:* **Howard Johnson's.** Just north of town. Pool, 24-hr. restaurant, bar.
Sheraton-Chateau Charles Motor Inn. Restaurant with first-rate French cuisine.

MANY. *Expensive:* **Toro Hills Resort.** At entrance to 300-acre Hodges Gardens. Full resort with pools, tennis courts, highly rated golf course.

MONROE. *Expensive:* **Ramada Inn.** Restaurant, grill, lounge, pool.

NATCHITOCHES. *Expensive:* **Holiday Inn.** Heated pool, 24-hr. restaurant, bar.
Moderate: **Best Way Motor Inn.** Color TV. No frills. Restaurant across the street.

SHREVEPORT. *Expensive:* **Chateau.** Downtown, near Shreve Square.
Holiday Inn. Four locations.
Hilton-Bossier. Near Louisiana Downs.
Ramada Inn. Pool, restaurant, lounge with dancing.

 DINING OUT in Louisiana often means the same fine Creole cooking you can experience in New Orleans. Price categories and ranges, for a complete dinner, are as follows: *Expensive:* $15 and up; *Moderate:* $10–15; *Inexpensive:* under $10. Drinks, tax and tip not included.

ALEXANDRIA. *Moderate:* **Herbie K's.** Specialties: oysters on half shell, other seafood, and steaks.

BATON ROUGE. *Expensive:* **Chalet Brandt.** Chef-owned, has à la carte menu and *prix fixe* meals, excellent local reputation.
Mike and Tony's. Tempting steaks and seafood à la Louisiane.
Moderate: **Piccadilly Cafeteria.** A local favorite.
Inexpensive: **Village.** Italian-American cuisine in old world atmosphere.

LAFAYETTE. *Expensive:* **Jacob's Restaurant.** Creole-Cajun cuisine featuring fresh Gulf seafood. Jackets and ties required after 5 P.M. Reservations recommended.

LAKE CHARLES. *Moderate:* **Chez Oca.** A delightful mixture of Creole, Cajun, French, and Basque cuisine.

OPELOUSAS. *Moderate:* **The Palace.** Gumbo, crawfish, seafood, and steaks are specialties.

SHREVEPORT. *Expensive:* **Don's Seafood House.** Excellent seafood.
Firenze. Continental Cuisine.
Sansone's. International cuisine. Bar, floor show, dancing.

MISSISSIPPI

Heartland Dixie

Exploring Mississippi is easy via north-south or northeast-southwest routes, following United States and some portions of interstate highways. The easternmost of the north-south itineraries begins on US 45 in Corinth, a vital railroad junction during the Civil War. By the time you reach Biloxi, heart of Mississippi's 65-mile seaside playground on the Gulf of Mexico, your tour will have included such places as Tupelo, on US 78, and its three nearby national battlefield sites; Columbus, on US 82, with its tree-lined streets and beautiful antebellum mansions; and Meridian, a leading industrial center at the intersection of US 45, US 80 and Interstates 20 and 59.

Highlights of a midstate, north-to-south tour are Holly Springs, Oxford, Jackson, Vicksburg and Natchez. Holly Springs, where US 78 and State 7 converge, is one of the state's antebellum jewels and was once known as the Athens of the South. Restored mansions now reflect the gracious living which characterized that era and many are open to the public during the April pilgrimage. The Kate Freeman Clark Art Gallery is located here, with many of her most important paintings on display.

Oxford, 27 miles south of Holly Springs on State 7, is the site of the University of Mississippi (Ole Miss). It was also the home of the late William Faulkner, 1949 Nobel Prize winner for literature, and is the "Jefferson" featured in so many of his novels. Medals and prizes awarded to Faulkner and interesting historic relics are on display in the Mississippi Room of the Library on the Ole Miss campus.

Jackson, Mississippi's capital, on US 51 and Interstate 20 and 55, and US 80 and 49, is well worth investigation. It played an important role in the Confederacy until 1863, when the Federal Army captured,

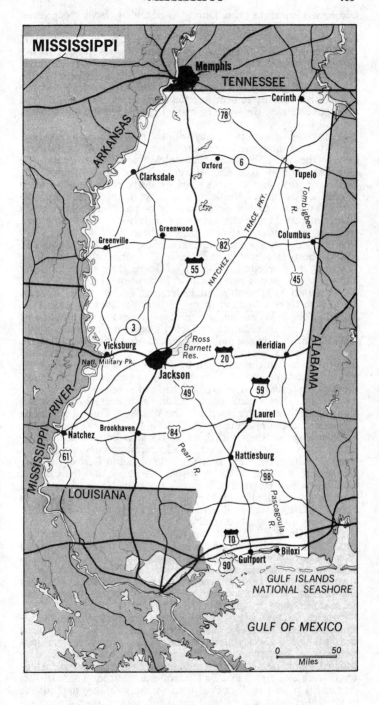

burned and looted the town. During its rebuilding, Jackson contended with hordes of carpetbaggers, indicative of the entire South's problems, and it was here that Jefferson Davis last spoke to a vanquished South. Buildings connected to the past and present state government are important attractions. The Old Capitol, which houses the State Historical Museum and is an excellent example of Greek Revival architecture, has been completely restored. You can inspect the reconstructed governor's office with its ornate, authentic period furnishings, as well as the Hall of Representatives, the scene of many important events in state and national history.

Few cities live more intimately with the past than does Vicksburg, on US 61 and Interstate 20, the site of one of the Civil War's fiercest battles. Today the Vicksburg National Military Park surrounds the city. Two main avenues, Confederate and Union, wind through the 1,330-acre park, following the main defensive position of Southern forces and the lines of Northern troops. At the park's entrance, the Visitors' Center offers a motion picture of the 47-day battle which ended with the Confederate surrender on July 4, 1863. On the park grounds, you can examine 898 historical tablets, 274 markers, 230 commemorative monuments, nine memorials, three equestrian statues, 150-odd busts and relief portraits, and 128 cannons.

Among the antebellum houses in Vicksburg, three are of particular interest. McRaven was owned by John Bobb when General U.S. Grant marched into Vicksburg. When Federal troops refused to leave his yard, Bobb threw a brick at them. He later was shot to death while walking alone in his garden, and this first incident of violence against the civilian populace during Vicksburg's occupation caused an outraged Grant to have the guilty soldiers court-martialed and hanged. Cedar Grove is a restoration project of the Little Theater group, and mute testimony to the siege can be seen in its walls where Federal warships attempted to level the house with cannonballs but failed. Planters Hall, the third showplace, has had a varied career. It was erected in 1832 as a bank, converted into a residence by the McRae family in 1848, and later bought by the Vicksburg Council of Garden Clubs for use as a museum.

Thirty miles south of Vicksburg on US 61 is Port Gibson. Tombstones in Port Gibson's cemeteries tell interesting tales of American history. Harmon Blennerhasset, associate of Aaron Burr in the Burr Conspiracy, is buried in the Protestant Cemetery, and the Catholic Cemetery holds the grave of Resin P. Bowie, inventor of the famed bowie knife, first used by his brother, Jim, of Alamo fame. Ten miles from Port Gibson on Old Rodney Road lie the ruins of Windsor, one of the most extravagant antebellum mansions of Greek Revival style in the state. Built in 1861 and consisting of five stories and an observatory, it burned in 1890, when a careless swain showing off a newfangled cigarette at a house party threw the glowing butt into a pile of shavings in the corner of the ballroom. Nearby is the ghost town of Rodney—a town which died when the river moved away. Not far from there is Grand Gulf Military Park near where Grant landed his troops and doomed Vicksburg by taking it from the rear.

Natchez, farther south on US 61, is your introduction to an antebellum town where time seems to have stood still. The past is treasured here, but this is also a manufacturing center, and modern buildings mingle with the dominating 18th- and 19th-century structures. Undoubtedly more people visit Natchez during its annual Spring Pilgrimage (March and April) and Fall Pilgrimage (October 5 through 22) than at any other time. The Pilgrimages were established in the 1930s by farsighted ladies, and many antebellum houses are open daily, some only during the Pilgrimages. The rest of the year a roster of mansions rotate the duty of staying open for visitors so that some are always available. For details, contact the Natchez-Adams County Chamber of Commerce, 300 N. Commerce St., zip 39120. On Ellicott's Hill stands Connelley's Tavern, reputedly the spot where Aaron Burr planned his defense against a charge of treason. A treacherous attorney in the pay of bandits also supposedly hung about the tavern to pick up from careless conversation hints of loot to be lifted from travelers on the Natchez Trace by his gang. Beginning about 10 miles north of Natchez on US 61 is a long segment of the old Natchez Trace now paved and maintained as a part of the federal park system. Along the Trace are Mount Locust, a restored hostelry, Emerald Mound, a magnificent 12-acre Indian mound, and the ghost town of Rocky Springs.

Mississippi's sixty-five-mile stretch of coast bordering the Gulf of Mexico runs from the Alabama line to Louisiana and affords the state its own playground in the sun. US 90, a four-lane highway from Pascagoula to Bay St. Louis, follows the old Spanish Trail that ran from St. Petersburg, Fla., to Mexico and the Western Spanish colonies. If you are in a hurry, Interstate 10 runs from just west of Pascagoula into New Orleans. Along the blue waters of the gulf and its bayous grow colorful flowers, with dense green foliage hinting of the tropics, and moss-bearded giant oaks grow in profusion. The coast offers white sand beaches and water sports—swimming, water-skiing, fishing and boating.

Entering Mississippi from Alabama, your first stop is Pascagoula, a region of former French-Spanish domination. A shipbuilding center, Pascagoula also has joined the growing number of cities holding spring pilgrimages for visits to antebellum houses. Ocean Springs, which has gained nationwide popularity as a resort, lies due west. It was there that the Sieur d'Iberville in 1699 established a French colony, the first white settlement in the Mississippi Valley. Neighboring Biloxi, with its historic Jefferson Davis Shrine, is noted also for seafood production and resort hotels. Between Biloxi and Gulfport is the site of the first stretch of beach in North America out-of-bounds to people during the Least Tern nesting season to protect eggs and fledglings. At Gulfport is one of the world's largest banana terminals and a major Gulf Coast recreation center. Offshore about 12 miles lies the Gulf Islands National Seashore, a federal park that includes in its Mississippi section Petit Bois (pronounced "petty boy") and Horn Islands which are kept in primitive wilderness, and the more developed Ship Island on which stand the ruins of Fort Massachusetts. Excursion boats go from the mainland to Ship Island during spring and summer. To reach the wilderness islands, you must charter a private trip.

PRACTICAL INFORMATION FOR MISSISSIPPI

HOW TO GET THERE. *By air: Delta, American and Republic* have direct service into many cities in the state. *Royale* flies New Orleans—Natchez—Jackson. *By car:* I-55, US 45 and US 61 go from north to south; US 82, I-20, US 84, I-10 and US 90 run from east to west. *Car rental: Avis, Hertz, Budget,* and *National* in major cities. *By train: Amtrak* from Chicago to New Orleans. *By bus: Greyhound* and *Trailways. By ferry:* from St. Joseph, La., to Port Gibson.

HOW TO GET AROUND. *By air: Republic. By car:* I–55, US 45 and US 61, north to south; US 82, I–20, US 84; I–10 and US 90 east to west. *By train: Amtrak* over the Illinois Central Gulf system north to south. *By bus: Greyhound, Trailways;* for eastern service from Mobile to St. Louis use *Gulf Transport.*

TOURIST INFORMATION. Contact the *Mississippi Dept. of Tourism Development,* P.O. Box 22825, Jackson, 39205; the *Mississippi Park Commission,* 717 Robert E. Lee Bldg., Jackson 39201; individual city chambers of commerce; and *Natchez-Adams County Chamber of Commerce,* 300 N. Commerce St., Natchez, re: antebellum homes open to public.

MUSEUMS AND GALLERIES. *Brice's Cross Roads Museum,* Baldwyn. *Winterville Indian Mounds Museum & State Park,* Greenville. *Grenada Historical Museum,* Grenada. *State Historical Museum,* in the Old Capitol, Jackson. *Old Spanish Fort,* Pascagoula. *Natchez Trace Parkway,* Visitor Center, Tupelo. *Park Museum,* Vicksburg National Military Park.

Art: *Kate Freeman Clark Art Gallery,* Holly Springs. *Municipal Art Gallery,* Jackson. *Mary Buie Museum,* Oxford. *Museum of Art,* Meridian. The *Lauren Rogers Memorial Library and Museum of Art* at Laurel deserves special mention for its houses many canvases of the Great Masters including Homer, Whistler, Corot, de Hoog and Daumier.

Special interest: *Mississippi Museum of Natural Science,* Jackson. *Military Museum,* Port Gibson. *Dunn-Seiler Museum* (geology) at Mississippi State University, Starkville. *Art Center Planetarium,* Jackson.

Others: *Old Country Store,* Lorman, *River Museum and Hall of Fame,* Vicksburg. *Florewood River Plantation State Park,* Greenwood. *Grand Village of the Natchez Indians,* Natchez.

HISTORIC SITES. *Brice's Cross Roads National Battlefield Site,* off Rte. 370, Baldwyn. *Beauvoir* (Jefferson Davis Shrine), Biloxi. *Friendship Cemetery,* Columbus. *Corinth National Cemetery,* Corinth. *Ship Island,* by excursion boats from Biloxi and Gulfport. *Tupelo National Battlefield,* Tupelo. *Vicksburg National Military Park & Cemetery. Grand Gulf Battlefield,* Port Gibson. *Emerald Indian Mound,* ghost town of *Rocky Springs,* Natchez Trace Parkway. *Old Spanish Fort,* Pascagoula.

TOURS. Schedules vary with seasons and days. *By boat: Sailfish Tour Boat,* 1½ hr. shrimping and oystering expedition from Biloxi. *Jefferson Davis Cruises,* from Vicksburg. *By train: Shrimp Train Tour,* from Biloxi lighthouse.

SEASONAL EVENTS. In every section of Mississippi *Annual Spring Pilgrimages* are held in early spring (Mar.-Apr.). Hoopskirted attendants greet visitors to the preCivil War mansions—filled with rare antiques and treasures of the antebellum past. These Pilgrimages can be enjoyed in the following cities: Aberdeen, Carollton, Columbus, Hattiesburg (homes featured here were built during the first years of the 20th century); Holly Springs, Jackson, Kosciusko, Monticello, Natchez, Oxford, Port Gibson, Raymond, Sardis, Vicksburg, Woodville. The *Gulf Coast Pilgrimage,* held during mid-March, covers 11 coastal cities. Tours are marked and are free. The Pilgrimage is sponsored by the Mississippi Gulf Coast Council of Garden Clubs.

February: Dixie National Livestock Show and Rodeo, Jackson. 2nd week.

March: During this month there are brilliant celebrations of *Mardi Gras* at Biloxi, Pascagoula, Pass Christian, and Natchez. From early Mar. to Sept. the *Dixie Showboat Players* present melodrama in Vicksburg.

April: Greenwood Arts Festival, with literary lions, all-day jazz, exhibits.

May: Armed Forces Day, Keesler Air Force Base, Biloxi. *Atwood Blue Grass Festival,* Monticello; *Jimmie Rodgers Festival,* Meridian.

June: Biloxi Shrimp Festival, the *Blessing of the Fleet,* and the *Shrimp King & Queen Pageant* (1st week).

July: Yachting Regatta, Biloxi. *Yachting Regatta,* Pass Christian (July 4th). *Mississippi Deep-Sea Fishing Rodeo,* Gulfport, 1st week of July. *Miss Mississippi Pageant,* Vicksburg Municipal Auditorium, Vicksburg. *Choctaw Indian Festival,* Philadelphia.

August: Outdoor Fishermen's Club Fishing Rodeo, Pass Christian (all month). *Faulkner International Conference,* Oxford. *Neshoba County Fair,* Philadelphia.

September: Delta Blues Festival, Greenville.

October: Invitational Golf Tournament, Pass Christian. *Mississippi State Fair,* State Fairgrounds, Jackson (2nd week). *Gumbo Festival,* Necaise Crossing.

November: Bird Dog Field Trails, Holly Springs (late Nov). *Frost-Bite Regatta,* Pass Christian (early Nov). *Antique Forum,* Natchez.

December: Shrimp Bowl Football game: Delta Band Festival & Winter Carnival. Greenwood (early Dec.). *Trees of Christmas,* Meridian. *Christmas at Florewood,* Greenwood. *Christmas at Natchez.*

NIGHTCLUBS AND DRINKING LAWS. Clubs along the Gulf coast: Biloxi: *Royal Terrace Room* and the *Trophy Lounge* (both in the Broadwater Hotel), the *Lafitte Lounge* in the Holiday Inn, *Leslee's,* and *Upstairs, Downstairs.* Ocean Springs: *White Pillar's.* Gulfport: *Sydney's Paradise Point, Nicholoff, Sugar Mill,* the *Shipwreck Lounge* in the Holiday Inn. Pascagoula: *Scranton's.*

Package stores and hotel and restaurant bars are legal on an optional basis. No Sunday package sales. The drinking age is 21, for beer 18.

SPORTS. *Swimming:* The world's longest man-made beach runs from Biloxi to Henderson Point. Other beaches are at Pascagoula, Ocean Springs, Bay St. Louis, Waveland and on offshore islands. *Boating:* Most towns on waterways have launching ramps. There is powerboating in the Mississippi Sound and many rivers and bayous. Small sailboat rentals are available in Biloxi. *Fishing:* Year-round saltwater and deep-sea fishing coast-wide. Freshwater fishing is excellent in the state's many streams and lakes, particularly good in reservoirs behind dams and spectacular in the oxbow lakes that border the Mississippi River.

SPECTATOR SPORTS. The *Shrimp Bowl* Football game is held at Biloxi in early December; football is king throughout the state all fall. Major golf tournaments are held at Pass Christian, Hattiesburg and Greenwood.

WHAT TO DO WITH THE CHILDREN. *Vicksburg National Military Park* and the *Park Museum* are teeming with mementos of the Civil War. At Biloxi is *Six Gun Junction* combined with the *Deer Ranch* where children pet the animals. At Gulfport is the *Marine Life Aquadome.* At Meridian and Tupelo are fish hatcheries with guided visits. The *Jackson Zoo* has a petting section and a Chimneyville Choo Choo train ride. At Vicksburg the Jefferson Davis boat ride follows the route of attacking Union gunboats.

HOTELS AND MOTELS. Along the Gulf Coast are several resort hotels with full beach and sports facilities. Inland hostelries are more modest. Hotels and motels are listed alphabetically within categories based on double-occupancy, in-season rates. Family rates are available at almost all listings. Rates run $3 to $4 higher during Pilgrimages. *Expensive:* over $50; *Moderate:* $30–50; *Inexpensive* under $30.

BILOXI. *Expensive:* **Broadwater Beach, Hilton, Royal d'Iberville** are luxury resorts with entertainment, dancing, heated pools, lifeguards, tennis and either full golf privileges or putting green.

Moderate: **Holiday Inn, Howard Johnson's, Quality Inn-Emerald Beach, Ramada Inn** are only slightly less opulent than the top rankers—and only slightly less expensive.

CLARKSDALE. *Inexpensive–Moderate:* Both **Holiday Inn** and **Best Western Up-Town** offer entertainment and other amenities unusual in houses charging so little.

COLUMBUS. *Moderate:* **Ramada Inn** has dancing and entertainment despite modest fees.

CORINTH. *Moderate:* **Holiday Inn** and **Ramada Inn,** kennels at former, entertainment at latter.
Inexpensive: **Econo Lodge** has cable television and restaurant.

GREENVILLE. *Inexpensive:* **Riverview Inn** has evening entertainment. **Holiday Inn** has modest but adequate amenities.

GREENWOOD. *Moderate:* **Holiday Inn** offers heated pool, kennel, entertainment and dancing. **Ramada Inn** has heated pool, entertainment, dancing.

GULFPORT. *Moderate:* **Best Western** (formerly Downtowner), **Holiday Inn** and **Sheraton Gulfport** somewhat more lavish than most motels in their respective chains.

HATTIESBURG. *Moderate:* **Holiday Inn** has a kennel for pets.

JACKSON. *Moderate:* **Coliseum Ramada Inn, Walthall, Regency, Holiday Inn–North, Holiday Inn–Southwest, Howard Johnson's,** and **Sheraton** are all considerably more luxurious than the average of their respective chains, all offer entertainment and dancing. **The Jacksonian** on I-55 North and **La Quinta** on I-20 West are reasonably priced and have enough comfort to make an excellent buy.

LONG BEACH. *Moderate:* **Ramada Inn,** entertainment, dancing, tennis, putting green.

MERIDIAN. *Moderate–Inexpensive:* Two **Holiday Inns, Howard Johnson's** and **Best Western,** typical comfortable chain operations. **Holiday Inn–Northeast** and **Best Western** sometimes offer entertainment and dancing.

NATCHEZ. *Moderate:* **Ramada Inn.** Entertainment and dancing. Superb view of Mississippi River.
Inexpensive: **Holiday Inn** and **Prentiss Motel,** entertainment and dancing. All Natchez inns add a few dollars to fees during Pilgrimage.

OCEAN SPRINGS. *Expensive:* **Gulf Hills.** Luxurious resort includes splendid 18-hole golf course, heated pool and lifeguard in summer, putting green, night tennis with instructors, stables, fishing, shuffleboard and usual resort entertainment and dancing. Advance reservations advisable because Gulf Hills sometimes closes for a time during the off season.

OXFORD. *Moderate:* **Best Western** and **Holiday Inn** offer usual chain amenities. **Rodeway Inn** has entertainment and dancing. Football weekends pose space problems.

PASCAGOULA. *Moderate:* **La Font Inn,** heated pool, lifeguard in summer, playground. Some rooms have sauna.
Also try the **Travel Motor Inn** and the **American Motor Inn** which offer considerably more comforts and amenities than usual at this level.

STARKVILLE. *Moderate:* **Holiday Inn** with heated pool and kennel for pets.

TUPELO. *Moderate–Inexpensive:* **Ramada Inn** with entertainment, dancing, beauty shop.

Inexpensive: **Natchez Trace Inn.** Playground, entertainment, dancing.

VICKSBURG. *Moderate:* **Holiday Inn** and **Ramada Inn** have music and dancing. **Rivertown Inn** houses the Old Southern Tea Room.

 DINING OUT. Mississippi offers many traditional Southern specialties, as well as all the standard American favorites. Along the Gulf coast, try shrimp prepared in the Creole manner, and hot gumbos or other seafood specialties. Among the Southern items to be found on many Mississippi menus: hush puppies, grits, country-style ham, and of course, Mississippi River catfish.

For other worthwhile restaurants, be sure to re-check hotel listings. Restaurants are listed in order of price category. Price ranges and categories for a complete meal without drinks are as follows: *Expensive:* $10–20; *Moderate:* $7–10; *Inexpensive:* under $7.

BILOXI. *Expensive:* **White Pillars.** Old South elegance in restored mansion, superb table.
Moderate: **Mary Mahoney's.** Chic surroundings, fine cuisine.
Inexpensive. **Baricev's.** Seafood plates from that same day's catch.
Sea 'n Sirloin. Try stuffed sirloin.

GREENWOOD. *Moderate:* **Giardina's.** Excellent Italian.
Lusco's. Still has curtained booths left from Prohibition days. A longtime favorite of locals.
Websters. Charming decor. Excellent food.

GULFPORT. *Inexpensive.* **The Landing.** Sporty atmosphere.

HOLLY SPRINGS. *Inexpensive.* **Hitching Post.** Steak and seafood.

GREENVILLE. *Expensive:* **Doe's Eat Place.** Far-famed for superb fare despite rundown appearance.
Moderate: **C & G Depot.** Splendidly converted railroad depot. Lunch buffet.

JACKSON. *Moderate:* **Cisco's** Mexican.
Dennery's. Oyster specialties.
Le Fleur's. Excellent raw oyster bar.
Sundancer. Lively ambience, good table
Inexpensive: **Palette.** In Art Museum. Nice surprise.

MERIDIAN. *Inexpensive.* **Weidman's.** A pleasant surprise.

MENDENHALL. *Inexpensive.* **The Hotel Mendenhall Revolving Tables.** Glorious old-style boardinghouse cooking.

NATCHEZ. *Moderate.* **Carriage House.** Southern cooking.
Cock of the Walk. Catfish in wicked old Natchez-Under-the-Hill.
Sidetrack II. Converted railroad depot overlooks Mississippi River.

OCEAN SPRINGS. *Moderate:* **Trilby's.** Creole menu. Seafood.

OXFORD. After years of mediocre-to-poor dining, the town now offers sound and inexpensive restaurants, **the Gin,** and **the Warehouse.**

PASCAGOULA. *Moderate.* **Tiki.** A strange decor, but the food is uncommonly good. Waterside location.

PORT GIBSON. *Inexpensive:* **The Old Depot.** Authentically restored turn-of-the-century railroad depot. Creole cooking.

TUPELO. *Inexpensive:* **Hunter's.** Man-sized portions.

VICKSBURG. *Moderate:* **Maxwell's.** Seafood including lobster.
Velchoff's. Seafood.
Walnut Hills. Lazy Susan roundtable.

NORTH CAROLINA

Blue Ridge, Smoky Mountains, and the Sea

North Carolina is divided into three major geographical regions: the coastal plains, the Piedmont Plateau, and western North Carolina.

A tour of the coastal plain—about 25,000 square miles including ocean beaches—can appropriately begin at Roanoke Island, site of the first English expedition in the New World. Lying between the mainland and long barrier islands called the Outer Banks, Roanoke Island has a visitors' center in Fort Raleigh. Near here (Manteo) visitors may see the *Elizabethan II*, a reproduction of the ships of 1585 that brought the first colonists to the New World. At Kitty Hawk are the sand dunes the Wright Brothers chose for their glider and airplane experiments. Wright Brothers National Memorial commemorates the 1903 first flight.

The Cape Hatteras National Seashore embraces seventy miles of oceanfront between Nags Head on Bodie Island and the village of Ocracoke on the southern tip of Ocracoke Island. Focal point of the National Seashore is Cape Hatteras itself, where the tallest lighthouse in the United States—208 feet—protects shipping from the treacherous Diamond Shoals. In earlier times Diamond Shoals was called the Graveyard of the Atlantic and, according to legends of the area, the original residents of Nags Head used to tie lanterns on the necks of their horses to lure ships into the shoals and then prey upon them for their profitable salvage.

Almost all of Ocracoke Island is on the National Seashore. Ocracoke and the central coast are virtually uninhabited Outer Banks of Portsmouth, Core, and Shackleford, destined for preservation in the natural state as the Cape Lookout National Seashore. The development of seaside beach and fishing resorts and the National Seashore has ended

471

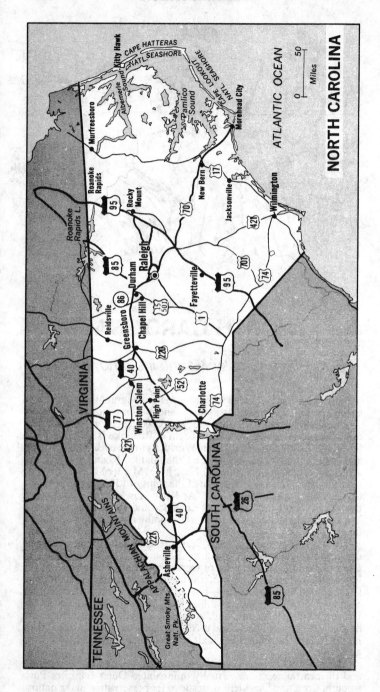

NORTH CAROLINA

NORTH CAROLINA

Blue Ridge, Smoky Mountains, and the Sea

North Carolina is divided into three major geographical regions: the coastal plains, the Piedmont Plateau, and western North Carolina.

A tour of the coastal plain—about 25,000 square miles including ocean beaches—can appropriately begin at Roanoke Island, site of the first English expedition in the New World. Lying between the mainland and long barrier islands called the Outer Banks, Roanoke Island has a visitors' center in Fort Raleigh. Near here (Manteo) visitors may see the *Elizabethan II*, a reproduction of the ships of 1585 that brought the first colonists to the New World. At Kitty Hawk are the sand dunes the Wright Brothers chose for their glider and airplane experiments. Wright Brothers National Memorial commemorates the 1903 first flight.

The Cape Hatteras National Seashore embraces seventy miles of oceanfront between Nags Head on Bodie Island and the village of Ocracoke on the southern tip of Ocracoke Island. Focal point of the National Seashore is Cape Hatteras itself, where the tallest lighthouse in the United States—208 feet—protects shipping from the treacherous Diamond Shoals. In earlier times Diamond Shoals was called the Graveyard of the Atlantic and, according to legends of the area, the original residents of Nags Head used to tie lanterns on the necks of their horses to lure ships into the shoals and then prey upon them for their profitable salvage.

Almost all of Ocracoke Island is on the National Seashore. Ocracoke and the central coast are virtually uninhabited Outer Banks of Portsmouth, Core, and Shackleford, destined for preservation in the natural state as the Cape Lookout National Seashore. The development of seaside beach and fishing resorts and the National Seashore has ended

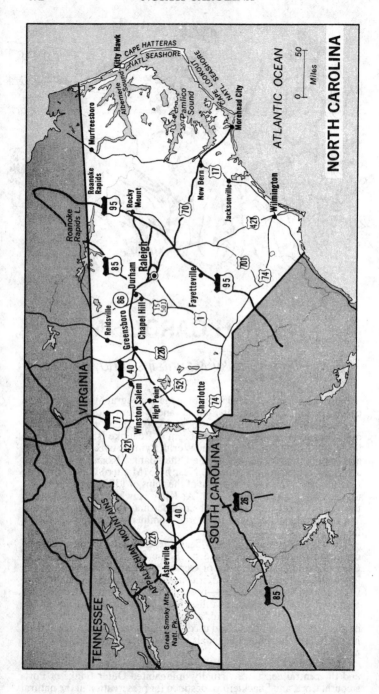

more than two centuries of isolation for the Outer Banks between Kitty Hawk and Ocracoke. Important fishing centers are at Oregon Inlet and Hatteras Village, the site of Gamefish Junction, where Gulfstream and cold northern currents meet, and where northern and southern species of fish abound. As to other natural endowments, within the National Seashore there is Pea Island National Wildlife Refuge on Hatteras Island, flocking point of shore birds and migratory waterfowl. Here over one half the world's population of greater snow geese can be seen between early November and late January.

The central coast swings southwest from Hatteras with Morehead City, one of the state's two ocean ports, the center of the maritime province of Carteret County. Morehead City has the state's largest fleet of charter fishing boats. Nearby resorts on Bogue Island offer advantages of both ocean and sound recreation activities. Wilmington, a historic port and permanent mooring of the battleship *USS North Carolina*, is a hub of beaches, plantations, and recreation for the southeastern coast. Wilmington greets Spring with its annual Azalea Festival. Wrightsville and Carolina beaches are a bit tamer than the Outer Banks but offer the same activities.

The Piedmont Plateau of central North Carolina begins a few miles east of Raleigh and rolls westward to the base of the Blue Ridge mountains. The Piedmont includes distinctive geographical features like the sand hills in the southeast, the Uwharrie and Sauratown mountains of the central area, and large rivers. The region is full of boating and fishing lakes, has parks and golf courses, and its tobacco farms, factories and textile mills form a combination of industry/tourist attractions.

Raleigh-Durham-Chapel Hill

Raleigh, the capital, is the southeastern apex of the Research Triangle Park formed by North Carolina State University in Raleigh, the University of North Carolina at Chapel Hill, and Duke University in Durham. Visitors can tour the historic capitol, the North Carolina Art Museum, Archives and History Building, the State Legislative Building, and the Museum of Natural History, and see the equestrian statue in Capitol Square honoring the three Presidents born in North Carolina: Andrew Jackson, Andrew Johnson, and James K. Polk. Durham is an industrial center, the home of Duke University, and a tobacco center spurred by the Duke family, which may be to the gold leaf what the Carnegies have been to steel. The University of North Carolina's famous alumnus Thomas Wolfe once described Chapel Hill as a place that "beats every other town all hollow." U.S. astronauts use the university's Morehead Planetarium in preparing for their space flights. North of Chapel Hill is historic Hillsborough, established in 1754 and the site of the hanging of six of the Regulators whose uprising against the British culminated in defeat at the Battle of Alamance on May 16, 1771.

Other major cities in the Piedmont are Charlotte, Greensboro, Burlington, High Point, and Winston-Salem, each important as trade and tobacco centers.

The natural areas of western North Carolina are what attract the most visitors—Mount Mitchell, highest peak east of the Mississippi, the Great Smoky Mountains, the Blue Ridge Parkway, and the reservation inhabited by Cherokee Indians. Asheville is the trade and tourism center for the areas and the final resting spot for writers Thomas Wolfe and O. Henry. Southwest of Asheville, in the Franklin, N.C. area, rockhounds may find more than 300 varieties of minerals and gems in various mines which are open to the public (small fee charged).

The Blue Ridge Parkway is a high-altitude route for pleasure travel between Shenandoah National Park in Virginia and the Great Smoky Mountain National Park entrance near Cherokee. The scenic drive illustrates the history, geology, and culture of the mountains. There are campgrounds, picnic areas, and scenic overlooks. Highest sections may be closed in winter.

Half of the Great Smoky Mountains National Park is within the state, with the Great Smokies Divide zigzagging from northeast to southwest for 71 miles along the North Carolina–Tennessee line. Sixteen peaks rise to more than 6,000 feet; the tallest is Clingman's Dome (6,643 feet). The park has paved main and secondary roads and over 700 miles of hiking trails. Campgrounds in the Great Smoky Mt. National Park are at Deep Creek, Smokemont, and Balsam Mountain.

Cherokee, at the end of the Blue Ridge Parkway, has the Oconaluftee Indian Village showing how the Cherokees lived two centuries ago. The shops lining Cherokee's Main Street get many of their mass-produced items from manufacturing concerns operating on the reservation and employing Cherokees.

Other western North Carolina spots to see are the Linville Gorge area in Pisgah National Forest, Blowing Rock resort area with its nearby developed ski areas, and the home of Carl Sandburg, a National Historic Site in Hendersonville.

PRACTICAL INFORMATION

FOR NORTH CAROLINA

HOW TO GET THERE. *By air:* Raleigh-Durham, Charlotte, Greensboro, Asheville, Fayetteville, Goldsboro, Hickory, Jacksonville, Kinston, New Bern, Rocky Mount, Wilmington, and Winston-Salem are all served from outside the state.

By rail: Amtrak goes to Rocky Mount, Wilson, Raleigh, Fayetteville, Hamlet, Southern Pines/Pinehurst, and Charlotte.

By car: I–95, I–85 and I–77 run north-south. I–40 goes east-west. I–26 comes in from South Carolina.

By bus: Greyhound and *Trailways.*

HOW TO GET AROUND. *By air: Delta, Eastern, Piedmont, Altair, United, Wheeler, US Air, Sunbird, Air Virginia,* and *Mid-South* have intrastate service. *By car:* All interstate and state roads are toll free. *By ferry:* State operated toll-free service from Currituck to Knotts Island, Hatteras Inlet, Pamlico River, at Bayview, and Neuse River, at Minnesota Beach. Toll ferry from Cedar Island to Ocracoke Island; Southport to Ft. Fisher.

By bus: Greyhound, Trailways, and *Seashore Transportation Co.*

TOURIST INFORMATION. *North Carolina Travel Division,* Dept. of Commerce, Raleigh, 27611. Call toll-free in US and Toronto, Can.: 1–800–VISIT; in Raleigh, NC, call 919–733–4171. *Park Superintendent,* Cape Hatteras National Seashore, Box 457, Manteo, 27954.

MUSEUMS AND GALLERIES. Historical: *North Carolina Hall of History,* Raleigh; *Cornwallis House,* Wilmington; *Museum of the Albemarle,* Elizabeth City. *Greensboro Historical Museum,* Greensboro.
Art: *Asheville Art Museum; Mint Museum of Art,* Charlotte; *Duke University Museum of Art,* Durham; *North Carolina Museum of Art,* Raleigh; *Piedmont*

Craftsman, Winston-Salem; *Southeastern Center for Contemporary Art,* Winston-Salem; *St. John's Art Gallery,* Wilmington.

Special-interest museums: *Country Doctor Museum,* Bailey; *Museum of the Cherokee Indian,* Cherokee; *North Carolina Maritime,* Beaufort; *World Golf Hall of Fame,* Pinehurst; *Discovery Place* (Science Museum), Charlotte.

HISTORIC SITES. *Thomas Wolfe Memorial,* Asheville; *Ft. Fisher State Historic Site,* Carolina Beach; *Wright Brothers Nat. Memorial,* Kill Devil Hills; *Roanoke Island Historical Park,* Manteo; *James K. Polk Birthplace,* Pineville; *Old Salem,* Winston-Salem.

TOURS. *By boat:* Southport-Ft. Fisher Ferry. Car and passenger ferry from Cedar Island—Ocracoke; Hatteras—Ocracoke; Swanquarter–Ocracoke.

DRINKING LAWS. Local option on county-by-county basis. In "wet" counties imbibers must be at least 21.

SUMMER SPORTS. *Water sports:* Bathing season begins in May and runs into late autumn on beaches, rivers, lakes. Intercoastal Waterway for 265 miles in state; consult Inland Waterway Guide, Ft. Lauderdale, Fla. *Fishing:* Deep-sea, salt-water centers at Nags Head, Morehead City, Oregon Inlet, Hatteras, Wrightsville, Southport, with blue marlin the big game. Freshwater requires a license.

Golf: Over 300 courses. According to *Golf Digest,* Pinehurst #2 in America's top 10, C.C. of North Carolina in top 30, Grandfather in Linville and Red Fox in Tryon in top 100.

Horseback riding and hiking all throughout the state: Appalachian Trail through Smokies. Pisgah and Nantahala Parks.

WINTER SPORTS. *Hunting:* Bear, boar, deer, small-game animals, ducks, etc. Consult *Wildlife Resources Commission,* Raleigh. *Skiing:* Appalachian Ski Mt., Hound Ears, Mill Ridge, Hawk's Nest, Sugar Mtn., Beech Mtn., all near Banner Elk. Also, Cataloochee Ski Slopes, Waynesville; Wolf Laurel near Mars Hill, Fairfield at Sapphire Valley; and Scaly at Scaly Mountain.

SPECTATOR SPORTS. *Charlotte Motor Speedway* in May and October and North Carolina Motor Speedway with NASCAR events. *Greater Greensboro Open* is a PGA tour stop. Duke, UNC, N.C. State, Wake Forest Davidson are among major colleges playing most sports.

SHOPPING. Outlet stores and mall featuring North Carolina products flourish along highways near Burlington, Southern Pines, Greensboro, Raleigh, Charlotte, Eden, Kannapolis, Lexington, High Point and Thomasville. You will recognize names such as Cannon, Burlington, Henredon, Haynes, Carter's, Van Heusen and many more. To organize an outlet shopping trip, we suggest you send for *The Central N. C. Outlet & Discount Guide* ($2.00), PO Box 2550, Greensboro, NC 27402. Personalized tour information, 1–800–334–6838.

WHAT TO DO WITH THE CHILDREN. *USS North Carolina* Battleship Memorial, Wilmington; *Tweetsie Railroad,* Blowing Rock; *Grandfather Mtn.,* Linville, with mile-high swinging bridge; *Caro-Winds,* theme park, south of Charlotte; *Discovery Place,* "hands-on" science museum, Charlotte; *Frontierland,* Cherokee; *Oconaluftee Indian Village, Cherokee Indian Reservation,* Cherokee; *Daniel Boone Railroad Park,* Hillsborough; *North Carolina Museum of Life & Science,* Durham; *Ghost Town* in Maggie Valley.

HOTELS AND MOTELS. Subject to change these infla-
tion-prone days, but generally predictable, are the following price ranges we've used: *Deluxe:* $75 and up;
Expensive: $60–75; *Moderate:* $40–60; *Inexpensive:* $40.

ASHEVILLE. *Deluxe:* **Grove Park Inn.** On Beaucatcher Mountain. Now
open year round. Resort hotel; outstanding service, magnificent view.
　Moderate: **Holiday Inn.** 3 locations. Pool, restaurant.

ATLANTIC BEACH. *Moderate:* **Atlantis Lodge.** Secluded oceanfront.
Kitchenettes, year-round.
　Ramada. At Pine Knoll Shores. Pools, restaurant, nice view, entertainment,
bar. All rooms oceanfront.
　Inexpensive: **Flemington.** Comfortable motel; very good restaurant. Year-
round.

BOONE–BLOWING ROCK. *Deluxe:* **Green Park Inn.** Open year round.
Resort is known for its golf course and excellent food.
　Hound Ears Lodge and Club. Golf course, ski slope. Exclusive resort.
　Moderate: **Azalea Garden Motel.** Comfortable and unpretentious.

CHAPEL HILL. *Deluxe:* **Hotel Europa.** Elegant surroundings, entertainment
nightly, gourmet dining.
　Moderate: **Carolina Inn.** Run by university.

CHARLOTTE. *Deluxe:* **Adam's Mark.** An uptown hotel. Raquetball, health
club.
　Moderate: **Holiday Inn.** Five locations in town.
　Inexpensive: **Days Inn.** Three locations: W. Woodlawn, Sugar Creek Rd., and
Tuckaseegee.

CHEROKEE. *Moderate:* **Boundary Tree Motor Court.** Operated by Chero-
kee Indians.
　Best Western Great Smokies Inn.
　Holiday Inn. Has trout fishing.

DURHAM. *Moderate:* **The Hilton Inn** at Duke Hospital. Lounge, good res-
taurant.
　Sheraton Center. On Hwy 15–501. Convenient location.
　Inexpensive: **Cricket Inn.** I–95 at Hillandale and Duke University.

GREENSBORO. *Moderate:* **Hilton Inn.** Downtown and airport.
　Holiday Inn-Four Season. I–40. Convention hotel; indoor-outdoor pool. One
of the finest facilities in the city.

NAGS HEAD. *Expensive:* **The Sea Ranch.** On ocean. Enclosed tennis courts
and pool.
　Moderate: **Carolinian Motor Hotel.** Oceanfront. Year-round.

PINEHURST. *Deluxe:* **The Manor Inn.** All facilities for sports.
　The Pinehurst Hotel. At village center. The home of the world famous #2
golf course.

RALEIGH. *Expensive:* **Marriott.** US 70 W. One of the finest accommodations
in Raleigh.
　N. Raleigh Hilton. US 1 N. Well-known lounge, one of the finest restaurants.
　Moderate: **Mission Valley Inn.** Near University.
　Inexpensive: **Comfort Inn.** Three locations: N. Hills, Crabtree area, and US
1N.

SOUTHERN PINES. *Deluxe:* **Mid Pines Club.** Golf Course. AP.
　Pine Needles Lodges and Country Club. All facilities. AP.

Moderate: **Charlton Motel.** US 1. Small, lakefront facility. Kitchenettes.

WILMINGTON AND WRIGHTSVILLE BEACH. *Expensive:* **Blockade Runner.** Oceanfront.
Hilton. Opposite battleship.
The Surf Motel. Ocean front, year round. Kitchennetes; seasonal rates.
Inexpensive: **El Berta Motel.** Year round.

WINSTON-SALEM. *Deluxe:* **Winston Plaza Stouffer Hotel.** Very plush convention ctr.
Expensive: **Hyatt Hotel.** Indoor garden with cascading waterfall; very good food.
Moderate: **Sheraton Motor Inn.** Good facilities and near shopping center and mini-mall.

DINING OUT IN NORTH CAROLINA. Prices are for a complete dinner but do not include drinks, tax or tip. *Expensive:* $25 and up; *Moderate:* $15–25; *Inexpensive:* under $15. Among North Carolina's specialties are country-cured ham, hot biscuits, chess pie, barbecue, strawberry pie, and candied yams.

ASHEVILLE. *Expensive:* **Jared's.** Excellent French restaurant; à la carte, reservations needed.
Moderate: **Stephen's.** International cuisine. Small, intimate, delightful. Reservations suggested.

BLOWING ROCK. *Moderate:* **The Farm House.** Delicious. Overlooks John's River Gorge. Season June-Nov. Singing waiters & waitresses.

BOONE. *Inexpensive:* **The Daniel Boone Inn.** Family style. Chicken, ham, biscuits, fresh vegetables are specialties.

CHAPEL HILL. *Moderate:* **Slug's at The Pines.** Excellent food; reservations advised.
Restaurant La Residance. 220 W. Rosemary St. Provincial French cuisine.
Spanky's. E. Franklin St. Lively night spot in the heart of Chapel Hill.
Savoy Restaurant. W. Franklin St. "Jazz in the Afternoon" Wed-Sat. Sat. night, dance to live music.
Inexpensive: **Carolina Coffee Shop.** Quaint atmosphere; good food.

DURHAM. *Expensive:* **Alexander's.** Excellent steaks and seafood.
Moderate: **Hartman's Steak House.** Famous for its steaks, banana peppers and Hartman's salad.
Inexpensive: **Bullock's Bar-B-Cue.** Specialty of the area.

GREENSBORO. *Moderate:* **Darryl's 1808.** Period restaurant and tavern. 2102 N. Church St.
The Pepper Mill. I-85 at Jamestown exit. Comfortable atmosphere, delicious food.
Inexpensive: **Stamey's Bar-B-Que.** Two locations. 908 S. Main St., and 2206 High Point Rd. Good eating.

HILLSBOROUGH. *Moderate:* **Colonial Inn.** W. King St. Revolutionary-era inn. Good homemade foods.

MONROE. *Moderate:* **Friendship Inn and Hilltop Restaurant.** Family restaurant featuring excellent southern style food.

RALEIGH. *Expensive:* **Sisters Garden of Eating.** N. Ridge Shopping Ctr. Creative cuisine at one of the finest restaurants in the city.
Moderate: **Neptune's Galley.** Good seafood, steamed oysters.

Inexpensive: **Bar-B-Que Lodge.** US 1 N. in Mini-City. Pork & chicken barbecue, Brunswick stew and cornsticks.

Hunam's. Excellent oriental food. In Fall's Village Shopping Ctr.

Piccolo Italia. Cameron Village Shopping Ctr. An excellent Italian restaurant. Veal a specialty.

WILMINGTON AND WRIGHTSVILLE BEACH. *Moderate:* **The Bridge Tender.** Steaks & seafood. Located on Inland waterway. Excellent Sunday buffet.

The Mediterranean. On beach. Seafood and Italian. One of the best.

Dry Dock. On Oleander Dr. between Wilmington and beach. Features seafood buffet.

Inexpensive: **Ballentine's** (Wilmington). Cafeteria with Southern specialties.

The Cotton Exchange. This is a restored waterfront area in Wilmington and houses several excellent eateries.

WINSTON-SALEM. *Moderate:* Salem Tavern. In Old Salem.

Staley's Charcoal Steak House. Steaks, chops.

Inexpensive: **Berry's.** Small restaurant, & the specialties are crêpes.

K&W Cafeteria. Breakfast, lunch, dinner.

Zeveley House. Quiche is one of the specialties of the house. Informal atmosphere. Enjoy brunch or lunch in one of the oldest restored houses in the city.

SOUTH CAROLINA

Charleston, Myrtle Beach, Hilton Head Island, and More

Charleston, important as a major seaport and industrial center, is above all the "Mother City of the South," a treasure trove of beautiful 18th- and 19th-century houses, gardens, and churches. Several exquisitely restored houses are open year-round. Many others welcome visitors during the annual month-long spring Festival of Houses. Also in spring, famous Cypress, Magnolia, and Middleton Place Gardens offer a feast of color. Brilliant in summer with oleanders, hydrangeas, hibiscus, roses, magnolias, and crape myrtle. All remain all open year. Middleton Place's Plantation Stableyards also offers fascinating glimpses at a working 18th-century plantation. Magnolia has a petting zoo with rare mini-horses. Nearby is Drayton Hall, considered the nation's finest example of untouched Georgian architecture. Boone Hall, on a 738-acre estate, is a beautiful plantation with original slave houses and ginhouse.

In broad and beautiful Charleston Harbor stands Fort Sumter, where the Civil War began. For Revolutionary War buffs there's Fort Moultrie on Sullivan's Island, site of the first decisive American victory over the British. Another permanent resident of this historic city, the aircraft carrier *Yorktown,* famed "Fighting Lady" of World War II, is berthed at Patriots Point across the Cooper River. Also here are the nuclear-powered *NS Savannah,* destroyer *Laffey* and submarine *Clamagore.*

Charles Towne Landing is a beautiful state park on the coastal site where the state's earliest English colonists settled in 1670. Archeological remnants of their first settlement have been unearthed, and a hand-

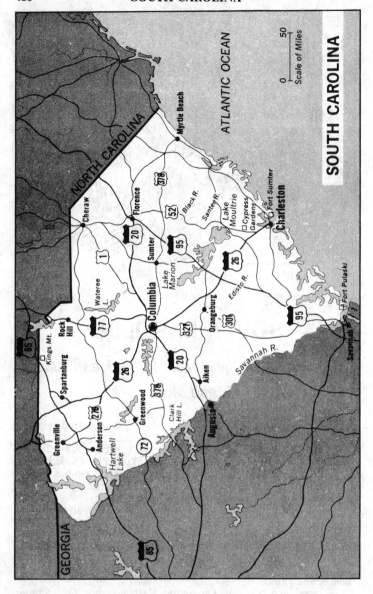

some contemporary visitor center vividly depicts three centuries of South Carolina history. Creatures indigenous to 1670s roam natural habitat Animal Forest. You may also board *The Adventure,* a replica of an 18th-century West Indies trading ketch, moored in the harbor.

Hub of the 55-mile stretch of broad, sun-splashed Atlantic beach known as the Grand Strand, Myrtle Beach is a popular family vacation center with a wide range of accommodations for your budget. You'll enjoy virtually every water-related activity, excellent golf courses, tennis, sports fishing, special events ranging from fishing tournaments to flower shows, plantation tours, and musical festivals.

Hilton Head, Fripp, Kiawah, Isle of Palms, Edisto, and Seabrook islands offer some of the eastern seaboard's finest and most famous resort facilities, many championship golf courses, superb tennis, horseback riding, children's programs, fully equipped marinas, and boat rentals—all in idyllic subtropical settings.

The state's second oldest city, dating from 1711, the lovely old port of Beaufort on the IntraCoastal Waterway, has many blocks of pre-Revolutionary and antebellum houses. An early center of rice, indigo, and—later—cotton production, it's now a thriving oyster and shrimp center. Hunting Island, 16 miles east, is a 5,000-acre state park offering palm-lined beaches, camping, picnicking, hiking trails, boating, fishing, swimming, and golf.

Located in the midlands, Columbia is the state capital and its largest city, as well as home of the University of South Carolina. Its three-story State House, still showing Civil War scars from General Sherman's artillery, has a statue of John C. Calhoun, famed antebellum statesman. Riverbanks Zoological Gardens, one of nation's most modern, is notable for habitat areas where creatures roam freely.

Hub of industrial Piedmont, "textile center of the world," prosperous Greenville is also a cultural center. Ultra-modern Greenville County Art Museum boasts the nation's most complete collection of Andrew Wyeth paintings. The art gallery of Bob Jones University has one of Southeast's major collections of religious art.

Francis Marion National Forest, on the coastal plains north of Charleston, was named for the "Swamp Fox," hero-general of the American Revolution. Indians, and Spanish and French explorers roamed the area, following waterways flanked by moss-covered gums, cypress, and tall loblolly pines. Camping, picnicking, boating, fishing, and hiking trails are available.

Cape Romain National Wildlife Refuge northeast of Charleston is an unspoiled island marsh and sea area, haven for shell collectors and bird watchers. Savannah National Wildlife Refuge, among the nation's oldest, teems with wildfowl, deer, raccoons, and alligators. Santee National Wildlife Refuge is a major sanctuary for thousands of Canada geese and other waterfowl.

PRACTICAL INFORMATION

FOR SOUTH CAROLINA

 HOW TO GET THERE. There's *air service* to Charleston, Columbia, Greenville–Spartanburg, and Myrtle Beach. *By car:* Principal routes through South Carolina are I-95, I-85, I-20, and I-26. US 17, the "coastal highway," parallels the shoreline. *By bus:* Greyhound and *Trailways* serve the state. *By train:* Amtrak goes into Dillon, Florence, Kingstree, Charleston, Yemassee, Clemson, Camden, Columbia, Denmark, Spartanburg, Greenville.

HOW TO GET AROUND. Car rentals can be arranged at all airports. Air and bus services link cities within the state.

TOURIST INFORMATION. The South Carolina Division of Tourism, Box 71, Columbia, SC 29202, will supply detailed information.

MUSEUMS AND GALLERIES. Charleston: *Charleston Museum* has fine collections of arts, crafts, furniture, and textiles from the state's early days. *Gibbes Art Gallery* displays notable Oriental collections, paintings, prints, sculptures, and miniatures. A replica of the Confederate submarine *Hunley* is displayed on the grounds. *Old Exchange and Customs House* includes the Provost Dungeon; award-winning documentary film, "Dear Charleston," is also shown here. *City Hall Council Chamber* is a mini-museum of relics and paintings, including Trumbull's famous portrait of George Washington.

Clemson: *Keowee-Toxaway Visitors Center* has fascinating ultra-modern three-dimensional energy displays, offers nature trails, picnicking along lake shore. Admission is free.

Columbia: *Columbia Museums of Art and Science* feature a fine collection of Renaissance art from Kress Foundation, and also include an aquarium, nature garden, and planetarium.

Rock Hill: *The Museum of York County* is one of the nation's finest regional natural history museums. Maurice Stans African Hall has the world's largest collection of mounted African animals in environmental settings.

HISTORIC SITES. Camden, the state's oldest inland town, is the site of *Historic Camden,* a restored Revolutionary-era settlement with lovely old houses, remains of forts, and a small animal farm.

Historic Pendleton District, dating from 1789, is a three-county area encompassing historic houses and an early agricultural museum. It includes *Fort Hill,* home of John C. Calhoun, on the Clemson University campus.

At *Cowpens National Battlefield,* the British sustained one of their worst disasters in the southern Revolutionary War campaign, starting Cornwallis on the road to ultimate defeat.

Kings Mountain National Military Park, site of the crucial Revolutionary battle, is off SC 21, just south of I–85.

Andrew Jackson State Park, north of Lancaster in heart of scenic *Waxhaw Hills,* is where "Old Hickory," seventh U.S. President, was born. The exact birth spot is disputed, however, and both Carolinas claim him!

TOURS. *Fort Sumter Tours* offers boat rides and also guided tours of the national monument. *Gray Line* has boat tours of Charleston harbor, plus several motorcoach tours of the city and area. There are several other bus, limousine, carriage, bicycle, cassette and individually guided tours of Historic Charleston.

DRINKING LAWS. Mixed drinks (sold by "mini-bottles") may be ordered in licensed restaurants, hotels, and motels. State package liquor stores sell by the bottle except Sundays and holidays. Legal age 21; 18 for beer and wine.

SPORTS. With 36 fine courses, the Grand Strand is one of the east coast's major *golf* centers. Add to this the dozen-plus fine championship courses of the resort islands and state resort parks, and duffer and pro alike can choose from miles of fairways, and hundreds of traps and hazards. In the state's mild climate, golf is a year-round activity.

For *fishing* buffs there are rainbow and brown trout in the mountainous areas of the western counties, and striped bass in the Santee-Cooper Lakes. Surf casting is popular all along the Grand Strand and in the islands, and charter boats offer deep-sea fishing in the Gulf Stream from Charleston and the islands.

Top spectator sports include the spring Carolina Cup and autumn Colonial Cup steeplechase events in Camden, the late March Sea Pines Heritage Golf Classic on Hilton Head Island and the Labor Day Southern 500 Stock Car Race in Darlington.

SHOPPING. Charleston has many fine antique and specialty shops and art galleries. Look for beguiling "Charleston bonnets" and smock dresses. *Historic Charleston Reproductions,* 105 Broad St., and *The Thomas Elfe Workshops,* 54

Queen St., have reproductions of Charleston furniture and accessories. An enclosed portion of the historic old City Market has many attractive small shops; this is a good place to buy distinctive, hand-woven seagrass and palmetto baskets. Also see the basketmakers at work, and buy their wares, at stands along U.S. 17 north of Charleston. Handcrafted hammocks can be found on Pawleys Island on U.S. 17.

SPECIAL EVENTS. Late May to early June, Charleston is the site of the annual *Spoleto Festival USA,* a major international festival of performing and visual arts, founded by famed composer Gian Carlo Menotti as a counterpart to Italy's Spoleto festival.

HOTELS AND MOTELS. Price categories and ranges, based on double occupancy, are: *Deluxe:* $75–160; *Expensive:* $55–75; *Moderate:* $35–55; *Inexpensive:* under $35. Even some of the more expensive resorts offer package plans and off-season rates which cut costs considerably.

BEAUFORT. *Moderate:* **Best Western Sea Island.** 1015 Bay St. Attractive motel facing the bay has color TV, swimming pool, restaurants.

Inexpensive: **Lord Carteret Motel.** 301 Carteret St. In the center of the city. Refrigerators, color TV, kitchenettes, free in-room movies.

Budget Host—The Pines Motel. Jct. US 21 and SC 170. Color cable TV, pool. Large, landscaped grounds. Hot sandwiches, soft drinks on premises; near restaurants. Pets.

CHARLESTON. *Deluxe:* **Battery Carriage House.** 20 S. Battery St. Delightful small luxury guest house has 10 beautifully furnished antebellum apartments, all with kitchen facilities. Color TV, continental breakfast, bicycles for touring the city.

The Coach House. 39 East Battery. First floor has bedroom with queen-size canopy bed, kitchen, dining area; second floor, twin beds, living room with queen-size pull-out sofa bed, piazza overlooking harbor. Continental breakfast, color TV and books on each floor, doghouse within the dog yard.

The Elliott House Inn. 78 Queen St. 1861 structure houses 26 rooms, each with distinctive 18th-century-style furnishings. Continental breakfasts brought to rooms on silver trays or served al fresco in bricked courtyard. Sip wine by the fountain at twilight as St. Michael's Church chimes toll the hour. Courtyard Jacuzzi; complimentary bicycles.

Indigo Inn. Pinckney at Meeting. In the heart of the historic district, the inn offers 18th-century ease, 20th-century comfort. Continental breakfast; daily newspapers are provided.

Lodge Alley Inn. Lodge Alley. Rooms, suites and two-bedroom penthouse with Colonial atmosphere. Oriental carpets, period reproductions, courtyard gardens. On premises are French Quarter Restaurant, Charleston Tea Party Lounge.

Mills House Hotel. 115 Meeting St. Antique furnishings and glowing chandeliers give unusual charm and ambience to this historic, reconstructed hostelry with its 20th-century amenities. Beautifully furnished lobby, guest rooms. Lounge, entertainment, pool. Part of Holiday Inn system.

Planters Inn. 110 N. Market St. Magnificently decorated with opulent fabrics and furnishings, including mahogany four-poster beds. Complimentary newspapers and Italian chocolates. There's a concierge, 24-hour room service. In the heart of Charleston's historic district.

Sheraton-Charleston Hotel. 170 Lockwood Dr., 1 blk. N of US 17. City's newest luxury hotel is elegantly furnished and has its own concierge. Dining rooms; entertainment in lounge.

The Sweet Grass Inn. 23 Vendue Range. Eight distinctively furnished guest rooms in completely restored 1800 ca. house. Rooms complimented with fresh flowers, fruit, morning newspaper. Relax around open-hearth living room fire or sun on the roof terrace on balmy days.

Swordgate Inn. 111 Tradd St. Several rooms available in the small, intimate inn off the courtyard of an 18th-century house. No credit cards.

Vendue Inn. 19 Vendue Range. Luxurious guest rooms feature canopied and poster beds, Oriental rugs, and 18th-century furniture. Complimentary wine and cheese are served in the courtyard. Continental breakfast.

Expensive: **The Francis Marion Ramada Hotel.** 387 King St. This conveniently located landmark hotel has been impeccably restored and refurbished. Extras, at no charge, include daily cocktail party, nightcap, morning paper at your door, full breakfast.

Moderate: **Days Inn.** 155 Meeting St. Color TV, pool, dining room, lounge with entertainment.

Heart of Charleston. 200 Meeting St. Pool, coffee shop, cocktail lounge.

COLUMBIA. *Deluxe:* **Columbia Marriott Hotel.** 1200 Hampton St. Indoor pool, whirlpool. 2 dining rooms, lounge.

Moderate to Expensive: **Holiday Inn.** Three locations: 630 Assembly St., jct. US 1 and I–26, US exit 1 at I–20. Pools, dining rooms, coffee shops, lounges.

Moderate: **Quality Inns.** 2 locations: I–20 at Broad River Rd.; I–20 at Two Notch Rd. Color cable TV, some kitchenettes. Pools, restaurants, lounges. Facilities for the handicapped.

Best Western Inn. 2 locations: US 76 and 378 E, I–26 and SC 302. Restaurants, lounges, some senior citizens' discounts, under 12 free in room with parents.

Inexpensive: **Days Inn.** Two locations: Jct. I–26, SC 302; and I–20, US 1. Both have pool, restaurant.

GREENVILLE. *Deluxe:* **Hyatt Regency Greenville.** 220 N. Main St. Brand-new luxury hotel has stunning eight-story atrium lobby, two elegant restaurants, two unusual lounges. Entertainment.

Moderate: **Holiday Inn.** Two locations: 27 S. Pleasantburg Dr.; and I–85 at Exit 46. Both have dining rooms, entertainment, pools, color TV, kennels. Golf, indoor tennis, racquetball, sauna.

Howard Johnson's South. US 25 & 291, N. of Jct. I–85. Cable TV (color), movies, pool. Seniors' discount.

HILTON HEAD ISLAND. *Deluxe:* **Hilton Head Inn.** Oceanfront. Accommodations in beautifully furnished rooms with contemporary decor, and in villas and cottages. Dining rooms, lounges, entertainment. Pool. Complete resort facilities of Sea Pines Plantation: superb golf, tennis, children's programs.

Hyatt at Palmetto Dunes. Oceanfront. Superb resort hotel has fine dining in elegant Hugo's, lounges, live entertainment, pool. Golf, tennis, all resort facilities at neighboring Palmetto Dunes.

Mariner's Inn–A Clarion Hotel. In Palmetto Dunes Resort. Large, luxurious ocean-view units all have kitchens. Pool, beach, sauna, fishing, golf, children's programs, health club. Lounge, entertainment.

Marriott's Hilton Head Resort. Oceanfront, in Shipyard Plantation. Dramatically beautiful new luxury hotel has spectacular five-story atrium lobby, fine dining rooms, lounges, pool bar, exercise rooms, saunas. Golf, tennis at adjacent Hilton Head Golf and Racquet Clubs.

Moderate to Deluxe: **Holiday Inn.** Oceanfront. Golf, tennis, marina privileges. Dining room, disco, lounge.

Moderate to *Expensive:* **Port Royal Inn.** Oceanfront. Inn rooms and villas. Dining, pool, golf, tennis, at Port Royal Plantation.

Sea Crest Motel. Oceanfront. Superb Captains Table dining room specializes in Continental European cuisine. Pool, wading pool, putting green, bicycles, golf and tennis privileges. Marina, rental and charter boats.

ISLE OF PALMS. *Deluxe:* **Wild Dunes Beach & Racquet Club.** Championship golf course, tennis, water sports, marina. Accommodations in ocean, golf, or marsh villas; fine dining at Edgar's. Cocktail lounge.

KIAWAH ISLAND. *Deluxe:* **Kiawah Island Inn.** Oceanfront setting on lush, wooded island. Accommodations in inn and villas. Excellent dining rooms, lounge, entertainment. Golf, tennis, children's programs, pools, bicycling, sauna, complete resort activities. Numerous vacation packages.

MYRTLE BEACH. *Moderate to Deluxe:* **Myrtle Beach Hilton Hotel.** Beachside, in Arcadian Shores. Luxury resort hotel has 14-story atrium lobby, Continental dining in elegant Alfredo's, lounges, entertainment. Shopping, social program, tennis, golfing on championship course. All rooms oceanfront.

Sheraton Myrtle Beach Inn. 7100 N. Ocean Blvd. Superb dining, dancing in Pinnacle Supper Club. Lounges, entertainment, tennis club, golf privileges. All rooms oceanfront.

The Breakers. Oceanfront at 21 Ave. N. Pools, fishing, children's program, tennis & golf privileges. Dining room, lounges, entertainment.

Moderate to Expensive: **Sea Mist Resort.** 1200 S. Ocean Blvd. Oceanfront & across from ocean. Pools, surf fishing, putting green, children's & social programs, playground. Golf privileges. Gift shop & arcade. Restaurant, cocktails.

Ocean Dunes. 74th–75th Ave., N. Oceanfront. Pools, fishing, children's program, tennis & golf privileges. Dining room, lounges, entertainment.

Moderate: **Casa Maria Motor Lodge.** 2703 N. Kings Hwy. Pool, tennis, golf privileges. Some refrigerators. Restaurant nearby.

Ocean Spray Motel. 1304 S. Ocean Blvd. Family oriented. Pools, restaurant adjacent.

Inexpensive: **Lakeside Motel.** 6805 N. Kings Hwy. Pool, playground, putting green, lawn games. Own lake, fishing, boating. Picnic tables. Family oriented. Restaurant nearby.

SEABROOK ISLAND. *Deluxe:* **Seabrook Island Club.** Luxurious accommodations in fully equipped villas and cottages on resort island. Beach Club and Island House—open to all guests—are centers for gourmet dining and leisure activities. Championship golf courses, tennis center, water sports, equestrian center, bicycling. Children's programs in season, many vacation packages.

 DINING OUT. Price ranges for semi–à la carte or complete dinners are: *Expensive:* $20 and up; *Moderate:* $10 –20; *Inexpensive:* under $10. Not included are drinks, tax, and tip. Coastal seafood is superb. Don't miss such Low Country specialties as she-crab soup, and benne (sesame) seed wafers!

CHARLESTON. *Expensive:* **Barbadoes Room.** Mills House Hotel, 115 Meeting St. Low Country/Continental cuisine in elegant setting.

The East Bay Trading Company, East Bay and Queen Sts. Stately brick structure, former warehouse, features seafood, continental and native cuisine on three levels wrapped around skylight-topped atrium. Antiques, artifacts, lavish greenery lend a warm, relaxed atmosphere.

Perdita's. 10 Exchange St. Small, elegant, low key, this is one of the South's best dining rooms. Reservations essential!

Silks. The Planters Inn. Takes its name from the collection of racing silks and equestrian paintings hung throughout the bar and dining room. Features grilled game, beef, lamb and seafood entrees. A superb collection of wines fills an entire wall.

Moderate–Expensive: **Colony House.** 35 Prioleau St. Low Country dishes, seafood, and steaks.

Moderate: **Henry's.** 54 Market St. Rambling, unpretentious restaurant is a great local favorite. Ask to be seated in the bar!

Inexpensive–Moderate: **The Lorelei.** Shem Creek, US 17 N. For family dining. Seafood is a specialty.

The Trawler. Shem Creek, US 17 N. Family dining, and seafood.

Inexpensive: **Harold's Cabin.** Meeting St. Piggly Wiggly. In-the-know Charlestonians drop by for lunch, and so should you. Ideal place to shop for take-home treats.

GREENVILLE. *Moderate:* **Ye Olde Fireplace.** 291 Pleasantburg Dr. Great steaks, seafood. Dancing, name entertainment in attractive supper club atmosphere. Dress code. Children's menus.

HILTON HEAD ISLAND. *Expensive:* **Fulvio's.** 33 New Orleans Rd. Continental dining with emphasis on Italian specialties.

Moderate: **The Boilers.** US 278, 1 mi. from bridge. Fine fresh seafood. Family favorite.

Hudson's. Shrimp docks, Skull Creek. Superb fresh seafood from their own docks. Local favorite.

MYRTLE BEACH. *Moderate—Expensive:* **Christy's.** US 17 North Myrtle Beach. Seafood and prime ribs specialties. Entertainment, dancing.

Slug's Rib. US 17 N. Superb restaurant serves only one entree—prime rib of beef.

Moderate: **Crab House.** US 17 N. on Restaurant Row. All-you-can-eat seafood. Casual dress.

The Rice Planters. 6707 Kings Hwy. N. Superb Low Country specialties in attractive rustic setting decorated with artifacts, antiques from rice-planting era.

Sea Captain's. 3002 N. Ocean Blvd. Superb seafood in charming ocean-front setting. Also at Murrells Inlet, S.C.

Inexpensive: **Morrison's Cafeteria.** Myrtle Square Mall. Fine home-cooked food, desserts. One of a regional chain.

Western Steer Steak House. Two locations: 512 Hwy. 17 S., 8000 Hwy. 17 N. Steaks, steak and seafood platters. Children's menu.

TENNESSEE

Nashville, Frontier Country, and the Lakes

Nashville has often been called the Athens of the South, a fitting name for a city known not only for its Greek Revival architecture, but for its special interest in the arts and education. The capital of Tennessee, Nashville was first settled in 1779 by James Robertson and a group of pioneers who built Fort Nashborough on the west bank of the Cumberland River—a log stockade that has now been reconstructed at First Ave. North and Church St.

By the 1830s, the log construction in Nashville was being replaced by limestone and marble, and the influence of Greek architecture began to be felt. In Centennial Park there's a reconstruction of the Athenian Parthenon.

Education plays an important part in Nashville life. Vanderbilt University, the George Peabody College for Teachers, Scarritt College, Belmont College, Meharry Medical College, and Fisk University are only a few of the many institutions in Nashville. Nashville also boasts several art galleries, including the Carl Van Vechten Gallery of Fine Arts, George Peabody College Museum, Vanderbilt University Gallery, and the Tennessee Botanical Gardens and Fine Arts Center.

The fine new Tennessee State Museum in the Polk Cultural Complex is highlighted by "Life in Tennessee" exhibits. The Cumberland Museum and Science Center on Ridley Avenue has displays of realistic animal homes from around the world, and offers frequent planetarium and laser light shows.

On Charlotte Ave., overlooking Memorial Plaza, the majestic Tennessee Capitol stands as a monument to the people of the Volunteer State and to its designer, William Strickland. The Governor's Residence on South Curtiswood La. in a beautiful residential area, is open

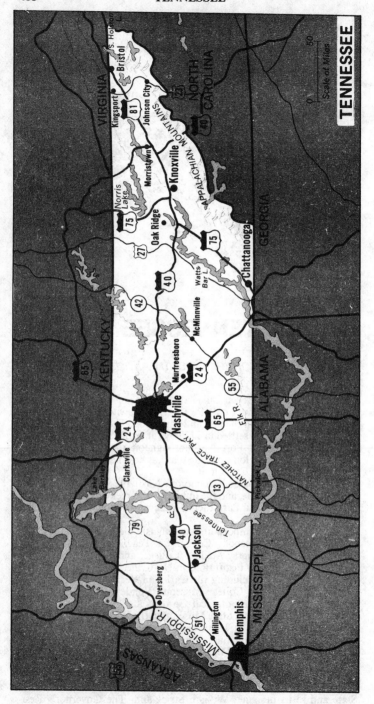

by appointment Tuesday and Thursday mornings. At 1908 Grand Ave. is The Upper Room, where the chapel has a polychrome wood carving of Leonardo da Vinci's painting *The Last Supper*.

Think of Nashville and the Grand Ole Opry comes to mind. At the dazzling Opry House, 2800 Opryland Drive about six miles from downtown, the lively "Grand Ole Opry" radio show is presented on stage each Friday and Saturday night. For tickets contact: Grand Ole Opry Ticket Information, 2802 Opryland Dr., Nashville 37214; tel. 615–889–3060. Opryland U.S.A. theme park next to the Opry House showcases American music, sprightly live entertainment, food, crafts, amusement rides, and family fun. Nashville's famous sound and some of its brightest stars are featured at the Country Music Hall of Fame and Museum, 4 Music Square East, the head of "Music Row" where more than half of all the record singles recorded in the nation are produced.

Outside town, off US 70S, you won't want to miss the estate of Belle Meade, once the site of the Dunham Station on the Natchez Trace and now a center of antiquity and a museum. This imposing Greek revival building, often called the "Queen of Tennessee Plantations," was constructed in 1853 by Gen. William Giles Harding. At one time the stables were famous for breeding some of the world's finest race horses.

In Hendersonville, is Music Village, U.S.A., now partially completed. Country music is the theme, with live performances by top stars, exhibits, and down-home food.

One of the most popular attractions in the Nashville area is The Hermitage, the hauntingly beautiful home of Andrew Jackson, thirteen miles east of Nashville on US 70. The interior furnishings are the original pieces used by Jackson and his wife Rachel, and the gardens have been maintained according to her design. The tombs of Old Hickory, Rachel, and other family members are in one corner of the formal garden.

South of Nashville along US 41 you will find other historical places —the Sam Davis Home in Smyrna, honoring the 19-year-old Confederate hero; the Stones River National Battlefield, site of the famous Civil War battle; and Murfreesboro, capital of Tennessee from 1819 to 1825, where Oaklands, one of the outstanding antebellum houses in Middle Tennessee, is located. Eighteen miles north on US 231 is the 8,300-acre Cedars of Lebanon State Park, with a forest of red cedar believed to be the largest in the nation.

Seventy miles west is the town of Hurricane Mills, owned by famed country singer Loretta Lynn and her husband Mooney. It includes a dude ranch, campground, restaurant, Western store, arts, and crafts shop, and Old Mill museum, with personal memorabilia of the "Coal Miner's Daughter."

PRACTICAL INFORMATION FOR NASHVILLE

HOW TO GET THERE. *By air:* Direct flights on *USAir, American, Delta, Eastern, Piedmont, Republic, TWA, United, Ozark,* and various commuter airlines. From Toronto, via *American Airlines. By car:* Interstate highways 24, 65, and 40 serve Nashville.

SPECIAL EVENTS. *May:* Second Saturday, Iroquois Steeplechase. *June:* International Country Music Fan Fair. *July:* Busch 420 Winston Cup Grand National Stockcar Race, Nashville International Raceway. *September:* Opryland Rock 'n' Roll Revival, Tennessee State Fair at Fairgrounds, Tennessee Grass Roots Days at Centennial Park. *November:* Tennessee Fall Crafts Fair. *December:* Cheekwood's "Trees of Christmas," Cheekwood Fine Arts Center.

MUSEUMS AND GALLERIES. *Tennessee Agricultural Museum, Ellington Center; Tennessee Game Farm Zoo,* 18 mi. NW off I–24 W, wild animals, including endangered species; *Tennessee State Museum,* 505 Deaderick St.; a general museum; *Travellers' Rest Historic House,* Farrell Pkwy just off US 31 S.; *George Peabody College Museum,* 21st Ave.; *Vanderbilt University Gallery,* on campus, West End Ave. at 21st; *Tennessee Botanical Gardens and Fine Arts Center,* Cheekwood, Cheek Rd., an art center and botanical gardens; *Country Music Hall of Fame and Museum,* 4 Music Square E.; *Ryman Auditorium,* 116 Fifth Ave. N., former home of Grand Ole Opry; *Country Music Stars Wax Museum and Mall,* 118 16th Ave. S.; *Nashville Parthenon,* Centennial Park, world's only replica of the famous Athenian temple; *Cumberland Museum and Science Center,* 800 Ridley Ave. in Fort Negley Park; *RCA's Original Studio B,* Corner Music Square W and Roy Acuff Place.

HISTORIC SITES. *Fort Nashborough,* 170 1st Ave. N., the 1780 replica of the first settlement at Nashville; *Belle Meade Mansion* on Leake Ave. off US 70 (Harding Road); *The Hermitage,* home of President Andrew Jackson, on Rachel's Lane, 13 miles east of Nashville.

SPECTATOR SPORTS. NASCAR stock car racing, Nashville Speedway at State Fairgrounds. May to October; Iroquois Steeplechase, second Saturday in May; Longhorn Classic Rodeo, Municipal Auditorium, August. All American 400 ASA/All Pro Stock Car Race, October.

TOURS. *Gray Line* of Nashville, 501 Broadway, offers tours featuring homes of the stars, Opryland, a Country Music Food and Fun Picnic Tour, Historic Nashville, and The Hermitage. *Opryland Travel Company* offers many Grand Ole Opry and country-music-oriented tours.

SPECIAL INTEREST TOURS. Riverboat replicas *Captain Ann* and *Music City Queen* cruise the Cumberland River, daytime and evenings Mar.–May, Sept.–Oct., departing from the foot of Broadway at 1st Avenue. Special tours of the State Capitol at Capitol Plaza downtown, and the Governor's Residence, 882 South Curtiswood, are also available.

HOTELS AND MOTELS. Listed in order of price. Based on double occupancy in peak season, price categories are as follows: *Deluxe:* $95–$150; *Expensive:* $75–$95; *Moderate:* $50–$75; *Inexpensive:* under $50.

Deluxe. **Opryland Hotel.** 2800 Opryland Dr., at Opryland USA. Colonial design, lavish decor, 614 rooms, pools, restaurants, lounges, dancing, entertainment, shops.

Expensive: **Hyatt Regency.** 623 Union St. Restaurants, bars, garage, liquor store, etc. The perfect headquarters for a Nashville stay. Stunning atrium lobby, 478 rooms.

Moderate: **Airport Hilton Inn.** International Plaza. At airport.

Holiday Inn. Six locations: 350 Harding Pl.; 230 W. Trinity Lane; 981 Murfreesboro Rd.; 2613 West End Ave., 2200 Elm Hill Pike at Briley Pkwy., I–24 and SR 96, Murfreesboro.

Inexpensive to Moderate: **Days Inn.** Four locations: I–65 and Trinity Lane; 1101 Bell Road; 321 Plus Park Blvd.; I–40 and Old Hickory Blvd.

Inexpensive: **Continental Inns of America.** Four locations: 710 James Robertson Pkwy., 711 Union, 303 Interstate Dr., 320 Murfreesboro Rd. All inviting.

La Quinta. 2001 MetroCenter Blvd., 4311 Sidco Dr. Members of excellent, fast-growing economy system. Restaurants adjacent.

Quality Inn Bell Rd. I–24 & Bell Rd. Restaurant, lounge, live entertainment nightly. Pool, golf and tennis nearby.

Ramada Inn. Four locations: 840 James Robertson Pkwy.; 709 Spence La. (Airport); I–65 and Trinity Lane; I–24 and Harding Pl.

RESTAURANTS. Listed according to price categories, for a complete dinner, as follows: *Expensive,* over $20; *Moderate,* $10–20; *Inexpensive,* under $10. Not included are drinks, tax and tip.

Expensive: **Hugo's.** Hyatt Regency Hotel, 625 Union St. American-Continental, posh.

Julian's. 2412 West End Ave. Classic French, chef owned, much flair.

Moderate: **Mario's.** 1915 West End Ave. Italian-Continental-American, elegant decor. "In" favorite of celebrities and locals.

The Brass Rail. 206½ Printers Alley. Steaks, ribs, flambé, in popular entertainment district.

Polaris. Atop Hyatt Regency Hotel, revolving restaurant, superb views.

Inexpensive: **B & W Cafeteria.** 3835 Green Hills Village Dr.

Morrison's. One Hundred Oaks Shopping Center; Rivergate Mall; Hickory Hollow Mall.

Po Folks. 3737 Nolensville Rd. Good home-style cooking in family atmosphere; four other locations.

EXPLORING TENNESSEE

Bristol, astride the Tennessee–Virginia line, is a popular gateway to the Volunteer State. Southward is a magnificent outdoor playground with beautiful mountains, and picturesque lakes impounded by massive TVA dams. A portion of the Great Smoky Mountains National Park, the most popular in the nation, lies in Tennessee.

Head down US 421 southeast to Mountain City, which provides arresting views of the lake impounded by Tennessee Valley Authority's South Holston Dam and the dam itself. Then take US 321 to Johnson City, a major tobacco-auction market with two TVA dams within easy driving distance, Boone and Fort Patrick Henry. South of Johnson City is Jonesboro, oldest town in Tennessee. On US 11E, near the little town of Limestone, is Davy Crockett Birthplace Park.

Gatlinburg, a charming resort community, abuts the entrance to the Great Smoky Mountains National Park, where great virgin forests and wildflowers of incredible beauty cover the mountains. Drive southeast on US 441 to Newfound Gap for one of the most beautiful views of the park. In town, enjoy Gatlinburg Sky Lift, a half-mile cable car ride up Crockett Mountain. In winter there is skiing at Ober Gatlinburg, and the town also boasts the American Historical Wax Museum, Christus Gardens with wax models of incidents in the life of Christ, and Smoky Mountain Trout Farms, where anglers can catch all the trout they want for free. In the National Park the Cades Cove Open-Air Museum is on the site of a former pioneer community. Camping and hiking are also offered visitors to the Park.

Six miles north of Gatlinburg is Pigeon Forge, where visitors of all ages enjoy Silver Dollar City, a replica 1870's mountain community with working craftsfolk, along with thrill rides, old-time music and shows. Then it's on to Knoxville.

Site of the gala 1982 World's Fair, Knoxville also played an important part in the Civil War. Its earliest link to the past is the Blount Mansion at 200 West Hill Avenue, built for the territorial governor William Blount. Six miles east on Thorngrove Pike is the first stone house in Knox County, Ramsey House, built in 1797. The University of Tennessee campus offers other attractions, including the Estes Kefauver Memorial Library, the Frank H. McClung Museum, and Neyland Stadium. Several homes of early settlers are open to visitors. Catalyst for unprecedented downtown urban renewal, the 70-acre World's Fair site is now an attractive permanent recreation area welcoming visitors to the heart of the city.

Before heading south to Chattanooga, visit Oak Ridge, once a top secret atom bomb town. There are guided tours, demonstrations, and exhibits at the American Museum of Science and Energy on Jefferson Circle, conducted by the U.S. Atomic Energy Commission. Nine miles south of Oak Ridge on State 95 is the Melton Hill Dam, a TVA dam finished in 1963. South of US 11, near Lenoir City, is Fort Loudoun Dam. Continuing south, plan to visit the mysterious underground Lost Sea near Sweetwater.

A lovely city set in the midst of steep mountain ridges, Chattanooga was the place where great Indian trails joined, and it became a Cherokee trading center called Ross's Landing. In 1837, Cherokee Indians being forcibly removed to lands west of the Mississippi embarked from here for the "Trail of Tears." Three important Civil War battles were fought in Chattanooga. Today Chattanooga offers a variety of attractions—the Chattanooga Choo Choo in the vintage Southern Railway Station converted to an attractive dining and shopping center, and the world's steepest passenger railroad to the top of Lookout Mountain, where the Battle above the Clouds was fought in 1863. Take the railroad or drive up Lookout Mountain to Point Park, where there is a museum and observatory. Opposite the Park is Lookout Mountain Museum, and nearby is Cravens House, built in 1856. Deep in the mountains are the twin caves of Ruby Falls–Lookout Mountain, and visitors may take an elevator down 1,120 feet. Nearby are the Rock City Gardens with spectacular scenery, and Confederama, at the foot of Lookout Mountain, with its miniature soldiers. There are several museums and galleries located in Chattanooga itself for the lovers of art and history, including Houston Antique Museum, Hall of Presidents Wax Museum, and the Tennessee Valley Railroad Museum.

Two TVA dams worth visiting are Chickamauga Dam on State 153, and Nickajack Dam seven miles west off US 41.

Leaving Chattanooga, you will pass Monteagle, where the summer months are given over to the arts; and Shelbyville, Tennessee's walking-horse country where each August the Tennessee Walking Horse National Celebration is held.

Memphis

Memphis, largest city in the state and hub of the Mid-South, is today the world's largest spot cotton market and hardwood lumber center. In PeeWee's Saloon on Beale Street, W.C. Handy blew those first lonesome notes and became the "Father of the Blues." And in a Memphis recording studio, the late Elvis Presley launched the career that made him "King of Rock 'n Roll."

Memphis is the home of numerous theater groups and nightclubs. The Brooks Memorial Art Gallery in Overton Park has an outstanding collection, and the Museum of Natural History and Industrial Arts, called the "Pink Palace" because of its unique Georgia pink marble exterior, has a distinguished African collection. The Magevney House, oldest pioneer home in Memphis, was home of an early schoolmaster. Children will be delighted with the Overton Park Zoo and Aquarium.

Recently opened on Mud Island in the Mississippi River is the impressive new $63-million Mississippi River Museum, a 50-acre complex dedicated to life on the Lower Mississippi.

Six miles south of Memphis is Chucalissa, a prehistoric Indian village which has been excavated, partially reconstructed, and is now open to the public.

From Memphis, drive northeast to Jackson, home of "Casey" Jones. The Casey Jones Home and Museum at Casey Jones Village contains nostalgic reminders of early railroading days.

Northeast of Jackson is Tennessee's biggest state-owned recreational area—Natchez Trace State Park. Continue on to Reelfoot Lake in northwestern Tennessee. This lake was created by the New Madrid earthquakes in 1811-12; the Mississippi River filled up the depression made by the quakes, and today weird shapes of the old forest emerge above the water.

Then on to Kentucky Lake, formed by the largest of the TVA dams, and Paris Landing State Park. US 79 then skirts the southern border of Land Between the Lakes—an elongated strip of 170,000 acres formed by a TVA dam on the Tennessee River and Lake Barkley, which is being developed as a national demonstration in outdoor recreation development. West of Dover you will come to Fort Donelson National Military Park, where Ulysses S. Grant captured first Fort Henry and then Fort Donelson.

Driving eastward to the Upper Cumberland country you can visit the minuscule town of Rugby, the last Utopian community in the United States, founded by a colony of British in the late 1800s. The Cumberland Gap National Historical Park commemorates Daniel Boone and the intrepid pioneers who hacked a road through the wilderness to the "dark and bloody grounds" of Kentucky. At Lincoln Memorial University in Harrogate, the South's largest collection of memorabilia about the Great Emancipator is on display.

PRACTICAL INFORMATION FOR TENNESSEE

HOW TO GET THERE. *By air:* Direct flights on several major national and regional airlines to Memphis, Nashville, Knoxville, Chattanooga. Interstate highways 24, 40, 65, 75, 81, and I–55 crisscross Tennessee to and from neighboring states. *By bus:* There is good service into the state from numerous bus lines.

By train: Amtrak serves Memphis and Dyersburg on the route between Chicago and New Orleans.

HOW TO GET AROUND. Many airlines operate between cities within the state, as do major bus lines. For an unusual carefree vacation, consider renting a houseboat to cruise the TVA Lakes. Boats may be rented from *Hixson Marina,* Big Ridge Rd., Chattanooga.

TOURIST INFORMATION. Fourteen welcome centers are conveniently located on the interstate highways entering Tennessee. Information about major attractions, events, state parks may be obtained from the Tennessee Department of Tourist Development, P.O. Box 23170, Nashville, TN 37202; about Great Smokies from Park Superintendent, Great Smoky Mountains National Park, Gatlinburg, TN 37738; about TVA lakes from Tennessee Valley Authority, Knoxville, TN 37902.

PARKS AND FORESTS. In addition to the Great Smoky Mountains National Park, outdoor recreational opportunities also abound in the Cherokee National Forest in East Tennessee. The state park system is one of the best in the nation. Attractive resort inns are located in several of the parks, including Fall Creek Falls Park near Pikeville in a rugged mountain area, and Pickwick Landing Resort Park at Pickwick Dam on the Tennessee River near Shiloh National Military Park. Besides the national and state parks, camping is available in the TVA's *Land Between the Lakes* recreational area and the *Cumberland Gap National Historical Park.*

TOURS. *By car:* Drive through *Reflection Riding,* 300 acres in Chattanooga with historical details and nature trails. Tape recorders are available for auto tours in the Great Smoky Mountains National Park, and may be obtained at Christus Gardens, Gatlinburg, and the Museum of the Cherokee Indian, Cherokee, N.C. *By bus:* Gray Line Tours of Chattanooga, Great Smokies (from Gatlinburg, Knoxville), Memphis. *By rail: The Incline Railway,* Lookout Mountain, Chattanooga.

By boat: The *Memphis Queen Line* Riverboats, Riverside Dr., Monroe: 1½ hour cruise of the Mississippi; *Delta Queen,* and *Mississippi Queen* offer cruises on the Mississippi River, which often include Memphis.

By chair lift: Aerial Tramway to Mount Harrison, Sky Lift up Crockett Mountain, both from Gatlinburg; double chair lift at Ober Gatlinburg Ski Resort.

SPORTS. With more than 600,000 acres of water and 10,000 miles of shoreline, the state offers limitless opportunities for *fishing, boating,* and *water-skiing. Hunting, horseback riding* and *golfing* are also popular sports. Skiing areas include *Ober Gatlinbu'g Ski Resort,* 1001 Parkway. In Memphis you can see two of the nation's top college football teams play in the Liberty Bowl, as well as the Memphis Blues baseball team and the Danny Thomas Memphis Classif golf tournament in May.

SHOPPING. Distinctive bowls, mugs, ceramic birds, and animals are sold at famed Pigeon Forge Pottery near Gatlinburg. At the Old Mill across the road, stone-ground corn meal can be purchased. Numerous craft shops on Gatlinburg's main street and along Highway 73 offer mountain handiwork; the shop at Arrowmont Craft School and Center is outstanding. Overton Square in Memphis highlights an assortment of galleries, specialty shops, boutiques.

HOTELS AND MOTELS in Tennessee run the full range from the oldest establishments in many of the downtown urban areas to the slick-looking motels along the major highways. As headquarters for the gigantic *Holiday Inn* chain, Memphis has six of those establishments alone.

Listings are in order of price category. Based on double occupancy in peak season, without meals, price categories and ranges are as follows: *Expensive:* over $80; *Moderate:* $45–$80; *Inexpensive:* under $45.

CHATTANOOGA. *Moderate:* **Choo-Choo Hilton Inn.** 1400 Market St. Some rooms in lavish railroad parlor cars.

Inexpensive: **Rodeway Inn.** 6521 Ringgold Rd. Dining room. Pool, playground.

Days Inn and Lodge. 1401 Mack Smith Road near junction US 41 and I–75. Restaurant, pool.

GATLINBURG. *Moderate:* **Park Vista Hotel** (formerly Sheraton Gatlinburg). Cherokee Orchard and Airport Roads. Mountain luxury, pools, dining room, entertainment, dancing, saunas.

Mountain View Hotel. On Parkway, junction highways 441 and 73. Old-fashioned resort hotel, new wing, pool, pleasant dining room, spacious grounds.

KNOXVILLE. *Moderate:* **The Knoxville Hilton.** 501 W. Church Ave. Two dining rooms, lounge, entertainment. Heated pool, garage parking.

Quality Inn Downtown. 401 Summit Hill Dr. Restaurant, lounge, live entertainment. Pool, tennis, golf, fishing nearby.

Inexpensive: **Hyatt Regency-Knoxville.** 500 Hill Ave. S.E. Large, lovely rooms. 11-story atrium.

Best Western Cherry Tree Inn. 1500 Cherry St. Restaurant, lounge, live entertainment. Pets. Senior citizens' discount.

Inexpensive: **Days Inn.** I–75/40 & Lovell Rd., Concord. Dining room, service station.

MEMPHIS. *Expensive:* **Hyatt Regency.** 939 Ridge Lake Blvd. Heated pool, restaurant, bar. 400 rooms.

Moderate to Expensive: **Holiday Inn Crowne Plaza.** 250 N. Main St. New luxury hostelry adjoins Cook Convention Center. Gourmet restaurant, lounge, live entertainment. Whirlpool, exercise room, sun deck.

The Peabody. 149 Union Ave. Famed landmark hotel, magnificently restored to its original grandeur. Health club, heated indoor pool. Two dining rooms, coffeeshop, lounges, entertainment.

Inexpensive: **Best Western Riverbluff Inn.** 340 W. Illinois St. Color TV, pool, pets. Coin laundry. Rooftop restaurant and buffet overlooking Mississippi River. Senior citizens' discount.

Days Inn. I–55 and Brooks Rd. Restaurant, pool.

La Quinta. 42 Camilla St., 2745 Airways Blvd. Both have 24-hour Kettle Restaurants adjacent.

Inexpensive: **Admiral Benbow Inn.** 4720 Summer Ave. Nicely decorated.

Best Western Lakeland Inn. Six mi. E. on I–40, exit 20. Color TV, pool, pets, playground. Restaurant. Senior citizens' discount.

ROGERSVILLE. *Moderate:* **Hale Springs Inn.** Oldest continually running inn in Tennessee, built in 1824, the gracious hostelry has hosted Presidents Jackson, Johnson and Polk. 8 rooms, elegantly decorated with period antiques, oriental type carpets. Canopied beds and fireplaces enhance the atmosphere.

 DINING OUT. Restaurants are listed according to their price category. Categories and ranges for a complete dinner are as follows: *Expensive:* $20 and up; *Moderate:* $10–20; *Inexpensive:* under $10. Not included are drinks, tax and tip.

CHATTANOOGA. *Moderate:* **Green Room.** The Read House, 9th and Broad Sts. Continental-American, beautiful atmosphere.

Inexpensive: **Town and Country.** 110 N. Market St. Quality service.

Magic Seasons Family Restaurant. 1305 Patten Rd.; take TN 58 and GA 157 5 mi. SW on Lookout Mountain. Informal, family-style restaurant encircles a large rock; children's menu.

GATLINBURG. *Moderate:* **Open Hearth.** 1138 Parkway. Pleasant and friendly.

Pioneer Inn. 373 Parkway. Good mountain cookery in historic log house beside Little Pigeon River.

The Burning Bush. At entrance to Great Smoky Mountains National Park. Famous bountiful breakfast runs the gamut from quail to country ham; fabulous lunch and dinner in serene setting with excellent service.

KNOXVILLE. *Expensive:* **The Orangery.** 5412 Kingston Pike. Rack of lamb, beef Wellington. Own baking. Closed Sun.

Moderate: **Regas.** 318 Gay, N.W. Informal, excellent food.

Inexpensive: **Morrison's.** West Town Mall. Pleasant cafeteria, Victorian atmosphere.

MEMPHIS. *Expensive:* **Justine's.** 919 Coward Place. Creole and French cuisine in elegantly restored antebellum mansion. One of the South's most famous dining rooms.

Moderate—Expensive: **Four Flames.** 1085 Poplar Avenue. American and Continental specialties in beautiful pre-Civil War home furnished with antiques.

Moderate: **Grisanti's.** 1489 Airways Blvd. North Italian cuisine. World's most expensive bottle of wine is here.

Inexpensive: **Morrison's** and **Britling's** Cafeterias at various locations throughout the city.

MONTEAGLE. *Inexpensive:* **Jim Oliver's Smoke House Restaurant.** Sewanee Rd. (just off I–24, exit 134). Fabulous barbecue, fried chicken, country ham, steaks, ribs, catfish and much more in attractive rustic setting. Adjacent trading post has specialty, handcraft, antique shops.

ILLINOIS

Surprising Colossus of the Midwest

A visit to Illinois should begin with Chicago, the nation's second largest city. Just mention that destination in some places and people will raise their eyebrows while visions of Elliott Ness, Al Capone and Bugs Moran in big, black Packards race through their imaginations. But, though that side of the city admittedly resurfaces occasionally, Chicago is a whole new scene.

After years of standing shyly on the sidelines nursing a Second City complex, Chicago has emerged as a glamorous, sophisticated Cinderella. Visitors are beginning to discover what locals have known all along: that Chicago is a special place with a vibrant, friendly personality all its own.

Many cities have allowed their waterfronts to become an unappealing clutter of piers, shabby warehouses, and dockyards. Fortunately Chicago had the good sense to prevent this and develop its lakefrontage. Yacht harbors, sand beaches, and beautiful parks stretch along the city's world-famed shoreline, creating an eye-opening backdrop for the tall buildings of its dramatic, ever-changing skyline. The lakefront extends north of the central area along the city's Gold Coast and past affluent suburbs. It extends south to a vast complex of steel mills, oil refineries and diversified industrial plants. Chicago is the only inland city with combined lake, river and ocean traffic. Freighters from all over the world, plying the St. Lawrence Seaway, meet Great Lakes carriers, river barges and other vessels from the Mississippi and many rivers and canals of the Inland Waterway.

Chicago continues to experience a building boom with skyscrapers reaching above the lower cloud levels. Sears Tower at the southwest edge of the Loop was the world's tallest building. It rises 110 stories

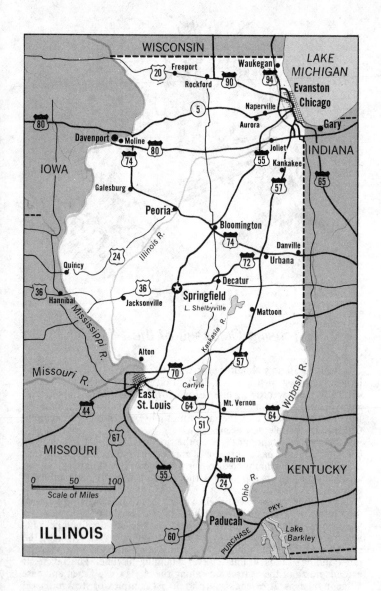

ILLINOIS

to a height of 1,454 feet, occupies a full city block of about 129,000 square feet, houses nearly 17,000 employees, and has a power capacity equal to the requirements of Rockford, the state's second largest city. It is the first building to use a modular construction system. It has an observation level 1,350 feet above ground level. Sears Tower is 100 feet higher than the New York World Trade Center, and nearly 325 feet higher than Chicago's John Hancock Center.

Hancock Center, known locally as Big John, at 875 N. Michigan Avenue, is the world's largest combined office and apartment building. It has 100 stories and reaches 1100 feet above ground level. The first 34 floors accommodate offices and parking space. Above these are 750 apartments on 49 floors, beginning with the 44th. An observation area facing all four directions is just below a restaurant on the 95th floor.

Another new skyscraper is the Standard Oil Building at 200 E. Randolph. It has 80 stories and a height of 1,136 feet, ranking it among the world's tallest buildings.

Breathing space has been provided by landscaped plazas built in connection with many of the giant buildings. The plaza at the Civic Center in the Loop is a popular strolling and resting place in the heart of the inner city. The plaza is dominated by a huge steel Picasso sculpture, which has caused much controversy and frequently gives rise to the question, "What is it?" Only Picasso knew for sure whether it was anything but a giant spoof, and he carried the secret to his grave. Plaza art has become an important part of city landscaping, with a 70-foot-long Chagall Mosaic at First National Plaza and two Calder conversation-pieces at Federal Center Plaza and Sears Tower Lobby, among several standouts.

The Loop is an area bounded by Wabash Avenue on the east, Wells Street on the west, and Van Buren and Lake Streets on the south and north. The loop of elevated tracks gave it its name.

Chicago is in the process of an explosion in imaginative building taking place on air rights over 83 acres of land between Randolph Drive and the Chicago River, Michigan Avenue and Lake Michigan. The Prudential Building, the Standard Oil Building, Hyatt Regency Hotel and other buildings already have been erected. More hotels and apartment and office buildings are going up.

In fact, for anyone interested in architecture, Chicago can best be described as an enormous outdoor museum evolved over the past century. Way back in 1883, "The Chicago School" of architecture started creating revolutionary new concepts in building, now world-famed, and many still stand to fascinate visitors on special architectural tours. Names like Sullivan, Adler, Jenney, Van der Rohe, and Frank Lloyd Wright set trends for the world to follow.

Chicago is noted for its excellent museums covering history, science, and art of many cultures and a wide range of periods and styles. A generous listing is provided under the heading "Museums and Galleries" in the Practical Information section.

Chicago's financial district is second in size only to New York's Wall Street. A visit to the fast-paced trading centers will appeal to many visitors. There is the Chicago Board of Trade, the world's largest grain exchange, at 141 W. Jackson Boulevard, the Midwest Stock Exchange at 120 S. LaSalle Street, and the Chicago Mercantile Exchange in a new building at 444 W. Jackson Boulevard.

The frantic pace of trading at the grain board will make little sense to the average person. However, a view from the visitors' gallery, watching millions of dollars of grain, soybean, and other futures contracts change hands in minutes, provides an exciting show. Friendly board officials will attempt to answer your questions, and every day

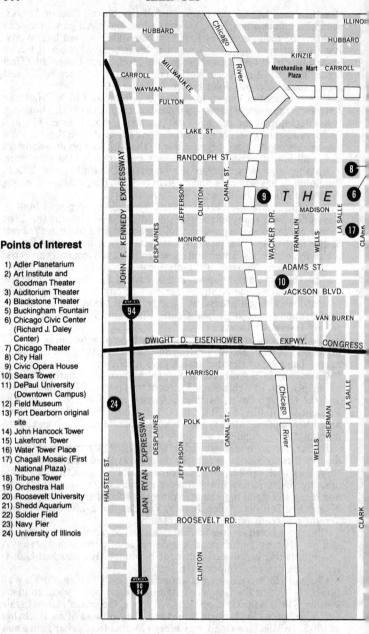

Points of Interest

1) Adler Planetarium
2) Art Institute and Goodman Theater
3) Auditorium Theater
4) Blackstone Theater
5) Buckingham Fountain
6) Chicago Civic Center (Richard J. Daley Center)
7) Chicago Theater
8) City Hall
9) Civic Opera House
10) Sears Tower
11) DePaul University (Downtown Campus)
12) Field Museum
13) Fort Dearborn original site
14) John Hancock Tower
15) Lakefront Tower
16) Water Tower Place
17) Chagall Mosaic (First National Plaza)
18) Tribune Tower
19) Orchestra Hall
20) Roosevelt University
21) Shedd Aquarium
22) Soldier Field
23) Navy Pier
24) University of Illinois

they show films that try to explain what the pandemonium is all about.

The stock exchange also is a great show from the gallery, which is open during trading hours. The Mercantile Exchange provides a superlative show, too, with fast and furious trading in such futures contracts

as frozen pork bellies (bacon) and other commodities. Their gallery also is open during trading hours.

Like all large cities, Chicago has many satellite communities, some with enough population to be classified as fairly large cities if they stood alone. Some are largely industrial in nature, and some are strictly bedroom communities. A growing number are becoming diversified as business, industry, and people move to the suburbs.

A drive along Sheridan Road through Evanston, Wilmette, Winnetka, Glencoe, and on up to Lake Forest, which reputedly has more millionaires per capita than any other community, will give you an idea of how really gracious living can be.

Evanston begins at Howard Street on Chicago's far north side. It is the home of the head of the Women's Christian Temperance Union, and until 1973 the city banned the sale of liquor. Howard Street became a beehive of liquor stores and taverns on the Chicago side of the street, drawing much of their patronage from Evanston, which, incidentally, also is the home of Northwestern University. In a revolutionary action, in 1973 the Evanston city council issued liquor licenses to a limited number of restaurants. It is worthwhile to note that the ice cream sundae was supposedly invented years ago in Evanston by a sodafountain owner to attract business that he lost because stringent "blue laws" banned ice cream sodas on Sunday.

In Wilmette you will find the Baha'i House of Worship, known the world over for the grandeur of the exterior and the simplicity of the interior. It is located atop a knoll on Sheridan Road at Linden Avenue. You can stroll through lovely gardens, ascend a series of stairs, and enter the nine-sided, domed building. The Baha'i religion was founded more than a hundred years ago in Persia (now Iran).

At Highwood, a largely Italian community, lies Fort Sheridan; and near Lake Bluff is the Great Lakes Naval Training Center, the Navy's largest inland center. Visitors are welcome at both installations.

PRACTICAL INFORMATION FOR CHICAGO

HOW TO GET AROUND. *By bus:* Chicago has an extensive bus system that will take you long distances for 90¢ (fares subject to change). For 10¢ extra you can get a transfer that allows you to spend an hour shopping or sightseeing before you ride back. CTA Culture Bus operates every Sun. and holidays Mid-April through September, on 3 routes departing the Art Institute for over 30 museums and cultural attractions. Fare: adults, $2.00; children, 70¢. 11 A.M. to 5:15 P.M., 836–7000.

By subway: Subway maps are available from the Chicago Tourism Bureau, and the same fare structure applies. If you need information on public transportation, call RTA 24-hour Information at 312–836–7000.

From the airports: O'Hare Airport, at Mannheim and Kennedy Expressways, is by far the most frequently used. For $6 *Continental Air Transport* will take you to downtown Chicago. The stops for the limousine are listed by hotels, so just get out at the hotel nearest your destination. A rapid-transit train now under construction will offer direct service to Chicago. Midway Airport is connected to Chicago by Continental Air Transport at $5 per person.

By taxi: Taxis charge $1 base fare and 90¢ for each additional mile. There is a 50¢ charge for each additional rider. **Note:** Taxi rates change often so check before you ride. A shared taxi system from O'Hare and Midway Airports identified by orange "Shared Ride" pennants is in operation. Minimum load is 2, maximum 3.

By car: Get a good road map and be wary of parking regulations; they are strictly enforced. Downtown State Street is now pedestrian mall closed to cars.

TOURIST INFORMATION. Contact the *Chicago Convention and Tourism*

Bureau, McCormick Place on the Lake, Chicago 60616, 312–225–5000. Their Visitor Eventline (225–2323) gives information on special events, theater, entertainment 24 hours daily. New *Chicago Visitor Information Center* is in Historic Water Tower. State maintains walk-in information center at 208 N. Michigan Ave. and the Conservation Dept. is at 160 N. LaSalle St. For information on facilities for the handicapped call 744–4016. *International Visitors Center* is at 116 S. Michigan Ave. (332–5875). In a language emergency call 332–1460. Chicago has nearly 50 foreign consulates. For weather information dial 976–1212.

SEASONAL EVENTS. *January* brings an ever-growing flurry of boat, travel, and outdoor shows, followed by a late *Feb.*-early *March* auto show. *March's* Medinah Shrine Circus is well attended, not to mention a grand and glorious St. Patrick's Day parade come rain, sleet or snow. They put dye in the Chicago River to turn it green for the day. Old Town Art Fair brings out artists and admirers in *June.* Lake Michigan's version of the Tall Ships depart for the Chicago to Mackinac race the third weekend in *July.* A special Olympics for the Handicapped is held in Grant Park during late summer. July's Taste of Chicago returns to tempt food enthusiasts with a sample of the city's cuisine. *November* brings the International Folk Fair at Navy Pier, focusing attention on dress and customs of our ancestors in their native lands. Santa Claus arrives for State St. parade, generally Thanksgiving weekend. Chicago is a parade town, and any occasion calling for a celebration gets a much applauded march downtown—everything from Mexican Independence Day to Columbus Day. Check locally.

MUSEUMS AND GALLERIES. The *Field Museum of Natural History,* in Grant Park at 12th St., is the world's largest museum of natural-history exhibits. It has a dazzling collection of precious and semiprecious stones. Trace the history of man through exhibits. Daily. Closed Xmas and Jan. 1.

Chicago Public Library founded after the fire of 1871, is noted for its Tiffany domes and mosaics. Recently restored as culture center with changing exhibits.

The *Oriental Institute* at the University of Chicago has exhibits dating back to 3000 B.C. Closed Mon. Artifacts from Egypt, Mesopotamia, Syria, Palestine.

Art Institute of Chicago is truly one of the great art museums of the world. Noted for its Impressionist collections, Thorne miniature rooms, garden restaurant, Children's Museum.

Adler Planetarium, near the Field Museum, is a great observatory on the lakefront, and offers the most dramatic view of the city's skyline.

John G. Shedd Aquarium, across Lake Shore Drive from the Field Museum, contains an impressive collection of freshwater and sea creatures. Daily. Facilities for the handicapped.

Chicago Historical Society, in Lincoln Park at Clark St. and North Ave., has everything to acquaint you with Chicago's history. Noted for its Lincoln collection and exhibits pertaining to Illinois pioneer life and the Chicago fire.

Chicago Academy of Sciences, 2001 N. Clark St., is well worth a visit. Daily. Closed Dec. 25. Free Mondays.

Museum of Science and Industry, in Jackson Park, 57th St. and Lake Shore Dr., is a magnet that attracts kids and senior citizens alike with its 14 acres of exhibits in engineering, industrial and medical progress. Tour a simulated operating coal mine, a Nazi submarine, an antique car display, Main Street of Yesterday. A must for all ages. You can spend days here. Daily.

Museum of Contemporary Art, 237 E. Ontario St., may give you a different viewpoint on art. Closed Mon. Elevator and ramp for handicapped.

Ukrainian Institute of Modern Art, 2320 W. Chicago Ave., has a permanent collection of work by Ukrainian artists in the West. Open daily except Mon., 12 to 4 P.M., free.

Polish Museum of America, 984 N. Milwaukee Ave., has notable stained glass, Polish art, sculpture, Paderewski and Kosciuszko rooms. Free.

Balzekas Museum of Lithuanian Culture, 4012 S. Archer Ave., has the largest amber and armor collections. Daily, 1–4 P.M.

DuSable Museum of African-American History, 704 E. 56th Pl., has rotating exhibits and documents about the history of Black Americans.

Ripleys Believe It or Not Museum, 1500 N. Wells St., shows fabulous exhibits of oddities collected by Robert L. Ripley during his foreign travels. Daily.

Frank Lloyd Wright Home and Studio in Oak Park. Guided tours. Suburban community where he lived and worked 20 years boasts over 2 dozen of his buildings. Chicago has 16 more, including Robie House, 5757 S. Woodlawn.

USS Silversides behind the Naval Armory at Randolph St. is city's first floating museum. Open from spring into winter. Restored WWII submarine.

 HISTORIC SITES. The picturesque *Water Tower* at Michigan and Chicago Avenues is one of the few buildings on the Near North Side that was not destroyed by the great Chicago fire of 1871, which made ruins of a large part of the city, including the central business district.

The Auditorium Theatre (1889) is one of the city's restoration jewels.

The *Pullman Community,* near 111th St. and Cottage Grove Ave., is a quaint reminder of the paternalistic outlook of the railway-sleeping-car inventor.

Fort Dearborn, the site of Chicago's first settlement, was just south of the Michigan Ave. Bridge. The city's early history is depicted on bronze tablets on the bridge.

Hull House, 800 S. Halsted, is part of the famed social settlement established in 1889 by Jane Addams. Two buildings have been restored and are National Historic Landmarks.

The lobby of *The Rookery,* 209 S. La Salle St., was designed by Frank Lloyd Wright in 1905. The building is the oldest remaining steel-skeleton skyscraper in the world and was built in 1886.

Old Town, running from 1200 to 1700 north on Wells St., includes some of Chicago's finest restored Victorian residences. It is a cosmopolitan area colored with distinctive shops, restaurants and pubs. The entrance to the famous 19th-century Piper's Alley at 1608 is marked by a large Tiffany lamp.

Prairie Ave. Historic District, former "Millionaires' Row," is now undergoing restoration. One gem, Glessner House, is a 35-room Romanesque mansion.

 TOURS. Chicago and nearby areas of interest are covered in tours offered by *Gray Line of Chicago,* 33 E. Monroe St., and *American Sightseeing Tours,* 530 S. Michigan Ave. They offer various specialized tours such as tours for women, nightclubs, the plush suburbs, after-dark, and Chinatown.

There are boating tours on Lake Michigan by the *Mercury Scenicruiser,* and the *Wendella Streamliner* with views of the photogenic shoreline and skyline. They leave from the Michigan Avenue Bridge and pass through locks at the mouth of the Chicago River into the lake. New 400-passenger *Star of Chicago* cruises city's scenic shoreline for lunch and dinner, offering varied entertainment. *Chicago Supernatural Tour* (735–2530) seeks out "haunted and legendary places." *Shoreline Marine Sightseeing* (864–3180) offers lake cruises from 3 locations.

 GARDENS. *Garfield Park Conservatory,* 300 N. Central Park Ave., offers exceptional flower shows and is considered the largest in the world under one roof. *Lincoln Park Conservatory* is well worth a visit. Its summer Grandmother's Garden dates to 1893 and features old-fashioned flowers. Both are open daily 9–5 and free. *Morton Arboretum,* 25 miles west of Chicago Loop on State 53 near the east-west tollway, offers an escape to the tranquil life. It's a nature lover's paradise with 4,800 species of living plants and trees. The conservatory has a plant clinic, lectures and field trips. Arboretum open daily 8-sunset. Spring garden walks are offered by many North Shore and city residential communities. Inquire locally. Impressive new *Botanical Gardens of Chicago Horticulture Society* are in the Skokie Lagoon area, north in suburban Glencoe. *Shakespeare Gardens* on Northwestern University's Evanston campus is planted with flowers Shakespeare wrote about in his plays.

MUSIC. The *Chicago Symphony* performs at Orchestra Hall. *Grant Park Music Concerts* are popular and free from late June to third week in Aug.; *Auditorium Theater* seats 4,000 for concerts and other musical events. Call 922–2110 for information.

The *Ravinia Music Festival* in Highland Park is justly famous as the home of varied musical fare from rock to jazz to symphony, presented in a lovely park setting. Many people picnic on the grass before or even during performances.

The *Lyric Opera* presents a variety of operas, top singers, beginning in late Sept. in the Civic Opera House. *Arie Crown Theater* at McCormick Place has varied programs. Free outdoor celebrity concerts are among entertainment scheduled daily in plazas at the Civic Center and 1st National Bank.

STAGE AND REVUES. Plays are booked at the Shubert, Blackstone, and the Arie Crown Theater at McCormick Place. "Off-Loop" theaters are increasingly popular. Goodman and Hull House theaters offer excellent shows. Both have children's theater. Marriott's Lincolnshire, Drury Lane, Pheasant Run are among many outlying theaters with name stars at times. There are noteworthy university and college theaters. See Second City, 1616 N. Wells St., for satire and spoofs on modern life.

HOT TIX half-price ticket booth sells day-of-performance tickets at 24 S. State St. downtown. Curtain Call hotline is 977–1755.

JAZZ. Jazz came to Chicago in the early 1920s and went on to become a national preoccupation. After a decline, jazz is staging a great comeback. *Andy's,* 11 E. Hubbard; *Back-Room,* 1007 N. Rush. *Rick's Cafe Americain, The Bulls, The Dairy, Leslee's* and *Manhattan* are among headliners. Jazz Institute hotline is 666–1881.

NIGHTCLUBS AND BARS. *Arnie's,* 1030 N. State and *Arnie's North,* 1876 1st St., Highland Park, are actually restaurants, but considered zingy "in" spots for a night on the town. *Holsteins!,* 2464 N. Lincoln, is a folk music favorite. *Wise Fools Pub,* 2270 N. Lincoln, attracts blues and jazz musicians, as does *Blues,* 2519 N. Halsted, with live music 7 nights a week. *Orphan's,* 2462 N. Lincoln, features jazz, folk, blues and rock.

Butch McGuire's, 20 W. Division, is still the singles scene. *Faces,* 940 N. Rush, is a current "in" spot; so is *The Raccoon Club,* 812 N. Franklin.

SUMMER SPORTS. *Bicycling.* Bike paths in major parks. Bike routes marked by signs on city streets, including some with heavy auto and truck traffic—exercise caution. American Youth Hostels has special tours. Many miles of trails utilize abandoned suburban railroad beds.

Boating. Big, broad and deep Lake Michigan is at the city's front door. Mooring slips taken long in advance in harbors. Launching ramps at Diversey Harbor, Burnham Harbor, Calumet Park, Rainbow Beach and Jackson Park. Two free launching ramps on Des Plaines and Calumet Rivers. Rowboat rental at Maple Lake and some other forest preserve lakes.

Canoeing. American Youth Hostel, 3712 N. Clark St., sponsors numerous trips. Canoe rentals at Chicagoland Canoe Base, Inc., 777–1489.

Golf. Chicago Park District has public courses, provides free winter golf school. Many courses are available for a greens fee in Chicago and suburbs.

Fishing. More than a score of lakes and rivers and park lagoon sites, not to mention Lake Michigan. Coho salmon are taken in Lake Michigan. License required. Charter boats available. Call Chicago Sport Fishing Assn. 922–1100.

Hiking and Horseback Riding. 200 miles of trails in forest preserves and parks. Riding instructors at most stables.

Racquetball. Pottawattomie Park, 7340 N. Rogers. 743–4313.

Scuba and Skindiving. Old shipwrecks lost in Lake Michigan lure divers.

Skeet and Target Shooting. At Lincoln Park Gun Club on shoreline of Lake Michigan.

Swimming. Chicago has miles of beautiful sand beaches fully staffed with lifeguards in season. Also many park district pools. Swimming from rocks along Lake Michigan or in unpatrolled area is not advisable.

Tennis. Park district has over 650 free tennis courts.

WINTER SPORTS. *Skating* on the park lagoons in cold weather can be dangerous. There are many neighborhood rinks. *Skiing.* Norge Hills, Fox River Grove is noted for ski jumping events. *Tobogganing,* James Park Winter Sports Complex in suburban Evanston.

SPECTATOR SPORTS. *Baseball.* Chicago Cubs play at Wrigley Field on the North Side, Chicago White Sox at White Sox Park on the South Side. *Basketball.* Chicago Bulls play at Chicago Stadium, which also is host to many college games and tournaments. Loyola, De Paul and Northwestern usually field strong, exciting teams. *Football.* Chicago Bears now play at Soldiers Field (Fall and Winter); Northwestern plays Big Ten and other teams at Dyche Stadium in Evanston. *Hockey.* Chicago Black Hawks play at Chicago Stadium. Chicago Sting soccer team, plays at Soldiers Field.

Horse racing. Flat racing at Arlington Park and Hawthorne. Harness racing, mostly nights, at Sportsman's Park and Maywood Park.

Tournaments. Western Open Golf Tournament is held in early summer. Sailors hope for a breeze the third weekend in July for Chicago-to-Mackinac boat race. Norge Ski Jump at Fox River Grove has slide tournament in January. Polo matches at the Chicago Armory and at Oak Brook.

SHOPPING. The Near North Side's Old Town section of Chicago, and farther north New Town, abound with antique shops and boutiques. Harper Court is Hyde Park's crafts center.

High-style centers such as *Saks Fifth Avenue, Lord & Taylor, Neiman Marcus* and *Bonwit Teller* offer the latest in expensive fashions. The budget-minded aim for cast-offs at many resale shops on Oak St.

The Maxwell Street Market is gone, but the surrounding area still offers good flea market-type bargains. Great department stores are on State St.

Glamour shops are on Michigan Avenue's Magnificent Mile from the bridge north to Oak St. Many present afternoon fashion shows. Water Tower Place is a favorite, with floors of imaginative shops.

By all means visit *Marshall Field & Co.,* 111 N. State St. You'll marvel at the chandeliers, polished mahogany, and the 13-floor inner court with a Tiffany-glass skylight dome. A good place to meet is at the famous clock outside.

Another of the architectural wonders is *Carson, Pirie, Scott & Co.,* with its intricate grillwork façade designed by Louis Sullivan.

Peacock's jewelry stock rivals its gorgeous bronze doors and marble interior.

WHAT TO DO WITH THE CHILDREN. *Colleen Moore's Doll House,* model trains, baby chicks, etc., get smallfrys' attention at the Museum of Science and Industry. Every child should see the *Adler Planetarium, Shedd Aquarium* and *Field Museum of Natural History,* all near Soldiers Field. *Art Institute* has a *Junior Museum. Lincoln Park Zoo* has a small operating farm. Both Lincoln Park and the *Brookfield Zoo* have children's zoos. *Lamb's Farm* near Libertyville also has children's farmyard, pet shop. *Marriott's Great America* north at Gurnee is the state's biggest new attraction.

HOTELS AND MOTELS in the Chicago area range from inexpensive to deluxe, and first-class establishments often offer deluxe extras such as sauna or steam baths, health club facilities, etc. We have listed establishments in the downtown area, some well-known ones away from the central business district, and selected motels and hotels in the nearby suburbs. There is also Bed and Breakfast–Chicago, PO Box 14088, 60614 (312–951–0085) offering varied accommodations.

The price categories in this section, for double occupancy, will average: *Deluxe*, $120–200; *Expensive*, $85–115; *Moderate*, $65–84; *Inexpensive*, under $65.

Deluxe: **Ambassador East and West.** 1300 N. State Pkway. Aristocratic, newly refurbished celebrity center. Noted for elegant service.

Barclay. 166 E. Superior. Low-key, London-style. Rooftop pool.

Chicago Marriott. 540 N. Michigan. Magnificent Mile location.

The Drake. 140 E. Walton at Michigan Ave. Baronial grandeur, lake view.

Hyatt Regency. 151 E. Wacker Dr. Waterfall lobby, underground garage.

Knickerbocker. 163 E. Walton Pl. Restored to pre-Playboy Towers glamour.

Mayfair-Regent. 181 E. Lake Shore Drive. Gracious, traditional beauty totally refurbished. Rooftop dining, lakeview. Accent on service. Afternoon tea.

Palmer House. State & Monroe Sts. A truly grand old hotel. Traditional.

Park Hyatt. 800 N. Michigan Ave. Delightful. Posh. Personalized.

Ritz Carlton. 160 E. Pearson. Grande luxe reputation.

Sheraton Plaza. 160 E. Huron. Dramatic rooftop pool.

Tremont. 100 E. Chestnut. Interior reminiscent of an English country home.

Westin. 909 N. Michigan Ave. Classy. Prestige address. Celebrity haven.

Whitehall. 105 E. Delaware Pl. Prestigious, understated. Very English.

Expensive: **Ascot House.** 1100 S. Michigan Ave. 9-story motel.

Americana-Congress. 520 S. Michigan Ave. Overlooks Art Institute.

Conrad Hilton. 720 S. Michigan Ave. Across from Grant Park. Reopening September 1985 after $150,000,000 transformation.

Continental (Former Radisson). 505 N. Michigan Ave. Excellent location.

Executive House. 71 E. Wacker Dr. Modern. Rooftop restaurant.

McCormick Center Hotel. 23rd St. & Lake Shore Dr. Convention hotel.

Raphael. 201 E. Delaware St. Luxurious. European atmosphere.

Moderate: **Allerton.** 701 N. Michigan Ave. Conveniently located. A find!

Avenue Motel. 1154 S. Michigan Ave. Far East décor.

Bismarck. 171 W. Randolph St. Garage, entertainment. Near Civic Center.

Essex Inn. 800 S. Michigan Ave. Rooftop pool, sauna. Bus to Loop.

Holiday Inn. 1 S. Halsted St.; motor hotel, 644 N. Lake Shore Dr., 300 E. Ohio St., 350 N. Orleans St., 7353 S. Cicero.

Hyde Park Hilton. 4900 S. Lake Shore Drive. Opened on lakefront in 1980.

The Lenox House. 616 N. Rush. Mostly suites, kitchens in all units. Refurbished.

Midland. 172 W. Adams St. Heart of financial district.

Ramada Inn Downtown. 506 W. Harrison St. All facilities.

Richmont. 162 E. Ontario St. Intimate size. Free Continental breakfast.

Inexpensive: **Blackstone.** 636 S. Michigan Ave. Popular with presidents since 1910.

Ohio House. LaSalle & Ohio Sts. Near Merchandise Mart. 2-story motel.

O'HARE AIRPORT AREA. *Deluxe:* **Hyatt Regency O'Hare.** 9300 Bryn Mawr Ave. A landmark, with copper, mirrorlike exterior, 1100 rooms.

O'Hare Marriott. 8535 W. Higgins Rd. Health club.

Expensive: **O'Hare Hilton.** Directly across from air terminals. Convenient.

Ramada-O'Hare Inn. 6600 N. Mannheim Rd. Health Club.

Moderate: **Holiday Inn.** 5440 N. River Rd.; Touhy Ave. & Mannheim Rd.; 1000 Busse Hwy, Elk Grove Village.

Howard Johnson's. 8201 W. Higgins Rd. Modern. 110 rooms.

EVANSTON. *Expensive:* **Holiday Inn.** 1501 Sherman Ave. 12-story motel.

Moderate: **Orrington.** 1710 Orrington Ave. Near Northwestern U.

ITASCA. *Expensive:* Hamilton-Stouffer. 3 mi. S. of Woodfield. Self-contained, resortlike facilities. Excellent restaurants, dramatic atrium. Sun. brunch.

LAKE FOREST. *Moderate:* **Deerpath Inn.** 255 E. Illinois Rd. Unique inn.

LINCOLNWOOD. *Moderate:* **Hyatt House.** 4500 W. Touhy Ave. Modern.

OAK BROOK. *Expensive:* **Drake Oakbrook.** Cermak & York Rds. Spacious, country setting. Golf, trap shooting, skating.

Oakbrook Hyatt. Spring Road. Circular 7-story lobby.
Stouffer's Oakbrook Inn. 2100 Spring Rd. Decor is Oriental.

SKOKIE. *Moderate:* **North Shore Hilton.** 9599 Skokie Blvd. Near Old Orchard Shopping Center.

 DINING OUT in Chicago can be exotic and memorable, expensive or inexpensive, depending on your taste and your purse. There are many great steakhouses. Over 6,000 restaurants in total.

Because of frequent price changes due to the changing times, costs are listed by category. Price categories are as follows: *Super Deluxe* will average $60 and up, *Deluxe* $50, *Expensive* $30–50, *Moderate* $15 to $25, *Inexpensive* under $15. These prices are for hors d'oeuvres or soup, entree and dessert. Not included are drinks, tax and tips. Restaurants are listed by type of cuisine.

American International

Deluxe: **Empire Room.** Palmer House. Gilded grande luxe. City's most elegant. Has the feeling of a European palace. Lunch weekdays, Sun. jazz, brunch.
Expensive: **The Bakery.** 2218 Lincoln Ave. Popular. Eat in the kitchen.
Cape Cod Room. 140 E. Walton Street. Seafood specialties, nautical décor.
Ciel Bleu. 181 E. Lake Shore Dr. Food is as good as the panoramic view.
Cricket's. 100 E. Chestnut. Very genteel atmosphere.
Pump Room. Ambassador East Hotel. Celebrities. Shiny new look.
Moderate: **Cafe Bohemia.** 138 S. Clinton St. Wild game. Unusual dishes.
Ireland's. 500 N. LaSalle St. Seafood favorite. Memorable clam chowder.
King Arthur's Pub. 200 N. LaSalle St. Rolls Royce delivery.
Miller's On Kinzie. 33 E. Kinzie. Dark wood panelling, stained glass.
Sally's Stage. 6335 N. Western. Conversation stopper. Waitresses on roller skates, mechanical bull for kids, games, contests. Special winter schedule.
Inexpensive: **Chicago Claim Company.** 2314 N. Clark. Gold rush setting.
Chapman Sisters Calorie Counters. 444 N. Michigan. Trendy. Lunch only.
Hamburger Hamlet. 44 E. Walton. Big on burgers, chili.

Chinese

Expensive: **House of Hunan.** 535 N. Michigan. Mandarin. Try corn crab soup.
Szechwan House. 600 N. Michigan. Both are unique and traditional.
Moderate: **Chiam.** 2323 S. Wentworth. Chinatown. Exotic atmosphere.

French

Super Deluxe: **Chez Paul.** 660 N. Rush St. Gracious, not pretentious.
Le Perroquet. 70 E. Walton St. French elegance. *Nouvelle* cuisine.
Ninety-Fifth. 172 E. Chestnut St. Panoramic view. Nouvelle cuisine.
Expensive: **Biggs.** 1150 N. Dearborn. Classic cuisine in a historic Victorian mansion. Goose often featured.
Moderate: **Gare St. Lazare,** 858 W. Armitage. Cozy fireplace, good menu.
L'Escargot. 701 N. Michigan. Excellent roast duck, memorable desserts.

German

Inexpensive: **Berghoff's.** 17 W. Adams. A German favorite since 1898. Lots of atmosphere. A slice of Heidelberg! Good dollar value. Locally popular.
Golden Ox. 1578 N. Clybourn. Munich mood, zither music.

Greek

Moderate: **Diane's Opaa.** 212 S. Halsted. Fun, good food.
Inexpensive: **Parthenon.** 314 S. Halsted St. Lamb is special.

Indian

Moderate: **Bombay Palace.** 50 E. Walton. Broad menu, great mango ice cream.

Italian

Moderate: **Agostino's.** 7 E. Delaware Pl. Tasty, old country style.
Italian Village. 71 W. Monroe St. Good. In heart of the Loop.

Como Inn. 546 N. Milwaukee. Mediterranean personality, fun place.
Inexpensive: **Pizzeria Uno.** 29 E. Ohio. Deep-dish pizza.

Japanese

Moderate: **Azuma Sukiyaki House.** 5120 N. Broadway. Japanese favorites.

Korean

Inexpensive: **New Korea House.** 4050 N. Lincoln.

Mexican

Moderate: **Su Casa.** 49 E. Ontario St. Popular. Hacienda style.
La Margarita. 868 N. Wabash Ave., near North Side. Celebrities. Hacienda atmosphere, with strolling musicians.
La Hacienda. 1945 N. Sedgwick St. Colorful. Strolling musicians.

Middle Eastern

Inexpensive: **Casbah** 514 W. Diversey Pkwy. Shish kebabs and cous cous.
Café du Liban. 5517 N. Clark. Hommos, felafel, baklava.

Polish

Inexpensive: **Patria.** 3030 N. Central. Excellent. Good dessert bar.

Polynesian

Expensive: **Kon Tiki Ports.** Hotel Continental. Colorful surroundings.
Trader Vic's. Palmer House. Atmosphere. Polynesian-Chinese menu.

Portuguese

Moderate: **Rio's.** 4611 N. Kedzie. Friendly. Tasty Portuguese-style menu.

Soul Food

Inexpensive: **Army & Lou's,** 422 E. 75th St. South side favorite.

Swedish

Inexpensive: **Ann Sather's.** 925 W. Belmont Ave. Busy.
House of Sweden. 5314 N. Clark St. Try pancakes with lingonberries.

Yiddish

Inexpensive: **The Bagel.** 3000 W. Devon. Kishke, kugel. Braille menu.

Yugoslavian

Inexpensive: **Golden Shell.** 10063 Avenue N. An ethnic neighborhood favorite. Serbian-American food. Try the Gypsy plate.

EXPLORING ILLINOIS

To begin a tour of the state from the Chicago metropolitan area, start north on US 12 to the 960-acre Chain O'Lakes State Park, the largest single concentration of lakes in the state, offering boating and fishing—even fishing through the ice in winter.

Going west, I–90 will lead you to Rockford, Illinois' second largest city, on the Rock River. The riverfront boasts Sinnissippi Park and its Sunken Gardens. You can browse among period furnishings in a preserved Civil War-era home which houses the Burpee Art Gallery. On the banks of the river you'll find the Robert H. Tinker Swiss Chalet, stocked with furnishings Tinker acquired in his travels.

West is Galena, the town that time forgot, once a bustling city whose lead and zinc deposits made the future seem limitless in the 1820s when Chicago was nothing more than a cluster of cabins. It climbed to a population of 15,000 by 1860 (by which time it had been far outstripped by Chicago) but now counts only about 4,000 residents. Much of the town was built on the bluffs, and most of the early buildings are still in use. This remarkably preserved slice of history is definitely worth a detour. Unlike other parts of the level-landed state, the rolling, almost "mountain-like" landscape enhances its architectural treasures.

Ulysses S. Grant lived briefly in Galena, tending his father's harness and leather store, before leaving to lead the North to victory in the Civil War. Grant's subsequent career as Commanding General of the Army, Secretary of War, and President gave him and his family little time to occupy the home local citizens presented him after the war. His son eventually deeded it to the state, which restored it and made it a state memorial in 1955.

The next stop is Rock Island, one of the Quad Cities—along with Moline, East Moline, and Davenport, Iowa—which constitute a busy commercial and industrial center on the Mississippi. Here you can tour Arsenal Island, a Civil War ordnance depot and prisoner-of-war camp, now housing, at Rock Island Arsenal, much of the nation's present small-arms stock. A replica of the blockhouse at Ft. Armstrong has been constructed. Inland to the east are Tampico and Dixon, the typically Midwest towns where President Ronald Reagan was born and grew up. His second floor birthplace at 111 Main St., Tampico, is undergoing restoration. There is a museum on the first floor and a "Reagan Country" gift shop selling souvenirs. Nearby Dixon's Chamber of Commerce at 74 Galena Ave. directs visitors past his former home at 816 S. Henepin and the park where he was a lifeguard. Melick Library at Eureka College in Eureka (between Bloomington and Peoria) where he attended college, has an 800-piece memorabilia collection chronicling his Illinois career and motion picture achievements.

Along the Mississippi, here and there winding its way into Iowa, runs a string of highways called the Great River Road. It passes through Nauvoo, one of the state's great historic sites. Joseph Smith led the main body of the Church of Jesus Christ of Latter Day Saints (Mormons) from Missouri to this point in 1839 and established it as the church's capital. In a few short years they had built a busy and prosperous community of 20,000, the largest in Illinois. But fear and suspicion of Mormonism was deep-seated in the countryside, and when Joseph Smith and his brother Hyrum were taken into "protective custody" in the Hancock County jail at Carthage in 1844, a lynch mob took them from the jail and killed them. Two years later Brigham Young led the Mormon community from Nauvoo on the long overland trip that led to the Utah Territory and Salt Lake City.

Three years later Etienne Cabet, a French lawyer and political figure with Utopian dreams, established a community of French and German followers known as the Icarians in Nauvoo. Although Cabet's dream of a Utopian community withered and died, the grape vines that his followers planted flourished, and do to this day, with a symbolic "Wedding of the Wine and Cheese" festival being held every Labor Day weekend.

The area along the Mississippi from Alton south to Chester is known as the American bottom, a fertile plain remarkable from early days for its bounteous crops. At Cahokia, where the Indian chief Pontiac, the guiding spirit in the French and Indian War, was killed, you'll find the exquisite vertical-log Church of the Holy Family, restored to its original appearance. Fort de Chartres State Park contains the partly reconstructed remains of the strongest of all in the string of forts the French built along the river.

You can follow the Mississippi to the state's southernmost point, Cairo ("KAY-ro"), passing many imposing old residences that bespeak the prosperity and wealth the river generated before the railroads branched out almost everywhere to move freight and people. In Cairo, at the junction of the Ohio and the Mississippi, is the Magnolia Manor, a showplace furnished with Victorian-era antiques, which was built when the general industrial trend indicated the town would become a giant.

Nestled in the area is the 211,000-acre Shawnee National Forest, whose Visitors Information Center is on State 3 in Gorham, offering details on activities, permits, and fees. Or write Forest Supervisor, Shawnee National Forest, Harrisburg, Ill.

The Land of Lincoln

The life of Abraham Lincoln is woven deeply and inextricably into the history of Illinois. Even more than Kentucky, where he was born in a log cabin, and Indiana, where he grew to manhood, Illinois claims Lincoln as its own. Aside from the centers of population and the usual reasons of business, education, culture and spectator sports that attract masses of people, the Lincoln story is the great key to Illinois as a tourist state. Almost every local throughout central Illinois boasts some Lincoln association.

The story begins on the west bank of the Wabash River across from Vincennes, Indiana, where young Abe's family entered the state on their way toward a farm site near Decatur, now the Lincoln Homestead State Park. And south of Charleston is the Lincoln Log Cabin State Park, graced by a reproduction of a two-room cabin Lincoln's parents built the year he left home to make his own way in the world.

The village of New Salem, now Lincoln's New Salem State Park, knew Lincoln as the gangly young man who arrived in 1831, his sole possessions the clothing he wore. Here he tended a store and the post office, studied surveying and law, and in 1837 was elected to the legislature, then moved to Springfield to establish himself as a lawyer.

Springfield is the heart of the land of Lincoln. Here he married and practiced law, except for the two years he spent in Congress. Many old buildings still stand, among them the Lincoln home, the building where he had his law office, the impressive restored Old State Capitol fronted by a mall, and others, including an old railroad station that recalls his moving farewell to neighbors and friends as he left for the national captial for the last time. His tomb in the Oak Ridge Cemetery is open to the public, for Lincoln does, indeed, "belong to the ages," as his Secretary of War, Stanton, said in the epitaph you will find there.

PRACTICAL INFORMATION FOR ILLINOIS

HOW TO GET THERE. *By car:* I–80, in the northern part of Illinois, and I–70, in the south, are major east-west highways. I–90 and I–94, north of Chicago, and I–57, south of Chicago, are the major north-south highways into Illinois. *By train: Amtrak* serves Chicago from major cities throughout the United States and connections from Canadian rail systems. Check for schedules and costs with your travel agent or nearest Amtrak passenger station. *By air:* Chicago's O'Hare airport is served by numerous major airlines including *Northwest, United, American, Delta, Trans World, Continental, Jet America, Capitol, Piedmont, US Air, Midway, Ozark, Republic, Eastern, Air Canada, Braniff, People Express,* and *Western.* Local ("trunk") airlines flying to Chicago are *Mississippi Valley, Simmons, Midstate, Air Wisconsin, Britt-Phillips, American Central, Air Midwest. By bus: Greyhound, Trailways,* and many other bus lines serve Illinois. Consult a travel agent or the carriers directly: *Greyhound* at 74 W. Randolph, *Trailways* at 20 E. Randolph, Chicago.

HOW TO GET AROUND. *By car:* If you are in a hurry, stay on the Interstate and state highway systems that connect all the major cities in Illinois. With the 55-mile-per-hour speed limit, however, you can get around almost as fast on the secondary roads, which will allow you to see much more of the countryside. *By train:* Amtrak connects Chicago with the rest of the country. *By air:* Within the state *Ozark Air Lines* flies to major cities. *By bus:* Nearly every town in Illinois is on a bus route.

TOURIST INFORMATION: The *Office of Tourism,* Department of Commerce and Community Affairs, 222 S. College St., Springfield, 62706, can be helpful. They also have offices at 2209 West Main St., Marion, and at the walk-in Illinois Adventure Center, 208 N. Michigan Ave. Chicago. Dept. of Conservation has a ground level office at 160 N. La Salle St., Chicago, as well as their main office at 524 S. 2nd St., Springfield 62706. *Springfield Convention & Visitors Bureau,* 624 E. Adams, offers a "Mr. Lincoln's Hometown Kit" with brochures and information. The Tourism Council of Greater Chicago has a *Visitors Information Center* in the historic Water Tower.

MUSEUMS AND GALLERIES. The Rock Island Arsenal houses the *John Browning Memorial Museum of Firearms,* including those developed by Browning. Wed.-Sun. 11–4, free. The *William Jennings Bryan Museum* in Salem was the birthplace of the golden-voiced orator. Daily except Thurs., 11–4, free. *Daughters of Union Veterans—Civil War,* 503 S. Walnut St., *G.A.R. Memorial Museum,* 629 S. 7th St., *Illinois State Museum of Natural History and Art* and the *Illinois State Historical Library* in the Old State House are among the many interesting museums in Springfield. *Illinois Railway Museum.* Union. Steam locomotives, interurban cars, old Chicago streetcars.

HISTORIC SITES. In Cahokia the state's first courthouse is a *State Memorial.* Daily 9–5, free. Cahokia also has some of the state's most important Indian mounds. In Carthage the *Old Jail* is a sober reminder of the lynching of two Mormon leaders, leading to the Mormon trek to Utah. In nearby Nauvoo, which the Mormons made into Illinois' largest and most prosperous community more than a century ago, many buildings have been restored. The Mormon story is shown in pictures and lectures at a new Visitors Center. Free guide service. Freeport has the *Stephenson County Historical Society Museum,* where, by appointment, you can view examples of farm machinery used by early settlers and mementos from the Jane Addams house. Almost all Galena is a historic site, including the U.S. Grant home. Carl Sandburg's birthplace is in Galesburg, Vachel Lindsay's home is in Springfield and the Lincoln legend worth a detour to intriguing New Salem and many treasured sites in Springfield, including Lincoln's home, law office, tomb, and the Old Capitol where he made his "house divided" speech. *Magnolia Manor* is a Cairo mansion, *John Deere's* restored blacksmith shop and house are in Grand Detour, *Edgar Lee Masters'* boyhood residence still stands in Petersburg.

DRINKING LAWS. Liquor can be purchased at any privately owned liquor store weekdays during regular business hours. Restaurants, bars and nightclubs have different closing hours depending on the license they hold. Minimum age for beer, wine, and hard liquor, 21.

SUMMER SPORTS. *Boating.* Boats can be rented in recreation areas throughout the state. For a cruise map of boating facilities write Illinois Dept. of Conservation, State Office Bldg., Springfield. *Bicycling.* Getting more popular every year. A growing number of communities are utilizing abandoned railroad beds and parks to develop routes. Inquire locally. *Canoeing.* More than 100 streams for paddlers; see Chicago listing. *Golf.* Public courses all over the state charge a fee. *Hiking.* Most state parks have extensive trails. *Swimming.* Many excellent beaches and sandbars are found along the rivers. *Fishing.* Many state parks offer excellent fishing and several Corps of Engineer projects in southern section of State have developed lakes (Crab Orchard, Rend, Shelbyville, Carlyle) that make fishing headlines. Lake Michigan and the Mississippi and Ohio Rivers are other fishing favorites.

WINTER SPORTS. *Hunting.* Deer hunting throughout state. Fine duck and goose hunting in southern Illinois. Write Dept. of Conservation for seasons, limits, license fees. *Skiing.* Chair lift at Chestnut Mountain near Galena. *Target shooting.* Public shooting grounds at Manteno.

SPECTATOR SPORTS. *Basketball.* Bradley University and the University of Illinois vie with Southern Illinois University at Carbondale and Northern Illinois University at DeKalb. *Football.* Northwestern University, the University of Illinois, Southern Illinois University and Northern Illinois University offer first-class teams. Saturdays, Sept.-Nov.

Horse racing. Thoroughbred racing at Cahokia Downs near East St. Louis and Fairmount Park in Collinsville. Harness racing at Springfield State Fair and many county fairs. *Tournaments.* State basketball tournament, the Sweet Sixteen, in March at Champaign-Urbana.

WHAT TO DO WITH THE CHILDREN. *Santa's Village* near Dundee is a popular spot for the kids. *Quinsippi Island,* in the Mississippi River at Quincy, has a small-gauge steam-train ride to the 130-acre recreation park. An excursion boat and cable car are in operation. *Lambs Pet Farm,* operated by the mentally retarded at Libertyville, includes summer barnyard zoo, pet store, farmers market and bakery. *Marriott's Great America* at Gurnee is the state's biggest new family attraction.

HOTELS AND MOTELS outside the Chicago metropolitan area cover a broad price range. Economy-minded chains are building low-cost motels along the interstates and other principal routes especially for the traveler who is not interested in extras. The price categories in this section, for double occupancy, will average: *Expensive:* $55–70, *Moderate:* $35–55, *Inexpensive:* under $35.

CHAMPAIGN-URBANA. *Moderate:* **Ramada Inn.** 1501 S. Neil. Putting green, sauna, 2 swimming pools, some kitchen units.
Howard Johnson's Motor Lodge. 222 S. State. Pool, sauna.

DIXON. *Moderate:* **Chalet.** A bargain in President Reagan's hometown.

GALENA. *Moderate:* **Chestnut Mountain Lodge.** Year-round river-view resort. Set high on bluffs overlooking the Mississippi. Resort activities.
Inexpensive: **Grant Hills Motel.** Late café nearby. Picnic tables at motel.

GALESBURG. *Moderate:* **Galesburg Travelodge.** 565 W. Main St. Pleasant.

ILLINOIS BEACH STATE PARK. *Moderate:* **Holiday Inn–Illinois Beach Resort.** Located on Lake Michigan shore in 2,485-acre park. Swimming, fishing, hiking, cross-country skiing.

LA SALLE. *Moderate:* **Starved Rock Lodge.** Woodsy, rustic setting; located in state park. Recently refurbished to accommodate handicapped.

OREGON. *Inexpensive:* **White Pines Lodge.** Old-style log cabins, picnic facilities. Surrounded by beauty of White Pines Forest State Park.

PETERSBURG. *Inexpensive:* **New Salem Lodge.** Attractive. Closed winters. Across from New Salem State Park. Rustic, frontier flavor.

ROCKFORD. *Moderate:* **Wagon Wheel.** Self-contained resort with rustic western lodge atmosphere, skating, curling, shops, air strip.

SPRINGFIELD. *Expensive:* **Springfield Hilton.** 700 E. Adams St.
Moderate: **Holiday Inn.** I–55 at Stevenson Drive and 625 E. St. Joseph St. **Howard Johnson's Motor Lodge.** 1025 S. 5th, and 3190 Dirksen Pkwy. **Mansion View Lodge.** 529 S. 4th St. Close to everything, including the capitol.
Inexpensive: **Days Inn, Motel 6** and **Regal 8** are budget pleasers. Off I–55.

WHEELING. *Deluxe:* **Marriott's Lincolnshire.** Self-contained resort has everything one expects in a luxury resort.

 DINING OUT reflects the state's fertile land bordered by fish-filled waters and German and Central European influence in the northern part of the state. Establishments are categorized according to the cost of a full-course dinner from the medium-price range of their menus: *Deluxe:* over $30; *Expensive:* $16–30; *Moderate:* $6–15; *Inexpensive:* under $6. Included are hors d'oeuvres or soup, entree and dessert; not included are drinks, tax and tips.

BLOOMINGTON. *Moderate:* **Central Station Restaurant.** New look for an old firehouse. Gift shop.

CHAMPAIGN. *Moderate:* **The Round Barn.** Actually a restored barn.

DUNDEE. *Moderate:* **Milk Pail.** On Fin 'n' Feather Farm. Good food, lots of it. Gift shops, Country Cupboard. Homemade bread.

EVANSTON. *Expensive:* **Café Provencal.** Hearty French country food served with classical music. Homey atmosphere, flavorful emphasis on fresh herbs.

GALENA. *Moderate:* **Stillman Manor Inn.** 1858 Victorian mansion. **The Kingston Inn.** Singing waiters serve a continental and American menu. Affordable wine list, classical and flamenco guitar entertainment.

GENEVA. *Moderate:* **Mill Race Inn.** Oodles of candlelit country atmosphere. Pastry kitchen a dessert delight.

GURNEE. *Moderate:* **Rustic Manor.** Large, rambling log restaurant built around re-created mill has appealing frontier décor with lots of antiques. Near Marriott's Great America.

JOLIET. *Moderate:* **The Sanctuary.** Stained glass and church pews remind diners restaurant was built on church property.
White Fence Farm. Country atmosphere, complete with corn fritters.

KANKAKEE. *Moderate:* **Yesteryear.** Located in house designed by Frank Lloyd Wright in 1900. Roast duck and quail are local favorites.

LINCOLN. *Moderate:* **Lincoln Depot.** In original train depot which was rich in Lincoln lore. Terrific soup and salad bar.

MARENGO. *Moderate:* **Shady Lane Farm.** Like visiting a friend's country place surrounded by manicured grounds.

MOLINE. *Moderate:* **Boar's Head.** Red snapper, beef. Old English mood.

OLNEY. *Moderate:* **Holiday.** Locally popular, bountiful Sunday buffet.

PETERSBURG. *Inexpensive:* **New Salem Inn.** State Park. Home-baked treats. Waitresses in Ann Rutledge costume. Marvelous Lincoln-era mood.

ROCKFORD. *Inexpensive:* **Bishop Buffet.** In Colonial Village Shopping Complex. Cafeteria. Colonial décor, super desserts prepared on the premises.

ST. CHARLES. *Moderate:* **Old Church Inn.** Unique setting is a historic church, vintage 1851. Meals also served outdoors, weather permitting.

SPRINGFIELD. *Moderate:* **Clayville Country Kitchen Restaurant.** 12 mi. W. on Rt. 125. Historic 150-year-old Stagestop, pioneer recipes. In Lincoln country.
Top of the Hilton. In the Springfield Hilton, 700 E. Adams St. Nice view of city.
Inexpensive: **Heritage House Smorgasbord.** 4 mi. S. on Rt. 66. A full plate of midwest favorites. Good for hungry families.

WHEELING. *Deluxe:* **Le Français.** Very famous, French and expensive.
Moderate: **94th Aero Squadron.** Pass old plane and ambulance to cross moat and sandbagged hallway. Can put on headsets and listen to takeoff and landing at Palwaukee Airport visible through picture windows.

WINNETKA. *Moderate:* **Indian Trail,** A North Shore favorite. Everything tastes homemade. Exceptional desserts and rolls.

WOODSTOCK. *Moderate:* **The Old Courthouse Inn.** Popular country kitchen in refurbished courthouse in the old square. Eat in the vault, browse boutiques after dessert.

INDIANA

Hoosier Heartland

Indiana is known for "Hoosier Hospitality," a warm spirit of friendliness that extends from the smallest towns to the largest city, Indianapolis.

The heart of Indianapolis is Monument Circle, adorned with the lofty Soliders and Sailors Monument, which has an observation platform at its top. From here, the web of streets fans out to include such worth while attractions as the John Herron School of Art, the Benjamin Harrison Memorial Home, Children's Museum, Scottish Rite Cathedral and James Whitcomb Riley home.

The city boasts many top-notch athletic facilities, including a new domed stadium with seating for over 60,000 fans. Indiana University's Natatorium hosts national and international swimming and diving competitions. Swimming, sailing, fishing, horseback riding and golf are some of the activities available at 4500-acre Eagle Creek Park and Reservoir, the largest city park in America.

Indianapolis's best-known attraction, however, is located five miles west of the center. This two-and-a-half-mile oval, the Indianapolis

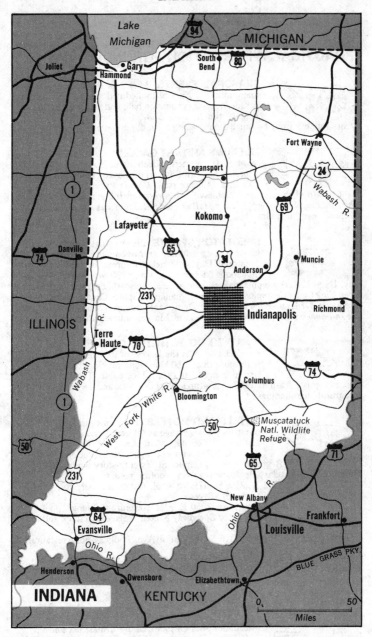

Motor Speedway, hosts the world-famous Indianapolis 500 every Memorial Day. During the "500" Festival, 30 days of hoopla preceding the big race, the city bustles with civic activities. Motels and hotels charge higher rates and are still jammed.

PRACTICAL INFORMATION FOR INDIANAPOLIS

 SEASONAL EVENTS. May 1 is the opening of the mammoth *500 Festival.* Scheduled activities include a parade, queen's coronation ball, and arts festival. In late August the *Indiana State Fair* gets underway with events ranging from hot-air balloon racing to fiddling contests.

 MUSEUMS AND ART GALLERIES. *Indianapolis Museum of Art.* Varied collections of European, Oriental, America, and primitive art displayed among three pavilions in a 140-acre park. *Connie Prairie Pioneer Settlement,* north of the city near Noblesville, is a restored Indiana village of 1836. *The Indianapolis Motor Speedway Hall of Fame Museum* has a large collection of classic cars, including 500 winners.

 SPECTATOR SPORTS. Biggest single spectator sport by far is the world-famous *Indianapolis 500,* held every Memorial Day. For ticket information, write the Indianapolis Motor Speedway, 4790 W. 16th St., Speedway, IN 46224. Top tennis players from around the world compete in the *U.S. Open Clay Court Championships* at the Indianapolis Sports Center the first week of August. NFL fans pack the Hoosier Dome for *Indianapolis Colts* football, and the *Indiana Pacers* provide NBA action at Market Square Arena.

 WHAT TO DO WITH THE CHILDREN. The *Children's Museum* is the largest of its kind in the nation, with more than 30,000 exhibits ranging from an Egyptian mummy to an original log cabin. The *Indianapolis Zoo,* in George Washington Park, features over 500 exotic and domestic animals in natural surroundings.

 HOTELS AND MOTELS. Price categories for double occupancy will average as follows: *Deluxe:* $50 and up; *Expensive:* $40–49; *Moderate:* $33–39; *Inexpensive:* under $32. Rates may be higher during the 500 Festival.

Deluxe: **Hyatt Regency.** 1 South Capitol St. Twenty-story landmark hotel. Huge lobby, with glass elevators; revolving rooftop restaurant.

Marriott Inn. 7202 E. 21st St. Heated pool, restaurant, bar, golf putting green, racquetball and tennis privileges.

Expensive: **Rodeway Inn East.** 7050 E. 21st. Restaurant, lounge, pool.

Moderate: **Indianapolis Motor Speedway Motel.** Adjacent to track and museum. Restaurant, lounge, pool, golf course.

La Quinta Inn-Airport. 5316 W. Southern Ave. Pool; 24-hour restaurant adjacent.

Inexpensive: **Red Roof Inn.** 5221 Victory Dr., at I–465 Emerson St. exit.

Susse Chalet Motor Lodge. 6990 Pendleton Pike. Pool. Five miles from state fairgrounds.

 DINING OUT. Price categories are as follows: *Deluxe,* over $20; *Expensive:* $15–20; *Moderate:* $8–14; *Inexpensive:* under $8. Not included are drinks, tax and tips.

Deluxe: **Chanteclair.** 2501 S. High School Rd. French menu. Extensive wine cellar.

New Orleans House. 8845 Township Line Rd. Lavish seafood buffet.

Expensive: **King Cole.** 7 N. Meridian St. Consistently excellent. Continental dishes.

La Tour. 1 Indiana Sq. Splendid view. French cuisine.

Moderate: **Iron Skillet.** 2489 W. 30th. Family-style dining in 19th-century homestead.

James Tavern. 8601 Keystone Crossing. Prime rib, roast pork, seafood. Rustic décor.

Inexpensive: **Paramount Music Palace.** I–465 and E. Washington St. Unusual family pizza restaurant with restored 1930s theatre pipe organ.

Shapiro's Deli-Cafeteria. 808 S. Meridian. Large selection of traditional deli foods.

EXPLORING INDIANA

Of Indiana's many natural areas, the most unusual is Indiana Dunes National Lakeshore and State Park, a 12-mile stretch of white sand dunes, beaches, and wooded hills along Lake Michigan. More than a thousand varieties of plants, trees, and exotic wildflowers thrive here, making it popular for nature hikes as well as sunning and swimming. The area is also directly in the migration path of thousands of birds.

A good portion of the well-kept farms in the lake country belong to Indiana's sizable Amish and Mennonite sects. Picturesque towns such as Middlebury, just east of Elkhart, feature Amish shops and restaurants. Amish Acres, a restored living-history farm in nearby Nappanee, offers a firsthand look at Amish traditions. Guided tours are available year round.

To the east is the heart and shopping mart for the Indiana lake district, bustling Fort Wayne. History comes alive here at an authentically reconstructed fort that depicts Indiana's last frontier military outpost. Fort personnel speak and dress in the style of 1816, playing roles that recreate the daily lives of early soldiers and settlers.

Known as "the covered bridge capital of the world," Parke County in west-central Indiana maintains 35 of these rustic structures. In October thousands of people visit the Covered Bridge Festival for tours, art shows, entertainment and, of course, splendid autumn scenery. Billie Creek Village, also in Parke County, is a cluster of turn-of-the-century shops and buildings where craftspeople demonstrate weaving, blacksmithing, and other old-time arts.

Most of Terre Haute sits atop a large plateau on the east bank of the Wabash River, a fact duly noted by early French fur traders who gave the town the name—"High Land." Terre Haute is the birthplace of two of Indiana's most famous, if dissimilar, sons: Eugene V. Debs, five-time presidential candidate of the Socialist Party, and Paul Dresser, composer of the state song. Both homes are open to visitors.

Harmony, a History of Idealism

Just southwest of Vincennes at the Illinois state line is the little town of New Harmony. Robert Owen bought the land in 1825, and began his program for a Utopian society here. He brought in distinguished educators, men of science, progressive artists, and social reformers from all over the world. In no time, New Harmony boasted a kindergarten (first in the U.S.), trade school and free public school system, free library, and civic drama club. The town was a-bustle with activity.

Yet in spite of these accomplishments, the great plan failed. Many reasons are given for its demise, but the main fault was that a large percentage of the community were freeloaders who had come seeking an easier way of life.

Today many of the original buildings and homes have been restored; prominent architects have added a number of notable modern structures.

Lincoln Land

From 1816 to 1830 young Abraham Lincoln lived in the southern
Indiana hills. The *Lincoln Boyhood National Memorial* in Spencer
County preserves the original family tract, which includes Nancy
Hanks Lincoln's grave and a working pioneer farm. The visitors' center
houses a museum and auditorium.

Of the historic towns along the Ohio River in southeastern Indiana,
none captures the charm of the steamboat era better than Madison.
Several hundred well-preserved 19th-century homes line the city's
streets.

Located in Bloomington is the nearly 2,000-acre campus of Indiana
University, cultural center for thousands of Hoosiers and visitors from
neighboring states who attend the numerous concerts, operas, and
plays performed by students and world-renowned artists. Brown County, east of Bloomington, is home to one of the Midwest's best known
art colonies. In the fall *Brown County State Park* and the rustic community of Nashville are flooded with visitors, who come to enjoy the bright
autumn colors in the hills and to visit Nashville's art galleries, museums, and crafts shops.

PRACTICAL INFORMATION FOR INDIANA

HOW TO GET THERE. *By car:* Seven interstates crisscross Indiana, connecting with an excellent network of
U.S. and state highways. Highways, towns and other
points are well marked, so getting around the state by
car is never a problem. *Hertz, Avis, National, Budget* and other rental car
agencies are found in most major cities and at airports.

By bus: In addition to *Greyhound* and *Trailways,* there are several smaller
carriers such as *Indiana Motor Bus.*

By air: Indianapolis International is served by *American, Delta, Eastern,
TWA* and other major airlines. Various regional and commuter carriers serve
cities around the state.

By train: Indiana fares well in national *Amtrak* passenger rail service with
trains from Indianapolis, Fort Wayne and other cities to both the East and West
coasts and other points. Routes are under review and are subject to change.

TOURIST INFORMATION SERVICES. For general travel information
write to the *Tourism Division,* Indiana Department of Commerce, 440 N.
Meridian St., Indianapolis 46204. For detailed recreational guide, write the
Indiana Dept of Natural Resources, 616 State Office Bldg., Indianapolis 46204.

MUSEUMS AND ART GALLERIES. Bloomington:
Designed by I.M. Pei, the *Indiana University Art Museum* houses thousands of works from around the world.
Fort Wayne: The *Lincoln Library and Museum* has the
world's largest private collection of Lincoln lore and memorabilia. Jeffersonville: *Howard Steamboat Museum* is a Vistorian mansion filled with steamboat
models, trophies and other treasures of the riverboat era. Peru: *The Circus
Museum,* with its vast collection of circus memorabilia, reflects Peru's heritage
as the winter home of some of America's greatest circuses.

SUMMER SPORTS. *Boating* and *water-skiing* are
popular at larger lakes and reservoirs; one of the best is
11,000-acre Lake Monroe near Bloomington. *Fishing* is
good in the south-central area where trout are often
cooperative in many clear streams. The state also stocks hundreds of miles of

streams and lakes with fish. *Riding* is another popular sport, particularly in the many state parks. Although Indiana has dozens of scenic *canoeing* routes, few surpass the natural beauty of Sugar Creek, which winds through the wooded bluffs of Turkey Run State Park.

WINTER SPORTS. Major college *football* and *basketball* draw huge crowds at Notre Dame, Purdue and Indiana University. *Downhill skiing* is a thriving sport at such areas as Ski World near Nashville and The Pines near Valparaiso. Seven state parks in northern Indiana have trails and equipment rentals for *cross-country skiing.*

WHAT TO DO WITH THE CHILDREN. Evansville: *Mesker Park Zoo* keeps most of its animals behind hidden moats, eliminating cages and bars. Fort Wayne: *The Children's Zoo* includes a 22-acre African veldt where you can watch free-roaming animals from safari cars.

Santa Claus: Rides, circus performers, a petting zoo, and Santa's toy shop are part of the fun at *Santa Claus Land,* a theme park about 40 miles northeast of Evansville.

DRINKING LAWS. Alcoholic beverages may be purchased by the drink or bottle Monday through Saturday from 7 A.M. to 3 A.M. No sales on Sunday except by the drink at establishments serving meals. Legal drinking age is 21.

HOTELS AND MOTELS. Price categories for double occupancy average as follows: *Deluxe:* $50 and up; *Expensive:* $40–49; *Moderate:* $33–39; *Inexpensive:* $32 or less.

BLOOMINGTON. *Deluxe:* **Fourwinds-A Clarion Resort.** On Lake Monroe. Private beach, marina, tennis courts, pool. Restaurant, lounge.

EVANSVILLE. *Moderate:* **Executive Inn.** 6th & Walnut. Indoor pool, tennis and racquetball courts. Buffet dining, lounge, entertainment.
Inexpensive: **Regal 8 Inn.** 4201 Highway 41 N. Indoor pool, restaurant.

FORT WAYNE. *Deluxe:* **Holiday Inn Downtown.** 300 E. Washington St. Restaurant, lounge, sidewalk cafe. Indoor pool, health club.
Inexpensive: **Red Roof Inn.** 2920 Goshen Rd. Restaurant adjacent.

GARY. *Deluxe:* **Holiday Star Resort.** Merrillville. Restaurants, lounges, Holidome facilities. Top entertainment in adjoining Holiday Star Theatre.
Moderate: **La Quinta Inn.** Merrillville. Pool. Supper club adjacent.

NEW HARMONY. *Moderate:* **New Harmony Inn.** E. North St. Indoor pool. Restaurant adjacent.

SOUTH BEND. *Expensive:* **Morris Inn.** On Notre Dame campus. Restaurant, lounge, golf course.
Moderate: **Days Inn.** 52757 US 31N. Pool, playground.

TERRE HAUTE. *Expensive:* **Howard Johnson's.** 3033 Dixie Bee Rd. (US 41). Indoor pool, sauna, restaurant, lounge.

Indiana's six *State Park Inns* offer attractive, completely modern accommodations at inexpensive rates. They are especially popular in the summer so reserve early. For information write the Dept. of Natural Resources, Division of State Parks, 616 State Office Building, Indianapolis, IN 46204.

DINING OUT. Price categories for a complete dinner average as follows: *Expensive,* over $15; *Moderate,* $8–15; *Inexpensive,* under $8. Not included are drinks, tax and tips.

BLOOMINGTON. *Moderate:* **Fireside Inn.** 4501 E. 3rd. Good steaks, seafood.

EVANSVILLE. *Expensive:* **Damien's.** 4701 Powell. French-Italian menu.
Inexpensive: **Wolf's.** 6600 1st Ave. In the barbecue business since 1927. Delicious beef, pork, mutton, chicken.

FORT WAYNE. *Expensive:* **Café Johnell.** 2529 S. Calhoun. A true gem.

MIDDLEBURY. *Inexpensive:* **Das Dutchman Essenhaus.** 240 US 20. Amish country kitchen specializing in family-style meals.

MORRISTOWN: *Moderate:* **The Kopper Kettle.** US 52. Noted for home cooking, generous portions. Between Indianapolis and Rushville.

NASHVILLE. *Moderate:* **Nashville House.** Van Buren St., 2 blocks N. of State 46. Home-style Hoosier cooking.

SOUTH BEND. *Moderate:* **Captain Alexander's Wharf.** 300 E. Colfax. Fresh seafood, steaks. Overlooks St. Joseph River falls.
Inexpensive: **Bishop Buffet.** Ireland Rd. at Miami St. Generous selection of homecooked foods.

TERRE HAUTE. *Moderate:* **Gasthaus–Stephan.** 3377 Dixie Bee Rd. (US 41). Continental cuisine. Grill room.

VINCENNES. *Inexpensive:* **Marone's Formosa Gardens.** 101 N. Second St. Chinese and American specialties.

IOWA

The Beautiful Land

From the Missouri River on its western border to the Mississippi River on the east, Iowa stretches out in a patchwork of fertile plains and forested hills. Des Moines, its largest city, is the commercial and cultural heart of the state. Begin with a tour of the capitol, which overlooks the city. The gilded dome, one of the largest of its kind, rises 274 feet above the ground floor. Carved stone and wood, the work of individual skilled craftsmen, decorate the interior in unexpected places. Art work, mural paintings, intricate mosaics, and a huge post-World War I mural photograph ornament the walls. Across the street is the Iowa State Historical Museum and Archives. Organized in 1892, the department's fine collection of historic artifacts preserves Iowa history from the earliest geological time, through the days of the Indians and pioneers, to the present. The building also houses important genealogical, medical, and historical collections.

Other points of interest in Des Moines include the Heritage Village at the Iowa State Fairgrounds; the handsome Civic Center, with its fountains and its giant iron umbrella, the work of Claes Oldenburg; the geodesic-domed Des Moines Botanical Center and Terrace Hill, a restored 1869 Victorian mansion, now the Iowa governor's residence. Just outside the city are the Living History Farms, authentic working farms that portray the history of agriculture from pioneer days to modern times.

Just north is Ames and Iowa State University. Founded in 1868, the university is known for its outstanding programs in agriculture, the basic sciences, home economics, engineering, and veterinary medicine.

Traveling southeast from Des Moines on IA–163 will take you to Pella, settled by Dutch refugees in 1847. Wyatt Earp grew up here, and

523

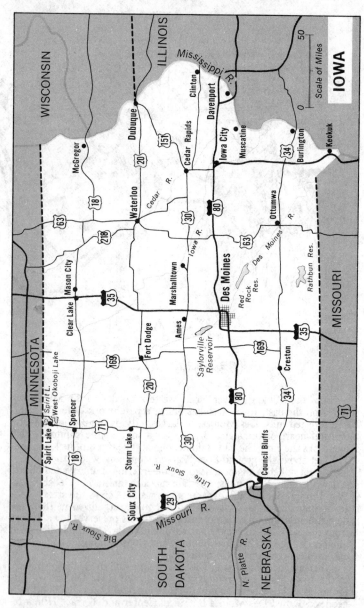

his boyhood home is part of the Pella Historical Village. The Kalona area in Washington County is Amish country. Known as "the plain people," the Old Order Amish live much as their ancestors did a century ago, rejecting most modern conveniences. Motorists should watch out for horse-drawn vehicles on area roads.

Farther north on IA–1 is Iowa City where the state's first permanent capitol was built in 1840. Now a National Historic Landmark, it stands at the center of the University of Iowa campus. Plum Grove, the historic home of Robert Lucas, first governor of the Territory of Iowa, was purchased by the State of Iowa in 1940 and restored.

The Banks of the Mississippi

Take a tour up the Great River Road, which hugs the banks of the Mississippi River. At Keokuk, the River Museum is housed aboard an old double helical paddle-wheel towboat, the *George M. Verity,* dry-docked on the riverfront. The Keokuk Dam, completed in 1913, has 119 spillways, and the locks are the largest on the Upper Mississippi. The locks and powerhouse are open to visitors during summer, free of charge. Mark Twain lived and worked briefly in Keokuk, and the only existing oil painting of the great author, along with other Twain memorabilia, is housed at the Keokuk Public Library.

The next principal city upriver is Burlington, which bursts into full river-town blossom each June with Steamboat Days. A marker stands where the governments of what were then the Wisconsin Territory and the Iowa Territory met in the Old Zion Church. Crapo Park and adjoining Dankwardt Park include 170 acres of natural stone bluffs, deep ravines, and majestic panoramas of the Mississippi River and the hills of Illinois in the distance. The park features formal gardens, an illuminated fountain, recreational facilities, nature trails, and a spring named for Chief Black Hawk, who once roamed this area with his tribe. Other Burlington highlights: Snake Alley (Ripley called it the world's crookedest street) and Phelps House, a restored Victorian mansion.

Northeast Iowa

Beautiful northeast Iowa is known for its tree-studded hills and rushing trout streams, some of the state's best canoe routes. Traveling north from Davenport along the Great River Road takes you to Le-Claire, the birthplace and early home of William F. "Buffalo Bill" Cody. A museum dedicated to Indians, pioneers, and steamboat days sits along the waterfront adjacent to the dry-docked sternwheeler *Lone Star,* restored to its original condition as a working barge, and open for tours. The museum contains displays associated with Buffalo Bill's Wild West shows, Cody's rifles, Indian artifacts, and memorabilia of riverboat days.

At Clinton, the completely restored triple-deck sternwheeler *City of Clinton* serves from May to October as a theater for summer stock. The 193-foot showboat was acquired from West Virginia in 1966. Its steam-driven engines, turbines, generators, and huge paddle-wheel shafts are intact and open for inspection. Follow the river to Dubuque, an early boat-building center, for a tour of the *William M. Black,* a restored steam-powered sidewheeler.

If you head west from Davenport on I-80, stop at West Branch to visit the Herbert Hoover Presidential Library–Museum. It houses papers, personal correspondence, books, manuscripts, audio-visual materials, and memorabilia of the first president born west of the Mississippi River. The Research Library has 8,000 volumes on the economic, political, and social history of America in the 20th century. In the auditorium films are shown several times daily during the summer.

Adjoining the grounds of the library-museum is Herbert Hoover National Historic Site. Here, the two-room Hoover Birthplace Cottage, restored in 1938 to its original appearance, holds many possessions of the Hoover family. The cottage, built in 1871, remains on its original site, and a replica of the blacksmith shop operated by the president's father stands behind the cottage. Across the street is the old Quaker Meeting House Herbert Hoover attended as a boy, and the graves of President and Mrs. Hoover are on a hillside southwest of the birthplace cottage.

Continuing westbound on I–80, a key stopover is the Amana Colonies, seven Old World villages. Amana was founded in 1854 in the Iowa River Valley by the Inspirationalists under the leadership of Christian Metz. The Inspirationalists established their own industries to provide the villages with all the essentials of life, and Amana products soon attracted national attention. Tours are provided through Amana factories and workshops, which produce fine woolens, furniture, baked boods, wines and meat specialties in the Old World tradition. Amana restaurants are famous for excellent meals served family style. The Amana refrigerator and other appliances are also manufactured here.

Guided tours are available of the Amana Heim and Blacksmith Shop Museum Complex. The house ("heim) features antique Amana furniture and household items. Another fine attraction, the Museum of Amana History shows a film every hour on the history of the Colonies. The Community Kitchen, Cooper Shop and Hearth Oven Museum in Middle Amana preserves the workplace of the past.

Western Iowa

In northwest Iowa, Fort Dodge is a good starting place. The Fort Dodge Historical Museum, Stockade, and Fort include a replica of a government fort built in 1850 as quarters for the U.S. Sixth Infantry, which protected the early settlers from hostile Sioux. The replica was built to the exact specifications of the original drawings. Two original log cabins, the first hotel, and the first post office in Fort Dodge were used in recreating the old fort.

The Estherville area is the gateway from the east of Iowa's leading resort area—the Iowa Great Lakes—consisting of Spirit Lake, West Okoboji and East Okoboji. Dozens of smaller lakes dot this region; all are of glacial origin, dating back about 12,500 years. There are ample tourist facilities as well as camping and other outdoor recreational areas.

Two excellent state parks are the Lewis and Clark south of Sioux City and Lake Manawa near Council Bluffs. Ample camping facilities are available in these parks as well as at Wilson Island near the DeSoto National Wildlife Refuge, west of the town of Missouri Valley. The refuge is a public-use area, and a major feeding and resting place for waterfowl migrating along the Missouri River Valley. Thousands of ducks and geese congregate here during their long spring and fall flights. Artifacts recovered from the sunken steamboat *Bertrand* (1865) are on display in a visitors' center and museum.

Bordering much of the Missouri River are the Loess Bluffs, a series of hills, terraces and ridges formed over 30,000 years ago when glacial streams deposited loess (loose soil) along the river valley. This unusual topography exists nowhere else in the world except China.

A big event in southwest Iowa occurs every August in Sidney and reflects the heritage of cattle-raising in the area. Riders gather from all parts of the country for the Sidney Championship Rodeo, a six-day exhibition that captures the spirit of the Old West.

PRACTICAL INFORMATION FOR IOWA

HOW TO GET THERE. *By car:* Interstate 80 from the east and west, Interstate 35 from the south and north through the center of the state, and Interstate 29 from the south and north through the western section of the state. *By air:* The main carriers to Des Moines are *United, Republic, T.W.A., Frontier, Ozark,* and *American Central. By bus: Trailways, Greyhound* (east and west) and *Jefferson* (north and south) have very good coverage throughout the state.

HOW TO GET AROUND. *By car:* The state has an excellent network of U.S. and state primary highways, paved secondary roads, and county highways, making even the most out-of-the-way place easily accessible. Maps are available by writing the Dept. of Transportation, 826 Lincolnway, Ames, Iowa 50020. *By air: Ozark Air Lines* is the major intrastate carrier. It flies to: Davenport, Des Moines, Waterloo, Cedar Rapids, and Sioux City. *By train:* Amtrak has service to Ottumwa, Osceola, Mt. Pleasant, Creston, Burlington, and Fort Madison. *By bus:* Besides *Trailways, Jefferson* and *Greyhound* there are numerous smaller carriers operating in Iowa.

TOURIST INFORMATION. Tourism Division, *Iowa Development Commission,* 250 Jewett Building, Des Moines, Iowa 50309. For a guide map and business directory to the Amana Colonies: *Amana Colonies Travel Council,* Amana, Iowa 52203.

WINTER SPORTS. *Hunting:* In addition to pheasant hunting, Iowa has good quail, partridge, grouse, duck, goose, woodcock, rabbit, squirrel, woodchuck, raccoon, fox, and coyote hunting open to both resident and non-resident hunters. Nonresident fees are substantially higher than resident fees, but not excessive for the amount of game available to the hunter.

Unfortunately, neither the deer nor turkey hunting is open to nonresidents. Complete information on hunting seasons, bag limits, and licensing requirements and fees is available from the Superintendent of Information and Education, *Iowa Conservation Commission.* Wallace State Office Bldg., Des Moines, Iowa 50319. Specify the type of game you are interested in, and they will provide handy pamphlets on where to find and how to hunt it.

Skiing (Alpine and cross-country), *snowmobiling* and *ice fishing* are also available in the state.

SUMMER SPORTS. *Fishing, boating, water-skiing,* and *sailing* have long been popular in the Iowa Great Lakes Region in upper northwest Iowa, and at Clear Lake in north-central Iowa. They have also taken hold at such large reservoirs as Red Rock near Knoxville, southeast of Des Moines; Lake Rathbun near Centerville, in south-central Iowa; Saylorville near Des Moines, and Carolville near Iowa City. The state's many major rivers also offer excellent fishing, boating and water-sport opportunities.

Canoeing: Canoe rentals are available in many cities around the state adjacent to the more easily accessible rivers. Overnight camping at state and privately-operated camping areas adjacent to the state's rivers.

Information on fishing, boating, sailing, water sports, and canoeing Iowa rivers is free from the Superintendent of Information and Education, *Iowa Conservation Commission,* Wallace State Office Bldg., Des Moines, Iowa 50319, and from the Tourism Division, *Iowa Development Commission,* 250 Jewett Building, Des Moines, Iowa 50309.

SPECTATOR SPORTS. *Baseball* thrives in Des Moines, where the *Iowa Cubs* of the American Association take to the diamond each spring. *Football, basketball* and top-ranked collegiate *wrestling* are available at the University of Iowa (Big Ten) at Iowa City, at Iowa State University (Big Eight), Ames, and the University of Northern Iowa, Cedar Falls. Drake University in Des Moines not only has Missouri Valley Conference sports, but is the site each April of the nationally prominent Drake Relays featuring top amateur university, college and high school *track and field* events.

MUSEUMS AND GALLERIES. The *Cedar Rapids Art Center* houses the world's largest collection of works by Iowa native Grant Wood, as well as many other contemporary paintings and prints.

The *Davenport Municipal Art Gallery* has a notable Grant Wood collection on permanent display in addition to numerous changing exhibits.

The *Davenport Putnam Museum* features a riverboat section, a pioneer room, and other exhibits on American history.

The *Des Moines Art Center* has an excellent collection of 19th- and 20th-century American and European art. The *Center* itself is by Eliel Saarinen. An addition, designed by I.M. Pei, houses contemporary sculpture.

The *Des Moines Center of Science and Industry* offers exhibits on space, environment, photography, and science, plus the *Sargent Planetarium.*

The *Salisbury House* in Des Moines is a replica of a King's Country House in Salisbury, England. It was built by a Des Moines millionaire descended from a 16th-century mayor of Salisbury; most of the interior materials were taken from the ancestral home in England. The rooms are filled with authentic Tudor furnishings, tapestries and artworks.

Each of the state universities also has art galleries open to the public.

DRINKING LAWS. State-run liquor stores are open daily except Sunday and legal holidays. Beer may be purchased in grocery stores during normal operating hours until 2:00 A.M. except Sundays when hrs. are noon to 10 P.M. Bars and restaurants are permitted to sell mixed drinks and beer on Sunday from noon to 10 P.M. The legal drinking age in Iowa is 19.

WHAT TO DO WITH THE CHILDREN. *Living History Farms* on I-80 west of Des Moines features a pioneer village and three working farms: the Pioneer Farm of 1840, the Horse-Powered Farm of 1900, and the Farm of Today and Tomorrow. There are crafts demonstrations, hayrides, and special events every weekend. *Adventureland,* just east of Des Moines, is a theme park with over 100 rides and daily live entertainment. Des Moines, Davenport, and Waterloo have children's zoos.

HOTELS AND MOTELS in Iowa are easy to find, but it is wise to make reservations early. Large motel chains with swimming pools operate throughout the state. However, there are numerous fine family-operated motels which provide a personal warmth only an individual innkeeper can give.

For free accommodations guide write the *Iowa Hotel & Motel Association,* 515 28th Street, Des Moines, Iowa 50312, or *Iowa Development Commission,* 250 Jewett Bldg., Des Moines, Iowa 50309.

The price categories for double-occupancy, one bed, will approximate: *Deluxe:* $45 and up; *Expensive:* $39–44; *Moderate:* $33–38; *Inexpensive:* under $32. (Hotel-motel tax in some cities.)

AMANA COLONIES. *Deluxe:* **Holiday Inn.** Off I-80 in Little Amana Complex. Restaurant, Amana shops, indoor pool

Inexpensive: **Die Heimat County Inn.** In village of Homestead off I-80. Restored 1858 hotel, furnished with antiques and handcrafted Amana furniture. Small, family-operated. Continental breakfast available.

AMES. *Deluxe:* **Holiday Inn Gateway Center.** US 30 Restaurant, lounge, live entertainment, pool.

Inexpensive: **Iowa State Memorial Union.** ISU campus, Iowa State Center exit. Restaurants, lounge, game rooms, browsing library.

Silver Saddle. US. 69 and Jct. US 30. Several restaurants nearby. Pool.

BETTENDORF. *Deluxe:* **Jumer's Castle Lodge.** I–74 at Spruce Hills Dr. One of Iowa's outstanding motels. Bavarian décor. Two lounges. Excellent restaurant. Pool and sauna.

BURLINGTON. *Expensive:* **Best Western Pzazz Motor Inn.** 3001 Winegard Dr. Indoor pool. King- and queen-sized beds. Lounge with live entertainment. Two miles from Crapo Park on Mississippi River.

The Holiday. 2759 Mt. Pleasant. Indoor pool, restaurant, lounge. Putting greens and game room.

CEDAR RAPIDS. *Deluxe:* **Stouffer Five Seasons Hotel.** 350 First Ave. Part of convention and entertainment complex. Heated pool, exercise equipment. Saunas. Rooftop restaurant.

Moderate: **Executive Motor Inn.** 3100 16th Ave. SW. Restaurant, lounge, pool.

CENTERVILLE. *Moderate:* **Motel 60 & Villa.** On Highway 5, seven miles from Lake Rathbun. Some efficiency suites, also rooms with steam baths. Fish-cleaning facilities.

CLEAR LAKE. *Moderate:* **Best Western Holiday Motor Lodge.** Near lake. Very popular five-story motor lodge. Good restaurant, lounge, entertainment. Indoor pool, sauna.

COUNCIL BLUFFS. *Moderate:* **Best Western Frontier Motor Lodge.** Restaurant, pool, whirlpool, sauna.

DAVENPORT. *Expensive:* **Clayton House.** 227 LeClaire St. Restaurant, lounge, indoor and outdoor pools. Overlooks the Mississippi.

DES MOINES. *Deluxe:* **Airport Hilton Inn.** 8 min. from downtown. Indoor pool and putting green, whirlpool, sauna. Sidewalk café. Good restaurant. Indoor tropical courtyard.

Hotel Fort Des Moines. A downtown landmark on the National Register of Historic Places. Restaurant, wine bar, lounge with live entertainment.

Capitol Plaza Holiday Inn. Downtown, 1050–6th Ave. Lounge, live entertainment, pool, roof-top restaurant. Near Veteran's Auditorium and Drake University.

Expensive: **Adventureland Inn.** Very nice with tropical décor. Adjacent to Theme Park. Reservations advised. Summer rates are higher.

Moderate: **Peppertree Inn.** 3809–109th St. Good restaurant, pool.

Best Western Bavarian Inn. NE 14th St. Pool, whirlpool. Restaurant, lounge.

Inexpensive: **Redwood Motel.** 3411 Hubbell, Hwy 6 and 65. Small. Family-owned. 3 mi. from Adventureland Theme Park; ¾ mile from State Fair Grounds.

DUBUQUE. *Deluxe:* **Midway Motor Lodge.** 3100 Dodge St. Large recreation area under bubble dome for suntanning, swimming, whirlpool and games. Excellent food in Hoffman House restaurant; live entertainment in bar. Mississippi River and river boat excursions nearby.

Inexpensive: **Julien Motor Inn.** 200 Main St. Restaurant, riverboat lounge. Overlooks the Mississippi.

FORT DODGE. *Expensive:* **Best Western Starlite Village Motel.** Jct. Hwy. 169 and 7. Restaurant, lounge, live entertainment, indoor pool, saunas.

Moderate: **Holiday Haus Motel.** Jct. Hwy. 169 and 20. Pool. Restaurant and lounge with live entertainment.

IOWA CITY. *Deluxe:* **Best Western Cantebury Inn.** King and Queen canopied beds. Old World atmosphere. Some rooms with fireplaces. Indoor pool. European steakhouse and lounge.

Expensive: **Highlander Inn & Supper Club.** I–80 and Highway 1. Near university campus. Restaurant, lounge, indoor pool.

KEOKUK. *Moderate:* **Keokuk Motor Lodge.** On US 218. Picturesque grounds. Mississippi River and dam 2¾ miles away. Restaurant nearby.

OKOBOJI. *Deluxe:* **Brooks Beach Resort.** On East Okoboji Lake. Family-owned. Rec. facilities. Sand beach, lakeshore fishing, tennis, playground, boat ramp and slips, swimming pool. Golf course nearby.

New Inn. On West Okoboji Lake. Restaurant, supper club, Hawaiian lounge, indoor and outdoor pools, tennis, 9-hole golf course, lakeshore swimming.

SIOUX CITY. *Expensive:* **Howard Johnson's Motor Lodge.** Restaurant, lounge, pool, tennis court. Also, sauna, whirlpool; guest laundry.

WATERLOO. *Moderate:* **Conway Inn Motel.** W. 5th and Jefferson. Restaurant, lounge. Near Civic Center.

 DINING OUT in Iowa is a total experience. The selection ranges from old-fashioned home cooking to international cuisine. Iowa's famous beef and pork are on almost all menus. Restaurant price categories for a complete dinner will average as follows: *Expensive,* $15 and up; *Moderate,* $10–15; *Inexpensive,* under $10. Not included are drinks, tax and tips.

AMANA COLONIES. *Inexpensive.* **Colony Market Place.** Charming Old World rathskeller. Delightful German-American food.

Ox Yoke Inn. Bavarian motif accented by a fireplace re-creates old Europe. German and American entrees.

Ronneburg. In summer you can eat and drink on roof. Family style, German cuisine. Specialties include sauerbraten and Wiener schnitzel.

BURLINGTON. *Moderate-Expensive:* **Pzazz! Back Porch.** 3003 Winegard Dr. Gourmet dining. Prime rib and steak Diane are specialties.

CEDAR FALLS. *Moderate:* **The Broom Factory Restaurant & Lounge.** US 20 and N. Main. Prime rib, steaks, and seafood. Building is on the National Register of Historic Places.

CEDAR RAPIDS. *Moderate:* **The Amalgamated Spirit & Provisions Company.** 3320 Southgate Ct. SW. Prime rib, fresh seafood.

Inexpensive: **Bishop Buffet.** In Lindale Mall, and Westdale Mall. Large selection of homecooked foods at reasonable prices in these cafeterias.

DAVENPORT. *Moderate-Expensive:* **Gay Nineties.** 227 E. LeClair St., Clayton House. Prime rib, steak, lobster. Charming 1890s decor.

DES MOINES. *Moderate:* **Babe's.** 417–6th. A tradition. Italian/American cuisine at its best.

Bavarian Haus. 5220 NE 14th St. An experience in the higher art of German cooking.

Chicago Speakeasy. 1520 Euclid. Steaks, prime rib. Excellent salad bar. Clever Prohibition-era décor.

Inexpensive: **Bishop Buffet.** In Merle Hay Mall and Wakonda Shopping Center. Large selection of home-cooked foods. Cafeteria service.

DUBUQUE. *Moderate-Expensive:* **Ryan House.** Excellent restaurant in charming Victorian mansion with some of its original elegant appointments intact. Specialties are beef Wellington, roast duckling, seafood Newburg.

Moderate: **Leiser's Supper Club.** Three miles north of Dubuque on US 52. Pleasant country stop with good view. Prime rib, lobster tails, chicken, and catfish.

IOWA CITY. *Moderate:* **Iowa River Power Company.** 501 First Ave., Coralville. Outstanding food served in unusual surroundings of a converted power plant. Hoover Presidential Library not far away.

MALCOM. *Inexpensive:* **Dickey's Prairie Home.** I–80 and Highway 63. Hearty down-home cooking. All-night breakfast bar.

OKOBOJI. *Moderate:* **Lakeview Room.** At New Inn, overlooking the lake. Seafood, steaks; live entertainment and dancing nightly except Sundays.

STORM LAKE. *Inexpensive:* **Cobblestone Inn.** Good food in an early American environment.

Ken-a-Bob Buffet. Excellent cafeteria, noted for homecooking.

MICHIGAN

Detroit and the Land between the Lakes

The top of the downtown Renaissance Center (RenCen) is a good place to get a feel for this river city. The Metropolitan Detroit Convention and Visitors' Bureau is below you at Suite 1950, 100 Renaissance Center. The Visitor Information Center is on the street below near Hart Plaza.

A minibus stops at RenCen on its regular run through the downtown area. Old English streetcars pass nearby. People Mover, a 2.9-mile monorail, is being built downtown.

Six blocks north of the RenCen is a small area called Greektown, a favorite downtown spot for Greek food, belly dancing, nighttime street life, and little ethnic shops. A major restoration of Trapper's Alley is underway, including shops, artist studios and restaurants. About three miles north at Grand Boulevard and Woodward Avenue is the New Center, site of the Fisher Theatre and General Motors world headquarters.

The Cultural Center

A few blocks south of the New Center, Wayne State University shares the Woodward Avenue area with a dozen cultural institutions most of them free. The Detroit Institute of Arts, which celebrates its centennial this year, has many special events as well as 35,000 works in 101 galleries, including two contemporary wings. The Detroit Public Library has its own walking tour, which includes the Burton Historical Collection and the National Automotive History Collection. You can walk along 18th- and 19th-century streets in the Detroit Historical Museum at Woodward and Kirby. Kirby is also the site of the Chil-

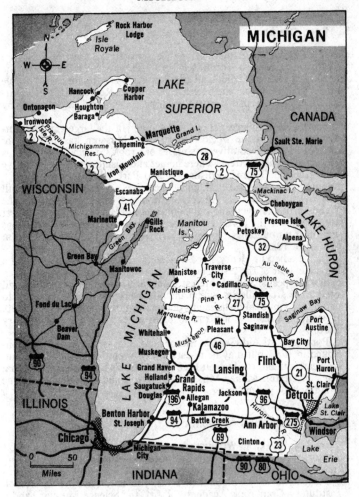

dren's Museum and the International Institute. Other cultural stops in the area include Your Heritage House, a Black museum; Detroit Community Music School; and the Detroit Science Center. The Afro-American Museum is located at 1553 West Grand Blvd.

Belle Isle

Belle Isle, east along Jefferson Avenue, has been a favorite place for family picnicking, canoeing, and ball games for a century. It includes a conservatory, aquarium, nature center, carillon, the Dossin Great Lakes Museum and the exciting Safari Trail Zoo for children.

Ford Country

Michigan Avenue runs twelve miles west to the heart of Dearborn (to travel faster take the Edsel Ford Freeway, I–94 West). On the northwest corner of Michigan and Southfield is a monorail or "people mover" running from the bronzed glass Hyatt Regency Hotel to Fairlane Town Center, one of North America's newest and largest shopping centers.

Southwest of this corner is the "skyline" of the largest indoor-outdoor museum in the world. Henry Ford Museum has 14 acres of technology and decorative arts under one roof. Greenfield Village has 260 acres of village streets where homes and businesses of the past have been restored. Thomas Edison's Menlo Park laboratory is one of a hundred reconstructed buildings. There are a 17th-century windmill and Pilgrim house; the 19th-century homes of famous Americans; the Wright brothers' cycle shop; the birthplace of Henry Ford and the first auto factory of the Ford Motor Company; plus a variety of craft shops and business buildings typical of early America. The Firestone Farm opened in 1985.

In the adjacent Henry Ford Museum, visitors can walk through a one-hour tour of the artifacts of early American technology and then explore a specific area of interest: home arts, automobiles, planes, and decorative arts galleries which include everything from furniture to ceramics to musical instruments chosen from the period 1670 to 1930. Upstairs is a display of personal mementoes from the life of Henry Ford.

Popular Ford and General Motor auto company tours were discontinued in 1980, but may be re-established eventually, so check it out. You can still tour the Detroit Free Press, Stroh's Brewery, the National Bank of Detroit Money Museum in Detroit and Leader Dog for the Blind School in Rochester.

Other Suburban Attractions

In Royal Oak, at Woodward and Ten Mile Road, is the Detroit Zoological Park with 122 beautifully landscaped acres containing thirty large, barless animal exhibits.

Farther north, in Bloomfield Hills, you may tour the Cranbrook Institutes—Cranbrook Academy of Art, the Science Museum, and a fine Planetarium.

North off I–75, at Oakland University, is Meadow Brook Music Festival (summer) and the Meadow Brook Theater (fall and winter). Also at Oakland is one of America's grand old houses, Meadow Brook Hall, open for public tours.

PRACTICAL INFORMATION FOR DETROIT

HOW TO GET AROUND. *By car:* Always refer to current highway numbers and a current map. Names associated with highways are: I–75, south to north, is the Seaway Freeway, Fisher Freeway, Chrysler Freeway. I–94 is the Edsel Ford Freeway. U.S. 10, the John Lodge Freeway, merges with Northwestern Highway and with I–696, Walter Reuther Highway. I–96, the Jeffries Freeway, joins I–275 (no name) for a few miles. M–85 is Fort Street; M–1 is Woodward Avenue; M–3 is Gratiot; M–102 is, east to west, Vernier,

Base Line, Eight Mile, Grand River and M–102 Expressway. U.S. 24 is Telegraph Road.

By bus: Maps of bus routes are obtainable at the Visitor Information Center. The booth also has general maps of the area.

By taxi: The taxi rate is $.90 the moment you get into the cab and $1 for each additional mile.

From the airport: Shortway Lines buses run from Metro airport to downtown hotels and cost $6 one-way, $11 round-trip. The trip takes about 45 minutes. There's limousine service to many of the suburban hotels at a considerably higher rate.

By train: There are no local trains. *Amtrak* runs three times daily to Chicago via Ann Arbor, Jackson, Albion and Kalamazoo; also daily to Toledo for connections east to New York City. Regular service from Detroit or Windsor to Toronto.

TOURIST INFORMATION. *Visitor Information Center,* 2 East Jefferson. (313) 567–1170.

MUSEUMS AND GALLERIES. The *Detroit Historical Museum* centers its displays around the city of Detroit: Here you may see the city as it existed 100 years ago reflected in the exhibits and pictures.

Also in the city is the *Detroit Institute of Arts.* World famous, this excellent gallery has examples from almost every culture of note in the world. The south wing houses a permanent African art and artifacts exhibit. Kresge Court dining area, with regular concerts, was recently renovated.

In Dearborn is the *Henry Ford Museum,* and *Greenfield Village,* a reconstructed 19th-century outdoor village.

At Bloomfield Hills are the *Cranbrook Institutes,* including the museum of the Cranbrook Academy of Art. Here you will find an excellent collection of fine arts, well displayed and featuring many of the contemporary artists of the area. *Cranbrook Science Museum* is a fine stop for adults and children.

HISTORIC SITES. At 6325 W. Jefferson, is the *Fort Wayne Military Museum.* The military feeling of 100 years ago is captured in the exhibits and fortifications in this unique museum. The actual stone barracks and the small museum with Indian memorabilia are just two of the many excellent displays which you may see.

TOURS. *Gray Line* offers three-to-seven hour tours, $15 to $19, mid–June through September; one includes *Greenfield Village.* Other tour companies, for groups only, include *Action, D-Tours, Tower Bus, Artours,* and *Shopping Spree Tours.*

Several summer cruises run daily to Boblo Island Amusement Park, with its picnicking, zoo, historic sites, and theme park. The ride down the river affords an excellent view of the Detroit skyline.

Trolleys tour downtown, including the only double-decker open-air trolley in the U.S.

MUSIC. The Detroit Symphony Orchestra performs at the Henry and Edsel Ford Auditorium at 20 Auditorium Drive. In the summer they play at Meadow Brook Music Festival, Oakland University, Rochester. In town, check Music Hall, Orchestra Hall, and Premier Center. North in Clarkstown, Pine Knob holds concerts in summer.

WHAT TO DO WITH THE CHILDREN. The *Belle Isle Zoo and Aquarium* has a Safari Trails Zoo; and children may ride a miniature railroad through naturalistic terrain at the *Detroit Zoological Park* in Royal Oak. Visit *Detroit Science Center,* downtown, and *Kensington Children's Farm and Village,* adjacent to Kensington Metro Park northwest of the city.

HOTELS AND MOTELS in metropolitan Detroit cater to the automobile industry. They range from sophisticated through full-service contemporary to a few family motels (accommodations also in Windsor, Canada). The price categories in this section, for *double* occupancy, will average: *Deluxe:* $120; *Expensive:* $60, *Moderate:* $45; *Inexpensive:* $35.

DOWNTOWN. *Deluxe:* **Westin.** Renaissance Center. Spectacular 73-story atrium hotel. Riverfront. Revolving restaurant, The Summit; also for dining, La Fontaine.

Pontchartrain. 2 Washington Blvd. Next to Cobo Hall overlooking river. Rooftop jazz in summer.

St. Regis. 3071 W. Grand Blvd., New Center opposite G.M. World Hqtrs. Old glamour renovated by Britain's Rank Hotels.

Expensive: **Mariner.** 231 Michigan Ave. High rise motel.

Moderate: **Shorecrest Motor Inn.** 1316 E. Jefferson, two blocks east of Renaissance Center. 54 rooms.

DEARBORN. *Deluxe:* **Hyatt Regency.** Fairline Town Center. Stunning atrium hotel; monorail to Fairlane shopping center. Ford Motor country! La Rotisserie restaurant is stunning.

Expensive: **Dearborn Inn.** 20301 Oakwood Blvd. Early American. Built by old Henry Ford opposite Greenfield Village. Piano bar, dining room, café. Comfortable and historic.

Holiday Inn. 22900 Michigan Ave. Near Greenfield Village and Ford Museum. Chambertin restaurant. Indoor, outdoor pools; whirlpool; sauna.

Moderate: **Dearborn TraveLodge.** 23730 Michigan. Families. Pool, movies; well-located.

Fairlane Inn. 21430 Michigan Ave. Good location, no restaurant/bar facilities. Motel.

PLYMOUTH. *Moderate:* **Mayflower Bed and Breakfast Hotel.** 827 W. Ann Arbor Trail. Historic hotel, well-kept, and interesting.

SOUTHFIELD. *Expensive:* **Holiday Inn.** 26555 Telegraph. Revolving restaurant tower. Near expressways.

Michigan Inn. 16400 J.L. Hudson Dr. Near most expressways. Fine dining at The Benchmark.

Hilton Southfield. 17017 W. 9 Mile Rd. Near expressways and old Northland shopping center.

Moderate: **Ramada Hotel.** 28225 Telegraph. Close to shopping and expressways.

BIRMINGHAM. *Moderate:* **Barclay Inn.** 145 S. Hunter. Central to elegant suburban main street.

Village Motor Inn. 300 N. Hunter Blvd.

BLOOMFIELD HILLS. *Expensive:* **Kingsley Inn.** 1475 N. Woodward. Comfortable rooms; balconies; restaurant and lounge; gift shop and art gallery. Restaurant, coffee shop, piano bar.

FARMINGTON HILLS. *Moderate:* **Botsford Inn.** 28000 Grand River. Old historic clapboard inn, American dining.

ROYAL OAK. *Inexpensive:* **Sagamore Motor Lodge.** 3220 N. Woodward. Free continental breakfast. Between Detroit and Birmingham.

TROY. *Expensive:* **Northfield Hilton.** 5500 Crooks at I–75. Extreme north edge of Metro area. Charley's Crab restaurant. Popular lounge.

Somerset Inn. 2601 W. Big Beaver. In elegant shopping center.

Moderate: **Drury Inn.** 575 W. Big Beaver. New high rise.

DINING OUT in metropolitan Detroit can be sophisticated, ethnic, varied. Restaurants cluster downtown, and in east, west, and especially north suburbs. Restaurant price categories: *Deluxe:* $25–35; *Expensive:* $12–25; *Moderate:* $8–12, *Inexpensive:* $5–8. Prices are for a complete dinner but do not include drinks, tax and tip. See also restaurants mentioned in hotel/motel listings. Check Windsor restaurants across the river in Canada.

Super deluxe: **London Chop House.** 153 W. Congress, downtown. World famous, elegant, crowded.

Restaurant Duglass. 29269 Southfield (north). Notorious chef, glamorous setting.

Van Dyke Place. 649 Van Dyke (east). Romantic, elegant. Glorious French food. Near Jefferson. Reserve weeks ahead!

Expensive: **Caucus Club.** 150 W. Congress. Same owners as London Chop House. Paneled piano bar. Fine menu.

Chambertin, in Holiday Inn Dearborn (west). Same good kitchen serves dining room, music bar, coffee shop. Excellent wine list.

Golden Mushroom. 18100 W. Ten Mile, Southfield (north). Popular suburban lunch spot.

Joe Muers. 2000 Gratiot, downtown east. No reservations. Fine fish.

Midtown Cafe. 139 N. Woodward, Birmingham (north). Trendy. Tasty. Balcony tables.

Money Tree. 333 W. Fort, downtown. French "sidewalk cafe" indoors behind glass.

Pontchartrain Wine Cellers. 234 W. Larned, downtown. French menu. Panelled intimacy. Excellent wine list.

Rhinocerous. 265 Riopelle. Artistic renovation of old stable in warehouse district east of RenCen.

Moderate: **Marios.** 4222 Second. Northern Italian cuisine. Go for lunch.

Peabody's. 154 S. Hunter, Birmingham (north). Hearty, informal, bargain prices. Expect a wait.

Inexpensive: **Chi-Chi's.** Popular Mexican restaurant. Several locations. The after-work crowd loves the drinks and snacks.

Hellas. 538 Monroe, Greektown near RenCen, in Detroit's favorite latenight ethnic neighborhood.

Magic Pan. Five locations, some in shopping malls, crepes, wine.

Olga's Kitchen. Renaissance Center, and malls citywide. Plants everywhere. Beef and lamb on Greek bread.

Traffic Jam and Snug. 4268 Second. Campus favorite. Fresh bread, quiche.

Sindbad's. 100 St. Clair, Detroit. No reservations, where socialites, sailors, and just plain folks mix. East on riverfront.

Soup Kitchen Saloon. Downtown in warehouse district. Blues and jazz entertainment.

Chuck Muer's seafood restaurants are excellent—all over Detroit and the suburbs, each one different, but all comfortable and with good food. *Expensive:* **Charley's Bar,** Hotel Pontchartrain. **Gandy Dancer,** Ann Arbor. *Moderate:* **Charley's Crab,** Troy. **Bloomfield Charley's,** Bloomfield. **Fairlane Charley's,** Dearborn. **Northville Charley's,** Northville. And there are others.

EXPLORING MICHIGAN

Michigan is two huge peninsulas washed by four of the five Great Lakes. The Algonquin Indians called it "Michigamea," land of great waters. These waters brought explorers to Michigan as early as 1618, and soon carried fur traders, miners, lumber barons, farmers, and eventually, iron ore to feed Detroit's automobile factories. Today huge lake freighters pass the spot where Cadillac founded a city in 1701 and called it *d'etroit,* literally "the straits."

Even a sampling of Michigan, the twenty-third largest state, should include stops in Detroit, in the lower peninsula, and the upper one. A corridor of cities runs westward from Detroit to Lake Michigan: Lansing, Ann Arbor, Battle Creek, Grand Rapids, Kalamazoo, Muskegon. A shorter corridor runs north through the General Motors complex at Flint to the tri-city area of Saginaw, Bay City, and Midland. Above the Bay City-Midland line, small towns and inland lakes dot the highways running to the Mackinac Bridge. Beyond the bridge is the Upper Peninsula, a proud and sparsely settled region of forested recreation areas. The land gets hillier and rockier going north, and by the time you hit the Lake Superior shore on the northern side of the upper peninsula, you are in the land of the Pictured Rocks and of Isle Royale National Park.

Traveling Toward Lake Michigan

Ann Arbor, 40 miles west of Detroit, is an ongoing fiesta of music, theater, art, and special-interest lectures, all related to the University of Michigan. A monthly calendar, available city-wide, lists these as well as events at the Matthae Botanical Gardens. Tour the campus, dine in the many student hangouts or sophisticated eateries, and check out the fine shopping.

Another university town, Lansing, is also the state's capitol and plays a vital part in automobile manufacturing. Michigan State University in nearby East Lansing has one of the nation's most beautiful campuses. It is the state's first land grant college. From Lansing travel west on I–96 to Grand Rapids, known once for furniture and now for its outdoor sculpture and exciting downtown renewal. Grand Rapids is hometown of former President Gerald Ford and the new Gerald Ford Museum.

West of Grand Rapids, the city of Holland is home of an annual Tulip Time Festival. For four days in May the city remembers its Dutch heritage. There are parades, pageants, wooden shoe dancing, and townspeople dressed in authentic Dutch costumes scrubbing streets with longhandled brooms. With good luck and good weather you may see the city's thousands of tulips in bloom.

Farther south on I–94 are the cities of Battle Creek—home of Kellogg's cereals—Kalamazoo, home of two of Michigan's finest universities and a great spot for antique hunters, and Jackson, with its Michigan Space Center and its computerized musical fountain. Driving West, you arrive at the major industrial cities of Muskegon and Benton Harbor. You have reached Lake Michigan.

This is boating and summer home country, whether you drive south towards Benton Harbor and on past the Indiana lakeshore dunes to Chicago, or north through Muskegon, Ludington, and Manistee to the hiking, camping, and glorious sand dunes of Sleeping Bear National Lakeshore. You can ride dune buggies outside the park.

The Sleeping Bear Dunes National Lakeshore leads you north to Michigan's busiest resort area. Follow the tiny towns, ferries, roadside fruit stands, and fruit farms around the Leelanau Peninsula to Traverse City, which celebrates a cherry festival in summer and a frozen cherry festival in winter. From this city overlooking the sailboats and swimmers of Grand Traverse Bay, you can reach the eleven main Lower Peninsula ski resorts and you can drive north along the shore through Charlevoix to Petosky and Harbor Springs.

At Interlochen, 15 miles southwest, more than 1,500 music students from across the nation gather to study music, drama, and dance. Travelers may attend their daily concerts and other performances.

Charlevoix is a lake city surrounded by 2-story Victorian cottages built at the turn-of-the-century by wealthy Chicagoans. Ernest Hemingway summered near here.

Take a ferry boat from here to Beaver Island, 35 miles out in the lake. This island was once the kingdom of James Strang, a self-proclaimed monarch who ruled his Mormon colony for nine years. When he decreed that all women must wear bloomers, he had gone too far. Someone shot him and ended the only kingdom to exist on U.S. soil.

Continue north through other resort cities (Petoskey, Harbor Springs), past rentable Victorian homes, boathouses, fish restaurants. You'll reach the Indian church and graveyard at Cross Village and restored Fort Michilimackinac in Mackinaw City. Take the ferry to Mackinac Island. Dominated by the long, white pillared porch of the Grand Hotel, the island was a fur-trading post operated by John Jacob Astor. An English military fort can be visited by rented bicycle, horse and carriage, or saddle horse. No cars are allowed on the island.

The Upper Peninsula

Fur traders, missionaries, miners, and lumberjacks discovered the ancient rocks and trees of the Upper Peninsula (UP) centuries before Henry Ford started making cars in Detroit. This is a mecca for those who love the wilderness. Tourist highlights include Isle Royale National Park, offshore in Lake Superior; a number of waterfalls: Laughing Whitefish, Douglas Houghton, and especially Tanquamenon Falls; and the photographers' paradise, the Pictured Rocks. There are eight major ski areas and the National Ski Hall of Fame. In the summer, visit the mines; mine tours include: Arcadian Cooper Mine, Hancock, and Adventure Copper Mine Greenland.

The UP is a wonderful place to camp—in the national forests, state parks, or on private grounds. Especially look into camping at Lake of the Clouds, Powder Mt. State Park, and Fayette State Park, a restored iron smelting community.

Lake Huron, the Eastern Shore

Drive back to Detroit on US 23 around Lake Huron, with its wide sandy beaches. Alpena and Rogers City, homes of Great Lakes sailors, are among the towns reflecting the lumbering, fishing, and boat-building side of Michigan's history.

South is Saginaw Bay where Saginaw, Bay City, and Midland comprise an industrial area mixed with recreational year-round opportunities. On Route 21, Port Huron, site of the Blue Water Bridge, is where the river towns take over. Boating is the major industry and recreation. At Harsen's Island, self-unloading ore boats plod up and down the dredged Detroit River, carrying an important part of the world's goods.

You have now returned to I-75. An hour's drive will take you back to Detroit after a "grand circle tour" of the state of Michigan.

PRACTICAL INFORMATION FOR MICHIGAN

HOW TO GET THERE. *By car:* Major routes into Michigan I-75, I-94, and Canada's Rte. 401; which approaches from Toronto and the east. *By train:* Amtrak runs from Chicago to Detroit via Kalamazoo, Battle Creek, and Jackson; it also runs to Toronto, Port Huron, and New York City. Canada's *ViaRail* runs from Windsor to Toronto and to New York City via Toledo.

By bus: Direct *Trailways* service will get you to Detroit only. *Greyhound* has fairly extensive routes into Michigan. The southern third of the state is so thickly settled that intrastate lines pick up where the Big Two leave off.

By air: Twenty Michigan cities have regularly scheduled flights in and out. Commuters include *Wright, Freedom* and *Simmons Airlines,* which works hand-in-hand with *Republic,* now headquartered in Detroit. Most major airlines fly to Detroit.

HOW TO GET AROUND. *By car:* Glance at a road map and you'll see that the southern third of Michigan has by far the most miles of divided highway. If you're planning to drive into the north country between October and April, it would be wise to check road conditions with the AAA or Highway Patrol.

By bus: The three widest-ranging bus lines within Michigan are *Shortway, North Star,* and *Indian Trails.*

By air: From Mackinac Island to Pellston, take *Phillips Flying Service.*

TOURIST INFORMATION. *Michigan Travel Commission,* P.O. Box 30226, Lansing 48909. Instate call 1–800 –292–2520. *Travel and Tourist Assn. of Southeast Michigan,* 64 Park St., Troy 48084. *West Michigan Tourist Assn.,* 135 Fulton East, Grand Rapids 49503. *East Michigan Tourist Assn.,* 1 Wenonah Park, Bay City 48706. *Upper Peninsula Travel and Recreation Assn.,* Box 400, Iron Mountain 49801.

MUSEUMS AND GALLERIES. *Gerald R. Ford Presidential Museum* in Grand Rapids; also the magnificent new *Grand Rapids Art Museum.* The tiny *Besser Museum* of natural history in Alpena; *Hackley Art Gallery,* Muskegon; the *Ski Hall of Fame,* Ishpeming, in the Upper Peninsula; a music museum at Interlochen and interesting museums at the universities statewide. *Michigan Space Center* in Jackson has space modules and displays from Apollo, Mercury, and Gemini flights, plus a Moon Room and Astrotheater.

HISTORIC SITES. Perhaps the most unusual historical fact concerning Michigan is that at one time *Beaver Island* in Lake Michigan was ruled by a "king"! This tiny monarchy of more than 100 years ago still shows evidences of its Mormon ruler.

Another deserted community is the *ghost town* of Fayette, now being restored as a state park.

The bloody Indian wars which erupted in this area are still remembered: there are no fewer than five restored or preserved forts in the state. Three historic state parks are Fort Michilimackinac, Fort Mackinac, and Mill Creek.

TOURS. Pre-scheduled tours are available through *Tower Bus Inc.,* Mount Clemens and Detroit, as well as *Indian Trails,* Owosso. Sterling is the home base for canoe trips down the Rifle River. Michigan has hundreds of places where canoes can be rented, along streams with names like Tittabawassee, Mainstee, Pere Marquette. One of the country's famed trout streams, the Au Sable, probably has more canoe traffic than any other.

If you want a little more boat between you and the water, take the two-hour cruise down the Au Sable River on the *River Queen,* a paddlewheeler from the days when they trafficked up and down the river in great numbers. The boat leaves from the Five Channels Dam near Oscoda. It is advisable to make reservations a few days in advance.

DRINKING LAWS. The legal age is 21. Sales by the drink or in package stores are allowed 7 A.M.–2 A.M. except Sunday, when at local option, they may begin at 2 P.M.

SUMMER SPORTS. *Water sports, golf,* and *tennis* are all enjoyed by millions each year. Trails for *hiking, biking,* and *horseback riding* are becoming more abundant, and *gliding* and *skydiving* also are gaining adherents. More than any of those, *hunting* and *fishing* are the recreations that attract people to the state because of the species that abound here.

WINTER SPORTS. *Skiing* and *snowmobiling* are the biggest cold-weather favorites and land-development patterns reflect this fact. Some *hunting* seasons occur with snow on the ground, and *ice-boating* and *ice-fishing* demonstrate that Michigan's thousands of lakes are never wasted.

SPECTATOR SPORTS. The most popular college and professional team sports are *baseball, football, basketball,* and *hockey.* Fast-proliferating rival tours in *golf* and *tennis* as well as *track and field,* all kinds of *auto racing,* and *winter Olympic sports* keep the fan busy. The new *Cherry Bowl* features college football in December at the Silverdome in Pontiac.

WHAT TO DO WITH THE CHILDREN. There's no end of historic sites and amusements for children outside the Detroit area. *Fort Michilimackinac* in Mackinaw City, with its remains from the fur trading and Indian days, is a wonderful place to take them. A little to the south, at Ossineke on the northeastern shore of Lake Huron, they may wander through a *prehistoric forest* which includes full-sized dinosaurs. South of Baldwin is a gigantic statue of *Paul Bunyan,* with displays of early logging days. In the southwestern corner of Michigan, the twin cities of St. Joseph and Benton Harbor have beaches, *Michigan Space Center* in Jackson is a must for the kids. Coloma has a *Deer Forest.* The little town of Holland has lots of transplanted Dutch people and customs which are interesting; the children will surely enjoy the *Dutch village,* the wooden-shoe factory, *Windmill Island Park,* and *Deerland Zoo.* At *Deer Acres,* near Bay City, children can feed the deer and also enjoy the Mother Goose characters and a fire engine ride.

Historic Village and Huckleberry Railroad, just north of Flint, operated by the Genesse County Parks & Recreation Department. This is a bona fide reproduction village, and the railroad ride is one of the few left in Michigan.

HOTELS AND MOTELS in outstate Michigan include such diverse establishments as the resorts of Mackinac Island and the state's simple but nicely furnished accommodations along the highways. The price categories in this section, for double occupancy, will average: *Deluxe:* $75 and up; *Expensive:* $60; *Moderate:* $45; *Inexpensive:* $30.

ANN ARBOR. *Expensive:* **Campus Inn.** 615 E. Huron, downtown. View of either campus or river. Small, good.

Ann Arbor Inn. 100 S. Fourth. Recently restored. Roof restaurant and pool.

Weber's Inn. 3050 Jackson at I-94. Large, with good restaurant and meeting rooms. Pool, sauna, lounge, dancing.

Moderate: **Bell Tower Hotel.** 300 S. Thayer, near central campus. Small, popular. Good restaurant.

Howard Johnsons's. 2380 Carpenter at US 23. Beautiful indoor pool.

Inexpensive: **Best Western Wolverine Inn.** 3505 S. State at I-94. Sauna.

Lamp Post Motel. 2424 E. Stadium Blvd. W. of US 23. Homey, attractive.

BATTLE CREEK. *Expensive:* **Stouffers.** 50 Capital Ave. S.W. Downtown. New highrise. Pool, Rooftop restaurant.

Moderate: **Comfort Inn.** Heated Pool. Downtown.

BAY CITY. *Moderate:* **Bay Valley Hotel and Resort.** Resort for golfers, tennis enthusiasts, tourists, diners. Meeting facilities.

BELLAIRE. *Expensive:* **Hilton Shanty Creek.** Ski and year-round resort overlooking lake. Good food.

CEDAR. *Moderate:* **Sugar Loaf Mountain Resort.** Skiing, golf, tennis, boating.

COPPER HARBOR. *Expensive:* **Keeweenaw Mountain Lodge.** Log cabins, lodge, golf. Rustic elegance.

GAYLORD. *Moderate:* **El Rancho.** Ranch facilities, water sports.
Chalet Center Motor Lodge. I–75 and M–32. Pools, tennis, restaurant.

GRAND RAPIDS. *Expensive:* **Grand Plaza Amway.** Restored elegance, downtown.
Marriott Hotel. 5700 28th St. S.E. New Ten minutes from downtown in Centennial Park.
Inexpensive: **Dillon Inn.** Near airport, I–96. Restaurants.

HARBOUR SPRINGS. *Moderate:* **Harbour Inn.** 19th-century lakeside resort being restored.

HOLLAND. *Expensive:* **Point West.** In nearby Macatawa. Year-round resort.

HOUGHTON. *Moderate:* **King's Inn.** US41. Downtown, near Isle Royale boat docks. Valley view. Whirlpool baths.
Main St. Inn. 820 Sheldon. Seven-story full-service hotel. Great dining room view. Whirlpool suites. Near Isle Royal dock and snowmobile trails.

KALAMAZOO. *Expensive:* **Hilton.** Adjacent to Kalamazoo Mall. Live theater, shopping, entertainment, dining.

LANSING-EAST LANSING. *Expensive:* **Harley Hotel.** 3600 Dunckel. Luxurious.
Moderate: **Capital Park.** Near Capitol.
Hilton. 7501 W. Saginaw Hwy. Modern. West side.

MACKINAC ISLAND. *Deluxe:* **Grand.** Complete summer resort.
Moderate: **Island House.** Old clapboard inn, a "little Grand."

MACKINAW CITY. *Expensive:* **Prince Timoa Inn.** Adjacent to ferry dock.

MARQUETTE. *Moderate:* **Holiday Inn.** Disco restaurant.
Ramada Inn. 412 Washington. Full-service.
Tiroler Hof. Restaurant and cocktails. Chapel, trout pond, ski slope.

PETOSKEY. *Moderate:* **Hayner's Motel.** US 31 and 131. Full service. Restaurant.
Stafford's Bay View Inn. Lovely restored rooms and dining room overlooking lake. Registered historic site.

ST. CLAIR. *Deluxe:* **St. Clair Inn.** Beautiful renovated inn on the river.
Chuck Muer's River Crab. Motel on the river. Fine seafood restaurant, breakfast and newspaper in bed!

ST. IGNACE. *Moderate:* **Straits Breeze Motel.** Lake view.

SAULT STE. MARIE. *Moderate:* **Ramada Inn.** Restaurant.

DINING OUT. Fine German and Scandinavian restaurants and dining rooms serving fresh fish from Michigan's abundance of waterways are almost everywhere. Restaurant price categories are: *Expensive:* $12 and up, *Moderate:* $9, *Inexpensive:* $9 and under. These prices are for hors d'oeuvres or soup, entree, and dessert. Not included are drinks, tax, and tips.

ANN ARBOR. *Expensive:* **Gandy Dancer.** 401 Depot. Clam-bake bucket.
Moderate: **Maudes.** 314 S. 4th. Carrot soup you'll die for. Crisp salads.
Old German. 120 W. Washington. Gemütlichkeit. Home cooking.

BENTON HARBOR. *Inexpensive:* **Holmsted.** 1919 Pipestone. Holm cooking.

CHARLEVOIX. *Moderate:* **Grey Gables Inn.** Dinner only.

CLARE. *Moderate:* **Doherty's.** Famous Sunday brunch in busy downtown.

ESCANABA. *Moderate:* **House of Ludington.** Once a grand hotel, now renovated as an elegant turn-of-the-century dining room. Lodging.

FRANKENMUTH. *Moderate:* **Zenders** and **The Bavarian Inn.** Both famous for chicken in this historic German village.

GRAND RAPIDS. *Expensive:* **Sayfee East.**
Moderate: **Great Lakes Shipping Co.** Dress up or down.
Inexpensive: **Schnitzelbank.** Oompa-pa good.

HOLLAND. *Moderate:* **Point West.** Lake view.

HOLLY. *Expensive:* **Holly Hotel.** Centerpiece of restored Battle Alley.

HOUGHTON. *Expensive:* **Main St. Inn.** Highrise dining room, good food, great view.
Moderate: **The Library.** Locals and university students love the sandwiches.
Inexpensive: **Ruohonen's Suomi Bakery & Restaurant.** Fresh pasties daily. Breakfast all day.

KALAMAZOO. *Expensive:* **Black Swan.** 3501 Greenleaf. Very elegant; good food. Wide-window view of swans.

LELAND. *Moderate-Expensive:* **The Cove.** By an old dam. You'll love it. Seafood specialties.
Bluebird Cafe. Family owned, unpretentious. Best fish in town.

MACKINAW CITY. *Expensive:* **Damsite Inn.** Overlooks a dam.

MARQUETTE. *Moderate:* **Northwood Supper Club.** Country setting, overlooking fish pond and woods. Patio in season. Sunday brunch special.

MARSHALL. *Expensive:* **Win Schulers.** Editor's Choice for best food, service, atmosphere in Michigan. Tiny historic town. You'll find Schulers elsewhere now, but not up to the original.

McMILLAN. *Moderate:* **Helmer House.** In Manistique Lakes area of Upper Peninsula. Turn-of-the-century roadhouse. Eat fresh fish, surrounded by antique clocks. Five hotel rooms available.

PETOSKY. *Expensive:* **Staffords Bay View Inn.** A classy old place with antiques and good food.

ST. JOSEPH. *Expensive:* **Tosi's.** Italian in the grand style. Suburban Stevensville.

Moderate: **Holly's Landing.** Rustic. Comfy.

SAULT STE. MARIE. *Moderate:* **Knife and Fork.** Ramada Inn. Wednesday smorgasbord.

Inexpensive: **The Antlers.** Bells ring, noisemakers blare, kids clap. Fish, steak and mounted animals.

MINNESOTA

Twin Cities and 15,000 Lakes

Minneapolis and St. Paul, Minnesota, may be directly across the Mississippi River from each other, but in no way are they "Twin Cities." Local residents consider them about as much alike as New Orleans and New York, San Francisco and Des Moines, or Tokyo and Leningrad.

St. Paul, the older city, is the state capital. It is Irish and Catholic. It is a smaller version of Boston, and fairly conservative, with the older Yankee influences still dominating the town. It is the end of "the East."

Minneapolis is a beautiful city. It has 11 lakes within the city limits, and they are still clean enough for swimming. Minneapolis has one of the finest park systems in the U.S., and its 156 parks are havens of greenery. They contain bikeways and hiking paths, flower gardens, wildlife areas, and numerous athletic facilities. Minnehaha Falls, in Minnehaha Park, was made famous by Henry Longfellow in his poem, *Song of Hiawatha* (though he'd never actually seen it himself). Minneapolis has twice been voted an "All-American City." Its combination of enlightened urban renewal, industrial progress and cultural pursuits is matched by few cities.

St. Paul is more small-town and more beautiful in some ways than Minneapolis. You can take a drive down Summit Avenue, a boulevard lined with stately old mansions cum apartments. It is on this street that F. Scott Fitzgerald ran down the steps of his home, raced along the avenue, and shouted, "It's done! It's finished!" He was talking about *This Side of Paradise.*

The theatrical scene in Minneapolis and St. Paul is hard to beat. For example, there are the renowned Guthrie Theatre, one of the nation's foremost repertory organizations; the Chanhassen Dinner Theater, with four live productions (including musicals) staged under the same roof nightly; the satirical Dudley Riggs Brave New Workshop; the acclaimed Children's Theater Company; numerous community theaters; and the Old Log Playhouse, on the shores of beautiful Lake Minnetonka.

The art scene is top-notch, too. Minneapolis has two major art galleries—the Walker Art Center and the Minneapolis Institute of Art, as well as the American Swedish Institute. St. Paul has the Science Museum of Minnesota, which, besides housing the Chimera Theater, where live productions are staged, boasts the McKnight 3M Omni-theater, where computer-operated projection equipment flashes cineramic films on a spherical screen that encircles the audience, to create the most advanced experience of its kind in the world.

Both cities have a campus of the University of Minnesota, one of the largest universities in the nation. Minneapolis can also boast the biggest summer festival in the U.S.—the Minneapolis Aquatennial, featuring over 200 land and water events. St. Paul offers the gala Winter Carnival in January each year. Just as they are major league in culture, the Twin Cities have become major league in sports, too, with the Vikings, Twins, Strikers, and North Stars.

Musically, the cities are mutually proud of the Minnesota Orchestra, which performs in Orchestra Hall; the St. Paul Chamber Orchestra, and the Minnesota Opera Company. Jazz, too, has found a home in the tiny suburb of Mendota, site of the Jazz Emporium.

PRACTICAL INFORMATION
FOR THE TWIN CITIES

HOW TO GET AROUND. *By car:* The Belt Line (I–494 and I–694) encircles the Twin Cities, while I–35 bisects the metro area from north to south. Minneapolis streets follow in numerical or alphabetical order, but there is no such logical order to St. Paul streets. *By bus:* The basic fare is 60¢. Trips between the cities or to suburbs cost 60¢ to $1.25. Downtown shuttle: 10¢. Surcharge for express (10¢) and rush hour (15¢). Children and senior citizens ride for less at specified times. Call 612–827–7733 for information. Exact change required. *By taxi:* The base rate is $1.95 for the first mile and $1.10 per each additional mile.

From the airport: Limousines stop at all the major downtown hotels and many suburban hotels, especially along I–494 near the airport.

MUSEUMS AND GALLERIES. The *Walker Art Center* in Minneapolis features a quality collection of modern American art. *The Minneapolis Institute of Arts* at 2400 3rd Ave. S. contains local and international paintings, sculpture, and artifacts from many periods. Private galleries, open to the public, that sell works by regional and international artists include Minneapolis' *WARM Gallery, Dolly Fiterman Art Gallery, Thomson Gallery, John C. Stoller Gallery, Groveland Gallery,* and *Peter M. David Gallery.*

In St. Paul's *Minnesota Historical Society,* at 690 Cedar Ave., the days of the pioneers graphically come to life. Nearby is the fascinating *Science Museum of Minnesota,* where live demonstrations are often scheduled.

HISTORIC SITES. *Sibley House* and *Faribault House* in Mendota, and the *Alexander Ramsey House* in St. Paul represent the Northwest in the mid-1800s. The *Gibbs Farm Museum,* 2097 W. Larpenteur Ave., St. Paul, displays facets of mid-19th-century farm life. The *F. Scott Fitzgerald home,*

599 Summit Ave., St. Paul, is not open to the public, but do drive by. At *Fort Snelling,* perched on the bluffs at the confluence of the Mississippi and Minnesota rivers, visitors are greeted by persons who dress and speak exactly as if they were living in the 1800s. The *Minnesota Valley Restoration Project,* southwest of the Twin Cities near Shakopee, is a collection of original buildings gathered from various areas of Minnesota in which period items and crafts are displayed.

TOURS. Regularly scheduled tours of the Twin Cities are offered. Several cultural centers such as the *Orchestra Hall* and the *Walker Art Center* offer tours. Reservations are suggested. At the Information Center in the IDS Crystal Court, pick up a brochure that lists local businesses that offer tours of their facilities, ranging from the Grain Exchange to Medtronic, Inc. You can also cruise the Mississippi aboard the sternwheelers *Jonathan Padelford* or *Josiah Snelling,* or choose from the *Queen of the Lakes* sternwheeler on Lake Harriet or *Lady of the Lake* on Lake Minnetonka.

MUSIC. *The Metropolitan Opera* comes to the University of Minnesota in Minneapolis every spring. The Twin Cities have their own opera company as well—the *Minnesota Opera Company.* The *Minnesota Orchestra,* one of the best orchestras in the country, performs in the spectacular Orchestra Hall, near Loring Park, in Minneapolis. The strikingly modern hall offers what has been called "the finest acoustics in the United States." St. Paul boasts its Chamber Orchestra, which performs in opulent Ordway Music Theatre.

Hall Brothers Emporium of Jazz, 400 D St., Mendota, is the place to hear real New Orleans jazz.

STAGE AND REVUES. Theaters in the Twin Cities offer a wide range of excellent productions. Not only is there the famous *Guthrie Theatre,* 725 Vineland Place, Minneapolis, but the *Chanhassen Dinner Theater,* the *Old Log Theater* in Excelsior, the *Children's Theater,* 2400 Third Ave. S., Minneapolis, and several community theaters as well.

The *Minnesota Dance Theater* and the Nancy Hauser Dance Company are leaders in classical and modern dance.

WHAT TO DO WITH THE CHILDREN. Visit the "Touch and See" room of the *Bell Museum of Natural History,* 17th and University Aves. S.E., Minneapolis; *The Children's Museum,* Bandana Square, St. Paul; *The Science Museum of Minnesota,* and the *McKnight 3M Omnitheater,* 30 E. 10th St., St. Paul; The *Minneapolis Institute of Arts,* 2400 3rd Ave. S., Minneapolis, home of the Children's Theater; the *Minnesota Zoological Garden* in suburban Apple Valley; the *State Capitol* or *Gibbs Farm Museum* in St. Paul; *Valleyfair Amusement Park* or the *Minnesota Valley Restoration Project* near Shakopee; *Ft. Snelling,* off Highway 55; and St. Paul's *Como Zoo and Conservatory.*

HOTELS AND MOTELS in the Twin Cities are numerous and varied. The price categories, for double occupancy, average as follows: *Deluxe:* $95 and up, *Expensive:* $65–$94, *Moderate:* $45–$65, and *Inexpensive:* under $45. Some *deluxe* hotels have weekend rates at 25–50% off.

MINNEAPOLIS. *Deluxe:* **Amfac Hotel.** 30 S. 7th St. Newest luxury hotel in the heart of downtown, adjacent to City Center.

Hyatt Regency. 1300 Nicollet Mall near Guthrie Theatre and Orchestra Hall.

L'Hotel Sofitel. 5601 W. 78th St., Bloomington. An elegant, modern French hotel. Fine rooms. Near airport. Superb cuisine.

Nicollet Island Inn. 95 Merriam St. A remodeled 1893 limestone factory-turned-inn on Mississippi River near restored waterfront development. Twenty-four rooms furnished with antique reproductions.

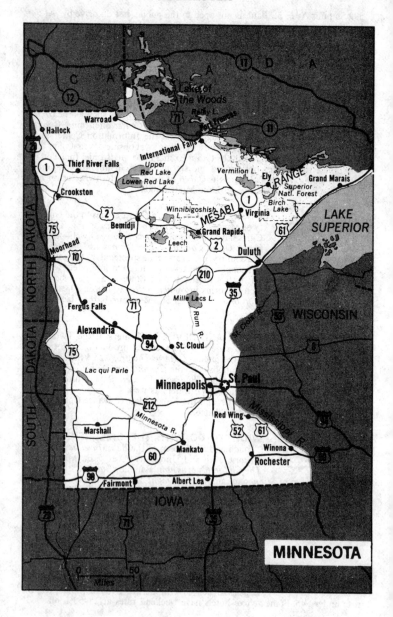

Marquette Inn. 710 Marquette. Large, beautiful rooms with contemporary decor.

Radisson Northstar Inn. 618 2nd Ave. S. Gorgeous rooms with traditional decor. Fine restaurant.

Radisson South Hotel. At Highways 494 & 100. Elegant hotel near airport. Several good dining rooms. Center atrium and pool.

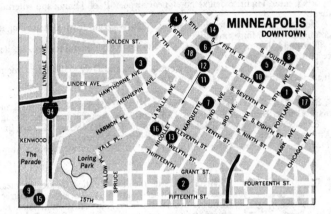

Points of Interest

1) Armory
2) Auditorium and Convention Hall
3) Bus Terminal
4) Butler Square
5) City Hall
6) Federal Reserve Bank
7) Foshay Tower
8) Grain Exchange
9) Guthrie Theater
10) Hennepin County Government Center
11) IDS Center
12) Nicollet Mall
13) Orchestra Hall & Peavey Park
14) Public Library
15) Walker Art Center
16) YWCA
17) Hubert H. Humphrey Metrodome
18) City Center

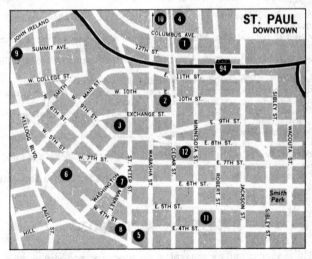

Points of Interest

1) Armory
2) Science Museum of Minnesota (McKnight/3M Omnitheater)
3) Assumption Catholic Church
4) Centennial Building
5) City Hall
6) Civic Center and Roy Wilkins Auditorium
7) Landmark Center, Ordway Music Theater, and Rice Park
8) Minnesota Museum of Art
9) St. Paul Cathedral
10) State Capitol
11) Sugarman Sculpture
12) Town Square

The Registry Hotel. 7901 24th Ave. So., Bloomington, across from the Met Sports Center. Highrise deluxe hotel, near airport. Pool. Dining and entertainment.

Moderate: **Ambassador Motor Hotel.** 5225 Wayzata Blvd. Outstanding accommodations. Many amenities.

Normandy Motor Inn. Downtown at 405 S. 8th St. Tasteful rooms. Excellent restaurant. Free parking.

Inexpensive: **Cricket Inn of Plymouth.** I–494 and Hwy. 55. Modern rooms. Includes continental breakfast. Restaurant adjacent.

ST. PAUL. *Deluxe:* **The Saint Paul Hotel.** 350 Market St. Near the Landmark Center. Beautifully restored, Old World touches and excellent dining.

Expensive: **Radisson St. Paul.** Downtown at Wabasha Ave and Kellogg Blvd. Attractive rooms. Revolving restaurant on top with view of river.

Moderate: **The Inn–Civic Center.** 175 W. 7th St. Convenient to downtown. Free parking.

 DINING OUT in the Twin Cities frequently means steaks, although there are plenty of exotic restaurants featuring everything from sukiyaki to moussaka. Restaurant price categories are as follows: *Super Deluxe* $25 and up, *Deluxe* $20–25, *Expensive* $15–20, *Moderate* $10–15, and *Inexpensive* under $10. Prices are for a complete meal, excluding drinks, tax, and tip.

Super Deluxe: **Le Café.** L'Hotel Sofitel, 5601 W. 78th St., Bloomington. Superb French food. Excellent.

The Willows. In Minneapolis' Hyatt Regency. Features fabulous salad bar with scrumptuous desserts. Superb dining with excellent service.

Deluxe: **Blue Horse.** 1355 University Ave., St. Paul. Fabulous French, Continental cuisine.

Forepaugh's. 276 S. Exchange. St. Paul. Classic French fare in restored mansion.

Expensive: **Edgewater Inn.** 2420 Marshall Ave. N.E., Minneapolis. Full menu.

Fuji-Ya. 420 S. 1st St., Minneapolis. Features Japanese cuisine in choice of booth, high table, or low table seating. Overlooks Mississippi River.

Jax Café. 1928 University Ave. N.E., Minneapolis. American food. Delightful ambience.

Lexington. 1096 Grand Ave., St. Paul. Delicious steak, prime ribs.

Szechuan Star Restaurant. 3655 Hazelton Rd. Excellent Chinese specialties. Special Chinese Smorg, Sundays through Thursdays (evenings).

Moderate: **The Nankin.** 2 S. 7 St., Minneapolis. Splendid Cantonese fare.

Venetian Inn. 2814 Rice St., St. Paul. Southern Italian pasta at its best.

Inexpensive: **The Chocolate Mousse.** 498 Selby Av., St. Paul. Features excellent mousses, from salmon to amaretto.

Ediner. 3669 W. 69 St. (in the Galleria). Features sandwiches and salads, in 1940s-style diner.

LePeep. 89 S. 10th St., Minneapolis. Known as the "Brunch Specialists."

EXPLORING MINNESOTA

The strongest pull for the typical vacation visitor to Minnesota is the still-unspoiled North Country, where the fish come big and the fish stories bigger, and the local lore is a mixture of Indian legends and tales of Paul Bunyan.

Traveling northeast from the Twin Cities, a North Country tour begins at Duluth, the international port city on Lake Superior. On a warm summer day, you'll suddenly feel a cool caressing breeze. That's the first dividend of the North Country—natural air conditioning.

Duluth itself has some interesting sights for those who tarry before heading northward. The city shoreline on Lake Superior runs 24 miles,

MINNESOTA 551

and the buildings here seem to spill downhill from the bluffs that rise 600 feet above the lake.

Duluth attractions include the Alworth Planetarium, Tweed Art Gallery, Skyline Drive, Glensheen Mansion, Harbor cruises, Duluth Zoo, the Canal Park Marine Museum next to the Aerial Lift Bridge, and St. Louis County Heritage and Arts Center.

Less than an hour's drive from Duluth is Two Harbors, Minnesota's first iron-ore port. Massive ore-loading docks contrast in size with the diminutive Three Spot, the 1887-vintage woodburning steam locomotive that is enshrined near the railway station.

Continuing on, you'll pass Gooseberry Falls on your way to Split Rock Lighthouse perched on a sheer cliff just short of Beaver Bay. Now a state park, Split Rock Lighthouse is being restored to its 1930s appearance.

Further on, at the halfway point to the Ontario border, a high curving bridge crosses the Manitou River. From here, a footpath leads to a mighty 80-foot waterfall, crashing down a deep gorge.

Some of the region's outstanding scenery is in Cascade State Park. The Cascade River flows through the beautiful 2,300-acre park and pours into Lake Superior over a series of dazzling waterfalls.

Grand Marais, 11 miles ahead, is a fishing and tourist center. It also serves as a jumping-off point for a delightful shunpike over the Gunflint Trail into a wilderness area of Superior National Forest. Beyond Grand Marais is Hovland, where there's a junction with another wilderness trail offering a side trip into Superior National Forest.

Minnesota has extensive national parks and forests. Voyageurs National Park, the state's first, is on the Kabetogama peninsula, just south of International Falls. Isle Royale National Park, actually located in Michigan, is more easily reached from harbors in Minnesota. At Isle Royale, visitors will find over 100 miles of trails for hikers (no automobiles are transported to the island), as well as boating excursions.

Chippewa National Forest, with over 641,000 acres, has over 2,000 lakes, including some of the largest in the state. For information, write to: Forest Supervisor, Chippewa National Forest, Cass Lake, Minnesota.

Superior National Forest covers more than three million acres and has close to 2,000 lakes. It borders on Canada's Quetico Provincial Park, and the two regions cover 3,400 square miles. For information, write: Forest Supervisor, Superior National Forest, Duluth, Minnesota.

Within Superior Forest is one of the famed, relatively new National Forest Wilderness areas. The name is apt; there are no public roads, no big recreation areas, no timber-cutting operations. The Superior Wilderness contains the Boundary Waters Canoe Area, possibly the most famous of the country's canoeing regions. It runs for nearly 200 miles along northeastern Minnesota's boundary with Canada. Travel permits are required.

State parks include Interstate State Park, south of Taylors Falls; Itasca State Park, north of Park Rapids; Judge C. R. Magney State Park, east of Grand Marais; Mille Lacs Kathio State Park, west of Onamia, Savanna Portage State Park, north of McGregor; Minneopa State Park, west of Mankato; and Camden State Park, southwest of Marshall.

Grand Portage Trail

At the easternmost point of Minnesota's North Shore is Grand Portage State Park. The first white settlement in Minnesota, the village of Grand Portage is steeped in regional history. The Grand Portage

Trail, carved through the heart of the park, is for hikers and cross-country skiers who wish to tread the path of the old-time voyageurs.

From Grand Portage, visitors can head for Isle Royale, Michigan, one of the nation's most primitive national parks. Twenty-two miles from the Minnesota mainland, the island is a paradise for nature lovers. Wildlife is abundant; the largest herd of moose in North America resides here.

The last five miles of scenery on US 61 to the Ontario border are especially magnificent. The 108-foot waterfall at Pigeon River is the most spectacular of all the North Shore waterfalls, providing a dramatic climax to this drive.

Turning west, you'll wind up in the middle of Minnesota's Arrowhead Country. From here, you can head for, and drive through, splendid Superior National Forest. The 61-mile drive will take you to Ely, where canoeing is the big business. It is also the takeoff point for most of the modern-day voyageurs.

From Ely, go on to the magnificent Mesabi (Indian for "giant") Iron Range. Years of strip mining have turned the range into an awesome panorama of man-made canyons. Beyond is Chisholm, where the story of the many ethnic groups that worked the iron mines is told in life-size displays and tape recordings at the Iron Range Interpretative Center on the edge of the inactive Glen open-pit mine.

Sportsman's Paradise

A major port of entry between Canada and Minnesota, International Falls is a crossroads for sportsmen traveling to and from the great walleye-populated waters of Rainy Lake, the isolated smaller lakes on both sides of the border, and huge Lake of the Woods, famous for its walleyed pike and muskies.

Bunyan Playground

Bemidji, originally a trading post, is located at the foot of Lake Bemidji, southwest of International Falls. This city is the home of Bemidji State College, a fine historical and wildlife museum, and Minnesota's oldest professional summer theater—the Paul Bunyan Playhouse.

Southward, in Itasca State Park, millions of tourists have "walked across the Mississippi without getting their shoes wet." Here at Lake Itasca, the Mississippi River begins its journey to the Gulf of Mexico as a narrow stream bubbling over a few rocks.

Close by is Park Rapids, surrounded by 400 lakes offering more fishing and 200 resorts. Walker, to the east, is known as Paul Bunyan's Playground. Located on the southwest shore of Leech Lake and adjacent to Chippewa National Forest, Walker attracts outdoors enthusiasts. Enormous walleyes, northerns and muskies make it a fisherman's heaven, and snowmobiling is popular, too.

At the geographic center of the state is Brainerd, another leading resort region and the self-styled hometown of Paul Bunyan. The Brainerd–Twin Cities route passes through the scenic Mille Lacs region and Little Falls, the boyhood home of Charles Lindbergh.

A Southeastern Minnesota Circle Tour

The 90-mile stretch southeast from the Twin Cities—along US 61—extends through the Minnesota Memorial Hardwood State Forest and a scenic part of the Hiawatha Valley to a point across the Mississippi from La Crosse, Wisconsin. Some of the highlights of this route are Lake City, where the Mississippi River widens to form Lake Pepin, known for its scenery, waterskiing, and fishing; Red Wing, surrounded by 400-foot bluffs from which you can enjoy a dramatic view; and La Crescent, center of the apple-growing region. East of this drive is Rochester, home of the Mayo Clinic and a good base from which to explore the area.

Rochester and the Mayo Clinic

Rochester has come a long way since Dr. William W. Mayo settled here in 1855. Besides taking a tour of the huge clinic and its fascinating medical museum, you can visit Mayowood, the home of Drs. C. H. and C. W. Mayo. This handsome mansion, set on 10 acres, contains period antiques and mementos. Guided tours are arranged through the Olmsted County Historical Center and Museum; call in advance. Mayo Park houses the Rochester Art Center, Civic Auditorium, and Civic Theatre; professional dramatic productions, children's theater, and concerts are scheduled. Within a short distance of Rochester are parks and recreation areas for sports activities and picnicking.

PRACTICAL INFORMATION FOR MINNESOTA

HOW TO GET THERE. *By car:* The two main east-west arteries are I–90, which skirts the southern border, and I–94, running diagonally from Fargo, North Dakota, in the northwest, through the Twin Cities to Eau Claire, Wisconsin, in the southeast. I–35 runs north to south through the Twin Cities. *By air: Northwest Orient, Western, United, US Air, Eastern, Ozark, Mississippi Valley, Air Wisconsin, American, Pan American, Continental, Delta, Midway, Frontier, People Express,* and *Republic. By bus: Greyhound* and *Jefferson* are the transcontinental lines serving this area. *By train:* Two *Amtrak* routes cross Minnesota: the *Empire Builder,* from Winona through St. Paul to Fargo, ND; and the *North Star,* from St. Paul to Duluth.

HOW TO GET AROUND. *By car:* The interstate system is useful for getting there quickly, but if you're looking for the real Minnesota, stay on the two-lane state roads. *By air: Republic, Ozark, Mesaba,* and *Mississippi Valley* are the main local carriers.

By bus: Intrastate bus lines include: *Greyhound* and *Jefferson* bus lines.

By train: Minneapolis, St. Paul, Winona, Red Wing, Duluth, Cambridge, Sandstone, Willmar, St. Cloud, Staples, Detroit Lakes, Morris and Breckenridge are on the *Amtrak* line in Minnesota.

TOURIST INFORMATION. The *Minnesota Tourist Information Center,* 419 N. Robert, 240 Bremer Bldg., St. Paul 55101, can furnish you with information about the state and its tourist facilities. Contact individual chambers of commerce for more specific information.

Tourist Information Centers, run by the Minnesota Dept. of Transportation, are located at Thompson Hill (near Duluth); Dresbach, just north of LaCrescent on I–90; Moorhead, at the North Dakota–Minnesota border on I–94, Beaver Creek on I–90; and south of Albert Lea on I–35.

MUSEUMS AND GALLERIES. At the *St. Louis County Heritage and Arts Center* in Duluth, 2222 East Superior St., you can see relics from the history of Duluth. Visitors can view the inactive Glen open pit mine from a glass-enclosed walkway extending out over the mine at the *Iron Range Interpretative Center* on Hwy. 169 southwest of Chisholm. At 1832 East 2nd St., Rochester has the *Mayo Medical Museum.* Life-size dioramas of Indian life are featured in the *Mille Lacs Indian Museum* in Onamia. Minnesota's interpretive centers are excellent. Each contains documents, period items, photographs and slide presentations on particular persons or eras. Centers are located at *Fort Ridgely,* south of Fairfax; *Grand Mound,* west of International Falls; *Lindbergh House,* in Little Falls; and the *Lower Sioux Agency,* east of Redwood Falls.

HISTORIC SITES. The lives of several of Minnesota's famous citizens are recorded in several restored homes: the *Mayo House* in Le Sueur, the *Folsom House* in Taylors Falls, the *Comstock House* in Moorhead, and the *Kelley Farm* southeast of Elk River. Other sites range from the prehistoric *petroglyphs* etched in rock near Jeffers to the *Harkin Store,* northwest of New Ulm, with its shelves stocked with 1800s wares, to the *North West Company Fur Post* near Pine City to the *Grand Portage National Monument,* northeast of Duluth, the home ground of the French voyageurs. In Northfield, one can see the last bank robbed by the James Gang before Jesse, Frank, and the Boys were put out of commission.

DRINKING LAWS. Legal age is 19 and cocktail lounges and bars close at 1 A.M.

SUMMER SPORTS. Minnesota, "land of sky blue waters," is a little bit of heaven for the avid sportsman. So extensive are its forest and prairie and so numerous are its lakes that the hunter can always find new trails to traverse, and the fisherman can fish for a lifetime without visiting all the lakes. The sportsman can enjoy every kind of water sport in addition to riding, camping, hiking, tennis and golf.

Northern Minnesota's low mountains are heavily wooded, while the middle and southern sections are gentle hills and prairies. The Arrowhead District of the northeast, so called because of its shape, is a renowned resort and sports area. The Detroit Lakes section, in the west, is famous for its excellent fishing.

Every kind of *freshwater fish* can be found in Minnesota waters. There is even deep-sea fishing for lake trout in Lake Superior.

Hunting is excellent. The hunter can find deer, pheasant, grouse, and other small game.

The *Department of Natural Resources,* Centennial Building, St. Paul, can supply information on all sporting activities in the state parks.

One of the United States' great areas for *canoeing* is the Quetico Reserve in the Superior National Forest. The Chippewa National Forest is also a wooded land of many lakes.

Visitors to the Twin Cities will find an assortment of sports activities throughout the year. Both cities are on the Mississippi and have lakes within their limits. Nearby are Lake Minnetonka and White Bear Lake. The cities offer *golf* courses and nature reserves, as well as *hiking* and *cycling* along scenic woodland park trails.

WINTER SPORTS. In this state, winter sports rival the summer ones for popularity. *Ice skating* and related sports such as *hockey, skiing, ski touring, bobsledding, curling, sleigh riding, snowshoeing, ice boating, ice fishing, sled dogging* and *snowmobiling* are enthusiastically enjoyed by residents and visitors alike.

For details on where you can enjoy these sports, send for the free *Minnesota Winter Guide.* Write to Department of Economic Development, 419 N. Robert, 240 Bremer Bldg., St. Paul 55101.

HOTELS AND MOTELS in Minnesota run the gamut from deluxe resort-style facilities in the lake regions to commercial hotels in the larger cities to comfortable, family-run motels. The price categories in this section, for double occupancy, average as follows: *Deluxe* $55 and up, *Expensive* $45–55, *Moderate* $35–45, *Inexpensive* under $35. Rates vary by season in resort areas.

ALEXANDRIA. *Deluxe:* **Radisson Arrowwood.** Resort complex on lake with complete recreational facilities from riding stables to golf course.

BEMIDJI. *Moderate:* **Edgewater Motel.** Pleasant rooms. Beach.

BRAINERD. *Expensive:* **Madden Inn.** Resort complex including tennis and golf. On Gull Lake.

DETROIT LAKES. *Moderate:* **Holland Motel.** Pool and attractive rooms.

DULUTH. *Deluxe:* **Radisson-Duluth.** 505 W. Superior St. Downtown. Attractive, clean rooms. Rooftop dining room rotates for 360° view of city and harbor.
Normandy Inn. Excellent rooms with poolside cabanas available. Near Auditorium.
Expensive: **Edgewater East Motel.** 2330 London Rd. Very attractive, large rooms.
Inexpensive: **Spirit Motor Inn.** Convenient to Spirit Mountain ski slopes and airport.

GRAND RAPIDS. *Expensive:* **Holiday Inn.** Pool, excellent dining and entertainment.
Moderate: **Rainbow Inn.** 1300 Highway 169. Very nice, comfortable accommodations.

MANKATO. *Expensive:* **Holiday Inn.** Two locations: Downtown and North. Pool and fine accommodations.

PARK RAPIDS. *Moderate:* **Vacationaire.** Cottages, lodge, and excellent restaurant on Island Lake.

RED WING. *Deluxe:* **St. James Hotel.** Restored Victorian hotel with period rooms, restaurant and lounge.

ROCHESTER. (Many of the hotels here have provisions for the handicapped and free transportation to the Mayo Clinic.) *Deluxe:* **Kahler.** Excellent accommodations and dining. Rooftop pool.
Moderate: **Connolly's Downtown.** 424–3rd St. Clinic a block away.
Brentwood Motor Inn. New, attractive rooms, 2½ blocks from Mayo.
Plaza Internationale. All amenities. Old World decor.
Inexpensive: **Carlton.** 1st Ave. N.W. & Center St. Good, older hotel.

DINING OUT. Minnesota's rivers and "10,000 lakes" abound with good things to eat—pike, trout and bass. Many restaurants are situated along the water's edge, nature thus providing beautiful views as well as good food. But if North Woods freshwater fish is not to your taste, this is a land of farms, too, and the Minnesotans know how to bake and how to broil steaks.
Restaurant price categories (average) are as follows: *Super Deluxe* $20 and up, *Deluxe* $15–20, *Expensive* $10–15, *Moderate* $8–10, and *Inexpensive* under $8. Prices are for complete meal, excluding drinks, tax, and tip.

BEMIDJI. *Expensive:* **Union Station.** Full menu in renovated railroad station. Entertainment.

DETROIT LAKES. *Expensive:* **Fireside Supper Club.** Dinner only. Beef, seafood.

DULUTH. *Expensive:* **The Chinese Lantern.** Renowned for prime rib.
Highland Supper Club. 1301 Miller Trunk. Lobster, steak. Live entertainment.
Moderate: **The Pickwick.** Full menu, with lake trout as specialty. Ask for table with view of Lake Superior.
Inexpensive. **Grandma's Saloon and Deli.** Fun atmosphere among antiques. Great sandwiches and ice cream drinks.

FARIBAULT. *Moderate:* **Lavender Inn.** Full menu, including homemade pies and combo platter with any two entrees.

GRAND MARAIS. *Expensive:* **Birch Terrace Supper Club.** Steak, beef. Restored 1889 home.

GRAND RAPIDS. *Expensive:* **The Cedars** in the Holiday Inn. Varied menu.
Rainbow Inn Motel. E. Hwy. 169, Grand Rapids. Beef, seafood specialties.

MANKATO. *Expensive:* **Century Club.** Full lunch, dinner, and children's menu.

PRIOR LAKE. *Moderate:* **The Wilderness.** Wild game and conventional dishes in log hunting lodge with rustic furniture and flagstone fireplace.

ROCHESTER. *Deluxe.* **Michael's.** Greek dishes on varied menu.
Expensive: **Hoffman House.** Full menu with excellent salad bar amid Bavarian décor.

OHIO

Cleveland, on the North Coast

Situated on the shores of Lake Erie at the mouth of the Cuyahoga River, within 500 miles of half of the populations of the United States and Canada, the second largest city in Ohio was founded by Moses Cleveland in 1796. The Civil War occasioned a great need for iron and steel, and set Cleveland on its way to industrial preëminence. Ore deposits in the upper Great Lakes and vast nearby fields of coal made the fantastic growth of the city inevitable. The Irish were the first to arrive, followed by the Welsh and English, a few French and Dutch. Then came masses of Poles, Germans, Czechs, Hungarians, Jews, Serbs, Italians, Slavs and more, until 63 different cultures were represented in Cleveland, each with its own customs, languages, costumes and foods.

The nation's 11th largest metropolitan area sprawls along the lake for forty-five miles on either side of the Cuyahoga and runs inland for an average of ten miles.

The Cleveland Art Museum is the leading attraction of the park-like University Circle area. Here are also found the Museum of Natural History; Severance Hall, the acoustically perfect home of the renowned Cleveland Orchestra; Western Reserve Historical Museum; and Case Western Reserve University. Still other points of interest are: the Health Education Museum, first in the nation; Dunham Tavern, a converted stagecoach house now filled with antiques; the Cleveland Metroparks Zoo, one of the country's top five; NASA Visitor Center; West Side Market; downtown Arcade; and Terminal Tower observation floor.

In addition to 2-hour boat tours up the Cuyahoga River and through the harbor and lake, there are guided tours of the city by Best Conventions, North Coast Tours and Trailways. The Cleveland Play House houses a professional repertory company and three theaters. The Hanna Theater and the interracial Karamu House are frequently visited by Broadway road companies, and Cleveland is also the home of Playhouse Square, three elegantly restored 1920's theaters: State, Ohio, and Palace. For those whose tastes run to things musical, there are the arena-style Front Row Theater; the Blossom Music Center, summer home of the Cleveland Orchestra, which also presents excellent rock, jazz and popular concerts; and the Beck Center for the Cultural Arts in Lakewood. And for sports fans Cleveland offers more than twenty public and semi-private golf courses, thoroughbred and harness racing, ski areas, boat launching ramps, and plenty of fine tennis courts, riding areas, wildlife sanctuaries, and other recreational facilities.

Baseball and football fans may watch the Indians or the Browns compete at Cleveland's Lakefront Stadium. The NBA's Cleveland Cavaliers play at the Coliseum in Richfield, as do the Cleveland Force Soccer team.

Twelve major parks totalling 16,000 acres and connected by a 74-mile circular park boulevard comprise one of Cleveland's major attractions. But you'll have to go 30 miles beyond the city before you find decent lake swimming, perhaps westward to Cedar Point and the best beach on Lake Erie. With a mile-long sandy beach, Cedar Point has been a popular resort since 1882, and its amusement park has been expanded and renovated in recent years to resemble Disneyland. Millions of Ohioans come each year to stay in the old Breakers Hotel, swim along the beach, and ride the Blue Streak roller coaster and Frontiertown train.

Northwest of Sandusky and linked to it by the Bay Bridge is the Marblehead Peninsula, a little piece of New England on Lake Erie, full of narrow village roads and surf-pounded shores. Spread over the entire peninsula are hundreds of acres of inland orchards that yield rich harvests of peaches, apples, and pears. The road leads visitors past picturesque boat liveries, bathing beaches, and even a lighthouse to complete the picture of a small coastal village in New England. All that's missing is the smell and taste of salt in the air.

PRACTICAL INFORMATION FOR CLEVELAND

HOW TO GET THERE. There are several good ways to get to and from Cleveland. Interstates 71, 77, 80 and 90 are excellent. *Amtrak* serves Cleveland with rail service; *Greyhound* and *Trailways* provide bus service. Cleveland is served by 16 major airlines operating in two airports, Burke Lakefront and Cleveland Hopkins International.

HOW TO GET AROUND. *By taxi:* In downtown Cleveland, taxis are readily available on the street. *By bus:* A ride on the downtown shuttle bus (marked "Local") is 25¢. The longer-range "Express Service" costs more. *From the airport:* Public Rapid Transit operates between the airport and downtown Cleveland. The trip from Hopkins International to Public Square takes about twenty minutes and costs $1. A cab ride from the airport to downtown will cost you about $16.

TOURIST INFORMATION. The *Convention and Visitor Bureau of Greater Cleveland*, 1301 E. 6th St., Cleveland 44144, (216) 621-4110, has information on all facets of Cleveland life. Group tours can be arranged by contacting the bureau. For current tours, events, and shows, call (216) 621-8860 for a recorded message.

MUSEUMS AND GALLERIES. The *Cleveland Museum of Art*, 11150 East Boulevard, overlooks the Fine Arts Gardens in University Circle. It is the second wealthiest museum in the nation, topped only by the Metropolitan Museum in New York. Closed Mon., July 4, Thanksgiving, Christmas and New Year's Day.

Cleveland Health Education Museum, 8911 Euclid Ave., first health museum in the U.S., opened in 1940. Exhibits show how the human body works, the transparent woman, and model of electronic human brain brought from New York World's Fair. Closed Thanksgiving, Christmas, and New Year's Day.

Also in Cleveland are the *Temple Museum of Jewish Religious Art & Music*, the *Howard Dittrick Museum of Historical Medicine*, the *Natural Science Museum*, the *Romanian Folk Museum*, the *Dunham Tavern Museum*, the *Western Reserve Historical Society Library & Museum*, *Crawford Auto-Aviation Museum*, and the *Afro-American Cultural and Historical Society*.

Short trips from Cleveland will take you to *Geauga County Historical Museum* in Burton, *Fairport Harbor Museum* (Fairport), *Pioneer Farm and Home Museum* and the *Dudley Peter Allen Memorial Art Museum* in Oberlin, the *Great Lakes Historical Museum* in Vermilion, and the Museum of *Lake Erie Junior College* in Bay Village.

GARDENS. For *Cleveland Cultural Gardens*, enter at East Blvd. and Superior Ave., continue toward St. Clair on East Blvd. in Rockefeller Park. Open all spring, summer, and fall. A chain of 19 cultural gardens that combine landscapes and sculpture typical of the cultures of the Polish, German, Hebrew, Italian, Lithuanian, Slovak, Yugoslav, Czech, Hungarian, Greek, Russian, Irish, American Colonial, Ukrainian, and Finnish who represent the national backgrounds of Cleveland's citizenry. The gardens were inspired by the success of the first, a *Shakespearean Garden*, dedicated Apr. 14, 1916, oldest Shakespeare garden in the country. Free.

Also in Cleveland are the *City Greenhouse* and the *Cleveland Fine Arts Garden* and the *Garden Center of Greater Cleveland*.

MUSIC. *The Metropolitan Opera* season in Cleveland is usually in April or May. Performances are given at Playhouse Square. The *Cleveland Orchestra* appears in Severance Hall, Euclid Avenue and East Boulevard, on Thursday, Friday and Saturday nights from September to May. *The Cleveland Ballet* performs at Playhouse Square Center.

The summer home of the *Cleveland Orchestra* is the Blossom Music Center. Rock groups, film festivals and pops concerts are staged almost every night at the Center throughout June, July and August. It is located south of Ohio Turnpike Exit 12 at 1145 West Steel Corners Road in Cuyahoga Falls.

STAGE AND REVUES. The *Hanna*, 2067 E. 14th St., presents road shows of Broadway plays evenings except Sundays, 8:30 P.M. Matinees Wed. and Sat. *The Cleveland Play House*, a renowned community theater with resident professional staff, 8500 Euclid Ave., features 3 theaters: Brooks, Drury, and Bolton. Usually evenings except Mon. from Oct. thru May, and Wed. thru Sat. rest of year. *Karamu House*, 2355 E. 89th St., is a unique, nationally known interracial community institution in a modern $500,000 center which includes a theater-in-the-round. *Great Lakes Shakespeare Festival* is an all-professional, nonprofit cultural repertory theater located in Playhouse Square Center. From mid-June to Oct. *Chagrin Valley Little Theater*, 40 River St., Chagrin Falls, is one of Cleveland's oldest community theaters. It offers live comedy, drama, and musical theater yearround. *Lakewood Little Theater* is another fine community-

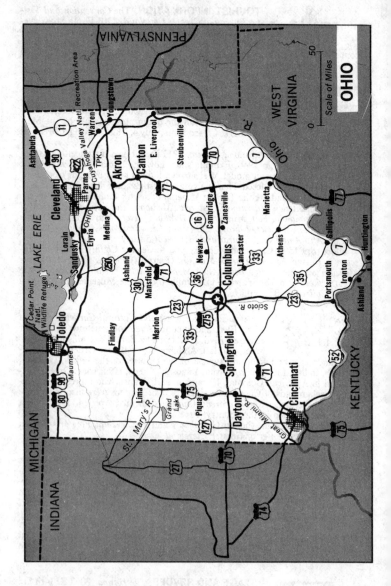

theater group, at 17823 Detroit Ave. Sept-May. Listing of all *summer theater* fare in northern Ohio is available free every summer at the Cleveland Press.

SPECTATOR SPORTS. In baseball, the *Cleveland Indians* represent the American League, and in football there are the *Cleveland Browns,* who play at Lakefront Stadium. In basketball, there are the *Cleveland Cavaliers;* and in soccer, the *Cleveland Force. Thistledown Race Track* is located on Warrensville Center Road. *Northfield Race Track* has trotters.

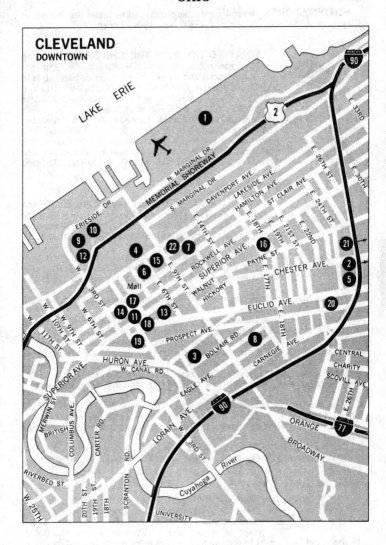

CLEVELAND
DOWNTOWN

Points of Interest

1) Burke Lakefront Airport
2) Case Western Reserve University
3) Central Market
4) City Hall
5) Cleveland State University
6) Cleveland Convention Center
7) Erieview Towers
8) Grays Armory
9) Horticultural Gardens
10) Lakefront Garden
11) Light of Friendship
12) Municipal Stadium
13) The Arcade
14) Old Stone Church
15) Public Auditorium
16) St. Peter's Church
17) Society National Building
18) Soldiers/Sailors Monument
19) Terminal Tower
20) Trinity Cathedral
21) Wade Park
22) Willard Park

WINTER SPORTS. Several good skiing areas can be found just outside of Cleveland in the nearby *Cuyahoga Valley* and *Alpine Valley.*

WHAT TO DO WITH THE CHILDREN. *Cleveland Metroparks Zoo,* in Brookside Park off W. 25th St., features lions and tigers without cages or bars, birds in natural habitat, Children's Farm, Kiddieland Park and touring trains. Open daily year-round 9:30 A.M. to 5 P.M. Sundays and holidays in summer to 7 P.M. Admission $2, $1 for children aged 2–11.

Sea World features the world's first trained killer whale, Penguin Encounter, plus dolphin and seal shows. Located SE of the city on State 43, 7 miles off Ohio Turnpike Exit 13. Open daily 9 A.M. to 10 P.M., Memorial Day to Labor Day.

Geauga Lake Amusement Park has over 100 rides, live stage shows, and water flumes. Memorial Day–Labor Day. Located off SR 43, Aurora, OH, next to *Sea World.*

HOTELS AND MOTELS in Cleveland are plentiful and afford the traveler any kind of accommodation he or she may desire. Downtown hotels, offering good locations and all facilities, compete with motels in and around the city.

The price categories in this section, for double occupancy, will average as follows: *Deluxe:* $50 and up, *Expensive:* $40–50, *Moderate:* $30–40, *Inexpensive:* under $30. For a more complete description of these categories see the Hotels & Motels part of *Facts at Your Fingertips.*

Deluxe: **Marriott Inn-Airport.** 4277 W. 150th St. Sauna and therapy pool. Dancing and entertainment.

Expensive: **Holiday Inn-CSU.** 2160 Euclid Ave. Five minutes by car to downtown area. Facilities here are typical of the chain. Pool.

Moderate: **Best Western Cleveland Airport.** 15541 Brookpark Rd. Four minutes from Hopkins Airport, attractive dining room, coffee shop and cocktail lounge. Pool, free parking, courtesy car to airport.

Stouffer's Inn on the Square. 24 Public Sq. Indoor pool, coffee shop, health club, entertainment, dancing. Free airport service, morning coffee, and newspaper.

Sheraton Inn-Euclid East. 27982 Euclid Ave. 15 mi. NE on US 20 at I–90 Euclid Ave. exit. Indoor pool, sauna. Coffee shop. Lounge has entertainment.

Inexpensive: **Gold Coast Inn.** 11837 Edgewater Dr. One block from Lake Erie.

Lakewood Manor. 12019 Lake Ave., 5 mi. W., 1 block N. of US 6.

Red Roof Inn. 6020 Quarry Ln. 7 mi. S. at I–77 Rockside exit. Coffee shop next door.

DINING OUT in Cleveland can be exciting, and the quality of food served in those spots featuring entertainment competes favorably with that in restaurants specializing in cuisine only. There are several fine Italian kitchens, but beef seems to top the menus in establishments favored by Clevelanders.

For other worthwhile restaurants, check hotel and nightclub listings. If you plan to eat out on a holiday, make sure you call to see if the establishment will be open. Restaurants below are categorized according to a mid-priced meal in each.

Restaurant price categories are as follows: *Deluxe:* more than $25; *Expensive:* $15–25; *Moderate:* $10–15; *Inexpensive:* under $10. These prices include appetizer and dessert. Not included are drinks, tax and tips.

Expensive: **Au Provence.** 2191 Lee Rd., Cleveland Hts. French creole, crayfish in season.

The French Connection. 24 Public Sq. French menu, elegant. Jacket required.

Moderate: **Hofbrau Haus.** 1400 E. 55th St. Casual Old German ambiance, food, and polkas.

Hollenden Tavern. 610 Superior Ave. in Hollenden House Hotel. Elegant. Popular for steaks and seafood. Entertainment.

New York Spaghetti House. 2173 E. 9th St. Specialties of veal and spaghetti.

Pier W. 12700 Lake Avenue. Seafood. The lakeside setting permits a view of much of downtown Cleveland, as well as the breaking waves of Lake Erie. Food is the equal of the view.

Inexpensive: **The Greenhouse.** 2215 Adelbert Rd. Large variety of fresh seafood. Garden dining.

For complete selection of restaurants, call Visitors Bureau, 800–321–1001 (in Ohio, 800–362–5100).

EXPLORING OHIO

Cincinnati

With the start of the 19th century, Cincinnati became a boom town because of its strategic location on the increasingly busy Ohio River and the introduction of the steamboat to the waterways of the West. German influence is still strong in the Ohio Valley today, an area which brings to mind the Rhine wine country. The Queen City is an engaging mélange of mosaics that are partly Midwest, partly European, with a touch of the South added for accent.

Conservative politically and cosmopolitan socially, Cincinnati today is similar in many ways to San Francisco, even to being situated on many hills. Cincinnatians enjoy the good things, and their city's restaurants well deserve their national recogniation. The city is no laggard culturally, with fine collections housed in both the Taft Museum and Cincinnati Art Museum. The Cincinnati Summer Opera performs during the summer, and the Cincinnati Symphony Orchestra and Cincinnati Ballet Company perform during the winter. Many nightclubs here and across the river in Kentucky re-create the atmosphere of the French Quarter in New Orleans. Garden lovers will appreciate the Irwin M. Krohn Conservatory in Eden Park, and the Mount Airy Arboretum. And the hills come alive with the sounds of music during the traditional May Festival, a two-week program of symphonic and choral music. During the summer, the river steamboat *Delta Queen* takes passengers in air-conditioned comfort on five-, seven- and ten-day trips on the Ohio River and 20-day cruises all the way to New Orleans, and the *Showboat Majestic* presents comedy and musicals, both at the Public Landing at the foot of Broadway. At Riverfront Stadium, sports fans can watch the Cincinnati Reds and the Cincinnati Bengals. Arena sports, circuses and other performances are staged at Riverfront Coliseum.

Toledo

Toledo is the Glass Capital of the world, and is the home of one of the country's finest art museums and an equally outstanding zoo. The museum is known for its collections of glass, paintings, sculpture, and decorative arts. Attractions at the zoo include the Museum of Science and Natural History, a large freshwater aquarium and the children's Wonder Valley. Other attractions include historic Fort Meigs, Portside Festival Marketplace, and riverboat rides.

East of Cleveland

East of Cleveland along the shores of Lake Erie on US 20 or I–90 is one of Ohio's most historic areas. Long before the white man came to the wilderness, this route was known as the Iroquois War Trail, used by the hostile tribes of the Iroquois Confederacy of upper New York. Later these same foot trails became the main avenue for white settlement of northern Ohio. Villages sprang up by the dozens, and the settlers from New England gave these fast-rising communities the characteristics of their villages back home. Even today, the vestiges of this era remain to be seen in the city squares, buildings, churches, and general layout of such towns as Hudson, Burton, Chardon, Painesville, and many others. Remaining too are other reminders of this driving westward push, such as the many inns, taverns, and stagecoach stops that still serve travelers in the area today.

Three possible visits could include: Old Tavern on State 164 in Unionville, which dates back to 1805, a stopping spot for soldiers on the way to the War of 1812 and later an important hideout on the Underground Railroad for slaves escaping to Canada; Rider's Inn and Tavern on US 20 in Painesville, dating back to 1812, when it first served guests on the old Indian Trail, and patterned somewhat after Mount Vernon; and the Welshfield Inn on US 422 in Welshfield, built in 1842, an important stagecoach stop en route to Pittsburgh and also part of the Underground Railroad. Dating back to this era too is the first Mormon Temple built in the United States, at Kirtland Hills on State 306 within sight of I–90. Joseph Smith, who organized the Mormons in 1830, made Ohio his first stop long before he headed westward. Burton, Chardon, and Middlefield on the borders of Ohio's second largest Amish settlement offer tourists a variety of yearly festivals and special events. Burton sponsors a Butter Churn Festival in June, and the Apple Butter Festival in October. Chardon, maple syrup center of the state, celebrates with a big Maple Festival in April, while Middlefield's contribution to the fun is its annual Amish-tinged Swiss Cheese Festival, held in June.

Socialists and Settlers

Candy was one of the things that helped bring about the downfall of Ohio's onetime collective settlement at Zoar, just west of State 8 on State 212. Founded in 1817 by German Separatists, Zoar flourished for more than 75 years, and at one time the community's property was valued at more than a million dollars. Besides much farmland, it also included iron foundries, shops, stores, and even a fine hotel. The latter was blamed by many of the Zoarites for bringing outsiders into the community; they wore finer clothes than the simply dressed Zoarites, gave candy to the children, and caused discontent with the regulated life of the villagers. In time, the younger element grew weary of the stoical communal life and the society disbanded.

The hotel still remains, serving plain, family style meals. Remaining also are two of the better homes of the era—the Number One house, formerly the home of Joseph Baumeler, the Zoar leader, and now a fine little museum, and the Bimeler home, just around the corner, also a museum. The most attractive legacy left by the Zoarites is their formal garden, which occupies an entire block in the center of the village.

South of New Philadelphia is historic Schoenbrunn Village, site of the first settlement in Ohio. More than a dozen log cabins and other buildings have been reconstructed to show how the early German Moravian missionaries and Christian Indians lived together in peace. With increasing bitterness all around them between early pioneers and marauding Indians, the neutral villagers were forced to move just prior to the Revolutionary War and the village was destroyed. Visit the graveyard and read the aged epitaphs. Nobody simply died back then. They either "went to sleep," "visited the vast beyond," or "went to the well."

Country of Plain Folk

The Amish are divided into two sects: The severe Old Order forbids owning cars, using electricity and strongly opposes any ostentation, worldly pleasures and all forms of violence; the more progressive Mennonites may own automobiles and also avail themselves of modern conveniences and comforts. Theologically, however, there is little difference between the two.

You'll see crowds of both Mennonites and Amish throughout Holmes, Wayne and Tuscarawas counties, among the nation's finest agricultural sections, and the shrewd, hard-working and self-sufficient Amish have contributed much to this standing. Largest town in Holmes County is Millersburg, which is also the county seat. The town's business district accommodates its many Amish customers with long hitching rails to which the farmers tie their horses while they shop. The Amish also have country auctions, just about the only social activity they allow themselves outside of their weddings and wakes. During summer, these auctions are held on Tuesday afternoons in Farmerstown and on Thursday afternoons in Kidron. Mostly produce is sold at these auctions.

Columbus

Columbus, with its rapid growth in the last few years, has a change of pace and face in the downtown area. Buildings that stood since the Civil War have been torn down in recent years, replaced by new office buildings, hotels, and restaurants. One thing that hasn't changed is the staid old limestone capitol, considered the purest example of Greek revival architecture in the United States. Completed in 1861, the building is a national historic landmark. The Ohio Historical Center has a fascinating display of state archives and archaeological findings. The main branch of Ohio State University is located here with its 85,000-seat stadium, 900,000-volume Ohio State Library, and horticultural gardens. Blossom browsers enjoy the Park of Roses in Whetstone Park with its 35,000 plants, and the Franklin Park Conservatory, with its array of exotic tropical and sub-tropical flora. Ohio Village is a reconstructed Ohio county seat, vintage 1800–1850, with 14 buildings and demonstrations of commercial crafts of that era. Seven miles north of Worthington is the Ohio Railway Museum. Also north of the city on State 23 are the Olentangy Caverns, the only three-level caves in Ohio. Just a mile south of the center of Columbus is a restored German Village. Restaurants and sausage houses here offer regional food, and shops and bazaars sell hand-crafted items. During the summer months, thoroughbred racing is presented at Darby Downs in neighboring Grove City and harness racing at Scioto Downs. Golfers, anglers, hikers, ice skaters, and picnickers can pursue their own interests at the seven reservations in Columbus' Metropolitan Park System.

Dayton and Airplanes

There will be no doubt in your mind as you drive through the modern downtown area of Ohio's fourth largest city: Dayton is a progressive town. Her greatest contribution to the world came with the success of the Wright brothers. Their first experiments with flying machines here led directly to their historic flight in North Carolina at Kitty Hawk.

At the city's Carillon Park are many transportation exhibits, including a restored Wright brothers' plane, a Conestoga wagon, a Concord coach, and Newcom Tavern, Dayton's oldest building. The park includes an actual section of the Miami-Erie Canal, fitted with one of the original locks.

The Air Force Museum at Dayton's Wright-Patterson Air Force Base is located in Fairborn, 11 miles east of Dayton. More than 20,000 items are on display as well as more than 150 historic airplanes and spacecraft. These include such aircraft from World Wars I and II as the German ME 109, the Russian Yak and Japanese Zero. Animated displays explain how jets and rockets work.

Other attractions include the Dayton Museum of Natural History, which also houses a planetarium; the Paul Lawrence Dunbar Homestead, home of the famous black poet; and the Dayton Art Institute. The largest amusement park in the area is Americana, at Le Sourdesville, south of Dayton off I-75 on State 63. Tombstone Territory, a sky ride, and Mark Twain Showboats are several of the attractions there.

PRACTICAL INFORMATION FOR OHIO

HOW TO GET THERE. *By car:* The major east-west highways into Ohio are I-90, I-80 and I-70. On the north-south axis are I-77, I-71, and I-75. *By train: Amtrak* serves Cincinnati and Cleveland. For information on Amtrak tours write to Amtrak Travel Center, P.O. Box 474, Riverdale, Maryland 20840.

By bus: Greyhound and *Trailways* provide service from all over America to Ohio.

By air: Cleveland, Toledo, Akron, Columbus, Dayton, and Cincinnati are all served by major carriers.

HOW TO GET AROUND. *By car:* More than 10,000 miles of good highways lead into almost every niche of the state. The *Appalachian Highway,* which travels through scenic southern Ohio, is being upgraded through the efforts of the Appalachian Development Highway System. All of the major U.S. and well-traveled state highways are dotted with roadside parks and rest areas with charcoal grills, sanitary facilities and frequent tourist boards showing points of interest in the area. Speed limit is 55 m.p.h. The minimum age for drivers is 16 with driver's education, 18 without. Helpful information for turnpike travelers is available by writing to: Department of Information and Research, Ohio Turnpike Commission, 682 Prospect St., Berea, 44017.

By train: Cleveland and Cincinnati are on *Amtrak* routes to Chicago from the East Coast. Routes are under review and are subject to discontinuance.

By bus: Greyhound and *Trailways* provide service throughout the state, and a number of smaller lines and local big-city transit companies provide feeder service around almost all of the largest cities.

By air: Cleveland is served by 16 major airlines, Cincinnati and Columbus six, and there is scheduled air service to Akron–Canton and Toledo, plus nine other Ohio cities. There are also close to 200 smaller airports and landing fields. For a free copy of "Some Places To Fly In Ohio," write to: *Ohio Division of Aviation,* Don Scott Field, 3130 Case Road, Columbus, 43220.

TOURIST INFORMATION SERVICES. *Ohio Office of Travel and Tourism,* Box 1001, Columbus, 43216: information on Ohio's festivals, history, gardens, Mound Builders, farm vacations, historic inns and mills, highway maps and much more. *Ohio Division of Parks and Recreation,* Department of Natural Resources, Publication Center, Fountain Sq., Columbus 43224: *Guide to State Parks,* and camping information. *Lake Erie Islands and Peninsula*

Vacationland Association, Port Clinton: brochure containing tourist map of area pin-pointing attractions and listing cottage information in the area. In Cincinnati, the *Cincinnati Convention & Visitor's Bureau,* 200 West Fifth St., Cincinnati 45202.

MUSEUMS AND GALLERIES. Canton has the *National Pro Football Hall of Fame,* just north of Fawcett Stadium and Cincinnati has the new *College Football Hall of Fame,* north off I–75 at King's Island exit. In Dayton, see the *Air Force Museum,* Wright–Patterson Air Force Base. *Carillon Park,* on Patterson Blvd., is a series of historical exhibits dealing with early modes of transportation, displayed in a charming village museum. Others in Dayton are the *Dayton Art Institute* and the *Dayton Museum of Natural History.* The *Toledo Museum of Art* contains a world-renowned collection of glass. Toledo also has a good *Museum of Science and Natural History.* The *Jonathan Hale Homestead and Western Reserve Pioneer Village* depicts Western Reserve life from 1800 to 1850.

In Cincinnati there are: *Taft Museum,* an outstanding example of Greek Revival architecture. It houses a priceless collection of portraits; French Renaissance painted enamel plaques and dishes; jewelry and watches from many countries; and almost 200 Chinese porcelains. You may also visit the *Jewish Museum of Hebrew Union College,* the *Museum of Natural History,* the *Cincinnati Art Museum,* the *Cincinnati Fire Museum,* the *Contemporary Arts Center, Stowe House,* and the *Christian Waldschmidt House. Grant's Birthplace and Museum* is 15 miles east at Point Pleasant.

HISTORIC SITES. *Fallen Timbers Park,* on US 24 just southwest of Maumee; free. *Flint Ridge State Memorial,* 3 miles N. of Brownsville off US 40 on State 668; *Fort Recovery State Memorial* is on State 49 at the small town of Fort Recovery; *Schoenbrunn Village,* 2 miles S. of New Philadelphia on State 8 and US 250; *Roscoe Village,* an old canal town on the north edge of Coshocton; *Serpent Mound* (4 miles northwest of Locust Grove off State 73), built of stone and clay, curls like an enormous snake for 1,335 feet—the largest and most remarkable effigy mound in America; free *Zoar Village* on State 212 is in a small, peaceful community.

Ohio contains more remains of the ancient race of Indians known as the *Mound Builders* than any other state east of the Mississippi River. Eleven of these mounds are maintained as State Memorials by the Ohio Historical Society. One group is administered by the National Park Service as a National Monument. Serpent Mound, discussed above, is in this group. For a complete listing of Ohio's state memorials, write the *Ohio Historical Society,* Ohio Historical Center, Columbus, 43211.

CANALS AND COVERED BRIDGES. There are close to 175 covered bridges remaining in Ohio. A complete list of Ohio's covered bridges is available from the *Ohio Historical Center,* Columbus 43211. Preserved portions of the *Ohio and Erie Canal* and the *Miami–Erie Canal* can be seen at four locations. For more information about canals, write to the *Ohio Historical Society,* Ohio Historical Center, Columbus, 43211, or the *Ohio Department of Public Works,* Division of Real Estate, Canal Lands, 708 Ohio Departments Building, Columbus, 43215.

DRINKING LAWS. Bars remain open until 1 or 2:30 A.M. daily, including Sun., in most larger cities by local option. Liquor may be purchased by the bottle in state stores from 11 A.M. to 6 P.M. Mon.–Sat. In large cities, selected liquor stores may stay open later. Age limit is 21 years, except for beer, 19 years.

SUMMER SPORTS. There are more than 100,000 acres of inland lakes, 36,000 acres of Sandusky Bay, and 7,000 miles of streams where water enthusiasts can enjoy *boating, fishing, swimming, water skiing, canoeing,* and *scuba diving.* There are more than 200 *golf* courses available to visitors. *Hunters* roam 10 million acres of farm lands and a half-million acres of licensed shooting preserves. *Hikers* and *backpackers* use the 478-mile *Buckeye Trail.* There are 200 miles of bridle trails through state forests, as well as primitive campgrounds for *horsemen.* Special bikeways have been built for *cyclists* who want to take a self-guided tour through scenic and historic areas of the state.

WINTER SPORTS. There are at least ten small *ski* areas. Two of the best are *Snow Trails* and *Clear Fork Valley* near Mansfield. *Ice skaters* join *anglers* and *boaters* who use Ohio's many rivers and lakes for winter sports activities.

SPECTATOR SPORTS. During fall and winter, the *Cleveland Browns* and *Cincinnati Bengals* play professional *football.* In Columbus, the Buckeyes of Ohio State University draw huge crowds to their Big Ten college games. Other fine collegiate teams include *Miami, Bowling Green, Ohio University, Dayton, Case Western Reserve, University of Cincinnati* and *Xavier.* The Toledo Golddiggers offer professional *ice hockey.* A top winter game is *basketball,* which finds many college teams participating, while the *Cleveland Cavaliers* offer professional play.

In major league *baseball* are the *Cincinnati Reds* and the *Cleveland Indians.* The *Toledo Mud Hens* and *Columbus Clippers* are part of the International League. *Racetracks* are located in 16 Ohio communities, including Cincinnati, Cleveland, Columbus, Grove City, and state and county fairgrounds. The *Mid-America Sports Car Course* at Mansfield is rated as one of the most competitive in the country. Trapshooters come from all over the world to compete in the *Grand American Trapshooting Tournament* held at Vandalia in August.

WHAT TO DO WITH THE CHILDREN. Vacationers can drive their cars through *African Lion Safari* and see lions, zebras, and plains game near Port Clinton. *Sea World* features the world's first tame killer whale, aquatic shows, and a Hawaiian village. *Geauga Lake Park* offers amusement rides, live shows, and water-park rides. A miniature Disneyland is located at *Cedar Point* on Lake Erie. There are more than 200 things to do and see, including a cable car ride, riverboat cruises, stage shows, and crafts on the historic Frontier Trail. The *Toledo Zoo* features the nation's largest fresh water aquarium, a children's zoo, a 12-foot cobra in its Reptile House. In Cincinnati: the second oldest zoo in the country, the *Zoological Gardens,* is located at Vine and Erkenbrecher Streets. A miniature Eiffel Tower stands in the amusement park at *Kings Island,* located 23 miles north at the junction of Kings Mill Road and I–71. It features International Street, Oktoberfest, Rivertown, Coney Island and the Happy Land of Hanna-Barbera.

HOTELS AND MOTELS in Ohio, outside the metropolitan areas of Cleveland and Cincinnati, range from deluxe to inexpensive, and can provide the traveler with any kind of accommodation from the dignified, older downtown hotel to the brighter, newer motel along the roadside. The price categories in the section, for double occupancy, will start from following figures up: *Deluxe:* $50 or more; *Expensive:* $40–50; *Moderate:* $25–40; *Inexpensive:* under $25.

CINCINNATI. *Deluxe:* **The Clarion Hotel.** 141 W. Sixth St. Convenient location. Heated pool, restaurant, bar. Health club.

Hyatt Regency Cincinnati. 151 W. 5th St. Elegant atrium styling.

Marriott Inn. 11320 Chester Rd. Heated pools, bars, restaurant, many sports facilities, and sauna.

Omni Netherland Plaza. 5th & Race St. Elegantly remodeled in French Art Deco style.

Terrace Hilton. 6th and Vine Sts. Downtown. Award-winning Gourmet Restaurant.

The Westin. Fountain Sq. Elegant. Fine dining, view.

Expensive: **Carrousel Inn.** Reading Rd., 8 mi. E on US 42. One of Ohio's finest, most complete resort motels.

Hilton Inn. 15 mi. N on I-275 at US 42 exit. Fine hotel with excellent dining, indoor pool. Golf nearby.

Moderate: **La Quinta.** 11335 Chester Rd. Pool, coffee shop.

Quality Inn–Riverview. Kentucky end of I-75 bridge, 5 min. from downtown. Two restaurants.

Inexpensive: **Bargaintel Inn–Florence.** I-71 & I-75, exit 180.

COLUMBUS. *Deluxe:* **Hyatt Regency.** 350 N. High St. Entertainment, dancing, in-room movies. Shops. Café.

Hyatt on Capitol Square. State & Third St. Elegant. Restaurant, bar, health club.

Expensive: **Hilton Inn North.** 7007 N. High St. Heated pool, restaurant, bar. Views of river, near shopping center.

Holiday Inn. Several locations. Downtown, Fourth and Town Sts.; East, 4801 E. Broad St.; North, 1212 Dublin-Granville Rd.; Airport, 750 Stelzer Rd. Usual features of the chain.

DAYTON. *Deluxe:* **Stouffer's Dayton Plaza.** Opposite convention center.

Moderate: **Quality Inn.** Pool, restaurant.

LEBANON. *Moderate:* **The Golden Lamb.** 27 S. Broadway. Ohio's oldest hotel still accommodates a few guests in antique-furnished rooms, so phone ahead and relax in the peaceful atmosphere. Noted for its food.

MANSFIELD. *Moderate:* **Best Western Mansfield Inn.** 880 Laver Rd., 5 mi. W. on State 30.

PAINESVILLE. *Deluxe:* **Quail Hollow Inn.** 11080 Concord-Hambden Rd., 4 mi. S off State 44. Tennis, golf, skiing, pool, sauna.

Moderate: **Rider's Inn & Tavern.** One of Ohio's historic stagecoach inns, and a sparkling change of pace from the auto age.

 DINING OUT. While the Midwest is generally steak and fried chicken country, seafood and foreign dishes are also popular. Hot cinnamon rolls, watermelon pickles, and hash brown potatoes are part of the country cooking in the small-town restaurants throughout the state.

Restaurant price categories are as follows: *Deluxe:* more than $25; *Expensive:* $15-25; *Moderate:* $10–15; *Inexpensive:* under $10. These prices are for hors d'oeuvres or soup, entrée and dessert. Not included are drinks, tax and tips.

AKRON. *Moderate:* **Tavern In The Square.** 135 S. Broadway in the Quaker Square Hilton. Prime rib.

Tangier. 532 W. Market. American and Mediterranean specialties and their own baked goods.

BURTON-WELSHFIELD. *Moderate:* **Welshfield Inn.** On US 422. An historic inn serving lunch and dinner.

CANTON. *Moderate:* **Bender's.** They specialize in seafood; the décor is turn-of-the-century.

CINCINNATI. *Continental. Expensive:* **The Heritage.** 7664 Wooster Pike. The early American décor is left from the days as a country tavern, and the food is as good and plentiful as the history.

The Celestial. 1071 Celestial St., Mt. Adams in the Highland Towers. Near downtown. Fine food and hilltop river view.

American. Moderate: **La Normandie.** 118 E. Sixth St. Steaks, London broil, fresh fish flown in daily.

French. Deluxe: **The Gourmet Room.** Terrace Hilton Hotel. Elaborate food, elaborate tariff, but the standard is remarkably high.

Maisonette. 114 East 6th St. This is one of the premier dining spots in the country. Classic cuisine is perfectly prepared. Prices are quite good for a deluxe restaurant. Food and services unequaled.

COLUMBUS. *Expensive:* **Ziggy's.** 3140 Riverside Dr., 7 mi. N.W. on US 33. Elegant. French and Continental specialties. Own pastries. Jackets required.

Moderate: **One Nation.** 1 Nationwide Plaza. American and Continental specialties. Each room decorated in style of different parts of the country.

COSHOCTON. *Moderate:* **Old Warehouse.** Quaint dining room in restored Roscoe Village.

DAYTON. *Expensive:* **L'Auberge.** 4120 Far Hills Ave. French. Veal St.-Jacques, duck salad with truffles. Own baking.

Moderate: **King Cole.** 4 S. Main. Haute cuisine and fine wine list.

Top of The Plaza. In Stouffer's Dayton Plaza, 5th & Jefferson Sts. Beef Wellington, glazed duckling. Seafood, steaks.

MANSFIELD. *Moderate:* **Gourmet Room.** 1313 S. Main. Fine dining at reasonable prices. Own pastries.

MARION. *Inexpensive:* **Turoff's.** They do their own baking and specialize in stews and casseroles.

MILAN-NORWALK. *Moderate:* **Milan Inn.** A historic "Inn of Fine Foods" expresses the unhurried lifestyle of the locale.

OBERLIN. *Expensive:* **Oberlin Inn.** Locally popular.

SANDUSKY. *Inexpensive:* **Baxter's Stone House.** Dinners and Sunday lunch served in restored 150-year-old-home.

SMITHVILLE. *Moderate:* **Smithville Inn.** It opened in 1818 as a stagecoach tavern, now specializes in family-style chicken dinners. The original building is worth a visit. Six miles N.E. of Wooster.

WISCONSIN

Milwaukee and Lush Resortlands

Milwaukee, with a growing population fast nearing 700,000 within the city limits, is the state's center of trade. Built mainly by German immigrants, it also has a large Polish population as well as the usual big city potpourri of nationalities. But somehow it manages to retain a smalltown friendliness despite its changing skyline. Steel and glass highrises were late to arrive, and residents still value their carefully maintained, older neighborhoods as much as the new lakefront additions.

Its lakefront residential district is one of the most beautiful in the nation, and the city has long been known for its orderly good government and its comparative lack of crime. Milwaukee has a beautiful art center and war memorial in an unusual modern structure on the lake front, a fine zoo, an ornate old public library (considered to be, along with the capitol at Madison, one of the state's most impressive buildings), lovely parks, and boulevards.

It probably is best known, though, for beer and baseball. Two breweries—Pabst and Miller—offer a conducted tour through their plants with a frothy glass of free refreshment in an attractive tavern at the end of the trip. The Milwaukee Brewers of the American League play home games at County Stadium, which is also used for Green Bay Packer home games during the pro football season.

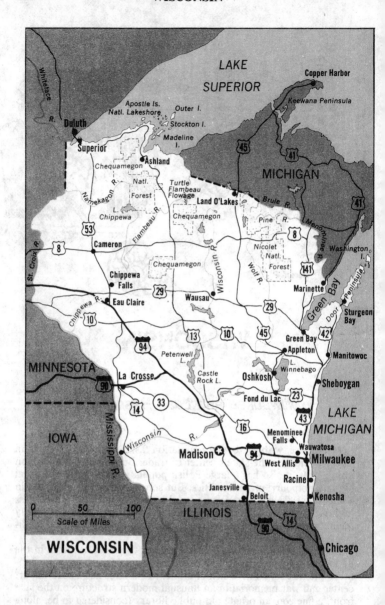

PRACTICAL INFORMATION FOR MILWAUKEE

HOW TO GET AROUND. *By bus:* The city-owned system operates around the clock throughout Milwaukee County, although runs are abbreviated after evening rush hours and weekends. They operate June-September city sightseeing tours. Call 344–4550 for information. Special wheelchair lift buses for handicapped. Call 344–6711. *By car: Avis, Budget,* and *Hertz* downtown and at the airport. *By boat: Iroquois Boatline* offers 1½-hour harbor cruises. Call 332–4194. *Emerald Isle Boatline* has dinner cruises, Sunday Brunch cruises, Happy Hour cruises and 1½-hour harbor cruises. Call 241–5631.

 TOURIST INFORMATION. The *Greater Milwaukee Convention and Visitors Bureau* is located at 756 North Milwaukee St., where visitors can obtain brochures on local attractions and special events. Two additional information centers are at 201 North Mayfair Rd., Wauwatosa, May to Sept., and the Main Level of General Mitchell Field. For daily listings of town events call the Milwaukee Fun Line, 799–1177, 24 hours a day.

 MUSEUM AND GALLERIES. *The Milwaukee Art Center and War Memorial,* 750 Lincoln Memorial Dr., a piece of art in itself, designed by Saarinen; *Science, Economics and Technology Center,* 818 W. Wisconsin Ave., features creative hands-on exhibits and The Great Electric Show; *Milwaukee Public Museum,* 800 Wells St., fourth largest natural history museum in the U.S., has a unique European Village representing Old World cultures; *Milwaukee County Historical Center,* 910 N. Third St., has everything from antique sleighs to fabulous toys. Be sure to see vintage dresses and the upstairs childrens' world. *Pabst Mansion,* 2000 West Wisconsin Ave., an extraordinary residential landmark of famed beer baron. *Villa Terrace,* formerly a private estate, is now a treasury of antiques.

 GARDENS. At the *Horticultural Conservatory* in Mitchell Park, 524 Layton Blvd., you can walk through several continents of gardens, and at *Alfred Boerner Botanical Gardens* in Whitnall Park, 5879 S. 92nd St., enjoy nature trails and formal gardens. *Schlitz Audubon Center,* 1111 Brown Deer Rd., covers 200 acres under development by National Audubon Society.

 MUSIC. For more than 40 years, Milwaukee has been staging an outstanding summer program, *Music Under the Stars.* Held from early June to Labor Day at various city parks, the programs range from the *Florentine Opera Company* to *Polka Concert Nights.* Free, but reservations required.

The annual Milwaukee *Summerfest* on the downtown lakefront presents a wide variety of musical events.

 STAGE AND REVUE. Top entertainment can be found at: the *Performing Arts Center,* 929 N. Water St., home of the city's repertory theater, ballet company, and symphony orchestra; *Glittering Pabst Theater,* 144 E. Wells St., has been lavishly restored to its 1895 elegance; and at *Marquette University* and *University of Wisconsin-Milwaukee. Melody Top Theatre,* 7201 W. Good Hope Rd., features Broadway musicals June into Sept.

 SPORTS. Milwaukee has variety for both spectator and participant. Professionally, there's the Milwaukee Brewers, *baseball;* the Milwaukee Bucks, *basketball;* and the Green Bay Packers, *football. Summer:* For the sportsman, there are *sailboat races* on Lake Michigan; supervised sandy *beaches* all along the lakeshore; *pleasure boat* rental, again along the lakefront; *fishing* (fighting coho salmon abound in Lake Michigan); nearly 30 *golf* courses; *scuba* and *skin diving; bike riding* on nearly 200 miles of trails and bikeways; *polo* at

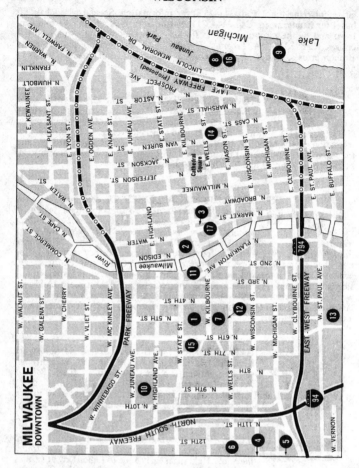

MILWAUKEE DOWNTOWN

Points of Interest

1) Auditorium-Arena
2) Center for the Performing Arts
3) City Hall
4) Pabst Mansion
5) Joan of Arc Chapel
6) Marquette University
7) MECCA-Convention Center
8) Milwaukee Art Center
9) Municipal Pier
10) Pabst Brewing Company
11) Pere Marquette Park
12) Public Museum
13) Railroad Station
14) Scottish Rite Cathedral
15) University of Wisconsin
16) War Memorial
17) Pabst Theater

Uihlein Field, North 70th St. at W. Good Hope Rd., and *auto racing* at Hales Corners and the State Fairgrounds.

    Winter: Rugby and *soccer* are popular. In October, pheasant *hunting—in November, deer hunting.* Fine ski slopes are within an hour's drive of the city, and *ice skaters* have numerous city and county parks to choose from.

WHAT TO DO WITH THE CHILDREN. The number one attraction is Milwaukee's *zoo* at 10001 Blue Mound Rd. Its construction keeps natural enemies apart—via hidden moats—yet it appears as if the animals are roaming common ground. Miniature train. Weekend lectures and movies are offered at the *Public Museum,* 800 W. Wells, and the *Central YMCA* also has an array of weekend programs. *Marriott's Great America* is popular day trip.

HOTELS AND MOTELS in Milwaukee are many and varied. Price categories (for double occupancy) start *up* from following figures: *Deluxe:* $70–90; *Expensive:* $55–70; *Moderate:* $35–55; and *Inexpensive:* under $35.

Deluxe: **Hyatt Regency.** 333 W. Kilbourn. Excellent location next to convention center. New, open-atrium lobby, revolving restaurant. Sophisticated setting.

Marc Plaza. 509 West Wisconsin Ave. Guests in their tower enjoy continental breakfast and happy hour in complimentary hospitality suite. A classy operation.

Pfister Hotel and Tower. 424 Wisconsin. Downtown. A 19th-century beauty lovingly maintained. Their English Room is dining standout.

Expensive: **Howard Johnson's Motor Lodge.** 2275 Mayfair Rd. Attractive.

Milwaukee River Hilton Inn. 4700 N. Port Washington Rd. Large rooms, view overlooking Milwaukee River.

Red Carpet Hotel. 4747 S. Howell Ave. Across from airport. Self-contained resort-style.

Moderate: **The Astor.** An old-fashioned hotel in prime Milwaukee location.

Golden Key Motel. 3600 S. 108th St. Pleasant. Free breakfast.

White Court Motel, 4400 S. 27th St. Very nice rooms.

Inexpensive: **Motel 6.** 5037 S. Howell Ave. Outdoor pool.

Safari Motel. 6798 W. Appleton. Pleasant rooms.

DINING OUT in Milwaukee reflects the varied ethnic make-up of the city. There is much good German food, as well as French and Italian. Seafood and good midwestern beef are staples. Restaurant price categories (averages) are as follows: *Expensive,* $17 and up; *Moderate,* $9–$17; *Inexpensive,* under $9.

Prices include a complete meal, excluding drinks, tax, and tip.

Expensive: **Fleur de Lis.** 925 East Wall St. Elegant French dining in landmark Cudahy Tower overlooking beautiful lakefront.

Melanec's Wheel House Restaurant. 2178 North River Boat Drive. Historic Milwaukee stained glass collection décor. Features veal, duck, fresh fish.

Moderate: **Bavarian Inn.** 700 W. Lexington Blvd. Try rouladen and Kassler ripchen.

John Ernst Café, 600 E. Ogden Ave. Superb German food. Since 1878.

Mader's. 1037 N. Third St. Medieval-style dining room, German menu.

Pieces of Eight. 550 N. Harbor Dr. Romantic Victorian atmosphere in Milwaukee's only lakefront restaurant.

The New Natatorium. 1646 S. 4th St. A conversation stopper in an imaginatively refurbished onetime city bathhouse. Giant hanging baskets, dolphin show.

Old Town Restaurant. 522 W. Lincoln. Well known for Serbian specialties.

Pandl's Whitefish Bay. 1319 E. Henry Clay St., Whitefish Bay. Broiled whitefish. Acclaimed since 1915. Save room for homemade dessert.

Ratzsch's. 320 E. Mason St. Best German food in town. Since 1904.

Inexpensive. **Casa del Lago.** 811 East Washington. Continental Mexican food.

EXPLORING WISCONSIN

Nearly 1.5-million choice acres compose the wilderness of the two national forests in Wisconsin, both of which are in the northern region.

Chequamegon National Forest is in the northwest and Nicolet National Forest is in the northeast.

Both forests offer the best in outdoor living and recreational activities. Contact the Forest Supervisor for details, road maps, literature, times, and schedules of events at Chequamegon, U.S. Forest Service, Park Falls, 54552; Nicolet, U.S. Forest Service, Federal Building, Rhinelander, 54501. Areas surrounding both regions are prime northwoods country rich in lumberjack legends and memories of French fur trappers. Today Hayward and Eagle River sit surrounded by a recreation utopia including literally thousands of lakes.

Lake Superior Shoreline and the Apostle Islands

Wisconsin has about 125 miles of shoreline on Lake Superior, which forms the northwest boundary of the state. The peninsula which thrusts out into the big lake, is heavily forested and little settled. It is here that the historic town of Bayfield is located. Once again coming to the fore as a fishing village, it is also the gateway to the Apostle Islands.

There are 22 Apostle Islands, chief of which is Madeline, settled first by the Chippewas, who stayed for 120 years, welcoming such notables as Father Jacques Marquette.

Madeline Island is the only one of the Apostles with a permanent settlement. Two ferries, each carrying nine cars and about 150 people, make frequent crossings from Bayfield.

These wild, remote, scenically spectacular islands are now part of the National Park service. Campfire lectures and nature walks are regularly conducted by park rangers in season.

Door County

The Door County peninsula extends about 70 miles right out into Lake Michigan. Swept by water-freshened breezes from all directions, it began to gain fame nearly 100 years ago as a naturally air-conditioned summer retreat. It remains so today, and the miles of narrow land are dotted with summer resorts and loaded with charm.

Often called the Cape Cod of the Midwest, Door County boasts a personality all its own—one with heavy Scandinavian overtones. Scandinavian restaurants and gift shops abound. There are an abundance of rustic fishing piers and old docks, beautiful shoreline drives, excellent golf, swimming, boating, and a very special mood.

Madison and the Dells

Touring Madison, you're bound to be impressed by the capitol, standing on a hill in the center of the city. It is one of the most resplendent of the domed edifices which characterize most state capitals. Here, too, is the gorgeous thousand-acre campus of the University of Wisconsin.

Madison itself is beautifully situated. It stands on a narrow neck of land between Mendota on the north, Lake Monona on the south, and Lakes Waubesa and Kegonsa to the southeast.

Although the Wisconsin Dells area 50 miles north is cluttered with a great concentration of commercial enterprises, the scenic portions of the river are virtually free of signs of civilization. The sightseeing is beautiful and unique. One example: In the Dells region of the Wisconsin River, the strong current has, over the centuries, gorged a 150-foot channel in the sandstone rock, cutting fantastic forms out of the soft rock.

The Greatest Show on Earth

"The Greatest Show on Earth" got its start in Baraboo, 10 miles south of the Dells. All that's left here now is the Circus World Museum, but it is one of the most interesting sights in the state. Opened in 1959, it is partly housed in the old buildings used by the Ringling Bros. Circus as winter quarters. From mid-May until mid-September the museum puts on a real one-ring show every day. And that isn't all! Many of the fabulous old circus wagons are here, as is John Zweifel's famous animated miniature circus and countless other priceless circus treasures. Bring your tape recorder . . . the circus music is remarkable.

The Great River Road

From Baraboo, if you drive a few miles south to the junction of US 12 and State 60, you should turn west on 60 for the 90-mile ride along the north bank of the Wisconsin River all the way to the Mississippi. It's one of the most beautiful drives in the state.

Then, when you reach Prairie du Chien, at the confluence of the two big rivers, you're not only in historic country, but on the threshhold of the Mississippi's most spectacular stretch as well.

Other Points of Interest

Starting again from Madison, take State 14. Eventually, you will come to Spring Green, where the late Frank Lloyd Wright's famed school Taliesen is still an architectural school and open to tourists. Spring Green's American Players Theatre tours the state, and from June to October performs classics locally in a beautiful outdoor setting. (For schedule and reservations contact them at Rte. 3, Spring Green 53588 [608] 588–7401.)

To the south, in a peaceful, wooded valley, is Little Norway—a combination of a Walt Disney production and a pioneer Norwegian homestead.

It would be a shame to end a tour without seeing Green County. You can leave the Norwegians and drive south right into "Switzerland." Monroe, the county seat of Green County, is the center of the state's dairying and cheese industry, the very heart of Wisconsin itself. If you have been driving all over the state to find the real Wisconsin, here it is, at last!

PRACTICAL INFORMATION FOR WISCONSIN

HOW TO GET THERE *By air:* The main carriers to Milwaukee are: *Ozark, Northwest Orient, Air Wisconsin, Continental, Comair, Eastern, Frontier, Midwest Express, Midway Metroliner, TWA, United, Republic, Simmons, Midstate,* and *Mississippi Valley. By bus: Greyhound* is the major long-distance carrier serving Milwaukee.

By train: Amtrak has scheduled service to Milwaukee, Portage, Tomah, Wisconsin Dells, and La Crosse and offers occasional package tours.

HOW TO GET AROUND. *By bus:* Every major municipality maintains an intracity bus line. The *Badger Coaches* run daily between Milwaukee, Madison, and other southern Wisconsin cities, and *Greyhound* maintains a regular schedule throughout the state.

By car: Avis, Budget, Dollar, and *Hertz* rent a variety of cars. Offices are maintained at all airports.

By air: Besides the major ailines mentioned above, commuter service is offered by *Air Wisconsin* of Appleton, *Midstate* of Stevens Point, and *Mississippi Valley* of La Crosse.

By bike: Wisconsin has the most extensive bicycle path in the country. Wisconsin Bikeway stretches 297 miles from Kenosha to La Crosse.

TOURIST INFORMATION. The *Wisconsin Division of Tourism* maintains information centers on main highways leading into the state and distributes detailed maps without charge, in addition to an assortment of literature on statewide attractions and accommodations. This information may also be obtained by writing to that office at Box 7606, Madison 53707.

MUSEUMS AND GALLERIES. The museum buff's first stop should be at the headquarters of the *State Historical Society of Wisconsin,* 816 State St., Madison. Free maps are available, listing more than 100 museums with their descriptions. Furthermore, the Society's museum is one of the best in the state and offers State exhibits from prehistoric times to the present.

In Green Bay, the *Neville Public Museum;* the *Packer Hall of Fame* highlights the glory years of Green Bay Packer football; and the *Rail America Museum* displays vintage railroad engines and cars.

The *Elvehjem Art Museum* on the University of Wisconsin campus in Madison, at 800 University Ave., is a beautiful small museum, with fine displays of historical and contemporary works; concerts on Sunday afternoons.

In Eau Claire, visit the *Paul Bunyan Logging Camp,* the one-room country *Sunnyview School,* the *Lars Anderson Log Cabin,* and the *Chippewa Valley Museum* in Carson Park.

Chalet of the Golden Fleece at 618 2nd St. in New Glarus contains Swiss antiques and jewelry, while the *Swiss Village Museum* at 6th and 7th sts. is a replica of a pioneer Swiss village with 12 buildings, including a cheese factory.

The *Little White School House* at Ripon is the birthplace of the Republican Party.

In conjunction with the *House on the Rock* on State 23 south of Spring Green is a museum with a number of unique collections including dolls, antique guns, model trains, and nickelodeons.

Madeline Island Historic Museum in the Apostle Islands has an intriguing, wide-ranging collection from beaded Indian deerskins to a horse-drawn sleigh-hearse.

Lovers of the sea will enjoy the *Manitowoc Maritime Museum and Submarine USS Cobia.*

Mid-Continent Railroad Museum at North Freedom attracts train buffs.

At Platteville, the *Mining Museum* and *Rollo Jamison Museum* offers mine tours and an outstanding collection of lead-mining memorabilia and native American artifacts.

Hayward's National Fresh Water Fishing Hall of Fame salutes fine fishing.

The *Peshtigo Fire Museum* at 400 Oconto Ave. re-creates the fire which claimed 1,000 lives the same day as the Chicago fire in 1871.

The *Rhinelander Logging Museum* in Pioneer Park on US 8 and State 47 has recreated an actual logging camp, complete with bunkhouse, kitchen, and lumberjack equipment. *New Civilian Conservation Corp. Museum* on site.

The Meteor is a whale of an attraction. This last remaining whaleback ship is a unique marine museum on Barker's Island near Superior.

Golden Rondelle at Johnson Wax headquarters in Racine was built for New York World's Fair and shows eye-opening free films; worth a detour.

Dard Hunter Paper Museum, 1043 E. South River, Appleton, portrays complete history of paper manufacturing.

Experimental Aircraft Association's *Aviation Center* and *Wisconsin Aviation Hall of Fame,* both now at Wittman Airfield, Oshkosh, house unique aviation collections.

HISTORIC SITES. Wisconsin lives with history. Among its plentiful attractions are: *The Circus World Museum* at Baraboo, located on the grounds of the first winter home of the Ringling Bros. Circus, offering daily circus acts (mid-May to mid-September), a circus train, restored old circus wagons.

The Old Ft. Crawford Military Hospital at Prairie du Chien traces development of medicine in this country from Indian and frontier times. Exceptional.

In Watertown is the famed *Octagon House,* completed in 1854.

Old Wade House, midway between Fond du Lac and Sheboygan on State 23, is an old stagecoach inn built by Sylvanus Wade. The complex includes the *Jung Carriage Museum,* featuring over 70 elegant carriages.

Galloway House and Village is located in Fond du Lac. The home is a farm house remodeled into a Midwestern version of an Italianate villa.

Villa Louis, overlooking the Mississippi at Prairie du Chien, is the lavish mansion of the state's first millionaire.

Old World Wisconsin, on a 565-acre site in Kettle Moraine State Forest, is an outdoor museum tracing the ethnic heritage of Wisconsin settlers.

Pendarvis at Mineral Point is a complex of restored Cornish miners' homes of the 1830s overlooking lead mines locally referred to as "badger holes."

Stonefield near Cassville is an 1890s village in Nelson Dewey State Park, onetime farm site of Wisconsin's first governor.

The *Old Indian Agency House,* a mile east of Portage off State 33 on Portage Canal Road, features Indian and early Wisconsin history in 1832 homestead.

Many historic houses are open to the public. Among headliners are Janesville's *Lincoln–Tallman Mansion,* Green Bay's *Heritage Hill State Park Complex,* and West Salem's *Hamlin Garland Homestead.*

SUMMER SPORTS. Nearly 15,000 lakes and over 1,700 river and streams make "outdoors" synonymous with Wisconsin. *Fishing* is the number one activity, but *scuba* and *skindiving* are gaining popularity. There's a *bikeway across the entire state,* and heavy *canoeing* on both quiet- and white-water rivers. Information on both is available from the *Wisconsin Division of Tourism,* Box 7606, Madison 53707.

The *hiker, camper,* and *backpacker* will find a bit of heaven throughout the state, and the *golfer* will find ample opportunity to swing.

WINTER SPORTS. Winter means one thing in Wisconsin and that's snow. When the white stuff falls, the sportsmen rise to meet its challenges. *Ice hockey* runs (rather skates) rampant. Big game *hunting*—whitetail deer and black bear—is popular.

There are more than 50 *ski* locations within the state and ever-growing numbers of public and private cross-country ski trails (30 state parks and forests offer over 400 miles), as well as extensive *snowmobile* trails. *Wisconsin Division of Tourism,* Box 7606, Madison 53707, will forward facts.

HOTELS, MOTELS, AND RESORTS throughout Wisconsin range from glamorous old-line hotels and plush resorts to new motels and homey family-owned establishments. Most resort areas have facilities which operate on various plans—European, Modified American and American. The price categories in this section, for double occupancy, will start and range up as follows: *Deluxe:* $70 and up, *Expensive:* $55–70, *Moderate:* $35–55, *Inexpensive:* under $35.

ALGOMA. *Moderate:* **Algoma Beach Resort/Motel.** On-the-water comfort.

BAILEY'S HARBOR. *Deluxe:* **Gordon Lodge.** Scenic view of Lake Michigan. Large lodge rooms and pleasant cottages, some with fireplaces.

BAYFIELD. *Moderate:* **Old Rittenhouse Inn.** Lumber baron's former summer home, decorated with antiques. Exceptional dining rooms.

CABLE. *Expensive:* **Telemark.** Four-season, family-oriented resort. Cross-country, downhill skiing; golf, tennis, horseback riding. Northwoods flavor.

DELAVAN. *Moderate:* **Lake Lawn Lodge.** Tennis, horses, wonderful rustic mood. Longtime favorite with modern additions. Attractive woodsy setting.

EAGLE RIVER. *Expensive:* **Chanticleer Inn.** Both motel and cottage units overlooking lake. Lots of activities.
Eagle Waters Resort. Beautifully situated on lake, with cottages and rustic cabins. Exceptional food.

GREEN BAY. *Moderate:* **Best Western Downtowner Motel.** Large comfortable rooms. Wide variety recreational facilities.

KOHLER. *Deluxe:* **The American Club.** A gracious village-inn atmosphere with Old World charm. Setting reminiscent of a private estate.

LAC DU FLAMBEAU. *Expensive:* **Dillman's Sand Lake Lodge.** Tranquil Northwoods setting with lodge and modern cottages. Good food.

LAKE GENEVA: *Deluxe:* **Americana Resort** (formerly Playboy Resort).

LAND O' LAKES. **Sunrise Lodge on Lac Vieux Desert.** The genuine article. A traditional Northwoods resort with meticulously maintained cottages, vast timbered grounds and an exceptional dining room. Physical fitness trail.

MADISON. *Deluxe:* **Concourse.** Normandy Restaurant excellent.
Expensive: **Edgewater Hotel.** On Lake Mendota; outdoor bar; exceptional dining room.
Sheraton Inn and Conference Center. Across from Coliseum.
Moderate: **Best Western Midway Motor Lodge.** Tasteful rooms.
Inexpensive: **Trails End.** Comfortable, some efficiencies.

NEW GLARUS. *Inexpensive:* **Swiss-Aire Motel.** Very nice, pleasant rooms.

OCONOMOWOC. *Deluxe:* **Olympia Resort & Spa.** Complete resort with spa facilities.

OSHKOSH. *Moderate:* **Pioneer Inn.** Year-round lakeside resort, 200-passenger paddlewheeler excursion boat, and full-service marina. Excellent food.

PORT WASHINGTON. Moderate: **Harbor Side Motor Inn.** Excellent.

RHINELANDER. *Moderate:* **Holiday Acres Resort.** On Lake Thompson. Cozy cottages, some fireplaces. Good cross-country skiing, snowmobiling.

SAINT GERMAIN. *Moderate:* **Idle Hours Resort.** On Little St. Germain Lake. Modern housekeeping cottages, good for families. Scenic setting.

SISTER BAY. *Moderate:* **Helm's 4 Seasons.** On Rt. 42 1 blk. from village center. Cottages and motel overlooking bay.

THREE LAKES. *Expensive:* **Northernaire.** North country classic.

WISCONSIN DELLS. *Deluxe:* **Chula Vista.** Resort in beautiful surroundings. Heated pool, bar, restaurant, many sports activities. Closed Dec.-Mar.
  Moderate: **Birchcliff Lodge.** Wooded grounds, fine accommodations.
  Mayflower Motel. Large rooms, 3 pools, whirlpool.

 DINING OUT in Wisconsin covers the gamut of eating establishments, from Scandinavian to lumberjack, from country cafés to elegant restaurants. Restaurant price categories are as follows: *Expensive:* $15–25, *Moderate:* $9–15; *Inexpensive:* $6–9. Price includes complete meal, excluding drinks, tax, and tip.

BOULDER JUNCTION. *Moderate:* **Outdoorsman Restaurant.** Local gathering place; dishes up one of best omelets in state.

CONOVER. *Moderate:* **The Fireside.** On Hwy. 45. Unpretentious exterior but worth a detour for the quality of the food.

DOOR COUNTY PENINSULA. Inquire locally about traditional outdoor fish boils scheduled in communities from summer into fall.

EAGLE RIVER. *Moderate:* **Czecho Club.** 3 mi. E. on Hwy. 70. Roast duck a standout; almond vanilla cheese cake a favorite.
  Pine Gables Gast Haus. On Hwy. 70. Quality German food served in log cabin setting.

ELKHART LAKE. *Moderate:* **Siebkins.** A summer find, open May–Sept. Genuine home cooking. Try German chocolate cherry cake and rye bread fresh from oven.

FORT ATKINSON. *Moderate:* **The Fireside.** Dinner theater and restaurant. Excellent food and entertainment.

GREEN BAY. *Moderate:* **Eve's Supper Club.** 2020 Riverside Dr. Overlooks Fox River. Fresh whitefish a specialty.
  Zuider Zee. 1860 University Ave. Try their prime ribs.

HAYWARD. *Inexpensive:* **Logging Camp Cook Shanty at Historyland.** All you can eat; better come hungry. Checkered tablecloths, tinware, mountains of food. Summer. A fun place with lumberjack atmosphere.

LAKE GENEVA. *Moderate:* **The Hayloft.** 1½ mi. from town on County BB. Fun place in stables of Old Lorimar estate.

MADISON. *Moderate:* **The Mariner's Inn.** Noted for steak, cheesecake.
  The Monastery. 4 blks from capital. Italian food served in former monastery. Good pasta.
  Namios. Gigantic T-bone steaks. Simple setting, hearty helpings.
  Ovens of Brittany. Traditional gourmet cuisine. Award-winning pastries.
  Quivey's Grove. Off Hwy. 18 and 151 on Nesbitt Rd. Restored farmhouse dining rooms are connected by tunnel to bar in barn. Outdoor fish boil in summer.

MANITOWISH WATERS. *Moderate:* **Little Bohemia.** 2 mi. S. of US 51. Stop for a meal or a cocktail at the lakefront resort where John Dillinger once hid out. Personal belongings left behind when he escaped lawmen are still there.

MINOCQUA. *Inexpensive:* **Paul Bunyan Lumberjack Restaurant.** 1 mi. N. on Rt. 51. Recaptures flavor of state's lively logging past. Good food, lots of it.

PORT WASHINGTON. *Moderate:* **Smith Bros. Fish Shanty.** On St. 32 at lakefront. Longtime favorite noted for seafood and atmopshere.

SAINT GERMAIN. *Moderate:* **Giese's Indian Lodge** on Hwy. 70. Unique log supper club with sophisticated menu.

SISTER BAY. *Moderate:* **Hotel du Nord** dining room. North Bay Shore Dr. Distinctive setting. Summer only. Home baking a specialty.

SPRING GREEN. *Expensive:* **Spring Green.** Charming restaurant designed by Frank Lloyd Wright. Overlooks scenic bend in Wisconsin River.

STAR LAKE. *Moderate:* **North Star Lodge.** Originally built at lumber camp. Cozy frontier flavor; homecooking would satisfy hungry loggers!
Inexpensive: **Star Lake Saloon & Eatery.** Worth the trip for their French toast and snowmobiler/lumberjack breakfast.

WISCONSIN DELLS. *Expensive:* **Fischer's Supper Club.** Delicious food. **Ishnala.** Rustic atmosphere on Mirror Lake. Closed in winter. **Jimmie's Del Bar.** Spectacular Fri. smorgasbord.
Inexpensive: **Paul Bunyan Lumberjack Restaurant.** Nostalgic old logging camp atmosphere. All you can eat, family-style. Closed in winter.

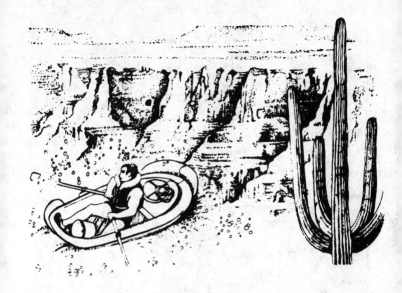

ARIZONA

Phoenix, Tucson, and Shangri-la

Phoenix, with surrounding Maricopa County, is the heart of Arizona. The main points of interest in the city are midtown Encanto Park, Pueblo Grande, Papago Park with the Phoenix Zoo and Desert Botanical Garden, the State Capitol, South Mountain Park, Civic Plaza, and several museums, including the noted Heard Museum, devoted to different aspects of Arizona's art, anthropology, Indian culture, and history.

Adjacent Scottsdale is so closely wrapped up in the Phoenix resort picture as to be an integral part of it, and, in addition, it is a thriving art and crafts center with posh homes, town houses, hotels, smart stores, art galleries, craft shops, and outstanding restaurants.

Traveling via routes I–19, US 89 and 89A not only reveals the many diverse landscapes, from southern deserts through the higher plateaus and grass prairies to pineclad mountains, but also is a key to many of the state's major cities, unusual sights, sports, and historic locales. The routes run north from the Mexican border at Nogales through Tucson, Phoenix, and Prescott, thence past cattle lands, ghost towns, piney mountains, and Oak Creek Canyon to Flagstaff, and then across the Navajo Reservation to Page and Glen Canyon Dam. No other Arizona highways match their variety and magnitude of lures.

In the northwestern section of Arizona, the Lake Mead National Recreation Area attracts millions of visitors annually. The interior of 726-foot-high Hoover Dam, one of the world's largest, can be toured, as can its power plant.

Side roads lead to developed sports sections like Temple Bar and Willow Beach. If desired, take US 93 to Kingman, then south on I–40 to State 95 and Lake Havasu. A prime lure is Lake Havasu City, where

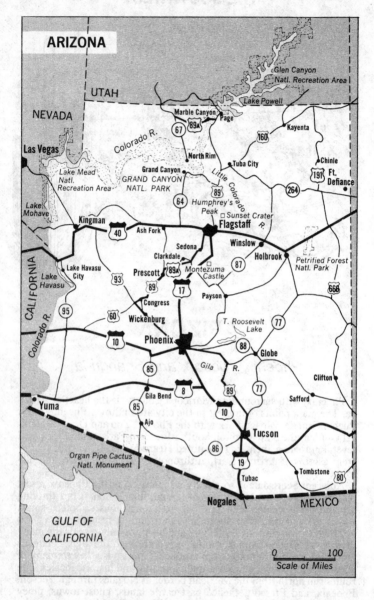

London Bridge has been reconstructed with an adjoining "English Village"; state park facilities, water sports, and other recreation add much appeal.

Northeast of Kingman stretches the million-acre Hualapai Indian Reservation, whose headquarters and trade center, on Old Route 66, is Peach Springs. Near Ash Fork, the highway joins I–40 and enters Kaibab and Coconino National Forests, which have some of the state's loveliest stands of ponderosa pine and aspen.

Northward, Glen Canyon National Recreation Area contains 186-mile Lake Powell with a shoreline of about 1,800 miles, much of it accounted for by an incredible number of side canyons that create imposing landscapes for boaters. The lake has both pleasure boating and sightseeing trips, as well as excellent fishing.

US 160 running northeastward to the Four Corners area (the only place in the United States where four state lines meet) rolls over vast, lonely expanses dotted with occasional Navajo hogans and sheep herds.

Six-hundred-acre Navajo National Monument contains two of the biggest and most intricate of the state's 13th-century cliff dwelling ruins. Easiest to reach is the Betatakin ruin, in a spur of Segi Canyon, where a steep trail of slightly more than a mile leads from the monument Visitor Center to a prehistoric apartment house that probably had 135 rooms.

In central Arizona, the old territorial capital of Prescott still reflects the mining, farming, and ranching endeavors that made it important in the late 1800s. Indians and cowboys are common sights in town, and the Smoki Ceremonials and Frontier Days Rodeo each summer intensify the atmosphere of yesteryears. The old section—with the log Governor's Mansion, Old Fort Misery, Sharlot Hall Museum, and other lures—is one of the state's foremost centers for viewing the paraphernalia of frontier days in a setting where the first Territorial Legislature met over 120 years ago.

Southward, just outside Coolidge, Casa Grande National Monument is one of the choicest surviving remnants of the Hohokam culture that flourished more than six hundred years ago. The main ruin, a four-story apartment house-watchtower, is protected by a huge steel umbrella. Self-guided tours through this Big House reveal such things as calendar holes, strange designs, pioneer inscriptions and the waist-high passageways between the maze of rooms. A deep appreciation of the area, its people, and their civilization can be obtained by examining exhibits in the monument's museum in the Visitor Center.

Tucson

The vacation lures of southern Arizona—for which Tucson is the touring center—are much more concentrated, the majority of them being located in and around Old Pueblo's environs, and in the region southeastward. Many of them are along or quite near the principal routes: Interstate 10 and 19; US 80 and 89. In Tucson the Spanish influence can still be seen and felt despite the rapid development as a winter resort and its ranking as Arizona's number-two city. Many sections of Tucson are browner than any in Phoenix since there is not the same widespread irrigation system. The desert comes closer to the city's mid-section, yet it's a pleasing, not harsh, meeting. Tucson's central area has the greenest look, and one of the nicest spots is the 312-acre University of Arizona campus. Points of interest on the campus are the Arizona State Museum, with its comprehensive archeological exhibits; the University Art Gallery, which features the Kress Collection of Renaissance Art; The Grace Flandrau Planetarium; and the Mineral Museum, with a collection of specimens from all over the world. Across from the campus, the Arizona Historical Society offers a complete Southwestern research library and pioneer museum. Nearby is the University's Center for Creative Photography, the nation's first such place with library, memorabilia and pictures by famous photographers.

Around the downtown section, some of the adobe buildings from the early American period—when architecture more closely reflected the heritage from south of the border—still stand. The most famous, The

Old Adobe Patio, now a historic site, was erected in 1868 and still shows the charm of pioneer patio-style living.

Tucson is a town for exploring, especially around the fringes, where a small bonanza of sights and pastimes awaits. The Santa Catalina Mountains, rising to the 9,157-foot summit of Mt. Lemmon, and their foothills, hide a wealth of vacation pursuits. Beneath the summit lies rocky Sabino Canyon, where tall pines shade trout pools, a cool clear stream, picnic and camp facilities, and nature trails that give intimate glimpses of the countryside. Tucson's old Fort Lowell, a key point in the Apache warfare during the 1870s and 1880s, has been partially restored, though many adobe walls still stand. Artist Ted DeGrazia's Mission in the Sun, constructed by him and Yaqui Indians entirely from desert materials, is an expression of both artistic ability and religious faith. The mission is part of the deceased artist's gallery.

On the Tucson west side, at the Arizona-Sonora Desert Museum, emphasis is placed on desert life. Larger animals are kept in open paddocks while smaller ones—insects, reptiles, and the like—are shown in three-dimensional dioramas. Trails lead through a desert garden, a walk-in aviary, along Water Street, through the above- and underground Beaver-Otter-Bighorn Sheep complex, the Congdon Earth Sciences Center (underground cave geology), and into the tunnel exhibit, where visitors can watch various animals living underground as they normally do. Nearby is Old Tucson, a popular family fun park and Old West film set.

Mission San Xavier del Bac, the White Dove of the Desert, founded about 1700 by Father Kino, represents a major breakthrough in early missionary work, and has remained important ever since it was created. The present structure dates to 1783 and is a gem of Spanish Colonial architecture, with carved stone portals, Indian-painted murals, and elaborate altar. It fell into disrepair in later years, but now has been faithfully restored.

PRACTICAL INFORMATION FOR ARIZONA

HOW TO GET THERE. *By car:* Major routes are: *east-west*—Interstate 40, 10 and 8, US 60, US 70; *north-south* —US 666, US 89, Interstate 17 and 19, US 93 and State 95.

By air: Phoenix is served by *American, Continental, Delta, Eastern, Frontier, Northwest, Pan Am, PSA, Republic, TWA, United, US Air* and *Western.* There are intra-state lines serving areas from Tucson and Phoenix. Airport terminal facilities for handicapped persons are excellent.

By bus: Greyhound and *Continental Trailways* have northern, central, and southern passages across the state.

By train: Amtrak's *Sunset Limited* stops in Benson, Tucson, Phoenix, and Yuma. Its *Southwest Limited* serves Winslow, Flagstaff, Seligman, and Kingman.

HOW TO GET AROUND. *By car:* Rental agencies are located in important tourist centers, and some companies offer special packages for a weekend, week or longer.

By bus: For local sightseeing, via 2½ hour or two-day escorted tours, the main source is Gray Line, Phoenix (600 E. Jefferson St.), Tucson (P.O. Box 1991) and Flagstaff (Box 339).

By air: Within Arizona, air service is provided by *Cochise, Frontier, Havasu, Sky West, Sun Aire, Scenic* and *Republic.* There are also charter services and local sightseeing flights.

TOURIST INFORMATION. State of Arizona Office of Tourism, 1480 E. Bethany Home Rd., Phoenix, AZ 85014 (602–255–3618).

MUSEUMS AND GALLERIES. There are worthwhile museums of Arizona's natural features, Indian culture, and white man's history in Flagstaff, Prescott, Tombstone, Tucson, Yuma, Jerome, Willcox, Window Rock, Wickenburg, Kingman, Ganado, Bisbee, Patagonia, Page, Fort Huachuca, and Camp Verde, in addition to the important museums and galleries concentrated in Phoenix and in numerous National Park preserves.

HISTORIC SITES. Twenty national parks, monuments, historic sites, and memorials protect exceptional scenic and geological areas, rare and beautiful plants, and outstanding Indian cultural remains. Nineteen state parks present relics of pioneer days, abundant recreational outlets, and unusual scenery.

TOURS. In Tucson there is *Gray Line,* 180 W. Broadway Blvd., Phoenix has *Gray Line,* 600 E. Jefferson, and the Sept.-May travelcades of the low-cost non-profit *Phoenix Dons Club,* P.O. Box 13493; Phoenix 85002. Flagstaff has *Gray Line (Nava-Hopi Tours),* 401 Malpais Lane.

DRINKING LAWS. Legal drinking in any licensed bar, restaurant, hotel, or inn from 6:00 A.M. to 1:00 A.M. weekdays, noon to 1:00 A.M. on Sundays. Most package stores close by 11:00 P.M. There are no state liquor stores. Minimum legal age is 21. Many markets and drugstores also sell alcoholic beverages.

SUMMER SPORTS. These include *archery, camping, horseback riding, boating, bowling, fishing, golf, hiking, swimming, surfing, scuba diving, snorkeling, river tubing, water skiing, soaring, hang-gliding, ballooning,* and *tennis.*

WINTER SPORTS. *Skiing:* The *Arizona Snow Bowl* near Flagstaff; *Mount Lemmon,* an hour's drive from Tucson; *Sunrise Ski Area* outside Spingerville. Season and conditions vary widely. *Hunting:* Big game in fall and winter; predatory and small game year-round.

SPECTATOR SPORTS. *Baseball:* Major league ball in exhibition games in Cactus League in Mar. to Apr. *Cleveland Indians* train in Tucson, *San Francisco Giants* at Scottsdale and the *Oakland A's* at Phoenix, *Chicago Cubs* in Mesa, *Milwaukee Brewers* at Sun City; *Seattle Mariners* at Tempe, and *San Diego Padres* at Yuma. *Basketball:* Phoenix Suns of MBA, also college games. *Boxing:* Phoenix and Tucson offer bouts. *Racing dogs:* Parimutuel betting at Phoenix. Other tracks near Apache Junction, Amado, Black Canyon, Tucson and Yuma. *Horse racing:* summer meets at Prescott and at county fairs. Fall, winter, and early spring racing at Turf Paradise, Phoenix, and Rillito Downs, Tucson. *Horse shows:* Tucson and Valley of the Sun regularly host shows during the winter. *Auto racing:* Tucson: Corona Speedway, Tucson Dragway. Phoenix: Beeline Dragway, Manzanita Park, Phoenix Dragway, and Phoenix Int'l Raceway. *Rodeos:* There are many sites throughout Arizona but the most important are in Prescott and Payson. *Events:* The Fiesta Bowl is a major month-long series of sporting events (about 33) culminating in the nationally televised Fiesta Bowl football game on New Year's Day.

WHAT TO DO WITH THE CHILDREN. *Tombstone's* famous landmarks are the *OK Corral, Wells Fargo Office, Boot Hill,* and many others around which stories have been told and retold.

Indian villages always interest children, particularly those of the *Hopi Indians,* where tribal dances are staged frequently.

There are also the ghost towns, various frontier forts, the old jails like those in *Wickenburg, Clifton* and *Yuma,* the *Smoki Museum* at *Prescott. Old Tucson,* a converted movie set outside Tucson, and *Rawhide,* north of Scottsdale, offer various Western-style amusements and staged gunfights in the streets. The *Arizona Sonora Desert Museum* in Tucson has special appeal for any age.

HOTELS AND MOTELS. The price categories in this section, for double occupancy, will start at the following prices: *Super deluxe:* $60, *Deluxe:* $45–60, *Expensive:* $30–45, *Moderate:* $25–30, and *Inexpensive:* below $25. Rates are for the winter season; off-season, in summer, southern area prices may be 25–50% lower.

FLAGSTAFF. *Deluxe:* **Best Western Little America.** Best in town.
Expensive: **Holiday Inn.** 1000 W. Highway 66.

GRAND CANYON PARK. *Deluxe:* **Grand Canyon Lodge.** At north rim entrance to Grand Canyon. Rustic cabins and motel complex.

LAKE HAVASU CITY. *Super Deluxe:* **Nautical Inn Resort.** On the lake. Restaurant, 2 lounges, heated pool, tennis and golf.
Expensive: **Best Western Lakes Place Inn.** Pool, coffee shop, cocktail lounge.
Moderate: **Sandman Inn.** Pool, some housekeeping units, good for families.

PHOENIX. *Super Deluxe:* **Phoenix Hilton.** Downtown near Civic Plaza. Full hotel facilities plus old bar from historic Adams Hotel.
Arizona Biltmore Hotel. One of America's finest resort hotels, located on 39 acres. Shops, golf, tennis, other sports, entertainment.
Doubletree Inn. Suites, fine dining, midtown, near shopping and business, and sports outlets.
Granada Royale Hometel. Five locations, elegant suites for couples or families. Informal mood. Pool and other sports. Free daily evening cocktails and breakfasts.
Hyatt-Regency. Another splendid example of this chain's hotels, which have become tourist targets even for people not staying at them.
The Pointe. One S. Phoenix and two N. Phoenix locations. Full facilities from golf to horseback riding, excellent dining and service, shops.
Townhouse Ramada. Heated pool, restaurant, bar. Big rooms and beds. That air of luxury you want.
Deluxe: **Ramada Inn—Downtown.** Fine motel of national chain. Three more in Phoenix.
Rodeway Inn. Top unit is a national chain. Near airport location. Two more in Phoenix.
Sheraton Greenway Inn. Adjacent to I–17. Fine hotel with sauna and whirlpool. Good dining, cocktail lounge, evening entertainment.
Expensive: **Western Village Motor Hotel.** 1601 Grand Ave. Attractive western-motif units, good dining.
Inexpensive: **Cocoanut Grove.** Small motel, family units.
Motel 6. 2 levels, very modern. Six locations.

PRESCOTT. *Expensive:* **Auto Rest Motor Motel.** Nearest in-town. Nice family units.
Best Western Prescottonian Motel. 120 units, Prescott's newest deluxe accommodation.

SCOTTSDALE. *Super Deluxe:* **The Cottonwoods.** A Stouffer resort. On Scottsdale Road with excellent facilities, pools, tennis, other sports, convenient shops. Spanish-style dining and cocktail rooms.
The Inn at McCormick Ranch. Posh units overlooking lake and golf courses. Fine dining.
Mountain Shadows. (Marriott's). Famous year-round resort.
Marriott's Camelback Inn. Heated pools, restaurant, bar. Many social and sporting activities, entertainment. Beautiful grounds, lots of room.

Scottsdale Registery Resort. Big 76-acre resort, large rooms with color TV and other amenities, restaurants, cocktail lounge, pool, tennis, golf, health club.

Safari. Elegant resort hotel. Studios and suites with kitchens.

Sunburst Hotel. All-year resort hotel, suites, and kitchenettes.

SEDONA. *Super Deluxe:* **Poco Diablo Resort.** Attractive rooms and villas, full facilities, pool, tennis, other sports. On 22 acres. Fine dining. Scenic near-town setting. Off-season here is April–October.

TUCSON. *Super Deluxe:* **Arizona Inn.** Rooms in cottages and lodge. Heated pool, restaurant, bars. Some sports. Beautiful, flower-bedecked grounds.

Hacienda del Sol. Adobe buildings in desert setting. Dude ranch. Pool, tennis.

Tanque Verda Guest Ranch. Top-grade, friendly rustic atmosphere in historic stage station and ranch. Full amenities plus nearby golf. AP. Informal but elegant.

Marriott Hotel. Heated pool, restaurant, bar. Convenient location. 311 rooms.

Smuggler's Inn. Attractive units with balconies or patio. Excellent dining.

Deluxe: **Westward Look.** 215 rooms, luxurious accommodations, 2 pools, 8 tennis courts. Spectacular view.

Best Western Ghost Ranch Lodge. Medium-size motor hotel with wide choice of rooms.

Holiday Inn. Three locations. Pleasant. Jacuzzi, pool.

Expensive: **Desert Inn.** 1 N. Freeway. Modern hotel, family rates.

Rodeway Inn. Three locations. Clean and comfortable.

TraveLodge. Tastefully furnished.

WICKENBURG. *Super Deluxe:* **The Wickenburg Inn.** Tennis and guest ranch with homey casitas and large nature preserve. Stables. Pool. Delightful informal mood. AP.

 DINING OUT in Arizona means chiefly American or American-Continental cuisine, but it can also mean Mexican, German, Chinese, Italian, Polynesian, and many other types. Restaurant price categories are as follows: *Deluxe:* $15 and up, *Expensive:* $10–15, *Moderate:* $5–10, and *Inexpensive:* under $5. These prices are for salad or soup and entree. Not included are drinks, tax, and tips.

CAVE CREEK. *Expensive:* **Trois Amis.** Delightful, homey cottage café. Fare is French provincial.

JEROME. *Expensive:* **House of Joy.** This restaurant, in the ghost town of Jerome, is known for its excellent food and service. Make reservations two weeks in advance. Open Fri., Sat., Sun. only.

NOGALES. *Moderate:* **Cavern Café.** Part of restaurant is in a cave, a former gold mine and jail in which Geronimo was imprisoned. In Mexico.

Inexpensive: **Zula's.** Mexican and American menu.

PHOENIX. *Expensive:* **Asia House.** Chinese, Japanese, and Mongolian, with decors and waitresses to fit the cuisines.

American-Continental. **Pointe of View.** At Pointe Resort. City views while dining on specialties like New York steak stuffed with crab, shrimp skewer and Dungeness crab. Bar. Locally popular.

Moderate: **Carlos O'Brien's.** Mexican–American menu. Generous portions. Popular spot.

The T-Bone Steak House. Huge steaks charcoal broiled before your eyes with an incredible view of the valley. The portions are generous, though totally unadorned, salad bar, beans and bread, and the food is excellent. Off-the-beaten-track and a real find.

SCOTTSDALE. *French. Expensive:* **Etienne.** One of Scottsdale's best restaurants. French cuisine prepared in the grand manner. Good wine list and better-than-average service.

Mexican. Moderate: **Los Olivos Mexican Patio.** A full range of Mexican dishes in a wonderfully evocative atmosphere, and American dishes for the less adventurous in the crowd.

American. Expensive: **Jed-Nolan's Music Hall.** Old-fashioned food, singing waiters, and old-time music.

Western. Moderate: **Reata Pass Steak House.** Take a step back into Arizona's past. Known for large cowboy steaks. Western music.

TUCSON. *Continental. Deluxe:* **Tack Room.** A visit here is usually a night out all by itself. One of the West's top dining spots.

Iron Mask. This restaurant and its owner-chef have proved themselves over many years. Consistently a favorite.

American. Expensive: **Solarium.** Fresh fish and seafood.

Expensive: **Saguaro Corners.** Fine American-Continental cuisine in a wildlife setting where desert birds and animals come close to picture windows.

Western. Expensive: **Pinnacle Peak.** Steak, pinto beans, and own baked bread are the staples, and they are well prepared on a grill over a deep pit and a true mesquite fire. Casual. Nice Western atmosphere.

Mexican. Moderate: **La Fuente.** A south-of-the-border flavor with specialties like margaritas, carne à la Tampiqueña, pastel Azteca, and mole poblane.

Spanish. Expensive: **El Parador.** Spanish, and Mexican, with some American dishes. Lots of greenery, like eating outdoors.

ARKANSAS

Land of Opportunity and the Ozarks

Before you visit Arkansas, make up a list of all the places you should see and the things you should do. Then try and find the time to do at least half of them.

There are the mountains in the north and west—the Ozarks and the Ouachitas. You will find scenic beauty, relaxation, and delightful people there in the hills; and lakes and rivers where the fishing is great and the going rugged.

Almost at an hour's notice you can exchange the hills for the flatlands and be in the land of cotton and the flooded paddies of the Grand Prairie. There you will find catfish farming, rice growing just as in China, and the finest duck hunting in the country.

Along the eastern border flows the Mississippi, and across the western border lies the great southwest and its memories of frontier days.

There is history to be accounted for. Fort Smith was a jumping off place for wagon trains heading west. The reconstructed Fort Smith National Historic Site, a national project, is a must. And the Arkansas Post National Memorial on the Arkansas River near Gillette carries the story of the visits of DeSoto, La Salle, Father Marquette, Joliet, de Tonti; almost 450 years of history.

Be sure to include Hot Springs. The attractive resort city and health spa almost surrounds 4,700-acre Hot Springs National Park. There's the Pea Ridge National Battlefield in the northwest; the Crater of Diamonds State Park near Murfreesboro; Dogpatch U.S.A. in the Ozarks; and Little Rock at the center, with its beautiful Arkansas Territorial Restoration, imposing Greek Revival Old State House, and handsome marble State Capitol nearby.

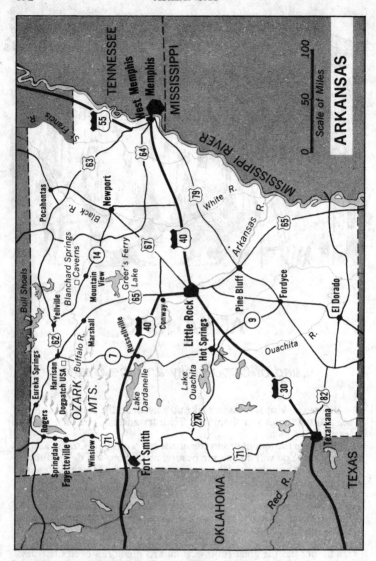

There's fried catfish, fried chicken, barbecue, hush puppies, corn-pone, black-eyed peas and huckleberry pie. Let's go!

Fort Smith, with its blend of Deep South and Far Western atmo-sphere, is a fascinating starting point. It gives you a choice of a diagonal Arkansas River run or a more comprehensive loop over the Ozark Mountains or the vast pine country of the scenic Ouachitas. Around and near the shady courthouse square, tourists stroll along reading historical markers depicting the time when 5,000 gold seekers gathered before crossing the nearby Poteau River and heading west to California in 1849. Other markers designate sites of the last encampments of

Cherokees east of the Arkansas at what is termed "End of the Trail of Tears." Bronc riders and roundup clubs bring the Old West to exciting life at Fort Smith's Harper Stadium and along historic Garrison Avenue in late May and early June.

A Fort Smith institution aimed directly toward additional enjoyment for tourists is Old Fort Days during the late May and early June Arkansas-Oklahoma Rodeo. The special days include authentic exhibition riding, shooting and saber action on horseback by Texas Cavalrymen, a reenactment of the 1896 trial of Cherokee Bill and his hanging, and tours of pre-Civil War and post-Civil War homes in the restoration area of historic old Belle Point.

The famed Judge Parker Courtroom, the "Dungeon Jail," and the hanging gibbet are included in Fort Smith National Historic Site. Adjoining, at 320 Rogers Ave., is the Old Fort Museum, with fine collections of Indian and pioneer artifacts, changing exhibits.

East of this historic river city, you have the choice of a circular junket across the Boston Mountains or a central run through the state. Both routes offer abundant scenery and history. Try I-40 first, skirting the Arkansas River Valley and beautiful Lake Dardanelle, for the central diagonal run. Just east of Ozark is St. Mary's Mountain, where grape-growing and wine-making have been traditional among the descendants of Swiss and German immigrants for almost a hundred years. Tour the Wiederkehr Wine Cellars and enjoy food and refreshments at the Wein Keller Café.

East of Russellville, in Pottsville, is one of the most impressive antebellum restorations in the state, the former home of Kirkbridge Potts, for whom the town was named. The large two-story house, with its tall brick chimneys and nearby wellhouse, stands on a rise overlooking a tiny business district which has just about faded away.

Petit Jean State Park is about seventeen miles southwest of Morrilton. The mountaintop park offers a lodge, cabins, and camping facilities. Nearby, the Museum of Automobiles displays vintage and classic cars.

Returning to I-40, you will travel through rolling pasture and farmland to Conway, then turn eastward across the flatlands with their cotton fields and the Grand Prarie rice paddies. Beyond, toward the Mississippi and Memphis, is the route of the Great River Road, which follows and often provides a view of the Father of Waters itself. This will make the end of your central run through Arkansas. A longer, more comprehensive loop will take you across the northwestern mountains, and then in a long swing back to Little Rock and Hot Springs.

Start at the Alma exit of I-40 and head north via US 71. The highway climbs and dips over cedar ridges to the western Ozarks like a ribbon blown in the mountain wind. Far below shine the waters of Clear Creek and the white span of Silver Bridge. Mountainburg, a quaint old town of stone and brick, nestles at the foot of a steep mountain slope where wagon trains of pioneer settlers crossed "The Narrows" and came down to better farming land.

Eureka Springs is probably Arkansas' most unusual city. Dozens of streets loop their way about the mountainsides below businesses and homes which have been constructed in tiers on sites literally blasted out of the cliffs. The main traffic artery is Spring Street, a narrow, picturesque thoroughfare where houses, and staircases ascending to dwellings further up, seem to lean out over the streets. The Historical Museum has local 19th-century items on display, while the Miles Mountain Musical Museum exhibits old musical instruments, as well as historic items. The last home of temperance crusader Carrie Nation contains personal memorabilia.

The *Christ of the Ozarks* statue atop Magnetic Mountain is seven stories tall, and depicts Christ standing with outstretched arms. In an amphitheater nearby, *The Great Passion Play* is performed nightly during the warmer months, and on US 62 you will find the Christ Only Art Gallery, with an enormous collection of documents in foreign languages—some dating to before Christ.

Eastward from Eureka Springs is Berryville, a gem of a little mountaintop city, with a panoramic view of neighboring mountains. There's good fishing in the nearby Table Rock Lake area, and also in Greers Ferry, Beaver and Norfork Lakes.

Bull Shoals Lake is another of the finer recreational areas of Arkansas; from there, wind your way through the hills to Yellville and southward on State 14 through rugged mountain country along the Buffalo National River, which stretches some 150 miles between magnificent, bluff-lined vistas and is considered by many to be the most beautiful free-flowing stream in the United States. Limestone bluffs tower above most of its length, and the white rapids of the mountain stream offer a challenge to canoeists and floaters. High on a bluff above the river, just off State 14, is Buffalo River State Park. Relax in the shade along natural beaches, swim in the blue pockets of water or enjoy such sites as Pebble Springs and the Indian Rock House, a gigantic overhanging cliff.

America's greatest new cave find is Blanchard Springs Caverns, one of the largest and most amazing subterranean wonderlands in the world. Guided tours leave every 20 minutes for a visit to the cavern's Cathedral Room and Coral Room. Stalagmites and stalactites, formed over millions of years by the continuous action of water and mineral deposits, create an eerie and beautiful masterpiece in each room.

Fifteen miles south of Blanchard Springs, the Ozark Folk Center at Mountain View offers a lively showcase for traditional country music. During peak visitor seasons, performances are held each evening except Sunday in the center's 1,060-seat auditorium. Authentic Ozark arts and crafts are exhibited in the Center's 15 buildings, and if it's real mountain food you're looking for, try buttermilk biscuits, Arkansas corn bread, fried catfish, or home-cured ham and black-eyed peas in the 150-seat restaurant on the grounds. In late April the Center has the famed Arkansas Folk Festival. The gala Family Harvest Festival is held there mid-October to early November, as autumn burnishes the surrounding woodlands.

Little Rock and Hot Springs

The elegant city of Little Rock stands between the northwestern mountains and the flatlands to the southeast, almost exactly at the state's topographical center. Recreational and historical attractions are abundant both in and around the city, and three municipal parks add to the state capital's congenial atmosphere.

At Third and Cumberland Streets, in a unique complex, stands the Arkansas Territorial Restoration, a magnificent courtyard landscaped with flowers, trees, and smaller shrubbery. One of its structures, the cypress-covered log Hinderliter House—oldest building still standing in Little Rock—was last used as a meeting place of the Territorial Legislature in 1835. When Arkansas became a state the next year, the seat of government moved to the Old State House in the Quapaw Quarter. This historic in-town district, an area first settled along the northern shore of the river about 1821, features restored old homes of territorial, antebellum, Victorian and early 20th century styling.

An hour's drive from Little Rock is Hot Springs National Park. Any season is good for visiting this city of spas and thermal baths, but those who want to catch horse racing season at Oaklawn Park had better come early February to early April. A showplace is the magnolia-bordered Bathhouse Row at the foot of the Hot Springs Mountain. Other diversions are boating, fishing, swimming, and water-skiing on the surrounding chain of lakes, and hiking or auto tours to the lookout tower atop Hot Springs Mountain.

Many special events during the year include an Easter Sunrise Service; the Arkansas Fun Festival in early June; the Arkansas Oktoberfest; and the Christmas Pageant, early December.

PRACTICAL INFORMATION FOR ARKANSAS

HOW TO GET THERE. *By air:* There are airports at Little Rock, Fayetteville, Harrison, El Dorado, Jonesboro, Pine Bluff, Hot Springs and Ft. Smith. *By car:* I–55 enters Arkansas from Missouri; I–40 from Tennessee on the east and from Oklahoma on the west; I–30 from Texas; US highways bring travel from all surrounding states: Missouri, Tennessee, Mississippi, Louisiana, Texas, Oklahoma.

By bus: Major bus lines serving Arkansas include *Trailways, Greyhound, Arkansas Motor Coaches, Great Southern Motor Coaches* and *Oklahoma Transportation Lines.*

By rail: Amtrak serves Walnut Ridge, Newport, Little Rock, Malvern and Texarkana.

HOW TO GET AROUND. *By air:* Within the state service is provided by *American, Delta, Frontier, Continental, Republic, TWA,* and several commuter airlines. There are also air taxis at Little Rock and Hot Springs, and Fort Smith now features commuter flights on "Scheduled Skyways" planes.

Car: All of Arkansas' interstate highway system is complete.

Car rentals: Avis and *Hertz* have offices in El Dorado, Fayetteville, Fort Smith, Hot Springs, Jonesboro, Little Rock, Pine Bluff, Texarkana, Stuttgart, Batesville and No. Little Rock. *Budget Reni-a-Car* has an office in Little Rock; *National* at Blytheville, Fayetteville, Ft. Smith, Hot Springs, Little Rock, Marked Tree and Texarkana; *Thrifty* at Harrison, Little Rock and Fort Smith.

Taxi service: You will find the Black & White Cab Co., Checker Cab Co., and Dixie Cabs in Little Rock and Fort Smith.

TOURIST INFORMATION. Arkansas Dept. of Parks & Tourism, One Capitol Mall, Little Rock, 72201; Hot Springs Chamber of Commerce, P. O. Box 1500, Hot Springs National Park, 71901. Tourist Information Centers on major highways leading into the state are centers at Ashdown (US 71–59); Texarkana (I–30); Bentonville (US 71); near Corning (US 67); Fort Smith (I–40); near El Dorado (US 167); Lake Village (US 65); Blytheville (I–55); and West Memphis (I–40). The Arkansas State Police, with district headquarters all over the state, is also a dependable source of information. In addition, local resort areas often provide tourist information conveniently placed along major routes.

MUSEUMS AND ART GALLERIES. Historical: *Saunders Museum,* 314 E. Madison, Berryville, one of world's largest historic gun collections; *Greathouse Home,* ca. 1830, restored farmhouse, inn, Conway; *Eureka Springs Historical Museum,* 95 S. Main St.; *University of Arkansas Museum,* U. of Arkansas, Fayetteville, is a natural history museum. In Fort Smith, *Old Fort Museum,* 320 Rogers Ave., displays Indian, pioneer artifacts; *Robinson Heritage Center,* on US 65SE.; *Museum of Automobiles,* atop Petit Jean Mtn., Morrilton; *Jimmy Driftwood Barn and Folk Hall of Fame,* Mountain View; *Lum & Abner Museum,* Pine Ridge; *Daisy International Air Gun Mu-*

seum, US 71 S, Rogers; *Arkansas County Agricultural Museum,* 921 E. 4th & Park Ave., Stuttgart; *Hampson Museum* (Indian relics, artifacts), Wilson.

Art: *Christ Only Art Gallery,* Mt. Oberammergau, off US 62, *Miles Musical Museum,* US 62 W, both in Eureka Springs. *Fine Arts Center,* University of Arkansas campus, Fayetteville. *Fort Smith Art Center,* 423 N. 6th St. *Southern Artists Assoc. Fine Arts Center,* 815 Whittington Ave., Hot Springs, which also stages productions of the Community Players. *The Arkansas Arts Center,* MacArthur Park, Little Rock; *Southeastern Arkansas Arts & Science Center,* 8th St., Pine Bluff.

HISTORIC SITES. *Fort Smith National Historic Site,* 1839–71, soldiers' barracks and commissary, "Hanging Judge Parker's" courtroom, Rogers and S. 2nd. Sts., Fort Smith. *Arkansas Post National Memorial,* south of Gillette; via Rtes. 1 and 169. *Old State House,* Markham and Center Sts., Little Rock, capitol of Arkansas from 1836 to 1912. *Arkansas Territorial Restoration,* 214 E. 3rd St., Little Rock. Buildings portray life in the 1820's. *Pea Ridge National Military Park,* adjacent to US 62, near Rogers. *Johnson's Mill,* just west of Highway 71 between Fayetteville and Rogers. Converted into gourmet restaurant. Buildings and millrace about 150 years old. *Old Washington State Historic Park,* Washington, state's Confederate capital from 1863–1865.

Historic houses. *Clayton House,* 514 N. 6th St., Fort Smith, headquarters of Belle Grove Historic District; *Wildwood,* 808 Park Ave., Hot Springs, handsome Victorian mansion. *Villa Marre,* 1321 Scott St., Angelo Marre House, 1881 Little Rock—Italianate Victorian home is headquarters of Historic Quapaw Quarter. *Du Bocage,* 4 Ave. & Linden St., Pine Bluff. Greek Revival Mansion. *Martha Mitchell's Home,* W. 4th Ave. & Elm Sts., Pine Bluff.

Pott's Tavern, I–40 & US 64, Pottsville, home of early settlers. Annual *Belle Fort Smith Tour* of beautifully restored antebellum and mid-Victorian homes occurs last of April and first of May in Fort Smith, and Little Rock's *Quapaw Quarter Spring Tour* is also late April-early May.

TOURS. *Bus: Trailways* and *Greyhound* provide coach tours of many popular visitor areas. *Gray Line Sightseeing Tours* offers a wide variety of trips from Eureka Springs, Hot Springs and Little Rock. Some resorts also will arrange area sightseeing packages.

Boat: In Little Rock, *Allison Queen Cruises* runs day cruises on the Arkansas River aboard an 18-passenger "party barge." *The White Ducks* are amphibious landing craft rebuilt for touring the Hot Springs and Lake Hamilton area. *Floating down the White River:* Float trips in 20-foot, flat-bottomed wooden boats have been popular with Arkansas fishermen since shortly after the turn of the century. Today, some 20 concerns operate 200 boats.

SUMMER SPORTS. *Boat rentals:* You'll find Arkansas lakes, such as Bull Shoals, Norfork, Dardanelle, Beaver, and Greers Ferry, complete with marinas. Boat-rental fees are moderate.

Fishing: License required; write Arkansas Game and Fish Commission, 2 Natural Resources Dr., Little Rock 72201. Some 30 species of fish swim in the state's many lakes. Float fishing is popular on streams, particularly the White River and Buffalo National River. Unusually large catches and individual fish have been taken from Bull Shoals, Blue Mountain, Chicot, Norfork Lakes.

Fishing, boating and water sports can be combined effectively at Hamilton, Norfork, Greers Ferry, Dardanelle and Gresson Lakes.

Hunting: License required; write Arkansas Game and Fish Commission, 2 Natural Resources Dr., Little Rock 72201; deer, quail, duck, turkey. Some wild boar hunts on private property in Pope and Newton Counties. Stuttgart, in the Grand Prarie, is known as the duck hunting capital of the country.

Golf: Seven courses are recommended by *Golf Digest:* the *Hot Springs G. & C.C.; Hot Springs Village C.C.;* also in Hot Springs, *Belvedere C.C.;* The *Dawn Hill C.C.,* Siloam Springs; *Paradise Valley G.C.,* and *Cherokee Village G.C.,* in Fayetteville; *Eden Isle G.C.,* Little Rock.

Horseback riding: Devil's Den State Park, Bull Shoals, Eureka Springs, Hot Springs, Blanchard Springs and Little Rock all have stables. Roundup-club trail rides also in abundance out of Fort Smith, adjoining Van Buren and the community of Bond Special to the 60-mile-long free-flowing Big Lee Creek where blue channel cat fishing is superb. Rides mostly during Arkansas-Oklahoma Rodeo period in May and early June.

SPECTATOR SPORTS. *Sailboat racing* on Lake Ouachita, from Brady Mountain Point, off State 270. *Outboard Racing* on Lake Hamilton. *Car racing,* Stuttgart Municipal Airport, State 11. *Stock car racing* in West Memphis. *Thoroughbred racing,* Oaklawn Jockey Club, Hot Springs. *Greyhound racing* at West Memphis. *Golf:* Open Invitational, Hot Springs Country Club in May. *Arkansas-Oklahoma rodeo,* Fort Smith, end May and beginning June at Exposition Park. *State Fair Rodeo,* Little Rock, on W. Roosevelt Rd., a part of the Arkansas Livestock Exposition in early Oct.

Collegiate games: The Razorbacks of Arkansas University play a regular schedule of Southwest Conference *football* either in War Memorial Stadium in Little Rock or at Razorback Stadium in Fayetteville. *Wrestling* at Robinson Auditorium; *basketball games, horse shows* at Barton Coliseum, Little Rock.

WHAT TO DO WITH THE CHILDREN. In Fort Smith: *Ben Geren Park,* just off State 22T; *Central Mall,* at the junction of old State 22 and Waldron Rd; *Tilles Park* on Grand Ave.; *Creekmore Park,* just off Jenny Lind Rd.

Hot Springs: *Arkansas Alligator Farm,* 847 Whittington Ave. *Mid-America Center Museum,* 400 Mid-America Blvd.; lively "hands-on" exhibits. *Tiny Town,* 374 Whittington Ave. Completely mechanized, animated village, farm, sawmill, Indian and Wild West towns, blacksmith shop, park. Open Apr. 1–Oct. 1. *Tussaud Wax Museum,* 250 Central Ave. *I.Q. Zoo,* 380 Whittington, performances by trained small animals. *Magic Springs Family Fun Theme Park,* US 70 E, rides, shows, arts and crafts, restaurants, shopping, new looping roller coaster.

In Little Rock: the zoo in *War Memorial Park* and the adjacent amusement park; *Arkansas Arts Center* in MacArthur Park, with a special gallery geared to young visitors; next door the *Arkansas Museum of Science and History* has a planetarium and special exhibits.

In Malvern: *Reader Railroad* offers rides on woodburning steam train May-Oct.

In the Ozark National Forest: *Blanchard Springs Caverns.* National Forest Service conducts guided tours of underground passageways.

DRINKING LAWS. Sold by individual drink and by package, under local option. No Sunday sales. No alcohol may be brought from another state. Legal age 21.

HOTELS AND MOTELS. Hotel rates are based on double occupancy. *Expensive:* $50 and up, *Moderate:* $30–50, *Inexpensive:* under $30.

ARKADELPHIA. *Moderate:* **DeGray Lodge.** DeGray State Park. Redwood & stone lodge overlooks lake. Golfing, tennis, swimming, sailing, houseboats. Good dining room. Gift shop.

BERRYVILLE. *Inexpensive to Moderate:* **Fairway Motor Inn.** US 62W. Color TV, pool. Golf course adjacent. Dining room.

BULL SHOALS RESORT AREA (12 mi. W. of Mountain Home). *Moderate –Expensive:* **Crow-Barnes Resort.** Overlooking Bull Shoals Lake. Fishing, float trips, golf privileges. Dining room, cocktails.

Moderate: **Bay Breeze Resort.** ARK 178. Playground, pool, lawn games, pony rides. Restaurant nearby.

EUREKA SPRINGS. *Moderate–Expensive:* **Best Western Inn of the Ozarks.** US 62W. Miniature golf, tennis, pool. Dining room, cocktails.

Crescent Hotel. US 62–B. Landmark turn-of-the-century hotel has been beautifully restored and furnished in period. Pool, tennis, shuffleboard. Excellent dining room, cocktails, entertainment.

1876 Inn. US 62S. Color cable TV, pool, gift shop, art gallery. Dining room features international menu at reasonable prices.

Inexpensive–Moderate: **Travelers Inn.** 1 mi. S on US 62.

FAIRFIELD BAY. *Expensive:* **Fairfield Bay Resort.** Fine, 14,000-acre family resort offers golf, tennis, fishing, nature program, horseback riding; 3 pools, beach, saunas, marina, restaurants, cocktail lounge. Some 2- and 3-bedroom units. Home of Arkansas PGA and Walter Hagen golf tournaments, John Newcombe Tennis Center.

FAYETTEVILLE. *Moderate:* **Best Western Inn.** US 71 Bypass & US 62B. Color TV, handicapped facilities. Dining room, swimming pool. Senior citizen rates, under 12 free in room with parents.

FORT SMITH. *Moderate:* **Holiday Inn.** 301 N. 11th St. Color TV, pool, kennel. Dining room, taproom, private club.

Ramada Inn. 5101 Towson Ave. Pool, free in-room movies, dancing, lounge. Near golf course. Seniors program. Pets.

Inexpensive: **Motel 6.** 6001 Rogers Ave. Pool. Restaurant nearby.

HEBER SPRINGS. *Expensive:* **Red Apple Inn.** At Eden Isle Resort on Greers Ferry Lake. One of state's best known resorts has championship golf, tennis, fishing, bicycling, sauna. Marina offers many water sports, is home of one of the South's finest sailing schools. Award-winning dining room, cocktail lounge.

HOT SPRINGS. (All rates higher during racing season.) *Moderate to Expensive:* **Arlington Resort Hotel & Spa.** Central Ave. & Fountain St. Popular large resort with some studios and suites. Complete social program; dancing in season. Thermal baths, pools (heated). Shops. Excellent food.

Holiday Inn-Lake Hamilton. Boating, tennis, playground. Marina, fishing, boat rental. Rooftop sun deck. Restaurant, bar; dancing, entertainment some nights. Airport transportation. Seasonal rates.

Moderate: **Best Western Sands Motel.** 1525 Central. Dining room, cocktail lounge, swimming pool. Senior citizen rates; under 12 free in room with parents.

Downtowner Motor Inn. 135 Central Ave. Pool, thermal baths, beauty shop. Restaurant, lounge.

Buena Vista Resort. On Lake Hamilton. Pool, marina, fishing, lighted tennis, playground. Motel-type & cottage units; some have refrigerators, kitchens.

Majestic Hotel-Bath House Resort/Spa. Park & Central Ave. Pool, wading pool, social program, playground, mineral baths. Dining room, coffee shop, cocktails. Hotel also has lodge on Lake Hamilton.

Holiday Inn East. 1125 E. Grand. Heated pool, playground, game room, hiking trails, tennis, golf. Dining room, lounge, live entertainment.

Inexpensive: **Brady Mountain Lodge.** On Lake Ouachita. Perfect for families. Pool, water sports. Pets allowed. Restaurant. Some cottages.

LAKEVIEW. *Moderate:* **Gaston's White River Resort.** ARK 178, on White River. Marina, trout fishing, tennis, pool, float and camping trips. Golf nearby. Dining room, cocktails. Cottage units.

LITTLE ROCK & NORTH LITTLE ROCK. *Expensive:* **Camelot Inn.** Markham & Broadway (Markham exit from I-30). Large facility with restaurant, bar, & entertainment. Pool (heated). Free parking. Pets allowed.

Little Rock Excelsior. 3 Statehouse Plaza. State's most luxurious new hotel has spectacular 18-story glass atrium lobby, lavishly appointed guest rooms. Six cocktail lounges and restaurants include Pinnacle rooftop lounge, La Petite Roche gourmet restaurant. Facilities for handicapped.

Moderate–Expensive: **Holiday Inn.** Four locations. All have pools, restaurants. **South:** 2600 W. 65th St. Golf, tennis.; **Downtown:** 617 S. Broadway. Current movies in rooms. Entertainment; **North:** 111 W. Pershing Blvd., I-40,

US 65 and St. 107. Tennis, sauna; **Airport East:** 3201 Bankhead Dr. Free airport transportation. Whirlpool, hot tub, game room.

Moderate: **Coachman's Inn.** E. Capitol & Ferry Sts. (6th St. exit from I–30). Excellent facilities. Free airport transportation. Restaurant, bar, entertainment. Pool (heated). Some pets.

Sam Peck Hotel-Motel. 625 W. Capitol. Nice selection of rooms, some with balconies. Friendly atmosphere. Locally popular. Restaurant, bar. Color TV. Fine parking. Free airport transportation. Pool. Pets allowed.

Days Inn. Two locations: 2508 Jacksonville Hwy., N. Little Rock; 3100 N. Main, N. Little Rock. Both have restaurants, allow pets. Service stations. September Days Club honored.

Inexpensive: **Motel 6.** I–30 E, take frontage road West exit. Pool, pay TV, free crib. Restaurant nearby.

MENA. *Moderate:* **Queen Wilhelmina Inn.** Queen Wilhelmina State Park, ARK 88. Handsome stone lodge originally named for Queen of the Netherlands offers royal retreat for guests. Picnic area, nature trails, scenic overlooks, animal park, miniature golf, scenic railroad. Good dining room. Campsites.

MOUNTAIN HOME. *Expensive:* **Scott Valley Dude Ranch.** Rt. 2, via ARK 5. In the Ozarks. Open mid-Mar. to Dec. 1. Heated pool, boats, fishing, tennis, horseback riding. Good food.

MOUNTAIN VIEW. *Moderate:* **Ozark Folk Center Lodge.** ARK 382. Modern motel-type units on grounds of state-operated Folk Center. Pool, color TV, recreation room. Two units for handicapped. Pets. Good down-home dining in handsome contemporary lodge.

DINING OUT in Arkansas can be a lot less expensive than in the more heavily populated states. Look for Arkansas favorites such as fried chicken, barbecued meats, catfish and hot apple or huckleberry pies.

Restaurants are listed in order of price category, based on price of a complete dinner without drinks. *Expensive:* over $20; *Moderate:* $10–20; *Inexpensive:* under $10.

ALTUS. *Moderate:* **Wiederkehr's Wein Keller.** German-Swiss cuisine, good Arkansas wine in Alpine chalet on grounds of operating winery. On National Register of Historic Places.

BULL SHOALS RESORT AREA. *Moderate:* **Gaston's White River Resort,** Lakeview, AR. Prime rib, trout dinners, barbecued ribs.

EUREKA SPRINGS. *Moderate:* **Bowen's Ozark Gardens.** US 62, ARK 23 SE. Local fish dishes and home baking.

The Barn Steak House. 8 mi. N. on Holiday Island. Open pit cooking of steaks, ribs, shish kebab, in rustic setting of 80-year-old former stable. Live entertainment, dancing in Saddle Club.

Ozark Village. US 62 SE. Luscious fried chicken, fresh vegetables, homemade fruit cobbler, pies. Lavish buffets.

FAYETTEVILLE. *Moderate:* **The Old Post Office Gathering Place.** 1 Center Square. Crepes, quiche, steak, eggs benedict in 1909 post office. Benches, flowers, brass rails, and golden oak lend an aura of charm and freshness.

FORT SMITH. *Moderate:* **Emmy's German Restaurant.** 620 N. 16th St. Hearty German specialties, locally popular. Children's menu.

Seaman's Store Company Restaurant. Excellent seafood. Fourth and Garrison, near Arkansas River waterway. Part of historical restoration.

Talliano's. 201 N. 14th St. Outstanding Italian specialties in beautifully restored Victorian-era residence.

Inexpensive: **Furr's Cafeteria.** US 71 S. Roast beef, seafood, own baking.

Lewis Cafeteria. 3400 Rogers Ave., in Park Plaza Shopping Center. Well-prepared food, good salads, desserts.

HEBER SPRINGS. *Moderate to Expensive:* **The Red Apple Inn.** On Greers Ferry Lake. Prime rib, steak Diane, crabmeat souffle are specialties of this superb 4-star dining room.

Moderate: **The Stockholm Restaurant.** 600 W. Main St. Wide selection of salads and entrees; sumptuous Friday night seafood buffet.

HOT SPRINGS. *Moderate:* **Coy's Steak House.** US 70 E. Oyster bar and steaks as you please. Rustic decor. Extremely popular.

Hamilton House. US 7 S. Enjoy outdoor dining, dancing, fabulous views at this magnificent old estate on Lake Hamilton. Specialties include leg of lamb, seafoods, steaks-as-you-like.

Miller's Chicken & Steak House. S on ARK 7. Friendly atmosphere. Mouthwatering fried chicken. Children's portions.

LITTLE ROCK & NORTH LITTLE ROCK. *Expensive:* **Jacques and Suzanne.** 30th Floor First National Bank Bldg., Capitol Ave. & Broadway. Superb continental cuisine, fine city views. Atmosphere is elegant, sophisticated; strict dress code. Background music, weekend entertainment.

Moderate to Expensive: **Tony's Dog House.** 3614 W. Roosevelt Rd. Lively atmosphere, excellent steaks, seafood, Southern specialties. Great local favorite.

Moderate: **Browning's Mexican Foods.** 5805 Kavanaugh. In a Mexican mood? Here's your answer for atmosphere and good food. Children's portions. Open for lunch & dinner. Takeout orders filled.

Bruno's Little Italy. 1309 Old Forge Rd. Locally popular Italian restaurant also has American food. Children's plates.

Cajun's Wharf. 2400 Cantrell Rd., on Arkansas River. Fresh seafood, entertainment, Old Cajun atmosphere.

Inexpensive: **The Old Train Station.** Markham & Victory Sts. Enjoy soup and salad at **Buster's;** soup, sandwiches, game room at **Slick Willey's.** They're all in Little Rock's restored train station.

Inexpensive: **Franke's Cafeteria.** 300 S. University. Luscious fresh vegetables, own baking. Locally popular.

Golden Host Cafeteria. First National Bank Bldg. Roast beef a specialty. Own baking. Very popular.

SPRINGDALE. *Moderate:* **A Q. Chicken House.** US 62 N. In the heart of chicken country, a famous chicken restaurant. Also steak, mountain trout.

Heinie's Steak House. 2407 S. Thompson (US 71). Low key, down home atmosphere, fine Italian, German specialties as well as steaks, seafood. Nationally known.

Mary Maestri's. ARK 68 W at Tontitown. Superb Italian-American menu inclues lasagne, chicken cacciatore, tortellini. Extremely popular.

WINSLOW. *Inexpensive:* **Burns Gables.** On a mountaintop. Country ham and sausage, trout, huckleberry pie. Closed Dec.-Feb.

KANSAS

Center of Middle America

Kansas lies in the approximate geographical center of the contiguous U.S. The exact geographical center is two miles NW of Lebanon.

When Kansas became a territory in 1854 (pop. 700), it had been home of the Wichita, Pawnee, Osage and Kansa Indians, and had been traded back and forth between France and Spain in a real life Monopoly game.

Today Kansas City alone has a population of about 174,000. The twin sister to Kansas City, Mo., Kansas City is a major livestock marketing center.

The oldest Army post west of the Mississippi River is Fort Leavenworth, situated on a bluff overlooking the Missouri River. It was established in 1827 for protection against Indians and as a starting point for wagon trains, eventually becoming the fountainhead for the Oregon and Santa Fe trails. Relics from from its early era can be seen in the Post Museum, which features an excellent exhibit of 19th-century horse-drawn vehicles, including one in which Lincoln rode.

The adjoining city of Leavenworth, where Buffalo Bill Cody grew up, has numerous historical buildings, such as the magnificent mansion built by restaurateur Fred Harvey or the elegant Victorian home now housing the Leavenworth Historical Society Museum. A federal prison also is in Leavenworth.

The museum containing thousands of mementos of Gen. Eisenhower's military and political career is situated in Abilene, where the late President and his brothers were reared. The Eisenhower Center is the official U.S. memorial to the late Dwight D. Eisenhower, and contains his home, library and "The Place of Meditation" burial site of the

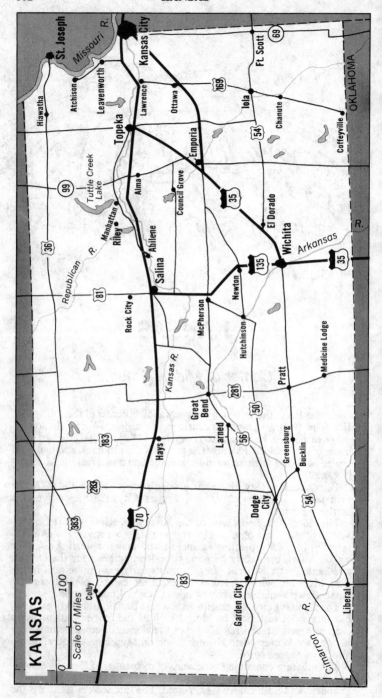

former President. Near the center is an attraction of a different type, the reconstructed wild west town, "Old Abilene Town."

For those with an interest in Indian lore, between Abilene and Salina (four miles E. of Salina) are the Indian burial grounds and museum. Other relics are displayed at Smokey Hill Historical Museum in Oakdale Park in Salina.

Travelers hungry for fried chicken and hot biscuits should detour 14 miles west of Salina on Hwy 140 to Brookville. The Brookville Hotel Dining Room, built in 1870, is famous for its fried chicken served family-style in a frontier atmosphere. Reservations are suggested. After filling up on the bountiful country fare, visitors may go upstairs to see a parlor and bedrooms furnished in Kansas frontier period furniture. For over 100 years, until 1972, the hotel also was in operation, and it is said that Buffalo Bill stayed in Number 7.

Topeka, the state capital (population approximately 140,000), boasts a Statehouse with murals by John Steuart Curry and grounds dotted by statues depicting its pioneer past. It is also home of the Kansas State Historical Society Museum with its collection of aircraft, autos, and stagecoaches, and is the site of the famed Menninger Clinic.

Northwest of Topeka is the village of Wabaunsee where abolitionist Henry Ward Beecher spewed fire and brimstone from the pulpit of the Beecher Bible and Rifle Church—which still stands today, serving its congregation.

Also Northwest of Topeka is the original capital of Kansas, Manhattan. Ft. Riley was established between Manhattan and Junction City— the junction of the Republican and Smokey Hill rivers—in 1853. The Ft. Riley Museum contains memorabilia of military history.

William Allen White, the well-known editor and founder of the *Emporia Gazette*, lived in Emporia, south of Topeka on the Kansas Turnpike. A memorial sculpture in his honor is in Peter Pan Park, and his mementos are in the William Allen White Library on the campus of Emporia State University.

Wichita, profiting from the advent of the railroad in a "cow town boom," grew rapidly and is the state's largest city, with a population of 270,000. In memory of its beginnings, there is a "Cow Town," containing replicas of 1872 Wichita with many original buildings. Wichita is proud of its historical museums, art galleries, some 28 parks and a very fine zoo. Also based here is the Wichita State University, Sacred Heart College and the McConnell Air Force Base. Beech, Boeing, Cessna and Lear jet plants are located in Wichita, making the city a world leader in manufacture of private airplanes and an important military aircraft manufacturing center. Tours of some plants are available.

If you'd like to "wet your whistle," stop by the Long Branch Saloon in Dodge City, on US 56, where every night from June 1 to Labor Day, Miss Kitty and her can-can girls entertain while visitors drink sarsaparilla and red-eye. You'll probably also find Doc Holliday, Wyatt Earp and Bat Masterson ambling along the Old Front Street of the authentic frontier town that was known as the "Cowboy Capital of the World" because millions of Texas longhorns were driven through in the late 1870s and 80s. Another title it earned was "The Wickedest Little City in America" because of the mixture of soldiers, railroaders, hunters, trail drivers and settlers who came to town. Some are remembered in the Boot Hill Memorial Cemetery, built on the site of the original Boot Hill.

Another city along US 56, Council Grove, preserves its part in history, too. It is the site of the Post Office Oak, a huge tree where letters were "mailed," awaiting pickup by passing wagon trains. While there, drop by the Kaw Indian Mission, once an Indian school, now a museum.

PRACTICAL INFORMATION FOR KANSAS

HOW TO GET THERE. *By air: United, TWA* and *Continental* fly into Wichita and Kansas City (Mo.). *By train: Amtrak. By bus:* Kansas is served by *Trailways, Greyhound* and numerous other smaller lines, including *Short Way, North Star* and *Missouri Transit.*

HOW TO GET AROUND. *By car:* Most roads run either north-south or east-west. The Kansas Turnpike runs northeast from Wichita to Topeka. *By air:* There are smaller airports in Parsons, Liberal, Garden City, Goodland, Hays, Manhattan, Salina and Topeka, besides the larger ones in Kansas City (Mo.) and Wichita. *Frontier* does the short hop flying. *By bus:* Midwesterners depend upon good bus service. *Trailways, Greyhound, Short Way, Missouri Transit* and numerous other small lines provide good coverage. *By train: Amtrak* has stops in Lawrence, Garden City, Dodge City, Hutchinson, Emporia, Topeka, Lawrence, Newton, Wichita, and Arkansas City.

TOURIST INFORMATION. You may write *Kansas Department of Economic Development,* 503 Kansas Avenue, Topeka, 66603, or call (913) 296–3481; or chambers of commerce in major cities. State universities at Lawrence and Manhattan have information on sports events, museums, drama, lectures. Write the president's office.

MUSEUMS AND GALLERIES. *Clark County Pioneer Museum,* Ashland; *Baker University Old Castle and History Museum, Baker University Quayle Collection* (a 17th-century room from Urishay Castle, England), Baldwin; *Safari African Museum* (items from expeditions of explorers Martin and Osa Johnson), Chanute; *Beeson Museum* (pioneer and Indian relics), *Boot Hill Museum,* Dodge City; *Ft. Scott Historical Museum* (old dresses), Ft. Scott; *Bridget Walker Art Collection* (works of John Steuart Curry and Henry Varnum Poor), Garnett; *Ft. Larned National Landmark* (military & Indian relics), Larned; *University of Kansas Wilcox Museum* (Greek & Roman antiquities), Lawrence; *Pony Express Museum,* Marysville; *Dalton Gang Hide-out Museum,* Meade; *El Quartelejo Kiva Indian Museum* (Cheyenne & Pueblo), Scott City; *Menninger Foundation Museum and Archives* (psychiatry museum), Topeka; *Mid-American All-Indian Center Museum,* Wichita.

HISTORIC SITES. In addition to those already mentioned are the *Madonna of the Trail* statue at Council Grove which was the last stop on the Sante Fe Trail; the *Pioneer Adobe House and Museum* in Hillsboro, a replica of the Mennonite pioneer homes; *W.T.C.U. Museum* in Medicine Lodge, hometown of the spirited (and anti-"spirits") Carry Nation.

DRINKING LAWS. Liquor may be purchased in package stores. Private club membership may be obtained for a nominal fee through some hotels and motels.

SPORTS. *Fishing* at numerous federal, state and county lakes. *Hunting* in season. *Trap shooting* at Winchester Center, Bucyrus, 30 mi. S. of Kansas City. All *water sports* at Lake Waconda.

CAMPING OUT. There are camping facilities at the state parks in: Fall River near Chanute, Elk City near Independence, Milford near Junction City, Meade near Liberal, Tuttle Creek near Manhattan, Lovewell near Mankato, Lake Crawford near Pittsburg, Wilson near Russell, Lake Scott near Scott City, Perry near Topeka, Cedar Bluff near Wakeeney, Cheney near Wichita, and Toronto near Yates Center.

WHAT TO DO WITH THE CHILDREN. The major cities have interesting *zoos.* The *wild west towns* at Abilene and in Dodge City provide background for shoot-'em-up fantasies, complete with stagecoach rides. *Old Cow Town* in Sims Park, Wichita, has 1875 log cabin, saloon and blacksmith shop.

HOTELS AND MOTELS. You'll have your choice, from comfortable old-style hotels to modern motels. The price categories in this section average: *Deluxe:* over $55; *Expensive:* $45–55; *Moderate:* $25–35.

ABILENE. *Moderate:* **Best Western Inn.** 2210 N. Buckeye. Excellent. 64 rooms.

DODGE CITY. *Moderate:* **Silver Spur Lodge Best Western.** 1510 W. Wyatt Earp. Excellent. 122 rooms.

JUNCTION CITY *Moderate:* **All Seasons Motel.** 1 blk n. of I–70. Indoor and outdoor pool, laundry facilities, free continental breakfast.

KANSAS CITY/OVERLAND PARK. *Deluxe:* **Doubletree Hotel.** 10100 College, Overland Park. Large, new facility.

TOPEKA. *Expensive:* **Ramada Inn and Tower.** 420 E. 6th Ave. Club. Restaurant. Excellent. 340 rooms. Downtown.

WICHITA. *Deluxe:* **Wichita Royale.** 125 N. Market St. Excellent. 137 rooms.

DINING OUT in Kansas means plenty of good country food. Restaurant price categories are: *Expensive,* over $12, *Moderate,* $7–12, *Inexpensive,* under $7.

JUNCTION CITY. *Moderate:* **Cohen's Chicken & Steak House.** Grandview Plaza.

KANSAS CITY/OVERLAND PARK. *Moderate:* **Leona Yarbrough's.** 2800 W. 53 St. Home-cooked meals. Family atmosphere. Excellent.
Inexpensive: **Hayward's Pit Bar-B-Que.** 11051 Antioch. Popular casual spot for hickory smoked meats.

SALINA. *Moderate:* **Brookville Hotel Dining Room.** Brookville. Family-style chicken dinners. Family owned and operated. Excellent.

TOPEKA. *Expensive:* **Le Flambeau Club.** 420 E. 6th St., in the Ramada Inn. French cuisine. Club. Gracious atmosphere.

WICHITA. *Moderate.* **Brown's Grill East.** 545 N. Hillside. Family atmosphere.

MISSOURI

St. Louis, Kansas City, Ozarks and More

A new spirit pervades St. Louis, one of the most historic communities in the nation. The St. Louisan of today walks with a brisk stride, proud of recent civic accomplishments, foremost of which has been the construction of the Gateway Arch—sometimes called the "Giant Wicket"—of the Jefferson National Expansion Memorial. Towering 630 feet above the city's riverfront redevelopment area, it is the nation's tallest monument, and was designed by Eero Saarinen.

This arch, built of stainless steel, commemorates the westward march of America. Each leg houses a stairway and trains. Carrying forty passengers at a clip, the trains rise to the top of the arch to give passengers a panoramic view of St. Louis from an observation deck.

The Old Cathedral, the Basilica of St. Louis, completed in 1834, still stands and receives worshippers near the Jefferson National Expansion Memorial grounds. St. Louis' Old Courthouse, of Greek Revival architecture, is also near the Gateway Arch. Here slaves stood on the auction block and in 1847 Dred Scott's lawyers first pleaded for his freedom from slavery. Five miles away is the new, St. Louis, Cathedral, whose golden dome covering the main altar reflects the images of the twelve apostles ranged on its interior. A large dome rises 207 feet above the surface of the church and is visible from the exterior. The mosaics that adorn the cathedral's interior are masterpieces of their kind—and the collection is reported to be one of the largest in the world.

Inside Forest Park are the St. Louis Art Museum and the Missouri Historical Society in the Jefferson Memorial building, which features the Charles A. Lindbergh Gallery. So is the McDonnell Planetarium, one of the nation's finest for research and study of the stars, and an 83-acre zoo, with over 2,000 animals in habitat settings. The park has a major skating rink too, for rollers in summer and ice skaters in winter. The St. Louis World's Fair of 1904 was held in Forest Park.

Southeast of here is another unique attraction, the Missouri Botanical Garden. In a geodesic-domed greenhouse visitors may view a variety of flora and see special displays year-round. The largest traditional Japanese Garden in the U.S. is the newest attraction. The site is often referred to as Shaw's Botanical Garden after its founder, Henry Shaw, whose restored home is open for viewing.

PRACTICAL INFORMATION FOR ST. LOUIS

HOW TO GET THERE. *By car:* I–70 (US 40) runs east-west through St. Louis. Points of reference on I–70 are Terre Haute, Indiana, to the east and Kansas City to the west. On a north-south axis, I–55 begins at Chicago, passes through St. Louis and enters Arkansas near the juncture of Missouri, Arkansas and Tennessee. I–44 runs from the northeast corner of Oklahoma to St. Louis.

By train: St. Louis has regular *Amtrak* service.

By bus: As a gateway to the west, St. Louis is a major bus terminal. It is served by *Trailways, Greyhound,* and several local lines.

By air: St. Louis is served by ten major airlines including *American, Delta, Eastern, Frontier,* and *TWA.*

By boat: The *Delta Queen* and the newer *Mississippi Queen* use St. Louis as a point of departure and/or return on Delta Queen Steamboat Co. Mississippi River cruises.

HOW TO GET AROUND. *By bus:* St. Louis has an extensive bus system that covers both the downtown area and the suburbs. Maps of the system are available from Bi-State Transit Co. at 3869 Park Ave. *By taxi:* The taxi fare is comparable to fares in other large cities.

From the airport: Limousines run from Lambert-St. Louis International Airport to downtown hotels on a regular schedule. Taxis are also available.

TOURIST INFORMATION. The *Convention and Visitors Bureau of Greater St. Louis,* Suite 300, 10 S. Broadway, (314) 421–1023, has maps and information of all kinds for the visitor.

MUSEUMS AND GALLERIES. The *St. Louis Art Museum* in Forest Park has a wide range of paintings, sculpture, drawings and prints. There are also Oriental and African collections. The *National Museum of Transport,* at 3015 Barrett Station Road, displays more than 50 locomotives and cars, streetcars and buses and other types of transport spanning the last century. *Steinberg Art Gallery* at Washington University has a fine collection of modern art, as well as changing exhibits. The *Missouri Historical Society,* at Lindell Blvd. and De Baliviere Ave., has a collection of frontier artifacts and the Lindbergh collection. The USS *Inaugural,* at Wharf St. near the Gateway Arch, is now a naval museum.

HISTORIC SITES. The *Jefferson National Expansion Memorial,* better known as the "Gateway to the West," ranks with New York's Empire State Building and Houston's Astrodome as one of the most familiar landmarks in an American city. The 630-foot arch, designed by Eero Saarinen, is open every day, except Thanksgiving, Christmas and New Year's. Also see the *Old Courthouse,* in the Jefferson National Expansion Memorial, the *Old Cathedral* nearby, and the birthplace of poet Eugene Field. *Grant's Farm,* at Grant and Gravois Rds., contains a log cabin built by Ulysses S. Grant when he lived here as a farmer from 1854 to 1860. Also, *Jefferson Barracks Historical Park,*

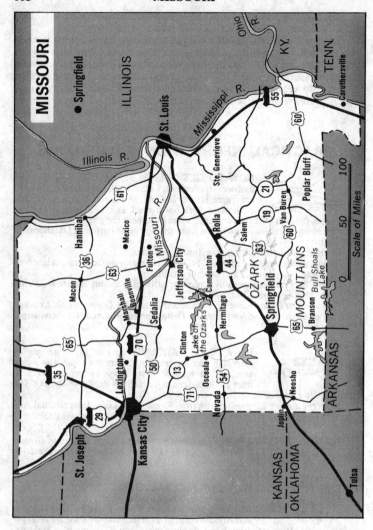

south of St. Louis on Grant Rd. at Kingston, was one of the pioneer military establishments of the west, in use from the early 19th century through World War II. Now it's a county park with restored buildings containing two military history museums.

 GARDENS. The *Missouri Botanical Garden* is the oldest in the U.S., dating from 1858. It boasts the Climatron, a large, domed greenhouse which permits tropical flowers and trees to grow in profusion, and the largest traditional Japanese Garden in the U.S. The *Jewel Box Floral Conservatory* in Forest Park has displays throughout the year, but is particularly pleasant at Christmas time.

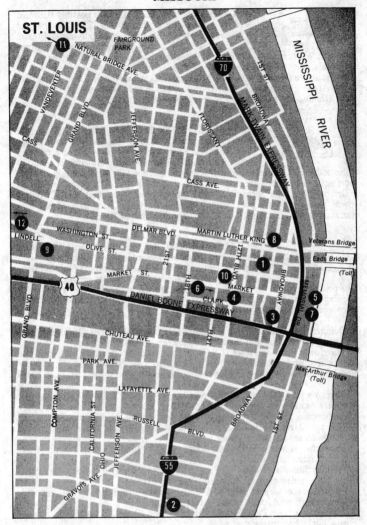

ST. LOUIS

Points of Interest

1) American Theater
2) Anheuser-Busch Brewery
3) Busch Memorial Stadium
4) City Hall
5) Gateway Arch
6) Henry W. Kiel Auditorium
7) Old Cathedral
8) St. Louis Gateway Convention & Exhibition Center
9) St. Louis University
10) Soldiers Memorial Building
11) University of Missouri
12) Washington University

MUSIC. *Powell Symphony Hall,* originally constructed in 1925, was renovated in 1967 and is now the home of the St. Louis Symphony Orchestra. The orchestra is in residence during the winter months. In late summer and early fall the *Municipal Opera* performs at Forest Park in the outdoor amphitheater. The company specializes in musical comedy and light opera.

SPECTATOR SPORTS. St. Louis is possibly the most *soccer*-conscious city in the country. The University of St. Louis almost always has a nationally-ranked team. The St. Louis Steamers play professional soccer at Francis Field, Washington University. Busch Memorial Stadium is the home for the Cardinals, both *baseball* and *football* teams. Incidentally, the Sports Hall of Fame is at the Stadium, too. The National *Hockey* League St. Louis Blues play at the Arena. Fairmount Park, 10 minutes east of the Gateway Arch in Collinsville, Illinois, has harness and thoroughbred horse racing.

WHAT TO DO WITH THE CHILDREN. The zoo and children's zoo at the *Zoological Gardens* have about 3,000 animals. There are animal shows, and a railroad circles the zoo. *Six Flags Over Mid-America* is about 30 miles southwest of the city in Eureka, Mo.; but the kids will certainly think it worth the trip. There are over 80 rides, including one of the world's famous roller coasters, The Screamin' Eagle, puppet shows, re-creations of frontier towns and a porpoise pool, among other attractions. *Strekfus Steamers* has narrated sightseeing harbor cruises on the Mississippi River.

HOTELS AND MOTELS in St. Louis range from quite simple but clean and comfortable to luxurious with many amenities. Some of the older, more famous establishments have excellent restaurants on the premises. The price categories, for double occupancy, average as follows: *Deluxe:* $75 and up; *Expensive:* $55–75; *Moderate:* $45–55, and *Inexpensive:* below $45. Some offer weekend packages or family rates.

Deluxe: **Chase Park Plaza.** N. King's Hwy. at Lindell Blvd. One of the focal points of city's social and business life. Several restaurants, pool.

Marriott's Pavilion Hotel. 1 S. Broadway. A 24-story tower built atop the former Spanish Pavilion (moved to St. Louis from the N.Y. World's Fair). Near Busch Memorial Stadium. Dining rooms, night club, and theater with entertainment, pool.

Sheraton St. Louis (at Convention Plaza). 910 N. 7th. Downtown's newest, this ultra-modern hostelry is part of the city's new convention center complex with shopping mall and parking garage. Restaurants, health club, pool.

Deluxe: **Clarion Hotel.** 200 S. Fourth St. Restaurants, one revolving atop hotel tower, entertainment, pool.

Expensive: **Henry VIII Inn and Lodge.** 4690 N. Lindbergh Blvd. 5 min. from airport. Kitchenette available.

Holiday Inn-Riverfront. 300 Fourth St. Restaurant with dancing, entertainment, pool, putting green. Adjacent Gateway Arch.

Park Terrace Airport Hilton. 10330 Natural Bridge Rd. Restaurant with entertainment, pool, one tennis court, playground.

Moderate: **Forest Park Hotel.** 4910 W. Pine Blvd. Quiet atmosphere near Forest Park. Free parking.

Inexpensive: **Days Inn.** 4545 Woodson Rd. Near airport, with shuttle bus. Restaurant, pool.

DINING OUT in St. Louis can mean an enjoyable evening in the elegant atmosphere of the city's downtown restaurants or fine food in one of the city's more casual, ethnic spots. Although St. Louis is noted for its German traditions, it has surprisingly few restaurants specializing in German cuisine. German restaurants listed here also serve American-International food.

Price categories are as follows: *Deluxe* $20 and up, *Expensive* $12–20, *Moderate* $7–12, and *Inexpensive* $7 and below. Not included are drinks, tax and tips.

Deluxe: **Al's Restaurant.** First and Biddle Sts. One of the city's best. Dinner only.

Anthony's. 10 S. Broadway. Elegant dining on Continental specialties in the Equitable Life Building. Reservations required.

Dominic's. 5101 Wilson Ave. First-rate Italian food. Owned and operated by a family.

Tony's. 826 N. Broadway. Local landmark. Italian food, stylish ambience. Dinner only.

Expensive: **Balaban's.** 405 N. Euclid Ave. Casual, Victorian atmosphere with Continental menu.

Bevo Mill. 4749 Gravois. German and American fare in what looks like a Dutch windmill. Good for families.

Busch's Grove. 9160 Clayton Rd. Continental cuisine and prime ribs served in rustic dining room or in individual screened log cabins in summer. Open since 1890.

Nantucket Cove. 40 N. King's Highway. Yankee seafaring atmosphere. Seafood flown in daily.

Moderate: **Catfish & Crystal.** 409 N. 11th St. Families enjoy this small, comfortable establishment in the heart of downtown. Varied cuisine in nineteenth century setting.

Inexpensive: **Miss Hulling's Cafeteria Downtown.** Open 'til 8 P.M.

EXPLORING KANSAS CITY

Kansas City, "The Heart of America," is progressive. For example, city fathers claim that there is more per capita construction here than in other U.S. cities. They cite the ultra-modern $250,000,000 Kansas City International Airport, a 5,000-acre facility of revolutionary design, and the unique twin-stadium Harry S. Truman Sports Complex, with a combined seating capacity of nearly 120,000. Crown Center, a short distance from the heart of downtown, is a long-range $350,000,-000, 85-acre shopping, residential, business and hotel complex. Another major hotel and office building recently were completed adjacent to Crown Center.

Before beginning your tour around the city, you may want to get an overall view. Perhaps the most impressive is that from the top of the Liberty Memorial, a 217-foot shaft erected on a hill overlooking the downtown area in front of Union Station. Built in memory of those who served in World War I, it was dedicated in 1921 by Marshal Foch of France, Admiral Beatty of England, General Jacques of Belgium, General Dias of Italy, and Missouri's own General "Black Jack" Pershing.

Maybe you'll want to spend part of the day visiting the Courthouse or going to the top of the 423-foot-high City Hall for a view of the city's expanse. A building boom is changing the character of downtown. Petticoat Lane (11th Street), once the center of the shopping district, is giving way to high-rise office buildings under construction. A few blocks south is the new H. Roe Bartle Exposition Hall and a 1930s-style Municipal Auditorium which provides space for conventions and exhibits.

From here, take the Southeast Freeway or Truman Road east to Independence. There, you can see the Harry S. Truman Home, the Truman Memorial Library and the Jackson County Jail of frontier days. The Reorganized Church of Jesus Christ of Latter Day Saints has its headquarters in Independence. One of the largest houses of worship in the world, its auditorium has a magnificent pipe organ, which is used for annual recitals of the *Messiah* at Christmas. Also here is the site on which the church members believe the Temple of Zion will be built.

Northeast of Independence a few miles, at Sibley, is restored Fort Osage, a former outpost of the early 19th century. Blockhouse, barracks, store, and stables are all here to see.

When you leave the Independence area, after returning from Fort Osage, drive south to 63rd Street in suburban Raytown. From here, you can drive west to Swope Park, one of the largest municipal parks in the nation. Here is a progressive zoo, with a special children's zoo and an African veldt area.

After you leave Swope Park, you can drive west on 63rd Street to Brookside Boulevard and head north. Now you may visit the University of Missouri at Kansas City, its Linda Hall Library (one of the largest technical and scientific library in the country), and tour the nearby cultural center, which features a group of sculptures by Carl Milles, the Swedish artist. His last work, this centers around a fountain in which is an equestrian St. Martin of Tours. Also on the south side of the mall, at the heart of this center, is the Midwest Research Institute, one of the country's better-known nonprofit foundations. On the west is famed Country Club Plaza, a world-renowned shopping center of distinctive Spanish architecture, with attractive fountains and parkway greenery. Many of the fountains were sculpted in Italy. One of the most impressive is the huge one at the corner of 47th Street and Broadway, a memorial to J. C. Nichols, creator of the Plaza. The first totally planned shopping center in the United States (1922), it is still considered by many to be the most beautiful. The Plaza was devastated by flooding in 1977, and it was feared that the place would never recover from the destruction. Within a matter of months, however, the damage was repaired and now the Plaza is more beautiful than ever. Its display of Christmas lights is spectacular and an excellent subject for camera fans. Luncheon on the Plaza is a popular pastime for Kansas Citians and tourists alike. At 46th and Main there is the Community Christian Church, designed by Frank Lloyd Wright.

After lunch, you should visit the Nelson-Atkins Museum of Art, two institutions combined into one magnificent building at the north end of a sweeping mall. The museum is known for its especially fine collection of Chinese art (the tomb figures in particular). It also has a fine assortment of European and American works and an ambitious educational program. Next door is the Kansas City Art Institute, which also has galleries open to the public.

South of the Plaza are Kansas City's most impressive residential districts, areas which Francois Mauriac was thinking of when he called Kansas City "the most beautiful city in the world." Loose Memorial Park and its adjoining residential districts show the older influence; Mission Hills, Kansas, across the border, boasts elegant mansions and has continuously ranked among America's premier residential areas. Also on the Kansas side (the state line is a street, named "State Line"), you can visit the historic Shawnee Indian Mission in Fairway.

Back on the Missouri side, head north on Ward Parkway through the Country Club Plaza. North of the Plaza on Westport Road between Pennsylvania and Broadway is the Old Westport Square, an area of restored historic buildings with many shops and restaurants. The buildings date to the 1830s when Westport was a booming pioneer town. The Nathan Scarrit residence at 4038 Central and the Col. John Harris Home at 4000 Baltimore are restored, and one of the earliest buildings in Westport, built about 1853, is the Albert G. Boone Store, called Kelley's. It is a favorite casual nightspot for the city's young adults.

Heading downtown on the Southwest Trafficway turn west on the 12th Street Viaduct to reach the stockyards, one of the country's prime marketing areas and site of the American Royal Horse Show. The 1976 Republican National Convention was held in Kemper Arena, part of the American Royal Center complex, the city's second area for conventions. A superb steak dinner at a fine stockyards restaurant can bring a day's touring to a fine finish.

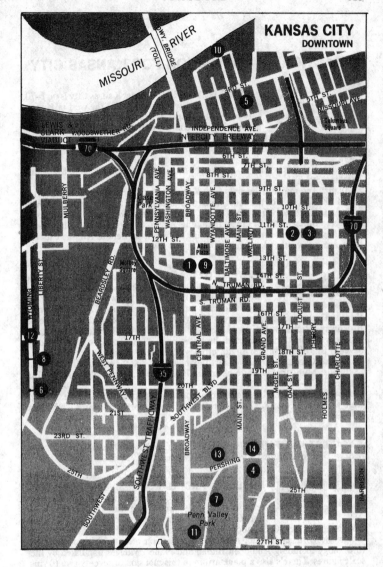

Points of Interest

1) H. Roe Bartle Exposition Hall
2) City Hall
3) Civic Center
4) Crown Center
5) Kansas City Market
6) R. Crosby Kemper Arena & American Royal Building
7) Liberty Memorial and Museum
8) Livestock Exchange
9) Municipal Auditorium
10) Municipal Wharf
11) Pioneer Mother Monument
12) Stock Yards
13) Union Station
14) Washington Monument

PRACTICAL INFORMATION FOR KANSAS CITY

 HOW TO GET THERE. *By car:* Kansas City is on I–70, an important east-west highway. To the west of Kansas City on I–70 is Topeka, Kansas, and to the east, across Missouri, is St. Louis. From the north, I–35 runs from Des Moines, Iowa, to Kansas City, and from Oklahoma City in the south, I–44 connects with US 71 near Carthage, Missouri, to head due north for Kansas City.

By train: Kansas City is on the *Amtrak* line; the station is at Main and Pershing Sts. Tel.

By air: Ten major airlines fly into Kansas City International Airport (often called "KCI"), one of the most modern and convenient in the country. These include *Continental, Frontier, Ozark, TWA,* and *United.* Ozark has extensive service to other Missouri cities, including Joplin, St. Louis, and Columbia.

By bus: Trailways and *Greyhound* are the major carriers to Kansas City but there are many other local lines.

 HOW TO GET AROUND. *By car:* Driving around Kansas City is slightly complicated by the Kansas and Missouri Rivers, which lie to the west and north of the city. The Missouri separates Kansas City from North Kansas City. Main bridges across the Missouri are the Broadway Bridge on Broadway (Richards Rd. in N. Kansas City), the A.S.B. Bridge on U.S. 71 Business (Burlington Ave.), and the Paseo on I–29–35 To the west of the city, Seventh St., off Southwest Blvd., crosses the Kansas River.

By taxi: Cab fare is $1.00 to start the meter and 80¢ for each additional mile.

By bus: Municipal bus fare begins at 70¢. For assistance call the Metro Bus system at 221–0660.

From the airport: A bus from the airport to downtown hotels or the Country Club Plaza will cost $8.50; a taxi ride from the airport to Country Club Plaza will run about $20.

TOURIST INFORMATION SERVICES. The *Convention and Visitors Bureau of Greater Kansas City* is at 1100 Main, (816) 221-5242.

 MUSEUMS AND GALLERIES. The *Nelson-Atkins Museum of Art* is one of the country's most impressive settings for a justly famous and wide-ranging art collection. Chinese and Japanese rooms outstanding. 45th and Oak Sts. (near US 50, 56) about 4 mi. S. of midcity. The *Kansas City Museum,* Gladstone Blvd. at Indiana Ave., has a collection of natural history and anthropology including American Indian and pioneer villages populated by life-scale figures. There's also a planetarium in this mansion of seventy-two (!) rms. The *Kansas City Art Institute,* almost next door to the Nelson Gallery, holds its own with a permanent roster of painting and sculpture, complemented by periodic shows.

 FOUNTAINS AND GARDENS. Kansas City points pridefully to the sculptures adorning its many fountains. One of the most notable is by Carl Milles and is named after the eminent philanthropist William Volker. The fountain at Country Club Plaza has figures cast in 1911 and was imported from Worcestershire. Loose Memorial Park has a Garden center with a beautiful rose garden and an expertly-staffed horticultural library.

MUSIC. The *Kansas City Symphony* winter season utilizes the Music Hall. Kansas City spawned some great jazz bands and soloists between the World Wars. Count Basie formed his band here and a native son, Charlie Parker, is thought by many to have been Louis Armstrong's only equal among players. The Vine St. district near 12th St., where it all used to happen, is hardly recognizable now. You'll have to search out your own spots to hear jazz nowadays, but good bets are major hotel cocktail lounges.

STAGE AND REVUES. Productions of good quality may be seen at the *Missouri Repertory Theatre,* 51st and Holmes Sts. on the University of Missouri–Kansas City campus. *Starlight Theatre,* Swope Park, stages musicals with top-name entertainers outdoors during the summer. Dinner theater productions may be enjoyed at *Tiffany's Attic,* 5028 Main, or at *Waldo Astoria Playhouse,* 7428 Washington.

SPORTS. *Swope Park* has two 18-hole golf courses. For spectators, Kansas City has acquired major franchises in *baseball* (Royals), *football* (Chiefs), *indoor soccer* (Comets) and *basketball* (Kings) in the last two decades. Baseball and football are played in the Truman Sports Complex; basketball in Kemper Arena. *K.C. Rodeo* at Benjamin Stables, 6401 E. 87 St., in mid-summer. In early November the *American Royal Horse Show* brings top show horses and riders to the city to compete in matinee and evening performances.

WHAT TO DO WITH THE CHILDREN. *Worlds of Fun,* at I–435 and Parvin Rd., has rides and entertainment of all kinds for the kids. One admission price. Open April to October. Nearby *Oceans of Fun* is open during the summer months. Riverboat tours on the Missouri River in summer. Phone 842-0027.

HOTELS AND MOTELS in Kansas City cover the gamut from the inexpensive to the luxurious. Price categories are divided as follows: *Deluxe:* $70 and up, *Expensive:* $50–70, and *Moderate:* $35–50. For a more complete explanation of these categories see the *Hotels and Motels* section of *Facts at Your Fingertips.*

Deluxe: **Alameda Plaza.** Wornall Rd. at Ward Parkway. Lovely grounds and handsome Spanish decor with many amenities. Rooftop dining room, pool.

Westin Crown Center. 1 Pershing Rd. A luxury hotel, part of a new multi-million dollar shopping/entertainment complex. Restaurants with entertainment, pool, tennis, putting green, sauna.

Embassy on the Park Sheraton. Refurbished older establishment. Connected to Bartle Hall.

Hilton Airport Plaza Inn. I–29 at exit 112 St. Near KCI airport, with airport bus. Restaurant with entertainment, tennis, putting green, pools, indoor and outdoor pool, sauna.

Hilton Plaza Inn. 45th & Main Sts. Well-kept, attractive hostelry near Country Club Plaza shopping. Restaurants, with entertainment, pool.

Hyatt Regency. 2345 McGee, adjacent to Crown Center. 5-story lobby. Revolving rooftop restaurant.

Marriott. Off I–29 at KCI Airport. On a small lake, with boating, indoor pool, restaurant with entertainment.

Radisson Muehlebach. Baltimore and Wyandotte at 12th St. A well-known, established downtown hotel near convention center. Restaurants with entertainment, rooftop pool.

Raphael. 325 Ward Parkway. Many suites, gracious atmosphere. Walking distance from Country Club Plaza shops and restaurants.

Sheraton Royal. 9103 E. 39th St. off I–70. Near sports complex. Saunas, tennis, pool, restaurant with entertainment.

Vista International Hotel. 200 W. 12th at Baltimore. Newest downtown hotel, dubbed the "Miracle on 12th Street," because of boost to area. Shops, restaurants, health club.

Expensive: **Americana Hotel.** 1301 Wyandotte St. at 13th St. Convenient to new downtown convention center and Muncipal Auditorium complex. Revolving rooftop restaurant with entertainment, pool.

The Inn at Executive Park. 1601 N. Universal off I-435 N. Near Worlds of Fun. Heated indoor/outdoor pool, tennis, health club, restaurant.

Moderate: **Holiday Inns.** Seven serve the Greater Kansas City area. All are moderate. Pools, restaurants, and services geared to the traveler are typical of the chain. Here are three: **Northeast,** 7333 Parvin Rd. off I–435 and near Worlds of Fun; **Sports Complex,** Blue Ridge, 20 mi. SE; **Southeast,** 8500 Blue Parkway, 11 mi. SE; (see also Kansas City, Kansas).

Howard Johnson's. 1600 NE Russell Rd. Indoor pool, 24-hr. restaurant, airport bus.

Howard Johnson Motor Lodge. 6th and Main Sts. Pool, restaurant.

Stadium Inn. I–435 at I–70 Interchange. Restaurant, lounge, indoor pool, whirpool. Close to baseball and football stadiums.

 DINING OUT in Kansas City means steak and the cut doesn't matter as long as it's "Kansas City steak." A real "KC" steak is a strip sirloin. There are a number of restaurants specializing in other types of food but when you order steak in this town you will generally not go wrong. Price categories are divided as follows: *Deluxe:* over $25; *Expensive:* $15–25; *Moderate:* $10–15, and *Inexpensive:* below $10. Not included are drinks, tax and tips. For a more complete explanation of restaurant categories refer to *Facts at Your Fingertips.*

Note: *For other nearby restaurants see Kansas City, Kansas.*

Deluxe: **American Restaurant.** 2450 Grand. One of Kansas City's best, with splendid service, finest cuisine, innovative menus, plus excellent décor and a view.

Alameda Plaza Roof. Wornall Road & Ward Parkway, in hotel. Atmosphere is traditional Spanish, complete with strolling guitars. Unusual beef and fish specialties. Good wine list.

La Mediterranée. 4742 Pennsylvania. Call early for a reservation. Try bouillabaisse, the Friday specialty, min. 4 persons.

Jasper's. 405 West 75th Street. Lavish décor, northern Italian food is equal to the ambiance. Excellent veal dishes make up backbone of menu. Good wine list. Service is first rate.

Expensive: **Plaza III.** 4749 Pennsylvania on Country Club Plaza. Continental cuisine, famous steak soup.

Moderate: **Colony Steak House.** In Union Station, Pershing and Main Sts.

Gaetano's 600 E. 8th St. Salad excellent, as is pasta.

Golden Ox. 1600 Genessee. Nothing very fancy in this big, noisy stockyard environment, but basics are attended to with real verve. Steaks and prime ribs are favorite.

Hereford House. 20 E. 20th. Fine charcoal-broiled steak in western atmosphere.

Imperial Palace. 103rd and State Line. One feature is 7-course Da–Yen Chinese feast.

Stephenson's Apple Farm Restaurant. 40 Hwy. E at Lee's Summit Rd. Farm products including many apple dishes. Hickory-smoked dinners. Real country dining keeps it popular with the local folk.

Inexpensive: **Gold Buffet.** 503 E. 18th Ave., North K.C. 80 items and tantalizing dessert cart.

Putsch's Cafeteria. 300 W. 47th St. Tasty simple food. Baking on the premises.

Putsch's Coffee House. 333 W. 47th St. Baking done on premises. Charming sidewalk café.

Seafood. Deluxe: **Savoy Grill.** 9th and Central. Old-line eating place. Chops and beef as well as seafood. Lobster flown in daily.

EXPLORING MISSOURI

Of all Missouri's delightful and unusual communities, one merits special attention—the friendly Mississippi River town of Hannibal. Samuel Clemens was born near here (at Florida, 30 miles away, west on US 24 and south on State 107), and grew up here in an environment that provided a rare assortment of childhood experiences. The river front, woods, caves, and slopes of Hannibal gave Clemens a natural setting for his stories about Tom Sawyer and Huck Finn. Clemens, who took the name Mark Twain, became one of America's first literary giants.

Today, Hannibal loves to recall the Twain heritage. A steamboat still anchors at the riverside dock, and occasionally other traffic up and down the mammoth stream recalls the paddlewheel days. A city of nearly 20,000, Hannibal has achieved significant industrial rank, but the recollections of Mark Twain still remain its primary claim to national attention. In fact, a popular annual event is Tom Sawyer Days, with a fence painting contest, raft races, etc., held early in July.

Southeast Missouri

An area of Missouri with the atmosphere of the Old South may be found in the southeastern Bootheel region. Cotton is grown here in what seems like Mississippi Delta country.

Ste. Genevieve, Missouri's oldest town, was founded by the French in the 1720s. By that time, lead miners had already been in the area for a number of years. Many of the town's old buildings date back to the 1700s and are open for modern visitors. Every August Ste. Genevieve holds "Jour de Fête," a commemoration of the town's French heritage.

Journey to the Springs

Missouri's diverse and beautiful scenery can be especially enjoyed on a tour of the south central region that might be termed "a journey to the springs." Missouri's range of ancient mountains, now shrunken by geologic metamorphosis, left behind a rich legacy of springs, caves, cliffs, and bluffs.

Just 55 miles southwest of St. Louis on I-44 are some of America's most popular caverns, the Meramec Caverns, in Stanton. Famous as a hideout of the Jesse James gang in the 1870s, this attraction claims to be the only five-story cave in the world. There are an underground river, a cave called the "Jungle Room," an onyx mountain, and groupings of rocks which look like stage curtains, subterranean gardens, and grapes, not to mention a wine table, all in a nature-controlled year-round temperature of 60 degrees. Nearby is Meramec State Park, second largest in Missouri, for boating, fishing, swimming, and camping.

America's first scenic riverway, the Ozark National Scenic Riverways preserves rivers in the region in their natural state. Among those directly concerned with this conservation program are Missouri's float fishermen. Float fishing is as typical of Missouri as mules, and the best-known float rivers are in the Big Springs region. Rivers such as the Current, the Jacks Fork, and the Eleven Point are well-known for float trips. These pleasant, peaceful journeys, by canoe or John Boat (a long, flat-bottom boat), can take one day or several, and they offer the beauty and isolation of the Ozark backwoods, all wrapped up in a simple fishing trip.

The Capital and a Big Dragon

Jefferson City ranks as one of America's finest capital cities. The massive state capitol, built of native Carthage marble, has long been a Missouri River landmark. The capitol building houses a museum that recalls the state's history and has many craft, geographical, and industrial exhibits. Near the capitol is the Cole County Historical Museum and the restored mercantile buildings of the Jefferson Landing Historic Site. You also may want to visit the governor's mansion nearby.

Continuing south from the capital, you reach the huge Lake of the Ozarks, also known as the Big Dragon. The lake has become a year-round attraction for Missourians and visitors alike. Near Camdenton are Bridal Cave (where many weddings have taken place), and Ozark and Stark caverns, farther north.

Southwestern Missouri

Missouri explorers also may consider a tour of the western and southwestern sections of the state and their several major lakes and prime resort areas. A section of the nearly 1.5 million acres which now comprise the Mark Twain National Forest is near Rolla. This area boasts almost 800,000 acres of oak and pine, clear waterways for float trips (fishing or just relaxing) and some small game. Some other sections are south of Springfield, including the popular Table Rock area which borders on Arkansas.

Joplin began as a 19th-century lead-mining camp. But as the lead deposits began to run out, the residents turned to above-ground commerce. Today Joplin is a growing, thriving city with modern shopping areas, many parks, and a large number of recreation opportunities. A mineral museum here is open to the public. Famous Missouri artist Thomas Hart Benton painted a mural for the city's centennial in 1973. It is displayed in the city's Municipal Building. Near Joplin is Carthage, a community where fine stone and marble have been quarried for years (some of it is in the state capitol building at Jefferson City).

From Carthage head back north toward Kansas City on US 71. Most tourists like to stop at Lamar to visit the birthplace of former President Harry S. Truman. The small cottage tells a great deal about the "rags-to-riches" success story of President Truman, who once was a Missouri farm boy.

St. Joe and Jesse James

St. Joseph was one of the authentic frontier towns of a century ago. It was a rendezvous of Jesse James, the outlaw who roamed over much of this area. Visitors may visit the cottage in which Jesse was shot in the back in 1882. St. Joe also has the Pony Express Stables Museum, located on the spot where the original express mail service to the West began. Lewis and Clark State Park on the Missouri River is southwest of St. Joseph.

For a taste of home cooking in a quaint atmosphere a detour east of St. Joseph on Hwy 6 to Gallatin is well worth the scenic drive. In 1931 the McDonald Tea Room was opened by a Texas transplant named Virginia McDonald who had grown up with southern cooking and southern tradition. She died in 1969 and Jim and Dottie Stotts bought the restaurant in 1979. Glazed ham, fried chicken and catfish taste as good as in Mrs. McDonald's day, and the homemade pastries are delicious. The main dining room retains its 1930s aura with a checkerboard floor, Roseville pottery and plants. Reservations are suggested on weekends and in summer.

PRACTICAL INFORMATION FOR MISSOURI

HOW TO GET THERE. *By Car:* I–70, from Vandalia in central Illinois, enters the state at St. Louis and connects it with Kansas City via Fulton, Columbia and Boonville. It continues to Topeka, Kansas, and beyond. From Oklahoma City and Tulsa, take I–44 to Joplin, Springfield, Rolla and St. Louis. I–55 follows the undulations of the Mississippi River from Memphis to St. Louis, looking in on Cape Girardeau and Ste. Genevieve; then it veers northeast to Springfield, Illinois. Motorists bound for Bull Shoals or Lake of the Ozarks from Little Rock may use US 65, which continues to Springfield. Southeastern Missouri is served by US 67, also out of Little Rock. It goes to Poplar Bluff and joins I–55 at Festus. In the northwest quadrant, Kansas City is express-linked to Omaha and Des Moines by I–29 and I–35 respectively.

By air: After St. Louis and Kansas City the busiest airports are at Springfield and Joplin, both of which have direct service from cities in neighboring states. Most of this service is provided by *Ozark Airlines,* complemented by *Frontier* and *Delta.*

By train: Amtrak has daily connections between Kansas City and St. Louis, and has service linking St. Louis and Chicago.

By bus: Coast-to-coast *Greyhound* and *Trailways* expresses stop in St. Louis, Springfield and Joplin. Kansas City and northern Missouri are on east-west routes that stretch through Chicago and Omaha. Trailways has a diagonal route from Memphis serving Thayer, Cabool, Springfield, Osceola, Warrensburg and Kansas City.

HOW TO GET AROUND. *By car:* Missouri has fine highways reaching every corner, crossing every tier. St. Louis, Kansas City and Joplin form a triangle of interstate service. Across the southern portion, US 60 goes from Springfield to Sikeston. In the north US 36 crosses from Hannibal to St. Joseph, and farther up, near the Iowa border, is US 136. The north-south routes—US 71, 65, 63, 61—are evenly spaced from west to east, respectively.

By train: Amtrak connects Kansas City with St. Louis and, on its other right of way, with Fort Madison, Iowa.

By air: Commuter and interstate airlines combine to connect Missouri's airports. *Ozark* is the busiest major carrier and the commuters are *Air Illinois, Trans Mo, Semo* and *Skyway.*

By bus: Some of *Greyhound's* routes along federal highways include St. Louis to Memphis. *Trailways* has, among others, a run from Hannibal to Kansas City. Regional lines are especially numerous in the state. You may find yourself riding *Missouri Transit, Trenton-St. Joseph, V-K* or *Conner.*

TOURIST INFORMATION SERVICES. The larger offices offering information are *Missouri Tourism Commission,* Box 1055; *Missouri Dept. of Conservation,* Box 180; and *Missouri Division of Parks & Recreation,* Box 176; all are in Jefferson City, Missouri 65101.

MUSEUMS AND GALLERIES. The *Springfield Art Museum* has American sculpture and paintings and relics of the westward movement. St. Joseph reflects its former role as the first point of the Pony Express route and Missouri's first railroad. *The Pony Express Stables Museum* and the *Doll Museum* are open to the public during the summer. Students of history and architecture will want to spend time at the *Winston Churchill Memorial and Library,* on the campus of Westminster College in Fulton. Here the British statesman delivered his "Iron Curtain" address just 10 months after the Allies had triumphantly entered Berlin. A London, England, church was moved here, stone by stone, and reconstructed in 1966. The church had been restored by Sir Christopher Wren in 1666, when it was already 500 years old. The library proper contains manuscripts, letters and paintings by Sir Winston.

 HISTORIC SITES. In Sibley, off US 24, visit the *Fort Osage Restoration.* A trading post and barracks for defense against Indian attacks, it was established in 1808 by William Clark after his return from exploring the Louisiana Territory. The *Harry S. Truman Shrine Birthplace* in Lamar has the restored family home, through which guided tours are available. Independence is where the *Truman Library and Museum* is located.

As one might expect, there are more historic houses in the state's oldest permanent community, *Ste. Genevieve,* than in any other community except Kansas City and St. Louis. The *George Caleb Bingham House* near Arrow Rock is open during the summer. Mark Twain, Bingham's contemporary, is, of course, the most famous citizen of *Hannibal,* and the Samuel Clemens Boyhood Home preserves local relics and family memorabilia. One of the state's most beautiful ante-bellum mansions is Linwood Lawn in *Lexington,* huge and elaborate with over 230 acres of grounds. *Defiance* is the site of the Daniel Boone Home. Daniel oversaw the building of this home and lived here the last 10 years of his life.

 TOURS. Sightseeing tours within individual communities in Missouri often focus on lakes and rivers. Lake Taneycomo in the southwestern region offers a Pirate Cruise from the Sammy Lane dock in Branson. A similar excursion on the *Lake Queen* puts out from Fisherman's dock, also in Branson. The huge Lake of the Ozarks has its cruise boats too, and they leave from Casino Pier near Bagnell Dam. Daytime trips and evening dance socials are available. Hannibal has sternwheeler tours on the Mississippi River and a "trackless" train ride around town. These all operate in warm-weather months. Tourists also enjoy a free tour year-round of Bagnell Dam in Lake Ozark. The dam, completed in 1931, formed one of America's largest man-made lakes, the Lake of the Ozarks.

 DRINKING LAWS. Liquor laws vary from town to town. Generally, liquor may be bought by the drink from 6 A.M. to 1:30 A.M. except Sunday, when the hours are 1 P.M. to midnight. Package sales are prohibited on Sunday; other days they are legal from 6 A.M. to 1:30 A.M. Legal drinking age is 21.

 SUMMER SPORTS. There are a number of fine courses: Lake Valley, near Camdenton, is public, and the Lodge of the Four Seasons Course, on the Lake of the Ozarks, is a layout by that Michelangelo of course design, Robert Trent Jones. The fishing in Ozark waters is famous, with walleye, rainbows, panfish, bluegill and bass the prized catches. Waterskiing and rowboating are available on the region's lakes, and canoeing, too, is healthy and relaxing, especially on the beautiful, quiet streams that lace the southern tier. Horseback riding is among the activities available at some resorts and state parks.

 WINTER SPORTS. Include the fall and you've got tremendous opportunities for hunting, if that's what you like; small game roams in great abundance: squirrel, rabbit, skunk, raccoon, fox and varieties of fowl. There are several Ozark resorts now offering ski slopes, but if you're used to Colorado or Switzerland, it might seem a little tame.

SPECTATOR SPORTS. Horse and auto races, with no regular seasons in rural Missouri, are special events for state and county fairs. Of course the

University of Missouri, Columbia, has a full athletic program, including football, basketball, track, swimming and wrestling.

WHAT TO DO WITH THE CHILDREN. Missouri's most unique natural attraction is its extensive series of caves. Nevada has the *Bushwhacker Museum,* a former jail complete with inmates' graffiti and cuts, scraping, chippings and holes recording their efforts at escape. Mementos of two famous native sons may interest youngsters. The *George Washington Carver National Monument,* off County Rd. V, southwest of Diamond, has exhibits and a diorama plus a self-guiding pathway through the neighborhood where Carver grew up. Hannibal has several houses, exhibits and events of interest to readers of Mark Twain. Near Excelsior Springs, in *Watkins Mill State Park,* visit the woolen factory and see the equipment used over 100 years ago. By all means, plan on a day's entertainment at the state's two major theme parks: *Six Flags Over Mid-America* near St. Louis and *Worlds of Fun* in Kansas City.

HOTELS AND MOTELS outside St. Louis and Kansas City range from the lavish Lodge of the Four Seasons in the Lake Ozark region to clean and comfortable establishments in smaller towns. Price categories for double occupancy average as follows: *Deluxe* $70 and up; *Expensive* $50–70; *Moderate* $35–50; *Inexpensive* below $35.

COLUMBIA. *Expensive:* **Hilton Inn.** Heated pool, restaurant, bar.
Ramada Inn. Pool, restaurant, bar, sauna. Airport bus.

HANNIBAL. *Inexpensive:* **Best Western Mark Twain Motor Inn.** Restaurant next door. Pool.

JEFFERSON CITY. *Expensive:* **Holiday Inn.** Downtown. Pool, restaurant, bar. Airport bus.
Ramada Inn. Pool, restaurant, bar, cinema theater.
Moderate: **Rodeway Inn.** Pool, restaurant, bar.

JOPLIN. *Moderate:* **Howard Johnson's.** Heated pool, restaurant, bar. Many sports facilities available.
Ramada Inn. Heated pool, restaurant, bar.
Inexpensive: **Capri.** Comfortable setting. Pool, restaurant.

LAKE OZARK. *Deluxe:* **Lodge of the Four Seasons.** Luxurious. Many activities.

OSAGE BEACH. *Deluxe:* **Tan-Tar-A Golf & Tennis Resort.** Many sports facilities both indoors and out, including boating, horseback riding, and ice skating.

STE. GENEVIEVE. *Moderate:* **Inn St. Gemme Beauvais.** Restored 17th-century dwelling furnished with antiques.

ST. JOSEPH. *Moderate:* **Pony Express.** Large, comfortable rooms. Pool, restaurant.

DINING OUT in Missouri can provide unique experiences to anyone willing to go off the beaten track. Eating in a plush dining room overlooking the Lake of the Ozarks is a real pleasure, as is sitting down to a plain table of simple, good food. Price categories are divided as follows: *Deluxe* $10 and up, *Expensive* $7–10, *Moderate* $5–7 and *Inexpensive* below $5. Prices are for complete meals, excluding drinks, tax and tip.

ARROW ROCK. *Moderate:* **The Old Tavern.** A museum and restaurant on the old Santa Fe Trail built in 1834 and furnished in the style of the period. Reservations required.

JEFFERSON CITY. *Expensive:* **Oscar's Steak House.** 1441 Christy. Generous cuts of beef are special.

STE. GENEVIEVE. *Moderate:* **Old Brick House.** 3rd & Market. German and American bill-of-fare served in charming 200-year-old restored building. Liver dumplings and kettle beef are specialties.

ST. JOSEPH. *Expensive:* **Pony Express.** Elwood. Well established for pleasant American dining.

SPRINGFIELD. *Expensive:* **Shady Inn.** 524 W. Sunshine. and 1364 E. Battlefield.
Inexpensive: **Heritage Cafeteria.** 1310 S. Glenstone, 210 E. Sunshine and 1364 E. Battlefield. Popular for simple American cooking, homemade bread.

NEW MEXICO

Santa Fe, Albuquerque, and Indian Country

The best (but expensive) base for seeing New Mexico is Santa Fe (pop. 50,957), but the many affluent summer people who flock in for the cool climate and the Santa Fe Opera make reservations essential.

The Plaza is worth several hours. Its north side is formed by the Palace of the Governors. Under this block-long porch, Indians from nearby pueblos traditionally hold a daily open-air market, spreading their silver-and-turquoise jewelry, pottery, leather goods, and other handicrafts on the brick sidewalk. The Palace is now part of the Museum of New Mexico. Its cool, dim, thick-walled rooms are filled with exhibits displaying the panorama of the state's history and prehistory. A superb example of adobe construction, with walls up to six feet thick, it was the official residence of one hundred appointed governors—Spanish, Mexican, and U.S.—from 1610 until 1910, and is by far the oldest public building in the country. Its exhibits offer a pleasant way to get a feeling for New Mexico's Indian, Spanish, and Anglo-American cultures.

Just down Palace Avenue from this historic structure is the state's Fine Arts Museum, housed in Pueblo-style architecture.

In the block up Palace Avenue from the Palace of the Governors is Sena Plaza, the palatial former home of the Sena family. Stand at the fountain in its interior courtyard to get some feeling how the rich lived in days gone by.

Just across Palace are the grounds of St. Francis Cathedral, a 19th-century Romanesque structure begun by Archbishop Jean Baptiste Lamy in 1869. The cathedral's Sacred Heart Chapel houses *La Conquistadora*, a statue of the Blessed Virgin Mary that Captain-General

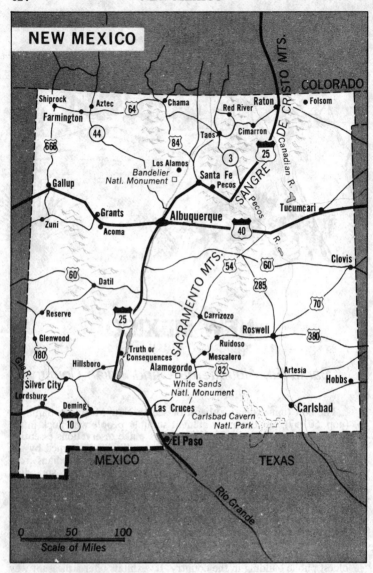

NEW MEXICO

Shiprock Aztec 64 Chama COLORADO
Farmington   Red River Raton Folsom
44   Taos Cimarron
666   84 25
          Los Alamos   SANGRE DE CRISTO MTS.
          Bandelier Santa Fe 3   Canadian R.
Gallup   Natl. Monument Pecos
                          Albuquerque Pecos R. Tucumcari
Grants   40
Zuni Acoma
                                      60 Clovis
60 Datil   54 285
                                      70
Reserve   Carrizozo
          Truth or   Roswell 380
Glenwood Consequences Ruidoso
180 Hillsboro Alamogordo Mescalero 82 Artesia
Silver City   White Sands   Hobbs
Lordsburg   Natl. Monument
     Deming Las Cruces Carlsbad Cavern Carlsbad
10   Natl. Park
          El Paso
     MEXICO   TEXAS
                    Rio Grande

0   50   100
     Scale of Miles

Don Diego de Vargas brought with him when he reconquered Santa Fe from the Indians in 1692.

Around the corner from the cathedral is another of Santa Fe's interesting churches—the tiny Loretto Chapel, modeled after the church of Sainte-Chapelle in Paris and best known for its beautiful staircase that climbs in a tight spiral to its choir loft. According to local legend, a stranger appeared when the church was nearing completion, performed this superb piece of carpentry, and then vanished without being paid.

Santa Fe's "Oldest Church" is two blocks away across the Santa Fe River. The Mission of San Miguel was built in 1636, burned by Indians in 1680, and rebuilt after the reconquest.

Adjoining this chapel across De Vargas Street is what may be the oldest house in the United States, an often-restored structure of puddled adobe which houses a curio shop.

A block west down the Santa Fe River Park on narrow De Vargas Street and you are on the State Capitol grounds. The Executive-Legislative Building is a controversial building which locals call "The Roundhouse"; it's the nation's only round capitol building, and a symbol of what happens when a state tries to compromise between modern and traditional.

Canyon Road, on the south side of the Santa Fe River, is the center of Santa Fe's art colony. The street is lined with the studios and galleries of painters, sculptors, and craftsmen. Browsers are welcome (and buyers even more so). An association of Canyon Road artists usually has an updated map available at hotels and the Chamber of Commerce office.

Just off Canyon is Cristo Rey (The Church of Christ the King), the largest adobe structure in the United States, with stark white walls and a high ceiling supported by wooden *vigas*. The screen behind the altar was carved in stone in 1751 and is considered a priceless example of Spanish-colonial religious art.

The Museum of International Folk Art and the Wheelwright Museum of the American Indian are on the southeast side of the city.

The Folk Art Museum, one of the very few of its kind in the world, is devoted to the beauty found in everyday costumes, carvings, furniture, toys, weapons, and tools of common people.

The Wheelwright features exhibits that interpret Native American arts and crafts in terms of tribal heritage. Downstairs the Case Trading Post offers Indian arts and crafts for sale.

Santa Fe is also an excellent base for brief side excursions. A few hours of round-trip driving will take you through colonial-vintage villages in the mountains, ghost towns, thriving Indian Pueblos, a ski basin complete with Hudsonian Life Zone fir, spruce, and aspen—and a rushing stream cold enough to numb your hand on the hottest day of summer.

Albuquerque and the Rio Grande Valley

Another excellent base for exploring is Albuquerque (pop. 341,978), New Mexico's only large city.

Albuquerque is unusual in several respects: nearly all of its growth is new; it is almost solidly middle class; and it has an extremely high percentage of people who make their living exclusively with their brains. The University of New Mexico, with twenty-three thousand students and a faculty of 1,200, is in the center of the city in buildings of modified Pueblo Indian architecture.

The Old Town Plaza looks pretty much as it did when Albuquerque began. The fortresslike San Felipe de Neri Church, along with its convent, makes up its north side. Inside is a choir-loft stairway that spirals its way around the trunk of a spruce tree. Mass has been said in the building every day since it opened in 1706.

The city's most spectacular attraction is the Sandia Peak Aerial Tram with a view that defies description. The altitude is 10,678 feet and all of north-central New Mexico lies around and below you: Albuquerque and some 10,000 square miles of river valley and mountain ranges. You can also see Santa Fe and, if the weather is as clear as it usually is, mountain ranges as far north as Colorado, into the Navajo country near Arizona, and stretching southward toward Mexico.

The Rio Grande needs a word of explanation. During most summers it is bone-dry; throughout the middle reaches of its 1,885 miles virtually all of its water is diverted into irrigation channels. In the autumn, after irrigation, the main bed carries a small stream. In spring, during the snow-melt season, it can become a roaring torrent.

Exploring westward from Alburquerque takes one into Indian country and the eroded mesa-and-butte landscape of the Colorado Plateau. This is a drive that features views of a vast landscape almost empty of people.

Acoma, one of the most remarkable settlements in the Western Hemisphere, may be the oldest continuously occupied town in the United States. It is a tidy and compact village atop a sheer-walled table of stone that juts out of surrounding grazing country for 357 feet, the height of a 40-story skyscraper. A look at the great mission church, the neat row of houses, and the natural cistern that provides the residents with their water supply on their flat sandstone perch is something to remember.

The landscape on the Acoma Reservation, and through much of this part of New Mexico, features great sandstone cliffs; pink, white, gray, salmon-colored, and bloody red, carved into grotesque shapes, or streaked with all the shades of red and often undercut into echo caves.

The colorful old art colony of Taos is an ideal base for exploring the northern mountain portion of New Mexico. It's an almost purely adobe place, easy to tour on foot. Its galleries and studios are nearly all centered within a few blocks of the plaza. The D. H. Lawrence ranch is maintained by the University of New Mexico and is open to visitors. It offers a superb view, of which Lawrence wrote: "I think the skyline of Taos the most beautiful of all I have ever seen in my travels around the world."

The Kit Carson House, where the famous frontiersman lived, is now a museum. (Carson, incidentally, is considerably less idealized in these days of Indian militancy. The Navajos remember his role in the scorched-earth campaign that starved them from the Dinetah and led to their infamous "Long Walk" into exile.)

Taos Pueblo, just north of Taos, is the northernmost of the pueblos. It is a thriving village of some nine hundred people and is dominated by its principal five-story apartment building which was ancient when the white men first saw it in the 16th century. It hasn't changed since.

St. Francis of Assisi Mission, at Ranchos de Taos, a suburb village four miles south, is probably the most-depicted church this side of St. Patrick's Cathedral in New York. Made of adobe, with massive abutments and buttresses, it has an odd, stark beauty that neither painters nor photographers seem able to resist.

Just north of Taos is some of the West's most beautiful mountain scenery. The lay of the land makes it possible to see a lot of it in a circle drive of 90 miles via US 64 over Palo Flechado Pass, then via State Road 38, Red River Pass, and Questa. The route is spectacular.

US 84 and State 17 bring you to Chama, an old lumber, sheep and railroad town; it is also the departure point for the Cumbres and Toltec Scenic Railroad, an ancient narrow-gauge railroad formerly operated by the Denver and Rio Grande as a freight line and now purely a sightseeing train. The old steam engines puff their way up Cumbres Pass, 10,022 feet above sea level, and then across the lush, high meadows of Wolf Creek into the Los Pinos River canyon, through Toltec Gorge and onto the Rio Grande plateau at Antonito, Colorado. It's a wonderful ride. There are picnic and photography stops, and since some of the round trips sell out early, check in advance on tickets and schedule (brochures from the State Tourist Bureau).

Aztec Ruins National Monument is just north of US 550 and shouldn't be missed. Here, about A.D. 1106, Indians built one of their largest pre-Spanish pueblos beside the Animas River. It's a massive (Pueblo III Period) five hundred-room apartment complex, with the largest underground kiva (forty-eight-foot diameter) ever excavated. No one knows why the great pueblo was abandoned about 1300.

Gallup (pop. 20,440) calls itself the "Indian Capital of the World" with considerable justification. A former coal and railroad town, it has gradually become the trading center for the most populous part of the Navajo nation, Indians from the nearby Zuni Reservation and from the other western pueblos. It's another good place to buy Indian-made articles.

If you happen to be in New Mexico early in December, check on the schedule of the Zuni "Shalako," the annual return of the Zuni "Council of the Gods" to the Pueblo. This is the most dramatic and colorful ceremonial in the Western Hemisphere. The council is accompanied by its six messenger birds (the Shalako) personified by Zunis wearing great bird-form masks ten feet tall; the event is the occasion for 24 hours of dancing and feasting and annually draws thousands of spectators. The hospitable Zunis try to feed and provide for everyone. You are welcome at all such ceremonials (at Zuni and the other Pueblos), but photography is absolutely forbidden, and so are sketching and the making of tape recordings.

The emptiest part of New Mexico is the southwest. In the 19th century this country buzzed with mining fever, but today the lodes are exhausted and the towns have fallen into ruin.

Silver City, where Billy the Kid became a juvenile delinquent and killed his first man, now survives on copper, cattle, and on New Mexico Western University. It's the center of a complex of mining communities —Bayard, Santa Rita, Hurley, Central, Hanover, and Tyrone. It also serves as the entrance to the Gila Wilderness Area—the oldest and most isolated in the nation. While no roads or wheeled vehicles are allowed in a Wilderness, this one wraps around a pre-existing access route to the Gila Cliff Dwellings National Monument. The route takes you through the old mining town of Pinos Altos, and then through 37 miles of empty, untouched forests.

If you turn toward the river at San Marcial, you pick up old US 85 which leads to the Bosque del Apache Wildlife Refuge. Here the ancient San Marcial marshes, once a favored wintering place for Apache war parties, have been converted into a sanctuary that attracts ornithologists from around the world. It's one of the few nesting places for the rare Mexican duck. The winter bird count soars past the half-million level, including the majestic whooping crane, Sandhill cranes, immense flocks of Canada and Snow geese, and scores of other bird species. The old marsh is also home for deer herds, beaver, coyotes and other wildlife.

At Lincoln the old Lincoln County Courthouse from which Billy the Kid escaped after killing two guards is now a state monument. The young outlaw and 18 companions shot it out with some 40 lawmen of the Murphy-Dolan faction, using the Alex McSween house as their fortress. Seven died in that scuffle; Billy was credited with killing 21 before he was shot to death at age twenty-one. The museum here is intriguing for those interested in frontier badmen.

US 70 leads down off the mountain to Tularosa and the Tularosa Basin. The big town is Alamogordo (pop. 25,475), an attractive little city. Its big tourist appeal is White Sands National Monument, 230 square miles of snowy white gypsum dunes, some as high as one hundred feet. The back side of these great dunes is hard because it is carved endlessly by the southwesterly winds. The face is as soft as fine sand, great for rolling down (if you're in a playful mood).

The Carlsbad Caverns

The caverns have to be seen to be believed, and the best way to see them, if you don't mind walking, is by taking the guided tour all the way from the outside entrance—a four-hour, three-mile trip. (Wear a jacket, because the temperature is always 56 degrees Fahrenheit.) If walking is not your thing, there's an elevator in the park headquarters that drops you 750 feet straight down into a cavern chamber. Here you can have lunch and you can also explore a smaller portion of this incredible cave.

PRACTICAL INFORMATION FOR NEW MEXICO

HOW TO GET THERE. *By car:* There are good roads into and across New Mexico from all the bordering states. *By air:* Albuquerque has direct service from the country's half-dozen major air centers. *By bus:* The New York-Los Angeles express buses of *Trailways* and *Greyhound* serve Tucumcari, Albuquerque and Gallup, along I-40. North-south expresses are Trailways' buses from Durango, Greyhound buses from Pueblo, Colorado. *By train: Amtrak's Super Chief* goes via Albuquerque and Santa Fe, and the *Sunset Limited* via Deming and Lordsburg.

HOW TO GET AROUND. *By car:* Hertz has offices in 14 of the state's cities and towns. If you do want to drive the back country, the Highway Patrol is the best source of advice on road and weather conditions. *By air:* Las Cruces, Albuquerque, Gallup, Farmington, Los Alamos, Hobbs, and Roswell all have intrastate service. *By bus:* The carriers listed above provide service within New Mexico, though neither goes into the small mountain settlements.

TOURIST INFORMATION. Write to Department of Development, Bataan Memorial Bldg., State Capitol, Santa Fe, N.M. 87501. Phone: (505) 827-5571.

MUSEUMS AND GALLERIES. Santa Fe is the museum capital by virtue of the *Museum of New Mexico's* five units: The *Palace of the Governors, Fine Arts Museum, Museum of International Folk Art, Wheelwright Museum of the American Indian.* All museums are open daily, May to September.

Many other special-interest museums enrich the state: in Albuquerque the *Museum of Albuquerque,* the University of New Mexico's *Maxwell Museum of Anthropology, Geology Museum, Meteorites Museum, Fine Arts Gallery* and *Jonson Gallery,* The *National Atomic Museum* at Kirtland Air Force Base features films, and demonstrations depicting history of the atomic age, *Indian Pueblo Cultural Center* contains exhibits of Pueblo life, arts and crafts; at Abiquiu, *Ghost Ranch;* the *Old Mill Museum* and *Ernest Thompson Seton Memorial Library,* at Cimarron; the *Pancho Villa Museum,* at Columbus; the *Los Alamos Historical Museum* (for atomic-science buffs); and the *Confederate Air Force Museum,* at Hobbs.

HISTORIC SITES. In addition to the pueblo missions, there are several other churches of great antiquity and historical value: *Church of St. Francis of Assisi* at Ranchos de Taos, *San Miguel Mission* and *St. Francis Cathedral* in Santa Fe, the *Church of San Felipe de Neri de Albuquerque,* the *Mission of San Miguel* at Socorro, the *Chimayo Santuario* and the *Church of the Twelve Apostles* at Las Trampas. The *Palace of the Governors* in Santa Fe was built in 1610 and is the oldest public building in the United States.

 TOURS. Both *Gray Lines* and *Thunderbird Tours* offer a list of regular sightseeing tours to various parts of New Mexico. Albuquerque and Santa Fe are the main centers; tours cover both the cities themselves and large areas around them.

DRINKING LAWS. Liquor, beer, wine retailers and dispensers are open daily except Sundays. Age limit is 21, or 18 when accompanied by parent, legal guardian, or spouse of legal age. (Sundays, by local option, by drink only, noon to midnight.)

 SPORTS. In lakes administered by the Department of Game and Fish, *boating* without motors is permissible. Some of these lakes are: Clayton Lake, twelve mi. N of Clayton on State 370; Fenton Lake, twenty-four mi. N of Jemez Springs on State 126; Bear Canyon Dam, six mi. NW of San Lorenzo on State 61; Lake Van, two mi. E. of Dexter on State 190. *Golf* courses are in Santa Fe, Los Alamos, Albuquerque, Cloudcroft, Hobbs, Carlsbad, Farmington, Las Cruces, and Roswell.

Horseback riding instructions, *hay rides, pack trips,* and *hunting safaris* are available at dude ranches, resorts, and riding academies.

Skiing: twelve ski areas attract buffs from all states and from Europe. Generally, it's a Thanksgiving-to-Easter season.

 SHOPPING. Because of the peculiarities of its culture, some parts of New Mexico offer unusual opportunities for the shopper. Taos offers dozens of galleries and studios and is an ideal town for the walking-browse. Santa Fe offers a somewhat similar situation along its Canyon Road. It is also well supplied with interesting little shops selling imports.

Albuquerque is one of the best places in the world to buy *Indian arts and crafts.* Some of the better shops are along Central Avenue and around Old Town Plaza. At both Albuquerque and Santa Fe the Indians hold their own sidewalk markets on the plazas. It is also possible to buy directly from the Indians at several of the pueblos and at trading posts on the Navajo and Apache Reservations. At Zuni, the tribe operates its own jewelry shop. Gallup is also a thriving Indian trading center. (Don't overlook the pawn shops. Pawned jewelry, made for the maker's own use, often tends to be the highest quality.)

New Mexican law requires proper marking of Indian-made goods to protect the consumer from counterfeit products. Nonetheless, when buying turquoise jewelry, it's wise to be suspicious. There are ways to make poor-quality stones take on a rich color temporarily, and some craftsmen aren't above using them. If the purchase is major, it's a good idea to ask someone who knows.

 WHAT TO DO WITH THE CHILDREN. In Carlsbad, in addition to the caverns, are the *Zoological and Botanical Gardens* and the *President's Park* (which has an old paddlewheel steamboat and miniature train). North of Abiqiu is the *Ghost Ranch Museum;* it is devoted particularly to local animals, plants and geology. In Albuquerque is the *Rio Grande Zoological Park,* where exotic species please the children and adults alike. The *Cumbres & Toltec Scenic Railroad* is a narrow-gauge train pulled by a steam locomotive.

HOTELS AND MOTELS. Accommodations range from American-Standard in towns of little tourist interest to colorful, charming, and unique in places like Taos and Santa Fe.

In all these places, however, it's a good idea to have reservations.

The price categories in this section, for double occupancy, will average as follows: *Super Deluxe:* $75–125; *Deluxe:* $60–75; *Expensive:* $50–60; *Moderate:* $30–50; *Inexpensive:* under $30.

ALBUQUERQUE. *Super Deluxe:* **Clarion Four Seasons Motor Inn.** I–40 at Carlisle, N.E. Indoor-outdoor central pool and patio, popular restaurant and bar.

The Classic. 6815 Menual, N.E. Convention facilities, vintage auto display, restaurants, bar, pool. Close to shopping centers.

Sheraton–Old Town Inn. 800 Rio Grande, N.W. Heated pool, restaurants, bar. Tennis. Convenient location.

Expensive: **Best Western Winrock Inn.** Part of New Mexico's second largest shopping center.

Moderate: **Dollar Inns of Albuquerque.** Non-smokers' section. Pool. Near intersection I–40 and I–25.

SANTA FE. *Super Deluxe:* **Bishop's Lodge.** A charming ranch resort.

Rancho Encantado. In nearby Tesuque, convenient to Santa Fe Opera. Tennis courts, horseback riding, romantic southwest bar.

Deluxe: **Inn at Loretto.** Pueblo style with large attractive rooms. Excellent location for sightseeing. Restaurant, bar, pool, shops, convention facilities.

Expensive: **La Posada de Santa Fe.** Small, secluded, individual units in landscaped grounds.

Inn of the Governors. A lovely example of what can be done with Santa Fe's historic architecture.

Moderate: **Stagecoach Motor Inn.** Caters to families. Quiet.

TAOS. *Deluxe:* **Holiday Inn.** Heated pool, restaurant, bar. Usual amenities.

Expensive: **Kachina Lodge and Motel.** Superb Pueblo-style architecture.

Sagebrush Inn. A beautiful, peaceful old place with a spectacular view of the Taos Mountains.

Taos Inn. Old Spanish hacienda on North Pueblo Road.

DINING OUT. In theory, traditional dishes of New Mexico are Mexican. Actually, the years have brought a totally unique evolution to New Mexican recipes, and traditional dishes have come to blend Spanish, Indian, and Anglo-American styles.

Some items that should be tried:

Chili. This is not to be confused with the commercial "chili con carne." It is a bowl of puree of green chili peppers, piquant and hot and delicious. You can also order the dish under the same name, but with dried chilies used.

Enchiladas. Cheese, chicken, or beef with a chili sauce, served either wrapped in a tortilla (a thin, fried pancake of corn meal) or served with garnish on a flat tortilla. Tortilla, incidentally, can mean either a soft, white bread, or a tough, brown one.

Frijoles refritos. Literally, refried beans—usually pintos, which have been boiled, mashed into paste, seasoned, and recooked in a skillet.

Tacos. Ground beef, pork, chicken, or cheese, topped with chopped lettuce, tomatoes, etc., and wrapped in a tortilla.

Tamales. Highly seasoned (with chili) meat, boiled in a corn meal dough, held together in the traditional corn husk.

Other popular items you'll be seeing on the menus (usually among the lowest-priced items, by the way) include guacamole, a salad of mashed avocados; arroz espanol, boiled Spanish rice; chili rellenos, green chili peppers (not bell peppers) filled with cheese and dipped in egg batter; tostadas, crisp-fried bits of tortilla; sopaipillas, deep-fried puffs of bread; bisochitos, anise-flavored cookies; empanaditas, fried pies filled with anything from nuts to meat; cabrito, barbecued goat; and posole, a stew of pork, hominy, and red chili.

Restaurant price categories are as follows: *Deluxe* $15 and up; *Expensive* $10–$15; *Moderate* $5–10; *Inexpensive* $5 and under. These prices are complete dinner. Not included are drinks and tips.

ALBUQUERQUE. *Deluxe:* The **Crystal Room** at the Clarion Four Seasons Motor Inn. Elegant dining.

Expensive: **Al Monte's.** Another gourmet place with a good wine list, a congenial host, logs blazing in the bar fireplace and well-prepared, moderately expensive Continental cuisine.

Luna Mansion. Interesting building. Historic southern colonial adobe. Standard menu well-prepared. Walk up the staircase to the bar.

Minato. Downtown. Japanese cuisine, fresh seafood, sushi, tempura amid charming décor. Excellent service. Open seven days.

Moderate: **Big Valley Ranch Company.** Steakhouse and lounge. Short menu but good food, moderate prices, and an excellent salad bar.

El Pinto. For years a favorite of local folks who love good and authentic Mexican food.

CARLSBAD. *Inexpensive:* **Cortez Café.** Excellent New Mexican foods.

ROSWELL/RUIDOSO. *Moderate:* **Tinnie's Silver Dollar.** One of the West's most colorful, in the old Tinnie Mercantile Building beside US70/80. Like dining in 1880. Open 5 to 10:30 P.M. Other 19th-century frontier re-creations by the same operator and about as good are the **Double Eagle** in Mesilla (near Las Cruces), the **Palace** in Raton and the **Maria Teresa** in Albuquerque.

LAS CRUCES. *Moderate:* **La Posta.** One of New Mexico's famous old restaurants. Patios, birds, flowers, and a good Mexican menu. Wine and margaritas. Closed Mondays.

RANCHO DE CHIMAYO. The historic Jaramillo rancho provide beautiful surroundings, and the Jaramillo family cooks beautiful food. It's in the 18th-century village north of Santa Fe with a wine list and fine service. Try a tequila in apple cider cocktail.

Moderate–Expensive: **El Paragua.** On the Santa Cruz highway in Espanola. Outstanding Mexican food. Try the gazpacho!

SANTA FE *Deluxe:* **The Haven.** This restaurant on colorful Canyon Rd. features an international menu. Good seafood and curry.

Expensive: **Plaza Ore House.** Conveniently located on the Santa Fe plaza. Nightly seafood specialities.

The Pink Adobe. New Orleans cooking in a 250-year-old adobe. An old favorite of New Mexicans.

The Steaksmith. An old hotel dining room that has been restored to resemble an old forge. Steaks are obviously the feature; racks of beef are in evidence at all times.

Moderate: **El Farol.** An excellent menu. Santa Fe atmosphere.

La Tertulia. Operated by an old Santa Fe family in the former Guadalupe Parish buildings. Delicious Mexican food, fine décor, fine service.

TAOS. *Deluxe.* **Casa Cordova.** Nationally recognized gourmet restaurant on the road to the famed Taos Ski Area. Continental and New Mexican specialties served in a hacienda atmosphere. Cocktail lounge. Closed Sundays.

Expensive: **The Taos Inn.** Good food and a varied menu. Locals love the seafood specials.

Moderate: **Michael's Kitchen.** Fresh baked breads, excellent desserts with generous helpings of home-cooked foods. Breakfast is terrific.

OKLAHOMA

"Home of the Indians"

Oklahoma City was settled overnight, during the homesteading "run" of April 22, 1889. Thousands of pioneers waited at the border for the signal to rush in and stake their claims to a portion of the land confiscated from the Five Civilized Tribes. (The land had been confiscated by the U.S. government as punishment for the five tribes' support of the Confederacy during the Civil War.) Oklahoma became our 46th state in 1907, and in 1910, Oklahoma City became the state capital.

In the early days, Oklahoma City's economy was built on livestock and agriculture. At the turn of the century, though, the city, like the state as a whole, underwent a drastic economic change when oil was discovered. Development of Oklahoma City's oil pool began in 1928, and the city quickly became the center of a leading, rich oil-producing area, with oil fields lying within the city limits.

Today oil wells surround the capitol building in the square at Lincoln Boulevard and 23rd Street; one is a "whipstock" well, drilled at an angle to tap the oil pool directly beneath the capitol building.

History and the Cowboy Hall of Fame

Many Indian artifacts and other items from Oklahoma's rich history are found across the boulevard from the capitol, at the State Museum of Oklahoma. Other facets of the state's history are documented and displayed at the National Cowboy Hall of Fame and Western Heritage Center—the world's largest museum of Western heritage and art—the Forty-Fifth Infantry Museum, the National Softball Hall of Fame, the

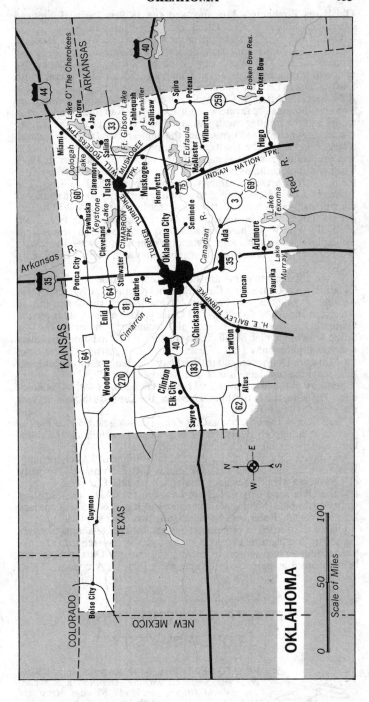

OKLAHOMA

Scale of Miles

0   50   100

Oklahoma Firefighters Museum, and the 1889ers Harn Homestead Museum. (All are located within five miles of each other.)

One of the West's most famous museums is the Western Heritage Center. This unique institution, dedicated to the memory of the heroic pioneers of the Old West, was established through the cooperative efforts of seventeen states: Texas, Oklahoma, Kansas, Nebraska, South Dakota, North Dakota, Montana, Wyoming, Nevada, Utah, Colorado, New Mexico, Arizona, California, Oregon, Idaho, and Washington. Life-size dioramas re-create an Indian camp, a roundup chuck wagon camp, and the frontier cavalry. A taped narration capsules the pioneer history as synchronized lights trace the pioneers' westward trek across a large relief map. The Heritage Center opened on June 26, 1965, and was proclaimed a national memorial by an Act of Congress in 1967. The institution contains books and documents on the frontier development, western art, and exhibits of early clothing and vehicles. The Rodeo Hall of Fame is devoted to exhibits commemorating the national championships. Although better known for his rope tricks, Will Rogers got his start in show business by capturing a rampant steer from Zach Mulhall's Wild West Show in Madison Square Garden; show was from Mulhall, Oklahoma. Another Oklahoma company, Pawnee Bill's Wild West Show, toured the world in combination with Buffalo Bill Cody's show.

Other notable museums are the Oklahoma Museum of Arts, the Oklahoma Art Center, and the Kirkpatrick Center which houses three unusual art galleries—the Sanamu African Gallery, the Center for the American Indian, and the Oriental Gallery. Also at the Center are the Omniplex, a "hands-on" science and technology museum; the Air Space Museum, which highlights the history of U.S. aviation; the International Photography Hall of Fame; the Green Arcade Greenhouse; the Minature Dollhouse; and the Kirkpatrick Planetarium, a space and time machine that lets visitors discover the universe.

Statuary in the downtown mall honors Oklahoma's 45th "Thunderbird" Division, the battleship *Oklahoma,* the Land Rush Pioneer, and the Five Civilized Tribes.

Next door is the Oklahoma City Zoo. The Aquatic Science Park is packed with dolphin shows, fresh- and salt-water exhibits and a simulated Oklahoma lake with natural inhabitants.

Oklahoma City also has its share of institutions of higher learning. It is, for example, the home of Oklahoma City University, University of Oklahoma Health Sciences Center, Oklahoma Christian College, and the Oklahoma City College of Law. On the Oklahoma Christian College campus (Memorial Rd. and Bryant), a 60,000-square-foot learning center, Enterprise Square, USA, was erected in 1982.

Once a city settled by pioneers, it has not lost the Oklahoma pioneering spirit. One form that spirit is taking today is research into alternative techniques and sources of energy, and one day Oklahomans may be recognized as pioneers in helping solve the energy crisis.

PRACTICAL INFORMATION

FOR OKLAHOMA CITY

HOW TO GET THERE. *By air: American, United, Eastern, Delta, Southwest, Frontier, Northeastern, Republic, Trans World Airlines, Sun World, Skyways, Metro, Air Midwest,* and *American West* serve Oklahoma City.

There are direct flights to Oklahoma City from both coasts. *By bus: Greyhound* and *Trailways* both have through service from other states. The best regional service is provided by *M.K.&0.* and *Oklahoma Transportation.*

HOW TO GET AROUND. *By car: Rent-A-Car* facilities are available from *Avis, Hertz, Budget, Cable, Dollar, National, Thrifty,* and independent dealers.

TOURIST INFORMATION. Tourist brochures and information can be obtained by writing to the *Oklahoma Tourism and Recreation Department,* 500 Will Rogers Building, Oklahoma City 73105, or from the information center in the Capitol Rotunda. A traveler information center is also located on I–35 at the intersection with NE 50th Street. The *Oklahoma City Convention and Tourism Bureau* also has information on current happenings in the city. Four Santa Fe Plaza, Oklahoma City 73102, telephone 405–278–8912. Daily events can be discovered by calling 405–232–2211.

Three major events in Oklahoma City are the *Festival of the Arts* every April, *Oklahoma State Fair,* in September, and the *Quarter Horse Show* held each November.

TRAILER TIPS. Trailer park facilities are available at many private and most state parks.

MUSEUMS AND GALLERIES. *Firefighters Museum,* 2716 NE 50; *National Cowboy Hall of Fame & Western Heritage Center,* 1700 NE 63; *National Softball Hall of Fame,* 2801 NE 50; and the *Kirkpatrick Center,* planetarium and fascinating science complex, at Lincoln Park, home of the city's fabulous zoo; all of the foregoing are clustered within a square mile in the city's northeast quadrant. The *State Museum of Oklahoma* is a few steps southeast of the south door of the State Capitol Building. The *Oklahoma Art Center,* Fairgrounds, and the *Oklahoma Museum of Art,* 7316 Nichols Road. *Air Space Museum* (at Kirkpatrick Center, 2100 NE 52nd St.) relives the history of aviation.

HISTORIC SITES. *Oklahoma Heritage House,* near the State Capitol Building, in the historic preservation area, was the home of an early-day city father and contains many antiques and imported items. Mon.-Sat. 9–5, Sun. and holidays 1–5. The *State Capitol,* NE 23rd St. at Lincoln Blvd., is the only statehouse with working oil wells right on its grounds. Guided tours available. *Harn Gardens & 1889er Museum,* 301 N.E. 16th St., 10 A.M.–4 P.M. Tues.-Sat, is free.

BOTANICAL AND ZOOLOGICAL GARDENS. *Will Rogers Park Rose Garden and Conservatory,* at NW 36th St. and Grand Blvd., has a delightful year-round display. The *Lincoln Park Zoo* features one of the nation's largest collection of hoofed animals and unique mountain gorillas. Also children's zoo.

MUSIC. The *Oklahoma Symphony Orchestra* (performing at the Civic Center Music Hall, 201 N. Dewey) has a fine season's offerings, including a series of classic and pops concerts, and features many outstanding international personalities. Season runs September through April.

STAGE AND REVUES. The *Stage Center* at Myriad Gardens, a strikingly modern downtown structure, offers live theater from fall through spring. *Theater in the round* is performed at The Jewel Box Theatre, 36th and Walker; *summer musicals* are produced by the Lyric Theatre at Oklahoma City University.

SHOPPING. Most of Oklahoma City's shopping will be found in four regional shopping centers—*Crossroads Mall,* 7000 S. Interstate 35; *Penn Square,* NW Expressway & Pennsylvania; and *Shepherd Mall,* NW 23rd & Villa. Unusual stores elsewhere include *Shepler's Western Wear,* just south of I–40 on Meridian, *Northpark Mall,* 12100 North May; and *Tener's,* south of I–40, at Reno and Meridian. Farther north, the new energy-efficient *Quail Springs Mall* features 140 stores. 2501 W. Memorial.

HOTELS AND MOTELS. The price categories in this section, for double occupancy, will average: *Deluxe:* $40 and up, *Expensive:* $30–40; *Moderate:* $25–30; *Inexpensive:* under $25. Most have private clubs.

Deluxe: **Hilton Inn West.** 401 S. Meridian. Convention property with resort atmosphere. Limousine service.

Lincoln Plaza Inn. 4445 N. Lincoln. Meeting rooms, sauna, pool, live entertainment.

Sheraton Inn Airport. 6300 E. Terminal. Hot tub, meeting rooms.

Skirvin Plaza. One Park Av. Turn-of-the-century charmer. Full-service hotel complete with concierge.

Expensive: **Hilton Inn. NW.** 3535 NW Expressway.

Holiday Inn. Four locations. All with dining on premises and recreational facilities.

Howard Johnson's Motor Lodge North. NE Expressway at Lincoln Blvd. (US 66). **Howard Johnson's West.** I–40 at Meridian. Both with dining and entertainment.

Quality Central Hotel. Convenient location. Exercise room.

Moderate: **Los Cuartos Inn South.** 7800 CA Henderson Blvd. Free continental breakfast and popcorn. Pool.

La Quinta Motor Inn. 8315 S. I–35. Free morning coffee and non-smoking rooms available.

Inexpensive: **Sands Motel.** 721 S. Rockwell Ave. Fast foods, free cable TV.

DINING OUT. The price categories in this section are for a complete dinner without drinks, tax or tip and will average: *Deluxe:* $15 and up; *Expensive:* $10–15; *Moderate:* $5–10; and *Inexpensive:* under $5.

Deluxe: **Chez Amis.** 3009 N. Classen. Dinner only. French farmhouse setting, and cuisine featuring trout, duck, veal, and filet.

Les Caveau. 1200 N. Shartel. Elegant dining in a Victorian mansion. Lunch and dinner. Reservations only.

Newport Restaurant. 1200 N. Shartel. Continental cuisine, elegant surroundings.

Raffles, 3103 NW Expressway. Lunch, dinner. Continental cuisine, dancing, svelte atmosphere.

Expensive: **Cowboy's Saloon, Dance Hall and Restaurant.** 4300 W. Reno. Steak and quail cooked over mesquite. Western atmosphere.

Molly Murphy's. 1100 S. Meridian. Steak and seafood. Costumed characters wait on table and also entertain. Dinner only.

Moderate: **Cappuccino's Café 7 Club.** 6418 N. Western. Great quiches in attractive setting. Veal cordon bleu, seafood.

Cattleman's Cafe. 1309 S. Agnew in Stockyards City. Open round the clock. Charbroiled steaks and home-style cooking. Where the cowboys chow down.

Classen Grill. 5124 Classen. Soup, sandwiches, and unusual specialties.

Dakotas. 2801 NW 122nd. Lots of fun. Features brisket, fajitas, and just plain burgers.

Furr's Cafeteria. 2842 French Market. Take your pick in this place with a homey atmosphere.

Queen Anne Cafeteria. Ground flr., United Founders Life Tower (just NW of NW Expressway & May Avenue intersection). Widely varied menu, pleasant atmosphere.

63rd Street Grill. 4217 NW 63. Lunch, dinner and great breakfasts. Interstating variety of food.

Sleepy Hollow. 1101 N.E. 50th. Family-style chicken, good country cooking. Old, established reputation.

Inexpensive: **Johnie's Charcoal Broiler.** 2652 W. Britton Rd. Some of the best hamburgers in town.

Lady Classen Cafeteria. 6903 N. May Ave. Local hangout featuring Dutch apple pie, country-style fried chicken and old-fashioned roast beef. Colonial atmosphere.

EXPLORING OKLAHOMA

Oklahoma, a land of lakes sprinkled with many state parks, is the home of 67 Indian tribes. Remnants of numerous tribes pushed from their original homes by white conquest finally settled in the state; several towns still bear tribal names.

The Five Civilized Tribes—Cherokee, Chickasaw, Choctaw, Creek, and Seminole—were granted most of the eastern half of the state. In Tahlequah, once capitol of the Cherokee Nation, is Tsa-La-Gi, a restored Cherokee village. Each summer *The Trail of Tears,* an outdoor drama about the tragic forced march of the Cherokees to Oklahoma, is performed here.

Sequoyah State Park is named for the Cherokee Indian leader who devised an alphabet for the Cherokee language. (California's great Sequoia redwoods are also named after him.) His cabin is preserved in Sallisaw.

Although each area has its local Indian festivals, Indians from all over the nation converge on Anadarko the third week in August for the annual American Indian Exposition. The city also houses the permanent exhibits of the American Indian Hall of Fame, the Southern Plains Indian Exhibit and Craft Center, and Indian City, U.S.A., with re-created authentic Plains Indian huts and dwellings.

Tourist Lures

The campus of Oral Roberts University with its futuristic architecture draws tourist attention. Adjacent is the City of Faith Medical Center, with a 60-story clinic, 20-story research facility and 30-story hospital. The Philbrook Art Center and the Gilcrease Institute of American History and Art are both legacies of prominent Tulsa oilmen. The Gilcrease collection features art, artifacts, rare books and documents that capture the development of America from the preColumbian era to the works of Frederic Remington, Charles M. Russell, George Catlin and others. On display is the first letter written from the North American continent, by Diego, Christopher Columbus' son.

Will Rogers Remembered

The life and works of Will Rogers are commemorated with dioramas, exhibits, and voice recordings at the Will Rogers Memorial and at the Will Rogers Hotel. Both are in Claremore. The Will Rogers Memorial Rodeo is held in Vinita in mid-August.

If Oklahoma has Indian settlements, it also has forts. Fort Gibson, once the westernmost outpost of the United States, has many of its original buildings remaining; others have been rebuilt. A grave in the nearby National Cemetery is said to be that of Tiana Rogers, Sam Houston's Cherokee wife.

General W.B. Hazen put down the Kiowa and Comanche rebellion from Fort Cobb, where there is now a lake and recreation area. At Fort Sill, the guardhouse where Geronimo was prisoner still stands. And General Custer attacked the Arapaho, Cheyenne and Kiowa Indians from For Supply. At that time the land around the fort was arid; today it contains the third largest lake in western Oklahoma.

Oklahoma's largest lake is Lake Eufaula in east central Oklahoma with 102,500 acres. Lake Texoma on the southern border of the state boasts a 93,000-acre lake and 2,600-acre Lake Texoma State Park are one of Oklahomans' favorite recreational areas.

Alabaster Caverns State Park, in the northwest, has the world's largest known alabaster cave open for public tour. Throughout its many chambers, special lighting effects enhance the transparent beauty of the marble-like rock.

The panhandle, once a no-man's-land, has an exciting heritage. Northwest of Boise City is the dramatic Black Mesa; nearby Kit Carson built Fort Nichols, now in ruins, and the bandit leader Coe hid out on Robbers Roost Mountain. Archaeologists have found this area to be rich in dinosaur bones and tracks.

Other archaeological finds in Oklahoma include the mounds of preColumbian Indians at Spiro, and the runestones left by Viking explorers at Poteau Mountain near Heavener.

Oklahoma means "red people" in the Choctaw tongue, and many Oklahomans today have Indian blood in their veins, and are proud of it.

PRACTICAL INFORMATION FOR OKLAHOMA

HOW TO GET THERE. *By air:* There are direct flights to Tulsa via *Air Midwest, American, Delta, Frontier, Muse, Ozark, Republic, Southwest, TWA, United, Western,* and *Scheduled Skyways.*
By bus: Greyhound, *Trailways* and *Jefferson* serve Tulsa.

HOW TO GET AROUND. *By car: Thrifty, National* and *Budget* as well as independent dealers, offer rental cars. *By bus:* In addition to *Trailways* and *Greyhound,* regional schedules are maintained by *M.K.&0., Oklahoma Transportation, Jefferson* and smaller companies.

TOURIST INFORMATION. Brochures and information are obtainable from the *Oklahoma Tourism and Recreation Department,* 500 Will Rogers Building, Oklahoma City 73105. There are also eleven traveler information centers along major highways.

In Tulsa, the *Visitor Information Center* (located near Will Rogers Turnpike gate on I–44) is operated by the Oklahoma Tourism and Recreation Department. Metropolitan Tulsa Chamber of Commerce operates a Visitor Information Center downtown at 616 South Boston, 918–585–1201.

MUSEUMS AND GALLERIES. *Aline and Cleo Springs:* Sod House Museum. *Alva:* Cherokee Strip Museum and Northwestern Oklahoma, State University Museum. *Beaver:* Beaver City Museum. *Blackwell:* Cherokee Outlet Museum. *Buffalo:* Graff Rock Museum. *Canton:* Cheyenne-Arapaho Museum and Archives. *Chandler:* Lincoln County Historical Society Museum of Pioneer History. *Claremore:* J.M. Davis Gun Museum, Will Rogers Memorial and Museum. *Cleveland:* Triangle Oil and Historical Museum. *Clinton:* Western Trails Museum. *Coalgate:* Coal County Historical & Mining Museum. *Collinsville:* Collinsville Depot Museum. *Coweta:* Mission Bell Museum. *Cushing:* Cimarron Valley Railroad Museum. *Dewey:* Dewey Hotel and Tom Mix Museum. *Drumright:* Drumright Community Historical Society in old Santa Fe Depot. *Durant:* Fairchilds Gallery, Navajo art. *Edmond:* Central State University Museum on campus. *Gate:* Gateway to the Panhandle Museum. *Gore:* Cherokee Courthouse. *Granite:* Ford's Museum. *Guthrie:* Oklahoma Territorial Museum. *Haworth:* Henry Harris home built in 1867. *Healdton:* Healdton Oil Museum. *Heavener.* Peter Conser House. *Indianola:* Old Choate House. *Leedey:* Boswell Museum. *Lindsay:* Murray-Lindsey Mansion begun in 1879. *Medford:* Grant County Museum. *Millerton:* Wheelock Mission Church built in 1846. *Muskogee:* Antiques, Inc., Bacone College Indiana Museum, Five Civilized Tribes Museum, Thomas-Foreman Home, *Newkirk:* Newkirk Community Historical Museum. *Norman:* University of Oklahoma Museum of Art, Stovall Museum of Science & History, Cleveland County Historical Museum. *Nowata:* Nowata County Historical Museum. *Okemah:* Territory Town Museum. *Oklahoma City:* The Arts Place, 6 Santa Fe Plaza; Eighty-Niners Museum, NE 17th & Sts.; Kathleen's Original Dollhouse Museum, 7512 N. Western; National Softball Hall of Fame and Museum; Oklahoma Heritage Center, 201 NW 14th; Oklahoma Museum of Art, 7316 Nichols Road; Overholser Mansion, 405 NW 15th. *Oologah:* Will Rogers Birthplace, Will Rogers State Park. *Pauls Valley:* Washita Valley Museum. *Perry:* Cherokee Strip Museum. *Ponca City:* Ponca City Cultural Center & Indian Museum. *Purcell:* McClain County Historical Museum. *Sapulpa:* Sapulpa Historical Museum. *Shawnee:* Museum of Special Interest Cars, Pottawatomie County Historical Society Museum, St. Gregory's Abbey & College Gerrer Collection. *Swink:* Old Choctaw Chief's House. *Tishomingo:* Arrowhead Museum, Chickasaw Council House. *Tonkawa:* A. D. Buck Museum of Science & History. *Tulsa:* Rebecca & Gershon Fenster Gallery of Jewish Art, 17th Place & Peoria; Tulsa County Historical Society Museum, 2501 W. Newton, on the Gilcrease Museum grounds. Alexandre Hogue Gallery of Art, Tulsa University. *Walters:* Walters Museum. *Warner:* Connors College Museum, *Watonga:* T.B. Ferguson Home. *Waurika:* Chrisholm Trail Historical Museum. *Wewoka:* Seminole Nation Museum. *Woodward:* Pioneer Museum. *Wynnewood:* Eskridge Hotel Museum. *Yale:* Jim Thorpe Home.

HISTORIC SITES. *Ada:* U.S. Senator Robert S. Kerr's Log Cabin Birthplace. *Anadarko:* Indian City, USA, authentic restoration of Plains Indians' villages. *Cheyenne:* Washita Battlefield. *El Reno:* Fort Reno and General Sheridan cabin. *Fort Gibson:* Fort Gibson Stockade, 1824. *Fort Supply:* Established by Custer, *Fort Towson. Gore:* Cherokee Council House. *Guthrie:* Territorial Capital of state with numerous landmarks. *Heavener:* runestones thought to be carved by early Viking explorers. *Hugo:* winter quarters for circuses. *Lawton:* Fort Sill National Historic Landmark, grave of Geronimo. *Madill:* Fort Washita established by Zachary Taylor as area Confederate headquarters during Civil War. *Okmulgee:* Creek Council House Museum. *Pawnee:* Ranchhouse-museum, former home of Pawnee Bill who with Buffalo Bill Cody took wild west shows to Europe. *Ponca City:* Marland mansion. *Rose:* Salina County Courthouse. *Salina:* Choteau Memorial. *Sallisaw:* Cabin of Sequoyah, inventory of Cherokee (the only) Indian alphabet. *Spiro:* Prehistoric Indian Mounds built between A.D. 800 and 1350. *Tahlequah:* Landmarks of Cherokee National Capital and Murrell House, antebellum mansion. *Tishomingo:* Chickasaw Council House erected in 1856. *Tulsa:* Creek Council Oak Tree where tribal councils were first held in 1836. *Tuskahoma:* Choctaw Council House. The state is dotted with nearly 2,000 ghost towns. Information available through the Dept. of Tourism. *Watonga:* T.B. Ferguson Home.

DRINKING LAWS. Liquor is available in package stores, 10 A.M.–10 P.M. except Sundays, holidays, and election days. Private club membership is available through hotels and motels, or by paying a modest fee. Where mixed drinks are not served, you may "bring your own bottle."

SPORTS. In Tulsa, there is almost limitless opportunity for *water sports;* dozens of *golf* courses, and ample *tennis* facilities.

SHOPPING. In Tulsa: *Utica Square,* 21st & Utica; *Southland* and *Southroads,* both at 41st & S. Yale: *Country Plaza,* 51st & Harvard; *The Farm,* a charming rustic shopping center at 5321 S. Sheridan Rd.; *Williams Forum,* downtown; *Woodland Hills Mall,* 71st and Memorial; *Kensington Galleria,* 71st and Lewis.

WHAT TO DO WITH THE CHILDREN. Tulsa has an excellent zoo with a separate Children's Zoo featuring Nocturnal Animal Building, Chimpanzee Colony, and African Savanna. The Robert J. LaFortune North American Living Museum is the newest zoo facility with Indian artifacts, fossils, and minerals. Children's playgrounds exist in almost all state parks and municipal parks.

 HOTELS AND MOTELS. Many have private clubs (the Oklahoma version of a bar) on the premises; guests automatically become members upon registering. The price categories in this section, for double occupancy, will average: *Deluxe:* $40 and up; *Expensive:* $30–40; *Moderate:* $20–30; and *Inexpensive:* under $20. Most have private clubs.

AFTON. *Deluxe:* **Shangri-La.** Resort hotel on Monkey Island, Grand Lake. Airstrip. Horseback riding, hay rides, golf.

ALTUS. *Expensive:* **Ramada Inn.** 2515 E. Broadway. Club, pool, meeting facilities.

ARDMORE. *Moderate:* **Lake Murray State Resort.** 7 mi. S. in Murray State Park. Abundant outdoor trails.

CHECOTAH. *Deluxe:* **Fountainhead State Resort.** In Fountainhead State Park. Overlooks Lake Eufaula. Popular with golfers because of 18-hole course, putting green and pro shop.

CLINTON. *Expensive:* **Tradewinds Best Western.** 2128 Gary Freeway. Hot tub, pool, restaurant on premises.
Moderate: **Silver Cloud.** 1413 Neptune. Restaurant, kitchenettes in rooms.

ENID. *Moderate:* **Lazy H.** 1610 S. Van Buren. Free coffee, pool.
Midwestern Inn. 200 N. Van Buren. Private club, tennis.

LAWTON. *Expensive:* **Montego Bay.** 1125 E. Gore. Captains Cabin Cafe, two pools, saunas, exercise room.

McALESTER. *Expensive:* **Arrowhead State Resort.** 18 mi. N. on Hwy. 69. Blends with forest's natural beauty on Lake Eufaula.

SHAWNEE. *Moderate:* **Cinderella Motor Hotel.** 623 Kickapoo Spur. Pool, whirlpool, supper club.

TAHLEQUAH. *Expensive:* **Tsa-La-Gi Inn.** S. of city on Hwy. 62. Club, restaurant.
Moderate: **Oak Park.** 706 E. Downing St. A great picnic spot complete with grills.

TULSA. *Deluxe:* **Camelot Hotel.** 4956 S. Peoria at Hwy 44. Restaurant.

Hilton Inn. 5000 E. Skelly Dr. Nice dining room, plenty of meeting space, game room.

Lexington Hotel Suites. 8525 East 41 Street. Nice lobby with plenty of plants, heated pool, free breakfast.

Tulsa Excelsior Hotel. Adjacent to Assembly Center. Cable television, spa, restaurant, and concierge.

Williams Plaza. 320 S. Boston. In Williams Center downtown.

Expensive: **Holiday Inn West.** 6109 New Sapulpa Road (I–44). Pool, restaurant.

Trade Winds Central Motor Hotel. 3141 Skelly Dr. Pool, restaurant.

Moderate: **Roadway Inn.** 11521 E. Skelly.

WAGONER. *Expensive:* **Western Hills Guest Ranch.** 9 mi. E. of city on Hwy. 51.

WATONGA. *Expensive:* **Roman Nose State Resort.** 5 mi. N. of city on Hwy. 8. Located on a vast canyon.

WOODWARD. *Moderate:* **Holiday Inn.** US–27 O E. Cable television, restaurant.

DINING OUT. Price categories in this section are for a complete dinner without drinks, tax or tips and will average: *Deluxe:* $15 and up; *Expensive:* $10–15; *Moderate:* $5–10; and *Inexpensive:* under $5.

Note: The lodges listed for Altus, Ardmore, Checotah, McAlester, Wagoner and Watonga are state-owned resorts with restaurants serving generally good food at moderate to expensive prices.

ARDMORE. *Inexpensive-Moderate:* **Bill and Barb's Restaurant.** 1225 N. Washington. Emphasis on Mexican cuisine.

Moderate: **El Palacio.** In the Chief Motel, 914 S. Commerce. Mexican/American cuisine.

BARTLESVILLE. *Expensive:* **The Embers.** 2933 E. Frank Phillips Blvd. Charbroiled steak.

BLACKWELL. *Inexpensive–Moderate:* **Hickory House Family Restaurant.** 213 W. Blackwell. Smoked meats top the menu of steak and chicken treats.

CLAREMORE. *Moderate:* **Hammett House.** 1616 W. Will Rogers Blvd. "Pampered" fried chicken, steak, homemade pecan pie.

EDMOND. *Deluxe:* **Roosevelt Grill.** Main and Broadway. French cuisine, roast duckling and veal specialties. Elegant atmosphere.

ENID. *Moderate:* **Richill's Cafeteria.** Downtown at 221 W. Randolph. Excellent, varied menu.

LAWTON. *Expensive:* **Martins Restaurant.** 2107 Cache Rd. Seafood and steak.

MARIETTA. *Moderate:* **McGeehee's Catfish Restaurant.** 2½ m. W. of town on Hwy. 32, then S. 3 mi.

McALESTER. *Expensive:* **Gia Como's.** 1 m. SE on 69 Bypass at cloverleaf. Charbroiled steaks.

WC Place. 21 E. Monroe. Surf-and-turf menu. Great steaks.

NORMAN. *Expensive:*

Legends'. 1313 W. Lindsey. French, American cuisine. Steak and seafood, baking on premises.
Moderate: **The Red Parriot.** 201 S. Crawford. Reasonably priced eatery with good selection.

PRYOR. *Moderate:* **Thomas'.** 215 S. Mill St. Excellent food and service. Baking on premises.

SHAWNEE. *Expensive:* **Mandarin Garden.** 1814 N. Harrison. Superb Cantonese cuisine.
Moderate: **LaPaloma Garden.** 506 S. Beard. Restaurant encircles ancient elm tree, local favorite. Mexican cuisine.
Van's Pig Stand & Charcoal Room. 717 D. Highland.

TAHLEQUAH. *Expensive:* **Restaurant of the Cherokees.** 4 mi. SW on 62, is owned and operated by Cherokee Nation; specializes in game and fried chicken.
Moderate: **Big Apple Restaurant.** 1001 E. Downing. Charburgers are featured at this home-style restaurant.

TULSA. *Deluxe:* **Benihana of Tokyo.** 3324 E. 51 St. Magical preparation of Japanese favorites at table-side hibachi.
The Chalet. 3030 S. Harvard. Continental.
Montague's. In Williams Plaza. Features Beef Wellington, pheasant vinter, and stuffed lobster tails.
Expensive: **Fountains.** 6540 S. Lewis. Elegant atmosphere, fine rack of lamb, roast duck, homemade breads.
Shadow Mountain Inn. 6151 S. Sheridan Rd. Steak and lobster; great city view.
The Spudder. 6536 E. 50th. Charbroiled steaks, chops, shrimp.
Moderate: **Glass on the Green.** In the Williams Plaza in Williams Center. Continental cuisine, steak and seafood. House carrot cake memorable.
Heritage House Smorgasbord. 3637 S. Memorial Ave. Everything under the sun in nice atmosphere. American cuisine.
Peking Garden. 6625 S. Lewis. Mandarin and Szechuan cuisine.
Inexpensive: **Grandy's Country Cookin.** 6801 E. Admiral Place. American eaterie, serves three meals every day.

WOODWARD. *Inexpensive:* **Buffy's Buffet.** 2704 Williams. Barbecued ribs, broasted chicken. Local hangout.
Rib Ranch. US–270 S. Barbecue in appropriate atmosphere.

TEXAS

Big Cities, Big Parks, Big Everything

Since Houston is the largest and most cosmopolitan city in Texas, it seems only fitting that its two most important sightseeing attractions are massive, both in size and in social implication. The one—the National Aeronautics and Space Administration's Lyndon B. Johnson Space Center—played a key part in the nation's space missions, from the early Mercury flights to the orbiting Skylabs and now is the nerve center for the space shuttle program; the other—Astrodomain, comprising Astrohall, Astroarena, and Astrodome—plays a huge role in entertaining Texans and those who are young of heart, for it is a play world of huge proportions and scope.

Astrohall, one of the world's largest exhibition centers, is a home-away-from-home for conventions, while the $53 million, 66,000-seat Astrodome is home to baseball's Houston Astros and football's Houston Oilers. It hosts the annual Livestock Show and Rodeo in February, and just about any attraction promotion-minded Houstonians can conceive. With its cushioned seats, air-conditioning, private suites, and dining rooms, it truly is fabulous.

Astroworld, now a part of the Six Flags family, is among the nation's outstanding parks for rides, shows and attractions for the entire family, along with Water World, a wet playground especially for the teens.

But it is growth to which Houston's future seems most attuned. The nation's fourth largest city is still considered one of the fastest growing areas in the country. With a projected population of 3.3 million in 1990, concern continues as to where everyone will settle in a county area encompassing only 1,777 square miles.

Fly Me to the Moon

If your first question about NASA's Lyndon B. Johnson Space Center is "Can I see the Mission Control Center?" the answer is "Yes." Several phases of NASA's remarkable operations off I–45 South, 25 miles from downtown, may be visited without special arrangement, or you may pick up a pass at the information desk for a guided tour.

On a self-guided tour you will see moon rocks, spacecraft, skylab trainers and training programs leading to the space shuttle. Tours are free. Tel: (713) 483–4321.

Much of Houston's considerable culture opulence is downtown in the Buffalo Bayou and Allen's Landing area. Here, within a few blocks, will be found the surrealistic Civic Center; the magnificent Jesse H. Jones Hall for the Performing Arts, home of the Houston Symphony Orchestra, the Houston Ballet and the Grand Opera; Sam Houston Historical Park, Tranquility Park, and the renowned Alley Theater and Old Market Square, a renovated collection of old buildings now housing restaurants. A new convention center is scheduled for completion in the late 1980's, not far from Houston's oldest building at 813 Congress.

And you will want to see Houston's famed ship channel. The best views are from the Sam Houston free excursion boat and at the turning basin observation tower in Buffalo Bayou.

A bit to the south of downtown is the University of Houston—second in size only to the University of Texas—which shares academic honors in the city with Rice University.

Houston has not taken a back seat in the field of medicine either. The Texas Medical Center comprises 29 institutions, hospitals, and research centers. The University of Texas' M.D. Anderson Hospital and Tumor Institute is foremost in the nation as a cancer research hospital, while The Methodist Hospital continues making strides in the study of heart disease following the famous 1968 heart transplant performed by Dr. Michael DeBakey.

Half an hour's ride from downtown Houston brings you to the San Jacinto battleground, where a gigantic iron and concrete pinnacle, the tallest masonry monument in the world, rises to a height of 570 feet to commemorate the spot where Sam Houston valiantly conquered Mexico's Gen. Santa Anna. Elevators take visitors to the observation deck. The Museum of Regional History at the base is free, fee for elevator. In the ship channel nearby, the Battleship *Texas* is moored.

PRACTICAL INFORMATION FOR HOUSTON

HOW TO GET THERE. *By car:* Houston, like Dallas, is a focal point of many major roads. Clockwise from the north use: I–45 (Dallas, Huntsville); US 59 (Texarkana, Shreveport, La); I–10 (Beaumont, Port Arthur; I–45 (Galveston); I–10 (San Antonio); US 290 (Austin).

By air: Houston has two airports, the busy Intercontinental and older William P. Hobby. There are direct flights from such world points as Amsterdam, London, Toronto, and Paris. There is a comprehensive service to major cities in the world. Over a dozen cities within Texas are directly linked, and the 50-minute run to and from Dallas takes place 50 times each week day. *Trailways* provides transportation ($6 one way) to and from Intercontinental; limousine service available ($4 and up) from Hobby.

By train: Houston is served three times a week by Amtrak's *Sunset Limited* to New Orleans and westbound to Los Angeles.

HOW TO GET AROUND. *Bus:* Basic charge for the rapid transit bus line is 40 cents with an additional 10¢ for each zone entered. Within the downtown area the fare is 10¢ for shoppers on the buses that run up and down Main St. *By taxi:* Cabs charge $2.10 for the first mile, 88¢ for each succeeding mile.

TOURIST INFORMATION. For literature, information, and directions about the numerous attractions in Houston, visit the *Greater Houston Convention and Visitors Council,* 3300 Main. Tel. (713) 523–5050, or toll free (800) 231–7799 in U.S.; (800) 392–7722 in Texas. There is drive-in service.

MUSEUMS AND GALLERIES. The *Museum of Fine Arts,* established in 1900, houses some of the finest examples of world art and attracts over 750,000 visitors annually. The multistoried, glassfronted *Brown Pavilion* surveys contemporary architecture. Open daily except Monday, guided tours by arrangement. 1001 Bissonnet. Free.

Bayou Bend: early American furnishings from the former home of the late Miss Ima Hogg, daughter of the first native-born governor of Texas, part of the Museum of Fine Arts collection and located at 1 Westcott St. *Contemporary Arts Museum:* contemporary statements in art and industrial design, 5216 Montrose Blvd. *Museum of Medical Science,* a world first in exhibits, displays animated models of the human body. Part of the *Museum of Natural Science* in Hermann Park. Tours at all museums. All museums are free.

HISTORIC SITES. Allen's Landing, where Houston orginated. Shortly after the Battle of San Jacinto, brothers August and John Allen of New York founded a town-site on Buffalo Bayou naming it after the victorious Gen. Sam Houston; Main and Commerce. Christ Church Cathedral, founded 1839, on its present site, 1117 Texas Ave., Sam Houston Park, an outstanding work of the Harris County Heritage Society displaying historical buildings. (Fee for tours offered daily except Monday.)

TOURS. *7K Transit, Adven-Tours,* and *Gray Line Tours* operate daily schedules to popular points. Metropolitan Transit Authority operates Astrodome runs.

HOTELS AND MOTELS. The lodging you select may be new. Houston continues its building trends with new hotels and motels opening at an alarmingly rapid rate in every sector of the city. Listings are in order of price category and are for double occupancy: *Deluxe:* $85 and up; *Expensive:* $65–85, *Moderate:* $40–65, and *Inexpensive:* under $40.

Deluxe: **Adams Mark.** 2900 Briarpark at Westheimer. New. 600 rooms.

Doubletree Hotel. 15747 Drummet. Pool, spa, restaurant, and lounge. Near Intercontinental Airport.

Four Seasons. 1300 Lamar. In Houston Center, connected to new downtown mall, The Park.

Guest Quarters. 5353 Westheimer. Neighbor to the Galleria.

Hotel Meridien. 400 Dallas in Allen Center. Overlooks downtown park.

The Houstonian. 111 N. Post Oak Lane. Resort on Buffalo Bayou. Near Galleria.

Hyatt Regency. 1200 Louisiana. All the luxuries, 1,000 rooms.

Marriott. 2100 S. Braeswood at Greenbriar. Astrodome, Texas Medical Center close.

Stouffer's Greenway Plaza. 6 Greenway Plaza.

The Warwick. 5701 Main. Also, **The Warwick Post Oak.** 2001 Post Oak.

Westin Galleria. 5060 W. Alabama. Prestigious companion to the Galleria Mall. **Westin Oaks.** 5011 Westheimer. Also in Galleria.

Expensive: **AstroVillage Hotel.** 2350 S. Loop W. Next to Astrodome and Astroworld.

Holiday Inn-Downtown. 801 Calhoun. Southeast of downtown.

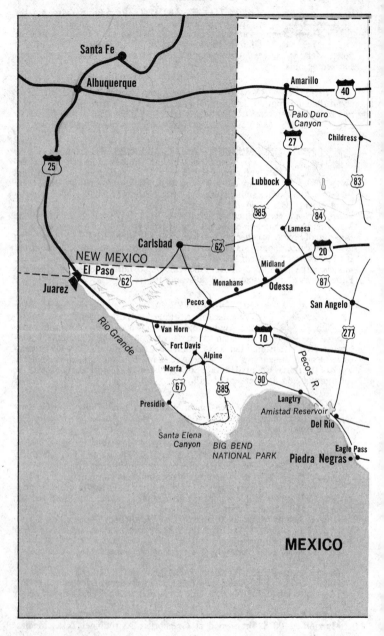

Marriott-Houston Airport. 18700 Kennedy Blvd. 576 rooms at airport.
Shamrock Hilton. 6900 Main at Holcombe Blvd. Trader Vic's dining, lighted tennis complex.
Sheraton Crown Hotel and Conference Center. 15700 Drummet Blvd. Health spa, pools, game room, dining. Near airport.
Sheraton Houston. 777 Polk. Downtown. Big and very good.

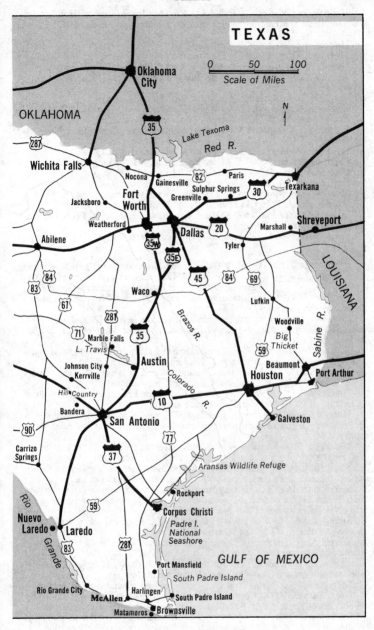

TEXAS

0   50   100
Scale of Miles

N

Oklahoma City

OKLAHOMA

35

Lake Texoma

Red R.

287

Wichita Falls

Nocona

Gainesville

82

Paris

Sulphur Springs

Texarkana

30

Jacksboro

Fort Worth

Greenville

Dallas

Shreveport

LOUISIANA

Weatherford

35W

20

Marshall

Abilene

35E

Tyler

84

45

84

69

83

Waco

Lufkin

67

281

Brazos R.

Woodville

71

Marble Falls

35

Big Thicket

Sabine R.

L. Travis

59

Johnson City

Austin

Kerrville

Colorado

Beaumont

Houston

Port Arthur

Hill Country

10

R.

Bandera

San Antonio

Galveston

90

77

Carrizo Springs

37

Aransas Wildlife Refuge

Rockport

59

Rio Grande

Nuevo Laredo

Laredo

Corpus Christi

Padre I. National Seashore

281

Port Mansfield

GULF OF MEXICO

South Padre Island

83

Rio Grande City

Harlingen

McAllen

South Padre Island

Matamoros

Brownsville

Sheraton Town & Country. 910 W. Belt. Adjacent to mall.
Westchase Hilton. 9999 Westheimer. On the city's west side.
Moderate: **Allen Park Inn.** 2121 Allen Pkwy. View of the Bayou.
Best Western Savoy. 1616 Main. Convenient to shuttle bus.
Dunfey Houston. 7000 Southwest Frwy. Also Dallas location.

Holiday Inn-NASA. 1300 NASA Rd. At Space Center. **Holiday Inn Memorial.** 2100 Memorial. Fringe of town. **Holiday Inn Eastex.** 10525 Eastex Hwy.

Howard Johnson's. 7901 Southwest Frwy.

La Quinta Greenway. 4015 Southwest Frwy. Near Summit.

Quality Inn. 6115 Jetero Blvd. Resort near Intercontinental Airport.

Ramada Inn–North. 4225 North Frwy; **Ramada Hotel.** 7787 Katy Frwy. West side of Houston.

Sheraton Town & Country. 910 W. Belt. Handy to mall.

Tidelands. 6500 S. Main. At Medical Center.

TraveLodge–North. 9025 I–45 N. Pool, wheelchair aids.

Inexpensive: **Crestwood Motel.** 9001 S. Main. Newly remodeled. Near Astrodome.

Days Inn–Webster. 1001 NASA Rd. One. Near Space Center.

Grant Motor Inn. 8200 S. Main. Pool, patio, near restaurants.

Greenway Inn. 2525 Southwest Fwy. 24-hr. coffee shop.

La Quinta–Wirt. 8017 Katy Frwy. Take Wirt exit. Food.

Manor House Motor Inn. 14833 Katy Fwy. 24-hr. restaurant.

Ranger Motel. 2916 Old Spanish Trail. Additional guests $5 each.

Roadside Motor Inn. 8500 S. Main. Group rates 260 rooms. Pool, TV, near Astrodome, Medical Center.

Texas State Hotel. 720 Fannin. Commercial rates. Large.

 DINING OUT. Your Houston dining experience can take in the world. Delicacies from a score of nations head the menu in many famous restaurants while our own favorites lure their followers. Most establishments offer children's servings.

Price categories for a complete dinner range from *Deluxe* $20 and up, *Expensive* $12–20, *Moderate* $7–12, and *Inexpensive* under $7. Not included are drinks, tax or tip.

Deluxe: **Brownstone.** 2736 Virginia. Dine in a setting of candlelight, antiques and the entertainment of a harpist. Located near the Summit.

Charley's 517. 517 Louisiana. Continental cuisine accorded many honors over the past years. The seafood will be long remembered.

Foulard's. 10001 Westheimer. A tradition in fine French cuisine. Member of Academy of Chefs of America. Intimate setting.

Harry's Kenya. 1160 Smith. Continental cuisine in this most unusual downtown spot. African wildlife mounting blend with art to create unusual atmosphere.

The Palm. 6100 Westheimer. Celebrity haven and a must for lobster lovers. Informal atmosphere with a New York speakeasy flair.

The Rivoli. 5636 Richmond. Awards and kudos are common in the Continental place. Superb dining and with elegant service. Piano music.

San Jacinto Inn. Rt. 1 Battleground Road. For the ravenous fresh seafood buff. Since 1917 a historical host to the world. All you can eat at one price. Houston ship channel in San Jacinto State Park.

Shanghai Red. 8501 Cypress on Brady Island. Tugs and ocean vessels pass while you dine in a barnlike structure.

Tony's. 1801 S. Post Oak. When other restaurants are considered deserving they often are awarded "Tonys." Class throughout.

Expensive: **Brennan's.** 3300 Smith. Open seven days and famed for all the specials and great food of the New Orleans banner bearer.

Gaido's. 9200 S. Main. Steaks, chicken, seafood. Founded in 1911.

Great Caruso. 10001 Westheimer. Just one other place like it—in Paris. Old World opera house décor. Excellent cuisine. Fine evening of entertainment.

La Colombe d'Or. 3410 Montrose. Early mansion converted to delightful dinner spot in the world's smallest deluxe hotel. French nouvelle cuisine.

La Hacienda de las Morales. 10440 Deerwood. Dining in the splendor of an 18th-century Spanish hacienda. Continental cuisine.

Look's Sir-Loin Inn. 9810 S. Main. Prime ribs a specialty of Houstonians for years, along with fine seafood. Live entertainment in club atmosphere, Old English décor.

Vargo's. 2401 Fondren. The fun of family-style dining overlooking lush colonial gardens and lake. Flamingos, peacocks, and animals roam in the native habitat. Prime rib is the specialty.

Moderate: **Athens Bar & Grill.** 8037 Clinton. Exciting Greek specialties. Nightly entertainment in seaport atmosphere. Attractive prices and a must for the adventurer. Across from Port of Houston.

Birraporetti's. 1977 W. Gray. Hand-flown New York style pizza and an assortment of pasta dishes. Several locations.

Bono. 5055 Woodway. Sonny Bono-style Italian food. Fresh homemade pasta with innovative daily specials.

Cody's. 3400 Montrose. View from a tenth-floor dining room with indoor and outdoor service. Enjoy the best of jazz band music. Informal.

Fat Ernie's. Plaza of One Allen Center. Downtown deli with sidewalk café featuring super sandwich lundh. European restaurant and bar provide cozy setting.

Kaphan's. 7800 S. Main. A Houston tradition for fresh Gulf seafood and fish specialties. Try the "Dichotomy of Oysters." Delightful garden room.

The Railhead. 6400 Richmond. Old railroad station replica presenting show bands and dancing. Heavy aged beef and Gulf seafood dishes.

Renata's. 2006 Lexington. Tasty northern Italy recipes, personalized service. Live entertainment in garden surroundings.

Tokyo Gardens. 4701 Westheimer. Well-rounded Japanese menu with authentic sushi-sashimi for the seafood buff. Also American preparations. Dances regularly presented.

Inexpensive: **Bavarian Gardens.** 2926 Feagan. It's always Oktoberfest with plenty of the German food favorites with 37 brands of beer.

China Garden. 1602 Leeland. Downtown. For over ten years a Houston favorite.

Butera's on Montrose. Deli-style everything from corned beef sandwiches to hot, café-style meals. A lunch favorite.

EXPLORING DALLAS AND FORT WORTH

As you move down from the northeast, Dallas's skyline rises out of the prairies. Once in the downtown area, you'll have to detour repeatedly around building construction—for Dallas is determined to maintain a respectable lead in business district expansion.

Dallas is second in size only to Houston, and, with Fort Worth, anchors an 11-county Standard Metropolitan Statistical Area comprising 8,360 square miles and 144 incorporated municipalities. Combined population is estimated at 3 million.

Dallas is the Southwest's largest banking center, ranks second nationally in home-based insurance companies, and is one of the nation's top three fashion centers. It also ranks among the first three cities nationally as a convention site.

Sprawling Dallas–Fort Worth Regional Airport, physically the largest in the United States and the world's fourth busiest in scheduled operations, is a partnership of the two cities. Almost a decade after its dedication, the airport has been lauded by the Aviation Safety Institute as one of the five safest in the world. Meanwhile, $200 million is being spent on additional runways. Ten railroads, including Amtrak, serve the area, as do 38 truck lines. Greyhound Lines and Trailways Bus System make intrastate stops on their national schedules.

As Houston is the Gateway of the Southern Tier, Dallas–Fort Worth is the Gateway to the North.

An impressive jewel in the Dallas skyline is the 570-foot Reunion Tower and adjoining 1,000-room Dallas Hyatt Regency Hotel. Atop the 50-story tower is a dazzling sphere, 118-feet in diameter and lighted at night, which streams myriad light designs over the city. A revolving restaurant rides atop the tower, reached by glass-enclosed elevators which whisk diners, bar patrons, and sightseers to an observation deck.

A few blocks east is the new Dallas City Hall and Park Plaza, and the expanded Dallas Convention Center. This area, extending the downtown west and south, includes a new sports arena for basketball, tennis, and other events, plus a library.

In the "heart" of downtown is Thanks-Giving Square, a triangular block at Pacific, Ervay, and Bryan, where three large bronze bells are positioned in a 50-foot tower. Fountains, waterfalls, and carpeted lawns offer the visitor sanctuary. The Chapel of Thanks-Giving, a circular structure of white marble, and a Hall of Thanks-Giving add to the solemn beauty.

It's thoroughly in keeping with Dallas's mercantile standing that the Dallas Market Center—a complex of eight unique buildings on some 175 acres within five minutes drive of downtown—should majestically reign as the world's largest wholesale mart, attracting more than a half-million buyers annually.

Imposing Loews Anatole hotel sits, directly across, fronting Stemmons Freeway, and connects with Market Center via an underground walkway. Southward, new and eye-catching expansion sparkles with a high-rise lodging establishment and a Shubert-operated theater. Prestigious shops and inviting restaurants add their charm to the area's attractions.

Plaza of the Americas at Pearl Blvd. and Olive St. is a 442-room deluxe hotel in the European tradition and operated by Truste Houses Forte. With two multi-story office towers it forms a 15-story atrium sheltering an ice arena and two levels of shops and restaurants.

The development has encouraged an expansion in the northeast quadrant of Dallas featuring several highrise office towers.

The development boom has reached the arts in Dallas, as well. An impressive $30 million Dallas Museum of Art opened in January 1984, housing a library, permanent holdings and special exhibitions, including facilities for public educational activities.

Hundreds of people—often busloads of out-of-town school children —daily come to gaze at the former Texas School Book Depository building and walk the grounds of Dallas's Triple Underpass where President John F. Kennedy was assassinated while riding in a motorcade. A polished granite marker is implanted on the approximate site where he was struck down, and nearby is John F. Kennedy Plaza, a 30-foot-high, 50-foot-square cenotaph in memory of the 35th President.

From its highrise structures and observation decks, Dallasites and their visitors can view, and of course visit, Old City Park, a museum of Living History where turn-of-the-century homes, buildings and churches have been assembled and function as an active community. Over 26 buildings, some dating to 1854, are open to guests Tuesday through Friday 10 A.M. to 4 P.M. and afternoons Saturday and Sunday. The park is located south of downtown on St. Paul St. Admission.

Playground of the South

Spend a day—or several—at Six Flags Over Texas, a spacious park attractive to all the family. One can leisurely stroll walks, enjoy shopfronts reflecting Texas history, view happenings from comfortable benches, or browse souvenir shops, all in air-conditioned comfort. Over 100 thrill rides to excite tots to teens, along with live entertainment shows. Uniformed college students are everywhere to assist visitors, and the park is scrupulously clean. Six Flags Over Texas is the state's top tourist magnet, attracting some 2.5 million fun-seekers annually.

Other tourist interests near to Six Flags include International Wildlife Park—where visitors may drive through and see wild animals in a natural habitat—and the Wax Museum of the Southwest, where the likenesses of famous people of Texas, the gunmen, and a new display of religious events may be seen. For the sports minded, Arlington Stadium, home of the Texas Rangers of the American Baseball League, is just up the road. These attractions are located directly off I–30 between Dallas and Fort Worth in the city of Arlington. There are also two water sports parks and the Texas Sports Hall of Fame located along the highway.

Gardens and Other Delights

In Fort Worth, a do-it-yourself auto tour, marked with distinctive blue road signs and printed in English, French, Japanese, and Spanish, directs visitors to nearly 20 points of interest. Some of these are: Fort Worth Water Garden Park, three water features in a park of greenery; the Japanese Gardens, so authentic as to have been acclaimed by a visiting group of Japanese journalists; the Botanic Garden, a delight for beauty seekers, and with an unusual "Garden for the Blind"; and venerable but hardy Will Rogers Memorial Center, a many-faceted complex which is the home of the Southwestern Exposition & Fat Stock Show, granddaddy of such shows in a state where rodeo rides a year-long circuit.

And, North Fort Worth, where cattle buying and shipping once flourished, seeks to renew a past, with tourist interest, rodeos in Cowtown Coliseum, western shops, restaurants, and bars. Fort Worth continues to rank as a major ranchman's and oil man's supply center, with a sprinkling of 10-gallon hats and high-heeled boots still to be seen.

PRACTICAL INFORMATION
FOR DALLAS AND FORT WORTH

HOW TO GET AROUND. Dallas: *By bus:* 50 cents fare, charge for additional zones to maximum of $1.25. Exact change required. Bunny-marked Hop-a-Bus operates downtown, 25 cents. Information: Dallas Area Transit (DART), tel. 979–1111.

Fort Worth: City-operated Citran buses charge 75 cents fare. Exact change required. Any bus downtown area free. Texas Motor Coaches operate between the two cities.

By taxi: Dallas boarding fare is $1.30 for first 1/10 mile and 10 cents for each additional 1/10 mile. Fort Worth is $1.30 first ¼ mile, 20 cents each additional ¼ mile. *Airport:* Surtran buses serve both cities and charge $5 to terminal or $7 to hotel.

TOURIST INFORMATION: Dallas: *Visitors Information Center,* Union Station, Houston at Young streets. Phone (214) 747–2355. Fort Worth: *Visitor Information Center,* 700 Throckmorton, phone (817) 336–2491. Arlington: *Convention & Visitors Bureau,* 1801 Stadium Drive East, Tel. (817) 265–7721.

MUSEUMS, GALLERIES AND LIBRARIES. Dallas. Several important museums are at *Fair Park. Texas Hall of State,* erected in 1936 to serve the Texas Centennial, is a stately edifice that displays 400 years of history; the new $30 million *Dallas Museum of Art,* an impressive building with equally impressive displays. *Dallas Health and Science Museum,* instructive displays; *Museum of Natural History* and the *Age of Steam Museum.* All open daily.

Owens Art Center at Southern Methodist University houses the *Bob Hope Theatre,* provided by gifts from the famous entertainer; the *Meadows Museum* (Owen Arts Center) displays 16th-20th-century Spanish paintings, drawing and prints. Mon., Sat. 10–5, Sun. 1–5. Free. and the *Pollock Galleries* features changing art exhibits. The *Meadows Sculpture Garden* displays works of leading 20th-century sculptors. Open daily. Free. Tours arranged.

Fort Worth: *Kimbell Art Museum.* Very impressive. Paintings, drawings, ceramics, and sculpture. Traveling exhibits are often shown. Free. *Fort Worth Art Museum* features 20th-century works. Also home of the *William Edrington Scott Theatre,* presenting Community Theatre offerings. *Museum of Science and History* has the largest children's museum in the Southwest; also a *Planetarium,* with admission to the latter. *Amon Carter Museum of Western Art.* Nationally known and featuring works by Frederic Remington and C.M. Russell. Free.

HISTORIC SITES. *John F. Kennedy Plaza,* Main and Market Sts. block-wide area containing 30 ft. high, 50 ft. square concrete memorial to the 35th President near the site of his assassination in Dallas Nov. 22, 1963.

John Neely Bryan Cabin, Elm and Market Sts., honors the first citizen of Dallas and was built in 1841 of handhewn logs.

Old City Park, Gano St. from 1600 block S. Ervay. Ervay Street bus or by auto south and on St. Paul. An assemblage of renovated homes and buildings and stores open to visitors. Admission.

Fort Worth, founded June 6, 1848, on bluff overlooking Trinity River by small military detachment to protect settlers. Now Heritage Park Plaza.

TOURS. The *Gray Line* operates daily 2½-hour morning and afternoon tours to points of interest in Dallas and Fort Worth and full-day combinations of those tours which originate from hotels in the separate cities. Fares range upward from $11.50 for adults and $5.75 (children under 11) for the half-day tours. *Silver Cloud Tours, Texas Express Tours, Texas Connection,* and *Tours by Stan* offer similar tour schedules at similar prices. There are also special tours to surrounding points like J.R. Ewing's Southfork Ranch. Brochures are available at hotels.

During baseball season the Texas Rangers will run buses to the park from downtown points.

Texas Stadium at Irving, home of the Dallas Cowboys professional football team, is open to tours beginning April 1 through Oct. 31 at 10 A.M. and 2 P.M., Mon.–Fri., and at 11 A.M., 12:30 P.M., and 2 P.M., Sat.–Sun. and holidays. Charges are adults $2 and $1.50 for children under 12. Groups of 25 or more can arrange special tours by phone. Also, special tours may be arranged after Oct. 1.

SPECTATOR SPORTS. *Baseball:* Texas Rangers, American League, play at Arlington Stadium.

Basketball: Dallas Mavericks play in Reunion Arena.

Football: Dallas Cowboys play at Texas Stadium off US 183 at Loop 12.

Golf: The Byron Nelson Golf Tournament is played at Las Colinas Sports Club in Irving. In Fort Worth, the Colonial Invitational is at Colonial Country Club. The Mary Kay Classic (LPGA) play is in Dallas.

Rodeo: The Mesquite Rodeo performs Friday and Saturday night, April through September. The arena is at Military Parkway and I–635 (LBJ). Cowtown Coliseum in the Fort Worth stockyards is the setting Saturday nights for amateur rodeo performers in a September-June indoor season.

Soccer: Dallas Sidekicks play in Reunion Arena November–April. Tickets $3–$7.50.

Tennis: World Championship Tennis Finals at Reunion Arena. Avon Championships (Women) with play at Southern Methodist University.

Wrestling: Matches are staged Sundays at the sportatorium at Corinth and Industrial in Dallas, and on Mondays at Will Rogers Coliseum in Fort Worth.

Texas Sports Hall of Fame, I–30 at Belt Line exit in Grand Prairie. Both the rookie and the old pro will enjoy this. Open daily except Monday. Fans can participate. Adults $3, children through age 12 $1.50.

SHOPPING. On weekdays, noontime turns Dallas into a street fashion-show as thousands of working women leave their jobs for lunch, and, most days, to get in some shopping. The most style-conscious shoppers will be seen toting packages from merchants such as Sanger-Harris, Joske's, Neiman-Marcus, Dillard, Cox, and Stripling. Shoppers also flock to Tandy Center in Fort Worth for its many stores, ice rink, and subway to customer parking lot.

While these stores still have their noontime faithful, they have also developed hardy offspring in suburbia and now extend their greetings from variously designed and architecturally different shopping centers and malls. Among these Fort Worth counts Hulen, Northeast, North Hills, Ridgmar and Seminary South, while Dallas has NorthPark, Town East, Red Bird, Valley View, Galleria and Prestonwood Mall. In Arlington, the Six Flags Mall, 2801 E. Division, and Forum 303 at the intersection of Texas 303 and 360, are exciting.

 WHAT TO DO WITH THE CHILDREN. *Six Flags Over Texas,* I–30 at Arlington between Dallas and Fort Worth. Over 100 rides and shows, all for a single admission price. The Texas Cliffhanger and Roaring Rapids lure the thrill-ride brigade, with Pac-Man Land providing special fun for the younger set. Group rates and two-consecutive-day rates.

Sandy Lake at Carrollton, north of Dallas on I–35, take Sandy Lake Road exit. Some 20 rides, including stagecoach, ponies, train, miniature golf, paddle boats, arcade.

Penny Whistle Park for the under-12 set. Thursday through weekends. 10717 E. Northwest Hwy. at Plano Road.

Carousel Raceway, Jupiter at Garland Road. Indoor race course, with electric go-carts, coin-operated arcade, billiards.

Midway rides and games are open Fri., Sat., Sun. during the summer at *Fair Park,* Second Ave. and Parry Ave. Kiddie rides are featured in a special section. Free admission to park except during State Fair of Texas in October. Other park attractions include the Aquarium, with over 300 species of amphibians, fish, and reptiles; Age of Steam Railroad Museum, early freight and passenger cars, engines and original Dallas passenger station. Open Sundays. Admission.

Antique fire-fighting equipment, including a steam pumper from the days when, are displayed on Parry Ave. across from the Fair Park entrance. The museum is housed in a working fire station which has a little history of its own. Open daily.

Dallas Zoo in Marsalis Park at 621 E. Clarendon is "home" to rare and interesting animals and birdlife. Open daily. Petting zoo for the small fry.

International Wildlife Park, 601 Wildlife Pkwy., off I–30 in Grand Prairie. A drive-through animal park. Entertainment, rides, paddle boats, souvenirs, snack bar, and picnic area. Open daily March through November.

Wax Museum of the Southwest, 601 E. Safari Pkwy., off I–30 in Grand Prairie. Famous history-makers appear, life-size, in wax. See Alamo heros, war leaders, Indians, gunmen, marshals, outlaws, politicians. Religious scenes are outstanding and include the Last Supper.

Fort Worth boasts of its zoological park with aquarium, herpetarium, and rain forest housing exotic birds. There's a special zoo for the children. Exit off I–20 at University Drive south.

Forest Park Rides. Miniature train in Forest Park runs five-mile course.

Children's Museum, 1501 Montgomery. Large cultural center designed primarily for children.

Kow Bell Rodeo at Mansfield, south of Fort Worth, 8 P.M. every Saturday in indoor arena. Children join in audience participation.

Sesame Place, off Hwy. 183 at Esters Rd. in Irving. More than 30 indoor/outdoor activities for parents and children, geared toward learning through participation. Based on famous PBS TV show, "Sesame Street." Admission: children (over age 2) $7.50, adults $5.50. Open daily in the summer and Wed.–Sun. in the fall.

Stockyards in North Fort Worth. Walk the area made famous by cowboys, attend a cattle auction Mon.–Thurs. at the Stockyards Exchange Bldg.

Trader's Village Flea Market, 2602 Mayfield in Grand Prairie. Famous Texas flea market and RV park with special family-oriented events. A real biggie in the Arlington entertainment area.

HOTELS AND MOTELS in the metropolitan area include those in Dallas, Fort Worth and Arlington, which lies between the two and where lodging generally caters to visitors to Six Flags Over Texas.

Price categories, for double occupancy, will average: *Deluxe:* $85 up; *Expensive:* $65–85; *Moderate:* $40–65; *Inexpensive:* under $40.

DALLAS. *Deluxe:* **The Adolphus.** 1321 Commerce. Open following interior and exterior revamping.

AMFAC Hotel. Dallas/Fort Worth Regional Airport. Largest airport hotel in the nation. Full service restaurants, lounges, discotheques.

Doubletree Inn. 8250 N. Central Expressway. Gleaming 302-room hotel to side the gold towers of Campbell Centre.

Fairmont. Ross and Akard Sts. Venetian Room presents name entertainment while Pyramid Room recipient of many restaurant awards.

Hyatt Regency Dallas. 300 Reunion Blvd. Thirty stories showcased around 19-story atrium. Dining, lounges. Conventions.

Loews Anatole Dallas. 2201 Stemmons Frwy. Two impressive atria. Restaurants, lounges, one thousand rooms., suites. Spacious, lighted, parking.

The Mansion. 2821 Turtle Creek Blvd. Exclusive restaurant-club and 120-room luxury hotel operated by Club 21 management.

Marriott. 2101 Stemmons. 500 rooms, suites. Across from Market Center.

Plaza of the Americas. 650 N. Pearl St. Complex includes 442-room hotel, office towers, ice arena, restaurants.

Sheraton–Dallas Hotel. Southland Center at Olive and Pearl sts. Recently remodeled.

Expensive: **Dallas Hilton.** 1914 Commerce. Downtown convenience. Also **Hilton LBJ,** 4801 LBJ (I–635) Frwy. Restaurant, lounge, pools.

Marriott Airport. 7750 LBJ Frwy. New.

The Plaza Hotel. 1933 Main at Harwood. Across from Old City Hall. Restaurant, lounge, beauty shop.

Summit. 2645 LBJ. A leader in the move for luxurious lodging out from downtown. Lounge-club active in entertainment.

Moderate: **Grenelefe Hotel.** 1011 S. Akard. Top-floor dining affords city view. Lounge, pool.

Holiday Inn-Downtown. 1015 Elm. Dining, lounge, pool, entertainment. Fourteen area locations.

Inexpensive: **Days Inn.** 9386 LBJ Frwy. (I–635). Restaurant, September Days Club. 290 units. Eight area locations.

Rodeway-Central. 4150 N. Central Expressway. Near downtown. Three other area units.

Town House Motor Hotel. 2914 Harry Hines Blvd.

FORT WORTH. *Expensive:* **Americana–Fort Worth.** 200 Main St. Two- and three-room suites.

Hilton Inn. 1701 Commerce. Gourmet dining, lounge, disco, patio bar. Plus pools, sauna, airport car.

Hyatt Regency Fort Worth. 815 Main St. Adjacent to Convention Center.

Moderate: **Best Western Metro Center Hotel.** 600 Commerce St. **Best Western Green Oaks.** 6901 W. Freeway. I–20 and US 183. Restaurant, lounge, pool, near golf, lively.

The Blackstone. 501 Main. Downtown, two-, three-rm. suites.

Holiday Inn Midtown. 1401 S. University. University exit south off I–30. Restaurant, lounge. Botanic Gardens adjacent. Also **Holiday Inn Northeast,** I–820 and US 183.

Howard Johnson's. 5825 S. Freeway (I–35W). 24-hour restaurant.

Ramada Inn-Central. 2000 Beach. Pool, golf, tennis, exceptional lounge, heliport, health spa, babysitting. Also 4201 S. Freeway.

Inexpensive: **Days Inn.** I–35W at Felix St. Also at I–20 and Las Vegas. Dining, gasoline both locations. Pets.

Downtown Motel. 600 N. Henderson Two-rm. suites also available.

Motel 6. 6401 Airport Frwy. Also locations north, south, and west city areas.

Quality Inn South. 4201 S. Freeway

Rodeway. 1111 W. Lancaster. Restaurant, entertainment, golf.

TraveLodge. 6855 E. Lancaster on US 80. Dining, lounge, pool, entertainment.

ARLINGTON: *Moderate-Expensive:* **Best Western Great Southwest Inn.** 3501 E. Division. Also **Best Western Turnpike Motor Lodge,** 2001 E. Copeland. Full services.

Flagship Inn. Texas 360 exit north off I–30 to Ave. H East. Golf, lighted tennis.

Moderate: **Caravan Motor Hotel.** 908 E. Division. Pool, dining, lounge.

Holiday Inn of Arlington. 903 N. Collins. Restaurant, pool, club.

Kensington Apts. Motor Inn. 1220 W. Division. 76 units. (Formerly Lexington Apts.)

Kings Inn. 1717 E. Division. Kitchenettes included among over 100 units.

Metro Park Inn. 1000 N. Watson Rd. 176 units. Dining.

Ramada. 700 E. Lamar off I–30 and FM 157. Dining, lounge, pool, tennis. Handicapped facilities.

Red Carpet Inn. 1175 N. Texas 360. Full services.

Rodeway Inn. Texas 360 at I–30. Lounge, entertainment. Conference rooms. 350 units. Two pools.

Inexpensive: **Friendship Oasis Motel.** 1818 W. Division. Restaurant near. Pool.

La Quinta. 1410 NW 19th. Take 19th exit off I–30. 24-hour restaurant, 122 rms.

Mayflower Motel. 1003 W. Division. Some kitchenettes.

Quality Inn—Arlington. 1601 E. Division. Restaurant, lounge, golf adjacent.

Days Inn. 1195 N. Watson Rd. Six Flags one mile.

Value Inn. Texas 360 at Six Flags. Fifty efficiencies among 114 units.

 DINING OUT. In Dallas many restaurants tend to locate along certain streets. Some of these streets are Greenville Ave., McKinney, Mockingbird and Northwest Hwy. Reservations generally needed at Deluxe and Expensive places. Fort Worth has some new restaurants in the stockyards area.

Prices for salad, entrée, and vegetable range from *Deluxe:* $20 and above, *Expensive:* $12–20, *Moderate:* $7–12, and *Inexpensive:* under $7. Not included are drinks, tax and tips.

DALLAS. *Deluxe:* **Café Royal.** Plaza of Americas. 650 N. Pearl. An experience in elegant dining.

Calluaud's. 2619 McKinney. Try Guy Calluaud's braised duck.

French Room. Adolphus Hotel, 1321 Commerce. Old World charm.

Jean Claude. 2404 Cedar Springs. Superior food. One price.

Il Sorrento. 8616 Turtle Creek. Décor, view exciting. Wonderful Italian food.

L'Ambiance. 2408 Cedar Springs. Bringing a new taste to food.

The Mansion. 2821 Turtle Creek. Club 21 dining touch. Lodging.

Old Warsaw. 2610 Maple. Lamb or veal in lemon sauce keeps followers coming back. Many delectable offerings.

Expensive: **Antares.** Reunion Tower. Dine in the sky.

Arthur's. 8350 Campbell Centre. Known for the steaks.

L'Entrecôte. Loews Anatole, 2201 Stemmons. Luxurious.

Old San Francisco Steak House. Stemmons to Walnut Hill to 10965 Composite. See Girl in Red Velvet Swing.

Patry's. 2504 McKinney. French-style pepper steak.

Pyramid Room. Ross and Akard in Fairmont Hotel. the complete place to dine. Numerous awards.

Royal Tokyo. 7525 Greenville. Sushi bar a showplace. American touch to Japanese customs.

Ruth's Chris. 4940 Greenville. Might be the town's best steak buy at $17.50 per.

Southern Kitchen. 6615 E. Northwest Hwy. Family operation. All-you-can-eat shrimp. Chicken, steaks. Also 2356 W. Northwest Hwy.

Trader Vic's. Dallas Hilton Inn, N. Central at Mockingbird. The Trader's Polynesian delights.

Moderate: **Cattleman's.** 2007 Live Oak. Downtown. Steaks naturally.

Crackers. 2621 McKinney. Balcony dining often enjoyable.

Jozef's. 2719 McKinney. Unusual seafood offering.

Kirby's. 3715 Greenville. Ask about the Pig Stands days.

Rib. 5741 W. Lovers La. Barbecue. Pittsburgh Steelers hangout in season.

Sahib. 9100 N. Central Expressway. Indian cuisine at its best.

Stuart Anderson Cattle Co. 7102 Greenville. A newcomer to the Dallas scene with a bargain in steaks.

Inexpensive: **Café Cancún.** 4131 Lomo Alto. Flavor of the Mexican resort.

China Star. 5027 W. Lovers Ln. Interesting selection of Cantonese dishes.

Highland Park Cafeteria. 4611 Cole. War II days favorite. Usually crowded.

Old Spaghetti Warehouse. 1815 N. Market. Downtown. Lunch, dinner. Kids love it.

The Shed. 9600 Overlake. Eat all you want. Steak.

Frank Tolbert's Original Texas Chili Parlor. 4544 McKinney. Widely known newspaperman has a hot story about chili.

FORT WORTH. *Expensive:* **The Balcony.** 6100 Camp Bowie. Luncheon menus change through week. The chef goes continental at night.

Carriage House. 5136 Camp Bowie. Seafood, prime beef specials. Wine list.

Cattlemen's. 2458 N. Main. Years of followers, long lists of awards. Charcoal-broiled steaks, barbecue ribs.

Courtyard. 5718 Locke. Exciting lunch. Dinner reservations helpful.

Lombardi's. Sundance Square. Famous Italian dishes, patio dining.

London House. 4475 Camp Bowie Blvd. Prime rib, steaks, seafood.

Texas Tumbleweed. 1800 N. Forest Park Blvd. Western-style family atmosphere where all steaks are cooked over mesquite.

Moderate: **Bill Martin's 3rd Edition.** Lobsters, catfish, oysters.

Bogard's Bar & Bistro. West Side. New. Excellent appetizers. Beef entrées.

Burgundy Tree. 1015 University. Lunch, dinner daily. Open until 2 A.M.

Caravan of Dreams. Downtown Houston St. New cultural restaurant.

Four Winds. 5650 E. Lancaster. Owner Joe Daniel. Excellent food.

Joe T. Garcia. 2201 N. Commerce. Mexican food served family style.

Petta's. 4255 Camp Bowie. New. Family place. Dinner on order.

Sammy's. 300 W. Central. Just off North Main. Late-night spot.

The Star Cafe. 111 W. Exchange. Hamburgers and lemon-buttered steaks.

Winfield '08. 301 Main in Sundance Sq. New and popular.

Inexpensive: **Angelo's.** In White Settlement area. Famed for ribs.

Calhoun Street Oyster Company. 210 Eighth St. at Calhoun. Fresh oysters daily.

Mi Charrito Ray, 5693 Westcreek. Mexican and very good.

Old Spaghetti Warehouse, 600 E. Exchange. Garlic comes to the stockyards.

Terry's. 902 Houston. Luncheon spot favored for chocolate pie.

EXPLORING EL PASO

El Pasoans consider their city a crossroads and oasis for travelers—some of whom will decide to stay—and this has proved to be true ever since Spanish gold-seekers first trekked to the area in 1581. The city was the site of outposts of European civilization long before the Pilgrims set sail from England. Several early missions still stand. One of these, Ysleta, is the base of Texas' oldest ethnic community, the Tigua Indian Reservation. International bridges connect El Paso with Juarez, a few steps across the Rio Grande.

A three minute cable-car ride carries sightseers 5,632 feet to Ranger Peak atop the Franklin Mountains. From that vantage point one may view three states and two nations, along with the rapidly spreading outlines and contours of El Paso and Juarez themselves.

PRACTICAL INFORMATION FOR EL PASO

HOW TO GET AROUND. *Bus.* Within the city the fare is 50¢, higher in the outlying areas. *Taxi:* Boarding fare is $1, plus 70¢ per mile. *Airport:* limousine $8, less at Juarez International Airport.

MUSEUMS AND GALLERIES. *Wilderness Park Museum,* Trans-Mountain Rd. and Gateway South. Sketches of the life of early man in the region. Indian artifacts. *El Paso Museum of History,* 12901 Gateway West, exhibits of early pioneers. *El Paso Museum of Art,* 1211 Montana Ave., shows works of European masters.

HISTORIC SITES. *Fort Bliss* was originally established in 1848 as a defense post against hostile Indians. It was headquarters for thee Confederate forces in the Southwest. Today it is the site of the U.S. Army Air Defense Center. A replica of the original adobe fort is maintained as a museum of the frontier military era. The *Ysleta, Socorro,* and *San Elizario missions,* built in the 1600s, are still in use. The *Tigua Indian Reservation* represents Texas' oldest identifiable ethnic group. All are located in the El Paso Lower Valley. Visitors are welcome.

TOURS. Several carriers operate morning and afternoon tours to Juarez, including special tours to the bullfights and dog races. There are also bus tours of El Paso. Do-it-yourself driving and walking tour maps may be obtained at the Convention and Visitors Bureau, Five Civic Center. Tel. (915) 534–0600. Passports are not necessary to visit Juarez.

SPORTS. *Parimutuel horse racing.* Betting is illegal in Texas, but there is a winter and spring racing season at Sunland Park, New Mexico, six miles from El Paso and at Juarez Sat. and Sun. afternoons when Sunland moves to Ruidoso, N.M. Dog racing at night. *Dog races,* and the chance to bet on them, are a favorite across-the-border sport, along with the national attraction, bullfighting. The Sun Bowl *football* game in El Paso at end of the year is nationally televised.

WHAT TO DO WITH THE CHILDREN. *Western Playland,* in Ascarate Park and *Magic Landing,* El Paso's answer to Disneyland. Out I–10 East, just past Avenue of Americas, *El Paso Zoological Park,* 4201 Paisano; *Hueco Tanks State Historical Park,* 32 miles northeast on US 62, 180 and Ranch Road 2775, Indian markings and drawings, ruins, picnic area; *Indian Cliff Ranch,* I–10 east 35 miles to Fabens exit, turn left and drive north five miles to ranch. Overnight family trail rides and seven-hour wagon train rides. Restaurant at ranch. *Insights,* 303 N. Oregon. Special learning exhibits of interest to children.

HOTELS AND MOTELS in El Paso perhaps are not as flashy, nor as expensive, as some of their bigger city counterparts, but they are comfortable and convenient. Prices, for double occupancy, are compareed with a state average as follows: *Deluxe:* $85 up; *Expensive:* $65–85; *Moderate:* $40–65; and *Inexpensive:* under $40.

Expensive: **Airport Hilton Inn.** Across from International Airport, 10 minutes to town. Conventions to 800. Restaurant, disco, five pools, putting green, tennis.

Granada Royale. 6100 Gateway east. Consists entirely of three-room suites with kitchenettes. Penthouse restaurant, pool. Therapy pool, sauna. Golf, tennis arranged. Embassy suites available. Limo service.

Moderate: **The Brock.** Airway and Montana. Just opened with suites and kitchens only. Pool, sauna. Residential style.

El Presidente. Centro Commercial ProNaf. Complete services. In Juarez.

Holiday–Airport. 6655 Gateway west; **Holiday-Downtown.** 113 W. Missouri. Live entertainment, dancing, restaurants at both locations.

Holiday–Midtown. 4800 Gateway East. New.

Marriott. 1600 Airway Blvd. Pool, sauna, exercise facility, gourmet restaurant. Airport courtesy car.

Ramada-Airport. 6099 Montana. 24-hour restaurant, disco, lounge, playground. Airport courtesy car.

Inexpensive: **Best Western Caballero Motor Hotel.** 6400 Montana and **Econ-Lodge,** out Dyer, near Ft. Bliss.

Colonia Motor Hotel Best Dollar. 8601 Dyer. Pool, restaurant, lounge, kitchenettes at Colonia. Truck parking.

Del Camino Motor Hotel. 5001 Alameda Ave. near river.

Executive Inn. 500 Executive Center. Fine restaurant, lounge, pool, pets.

Hotel Gardner. 311 E. Franklin. Very inexpensive. Color TV only extra.

Howard Johnson's. 8887 Gateway east. 24-hour restaurant, lounge, pool, meeting rooms. Courtesy car.

La Quinta. 6140 Gateway East. 24-hour restaurant, lounge. Baby sitting. Meeting rooms. Also at 11033 Gateway West, and I–10 in Mesa (new).

Rodeway. 6201 Gateway west. Restaurant, lounge, golf, tennis near. Facilities for handicapped. Pets. Shopping center across street.

Sheraton El Paso. 325 N. Kansas. 117 rooms, suites. Restaurant, lounge, heated pool.

Texan Motor Inn. I–10 near Farah's. Brand new.

TraveLodge Central. 409 E. Missouri. Restaurant, pool. Wheelchair aids.

TraveLodge Downtown. 1301 N. Mesa; also 6301 Montana. Both have pools, coffee only on Montana.

Tom Penny Inn. 7144 Gateway E. Pool, restaurant.

 DINING OUT in El Paso is enhanced by the Mexican influence on most menus or by simply crossing into Juarez to patronize one of the excellent restaurants there. One surprise is authentic German food brought about by the presence of German troops training there. Price categories are as follows: *Deluxe* $20 up, *Expensive* $12–20, *Moderate* $7–12, and *Inexpensive* under $7. Prices are for a complete dinner but do not include drinks, tax or tip.

Expensive: **Cooper's at Stanton.** 508 N. Stanton. Gourmet continental cuisine. Reservations required for dinner. Cooper's adjoining café/bar is less expensive.

Moderate: **Billy Crew's.** 3614 Doniphan. Steaks are the house specialty. Excellent service.

Buck's Bar-B-Q. 9496 Dyer. Barbecue spot is a favorite with El Pasoans.

Carlos and Mickey's. 1310 Magruder. Mexican dishes with variety. Big steaks.

The Cinders. 2280 Trawood. Charcoaled prime rib, steaks. Seafood. Fireplaces. Piano bar, lounge. Appetizers.

Cattleman's Steak House. I–10 southeast at Indian Cliffs Ranch, a 30-minute auto drive. Ranch surroundings add to good dining atmosphere. And the steaks are big.

Gunther's Edelweiss. 11055 Gateway W. Oktoberfest all the time.

Happy Bavarian. 8168 Alameda. German food. Reservations a day ahead.

Iron Tender. 1270 Giles and west side on Executive Blvd. Steaks and seafood. Bar entertainment.

Miguel. 600 N. Oregon downtown. Dancing; steaks and seafood.

Moon Garden. 4675 Montana. Cantonese cuisine, along with American fare.

Pelican's. 9077 Gateway E. and 130 Shadow Mountain. Seafood.

Peppertree. 5411 N. Mesa. Crêpes are specialties, also steaks, seafood.

State Line. 1222 Sunland Park. Brisket, ribs, sausage served in generous portions with potato salad, coleslaw.

Inexpensive: **Fortis' Mexican Elder Centro.** Premier Tex–Mex eatery.

Griggs. 9007 Montana. Mexican food enthusiasts are in for a treat and a new taste.

Leo's Mexican Food. Six locations, and the food is uniform and plentiful.

In Juarez: Moderate: **Casa de Sol.** Many delights for across-the-border visitors. ProNaf Center.

Florida. Serving five generations of Mexicans and Gringos.

Shangri-La. 133 Ave. de las Americas. A variety of Cantonese and Chinese dishes served in rich Oriental setting.

EXPLORING SAN ANTONIO

San Antonio is Spanish and Mexican, not only in its heritage, but in its daily routine. But while its setting is palm trees and banana plants, and parts of the city seem basically sleepy in its outlook on 20th-century life, the lure of San Antonio lies in its resistance to easy description. It is an amalgam of old and new, of ox-cart and intercontinental missile, of broiled cabrito and steaks tartare; and to understand the city you must accept the contradictions. Indeed, San Antonio deservedly is called one of America's "four unique cities."

Your tour of San Antonio—whether you choose a sightseeing bus, your own car, or a walking visit to downtown points—will begin, of course, with the Alamo, alive with the story of Travis' arrogant defiance of the Mexicans, of Crockett and Bowie and the rest of the reckless and valiant 188 men who made a shambles of a mighty army before they fell under sheer weight of numbers.

From the Alamo you'll find the River Walk, or Paseo del Rio, as it is now referred to, with due regard for the melodious Spanish equivalent. If you have an eye for tropical splendor, walkways bordered by quaint shops, art galleries and eating places, you'll love the Paseo del Rio. The cuisine features Mexican, Italian, and French food and a couple of elegant steak houses, not to mention the dining rooms of several fine riverside hotels. Outdoor dining is enjoyable every month of the year.

You can hire a pedal boat—and pedal yourself up and down the river, seeing all its sights at leisure—or board one of the many sightseeing boats for relaxed enjoyment or to make an impressive entrance at the city's Convention Center. Again, you may relish an evening of dining on the boats serenaded by Mexican musicians.

You'll especially enjoy the Arneson River Theater, where performers undertake every kind of production on one side of the river, and the audience applauds from the other. Some of the most dramatic speaking parts are interrupted from time to time by the passage of some kind of riverboat—but this only adds to the gaiety.

It's still walking distance to La Villita—where you'll cross suddenly over into 18th-century Spanish Texas. La Villita (pronounced Lah Vee-YEE-tah) is a charming city within a city, standing in the very shadow of downtown skyscrapers, a block-square restoration of San Antonio as it was in the time of Bowie and Travis or even before. Many of the skills and crafts of the very early San Antonio days are still practiced at La Villita—and if you have an eye for blown glass, pottery bowls and the like, you'll find a beautiful assortment here. Free brochures describe nearly 20 fascinating structures, sites and places of interest.

On Military Plaza, directly behind City Hall, is the old Spanish Governor's Palace; a statue of Texas pioneer Moses Austin stares down on the palace. Inside the adobe walls that surround the palace the

Spanish governors of Texas brightened a wilderness frontier with fantastically colorful balls and parties.

On the southeast corner of HemisFair Plaza in a modern structure stands the impressive Institute of Texan Cultures, a living tribute in sight, sound, and often taste, to the 26 ethnic groups that make up present-day Texas. Free parking and admission except during the Texas Folklife Festival in early August.

The Mexican Cultural Institute and the San Antonio Museum of Transportation are in HemisFair.

The Hall of Texas History Wax Museum (formerly at the Hemisphere) and the outstanding Buckhorn Hall of Horns are located at the nearby Lone Star Brewery, 600 Lone Star Blvd. Both are open daily; minimal admission.

You need walk north from Villita St. only one block on St. Mary's to Market St. to see another of the wildly improbable attractions that make San Antonio world-famed. This is the much admired Hertzberg Circus Collection, housed in the original Public Library. The collection includes circus artifacts from every period of American development. The collection begins with the circus pretensions of King George III of England, and continues through the heyday of Phineas T. Barnum to the present time. Here you'll find Tom Thumb's original carriage—and, in one room, a complete circus, in miniature.

El Mercado, Mexican market area on W. Commerce St., exudes charm with a variety of shops and restaurants, among the latter an inviting indoor-outdoor oyster bar housed in a restored turn-of-the-century building on Produce Row. The City of San Antonio and private enterprise separately are active in a blending of early-era structure renovations and new construction in several areas. An example is the affluent and prestigious San Antonio Museum of Art, taking up quarters in a nearly 100-year-old renovated brewery. Several new or expanded hotels also add to visitor comfort.

And, tying the downtown points together, small, colorful streetcars run on ten-minute schedules with passengers boarding for a dime.

Leaving downtown, you should find time to visit the Sunken Garden in Brackenridge Park, and the adjacent and widely renowned San Antonio Zoo. At Brackenridge Park, too, is the splendid Witte Museum, and farther out, the McNay Art Institute showing graphic art, sculpture and tapestries among other objects. The military influence upon San Antonio culture and growth is great and there are worthwhile military-related museums open to the public without charge at Fort Sam Houston, Brooks Air Force Base, and Lackland Air Force Base. The South Texas Medical Center in northwest San Antonio assumes a vital role in the area's economic, health and educational life.

Starting with the Alamo, you'll want to see all of the missions Concepion, San Juan Capistrano, San Francisco de la Espada, and San Jose—reflecting their 18th-century glories.

PRACTICAL INFORMATION

FOR SAN ANTONIO

HOW TO GET AROUND. *By bus:* VIA Metropolitan Transit Service (tel. 227-2020) will provide schedule information on city routes. Fare is 40 cents and 10 cents extra for outlying zones. San Antonio streetcars operate downtown for 10-cent fare.

By taxi: $1.85 first mile, 80 cents each added mile. *Airport:* Taxi $8.25. Airport express buses operate 5:43–9:21 A.M. (no mid-day service) and 3:57–6:19 P.M.

TOURIST INFORMATION. Complete details on city attractions, special events, tours and other data are available from the San Antonio Convention & Visitors Bureau, P.O. Box 2277, San Antonio 78298. Call toll free (800) 531–5700 outside Texas and (800) 292–1010 inside Texas. Across from the Alamo, a Visitor Information Center provides maps and directions. Tel. 299–8155.

SEASONAL EVENTS. Perhaps more accustomed to sombreros, San Antonians don cowboy hats the second weekend in February for a 10-day Livestock Show and Rodeo at Joe Freeman Coliseum, held annually for three decades. Fiestas are held for any occasion, and so St. Patrick's Day is celebrated —for a week—with green dye coloring the San Antonio River, the city's Irish parading, and bartenders serving green-colored beer. Then paints, brushes, and easels are in style for the Starving Artists Show on the River Walk. April finds the socially-elite in jodhpurs and proper raiment for the annual Charity Horse Show. For ten days around April 21, Fiesta San Antonio's parades and pageantry noting Sam Houston's victory at San Jacinto attract national attention. The San Antonio Festival, an international performing arts festival, takes place at theaters downtown during June. Fiesta Noche del Rio takes the Arneson River Theater stage Tuesday, Friday and Saturday nights in June and July, along with Sunday night performances by the Ballet Folklorico. July fun is increased with Fun-Tier Nights musical programs in La Villita each Wednesday. August brings the statewide ethnic attraction Texas Folklife Festival to the Institute of Texan Cultures, and September is highlighted by Diez y Seis de Septiembre (September 16), Mexico's Independence Day. A River Art Show in October attracts statewide entries; and then San Antonio interests focus on the Christmas season and programs at El Mercado, home pilgrimages, Riverwalk decorating, processions depicting the Holy Family's travels, and Fiesta de las Luminarias with candles lighting the river.

MUSEUMS AND GALLERIES. *San Antonio Museum of Art,* 300 W. Jones Ave., in a renovated brewery complex going back nearly 100 years. *Witte Museum,* 3801 Broadway, now directed to the preservation and display of Texas and area history. *Buckhorn Hall of Horns,* and *Hall of Texas History Wax Museum,* 600 Lone Star Blvd. Outstanding, and impressively displayed, collection of horns, antlers, tusks of Texas-area big game, along with exhibits of fins and feathers of fish and fowl. *Museum of Transportation,* the automobile then and now; *Institute of Texan Cultures,* representing the 26 ethnic cultures of Texas; *Mexican Cultural Institute,* work of artists of Mexico. All in Hemis-Fair Plaza. *McNay Art Institute,* 6000 N. New Braunfels. A private museum showing priceless works.

HISTORIC SITES. The Alamo, built in 1718 and often referred to as the "Cradle of Texas Liberty," is in the downtown area. Other missions of circa 1700 are to be found along "mission row." The Spanish Governor's Palace, an 18th-century structure is typical of the buildings in Colonial Spain. Moses Austin came here in 1820 for permission to bring a colony of U.S. citizens into Spanish Texas. King William Historic District at King Williams St., and S. St. Mary's St., comprises restored Victorian and early Texas homes of the 1870s. Jose Antonio Navarro State Historic Site, 228 S. Laredo, home of the Texas patriot and signer of the Texas Declaration of Independence. La Villita, where the past lives on.

MUSIC. The Symphony Society of San Antonio sponsors the Grand Opera Festival, presenting the great operas with internationally known performers, and the San Antonio Symphony Orchestra.

TEXAS

662

SPORTS. The San Antonio baseball team performs in the Texas league; the San Antonio Spurs perform in the National Basketball Association; and the San Antonio Gunslingers participate in the United States Football League. Four 18-hole public golf courses are available. The Texas Open Golf tournament in September is the state's oldest. The San Antonio Recreation Dept. maintains McFarlin Tennis Center, offers 22 lighted courts.

WHAT TO DO WITH THE CHILDREN. Brackenridge Park, 2800 block N. Broadway, is an adventure for a full day or several. There are 343 acres and something exciting with every step—the Aerial Skyride, the Brackenridge miniature train that runs for three miles. And the San Antonio Zoo is right at hand and rated one of the best in the country. Some 4,500 animals, birds, and reptiles. The Hertzberg Circus Collection, 210 W. Market, is for circus lovers of all ages. The collection includes 20,000 items, making up a complete miniature circus right down to the various wagons, sideshow tents and big top. The carriage of performer Tom Thumb is displayed.

HOTELS AND MOTELS in San Antonio range from the storied Menger to the palatial Hilton, and include new or expanded La Villita and river-area lodgings. Price categories, for double occupancy, are: *Deluxe:* $85 up, *Expensive:* $65–85; *Moderate:* $40–65; *Inexpensive:* under $40.

Deluxe: **Four Seasons.** 507 E. Nueva. Pool. Handicapped aids.
Gunter Hotel. 205 E. Houston. The "Grand Duchess" triumphantly returns.
Hilton Palacio del Rio. 200 block Alamo St. Balcony views.
Hyatt Regency. 123 Losoya. Rims exciting river turn. 633 rooms. New. River flows *through* hotel!
Marriott Hotel. 711 E. Riverwalk. Dining and lounges overlook the river.
St. Anthony Intercontinental. 300 E. Travis. On the scene since 1909; just remodeled.
Expensive: **La Mansion del Norte.** Loop 410 at McCullough. Near airport.
La Mansion del Rio. 112 College St. On the river, 353 rooms.
Moderate: **El Tropicana.** 110 Lexington, on river downtown.
Granada Inn. 402 S. St. Mary's St. by the river. Pool, dining.
Holiday Inn-Airport. 77 NE Loop 410. Exit Airport Blvd.
La Quinta Downtown. 1001 E. Commerce. Home base for the La Quinta chain started in San Antonio in 1968 and now counting eight other city locations.
Marriott Inn. 6111 NW Loop 10. New night club.
Menger. 204 Alamo Plaza. Teddy Roosevelt recruited Rough Riders here.
Sheraton San Antonio. 1400 Austin Hwy. Golf, tennis.
Inexpensive: **Park Plaza.** 2908 Broadway. Near Brackenridge Park.
Ramada North. 1131 Austin Hwy., south of Loop 410. Pool.
Rodeway Downtown. 900 N. Main. Three additional locations.

DINING OUT. Whether it's dinner on a riverboat, at one of the many charming places along the Riverwalk or at El Mercado (the market), you'll likely be delighted. Complete dinner prices average: *Deluxe:* $20 up, *Expensive:* $12–20, *Moderate:* $7–12, and *Inexpensive:* $7 under. Drinks, tax, tip not included.

Deluxe: **Anaqua Room.** Four Seasons Hotel, 555 S. Alamo. French cuisine served perfectly.
Fig Tree. 515 La Villita. Beef prevails. Garden dining a delight.
San Angel Room. La Mansion del Norte Hotel. Local favorite.
Expensive: **Arthur's.** 4001 Broadway. Continental cuisine with some divine touches.
Chez Ardid. 7701 Broadway. Family influence kitchen to table.
Crystal Baking Co. 1039 NE Loop 410. Continental food, tasty treats.
La Louisiane. 2632 Broadway. Creole cooking for old and new friends.
La Provence. 206 E. Locust. French cuisine flavored to perfection.
Old San Francisco. 10223 Sahara. Steaks and the girl in the swing.
Moderate: **Bayou's Riverside.** 517 N. Presa. Seafood with a Cajun flavor.

Checkers. 4901 Broadway. American fare simplicity.
Crumpets. 5800 Broadway. American menu with some special delights.
Mama's Cafe. 9903 San Pedro. Large steaks, filling side dishes.
Naples Italian. 3210 Broadway. Around for a long time.
Night Hawk. 7202 San Pedro. Plain American food popular here.
Paesano's. 1715 McCullough. Italian fare, some seafood surprises.
Red Carpet. 107 E. Main. Continental dishes. Wonderful shrimp sauce.
Inexpensive: **Little Bavarian.** 2102 S. Presa. German, fittingly near brewery.
La Margarita. 120 Produce Row. Mexican fare in the market area.
Mario's. 325 S. Pecos. Mexican menu covers breakfast, lunch, dinner.
Mi Tierra & Bakery. 218 Produce Row. Nachos, pastry.

EXPLORING THE REST OF TEXAS

Interstate 35 south from Dallas brings you to Waco, home of Baylor University, established as a Baptist school in 1845. The university is known for its College of Medicine in Houston, College of Dentistry in Dallas, and School of Nursing in Waco and Dallas. It was in Waco that the soft drink, Dr. Pepper, was concocted. I–35 bypasses the city but goes by Fort Fisher Park and the Texas Ranger Hall of Fame. The Waco Tourist Information Center is located at Fort Fisher. Nearby, the riverboat *Brazos Queen* makes pleasure and dinner cruises April through early September. If university sightseeing is an attraction, take Texas 6 southeast from Waco to Bryan-College Station and the campus of Texas A&M University some 85 miles distant. Waco's Brazos River Festival each April re-enacts a Civil War battle.

Westward Ho

Moving west from Dallas through Fort Worth on I–30 (the former toll road), you'll pick up US 80, 181, and I–20, the latter having circled south of Dallas. Sticking to US 180, you'll shortly arrive in Weatherford, the home town of actress Mary Martin. Near the courthouse citizens have erected a statue of her as Peter Pan.

Northward from Weatherford brings you to Wichita Falls, scene of Indian massacres and the U.S. Cavalry riding to the rescue. Indians are not longer a threat, and the Cavalry is long dismounted, but the city has a stout defender in Sheppard Air Force Base, one of the nation's largest training centers. Devastating tornados struck in 1964 and 1979 taking 52 lives.

Just 150 miles southwest of Wichita Falls lies Abilene, itself a strange mixture of modern enterprise and Old West flavor. Three denominational colleges call the city home: Hardin Simmons University (Baptist), McMurry College (Methodist), and Abilene Christian University (Church of Christ). The city also has an outstanding zoo, as well as the ruins of Fort Phantom Hill. Abilene takes its name from the Kansas cattle drive and railroad center.

Moving up from Wichita Falls on US 287 past Childress, brings you into the Panhandle Plains which, until 1870, supported no human life at all. Here the Conquistadores searched for the mythical Seven Cities of Cibola, and the last of the food-giving bison was slaughtered.

Modern-day taming of the Panhandle, and the booming of Amarillo, began with the discovery of oil and natural gas. Today the city claims title as "helium capital of the world," and a Futuristic Helium Monument with Time Capsules is a sightseeing attraction. Lake Meredith is a recreational paradise and the Alibates Flint Quarry National Monument an historical treasure trove. Nearby Boy's Ranch is nationally known.

Twenty-seven miles southeast and you come to the university and museum-famed town of Canyon, gateway to 120-mile-long Palo Duro Canyon, a breathtaking color spectacular and the largest—15,103 acres —of the state's parks. There are camping areas, restrooms, showers, hiking trails, riding stables, and a miniature train for exploring the 1,000-foot-steep canyon floor. The popular outdoor historical musical "Texas," is performed nightly, except Sunday, in the park amphitheater from mid-June through mid-August. "Palo Duro," a light-and-sound production, follows for a month in September.

And on, via I–27, to Lubbock, where, so the story goes, a group of buffalo hunters around a campfire in 1878 took turns making up phrases to the song we now know as "Home on the Range." Regardless, Lubbock is "home" to the prairie dog, with Prairie Dog Town at MacKenzie State Park. It is also home to some 22,000 students attending Texas Tech University. The Ranching Heritage Center at the university is an assemblage of over 20 ranch homes and buildings tracing early life.

There is a story that the city of Midland actually grew from an industrious hunter's selling of antelope meat from an abandoned boxcar. However, it was to be oil, not antelope meat, that would mean prominence and prosperity for Midland and its neighbor city, Odessa. Both are south of Lubbock via US 87 and passing Lamesa, an oil, ranching, and agricultural community, and Big Spring, where Indians once battled for control of the life-giving spring.

The huge Permian Basin oil discovery was made in 1923 and takes its name from a prehistoric inland sea, the Permian. Grateful citizens have erected the Permian Basin Petroleum Museum, Library and Hall of Fame to tell the story of this development. A simulated oilfield fire is a thriller. It is located on I–20.

Down the road a piece is Odessa and a replica of William Shakespeare's original Globe Theatre, where the bard's plays are presented each spring in professional and student productions. Other dramatic presentations enhance the season. The theater, which opened in 1968, was the dream of an Odessa teacher and her student and has entertained audiences of over 250,000. Contrasting civic pride in Shakespeare, Odessans also ballyhoo—with a highway sign—native jackrabbits as the world's largest.

Moving southward from Odessa along I–20 you come to a 4,000 acre sandpile with dunes reaching as high as 70 feet where adults and children happily cavort. Monahans Sandhills State Park has many attractions. Legend holds there's a treasure in gold lost somewhere in the windblown sand, buried seconds before an Indian massacre. And there is treasure—an operating oil well.

The Pecos

Bearing on southwestward, you'll cross the Pecos River and see the town where early-day cowboys engaged in shoot-'em-ups just to relieve the monotony, and the site in 1883 of the nation's first rodeo. Beyond Pecos the land roughens, and purple mountains rise out of the plain. I–10 continues west through Sierra Blanca, then forks right to begin a gradual descent into El Paso (described earlier).

Southeastward from I–10 on Texas 17 and Texas 166, you can probe the Davis Mountains, with history and geology fully recorded on roadside markers. Old Fort Davis National Historical Site and the McDonald Observatory, both inviting visitors, are near. Here Texas 118 takes you to Alpine and further south to Big Bend National Park.

To visit the stamping grounds of Judge Roy Bean, storied "Law West of the Trinity," take US 90 from Alpine to Langtry and a look at the judge's Jersey Lilly Saloon. The state maintains a visitor center there. South on US 90 takes you to Amistad Reservoir, the first of two Rio Grande projects operated by the U.S. and Mexico.

Gateway to Mexico

Highly-spiced Laredo offers almost every form of tourist attraction you can find in Texas. Walking through American Laredo, everything you see reveals a profound Mexican and Spanish background. The Mexican city of Nuevo Laredo is just a short walk over a majestic bridge spanning the Rio Grande. Laredo and Nuevo Laredo observe George Washington's Birthday each February with four days of colorful pageantry, attracting national attention. Nuevo Laredo now offers horse and dog-track betting. Bets can also be placed on U.S. sports events.

Lower Rio Grande Valley

Continuing south from Laredo you pass Falcon Reservoir, the second flood control and water conservation facility benefitting the two neighbor countries. On the American side, Falcon State Recreation Park operates all year and deer and white-winged dove lure hunters in season. Fishing is excellent. Licenses are required.

You are now in the world of the citrus- and vegetable-rich Rio Grande Valley, for a bevy of charming little communities lining the river for 150 miles and catering to visitors from the North. McAllen, Harlingen and Brownsville lead the parade with across-the-border neighbors Reynosa and Matamoros. Hotels and motels, mobile home and recreation vehicle parks abound.

Harlingen, base for the Confederate Air Force (CAF), boasts 1,000 or more former World War II pilots, crewmen and others who are dedicated to the restoration and flying of military aircraft of the period —both American and enemy. These planes—and their history—are displayed at Rebel Field.

And in Brownsville don't miss the world-renowned Gladys Porter Zoo. Some of the many scenic points in and about Brownsville include shrimp trawlers at the port and the delights of Matamoros across the Rio Grande. Port Isabel Lighthouse (built in 1853) State Historic Site toward Padre Island lures photographers.

Of course you'll want to see Padre Island, one-time pirate hangout and a "graveyard" in past years for craft swept ashore by vicious winds and currents in the adjoining Gulf. Despite its association with pirates and shipwrecks, the island took its name from a padre who operated a ranch there in the early 1800s.

Until a couple of decades back, South Padre was left more or less to the hardy—fishermen and some vacationing campers.

You reach South Padre Island via the three-mile Queen Isabella Causeway from Port Isabel. Your introduction to this two-mile-wide sandstrip is a maze of luxurious hotels (the Hiltons and Holidays), condominiums, apartments, beach houses and what not—over 45 establishments having 2,256 rooms. Padre Island is ideal for fishing, boating, swimming and beachcombing. Two county parks and a state park provide camping facilities.

Of Horses and Ships

Leaving Padre and back on 77 north you can visit the largest ranch in the world—the King Ranch, whose headquarters 2 ½ miles from Kingsville anchor a 12-mile road along which ranch points of interest are spaced. Northeast of Kingsville leave 77 and turn right on Texas 44 for a 20-mile breeze into Corpus Christi.

A crisp, clean city of mostly white buildings and smart shops at an upper level, while imposing hotels, motels and restaurants rim the blue waters of the bay, Corpus Christi is a wild combination of industrial vitality and beachfront lassitude. In the bay itself, hundreds of craft of all sizes and values bob restlessly at their moorings, and pleasure cruise and fishing boats invite passengers.

With a new 2,500-seat Bayfront Plaza Convention Center large gatherings are welcomed. Corpus Christi's port, ranked ninth nationally, and spectacular Harbor Bridge attract sightseers. Auto trip maps help you explore Mustang Island and North Padre Island.

Reached by the Kennedy Causeway, a short drive from downtown, Padre opens on a county park and immediately confronts a fabulous development of hotels, condos, country club and golf and residences. Some 14 miles south the visitor comes upon Padre Island National Seashore and Malaquite Beach. Malaquite includes a refreshments pavilion renting all sorts of beach equipment. There is paved parking.

Two routes are open to the driver returning to San Antonio. One shoots north on I-37 to join US 281 coming up from the Valley. The second crosses Harbor Bridge and up 181 and through Floresville, home of former Gov. John Connally.

Again in San Antonio, Texas 16 northwest leads you through scenic hill country to Bandera, center for a spread of fabulous guest ranches. Visit one if you can. Texas 173 cuts north to Kerrville, passing Camp Verde where the U.S. Army once tried camels for transport. An Arts and Crafts Fair each May brings thousands of people to Kerrville. Picking up Texas 16, it is a short drive to Fredericksburg, where the Admiral Chester W. Nimitz Center honors the World War II hero.

US 290 slices east to Austin, but you'll want to stop at Stonewall and Johnson City to see the ranch and boyhood homes of the late President Lyndon B. Johnson.

Another choice from San Antonio is I-10 north to Boerne, site of Cascade Caverns and the Civil War-era Kendall Inn, then east over Texas 46 to New Braunfels, famed for its Wurstfests each November and the nearby Natural Bridge Caverns. Take I-35 to Austin, but plan to see Aquarena Springs and Wonder Cave at San Marcos.

Whatever your route, pack plenty of film for the camera.

A Capital City

Capital city and home base for the rapidly spreading University of Texas system, Austin sits in the very center of the state, rated by environmentalists as among the nation's most livable areas and cited for moderate living costs.

A chain of seven lakes extends north 150 miles.

The city's population is estimated at 352,000 in a state of 14,152,339 souls. Principal landmarks are the red granite Capitol, the University of Texas tower, and the Lyndon Baines Johnson Memorial Library, a leading attraction among scholars and tourists.

Austin is a city worth knowing, so spend as much time as you have to get acquainted. Many interesting points on a walking tour are convenient from downtown lodging. The original section of the Driskill

Hotel, built in 1885 and always popular with the political crowd, at times seems to function as an "unofficial" state capital. There are tours of the governor's mansion.

East from Austin, along US 290 on the way to Houston, you will cross the Brazos River. It was at Washington-on-the-Brazos, a few miles north, where a group of Texans gathered in March 1836 to declare independence from Mexico and approve a Constitution.

The Strand, an old section of Galveston known in the 19th century as the "Wall Street of the West," is getting that gleam again, and at Galveston Island State Park an adopted Texan named Sam Houston is kicking up an old ruckus as principal figure in an outdoor summer drama, "The Lone Star," presented nightly except Monday, late May through August. "Annie Get Your Gun" plays alternate nights.

The new attractions complement Marineworld, the multimillion dollar showplace with performing fish and animals and displays of birds and fowl in their natural habitat. Large water slides and county "pocket" parks, with picnic tables and showers, round out the fun that can be found along the 30 miles of beach. Historic homes, the Bishop's Palace, and the archives and view of Galveston from the 20-floor American National Tower add to the lure of this charming old city.

I–10 from Houston takes you to Beaumont, known for its port—the state's third largest in tonnage—and as the site of the Lucas oil well gusher, which blew in at Spindletop on January 10, 1901 to change the way of life of a state and nation. The Lucas Gusher Monument, a national historic landmark, is located at Gladys City-Spindletop Boomtown, the latter a living replica of an oilfield boomtown, at Cardinal and University Drives.

From Beaumont, US 69 and 287 to Woodville and US 190 (left turn) takes you to the Alabama-Coushatta Indian Reservation, open daily June through August. *Beyond the Sundown,* an outdoor historical drama, is presented nightly except Sunday, mid-June through August.

Leaving the reservation, follow US 190 to Livingston and go north on US 59 to historic Nacogdoches, over to Carthage, and Marshall and Jefferson and Texarkana again.

PRACTICAL INFORMATION FOR TEXAS

HOW TO GET THERE. *By car:* Interstate and U.S. highways enter Texas from the west, north, east, and from Mexico. *By air:* Dallas-Fort Worth, Houston, Brownsville, San Antonio, and El Paso boast regional or international airports. Service is worldwide, often direct. Many carriers fly intrastate. *By bus: Greyhound* and *Trailways Bus System* serve Texas.

HOW TO GET AROUND. *By car:* Texas has more than 70,000 miles of outstanding state and federal highways which are remarkably well maintained, as are the smaller farm to market and ranch roads. The State Department of Highways and Public Transportation has devised a series of "Texas Trails," maps which suggest 500–700 miles off-the-main highway side trips. They are clearly marked.

By air: Texas has more landing fields (over 1,300 according to the Texas Aeronautics Commission) than any other state. Nearly 270 of these fields are publicly owned, and there is service to over 30 cities by commercial airlines.

By bus: Regular bus service reaches 1,100 Texas communities according to the Texas Railroad Commission, many of which do not have any other form of public transportation. These communities and cities are served by nearly 30 bus companies, the largest of which are *Greyhound* and *Trailways.*

TOURIST INFORMATION. The State Department of Highways and Public Transportation maintains tourist bureau stations at Amarillo, Anthony, Austin, Denison, Gainesville, Langtry, Laredo, Orange, Texarkana, the Valley, Waskom and Wichita Falls. They provide maps and information about roads, camper and trailer regulations, the latest weather advisories, and location of state-maintained roadside rest areas, state parks and campsites.

For advance planning, write Texas Tourist Development Agency, Box 12008, Dept. DB, Austin, Texas 78711. They will send you free, colorful material about vacationing in Texas.

MUSEUMS AND GALLERIES. Whether in a city or a crossroads hamlet, Texans pridefully preserve the history, events, and customs which affect their culture. Some displays are housed in contemporary structures such as San Antonio's famed Institute of Texan Cultures, which recognizes the state's 26 different ethnic groups; others may flourish in an abandoned courthouse, deserted jail, railroad depot, or early-day barroom.

Larger museums usually are open 10 A.M. to 5 P.M. weekdays, and afternoons on weekends. Admission, if any, is nominal. In the smaller locales the visitor may have to look up a responsible citizen to open the quarters. Following are some samples, listed alphabetically by location.

Alpine, *Sul Ross State University Museum of Big Bend.*

Amarillo, *Helium Monument,* erected in 1968 of stainless steel and stretching six stories skyward, commemorates world's largest supply of this resource. An Exhibits Pavilion is nearby.

Austin, *LBJ Library and Museum,* Manor Road-Memorial Stadium exit off I–35, honors the late President Lyndon Baines Johnson. "Museum" was added to name because of the expanding exhibits. Popular with tourists. *Texas Archives and Library Bldg.,* on State Capitol grounds, has artifacts, documents, relics.

Beaumont, *Spindletop Museum* reviews thrilling era of 1901 oil discovery. *Gladys City Spindletop Boomtown.* Replica of town.

Bonham, *Sam Rayburn Library.* Collection of books, papers, and mementos of the late Speaker of the House of Representatives.

Canyon, *Panhandle Plains Museum* on West Texas University campus.

Corpus Christi, *Art Museum of South Texas.* Area artists' works.

Dallas, *Hall of State,* other museums at Fair Park. Also downtown.

Del Rio, *Whitehead Memorial Museum* located in early trading post. Grave of Judge Roy Bean on grounds.

Hillsboro, *Confederate Research Center,* Hill Junior College campus.

Jefferson, *Historical Society Museum.* Old Federal Bldg. Paintings, sculpture, pioneer furnishings.

Kilgore, *East Texas Oil Museum.* New. Dioramas, films. Admission.

Midland, *Permian Basin Petroleum Museum* dramatizes the Permian Basin formation and oil development.

Pecos, *West-of-the-Pecos Museum.* Old hotel and saloon is showcase for authentic displays of 1800s.

Waco, *Texas Ranger Hall of Fame.* Take Fort Fisher exit off I–35.

TOURS. *Air:* Major airlines seasonally participate with tourist areas, hotels and travel agencies in fly/drive tours. *Train:* Check with *Amtrak. Bus: Gray Lines* operates sightseeing tours in major cities and arranges charter tours. *Boat:* Fishing and sightseeing excursions are offered from Gulf points. Additionally, tourist agencies and tour brokers can be of assistance. Tour agencies in Dallas and Houston operate guided trips to state points for seasonal and special events.

DRINKING LAWS. Legal age for purchase of spirits is 19. Hours for legal sales are set by state law, but each county—even precincts within counties—can determine by local option election whether to permit sales. Such elections also decide what spirits may be sold. For instance, some counties or precincts may limit sales to beer and wine only and decide if they may be consumed at the place of sale. Liquor by the bottle is sold only at package stores, and on-premise consumption is unlawful. Package stores are open between 10 A.M. and 9 P.M. Monday through Saturday. In legal areas, restaurants and taverns may sell spirits between the hours of 7 A.M. and midnight Monday through Friday and until 1 A.M. Sunday. Legal hours for Sunday sales are from noon until midnight. Restaurants and taverns in the major cities may purchase special permits allowing operation until 2 A.M. daily. Generally, beer, wine, and liquor can be purchased in the larger cities, but you may do well to ascertain the laws in the town ahead. A case of beer or a quart of liquor can be legally carried in your car.

SPORTS. Most every city has its public tennis courts, golf courses and swimming pools. 600 miles of coast beaches and over 100 public lakes challenge the angler, water skier and scuba diver. State and national forests welcome the camper, hiker or backpacker. The hunter will find ducks in the Rio Grande Valley, white-tailed deer, and big-game hunts on some ranches. Hunting and fishing licenses are required.

WHAT TO DO WITH THE CHILDREN. *Six Flags Over Texas,* the entertainment and history-tuned theme park between Dallas and Fort Worth, attracts over 2.5 million guests during a March-into-November season. *Astroworld* at Houston, now in the Six Flags family and patterned after the Dallas park. *Innerspace Cavern,* I–35 northeast of Austin, discovered while building the Interstate. Other commercial caverns: *Longhorn Cavern* near Burnet; *Wonder World* at San Marcos; *Natural Bridge Caverns* between New Braunfels and San Antonio; *Cascade Caverns,* I–10 and US 87 northwest of San Antonio. *Aquarena Springs,* San Marcos, theater submerges for spectacular underwater show; glass-bottom boat rides, skyride. *Sea-Arama,* Galveston, glass-encased sealife displays, amphitheater water show, exotic birds in tropical habitat. *Alabama-Coushatta Indian Reservation* at Livingston. *Prairie Dog Town,* Lubbock. *Gladys Porter Zoo,* Brownsville. *Brackenridge Park and Zoo* in San Antonio. Also in San Antonio, the *Institute of Texan Cultures, Texas State Railroad.* Restored steam engines, cars operate in summer between Rusk and Palestine.

HOTELS AND MOTELS. Outside the larger cities you may find more time to enjoy the accommodations. Pools and air conditioning are generally offered, and there will be a restaurant on the premises or nearby. You will find management helpful in making reservations ahead for you as your trip progresses. Rates for double occupancy are based on a state average: *Deluxe:* $85 up; *Expensive:* $65–85; *Moderate:* $40–65; *Inexpensive:* under $40.

ABILENE. *Inexpensive:* **Holiday Inn.** Near airport. Restaurant, lounge, pool.
Hotel Windsor. 4th and N. Pine. Restaurant.
Sheraton Inn. 505 Pine. Restaurants, lounge, pool, wheelchair facilities.
Best Western Colonial Inn. 3210 Pine. Near Hardin Simmons. Restaurant.
Mid-Continent Inn. Restaurant, pool.

AMARILLO. *Moderate:* **Best Western Villa.** I–40, Grand exit. Restaurant, patio dining, heated pool.
Howard Johnson's Motor Lodge. I–40 West.
Inexpensive: **Concourse Motor Inn.** 321 S. Polk. Civic Center area.
Rodeway Inn. 2015 Paramount.
TraveLodge. 2035 Paramount.

ATHENS: *Moderate:* **Holiday Inn.** Highway 31 East.

AUSTIN: *Deluxe:* **Marriott Hotel.** I–35, US 290. 300 rooms, car, taxi service. Pool, shopping.
Expensive: **Austin Hilton.** I–35 at US 290. Caters to conventions.
Bradford-Austin. Formerly Stephen F. Austin. 7th and Congress.
Moderate: **Best Western Villa Capri.** 2400 N. I–35. Fine restaurant.
Driskill Hotel. Downtown. From 1885, Austin's landmark showplace.

Holiday Inn at Town Lake. Circular design.
Sheraton Crest. 1111 First St. Overlooks Town Lake.
Inexpensive: La Quinta Motor Inn. I–35, US 290 near Mall.

BEAUMONT. *Moderate.* Howard Johnson's Motor Lodge. 3985 College.
Ramada Inn. 1295 N. 11th. Convenient for travelers to Orange.
Red Carpet Inn. 55 I–10 North.
Sheraton Spindletop Hotel. 2525 N. 11th. New. 200 rooms.
Inexpensive: Days Inn. 1–10 at Rusk. Handicapped aids.
La Quinta Motor Inn. 220 I–10 North.

BROWNSVILLE. *Expensive:* Rancho Viejoa Resort. 6 miles NE on Expressway.
Moderate: Best Western Fort Brown. Beautiful.
Inexpensive: Colonial Inn. 1147 E. Levee. Downtown.
La Quinta Motor Inn. 55 E. 12th. Near Matamoros.
Ramada Inn. 715 N. Frontage. Dependable.
Rodeway Inn. One mile downtown.

CORPUS CHRISTI. *Expensive:* Holiday Inn-Emerald Beach. 1102 S. Shoreline. Entertainment.
Sheraton Marina Inn. 300 N. Shoreline. Two restaurants, entertainment.
Moderate: La Quinta Royale. 601 N. Water. Cantina entertainment.
Quality Inn. 411 N. Shoreline. 99 units.
Ramada Inn Bayfront. 601 N. Shoreline. Recommended.
Inexpensive: Econolodge/Airport. 6033 Leopard St. 126 units.
Hoover Motor Lodge. 1301 N. Chaparral.

GALVESTON. *Deluxe:* Flagship Hotel. Sleep over Gulf waters.
Expensive: Marriott's Hotel Galvez. An old queen back in full glory.
Moderate: Commodore Motel. Walk across Seawall to beach.
Gaido's Motor Inn. Near the fun.
Holiday Inn. 244 rooms on The Strand.
Inexpensive: Anchorage Motor Hotel. Beach. Beach site.
Seawall Motor Inn. On seawall.

HARLINGEN. *Inexpensive:* Holiday Inn. 1901 W. Tyler. Newly remodeled. Restaurant.
Ramada Inn. 1800 W. Harrison. Lounge, entertainment.
Rodeway Inn. 1821 W. Tyler. Some family units.

LAREDO. *Moderate:* La Posada Hotel. Miramba band.
Hilton Inn. Downtown, 200 rms.
Sheraton Inn. Off I–35. 133 rooms.
Inexpensive: New Hamilton Hotel. Downtown, 300 rooms.
TraveLodge. Near Convention Center.

LUBBOCK. *Moderate:* Hilton Inn. 505 Avenue Q. Convention Center.
Ramada Inn. 5845 Avenue Q. Lounge, pool.
Inexpensive: Best Western Coronado Inn. 501 Amarillo Hwy. Restaurant.
Executive House Motel. Near International airport.
Howard Johnson's. 6011 Avenue H. Traffic circle.
Lexington Motor Inn. 4521 Brownfield Rd. Kitchenettes, TV, pool.
TraveLodge. 714 Avenue Q. Convention Center.

MARSHALL. *Inexpensive:* Holiday. I–20, US 59. Marshall Civic Center 2 mi.
Ramada Inn. US 59 south of I–10. Restaurant.

MIDLAND. *Moderate:* Sheraton Inn. Downtown, 120 rooms.

ODESSA. *Moderate:* Inn of the Golden West. Fourth and Lincoln. 157 rooms.

SOUTH PADRE ISLAND. *Deluxe to Expensive:* **Bahai Mar Resort.** Weekly, monthly rates, 300 rooms. Resort.

Hilton Resort Hotel. A hotel and condominium totaling 235 units including apartments and suites.

Expensive: **Holiday Inn.** Gulf view and Island view accommodations.

Inexpensive: **Sandy Retreat Motor Inn.** Some doubles with kitchen.

TEXARKANA. *Inexpensive:* **La Quinta.** 5201 State Line. North of city.

TYLER. *Moderate:* **Holiday Inn.** Can seat 200, 132 rooms.

Sheraton. Loop 323.

Inexpensive: **Best Western Kingsway.** Restaurant, pool.

Ramada Inn. Restaurant with buffet.

Red Carpet. Northwest area.

Rodeway Inn. Restaurant, club.

WACO: *Moderate:* **Sheraton Inn.** 801 S. 4th.

Inexpensive: **Best Western Old Main Lodge.** I–35 at 4th. Baylor exit.

Holiday Lodge. 4909 W. Waco. Near Baylor Stadium.

Ramada Inn. 4201 Franklin.

WICHITA FALLS. *Moderate:* **Gateway Inn.** 1211 Central Expressway. Restaurant, club, playground.

Holiday Inn. Downtown, near university. Restaurant, lounge.

Inexpensive: **Best Western Towne Crest.** Near US 277, 287.

La Quinta. Maurine exits off 287, 281.

 DINING OUT. With modern highways tending to skirt many of the smaller cities and towns, good access-road franchise operations offer fast food or complete menus in comfortable, air-conditioned surroundings. Yet it's often exciting to drive into town and get a townsman's recommendation. Statewide price categories for dinner average: *Deluxe:* $20 up, *Expensive:* $12–20, *Moderate:* $7–12, and *Inexpensive:* under $7. Drinks, tax, tip not included.

ABILENE. *Moderate:* **The Outpost.** 3126 S. Clack. Steak, seafood, quail.

Pelican's. 3130 S. Clack. Prime rib, shrimp.

Steak & Ale. 1882 S. Clack. Known throughout Texas. Reputable.

Inexpensive: **Gardski's Loft.** 3370 N. First. Varied menu, including gourmet hamburgers.

AMARILLO. *Expensive:* **Maison Blanche.** 2740 W. Haven Village. Elegant dining, superb cuisine.

Moderate: **Big Texan Steak Ranch.** 7701 E. I–40. Widely known.

The Country Barn. 1805 Lakeside. Steak, barbeque.

Inexpensive: **Best Western Tradewinds.** 1001 N. Pierce. Breakfast, lunch, dinner.

AUSTIN. *Expensive:* **Green Pastures.** 811 W. Life Oak. An Austin landmark.

Moderate: **Convict Hill.** US 290 and Oak Hill. Fireplace dining.

Hoffbrau. 613 W. Sixth. Steaks fried in lemon butter.

Dan McKlusky's. 419 E. Sixth. Steaks cut to order.

Magic Time Machine. 600 E. Riverside. Dinner groups come alive at this fun place.

Inexpensive: **Night Hawk.** 336 W. Congress. Favorite with students.

Scholz Garden. 1607 San Jacinto. Around since 1866. German food.

BEAUMONT. *Expensive:* **Patrizi's Other Place.** 2050 I–10 South. Vic Patrizi a former president of state restaurant association.

Moderate: **Don's Seafood.** 2920 I–10 south. Popular. Gumbo is an excellent choice.

Hoffbrau. 2310 N. 11th. Steaks any way you want them.

Inexpensive: **Carlo's.** 2570 Calder. Italian cuisine. Entertainment.

BROWNSVILLE. *Expensive:* **Valley Inn & Country Club.** Expressway north of town. Food, lodging, sports.
Moderate: **Fort Brown.** 1900 E. Elizabeth. Excellent service. Complete menu.
Inexpensive: **Miguel's.** 2605 Boca Chica. Popular.

CORPUS CHRISTI. *Expensive:* **The British Sideboard.** 3166 Reid Drive. Elegant, intimate dining in 18th-century atmosphere.
Moderate: **Black Diamond Oyster Bar.** 5712 Gollihar and 7202 S. Padre Island Drive. Half–shell oysters, frog legs, shrimp.
Captain Boomer's. Peoples St. T-Head in the marina. A floating barge restaurant featuring a wide variety of seafood.
Cooper's Alley Saloon. 15 Gaslight Square. Lots of atmosphere.

GALVESTON. *Expensive:* **Gaido's.** 3828 Seawall. Long a favorite for great seafood.
Café Torrefie. 22nd and Strand. International cuisine.
Cattlemen's. 2406 61st St. Barbecue aroma gets you hungry.
The Original Hill's. 1502 Seawall. Try flounder and potato.
Moderate to expensive: **Balinese Room.** On the pier. Memories for many.
Wentletrap. 2301 The Strand. Excellent food.
Inexpensive: **Shrimp & Stuff.** 6801 Steward Road and 3901 Avenue O. Try shrimp po–boy.

LUBBOCK. *Moderate:* **Bigham's Smokehouse.** 3310 82nd. The usual treats.
Catfish Station. 2414 4th St. All-you-can-eat.
Harrigan's. 3801 50th St. Continental menu.
Inexpensive: **El Charro.** 1608 19th. The Mexican dishes are homemade.

LAREDO. *Moderate:* **Bernardo's.** 7060 N. San Bernardo. Authentic Mexican dishes.
Hungry Farmer. 802 Juarez. 24-oz. T-bone special.
Inexpensive: **La Hacienda.** 4801 Gallagher. Cabrito, Mexican fare.
La Fonda Restaurant. 3702 San Bernardo. Home cooking.

TEXARKANA. *Moderate:* **Acadian Seafood House.** 114 E. Broad. Cajun cooking at its best.
Hush Puppy Restaurant. Hwy. 71 North. Catfish the specialty.
Inexpensive: **La Casa Rosa.** 1824 State Line. Mexican dishes, tortillas made fresh daily.

TYLER. *Expensive:* **Red Ackers Steakhouse.** 2500 E. Fifth. Steaks for every appetite.
La Rose European Restaurant. 3333 Troup Hwy. Continental cuisine.
Moderate: **Catfish Cove.** Hwy 69 South. Seafood specializing in fried catfish.

WACO. *Expensive:* **Nick's.** 4508 W. Waco. Steaks, Greek food specialty.
Moderate: **The Sirloin.** 2803 Franklin. Steak and seafood.

COLORADO

Denver, Mining Towns, and Ski Paradise

Perhaps the best place to start a tour of the mile-high city of Denver is the Colorado Visitor's Bureau at 225 West Colfax Avenue, across from the city hall (known as the City and County Building), where visitors can find information about the city and the state.

North of the City and County Building is the United States Mint, where automatic machinery stamps out pennies, nickels, dimes, quarters, and half dollars. Tours all year except mid-June–July 1.

From the City and County Building a grassy mall, dotted with shade trees, stretches eastward to the gold-domed Colorado State Capitol. The capitol, constructed of Colorado gray granite, is a miniature version of the U.S. Capitol in Washington, D.C. Fountains, a Greek theater for public gatherings, and monuments to Colorado pioneers grace this popular public area.

On Bannock Street is the Denver Art Museum, noted for its contemporary and traditional American, European, and Oriental exhibits. This strikingly modern building, next to the Civic Center, is composed of more than one million faceted-glass tiles. Across from the museum is the Denver Public Library. The library's western history department is considered one of the nation's best. And directly opposite the Main Library, also on Broadway, you'll find the Colorado Heritage Center, with its displays on state and western history.

The State Capitol was completed in 1896. Its dome is covered with Colorado gold leaf that cost nearly $200,000. The thirteenth step of the Capitol's west entrance is exactly one mile above sea level.

Capitol Hill, once the site of luxurious homes of mining tycoons, still has a number of mansions that can be visited. Among them is Molly

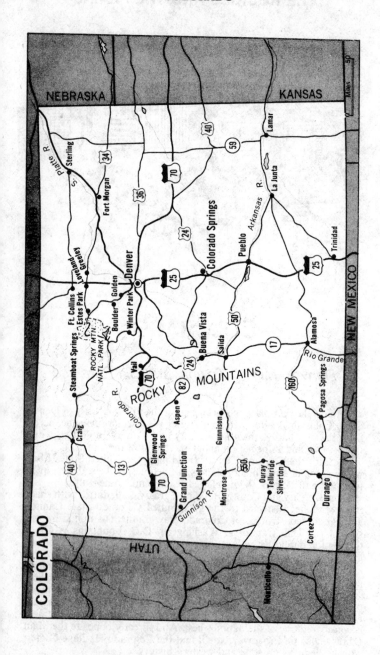

COLORADO

Brown's House, which was the home of the real-life folk heroine of "The Unsinkable Molly Brown."

At 16th and Lawrence Streets is Tabor Center, a new mall featuring over seventy shops and restaurants.

East of the downtown area is the Denver Museum of Natural History situated in the 640-acre City Park. You can view fossilized bones of prehistoric animals found in the Rockies, and visit Gates Planetarium and the four-and-a-half-story-high Imax Theater. Other exhibits show Rocky Mountain, Arctic, and South American animals mounted in lifelike dioramas. City Park itself has a large zoo. Also in east Denver, adjoining Cheesman Park, are the Denver Botanic Gardens, featuring a million-dollar conservatory for tropical flowers and plants.

In the northwest, on 44th Avenue, near Golden, is the Colorado Railroad Museum, which appeals to the rail buff.

PRACTICAL INFORMATION FOR DENVER

HOW TO GET AROUND. *By bus:* RTD buses running centrally and into the suburbs. *By taxi:* cabs are plentiful. *From the airport:* Airport taxi; airport limousine service to major hotels.

TOURIST INFORMATION. *Denver & Colorado Convention & Visitor's Bureau,* 225 W. Colfax Ave., Denver 80202. Telephone: (303)892–1112.

SEASONAL EVENTS. *January:* National Western Stock Show and Rodeo. *April:* Easter Sunrise services at Red Rocks. *May:* Lakeside Amusement Park and Elitch Gardens open for summer. *June:* Greyhound Racing at Mile High Kennel Club throughout the summer. *August:* International bicycle race. *October:* Larimer Square Oktoberfest. Denver Symphony begins its season. *December:* Denver Civic Center Christmas Display; Larimer Square annual Christmas Walk; 16th St. Mall "Parade of Lights."

MUSEUMS AND GALLERIES. *Denver Museum of Natural History* in City Park has realistic dioramas of prehistoric and present-day animals. *Colorado Heritage Center,* 1300 Broadway, for Colorado artifacts and photo exhibits. *Denver Art Museum,* on 14th Ave. *Arvada Center for the Arts and Humanities,* 6901 Wadsworth Blvd., on hill overlooking city.

HISTORIC SITES. The *Governor's Mansion,* 400 East 8th Ave. *The Molly Brown House,* 1340 Pennsylvania St.

TOURS. *Best Mountain Tours* and *Gray Line Tours* offer daily excursions. *Historic Denver Walking Tours,* 1340 Pennsylvania, organizes city walks and guided tours of Capitol, weekdays.

The most famous special-interest tour is of the *U.S. Mint* at Colfax and Delaware Sts.

GARDENS. The *Denver Botanic Gardens* are among the best in the western U.S. The library and greenhouse open to the public.

MUSIC. During summer, outdoor band concerts in City Park. The Denver Symphony performs three times a week in fall and winter in the Boettcher Concert Hall of the Denver Center for The Performing Arts (DCPA) at 14th and Curtis.

STAGE AND REVUES. Elitch Gardens is home of America's oldest summer theater. Bonfils Theatre has several productions throughout the year. The DCPA hosts a number of national companies of Broadway productions. Comedy Works offers performances nightly.

SUMMER SPORTS. Two dozen public golf courses; tennis in city parks. Sloans Lake, nearby Cherry Creek Reservoir and Chatfield Dam, farther away, have boating and water-skiing facilities. Jogging paths wind through many of the parks and bicycle routes are plentiful.

WINTER SPORTS. Major skiing at more than thirty Colorado areas and resorts.

 SPECTATOR SPORTS. Bandimere and Colorado National Speedways offer drag and sports car racing. Denver Bears in AA baseball league. Denver Nuggets, basketball. Denver Broncos, NFL football; Denver Gold, USFL football. National Western Stock Show and Rodeo in January. Horseracing at Arapahoe Park Race Track; dog racing at Mile High Kennel Club.

 WHAT TO DO WITH THE CHILDREN. The *Children's Museum* and *City Park* with its zoo, children's zoo, and the Denver Museum of Natural History and Planetarium. The *Forney Transportation Museum* and the *Wax Museum* are of interest. The *Colorado Railroad Museum* is good for exploring. *Elitch Gardens* has a kiddie area, and Lakeside Amusement Park features rides for all ages.

 HOTELS AND MOTELS. Price categories, for double occupancy, will start *upward* from the following: *Super Deluxe:* $120–165; *Deluxe:* $60–119; *Expensive:* $45–59; *Moderate:* $30–44; *Inexpensive:* $18–29.

Super Deluxe: **Fairmont Hotel.** Welton & 18th Sts. Sleek, Old World hotel. Elegant restaurants.

Brown Palace. Tremont and 17th. One of the west's most renowned.

Deluxe: **Cherry Creek Inn.** 600 S. Colorado Blvd. In southeast Denver. Relaxing atmosphere.

Clarion Hotel. 3203 Quebec St. All the amenities. Close to airport.

Executive Tower. 1405 Curtis St. Downtown skyscraper hotel.

Radisson Hotel Denver. 1550 Court Pl. Heated rooftop pool; sauna; conventions.

Stapleton Plaza. 3333 Quebec St. Heated pool, restaurant, bar.

Expensive: **Ramada Inn Foothills.** 6th Ave. & Simms. Good location at foot of the mountains.

Moderate: **Broadway Plaza.** Broadway at 11th Ave. Near Capitol.

Quality Inn Downtown. 2601 Zuni, I–25 and Speer Blvd.

Inexpensive: **American Family Lodge West.** 4735 Kipling. Chain motel.

Anchor. 2323 S. Broadway. Good value.

 DINING OUT Price categories are: *Super Deluxe;* over $28; *Deluxe:* $18–27; *Expensive:* $13–17; *Moderate:* $10–12; *Inexpensive:* $4–9. Drinks, tax, and tips not included.

Deluxe: **Normandy Restaurant Francais.** 1515 Madison St. Quiet French dining.

Palace Arms. At Brown Palace Hotel. American menu including good steaks.

Tante Louise. 4900 East Colfax. Elegant, European ambience.

Expensive: **Buckhorn Exchange.** 1000 Osage. Historical Western restaurant.

The Fort. Off 285 near Morrison. Buffalo, elk, and beef.

Golden Dragon. 1467 Nelson. Mandarin and Szechuan cuisine.

Josephinas. 1433 Larimer. Italian restaurant in historic building.

Quorum. 233 East Colfax. Continental dining across from State Capitol.

Ridgeview Inn Gasthaus. W. 44th & Garrison. Authentic German.
Wellshire Inn. 3333 S. Colorado Blvd. Varied menu. Pastoral atmosphere.
Moderate: **Gasho.** At Denver Tech Center and downtown location. Hibachi-style food.
North Woods Inn. 6115 S. Santa Fe. Cowboy-style food.
Yuan Mongolian Barbeque. 7555 East Arapahoe Rd. and 1515 S. Albion St. Four Oriental cuisines plus Mongolian barbecue.
Inexpensive. **Casa Bonita.** 6715 W. Colfax Ave. Mexican and American food.
Le Central. 112 E. 8th Ave. Genuine French; bargain priced.
White Fence Farm. 6263 W. Jewell. American family restaurant.

EXPLORING COLORADO

A number of attractions and scenic areas are within range of one-day excursions from Denver.

As you approach Boulder, home of the University of Colorado, the tilted slablike rocks of the Flatirons tower to your left. Head west from Boulder, up Boulder Canyon and along the edge of Barker Reservoir, to the mountain town of Nederland. State 72, the scenic Peak to Peak Highway, winds through lodgepole pine forests toward Estes Park, a recreation gateway to Rocky Mountain National Park. On the other side of the Continental Divide is Granby, noted for its lakes and abundance of dude ranches.

From Golden, site of the first territorial capital and home of the Colorado School of Mines, a good highway leads to Central City, an old gold-mining town whose Opera House, Teller House Hotel, and private Victorian homes have been preserved and restored. Opera companies and Broadway shows perform here each summer. Well-maintained highways to Idaho Springs and gemlike Echo Lake at 10,600 feet provide breathtaking views. For the adventuresome there is a further drive up Mount Evans on the nation's highest automobile road.

South from Denver are Colorado Springs and Pikes Peak. At Castle Rock, en route, there are mountain views in all directions. Various areas of the Air Force Academy are open to the public; best known is the many-spired glass and aluminum chapel. Colorado Springs is the state's second largest city, long famous as a summer resort. There is a Fine Arts Center with collections of southwestern art, modern photographs; Colorado Springs also has a Pioneer Museum. The nearby Garden of the Gods is noted for its beautiful red rock formations. Pikes Peak looms above Colorado Springs. A cog railway also ascends the mountain from Manitou Springs. In the hills behind Pikes Peak are the once-booming gold-mining towns of Cripple Creek and Victor—now home to only a few hundred people but visited by many tourists during the summer months.

On a longer, several-day tour of Colorado, head southwest from Denver through the Kenosha Pass to Fairplay. This pass affords a magnificent panorama of the broad South Park valley. From Fairplay drive north to the Dillon Reservoir and turn west toward Vail. Vail, created out of a sheep meadow in 1962, is fast becoming a year-round vacation center. Former President Ford's selection of Vail for skiing and golf helped create a resort metropolis.

Continuing west, the road parallels the Eagle River, which joins the Colorado in Dotsero, and follows spectacular Glenwood Canyon—a 1,000-foot chasm between slate-colored cliffs—to Glenwood Springs, famous for its vapor caves and hot springs. North of the Colorado lies the White River wilderness area, heavily wooded and virtually unscarred by roads.

South of Glenwood Springs is Aspen, Colorado's top ski center and an old silver-mining town transformed into a mountain cultural mecca. The summer Aspen Music Festival and School is widely known. The surrounding area has trout lakes and streams, plus countless miles of hiking and riding trails.

Farther west is Grand Junction, important as a uranium center and western Colorado's largest city. Ten miles outside of town is Colorado National Monument, an area of dramatically eroded stone spires, canyons, and fossil beds.

In the southwest corner of the state is Mesa Verde National Park. In canyons gashing the plateau which gives the park its name (Mesa Verde means "green table" in Spanish) early Indians built apartment-like dwellings under overhanging cliffs and designed primitive irrigation systems for agriculture. The National Park Service has tours of the ruins, including Cliff House, a settlement of 200 "rooms" on eight levels.

You can return to Denver by way of Durango, where a narrow-gauge train drawn by a steam locomotive makes a 45-mile run to Silverton; nearby Ouray is known as the heart of the "Switzerland of the Rockies"; don't miss the Black Canyon of the Gunnison National Monument on your way back to Denver; Canon City, location of Royal Gorge, where the world's highest suspension bridge crosses the 1,000-foot-deep gorge of the Arkansas River; and Pueblo, center of the state's steel industry. Or, swinging farther south, travel to Alamosa in the center of the richly productive San Luis Valley to the Great Sand Dunes National Monument at the foot of the lovely Sangre de Cristo Mountains.

Two major areas have not been included in this tour: the eastern plains with the rich agricultural South Platte and Arkansas river valleys; and the sparsely populated northwest, a region with trout fishing streams, skiing at Steamboat Springs, and Dinosaur National Park, where one can see paleontologists at work unearthing dinosaur fossils.

PRACTICAL INFORMATION FOR COLORADO

HOW TO GET THERE. *By air:* Denver, Colorado Springs, Pueblo, and Grand Junction have major service. *By rail:* Amtrak from Chicago, San Francisco, Los Angeles, Seattle, and Portland to Denver. *By car:* I–25 from Wyoming in the north and New Mexico in the south; I–70 from Utah in the west and Kansas in the east; and I–80S/I–76 from Nebraska in the northeast.

By bus: Greyhound and *Trailways.*

HOW TO GET AROUND. *By air:* Steamboat Springs, Grand Junction, Aspen, Montrose, Gunnison, Cortez, Durango, Alamosa, Lamar, Pueblo, Eagle, Colorado Springs and Denver are intrastate terminals.

By train: Amtrak has passenger service between Denver and Grand Junction and between Denver and Trinidad.

By bus: Trailways, RTD Bus Co., and *Greyhound.*

By car: Good highways throughout state.

TOURIST INFORMATION. *Denver & Colorado Convention & Visitor's Bureau,* 225 W. Colfax Ave., Denver 80202. Telephone: (303) 892–1112.

MUSEUMS AND GALLERIES. The *University of Colorado Museum and Art Gallery* and the *Boulder Center for the Visual Arts*. Central City has the *Opera House* and the *Gold Mine Museum*. Colorado Springs has the *Fine Arts Center, Prorodeo Hall of Champions,* and the *National Carvers Museum. Matchless Mine and Tabor Opera House* in restored Leadville. Vail built the *Colorado Ski Museum*.

 HISTORIC SITES. *Old Fort Garland,* west of Walsenburg, is a restored Army post once commanded by Kit Carson. *Fort Vasquez,* an 1830s fur-trading post, is near Platteville. Colorado has more than 300 mining ghost towns; the best known are in the Central City—Black Hawk region, Nevadaville, Apex, and the Cripple Creek—Victor region.

TOURS. *Best Mountain Tours,* in Denver, and *Gray Line Tours* in Denver and Colorado Springs.

DRINKING LAWS. Over 18 for "3.2" beer. The age for hard liquor and regular beer is 21.

 SUMMER SPORTS. Fishing, especially for trout, is a big seasonal sport. Nonresident licenses are obtainable. Mule deer and elk are major hunting quarry. Boating, water skiing, and rafting on lakes and rivers. Colorado also attracts hikers and backpackers. Most campsites are available on a first-come, first-served basis.

 WINTER SPORTS. Aspen is one of the largest ski complexes in the country. Ski areas close to Denver are Loveland Basin and Winter Park. Other major sports centers include Keystone, Breckenridge, Arapahoe Basin, Copper Mountain, Steamboat Springs, and Vail.

 SPECTATOR SPORTS. *Auto racing:* the Pikes Peak Auto Hill Climb every July 4. *Dog racing* at Cloverleaf Kennel Club in Loveland and at Rocky Mountain Greyhound Park in Colorado Springs. *Rodeos* in Colorado Springs, Pueblo, Estes Park, Steamboat Springs, Canon City, Boulder, Glenwood Springs, and in most smaller communities.

 WHAT TO DO WITH THE CHILDREN. Colorado Springs has the *Cheyenne Mountain Zoo,* the *North Pole* and *Santa's Workshop,* the *Garden of the Gods* and *Cave of the Winds.* From Antonito, Colorado, to Chama, New Mexico, runs the *Cumbres & Toltec Scenic Railroad.*

 HOTELS AND MOTELS. Peak season price categories for double occupancy, average: *Deluxe:* $60–125; *Expensive:* $45–59; *Moderate:* $30–44; *Inexpensive:* $18–29.

ASPEN. *Deluxe:* **Aspen Meadows.** West edge of town. Chalet accommodations with hotel services.
Expensive: **Maroon Creek Lodge.** 2½ miles southwest on Maroon Creek Road.

BOULDER. *Expensive:* **Golden Buff Motor Lodge.** 1725 18th, near campus.
Moderate: **University Inn.** 1632 Broadway, near downtown.

COLORADO SPRINGS. *Deluxe:* **Broadmoor Resort.** World famous; 5,000 acres; all facilities.
Expensive: **Holiday Inn.** Convenient to downtown.

Moderate: **Imperial 400.** At 714 N. Nevada. Chain motel.

CRIPPLE CREEK. *Moderate:* **Cripple Creek Motel.** On SR 67. Coffee shop.

DURANGO: *Moderate:* **General Palmer House.** Gay 90's restored hotel. *Inexpensive:* **Silver Spruce.** Comfortable motel.

ESTES PARK. *Deluxe:* **Longs Peak Inn and Guest Ranch.** Lodge, cottages, duplex chalets. Glass-walled dining room; lounge. Pool; horses; fishing.
   Moderate: **Best Western Lake Estes Motor Inn.** Restaurant. Swimming, wading, therapy pools.
   Trail Ridge Motel. Some efficiencies.

GLENWOOD SPRINGS. *Deluxe:* **Hotel Colorado.** Historic hotel.

VAIL. *Deluxe:* **Holiday Inn at Vail.** US 6 at Vail Village Rd. All the conveniences.
   Marriott's Mark Resort. South Frontage Rd. at Lionshead. With large health club.

 DINING OUT. Price categories are *Deluxe:* $25 and up; *Expensive:* $14–24; *Moderate:* $10–13; *Inexpensive:* $5–9. Drinks, tax, and tips not included.

ASPEN. *Deluxe:* **Copper Kettle.** On Dean St. International and exotic.
   Expensive: **Guido's Swiss Inn.** At Galena and Cooper Sts. Mountain chalet, drinks.
   Moderate: **Chart House.** Steak and salad bar.

BOULDER. *Expensive:* **Flagstaff House.** On Flagstaff Mountain. Continental and American. Lovely view.
   Inexpensive: **Tico's.** 1101 Walnut St. Mexican and American.

CENTRAL CITY. *Expensive:* **Black Forest Inn.** Chalet with beer garden. German food.
   Teller House. Restored from earlier days.

COLORADO SPRINGS. *Deluxe–Moderate:* **Broadmoor Hotel Dining Rooms.** Several restaurants in various price categories.
   Inexpensive: **Flying W Ranch Chuckwagon.** Western-style dinner with show. Summers only.

DURANGO. *Deluxe:* **Canyon Restaurant–Tamarron.** Continental. At resort 18 miles from town.
   Expensive: **The Palace.** Gourmet. Overlooks historic Narrow Gauge train depot.

ESTES PARK. *Expensive:* **Old Plantation.** Yankee pot roast and rainbow trout are specialities.

GRAND JUNCTION. *Expensive:* **Cork & Embers.** Steakhouse.

VAIL. *Deluxe:* **Gasthof Gramshammer.** Austrian specialties.
   Expensive: **Watch Hill Oyster Club.** Fine seafood.

IDAHO

White Water Adventures

Boise is the capital and largest city of Idaho. A flourishing agricultural, horticultural, and stock-raising region lies about the city, and rich mines abound in the surrounding mountains. It is also one of the most important wool-trade centers in the U.S.

Among the unique points of interest in Boise is the Basque dancing, a feature here, because the state of Idaho still has more Basques than any place other than their homeland.

There is also the classical state capitol, historical Ft. Boise, and Julia Davis Park containing the Idaho Historical Museum, Boise Art Gallery, and Pioneer Village.

Coeur d'Alene's Lovely Lake

This particular drive ought to be made slowly, for there is enchantment every yard of the winding overlook. The lake is lovely to the point of disbelief. No lake in all the Northwest evokes such imagery, has such color range, seems so ethereal.

Excursion boats operate in the summer months from the City dock for short cruises on the lake; seven- and eight-hour boat journeys available Sun. and Wed. Seaplane flights of 20 minutes from 1st St. Dock.

Located at the lowest point in the state, 738-foot elevation, Lewiston is at the confluence of the Snake and Clearwater Rivers, and is flanked by steep hills. A trading center for the rich grainlands and fruit orchards, it is also Idaho's only "seaport."

There is much to see and do here. Potlatch Forests offers free tours. Luna House Museum, a pioneer residence, displays ancient Indian

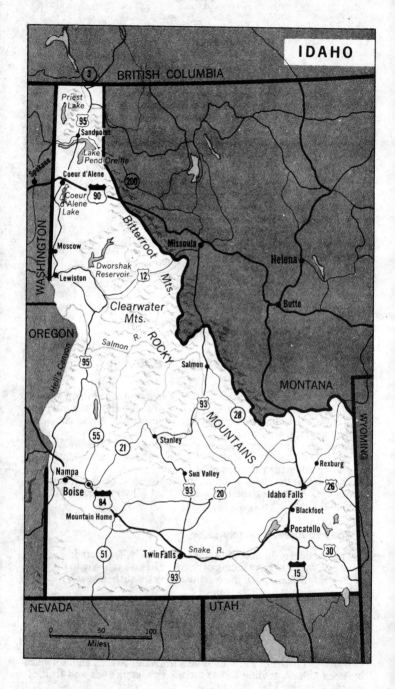

artifacts, and one of the more famous Western rodeos, the Lewiston Roundup, is held here the first weekend after Labor Day.

One of the outstanding riverboat trips in the West begins and ends in Lewiston. Tourist boats go up the Snake River to within 17 miles of Hells Canyon. Shorter trips and cruises are also available. For information contact the Greater Lewiston Chamber of Commerce.

An Eastern Tour

An Eastern tour of the state will take you to Gooding, the gateway to Mammoth Cave, Shoshone Ice Caves, Sun Valley, and Craters of the Moon; Thousand Springs, where waterfalls cascade down the glistening banks above the road; Twin Falls, south-central Idaho's largest city; and Shoshone Falls, a spectacle in the spring when the Snake takes a sheer 212-foot drop over the basaltic horseshoe rim nearly 1,000 feet wide.

If you continue eastward, you'll come to Pocatello, eastern Idaho's largest city, and Ft. Hall, agency headquarters for the Shoshone, Bannock, and other tribes of the Ft. Hall Indian Reservation. Two Sun Dances are held in July on the Ft. Hall Reservation, and in August, on the same reservation, there is the four-day Shoshone-Bannock Indian Festival. All three include a buffalo feast. Palefaces admitted.

A World-Famous Resort

Long recognized as one of the world's famous winter resorts, Sun Valley has, for some years, also been popular as a summer playground. In addition to the usual ice skating, swimming, riding, tennis, and fishing, there are mind-shattering trips into the wilderness.

Beyond Sun Valley is Craters of the Moon National Monument. This utterly desolate 83-square-mile area is a fantastic, grotesque Dante's inferno of basaltic features. A seven-mile loop drive passes by some of the volcanic landscapes, while a variety of trails leads to others.

National Forests

Several words about Idaho's national forests: fascinating, unique, unparalleled, fantastic, adventurous, and beautiful.

Eight national forests lie entirely within the boundaries of Idaho and seven others partly within, giving the state more than 20 million acres of National Forest lands.

Major forests include: *Boise,* the state's largest; *Caribou, Challis, Clearwater, Coeur d'Alene, Kaniksu, Nez Perce, Payette, Salmon, St. Joe National Forest,* and *Targhee.*

PRACTICAL INFORMATION FOR IDAHO

HOW TO GET THERE. *By air: United* serves Boise from Portland, San Francisco, and Salt Lake City. *Cascade* serves Boise, Idaho Falls, Pocatello, Lewiston, and Moscow. *Western* serves Boise from Salt Lake City. *Frontier* serves Boise from Denver. *Horizon* serves Boise, Idaho Falls, Twin Falls, Pocatello, Lewiston, Sun Valley, and Moscow. *Alaska Airlines* serves Boise from Seattle. *By bus: Greyhound* or *Trailways. By train: Amtrak.*

HOW TO GET AROUND. *By air: Cascade* and *Horizon. Car rental: Avis* and *Hertz* have offices throughout the state. *By bus:* A dozen bus lines operating in the state. *By train:* The daily *Empire Builder* stops at Sandpoint on the Seattle-Chicago run. The *Pioneer* on the Salt Lake City–Portland run, stops daily at Pocatello and Boise.

TOURIST INFORMATION SERVICES. Best source: *Idaho Tourism,* Room 108, State House, Boise, (208) 334–2470. For hunting and fishing information write: *Idaho Fish & Game Dept.,* P.O. Box 25, Boise 83707.

MUSEUMS AND GALLERIES. Historical: *Idaho State Historical Museum,* Boise; *Blaine County Historical Museum,* Hailey, contains an American Political Items Collection; *Luna House Museum,* Lewiston, displays Indian artifacts; *Pioneers Historical Museum,* Montpelier; *Bannock County Historical Museum,* Pocatello; *Lemhi County Historical Museum,* Salmon; and *Twin Falls County Historical Museum,* Twin Falls. Art: *Boise Gallery of Art* and *Herrett Arts and Science Center,* Twin Falls.

HISTORIC SITES. Many of Idaho's historic sites parallel the trails of history through the state—the *Oregon Trail* in the south, *Lewis and Clark Route* in the north-central section, and *Mullan Road* in the panhandle. The visitor may retrace these famous routes on modern highways.

Other sites include the gold ghost towns of Centerville, Placerville, and Pioneerville, and a replica of Ft. Hall, built in 1834, in Pocatello.

TOURS. *By boat:* Boat trips from Lewiston go into Hells Canyon. The adventurous can go down the Snake through Hells Canyon or down the Middle Fork of the Salmon, the "River of No Return," on float trips or jet-boat excursions. For detailed information write: *Idaho Outfitters and Guides Association.* P.O. Box 95, Boise 83701.

SUMMER SPORTS. Idaho is sheer heaven for the outdoor sportsman. *Fishing:* The fishing is good in all parts of Idaho. Record-size trout, steelhead, and sturgeon. *Boating:* The lakes, rivers, and streams provide water highways for small boat operators. Special thrills are offered on the white-water trips down the Snake, Salmon, and Selway. *Hunting:* Small and big game, with the many miles of wilderness and forests providing a special opportunity for hunting big game.

WINTER SPORTS. In a word, skiing. For all information contact *Idaho Tourism,* Room 108, State House, Boise.

DRINKING LAWS. Minimum drinking age is 19.

SPECTATOR SPORTS. Rodeos are scheduled in Idaho throughout summer and fall. Motorcycle and drag races are held throughout the state and there is horse racing during the summer.

WHAT TO DO WITH THE CHILDREN. In a state abounding with lakes, streams, and trails, children will find activity nearly every time the family car pauses. In addition, there's the *miniature power station* in Trenner Memorial Park at American Falls, and the *Island Park Music Circus,* at Macks Inn, in Idaho's legendary *Mountain Man* country.

HOTELS AND MOTELS. Based on double occupancy, categories and price ranges are as follows: *Deluxe:* $35–70; *Expensive:* $25–35; *Moderate:* $20–25; *Inexpensive:* under $20.

BOISE. *Deluxe:* **Red Lion Motor Inn/Riverside.** Large. dining room; 2 restaurants; heated pool.
Rodeway Inn. Luxurious units on lovely award-winning grounds. Skiing, tennis, golf available. 24-hour coffee shop.
Expensive: **Owyhee Plaza.** Large, multi-story; some rooms with balconies. *Holiday* magazine award-winning Gamekeeper Room.
Red Lion Inn/Downtowner. Restaurant, coffee shop; lounge.
Shilo Inn. Pool, saunas, movies, game room. Private patios, continental breakfast.
Moderate: **Cabana Inn.** Attractively furnished, close to downtown.
Seven K Motel. Family motel on lovely landscaped grounds, with nearby grassy play area for children.
Super 8 Lodge. Rooms for handicapped. Free coffee lounge.
Idanha Hotel. Modern and antique decor. An historic air.
Skyline. Comfortable, lovely grounds. Genteel and rustic.

COEUR D'ALENE. *Expensive:* **Holiday Inn.** Very large; family units available.
North Shore Resort Hotel. Beautiful lakefront motel, with 3 heated pools, marina, playground.
Sandman Hotel. Cozy, nice ambiance.
Moderate: **Pines Motel.** Quiet; well back from highway.
Inexpensive: **Motel 6.** Convenient, comfortable, and clean.
Travels 9 Motel. Efficiency with a flair.

IDAHO FALLS. *Expensive:* **Littletree Inn.** All units with king- or queen-size beds. Charming landscaped courtyard. They make you feel wanted.
Best Western Stardust Lodge. Huge motel located on river bank, offering a fine view of LDS Temple.
Driftwood–Falls View Motel. Large motel overlooking river and falls.
Moderate: **Evergreen Motel.** Kitchenettes; play area for kids.
Motel West. Recreation area. Latchstring welcome.
Westbank Quality Inn. Lovely view of park and falls.

KETCHUM–SUN VALLEY. *Deluxe:* **Christiania Lodge.** In center of Ketchum; variety of accommodations. Four golf courses within one mile.
Bald Mountain Hot Springs Motel. Easy access to ski areas; adjacent to restaurants and shopping; Olympic size natural hot water pool; charming rooms.
Sun Valley Resort. World-renowned. All the trimmings. If you need to ask about rates, this is not the place for you.
Heidelberg Inn. Built in Bavarian-style. Golf course across the way; easy walk to front stream.
Tamarack Lodge. Enclosed courtyard, private balconies or patios. Heated pool. Fireplaces.
Expensive: **Ski View Lodge.** Looking out to Baldy Mountain ski lift. Kitchenettes, heating, in all units.
Tyrolean Lodge. Convenient medium-size motel; Continental breakfast. The Alps in Idaho.
Moderate: **Wood River Motel.** Rustic log cabins, kitchenettes, close to lifts and town.

LEWISTON *Expensive:* **Pony Soldier Motor Inn.** Heated pools, kitchens, air-conditioned.
Tapadera Motor Inn. Comfortably furnished rooms.
Moderate: **El Rancho Motel.** Quiet, modest-size motel with heated pool.
Hillary Motel. Kitchenettes, weekly rates available.
Sacajawea Lodge. Large motel with variety of units. Restaurant, lounge.

POCATELLO. *Deluxe:* **Cottontree Inn.** Large motel with heated pool, restaurant, and lounge. Tennis.

Littletree Inn. Complimentary breakfast, cocktails, and airport limo. Elegant.

Expensive: **Holiday Inn.** Huge motel with variety of units; free transportation from airport. Their usual efficiency.

Moderate: **Bidwell Motel.** Medium-size motel across from Idaho State University. Kitchens. Indoor heated pool.

Idaho Motel. Across from Idaho State University. Insulated. Some kitchens.

Imperial "400" Motel. Casual. Across from Idaho State University.

Laab's Motel. Medium-size. Kitchenettes. Homey.

Sundial Inn. Sparkling, attractive. Cheerful service.

Thunderbird Motel. Heated pool, relaxed air, guest laundry.

SALMON. *Expensive:* **Stagecoach Inn.** Medium-size motel with heated pool; cafe nearby.

Moderate: **Suncrest Motel.** Some kitchen units; playground for youngsters; near cafe.

SANDPOINT. *Expensive:* **Edgewater Lodge.** On shore of Lake Pend Oreille with private patios offering magnificent views of lakes and mountains.

Lakeside Motel. Easy access to city beach and park. Some kitchens.

Moderate: **Whitaker House Bed & Breakfast.** Hospitable; comfortable rooms; hearty food.

TWIN FALLS. *Expensive:* **Apollo Motor Inn.** Medium-size motel with heated pool. Golf. Cafe nearby. Seasonal rates.

Canyon Springs Inn. Formerly Littletree Inn. Poolside dining, nightly entertainment, seasonal rates.

Holiday Inn. Health club facilities, cafe, dining room, bar, dancing, entertainment.

Weston Lamplighter. Large, heated pool, free coffee.

Moderate: **Capri Motel.** A medium-size, feel-at-home place.

Dunes Motel. Top flight with sweet touch.

Holiday Motel. Small, comfortable, coin laundry, picnic facilities.

Monterey Motor Inn. Quiet, medium-size, on spacious grounds; family units, heated pool; picnic and playground areas.

WALLACE. *Moderate:* **Stardust Motel.** Downtown, medium-size, family units, ski-waxing room. Free coffee.

WEISER. *Moderate:* **Colonial Motel.** Comfortable units; some kitchens; close to restaurant and coin laundry.

 DINING OUT. Restaurants are listed by categories. *Expensive:* $10–15; *Moderate:* $5–10; *Inexpensive:* under $5. Drinks, tax and tip are not included.

BOISE. *Expensive:* **The Gamekeeper.** Located in the Owyhee Plaza Hotel. Top quality steaks, seafood, wines. A regular award winner.

Moderate: **Bonanza Restaurant.** All you can eat. Children's menu.

La Fiesta. Delightful Mexican food.

Stuart Anderson's. Steak at its best.

COEUR D'ALENE. *Expensive:* **The Cedars.** Floating restaurant on Lake Coeur d'Alene.

Moderate: **North Shore Plaza Restaurants.** Lakeshore complex, with plush rooftop dining, casual atmosphere of Shore Restaurant, or chicken-to-go from Templin's.

IDAHO FALLS. *Moderate:* **Italiano.** The taste and atmosphere of Old Italy.

Stardust Restaurant. Well patronized. Westbank Coffee Shop. Varied menu and exhilarating river view.

KETCHUM–SUN VALLEY. *Moderate:* **The Ore House.** On the mall. Make-it-yourself salads.

Warm Springs Ranch Restaurant. Outdoor dining with a mountain view.

LEWISTON. *Moderate:* **Cedars III.** Famous for hand-cut steaks and crisp salad bar.

The Helm. Mouth-watering prime ribs, steaks, and shrimp. Children's menu.

POCATELLO. *Moderate:* **Elmer's Pancake and Steak House.** Twenty-one varieties of pancakes. Located across from Idaho State University.

SANDPOINT. *Moderate:* **Garden Restaurant.** Outdoor dining; specialties range from fresh seafoods to roast duck and Oriental-style dishes.

TWIN FALLS. *Moderate:* **Depot Grill.** Popular since 1927. Smorgasbord in the Caboose Room. 55 different specialties. Children's prices. Local flavor.

MONTANA

Yellowstone and Riches of the Earth

The Yellowstone River has been the dominant highway of the region for years. Generations of Montanans have looked to it for protection, direction, and a sometimes reliable drink for man, cow, or crop.

The Tongue River forks into the Yellowstone at Miles City, and just north of Miles City you can see the Fort Peck Dam and the Missouri River where Lewis and Clark first entered Montana.

Custer's Last Stand is the Montana incident most familiar to Americans, and at Custer Battlefield National Monument, 15 miles southeast of Hardin, a government museum tells the story of the ill-fated Yellow Hair, as the general was called.

Billings, northwest of the Custer Battlefield, is the largest city in Montana. Named for Frederick Billings, president of the Northern Pacific Railway that gave it life, Billings has sugarbeet and oil refineries, livestock yards, and two small colleges.

Among the Billings sights is the statue of the Range Rider of the Yellowstone, posed for by William S. Hart, cowboy hero of silent movies. This is along Black Otter Trail, which follows the rim above the city to the north. Five miles from Billings, a Pictograph Cave contains the most important scratchings of prehistoric man on the Great Plains.

From Billings, a breathtaking ride along the Beartooth Scenic Highway cuts through the western portion of Custer National Forest.

Bozeman, settled in 1864, is the home of Montana State University with its 11,300 students, headquarters for the 1,700,000-acre Gallatin National Forest, and the center of purebred livestock, small grain, and dairying. The college fieldhouse and the museum on the campus are worth a side trip.

...es City, highlights the days of the open range. *The Museum of the Plains* ...ians in Browning features artifacts of Indian tribes.

HISTORIC SITES. *Fort Union Trading Post National Historic Site,* 23 miles north of Sidney, is a fort built in 1828 by the American Fur Company. *Custer National Monument,* southeastern Montana, is the scene of the ...ous last stand. *Pompey's Pillar,* near the town of the same name, is a ...ering sandstone rock that was a Lewis and Clark Expedition landmark. ...ntana Territorial Prison, Deer Lodge, was the first of its kind in the Western ... It's now a museum. *Original Montana Governor's Mansion,* Helena, was ...t in 1885 and has housed nine governors since 1913. *St. Mary's Mission* in ...ensville is the oldest church in the Pacific Northwest. *Virginia City,* south- ...t of Bozeman, is a restored pioneer mining boom town and political capital.

TOURS. *Glacier Park, Inc.* offers two- to six-day tours of Glacier National Park and Waterton Lakes National Park, Canada. For complete information write Glacier ...cier Park Inc., Greyhound Tower, Phoenix, AZ, 85044 (Sept.-May).

DRINKING LAWS. Legal drinking age is 19 and bars are open until 2 A.M.

SUMMER SPORTS. *Fishing.* Almost every type of fish can be caught in Montana. The season usually starts in May and ends around Nov. 30. Local inquiry to the State Fish, Wildlife & Parks Dept. will yield information ...ut laws, and locations of the types of fish you want.
...*Hunting:* Hunting licenses for nonresidents vary. A license entitles you to a ...ety of game, but the nonresident must put in for drawings, by regions, in ...er to get the appropriate tags. Most areas also require that you hunt with ...esident who can double as guide.
...*Golfing:* There are three dozen courses in Montana, in most principal cities.
...*Riding:* At any of the many guest ranches. For an up-to-date list of riding ...ches, contact the Montana Travel Promotion Division, Helena, Montana ...20. Also, the bigger towns have saddle clubs which can help you find riding ...ilities.
...*Rock hunting:* Montana is a rockhound's paradise. The Travel Promotion ...ision has a special pamphlet on the subject.
...*Boating:* Water-skiing and power-boating are common on the larger lakes ...reservoirs. River rafting is also in fashion.

WINTER SPORTS. *Skiing:* Write for a complete guide on skiing from the Travel Promotion Division, Helena, Mont. 59620, or phone 1-800-548-3390. Major ski areas are as follows: *Big Sky,* located 45 miles from ...zeman, in the heart of the Gallatin Valley; *Big Mountain Ski Area,* Whitefish, ...l *Red Lodge Mountain,* 65 miles southwest of Billings.

WHAT TO DO WITH THE CHILDREN. The oppor- tunities to see animals in their natural habitats are excel- lent. Near Ronan, the *Ninepipe* and *Pablo National Wildlife Refuges* are particularly good spots to see ...terfowl. At the *National Bison Range,* 300–500 head of buffalo roam over an ...000-acre range. Maiden, Kendall, and Gilt Edge, all near Lewistown, are ...ost towns left over from the mining days of the 19th century. Helena's *Frontier ...wn* is a replica of a pioneer village, hewn out of solid rock and cut from giant ...s. Virginia City is a restored *gold boom town,* and the Nevada City Depot ...a *railroad museum* with antique engines and cars. *Glacier National Park* is ...r country—be sure to read a bear information folder.

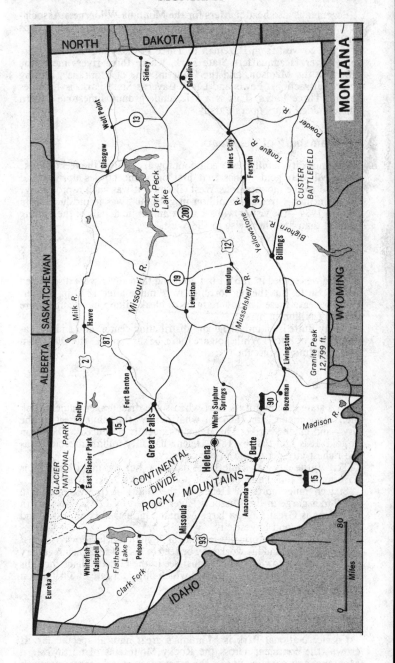

Bozeman is also headquarters for the Montana Wilderness Association, which every summer conducts numerous walking and riding trips for visitors into the wilds of the state.

If you go west from Bozeman to Three Forks, you'll find the Missouri River Headquarters State Park, where three rivers meet: the Jefferson, the Madison, and the Gallatin. One of Montana's leading natural attractions, Lewis and Clark Caverns State Park, is 13 miles beyond Three Forks. This is a safe, underground limestone cavern where guided tours operate daily.

Williamsburg of the West

Virginia City, a fully restored boom town, captures the feel of those post-Civil War gold rushes that first drew the hordes upriver and overland to the mountainous West. Because it was such a productive mining center—over $300 million in gold dust was found here from 1863 to 1937—the visitor will see more authentic details of the mining frontier than anywhere else in the West.

Butte

Butte was settled in 1864. First gold and then silver were discovered around Butte, but the big fortunes were made after 1870 in copper. From beneath these five square miles of bleak hilltop have come more than $17 billion in ores.

Today Butte is an industrial and distributing center, and an international Port of Entry. While you are there, be sure and see the Old Town and the Mining Museum.

Helena

This state capital got its start when some discouraged miners took their "last chance" in 1864 on what is now the main street of the city—and made a strike. The area subsequently produced $20 million in gold. It is said that by 1888 Helena had fifty millionaires and was the richest city per capita in the country.

Today, the city has some large industry, but the main business is government, and the trappings of politics are the real attraction.

Sixteen miles north of Helena is the Gates of the Mountains, a 2,000-foot gorge in the Missouri River, named by Lewis. Also north of Helena is Great Falls, a large Montana industrial boom town and the State's second largest city.

Great Falls is historically famous as home base for cowboy artist Charlie Russell, and his work may be seen in his old studio cum gallery in the center of town. Another must-see in the Great Falls is the falls themselves, and the nearby springs which flow at a rate of 388 million gallons daily.

National Parks and Forests

Glacier National Park is Montana's great natural spectacular. It crowns the continent across the Rocky Mountains of northwestern Montana, and contains one of the most spectacularly scenic portions of the entire range. Covering over 1,500 square miles, it is the U.S. section of the Waterton-Glacier International Peace Park. For full details, see "Glacier N.P." section in *Distinctively American Vacations*, earlier in this book.

Some of Montana's other national parks and forests [Yellowstone National Park (described earlier in this book[ ]National Forest, west of the Divide in southwestern Mon[ ]National Forest, in southeastern Montana; Deerlodge Nati[ ]Butte; Flathead National Forest, southwest of Glacier Pa[ ]National Forest, in south central Montana; Helena Nation[ ]west central Montana, and Lewis and Clark National For[ ]central Montana.

The major state parks include: Lewis and Clark Caverns[ ]east of Butte; Giant Springs State Park, four miles northe[ ]Falls; Medicine Rocks State Park, north of Ekalaka, and[ ]State Park, near Glendive.

Flathead Lake and the Mission Valley

Flathead Lake is the largest freshwater lake west of the [ ]28 miles long and from 5 to 15 miles wide. On the east sh[ ]nestles up to the white-topped Mission Range; on the we[ ]into the foothills of the Cabinet Mountains. On the east [ ]find a state park and the Montana State University Biolog[ ]on the west shore, two state parks and many resorts.

Just south of the lake is the heart of the Mission Valle[ ]Flathead Indian Reservation. And southwest of this is t[ ]Bison Range, with headquarters at Moiese. During [ ]months, there are self-guided auto tours to search out the [ ]and their accompanying bands of deer, antelope, elk, [ ]sheep. The range covers 19,000 acres, and is one of the ol[ ]preserves in the country.

PRACTICAL INFORMATION FOR MON

HOW TO GET THERE. *By air: Western,* [ ]*neer,* and *Northwest Orient.* By train: *Am* [ ]service to Glacier National Park and H [ ]*Trailways* and *Greyhound.*

HOW TO GET AROUND. *By air: Fron* [ ]*Northwest Orient,* and *Big Sky.* By train: [ ]rail system—the "Empire Builder" (which [ ]2). *By bus: Greyhound, Trailways, Intermo* [ ]portation, Glacier Transportation, and *Brown Bus Lines* (in som[ ]

TOURIST INFORMATION SERVICES. For information or [ ]hostelries, and activities, call (800) 548-3390 or write to *Montan[ ]Commerce* P.O. Box 1730, Helena, Montana 59624.

MUSEUMS AND GALLERIES. The *Mo[ ]cal Society & C. M. Russell Art Gallery,* He[ ]a capsule history of Montana and a collec[ ]Russell's art. *Charles M. Russell Origina* [ ]*Museum,* Great Falls, exhibits Russell's works as well as his own [ ]Indian costumes and gear. *J. K. Ralston Museum & Art Center,* [ ]lights historical artifacts from the region and original Ralston p[ ]*Museum of the Rockies* in Bozeman, has permanent and changing [ ]depict the physical and social heritage of the northern Rockies. *W[ ]of Mining,* Butte, shows mining relics. *Big Sky Historical Museum[ ]displays Western frontier guns and Indian artifacts. *Range Ride[ ]

HOTELS AND MOTELS. The price categories in this section, for double occupancy, will average as follows: *Deluxe:* $55–90; *Expensive:* $46–54; *Moderate:* $35–45; *Inexpensive:* $18–34.

BILLINGS. *Expensive:* **Best Western Northern.** B'way, & 1st Ave. N.
Ponderosa Inn. Heated pools, 24-hour café. Best Western.
Moderate: **Dude Rancher Lodge.** 415 N. 29th. Movies, coffee shop.
War Bonnet Inn. 2612 Beknaj Ave. Pool, dancing, entertainment. Heated pool.
Inexpensive: **Regal Inn.** 5353 Midland Rd. Pool.

BOZEMAN. *Expensive:* **Holiday Inn.** Off the interstate highway. Modern.
Voss Inn Bed & Breakfast. Restored Victorian mansion.
Inexpensive: **Imperial 400 Motel.** 122 W. Main Street. Downtown.

BUTTE. *Expensive:* **Copper King Inn.** Close to airport. Indoor pools, sauna.
War Bonnet Inn. Heated pool, café.
Moderate: **Thrift Inn.** Pool, cafe.
Inexpensive: **Mile–Hi Motel.** Heated pool, restaurant adjacent.

GLACIER NATIONAL PARK. *Expensive:* **Glacier Park Lodge.** On MT. 49. All amenities and sports.
Many Glacier Hotel. US 89. Reservations essential. Summer only.
Inexpensive: **Swiftcurrent Motor Inn and Cabins.** On lake with camp store, resort activities.

GREAT FALLS. *Deluxe* to *Expensive:* **Heritage Inn.** Indoor pool, café, entertainment. 232 rooms. Best Western.
Holiday Inn. Heated pool, dancing, entertainment.
Sheraton Great Falls Inn. Seven stories. Restaurant.
Moderate: **Triple Crown Motor Inn.** Cafe nearby.

HELENA. *Expensive:* **Best Western Colonial Inn.** All amenities.
Coach House. Health spa, lounge, café.
Park Plaza. Elevator, restaurant, entertainment.
Inexpensive: **Motel 6.** Cafe nearby.

MILES CITY. *Moderate:* **Best Western War Bonnet Inn.** Free Continental breakfast. Best Western chain.
Inexpensive: **Super 8 Motel.** At US 59 and I–94.

MISSOULA. *Expensive:* **Best Western Executive Motor Inn.** Heated pool, café. 3 stories.
Village Red Lion Motor Inn. All luxuries.
Moderate:
Ponderosa Lodge. Close to town and university.
Royal Motel. Central location.
TraveLodge. Family restaurant.

VIRGINIA CITY. *Moderate:* **Nevada City Hotel.** On US 287. Gold rush style.
Inexpensive: **Fairweather Inn.** On US 287. Old West décor.

DINING OUT. Steak, prime ribs, lobster and local game are the big favorites in this area. Restaurant price categories are for a complete dinner but do not include drinks or tip: *Deluxe:* $21 and up; *Expensive:* $18–20; *Moderate:* $11–17; and *Inexpensive:* $6–10.

BILLINGS. *Expensive:* **Golden Belle.** In Best Western Northern Hotel. Specializing in steak and seafood.
Moderate: **Black Angus.** Locally popular.

BOZEMAN. *Expensive–Moderate:* **Overland Express Restaurant.** In Bozeman Hotel. Steak and lobster.
Inexpensive: **Union Hall.** Located in former art studio.

BUTTE. *Expensive:* **Lydia's.** Excellent steak and Italian cuisine.
Inexpensive: **4 B's.** Popular with the local crowd.

GLACIER NATIONAL PARK. *Moderate:* **Glacier Park Lodge.** Complete dinners served with home-baked goods.
Many Glacier. Prime rib, steak, trout.

GREAT FALLS. *Moderate:* **Black Angus Steak House.** Prime rib, steak.
Gordon's. Prime rib.
Inexpensive: **4 B's.** Family place.

HELENA. *Expensive:* **Overland Express.** Good meats.
Inexpensive: **Jorgenson's.** In Best Western Holiday Motel.

KALISPELL. *Inexpensive:* **Pancho Villa's.** Mexican.

MISSOULA. *Moderate:* **4B's Restaurant.** Good value.
Inexpensive: **King's Table.** Buffet style.
Ming's. Chinese-style dinners.

NEBRASKA

The Great Plains State

Nebraska has long been known as a corridor to the West, for the Mormon Trail, Oregon Trail, Lewis and Clark Trail and Pony Express all crossed through the state, using the flat terrain of the broad Platte Valley.

The romantic figures of the Old West also knew Nebraska well—Buffalo Bill, Wild Bill Hickok, Chief Red Cloud, the James Boys, just to name a few.

The railroad was a vital force in Nebraska's settlement and expansion, and the Union Pacific was of primary importance. It was in Omaha, in 1863, that ground was broken for the eventual joining of rails to the West Coast. Headquarters for the Union Pacific are in Omaha and a museum operated by the company houses many souvenirs from the railroad's history.

The past is commemmorated at several fine museums in Omaha. Joslyn Art Museum, an imposing structure of pink marble, is considered one of America's foremost centers of Early West art. The Western Heritage Museum, in the old Union Station, also traces Omaha's earliest history. In nearby Bellevue is located the Strategic Aerospace Museum, a collection of aircraft and missiles dating from World War II. The museum sits on an unused runway connected with the Strategic Air Command's top-secret underground control center. West of the city is famed Father Flanagan's Boy's Town, "the city of little men" made famous by a movie starring Spencer Tracy and Mickey Rooney.

Lincoln, 50 miles southwest of Omaha, has the state capitol, a building long recognized as one of the world's architectural masterpieces. Here also are the University of Nebraska, with the State Museum, the State Historical Society Museum (housing outstanding pioneer and

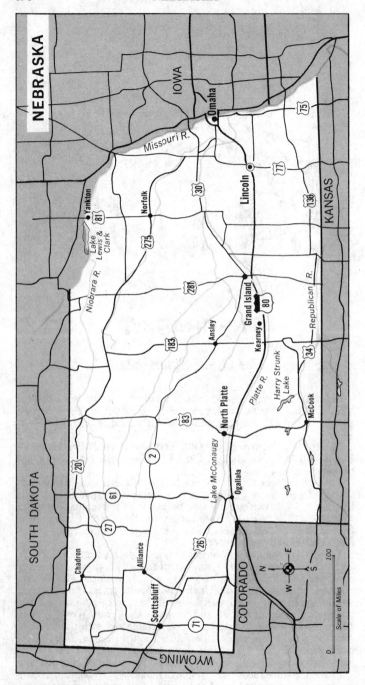

Indian exhibits), and the Sheldon Art Galleries. Also in Lincoln is the home of the famous orator, William Jennings Bryan.

Heading west from Lincoln, several museums capture the lore of the West and Pioneer days. Outstanding is Pioneer Village in Minden, where 30,000 antique items are on display in 24 buildings, many of which are authentic reproductions or originals. In nearby Hastings is the Hastings Museum (House of Yesterday) which also specializes in Pioneer and Indian history. In Grand Island, the Stuhr Museum of the Prairie Pioneer is housed in a unique building designed by Edward Durrell Stone and surrounded by a watery moat. Exhibits include a large antique vehicle collection. The adjacent area has been developed into a 19th-century prairie town with original buildings. The town is complete with early post office, stores, churches, refurbished homes, depot, and a train that provides rides over a 1½-mile track.

Many early military forts were established in the state, and many have either been preserved or restored, including Fort Kearny, near the town of Kearney. The fort was an important deterrent to Indian troubles, and provided protection for wagon trains.

Fort McPherson, near Maxwell, has been declared a National Cemetery; Fort Robinson, where the great Sioux Chief Crazy Horse was mortally wounded, has become one of the major state parks, with overnight accommodations in original fort buildings and various outdoor recreational activities in the rugged lake and stream-dotted terrain. Fort Niobrara, near Valentine, is now a National Wildlife Refuge.

A unique art form in Nebraska is its 450-mile-long sculpture garden. A project of the Bicentennial, a dozen sculptures of abstract design commissioned to commemmorate the state's history are located at rest areas along I–80.

PRACTICAL INFORMATION FOR NEBRASKA

HOW TO GET THERE. *By air: Republic, Western, American, America West, United, Continental, Eastern, TWA, Northwest Orient, Ozark, Frontier,* and five commuter airlines all serve Omaha. *By train: Amtrak. By bus: Continental Trailways* and *Greyhound.*

HOW TO GET AROUND. *By air: Frontier, United, Air Midwest,* and *American Central. By train: Amtrak* stops at Omaha, Lincoln, Hastings, Holdrege, and McCook. *By bus: Arrow, Black Hills Stage Lines, United Motorways, Chief, Continental Trailways,* and *Greyhound.*

TOURIST INFORMATION. For information concerning touring, events, convention facilities or business opportunities, contact *Dept. of Economic Development,* 301 Centennial Mall, Lincoln 68509. Specific information about outdoor activities is available from *Games and Parks Commission,* and *Nebraskaland,* 2200 N. 33rd St., Lincoln 68503. *Douglas County Tourism Dept.,* Omaha/Douglas County Civic Center, Suite 1200, 1819 Farnam St., Omaha, NE 68183.

CAMPING OUT. Nebraska has more than 60 state recreation areas, as well as another 150 special-use and wayside areas. The following are some of the larger campgrounds: Branched Oak Lake, 3 mi. N of Malcolm; Fremont Lakes, 3 mi. W of Fremont; Lewis & Clark, 15 mi. N of Crofton; Two Rivers, 1 mi. W of Venice; Lake McConaughy, 9 mi. N of Ogallala.

MUSEUMS AND ART GALLERIES. The *Stuhr Museum of the Prairie Pioneer,* is located on the outskirts of Grand Island. The *Museum of the Fur Trade,* E. of Chadron, traces American fur trading. The *Hastings Museum,* Hastings, has wildlife, Indian, and natural history exhibits. *Joslyn Art Museum,* Omaha, is a magnificent marble structure housing a varied collection of art. Also in Omaha are the *Union Pacific Historical Museum, Strategic Aerospace Museum,* and *Western Heritage Museum.*

At the University of Nebraska at Lincoln are several significant museums: the *University of Nebraska State Museum,* displaying geology and wildlife of the Great Plains; the *State Historical Society Museum,* and *Sheldon Memorial Art Gallery and Sculpture Garden.*

 HISTORIC SITES. *Agate Fossil Beds National Monument,* 9 mi. NW of Scottsbluff on US 26 to Mitchell, then 34 mi. N. on State 29, is an area where the fossils of animals alive 20 million years ago are concentrated. *Homestead National Monument,* 4 mi. NW of Beatrice, site of the first homestead claim in the U.S. *Chimney Rock National Historic Site,* 3½ mi. SW of Bayard, early pioneer beacon. *Scottsbluff National Monument,* at Scottsbluff, prominent 800-foot-high escarpment that was a pioneer landmark. *Toadstool Park,* 18 mi. NW of Crawford, badland area of weird carvings by nature. *Arbor Lodge State Historical Park,* Nebraska City, is Nebraska's oldest state historical park. *Fort Kearny State Historical Park,* 8 mi. SE of Kearney on State 10, re-creates the frontier outpost as it was a century ago. *Buffalo Bill Ranch State Historical Park,* at North Platte, was William F. Cody's ranch and winter quarters. Also worth a visit are the *Willa Cather Pioneer Memorial and Museum* in Red Cloud; the *Harold Warp Pioneer Village* on State 10 in Minden; and the *State Capitol Building* in Lincoln.

DRINKING LAWS. Liquor is sold by the drink or the bottle from 6 A.M. to 1 A.M. No package liquor sales may be made on Sunday except beer and wine. Liquor sale by the drink is subject to local option. Minimum drinking age is 21.

 SUMMER SPORTS. *Fishing:* Game fish are so abundant in Nebraska that a fisherman may indulge himself all year and catch black bass, trout, northern pike, walleye and catfish. *Hunting:* Pheasant, quail, turkey, prairie chicken, ducks, and geese are prime targets, but there are seasons on other large and small game. The State Game and Parks Commission in Lincoln has information regarding seasons and licenses.

Boating, swimming, water skiing. Dams have backed up several rivers and formed large lakes well-suited to water sports.

 SPECTATOR SPORTS. *Rodeo.* These events take place all over Nebraska during the summer and fall. The Buffalo Bill Rodeo, combined with Nebraskaland Days, held in North Platte on the third week of June, is one of Nebraska's biggest annual outdoor events. *Horse Racing.* Pari-mutuel thoroughbred racing starts off in Grand Island in early March, then moves to Ak-Sar-Ben in Omaha May–August; Ato-Kad in S. Sioux City, May–July; Columbus, Aug.–Sept., Lincoln, Sept.–Nov.

WHAT TO DO WITH THE CHILDREN. In Lincoln, visit the Children's Zoo, the prototype for many similar ventures in the U.S. In Brownville, cruise the Missouri River via the *Belle of Brownville.* In Omaha, the Children's Museum, Henry Doorly Zoo and Peony Park offer interesting entertainment.

 **HOTELS AND MOTELS.** The price categories in this section, for double occupancy, will average as follows: *Deluxe:* $60–80; *Expensive:* $45–60; *Moderate:* $35–45; *Inexpensive:* under $35.

ALLIANCE. *Moderate:* **Best Western West Way Motel.** 1 story, 44 rooms. Queen-size beds.

BELLEVUE. *Moderate:* **White House Inn.** Queen-size beds, large rooms, some water beds. 2 stories, 40 rooms.

GRAND ISLAND. *Moderate:* **Ramada Inn.** Jct. US 34 & SR 2. 2 stories. Indoor pool, 182 rooms, game room, tennis court, play area, Jacuzzi, two saunas, king-size and water beds.
I-80 Holiday Inn. Jct. US 34 & 281. Indoor & outdoor pools, sauna, whirlpool. Pets.

KEARNEY. *Expensive:* **Holiday Inn.** I-80 exit Kearney. 210 rooms, indoor rec area with heated pool, sauna, playground.
Moderate: **Quality Inn.** 67 rooms. Heated indoor pool, coin laundry, sauna, miniature golf.
Best Western Tel-Star Motor Inn. 63 rooms. Heated outdoor pool, queen-size beds, playground.
Inexpensive: **Fort Kearny Inn.** Jct. I-80 & SR 10. 3 stories, 107 rooms. Outdoor pool, extra long beds.
Hammer Budget Inn. 1 mi. W on US 30. 34 rooms. 4 2-bedroom suites, heated pool.

LINCOLN. *Deluxe:* **Lincoln Hilton.** 9th & P Sts. 233 rooms, indoor pool.
Moderate: **Airport Inn Best Western.** 3200 NW 12 St. 5 stories, 127 rooms. Heated outdoor pool.
Best Western Villager Motel. 5200 O St. 190 rooms. Heated outdoor pool, putting green.
Ramada Inn. 2301 N.W. 12th St. 2 stories, 140 rooms, pool, in-room movies.
Inexpensive: **Great Plains.** 2732 O St. 42 units, 6 efficiencies.
Congress Inn. 2801 West O St. Swimming pool, 53 rooms.
Day's Inn. 2400 NW 12 St. 142 rooms.

NORTH PLATTE. *Moderate:* **Best Western Circle C South.** 77 rooms, 2 stories. Heated indoor pool, queen-size beds.
Howard Johnson's Motor Lodge. Jct. I-80 & US 83. 80 rooms, heated pool, coin laundry.
Inexpensive: **Dunes Motel.** 1 story, 47 rooms. Heated outdoor pool.
Rambler Friendship Inn. Near rodeo grounds and Buffalo Bill Ranch. 1 story, 25 rooms.

OGALLALA. *Moderate:* **Ogallala Stagecoach.** Jct. I-80 & US 26. 2 stories, 100 rooms. Outdoor pool, coin laundry, playground.
Lee's I-80 Inn. Jct. I-80 & US 26. 1 story, 40 rooms. Heated outdoor pool.

OMAHA. *Deluxe:* **Omaha Marriott.** 10220 Regency Circle. Heated indoor-outdoor pool, whirlpool, restaurants.
Moderate: **Best Western Immanuel Plaza Motel.** 6801 N. 72 St. 47 rooms. Indoor pool, suana, whirlpool, coin laundry.
LaQuinta Motor Inn. Maple St. and I-680. 2 stories, 130 rooms. Pool.
New Tower Inn Best Western. 7764 Dodge St. 2 stories, 336 rooms. Solar dome with heated pool, sauna, whirlpool.
Oak Creek Inn. 2808 S. 72 St. 2 stories, 104 rooms. In-house movies, heated pool, suana, whirlpool, some suites.
Inexpensive: **Best Western Shamrock.** 12000 W. Dodge Rd. 1 story, 47 rooms.
Budgetel Inn. 10760 M St. King-size beds, 96 rooms.
Thrifty Scot. 7101 Grover. 6 stories, 84 rooms.

SCOTTSBLUFF. *Moderate:* **Candlelight Inn.** 2 story, 56 rooms, heated outdoor pool.
Inexpensive: **Lamplighter Motel.** 40 rooms. Heated indoor pool. Two stories.
The Sands Motel. 19 rooms.

SOUTH SIOUX CITY. *Inexpensive:* **Best Western Marina Inn.** 108 rooms. Indoor pool, saunas, queen and king size beds. Four stories.

 DINING OUT. Restaurant price categories are as follows: *Deluxe:* $15 and up; *Expensive:* $10–15; *Moderate:* $5–10; *Inexpensive:* below $5. Prices are for a complete meal without drinks, tax or tip.

GRAND ISLAND. *Expensive:* **Atch's Grand Restaurant.** Prize steaks and prime rib in the heart of cattle country.

Dreisbach's. Steak is king—in size of portions and in quality—from their own aged beef.

KEARNEY. *Expensive:* **Cattleman's Mining Co.** Old West atmosphere. Superb steaks, prime rib, and specialty dishes.

Moderate: **Grandpa's Steak House.** Steaks, seafood in family atmosphere.

LINCOLN. *Deluxe:* **Misty III,** 63rd & Havelock Ave. Famous for prime rib, especially the "regal cut."

Expensive: **Crockett's Restaurant & Lounge.** 3201 Pioneer Blvd. Outstanding salad bar and tops in prime rib.

Misty Edgewood. 5508 S. 56th St., Suite 5. Specializing in steaks and prime rib.

P. O. Pear's. 329 South 9th St. Unique décor in a myriad of themes. Excellent menu, emphasis on beef.

Tony & Luigi's. 5140 O St. Beef and Italian specialties in a decor of stained glass.

Moderate: **Bishop Buffet.** Gateway Shopping Center.

K's Restaurant. 1275 S. Cotner. Family dining.

NEBRASKA CITY. *Moderate:* **The Embers.** Tasty beef. Cozy Atmosphere.

NORTH PLATTE. *Expensive:* **The Circle C.** Excellent steaks.

Moderate: **Merrick's Ranch House.** Family style dining.

OMAHA. *Deluxe:* **The Blue Fox.** Excellent seafood, continental cuisine, and extensive wine list.

Maxine's. Atop Red Lion Inn downtown. Excellent continental dining in elegant atmosphere.

The French Café. 1017 Howard St. Glamorous dining, outstanding French cuisine. In Old Market area.

Expensive: **Salvatore's.** 4688 Leavenworth St. Authentic northern and southern Italian cuisine.

Moderate: **Bohemian Cafe.** 1406 S. 13 St. Kraut, dumplings, veal, sausages.

House of Genji/House of Cathay. 8809 W. Dodge Rd. Two restaurants in one building. Japanese teppan cooking on one side, authentic Cantonese Chinese on the other.

Jack & Mary's. 639 N. 109 Court. Chicken is the favorite, but steaks are good, too.

Johnny's Cafe. 4702 S. 27 St. Outstanding steaks at the stockyards.

Mr. C's. 5319 N. 30 St. Italian and beef specialties in a "Christmas all year" atmosphere. Strolling string musicians.

Mother Tucker's, 7505 Dodge St. City's best salad bar; prime rib a specialty.

Ross' Steakhouse. 909 S. 72 St. One of Omaha's most popular steak houses, a reputation well earned.

Inexpensive: **El Hombre.** Excellent Mexican food in authentic setting. Some American dishes, too.

SCOTTSBLUFF. *Expensive:* **Gaslight.** Terrytown. Very popular with locals featuring excellent steaks and prime rib.

The Loft. Excellent salad bar, homemade bread and soups, prime steaks, shish kabobs, seafood, "paddock-style" rooms in a converted stable. Beef, smoked ribs, and "brandied" chicken.

Moderate: **Oriental House.** Excellent Cantonese cuisine.

NORTH DAKOTA

Roughrider Country

North Dakota is known as Roughrider Country because of the horseback antics of Teddy Roosevelt, the state's well-remembered "temporary" resident.

Fargo is the main portal to this broad plainsland via I–94. It is the state's largest city, with a population of more than 60,000, almost twice that of its sister city of Moorhead, Minnesota, just across the Red River. It was named for William G. Fargo of the Wells Fargo Company, and features the 2,100-acre campus of North Dakota State University.

West on I–94 is Jamestown, site of the popular Jamestown Dam Recreation Area with its 14-mile lake. Upstream thirty miles, the Arrowwood National Wildlife Refuge is a nesting and feeding ground for migratory birds and various kinds of wildlife. Twice a year the skies over Jamestown are almost blackened by millions of migrating ducks and geese. To the southwest, Gackle is known as the "Mallard Capital of the World."

The West truly begins at Bismarck where the skyscraper state capitol rises 18 stories above the prairies. Across the Missouri River is Mandan, and five miles to the south is Fort Abraham Lincoln from which Lt. Col. George A. Custer and the Seventh Cavalry began their ill-fated trek to disaster at Little Big Horn.

One hundred miles to the west lies the most spectacular part of North Dakota. The Badlands extend throughout the Little Missouri National Grasslands and also include Theodore Roosevelt National Park. Here one can see wild horses or perhaps bighorn sheep, as well as buffalo, deer, and antelope. The landscape has a strange and wild

702

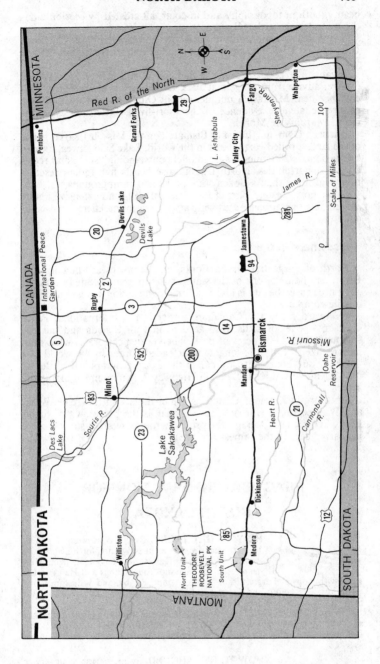

NORTH DAKOTA

MINNESOTA

CANADA

MONTANA

SOUTH DAKOTA

Red R. of the North

Pembina

Grand Forks

Devils Lake

Devils Lake

L. Ashtabula

Valley City

Fargo

Wahpeton

Sheyenne R.

James R.

International Peace Garden

Rugby

Des Lacs Lake

Souris R.

Minot

Jamestown

Bismarck

Mandan

Missouri R.

Oahe Reservoir

Heart R.

Cannonball R.

Lake Sakakawea

Williston

North Unit

THEODORE ROOSEVELT NATIONAL PK.

South Unit

Dickinson

Medora

Scale of Miles

0   100

N E S W

29 2 3 5 52 200 14 20 23 83 85 21 12 94 281

beauty, both in topography and in color, all created by erosion along the meandering Little Missouri River.

There are two major units in the Roosevelt National Park. The South Unit borders I–94. The North Unit is a half-hour drive to the north on US 85.

Because a large segment of the Badlands is still wild, visitors should first get advice from rangers at Park Headquarters at the South Unit entrance near Medora, a unique, rebuilt Old West cowtown. Here a restored chateau is evidence of the short-lived cattle dynasty of the fabled Marquis de Mores.

Garrison Dam, northwest of Bismarck on the Missouri River, is one of the largest rolled-earth dams in the world. Lake Sakakawea, formed by the dam, is 200 miles long and offers outstanding fishing and recreational opportunities. North Dakota also boasts five Indian reservations and more than a dozen state parks and campgrounds.

In the northwestern part of the state, oil wells and extensive lignite coal mining operations are growing attractions in this energy-conscious country.

Elsewhere in the State

North of Fargo lies Grand Forks, on the northward-flowing Red River, and home of one of the state's two universities. Site of a major Air Force base, the city is also near one of the nation's most important missile complexes.

Westward along the Canadian border is the International Peace Garden, a series of landscaped gardens in both Canada and the US, surrounded by 2,000 acres of park. The Garden celebrates what both nations like to call "the longest undefended border in the world."

About one hour south by car is the exact geographical center of North America, at Rugby, on US Highway 2. A monument marks the spot.

Strasburg in Emmons County is the birthplace of Lawrence Welk, and Wimbledon, northeast of Jamestown, is the hometown of singer Peggy Lee. Louis L'Amour, the prolific writer of western stories, spent his early years in the Jamestown area.

PRACTICAL INFORMATION FOR

NORTH DAKOTA

HOW TO GET THERE. *By air: Northwest, Republic, Western,* and *Frontier* airlines fly into North Dakota. *By train: Amtrak* passenger service is available from Minneapolis in the east and from Billings and Havre in the west, with stops at Fargo, Grand Forks, Minot, Rugby, and Williston.

By bus: Greyhound and *Interstate Transportation Company* are the major interstate carriers in North Dakota.

By car: I–94 and US 2 provide access to the state from Minnesota in the east and from Montana in the west. US 85, 83, 281 and 81 reach the state from South Dakota in the south. I–29 and US 281 are major routes to and from Manitoba.

HOW TO GET AROUND. *By air:* Intrastate air service is very limited; check locally. *By train: Amtrak* has one line crossing the state with limited stops. *By bus:* In addition to the service provided by *Greyhound* and *Interstate Transportation Co., Star Bus Lines* serves Grand Forks, Devils Lake, and Minot.

By car: I–94 is the major east-west route across the southern portion of the state and US 2 across the northern. I–20 and US 281 are the principal north-south arteries.

TOURIST INFORMATION. An annual colorful guide to North Dakota gives a particularly useful summary of the principal attractions, parks, campgrounds, museums, and events in the state. Available from North Dakota Tourism Promotion Division, Economic Development Commission, Bismarck 58505. A national WATS line is available: 1–800–437–2077.

MUSEUMS AND GALLERIES. Historical: *Bismarck*—**Heritage Center,** on the capitol grounds; *The Camp Hancock Museum, Medora—De Mores Interpretive Museum.* Art: *Grand Forks—University Art Gallery,* U. of North Dakota. *Medora—Gallery of Western Art.*

HISTORIC SITES. Many sites and remnants of forts remain from the Indian wars. Custer commanded the 7th Cavalry at *Fort Lincoln,* near Mandan. Sitting Bull surrendered at *Fort Buford,* 5 mi. west of Williston. In the same vicinity is **Fort Union,** once the largest fur-trading post on the Missouri River. The Fort Mandan Historic Site overlooks the site of the *Lewis and Clark winter camp. Fort Abercrombie* was one of the first federal forts in the region.

The *Whitestone Battlefield Historic Site,* near Ellendale, was the site of the largest major battle between U. S. troops and Sioux Indians east of the Missouri River. Fort Totten, near Devils Lake, is one of the best preserved forts of the Indian period.

DRINKING LAWS. Liquor can be purchased by the drink at bars and by the bottle at liquor stores from 8:00 A.M. to 1:00 A.M.

TOURS. *Theodore Roosevelt National Park,* located in the western North Dakota Badlands, has a 49-mile circle drive through spectacular scenery in both North and South units.

Lewis and Clark Trail parallels Lewis and Clark's famous Missouri River expedition.

SPORTS. *Fishing:* Major year-round sport. Many species available. Huge Lake Sakakawea behind Garrison Dam is especially productive. *Hunting:* Whitetail deer throughout state; mule deer in west, antelope in southwest. One of the best duck areas in the country. *Golf:* Challenging courses at or near all major cities. Sand greens in west. *Skiing:* There are six areas scattered throughout the state. Cross-country skiing is booming.

SPECTATOR SPORTS. *Rodeo* is a big event here, and many towns sponsor one or more throughout the year. *Auto racing:* Stock car racing takes place at the Grand Forks Speedway from mid-May to mid-Sept.

WHAT TO DO WITH THE CHILDREN. In Bismarck, the *Sertoma Riverside Park* is located near the Missouri River. Next to the Park is the *Dakota Zoo,* with over 100 species of native animals. Jamestown features the world's largest buffalo (in concrete and steel) and *Frontier Fort* for the children.

HOTELS-MOTELS. The price categories in this section for double occupancy, will average as follows: *Expensive:* $35 and up; *Moderate:* $25–35; and *Inexpensive:* $16–25. (Larger cities and towns now have a number of economy motels such as *Super 8, Econ-O-Inn, Thrifty Scot,* etc. Check locally. Some of the larger facilities include a casino.)

BISMARCK. *Expensive:* **Best Western Kirkwood Motor Inn.** Elegant Bavarian decor.
Holiday Inn. Wide range of services; near capitol.
Town House Motor Inn. Quality accommodations; near capitol.
Moderate: **Bismarck Motor Hotel.** Medium-sized, family rates.
Fleck House Motel. Downtown, large, attractive. A Best Western facility.
Gateway Comfort Inn. Well-rated, with heated indoor pool; restaurant nearby.

BOTTINEAU. *Moderate:* **Norway House.** Near International Peace Garden. Pleasant with lounge and restaurant.

DEVILS LAKE. *Moderate:* **Artclare Motel.** Indoor pool. Lounge and restaurant.

DICKINSON. *Moderate:* **Best Western Prairie Wind Inn.** Typical of the Best Western affiliates.

FARGO. *Expensive.* **Best Western Doublewood Inn.** Living in high style.
Holiday Inn. Large facility with fine services.
Moderate: **Oak Manor.** Nicely landscaped; restaurant and lounge.

GARRISON. *Moderate:* **Econo-O-Inn.** Access to Lake Sakakawea.

GRAND FORKS. *Expensive:* **Best Western Townhouse Motor Inn.** High quality, extensive services.
Ramada Inn. One of their top-rated inns.
Moderate: **Roadking Inn.** Nearest to University. Restaurant opposite.

JAMESTOWN. *Expensive:* **Holiday Inn.** Adjoining Civic Center.
Moderate: **Tumbleweed.** Restaurant and lounge; heated indoor pool.

MANDAN. *Expensive:* **Seven Seas Inn.** Across river from state capitol.

MEDORA. *Moderate:* **Badlands Motel.** In unique Badlands town.

MINOT. *Moderate:* **Best Western Thunderbird Motel.** Across from N. Dakota Fairgrounds.

WAHPETON. *Moderate:* **Travel Host Motel.** Dining room and coffee shop.

WILLISTON. *Expensive:* **El Rancho Best Western.** Quality accommodations. Near Lake Sakakawea and historic sites.

 DINING OUT. Dining in North Dakota ranges from highly sophisticated to simple ranch-country fare. Restaurant price categories are as follows: *Deluxe:* $15 and up; *Expensive:* $7–15; *Moderate:* $4–7; and *Inexpensive:* under $4. Not included are drinks, tax, and tip. Numerous fast-food chain facilities are available along interstates and in larger cities and towns.

BISMARCK. *Expensive:* **Der Mark.** Elegant food service in the Kirkwood Motor Inn.
Moderate: **Kroll's Kitchen.** Family dining treat, German specialties.

BOWMAN. *Moderate:* **Gene's Restaurant.** Family dining.

DEVILS LAKE. *Moderate:* **The Ranch.** In remodeled barn.

DICKINSON. *Moderate:* **El Comedor.** Fine dining at the Ramada Inn.
Sims Restaurant. Family dining; bakery specialties.

FARGO. *Expensive:* **Cork N' Cleaver.** Excellent steaks.
The Grainery. Yesteryear agricultural motif.
Moderate: **English Café.** Sixty years in business serving beef "fit for a king."
Haugen's Ice Cream Parlor. Two locations. Has extensive restaurant menu, too.
The Old Broadway. Vintage décor and tantalizing menu.

GRAND FORKS. *Expensive:* **The Palace** (Westward Ho Motel). Award-winning French cuisine in a Victorian atmosphere.
Moderate: **The Bronze Boot.** Features steaks, chops, Chinese food.
La Campana. Mexican dishes in appropriate decor.

JAMESTOWN. *Moderate:* **Wagon Masters.** Near the "world's largest buffalo." Unique atmosphere.

MANDAN. *Moderate:* **Gourmet House.** Charming, widely known, features pecan pie. Across Missouri River from Bismarck.

MINOT. *Moderate:* **El Tios Mexican Restaurant.** American entrées also available.
The Roll'n Pin. Family dining. Large breakfast menu.

RUGBY. *Moderate:* **Andrews Steak House.** Featuring North Dakota beef; near Center of North America monument.

VALLEY CITY. *Moderate:* **Post Specialty Restaurant.** Well-recommended for casual dining.

WILLISTON. *Moderate:* **Bavarian Inn.** German-American restaurant and lounge; in oil, lignite coal region.
Red Fox Restaurant. Family dining, full menu.

SOUTH DAKOTA

Black Hills, Badlands, and Prairies

South Dakota is unique among the 50 states in its capacity to test the timbre and temperament of those who have called it home. It has been dubbed a "land of savage extremes," with temperatures ranging from 40 degrees below zero to 116 or more above. That is why the nickname *The Challenge State* is so appropriate and inspiring. It describes and dramatizes the continuing struggle for an unshackled life by Indians, homesteaders, farmers, and entrepreneurs who have pitted themselves against nature on the prairie arena. The state is 16th among the 50 in size, 45th in population, first in the production of gold, and its people are noted for their longevity.

The major geographical features are the broad prairies, the Black Hills, the Badlands, and the Missouri River. Of the four, the historic stream undoubtedly has had the greatest effect on the most citizens over the longest period of time. Today the dam-harnessed river divides the state into two distinct sections geographically and philosophically.

Sioux Falls, the largest city, is the bustling home of more than 80,000 residents on the eastern border. Yankton, in the southeastern corner, is called the Mother City of the Dakotas and is near Gavins Point Dam, southernmost of the four barriers on the Missouri which create the Great Lakes of South Dakota. South Dakota State University at Brookings specializes in agriculture, engineering, and sciences. The University of South Dakota at Vermillion features law, medicine, and liberal arts. Mitchell is the site of the "world's only" Corn Palace, and Wall, near the Badlands, boasts one of the world's most unusual drug stores. Pierre (pronounced "Peer") is the state capital and is in the middle of ranching country on the Missouri. De Smet in Kingsbury County is the location of Laura Ingalls Wilder's famed "Little House on the Prairie."

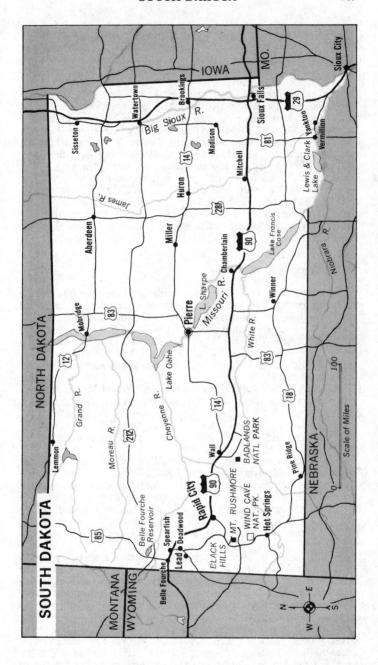

The Badlands

From the city to the Badlands is an incredible contrast. The latter are reached by turning south off I–90 on SD 240, just eighteen miles west of Kadoka. The headquarters are at Cedar Pass, nine miles southwest, where exhibits and audio-visual programs illustrate this fantastic area of wind- and water-eroded rocks. Millions of years ago, this jagged and desolate area was a flat grassland and the home of prehistoric beasts such as the saber-toothed tiger and hairy mammoths. Then the earth's crust rose and volcanic ash drifted down. Rivers carved gorges, and the winds of thousands of centuries slowly wore away the softer rock and left sharp spires, rounded cones, and grotesque designs. The Badlands are a rich fossil bed, but it is illegal to remove specimens. Picture-taking, however, will provide a thrill almost equal to the finding of a tiger bone. Subtle colors, especially striking in early morning and late afternoon, are difficult to capture but are worth many hours of trying. As for the fossils, see them under plexiglass along the fossil trail.

The Black Hills

The fabled Black Hills—so named because of the ebon hue created by thick growths of various coniferous trees—are entered from Rapid City, rebuilt following a tragic flood in 1972 which claimed 238 lives. The city's growth was stimulated during World War II by the establishment of Ellsworth Air Force Base on the flatlands to the east. The Dahl Arts Center near mid-city is noted for its 200-foot mural of U.S. progress. The Chapel in the Hills is a replica of Norway's eight-centuries-old nail-less Stavkirke.

The Black Hills National Forest consists of nearly 1 ¼ million acres, featuring towering spires, magnificent forests, and dramatic scenery. Harney Peak, at 7,242 feet, is the highest mountain. A whole spectrum of year-round recreational activities is available. The two-hour 1880 train ride from Hill City to Keystone is a special treat. So is a drive on the spectacular Needles Highway.

In 1876 the region was populated virtually overnight after the Custer Expedition revealed the discovery of gold. Today, after more than a century of operation, the Homestake Mine in Lead (pronounced "Leed") still produces more gold than any other mine in the Western Hemisphere. Tours are conducted, but only at ground level. Just four miles away the historic "naughty" city of Deadwood features Mount Moriah Cemetery where Wild Bill Hickok and Calamity Jane are buried.

Mount Rushmore, about 25 miles southwest of Rapid City on US 16, is the area's leading man-made attraction. Carved into the granite face of the mountain is the "Shrine of Democracy," 60-foot-high likenesses of Washington, Jefferson, Lincoln, and Theodore Roosevelt. This masterpiece of sculptor Gutzon Borglum is a "must" stop for everyone, especially on the first trip to the Hills.

South of Mount Rushmore is Custer State Park, where one of the largest buffalo herds in the country can be viewed. The Game Lodge, once President Coolidge's Summer White House, is also located in the park. West of Custer, Jewel Cave National Monument is a 1,300-acre area covered with ponderosa pine and wild flowers. Jewel Cave itself consists of a series of subterranean chambers and limestone galleries whose calcite crystals produce unusual effects. Guided tours and picnicking facilities are available.

Spearfish, home of the internationally famous Passion Play, is the logical place of departure from the Black Hills going north or west. Hot Springs, which features the largest indoor natural warm-water pool in the world, is the southern exit. North of the historic spa city is Wind Cave National Park, where rangers conduct safe tours of the vast underground caverns, seven miles of which have been explored. Above ground, buffalo, deer, antelope and prairie dogs inhabit the park.

Other South Dakota Attractions

Custer National Forest is north of the Black Hills and extends into Montana. This vast expanse of rolling hills and grasslands offers camping areas, picnic facilities, and hiking trails. The site of the Battle of Slim Buttes (1876) is in Harding County.

Bear Butte State Park, northeast of Sturgis, is dominated by a huge volcanic bubble which rises abruptly 1,400 feet above the plains, and offers unusual photographic possibilities. Indians still regard it as a religious shrine.

Fort Sisseton State Park, in the lake region of the northeastern corner of the state, is the site of an excellent example of a frontier stone military installation built in 1864.

North of Sioux Falls, near Garretson, is the Earth Resources Observation Systems project (EROS), a data center for recording and disseminating information received from orbiting satellites.

Huron is the home of the South Dakota State Fair and is in the center of the pheasant hunting country.

The Mammoth Site at Hot Springs is one of the most remarkable concentrations of skeletons of these giant prehistoric mammals in North America.

PRACTICAL INFORMATION
FOR SOUTH DAKOTA

HOW TO GET THERE. *By air:* Air service to South Dakota is limited beyond Sioux Falls, Pierre, and Rapid City. Check current scheduling for carrier availability to other locales. *By bus: Greyhound, Continental Trailways,* and *Jack Rabbit Lines* provide the bulk of the passenger service into the state, serving Sioux Falls, Aberdeen, Rapid City, Pierre, and other towns.

By car: I–90 enters South Dakota from Minnesota in the east and from Wyoming in the west. I–29 is the principal access from Nebraska and Iowa in the south and from North Dakota in the north.

HOW TO GET AROUND. *By air:* The principal cities and towns have good airports, but commercial schedules are limited. South Dakota has no passenger rail service. *By bus: Jack Rabbit Lines* offers extensive service within the state serving all of the key cities and towns and many smaller ones, including Sioux Falls, Yankton, Mitchell, Rapid City, Huron, Pierre, and Aberdeen.

By car: The principal east-west routes are I–90 across the lower half of the state and US 212 across the upper half. The key cities and towns served by I–90 are Spearfish, Sturgis, Rapid City, Kadoka, Kennebec, Murdo, Chamberlain, Mitchell, and Sioux Falls. US 81, 281, and 83 run north-south, and I–29 runs north-south through Watertown, Brookings, and Sioux Falls.

TOURIST INFORMATION. Free travel information and leaflets are available from the South Dakota Division of Tourism, Pierre 57501, which also has a national WATS line: 1–800–843–1930.

MUSEUMS AND GALLERIES. The *Museum of Geology* in O'Harra Memorial Building on the campus of South Dakota School of Mines and Technology in Rapid City, has excellent exhibits of rocks and minerals from the Black Hills and fossils from the Badlands.

Prairie Village at Madison is a "living museum" which features turn-of-the-century buildings and pioneer activities.

The *Robinson Museum* opposite the State Capitol in Pierre has pioneer, Indian and historic exhibits and houses the *South Dakota State Historical Society,* a repository for genealogical study.

There are antique auto museums at Alcester, Custer, Mitchell, Murdo, and Rapid City.

Shrine to Music, Vermillon, contains the nationally renowned Arne B. Larson collection of antique and foreign musical instruments.

South Dakota Memorial Art Center, in Brookings, features a collection of Harvey Dunn paintings. The major collection of paintings by the Sioux artist, Oscar Howe, is at the *W. H. Over Dakota Museum* in Vermillion.

Not to be overlooked are the *Blue Cloud Abbey Museum,* Marvin; *Buechel Memorial Lakota Museum,* St. Francis; *Pettigrew Museum,* Sioux Falls; *Agricultural Heritage Museum,* Brookings; *Museum of Pioneer Life,* Mitchell; *Adam West Museum* and *No. 10 Saloon,* Deadwood.

HISTORIC SITES. *Mount Rushmore,* the massive "Shrine of Democracy," is a most impressive sight by day or by night. Meanwhile, at *Thunderhead Mountain,* 5 mi. N. of Custer off US 16, 385, the family of Korczack Ziolkowski carries on the late sculptor's dream of carving the world's largest statue. It will depict the fabled Sioux chief, Crazy Horse.

The *Sitting Bull Monument,* on a hill near Mobridge overlooking the Missouri River, marks the controversial burial site of the famous Sioux leader.

The *Dells of the Sioux* near Dell Rapids feature craggy formations of red rock known locally as "Sioux Falls granite."

South Dakota has six Sioux Indian reservations within its borders. Check locally for touring conditions. Accommodations are limited.

TOURS. *Gray Line, Stagecoach West,* and *Jack Rabbit* offer a varied program of tours of the Black Hills and Badlands, including the Passion Play. Pickup and return to hotels and motels is available. *Golden Circle Tours* visit points of interest in the southern Black Hills, including an evening schedule to the lighting program at *Mount Rushmore.*

DRINKING LAWS. Liquor may be purchased both by the bottle (in stores) and by the drink. Liquor may be sold in stores from Mon. to Sat., 7:00 A.M. to midnight; by the drink to 2:00 A.M.; Sun. 1:00 to 10:00 P.M., subject to local option.

SUMMER SPORTS. *Fishing:* The four huge lakes created by damming the Missouri River have made South Dakota one of the finest sport-fishing areas for walleye. The reservoirs and streams of the Black Hills offer excellent trout fishing, and there are many largemouth bass in stock ponds across the state. *Hunting:* Many consider South Dakota the Pheasant Capital of the World; and grouse, prairie chicken, quail and partridge are plentiful. There is almost an over-supply of deer and antelope. *Water Sports:* The same four reservoirs on the Missouri which offer exciting fishing provide ample space for boating, skiing, and swimming as do various lakes around the state. *Golf:* There are numerous courses, although many are 9-hole, and some still have sand greens. *Gold-panning* and *Rock-collecting* are interesting Black Hills diversions. *Motorcy-*

cling: The annual rally at Sturgis attracts thousands of bikers from all over the U.S.

WINTER SPORTS. *Skiing:* Best known of South Dakota's ski areas is Terry Peak in the Black Hills, whose 1,200-foot vertical drop from over 7,000 feet makes it the highest ski area east of the Rockies. Facilities include chair lifts and cross-country trails. Other areas include Great Bear Ski Valley near Sioux Falls and Deer Mountain near Lead. Ski season generally runs from Thanksgiving to April. *Snowmobiling* and *cross-country skiing* are popular statewide.

SPECTATOR SPORTS. *Horse racing:* A parimutuel circuit includes Ft. Pierre, Aberdeen, and Rapid City, but check locally for dates. *Greyhound racing:* The Black Hills track at Rapid City and Sodrac Park in N. Sioux City have races from June to Sept. *Drag racing:* Thunder Valley Dragway at Marion. *Rodeos:* Check with state tourism for an extensive schedule in various locations.

SHOPPING. Authentic Indian items are available throughout the state. *Al's Oasis,* across the Missouri River near Chamberlain, is a favored mid-state stop on I–90 for souvenirs and necessities. Giftshops at Rushmore Memorial, Hill City, Keystone and other Black Hills towns offer wide selections. The unique Wall Drug Store on the edge of the Badlands has "everything."

WHAT TO DO WITH THE CHILDREN. Sioux Falls is a good place to bring children because the small but excellent *Great Plains Zoo* is next to *Dennis the Menace Park.* A short drive leads to *Terrace Park,* where children may fish in a stocked lake. In Rapid City, *Dinosaur Park* on Skyline Dr. has life-size models of prehistoric dinosaurs; eons ago these beasts romped on this spot. At Aberdeen is the fabled *Storybook Land.*

At *Reptile Gardens,* 6 mi. S. of Rapid City on US 16, children may view an extensive reptile collection which includes an underground snake den. There are performing animals, and children may ride giant tortoises. *Bear Country U.S.A.* has a "babyland" and children's zoo. The Flintsones come alive at *Bedrock City,* Custer. The aquarium at the *Gavins Point National Fish Hatchery* is fascinating.

HOTELS AND MOTELS in South Dakota, because they are generally smaller than those in the east or west, offer a homey, friendly atmosphere. A tip: when traveling in the sparsely populated interior, make advance reservations. Out-of-season rates are usually available, particularly in the Black Hills region.

The price categories in this section, for double occupancy, will average as follows: *Expensive:* $35 and up; *Moderate:* $25–35; and *Inexpensive:* $16–25.

ABERDEEN. *Expensive:* **Sheraton Inn.** Out of the swirl, on city's edge. *Moderate:* **Breeze-Inn Motel.** Small but comfortable and accommodating.

BROOKINGS. *Moderate:* **Staurolite Inn.** Indoor pool, restaurant and lounge. S. Dakota State University nearby.

CHAMBERLAIN. *Moderate:* **Lake Shore Motel.** Pleasant mid-state stopover. Close to good fishing.

CUSTER. *Moderate:* **Bavarian Inn Motel.** Old World décor on heights above historic city.
Dakota Cowboy Inn. Western motif. Includes family units. Restaurant adjoining.

CUSTER STATE PARK. *Deluxe:* **State Game Lodge.** President Coolidge slept here!
Moderate: **Blue Bell Lodge & Resort.** Black Hills scenery and recreation accessible.
Sylvan Lake Resort. Off the beaten path in picturesque setting.

DEADWOOD. *Moderate:* **Franklin Hotel and Motor Inn.** In historic downtown area, easy walk to museums, Gold Rush-era attractions.

KADOKA. *Moderate:* **Cuckleburr Motel.** On I–90 near entry to the Badlands.

KEYSTONE. *Moderate:* **Four Presidents Motel.** Best Western. Near tourist attractions.

MITCHELL. *Expensive:* **Holiday Inn.** Quality accommodations and services.
Moderate: **Thunderbird Lodge.** Accessible to the Corn Palace.

MOBRIDGE. *Moderate:* **Wrangler.** Overlooking Lake Oahe. Has indoor pool and adjoining restaurant.

MURDO. *Expensive:* **Best Western Graham's.** Near outstanding antique auto exhibit.

PIERRE. *Moderate:* **Best Western Kings Inn.** Very popular, not far from state capitol, museum.
Inexpensive: **State Motel.** Well-rated. Near state capitol, official buildings.

RAPID CITY. *Expensive:* **Alex Johnson Hotel.** Fine old downtown hotel, nostalgic luxury.
Best Western Gill's Sun Inn. Wide variety of well-maintained, attractive units, with restaurant and lounge.
Holiday Inn. With Holidome, on edge of city.
Sands of the Black Hills and **Plaza Sands.** Both well managed.
Town 'n Country. Best Western. Two heated pools.
Moderate: **Prime Rate Motel.** Heated pool, restaurant adjacent.
Tip-Top Motor Hotel. In downtown location.

SIOUX FALLS. *Expensive:* **Holiday Inns, Downtown** and **Airport.** Holidome fun centers.
Ramada Inn. Fine accommodations, all services.
Moderate: **Lindendale Motel.** Quiet country setting.
Inexpensive: **Westwick Motel.** Small but well rated.

SPEARFISH. *Expensive:* **Best Western Luxury Lodge.** Near Passion Play.
Moderate: **Downtown McColley.** Convenient central location.

STURGIS. *Moderate:* **Outlaw Inn.** Has heated indoor pool and adjacent restaurant.

VERMILLION. *Moderate:* **Best Western Tomahawk Motel.** Near University.

YANKTON. *Expensive:* **Sheraton Yankton.** Top level accommodations, with Sternwheeler Restaurant.
Moderate: **Skyline Motel.** Lounge and café, in historic city.

DINING OUT. The number of tourists visiting South Dakota has increased dramatically in recent years, and as a result many of the newer restaurants have been built in conjunction with the motels intended to accommodate this influx of visitors. But there remain a number of restaurants not associated with any lodging establishments which serve good, moderately priced food.

Restaurant price categories are as follows: *Deluxe* will average $15 and up; *Expensive:* $7–15; *Moderate:* $4–7; and *Inexpensive:* under $4.

ABERDEEN. *Moderate–Expensive:* **The Lumberyard.** As the name implies, a converted structure.
Moderate: **Centurion Family Restaurant.** Has an appealing menu for all ages.

CUSTER. *Expensive:* **State Game Lodge.** Specialty is buffalo; in state park.
Moderate: **Skyway Cafe.** Steaks, seafood, well-prepared dishes.

HILL CITY. *Moderate.* **Chute Roosters.** Old barn, a dining treat.

HOT SPRINGS. *Moderate:* **Wishing Well Restaurant.** Located in historic Braun Motor Hotel. Pleasant surroundings.

KEYSTONE. *Moderate:* **Buffalo Room.** At Mt. Rushmore National Monument—a chance to eat, relax, and enjoy the massive sculpture.
Ruby House. Excellent steaks in unique Old West atmosphere.

MURDO. *Moderate:* **Star.** Wholesome food, steak the specialty.

OACOMA. *Moderate:* **Al's Oasis.** Popular mid-state stop featuring buffalo-burgers.

PIERRE. *Expensive:* **The Bunkhouse.** Outstanding prime ribs.
Moderate: **Kings Inn.** Walleye a house specialty.
Inexpensive: **State Capitol Cafeteria.** In basement of statehouse building.

RAPID CITY. *Deluxe:* **The Pyrenees.** Luxurious rooftop restaurant.
Expensive: **Landmark Restaurant.** In Alex Johnson Hotel.
1915 Firehouse Company. Old firehouse décor.
Moderate: **The Chuck Wagon.** Western décor, fun for children.
Dakota House Restaurant. Full line menu.
Tally's. In historic downtown Rapid City.

SIOUX FALLS. *Deluxe:* **Lafayette.** A touch of France on the prairie.
The Northlander. Outstanding menu. The building itself is an architectural treat.
Expensive: **First Edition.** Gourmet food, excellent service. Old-time newspapering décor.
Moderate: **Kirk's Restaurant.** Conventional fare. Near Great Plains Zoo.
Minerva's Corner Creperie. Specialties are Brittany crepes.
Stockyards Café. Eat well with ranchers and truckers.

SPEARFISH: *Expensive:* **The Sluice.** 21-page menu. Gold-mining décor.

SPRINGFIELD. *Moderate:* **Sandbar Marina.** Fish specialties, on scenic Lewis & Clark Lake backwater.

VERMILLION. *Moderate:* **The Cowboy Family Restaurant.** From soup 'n sandwiches to full-course meals near university campus.
The Prairie. Near Dakota Dome athletic facility.

WALL. *Moderate:* **Wall Drug Store.** Varied fare in unique setting, nationally known.

WATERTOWN. *Moderate:* **Millstone Family Restaurant.** Pleasant family dining as name implies.

YANKTON. *Expensive:* **Happy Jack's.** Where celebrities stop for good steaks.

The Library. Big-city style in old converted Carnegie building.

Expensive–Moderate: **The Black Steer.** Delicious barbecued ribs.

Russo's Ristorante and Sandwich Emporium. Italian cuisine.

Moderate: **JoDean's Steak House.** Large South Dakota steaks a specialty.

GRAND OPENING

Union Pacific

UTAH

Salt Lake City and Magnificent Vistas

Salt Lake City serves three essential functions. First, and eternally foremost, it is the headquarters—the Mecca, the Vatican, the Jerusalem—of an international religion: the three-million-member Church of Jesus Christ of Latter-day Saints. Next, but not necessarily in that order, it is Utah's economic drive wheel. Finally it is the state's capital city. From any approach to Salt Lake City, the setting is impressive.

Temple Square

Salt Lake City's greatest single attraction for visitors is the Temple Square area, the sacred ground of Mormonism. Here, on two 10-acre blocks flanking Main Street, in the middle of town, are the central religious shrines of Latter-day Saint worship. The Temple block, on the west, is surrounded by a 15-foot-high masonry wall. On the grounds stand the Temple, Tabernacle, Assembly Hall and Visitors Center. Visitors are welcome in all these buildings except the Temple, which is for sacred rites, such as marriages and devotional chores, known as "temple work," done by church members in good standing.

The Tabernacle houses the famous Temple Square pipe organ and hosts the Sunday concerts performed by the Mormon Tabernacle Choir. This is an elongated structure with rounded ends that resembles a grounded dirigible. The choir, 375 mixed voices, was organized in the early 1850s and can be heard during its Thursday evening rehearsals as well as on Sundays, when the formal program is presented in its entirety.

Overwhelming everything in Temple Square is the Temple itself. Although there are six other LDS temples in Utah, the Salt Lake City

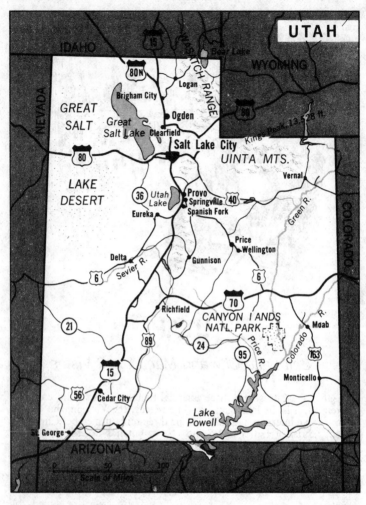

Temple has a majesty and singularity about it denied the others. Its architectural style is imprecise. Some have called it "Mormon Gothic." In appearance it is not unlike Europe's medieval cathedrals, yet it departs from that design, too. In any case, the building was dedicated in 1893, exactly 40 years to the day after ground was broken for the foundation. Granite for its 167-foot-high walls was quarried from the nearby mountains and first dragged by oxen and mules to the building site. Later, rails were used for transportation. At each end of the 163-foot-long, 100-foot-wide edifice rise three spire-tipped towers, the highest, 204 feet in the air, centered above the east facade. Balanced on that point is a gilded statue of the angel Moroni, heralding toward the east with a long-stemmed trumpet. According to Joseph Smith, it was Moroni (pronounced Mo-rown-eye) who led him to the golden plates engraved with hieroglyphics described as "Reformed Egyptian." Smith testified that with heavenly aid he was allowed to translate the record into English. Two years of laborious writing became the Book of Mormon. By 1830, Smith had six followers and the beginning of the Church of Jesus Christ, which eventually lengthened into the Church of Jesus Christ of Latter-day Saints.

At the corner of South Temple and State Streets are two buildings which originally served as office and residence for the church's second prophet, Brigham Young. They are the Lion House, his headquarters, and the Beehive House, appropriately named for the quarters he shared with his 26 wives and 56 children (at least some of them). Polygamy, of course, was the stigma that caused early Mormons their deepest trouble. It wasn't practiced by every LDS male, but, nonetheless, it had the first prophet's blessing; he said God willed that men take more than one wife. The indulgence had its practical value in the early days when husbands often died on the difficult way west and widows arrived in Utah without immediate prospects of support for themselves or their children. Still, America couldn't accept polygamy, even if—or perhaps especially if—it was approved by a Christian denomination. Congress denied Utah statehood until polygamy was purged, and, in late 1890, Church President Wilford Woodruff issued a manifesto removing plural marriages from Mormon sanction. Statehood followed along with perpetual prosecution of polygamous elders who could not or would not accept the prophet's word. Splinter groups still practice plural marriage in and around Utah. One thing is certain: plural marriage is enough to earn instant excommunication from the central LDS Church.

Capitol Hill

Salt Lake City is the state's capital city, and Capitol Hill is worth a visit. Completed in 1914, the copper-domed Capitol was designed for largely ceremonial uses, although it contained chambers for two houses of the bicameral legislature, the five-member State Supreme Court and the governor's office. The capitol's first-floor hallway is lined with showcases exhibiting the qualities of every Utah county, mostly by region. Though sometimes slightly outdated, the displays are accurate enough to be instructive.

Skiing Around Salt Lake City

Skiing is the area's chief winter pastime. East from the city, up two adjacent canyons, are four ski areas that rival any in the U.S. for snow depth and consistency. Salt Lake City residents have been skiing at Park City, on the east side of the mountains, for the last several years. Originally a mining town, Park City made a comeback from "ghost" status when its recreational potential was discovered. Downtown Park City has retained much of its old mining character. As a "Gentile" town, Park City differs markedly from other Utah communities. Its downtown streets are two-lane, it has more former saloons on Main Street, and its past is charred by horrendous fires that repeatedly leveled homes, stores, bars, churches and schools. Most of the mine owners, who took their riches from hills around Park City, lived in Salt Lake City.

The four ski areas nearest Salt Lake City are Brighton Ski Bowl, and Solitude, located in Big Cottonwood Canyon, and Alta and Snowbird, in Little Cottonwood Canyon. All offer excellent skiing conditions and facilities for the beginner and advanced skier, and reach altitudes from 8,500 to 10,000 feet.

Skiing season usually begins mid-Nov. and ends mid-May, depending on the weather.

PRACTICAL INFORMATION
FOR SALT LAKE CITY

HOW TO GET THERE. *By car:* I–80, probably the most heavily traveled transcontinental highway, passes through Salt Lake City. From the north I–80N runs southeast through Salt Lake from Portland, Oregon. I–15 comes from the Los Angeles area through Cedar City, Utah, and up to Salt Lake.

By air: Salt Lake City is the major terminal. Among the long-distance carriers serving it are *Frontier, Delta, American, United, Western* and *Continental.*

By train: Amtrak's *Rio Grande Zephyr* runs from Denver to Ogden, Utah, about 30 miles north of Salt Lake City. The *Amtrak Pioneer* connects Salt Lake City and Seattle, with stops at Ogden, Pocatello, Boise, and Portland in between.

By bus: Continental Trailways, and *Greyhound* are the major carriers to Salt Lake City, but the area is also served by numerous other lines.

SEASONAL EVENTS. *January:* The drama season is still in full swing, with productions at Promised Valley Playhouse, and Theatre 138. Utah's International Hockey League team, the Golden Eagles and National Basketball Assn., Utah Jazz are in mid-season at the Salt Palace. *June:* The Salt Lake City municipal band starts its Sunday concerts in Liberty Park. *July:* On the 24th the "Days of '47" parade is held in downtown Salt Lake City; rodeo at the Salt Palace. *August:* County fair time. *September:* The Utah State Fair is held at the state fairgrounds. *December:* Utah Symphony and Ballet West launch season. The Salt Lake Oratorio Society's annual performance of *The Messiah* is performed in the Salt Lake City Tabernacle.

MUSEUMS AND GALLERIES. The Utah Museum of Natural History, located on the University of Utah campus, houses prehistoric fossils and Indian relics. Also on the University of Utah campus is the University Fine Arts Museum, exhibiting a variety of art forms. Art exhibits may also be seen at the Bicentennial Concert Hall at the Salt Palace complex, downtown Salt Lake City.

HISTORIC SITES. Salt Lake City is packed with historic reminders. Prominent among them are *Lion House,* Brigham Young's office, and *Beehive House,* right next door, which was one of his homes. Also, there are the *"This Is the Place" Monument,* the *Daughters of the Utah Pioneers Museum and Council Hall.* The last two are on Capitol Hill.

MUSIC. The Tabernacle on Temple Square is the home of the world-famous Mormon *Tabernacle Choir.* A custom-built Bicentennial Concert Hall, on Salt Palace grounds in downtown Salt Lake City, is the Utah Symphony's home, as well as the site for touring concerts.

SPECTATOR SPORTS. The International Hockey League's *Golden Eagles* and National Basketball Association's *Utah Jazz* play at the Salt Palace, University of Utah intercollegiate sports are played at the campus in Salt Lake City. A similarly full range of athletic events occur at Brigham Young University, Provo; Utah State University, Logan; and Weber State University, Ogden.

Bryce Canyon National Park is located in the southwestern part of the state. Its multicolored layers of limestone and clay produce a quilted effect that is enhanced by the rays of the sun. Bryce Canyon itself is particularly impressive, as are Yellow Creek, Willis Point and Rainbow Point. At Zion, the emphasis is also on natural beauty. At the entrance, visitors pass between two enormous colored monoliths, indicators of what lies ahead. After entering the "gate," you can see in the distance the famous Bridge Mountain, so named because of a natural rock bridge high on the crest. Past this is a succession of rainbow-hued rock formations including Streaked Wall and the Mountain of the Sun. The green, wooded canyon and murmuring river combine with majestic temples and towers to make this a magnificent showcase of natural splendor.

PRACTICAL INFORMATION FOR UTAH

HOW TO GET AROUND. *By car:* The Interstates (I–70, I–80 and I–15) are the primary routes if there are long distances between towns. State roads crisscross the rest of the state except in truly desolate areas like the Great Salt Lake Desert to the west of Salt Lake City.

By air: From Salt Lake City, *Sky West* flies to St. George and Cedar City, and *Frontier Air Lines* serves Vernal. There is also charter service from Salt Lake City to local airports near Zion, Bryce and Canyonlands National parks.

By train: Ogden and Salt Lake City are on the *Amtrak* line. The only other passenger train service is the *Denver Rio Grande*, between Denver and Salt Lake City.

By bus: All major cities and towns in Utah have good bus service. *Greyhound, Trailways* and *Utah Transit Authority* between Salt Lake City and Ogden, are some of the carriers.

TOURIST INFORMATION. Detailed information about anything in the state may be obtained from the *Utah Travel Council,* Council Hall, 300 W. State St., Salt Lake City 84114, telephone (801) 533-5681.

MUSEUMS AND GALLERIES. *Pioneer Museum,* Provo, contains a particularly extensive assortment of pioneer utensils, tools and weapons used in the early West. The *Springville Museum of Art,* Springville, Utah County, is Utah's most well-known art center. Outdoor art festivals are held annually at many of Utah's resort areas. *Park City* closes its Main Street for such an occasion, usually sometime in August.

HISTORIC SITES. The state's oldest house, the *Miles Goodyear Cabin,* is on display in Ogden. Built around 1841, the log-hewn house was used by the first white family settling permanently in what became Utah. *Ghost town* prowling has become a popular Utah pastime, principally because there are so many abandoned settlements throughout the state and it's another enjoyable way to see the countryside. Stephen L. Carr, in a 1972 publication, listed 150 ghost towns marking Utah's landscape. Just outside Brigham City is the Golden Spike Historical Site, where on May 10 of every year the driving of the golden spike connecting the Transcontinental Railways is reenacted. It is easily reached by I–15 North.

OTHER PLACES OF INTEREST. *Lagoon Amusement Park,* Farmington, is a favorite fun spot of the people of Utah. 34 rides, including a roller-coaster; picnic areas, miniature golf, games, and a heated outdoor pool. Open daily from mid-May to Labor Day.

OTHER PLACES OF INTEREST. *Hanson Planetarium,* 15 South State Street, offers simulated journeys to the moon or anywhere in the universe. Excellent for the whole family. Group rates available.

Hogle Zoo, Emigration Canyon and Sunnyside Avenue, houses hundreds of specimens of wildlife. Children's Zoo, where some animals may be touched, has a Miniature Train and refreshment stands.

Trolley Square, 602 East 5th South, is a delightful shopping mall that used to house Salt Lake's trolley cars and buses. The many shops, stores, and restaurants include the Spaghetti Factory and even a "Farmer's Market." One square block blending the old Salt Lake with the new, it is recognized as a Utah Historical Site.

HOTELS AND MOTELS. Double occupancy rates for hotels and motels in Salt Lake City are: *Deluxe:* over $45, *Expensive:* $35–45; *Moderate:* $25–35; *Inexpensive:* under $25.

Deluxe: **Hotel Utah.** South Temple at Main St. Downtown location, close to shopping. Free in-room movies, first-class restaurant.

The Marriott. 75 S. West Temple. Salt Lake City's newest, with restaurants, lounges, liquor store, swimming pool and sauna, gift shop. Close to all downtown shopping areas and the Salt Palace complex. Special weekend rates are just below the deluxe range.

Expensive: **Holiday Inn.** 1659 West North Temple. 5 minutes from airport. Swimming pool, pleasant rooms with color TV.

International Inn. 206 South West Temple. Luxury suites, liquor store, gift shop, therapy pool and sauna. Across from Salt Palace.

Moderate: **Ramada Inn.** 999 South Main St. Near downtown area. 24-hr. restaurant, game room, liquor store. Disco dancing.

Inexpensive: **Country Club Motor Inn.** 2665 Parleys Way. Medium-sized, scenic view.

Scenic. 1345 Foothill Drive. Opposite convenient shopping center.

Temple Square Hotel. 75 W. South Temple. Downtown Salt Lake City, across from Temple Square. Has restaurant.

DINING OUT. Salt Lake City is beginning to acquire a distinctive cuisine, but the going is slow because of the conservative liquor laws. But specialty places, offering French, Spanish and German dishes, are increasing. Some of the best menus can be found up nearby canyons. Price categories are: *Expensive:* $10 and up, *Moderate:* $5–10 and *Inexpensive:* under $5.

Expensive: **La Caille.** 9564 Wasatch Blvd. Wealthy country atmosphere; game birds.

La Fleur de Lys. 165 S. West Temple. Elegant French cuisine, live music.

Log Haven. Millcreek Canyon. Mountain setting. Great omelets.

The Roof. Hotel Utah, South Temple and Main St. First-rate cuisine with a view.

Tri Arc 13th Floor. West Temple at 6th South. Great view, steaks and ribs.

Moderate: **The Dodo.** 680 S. 900 East. Slightly out-of-the-way, but a favorite of locals who appreciate a limited but specialized menu.

Finn's. 2675 Parley's Way. Unpretentious outside, but delectable meals inside.

Le Parisien. 417 South 3rd East. Excellent Dover sole. Wine list. Outdoor seating.

Inexpensive: **Spaghetti Factory.** 189 Trolley Sq. Fun family setting.

TOURIST INFORMATION. Information about Salt Lake City and its surrounding areas can be obtained from the Salt Lake Valley Convention and Visitors Bureau, Salt Palace, Suite 200, Salt Lake City, Utah 84101. Phone (801) 521-2822.

EXPLORING UTAH

Great Salt Lake is indeed a natural wonder. Approximately 1,500 square miles in area, it is the nation's largest inland sea. Twenty-five percent saline, the lake is five times saltier than any ocean. Utah's relationship with the lake has changed through the years, just as the waterline has fluctuated. Five years' worth of higher-than-average rain and snowfall has caused the lake to rise. Beaches and other shoreline recreation spots have been seriously affected.

It's true that a swimmer can bob on the lake surface "like a cork" without any effort. Until the lake's water level stabilizes, however, there will be no public accommodations for swimming in Great Salt Lake. Because of successful efforts to protect certain rail lines and interstate highway mileage along the lake's southern shore, it is possible to travel on ground which is lower than the surrounding lake surface.

Except for a species of tiny shrimp, no fish live in Great Salt Lake, so it had little practical value to the pioneers. Eventually, wood-hauling sternwheelers plied its waters. Some were converted to early-day cruise ships. Although most are no longer operating, lakeside resorts, dance halls and amusement parks have existed around Great Salt Lake's eastern and southern shores through the years. Most have either burned or been abandoned, but a smaller replica of the burned Arabian Nights-inspired Saltair has been rebuilt on the north shore, off I-15, with pavilion restaurant, and water rides.

Dinosaur National Monument, east of Vernal, is particularly fascinating. The area has supplied the largest collection of prehistoric vertebrates in the U.S. Entire skeletons have been excavated intact by several archeological institutions. Some are kept at a small museum for visitors to inspect.

Railroad Run

During summer months and also from Thanksgiving to New Year's Day, a steam engine, known as the Heber Creeper, hauls passengers from Heber City to Bridal Veil Falls in Provo Canyon. The round trip meanders through meadowland, along streams and reservoirs while penetrating a mountain pass. It's a quaint way to sightsee.

Bridal Veil Falls, a double cataract, splashes in steep descent down Provo Canyon's sheer mountain walls. It's viewable from alongside US 189, if that's the route selected out of Heber City. Provo Canyon is one of the prinicipal passes slicing through the Wasatch Range, and, most of the way it follows the Provo River, a premier trout stream. Also off US 189 in Provo Canyon is Sundance Resort, a development led by film actor Robert Redford. It features skiing during the winter and camping or horseback riding through the other seasons.

Provo and BYU

Located at the foot of 11,000-foot-high Provo Peak, the city of Provo is typically Mormon, with clean, wide streets and well-tended landscaping. It is a combination agricultural, educational and industrial center. The Mormon Church's biggest and best college campus graces Provo—Brigham Young University. Handsome and sprawling after a massive 1960s construction program, BYU (or "The Y," as it is colloquially called by many Utah admirers), attracts 25,000 students from

LDS families throughout the U.S. and foreign countries. Its rigid and obeyed code of conduct rivals its nationally-ranked athletic teams for far-flung recognition.

To the north, near Lehi, is Timpanogos Cave National Monument. Located in American Fork Canyon, the cleverly lighted caves were formed by a now-vanished underground river. The monument visitor center is open from May to October and the setting is spectacular. The cave is at the head of a long, uphill walk not recommended for the aging or infirm.

Colorado River Canyon Country

Capitol Reef National Park, 61 square miles in area, includes 20-mile stretches of cliff. A road along the base meets spurs and graded trails leading to impressive Grand and Capitol gorges, Chimney Rock, Hickman Natural Bridge, petrified forests and Indian petroglyphs engraved on stone 1,200 years ago.

The Capitol Reef escarpment marks the southern boundary of Wayne Wonderland, a desert region of canyons, basins and sheer cliffs, the most awesome work produced by natural upheaval and erosion. Here stand Cathedral Valley, Walls of Jericho, Hoodoo Arch and the surrealistic Valley of the Goblins. Ask about road conditions before exploring these sites in standard model cars.

East of Bluff, southeastern Utah's first white settlement, are the widely scattered prehistoric ruins of Hovenweep National Monument. The two Utah sections are reachable by partly paved, partly graded roads. South from Mexican Hat, on US 163, travelers enter the northern rim of the 25,000-square-mile Navajo Indian Reservation, largest in the U.S. Here, on the Utah–Arizona border is awesome, incredible Monument Valley. Mile after mile, the pavement passes huge red sandstone buttes, pillars, columns and needles soaring more than a thousand feet above the wide desert floor. The unforgettable shapes have been given such names as Totem Pole, Castle, Stagecoach, Brigham's Tomb and Mitten Buttes. Indians still spend summers amid these wonders, living much as their ancestors did centuries ago.

Arches and Towers

Crossing the Colorado, US 163 passes Arches National Park, featuring a 53-square-mile area with rock spires, pinnacles and narrow fins pierced by 88 naturally formed openings. One is a 291-foot bridge, the largest known natural arch. You may drive on paved roads to the finest specimens, but some walking is necessary to see the rock-formed skyscrapers of Park Avenue, Landscape Arch, The Devil's Garden and whimsical Delicate Arch. The last, called Schoolmarm's Britches by local cowhands, is the most beautiful and remarkable of the bunch. Rising more than 100 feet high, it stands alone and unsupported in a setting of slickrock domes, with the gorge of the Colorado River and the 12,000- to 13,000-foot peaks of the La Sal Mountains in the distance.

Farther South

Zion National Park is located directly south of Cedar City, off I–15 and then along state routes that take motorists through small prim Mormon settlements named Toquerville, La Verkin and Virgin. A tranquil, wooded camping site east of Cedar City off State 14 is Navajo Lake, cold enough for good trout fishing and big enough for boating.

Pioneer Village, in the Lagoon Amusement Park, includes reconstructed buildings, complete with furnishings from several periods of U.S. history, and stores stocked with original inventories. Enjoyable and educational. Free with paid admission to Lagoon.

Bonneville Salt Flats, near Wendover, is the home of the land speed records. For further information contact the Utah Travel Council.

TOURS. *Gray Lines* offers tours to Bryce Canyon National Park, Zion National Park and Cedar Breaks National Monument, as well as a Canyonland tour. *Trailways* schedules tours from Salt Lake City to Zion, Bryce, and Cedar Breaks National Monument. Boat tours are offered on Flaming Gorge Reservoir behind Flaming Gorge Dam by *Hatch River Expeditions.* Similar outings are available at *Lake Powell* behind Glen Canyon Dam, at Page in Arizona. For white-water river running on the Green and Colorado rivers, float trips are conducted by *Worldwide River Expeditions* at Vernal and Moab, with headquarters at 175 E. 7060 S., Midvale, Utah 84047. *Hatch Expeditions* has river-running headquarters at Vernal, Tag-a-long Tours is in Moab.

DRINKING LAWS. Utah's liquor control laws beg the visitor's tolerance. Beer is the only alcoholic beverage served in all public bars. Certain licensed restaurants also serve two-ounce "mini-bottles" of the most commonly preferred cocktail or highball liquor; but they can only be ordered with food. That applies to wine as well. Retail liquor is only sold in state stores or package agencies. The legal age is 21.

SUMMER SPORTS. Some 200 *fishing* waters are open year-round. The state's most popular and regularly caught fish is the rainbow trout. Frequently taken from many waters are brook, native cutthroat, brown, Kokanee salmon, Mackinaw or lake trout, grayling, largemouth and white bass, channel catfish and walleyed pike. Nonresident license fee: 1 day, $5; 5 day $15; season, $35, $3.30 additional for adults and $2.30 for youngsters under 16 fishing for trout.

There are 45 public *golf* courses in operation around Utah. Many are nestled in unique mountain or desert settings.

Hunting is widely practiced in Utah, whether for deer, elk, antelope, jack rabbits, badgers, woodchucks and gophers or quail, pheasant, chukar partridge, ducks and geese. A nonresident big game license costs $120 for one deer. Small game nonresident license is $30.

WINTER SPORTS. Utah's mountain winters are long, snow-covered and, though cold, often sunny for extended periods. The official state guide book lists 14 ski resorts, but not all excel. Snowmobiling and cross-country skiing are catching on in Utah's snow country. Both are allowed in certain areas of local canyons.

HOTELS AND MOTELS in Utah are relatively inexpensive. Highest rates are in effect for the "in-season" period, which, according to the locale, is either ski season (November to April) or the summer months that bring tourists to the national parks and forest lands. Based on double occupancy, the rate categories for Utah are: *Deluxe:* over $45, *Expensive:* $35–45; *Moderate:* $25–35; and *Inexpensive:* under $25.

ALTA. *Deluxe:* **Alta Lodge.** Scenic mountain atmosphere.

BRYCE CANYON. *Moderate:* **Ruby's Inn.** US Highway 63. Cafe, laundromat.

HEBER CITY. *Moderate:* **Homestead.** Many activities; including horseback riding.

MEXICAN HAT. *Moderate:* **Friendship Inn San Juan Motel.** Highway 163. Scenic tours; restaurant.

MONTICELLO. *Moderate:* **Navajo Trail.** 440 N. Main St. Family style.

PARK CITY. *Deluxe:* **Best Western Copper Bottom Inn.** Fireplaces. Restaurant and lounge. Sauna; hot tub.
  Expensive to Deluxe: **Blue Church Lodge.** Historic turn-of-the-century church converted to 1- to 4-bedroom apartments; some with fireplaces. Common lounge with fireplace; game room; Jacuzzi.

PROVO. *Moderate:* **Holiday Inn.** 1465 S. University Ave. 45 minutes from ski resorts; near municipal golf course.

 DINING OUT. Mormon cooking is neither different nor unique. It's possible to discover especially tasty fare in out-of-the-way locations, but don't count on it. Statewide restaurant quality has improved considerably, however, since tourism has developed into such a big, booming business. Price categories are for a complete dinner but do not include drinks, tax or tip. *Expensive:* $10 and up; *Moderate:* $5–10 and *Inexpensive:* under $5.

CEDAR CITY. *Moderate:* **Sugar Loaf Café.** Broasted chicken, steak.

HEBER CITY. *Inexpensive:* **The Hub.** Open 24 hours.

LOGAN. *Moderate:* **Country Kitchen.** Good family style.

OGDEN. *Moderate:* **Olde Country Bar.** Old-fashioned American food served family style.

PARK CITY. *Expensive:* **Adolph's.** Continental dining.

PROVO. *Moderate:* **Jedediah's Famous Dining,** at the Rodeway Inn. 1292 University Ave. Family diners and lunches.

ST. GEORGE. *Moderate:* **Atkins' Sugar Loaf Café.** Chicken, steak.

WYOMING

The Cowboy State

Wyoming sits in the lap of the broadest part of the Rocky Mountains. Rectangular in shape, on a plateau four to seven thousand feet above sea level, Wyoming is at a higher average altitude than all other states except neighboring Colorado.

A big loop tour of the state can begin at Sundance near South Dakota's Black Hills. Sundance is a trading center for surrounding ranches, and cowboys in high-heeled boots and cowboy hats give a sense of the Old West. About 27 miles to the northwest is Devils Tower National Monument, a stump-shaped cluster of volcanic rock columns 1,000 feet across at the bottom and 275 feet at the top. In 1906, it was set aside as America's first National Monument. Further west is Buffalo and nearby Indian-U.S. Cavalry battlegrounds and the Bradford Brinton Memorial Ranch near Big Horn.

Sheridan is the largest city in northern Wyoming and headquarters for Bighorn National Forest. Sheridan's rodeo in mid-July is an authentic relic of earlier frontier days. Over the Bighorn Mountains lies Cody, named after the scout, Buffalo Bill Cody. The town is packed with mementos of this famed westerner, including his boyhood home and an impressive historic center which also houses the entire Winchester Firearm Collection.

Laramie, in the southwest, is over one hundred years old and has flourished since its inception as a Union Pacific Railroad station. Nearby is Old Fort Sanders, a stopping place for Western pioneers and Mormons. Laramie is also home of the University of Wyoming.

Cheyenne, the state capital and now a peaceful prosperous community, was known as "Hell on Wheels" in the days of the Old West. Once a year, during the last full week of July, the spirit of the bygone era is

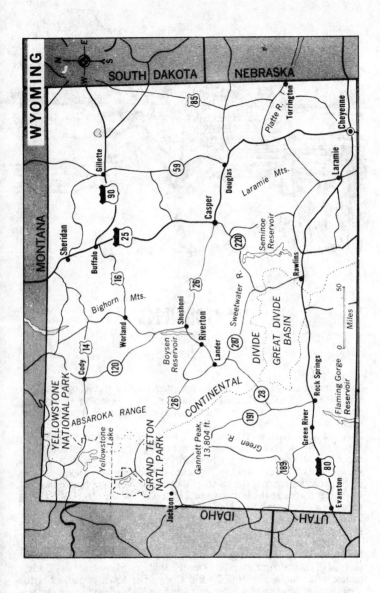

revived with Cheyenne Days, a festival of grade A rodeos, parades and cowboys playing cowboys.

From Cheyenne are three suggested day tours. The first tour takes in "Old Bedlam," Fort Laramie and the Oregon Trail National Historic Site. Indian, U.S. Cavalry and settler artifacts and remains are found along the way. A second loop tour takes in the Medicine Bow National Forest, Curt Gowdy State Park and Laramie. The third trip includes stops at Scotts Bluff National Monument, which commemorates a stopping point for both the Pony Express and Oregon and California bound settlers, Chimney Rock National Historic Site, and the Glendo Recreation area.

PRACTICAL INFORMATION FOR WYOMING

HOW TO GET THERE. *By air: Frontier* flies to Cheyenne, Casper, Riverton, Jackson, Laramie, Gillette, Sheridan, Cody, and Rock Springs. *Continental Airlines* services Gillette, Jackson, and Riverton; *Western* flies to Casper; *Rocky Mountain Airways* offers service to Cheyenne. *By car:* I–80 passes east-west in the southern part of state, I–90 in the north. I–25 from Colorado in the south. *By bus: Continental Trailways* and *Greyhound.*

HOW TO GET AROUND. *By air:* Airports in Jackson, Cody, Worland, Rock Springs, Riverton–Lander, Casper, Laramie, Sheridan, Gillette, and Cheyenne. *By car:* Good interstate roads. All toll free. *By bus: Greyhound, Trailways,* and *Jackson–Rock Springs Stages.*

TOURIST INFORMATION. *Wyoming Travel Commission,* Cheyenne 82002, (307) 777–7777.

MUSEUMS AND GALLERIES: In Cody, *Buffalo Bill Historical Center,* with *Buffalo Bill Museum* and *Whitney Gallery of Western Art. Bradford Brinton Memorial Museum,* near Big Horn, with western pioneer relics. *University of Wyoming Art Museum* in Laramie. The *Wyoming State Museum* in Cheyenne with artifacts, Indian and military collections. Cheyenne also has the *Frontier Days Old West Museum. Fremont County Pioneer Museum* in Lander.

HISTORIC SITES. *Fort Laramie* has been restored to the days when it served as Cavalry headquarters. *South Pass City* near Lander has rebuilt the authentic western gold ghost town from 1867–68. Most famous of the forts are: *Fort Bridger,* in Fort Bridger State Park, named after the famous trapper and guide; *Fort Phil Kearney* near Story in the Sheridan area; *Fort Caspar* in Casper. Best-known of pioneer sites are: *St. Mary's Stage Station,* near South Pass City, where 90 Mormons perished in a blizzard; *Buffalo Bill Statue* near Cody; and *Independence Rock* near Casper.

TOURS. *Jackson Lake Lodge* and *Yellowstone Park Co.* arrange tours of park areas. *Old West Tours* operates in Jackson.

DRINKING LAWS. Minimum drinking age is nineteen.

SUMMER SPORTS. *Boating,* rafting, canoeing, on lakes and reservoirs. State and national recreation areas are full of opportunities. Trout is most prevalent *fish* in 20,000 miles of streams and 264,000 acres of lakes. *Hunting* seasons for various animals—consult state Game and Fish Commission. Horseback *riding* and *pack trips* throughout the state. Mountain climbing is taught in the Grand Tetons.

WINTER SPORTS. Big *ski* areas at: Jackson and Grand Targhee in the Tetons; Medicine Bow near Laramie; Hogadon near Casper, *Sleeping Giant* at edge of Yellowstone National Park, *Meadowlark* in the Bighorns. *Snowmobiling* and *cross-country skiing* are available.

SPECTATOR SPORTS. More than 80 rodeos are held each summer in Cody, Jackson, Cheyenne, Casper, Lander, and other cities. Consult state commission for dates and times. Gillette has stock car racing. Polo tournaments on summer Sundays in Jackson.

SHOPPING. *Welty's Store* in Dubois is a large trading post. Most towns have shops selling leather and buckskin jackets, hunting and camping equipment. High-quality art galleries thrive in the larger towns.

WHAT TO DO WITH THE CHILDREN. All parks, of course, offer delights for children. Special *stage coach rides* for children from Town Square in Jackson as well as nightly "shootouts." See separate section on Yellowstone Park earlier in book.

HOTELS AND MOTELS. Based on single room, double occupancy, the rates are: *Deluxe:* $55–90; *Expensive:* $46–54; *Moderate:* $35–45; *Inexpensive:* $18–34.

CASPER. *Expensive:* **Holiday Inn.** Plush accommodations.
Ramada Inn. 347-room hostelry.
Inexpensive: **Travelier Motel.** Small and adequate.

CHEYENNE. *Deluxe:* **Best Western Hitching Post Inn.** Wyoming landmark. Near downtown. Gourmet restaurant.
Holiday Inn. Entertainment center. New.
Inexpensive: **Super Eight.** Downtown area, near Hitching Post Inn.

CODY. *Deluxe:* **Holiday Inn.** At Buffalo Bill Village.
Moderate: **Irma Motor Hotel.** Downtown. Old West landmark.

JACKSON/JACKSON HOLE. *Deluxe:* **Americana Snow King Resort.** Restaurant, bar. Pool, sauna, Jacuzzi. Sports shop and ski rental.
Sojourner Inn. Elegant and spacious. Restaurant, bar. Pool, sauna, Jacuzzi. Close to skiing, golf, tennis, water sports, horseback riding.
Moderate: **Virginian Motel.** Quiet spot at base of ski lifts. Restaurant, bar, entertainment. Pool. Golf nearby.

LARAMIE. *Expensive:* **Holiday Inn.** Large. Convention facilities.
Moderate: **Circle S Motel.** Pleasant rooms, heated pool.
Wyoming Motel. Across from University.

SHERIDAN. *Expensive:* **Sheridan Center Motor Inn.** Meeting and banquet facilities.
Moderate: **Trails End Motel.** Small, attractive.
Inexpensive: **American Inn.** Modern.

YELLOWSTONE NATIONAL PARK. *Moderate:* **Canyon Village.** All facilities; horses. Open summer.
Old Faithful Inn. Across from the geyser. Unique building. Open summer.
Inexpensive–Moderate: **Mammoth Hot Springs Hotel.** Open summer.

DINING OUT. Prices are for a complete dinner but do not include drinks, tax or tip: *Deluxe:* $20 and up; *Expensive:* $16–19; *Moderate:* $10–15; *Inexpensive:* $5–9.

CASPER. *Deluxe:* **Benham's.** Steaks and businessman's lunch.

CODY. *Moderate:* **Green Gables.** Western food.
Irma Grill. Steaks, ribs. Buffalo Bill's cherrywood bar.

EVANSTON. *Moderate:* **The Grand Manor Restaurant.** At Sheraton Inn.

GLENROCK. *Expensive:* **Paisley Shawl Restaurant.** Varied menu. National Historic Building.
  Moderate: **Jedediah's House of Sourdough.** Hearty fare and plenty of it.

JACKSON. *Deluxe:* **Alpenhof.** European gourmet restaurant at Teton Village.
  Inexpensive: **Lame Duck.** Oriental. Roast duck a specialty.

LANDER. *Deluxe:* **Miner's Delight.** In Atlantic City ghost town. Continental.

LARAMIE. *Moderate:* **Curt's.**
Diamond Horseshoe. Chinese and American.

YELLOWSTONE NATIONAL PARK. *Moderate:* **Canyon Village.** Prime ribs and seafood.
  Old Faithful Inn. Beautiful, unique rooms. Good food.

ALASKA

America's Last Frontier

Approaching Alaska by boat on the beautiful "Marine Highway," the first city is Ketchikan, at the base of 3,000-foot Deer Mountain. The town claims titles of "Salmon Capital of the World" and "Birthplace of the Alaska Pulp Industry." Along with timber and fish, Ketchikan banks on tourism, a molybdenum mine, and a hydroelectric project.

Visitors remember Ketchikan for its many carved Tlingit totem poles: at Saxman Totem Park just south of town; the Totem Heritage Cultural Center in town; and Totem Bight ten miles to the north.

And for fish, whether they observe them from platforms in the city park's sophisticated "fish factory," the Deer Mt. Hatchery, or go out and catch them. Clover Pass, 15 paved miles from Ketchikan; Yes Bay; and Bell Island Hot Springs, 45 air miles away, border some of the finest king-salmon fishing grounds in Alaska, as well as coho, or silver, salmon runs. There is also fabulous trout fishing.

To the north along the Inside Passage are more island villages. Wrangell thrived under British, Russian and American flags. A foot-bridge leads to Chief Shakes Island, where there is a replica of an Indian tribal house and totems. Petersburg has a Norwegian accent; Sitka retains its Russian one.

On Baranof Island, named after the guiding genius of Russian settlement in Alaska, Sitka was once the capital of Russian America. Crumbling headstones of the Old Russian Cemetery include that of Princess Maksoutoff, wife of the last Russian governor. The annual October 18 ceremony relives the transfer of Alaska to the United States in 1867.

St. Michael's Orthodox Cathedral, destroyed by fire in 1966, is an exact reconstruction of the 1844 – 48 building. Inside are rare relics and religious paintings rescued by the townspeople. Nearby is an origi-

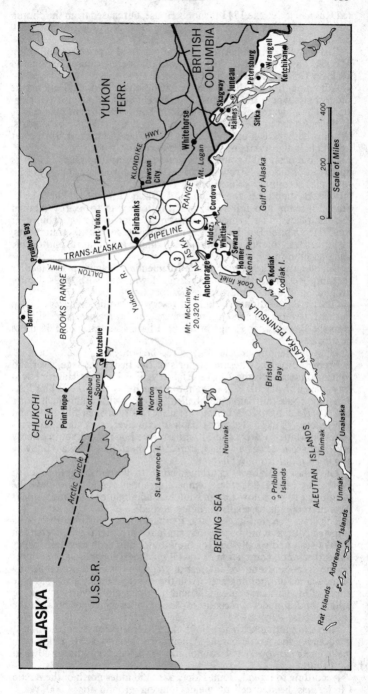

ALASKA

BRITISH COLUMBIA

YUKON TERR.

Petersburg
Wrangell
Ketchikan
Juneau
Skagway
Whitehorse
Haines
Sitka
KLONDIKE HWY.
Dawson City
Mt. Logan
RANGE
Gulf of Alaska

Scale of Miles
0   200   400

Fort Yukon
Fairbanks
Cordova
PIPELINE
TRANS-ALASKA
Valdez
Whittier
Seward
Prudhoe Bay
DALTON HWY.
Yukon R.
ALASKA
Anchorage
Homer
Kenai Pen.
Cook Inlet
Kodiak
Kodiak I.
Barrow
BROOKS RANGE
Mt. McKinley, 20,320 ft.
Kotzebue
ALASKA PENINSULA
CHUKCHI SEA
Point Hope
Kotzebue Sound
Nome
Norton Sound
Bristol Bay
Nunivak
St. Lawrence I.
Arctic Circle
BERING SEA
Pribilof Islands
ALEUTIAN ISLANDS
Unimak
Unmak
Unalaska
U.S.S.R.
Rat Islands   Andreanof Islands   Unmak

nal Russian jewel, the 1843 Bishop's House, purchased from the church and now on display after a long, meticulous restoration by the Park Service.

Russian, Indian, and American artifacts, and a priceless collection of books on early Pacific Northwest exploration are housed in Sheldon Jackson College, Alaska's oldest school.

Adjoining the city, the 54-acre Sitka National Historical Park marks the fort site where the Tlingits made their last stand against the Russians. The towering Governor Brady or Sonny Hat totem pole stands at the entrance to the Park, surrounded by Tlingit Wolf House posts. Within the Park is a unique "totem lovers' lane," and a visitor center in which Indian craftsmen may be observed at work.

Born out of an 1880 gold strike, Juneau, the state capital, is 151 miles northeast of Sitka. Narrow winding streets and wooden stairways lead to homes seemingly gouged out of the hillside.

Visitors should see the Indian and Eskimo artifacts at the Alaska State Museum, and follow the walking tour map to nearby marked historic places. The Visitor Information Center in the log cabin near the State Capitol Building has them. It will take you to monuments, historic sites, totems and vintage buildings, including a photogenic Russian church.

But the area's key attraction is Mendenhall Glacier, a spectacular receding ice river only 14 miles from downtown, with trails, campgrounds, and a fine, interpretive Visitors Center.

Glacier Bay National Park and Preserve, 3.28 million acres of deep fjords, tidewater glaciers, jutting icebergs, and rare species of wildlife, is in the Fairweather Range of the St. Elias Mountains, and 55 miles northwest of Juneau.

The 65-mile-long Glacier Bay is reached only by plane or boat.

From the two northernmost ports of the Inside Passage, overland routes connect with the Alaska Highway. The 159-mile Haines Highway joins at Mile 1016. It does not appear likely that the White Pass & Yukon route railroad, "mothballed" in 1983, will resume its historic trek overlooking traces of the "Trail of '98" between Skagway and Whitehorse, Yukon Territory capital. However, cars and motorcoaches continue to drive the 110-mile scenic but rugged summer-only highway from Skagway via Carcross to meet the Alaska Highway about 14 miles from Whitehorse.

The Alaska Highway continues north to its end at gold-founded Fairbanks, Mile 1523, where temperatures may range from above 90° in summer to 60° below zero in winter. A highlight of long midsummer days is midnight baseball, no lights needed.

The state's second-largest city, Fairbanks has grown because of its assorted roles as a military center, space research center, University of Alaska seat, and supply hub for the Interior and Arctic regions. After a breather upon completion of the oil pipeline, North Slope activity is on the increase. Renewed interest in gold has triggered the reopening of old claims and mining activity in the vicinity. Today's visitors note a mix of modern shopping malls and buildings along with vintage log cabins, and a modern, recently expanded, refurbished terminal at the International Airport.

North of Fairbanks, where the Yukon River makes its northernmost bend above the Arctic Circle, Athabascan Indians of Ft. Yukon still make fine beadwork, catch salmon in fish wheels, trap furs, and live in log cabins.

According to legend, Point Hope, over 150 miles north of the Arctic Circle, has been excellent whale hunting ground for 4,000 years. Whales up to 60 tons are caught here, and some giant whale jawbones have decorated the cemetery for a century.

The Native Land Claims Settlement Act passed in 1971 allowed for $900 million in cash and 40 million acres of land to be divided among Alaska's 60,000 native Indians, Aleuts and Eskimos. It is too soon to predict the full impact on Native ways, but there have been many changes. However, the Arctic is a most fascinating place to visit while it has its past still present.

Stand at Point Barrow, and you are at the northernmost tip of our continent, about 300 miles above the Arctic Circle. Kotzebue is about 30 miles above the Circle. Both Eskimo towns opt for developing tourism, and the natives are spending their money on fine hotels and other modern facilities. Since the coming of the snowmobile, dogs are less numerous. However, the Eskimos still hunt and fish for some of their food and prepare it in traditional ways. And they continue with their skills and games like ivory carving, blanket toss and dancing, partly for tourists, but mostly because they still want to.

Denali National Park, between Fairbanks and Anchorage and reached by highway and railroad, is one of the continent's outstanding wilderness areas. It is dominated by 20,320-foot Mt. McKinley, the highest mountain in North America. Traversing the 90-mile gravel highway in the 4,700,000-acre park and preserve is like being in a natural history museum of mountain, tundra, and wildlife. Almost 40 species of mammals dwell here, including caribou, moose, bear (grizzly and black), Canada lynx, red fox, Dall sheep, porcupine, and beaver. In summer, well-guided wildlife tours deep into the Park by bus allow visitors to see and photograph some of the more than 130 varieties of birds, animals, and wildflowers.

Private vehicles are restricted on the McKinley Park road now, but there is free shuttle bus service daily from Park Headquarters in summer. Camping is by reservation beyond the first three campgrounds. Reserve ahead to stay within the Park at the Denali Park Station Hotel at North Face Lodge, and Camp Denali, both near Wonder Lake. Be aware that excellent accommodations near the park entrance, such as McKinley Village Hotel, McKinley Chalets, KOA Kamp, and Denali Cabins (hot tub!), fill up fast in summer.

Modern, cosmopolitan Anchorage is Alaska's largest city. It is the financial and business metropolis of the state, as well as the focal point for the creative arts. The city is well into all phases of "Project '80s," aimed at building and beautifying while developing recreation and tourism.

Besides being an air crossroads of the world, Anchorage is a takeoff point for remote areas in Western and Northern Alaska: the Katmai; the semi-volcanic, treeless Aleutian Islands and the Bering Sea Pribilof Islands, fur-seal breeding grounds; Nome on the Bering Sea Coast; and Kotzebue, Barrow, and Prudhoe Bay on the Arctic Ocean.

From Anchorage, roads lead to Interior destinations, the Alaska Highway, and popular recreation areas on the game and fish-filled Kenai Peninsula.

Kenai, on Cook Inlet, and Kodiak Island, were both settled by the Russians during the last half of the 18th century. The city of Kodiak is the oldest permanent settlement in Alaska.

Perhaps Kodiak is most famous for the Kodiak brown bear and king crab. The continent's largest carnivore can weigh up to 1200 pounds. The sea monster may reach four feet, pincer to pincer.

PRACTICAL INFORMATION FOR ALASKA

HOW TO GET THERE. *By air:* Scheduled U.S. airlines jet direct to Alaska from gateway cities in the United States and Canada. Several foreign and domestic airlines touch down on international flights.

By land: The Alaska Highway is open year round. Car travelers should buy a guide to facilities and services, and despite the generally good road conditions, special precautions and preparations may be needed. U.S. citizens need no passport at the Canadian border, but some personal papers as proof are advisable. Bus systems serve major Alaskan cities from U.S. and Canadian points.

By sea: Alaska State Ferries operate year round between Prince Rupert, B.C., Seattle, Wash., and Southeastern Alaska ports along the Inside Passage. For schedules, fares, and reservations (needed in peak season summer travel): Alaska Marine Highway System, Pouch R, Juneau, AK 99811, (907) 465–3941. In Anchorage, (907) 272–7116; in Seattle, (206) 623–1970. Contact the B.C. Ferry Corp., 1045 Howe St., Vancouver, B.C. Canada V6Z 2A9, (604) 669–1211 about Canadian ferries operating between Vancouver, Vancouver Island, and Prince Rupert. Most cruise ships leave from Vancouver, B.C.; a few sail from San Francisco and Los Angeles. Combination land, air, and Marine Highway trips are popular.

HOW TO GET AROUND. *By air:* Many scheduled carriers link principal cities and towns. Bush pilots offer dependable service to isolated points. *By car:* Most of the main highways covering about a fifth of the state are paved. These include the Alaska Highway, Richardson, Glenn, Seward-Anchorage, Sterling, and George Parks (between Anchorage and Fairbanks). Stay alert for rough spots caused by annual freezing and thawing, and for road crews and equipment repairing them.

Car and recreational vehicle rental: All main agencies have offices in major cities and many smaller ones, usually at the airport and hotels.

By bus: Public bus systems and motorcoach sightseeing tours serve main cities, and there's scheduled service along most highways.

By rail: Though "mothballed" at this writing, railroad buffs hope the White Pass & Yukon Route will again carry passengers and freight between Skagway and Whitehorse. The Alaska Railroad travels to Fairbanks, Denali Park, Anchorage, and Whittier, ferry port on Prince William Sound.

By ferry: Ferries of the Southcentral Marine Highway System serve ports of Prince William Sound, Gulf of Alaska, the Kenai Peninsula, and Kodiak Island. The Southcentral and Southeastern systems do not interconnect.

Other: Dog sleds, snowmobiles, canoes and kayaks, plus bicycling, horseback and backpacking trips, and river rafting.

TOURIST INFORMATION SERVICES. Write the *Alaska Division of Tourism,* Pouch E, Juneau, AK 99811 for their free, annually updated "Alaska & Canada's Yukon Vacation Planner"; phone (907) 465–2010. Most communities have a tourist center dispensing information about overnight accommodations and attractions.

Alaska Highway travelers get hospitality (free coffee) and information every day from 7 A.M. to 10 P.M. at the Tok Information Center, Mile 1314.1; phone (907) 883–5667; write Box 335, Tok, AK 99780.

MUSEUMS AND GALLERIES. The *Anchorage Historical and Fine Arts Museum,* 121 W. Seventh Ave., exhibits arts and artifacts of Alaska, as do the *University of Alaska Museum* at Fairbanks, and Juneau's *Alaska State Museum.* Southeast Alaska Indian artifacts are featured at the *Tongass Historical Society* Museum and the *Totem Heritage Cultural Center.* The Dog Musher's Hall of Fame is at Knik, 50 miles from Anchorage in the Matanuska

Valley. The Kodiak Historical Society's *Baranof Museum* is in Erskine House, the oldest structure remaining in Alaska. In Nome the *Carrie McLain Memorial Museum* emphasizes the Gold Rush, Eskimo culture, and the region's natural history. More gold-rush memorabilia are featured in the developing *Rocker Gulch Park*. A fine bronze sculpture "Fisk" in front of the Clausen Memorial Museum portrays all of Petersburg's fish. *Sheldon Jackson College Museum* in Sitka has an interesting collection from Tlingit Indian and Russian-American times. The *"Trail of '98" Museum* and outlaw *Soapy Smith's Saloon Museum* are in Skagway. The *Living Museum of the Arctic,* with dioramas of Arctic life and environment, live Eskimo crafts and dance demonstrations, is in Kotzebue.

Art: Numerous galleries, from the University of Alaska Fine Arts Center, Fairbanks, to art-minded Homer near the tip of the Kenai Peninsula, represent Alaskan artists.

HISTORIC SITES. Over a hundred are listed in the National Register. Some are National Landmarks, such as the whole town of Eagle, where the Norwegian explorer Amundsen stayed in 1905. Many historic buildings are being restored, including Judge Wickerham's First Judicial Courthouse from 1901. Historic buildings surround the parade ground of Fort William H. Seward, adjacent to Haines.

Fairbanks hoards historic things from boats to buildings in 44-acre Alaskaland. The *Felix Pedro Monument* in *Pedro Creek Discovery Claim,* Mile 17 on Steese Highway, marks the beginning of the 1902 gold rush to the interior.

Juneau: The house museum of turn-of-the-century statesman and historian, Judge Wickersham, has an outstanding collection of Alaskana. (Admission charge.)

Kenai: Site of *Redoubt St. Nicholas,* a fortified Russian fur-trading post (1791). The *Russian Orthodox Church* (1894) is a Historic Landmark.

Ketchikan: *Totem Bright State Historical Site* contains excellent totems.

Sitka: The restored *Russian Bishop's House* (1843) and the reconstructed *St. Michael's Cathedral* portray the Russian era. *Sitka National Historical Park* with totem poles and Visitor Center commemorates site where Russians defeated Indians in the final "Battle for Alaska" in 1804.

Skagway and nearby ghost town Dyea: overland starting points for the rugged mountain and river route to Canadian goldfields, are part of the new *Klondike Gold Rush National Historical Park.*

TOURS. For a few days or up to several weeks, package tours cover big Alaska, using assorted land, sea, and air transportation. They allow for optional tours; add them as you plan, for savings. Most firms listed here have grown up with Alaska tourism. They work closely with airlines, cruise ships, ferries, motorcoaches, railroads, local Alaskans, and your local travel agent.

Alaska Exploration Holidays & Cruises, 1500 Metropolitan Park Bldg., Olive Way at Boren Ave., Seattle, WA 98101, round up the best of Alaska and the Yukon summer destinations ranging from far west Pribilof Islands to the Arctic. Their cruises of Alaska's Inside Passage feature Explorer Class ships visiting wilderness areas—especially Glacier Bay—and calling at both big and small ports. The fleet includes three specially designed American ships carrying fewer than a hundred passengers on round trips from Ketchikan. These boats boast unique bow landing facilities for debarking and exploring where bigger cruise ships cannot go. The 158-passenger Norwegian *North Star,* larger and with added amenities (swimming pool!), cruises from Prince Rupert, BC, Canada.

Kneisel Travel, Ste. 16, 6950 SW Hampton, Portland, OR 97232, long has offered "Mr. K's Alaska Treasure Chest" of air/sea tours for independent travelers, and the "Green Carpet" program for escorted groups. *Maupintour's* Alaska adventures are also escorted. Write Box 807, Lawrence, Kansas 66044. *TravAlaska Tours, Inc.* (and *Alaska-Yukon Motorcoaches*), 555 4th & Battery Bldg., Seattle, WA 98121, headed by Alaska travel pioneer Chuck West, feature economy all-season tours, plus custom-designed ones.

Princess Tours offers "The Alaska Vacation." All itineraries include an Inside Passage cruise, coming or going, aboard one of three sleek Princess ships. Treatment is royal throughout, including the 15-day escorted tour to the Arctic.

Westours, Inc. 300 Elliott Ave. West, Seattle, WA 98119, operate their own hotels at strategic places and their own sightseeing motorcoaches, for "Hyway

Holidays." Holland America ships sail the Inside Passage for them as far as Juneau. From there, Westours' mini-cruiser MV *Fairweather* runs daily in fjord-like Lynn Canal between Juneau and Skagway to connect with the Yukon and northern Alaska points.

Featuring small group wilderness trips are *Alaska Discovery,* Box 28, Gustavus, AK 99286; *Alaska Travel Adventures,* 200 No. Franklin St., Juneau, AK 99801; and *Questers,* 257 Park Ave. S, NY 10010. "Fish Our Alaska!" is the theme of *Alaska Sportfishing Packages,* Ste. 1320, 4th & Blanchard Bldg., Seattle, WA 98121; phone 800–426–0603.

Airlines flying to and within Alaska offer "promotions" featuring air travel bargains, such as stopovers for a small charge, special senior citizen rates, and low fares in connection with cruises and tours. Travel agents stay alert to such, and they are boldly advertised. Inquire at your nearest airline regional office, or the following: *Alaska Airlines,* Box 68900, Seattle, WA 98168; *Northwest Orient Airlines,* Tour Sales, Minneapolis–St. Paul International Airport, St. Paul, MI 55111; *Western Airlines,* 3830 International Airport Road, Anchorage, AK 99502; *Wien Air Alaska Airlines,* 4100 W. International Airport Road, Anchorage, AK 99503.

SUMMER ACTIVITIES To hunt and fish, all nonresidents must possess a valid license and tags. Write Public Communications, *Alaska Dept. of Fish & Game,* Box 3–2000, Juneau, AK 99802; phone (907) 465–4112 for current regulations. Major salmon derbies run from January through September.

Boating. Boats are available for rent or charter in some communities. Kayaking, canoeing, and rafting expeditions are offered on all kinds of rivers and lakes.

Scuba and *skin diving* are popular along the coast. *Swimmers* find coastal waters chilly, but lakes warm enough. Hotels in larger cities may have pools. Some towns have community swimming pools.

Hiking. Of about 500 miles of trails alone in the national forests, the most famous is the Chilkoot Pass Trail from Skagway.

Mountain climbing. From afternoon climbs to the highest peak in North America. But be prepared in every respect—and have guides on any extended climb.

Golf. 5 greens in the Anchorage area; 2 at Fairbanks; and a course at Soldotna on the Kenai Peninsula.

Glacier skiing. For die-hards, high on the Juneau Ice Field and in mountains behind Mt. Alyeska near Anchorage.

Flightseeing is offered by small air services throughout Alaska.

WINTER ACTIVITIES. Alaskans frequent many local ski runs and tows, but the best-developed ski area is *Mt. Alyeska Ski Resort,* about 40 miles from Anchorage, with heli-skiing and dogsledding, chairlifts, ski school, and restaurants. Two easily accessible ski slopes are near *Fairbanks. Juneau's Eaglecrest* ski area, across the bridge on Douglas Island, has a day lodge, chairlift and rope tows. *Turnagain Pass Area,* 59 miles from Anchorage on the Seward Highway, is popular with cross-country skiers and snowmobilers; snowfall frequently exceeds 12 feet. *Ice skating* and *ice fishing* are popular on many suitable frozen lakes, December through March.

Curling. This Scottish favorite is played in Anchorage, Fairbanks, and in Whitehorse, YT.

SEASONAL EVENTS. Alaskans are prone to celebrations year-round, and for almost any reason. January 3, 1984 marked Alaska's Silver Anniversary of Statehood, setting the theme for local celebrations all year. In the summer season, roughly May through September, you can count on being entertained by assorted continuous community "specials." For many more events and festivals and exact dates, write the area Chamber of Commerce and consult the listings in the Alaska Yukon Travel Planner, free on request from the Division of Tourism, Pouch E, Juneau, AK 99811.

February: Cordova holds an *Iceworm Festival;* Homer, a *Winter Carnival.* The Anchorage Fur Rendezvous features *World Championship Sled Dog Races.*

March: Fairbanks holds more *Championship Sled Dog Races.* Nome sponsors the 1000-mile Iditarod *Sled Dog Classic.*

April: Kotzebue holds the *Archie Ferguson Snowmachine Race.*

May: Petersburg's *"Little Norway"* Festival. Kodiak *King Crab Festival.*

June: Highlighting the solstice (the 21st/22nd): Nome's *Midnight Sun Festival;* Fairbanks's *Midnight Sun Baseball Game;* Anchorage's *Mayor's Midnight Sun Marathon;* Anchorage holds a *Renaissance Faire* and a *Basically Bach Music Festival;* Sitka revels in a three-week *Summer Music Festival,* and watches *all-Alaska Logging Championships;* and there are *whaling festivals* at Barrow and Point Hope.

July: The 4th of July is a bang-up celebration from Ketchikan to Kotzebue, where they follow it with the *Northwest Alaska Native Trade Fair; Loggers Rodeo,* Ketchikan; *horse races,* Palmer; *foot race* up Mt. Marathon, Seward; and all sorts of fun and *Eskimo games* in Arctic towns. Fairbanks's "Golden Days" are celebrated in late July with the *World Eskimo, Indian, Aleut Olympic Games.*

August-September: Gold Rush Days at Valdez, and *Silver Salmon Derbies* at Valdez and Seward. *Fairs* at Haines, Fairbanks, and Palmer, and a *Buffalo Barbecue* at Delta. *Outdoor drama* "Cry of the Wild Ram" at Kodiak, and also a *Rodeo and State Fair.* In Anchorage they celebrate a mid-September *Festival of Music.*

October: Alaska Day Festival (Oct. 18) at Sitka.

The rest of the year Alaskans celebrate the holidays; visitors are welcome to join in.

SHOPPING. The unique and best buys in Alaska are furs and products made by natives. In particular, look for ivory and soapstone carvings, parkas, paintings on skins, silver, jade, gold-nugget and ivory jewelry, mukluks, slippers, hats, small marks, souvenir skin boats and totem poles.

The state-wide, native-owned and operated *Alaska Native Arts and Crafts Cooperative* offers an extensive selection. There are also many fine gift shops that sell contemporary arts and crafts work along with native-made items. Look for the state symbols—a hand or a map—that indicate your purchase is authentic.

WHAT TO DO WITH THE CHILDREN. The gold mines, ghost towns, old forts, museums, sled dogs, sawdust floor saloons, ferry boats, glaciers, nights without darkness, sourdough breakfast, salmon bakes—in all these and more Alaska offers an unlimited opportunity for a child's delight and wonder.

At *Denali National Park,* free roaming wildlife, birds and flora will amaze and instruct. More animals are on view in the free museum at Elmendorf Air Force Base and at the *Alaska Children's Zoo* near Anchorage. *Alaskaland,* at Fairbanks, is designed for all ages.

Around and About Anchorage with Children, by the Anchorage Volunteer Service League, is full of ideas for fun. Ask at bookstores or write P.O. Box 3762-S, Downtown Station, Anchorage, AK 99510.

There will be memorable rides on the sternwheeler *Discovery* paddling gold trails from Fairbanks, or via the Alaska Railroad, as it tunnels through mountains or traverses wilderness spiced with glimpses of wildlife.

Fishing streams, especially those with salmon spawning, will attract the curious. Indians, Aleuts and Eskimos will leave indelible impressions.

DRINKING LAWS. Minimum age is 21. Watering holes are plentiful; many close only between 5 and 8 A.M. However, communities vote whether to be dry or wet. Check, especially before heading for native villages.

TIME. Though 4 zones geographically, the state settles for 2 now. Yukon Time (1 hour behind Pacific) prevails except in the farthest west Aleutian Islands (Hawaii Time, 2 hours behind). Most of the Yukon observes Pacific Time.

HOTELS & MOTELS. There's a variety, from frontier to plush. Alaska travelers used to expect to pay premium prices. Now they'll find costs on a par with—or less—than many other destinations. In smaller towns lodging may be less expensive than in the big cities, but fewer choices. Major credit cards are widely accepted. Fine, modern accommodations are included in package tours to destinations throughout Alaska. Other travelers may find space limited or lacking in remote areas such as the Arctic or at Glacier Bay. Reserve ahead in summer, unless you are self-sufficient with camper, trailer, or tent. Stop by visitor information centers and Chambers of Commerce for local lodging leads and prices. These are based on double occupancy. *Deluxe* might run $100 and up per night; *Expensive:* $80–$100; *Moderate:* $60–$80; and *Inexpensive:* under $60. Bed & Breakfast, available in many communities, is about $45–$50, double.

ANCHORAGE. *Deluxe:* Downtown, and mostly highrise, are the **Anchorage Westward Hilton;** the **Captain Cook; Sheffield House;** the **Sheraton.**
Expensive: **Best Western Golden Lion; Mush Inn; TraveLodge.**
Moderate: **Best Western Barratt Inn** and **International Inn,** near the airport. **Northern Lights Inn; Super–8 Motel.** Downtown: **Holiday Inn** and the **Voyager Hotel.**
Inexpensive: the **Inlet Inns;** the **Hillside Motel, John's Motel,** and **Johnson's Motel,** all with camper parks, in the suburbs.

BARROW. Deluxe prices buy the comforts at the new **Airport Inn** and **Top of the World,** which houses tour groups in summer.

FAIRBANKS. *Deluxe:* **Captain Bartlett Inn; Fairbanks Inn; Golden Nugget Motel;** and **Traveler's Inn.**
Expensive: **The Great Land Hotel; Golden North Motel; Polaris Hotel** and **Towne House Motel.**
Moderate: **Klondike Inn; Maranatha Inn; Super–8 Motel; Tamarac Inn Motel.**
Inexpensive: **Alaska Motel and Apartments; Aurora Motel** near the university campus. **Cripple Creek Resort,** with mining camp atmosphere, 11 miles from town. **Alaskan Motor Inn,** downtown.

HOMER. *Expensive-Moderate:* **Land's End Resort,** at end of Homer Spit. Open year-round. Fishing, clamming, crabbing charters; flight-seeing tours. Nearby is the **Best Western Bidarka Inn.**
Moderate: **The Baycrest Motel; Heritage Hotel;** and **Ocean Shores Motel,** on beach with view.
Inexpensive: **Anchor River Inn** (16 miles from Homer) and in Homer, the **Driftwood Inn,** near the beach.

JUNEAU. *Deluxe:* **Sheffield Baranof Hotel;** and **Sheffield House Juneau.**
Expensive: **Breakwater Inn; Prospector Hotel.**
Moderate: **Driftwood Lodge; Best Western Country Lane Inn; Super–8 Motel.**
Inexpensive: **The Bergmann Hotel; Alaskan Hotel; Summit Hotel.**

KETCHIKAN. *Expensive:* **Clover Pass Resort,** 15 miles from town.
Moderate: **Hilltop Motel; Gilmore Hotel** and **Ingersoll** right downtown; and **Super–8 Motel,** near Airport Ferry Terminal.

KODIAK. *Expensive:* **Sheffield House; Shelikof Lodge.**
Moderate: **Kodiak Star Motel; Kalsin Inn Ranch,** 30 miles from town, and **Road's End** have rooms, food, and campgrounds.

SITKA. *Expensive:* **Shee Atika Lodge.** Newest and biggest, opposite convention center, 80-room **Sheffield House** on waterfront downtown.
Moderate: **Potlatch House,** out of town; **Sitka Hotel** in heart of town.

SKAGWAY. *Expensive:* **Golden North Hotel; Klondike Hotel.**

Moderate: **Irene's Inn; Skagway Inn; Gold Rush Lodge; Wild Valley Lodge.**
Inexpensive: **Fifth Av. Bunkhouse,** $10 a night.

TOK. *Moderate:* **Golden Bear Motel; Tok Lodge; Tundra Lodge; Alaska North Motel; Gateway Motel.**

VALDEZ. *Expensive:* **Lamplighter Hotel.**
Moderate: **Sheffield Valdez; Totem Inn; Valdez Motel; Village Inn; Leitch Brothers' Lodge & Camper Park.**

YOUTH HOSTELS. A dozen in Alaska at $5 a night. Those in Anchorage, Fairbanks, Haines, Homer, and Soldotna are open year round. Others may be summer only. *The Alaska Division of Parks,* 619 Warehouse Ave., Suite 210, Anchorage, AK 99501 and National Offices, *American Youth Hostels,* 1332 I St. NW #800, Washington DC 20005, have information.

DINING OUT. You'll get your money's worth. Don't hesitate to ask the "natives" where they eat—when they want to splurge, and when they want to eat inexpensively, but well. Sometimes eating at "the only place in town" turns out to be delightful, friendly, and delicious. Sourdough and seafood are Alaskan specialties. Larger cities have infinite variety in cuisine, including chains like Colonel Sanders and H. Salt, McDonald's, etc., to aid the food budget. These categories will give a clue to the tab of complete dinners in a sampling of restaurants around the state. Not included are drinks, tax and tips. *Deluxe:* $30 and up; *Expensive:* $20–$30; *Moderate:* $15–$20, and *Inexpensive:* under $15.

ANCHORAGE. *Deluxe:* High dining in Captain Cook Hotel's **Crows Nest;** Hilton's **Top of the World; Josephine's** at the Sheraton; and also at exclusive **Stuckagain Heights,** and **Elevation 92.** At sea level, elegant entrees in **Sheffield's House of Lords;** the **Corsair** beneath the Voyager Hotel.
Expensive: **Clinkerdagger, Biggerstaff and Petts; Club Paris;** the **Marx Brothers; Nikko Garden** (Japanese–style, cuisine); and **Regina's** (French).
Moderate: Long-time quonset-hut favorite, **The Garden of Eatin';** another oldtimer, **Peggy's Airport Café** at Merrill Field. Go Italian at **Mazzi's** and at **Legal Pizza;** Oriental at the **Rice Bowl** and the **Tea Leaf;** healthful at the **Cauldron** and the **Downtown Deli;** old-fashioned at **Simon & Seafort's Saloon & Grill.**
Inexpensive: The **Balcony** in the University Center; **Huggebuns** at 6th and I St.; plus **Burger King** and **McDonald's** at several locations.

BARROW. *Expensive* (wherever you eat): **Pepe's** adjoining the Top of the World Hotel has good Mexican food and amazing decor; **Mattie's** in Browerville section is also popular.

FAIRBANKS. *Deluxe:* **Bear and Seal Restaurant,** at the Traveler's Inn; **Husky Room** at the Fairbanks Inn; and the **Lord Baranof Castle Inn.**
Expensive: **Club 11** out Richardson Highway; **Mine Room,** at Cripple Creek Resort 12 miles out Nenana Highway; **Ivory Jack's** on Goldstream Road; **Ranch Dinner House; Sourdough Dining Room** at the Captain Bartlett Inn.
Moderate: **Tiki Cove,** and **Sizzler** for steak; **Sombrero** and **Los Amigos,** for Mexican—Ole!
The Pump House. Atmospheric restaurant and saloon with genuine antiques. **Sandbar** and **Alaska Salmon Bake,** both at Alaskaland.
Inexpensive: **Arctic Pancake House** across from Log Cabin Visitor's Center. **Star of the North Bakery & Luncheonette.**

HAINES-PORT CHILKOOT. *Moderate:* **The Lighthouse; The Bamboo Room; Kitchen Restaurant** in the Chillkat Bakery; **Hotel Halsingland; Port Chilkoot Potlatch; Post Exchange.**
Inexpensive–Moderate: **Annie's Place; Dave & Barb's; Fog Cutter; Sidewalk Sandwich; 33 Mile Roadhouse.** Also fill gas tank; 92 miles until more.

HOMER. *Moderate:* They eat well in town and out at the **Willow Wind Restaurant, Porpoise Room** and **Land's End** on the Spit, **Sterling Cafe, Waterfront Bar and Dining** and **Connelly House** overlooking Kachemak Bay.

Inexpensive: **Parfait Shoppe,** and a new **McDonald's,** for hamburgers, shakes. **Soup Bowl Café & Deli,** Lakeside Mall; **the Reel House** for soup, sandwiches, and movies, and **Millie's Copper Kettle.**

JUNEAU. *Deluxe:* The **Woodcarver,** Sheffield House; **Gold Room** (French style), Baranof Hotel; and the **Diggings,** Prospector Hotel.

Expensive: **The Breakwater Inn;** for authentic Italian, **Bellezza E La Festa.**

Moderate: **City Café; El Sombrero** (in town), and **Fernando's** (on the Glacier Highway) for fine Mexican dishes; **Fiddlehead** and **Renovation Pantry** feature vegetarian and home-baked goodies; **Second Street** is across the bridge in Douglas; **Glacier Restaurant & Lounge** at the airport is newly remodeled; **Summit Café** serves only 18; (try the tempura and prawns),

Inexpensive: Local favorites are **Bullwinkle's Pizza;** the **Underground; Fisherman's Wharf** at Merchants Wharf; **Pattie's, Etc;** and the **Orpheum Restaurant** (great pastry) **& Theatre,** across from the Marine Park.

KETCHIKAN. *Expensive:* **Clover Pass Restaurant; The Helm & Spar Tree Lounge.**

Moderate: **Charley's Restaurant; Gilmore Gardens; Fireside; Hilltop; Kay's Kitchen;** the **Narrows Supper Club,** 1½ miles south of town.

Inexpensive: **The Galley; Harbor Inn; Angela's Delicatessen.** Also try **Jackie's,** Midtown Mall, **June's Cafe,** and **Stephanie's Seaplane Dock.**

KODIAK. *Expensive:* **Sheffield House** and **Harbor Room** at Shelikof Lodge.

Moderate: **El Chicano; Sollies; Towne Square.**

Inexpensive: **H.D.'s** at airport; **Sparky's;** and a big **Dairy Queen Brazier.**

KOTZEBUE. *Expensive* (wherever you eat): **Nul-luk-vik Hotel** serves excellent buffet lunch to tour groups. Try the **Arctic Dragon** for Chinese food. The farthest north **Dairy Queen Brazier** has steak and sea food at Arctic prices. Ask locally for other options; deli, hamburgers, pizza.

NOME. *Expensive:* **Fort Davis Roadhouse,** a bit out of town, has seafood, steak—even reindeer, and Starlight Lounge.

Moderate: **Polar Club** serves breakfast and lunch only. **Milano's Pizzeria** and **Nachos Mexican** are in the old Federal Bldg. Try the **Snack Shack** for a tasty light meal; **Ding How** for delicious Chinese food.

PETERSBURG. *Expensive:* **Viking Room** at Beachcomber Inn, 4 miles out.

Moderate: **Irene's** near Fisherman's Wharf. On Indian St., the **Harbor Lights** features pizza; the **Homestead,** healthful home cooking.

SITKA. *Deluxe:* Dining Rooms at **Shee Atika Hotel** and **Sheffield House.**

Expensive: **Channel Club; Staton's Steak House: Paul & Judy's Canoe Club.**

Moderate: **The Nugget Saloon,** airport; **Lori's Sitka Cafe; Revards** by Cathedral Circle.

Inexpensive: **Fish Factory; Marina Pizzeria.**

SKAGWAY. *Expensive:* **Chilkoot Dining Room** in the Klondike Hotel; **Golden North Restaurant; Irene's Inn,** Alaskan food.

Moderate: **Salmon & Sourdough Shedde** across from the Klondike; **Northern Lights Café; Sweet Tooth Saloon.**

VALDEZ. *Expensive:* **Lamplighter Hotel Dining Room; Sheffield House Dining Room. Pipeline Club** in Valdez Motel.

Moderate: **Hangar 9,** at airport; **Pizza Palace,** view of pipeline terminal site; and restaurants in the **Totem Inn,** and the **Village Inn.**

WRANGELL. *Moderate:* **The Dockside** in the Stikine Inn has fresh local seafood, especially tiny shrimp, in season; steak and seafood are mainstays in the **Timber Room** of the Totem Bar. The **Hungry Beaver** is at Wrangell's oldest site, now the Marine Bar. **The Roadhouse,** out of town, sends a courtesy car for diners. The **Better Way** has herb teas and vegeburgers. The **Wharf** features "home cooking and Alaska hospitality."

CALIFORNIA

The Ultimate Image

Those who come to Southern California thinking that they will spend all their time sightseeing within the city limits of Los Angeles are in for a pleasant surprise. Los Angeles proper is a microcosm. It is a large city—464 square miles—and there are countless things to see and do here. Furthermore, Los Angeles is merely the center of a much larger area—the Los Angeles basin—which extends into Los Angeles County, into Ventura, Orange, Riverside and San Bernardino counties and offers numerous scenic attractions.

Los Angeles has grown from a tiny settlement of 44 in 1781 to the second largest metropolitan area in the nation with a population of over seven million. It is notorious for its advanced case of urban sprawl. Transportation is mainly by auto, with rental car agencies servicing all major areas. Buses supply local and inter-urban transportation.

1984 was an exciting year in the history of Los Angeles and its emerging "new downtown." Work began on the massive $1.2 billion California Plaza, a complex featuring residential and office towers, and a new hotel. The first phase is expected to be completed by late 1985 and will include the Museum of Contemporary Art, the Bella Lewitzky Dance Gallery, and a 42-story office tower and garage. The historic Angels' Flight Funicular Railway will be installed later.

First Street and Grand Avenue is one of the country's most enlight-ened, municipally supported developments—the Music Center. Com-posed of three handsomely designed buildings, it is interconnected by a large landscaped plaza and crowned by Jacques Lipschitz's symbol of peace—an impressive sculpture entitled *Peace on Earth*.

The dramatic Dorothy Chandler Pavilion is the home of the Los Angeles Philharmonic, where opera, ballet, symphonies, and musical comedies are performed.

The Ahmanson Theater features the Civic Light Opera, musical dramas, and plays. The annual Academy Awards are held at the Music Center. The Mark Taper Forum features experimental and intimate theater.

To orient yourself to Los Angeles, you can go up to the 27th-floor observation area in the City Hall. On a rare day there is a panorama of the entire city—Mt. Wilson in the San Gabriel Mountains, the Pacific Ocean, and the Los Angeles Harbor. You may also ascend to the revolving lounge at the Bonaventure Hotel, or to one of several other high-altitude vantage points.

Nearby, facing the Plaza, is Olvera Street, a colorful block-long walkway with open booths, restaurants, and a light-hearted air reminiscent of Old Mexico. Walk and browse; they sell souvenirs, Mexican candies, and handicrafts. There are worthwhile bargains in candles, onyx bookends, and sandals. Frequently there is outdoor entertainment. This is the major tourist center of Californian-Mexican folklore.

Nearby, at First Street, is Little Tokyo, which celebrated its 100th anniversary in 1984. Visit the Cultural Center and its handsome theater and impressive gardens; sample sushi or dine Japanese style in a private tatami room. Shop at Weller Court or Japanese Village Plaza for traditional products.

Chinatown, located off North Broadway near College Street, is a collection of Chinese curio shops and restaurants. The restaurants range from mediocre to excellent. Some are so popular that long waits are required for tables, increasing the popularity of local picture galleries, curio shops, and the typical amusement-park entertainment. Travelers can find excellent values in fine silk (by the yard), brocades, lacquerware, soapstone and jade novelties, and kimonos. While not quite as exciting as the New York or San Francisco Chinese quarters, the Los Angeles Chinatown does have a lively aspect at night.

Stadiums and Museums

Major-league baseball games in Los Angeles are now all played at Dodgers' Stadium, a beautiful ball park situated on a bluff overlooking downtown Los Angeles. The view from the park is spectacular. The California Angels play in Anaheim (40 miles south) at modern Anaheim Stadium, which also hosts Rams football and California Surf soccer.

Equally noteworthy in the downtown Los Angeles Area, in Exposition Park at Exposition Blvd. and Figueroa St., is the Los Angeles Memorial Coliseum. Site of the 1932 Olympic Games, the Coliseum hosted many 1984 Olympic events. It is also home base for the Los Angeles Raider pro football team as well as collegiate football and soccer events.

Also situated in Exposition Park is the Sports Arena. Modern, completely enclosed and air-conditioned, the Sports Arena plays host to hockey games, ice extravaganzas, track and field events, as well as special exhibitions.

Opposite the Sports Arena is a pair of museums, the Natural History Museum of Los Angeles County and the California Museum of Science and Industry. The former has outstanding animal-habitat halls of mammals and birds from Africa and North America. Its fine displays of reconstructed prehistoric skeletons have been moved seven miles northwest to the magnificent George C. Page Museum in Hancock Park, site of the La Brea Tar Pits, original source of the skeletons. The

California Museum of Science and Industry has embarked on a $43 million expansion program. When completed, the museum will be second only to the Smithsonian as a cultural and educational museum complex. The Aerospace Building has already been constructed.

Across the street from Exposition Park is the University of Southern California, founded in 1876. It has several highly regarded graduate schools—medicine, dentistry, pharmacy—and an outstanding cinema department. Located on the campus is the Fisher Art Gallery—featuring sixteenth- and seventeenth-century Dutch and Flemish paintings.

Reaching northwest toward Hollywood, you pass the edge of Griffith Park, the country's largest city park, with over 4,000 mountainous acres. Griffith Park boasts an observatory-planetarium; the open-air Greek Theater (set in a natural canyon below pine-covered mountains) where summer performances play to capacity audiences; golf courses; five tennis courts; the fabulous new $15 million Griffith Park Equestrian Center. In the center of the park is the Los Angeles Zoo with its 2,000-plus animals. They are grouped by their five continental origins, in areas resembling their natural environments. There's also a Children's Zoo, and Travel Town, featuring vintage transportation. Here, children can explore a Victorian railroad station, antique trains, planes, cable cars, and a swimming pool. Ferndell, a lovely green spot, has paths shaded by ferns, sycamore and oak trees, waterfalls, running streams and a Nature Museum with plant and animal exhibits.

Barnsdall Park is an artistic confection sweetened by Frank Lloyd Wright's early handsome Hollyhock House, the Los Angeles Municipal Art Gallery (changing exhibits), and the Junior Arts Center workshops.

Hollywood

Hollywood is still synonymous with the movies and television. As the glamour capital of the world, it retains much magic because of the stars who work, live and play in this vicinity. For anyone who has not been into a large motion-picture studio, Universal Studios invites you into Never-Never Land (you can catch Hollywood in the act, for a price). Guided tours and free tickets are available from NBC, CBS, ABC and Metromedia to attend live television programs.

Hollywood Boulevard brings to mind visions of glamour and excitement few home-towns can equal. Some visitors are disappointed by its honky-tonk. Others are thrilled by famous names and places. The Walk of Fame is a roll call of entertainment's "greats," commemorated in concrete and bronze stars in miles of sidewalks. At Christmastime, the boulevard is transformed by the Santa Claus Lane parade, with scores of entertainment celebrities and colossal floats led by Santa Claus.

The celebrated Mann's Chinese Theater, 6925 Hollywood Boulevard, started the dramatic custom of preserving concrete footprints and handprints of theatrical personalities back in 1927 with Norma Talmadge. By now, millions of tourists have matched their footprints with those of leading cinema personalities.

Very little of Sunset Strip's early glamour remains. Today, it is a bustling boulevard of porno-flick houses and bookstores; punk rock and loud disco lounges; fast-food outlets; and motley pedestrians. However, one of the city's most elegant nightclubs, the art deco-decorated Roxy, is at 9009 Sunset Blvd.

In Highland Park, a suburb of Los Angeles, the Southwest Museum sits high on a hill overlooking the Pasadena Freeway. The museum contains extensive collections of Indian relics and artifacts from North, South, and Central America. It has an outstanding collection of California Indian baskets, material gathered by several archeological expeditions into the field in California, and Plains Indian materials. It plays host to a large number of Southern California schoolchildren who study the California Indians as a regular part of their curriculum.

The Los Angeles County Museum of Art is located at the edge of Hancock Park. It is evidence of the city's significance as an art center, for its exhibitions, lectures, films, and concerts are of great aesthetic and educational value to the community. It draws students, art lovers, and scholars from all over the world. The handsome three-building complex is surrounded by fountains and tree-lined plazas. Ahmanson Gallery displays the permanent collection, spanning over 5,000 years, from ancient to avant-garde works. Major traveling exhibitions accompanied by lectures, films, and special programs are shown in the Frances and Armand Hammer Wing. The Leo S. Bing Center has a cafeteria, art rental gallery, and the Bing Theater, which features various cultural programs.

West Los Angeles

The western section of the city includes Beverly Hills, Century City, Westwood, Brentwood, and Bel-Air. These suburbs became part of the vast Los Angeles metropolis in the early 1900s. Most visitors to Southern California have a great desire to see TV and movie stars, who frequent the chic shops, supermarkets, and celebrity haunts of these elegant communities. Starting from the early 1920s, many showpeople from the movie colony moved to these suburbs, and it is still a popular area among celebrities. An evening stroll along Wilshire Boulevard and posh Rodeo Drive in Beverly Hills is perfectly safe.

Century City is a pacesetter for urban development. It is a handsome, well-planned "city within a city." This complex includes Century Plaza Hotel, an elevated shopping mall, the ABC entertainment center, towering office buildings and apartments, the Shubert Theater, restaurants, and a hospital. The development is built on the grounds that were once Twentieth Century-Fox Studios.

Northwest of Los Angeles, near Beverly Hills in Westwood, is the sprawling campus of the University of California at Los Angeles, part of the statewide University of California complex. The school engages in many crosstown rivalries with the University of Southern California. U.C.L.A. has outstanding departments of chemistry, medicine, theater arts, and environmental design. For a special afternoon, take a stroll through the Franklin D. Murphy Sculpture Garden. Displayed in this lovely outdoor setting are twentieth-century works, all major in scale and quality, from the Rodin *Walking Man* of 1906 to the David Smith *Cubi XX* of 1964 (located at the north campus), and even later works. U.C.L.A. also offers the rare beauty of Japanese Gardens. Artisans and architects were brought from Japan to help create this authentic landscape. The Museum of Cultural History, in Haines Hall, displays contemporary and historical art, archeological and anthropological artifacts. It houses the renowed Grunwald Center for Graphic Arts.

From Pasadena to San Gabriel

Pasadena is located northeast of Los Angeles and is the well-known home of the annual Tournament of Roses (The Rose Bowl) each January 1. The city is famed for its fine residential district, the world-famous Huntington Library, art galleries and gardens, and the sprawling Huntington-Sheraton hotel, built at the turn of the century by railroad tycoon Henry E. Huntington.

The site of the Rose Bowl—open throughout the year in the bottom of the Arroya Seco just west of town—and of the California Institute

OREGON

Upper Klamath Lake
Medford
Klamath Falls
Goose Lake

KLAMATH MTS.
97

Klamath

Weed
5

LASSEN VOLCANIC NATL. PARK
Susanville
Honey Lake
Pyramid Lake

Eureka

Shasta Lake
Redding
36
Red Bluff
70
Oroville

"REDWOOD
101
Clear Lake
EMPIRE"

Mendocino

Sacramento R.
99
Yuba City
Sacramento
80
50
Lake Tahoe
Reno
Carson City

Mono Lake

Santa Rosa
Napa
Berkeley
Oakland
San Francisco Bay
San Francisco
Lodi
Stockton
San Joaquin Valley
YOSEMITE NATL. PARK
S i e r r a
N e v

San Jose
San Joaquin R.
99
Merced
Madera
Fresno

SANTA CRUZ MTS.
Santa Cruz
Monterey Bay
Monterey
Gilroy
Salinas
STA. LUCIA RANGE
Big Sur

C o a s t   R a n g e

5
101
San Luis Obispo

PACIFIC
OCEAN

N

CALIFORNIA

0   40   80
Scale of Miles

Santa Rosa I.

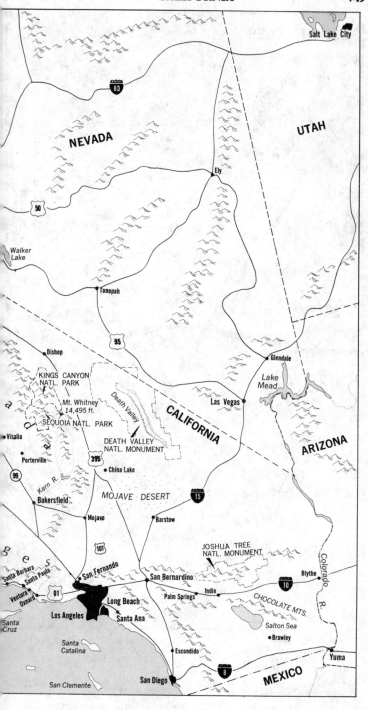

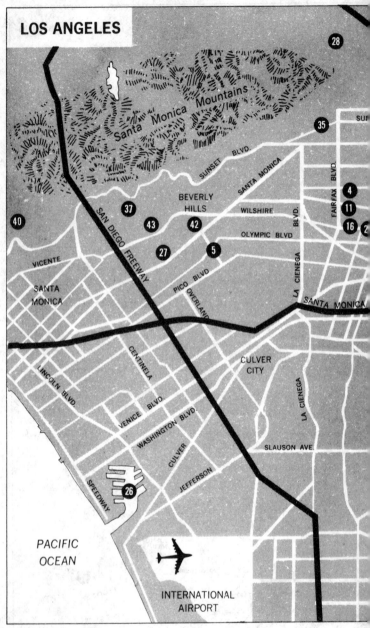

LOS ANGELES

Santa Monica Mountains

BEVERLY HILLS

SANTA MONICA

CULVER CITY

PACIFIC OCEAN

INTERNATIONAL AIRPORT

SUNSET BLVD.
SANTA MONICA
WILSHIRE
OLYMPIC BLVD.
PICO BLVD.
SANTA MONICA
VICENTE
SAN DIEGO FREEWAY
FAIRFAX BLVD.
LA CIENEGA
CENTINELA
LINCOLN BLVD.
VENICE BLVD.
WASHINGTON BLVD.
CULVER
JEFFERSON
SLAUSON AVE.
SPEEDWAY
OVERLAND

Points of Interest

1) Angelus Temple
2) Atlantic Richfield Plaza
3) California Museum of Science and Industry
4) CBS Television City
5) Century City, Shubert Theater
6) Chinatown
7) City Hall (Los Angeles)
8) Civic Center (Los Angeles)
9) Dodger Stadium
10) Exposition Park

11) Farmers' Market
12) Forest Lawn Memorial Park
13) Mann's Chinese Theater
14) Greek Theater
15) Griffith Park Zoo
16) Hancock Park
17) Hollywood Bowl
18) Hollywood Star Sidewalk
19) La Brea Tarpits, George C. Page Museum
20) Lawry's California Center
21) L.A. Convention Center

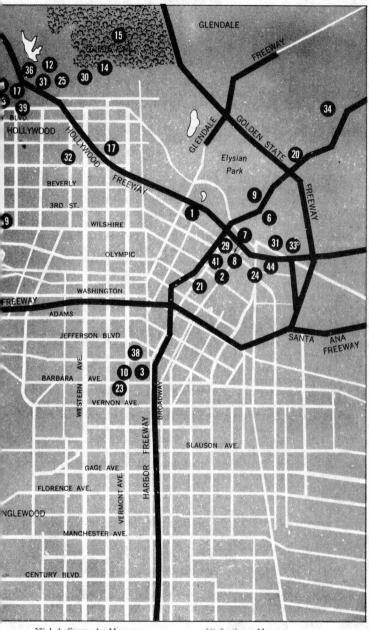

22) L.A. County Art Museum
23) L.A. Memorial Coliseum
24) L.A. Times
25) Burbank Studios (Warner Brothers)
26) Marina del Rey
27) Mormon Temple
28) Mulholland Drive
29) L.A. Music Center
30) Observatory and Planetarium
31) Olvera Street
32) Paramount Studios
33) Pueblo de Los Angeles State Historical Park

34) Southwest Museum
35) Sunset Strip
36) Universal Studios
37) University of California (UCLA)
38) University of Southern California
39) Wax Museum
40) Will Rogers State Historic Park
41) World Trade Center
42) Beverly Hills
43) Westwood
44) Little Tokyo

of Technology, on California Boulevard at Hill Avenue, Pasadena has become even more famous recently as the home of NASA's Jet Propulsion Laboratory. Many of the complicated moon- and Mars-scanning satellites sent aloft from Cape Canaveral in Florida were designed at Pasadena's Jet Propulsion Laboratory by local technicians. Pasadena is also the home of the magnificent Norton Simon Museum, the Pasadena Historical Museum, a 1905 mansion with Pasadena memorabilia, and the 1908 Gamble House.

In La Canada, five miles west, are lovely Descanso Gardens, 1418 Descanso Dr. Each month features floral beauties, from camellias in January to roses, begonias, and fuchsias in June. The 165-acre horticultural haven is part of Rancho San Rafael, located on a 1784 Spanish Land Grant. There are paths through the lovely woods, which are threaded by a running stream. More than 150 species of birds find refuge here.

To the east of Pasadena is Arcadia, home of the Santa Anita Race Track. Thoroughbred racing from December to April and October to November. One of the most beautiful race tracks in California, this one is lavishly planted with flowers. A local custom: gardeners dig up the plants and give them away on a first-come basis the day the season ends. The new year will see the track decorated with a fresh crop. Also in Arcadia is the Los Angeles State and County Arboretum. Formerly part of the old "Lucky" Baldwin estate, it was turned over to the two agencies as a growing ground for native and exotic plants. There is a palm-fringed lagoon that has been the setting in a hundred jungle-story motion pictures. A tram takes visitors on a tour of the site. Artists come here to paint the old Queen Anne Cottage, built by Baldwin, and to sketch the Hugo Reid abode, a Spanish-period structure which has been restored on the grounds and given a museum-display treatment.

Adjoining Pasadena on the south is San Marino, which is the home of the Henry E. Huntington Library and Art Gallery. Situated on a hillside and beautifully planted, this 200-acre site is the former home of Henry E. Huntington, railroad builder and real-estate developer. The home grounds and buildings have been converted into an extraordinary art gallery, displaying among its famous paintings *The Blue Boy* and *Pinkie*. The library has a renowned collection of rare books and printed manuscripts and draws visitors and scholars from all over the world. Among the works of general interest: a fifteenth-century Gutenberg Bible, Shakespeare's First Folio, and the original manuscripts of Benjamin Franklin and Edgar Allan Poe. The surrounding botanical gardens are famed for their camellias and desert plants. Reservations are required on Sunday.

Adjacent to San Marino is San Gabriel. The fine old San Gabriel Mission, founded in 1771 ten years before the settling of Los Angeles and completed about 1800, is still a parish church in the community. It has a fine mission garden, a rare set of Indian paintings depicting church history, and the oldest winery, now a museum. The great arrangement of ancient bells, high on the side of the mission wall, is often photographed. San Gabriel Mission was the fourth mission founded in California; San Diego, the Carmel site, and San Antonio de Padua, near King City, preceded it.

Hills and Mountains

Hills ring the Los Angeles basin. They are the barrier that keeps out the desert influences and makes Southern California a delightful place to live.

Immediately north of the basin are the Santa Monica Mountains, running north along the coast as far as Oxnard and sorting the seaward breezes.

In the Hollywood-Santa Monica area, homes have been placed on hundreds of lots whittled from hillside sites, which afford an aerial view of the Southland. By night and without smog it is a fairyland of lights and colors.

There are scenic drives that cross along this mountain area. Mulholland Drive is the most famous of these. It can be reached most easily from the Hollywood Freeway. Near the beginning of Mulholland Drive, in the area where the Hollywood Freeway cuts through the hills, is the Hollywood Bowl, which offers a gala summer season of rock to classical music. This natural amphitheater, designed by Frank Lloyd Wright, is built along a hillside and the acoustics are excellent. The Bowl's grounds are so inviting that picnickers tote gourmet suppers, complete with wine, candles and tablecloths.

The larger San Gabriel Mountain Range, which separates the Los Angeles basin from the Mojave Desert, is one of the state's most notable transverse ranges. The San Gabriels start at Interstate 5—the main freeway that reaches north and south through the center of the state— and stretch east for well over fifty miles. Rising to almost two miles at their tallest peaks, the San Gabriels are considered Los Angeles's mountain playgrounds and are within the Angeles National Forest, one of the most heavily used national forests in the United States, covering one-fourth of the area of Los Angeles County.

Along the Angeles Crest Highway (State 2)—the main road into the mountain area which starts at La Canada—there are a number of fine mountain campgrounds; Chilae, Charlton Flats, Buckhorn, Horse Flats, and a number of lesser picnic sites. Good paved roads and dirt roads crisscross the mountain country. Some of the mountain lands facing the Los Angeles basin are closed to public entry during the summertime because of high fire hazard.

The principal scientific outpost in the San Gabriel Mountains is the Mt. Wilson Observatory. A crude road up from Pasadena originally brought the astronomical equipment to this mountain site. It was chosen around 1904 because of the unparalleled viewing from the site— this was before smog. Here are a small astronomical museum, the giant 100-inch Hooker telescope, a smaller 60-inch telescope and a trio of solar telescopes. There is a good road to the observatory site from Red Box on the Angeles Crest Highway. The resort of Mt. Wilson will see many changes in the coming years, but the astronomical installation will remain undisturbed.

Valleys, Gardens and Show Farms

East of Los Angeles, the San Gabriel Valley, the Pomona Valley, and eventually the San Bernardino Valley, separated only by low ridges of hills, form the arm of the Los Angeles basin that reaches in that direction.

East of Pasadena is Claremont, noted for its collection of colleges— Scripps College, Claremont Men's College, Pomona College, Harvey Mudd College and Claremont Graduate School—and the exceptional Rancho Santa Ana Botanic Gardens, a wonderland of native plants.

In Pomona, the Los Angeles County Fairgrounds stage the Los Angeles County Fair each September. There are miles of vineyards in this corner of the Pomona Valley, around Cucamonga and Guasti. There are numerous wineries in the area, most with tasting rooms. It is a colorful sight in the fall to watch the grapes being harvested, and at the winery you can smell the perfume of new wine. At Pomona is

California State Polytechnic University and the Kellogg Arabian Horse Ranch, where demonstrations by the fine horses are given. Also to be seen in this eastern San Gabriel Valley-Pomona Valley-San Bernardino Valley complex are the last of the great groves of citrus that once blanketed all of this area. Each spring, San Bernardino hosts an 11-day National Orange Show.

Knott's Berry Farm, on Beach Boulevard in Buena Park, is an amusement center theme-park built up from the original industry of raising boysenberries and selling boysenberry jam and pies from a roadside stand. Today the spreading farm has restaurants, still featuring the famous berry pies, and a host of amusements. Shops and rides have a frontier motif. You can pan for gold. Holdups are staged on the narrow-gauge railroad. Its "Old-Time Adventures" include Ghost Town Fiesta Village, Independent Hall West, and the Roaring Twenties Airfield and Amusement Area. Official greeter is Charles Schulz's lovable beagle, Snoopy.

Also on Beach Boulevard is Six Flags' Movieland Wax Museum, a collection of more than 240 waxen images of famous motion-picture and TV stars in actual onstage settings. Military buffs will enjoy the *Museum of World Wars,* 8700 Stanton Avenue, the largest private military collection in the country.

Westward, beyond Point Fermin and Cabrillo Beach, is exciting Hanna-Barbera's Marineland of the Pacific, situated right on the ocean in an area where smugglers and pirates used to put ashore. Presented here are the antics of trained whales in a giant seawater tank. There is a larger tank, as well, with viewplates around its circumference at various levels. This vast tank contains all manner of Pacific Ocean fish. Divers frequently visit this large tank and hand feed the fish. Sharks and barracuda are among the residents.

Touch pools allow youngsters to pet and feed friendly dolphins. The Baja Reef offers visitors an exciting swim adventure in an underwater world alive with ocean fish. Swimwear and equipment available for rent. Of special interest is the Marine Animal Care Center, devoted to the care and rehabilitation of sick and wounded marine life. Film the family with Yogi Bear, Fred Flintstone, and other celebrated characters. There are regular shows in still another tank—a circus area with grandstands—featuring pilot and killer whales, dolphins, and sea lions.

North of Marineland, along the Pacific, are a number of beach communities: Redondo, with a marina and a fine fishing and restaurant pier; Hermosa, also with a fishing pier; Manhattan, likewise with a pier. Venice, once designed to look like the Old World site with canals and gondolas, has become the center of Punk Rock and New Wave exponents.

Santa Monica has many beaches, excellent sport- and pier-fishing and a Civic Auditorium, where many popular and classical productions are staged and contemporary music is presented.

In the community of San Fernando, in the heart of Los Angeles County's sprawling San Fernando Valley, is the Mission San Fernando Rey de Espana. Founded September 8, 1797, the mission today houses a carefully reconstructed museum. It was the seventeenth in the Franciscan chain of 21 California missions.

North, after the sprawling San Fernando Valley and into Ventura County, is Thousand Oaks. On the Pacific sand are Malibu, Oxnard, and Ventura.

PRACTICAL INFORMATION
FOR THE LOS ANGELES AREA

 HOW TO GET AROUND. *By air: PSA* and *AIRCAL* serve Orange County Airport, in addition to several major airlines using this airport. *Republic* has daily flights to Palm Springs, and San Francisco. *PSA* has daily flights on convenient schedules from Los Angeles International Airport, and also from Hollywood-Burbank Airport.

By car: Avis, National, Budget, Dollar-A-Day and *Hertz* have offices at all the airports, as well as dozens of other locations in the area.

By bus: Continental Trailways and *Greyhound* operate out of the central bus terminal, 6th and Los Angeles Sts., Los Angeles, and out of Hollywood and Santa Monica. *By train: Amtrak* has four departures daily to San Diego, and vice-versa. Stops at San Clemente, Santa Ana, Fullerton, San Juan Capistrano, as well as northern destinations.

 TOURIST INFORMATION SERVICES. *Greater Los Angeles Visitors and Convention Bureau,* 505 S. Flower St., offers a full range of brochures and information. Tel. 488–9100. For a 24-hour "Welcome to Los Angeles" recording of special current events, dial (213) 628–5857. *Anaheim Area Visitor & Convention Bureau,* 800 W. Katella Ave., Anaheim 92803. Tel. (714) 999-8999. *Beverly Hills Visitors and Convention Bureau,* 239 S. Beverly Dr., Beverly Hills 90212 (tel. 271–8126).

Automobile Club of Southern California (affiliated with the American Automobile Assn.) provides maps, brochures, booklets and information on highway conditions, special events, theaters, hunting and fishing. For ACSC and AAA members only. Offices in all major cities. Headquarters: 2601 S. Figueroa St. Los Angeles 90054.

Santa Monica Convention & Visitors Bureau, 2219 Main St. (tel. 392–9631), distributes information on sports, shopping, special-interest musuems, dining and nightlife. Also, there is a visitors' information booth in Palisades Park.

Buena Park Visitors & Convention Bureau, 6696 Beach Blvd., Buena Park, provides information on Knott's Berry Farm and nearby attractions and accommodations. Tel. 994–1511.

Where Magazine is a weekly distributed in the better hotel and motel lobbies.

Los Angeles Magazine, 1888 Century Park East, Los Angeles 90067. Complete listings of theatrical, film, art, music and sport attractions. Their "What's Doing This Month" covers all current offerings. The Reader's Service Desk will answer your questions.

Los Angeles *Sunday Times,* Calendar Section. This supplement to the Sunday *Times,* which comes out Saturday mornings, lists every interesting cultural event of the week to come, including free lectures, art exhibits, dance recitals, theater performances.

Key Magazine. A pocket-sized weekly guide, free, on counters everywhere.

 MUSEUMS AND GALLERIES. Los Angeles museums are lively and varied, maintaining fine permanent collections and displaying significant changing exhibitions. The interim home of the *Museum of Contemporary Art* —the "Temporary Contemporary," 152 N. Central, showcases the "art of our times"—the last four decades. Take your choice of museum displays such as science and natures, ethnic artifacts, fine arts, furniture, technology, crafts and designs. Call the museums, check the Los Angeles *Times,* or *Los Angeles Magazine,* for information on exhibits, lectures, films, dance and special museum programs, hours and admission fees. Gallery viewing may be done in Hollywood, West Hollywood, and in downtown galleries.

Art: *University Galleries,* University of Southern California, 823 Exposition Blvd. Paintings, sculpture, graphics, archaeology. The *Los Angeles Children's Museum,* 310 N. Main St., opened in 1979, offering a number of touching exhibitions for youngsters. Phone 687–8800 for hours. *Los Angeles County Museum of Art,* 5905 Wilshire Blvd., Hancock Park. Housed in three separate buildings. The Ahmanson Gallery is the main building. Traveling exhibitions can be seen in the Frances and Armand Hammer Wing. The Leo S. Bing Center has an Art Rental Gallery. *Otis Art Gallery,* 2401 Wilshire Blvd. Exhibits and sells the works of the students of the Otis Art Institute semiannually. The *Museum of Cultural History,* U.C.L.A., 405 Hilgard Ave. The *Fowler Foundation Museum,* 9215 Wilshire Blvd., Beverly Hills. *J. Paul Getty Museum,* 17985 Pacific Coast Hwy., Malibu (advance parking reservation suggested).

Norton Simon Museum, Colorado and Orange Grove Blvds., Pasadena. The nucleus of the permanent collection is 20th-century works. In addition, the museum showcases sculpture and paintings from the Norton Simon Foundation. There is a charming restaurant and bookshop. Noon–6 P.M., Thurs.–Sun.

San Marino: *Huntington Library, Art Gallery and Botanical Gardens,* 1151 Oxford Rd. Once the home of railroad magnate Henry E. Huntington, this estate and its buildings house many of the world's "only, finest, and earliest," including Thomas Gainsborough's painting *The Blue Boy,* the world's largest garden of desert shrubs and growths, one of the world's 47 copies of the Gutenberg Bible, early editions of Chaucer and Shakespeare, handwritten works by Benjamin Franklin, George Washington and Edgar Allan Poe.

George C. Page Museum, Hancock Park (Wilshire Blvd. next to Los Angeles County Museum of Art). Fascinating collection of Ice Age mammal skeletons (sabre toothed cats, mammoths) displayed at the site of the tar pits (still active) where they were trapped 35,000 or more years ago.

The Simon Weisenthal Museum and Center for Holocaust Studies, 9760 W. Pico Blvd. The first major Holocaust Center and Museum in North America, featuring electronic A/V presentations, graphic displays and a replica of Auschwitz–Birkenau camp.

Special Interest: The *Craft and Folk Art Museum,* 5814 Wilshire Blvd., features traditional and contemporary crafts created in clay, wood, paper, glass, metal and fiber. *Natural History Museum of Los Angeles County,* 900 Exposition Blvd. *California Museum of Science and Industry,* 700 State Dr., Exposition Park. Space show of missiles and capsules, scientific do-it-yourself gadgets, incubator that hatches 100 chicks. *Ferndell Ranger Station and Nature Museum,* 5375 Red Oak Dr. Collections of insects, reptiles, mammals, and birds, geology, local plants. *Southwest Museum,* 234 Museum Dr., Highland Park. Comprehensive collection of Indian artifacts from North, South, and Central America. *Mount Wilson Observatory,* Hwy. 2 to Mount Wilson Rd. Visitors are admitted for a view of the heavens through the 100-inch telescope. Exhibits of work done at Hale's Observatory.

Others: The *Briggs Cunningham Automotive Museum,* just west of Orange County Airport, Costa Mesa, is a treasure of classic automobiles dating from 1902 to the present. *Movieland Wax Museum and Palace of Living Art,* 7711 Beach Blvd., Buena Park. More than 200 waxen images of stars and scenes that made them famous. Tour the *Queen Mary* at War Exhibit as well as the luxurious liner (at the end of the Long Beach Freeway), Long Beach. Adjacent to the refurbished Cunard liner is Howard Hughes's famous *Spruce Goose* airplane housed in a 12-story aluminum dome. The *Roy Rogers and Dale Evans Museum* was moved to Victorville in 1980. Exhibits include Roy's horse, Trigger, and dog, Bullet, a handsome gun collection, big-game animal trophies, and movie mementos.

 HISTORIC SITES. *Avila Adobe,* 14 Olvera St., 1818 historic house. Antique furnishings. *The Lummis Home State Historical Monument* rock home of Charles F. Lummis, noted historian, is at 200 E. Avenue 43, east of N. Figueroa, L. A. *El Pueblo de Los Angeles,* Olvera St. and the Old Plaza, is a 42-acre state park, and the birthplace of the city of Los Angeles, with 30 historic buildings as well as famed Olvera St. and its Mexican marketplace.

OLD MISSIONS. *San Gabriel Arcangel,* on the outskirts of eastern Los Angeles at 537 W. Mission Dr. in San Gabriel, was the fourth mission to be founded (1771). It is famous for its bells and museum of religious and historical treasures of early California and holds regular church services. Handsome *San Fernando Rey de Espana* is in a valley two miles west of suburban San Fernando at 15151 Mission Blvd. It had one of the largest single structures of the Mission era.

San Juan Capistrano, the "Jewel of the Missions," founded in November 1776, is known the world over for the legend of its swallows, which supposedly return faithfully to the mission ruin every St. Joseph's Day (March 19th). The classic beauty of the mission, its gardens and its flocks of white pigeons attract visitors and photographers in great numbers.

 TOURS. *By bus: California Parlor Car Tours.* Three- to six-day tours of coastal areas, Hearst Castle, Lake Tahoe, wine country, Palm Springs, and Yosemite. Largest of the sightseeing companies in the Southland is *Gray Line Tours Company* of Los Angeles. There are offices, branches, and travel desks in hotels throughout Southern California. Listed under Sightseeing Tours in the yellow classified pages are many smaller companies offering individualized tours, multilingual guides, personal chauffeurs in your car or theirs, etc.

Gray Line will, for a large enough group and with enough advance notice, plan any special tour anywhere you want to go. All Gray Line tours make pick-ups at major hotels in Hollywood and Beverly Hills, then join up for a mass departure from the Gray Line, 1207 W. 3rd St., L.A.

Among the tours offered are: Pasadena and Huntington Library; Hollywood, Beverly Hills and Ocean; Universal Studio Tour (includes studio tour plus many of the things in Hollywood and Beverly Hills). Also goes to Forest Lawn; Los Angeles and Hollywood, and Marineland of the Pacific; San Diego and Tijuana, Mexico. Newest is their 2½-hour cruise to view the gray whales.

Starline Sightseeing Tours, 6845 Hollywood Blvd., Hollywood 90028, goes to moviestars' homes in Beverly Hills, as well as Universal Studios.

By boat: Sightseeing boat trips are available from the piers and docks at Malibu, Pierpoint Landing at the Port of Long Beach and at the foot of Mangolia Ave. in the City of Long Beach itself, and from Fisherman's Wharf at Redondo Beach.

Catalina Terminals, Inc., has tours via ship from San Pedro to Santa Catalina Island which include glass-bottomed boat, inland motor trips, seal colony, scenic drives.

Long Beach/Catalina Cruises offers one of three modern boats to Catalina Island. There are also harbor tours at Long Beach, including close-up water view of the *Queen Mary.*

Exciting Los Angeles —Long Beach Harbor helicopter tours lift off from San Pedro's Ports o' Call Village.

 SPECIAL INTEREST TOURS. *Stars' Homes Tours.* Starline offers a 2-hour bus tour, highlighting more than 60 stars' homes in Beverly Hills and Bel Air, Gray Line's Air. tour also visits the famed Farmers Market.

Architecture Buff's Tour. Everywhere you look, there are sleek, handsome high-rise buildings surging upward—that's L.A. today. However, intermingled with these new structures are older ones that reflect the tastes and styles of the city during different stages. Many are exceptional works and were designed by such world-famous architects as Frank Lloyd Wright and Richard Neutra. They have Spanish, Southern, New England and Far Eastern overtones. Here is a sampling of some of the most fascinating of these: Frank Lloyd Wright's Hollyhock House, built 1917–1920, Barnsdall Park; Bradbury Building, 304 S. Broadway, L.A., outstanding iron decoration; Cathedral of Saint Sophia, 1324 S. Normandie Ave., L.A., ornate, Byzantine architecture; Gamble House, Pasadena, Greene-designed, luncheon served and reservations are necessary, charming example of the California bungalow-style; La Casa Pelanconi, 33–35 Olvera St., first brick house in L.A., dates back to 1855, presently a restaurant; Lovel House, 4616 Dundee Ave., the 1929 home that established Richard Neutra's reputation; Queen Anne Cottage, 301 N. Baldwin, part of the Los

Angeles State and County Arboretum; fabulous Watts Tower, 33 years in the making, 1765 E. 107 St., L.A. Casa de Adobe, 4605 N. Figueroa St., L.A., duplicates a Spanish hacienda.

There is an annual home tour into private homes designed by master builders and architects. Check with information at the *Los Angeles County Museum of Art* to find out when this is scheduled.

Nature Tour. For a closer look at the gray whales migrating, there are scheduled excursion boats which leave the pier at Long Beach and San Pedro. Best time for whale sightings is Dec. and Jan., when 70 or 80 a day have been counted splashing and sounding their way south.

STUDIO AND ENTERTAINMENT TOURS. On the *Universal Studios Tour,* you'll enjoy the behind-the-scenes view of motion pictures and television. Guided tours aboard a tram wind through the back lots, TV sets, a sound stage, and you'll peek inside stars' dressing rooms, plus see two hours of animal and stunt shows, as well as the Stage 70 Video Tape Theater. You can also tour both NBC and Burbank Studios.

After you've seen the studios, you may be in the mood to see how other Los Angeles-area industry compares to that of the rest of the world. The Greater Los Angeles Visitors and Convention Bureau, 505 W. Flower Street, Los Angeles 90071, has a limited number of TV show tickets available on a first-come, first-served basis.

GARDENS. Los Angeles itself has two notable gardens. *Exposition Park Rose Gardens,* Exposition Blvd. between Figueroa St. and Vermont Ave., has 150 species of roses on 15,000 bushes in seven areas. They bloom with heavenly scent and color during spring and summer.

And there's *U.C.L.A. Botanical Garden,* southeast end of campus near Le Conte and Hilgard Aves. Printed trail guide available at entrance tells about each numbered tree and other flora and fauna. For botany buffs, a guided group tour may be arranged by calling U.C.L.A. Visitors' Center. The university also offers the serene and authentic Japanese Gardens, a most rewarding experience.

At the *Descanso Gardens,* in La Canada, camellias are in bloom from late Dec. thru March.

Pageant of Roses Garden features four acres of roses in 750 varieties. Some 7,000 roses are identified for you at Rose Hills Memorial Park, 3900 S. Workman Mill Rd., Whittier 90601.

MUSIC. Today the traveler to Los Angeles has a broad range of musical choices: at indoor auditoriums or amphitheaters, at the universities—recitals, opera, musical comedy, concerts, rock and jazz festivals, symphony. The *Los Angeles Philharmonic Season* starts in Jan. at the Dorothy Chandler Pavilion, in the modern Music Center. The *Ahmanson Theater* presents occasional dance attractions and musical dramas. From July to mid-Sept., *Hollywood Bowl,* 2301 N. Highland Ave., presents "Symphonies Under the Stars" with international artists. A recent innovation is the Hollywood Bowl Bach Festival. *Greek Theater,* 2700 Vermont Ave., Los Angeles, offers ten weeks of outdoor concerts, ballet and opera July through Aug.

Long Beach Civic Light Opera presents seasonal productions. *Bing Auditorium,* Los Angeles County Museum of Art, presents Monday evening concerts. *Wilshire Ebell Theater,* 4401 W. 8th St., Los Angeles, built in 1924, is a Spanish–Renaissance gem, with fine programs of dancers and quartets. Programs also at the newly redecorated *Pasadena Center Auditorium,* 300 E. Green St., Pasadena and *Callboard Theater,* 8451 Melrose Pl., Hollywood.

For rock and pop, look up the *Roxy,* 9000 Sunset Blvd.; *Troubadour,* Doheny Dr. and Santa Monica Blvd., *Studio One's Backlot,* 657 N. Robertson, W. Hollywood. Top country and western music may be heard at *The Palomino,* 6907 Lankershim Blvd. Universal Amphitheatre has summer concerts of popular recording stars. Concerts are big in Southern California (and Los Angeles) which is headquarters for the recording industry. Consult Sunday's calendar section of the Los Angeles *Times.*

The universities offer various programs by student, resident and visiting performers at: *Beckman Auditorium,* California Institute of Technology,

Pasadena; *Bovard Auditorium,* University of Southern California, Los Angeles; *Schoenberg* and *Royce Halls,* University of California at Los Angeles.

STAGE AND REVUES. There are several areas of theater in the Los Angeles vicinity—experimental, commercial, university, and little. All of them create stimulating, exciting and novel works. The commercial theaters are the ones you've heard of—the *Ahmanson Theater* in the Music Center; *The Mark Taper Forum,* adjacent; *Greek Theater,* Griffith Park, which presents outdoor performances of music, drama and dance June-Sept.; the *Hollywood Pantages* and the *Shubert* in Century City. What is playing at these theaters, as well as the lesser-known, is readily available in the theater section of the newspapers, especially the "Calendar" section of the Sunday Los Angeles *Times.* For tickets try the theater directly, a broker or Ticketron at all Sears, May Co., Broadway, and Montgomery Ward stores.

Lesser-known theaters whose works vary from satire to romantic, and from avant-garde to traditional: *L.A. Stage Company,* 1642 N. Las Palmas Ave., Hollywood; *Los Angeles Actors' Theater,* 1089 N. Oxford Ave.; *Melrose Theater,* 733 Seward St.; *Odyssey Theater,* 2111 Ohio St., West L.A.; *Cast Theater,* 804 N. El Centro Ave., Hollywood; *Century City Playhouse,* 10508 W. Pico Blvd.; the universities, and *The Westwood Playhouse,* 10886 LeConte Ave., Westwood.

The Comedy Store on Sunset Blvd., W. Hollywood, and *The Improvisation,* 8162 Melrose, offer fine entertainment.

BARS. Most of the hotels and restaurants have bars or lounges for a convivial cocktail—some are lively, others are intimate and secluded. You'll find them attractively decorated. Two new elegant Art–Deco lounges are *Tango,* Sheraton Grande Hotel, 333 S. Figueroa and *Rex II Ristorante,* in the landmark Oviatt Building, 617 S. Olive. *O'Shaughnessy's,* in the downtown Arco Plaza. *Café Rodeo,* 360 Rodeo Dr. Beverly Rodeo Hotel, Beverly Hills. *The Library Bar,* Beverly Hilton, 9876 Wilshire Blvd., is a quiet retreat for conversation and conviviality. *Polo Lounge,* Beverly Hills Hotel, Beverly Hills, Rangoon Racquet Club, 9474 Santa Monica Blvd., Beverly Hills.

NIGHTCLUBS. Most of the night spots in Los Angeles are for seeing and listening to top-name rock, pop, jazz, and country/western entertainers. The list includes after-dark "in spots," flamboyant clubs that have received lots of media publicity. *The Roxy,* 9009 Sunset Blvd., West Hollywood. *Troubador,* 9081 Santa Monica Blvd., West Hollywood. *The Central,* 8852 Sunset Blvd., West Hollywood. *Donte's,* 4269 Lankershim Blvd., North Hollywood. Top jazz entertainers.

The Palomino (country & western), 6907 Lankershim Blvd., N. Hollywood. *Little Nashville Club,* 13350 Sherman Way, North Hollywood. Country entertainment and dancing nightly. Dining Wed.–Sun.

The following is a list of places that have been popular for quite a while—not too many in this ever-changing city. *Ye Little Club,* 455 N. Canon Dr., Beverly Hills. An intimate spot, entertainers and cocktails. *Mulberry Street,* Studio City, offers the Beverly Hills Unlisted Jazz Band with George Segal; *Continental Room,* Bel-Air Hotel, Bel-Air. Cocktails, piano and vocal entertainment. *L'Escoffier,* Beverly Hilton Hotel, Beverly Hills. Dancing, elegant dining. For disco dancing: *Chippendales,* 3739 Overland Ave., West L.A. Male exotic dancers; punk, new wave, disco. *The Speakeasy,* 8531 Santa Monica Blvd., West Hollywood; *Rage,* 8911 Santa Monica Blvd; and *Fantasia,* Westin Bonaventure Hotel, 404 S. Figueroa, a trendy crowd in a futuristic disco.

Consult the "Calendar" section of the Sunday Los Angeles *Times* or *Los Angeles* or *California* magazines.

SPORTS. *Fishing:* You will find the best ocean sportfishing services at Malibu, Redondo Beach, San Pedro and Santa Monica.

Surfing: The entire city of Huntington Beach is directed toward surfing. Walk out on the Huntington Beach Pier, catch the Championship Meets in Sept., watch in amazement as they "shoot" (means "going through" in surfers' language) the pier pilings. The "Wedge" in Corona del mar is the most famous body-surfing beach in California—waves up to 20 feet! Malibu Beach is always crowded—the "real" surfers say that it has the best point break in California, meaning that the swell is in the right direction. At Leo Carrillo Beach in Malibu, the surfers take off next to 10-foot rocks and surf waves up to seven feet. The oceanfront is part of Leo Carrillo State Park; it has picturesque rocky-sandy beaches and camping areas.

Boating: There are boat marinas and yacht harbors in Playa del Rey just south of Santa Monica, in San Pedro, Long Beach, Newport Beach, Laguna Beach. An annual Grand Prix Power Boat Race takes place from Long Beach in Sept.

Golf: Many excellent courses are to be found throughout the Los Angeles area. Among the most notable are The Riviera G.C., at Pacific Palisades, and Los Angeles G.C., El Rancho is an excellent public course, and there is also one at Griffith Park.

Other courses in the Los Angeles area (all of them municipal) include Rancho Park G.C., Los Angeles; Brookside G.C., Pasadena; Costa Mesa. *Pala Mesa Golf and Tennis Resort,* in Fallbrook, near Escondido, also boasts one of the best courses in the U.S.

Jogging: Jogging has become a tradition in California. Here the emphasis is on physical fitness and trimness. You can join the jogging enthusiasts in any Southern California open spaces, along the waterfront at the beaches, on special paths in the parks, during the winter or summer. A favorite jogging stretch is along San Vincente Blvd., from the Pacific Palisades Park, along a wide grassy strip with coral trees through Brentwood. If you prefer the use of showers and other facilities, try the *YMCA,* 11311 La Grange, Westwood, Uniturf jogging track on roof; or the *YMCA,* 1553 N. Hudson, Hollywood, men and women, & 1/16th-mile roof track.

Bicycling: For information on bicycling clubs, contact the *American Youth Hostels,* 7603 Beverly Blvd.

Tennis: There are hundreds of free municipal and pay-for-play courts in Los Angeles, where tennis is more popular than any other sport. Also some of the top private tennis clubs in the country are here.

Racquetball: Enthusiasts have a wide range of courts to play from YMCA and local college facilities to membership clubs.

WINTER SPORTS. Ski areas offer all types of slopes. Rentals range from skis to snowmobiles, depending on location. Novice to expert runs can be found at Blue Ridge Ski Area, Holiday Hill Ski Lifts, which also has toboggan run, Kratka Ridge, Mt. Waterman and Table Mountain Ski area.

SPECTATOR SPORTS. The area offers a variety of year-long sports events, that begins with the kick–off football classic at the Rose Bowl each New Year's day.

Baseball: Dodgers, April through September, at Dodger Stadium in L.A.; Anaheim Stadium, Anaheim, seating 70,000 fans, offers California Angels, baseball, April-Sept.

Basketball: The modern Inglewood Forum, a 15,000-seat-capacity sports palace, is where the pros (Los Angeles Lakers) and the collegiates dribble. Track meets and other sports spectaculars show off here, plus circuses. UCLA's championship squad goes at it at Pauley Pavilion on the campus.

Football: The National Football League's Rams moved to the Anaheim Stadium in 1980. The big (100,000-seat) Memorial Coliseum, site of some of the 1984 Olympic games, is home to the L.A. Raider pros. The ambidextrous coliseum hosts the American Legion Fireworks and Thrill Spectacle, and many other events. In Exposition Park, 153911 S. Figueroa St. The Rose Bowl is held in Pasadena every New Year's Day and is also wheere the UCLA Bruins play their home games.

Golf: Glen Campbell-L.A. Open Golf Tournament, Rancho Golf Course. Annual February classic.

Auto Racing: A big sport in Southern California—very well-attended year-round at Ascot Park in Gardena and Riverside International Raceway, Riverside. The Long Beach Grand Prix is a popular new event.

Horse Racing: Santa Anita Racetrack, Arcadia, Dec.-early April. Oak Tree Thoroughbred Racing, Oct. Hollywood Park Race Track, Inglewood.

Thoroughbred racing April through July and night Harness Racing Sept. through Dec.

Ice Hockey: From October-March, fans are out at the Forum for the Los Angeles Kings.

Drag races are at Orange County International Raceway, Santa Ana Freeway at Sand Canyon Ave., and San Diego Freeway, Moulton Parkway. Also, monthly *motorcycle races* and the Super Bowl of Motocross, held annually at the Coliseum. In Sept., the Ontario Motor Speedway near Pomona is the site of the annual California 500.

 SHOPPING. In the vast Los Angeles area, shopping runs the gamut from high-priced quality department stores and trendy boutiques to inexpensive national chain stores. What has been called "urban sprawl" (decentralization of living away from a downtown section) has brought about shopping centers throughout Southern California. In them you'll find department stores (*Bullock's, I. Magnin's, Bonwit Teller, Robinson's, Saks, Broadway* and *May Co.*), chain stores, boutiques, bookstores—everything from health foods to furniture to garden shops—all grouped together around landscaped malls and plazas. Browse, shop, lunch, see a fashion show.

Beverly Hills is a mecca for shoppers: On Whilshire Blvd. starting at Beverly Dr. and running west you'll find *Tiffany and Co., Mark Cross, Cartier's, Georg Jensen, Saks Fifth Avenue, I. Magnin* and *J. W. Robinson's.* For shopping or being tempted, walk along Rodeo, Camden, Bedford Drives. Many of the stores are as handsome as their merchandise. For women's chic clothes, accessories and jewelry: *Gucci's, Courreges, Celine, Giorgio, Matthews, Amelia Gray, Edwards-Lowell Furs, Bally, Van Cleef and Arpels, Omega,* superb collection of pearls. Elegant men's clothiers: *Ted Lapidus, Bijan* and *Carroll & Co.* and *Battaglia.* Plus posh *Neiman Marcus, Gump's* and two *Abercrombie & Fitch* showplaces.

Miracle Mile, between La Brea and Fairfax, has branches of *May Co., Ohrbach's, Silverwood's* and *Desmond's.* Ohrbach's is famous for its copies of French-designed couturier clothes.

Westwood has *Bullock's Westwood, Desmond's* and many specialty shops and bookstores patronized by faculty and students from adjacent U.C.L.A.

Shopping Centers: *Century City,* 10250 Santa Monica Blvd., West L.A., is dominated by high rises, Bullock's, 80 specialty shops and the Broadway. Three-hour free parking in Century Square garage. Convenient shopping for moderately priced merchandise of all types. *Santa Monica Place,* 2nd & 4th, is a three-level mall with 160 fine stores and restaurants, including the Broadway and Robinson. *Marina Pacific Shopping Village,* 6346 C Pacific Coast Hwy, Long Beach. Over 100 shops, 6 restaurants located in the marina. *Fashion Square,* Sherman Oaks, in the San Fernando Valley. I. Magnin's and Bullock's. Good parking facilities.

Visit the *Japanese Village Plaza,* 327 E. Second St., in Little Tokyo, where two dozen specialty shops offer the best of Nippon.

 WHAT TO DO WITH THE CHILDREN. *Hanna-Barbera's Marineland,* recently renovated, offers a variety of fun attractions. In addition to their famed performing killer whales, trained dolphins and playful sea lions, meet Yogi Bear, Scooby-Doo and other Hanna-Barbera characters. Study mini-marine creatures at the Touch Tanks. Highly popular is the Adventure Swim; selected volunteer guests join 4,000 finny friends in a 500,000-gallon tank.

Knott's Berry Farm and Ghost Town, Beach Blvd. (Calif. 39), Buena Park, America's oldest (60th Anniversary) and third-largest theme park. Visitors will thrill to the exciting Corkscrew ride, pan for gold, ride ore cars, stagecoaches, a narrow-gauge railroad, burros and eat finger-lickin' chicken dinners.

Orange County Marine Institute, 35502 Del Obispo Street, Dana Point Harbor, is a free learning experience, with aquariums, tide pool, marine exhibits, museum shop.

Los Angeles Zoo, 5333 Zoo Dr., Griffith Park, reached via Ventura and Golden State freeways. Be sure to visit the Ahmanson Kpala House.

Queen Mary, Long Beach. Visit the Queen Mary at War Exhibit; tour the luxurious liner and dine and shop aboard. Adjacent is Howard Hughes' fabulous

Spruce Goose airplane exhibit. *Six Flags Magic Mountain,* Valencia, is a theme park with emphasis on thrill rides.

Ports o' Call Village, in San Pedro, is a charming mid-19th-century melange of shops, restaurants, entertainment, plus cruising and helicopter viewing.

And, of course, don't forget about *Disneyland.*

 HOTELS AND MOTELS. Listings are in several sections: first is the downtown (central) area of the city, followed by the leading outlying areas and distinctive neighborhoods, such as Hollywood, Beverly Hills, West Los Angeles and Santa Monica, listed in alphabetical order. Listings are in order of price category. Reservations are suggested. If possible, select accommodations in an area convenient to the tourist attractions you plan to visit. For a more complete explanation of hotel and motel listings, see *Facts At Your Fingertips,* earlier in this book.

Based on double occupancy, the price categories and ranges are about as follows: *Super deluxe:* $75 and up; *Deluxe:* $60 and up; *Expensive:* $50–60; *Moderate:* $40–50; *Inexpensive:* under $40.

DOWNTOWN LOS ANGELES. *Deluxe:* **The Biltmore.** 515 S. Olive. A Los Angeles historical landmark sporting a $35 million renovation.

The Bonaventure. At Fifth and Figueroa Sts., this impressive round-towered jewel of downtown is elegant with all the necessary amenities.

Hyatt Regency, 711 South Hope St., at Broadway Plaza. *Hugo's V,* gourmet dining, plus roof-top revolving restaurant and lounge.

Sheraton Grande. 333 S. Figueroa. New. European ambience; elegant decor; butler serves each floor.

Expensive: **The Ambassador.** 2400 Wilshire Blvd. A central, businessman's location with health club and fine restaurants as well as new tennis complex.

Los Angeles Hilton. 930 Wilshire Blvd. Typically Hilton. Six restaurants. Tour and convention-oriented.

Mayflower. 535 S. Grand Ave. Renovated charmer.

New Otani. 120 S. Los Angeles St. Garden luxury. Visit Weller Court and its 12 Oriental restaurants, in Little Tokyo.

Sheraton Town House. at 2961 Wilshire Blvd. Comfortable hotel for business people on the go. Tastefully decorated w/cafe, bar, entertainment, sauna, tennis courts.

Moderate: **Alexandria.** Spring St. at Fifth St. Restored 1905 hotel.

Figueroa Hotel. 939 S. Figueroa St. Pleasant, convenient.

Gala Inn Towne. 925 So. Figueroa St. Multilingual staff.

Inexpensive: **City Center Motel.** 1135 W. 7th St. Central. Tour bus.

Holiday Lodge. 1631 W. Third. Small. Good downtown location.

Oasis Motel. 2200 W. Olympic Blvd. Quiet, attractive.

WEST LOS ANGELES. *Deluxe:* **Bel-Air.** 701 Stone Canyon Rd. Resort, distinctive.

Westwood Marquis Hotel. 930 Hilgard Ave. All suites.

Expensive: **Bel-Air Sands.** 11461 Sunset Blvd., Westwood Village. Well-landscaped grounds. Recently renovated. **Le Parc.** 733 N. West Knoll, West Hollywood. All suites. Sauna, gym.

Holiday Inn-Westwood. 10740 Wilshire Blvd. Usual amenities.

Moderate: **L.A. West TraveLodge,** 10740 Santa Monica Blvd., Westwood Village. Complimentary extras.

ANAHEIM. *Superdeluxe:* **Disneyland Hotel.** 1150 W. Cerritos Ave. Monorail to Disneyland.

Deluxe: **Sheraton-Anaheim.** 1015 W. Ball Rd. Pool; entertainment; free bus to Disneyland.

Expensive: **Howard Johnson's.** 1380 S. Harbor Blvd. Opposite Disneyland.

Moderate: **Concord Inn.** 1111 Harbor Blvd. Pool, spa.

AVALON (CATALINA ISLAND). *Expensive:* **Las Casitas Resort,** 400 Avalon Canyon Rd. Memorial Canyon Dr. Newly renovated.

Pavilion Lodge. 513 Grescent Ave. Across from beach.

BEVERLY HILLS. *Super Deluxe:* **Beverly Hills.** 9641 Sunset Blvd. Beautiful grounds, quiet.

Beverly Hilton. 9876 Wilshire Blvd. Large. Restaurants and shops.

Beverly Wilshire. 9500 Wilshire Blvd. European atmosphere and decor.

L'Ermitage, 9291 Burton Way. "Hotel de Grande Classe." All suites. Intimate, gourmet Café Russe.

Deluxe: **Beverly Hillcrest.** 1224 S. Beverwil Dr. at Pico Blvd. Luxurious.

Beverly Rodeo. 360 N. Rodeo Dr. Elegant, convenient.

Westin Century Plaza. 2025 Avenue of the Stars. This hotel is handsomely decorated w/refrigerators, lanai and view in all rooms. Several restaurants. Elegant new 30-story tower.

Moderate: **Beverly House,** 140 S. Lasky Dr. Close to UCLA, Century City.

HOLLYWOOD. More expensive Hollywood motels generally are in the Sunset Strip area. Farther out, the rates are apt to be lower.

Expensive: **Hyatt on Sunset.** 8401 Sunset Blvd. Sunset Strip center.

Holiday Inn. 1755 N. Highland Ave. at Hollywood Blvd. Rooftop café.

Ramada Inn. 8775 Sunset Blvd. Attractive.

Moderate: **Best Western Hollywood Motor Hotel.** 6141 Franklin Ave., between Gower and Argyle St. Comfortable. Some kitchens.

Hollywood Highland Motel. 2051 N. Highland Ave. Near Hollywood Bowl, Mann's Chinese Theater. Free Chinese/Continental breakfast.

Vagabond. 5410 Hollywood Blvd. Family rates. Coffee shop.

NORTH HOLLYWOOD. *Expensive:* **Burbank Airport Hilton,** opposite Hollywood–Burbank Airport. Near TV & film studios.

Sheraton-Universal Hotel. 30 Universal City Plaza, Universal City. Large. Distinctive restaurant.

Moderate: **Beverly Garland's Howard Johnson's Resort Lodge.** Pool, tennis. 4222 Vineland Ave.

Sportsman Lodge. 12825 Ventura Blvd. Studio City. Resort complex.

HUNTINGTON BEACH. *Deluxe:* **Huntington Beach Inn.** 21112 Pacific Coast Hwy. Excellent. Superb dining.

Moderate: **Huntington Shores Motel.** 21002 Pacific Coast Hwy. Opposite beach. Coffeeshop. Pleasant. Restaurant nearby.

INGLEWOOD. *Deluxe:* **Marriott.** 5855 W. Century Blvd. Full services.

Hyatt Hotel-LAX. 6225 Century Blvd. At L.A. Airport.

Sheraton Plaza La Reina Hotel, 6101 W. Century Blvd. New, convenient.

Expensive. **Airport Marina.** 1, 8601 Lincoln Blvd. at Manchester Ave. Large.

Airport Park Hotel. 600 Ave. of Champions. Near Hollywood Park. Airport transportation.

Howard Johnson Motor Lodge. 5990 Green Valley Dr. 24-hr. coffeeshop.

Pacifica Hotel. 6161 Centinela Ave. Culver City. 3 miles from L.A. International Airport. Health spa.

Moderate: **Manchester House.** 901 W. Manchester. Free transport to Disneyland, Knotts Berry Farm.

LONG BEACH. *Expensive:* **Hyatt Long Beach.** 6400 E. Pacific Coast Hwy. Large rooms, picturesque surroundings.

Queen Mary Hotel. The famous old Cunard liner, now tied up permanently at Pier J. Her staterooms are the largest ever built on a ship. Restaurants, bar.

Queensway Bay Hilton. 700 Queensway Dr. Marina; sportfishing.

Moderate: **Beachtown.** 4201 E. Pacific Coast Hwy. Pool; whirlpool; sauna.

Best Western Queen City Motel. 3555 E. Pacific Coast Hwy. Pool; coffee shop.

Holiday Inn. 2640 Lakewood Blvd. at Willow St. Attractive, multi-story circular building.

Ramada Inn. 5325 E. Pacific Coast Hwy. Family rates. Restaurant.

MARINA DEL RAY. *Expensive.* **Marina International** 4200 Admiralty Way. The "in-scene" for locals and visitors.

NEWPORT BEACH-BALBOA BAY. (Reservations necessary in summer and during Easter Week, when teenagers take over the town.)
Deluxe: **The Newporter.** 1107 Jamboree Rd. Twenty-six-acre resort that's had a $10 million renovation.
Expensive: **Airporter Inn.** 18700 MacArthur Blvd. Large. Suites.
Marriott Hotel. Tennis, nearby golf, pool. 900 Newport Center Drive.
Sheraton Newport Beach. Near Orange County Airport. Lighted tennis courts. 4545 MacArthur Blvd.

PASADENA. (Reservations mandatory during Tournament of Roses and Rose Bowl Game on New Year's Day.)
Expensive: **Huntington-Sheraton.** 1401 S. Oak Knoll Ave. Picturesque old building.
Moderate: **Vagabond Inn.** 2863 E. Colorado Blvd. Heated pool; pets OK.
Inexpensive: **Saga.** 1633 E. Colorado Blvd. Restaurant near.

SAN JUAN CAPISTRANO. *Moderate:* **Best Western Capistrano Inn.** 27174 Ortega Hwy. Pool, whirlpool. Café adjacent.

SANTA MONICA. *Deluxe:* **Miramar-Sheraton.** Wilshire Blvd. at Ocean Ave. Tropical setting.
Huntley Hotel. 1111 Second Street. Smart hirise; rooftop dining.
Expensive: **Holiday Inn.** 120 Colorado Ave. at Ocean Ave. Free coffee.
Moderate: **Hotel Carmel.** 210 Broadway. Near new shopping plaza. 201 Broadway. Comfortable.
Shangri-La Hotel. 1301 Ocean Ave. Quiet, ocean view, garden.

 DINING OUT. Dining in the Los Angeles area has become sophisticated and international in accent. The gourmet can dine on superb continental cuisine in a variety of elegant settings—some quiet and intimate, others *a la Français,* with strolling musicians. There are the chic eateries that attract "the beautiful people," and there is the gamut of ethnic restaurants. So whether your preference is for Mexican, Polynesian, Greek, Japanese, Chinese, or just good, tasty traditional food, you'll be able to please your palate in the City of the Angels. It is advisable to call for reservations.
Restaurants are listed in order of price category within each type of cuisine. Price categories and ranges for dinner, without drinks, tax or tip, are: *Deluxe:* over $35; *Expensive:* $25–35; *Moderate:* $15–25; and *Inexpensive:* under $15. Restaurants featuring á la carte menus are more expensive. For a more complete explanation of restaurant categories, see *Facts at Your Fingertips* at the front of this volume.
Deluxe: **Carlos 'n Charlie.** *Continental.* 8240 Sunset Blvd. Seafood and barbe-cue chicken are specialties.
The Palms. *American.* 9001 Santa Monica Blvd. Manhattan mood and steak selection.
La Scala. *Italian.* 9455 Little Santa Monica Blvd. Considered by many to be top dining in Beverly Hills.
Scandia. *Scandinavian.* 9040 Sunset Blvd., W. Hollywood. perennial . . . favorite.
Expensive: **Bernard's.** *Continental.* Biltmore Hotel. Superb nouvelle cuisine; Fresh fish; creative desserts.
Francois. *French.* 555 S. Flower (Arco Plaza). Popular pre-theater dining. Rack of lamb; roast ducking, fresh fish selections.
Jade West. *Chinese.* 2040 Ave. of the Stars. Exquisite Szechuan cuisine.
Jimmy's. *French.* 201 Moreno Drive. Beverly Hills. Stylish clientele and classical specialties.
Maison Magnolia. *Continental.* 2639 S. Magnolia Ave. An undiscovered gem. Memorable dining in an art and antique filled residence.
Perino's. *Continental.* 444 S. Flower Street. The new $7.5 million dollar home of the renowned restaurant.

Verdi. *Italian.* 1519 Wilshire Blvd. Santa Monica. Handsome "ristorante di musica" features Northern Italian fare enhanced by staged musical programs.

Moderate: **Ginger Man.** *Continental.* 369 N. Bedford Ave. Trendy area (Rodeo Drive); popular and casual.

Homer & Edy's Bistro. *Creole.* 2839 Robertson. New Orleans favorites in a former home. Nightly jazz entertainment.

Mischa's. *Russian.* 7561 Sunset Blvd. Picturesque Hollywood restaurant with Gypsy and Russian entertainment nightly.

The Egg and the Eye. *Continental/American.* 5814 Wilshire Blvd. Fine choice for light fare; lunch and brunch omelets and crepes.

Yamashiro. *Continental/Oriental.* 1999 N. Sycamore Ave. Hollywood. This former estate boasts a superb view and pleasant dining.

Inexpensive: **El Cholo.** *Mexican.* 1121 S. Western Ave. Great margaritas; patio dining.

Gorky's. *Russian/American.* 536 E. Eight Street. High-tech mood in city's "Soho" district. Good food; great ambience. Open around the clock every day.

Hard Rock Cafe. *American.* 8614 Beverly Blvd. The "in" ribs, chili, and burger scene.

Mon Kee. *Chinese.* 170 N. La Cienega Blvd. Locals consider this one of the city's best. Also downtown at 679 N. Spring Street.

Nate 'n Al's. *Deli.* 414 N. Beverly Dr., Beverly Hills. Very popular; great sandwiches and desserts.

The Cheesecake Factory. *American.* 364 N. Beverly Dr., Beverly Hills. Great salads, hamburgers and 30 kinds of cheesecake.

ANAHEIM. *Expensive:* **Granville's.** *Disneyland Hotel.* American menu and mood in handsome setting.

Moderate: **Charley Brown's.** 1751 S. State College Blvd. Lunch, dinner. Bar. Children's menu.

WEST HOLLYWOOD. *Moderate:* **Alberto's.** 8826 Melrose Ave. Cannelloni, fresh fish. Also at Rancho Mirage.

Daisy's on Sunset. Hyatt on Sunset, 8401 Sunset Blvd. Sunday champagne brunch; try ginger fruit salad. Singing waiters evenings. Open daily.

BEVERLY HILLS. *Deluxe:* **L'Escoffier.** 9876 Wilshire Blvd., atop the Beverly Hilton Hotel. Extremely elegant.

La Bella Fontana. Fine French & Continental cuisine in an elegant atmosphere. Beverly Wilshire Hotel, 9500 Wilshire Blvd.

Expensive: **Chasen's.** 9039 Beverly Blvd. Renowned cuisine.

La Scala. 9455 Santa Monica Blvd. Area's best Italian food.

Mr. Chow. The best Oriental cooking in town. Show people go in droves. 344 N. Camden Dr.

Romeo and Juliet. 435 N. Beverly Dr. Elegant Italian specialties; try veal stuffed with prosciutto.

HOLLYWOOD. *Deluxe:* **An Petit Café.** Superb French cuisine. A hang-out for the "stars." 1230 Vine St. Reservations a must.

Moderate: **Butterfield's.** 8426 Sunset Blvd. Daily fish and veal specialties.

Cock 'n Bull. 9170 Sunset Blvd. Pub fare. Moscow Mule created here.

Sushi on Sunset. 8264 Sunset Blvd. Sushi bar, tempura, teriyaki.

SANTA MONICA. *Expensive:* **Jack's at the Beach.** 2700 Wilshire Blvd. Sample petrale sole or Catalina sand dabs.

Chinois on Main. 2709 Main St. French-Chinese haute cuisine.

Valentino. 3115 Pico Blvd. Continental classics; veal, baby spring lamb.

Moderate: **Knoll's Black Forest Inn.** 124 Santa Monica Blvd. Hearty German fare in a Bavarian-flavored atmosphere.

COFFEE HOUSES AND CAFES. Catering to the appetite needs of the "traveler on the go," they are conveniently located throughout the city near theaters, at the beaches, parks, and entertainment centers. Some stay open around-the-clock.

Two lively coffee houses with atmosphere are *Gorky's*, 536 E. 8th St., downtown and *The Intersection*, 2735 W. Temple St., a folk-dance café featuring ethnic foods and dancing. Both have excellent food, informal atmosphere.

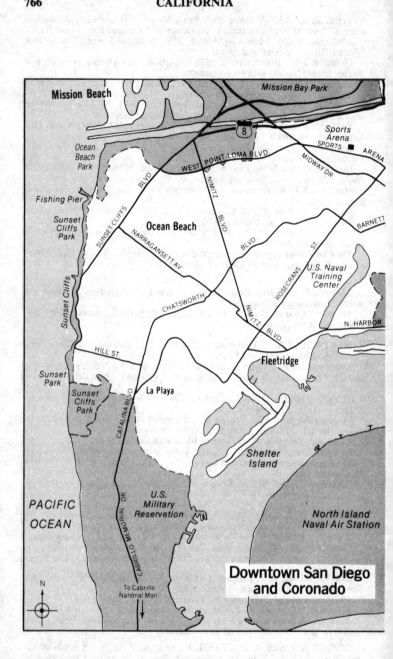

Downtown San Diego and Coronado

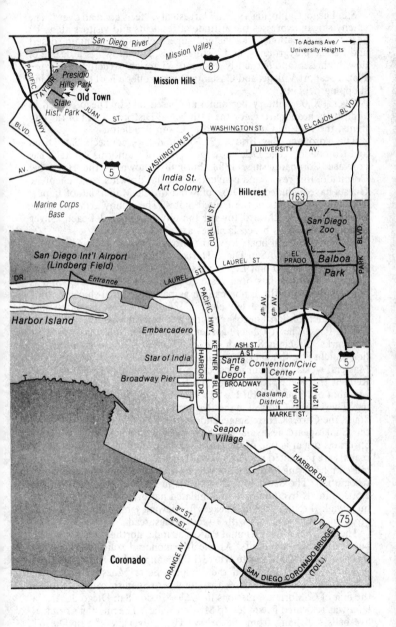

EXPLORING SAN DIEGO

San Diego, California's second largest city, "feels good all over." The catchy slogan expresses the attitude of residents and visitors alike. Its year-round vacation perks include superb climate, mountain, desert and Pacific playgrounds; and historic sites. Downtown is a dazzle of new highrises and elegantly restored Victorian structures. Horton Plaza, Seaport Village, and Gaslamp Quarter offer a host of dining and shopping delights.

Over 100,00 military personnel are based in San Diego, which in addition is headquarters for the 11th Naval District. North of the city limits, the Marine Corps is based at Camp Pendleton.

The Coronado Bay Bridge ($1.20 round trip) connects San Diego and Coronado. "The Del," dowager queen of California's hotels, has crowned Coronado since 1888. Formally known as the Hotel del Coronado, this resort and convention site has drawn a royal clientele. Guests have included the Duke of Windsor, the Maharajah of Jaipur, and eight Presidents of the United States. The skinny arm of barrier beach extends southward toward the city of Imperial Beach. Silver Strand State Park's beach facilities are along the route.

Harbor excursion boats leave the Broadway pier for one- and two-hour cruises around San Diego Harbor. The excursions head toward Shelter Island and Point Loma, passing cargo vessels and Navy ships. The *Star of India* has been restored to her best appearance and is moored alongside the Embarcadero as part of a three-ship maritime museum. The vessel was launched in 1863 and now is the oldest ship afloat. Much of San Diego's cultural and recreational life centers on Balboa Park. The 1,400-acre garden spot is one of the country's finest city parks. Gracious Spanish Baroque buildings house many attractions, including the Fine Arts and Timken Galleries, displaying Old Masters' works, Russian icons, exceptional changing exhibitions; the Reuben H. Fleet Space Theater and Science Center, Spanish Village, Museum of Man, Natural History Museum, and the Botanical Building. The Edison Centre for the Performing Arts includes the Festival Stage, the Carter Centre Stage, and the new Old Globe Theatre, where the Shakespeare festivals are held each summer. The 5,000-pipe Spreckels organ is one of the world's largest outdoor organs; Sunday recitals are presented regularly. The Hall of Champions is an all-sports museum honoring local athletes who have achieved national and world recognition. The San Diego Zoo also is in Balboa Park. Most of the 5,500 animals live outdoors in simulated nattural habitats. There are huge walk-through, free-flight cages for viewing some of the zoo's 2,850 birds, including condors with 10-foot wingspreads.

The San Diego Wild Animal Park is 30 miles northeast of downtown but still within city limits. An electric monorail train takes visitors through the 1,800-acre site where 1,000 animals live in near-natural habitats. Presidio Park and the Junipero Serra Muesum (historical relics of the Southwest) mark the site where Spanish padres founded the first of California's missions in 1769. Mission San Diego de Alcala later was relocated five miles up Mission Valley. The mission's original five bells still hang from the belfry. The University of San Diego's archaeological research is unearthing fascinating artifacts, on display in the mission's museum. Old Town State Historic Park is around the plaza below Presidio Park. Adobe buildings of the later Spanish rancho era and Early California restaurants dot Old Town.

PRACTICAL INFORMATION FOR SAN DIEGO

 HOW TO GET AROUND. *By air: Republic, American, Frontier, Air California, Pacific Southwest, United, Continental,* and *Western Airlines* serve San Diego.

By car: Avis, Budget, Dollar-A-Day, Hertz, and *National* have car rental offices in San Diego.

By bus: City buses are your best bet. You can take them up to La Jolla, down to the Mexican border, and to Coronado, Point Loma, La Mesa and El Cajon.

By train: Amtrak operates from Los Angeles, with several stops en route.

 TOURIST INFORMATION SERVICES. Write to or visit the *San Diego Convention & Visitors Bureau,* 1200 3rd Ave., Suite 824, San Diego 92101, for maps and booklets on tours, golf, restaurants, hotels, motels, and what to do and where to go in San Diego and vicinity. The *San Diego Union* and *Evening Tribune,* 350 Camino de la Reina, San Diego, hands out a San Diego Facts Book.

 MUSEUMS AND GALLERIES. *San Diego Historical Society, Serra Museum, Library and Tower Gallery,* 2727 Presidio Dr., Presidio Park honors the Franciscan founder of California's missions. Located on the site of the first mission, founded in 1769 by Fray Junipero Serra and Gov.-Capt. Gaspar de Portola. The museum contains relics and documents concerning the history of San Diego and environs. Setting and view are magnificent.

Whaley House, 2482 San Diego Ave., displays historical items.

Villa Montezuma, 1925 K St., is a restored Victorian era home.

In San Diego's 1,400-acre Balboa Park: the *Museum of Man* traces mankind's history with emphasis on the Indian cultures of the Americas; the *Natural History Museum* contains exhibits of birds, fish, reptiles, mammals and prehistoric animals; the $4 million *Reuben H. Fleet Space Theater and Science Center* features a futuristic space adventure shown on the largest projection dome in the U.S. and a scientific do-it-yourself exhibit hall; the *Hall of Champions* is a museum honoring local sports heros; the *Fine Arts Gallery* of San Diego features changing and permanent exhibitions of Flemish, Renaissance, Italian, Spanish and contemporary art. When visiting Balboa Park, you can obtain maps, brochures and information at Park Information Center, House of Hospitality.

Others: The San Diego Hall of Champions, containing memorabilia of local athletes, Balboa Park. There is a maritime museum (on the Embarcadero at the foot of Ash St.) which includes the merchant windjammer *Star of India,* 1800s ferryboat *Berkeley* and WWI-vintage yacht *Medea.*

HISTORIC SITES. In 1967, the state provided $2.5 million to buy six blocks in *Old Town,* the first European settlement in California. Presently, it covers 12 acres as well as near neighbor Heritage Park with its handsome refurbished Victorians. *Cabrillo National Monument* provides views of the Bay as well as the California and Mexican coastline.

 OLD MISSIONS. *Mission San Diego de Alcala,* the first of 21 links in the California mission chain stretching north along El Camino Real (The King's Highway) to Sonoma, was founded by the Franciscan padre, Junipero Serra. Today, peaceful gardens grace the site where the state's first palm and olive trees were planted. The mission museum contains religious relics and items from that era.

Mission San Luis Rey, about five miles east of Oceanside, was founded in 1798. The 18th and largest mission now is a seminary.

San Antonio de Pala, constructed in 1816 near Palomar Mtn., Hwy. 76, as an *asistencia* to San Luis Rey.

Santa Ysabel, an *asistencia* to Mission San Diego de Alcala, built in 1818, is southeast of Pala on Hwy. 79 near Julian.

 TOURS. San Diego offers a wide variety of tours and packages such as "golf" outings; San Diego Zoo and Sea World Trips. Write: San Diego Convention and Visitor's Bureau, 1200 Third Ave., Suite 824, San Diego 92101.

Bike Tours: Bike tours are a natural for Southern California. One possibility, covering approximately eight miles, combines "a ride back into California history" and a pleasant view of San Diego's surrounding bay, sea and landscape. Start at Pepper Grove Dr., in Balboa Park. Ride along El Prado, pedal to Upas St., ride west to a connection with Third Ave., continue along University Ave. and Ft. Stockton Dr. to Presidio Park—the site of the original mission. The view from this vantage point encompasses Point Loma, San Diego Bay and Mission Valley. Then ride down the slope to Old Town where you can relax in Old Town Plaza, follow the painted green line leading to historical sights, or lunch at one of the excellent Mexican restaurants.

A 3.6-mile *La Jolla bike tour* runs along the ocean. Start at La Jolla Cove, pedal along Coast Blvd., ride along Neptune Place, continue to Chelsea St., and follow the well-marked route to its end at Turquoise St. Stops along this tour will allow you to explore La Jolla caves, view charming seaside homes, and see Bird Rock (at times covered with flocks of sea gulls, pelicans and cormorants).

Horseback, sightseeing hikes and jeep tours: Available at *Anza Borrego Desert State Park.* Best season is Mid-January through April.

By boat: One- and two-hour excursions around the San Diego Harbor depart from the Broadway Pier. Whale-watching excursion boats depart from the San Diego Bay and Mission Bay piers, generally Dec. through April.

 ZOOS. *San Diego Zoo.* One of the world's largest zoos. Guided bus tour and Skyfari aerial tramway. Also children's zoo. *San Diego Wild Animal Park* is an 1,800-acre preserve within city limits. Exhibits, snack bars, shops and guided, five-mile monorail tour. *Sea World,* 1720 S. Shores Rd., Mission Bay, has daily shows, hydrofoil boat ride, Japanese Village, Skytower ride, the world's largest shark exhibit, and its new $7 million Penquin Encounter.

 MUSIC AND THEATER. San Diego now offers exciting year-round cultural experiences. The San Diego Opera's acclaimed June Verdi festival, outstanding premier productions of American vehicles and international stars draw enthusatic supports to the downtown *Performing Arts Center.* Meanwhile, in Balboa Park, the "new" Old Globe Theater, Cassius Carter Center and Festival Stage are all part of the $6.5 million *Simon Edison Center.* The refurbished *Fox Theatre* debuts as Symphony Hall in November; check the *Gaslamp Quarter Theater* and *San Diego Repertory Theater.*

 SPORTS. *Surfing* is popular along the 70 miles of beaches in the county, with La Jolla's Wind 'n' Sea Beach said to be the best this side of Hawaii. To learn where the surfing is good, telephone 619–488–WIND.

Fishing: If there's a fisherman's paradise, it's the San Diego area. Take your pick of fishing surface, bottom, surf, rock, bay, shell and freshwater for albacore, barracuda, bluefin tuna, bonita, grunion, mackerel, kelp bass, white sea bass, marlin, swordfish and yellowtail. Ocean sport-fishing services are offered year-round by a number of operators. For further information, contact the San Diego Convention and Visitors Bureau.

Boating: Boat marinas and yacht harbors ring Mission Bay, Harbor Island and Shelter Island.

Water sports: Full range of facilities are available at Mission Bay Park, Carlsbad, Shelter Island and Harbor Island.

Tennis: The La Jolla Beach & Tennis Club has eight championship courts. But tennis is booming everywhere, especially in this area with the Parks and Recreations Dept. operating 98 public courts, and 1,200-public courts counted in the county. Morley Field in Balboa Park has 25 two-tone cement courts, a stadium court, pro shop, and clubhouse. *Free* courts include those at Mesa,

Grossmont, Palomar, Mira Coast and Southwestern College, Escondido, Helix, Poway, Vista and Chula Vista high schools.

Golf: San Diego is "Golfland, U.S.A.," with 70 year-round courses. Among the many to be recommended are: Pauma Valley C.C., Pauma Valley; Torrey Pines G. C., S. La Jolla; and La Costa C.C., Carlsbad. All are ranked among the second fifty of America's great golf courses.

Bicycling: Most of the clubs are affiliated with the American Youth Hostels. For details, contact the A. Y. H., 1031 India St., San Diego.

Jogging: Groups for men and women: San Diego Parks and Recreation Dept.; Y.M.C.A., 1115 8th Ave.

SPECTATOR SPORTS. *Horse Racing* at Del Mar Race Track, 15 mi. north of San Diego. The season is mid-July to mid-Sept. Also horse and dog racing all year at Agua Caliente Race Track in Tijuana, which is 15 miles south of San Diego.

The San Diego Jack Murphy Stadium is home for the Padres (baseball), the Chargers (football), and the Sockers (soccer).

At Torrey Pines State Park you can watch the Annual Pacific Coast *Glider Soaring Championship* in late March or early April. Tijuana, Mexico, offers year-round jai alai and summer bullfighting.

Rough water swims: Sept. at La Jolla Cove, July 4 at Coronado, Oct. at Oceanside. *Golf:* Andy Williams San Diego Open, Torrey Pines late Jan.; the MONY Tournament, La Costa, May. *Tennis:* the 69th annual La Jolla Tennis Championships, late June. The world's largest, with over 40 events.

SHOPPING Specialty shops are concentrated at Heritage Park and Bazaar del Mundo in the Old Town and Seaport Village at the Embarcadero.

Shopping along La Jolla's Prospect or Girard avenues is special. High fashions for all the family, choice china, crystal, and furniture plus antiques and gems put our credit cards to use most easily.

San Diego's Mission Valley hosts a popular shopping sprawl, Fashion Valley, and Mission Valley Shopping Centers.

Hop the bright red "Tijuana Trolley" for the exciting 16-mile run to the Mexican border $1 one way). Explore the dramatic new Cultural Center, and discover duty-free imports and Mexican wares on the Avenida Revolucion and the attractive Plaza Rio Tijuana shopping center.

WHAT TO DO WITH THE CHILDREN. San Diego Zoo at Balboa Park is a five-minute ride from downtown. World's largest collection of rare and wild animals housed in enclosures duplicating their native habitat. Separate Children's Zoo. Seal shows, aviaries, guided bus tour; restaurant, refreshment stands, picnic areas, curio shop.

New is Seaport Village, 14 acres of downtown, transformed into a melange of Early California, Victorian, and Mexican charm. Shops; dining; a vintage 1880 merry-go-round, picnic area.

Visit the *Scripps Institution of Oceanography,* with its new T. Wayland Vaughn Aquarium Museum exhibiting local and tropical aquatic specimens. Inspect the San Diego-La Jolla Underwater Park (an ecological) reserve, extending nearly two miles along the shoreline) and view the television monitor for a Cousteau-view of aquatic life.

HOTELS AND MOTELS in the San Diego area are listed in order of price category. For double occupancy, categories and ranges are as follows: *Deluxe:* $75 and up; *Expensive:* $60–75; *Moderate:* $50–60; and *Inexpensive:* under $50. For a more complete explanation of hotel categories, see *Facts at Your Fingertips* at the front of this volume.

Deluxe: Hyatt Islandia. 1441 Quivira Rd. Heated pool, restaurant, bar.
Inter-Continental. 333 W. Harbor Dr. New, luxury high rise.
San Diego Hilton. 1775 E. Mission Bay Dr. Tennis resort; convenient.
Westgate. 1055 Second Ave. Downtown. Elegant decor, service.

Expensive: **Vacation Village.** Hotel. Mission Bay. 43-acre resort; 10 minutes from downtown.

Moderate: **Fabulous Inns of America.** 2485 Hotel Circle. Adjacent sports, restaurants.

Padre Trail Inn. 4200 Taylor St. Heart of historic Old Town.

Inexpensive: **Pacific Shore Motel.** 4802 Mission Blvd. Pool. Near beach.

TraveLodge, 412 Playa del Norte, La Jolla. Near beach; dining and shopping.

Vagabond Inn. 625 Hotel Circle. Mission Valley. On I–8; good location.

CARLSBAD. *Deluxe:* **La Costa Hotel and Spa.** Costa Del Mar Rd. A luxury resort with golf, tennis, health spa and fine restaurants.

Expensive: **Beach Terrace Inn–Best Western.** 2775 Ocean St. Beachfront facility with fireplaces, carports, private balconies; kitchens available.

 DINING OUT. San Diego offers an unusually broad range of choices for dining. The oceanside location of the city means a ready supply of fresh seafood, and the proximity to the Mexican border accounts for the spicy, Mexican influence. San Diego's eating establishments reflect a cosmopolitan heritage. Categories: *Expensive* $25 and up; *Moderate* $15–25; *Inexpensive* under $15. (Prices do not include wine or cocktails.) A la carte menus are more expensive. For more complete explanation of categories, see *Facts at Your Fingertips* earlier in book.

Expensive: **Anthony's Star of the Sea Room.** 1362 Harbor Dr. Gourmet dining from the sea.

Fontainebleau Room. 2nd Avenue & Broadway (in the Westgate). Very elegant. The kitchen here has been top-flight, and the Beef Wellington is super.

Moderate: **Bali Hai.** 2230 Shelter Island Dr. The emphasis is on Cantonese specialties, all served in a pleasant environment overlooking the bay. A long and exotic drink list complements dining. There's also a floor show.

Chart House at the San Diego Rowing Club. 525 E. Harbor Dr. The restored site of the club offers fine seafood and prime ribs in nautical surroundings.

Casa De Bandini. Old Town Plaza. Mexican mood and menu.

La Chaumine. 1466 Garnet, Pacific Beach. Fine French dining, reservations suggested.

Miki-San. 2424 5th Ave., Balboa Park. Japanese cuisine and entertainment.

Papagayo. Seaport Village. Seafood with a dash of Latino flair.

Reuben E. Lee. 880 Harbor Island Dr., near airport. Boat docked on San Diego Bay. Steak, seafood.

Inexpensive: **El Ranchero.** 7404 La Jolla Blvd., La Jolla. Tiny. Informal mood and menu.

Vieux Carré. 828 Fifth Ave., downtown. Creole specialities—gumbo, jambalaya.

EXPLORING SAN FRANCISCO

San Francisco owes much of its individuality to three natural endowments: its site, topography, and climate.

The city occupies a 44.6-square-mile fingertip between the Pacific Ocean and one of the world's greatest natural harbors. Such confinement has caused San Francisco, like Manhattan, to grow up rather than out, although its skyscrapers don't rival Manhattan's. Thus, it has kept its distinctive urbanity intact.

Its topography is, to put it mildly, uneven. The peninsula that forms the Golden Gate's southern portal undulates from sea level to an altitude of 925 feet. The downtown buildings rise in steep zigzags—rather as if some dauntless developers had tackled the Grand Tetons.

Just how many hills San Francisco covers is a moot question—enough, certainly, to provide a whole succession of spectacular views. Some sources list upward of 40. The main ones—Nob, Russian, Telegraph, Rincon, Twin Peaks, Mt. Davidson, and Lone Mountain—early earned it the Roman sobriquet "City of Seven Hills."

If San Francisco has a look of its own, it also has a climate of its own. Visitors invariably find it invigorating, like perpetual spring. Great, cleansing drafts from the Pacific set the air atingle. Since temperatures seldom rise above 75 F. or drop below 45 F., cool-weather clothing is comfortable for both summer and winter. The steady inshore breezes and summer fog combine to act as natural air conditioners and to give the city a sea-washed look. Even the fog can be exciting, tumbling and boiling over the coastal hills, as it sometimes does, in a 1,700-foot-high bank, or rushing in a single tendril down the center of the Bay.

San Francisco is the financial and insurance capital of the West, a dominant port in world trade and "The City" to the whole of Northern and Central California. The Pacific Coast's economic pulse can be felt along canyonlike Montgomery Street and read on the big board of the Stock Exchange at 301 Pine Street. Lower California Street, one block north, is the core of the shipping and banking industries. The reason for the city's international reputation for chic is readily apparent in the shopping district, the area of smart shops and equally smart shoppers fanning out around Union Square. The local flair for living is dramatically reflected in the show windows and showrooms of the Jackson Square quarter, where home furnishings wholesalers, retailers, and decorators have transformed a portion of the old Barbary Coast into a uniquely picturesque business enclave. It is also evident along outer Union Street, beyond Van Ness, where imaginative merchants have reclaimed old Cow Hollow residences, carriage houses, and barns.

Like all major business centers, San Francisco has many "bedrooms"; the city is the hub of a nine-county complex, and on workdays commuters pour into the city by train, bus, car and boat from Marin County to the north, the East Bay, and the Peninsula to the south. To them you can add a steady ebb and flow of out-of-state visitors.

Some of the best places for you to savor this maritime center's salty flavor are along the Embarcadero, where ships of all flags are constantly disgorging cargo; beside the Fisherman's Wharf lagoon in the late morning when the fishing fleet puts in; and looking shoreward from the deck of one of the sightseeing boats that cast off at frequent intervals from Pier 41. A backward glance at San Francisco's romantic seafaring past is possible at the National Maritime Museum at Aquatic Park, aboard the museum's three-masted *Balclutha* at Pier 43, or the turn-of-the-century coastal vessels berthed at Hyde Street Pier.

Across the street from the National Maritime Museum is Ghirardelli Square, a fascinating collection of shops, galleries, restaurants, and plazas concocted out of a 19th-century chocolate factory. Nearby at Fisherman's Wharf is The Cannery, a comparable complex housed in an old fruit-processing plant. A look at "The Coast" in Gold Rush days can be had at the Wells Fargo History Room at 420 Montgomery Street.

A significant clue to San Francisco's character is the fact that nearly one out of every two (44.3 percent) of the Bay Area's inhabitants was born outside of the U.S. or has at least one parent of foreign stock. The city known variously as the Paris of the West, Baghdad-by-the-Bay, Great City of the Golden Hill, and the Gateway to the Orient has some 30 foreign-language newspapers. Its culture has been enriched by the traditions and folkways of countless ethnic groups. Its cuisine is legend-

Points of Interest

1) Alcoa Building
2) Balclutha
3) Bank of America
4) Cannery
5) City Hall
6) Civic Center
7) Coit Tower
8) Curran Theater
9) Embarcadero Center
10) Ferry Building
11) Fisherman's Wharf
12) Flood Building
13) Geary Theater
14) George R. Moscone Convention Center
15) Golden Gate Center
16) Grace Cathedral
17) Hilton Hotel
18) Hyatt Hotel
19) Hyde Street Pier
20) Lotta's Fountain
21) Maritime Museum
22) Municipal Pier
23) Museum of Modern Art
24) Old U.S. Mint
25) Opera House
26) Pier 39
27) St. Mary's Cathedral
28) St. Patrick's Church
29) Stock Exchange
30) Transamerica Pyramid
31) Victorian Park
32) Visitor Information Center

ary. For those with an appetite for the exotic, there are restaurants serving the foods of France, Germany, Greece, Scandinavia, Russia, Italy, Switzerland, Spain, the near East, India, China, Japan, Polynesia, and Latin America.

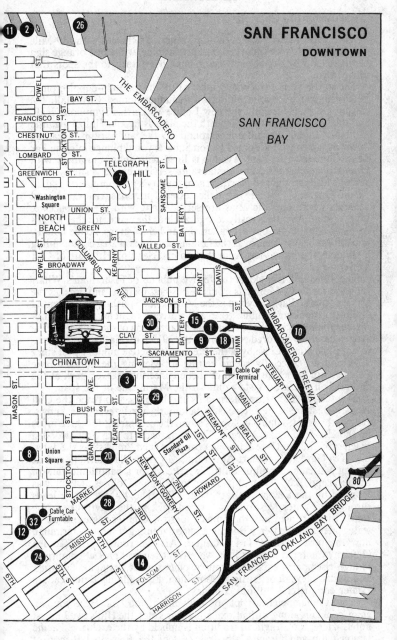

There are three distinct and captivating cities within the city: China-town, the largest settlement of its kind outside of Asia; North Beach, San Francisco's "Little Italy"; and Japantown, in the Post-Buchanan Streets sector, landmarked by the $15-million Japan Center.

Following the Seagull

An excellent introduction to San Francisco's charms is the 49-Mile Scenic Drive. It's well-marked. Follow the blue, white and orange sign of the seagull by car or sightseeing bus, then return to the spots that intrigue you.

The starting point is Civic Center, where the fountain-dappled plaza is surrounded by public buildings, including domed City Hall, the elegant Opera House and the new Louise M. Davies Symphony Hall, and the Civic Auditorium. Beneath the plaza is Brooks Hall, a gigantic exhibition arena linked underground to the auditorium. Heading downtown past well-groomed Union Square, you'll plunge into the Far East. Chinatown's Grant Avenue is lined with shops crammed with Oriental merchandise, and restaurants serving exotic dishes. Grant Avenue leads straight to North Beach, the city's predominantly Italian "Latin Quarter," dotted with delicatessens, pizzerias, ristorantes and cabarets where operatic arias are served along with the *Cappuccino*. Upper Grant Avenue is easily recognizable as the center for the Beach's free spirits by its far-out art galleries, handicraft shops, coffee houses, and offbeat bistros. Nearby is the famous observation area commanding a fabulous four-way view from the top of Telegraph Hill, site of Coit Tower.

The 49-Mile Drive skirts the festive hubbub of Fisherman's Wharf (best approach: by Muni bus from the business district) and brushes the Bay at Aquatic Park. Beyond is the Marina, a Spanish-style residential stretch overlooking a public green and a private yacht harbor. Continuing on, you'll catch sight of the terra-cotta rotunda of the Palace of Fine Arts, a carefully restored souvenir of the 1915 Panama-Pacific International Exposition. Close by is the Presidio, an active military post since 1776 and an especially scenic setting for viewing the Golden Gate Bridge. (For closer inspection of this engineering marvel, park at the Bridge Toll Plaza or Vista Point on the Marin side of the span.)

Eventually, via northwestern cliffs and beaches, you reach the Cliff House. Offshore is Seal Rocks, a landmark nearly everyone knows. Below, the Great Highway sweeps along the oceanfront for three miles to the Zoo and Lake Merced. Doubling back to the vast, wooded reaches of Golden Gate Park, you can visit such "musts" as the Japanese Tea Garden, Steinhart Aquarium, Morrison Planetarium, and de Young Museum. Continue on to Twin Peaks for a panoramic view of the city and Bay. Then dip down to Mission Dolores, which was founded by the Franciscan fathers in 1776. The 49-Mile Drive leads through the outer Mission district and back to the Bayfront via the James Lick Freeway and the Embarcadero. The latter passes the deep-water piers and the Ferry Building, once a teeming trans-Bay terminal, now the port's World Trade Center. Also en route is the Golden Gateway Center, a $150-million waterfront-renewal project comprised of high-rise apartments, townhouses, office towers, shopping facilities, and parks. Next door is the $150-million, five-building Embarcadero Center commercial-cultural complex.

From the financial district you may climb Nob Hill. Here you can enjoy cocktails along with intoxicating views atop the Hill's two highest hotels. Here, too, Anglican tradition is upheld by the exclusive Pacific Union Club and Grace Cathedral, seat of the Episcopal Bishop of California. The route back to City Hall, completing the loop, includes Gough Street's Victorian dwellings and the architecturally dramatic St. Mary's Cathedral, at Gough and O'Farrell Streets.

San Francisco's compactness is an advantage to sightseers; much of it can be seen conveniently on foot. It's a mistake, though, to try to telescope everything into a quick visit; there's too much to see and do. The 49-Mile Drive is a good preface, but there's much more to the San Francisco story. Russian Hill, for example, is laced with wooden lanes, and Pacific Heights is lined with fine mansions. The Powell and Mason and the Powell and Hyde cable-car lines returned to service in mid-1984 after a 20-month renovation. Both the Golden Gate and Bay bridges should be crossed, and the attractions of the opposite shores explored—not the least of which are Marin County's Mediterranean-like boating communities, with their many open-deck restaurants.

The East Bay Area

Even the casual observer would be amazed at how much the East Bay has changed within the past decade. Once the poor stepchild of San Francisco, Oakland has added some major attractions of its own. The Port of Oakland boasts excellent facilities. The attractive, huge Alameda sports complex is home to professional football and the Oakland Athletics. The arts are represented by the Oakland Museum, which is significant, and the Oakland Symphony, which has a beautiful performing center. Lake Merritt, in the heart of downtown Oakland, has excellent facilities; boats may be rented, and special events are held frequently.

Berkeley, Oakland's next-door neighbor, is the site of the magnificent University of California. Its impressive buildings include the Lawrence Hall of Science, Lowie Museum of Anthropology, and the University Art Museum.

The North Side of San Francisco Bay

Drive across the Golden Gate Bridge and you're in a different world. Sausalito (Little Willow) is situated on the Mediterranean side of the Golden Gate, eight miles north of San Francisco. Its rustic houses cascade down steep slopes to the bay; its shops and restaurants hug the waterfront; its winding, wooded streets look down on a thicket of masts and a colony of houseboats.

For the adventurous, Helicoptours suggests a new 30-minute, 100-mile aerial sweep of Sausalito, Tiburon, and Belvedere Island, plus low-level viewing of both the Oakland Bay and Golden Gate bridges, Alcatraz, and Fisherman's Wharf.

Tiburon (Shark) lies eight miles east of Sausalito on Raccoon Strait. Its villagelike Main Street is a blend of Cape Cod and early California. Its colorful harbor shelters the venerable Corinthian Yacht Club and a cluster of open-deck restaurants.

Angel Island (California's only island state park) looms like a pocket-size Corsica seven-eighths of a mile across the Raccoon Strait from Tiburon. The bay's biggest island, Angel has a crescent cove leading to a grassy rise, with picnic tables and 12 miles of roads and hiking trails.

To the delight of commuters, shoppers, and joyriders, the *Golden Gate* operates round trips daily year-round. The blue-and-white cruiser casts off from the north side of the San Francisco Ferry Building, at the foot of Market Street. She comes about in the shadow of the San Francisco-Oakland Bay Bridge, skirts the towering hulls of liners loading along the Embarcadero, and then strikes a course past Alcatraz. The crossing takes 30 minutes. Snacks are served on the saloon deck, and the bar is open all day. In Marin County, passengers disembark into the town plaza, a few steps from Sausalito's mainstream, Bridgeway.

San Francisco's inland sea resorts are apt to be as crowded as Carmel on weekends. The best time to sample the charms of the Willow, the Shark, and the Angel is during the week.

PRACTICAL INFORMATION
FOR SAN FRANCISCO

TOURIST INFORMATION SERVICES. General information is available from *San Francisco Convention and Visitors Bureau,* 201 Third; (414) 974–6900. For bus tours, contact: *Gray Line of San Francisco,* 420 Taylor St., San Francisco.

HOW TO GET AROUND. *By foot:* San Francisco is surprisingly compact. Many of its most interesting sights are within easy walking distance of each other. From Union Square, it's an easy stroll through Chinatown to Jackson Square and North Beach—and wherever you are there are things to see.

By car: If you are driving your car during your stay in San Francisco, there are three points to remember: 1) cable cars have the right of way, 2) cars parked on any grade or hill must have wheels set to the curb to prevent rolling, 3) watch parking signs—there are many tow-away zones during certain hours, and cars parked illegally are towed away.

By bus: The most economical ways to reach points in the city beyond walking distance are cable cars, street cars and buses. Bus maps are at the front of the Yellow Pages in the telephone book. Transfers are available at many points.

Beyond the city limits, trains and buses will carry you most anyplace. The *Bay Area Rapid Transit System* (BART) is now in operation; *Greyhound* offers regular commuter service to most points. *AC Bus Transit System* operates between San Francisco and many points in the East Bay.

By ferry: MV *Golden Gate* makes 10 round trips weekdays, seven on weekends and holidays, between Sausalito and San Francisco. The Tiburon-San Francisco commuter run is covered by ferries of *Harbor Tours, Inc.,* Pier 43 ½; it takes 35 min. Harbor Tours also operates cruises around the bay all year round. From April to October, the feature is the champagne dinner cruise from San Francisco to Tiburon on Thursday evenings.

By bridge: San Francisco-Oakland Bay Bridge is the world's longest: over eight miles. Golden Gate Bridge, accessible to autos and pedestrians, links San Francisco and the north.

By cable car: The city's 110-year-old cable car system reopened in 1984, after a 20-month, $60 million rehabilitation. Both the Powell–Mason (#59) and the Powell–Hyde (#60) terminate at Fisherman's Wharf. The California (#61) runs east–west from the Hyatt Regency to Van Ness Avenue. Fare: $1.00; free transfer.

MUSEUMS AND GALLERIES. There are four major art museums in the city. In the Civic Center is the *San Francisco Museum of Art,* which frequently changes exhibits. The *M. H. deYoung Museum* is in Golden Gate Park. Its spacious galleries enclose a landscaped court. Included are paintings by Rembrandt, El Greco, Titian and Rubens. Visit the new American Galleries, incorporating the collection of John D. Rockefeller III. The installation was planned by Alfred Frankenstein. Adjoining Asian Art Museum displays some of its priceless Brundage Collection and additional Asian treasures.

The *California Palace of the Legion of Honor* is in Lincoln Park, at the end of California Street. Emphasis on French paintings, sculpture, it offers a magnificent view of the city from the terrace. There's a small restaurant. The world-famous Achenbach Foundation for Graphic Arts is also housed in the Legion of Honor. The *Oakland Art Museum,* 10th and Oak Streets, displays a large collection of California art, including early engravings by the Spanish explorers, and Gold Rush paintings. Be sure to visit its new *Natural Sciences Gallery,* with special exhibits.

Arts and crafts may be seen at the Union Street galleries, between several unusual restaurants. *The Museum Shop,* on Fillmore near Union, is a tempting bazaar of one-of-a-kind treasures from the four corners. *Urban Antiques,* 1861 Union St., an old-fashioned fantasy of collectibles from art pottery to advertising memorabilia.

Other kinds of exhibits may be seen at the following museums: *Wells Fargo History Room,* in the Wells Fargo Bank at 420 Montgomery St., has a varied collection of objects that figured in the development of the West. There is the *Academy of Sciences* in Golden Gate Park, housing a collection of American and African mammal specimens, as well as the *Steinhart Aquarium,* with its Fish Roundabout, *Wattis Hall of Man and Planetarium.* The *Maritime Museum,* at the foot of Polk St., has seafaring exhibits with model ships, old figureheads, etc. *The Guinness Museum of World Records,* 235 Jefferson, is the newest museum at Fisherman's Wharf and will impress visitors of all ages.

The *Balclutha* is a museum ship, last of the square-sail fleet that sailed around Cape Horn to San Francisco in the late 19th century. Exhibits aboard include photo displays and relics. *Museo Italo Americano,* 678 Green St., exhibits 19th- and 20th-century works by Italian–American artists. Free. Wed–Sun., noon–5.The *Mexican Museum,* Fort Mason, is devoted exclusively to Mexican art. The *California Historical Society,* 2090 Jackson St., has a library and small museum housed in an 1896 red sandstone mansion.

HISTORIC SITES. San Francisco itself has the *Presidio,* the *Mission Dolores,* and the *Opera House,* important because it was the site of the official organization of the United Nations. *Fort Point National Site* offers guided tours of this Civil War station, a military museum, and is open daily. *Portsmouth Square* is a small historic park in Chinatown, where the U.S. flag was raised in July 1846. Short trips outside the city will take you to a few other historic spots. *Ft. Ross* is one. Ten miles north of the junction of State Highways 1 and 12 at Jenner, north of San Francisco, it is a 19th-century fort that was used by Russian fur traders. It's contained within a redwood stockade.

GARDENS. The sidewalk flower stands of San Francisco have been a tradition since the 1880s. Specialties are daphne in the spring, tiny Pinocchio roses in summer, chrysanthemums in fall and holly in winter. At Golden Gate Park, see the *Japanese Tea Garden,* with its camellias, magnolias and redleafed Japanese maples. It's a fairyland of cherry blossoms in the spring (usually at their best in early April). See also the *Conservatory.* Modeled after Kew Gardens in England, it's a fascinating hothouse in a fascinating setting—the sections of the building were brought around Cape Horn by clipper ship. Out front, a floral design honors contemporary events of local or national importance.

In Woodside, visit Filoli, a 16-acre estate operated by the National Trust. Phone 364–2880 for reservations. Tours are given by knowledgeable docents, who are able to identify most of the trees and plants.

In Watsonville, see *Rod McLellan Gardens,* at 2352 San Juan Road. There are orchids as far as the eye can see, as well as greenhouses filled with carnations, gardenias, anthuriums and poinsettias, all aligned in uniform rows under laboratory-like conditions. The gardens at *Sunset Magazine,* Menlo Park (down the Peninsula), have all the outstanding trees, shrubs and flowers native to all sections of the Pacific coast. There are tours, or you can stroll about on your own.

An hour south of San Francisco, visit Saratoga's Hakone gardens—a Japanese fantasy—and Villa Montalvo, a cultural center with formal gardens, amphitheater, and galleries.

TOURS. *Gray Line* offers a deluxe 3½-hour city tour of San Francisco several times daily; a *Chinatown Dinner Tour* and a *Chinatown After Dark* tour (nightly, all year); a tour across the Golden Gate Bridge to *Muir Woods,* the nearest redwood grove to San Francisco (daily, all year); a *Three-Bridge* tour combining Muir Woods and Oakland and Berkeley (daily in summer, three times a week the rest of the year); *Monterey-Carmel* and the *17-Mile Drive* (daily in summer, three times a week otherwise); a tour of the *Valley of the Moon* wine country April 1–Oct. 15 (three times a week); a *Night Life Party,* all year (except New Year's Eve). Gray Line also offers four-day tours combining *Yosemite, Monterey, and Carmel,* weekly, all year (reservations required).

The *Red & White Fleet* has been cruising the Bay since 1890. Its sightseeing boats make short (1¼-hour) cruises around San Francisco Bay constantly, every day, all year round. Departures are from Fisherman's Wharf. Weekly, from late April through October, one of the boats makes a Champagne Dinner Cruise to Tiburon, fare including the round-trip ferryboat ride, champagne party on board and dinner at your choice of excellent Tiburon restaurants.

Classic Wine Tours offers a full day of tasting and touring with guides trained in wine appreciation and history. Gourmet luncheon; luxury vans. Phone 391–8585 for information.

MUSIC. All year, there are free *band concerts* in San Francisco's Golden Gate Park on Sunday and holiday afternoons. Free jazz concerts in the Atrium Lobby of the Hyatt Regency; weekends. *San Francisco Opera* has two seasons; a 13-week international season which begins in mid-Sept. and the summer international season beginning in June. Tickets are extremely difficult to get; especially in fall. Phone 864–3330. *San Francisco Symphony,* Davies Hall, Civic Center, plays from September thru May. Internationally acclaimed guest conductors, vocalists, violinists, and pianists attract faithful followers. Tickets are scarce; phone 431–5400. During July and August, the symphony can be heard in a lighter role—in pops concerts. Sunday afternoons in summer, there's free opera, symphony or ballet in the *Sigmund Stern Grove,* out past Golden Gate Park, and also chamber music concerts at the *Paul Masson Vineyards* high on a mountaintop in Saratoga (down the Peninsula). *The Trident,* in Sausalito, presents jazz sessions every Sunday afternoon. This is a charming waterfront spot, open for luncheon, dinner and cocktails.

STAGE AND REVUES. The *American Conservatory Theater,* Geary Theater, is a resident repertory company with a regular season extending from late October into May. Both the Curran and Golden Gate Theaters offer the best-of-Broadway musicals and drama, as will the Orpheum, former home of the defunct Civic Light Opera. In June, the *San Francisco Ballet* takes part in the Summer Festival.

NIGHTCLUBS. Remember the fame of North Beach's Broadway, where Carol Doda established the decade of "topless" entertainment. Today, the area has slipped several more notches to its all-time low with seedy "encounter parlors" brash barkers and fellow misfits. Except for several long-time fine Italian restaurants and the perennial favorite, *Finocchio's* with its female impersonators, the area draws few nighttime strollers.

Night life is alive and well, however, in other parts of the city.

For sophisticated revues and name entertainers, try the elegant *Venetian Room* at the *Fairmont.* This is the town's top supper club—expensive, and reservations are a must. The town's top jazz palaces include *Kimball's, Earthquake McGoon's, Pier 23 Embarcadero, Wolfgang's,* and *The Palms.*

Escape to the *St. Francis' Oz*—a wizard of a disco; exotic décor, onyx dance floor. Discover tea dancing on Fridays at the *Hyatt Regency.*

For Greek folk dancing, seek out the *Greek Taverna.*

BARS. San Francisco is a city of super saloons. Each bar seems to radiate a special style. Take *Lord Jim's,* on Polk and Broadway. It's a dazzle of Boston ferns, original London pub mirrors, Victorian love seats, and acres of Tiffany glass. Add premium spirits, wine and beer, an eclectic audience and a charming, dynamic Greek proprietor. Result—a special watering hole.

Or the famed *Perry's.* A wall to wall people experience. Besides the fine libations, popular for tasty breakfasts and anytime cheeseburger.

For Irish coffee buffs, the *BV (Buena Vista)* is Mecca. Over 1,400 are served daily.

Gino and Carlo, 548 Green St., considered by many North Beach locals to be the most solid of mainstream Italian bars. Strong drinks, pool table, loud conversations.

The *Hyatt Regency's Equinox* is an 18-story-high revolving lounge with sensational viewing.

History majors survey the life-size portrait of Commodore Dewey surveying the scene at the *St. Francis' Dewey's,* in the Hotel St. Francis on Union Square. New is the *Compass Rose,* their art- and antique-filled restaurant-bar rendezvous.

Lefty O'Doul's is a family spot featuring a photo gallery of sports figures and a sing-along piano bar.

In North Beach, a favorite with media, political, and theatrical names is the *Washington Square Bar & Grill.* Ghirardelli Square's *Maxwell's Plum* is a Holywood-spangled production.

 SUMMER SPORTS. *Golf:* Among the many fine courses that dot the San Francisco region is the Olympic Club, one of the best in the nation. There are five public golf courses: Harding Park, Lincoln Park, Golden Gate Park, Sharp Park in Pacifica, and McLaren Park, Sunnydale, between Brookdale and Persia.

Tennis: There are more than a hundred tennis courts throughout the city. For information call McLaren Lodge: 415–558–3706. With the exception of the 21 courts located in Golden Gate Park, all are free.

Sailing: San Francisco offers sailing all year round, and there's also sailing in the Oakland Estuary, and on Lake Merced, Lake Merritt, Richardson Bay, and Tomales Bay, as well as at Palo Alto and Redwood City.

Fishing: Just go casting off San Francisco's municipal pier at Aquatic Park (all year, no license), or try Fort Mason, Piers 2 & 3.

 SPECTATOR SPORTS. Professional matches may be seen year-round: *football* games of the San Francisco 49ers in Oakland; the Giants and A's play *baseball* games; *basketball* matches feature the Warriors; and the Seals have *hockey* games. The Annual Open *Skeet and Trap Shoot* of the Pacific Rod and Gun Club takes place at Lake Merced in late April. For *horse racing,* Bay Meadows is the busiest race track in the west, with almost 200 days of racing each year—harness racing in winter; spring quarterhorse racing. There is also racing in the East Bay at Golden Gate Fields from February to June. See the Annual Pacific Coast International.

May headlines the *San Francisco Examiner* Bay to Breakers Race thru San Francisco to Ocean Beach.

Opening Day *yachting* parade is held the first Sunday in May. In addition, the Yacht Racing Association holds about 20 races a year, most of them in the Bay. Good vantage points are along the Marina or the Vista View area on the Sausalito side of the Golden Gate Bridge. *Tennis Championships* at the Berkeley Tennis CLub in September. *Rodeo* buffs will want to see the Grand National, in October.

SHOPPING. Try *Podesta & Baldocchi,* 2525 California, a floral shop that came to the rescue of the sidewalk flower vendors when they were threatened with extinction some years ago. It's always a fantasyland, especially during the Christmas season. The Grant Avenue shops and bazaars in Chinatown are fascinating, with their plastic jade and ivory-like collectibles, brocade material, basketry, and teak furniture.

Union Square and its environs is the center of an extensive, smart shopping area that includes large department stores and specialty shops for both men and women. *Alfred Dunhill, Bullock Jones, I. Magnin, Macy's,* and *Saks Fifth Avenue,* plus the new architecturally controversial *Neiman-Marcus.* On Post Street nearby are several luxury shops, including *Gump's, Shreve's, Brooks Brothers, Gucci, Celine,* and *Mark Cross.* They're all in the "200" block of Post. Gump's is unique for exotic and useful imports, with heavy accent on the Oriental (ask to see the jade collection, worth, in individual pieces, up to $100,000. It is kept behind locked doors but will be shown to anyone interested.). This store got its start as a bric-a-brac shop!

Fisherman's Wharf's 12 million yearly visitors have a new experience touring Pier 39, a $29-million turn-of-the-century showcase of over 100 shops, 20-plus restaurants, and marinas. Several interesting shops are located at The Cannery and Ghirardelli Square, which are must-sees. For *antiques,* try the Jackson Square area, Union Street, between Franklin and Steiner, and upper Sacramento Street. Among the best: *The Dolphin, John Doughty, Dillingham & Co., Bauer, Postlethwaite, Arbes, Fenton.* Auction aficionados seek out *Butterfield's,* 1244 Sutter St.; for information on upcoming sales, phone 673–1362.

For *fine art,* Sutter Street has several important galleries: *Walton-Gilbert, Maxwell, Wortsman Stewart, Galerie De Tours,* and, nearby, *John Berggruen,* and *Hansen.* Also worth a visit are *Vorpal* and *Conacher* galleries. You can also buy a thousand paintings of San Francisco, but many of them are turned out in assembly-line fashion.

Haagen-Dazs, 2066 Union, serves fabulous ice cream. And be sure to try a good selection of California wines; some of the best can be purchased only here in San Francisco or at the wineries; estate-bottled classics.

WHAT TO DO WITH THE CHILDREN. Stroll across the *Golden Gate Bridge.* Try to time your walk to coincide with the sailing of a ship beneath. Then you'll realize how very high you are (220 feet) and how very huge the bridge is. Take them aboard the *Balclutha,* the handsome old three-masted sailing ship near Fisherman's Wharf. They'll enjoy inspecting the wheelhouse, the red-plush chart house, the captain's cabin and the ship's galley. Take them *sailing* on easy-to-navigate Lake Merritt in Oakland or Lake Merced in San Francisco. Tour the *Fire Department Museum,* 655 Presidio Ave., displaying historical engines and memorabilia.

Take them to the *San Francisco Zoo.* Sightsee via the Zebra Zephyr, which makes frequent departures from the Giraffe Barn. Show them the buffalo in the paddock at Golden Gate Park; the buffalo seem to be roaming at large. If the children are very young, visit *Storyland,* with permanent exhibits including the Gingerbread House, Cinderella's Coach and the Old Lady's Shoe. (Storyland is open weekends January through mid-March; daily at other times.)

Marina Green is a grassy waterfront recreation area with a beautiful view of the Bay. *James D. Phelan Beach,* at 28th and Sea Cliff Avenues, is a six-acre park with beach frontage; it's a great place for sunbathing and picnics. Ocean Beach has plenty of sand and surf with a superb view.

HOTELS AND MOTELS. San Francisco's accommodations are many and varied. Catering to a wide variety of tastes, they range all over the compact city. San Francisco is a very popular city with tourists and convention groups, so be sure to reserve your rooms as soon as your travel plans are set.

Hotel rates are based on double occupancy. E.P. Categories determined by price start *up* from following price figures: *Super deluxe:* $100 and up; *Deluxe:* $80–100; *Expensive:* $70–79; *Moderate:* $60–69; *Inexpensive:* under $59. For a more complete explanation of hotel and motel categories, see *Facts at Your Fingertips* at the front of this volume. *Note:* Scheduled to be open in 1985 are the *Monach* at Fisherman's Wharf and the 32-story *Ramada Renaissance* near the downtown Airport Bus Terminal.

Super Deluxe: **Campton Place.** 340 Stockton. Luxurious. Elegant dining.

Clift/Four Seasons. Geary St. At Taylor. Restaurant, bar.

Fairmont Hotel and Tower. Atop Nob Hill at California and Mason. Restaurant, bar.

Hyatt on Union Square. Stockton and Post. Restaurant. Family plan.

Hyatt Regency San Francisco. 5 Embarcadero Center. Family plan. Atrium lobby, health club.

Meridien. 50 Third Street. New, French managed.

Ramada Renaissance. 55 Cyril Magnin St., two blocks from Union Square. New, 32-story luxury hotel.

Stanford Court. Nob Hill at California and Powell. Family plan. The city's most elegant.

Westin St. Francis. Union Square. International clientele.

Deluxe: **Holiday Inn—Union Square.** 480 Sutter. Movies. Free parking. Pets.

Huntington. 1075 California. Restaurant, bar. Kitchenettes.

Mark Hopkins. 1 Nob Hill at California and Mason. Family plan.

Marriot Fisherman's Wharf. New, fine dining in the elegant *Wellington's.*

Miyako. 1625 Post. Japantown. Sauna.

Sheraton at Fisherman's Wharf. Heated pool, restaurant, discotheque, bar.

Expensive: **Handlery Motor Inn.** 260 O'Farrell. Family plan. Pool.

Holiday Inn—Fisherman's Wharf. 1300 Columbus Ave. Family plan. Pool.

Kyoto Inn. 1800 Sutter. Japantown. Free parking.

The Mansion. 2220 Sacramento. Victorian hide-away.

Pacific Plaza. 501 Post Street. Elegant European ambience. Fine dining in "Donatello."

Sheraton Palace. 639 Market at New Montgomery. Family plan. Pets.

Sir Francis Drake. 450 Powell. Family plan.

TraveLodge at the Wharf. 250 Beach. Family plan. Pool.

Moderate: **Bedford.** 761 Post St. Central location, international clientele.

Beresford. 635 Sutter. Pets. Downtown.

Californian. 405 Taylor. Family plan.

Canterbury. 750 Sutter. Pets. *Lehr's Greenhouse* Restaurant.

Cartwright. 524 Sutter. One block from Union Square and shopping.

Chancellor. 433 Powell. Steps from cable cars.

Commodore International. 825 Sutter. Near Union Square.

Manx. 225 Powell. Movies. Family plan.

Mark Twain. 345 Taylor. Downtown, near theaters.

"New" York Hotel. 940 Sutter. Good location; refurbished with great charm.

Raphael. 386 Geary. New English pub, **Rosebud's,** adjacent.

Savoy. 580 Geary. Victorian ambience. Convenient.

Stewart. 351 Geary. Free parking. Pool.

Inexpensive: **Abigail.** 246 McAllister. Newly renovated, near Civic Center. English tea room.

Golden State. 114 Powell. Kitchenettes.

King George. 334 Mason, a block to Union Square. Tea room.

Oxford. Mason & Market. Downtown. Drive-in parking.

Victorian. 54 Fourth St. Near Moscone Convention Center.

Yerba Buena. 55 Fifth St. European style, brass beds in every room. Excellent value.

Embarcadero Y.M.C.A. Center. Men & women. 166 the Embarcadero. Pool, athletic facilities.

 DINING OUT. San Francisco's more than 2,600 restaurants offer visitors a round-the-world ticket to dining pleasure. Practically every ethnic taste can be satisfied at every price range. Among the unique regional foods to be sampled are abalone, Dungeness crabs, sand dabs, bay shrimp, crusty sourdough French bread, artichoke dishes and excellent cheeses. All these may be accompanied by fine California wines from vineyards within an hour and a half of the city.

Restaurants are listed according to the price of a complete dinner (drinks, tax and tip not included) starting *up* from following figures; *Super deluxe:* $30 and up; *Deluxe:* $25–$30; *Expensive:* $20–$25; *Moderate:* $12.50–$20; *Inexpensive:* under $12.50. À la carte will, of course, be more expensive. Add 50% to complete dinner prices above for à la carte super deluxe, deluxe, and expensive categories; double the price for moderate and inexpensive categories.

Deluxe: **Ernie's.** 847 Montgomery St. Lavishly decorated in Victorian era. Consistently hits the heights of culinary achievement. Unusually fine wine list.

Fournou's Ovens. Stanford Court Hotel. Continental; notable rack of lamb.

The French Room. Four Seasons Clift Hotel. Elegant; Legendary Sunday Brunch.

Imperial Palace. 919 Grant Ave. The most elegant and exclusive Chinese restaurant in the U.S.

L'Etoile. 1075 California. Superb French food, elegant decor, service.

Victor's. The Westin St. Francis. Outstanding California cuisine and wines.

Expensive: **Amelio's.** 1630 Powell St. Very posh. Northern Italian tradition is well served. Superb pasta is a special favorite.

Bentley's. 185 Sutter. Oyster bar and seafood specialties.

Donatello. Pacific Plaza Hotel. 501 Post. Elegant Italian dining.

Empress of China. 838 Grant Ave. Elegant Chinatown spot.

Gaylord. Ghirardelli Square. Northern Indian cuisine; Bay view; handsome decor.

Harris. 2100 Van Ness. Prime ribs and steaks served in an elegant atmosphere.

Jack's. 615 Sacramento St. This restaurant has been a civic landmark for 100 years. Very tasty American specialties are the featured fare.

Le Castel. 3235 Sacramento St. Superb food; expensive wines. Reservations.

Le Central. 453 Bush Street. Very popular bistro in financial district.

Le Trianon. 242 O'Farrell. Former White House chef's masterful cuisine.

Mandarin. 900 North Point (in Ghirardelli Square). Not only the best Chinese restaurant but the prettiest as well. The kitchen specializes in dishes from the Peking/Nanking axis; it's an inventive and challenging menu. Lovely view of the bay.

Maxwell's Plum. Ghirardelli Square. Lavish decor; view.

Modesto Lanzone's. 601 Van Ness. Opera Plaza. New; Italian specialties

Scott's. 2400 Lombard. Seafood, popular. No reservations. Suggest off-hour dining. New is **Scott's** at Embarcadero III.

Tadich Grill. 240 California. Steak, seafood.

Trader Vic's. 20 Cosmo Place. A San Francisco institution. Consistently excellent Polynesian food makes it still very much *the* place to have lunch. Lethal rum drinks are deservedly famous.

Moderate: **Castagnola.** 289 Jefferson St. on Fisherman's Wharf. Seafood.

New San Remo. 2237 Mason. Renovated Victorian serving seafood and Italian specialties.

North Beach. 1512 Stockton St. Italian food. Also **Basta Pasta,** 1238 Grant Ave., their new fish and pasta scene.

Sam's. 347 Bush. Downtown landmark. Superb fish. Dinner till 8:30 P.M. Reservations please.

Schroeder's. 240 Front St. German cuisine.

Scoma's. Pier 47 (at the foot of Jones St.). Make reservations well in advance. Don't leave the city without trying the Olympia oysters and the incredible crabs.

Vanessi's. 498 Broadway. Continental-American menu.

Washington Square Bar & Grill. 1707 Powell. Popular North Beach spot; saloon atmosphere. Fresh fish; pasta experts.

Yamoto. 717 California St. Perhaps the best Japanese restaurant in town. Serene, understated décor. Swift, deferential service. Superb sushi.

Inexpensive: **Hamburger Mary's.** 1582 Folsom. Funky décor; multimix of patrons. Great hamburgers.

Zuni Cafe. 1658 Market. Eclectic menu; very popular.

Enrico's. 504 Broadway. Salads, sandwiches.

Hog Heaven. 770 Stanyan St. Near Golden Gate Park. Memphis-style barbeque; funky porky art décor.

Salmagundi. Four locations. 442 Geary St., theatre district. Gourmet soups, salad, quiche, wines.

Tommy's Joynt. 1101 Geary St. Hofbrau, beer from 26 countries.

Also in the *Inexpensive* category are dozens of interesting Chinese restaurants in Chinatown, including *Tung Fong,* 808 Pacific; *Clay; Canton Tea House,* 1108 Stockton; and many others on Jackson, Clay and Washington, off Grant. All offer mostly Chinese cuisine in the Cantonese style, with individual dishes from $1.50 to $3 and up. Several good, inexpensive restaurants border the Japanese Cultural Center. Many of the Chinese restaurants in this category also can provide a good, filling Chinese rice dish from around $2.50.

Bay Park's 4,600-acre aquatic wonderland is a city-ow
between La Jolla and San Diego. The bay area, the mar
grassy, tree-lined coves, and the resort hotels offer boating
fishing, water-skiing, golfing, camping and trailer sites. Sea
ne of the highlights at Mission Bay. Trained dolphins per-
Theater of the Sea. Also on exhibit are elephant seals,
ler whales and demonstrations by Japanese pearl divers.
, take a skyride, a hydrofoil ride, and view the new $7
nguin Encounter.

rt of Palm Springs sprawls in the Colorado Desert, south-
Colorado's desert lands. With 39 grass golf courses, it has
own as the "Golf Capital of the World," attracting political
and television stars. The Chamber of Commerce issues a
e than 100 Hollywood celebrities living in Palm Springs.

ack Country"

California's "back country," as it is called, is Indian coun-
ate 8, heading inland from San Diego and at times touching
an Border, received a rating among veteran travel editors as
most scenic highways they had seen. Indians once warred
arm sulphur springs that still pour out 300,000 gallons daily
rner Springs Guest Ranch.
Varner Springs it's a 30-mile climb to the world's biggest
on Palomar Mountain. The giant silver dome is 12 stories
telescope, which can be viewed from a glassed-in balcony
eight stories high and weighs 500 tons. The 200-inch Hale
s so delicately mounted that a slight push can move it.
perial Valley, with El Centro as its largest city, claims the
pulation on earth living below sea level. Salton Sea sparkles
l Valley where crops are harvested in midwinter. Lush green
f alfalfa thrive in December. Farmers here get seven cuttings
rly. Winter farms are blue with flax flowers, red with mass
f tomatoes and carrots, and white with cotton. Melons go east
ads. In this area you'll frequently drive across irrigation
ich extend for more miles than the highways. It seldom rains
eys; schools may declare a "mud holiday" when a rare, heavy

and northward you'll explore the San Joaquin Valley, where
crops grow under irrigation. Cotton and potato fields and
eyards stretch by the mile. During harvest time the potatoes
the trainloads. During the early winter cotton harvest you
a cotton ball for a souvenir, follow a "train" of cotton trailers
watch seeds being picked from crops.
the northern part of the San Joaquin at Bakersfield, it's an
along California 178 to the Sierra Nevada Mountains. The
Lone Pine looks up at Mt. Whitney, 14,495 feet high, and
the United States only by peaks in Alaska. Close by are Mt.
on, 14,384 feet, Mt. Russell, 14,190 feet, and Mt. Muir, 14,015
ail which cost $25,000 to build climbs Mt. Whitney from the
auto road at Whitney Portal. Each summer thousands make
o the "attic" of the continental U.S., a near-plateau of three
res at the summit.

of Los Angeles

of Los Angeles and a few miles inland you'll find lemon groves
the valleys. The world's largest lemon grove, 1,800 acres, is
ta Paula, and known as the "Lemon Capital." Lemons are

COFFEE HOUSES AND OUTDOOR CAFÉS. San Francisco has a prepon-
derance of small cafés, many of which are charming and atmospheric, as well
as easy on the pocketbook. Particularly good areas for finding them are Broadway and Columbus (and surrounding side streets); Polk St. between Geary and
Union; the "1800" to "2000" blocks of Union St.; and Lombard St. between
Laguna and Broderick.

Good dependable counter-type restaurants include *The Hippo, Miz Brown's,
Zim's, Pam Pam East,* 398 Geary, in the Raphael Hotel, and *Clown Alley,* 42
Columbus, North Beach, reputed to serve the best hamburger and french fries
in town.

In Sausalito, check the patio at *Zack's,* Bridgeway and Turney Sts., for
charbroiled burgers and libations. For a grand outing take the ferry to the
waterfront community of Tiburon. Two-block long Main Street is bustling with
shops and restaurants. Join the recreational sailors on the deck of *Sam's, The
Dock,* or *Carlos O'Brian's* for a gin fizz and watch the sky turn pink at sundown.

EXPLORING THE REST OF CALIFORNIA

California abounds in attractions and the lures are not confined to
major cities. Today US 101 closely parallels the historic Mission Trail,
one of the state's most popular tourways. In 1768, when the Russian
interest in Alaska was seen as a possible prelude to southward expansion, King Charles of Spain ordered the colonization of California. His
decree launched the missions which provided the seminal growth for
California. Under the astute leadership of Father Junipero Serra and
Father Fermin Lausen (each founded nine missions) the gray-robed
Franciscans moved slowly northward. By 1823 a chain of 21 missions
extended 600 miles from San Diego to Sonoma along the coastal route,
El Camino Real (The King's Highway).

On California 76, a replica of Mission San Antonio de Pala, originally Asistencia, or outpost of the Oceanside Mission, still serves the
Indians' religious needs and provides schooling for seven neighboring
reservations. Thus, it is the only California mission still serving its
original purpose.

Mission San Buenaventura, at Ventura, was the ninth mission founded and the last to be dedicated by the Franciscan Padre, Father Serra.
The date was Easter Sunday, 1782, two years before his death.

Mission Santa Barbara, "Queen of the Missions," on a height overlooking sea and city, is considered the state's most photographed building. Its museums and gardens are outstanding. This is the only one of
California's missions never abandoned by the Franciscans. A candle
has been kept burning on the altar since December 4, 1786. Mission
Santa Ines, 35 miles north of Santa Barbara, is only a bell's call from
the Danish-inspired town of Solvang. The beautifully restored mission
housed California's first seminary, the College of Our Lady of Refuge.
Santa Ines was founded in 1804 and dedicated to the martyred Saint
Agnes. Still in use are carved wooden crucifixes, hand-hammered copper and silver altar pieces, and other religious articles crafted on the
premises by Indian neophytes. The original mural decorations are ri-
valed only by those at San Miguel.

Mission La Purísima Concepción is a faithful restoration of the impressive mission that was sadly neglected after the Mexicans sold it at
auction in 1854 for $1,000. When the mission was being restored in the
1930s, young men of the Civilian Conservation Corps (CCC) molded
more than 100,000 adobe bricks in the manner of the original Indian
builders. The mission was founded in 1787, but the original buildings
were destroyed in an 1812 earthquake. The hero of the earthquake,
Father Mariano Payeras, is buried on the premises.

San Luis Obispo de Tolosa, in the center of the city of San Luis Obispo, was Father Serra's fifth mission, dedicated in 1772. It is believed that tile roofs had their beginning here after the flaming arrows of Indians continually set fire to the original roofs of tule or rush. Father Serra's vestments and other rare religious items are preserved in the mission museum.

San Miguel Arcángel Mission, about 10 miles north of Paso Robles, adjacent to the town of San Miguel, is noted for its murals, arches and a donkey named Ramona. Founded in 1797, it is the sixteenth mission.

Other missions, with the town nearest each one, are: San Antonio de Padua, King City; Nuestra Senora de la Soledad, Soledad; San Juan Bautista, San Juan Bautista; San Jose de Guadelupe, San Jose; Santa Clara de Asis, Santa Clara; San Francisco de Asis, San Francisco; San Rafael Archangel, San Rafael; and San Francisco Solano de Sonoma, Sonoma.

State Parks

California counts its blessings in having 6 National Parks and 7 National Monuments, described earlier in this book in the *Distinctively American Vacations* section. Today, California's State Park system involves more than 275 units, with over one million acres of mountains, valleys, lakes and plateaus, rivers, forests, and beaches. It also embraces many landmarks of historical heritage.

Following are a number of noteworthy state parks.

Big Basin Redwoods State Park, the first of the redwood groves to be declared a protected state park, usually is visited en route to Carmel. You can hike, picnic, or camp here, take advantage of planned recreation facilities, or just enjoy the magnificent giant trees. Dogs allowed in campgrounds/day-use areas; overnight fee.

Caswell Memorial State Park is five miles west of US 99, 16 miles south of Stockton. The park is one of the few remaining primeval groves of valley oaks that once were abundant in the Great Central Valley. Swimming, fishing, camping, hiking trails, and picnicking.

Del Norte Coast Redwoods State Park (about 10 miles south of Crescent City), is a blaze of rhododendrons in spring; offers fishing, camping, hiking, picnicking. Closed winters. There are magnificent drives through rugged inland forest, with views of the Pacific from high points.

Henry Cowell Redwood State Park, just south of Felton, is another forest preserve. Picnic areas are outside the grove of big trees. Take a ride on the old train here.

East Bay Regional Parks are 8,200 acres of beautiful California countryside set aside for daytime recreation. The parks practically overlap each other with miles of hiking and bridle trails and picnic spots. Charles Lee Tilden Regional Park has the most recreational facilities. Try Lake Temescal Regional Park, Round Top, Redwood and Grass Valley.

Humboldt Redwoods State Park is 35 miles of forest bordering US 101 between Garberville and Redcrest. Highlights are the Rockefeller Forest, Founder's Grove, and the Avenue of the Giants, where you can drive on the wide pebble beach of the Eel River.

Mount Diablo State Park is behind Oakland. According to Indian superstition, the mountain was the dwelling place of an evil spirit, a puy. Bret Harte stated that the peak was named when a Mexican muleteer on a missionary expedition first espied it and cried: "Diablo!" (Devil). The Creek-Clayton Road gives the most diabolic impression—dark shadows in deep ravines, sharp and craggy contours.

Mount Tamalpais is back of Mill Vall Bridge from San Francisco. It's one of th town that can really be termed pastoral. also an easy hike. Part of the land is in M ment; the rest is state park.

Russian Gulch State Park is along the co It has a wave-scarred headland pocked w campsites, and the lure of skin diving for the summer. A more protected park a few mick Memorial State Park, is nine miles f and has camping facilities.

On the west shore of Lake Tahoe, 17 m Highway 89, D.L. Bliss State Park is a 1,2 offers camping, fishing, swimming, hiking, winter; elevation about 7,000 feet.

Sonoma Coast Beaches State Park is gr especially from the Russian River approac and Calif. 1 intersect.

Santa Catalina and the Beaches

In the southern part of the state, Santa offshore and accessible from San Pedro b Airlines offers a 20-minute helicopter fligh settlement on the island. It's a quiet villag fronting a crescent bay and scaling the slo (May to October) are, according to autho some growing to 18 inches. Glass-bottom fornia State Marine Preserve which covers a sea life.

Back on the mainland, and more southerl of annual September Surfboard Champion Harbor are next. Showplace homes with pr ways. Newport's boat population is more t yacht clubs and a regatta practically every

Next along the coast is Laguna Beach. studio-clustered and the area is being design

Missions, Sports, Stars

A few miles beyond is Mission San Juan (Spanish Franciscan padres in 1775. It gaine its flock of swallows always flew off on the r October 23, and returned "miraculously" o 19. An inquiring young priest studied swallo come and go at fairly regular dates, but the the local Spanish Californians' belief.

At La Jolla, north of San Diego, seven ca of the soft cliffs by waves over the centuries. an inland tunneled stairway and the other six ocean. La Jolla has been a tennis center for g La Jolla Tennis Tournament, held since 191 for all ages. The La Jolla Beach and Tennis (tennis courts. In the oceanside Marine Room lounge, picture windows of tempered plate g waves. The aquarium museum at Scripps Ins 8602 La Jolla Shore Dr., is one of two such Pacific and Baja marine life and a tidepool d Pines Mesa is the campus of UC–San Diego

Mission playgroun parks, the swimming. World is form at it trained ki While her million Pe

The res ernmost o become kn figures, fil list of mor

The "B

Souther try. Inters the Mexic one of the over the w at the Wa

From telescope high. The inside, is telescope

The Im largest po in Imperia sections o of hay ye harvests by trainle canals wh in the vall rain falls.

Inland large-scale grape vin go out by may pick to a gin,

Once i easy driv town of topped in Williams feet. A tr end of th the hike or four a

North

North covering near Sar

picked every six weeks and in a single year, a well-bearing tree may produce 3,000 lemons. Trees are trimmed, giving the impression of a uniform flat top, to increase the yields.

The stretch of freeway entering Santa Barbara is regarded as the most beautifully landscaped in the California system. Santa Barbara climbs the mountain slopes from the yacht harbor and more than 30 miles of unspoiled beaches. This was the gracious social center of old Spanish California. Today's residents, many of them wealthy, retired Easterners, attempt to retain the old atmosphere. The Spanish-Moorish County Courthouse is rated as one of the most beautiful public buildings in North America. The Santa Barbara Museum houses excellent exhibits of Greek, Roman and Egyptian sculptures. The Museum of Natural History, in a wooded canyon behind the Mission, is notable for, among other things, the mounted specimens of the California Condor, the largest flying bird in North America. A sanctuary for the last band of the 10-foot winged Condors is tucked in the mountains behind Santa Barbara.

Santa Barbara's many Spanish adobes were built with massive bricks made from local adobe clay. Follow the "Red Tile Tour"—12 blocks of fascinating historical landmarks. Stop in at the Casa De la Querra, once the social center of Alta (upper) California. The Spanish influence is quite apparent in the city. Streets bear such names as Indio Muerte (Dead Indian), Los Olivos (The Olives), and Camino Cielo (Street of the Sky). The University of California is up the coast a few miles. It overlooks the sea at Goleta and is a gem of California architecture. San Marcos Pass is an easy jump inland, offering panoramic marine views out over the coast and the chain of Channel Islands.

The village of Solvang, meaning "Sunny Valley," has sought to make itself a bit of transplanted Denmark. It was founded by Lutheran clergymen who called for Danes throughout the country to help establish an old-country "folk" school here. Danish festivals are held annually in September.

For a scenic and leisurely trip, drive along Route 1 to Pismo Beach, home of giant clams. Years ago the beach literally was paved with clams and farmers plowed them up for chicken and hog feed. Today there's a daily limit and no clam less than five inches in diameter can be taken. Local shops and motels carry schedules of the tide and limit.

San Luis Obispo is an old town, where you can walk through an eight-block area dotted with Queen Anne and shingle-style Victorians. This also is the home of the California State Polytechnic College, which has model stock farms worth a visit. The San Luis Obispo Nuclear Center has many exhibits and a nuclear theater presenting a 14-minute program on nuclear power.

About 40 miles due west of San Luis Obispo along Calif. 1, watch the mountains for the first sight of what appears to be a towered European castle. La Casa Grande is just that. It's the castle built by the late William Randolph Hearst and depository of millions of dollars' worth of his worldwide art collection. The 159-acre estate is a state historical monument, presented to California by the Hearst family. San Simeon crowns La Cuesta Encantada (the Enchanted Hill) in the Santa Lucia Range. Traveling by tour bus five miles, you'll pass through the former Hearst ranchland for Herefords and a game preserve of zebra, fallow deer, aoudads, axis, sambar deer and tahr goats. Scheduled tours visit some of the castle's 100 rooms (38 are bedrooms, 31 are bathrooms and 14 are sitting rooms). One of the floors of the castle is Pompeiian mosaic tile dating to 60 B.C. Some of the carved and decorated ceilings were dismantled in Europe and shipped here to be reassembled by European craftsmen. Reservations necessary in summer.

North of San Luis Obispo is the historic town of Monterey. The famous seventeen-mile drive between Monterey and Carmel offers spectacular scenery. Carmel itself is a charming town, filled with artists and shops selling locally made goods. The Big Sur Highway, running south of Carmel to Big Sur; is one of the most breathtakingly beautiful roads in the world.

Gold Rush Towns

The Mother Lode Country lies along a state route appropriately numbered 49. Running along the western slope of the Sierra from Mariposa to Sattley, much of this 266-mile stretch has reassumed the lazy, back-country look California must have had before the Gold Rush.

The most authentic and best restored of all the bonanza towns is Columbia. It's above Sonora on a side road just off 49. California keeps Columbia in its original Gold Rush Days state. It is officially a State Park. The yearly Fireman's Muster, in early May, parades antique fire engines and equipment. Summer theatre is housed in the restored Fallon House.

The Andes' Lake Titicaca in Bolivia is the highest lake in the world. Tahoe is the second highest. Nevada borders the eastern side of Tahoe and contributes gambling casinos to the lake's other resorty attractions. Crystal Bay and State Line are the towns with casinos. Their entertainment offerings rival those of Las Vegas. A 70-mile road around Tahoe provides an easy way to view the lake's many coves, forested peninsulas, and broad reaches of water.

From Tahoe City on the lake, Calif. 89 takes you to the 1960 Winter Olympic site—Squaw Valley. Ski lifts operate in summers here.

Sacramento and Nevada City

In Sacramento, California's capital, at 28th and K streets you'll see a reconstructed Sutter's Fort, where he ruled in the years preceding the Gold Rush. It's an entire little village. The State Capitol, on 10th Street between L and N streets, with a gold dome and elaborate legislative halls, has been lavishly restored to its nineteenth-century elegance. The old Governor's Mansion, at 16th and H streets, with turrets, towers, and gingerbread trim, is a popular stop for tourists.

East and northeast of Sacramento lie the Gold Rush towns with the most picturesque and the most improbable names. Some examples are You Bet, Confidence, Red Dog, Rough and Ready, Fairplay. Nevada City is another Gold Rush ghost town that looks the part perfectly. It's set on seven hills, has fantastically shaped houses and a typical old hotel.

Two great rivers, the Sacramento and the San Joaquin, form a maze of sloughs, canals, and marshes locally called the Delta. It's a favorite of San Francisco yachtsmen since it is only 50 miles northeast of San Francisco Bay. Its thousand miles of navigable waterways are plied by vessels from rowboats to ocean freighters. Some of the world's richest farmland lies on either shore. During the Gold Rush, sailing ships and side-wheelers carried miners and supplies to Sacramento, Stockton, and other jumping off points. At one time, there were 28 steamboats regularly moving up and down the river. The automobile and good roads announced the close of the era here. Within the Delta there are areas much like the early Everglades. Best known is The Meadows at Snodgrass Slough (north of Walnut Grove), a favorite gathering place for boaters and houseboat renters.

Mt. Shasta, a 14,162-foot-tall landmark, is visible for more than a hundred miles in each direction. Take Calif. 89 from Lassen to Mt. Shasta and on the way you'll pass McArthur-Burney Falls State Park, with picnic and camping facilities and a split waterfall fed by an underground river. US 99 takes you through Castle Crags, sheer rocks rising 6,000 feet, the Lake Shasta Caverns, open daily year-round, with guided tours, and the Shasta Dam.

At Redding, king salmon flip up fish ladders in the Sacramento, providing a great show. Pick up Calif. 299, which parallels the Old Trinity Trail—first an Indian Path, then a pioneer trail, then a Gold Rush wagon road. Within six miles you're back in gold country in the small town of Shasta. Today in the streams of this area you can still see prospectors panning the gravel. French Town is another "gold" mining town which sprang into existence overnight. But it was silver that supported this settlement. In 1965 the Whiskeytown-Shasta-Trinity National Recreation Area was created with the formation of three major dam-created lakes: Whiskeytown, Shasta, and Clair Engle (Trinity)-Lewiston lakes. Outdoor recreation is unlimited in this northern wonderland just 234 miles north of San Francisco. Boating, fishing, camping, hiking, and swimming attract summer crowds. Winter draws ski enthusiasts.

A colorful relic of early California is the Joss House at Weaverville. It is a state museum and one of the few structures recalling the role of the Chinese in the Gold Rush and the building of California.

From Junction City, it's 12 miles to Canyon Creek. From here you can hike through mining country to excellent fishing and picnic spots on the Canyon Creek Lakes. Another road strikes off from the Coffee Creek Ranger Station at the northern end of Trinity Lake. To really experience Trinity Alps, however, you should pack in. There are 15 major resort-ranches in the area, most of which offer pack trips. Guides will accompany your party or meet you at specified times. The Yurok, Karuk, and Hoopa Indians live in the town of Hoopa. Game laws permit the tribes to scoop-net the salmon from the falls in the ancient way.

At Klamath, you can camp in the redwoods and photograph the Roosevelt elk in Prairie Creek State Park. This is rugged country, battered by storms in winter, shrouded by fogs in summer. New Englanders first settled here to log and fish. The towns and mansions have a New England–Victorian look. Carson Mansion in Eureka is one of America's best preserved Victorian Gothic buildings.

At Pepperwood on 101, watch for the turnoff to the Avenue of the Giants, a spectacular 31-mile stretch of redwoods in the Humboldt Redwoods State Park. Near Redcrest is another turnoff leading to Rockefeller Redwood Forest, often called the "world's finest forest." You can drive through a giant tree near Leggett.

Fifty years ago, Mendocino was a dying, two-street town—there being no more call for ship-building timber. Now the town is having a rebirth, this time as an artists' colony. The tourist peak in this picturesque village runs from Memorial Day to Labor Day. At the beginning of the season, Mendocino is ablaze with azaleas, fuchsias, and rhododendrons. Art works of community residents are on display at galleries and at the Art Center on Little Lake Street. Three powerful lighthouses here are also open to visitors. Mendocino's ancestral heritage is traceable to New England through its architecture, a blend of both pure and improvised Victorian. Surf at most beaches is too rough for swimming, though skindiving for abalone is allowed.

Wine Country

Calistoga is an excellent central point from which to explore nearby wine country. California's almost 500 wineries produce 85% of the country's wine and host more than 5½ million people annually. There are approximately 60 wineries in Napa County and 50-plus in neighboring Sonoma County. Most give conducted tours. Sebastiani's stone cellars are on the oldest vineyard in Northern California, originally that of the Mission de Sonoma. Especially interesting are Inglenook, which gets its staves for its wine casts from German Black Forest oaks, and Beringer Brothers, where Chinese coolie labor dug out the tunnels in the hills where the barrels of wine are aged. Both are in Rutherford.

Newest in the Napa Valley is French-owned Domaine Chandon, just west of Yountville. (Elegant dining in their gourmet restaurant, but reserve ahead.)

East of Sonoma is the Buena Vista winery. The winery has ivy-covered stone walls and a tasting room that is candlelighted. Agoston Haraszthy, a Hungarian, was responsible for establishing Buena Vista. He brought the vine cuttings for planting from Europe's best vineyards.

The town of Sonoma is historical. Successors of the padre Junipero Serra built the last of the 21 missions here. In 1846 Americans proclaimed Californian independence from Mexico and the establishment of the California Republic. There are some European touches here; one of them is the Swiss Hotel where you can get an excellent meal. At "Train Town," one mile south of the Sonoma main square, steam powered locomotives make 15-minute runs through a reproduction of an old mining town. The country around Sonoma is enchanting. There are rolling hills, and one can wander amongst oak, eucalyptus and pine groves. Santa Rosa has a unique arboreal-architectual curiosity—a whole church built from the wood of one tree. The church is now the Ripley "Believe It or Not" Museum. Jack London State Park is in nearby Glen Ellen. London is buried beneath a giant boulder near the burnt ruins of his Wolf House. Luther Burbank, the famed horticulturist, grew grapes experimentally in the Santa Rosa region, but never drank. Today, tourists visit the gardens and the greenhouse, where he is buried under a cedar of Lebanon.

Back in the coastal area, Sebastopol is the sole survivor of five California communities that once bore this name. Sebastopol is apple growing country. An apple blossom festival and tour of the orchards takes place there every year near Easter. Just a bit north of Sebastopol is Guerneville, "capital" of the Russian River, a congested holiday center in summer. The Korbel winery is located here. One of the best producers of California champagne, it offers tours daily in the summer, or any time by appointment. Follow the river west, imagining the days when it teemed with Alaskan colonists. It brings you out to Jenner, a coastal fishing center.

Eleven miles north of here are the stout wooden buildings of Fort Ross. A state monument, it was the American outpost for Russian fur traders during the nineteenth century. They used it as a base for hunting sea otters and for raising crops to feed their Alaskan allies.

Continuing down the coast, you'll see a 10-mile stretch of spectacular beaches. The surf is treacherous and swimming is prohibited. Pebble collecting is great. Some lucky fossickers have uncovered jade pebbles. The beaches bear such names as Salmon Creek, Arch Rock, Portuguese, Shell and Goat Rock. They make up the Sonoma Coast Beaches State Park.

Angling west through pine forests and sand dunes leads you eventually to Point Reyes Lighthouse, the tip of California's only National

Seashore. There is swimming at Drake's Beach and four backpack camping sections. Retracing your steps from Point Reyes National Seashore, you can have the dubious thrill of knowing you're driving on top of California's infamous San Andreas Fault.

PRACTICAL INFORMATION
FOR THE REST OF CALIFORNIA

HOW TO GET THERE. *By air: Eastern, TWA, United, American Airlines, Delta, Pan Am, Continental, North- west* and *Republic* service both San Francisco and Los Angeles from various major points in the U.S. *Eastern, Western, Air France, KLM, Lufthansa, PSA, China Airlines, British Airways* and *Korean* also serve Los Angeles. Airlines and service from other points to Los Angeles are: *Pan Am,* Honolulu; *Delta,* Puerto Rico; *Air Canada,* Montreal and Toronto; *Western,* Calgary; *Aeromexico, Mexicana,* and *Western,* Mexico. *Qan- tas* from Sydney; *Thai Airways* from Bangkok; *Japan Airlines* from Tokyo; *Singapore Airlines* from Singapore; and *Air New Zealand* service Los Angeles International Airport. *PSA* and *United* service Sacramento. *Alaska Airlines* flies to San Francisco, Burbank, Ontario, and Palm Springs. *PSA* operates San Francisco-Long Beach. San Diego is served by several major airlines. *Los An- geles International Airport,* near Inglewood, is one of the busiest airports in the world. Other metropolitan Los Angeles airports serving major airlines are *Bu- rank-Glendale-Pasadena Airport,* 14 miles northwest; *Long Beach Airport,* 22 miles south; *John Wayne Orange County Airport,* 30 miles southeast in Santa Ana; and *Ontario International Airport,* about 40 miles east in San Bernardino County.

By car: Interstate 80 runs from the east to San Francisco, Interstate 5, from Washington through California. The main freeways delivering traffic through and into downtown Los Angeles are: Pasadena, from the San Gabriel Valley; Hollywood, servicing Hollywood and the San Fernando Valley; San Bernardino Freeway, from eastern areas, Riverside and San Bernardino counties. The Santa Ana Freeway reaches down toward beach communities and Orange County. The Santa Monica Freeway links Los Angeles and Santa Monica on the Pacific. The Harbor Freeway covers the San Pedro/Wilmington route. The Golden State Freeway runs toward eastern San Fernando Valley, Burbank and Glen- dale.

By train: Amtrak serves Los Angeles from limited points in the U.S. and Oakland-San Francisco. Amtrak also operates numerous daily trains between San Diego-Orange County-Los Angeles. By bus: *Greyhound* and *Continental Trailways* transportation to San Francisco and Los Angeles.

HOW TO GET AROUND. *Republic, PSA* and *Air Cal* have intrastate flights from San Francisco. Palm Springs has the largest airport in its area, with *Air Cal, American* and *Western Airlines* offering direct or connecting flights to other cities.

By car: Major firms, such as *Avis, Hertz, Budget, National* and *Dollar-A-Day* have rental offices in various cities and airports.

By bus: Continental Trailways and *Greyhound.*

On horseback: There are many pack trips available in Yosemite as well as in other parks and areas. Write to the *California Office of Tourism,* 1121 L St., Suite 103, Sacramento, CA 95814, for its *Packers and Pack Trips* booklet.

By boat: For a trip along the Sacramento River (the Delta), write: Houseboats, 11530 W. 8 Mile Rd., Stockton, 95209. The Delta's Rental fleet is 100 strong; *almost* all are rented by reservation.

By train: Three to eight hour trips via the Skunk winds through redwood forests between Fort Bragg and Willits. Another interesting train, the *Roaring Camp & Big Trees Railroad,* is one of the nation's few remaining steam rail- roads. Its one-hour, six-mile round trip operates out of Felton in the Santa Cruz Mountains.

TOURIST INFORMATION SERVICES. Most local Chambers of Commerce will send you material on their cities. The *San Francisco Convention & Visitors Bureau,* 201 3rd, has a supply of general information. Also in San Francisco, the *Redwood Empire Association* welcomes visitors at its office, One Market Plaza. Information on specific subjects is available from such services as these:

California Office of Tourism, 1121 L St., Suite 103, Sacramento 95814; Wine Institute, 139 Market St., San Francisco; *Shasta-Cascade Wonderland Association,* Redding; *Lake Tahoe Chamber of Commerce,* P.O. Box 884, Tahoe City; *Golden Chain Council of Mother Lode,* P.O. Box 206, Soda Springs, CA, and *Division of Beaches and Parks* (send $2 for its booklet), P.O. Box 2390, Sacramento 95814. For information on the *National Forest Campgrounds,* write the Regional Forester, 630 Sansome St., San Francisco 94111. For tour information, contact *Gray Line of San Francisco,* 420 Taylor St., San Francisco—or dial 771–4000. for visitor information. For a two-minute recorded message of daily special events and activities, dial 391–2000.

MUSEUMS AND GALLERIES. Hours and admission fees vary. Some exhibits are open only seasonally. It is advisable to check locally for up-to-date information. Atwater: *Castle Air Museum.* This free museum is housed in former barracks. Exhibits include photos, uniforms, and weapons dating from WW I to the present, plus 30 restored vintage planes.

Bakersfield: *Kern County Museum,* 3801 Chester Ave. Indian artifacts, firearms.

Berkeley: *Art Center,* 1275 Walnut St. Paintings and sculpture; films, gallery talks. *Judah L. Magnes Memorial Museum,* 2911 Russell St., houses an impressive collection of Jewish ceremonial art, rare books, a holocaust collection. *University Art Museum,* 2626 Bancroft Way, offers guided tours and gallery talks, paintings, sculpture, drawings, prints.

Carmel: *Weston Gallery,* 6th and Dolores Sts., exhibits the photographic works of Edward and Cole Weston and celebrated Ansel Adams.

Crescent City: *Del Norte County Historical Society,* 710 H St., is housed in an old jail building.

Death Valley: *Death Valley Museum,* Death Valley National Monument, Natural History Museum, charcoal kilns, Harmony Borax Works and Scotty's Castle.

Desert Hot Springs: *Cabot's Old Indian Pueblo,* 67–616 East Desert View, is a Hopi-Indian-style structure with a museum, art gallery and trading post.

Eureka: *Clarke Memorial Museum,* 240 E. St., has anthropology, archeology, costume, Indian lore and natural history exhibits.

Fresno: *Arts Center,* 2233 First, has a new gallery displaying Mexican masters. Saturdays free. *Kearney Mansion Museum,* 7160 W. Kearney Blvd., includes a blacksmith shop, carriage house, and 1890s home.

Jackson: *Amador County Museum,* 225 Church St. Gold mining exhibits are housed in this Victorian dwelling.

Laguna Beach: *Laguna Beach Museum of Art,* 307 Cliff Dr. Paintings by early Calif. artists.

Monterey: *Allen Knight Maritime Museum,* 550 Calle Principal. *History and Art Association,* 550 Calle Principal, offers guided tours of three historic buildings and its painting and costume exhibits. *Monterey Peninsula Museum of Art,* 559 Pacific St. *Old Monterey Jail,* Dutra St., Civic Center. *Robert Louis Stevenson House,* 530 Houston St. *United States Army Museum,* Presidio of Monterey, is housed in a 1908 cavalry-supply depot. New $40-million *Monterey Bay Aquarium,* Cannery Row. Major exhibits include a kelp forest and a stunning walk-through aviary. The complex marine life is all from Monterey Bay.

Palo Alto: *Stanford University Museum of Art:* Stanford family collection; Rodin sculpture.

Redding: *Museum and Art Center* specializes in Indian lore, crafts.

Sacramento: *California State Historic Railroad Museum & Central Pacific Passenger Station,* Old Sacramento; *Sutter's Fort & State Indian Museum; Crocker Art Museum; State Capitol.*

San Jose: *State University Art Gallery,* 20th-century painting, sculpture, graphics. *Civic Art Gallery,* 110 S. Market St. Regional artists. *Historical Museum,* 635 Phelan Ave. Mining, transportation, historic houses.

San Luis Obispo: *County Historical Museum,* 696 Monterey St.

Santa Barbara: The *Santa Barbara Museum of Art,* 1130 State St.

Stockton: *Pacific Center for Western Historical Studies,* Univ. of the Pacific. Western Americana, John Muir papers. *Pioneer Museum and Haggan Galleries,* 1201 N. Pershing Ave.

Special Interest: Bishop: *Laws Railroad Museum,* 5 miles N.E. on U.S. 6. Port Hueneme: *Civil Engineer Corps Seabee Museum,* a fascinating memorial to the U.S. Navy Construction Battalions, Naval Base. Palm Springs: *The Palm Springs Desert Museum,* 135 E. Tahquitz-McCallum Way, has exhibits devoted to the desert. Randsburg: *Desert Museum,* Butte St. Mineralogy collection. Santa Barbara: *Museum of Natural History,* 2559 Puesta del Sol Rd. *County Courthouse,* 1220 Anacapa & Anapamu Sts. Spanish-Moorish structure. Santa Paula: *The California Oil Museum,* 1003 Main St., is a gusher of oil information. Morro Bay: *The Museum of Natural History,* State Park Rd.

 HISTORIC SITES. Scattered along the 780-mile length of California are about 44 official State Historical Monuments and nearly 900 Historical Landmarks. There is also the "Father Junipero Serra Rosary" of 21 missions. *Columbia State Historic Park,* four miles from Sonora, is the best preserved of the Gold Rush towns. Its buildings are marked for easy identification and the town has an excellent museum.

Donner Memorial Park, two miles west of Truckee on US 40, has a very impressive monument, commemorating members of the Donner party who camped there during the winter of 1846–47.

San Juan Bautista State Historical Monument, off US 101 between Gilroy and Salinas, is a chapter of California history that ended with the coming of the railroad.

Sutter's Fort (Sacramento), where gold was discovered, has California's greatest collection of Gold Rush and Pioneer relics.

Be sure to visit Santa Barbara's adobe *Casa de la Guerra.* It houses the Chamber of Commerce in the center of El Paseo, a quaint restoration of an old Spanish shopping center at 19 E. de la Guerra St.

Hearst San Simeon Historical Monument has statuary, art treasures, historical structures, an indoor gold-inlaid Roman pool and magnificent gardens on its 159 acres. Reservations: Dept. of Parks & Recreation, 1416 Ninth St. Sacramento 95814. Cost: adults: $8.00; $4.00, children 6–12.

A note on Monterey: Visit the *Monterey State Historic Park* and follow the historic "Path of History."

Frontier Museum Historical Center, Temecula, is a museum celebrating the Old West. Open 7 days, 9:30–5:00.

 TOURS. *California Parlor Car Tours* has year-round four- and five-day circle tours of Yosemite, Monterey and Carmel. Six-day versions, offered in the summers only, include Lake Tahoe, Santa Barbara and Los Angeles. The *California Western Railroad* operates a small train, the Skunk, between Ft. Bragg and Willits. The 80-mile round trip runs through redwood forests, over 33 bridges and trestles and through two tunnels.

Western-Greyhound Lines offers four-day Redwood Empire tours monthly in July, August and September, covering Frank Lloyd Wright's Marin Civic Center, Sonoma, St. Helena, Santa Rosa, Mendocino, Ft. Bragg, the Avenue of the Giants, the Pacific Lumber Mill at Scotia, Eureka and the Rockefeller Redwoods State Park.

New is the Yosemite-in-a-Day tour and a Hearst Castle overnighter from San Francisco. Phone (415) 621–7738.

By boat: Some options are sightseeing excursions available from piers and docks at Santa Barbara and Newport Beach.

Cable car rides: Palm Springs Aerial Tramway, located at Tramway Dr., Chino Canyon, off Hwy. 111 north, operates seasonally. Adult and children prices. There also are special ride and dinner tickets.

DRINKING LAWS. The state rigidly enforces its drinking laws. You must be 21—if you're youthful looking, be sure to carry proof of your age. Legal hours for dispensing drinks in public places are from 6 A.M. to 2 A.M. daily.

SUMMER SPORTS. For *skiing* and *boating* in general, California is loaded with lakes. Some major ones are Clear Lake, Berryessa and Shasta. Year-round water sports may be enjoyed along California's southeast border, from Parker to Blythe, and among many places, at Salton Sea, Lake Gregory, Lake Arrowhead, Big Bear Lake and June Lake. You can dig for clams at Morro Bay; for giant clams at Pismo Beach.

Fishing: Inland, the lakes, reservoirs, rivers and mountain streams yield bluegill, bullheads, channel and white catfish, crappie and rainbow trout. There's trout fishing at Whitewater Canyon and Bishop. Salton Sea is populated with corvinas up to 15 lbs. Oxnard is a port for fishing the Channel Islands for halibut. There is good sport fishing at Catalina Island. Ocean sportfishing services are available at Santa Barbara, Avila Beach, Morro Bay, Port Hueneme, San Simeon and Ventura. There are many choice fishing spots at such places as Lake Tahoe, along the Upper Sacramento River and in the Castle Crags State Park area.

White water enthusiasts can run the Klamath, Rogue, and American rivers. For information contact The American River Touring Association, 1307 Harrison St., Oakland, Calif. 94612.

Golf: California is teeming with courses. The Palm Springs area alone has 40. Pebble Beach G. Links, Pebble Beach, ranks among the first ten of America's 100 greatest courses; Spyglass Hill, Pebble Beach, among the fourth ten, and Cypress Point Club, Pebble Beach, among the fifth ten. Some of the many others recommended by "Golf Digest" include: Lake Shastina, Mt. Shasta, a Robert Trent Jones course; Alameda, in Alameda, a renovated course with five artificial lake hazards; Pasatiemo, in Santa Cruz, overlooking Monterey Bay; Laguna Seca, Monterey, a Trent Jones course; Avila Beach, a resort course; Alisal, a resort course at Solvang; Ojai Valley, a resort course at Ojai; Soboba Springs, San Jacinto, a challenging Muirhead creation; Desert Island, Cathedral City, private Muirhead course; Pala Mesa Inn, Fallbrook, a championship course; San Vincente, Ramona, semi-private Tcd Robinson course; Rancho Santa Fe, north of San Diego, in a gorgeous horse-country setting.

Boating: California's most popular boating park is the Salton Sea State Recreational Area.

Surfing: Surfing is a big sport in Southern California. There are about 125 beaches between Morro Bay and San Diego. For exciting participation or observation, head for the beaches early—best time is between 6 A.M. and 9 A.M. You'll find lots of surfers during the summers in the arty community of Laguna; the main spot is at Thalia St. During the winters (it's a year-round sport) you'll see some of the world's best surfers at Rincon in Ventura and at Jalama State Park in Santa Barbara.

Bicycling: There are many bicycling clubs in Southern California, most of them affiliated with the American Youth Hostels.

Hiking: Sturdy shoes are recommended for trails at Andreas, Murray, Palm Canyons and up Mt. Whitney.

Pack trips: There are guided pack and saddle animal trails in summer at Mammoth Lakes.

WINTER SPORTS. *Skiing* is another big sport in California. Good areas are Squaw Valley, eight miles from Tahoe City with 25 chair lifts, moving 26,500 skiers an hour, Mammoth, with 21 chair lifts, tops every ski area in the nation with its ability to accommodate 31,000 skiers an hour. Down south, Snow Summit, at Big Bear Lake features cross-country Nordic Touring Center; night skiing. Sugar Bowl, Heavenly Valley, Kirkwood, Northstar-at-Tahoe offer a variety of apres-ski pleasures: day lodges, discos, heated pools, condominiums for a complete California-style ski experience.

SPECTATOR SPORTS. Rodeos: California is second only to Texas in number of rodeos. More than sixty are sanctioned each year by the Rodeo Cowboys Association. Major ones are at Red Bluff in April. The California Rodeo, the biggest of them all, is held at Salinas in July. Equestrian events: Some of the options are: the Interclub Horse Show at Carmel Valley Trail and Saddle Club in May; the Shasta Wonderland Three-Day Non-Competitive Trail Ride in July, and the Equestrian Trails and Western American Cup, preceded by a big, public breakfast and a parade at the Pebble Beach Stables in early September. Races: Ontario Motor Speedway, Ontario. California "500" Grand Prix Motorcycles. In Long Beach, Grand Prix, on downtown streets, in March. Riverside Raceway, Riverside. Five major races yearly. And in Indio, a few miles from Palm Springs, camel and ostrich races are held every winter during the National Date Festival. Tennis: The annual Ojai Tennis Tournament is held in April. Boating: The flight of the Snowbirds Regatta is held at Newport in July; "Character Boat Parade" in August.

Jai Alai. (pronounced *Hi Lie*): The betting is heavy and the crowds gather during scheduled weeknights at Fronton Palacio, Tijuana, Mexico, 16 miles below San Diego.

 WHAT TO DO WITH CHILDREN. *Marine World/ Africa U.S.A.* in 1986 premieres its new home in Lake Chabot Park, in Vallejo, 28 miles northeast of San Francisco. *Child's Estate Zoological Gardens,* Santa Barbara, is a unique park, playground and zoo. Its Sealarium has underwater portholes for viewing. A miniature railroad tours the 81-acre park.

Santa Monica Pier's restored 62-year-old carousel. The 4-minute spin on either one of the 44 dazzling steeds or in ornate chariots costs 25¢. It's a great bargain for a family outing.

Marriott's Great America, 45 miles south of San Francisco, is a 65-acre amusement park dedicated to recalling America's history (Orleans Place, Hometown Square, Yukon Territory). Debuted in 1976. World's largest and probably most beautiful carousel. Three super-sensational roller coaster chillers: Willard's Whizzer, the Turn of the Century, and the Tidal Wave. 30 rides and attractions, ditto eateries, plus a children's play area, Fort Fun, and The Cuddly Critters corral, with baby lambs, goats, and other tiny creatures to fondle.

Open late May-early Sept., daily. Check for other seasonal weekend opening days.

In *Happy Hollow Park,* San Jose, children may feed seals and pet the ponies, donkeys, lambs, goats and ducks. San Jose's *Winchester Mystery House* is a 160-room dwelling with trapdoors and secret passageways. Tours daily, including 2½-hour house and garden viewing.

Whale Watching. Approximately 10,000 California Gray whales migrate 5,000 miles from the Bering Sea to Baja California lagoons between mid-Dec. and Feb. two- to three- hour cruises (about $10) are offered. San Francisco: (415) 474–3385; Los Angeles: (213) 775–6111; San Diego: (619) 222–1144.

Another favorite spot with youngsters is Oakland's *Fairyland,* as well as the *Oakland Zoo* in Knowland State Park.

 HOTELS AND MOTELS. In *Northern California* accommodations range from plush seaside establishments to the cozy chalet-type digs found in Carmel, to the rustic and far-from-rustic rooms available in and around the national parks. Accommodations are plentiful in *Southern California,* where you are apt to find some good bargains. Motels compete vigorously for the tourist trade—most have one swimming pool, several have three. The luxury hotels are as elaborate as those in Florida, though not all of them are beachfront.

Based on double occupancy, prices throughout California start *upwards* from figures given as follows: *Super deluxe:* $60 and up; *Deluxe:* $50–60; *Expensive:* $40–50; *Moderate:* $30–40; *Inexpensive:* under $30.

For a more complete explanation of hotel and motel categories, refer to *Facts at Your Fingertips* at the front of this volume.

BAKERSFIELD. *Expensive:* **Rio Bravo Resort,** 12 miles north. All sports.

Moderate: **Best Western Casa Royale Motor Inn.** Dining room, entertainment.

Best Western Oak Inn. 889 Oak St. Pool; cable TV.

Downtowner Inn. Cable color TV.

Holiday Inn. Attractive rooms. Pets; pool.

Ramada Inn. Pool; entertainment

Inexpensive: **Plaza Inn TraveLodge.** 1030 Wible Rd. Pool, sauna, whirlpool.

BERKELEY. *Deluxe:* **Berkeley Marina Marriott.** Many amenities.

Expensive: **Best Western Berkeley House.** 920 University. Dining room; entertainment.

Hotel Durant. Downtown, near campus. Newly refurbished.

BIG BEAR LAKE *Moderate–Expensive:* **Forest Shores.** New condo units.

BIG SUR. *Moderate–Expensive:* **Big Sur Lodge.** In state park. Pool, cafe.

CLEAR LAKE. *Expensive:* **Konocti Harbor Inn.** Resort. Tennis pro. All water sports.

FRESNO. *Moderate:* **Best Western Tradewinds.** Landscaped grounds.

Best Western Water Tree Inn. Coffee shop.

Fresno Hilton. Downtown. Rooftop bar.

Piccadilly Inn Airport. Pool; restaurant.

Inexpensive: **Manchester Motel.** 3844 N. Blackstone. On Hwy. 41; route to Yosemite.

LAGUNA BEACH. (Reservations necessary during July–August Art Festival.)

Super Deluxe: **Ritz-Carlton.** Laguna Niguel. Opulent resort; 18-acre hilltop villa. Exceptional service, dining, and ambience.

Surf & Sand. S. Coast Hwy. Hotel services.

Moderate: **Laguna Hills Hyatt Lodge.** Restaurant nearby.

Vacation Village. S. Coast Hwy. Large familiy complex.

LAKE TAHOE AREA. *Deluxe:* **Best Western Station House Inn.** South Lake Tahoe.; near casino center. Ski package.

Caesar's Tahoe. South Shore. Six restaurants; health spa; 21 ski resorts nearby.

Expensive: **Harvey's Inn.** Stateline, Nev. Casino, restaurant.

Moderate: **Sierra House.** Park & Cedar Aves. Year round. Small pool, sauna.

MENDOCINO AND FT. BRAGG. *Deluxe:* **Heritage House.** Little River. Attractive. Many antiques.

Moderate: **Hill House,** Mendocino. Modern replica of Victorian inn.

Harbor Lite Lodge. Sauna. View of Noyo Harbor.

Little River Inn. 130-year-old farmhouse. Locally popular.

MONTEREY. *Deluxe:* **Doubletree Inn.** Resort hotel amenities. At Fisherman's Wharf.

Hyatt Regency. One Old Golf Course Rd. Large, gracious. Suites, cottages.

Stanford Terrace Inn. 531 Stanford Ave. Edge of campus.

OAKLAND. *Expensive:* **Claremont.** Resort. $14 million renovated Victorian "grande dame."

Hyatt Regency. Broadway. New, near convention center.

Oakland Hilton Inn. Near airport; pool.

Moderate: **Best Western Thunderbird Lodge.** Near Jack London Sq.

London Lodge. 423 7th St. Downtown; pool.

OJAI. *Deluxe:* **Ojai Valley Inn.** Popular for conventions.

PALM SPRINGS. *Super Deluxe:* **Ingleside Inn.** 200 W. Ramon Rd. Luxurious hideaway; antique-decorated.

Deluxe: **Sheraton Plaza.** 400 E. Tahquitz–McCallum Way. Large, resort property; attractive grounds.

Expensive: **Gene Autry.** 4200 E. Palm Canyon Drive. Popular convention hotel. Six tennis courts; three pools, plus two hot therapy pools.

Moderate: **Monkey Tree Hotel.** 2388 E. Racquet Club Rd. Kitchens. Pool.

PALO ALTO. *Deluxe:* **Rickey's Hyatt House.** Heated pools.

Moderate: **Best Western Flamingo Motor Lodge.** Restaurant.

Tiki Inn Motel. Near Stanford University campus.

Town House Motel. No pets.

SAN BERNARDINO. *Moderate:* **Villa Viejo.** Sauna, whirlpool. Movies.

SACRAMENTO. *Expensive:* **Capital Plaza Holiday Inn.** Old Sacramento. Newest deluxe hotel.

Red Lion Motor Inn. Resort-type; gardens.

Moderate: **Best Western Ponderosa.** Downtown, near capitol; Old Sacramento.

Mansion Inn. Opposite Governor's Mansion.

SAN JOSE. *Expensive:* **Hyatt San Jose.** Large. Gardens, patios.

Moderate: **Holiday Inn.** Two locations.

Howard Johnson's. Restaurant, lounge. Pool.

Vagabond. 1488 N. 1st St. Family rates. Pool.

SAN LUIS OBISPO. *Expensive:* **Madonna Inn.** Unusual decor. Reservations a must.

Moderate: **Discovery Motor Inn.** 1800 Monterey Dr. Heated pool, whirlpool, restaurant.

Best Western Somerset Motor Inn. Pool. Coffee shop.

Vagabond Inn. Coffee shop.

Inexpensive: **Villa San Luis. Comfortable.**

SAN SIMEON. (Reservations advisable during summer season, when tourists flock to see **Hearst's Castle.**).

Moderate: **Best Western Cavalier Inn by the Sea.** Attractive. Oceanfront.

Best Western Green Tree Inn. Near Hearst Castle.

Mariners Inn. Moonstone Beach, Cambria.

SANTA BARBARA. *Deluxe:* **Marriott's Santa Barbara Biltmore.** Resort overlooking ocean.

Sheraton Santa Barbara Hotel & Spa. Golf and tennis privileges.

Expensive: **Santa Barbara Inn.** On ocean. Disco.

Moderate: **Ambassador by the Sea.** Open all year.

Best Western Pepper Tree Inn. Full services.

El Prado Motor Inn. Downtown, near Performing Arts Center.

Sandpiper. Near shopping and restaurants. Weekly rates available.

Polynesian Motel. 433 W. Montecito. Pool, no pets.

SANTA CLARA. *Expensive:* **Marriott.** One mile to Great America Amusement Park, free transport.

SANTA CRUZ. *Expensive:* **Best Western Torch-Lite Inn.** 500 Riverside Ave. All sports and restaurants close by.

SAUSALITO. *Expensive:* **Casa Madrona.** 801 Bridgeway. Victorian landmark; imaginative decor.

TIBURON. *Moderate:* **Tiburon Lodge.** Many services.

DINING OUT. Restaurants throughout California are prepared to please all palates and pocketbooks. Generalizing is impossible as the array runs from gourmet to good, plain fare.

Price ranges for dinner start *upwards* from the following figures (drinks, tax and tip not included): *Super deluxe:* $25 and up; *Deluxe:* $20–25; *Expensive:* $15–20; *Moderate:* $10–15; *Inexpensive:* under $10. For à la carte meals, add 50% to above figures in top three categories, double the figure in bottom two categories.

For a complete explanation of restaurant categories, see *Facts at Your Fingertips* at the front of this volume.

BAKERSFIELD. *Moderate:* **Maison Jaussaud.** Gallic touch. Excellent.

BERKELEY. *Expensive:* **Santa Fe Bar & Grill.** 1310 University. Creative cooking. Art Deco ambience.
Moderate: **Siam Cuisine.** 1181 University Ave. Informal atmosphere with fine Thai specialties.
Spenger's Fish Grotto. Popular seafood restaurant.

BIG SUR. *Moderate:* **Nepenthe.** Hwy. 1. Great view of coastline; fireplace. Vegetarian, steak, chicken, al fresco omelette bar.

LAGUNA BEACH. *Expensive:* **Cordon Bleu.** 859 Laguna Canyon Rd. Elegant dining.
Moderate: **Andree's.** Swiss, French cuisine.
Ben Brown's Restaurant. In Aliso Creek Inn; secluded resort.
Gauguin's. 696 S. Coast Hwy. Continental fare; jazz.
Las Brisas. Mexican menu; overlooks ocean.

LAKE TAHOE AREA. *Expensive:* **The Dory's Oar.** 1041 Fremont Ave., South Lake Tahoe. Eastern seafood; steaks in charming cottage.
Moderate: **Caesar's Tahoe.** Route 50, Stateline. Lavish Evergreen buffet.

LOS GATOS. *Expensive:* **Il Nido.** 170 W. Main. Northern Italian pasta; fresh fish.
La Hacienda. Continental-American menu.
Villa Felice. Continental-American menu.

MONTEREY. *Expensive:* **Sardine Factory.** 701 Wave St. Seafood and steaks.
The Rogue. Wharf #2. Panoramic view of harbor and bay.

OAKLAND. *Expensive:* **Scott's.** Jack London Square branch of San Francisco favorite.
Trader Vic's. The original, in Emeryville. Superb dining, viewing.
Moderate: **Pacific Fresh,** 2203 Mariner Sq. Loop, Alameda. California decor and wines; excellent menu.

PALM SPRINGS. *Super Deluxe:* **Gaston's.** Bank of Palm Springs Centre. French cuisine with panache. Celebrity patrons.
Melvyn's Restaurant. 200 W. Ramon Rd. Gathering place for celebrities. Continental.
Las Casuelas/Nuevas. 70–050 Hwy. 111, Rancho Mirage. Fine Mexican cuisine. Guitar players and mariachis. Excellent margaritas.
Inexpensive: **Buddy's.** 401 E. Tahquitz–McCallum Way. New York Kosher style deli. Daily dinner specials.

SACRAMENTO *Moderate:* **Firehouse.** Old Sacramento. Victorian ambience.
Fish Emporium. 3800 J St. Fresh seafood and salads.
Toulouse Lautrec. 2711 Fulton Ave. French dining, Tues–Sat.

SAINT HELENÀ. *Expensive:* **St. George.** Elegant décor; luncheon favorite.

SANTA BARBARA. *Moderate:* **Harbor Restaurant.** Stearns Wharf. Live lobster, steak, homemade pastas.

SANTA CRUZ. *Expensive:* **Shadowbrook.** In Capitola, 4 miles south. Unusual wooded setting. Ride funicular down to restaurant. Reservations suggested.

SANTA ROSA. *Moderate:* **John Ash & Co.** California fare. Great wine selection.
Restaurant Matisse. 620 5th St. Mesquite-grilled seafood. Sonoma County wines.

SAUSALITO. *Expensive:* **Ondine.** Elegant dining. Superb views of San Francisco.
Casa Madrona. Historic hotel serving country French cuisine in a romantic atmosphere.

SOLVANG. *Moderate:* **Danish Inn.** Own baked goods.

SONOMA. *Expensive:* **Depot Hotel 1870.** French country inn; imaginative dinners. Reservations essential.
Moderate: **Au Relais.** 691 Broadway. Popular; attractive Victorian house; gardens.

VACAVILLE. *Moderate:* **Nut Tree.** Super breakfast, salad treats. A legend in Northern California.

NEVADA

Las Vegas, Reno, and Lake Tahoe

Las Vegas, which calls itself "The Entertainment Capital of the World," is truly one of the world's most exciting cities. Located in the Southern Nevada desert near the tip of the "Silver State," Las Vegas annually plays host to some 12 million visitors, who come to this famous resort to see the top stars of show business and try their luck in the city's numerous legal casinos. Although casino-style gambling was legalized in Nevada in 1931, the phenomenal growth of Las Vegas did not start until after World War II. But it has continued unabated since that time.

The largest concentration of luxury resorts is along the three and one-half mile "Strip." But another casino complex is located downtown, in what is called "Casino Center." The latter is along famous Fremont Street, the main street of the city when it was founded in 1905.

Today, Las Vegas is one of the country's leading convention cities. An 825,000-square-foot, one-level, air-conditioned Convention Center is the site of over 300 conclaves yearly, and also is used for a number of sporting and special events.

Boulder City & Hoover Dam

Stop at the Visitor's Center in Boulder City or at the headquarters of the Lake Mead National Recreation Area for exhibits, and a schedule of tours and other activities. If you want to explore on your own, start with the tour of Hoover Dam, then drive on to Willow Beach on the Arizona side of Lake Mohave. Here you will develop a fast appreciation for the effort it required to tame the rampant Colorado in such a rugged setting. Return to Hoover Dam and proceed along the

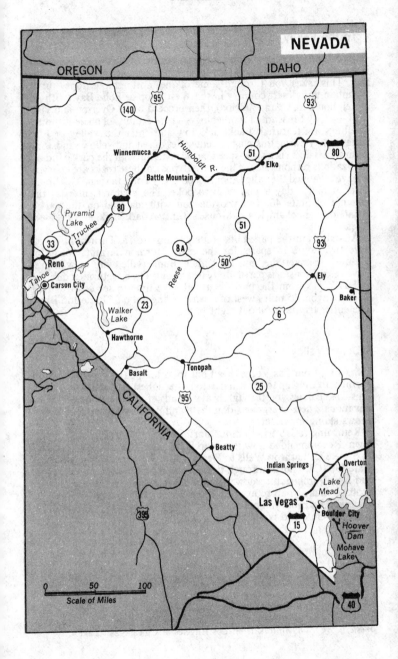

shore of Lake Mead to the marina for swimming, boat rides and sweeping views. (In March there are superb wildflower displays throughout the desert.)

To the Valley of Fire

Another tour begins with the drive to Henderson and onto the scenic highway built by the Lake Mead National Recreation Area to Echo Bay. This takes you through some of the most remote, topsy-turvy mountain and desert country in the West. Stop at Echo Bay (with its motel, houseboats, and marina), then proceed on to Overton and visit the Lost City Museum of Archeology, where exhibits of ancient Indian dwellings are featured. Backtrack now and enter the Valley of Fire State Park, viewing this magnificent series of red and yellow sandstone natural carvings via a slow-speed paved road through the park. (Indian civilizations responsible for the petroglyphs on these rocks are believed to have inhabited the valley about 1,500 B.C.) You can spend two hours here, or half a day if you wish to poke. The Visitor Center, at the junction of State 40, will provide you with material on the park's attractions: Elephant Rock, Mouse's Tank, Atlatl Rock, and the Bee-hives.

An exit from the park puts you on Interstate 15. Turn right if you have two hours to spare, for the early Mormon farming towns of Mesquite, Bunkerville, and Logandale. Bunkerville, with its well-preserved early houses, is particularly interesting. Or, by returning directly to Las Vegas from the park, you will have time to see colorful Red Rock Canyon, 15 miles west of town heading out on Charleston Blvd. The entire trip takes about eight hours.

Death Valley

Starting from Las Vegas, head out for a long day's drive on US 95 north, detouring up to Mt. Charleston, the highest range in the vicinity. This road carries you through heavy stands of yucca and cactus up to elevations where evergreens dominate and where substantial snowfall allows skiing in winter.

Returning to US 95, continue north to Beatty, another old mining town. Recommended now is a loop drive into Death Valley, reached on State 373, Lathrop Wells to Death Valley Junction. From here take State 190 (Cal.) north through this desolate basin to Scotty's Castle, an odd bit of architecture now open to the public as a museum. From Scotty's make your return via State 374 to Beatty and proceed to Tonopah. En route you pass through Goldfield, a pitiful remnant of the Tonopah-Goldfield boom 60 years ago.

PRACTICAL INFORMATION FOR LAS VEGAS

HOW TO GET THERE. *By air:* There are direct flights on 15 lines from major cities all over the U.S.; and from Canada by *Eastern, Republic* and *Western. By train:* Amtrak from Los Angeles or Chicago-Salt Lake City.

HOW TO GET AROUND. *By air:* Small planes can be rented or chartered at McCarran Int'l. Airport or at North Las Vegas Air Terminal. *By car: Hertz, Avis, National* and *Budget* car rental companies are at the airport; *Brooks Rent-A-Car* and other major rental agencies are on the main

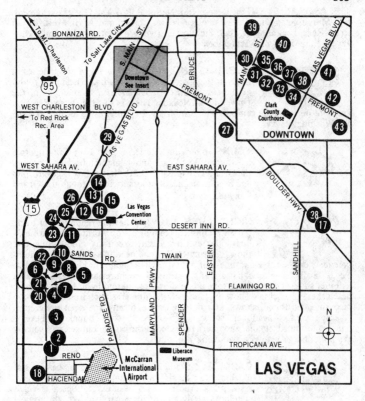

Resort Hotels and Casinos

1) Tropicana
2) Marina
3) Aladdin
4) MGM Grand
5) Barbary Coast
6) Flamingo Hilton
7) Maxim
8) Imperial Palace
9) Holiday Inn & Casino
10) Sands
11) Desert Inn
12) Riviera
13) El Rancho
14) Sahara
15) Las Vegas Hilton

16) Landmark
17) Nevada Palace
18) Hacienda
19) Dunes
20) Dunes
21) Caesar's Palace
22) Castaways
23) Frontier
24) Silver Slipper
25) Stardust
26) Circus-Circus
27) Showboat
28) Sam's Town

Downtown Hotels and Casinos

29) Vegas World
30) Union Plaza
31) Golden Gate Casino
32) Golden Nugget
33) Four Queens
34) Sundance
35) Las Vegas Club
36) Mint
37) Horseshoe
38) Fremont
39) Holiday Inn
40) California Hotel
41) Lady Luck Casino
42) El Cortez
43) Western Hotel

highway into town. *By bus: The Strip Bus* (#6) runs every 15 min. from the Hacienda Hotel (on the Strip) to the Downtown Casino Center.

TOURIST INFORMATION SERVICES. For Las Vegas information, hotel and show reservations, stop at the *Travel Center* on Interstate 15, southwest of the city, *Las Vegas Tourist Center* on Hwy. 95 southeast of town or at the *Greater Las Vegas Chamber of Commerce,* 2301 E. Sahara Av.

SEASONAL EVENTS. Desert Inn National Pro-Am Golf Tournament, mid-March; Alan King Caesars Palace Tennis Classic, mid-April; Mint 400 Off Road Race, beginning of May; Helldorado (western events, rodeo), mid-May; Jaycee State Fair, mid-September.

MUSEUMS AND GALLERIES. There are galleries in many of the Strip hotels. Shows are also held year-round at the *Grant Hall Art Gallery,* on the campus of the University of Nevada. There is also the *Desert Research Institute* on the same campus. The *Las Vegas Art Museum,* is located at 3333 W. Washington Av.

TOURS *American Sightseeing* and *Gray Line* operate bus tours of Las Vegas and its nightclubs, Hoover Dam, the Grand Canyon and Death Valley. *Las Vegas Airlines* and *Scenic Airlines* fly tours to and through the Grand Canyon.

NIGHTCLUBS. Las Vegas has the reputation of being the entertainment capital of the world. There are million-dollar extravaganzas, Broadway productions, and shows starring Hollywood headliners, all playing simultaneously on the three-and-one-half-mile stretch of boulevard known as the Las Vegas "Strip." The usual pattern among the showroom restaurants is to present a dinner show at about 8 P.M. then a late show around midnight; however, some hotels have a cocktail show in place of the dinner show. Reservations are recommended for all shows, and hotel guests naturally are given preference. Average cost for "headliner" shows is $25–30 per person. To make sure everyone is entertained, smaller shows are provided in the casino lounges, and usually the only charge here is a two-drink minimum.

CASINOS. Nevada is all one big gambling casino; slot machines are at airplane, train, and bus terminals, at restaurants, grocery stores, even gas stations. Las Vegas standouts along the Strip, a carnival-like glittering 3 ½-mile section, are *Caesars Palace, Circus Circus,* the *Desert Inn,* the *Dunes, Hacienda,* the *Flamingo Hilton,* the *Riviera,* the *Sahara,* the *Sands,* the *Stardust,* the *Frontier,* the *El Rancho,* the *Landmark,* the *Las Vegas Hilton,* the *Imperial Palace,* the *Maxim,* the *Marina,* the *MGM Grand Hotel,* and the *Tropicana.*

Games of chance include 21, craps, roulette, blackjack, poker, baccarat, and keno. Pretty cocktail waitresses hover about the tables, offering free drinks to the more serious-looking players. You don't have to order liquor; you can just have a soft drink if you would prefer. (There is something about the casinos that makes you terribly thirsty; you will be glad of this special service.) Most of the above-named casinos also maintain (very close to the playing rooms) bountiful buffet tables, where you can have breakfast, lunch, or dinner at very modest prices.

Outstanding casinos in downtown Las Vegas (Fremont St.) are the *Mint,* the *Union Plaza,* the *Fremont,* the *Sundance,* the *Las Vegas Club,* the *Golden Nugget* and *Binion's.* "Glitter Gulch," as this section is called, is only three blocks long, but the light is so bright from a dozen hotels that you can read a newspaper at 3 A.M.! This section of Las Vegas, because of the congestion of light, has been more photographed than the Strip and is the site of much of VEGAS' action. The big-name stars do not work here, but many tourists feel the casino odds are better than those on the more luxurious Strip.

SUMMER SPORTS. Golf is readily available. The best courses are at the Sahara Country Club, the Dunes Country Club, the Tropicana Country Club and the Desert Inn Country Club. Public courses are Winterwood, Craig Ranch, Las Vegas City and Paradise Valley.

WINTER SPORTS. Skiing is found at Lee Canyon (Mt. Charleston).

SPECTATOR SPORTS. Rodeos highlight *Helldorado,* the big annual Western pageant in Las Vegas in May.

WHAT TO DO WITH THE CHILDREN. In Las Vegas, children seem to enjoy the live circus acts at Circus Circus Hotel; and the electronic games rooms in all of the major hotels. The best are at the MGM Grand and the Las Vegas Hilton, which has its own children's hotel.

An excursion to *Lake Mead* for a picnic on the beach—with swimming, fishing, and water skiing—is a favorite pastime for children.

An excursion to Death Valley, about 140 miles north of Las Vegas, off Hwy. 95 is popular. *Warning:* Extremely hot during the summer.

Hoover Dam is an exciting sightseeing venture; guided tours leave from the dam every few minutes. (The huge dam was constructed in 1931–35 and backs up the Colorado River for 115 miles as Lake Mead.)

HOTELS. The famous Las Vegas "Strip" is the world's most concentrated area of luxury hotels. The hotels are designed to keep the guests inside and entertained 24 hours a day and so have a half-dozen restaurants each, many shops, varied entertainment—and no clocks. *Deluxe:* $60 and up; *Expensive:* $50–60; *Moderate:* $40–50; *Inexpensive:* under $40.

ON THE STRIP *Deluxe:* **Caesars Palace.** Luxurious rooms. Ultimate in service and atmosphere. Spacious grounds with fountains and Roman statues. Superstar entertainers. (731–7110)

Las Vegas Hilton. Largest resort hotel in the world. Top entertainment. 11 restaurants, children's hotel, next to Convention Center, 3000 Paradise Rd. (732–5111)

MGM Grand Hotel. A $100 million extravaganza designed to be Hollywood's dream of what a hotel should look like. Fine restaurants, lavish shows. (739–4111)

Desert Inn. Rambling inn and country club with beautiful gardens. Center of the strip. (733–4444)

Expensive: **Dunes.** 1,000 rooms and 100 luxurious suites. Restaurants, bar, and entertainment. Eighteen-hole golf course. (737–4110)

Flamingo Hilton. One of the larger of the Strip hotels with a wide choice of accommodations. Family rates. (733–3111)

Frontier Hotel. Colorful western motif. (734–0110)

Tropicana. The grounds are a sporting paradise: 18-hole golf course, putting green and driving range; tennis courts; pool. (739–2222)

Moderate: **Hacienda.** Rambling, garden-type hotel. (739–8911)

Stardust. Noted for its Lido de Paris Revue. (732–6111)

OTHER HOTELS AND MOTELS.

DOWNTOWN. *Moderate:* **Four Queens.** All rooms the same price.

Mint. Excellent buffet.

Sundance. Tallest building in Nevada.

Union Plaza. Dinner-theatre. Amtrak station.

Inexpensive: **Bali Hai.** Centrally located, off the Strip.

Mini-Price. Two locations in the city.

Motel 6. Near the Tropicana.

Orbit Inn. Located at the end of "Glitter Gulch."

Showboat. A large hotel with 110 bowling lanes. On Boulder Hwy.

DINING OUT. The offerings range from exotic and foreign gourmet cuisine to buffet budgeter's bonanzas. The restaurants vary in price and menus—you'll find moderately priced cafes, coffee shops, health food store counters, and pancake houses all around town. Food is served at all hours.

An average showroom dinner costs between $15 and $25, and a marvelous show is included. (Casual tourists should be prepared to stand in line for about an hour to be seated.)

The principal showrooms are at the *Caesars Palace,* the *Desert Inn,* the *Dunes,* the *Riviera, Sahara, Sands, Stardust, Frontier, Golden Nugget, MGM Grand, Hilton, Flamingo Hilton,* and the *Tropicana.* In "Casino Center" downtown, the *Union Plaza* has dinner-theatre with Broadway plays.

Restaurants are listed by price ranges of a complete meal, without drinks: *Deluxe:* $25 and up, *Expensive:* $15–25, *Moderate:* $10–15, *Inexpensive:* under $10.

Deluxe: **Ah-So.** Caesars Palace. A 10-course feast on a tabletop hibachi.

Aku-Aku Stardust Hotel. Large menu includes exotic drink list.

Bacchanal. Caesars Palace. Feel like one of the ancient Caesars. A Roman gourmet feast.

Dome of the Sea. Dunes Hotel. Considered by many the best seafood restaurant in Las Vegas.

Gigi's. MGM Grand Hotel. One of the best in the state. French cuisine.

Le Gourmet. Tropicana Hotel. Haute cuisine and elegant French setting.

Palace Court. Caesars Palace. The best food in Las Vegas in a luxurious garden setting.

The Library. Across the from Sahara. English manor house setting.

Expensive: **Alpine Village.** Swiss-German food. Across from Las Vegas Hilton and convention center.

Sabre Room. Aladdin Hotel. Excellent French menu.

State Street. In the Commercial Center. A favorite hangout of entertainment celebrities.

Moderate: **Battista's Hole in the Wall.** More fun than a barrel of opera singers.

Inexpensive: **Old Heidelberg.** Near the Sahara Hotel. Fine Bavarian cuisine.

Ricardo's. Best Mexican food in the city.

EXPLORING RENO, LAKE TAHOE, AND
NORTHERN NEVADA

If you can allow about nine days, a memorable trip covering every corner of the state awaits you. If you do not have nine days to spare, plan to make your base at any of the stopover points to be designated later and see as much as you can. For reference, consult any good map of the state, such as the official Nevada map that can be obtained by writing the *Nevada Department of Transportation,* 1263 S. Stewart St., Carson City, Nevada 89712.

Ichthyosaur, Anyone?

From Tonopah via US 6, drive through one of Nevada's characteristic and isolated interior basins, Smoky Valley. Detour on State 376 to see the semi-ghost towns of Manhattan and Belmont and, when you reach US 50, see a boomtown of a century ago, Austin. Continue west on US 50 past the famous Singing Sand Mountain, the rich ranching area fed by Lanhontan Dam, to your overnight stop at either Carson City or Lake Tahoe. A second route from Tonopah leads, via US 6–95, from Luning to Gabbs. Detour here to Ichthyosaur Paleontologic State Monument over an adventurous road, State 91. The remains of the ancient sea-going ichthyosaur lie near the bleak ghost town of Berlin.

Ichthyosaurs dominated the seas 160 million years ago, ages before the dinosaur. This deposit of fossilized bones in central Nevada is the only one of its kind in the world and is well worth visiting.

Shortest yet in terms of mileage, here is a route filled with sights and scenery you won't soon forget. Start at Lake Tahoe, around the northeast shore via State 28; travel through unspoiled stands of pine and cedar and enjoy breathtaking views of this vivid, blue freshwater

lake—6,000 feet high, second in size and altitude only to South America's Lake Titicaca.

Continue on to junction of State 431. Motor over the high-flung Mt. Rose highway for sweeping panoramas of Lake Tahoe and a bird's-eye view of Reno, Washoe Valley, and Washoe Lake, all memorable sights.

At Virginia City you are in one of the West's most fascinating towns. Boardwalks, sagging facades, Victorian mansions (several open to the public), and honky-tonk saloons vividly transmit the spirit of the Comstock days. Take a walking tour and really poke—you can spend two hours pleasantly, or an entire day, in this very lively ghost town.

In Carson City, visit the State Museum. See the impressive Indian and period exhibits and go through the realistic underground mine. Then take the tour of old houses and mansions of Nevada's capital, and have a quick look at the quaint old Victorian Capitol.

PRACTICAL INFORMATION FOR RENO, LAKE TAHOE, AND NORTHERN NEVADA

HOW TO GET THERE. *By air:* Reno is now served by nine major airlines. *By car:* via U.S. Hwy. 50 and I–80 from San Francisco and Sacramento; U.S. Hwy 395 from Los Angeles; I–80 from Salt Lake City and points east. *By train: Amtrak* has service to Reno from San Francisco and Chicago. *By bus: Greyhound,* and *Trailways* from all points.

HOW TO GET AROUND. *By air:* Service to South Lake Tahoe Airport by *Golden Gate Airlines. By car:* Major car rentals at the airport and *Econo-car* and *Fairway Rent-a-Car* nearby. *By bus:* Four routes on Reno Citifare from 6 A.M. to 6 P.M. *LTR* bus lines to Las Vegas, Tonopah, and Lake Tahoe Airport.

TOURIST INFORMATION SERVICES. *Reno: Reno Visitors Service,* 704 S. Virginia St. Sparks: *Sparks Chamber of Commerce,* 1880 Prater Way. Virginia City: *Virginia City Visitors Bureau,* South Virginia City. *Carson City: Carson City Chamber of Commerce,* 1191 S. Carson St.

MUSEUMS AND GALLERIES. *Nevada State Historical Society,* 1650 N. Virginia St., Reno. Early settlement days of Nevada, Indian artifacts, Victorian costume, mining artifacts. *Sierra Nevada Museum of Art,* 549 Court St., Reno. Local and regional artists and traveling exhibitions of national importance. *Fleischmann Atmospherium-Planetarium,* N. Virginia St., Reno. Star shows, 180-degree motion picture projection. Stunning presentations. *Nevada State Museum,* 600 N. Carson St., Carson City. Formerly a branch of the U.S. Mint. Mineral exhibits and a replica of a full-scale mine.

HISTORIC SITES. Historical markers, some three dozen in all, were erected throughout the state during the Centennial year of 1964. For a listing of locations, write the *Division of State Parks,* Carson City, Nevada 89710. *The Nevada Department of Transportation* also makes them easy to locate. Its official highway map, published annually, circles the major places of interest; by a dotted trail, the map also pinpoints the early pioneer trails and ghost towns.

Outstanding are *Virginia City,* the most tourist-conscious and once the richest city in America; *Manhattan and Belmont,* on State 376, are semi-ghost towns, relics of past glories and riches; *Austin,* on US 50, is an interesting ghost town of deteriorating old buildings (Stokes, Castle, Courthouse, churches, stores, and hotel); *Eureka,* US 50, is another relic of mining days, while *Tuscarora,* on State 226, also exhibits remains of an early mining camp.

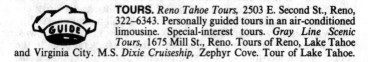

TOURS. *Reno Tahoe Tours,* 2503 E. Second St., Reno, 322–6343. Personally guided tours in an air-conditioned limousine. Special-interest tours. *Gray Line Scenic Tours,* 1675 Mill St., Reno. Tours of Reno, Lake Tahoe and Virginia City. M.S. *Dixie Cruiseship,* Zephyr Cove. Tour of Lake Tahoe.

DRINKING LAWS. There are no restrictions on hours for legal drinking, nor on where drinks and bottles can be ordered and consumed. Age minimum is 21.

SUMMER SPORTS. *Fishing* is best from November through April at Pyramid Lake (cutthroat and rainbow trout), Lake Tahoe (giant mackinaw, rainbow, and cutthroat), Walker Lake (cutthroat and Sacramento perch), lakes Mead and Mohave (bass, bluegill, catfish, black crappie, stripers, coho, and rainbow trout). Licenses are $10 for the special three-day visitor's permit or $20 annually. For Mead and Mohave there are also $3 special-use stamps.

Swimming, boating and water sports are year-round activities in southern parts of the state, but are enjoyed in the summer only at Lake Tahoe and other regions. Water skiing is especially good on Lake Tahoe, and on lakes Walker, Pyramid, Topaz, Mead, and Mohave.

Golf can be enjoyed readily. The best courses are: Brookside Municipal, 700 S. Rock Blvd., Reno; Washoe County, Highway 395 north; Lakeridge, 1200 Razorback Rd., Reno; Sierra Sage, Stead Turnoff, 8 mi. N. of Reno; Northstar at Tahoe, Hwy. 267 and Northstar Dr., Truckee; Wildcreek, 3500 Sullivan La., Sparks; Incline Village Championship, Incline Village.

Hiking is enjoyed throughout the state, particularly in the National Forest areas. Here are good, established trails awaiting the outdoorsman.

Horseback riding can be found at Stateline Stables, South Shore Lake Tahoe; Corky Prunty's Stables, 10199 Mogul Rd., Reno.

Hunting is richly varied. Deer hunting lasts from early October through mid-November; non-resident licenses cost $50, plus $50 for a deer stamp; state duck stamp is $2; pheasant stamp $2. Bow-and-arrow hunts can be held before the regular rifle season, usually the first three weeks of September; license is $10 with a $50 tag fee. Hunting seasons for ducks and upland game are mid-October until early January; mid-September to late January is the season too for small game, except mid-November for pheasant.

WINTER SPORTS. Skiing is excellent. In the Reno-Lake Tahoe area, more than a dozen large, well-equipped ski resorts lie within an hour's drive from Reno. Among the big ones are Alpine Meadows, Heavenly Valley, Mt. Rose, Northstar, Ski Incline, Squaw Valley and Tahoe Donner.

SPECTATOR SPORTS. Rodeos are the favorite. The Reno Rodeo, the state's richest, occurs in June. The Nevada Rodeo, the biggest and most traditional, takes place in Winnemucca in September.

HOTELS AND MOTELS. Prices are double occupancy in-season rates; winter rates are slightly lower. *Deluxe:* $60 and up; *Expensive:* $50–60; *Moderate:* $40–50; *Inexpensive:* under $40.

CARSON CITY. *Expensive:* **Ormsby House.** 202 rooms, casino.
Moderate: **Carson City TraveLodge.** Medium-sized chain member with fireplaces in some special units. Family rates.

DEATH VALLEY. *Expensive.* **Furnace Creek Inn.** Beautiful old inn which sprawls over several levels in the desert. Closed in the summer. *Moderate.* **Furnace Creek Ranch.** Large motel complex, open all year.

RENO. *Deluxe:* **MGM.** As extravagant as the movie company. World's largest casino.

Reno Hilton (formerly Sahara Reno). Twenty-one-story highrise, turn-of-the-century décor and 610 rooms.

Expensive: **El Dorado.** 411 rooms. Newly remodeled, four restaurants.

Circus Circus. Colorful circus atmosphere. Very unusual.

Harrah's Reno. Heated pool, restaurants, bars, health club, etc. The famous Harrah Automobile Collection (as well as some airplanes, boats, etc.) must be seen.

Peppermill Inn. 200 dramatically decorated rooms and the famed Peppermill restaurant.

Pick Hobson's Riverside Hotel. A Reno landmark with the tradition and hospitality of the Old West.

Pioneer. Downtown, 251 rooms, free parking.

Ramada Hotel. Custom designed rooms.

Inexpensive: **Reno TraveLodge.** Large member of the chain; family rates.

NORTH LAKE TAHOE. *Deluxe:* **Hyatt Lake Tahoe.** 500 luxury rooms and suits. Splendid panorama of the lake.

Expensive: **Cloud's Cal-Neva Lodge.** Nine-story hotel; every room with a panoramic view.

SOUTH LAKE TAHOE. *Deluxe:* **Caesars Tahoe.** 446 beautiful rooms with magnificent views of the lake. Marble hot tubs in most rooms.

Harrah's Lake Tahoe. 540 rooms, every one with a scenic view of the lake or the pine forest.

TONOPAH. **Mizpah Hotel.** Restoration of a turn-of-the-century hotel.

VIRGINIA CITY. *Moderate:* **Comstock.** Comfortable, small motel.

 DINING OUT. Dining out in Nevada often means dining and dancing and show-watching, especially in the gambling towns of Las Vegas and Reno. In Reno-Tahoe most of the hotels have buffets where you can eat all you want for a reasonable price. You should also try to sample the cooking of the Basque shepherds in northern Nevada; Elko and Gardnerville have good, representative Basque restaurants.

Restaurants are listed by price ranges of a complete meal without drinks: *Deluxe:* $25 and up, *Expensive:* $15–25, *Moderate:* $10–15, *Inexpensive:* $5–10.

CARSON CITY. *Moderate:* **Enrico's of Carson.** Italian-American cuisine.

ELKO. *Inexpensive:* **Nevada Dinner House.** Family-style dinner specializing in Basque food.

Star Hotel. One of the best Basque restaurants in Nevada.

GARDNERVILLE. This tiny town has two excellent and inexpensive popular Basque restaurants that serve dinner starting at 6 P.M. They are the *J. and T.* and the *Overland.*

GENOA. *Moderate:* **Sierra Shadows.** A century-old barn in Nevada's oldest settlement.

RENO. *Deluxe:* **Bundox.** Continental and American cuisine.

Gigi. In the MGM Grand. French cuisine in an elegant setting.

Moderate: **Miguel's.** Fine Mexican food. A landmark.

Vario's. Excellent service. Prime ribs and charcoal broiled steaks.

SOUTH LAKE TAHOE. *Expensive:* **Edgewood.** In Caesars Tahoe. Superior food, in an atmosphere of beamed oak and etched glass.

VERDI. *Moderate:* **Verdi Inn.** Historic inn. Continental gourmet food.

WINNEMUCCA. *Moderate:* **Winners Hotel.** Restaurant, bar and dancing.

OREGON

Portland, the Gorgeous Coast, and Wilderness

Portland is not only Oregon's largest, but also its sole metropolitan city. As such, it is the proper starting point for tours of the state. But first, Portland itself invites exploration.

The best way to see the "City of Roses" is to take the fifty-mile Scenic Drive, whose most convenient starting point is the Visitors Information Center (Chamber of Commerce Building) at S.W. Fifth and Taylor streets.

The Scenic Drive leads motorists to the summits of three hills—Council Crest, Rocky Butte, and Mount Tabor (an extinct volcano)—which afford awesome panoramas of Oregon and Washington. Clearly visible from these vantage points are Mount Rainier, the volcanic Mount St. Helens, and Mount Adams, all in Washington; and the great peaks of the Oregon Cascades: Mount Hood, Mount Jefferson, and the Three Sisters.

Other attractions on the route are the famed International Rose Test Gardens, Rhododendron and Azalea Test Gardens, and Peninsula Park's Sunken Gardens; Reed College, which has turned out more Rhodes scholars than either Yale, Harvard, or the University of Chicago and whose reputation for intellectual freedom is worldwide; the fun-in-learning Oregon Museum of Science and Industry (OMSI); the Western Forestry Center; the Portland Zoo, with its famed elephants and streamlined Zooliner, which carries riders on a mile-long journey through Washington Park; Japanese Gardens; Hoyt Arboretum; the opulent Pittock Mansion; and many old homes and some of the city's most beautiful neighborhoods.

The city's biggest event is its Rose Festival, an annual celebration since 1909. The fiesta, generally held the second week of June and as

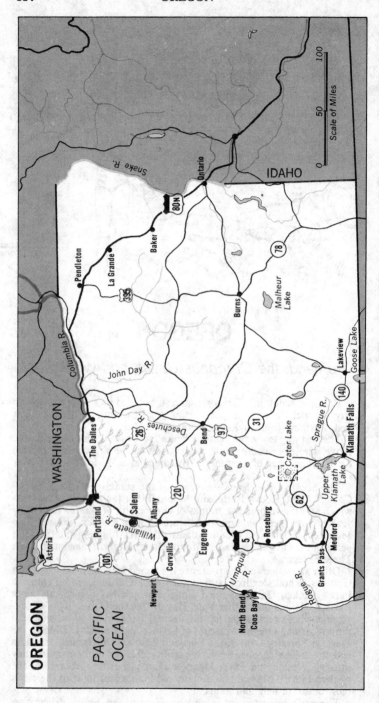

OREGON

colorful as a Mardi Gras, features the Rose Show; the Golden Rose Ski Tournament (on the slopes of Mount Hood, 62 miles east); and numerous cultural, carnival, and outdoor stage and entertainment activities—all climaxed by the Grand Floral Parade, which draws floats and bands from as far as 1,500 miles away.

PRACTICAL INFORMATION FOR PORTLAND

HOW TO GET THERE. *By air:* Portland, which has about half the state's population in its metropolitan area, is served by 18 airlines. From the city's modern international airport, DART buses take visitors to the downtown area. *By train: Amtrak* runs passenger trains from several West Coast cities and the East via Boise. *By car:* Route 1–5 runs to Portland from Washington and California. *By bus: Trailways* and *Greyhound* have continental service to Portland.

HOW TO GET AROUND. *By car:* Oregon has a fine, toll-free highway system. The main north-south route (Interstate 5) runs stoplight-free through the heart of the state. *By bus:* Portland's municipal bus system, Tri-Met, costs 75¢ in-city, with free transfers.

TOURIST INFORMATION SERVICES. In Portland, the *tourist center* is at Interstate 5 (north, near the Interstate bridge), 12345 N. Union Ave. 97217, (503) 285-1631. It is open from May 1 to Oct. 30. The *Portland Visitors Service* is at 824 S.W. Fifth Ave., in Chamber of Commerce Building.

SEASONAL EVENTS. The top attraction on Portland's crowded calendar of events is the *Rose Festival* in June. Other highlights include the *Pacific International Livestock Exposition,* an all-breed *dog show* in July and *Neighborfair* in mid-August.

MUSEUMS AND GALLERIES. Historical: *Oregon Historical Society,* 1230 S.W. Park Ave. The French Renaissance *Pittock Mansion,* 3229 N.W. Pittock Dr. Art: *Portland Art Museum,* 1219 S.W. Park Ave. Northwest Indian artifacts. Special Interest: *Oregon Museum of Science and Industry,* 4015 S.W. Canyon Rd.; *Western Forestry Center,* 4033 S.W. Canyon Rd.

TOURS. *The Gray Line* has tours to Mt. Hood, the Coast, the Mt. St. Helens volcanic country, and around Portland.

SPECIAL INTEREST TOURS. Portland Parks Bureau offers inexpensive hiking tours to the coast, hills and woods.

GARDENS. See *Washington Park* for the International Rose Test Gardens and Japanese Gardens. *Rhododendron Test Garden* at S.E. 28th Ave. and Woodstock, and *Sunken Gardens* in Peninsula Park, 6400 N. Albina.

MUSIC. *Music by Moonlight* program is held in Washington Park from late July through mid-August. The *Portland Opera Assn.* presents 4 operas during its Sept.–May season. The *Oregon Symphony Orchestra,* from Sept. through May, presents 6 sets of Sun.–Tues. evening concerts.

STAGE AND REVUES. Portland Civic Theatre, 1530 S.W. Yamhill, offers a varied fare of stage productions through the year.

NIGHTCLUBS. The current spots include *Darcelle XV, Last Hurrah, Flower Drum, Club Venus,* and *The The Great Gatsby's.* Top bars include the *Agate* in the Cosmopolitan Hotel at 1030 N.E. Union and *Panorama* at the top of the Hilton.

SUMMER SPORTS. There are 29 golf courses in the Portland area, most open to public play.

WINTER SPORTS. The largest ski crowds gather at Mt. Hood's *Timberline Lodge,* which has the most complete facilities in the area.

SPECTATOR SPORTS. A range of offerings from minor league *baseball* to pro *basketball, horse racing* at Portland Meadows and *greyhound racing* at nearby Gresham, in the summer.

WHAT TO DO WITH THE CHILDREN. The parks system has daily children's programs in the summer, the *zoo* is famous for its elephants, and the *Oregon Museum of Science and Industry* is a fun-in-learning wonderland.

HOTELS AND MOTELS. Hostelries listed here are given in price categories based on double occupancy without meals: *Deluxe:* $40 and up; *Expensive:* $30–$40; *Moderate:* $25–$30; *Inexpensive:* $25 and under.

Deluxe: **Westin Benson.** 309 S.W. Broadway. Large, elegant, downtown. Portland's oldest posh hostelry.

Rodeway Inn–Chumaree. 8247 N.E. Sandy Blvd. Near airport.

Cosmopolitan Airtel. 6221 N.E. 82nd Ave. Resort hotel at Portland International Airport. Posh.

Marriott Hotel. 1401 S.W. Front. Overlooks the Willamette River. Pools, sauna restaurants, bar.

Portland Hilton. 921 S.W. 6th Ave. Large, downtown, modern. Three restaurants. The leading convention hotel.

Portland Motor Hotel, 1414 S.W. Sixth St. Large, downtown. Sprightly.

Red Lion Inn/Lloyd Center. 1000 N.E. Multnomah. Large, near Lloyd Center.

Red Lion Motor Inn–Jantzen Beach. 909 N. Hayden Island Drive. View of Columbia River. Pools, boating, restaurants, lounge, entertainment.

Red Lion Motor Inn–Portland Center. Formerly Ramada Inn. 310 S.W. Lincoln. Large, near Civic Auditorium.

Riverside West Motor Hotel. 50 S.W. Morrison. Convenient to Morrison Bridge and downtown. Subdued, sophisticated air.

Sheraton Inn–Portland Airport. 8233 N.E. Airport Way. Large, heated pool, adjoining Portland International Airport.

Thunderbird Motor Inn–Coliseum. 1225 N. Thunderbird Way. Across from Memorial Coliseum.

Thunderbird Motor Inn–Jantzen Beach. 1401 N. Hayden Island Drive, off I-5. Lavish, glittering, on bank of Columbia River.

Cosmopolitan Hotel. 1030 N.E. Union. Near both downtown and Lloyd Center. Great view from "penthouse" tavern.

Holiday Inn At The Coliseum. 10 N. Weidler. Near Coliseum and Lloyd Center. Large motel with the many guest features offered by this chain. No extra charge for children under 12 in same room with parents. Heated pool. Coffee shop, dining room, cocktail lounge.

Holiday Inn–Holidome. 8349 N.E. Columbia. Comfortable.

Expensive: **Flamingo Motel.** 9727 N.E. Sandy Blvd. Large kitchen units. Swanky.

Hyatt Lodge. 431 N.E. Multnomah. Near downtown & Lloyd Center. Heated pool. Pets allowed.

Imperial 400 Motor Inn. 518 N.E. Holladay. Near Lloyd Center and Memorial Coliseum. Medium size motel with family units as well as one-room units. Heated pool. Restaurant nearby.

Jade Tree Motel. 3939 N.E. Hancock. In Hollywood shopping district.

Kings Way Inn. 420 N.E. Holladay. Near Lloyd Center. Therapy pool, sauna baths.

Shilo Inn–Lloyd Center. 1506 N.E. 2nd Ave. New facility near both Lloyd Center and Memorial Coliseum. Sauna. Restaurant near.

Shilo Inn–Portland Airport. 3828 N.E. 82nd Ave. Kitchen units, near airport.

Sunnyside Inn. 12855 S.E. 97th Ave. Near Kaiser Sunnyside Hospital.

Moderate: **Cameo Motel.** 4111 N.E. 82nd. Near airport. Cheery.

Caravan Motor Hotel. 2401 S.W. 4th. Good choice of rooms.

City Center Motel. 3800 N.E. Sandy Blvd. Family units.

Corsun Arms Motor Hotel. 809 S.W. King. Quiet, roof garden.

Continental Motel. 800 E. Burnside. Across bridge from city center.

Del Rancho Motel. 7622 S.E. 82nd Ave. Clean, kitchens.

Imperial Hotel. 400 S.W. Broadway. Well-kept, convenient.

Mallory Motor Hotel. 729 S.W. 15th Ave. At edge of downtown.

Portland Rose Motel. 8920 S.W. Barbur Blvd. Wheelchair units.

Wayside Motor Inn. 11460 S.W. Pacific Hwy. Equipped for handicapped. Sunny ambience.

Inexpensive: **Danmoore Hotel.** 1217 S.W. Morrison. Older, quiet.

Econo Lodge. 4810 N.E. Sandy Blvd. Family units, kitchens.

Motel 6. 3104 S.E. Powell Blvd. Comfortable.

 DINING OUT. Restaurants are listed in order of price category: *Deluxe:* $15 and up; *Expensive:* $10–15; *Moderate:* $6–10; *Inexpensive:* $6 and under. Drinks, tax and tip not included.

Deluxe: **Couch Street Fish House.** 3rd & Couch, in Old Town. Classic seafood dishes.

Genoa. 2832 S.E. Belmont. Northern Italian relative of L'Auberge.

L'Auberge. 2180 W. Burnside. Small; fine French food. Left Bank flair.

London Grill. In Benson Hotel, 309 S.W. Broadway. Continental, elegant.

Panorama. On 23rd floor of the Hilton Hotel. 921 S.W. 6th Ave. Fine food with a magnificent view.

Trader Vic's. Broadway and Stark. Downtown. Exotic Polynesian menu.

Expensive: **Benihana of Tokyo.** 315 S.W. 4th. Exquisite Japanese food in authentic setting.

Bush Garden. 121 S.W. 4th Ave. Authentic Japanese.

Hillvilla. 5700 S.W. Terwilliger Blvd. Good food, fine view.

Jade West. 122 S.W. Harrison. Fine Chinese food.

Jake's Famous Crawfish. 401 S.W. 12th Ave. Locally famous since 1892.

Old Country Kitchen. 10519 S.E. Stark. Portland's best beef.

Rian's. 729 S.W. Alder and 6620 S.W. Beaverton-Hillsdale Hwy. Relaxed, informal, huge portions.

Ringside. 2165 W. Burnside. Gourmet's delight.

Rusty Pelican, 4630 S.W. Macadam. River views.

Moderate: **Alexis.** 215 W. Burnside. Homemade Greek specialties, including Horiatiki salads.

Dan & Louis Oyster Bar. 308 S.W. Ankeny. Seafood in nautical-style dining room. Popular for all ages.

Old Spaghetti Factory. 126 S.W. 2nd. Zany atmosphere, fun, Italian favorites.

Old Wives' Tales. 1300 E. Burnside. Vegetarian. Children's playroom.

Rose's. 315 N.W. 23rd. and 12329 N.E. Glisan. Kosher. Homemade cakes.

Sumida's. 6744 N.E. Sandy Blvd. Authentic Japanese village atmosphere.

Tortilla Flats. 9010 S.E. 82nd Ave. Mexican food with authenticity.

Inexpensive: **Abou Karim.** 221 S.W. Pine. Authentic Lebanese cuisine.

North's Chuck Wagon. 10520 N.E. Halsey. All you can eat of great variety.

The Organ Grinder. 5015 S.E. 82nd Ave. Pizza to the accompaniment of the world's largest organ—and a surprise a minute.

The Pagoda. 3838 N.E. Broadway. Excellent Chinese cuisine.

The Sizzler. 3737 S.E. 82nd. Fantastic salad bar; all you can eat. Great senior menus.

EXPLORING OREGON

Heading inward from Oregon's famed coast (see section on this in *America's Travel Wonders,* earlier in this book), visitors may venture toward the Rogue River Valley. En route is Cave Junction, 14 miles above the California line. This is the gateway to Oregon Caves National Monument, "The Marble Halls of Oregon." The monument consists of a group of weirdly beautiful caverns at an elevation of 4,000 feet in the heart of the Siskiyou Mountains.

Grant's Pass, 30 miles east of Cave Junction, sits on the banks of the Rogue and is the takeoff point for runs down the frothing, wicked waters; runs range from a few hours to five days.

About 33 miles from the town of Rogue River, en route to Medford, is Jacksonville, Oregon's most picturesque historical settlement, founded on the heels of a gold rush in the early 1850's. Brought back to its previous state, the town is a nineteenth-century Western portrait.

Medford, the largest city in southern Oregon, is the center of a vast recreational area and of fruit-packing industries and orchards. Medford is also the most popular western gateway to Crater Lake National Park, Oregon's only national park. The lake, a deep brilliant blue, is encircled by lava cliffs. For details, see *Distinctively American Vacations* section of this book.

Ashland, home of America's first Elizabethan theater, is 12 miles south of Medford. The plays of the annual Oregon Shakespearean Festival are performed in a magnificent replica of the Globe Theater, in Lithia Park.

Oregon's second largest city, Eugene, is the seat of the University of Oregon. The Oriental Art Museum on campus is visited by scholars from around the world.

In the northern direction, on the banks of the Willamette, is Albany. Though the city is not a lumbering town of any real significance, it is host to the annual daredevilish World Timber Carnival. Virile contestants come from as far as Australia.

Albany is the gateway to a historic land of old: weather-worn towns, covered bridges, churches steeped in pioneer lore, and a Willamette river ferry (at Buena Vista).

Salem, the state capital, lies 24 miles north of Albany. Murals depict the state's history and from the capitol dome—above the murals—there is a marvelous overlook of the Willamette Valley and the Cascade foot-hills. On the grounds of the old Thomas Kay woolen mill, at Twelfth and Ferry Streets, stand what could be the two oldest buildings in Oregon: the Jason Lee House and Parsonage, both reputedly built in 1841.

Less than 40 miles from Salem is the state's most historic town, Oregon City. The municipality was first called Willamette Falls, the settlement having been located where the river drops 42 feet from a basaltic ledge. Oregon City was the first community incorporated west of the Missouri River and was Oregon's first provisional and territorial capital.

East from Portland, the first point of significant interest is Multnomah Falls, 24 miles from the city's heart. Second highest in the United States (620-foot drop in two steps), the falls are set in a sylvan glen against the cliffs of the Columbia River Gorge.

Eastern Oregon's largest City is Pendleton, home of the internationally renowned Pendleton Rodeo. The four-day affair, held each September, transforms the city into a Western camp. There are more events than most rodeos, with all the leading cowboys from the United States and Canada competing here.

Many regard Hell's Canyon as eastern Oregon's most spectacular attraction. Here black walls erupt from the river to a height of 2,000 feet, reach a bench, then soar 2,000 feet to a second bench. Hell's Canyon Park, on the reservoir en route to the canyon dam, has trailer-camper hookups with water and electricity. Jet boats, shooting the boiling rapids, penetrate the canyon for seven miles below the dam.

The town of Burns is the gateway to Oregon's "Big Sky" country, an immense area of sageland, great cattle ranches, rimrock buttes, and silent hamlets, spreading out from the slopes of the 50-mile-long, 9,000-feet-high Steens Mountains. Frenchglen, with 21 persons, is the largest settlement of the cattle country south of Burns.

Central Oregon is marked by the results of volcanic eruptions—the Lava Cast Forest, Lava River Caves State Park, Lava Butte Visitor Center, and the 9,000-acre Lava Butte Geological Area, encompassing Central Oregon's lava domain. The butte is the most popular site of Oregon's "Moon Country."

Another of the most impressive explorations in the state is Century Drive, also known as the Cascades Lake Highway. Taking off at the town of Bend, this 97-mile loop passes through high and rugged mountains, lava flow, lakes, reservoirs, and waterfalls.

Just 100 miles from Portland is Warm Springs, administrative center of Warm Springs Reservation. Turn north and drive ten miles to Kah-nee-ta, a resort operated by the Indians. In an Indian encampment, tepees are for rent. There are also a swimming pool complex, hiking trails, riding horses, a golf course, a fine restaurant, convention facilities, picnic grounds, and sites for trailers.

PRACTICAL INFORMATION FOR OREGON

HOW TO GET THERE. *By air:* Portland is served by 18 airlines (*American, Continental, Delta, Eastern, Northwest, Republic, TWA, United, Western, AirCal, Alaska, Frontier, PSA, Astor Air, Cascade, Horizon, Great American, Total Air*). *By train: Amtrak* runs passenger trains from Seattle, San Francisco, Oakland, Los Angeles, San Diego and from the East on the Union Pacific line. *By car:* From the east, Interstate 84 enters the state from Idaho at Ontario. From California, you can take Interstate 5 to the state line below Ashland or U.S. 101 along the scenic coast to Astoria. *By bus: Greyhound* and *Trailways* have service into the state.

HOW TO GET AROUND. *By air:* Almost every Oregon city of 10,000 or more has some kind of commercial air service. Private planes are for hire at scattered airfields. The state is served by two commuter airlines: *Horizon* and *Cascade*. *By car:* Oregon has a highway system that is among the best in the nation. The route for touring the coast is US 101, from California to Astoria at the mouth of the Columbia. From Portland, the most popular highways to the coast are US 26, Oregon 6, and Oregon 18. *By bus:* Nearly all the state's cities are reachable by bus.

TOURIST INFORMATION SERVICES. Headquarters for travel and tourist information is the *Travel Information Division,* in the Dept. of Economic Development Bldg., 595 Cottage St. N.E., Salem 97310. There are six port-of-entry *information centers* to aid travelers. *Tourist information services* are also offered at more than 45 Certified Centers located in local chamber of commerce offices throughout the state. Travelers can look for the blue direction-al signs adjacent to the major highways for reference to the centers.

 MUSEUMS AND GALLERIES. Several Oregon towns, some only a few ghostly buildings, are maintained as museums. They are scattered about the state.

Historical. Astoria: *Flavel Mansion.* Museum of Clat-sop County Historical Society in the home of a 19th-century sea captain.

Aurora: *Robert E. Newell House,* D.A.R. Museum.

Canyon City: *Herman and Eliza Oliver Museum.* Well-displayed relics of the gold rush days.

Haines: *Eastern Oregon Museum.* Wide assortment of 19th-century articles.

Jacksonville: *Jacksonville Museum.* Historical displays of famous gold coun-try and studio of great photographer, Peter Britt.

Klamath Falls: *Favell Museum of Western Art and Artifacts.* Beautifully displayed life of the Old West.

Salem: Archives of the *Oregon State Library* on the capitol mall—a wealth of precious documents and other historical materials.

Tillamook: *Tillamook County Pioneer Museum.*

Art. Eugene: *Museum of Art,* University of Oregon, Oriental collection; *Maude I. Kerns Art Center,* full schedule of arts and crafts exhibits.

Salem: *Salem Art Ass'n,* art gallery and collection of costumes.

 TOURS. Despite its many attractions and brisk tourist trade, Oregon has surprisingly few commercial travel tours. The visitor who drives to the state is best off with a do-it-yourself tour service—selecting specific areas or attractions, then plotting a course.

Launches circle Crater Lake or go to Wizard Island and Phantom Ship. A bus also makes daily trips around the lake. A thrilling way to view the Wallowa Mountains is to take the *High Wallowas Gondola Lift,* which rises 3,700 vertical ft. in 15 minutes to 8,020-foot Mt. Howard.

DRINKING LAWS. Nearly all bars in Oregon serve to the legal limit of 2:30 A.M. The minimum age for consumption of alcohol is 21. Motor Vehicles Dept. issues ID cards for those who don't have a driver's license.

 SUMMER SPORTS. *Swimming:* Most popular spa swimming is at Kah-nee-ta, on the Warm Springs Reser-vation. Most popular coastal swimming is at Seaside, and the most popular river swimming is at Rooster Rock State Park on the Columbia. *Boating:* All kinds on lakes and scenic rivers. Water skiing also popular. *Fishing* draws more than half a million fishermen a year to 15,000 miles of angling streams and hundreds of lakes.

Golf: Oregon boasts over 130 courses, active all year in mild western areas.

Hiking and packing: Natural sites in the numerous national forests and primitive areas. Indian-style hiking at Kah-nee-ta and at Rooster Rock State Park is available.

Horseback riding: Fine resources in all areas. Organized packhorse trips appealing to many through the mountainous country of center and eastern Oregon.

Hunting: The best game hunting is in the mountain country of central and eastern Oregon, and birds are also more plentiful east of the Cascades.

 WINTER SPORTS. Widely acclaimed for its fine pow-der snow and as training site for the 1972 Olympic team is Mt. Bachelor, 22 mi. west of Bend. Outstanding skiing and a breathaking panoramic view can be found at Hoo-doo Bowl Ski Area, 88 mi. southeast of Salem. Other areas: Mt. Hood, with the greatest concentration of ski areas in the state; Spout Springs in the Blue Mountains; Anthony Lakes Ski Area in the Elkhorn Range; and Mt. Ashland Ski area, south of Ashland.

SPECTATOR SPORTS. *Football:* Oregon plays its home games at Eugene and Oregon State at Corvallis.

WHAT TO DO WITH THE CHILDREN. Everything. The unlimited possibilities include: building sand castles, collecting driftwood and looking for Japanese glass floats, agates, and shells on the beaches of the coast; rockhounding throughout the state; swimming in lakes and rivers; hiking forest trails; looking at waterfalls and wildflowers and caves and canyons and Indian pictographs; splashing in Portland's *Forecourt Fountain;* angling for a trout at *Small Fry Lake* (14 is the upper age limit) seven mi. southeast of Estacada; goggling at the *Lakeview geyser;* tracing the steam to the hot mineral outlets at *Austin Hotel Springs,* on the Upper Clackamas River; watching the *fishing boats* come in at Astoria, Depoe Bay, Warrenton, Newport, and other ports; playing on an extinct volcano and walking through huge lava fields; rodeos, dune-buggy rides, and much more.

HOTELS AND MOTELS. Oregon has many fine local hotels and motels that complement those operated by, or under franchise with, the larger regional and national chains. While price and luxury generally go hand-in-hand, the traveler will frequently find excellent accommodations and facilities in the moderate and inexpensive price ranges. Seasonal price variations are more likely to be found along the coast and in a few other prime tourist areas than in the larger cities, where prices tend to be more constant the year round. Hostelries listed here are given in order of price category, highest first, within each city or town group. Cities are listed in alphabetical order.

Price categories are based on double occupancy without meals. *Deluxe:* $40 and up; *Expensive:* $30–40; *Moderate:* $25–30; *Inexpensive:* $25 and under. For a more complete examination of hotel and motel categories see *Facts at Your Fingertips* at the front of this volume.

ALBANY. *Moderate:* **Al-Ray Motel.** Attractive, heated pool.
Takeena Lodge (formerly Swept Wing Motor Inn).

ASHLAND. *Deluxe:* **Ashland Hills Inn.** Has many recreational extras.
Expensive: **Bard's Inn Motel.** Near Shakespearean Theater. Fit for a king.
Moderate: **Valley Entrance Motel.** Small, well-maintained. Courteous treatment.
Knight's Inn Motel. Medium-size, seasonal rates. Congenial.
Inexpensive: **Columbia Hotel.** Charming European style, old-fashioned elegance.

ASTORIA. *Expensive:* **Thunderbird Motor Inn.** Large, fine view of Columbia River.
Moderate: **Crest Motel.** On hilltop at edge of town, magnificent view of Columbia River.
Dunes Motel. Well-equipped units, seasonal rates.
Lamplighter Motel. Smaller, attractive.
Rosebriar Inn. Bed-and-breakfast; close to downtown.

BAKER. *Expensive:* **Sunridge Inn.** Large; beautiful grounds.
Moderate: **Eldorado Motel.** 24-hour service.
Oregon Trail Motel. Downtown; heated pool, saunas.
Royal Motor Inn. Comfortable, centrally located, pool.
Inexpensive: **Western Motel.** Small; playground area for youngsters, seasonal rates.

BANDON. *Moderate:* **Sunset Motel.** Medium-size; lovely ocean views.
Lakris Motel. Well-maintained.
Inexpensive: **Table Rock Motel.** Spic-and-span, on beach, some kitchens.

BEAVERTON. *Deluxe:* **Greenwood Inn.** Large inn. Pool, restaurant, lounge.
Expensive: **Nendel's Inn.** Between Portland and Beaverton. Large motel with restaurant, lounge, pool.
Moderate: **Royal Motor Inn.** Olympic-size pool, near restaurant.
Satellite Motel. Comfortable. Medium size. Some kitchens, pool.

BEND. *Deluxe:* **Inn of the Seventh Mountain.** 7 miles west of Bend on Century Drive. Beautiful resort. Breathtaking views of Cascade Mountains.
Sunriver Lodge. 15 miles south of Bend, off US 97. Outstanding resort in magnificent natural forest setting.
Expensive: **Entrada Lodge.** 4 miles west of Bend on Century Drive. Small immaculately clean. Alpine scenery.
Red Lion Motel. Comfortable, attractive.
Riverhouse Motor Inn. Large, luxurious, overlooking Deschutes River.
Thunderbird Motel. Large; restaurant, bar.
Moderate: **Maverick Motel.** Pool, restaurant. Quiet.
Royal Gateway Motel. Smaller, some kitchens, restaurant near.
Sportsman's Motel. Waterbeds, playground, pool.
Westward Ho Motel. Some kitchens; play area.
Inexpensive: **Edelweiss Motor Inn.** Some kitchen facilities.
Rainbow Motel. Some kitchens, playground area, coffee bar.

BIGGS. *Expensive:* **Dinty's Motor Inn.** Heated pool. Restaurant opposite.

BOARDMAN. *Moderate:* **Nugget Motel.** Comfortable units, heated pool, restaurant handy.

BROOKINGS. *Moderate:* **Brookings Inn.** Handy to ocean beaches and to rivers.
Spindrift Motor Inn. Sparkling clean rooms.

BURNS. *Expensive:* **Ponderosa Motel.** Heated pool. Pets okay.
Moderate: **Silver Spur Motel.** Smaller motel, comfortable. Folksy.

CANNON BEACH. *Deluxe:* **Surfsand Resort Motel.** Variety of one-room and larger units, some kitchens. Pool, playground, beach access.

CORVALLIS. *Expensive:* **Nendel's Inn.** Dining room, lounge, entertainment.
Moderate: **Shanico Inn.** Restaurant adjacent.

COTTAGE GROVE. *Deluxe:* **Village Green Motor Hotel.** Large, renowned, on spacious, beautifully landscaped grounds.

CRATER LAKE. *Expensive:* **Crater Lake Lodge.** Lodge-type, comfortable, activities.

EUGENE. *Deluxe:* **Eugene Hilton.** In center of town.
Greentree Motel. Quite impressive. Lounge.
Valley River Inn. Units with balconies overlook Willamette River.
Expensive: **Country Squire Inn.** Lovely grounds, 5 miles north of Eugene.
Holiday Inn of Eugene. Large, well-kept.
New Oregon Motel. Large, immaculate. Crisp cheeriness.
Ramada Inn. Excellent accommodations.
Shilo Inn. Big, sumptuous.
Thunderbird Motor Inn. Large; restaurant, bar.
Moderate: **TraveLodge.** Pool, restaurant, lounge, close to city center.
Downtown Motel. Near arty, culture-filled Downtown Mall. Sprightly.
The Timbers Motel. Convenient central location. Delightfully homey.
Inexpensive: **City Center Lodge.** Medium-size, close to downtown mall.
66 Motel. Medium-size, with comfortable units.

FLORENCE. *Expensive:* **Driftwood Shores Surfside Resort Inn.** All units face ocean.
    Moderate: **Le Chateau Motel.** Convenient; putting green.
    Inexpensive: **Park Motel.** Small, comfortable.

GLENEDEN BEACH. *Deluxe:* **Salishan Lodge.** The Taj Mahal and Shangri-La of the Oregon resorts.

GOLD BEACH. *Expensive:* **Jot's Resort.** Overlooking the Rogue River. Salmon and steelhead fishing. Restaurant.
    Tu Tu Tun Lodge. Seven miles up Rogue River.
    Moderate: **Ireland's Rustic Lodge.** Beautifully landscaped.
    Nimrod Motel. Comfortable; putting green.

GRANT'S PASS. *Expensive:* **Riverside Inn.** Large, overlooking Rogue River, boat dock, outdoor dining in summer.
    Moderate: **Bridge Motel.** Overlooking Rogue River, swimming pool.
    Redwood Motel. Small, comfortable, some kitchens, playground.
    Regal Lodge. Well-maintained; long beds.

JORDAN VALLEY. *Moderate:* **Sahara Motel.** In center of picturesque desert hamlet.

JOSEPH. *Moderate:* **Indian Lodge Motel.** Small, well-maintained.

KLAMATH FALLS. *Expensive:* **Thunderbird Motel.** Large, attractive rooms.
    Moderate: **Molatore's Motel.** Heated pool, restaurant.

LA GRANDE. *Expensive:* **Pony Soldier Motor Inn.** Very large; sauna, delightful courtyard.

LAKEVIEW. *Moderate:* **Hunters Lodge.** At site of perpetual geyser. Scenic, picturesque, quiet.

LINCOLN CITY. *Deluxe:* **The Inn at Spanish Head.** Huge, 10-story inn built against cliff on oceanfront.
    Shilo Inn. Large indoor swimming and therapy pool.
    Expensive: **Sailor Jack's Oceanfront Motel.** Medium-size, some kitchens, fireplaces, sauna.
    Moderate: **Coho Inn.** Overlooking ocean.
    Inexpensive: **Captain Cook's Motel.** Folksy atmosphere.

MEDFORD. *Expensive:* **Holiday Inn.** Large, well-maintained; putting green.
    Moderate: **Capri Motel.** Some kitchen facilities.
    Cedar Lodge. Medium-size; heated pool.
    Knight's Inn Motel. Downtown, comfortable.
    Rodeway Inn. Snazzy. Heated pool, 24-hour restaurant, airport transportation.

NEWPORT. *Deluxe:* **Embarcadero Resort Hotel.** Large, new; balconies overlook Yaquina Bay.
    Expensive: **Newport Hilton.** Ocean-view units.
    Moderate: **Moolack Shores.** Good access to beach.

NORTH BEND. *Moderate:* **Bay Bridge Motel.** At north end of Coos Bay Bridge.

ONTARIO. *Expensive:* **Tapadera Motor Inn.** Large, in garden setting.
    Moderate: **Holiday Motor Inn.** In-room movies, heated pool.
    Stampeder Motel. In north-center of town.

OREGON CAVES. *Moderate:* **Oregon Caves Chateau.** Beautiful mountain locale at Oregon Caves National Monument.

PENDLETON. *Deluxe:* **Red Lion Motor Inn–Indian Hills.** Large; dining room, lounge, heated pool.
Expensive: **Imperial 400 Motel.** Well maintained.
Moderate: **Chaparral Motel.** Kitchenettes, color TV, restaurant adjacent. Folksy place.
Pendleton TraveLodge. Medium-size facility, with standard comforts and heated pool.

ROSEBURG. *Expensive:* **Windmill Inn.** heated indoor pool. Whirlpool, sauna.
Moderate: **Hilltop Motel.** Comfortable, attractive, and modern.
Rose–Etta Hotel. Cozy, family atmosphere.
Inexpensive: **Shady Oaks Motel.** Small; spacious units.

SALEM. *Expensive:* **New Kings Inn.** Large; comfortable; saunas.
Moderate: **City Center Motel.** Medium-size, cozy.
Inexpensive: **Western Saver Motel.** Large, pool, neat.

THE DALLES. *Expensive:* **Mill Creek Motel & Trailer Park.** On Mill Creek. Kitchens, near restaurants. Jovial atmosphere.
Portage Inn. Near bridge crossing Columbia River.
Tapadera Inn. Multi-story motel at city center.
Inexpensive: **Shamrock Motel.** Small, close to city center, neat.

TIMBERLINE. *Deluxe:* **Timberline Lodge Resort.** On south slope of Mt. Hood, at 6,000-foot level.

UMATILLA. *Moderate:* **Columbia Court Motel.** Near water sports area of McNary Dam.
Tillicum Motor Inn. Large; comfortable units, kitchens, laundry, heated pool, restaurant, lounge, entertainment.

WARM SPRINGS. *Deluxe:* **Kah-nee-ta Village and Kah-nee-ta Lodge.** On Warm Springs Indian Reservation. Resorts.

 DINING OUT in Oregon means an opportunity to savor fresh salmon and other seafood, as well as river-fresh fish from the state's many streams. The all-time favorites— steak, fried chicken, and prime ribs—are also easily found. But there are also many foreign favorites that can be found here, and the exotic treats of Oriental, European, Middle East, and Polynesian cooks have made dining out in Oregon a cosmopolitan experience. Restaurants are listed in order of price category.

Price categories and ranges for a complete dinner are: *Deluxe:* $15 and up; *Expensive:* $10–15; *Moderate:* $6–10; *Inexpensive:* $6. Drinks, tax and tips not included. A la carte meals would cost more.

ASHLAND. *Expensive:* **Chateaulin.** Delightful French cuisine.

ASTORIA. *Moderate:* **Seafare Thunderbird Restaurant.** Attractively decorated. Fine selection of seafood and steaks.

BEAVERTON. *Expensive:* **Pavillion** (Greenwood Inn). Gourmet dining experience for any meal.

BEND. *Moderate:* **The Ore House.** Famous for steaks. Soup, salad, and bread bar.
Pine Tavern. Well known. Pleasant.

BURNS. *Moderate:* **Pine Room Cafe.** Delightful surroundings.

COTTAGE GROVE. *Expensive:* **Iron Maiden.** At Village Green Motor Hotel. Gourmet cuisine.
Moderate: **The Cottage.** Nourishing food in innovative solar building. Clean, courteous.

EUGENE. *Expensive:* **Coburg Inn.** 5 miles north of Eugene. Gas-lit atmosphere and unusual beef in 19th-century residence.
Moderate: **Original Joe's.** Fabulous Italian foods. Downtown.

GLENEDEN BEACH. *Deluxe:* **Gourmet Dining Room** in Salishan Lodge. Most exotic menu in state. Fantastic.

GOLD BEACH. *Expensive:* **Rod 'n Reel Club.** Great seafood dishes.

LAKEVIEW. *Moderate:* **The Indian Village.** Beautiful décor.

LINCOLN CITY. *Moderate:* **Mo's.** Best clam chowder in state; pungent atmosphere.
Road's End Dory Cove Restaurant. Enchanting.

MEDFORD. *Expensive:* **Mon Désir Dining Room.** Distinguished continental cuisine.

NEWPORT. *Expensive:* **The Moorage at Embarcadero.** Elegant food and Yaquina Bay views.
Moderate: **Mo's again.** The original site, where their clam chowder reputation was made.

NORTH BEND. *Expensive:* **Hilltop House Restaurant.** Dining with a bay view.

ONTARIO. *Moderate:* **Cheyenne Social Club.** Dine in another era.

PENDLETON. *Moderate:* **Circle S Barbeque.** Locally famous for steaks.

ROSEBURG. *Moderate:* **Duffy's.** Seafood, steaks.

SALEM. *Expensive:* **Prime Country.** A favorite of legislature lobbyists, who ought to know.

SEASIDE. *Moderate:* **Crab Broiler.** Splendid seafood, gorgeous atmosphere, within and without.

WASHINGTON

Seattle, Sound, Sea, and Mountains

From the Space Needle's observation tower, newcomers quickly can orient themselves to Seattle and its entire setting. Clockwise from Queen Anne Hill (north) are the marinas and houseboats of Lake Union with the University District behind them, Capitol Hill, Beacon Hill, the central business district, Elliott Bay and its shipping activity, and to the west, Puget Sound, its islands, and the Olympic Mountains as the backdrop. To the east are glimpses of the city's eastern boundary, 24-mile-long Lake Washington and, in the distance, the Cascade Range. On a clear day you can see 10,778-foot Mt. Baker, 14,410-foot Mt. Rainier, 12,307-foot Mt. Adams and 165 miles away, the active volcano, Mt. St. Helens. Mt. St. Helens is the state's newest attraction. The volcano exploded in May 1980, after a 123-year rest, and nobody knows how long it will remain active, or *how* active it may become.

Pioneer Square, at First and Yesler, gives its name to the district around the totem pole and south to Kingdome, the huge covered stadium. Here the city began in 1852 when Henry Yesler built, and skidded logs to, the first steam sawmill on Puget Sound. As business moved on uptown, the old hotels, taverns, and cafes became the haven of transient workers and people down on their luck. The area was called "Skid Road," and the name spread to other cities (where, lacking the same logging background, it often changed to "Skid Row").

Now protected by preservation ordinances, the Pioneer Historic District is full of small shops, galleries, and restaurants. A big attraction is Bill Speidel's Underground Tours through Seattle's past. Much of the tour is in passageways buried and long forgotten after streets were regraded and raised to second-story level.

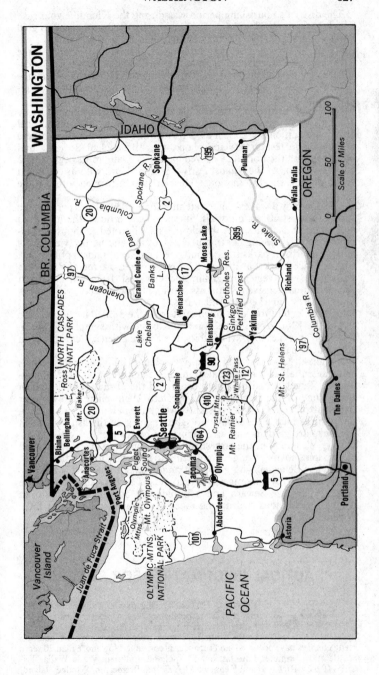

The district's flourishing period was during the Klondike gold rush which began in 1897 and was followed by stampedes to Alaska's gold strikes. Consequently it is the southern end of an unusual new "national park," which is actually international, running the route of the rush through Skagway, Chilkoot and White Passes, and north to Dawson City in the Yukon Territory. The National Park Service's Klondike Gold Rush National Historical Park has an interpretive center in Pioneer Square.

Up Yesler Way from Pioneer Square, in an area bounded roughly by 4th and 8th Avenues and Main and Lane Streets, is the International District, traditionally known as Chinatown. There are many Chinese and Japanese restaurants and shops, the "Benevolent Society" and buildings with their ornately carved balconies. Daily tours begin at 622 S. Washington. At the August festival of Bon Odori, with its costumed street dances, the International District is transformed into a huge bazaar.

The downtown waterfront, stretching some 20 blocks, is perhaps the greatest tourist attraction of all. Shipping moved down the harbor to more modern facilities, and the old piers are devoted to shops, restaurants, bars, sightseeing boats, a new aquarium, and harbor viewpoints in two waterfront parks (the second one being a path north of Pier 70).

Pike Place Market at Pike and 1st is a covered warren of shops and stalls deep with vegetables, fruit, and fish fresh from salt and fresh waters. At inexpensive restaurants overlooking the harbor, visitors can taste the fresh market-carnival wares.

Seattle Center (you look down on it from the Space Needle) was the site of the 1962 World Fair. It remains busy, with symphony, opera, stage and sports events, art exhibits, the Pacific Science Center, and an amusement park.

A short distance north of midcity lies Lake Union, with its marinas and residential houseboats. Lake Union is connected to Lake Washington and Puget Sound by a ship canal and the Hiram M. Chittenden Locks, one of the largest in the Western Hemisphere and another tourist attraction. Crowds constantly watch the parade of boats passing through the inland waterway and salmon going up the fish ladder. At the locks are gardens and an interpretive center.

Lake Washington, the largest of the metropolitan lakes, is spanned by two long floating bridges connecting to eastside suburbs, the largest of which is Bellevue, with a population of 70,000. The west side of the lake is dotted by moorages, playgrounds, beaches, and parks. The biggest parks are Seward and a brand new one at Sand Point. In August, the famous hydroplane races of Seafair are staged on Lake Washington.

PRACTICAL INFORMATION FOR SEATTLE

HOW TO GET AROUND *By air:* The number of foreign and domestic airlines serving Seattle-Tacoma International Airport can be determined only by a current count. Until 1979 there were 11, but since deregulation many changes have occurred, and turnover is constant. Now more than 20 serve Seattle and commuter lines fan out to Spokane, Pullman, Walla Walla, Tri-Cities (Pasco, Richland and Kennewick), Yakima, Bremerton, Whidbey Island, Bellingham, Port Angeles, and the San Juan Islands.

Air-taxi and charter service—available at Boeing Field, Lake Union, Renton and Paine Field (Everett).

Car rental: Avis, Hertz, and *National,* plus a dozen or more other firms.

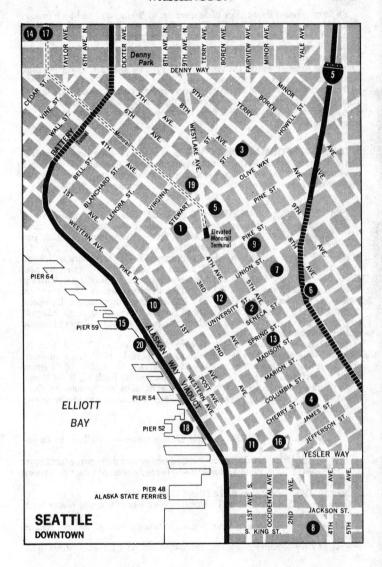

SEATTLE DOWNTOWN

Points of Interest

1) Bon Marche
2) Four Seasons Olympic Hotel
3) Central Bus Terminal
4) City Hall
5) Frederick & Nelson
6) Freeway Park
7) Hilton Hotel
8) King Street Station (Amtrak)
9) Seattle Sheraton
10) Pike Place Market
11) Pioneer Square
12) Post Office
13) Public Library
14) Seattle Center
15) Seattle Public Aquarium
16) Smith Tower
17) Space Needle
18) State Ferry Terminal
19) Westin Hotel
20) Waterfront Park

By ferry: From Pier 52, foot of Marion St. to Bremerton; and to Winslow, Bainbridge Island (bridged to the Kitsap Peninsula). From Fauntleroy, West Seattle to Vashon Island and to Southworth, Kitsap Peninsula. From Edmonds, north of Seattle, to Kingston.

Ferry service to Whidbey Island is via Mukeltio, two miles south of Everett. During the summer season, the venerable old *Princess Marguerite,* a cruise ship, makes daily voyages to Victoria and back.

By bus: Metro Transit serves city, surrounding county, and waypoints to Everett and Tacoma. No fare charged in the central business district.

A *monorail* whisks passengers from downtown to Seattle Center in less than three minutes.

TOURIST INFORMATION SERVICES. The *Seattle-King County Convention & Visitors Bureau,* 1815 Seventh Avenue provides schedules of events and brochure-maps of the four loop drives. For ferry information, write the *Washington State Ferry System,* State Ferry Terminal, Seattle, WA 98104

 MUSEUMS AND GALLERIES Historical: *Museum of History and Industry,* 2161 E. Hamlin. History, transportation, aerospace, fashion, furnishings, maritime and wildlife collections. Art: *Charles and Emma Frye Art Museum.* 704 Terry—Munich School paintings, 1850–1900; American School, 19th and 20th centuries. *Seattle Art Museum,* Volunteer Park—Asian art; pre-Columbia collection; European and American paintings. *Seattle Art Museum Pavilion,* Seattle Center—Rotating exhibits, generally contemporary. *Henry Art Gallery,* U. of Washington—19th- and 20th-century American and European paintings; contemporary prints; American ceramics; modern Japanese folk pottery. There also are more than a hundred recognized private galleries in Seattle and its suburban cities.

Special Interest: Seattle Center. *Pacific Science Center,* 200 2nd Ave. N. *Thomas Burke Memorial Washington State Museum,* U. of Washington—ethnology, geology, paleontology, zoology. *Fire Station No. 5,* foot of Madison Street, waterfront. *Wing Luke Memorial Museum,* 414 8th St. S.—Chinese history and culture. *Kirkland Historical Museum,* Kirkland (a suburb): three old ships. The *Museum of Flight,* a world-class museum on the southeast end of Boeing Field.

 TOURS. *Seattle Harbor Tours*—from Pier 56 downtown.

Canadian Pacific summertime daily cruise from Seattle to Victoria, B.C, via the *Princess Marguerite,* Lenora St. Terminal, Pier 69.

Boat to Tillicum Village, Blake Island (summer), Pier 56.

Gray Line of Seattle, 4th and University—a variety of tours by bus or boat, daytime and nighttime.

Bill Speidel Underground Tours—guided walking tour of Pioneer Square area. (682–4646 for reservations.)

Trident Tours—Four self-guiding, drive-yourself tours, following street signs.

GARDENS. *U. of Washington Arboretum,* Lake Washington Blvd. 250 acres including *Japanese Tea Garden. Woodland Park Zoological Gardens,* 95 acres including extensive rose garden. *Volunteer Park,* and its conservatory. *Carl S. English, Jr. Gardens,* Hiram M. Chittenden Locks.

 MUSIC. *Seattle Symphony Orchestra,* at Seattle Center Opera House. *Seattle Opera Association,* at Seattle Center Opera House. *Seattle Gilbert & Sullivan Society,* summer performances at Seattle Center Playhouse. There are also regular bookings of famous performers, chamber music concerts, children's symphonies and pop concerts. For scheduling see the *Seattle Guide* (free at hotels and motels) Friday newspapers; "Tempo" in *The Seattle Times;* "What's Happening" in *The Post-Intelligencer,* and *The Weekly.*

STAGE AND REVIEWS. *Seattle Repertory Theater, Seattle Center Playhouse. A Contemporary Theater (ACT).* U. of Washington playhouses: *The Showboat, The Hughes, Penthouse.* Others include *Empty Space, 2nd Stage, Bellevue Playbarn, Skid Road, Poncho, Langston Hughes Cultural Center. Pioneer Square Theater* is a leader in local, experimental productions. Children's productions at the *Piccoli Theater,* Seattle Center, and (interspersed with adult fare) at *The Bathhouse,* Green Lake.

Seattle's abundance of professional companies leaves slim pickings for groups in smaller cities within range of the metropolis, but many communities support theaters that are active seasonally, on week-ends, or for an annual production. The *Snoqualmie Falls Forest Theater,* Fall City, plays outdoors under the trees during summer. Edmonds is among the communities that have an active theater group, *The Driftwood Players.*

 SPORTS. *Boating:* See yellow pages, telephone directory, for rentals of rowboats, kickers, canoes, sailboats, cruisers and yachts for charter. *Bicycle Riding:* Miles of designated streets and paths. Best areas for bike rentals are Alki (West Seattle), Green Lake, University District, Seward Park, and Kenmore. *Fishing:* From downtown piers, in city lakes, and in Puget Sound. License required for freshwater and salmon. Boathouses at Ballard, West Seattle, and in suburban shore towns. They also rent gear. *Golf:* Municipal 18–27-hole courses in Seattle and a dozen other public links in the suburbs. *Hiking:* Many trails in and around the city. Myrtle Edwards Park is a 2-mile path along Elliott Bay. Nature trails in Arboretum-Foster Island; Seward, Schmitz, Lincoln, and Discovery Parks, Burke-Gilman Trail runs 12½ miles from Lake Union to Kenmore, north end of Lake Washington. (It's also for bicyclers.) *Picnicking:* In almost all city and county parks. *Swimming:* City and county beaches, very cold freshwater and saltwater. Twenty more comfortable public pools in city and suburbs. *Tennis:* Courts abundant in city parks, but with current tennis madness, call Seattle Parks & Recreation Dept. for reservation, 625–4672.

 SPECTATOR SPORTS. For schedules consult daily papers or Seattle Visitors Center. *Baseball:* Seattle Mariners, American League. *Basketball:* Seattle Supersonics, National Basketball Association; college contests. *Football:* Seattle Seahawks, NFL; U. of Washington Huskies. *Hockey:* Seattle Center Arena. *Soccer:* Arena. *Boxing:* Arena. *Auto Racing:* Pacific Raceways at Kent; Evergreen Speedway at Monroe; Puyallup International Dragway. *Horse Racing:* Longacres, Renton (mid-May–late September). *Hydroplane Racing:* Lake Washington, early August.

 WHAT TO DO WITH THE CHILDREN. There is an abundance of parks and beaches. The most unusual playground is the new Gas Works Park, north side of Lake Union. You'll never see another one like it, nor happier children as they clamber over and into what was once industrial equipment. Ferry rides and the Monorail appeal to the young. In Seattle Center are the Space Needle, Skyride, Pacific Science Center (with special exhibits for youngsters only), an amusement area, children's shows at Piccoli Theatre. Children also enjoy Tillicum Indian Village on Blake Island; the Lake Washington Ship Canal and locks; Woodland Park Zoo; and the waterfrong with its curio shops, fire station, fire boats, and Aquarium. They can fish from a pier at the downtown Waterfront Park.

 HOTELS AND MOTELS. Based on double occupancy, price categories and ranges are: *Deluxe:* $80 and up; *Expensive:* $60–$80; *Moderate:* $45–$60; *Inexpensive:* under $45.

Deluxe: **Doubletree Inn at South-Center.** Transportation to Sea-Tac Airport, pool.

Edgewater Inn. On the Waterfront. 2411 Alaskan Way, Pier 67.

Four Seasons Olympic. Fourth and Seneca. Refurbished grand old lady of Seattle's hotel community.

Hyatt House Hotel. 17001 Pacific Hwy S. International Airport, pool.

Marriott at Sea-Tac. S. 176th & 32nd Ave. A plush new addition to the Sea-Tac scene with atrium and Yukon theme.

Park Hilton. Sixth & Seneca. Another new one with an elaborate garden setting for a lobby.

Red Lion Sea-Tac Motor Inn. 18740 Pacific Highway S. Largest of airport hotels, with rambling wings and new tower. Convention center.

Seattle Hilton. 6th & University St. Convenient. Overlooks Freeway Park. Coffee shop, dining room. Lounge, entertainment.

Seattle Hilton Inn at Sea-Tac. 17620 Pacific Hwy S. Opposite International Airport. Pool, restaurants, bar.

Seattle Sheraton. Sixth & Pike. One of Seattle's newest and most luxurious.

The Westin Hotel. 5th & Westlake. Huge, downtown.

Expensive-Deluxe: **Camlin Hotel & Cabanas.** Pine St. bet. 8th & 9th Aves. Pool.

Continental Plaza Motel. 2500 Aurora Ave. N. Views, pool.

Holiday Inn of Sea-Tac. 17338 Pacific Hwy. S. International Airport, pool.

Holiday Inn (South). 11244 Pacific Hwy. S. Between Sea-Tac & Seattle, pool.

Ramada Inn. 2140 N. Northgate Way. Large, pool.

Sheraton-Renton Inn. 800 Rainier Ave. S., Renton. Large, pool.

Sixth Ave. Motor Hotel. 2000 6th Ave. Pool.

Sorrento Hotel. 900 Madison. A recently remodeled small hotel with one of the best views of Seattle.

Thunderbird-Bellevue. 818 112th Ave. NE, Bellevue. Large, pool.

Towne Motor Hotel. 2205 7th Ave. Convenient.

University Tower Hotel. 45th & Brooklyn Ave. Large, University area.

Vance Airport Inn. 18220 Pacific Hwy. Large, pool.

These are obviously only some of the better-known, large, expensive hotels. One can find nice but less costly smaller motels on "Motel Strip" along old Highway 99—Aurora Ave. north of the city and Pacific Highway to the south.

 DINING OUT. Price categories and ranges for a complete dinner are: *Deluxe:* $15 and up; *Expensive:* $10–$15; *Moderate:* $7–$10; *Inexpensive:* $6 or less. Not included are drinks, tax, and tip.

Deluxe: **Canlis.** 2576 Aurora Ave. Overlooks Lake Union. Seafood and steaks. First in the city to go modern posh and draw national attention.

Franco's Hidden Harbor. 1500 Westlake N., on Lake Union. Seafood dishes.

Le Provencal. Kirkland. French, of course, in a warm rustic setting.

Mirabeau. SeaFirst Building. Continental.

The Other Place. 319 Union. Fish and game from own farm served.

Rosellini's Four-10. 2515 Fourth. Old World recipes served with elegance.

These are far from all. Among others rated *Deluxe* or better are **Asuka's, Brasserie Pittsbourg, Mirabeau** on the 46th floor of the Sea-First Bank Bldg., and **Trader Vic's.** Hotel dining rooms also compete in this league.

Expensive: **Ivar's Captain's Table.** 333 Elliott Ave. W. At harborside, music.

Ivar's Salmon House. 401 N.E. Northlake Way. Indian-style barbecued salmon. Children's portions.

Ray's Boathouse. 6049 Seaview N.W. Fresh seafood, view of Shilshole Bay.

The Wharf. On Salmon Bay, 2 blocks from south end of Ballard Bridge. Clam chowder, seafood. Children's portions.

Windjammer. 7001 Seaview Ave. N.W. Maine lobster.

Moderate: **Andy's Diner.** 2963 Fourth Ave. S. A complex of railroad cars. Prime quality beef only.

Bruccio's. On Pier 52, foot of Marion St., in Seattle Ferry Terminal. Seafood specialties and meat. Children's portions.

Gasperetti's Roma Cafe. 220 Fourth St. Good Italian food and sports-fan clientele.

Ivar's Acre of Clams. On Pier 52, at foot of Marion St. Fried and steamed clams, baked salmon.

Smuggler and **Top of the Pier.** Both on Pier 70. Wide picture windows overlooking Elliott Bay.

Inexpensive: **Guadalajara.** Two largest (of four) at 1429 4th Ave. and 222 S. Main. Good Mexican food.

The Old Spaghetti Factory. Elliott Ave. at Broad Street in old warehouse full of antiques. Numerous special sauces. Dinner only, expect to wait your turn.

Orchid Villa. 4530 Union Bay N.E. Choice of Chinese or American menus in English Tudor setting.

Royal Fork (five in the Seattle area). Buffet style. Very popular with families.

Chinese. Moderate-Expensive: **Hong Kong.** Chinatown's oldest first-class restaurant.

Japanese. Expensive: **Benihana of Tokyo.** 5th & University, IBM Bldg. Tabletop cooking. Steak.

Bush Garden. 614 Maynard Ave. S. Authentic Japanese cuisine.

EXPLORING WASHINGTON

The capital is one gateway to the Olympic Peninsula. From Olympia it is less than a 30-minute drive up US 101 to Shelton, whose annual million-dollar crop of Christmas trees makes it the "Christmas Town." Shelton is headquarters for the Simpson Timber Company, and its plants can be toured in summer.

For 40 miles, US 101 is a marine drive along Hood Canal. In a dozen more miles it reaches Discovery Bay, an inlet from the Strait of Juan de Fuca. Here Wash. 20 splits right, to Port Townsend, a genuinely fascinating city. Its fine Victorian architecture dates from the days when Port Townsend was one of the most elegantly fashionable cities of the West Coast and, briefly, its busiest port. The Tourist Information Center provides a city guide that will route you to the points of interest. One, Point Wilson Lighthouse (1870), stands where the Strait of Juan de Fuca turns to form Admiralty Inlet, which leads into Puget Sound.

From Discovery Bay, it is 11 miles on US 101 to Sequim, the center of a pioneer farming area whose reputation as the peninsula's "sunshine belt" is bringing it retirement home subdivisions. A nearby attraction is the Olympic Game Farm. (See "What to Do with Children.")

Port Angeles, biggest city on the peninsula, has ferry connections to Victoria, B.C., lots of motels, Olympic National Park headquarters and Ediz Hook. The best views of the Olympic Mountains are from this long spit and from Hurricane Ridge, in the park, 20 miles from town.

Beyond Port Angeles, side roads from US 101 lead to Neah Bay, Makah Indian village famous for salmon fishing; to Lake Ozette and the farthest west point of the coterminous states; and to La Push, an Indian village on the outer coast.

The Rain Forest

There are rain forests in the river valleys all along the southwest side of the Olympics. Most accessible is the one up the Hoh River, 13 miles south of Forks. It's an 18-mile drive, but there is a visitor's center that explains the conditions that cause these distinctive and awesome jungles, where sunlight rarely penetrates the towering forest and limbs and ground are thick with moss and ferns.

Back on 101, it reaches the ocean at Ruby Beach and follows the shore for some dozen miles. Highway signs mark short trails to the beach. This stretch is in Olympic National Park.

The highway turns inland to Lake Quinault, where there are several resorts, including famous old Lake Quinault Lodge. After that, US 101 heads off for Hoquiam on Grays Harbor, 38 miles away.

North of Grays Harbor, from Ocean Shores to Moclips, are 25 miles of ocean beaches and small resort towns. They are tapped by Wash. 109 out of Hoquiam, and by several secondary roads from 101. From Hoquiam and Aberdeen, the Olympic loop may be completed by fast highway to Olympia and I–5.

If you go south of Grays Harbor, Wash. 105 takes you to Westport, almost totally devoted to deep-sea fishing for sport or profit, and 12 miles along the coast to Willapa Bay. Nineteen miles eastward along the bay, it reaches US 101 at Raymond.

These bayshores are kind to cranberries, and oysters thrive in Willapa's waters. If you follow US 101 south around the bay, you can explore the Long Beach Peninsula. Its ocean side is noted for miles of hard-packed, driveable beaches, a history as a summer playground, and surf-fishing. Two miles from Seaview, just inside the mouth of the Columbia, is Ilwaco, another center of charter and commercial fishing boats that go out after salmon and tuna.

Ft. Columbia State Park, at Chinook between Ilwaco and Megler, was one of three military posts established at the mouth of the Columbia River during the Spanish-American War. The park includes old buildings and gun batteries as well as a museum containing Indian and pioneer relics and a D.A.R. House Museum. At Megler a four-mile-long toll bridge crosses to Astoria, Ore.

Ferry to the San Juan Islands

A variegated fleet of ferry boats, most of them operated by the state, connects the Washington mainland with a dozen islands, the Kitsap and Olympic peninsulas, and Vancouver Island (British Columbia).

Anacortes is the ferry gateway to the San Juan Islands. There you can visit San Juan Island National Historic Park, where a war between the British and the Americans was almost fought. There are resorts on San Juan, Lopez and Orcas Islands. Rosario Resort, on Orcas, is situated on a 1,300-acre estate once owned by a millionaire. It includes a "boatel" for guests arriving by sea.

Back in Anacortes, you can go east to Mount Vernon or Burlington, both on I–5. If you're southbound, a more interesting route than the freeway is Wash. 20, which crosses a bridge onto Whidbey Island. The 50-mile drive goes through Coupeville, a preserved historic town, and ends at Columbia Beach, where you catch the ferry to Mukilteo, near Everett.

Northbound from Mount Vernon, much of the tourist traffic is headed for Vancouver, B.C. Bellingham is the biggest city on the way, and it caters to Canadians headed the other direction.

Bellingham, which overlooks Rosario Strait and the San Juan Islands, is within view of both the Olympic Mountains and the Cascades. It celebrates its reputation as a flower-area hub with a Blossomtime Festival in mid-May. (In season, drive out to the tulip fields around Lynden and Everson.) The most scenic trip out of Bellingham is to Mt. Baker, 58 miles east. Mt. Baker, 10,778 feet, dominates the view until you get to road's end and discover 9,127-foot Mt. Shuksan in behind it. Shuksan thereupon steals the scene.

Grand Coulee Dam

Grand Coulee Dam is such a man-made wonder, it has become an unofficial national monument. The Bureau of Reclamation built a shaded grandstand at the dam for the comfort of visitors and gives lectures at a nearby small-scale model of the project. The dam is 4,173 feet across and rises 550 feet from bedrock. Nearly half of its volume is below the waters of the river. Construction took from 1933 to 1941. Its reservoir, named Franklin D. Roosevelt Lake, stretches 151 miles behind the dam to the Canadian border, and for most of the distance its shores are in the Coulee Dam National Recreation Area.

The dam is situated at the head of the Grand Coulee, a chasm 52 miles long and up to five miles wide. Its rock walls, streaked in red and green, tower a thousand feet high in some places along its length. The coulee, or channel in the rock, was formed by the flood waters of a mighty glacier which once blocked the bed of the Columbia River and forced it to carve a new channel. When the glacier receded, the river returned to its old course and size, leaving the coulee dry. The dam is at the point where the river originally broke through to form the coulee. Its mammoth pumps irrigate about 2,000 square miles of land with waters from the huge reservoir.

The road south from the dam, Washington 155, follows the Grand Coulee, now a reservoir, to Coulee City, 30 miles away on US 2. Two miles southwest of Coulee City on Wash. 17 one can visit a fascinating geological phenomenon—the sheer cliffs of Dry Falls. A cataract many times greater than Niagara Falls, created by the enormous glacial runoffs, once thundered here and eroded the coulee below. An excellent interpretive center gives you the vast picture.

Spokane

Spokane is known as "the Hub of the Inland Empire." Indeed, it is not only second largest city in Washington (1981 estimate, 180,000) but the biggest one between Seattle and Minneapolis—or south to Salt Lake. Lakes and streams surround the city. Northeast by 30 miles is the highest point in the "Inland Empire"—a 5,878-foot peak at the center of Mt. Spokane State Park. The park, the largest in the state, with almost 21,000 acres, offers views in the summer, sports in the winter.

Spokane itself has more than 60 parks and gardens, including the famous Duncan Gardens and Japanese Tea House in Manito Park. The 100-acre city-center site cleared by the city for its Expo '74 World's Fair is on riverbanks and islands by the waterfalls of the Spokane River. Spokane's museums include Cheney Cowles Memorial Museum, a history museum of plateau Indian art and culture, and also an art gallery; Ft. Wright College Historical Museum, with items relating to the military occupancy of the fort (1899–1958); Clark Mansion, elegant old residence with Tiffany glass, carved woodwork, murals and period furniture. Adjoining Cheney Cowles Memorial Museum is Campbell House, a late 19th-century mansion of 19 rooms and 10 fireplaces that has been restored to its former glory. Pacific Northwest Indian Center is one of the best of its field.

Walla Walla

Walla Walla, the largest city in southeastern Washington, derives its name from an old Indian word meaning "many waters." It has been said that Walla Walla was misplaced from New England, but the town's history has been thoroughly Western—military outpost, trade center during Idaho gold rushes, and all. Whitman College, founded in 1859, was named after Dr. Marcus Whitman, who, with his wife and 12 other persons at their mission, was slain by Cayuse Indians in 1847. Ft. Walla Walla Park, at the edge of the town, contains a replica of the fort built in 1856, with the pioneer building of the village furnished in period style.

Six miles from town, on US 12 there is a turnoff to Whitman Mission National Historic Site. This is where the Whitman established Wai-i-lat-pu Mission in 1836. The mission ruins have been excavated, a millpond and irrigation ditch have been restored, and excavated articles are displayed in a museum at the site.

Yakima Valley

Apples and soft fruits from this area—including wine grapes—long ago gained a national reputation. Yakima is the agricultural capital of the rich region, and its abundant motels feature swimming pools for sun-seeking residents of Western Washington. In 1974, Yakima broke into the U.S. census list of "Standard Metropolitan Areas" credited with 151,000 population (city itself, 46,000), which made it No. 4 in the state.

At the lower end of the valley, on the Columbia River, are Pasco, Kennewick, and Richland, door-to-door but showing separate populations, and combined under the unofficial but generally used name "Tri-Cities."

The largest of the three, Richland, owes its existence to atomic energy and the nearby Hanford Works, which began during the Second World War. Hanford's Science Center in Richland explains this history and what goes on now.

PRACTICAL INFORMATION FOR WASHINGTON

HOW TO GET THERE. *By air: United, Northwest, Alaska, S.A.S., Western, Republic, Pacific Western, Pan Am, Eastern, Continental, British Airways, Delta, Republic, Mexicana, National, Reeve Aleutian, Thai, Transworld, Wien Air Alaska, Finnair* and *Evergreen International* provide regular schedules to Seattle-Tacoma International Airport. (Also see airport information under Seattle.) *Northwest, United* and *Republic* touch down in Spokane, which is also served by *Frontier.*

By train (Amtrak): From the east, to Spokane and Seattle; West Coast route from San Diego to Seattle.

By car: The main east-west route, Interstate 90, enters from Idaho just east of Spokane. US 101 enters at Astoria, Ore., and the main arterial, I–5, at Portland or from British Columbia. From the southeast (up through Boise, Idaho, and Pendleton, Ore.) I–80N splits north as I–82 to follow the Yakima Valley, then head north to meet I–90 at mid-state Ellensburg.

By bus: Greyhound, Trailways.

By ferry: Black Ball between Victoria (British Columbia) and Port Angeles. *Alaska State Ferries* run once a week summers, twice weekly in winter, between Southeast Alaska and Seattle.

HOW TO GET AROUND. *By air:* Spokane is served by *Northwest, Alaska, Cascade Airways, United,* and (to Montana and Denver) by *Frontier.* (See also Seattle-Tacoma. Some of the new ones at Sea-Tac also have added Spokane.)

By car: I–90 and US 2 cross the state between Spokane and Seattle. Expect heavy snow in late fall and winter in mountain passes. Interstate 5 is the principal north-south route. US 101 weaves along the coast and encircles the Olympic Peninsula. Scenic US 2, US 12 and Wash. 410 also cross the Cascades. The most spectacular east-west route is the new North Cascades Highway (Washington 20). US 97 runs north and south in the eastern foothills of the Cascades. US 395 connects Spokane with the Tri-City area and also runs north to Canada.

Car rental: Hertz, Avis or National have offices in many of the smaller cities.

By bus: Greyhound connects cities on the main arterials. Area bus lines run out of Spokane, Grays Harbor, and several other centers. Small cities have transit lines offering services to those who are lucky enough to be at a stop on the rare occasion when a bus comes along. In Seattle, tax-supported buses charge no fare in the mid-town zone, and will carry you anywhere up to 65 miles in King County for a modest fare.

By ferry: In the Puget Sound region, state ferries are part of the highway system, their fares being the equivalent of tolls. They act as bridges across the Sound and to major islands. Their routes connect with arterial highways and more-literal bridges, so motorists have a great number of loop choices taking anywhere from a few hours up to three days around the Olympic Peninsula.

These loops can be started anywhere, but going or coming they will pass through one to four of these ferry terminals: Fauntleroy (West Seattle), downtown Seattle, Edmonds, Mulkilteo, Columbia Beach or Keystone on Whidbey Island, Port Townsend, Kingston (opposite Edmonds), Winslow on Bainbridge Island, Bremerton or Southworth (across from Fauntleroy).

Tacoma figures in these loops because the Tacoma Narrows Bridge is the only crossing independent of ferries. Using it, a loop might include only one ferry trip. However, you can ferry from Tacoma to Tahlequah on the south end of Vashon Island, drive to Vashon's north end, and ferry either west to Southworth or east to Fauntleroy.

State ferries encourage their use as sightseeing boats by offering walk-ons an excursion fare. Ride the round-trip or stopover for up to five hours.

Longest ferry route is from Anacortes through the San Juan Islands to Sidney, B.C. See text under that heading.

By boat: Boat rentals and charters for fishing or sightseeing in most saltwater ports, both on inside waters and along the Pacific coast. Several riverside cities offer similar opportunities.

On horseback: Pack trips through the Cascades and in Eastern Washington. For guides—U.S. Forest Service, State Travel Development Division, or local chambers of commerce.

On foot: Innumerable miles of mountain trails in national forests and the three national parks. Hundreds of miles also are designed for a milder form of hiking, nature walks, and pedestrian exercise. These are in and around even the biggest cities. Then, too, some urban features such as Seattle's central waterfront are best seen by walking for as long as feet hold out.

 TOURIST INFORMATION SERVICES. There are *Visitor Information Centers* at border points and chambers of commerce throughout the state. *Travel Development Division,* General Administration Building, Olympia, WA 98504—tourist attractions. *U.S. Forest Service,* Regional Office, P.O. Box 3623, Portland, OR 97208—camping. *Washington State Dept. of Natural Resources,* Public Lands Bldg., Olympia, WA 98501—camping. *Superintendent, Mt. Rainier National Park,* Ashford, WA 98304. *Superintendent, Olympic National Park,* Port Angeles, WA 98362. *Superintendent, North Cascades National Park,* Sedro Woolley, WA 98284. *State Parks and Recreation Commission,* P.O. Box 1128, Olympia, WA 98504. *Washington State Dept. of Fisheries,* General Administration Bldg., Olympia, WA 98504—saltwater fishing. *Washington State Game Dept.,* 600 N. Capitol Way, Olympia, WA 98504—hunting and freshwater fishing.

 MUSEUMS AND GALLERIES. Some of these have been mentioned in connection with Seattle and Spokane. Almost all of the 39 counties have their historical societies and a museum, usually at the county seat. Inquire locally for the address. Exhibits run from the usual heirlooms of local pioneer families to some rather impressive collections.

Other museums worthy of note are *Fort Lewis Military Museum; Olympia State Capital Museum,* 2111 W. 21st Ave.; *Port Townsend Rothschild House,* 19th Century furnished, a State Parks operation; *Vantage, Gingko Petrified Forest State Park Museum;* Tacoma, *Washington State Historical Society Museum,* 315 N. Stadium Way; *Tacoma Art Museum,* 12th & Pacific; *Handforth Gallery,* Tacoma Public Library, 1102 S. Tacoma.

Fair to excellent handcrafts and paintings appear in small shops and galleries in the most unexpected places. Somehow an "art colony" (or an outstanding individual) has developed there. Gig Harbor, Langley on Whidbey Island, Stanwood, and Anacortes are a few examples. Best guide to these is to look for them where you find them.

HISTORIC SITES. Lately, these proliferate (in recognition) as Americans become conscious of their heritage. Included are Ellensburg: *Olmstead Place Heritage Site,* 4 miles east of town. 1875 log cabins.

Olympia: *Crosby House,* Des Chutes Way, built in 1860.

Port Townsend: *Fort Worden,* 1 mile north of town. Site of *Old Fort Townsend,* 3 miles south of town. Rosalia: *Steptoe Battlefield.*

Spokane: *Site of Spokane House,* 1810. fur-trading post.

Vancouver: *Fort Vancouver* (founded in 1824) replica being built on the site. Wallula: *Site of Fort Walla Wall.* Blaine: *International Peace Arch.* White Swan: *Fort Simcoe. Port Gamble,* where the whole town is registered as a National Historic Site; Suquamish, Chief Seattle's grave and site of *Old Man House,* a 600-foot-long, pre-white Indian "condominium."

TOURS. *Gray Lines* runs sightseeing tours the year-round in Seattle, and during the summer in Spokane and Port Angeles. Summer excursion boats in the harbors and lakes of Seattle. Excursions into the Snake River's Hell's Canyon start in Clarkston. River float trips on the Skagit, and out of Spokane.

DRINKING LAWS. Bars, all in conjunction with a restaurant, can stay open until 2 A.M. every day. Taverns dispense beer and wine, which is also sold by the bottle in grocery stores. Hard liquor at state stores, usually open 10 A.M.–8 P.M. closed Sundays. Some big-city stores stay open later and also on holidays (except Christmas). Minimum drinking age, 21.

SUMMER SPORTS. Bicycle riding, swimming, tennis are found throughout the state. *Golf:* Courses can be found at all resort areas and at cities of any size. Those near small towns tend to be nine holes. *Fishing:* River fishing—licenses required for steelhead. Lakes—8,000, with trout, bass, and other whitefish. Saltwater—salmon in summer. Charter boats and equipment at Westport (Grays Harbor), Ilwaco (mouth of Columbia River), Neah Bay and Sekiu (outer end, Strait of Juan de Fuca), Port Angeles and other coastal towns. *Clam digging*—Pacific beaches.

No license is needed in national parks.

Hiking: Trails within an hour of all cities. Longest are Cascade Crest Trail and Olympic National Park trails crossing Olympic Peninsula.

Horseback Riding: inquire locally.

Hunting: Deer, elk, black bear, mountain goats. Pheasants, ducks, geese, grouse, quail and partridge, rabbits. Licenses are purchased from sport stores or request application from the Game Department.

Mountain Climbing: Mountains cover half the area of state, some with glaciers. (A guide is required at Mt. Rainier.)

WINTER SPORTS. *Skiing.* November to mid-May. Outstanding areas are Alpental, Snoqualmie Summit and Ski Acres, 46 to 50 miles E. of Seattle on I–90; Crystal Mountain, 64 miles S.E. of Tacoma on Wash. 410; Stevens Pass, 60 miles east of Everett on US 2; White Pass, 50 miles W. of Yakima on US 12; Mt. Baker, 60 miles E. of Bellingham on Wash. 542; Mt. Spokane, 34 miles northeast of Spokane; 49° North at Chewelah (45 miles N. of Spokane on US 395); Mission Ridge, 12 miles S. of Wenatchee. There are numerous others.

"Ski-erized' rental cars are available at Sea-Tac and Spokane International Airports and regional airports at Wenatchee and Yakima. Many ski resorts can be reached by bus.

Skating: Unique to the state is the outdoor Pavilion in Spokane's Waterfront Park. Open mid-November to mid-April. Indoor rinks are found in a few other cities.

SPECTATOR SPORTS. (Other than in Seattle area). *Baseball:* Pacific Coast League baseball in Tacoma, Spokane. Northwest League includes Bellingham, Walla Walla, and Aberdeen-Grays Harbor. *Football:* Washington State U and other university and college games. *Basketball:* Collegiate games—Washington State U and other universities and colleges. *Horse Racing:* Playfair at Spokane—July to late Oct. Yakima Meadows—March to early May; Oct. to end of Nov.

WHAT TO DO WITH THE CHILDREN. Most large cities have zoos, parks, and playgrounds. Along the coast, nothing beats *beachcombing. Gingko Petrified Forest* at Vantage, on the Columbia River, displays stone logs at its interpretive center.

Tacoma: *Point Defiance Park*—Aviary, Never-Never Land, Old Ft. Nisqually, Aquarium; *Children's Farm Animal Zoo.* Steam Shea Locomotive at *Camp Six,* replica of logging camp. Totem Pole.

Lake Chelan: *Boat ride.*

Largest zoo is in Seattle. Spokane has developed a cageless zoo. *Northwest Trek* at Eatonville is a branch of the Tacoma zoo. Animals roam freely, viewed from quiet motor trams. Near Sequim is *Loboland,* with many species of wolf, and *Olympic Game Farm,* where famous animal characters are kept and filmed for TV and Disney "nature" movies. Walk through with guide or ride around the extensive compound.

Throughout the state, children can climb, swim, throw snowballs in August, watch rodeos, dance to Indian drums, ride horses, and have a good chance of seeing animals in the forest. The state is a children's playground.

HOTELS AND MOTELS. Price ranges are based on double occupancy, without meals, and apply to Washington cities other than Seattle. *Deluxe:* $35 and up; *Expensive:* $30–35; *Moderate:* $22–30; *Inexpensive:* $22 and under. Listings are in order of price category.

ABERDEEN. *Expensive-Deluxe:* **Red Lion Motel.** Some kitchenettes. Pool. Pets allowed.
Expensive: **Olympic Inn.** Some suites and kitchenettes.

ANACORTES. *Expensive:* **San Juan Motel.** Housekeeping.
Moderate: **Anacortes Inn.** Some two-room units.

BELLINGHAM. *Moderate–Expensive:* **Leopold Hotel.** Cabana units, three dining rooms.
Pony Soldier. Pool, restaurant.

BREMERTON. *Moderate–Deluxe:* **Bayview Inn.** Large hotel. One or two-room units. Indoor pool, playground. Restaurant on premises.

CHELAN. *Deluxe:* **Campbell's Lodge.** Resort. Beach, boat dock.

COULEE DAM. *Expensive:* **Coulee House Motel.** 1 block from Columbia River bridge. Pool, restaurant, sauna.

ELLENSBURG. *Expensive–Deluxe:* **Holiday Inn.** Large motel. Coffee shop, dining room, lounge with entertainment. Pool, playground.

MANSON. *Expensive.* **The Inn at Wapato Point.** Motor inn, resort and condominium complex on Lake Chelan. Some kitchenettes, pools, beach and marina.

MOSES LAKE. *Expensive:* **Moses Lake TraveLodge.** Some suites, some wheelchair units. Adjacent to park, restaurant near.

MT. RAINIER NATIONAL PARK. *Moderate–Expensive:* **Paradise Inn.** Star Route, Ashford. 22 miles from S.E. entrance. Restaurants. Seasonal.
  Inexpensive: **Mountain View Lodge Motel.** Box 525, Packwood. ½-mile E. of Packwood, US 12.

OLYMPIA. *Deluxe:* **Westwater of Olympia.** Restaurants, cocktails, entertainment, pool.
  Expensive–Deluxe: **Vance Tyee Motor Inn.** Very large with many amenities. Pools, restaurants, lounge and entertainment.
  Expensive: **Olympia-Aladdin Motor Inn.** Pool, restaurant.
  Moderate: **Golden Gavel.** Older motel. (Best Western affiliate.) No pets.

OLYMPIC NATIONAL PARK. *Expensive–Deluxe:* **Lake Crescent Lodge.** On US 101. Swimming, restaurant. Seasonal
  Moderate–Expensive: **Lake Crescent Log Cabin Resort.** On west side of lake. Lodge and cottages, dining, kitchenettes, boats. Extra fee for pets. Reservations advised.

PASCO-RICHLAND. *Deluxe:* **Hanford House.** (Richland). On shore of the Columbia River. Wide choice of units. Coffee shop, dining room, lounge with entertainment. Recreational facilities and pool.
  Red Lion Motor Inn. (Pasco) Large motel. Coffee shop, dining room, room service. Lounge, entertainment, dancing. Pool.
  Expensive: **Nendel's.** Large downtown Richland motel. Pool. Pets extra.
  Pasco TraveLodge. Pool. Restaurant opposite.

PORT ANGELES. *Deluxe:* **Red Lion Bayshore Inn.** Pool, restaurant.
  Moderate–Deluxe: **Aircrest Motel.** Smaller motel on east side of town.
  Uptown Motel. One- and two-room units, away from highway.

PORT TOWNSEND. *Moderate–Expensive:* **Port Townsend Motel.** Seasonal rates. Also several bed-and-breakfast homes.

SPOKANE. *Deluxe:* **Red Lion Motor Inn.** Restaurant, coffee shop, lounge, pool.
  Sheraton-Spokane Hotel. Restaurants, pool, shops. Near Riverfront Park.
  Expensive–Deluxe: **Davenport Hotel.** Pool.
  Ridpath Hotel and Motor Inn. Restaurants, pool.
  Expensive: **Holiday Inn Downtown,** and **Holiday Inn West** (at airport). Pool.

TACOMA. *Expensive-Deluxe:* **Lakewood Motor Inn.** Some suites. Restaurant, lounge. Pool.
  Moderate–Expensive: **Doric Tacoma.** Large downtown motel. Some suites. Coffee shop, dining room, lounge. Pool.
  Wendel's. Large, comfortable motel. Dining room, lounge with entertainment. Pool.
  Moderate: **Sherwood Inn.** 8402 S. Hosmer St. Coffee shop, dining room, entertainment.

VANCOUVER. *Deluxe:* **Thunderbird Inn at the Quay.** Restaurants, cocktails, entertainment, pool.
  Expensive–Deluxe: **Vancouver TraveLodge.** Downtown motel. Some 2-room units. No pets.

WALLA WALLA. *Expensive–Deluxe:* **Black Angus Motor Inn.** Midtown. Pool.

Walla Walla TraveLodge. 421 E. Main St. Pool. Restaurant nearby.

WENATCHEE. *Deluxe:* **Thunderbird Inn.** Attractive units, some suites. Restaurants, lounge with Pool. Seasonal rates.

Expensive: **Chieftain Motel.** Some 2-room units and suites. Well-known restaurant on premises. Lounge and entertainment. Pool. Sitter list.

Moderate: **Imperial 400 Motel.** Comfortable units, one with kitchenette (extra). No pets. Restaurant near.

YAKIMA. *Deluxe:* **Thunderbird Motor Inn.** Pool, restaurants, entertainment, cocktails.

Expensive: **Red Lion Motel.** Pool, restaurant near. (Member of Best Western.)

Moderate: **Bali Hai Motel.** Pool.

 DINING OUT. Price ranges for a complete dinner are: *Deluxe:* $18 and up; *Expensive:* $15 and up; *Moderate:* $8–10; *Inexpensive:* under $7. Drinks, tax, tip not included. À la carte meals will cost a bit more.

ABERDEEN. *Moderate:* **Nordic Inn Restaurant.** Pleasant "Viking" décor. Wide variety of entrées. Children's menu. Lounge.

BELLINGHAM. *Moderate:* **Johnson's Restaurant.** Family-type restaurant. View of Mt. Baker from dining room. Large servings. Children's menu. Lounge.

La Creperie. Interesting restaurant in Fairhaven Village, a restored section of old Bellingham. Taproom with beer and wine.

BREMERTON. *Expensive:* **The Hearthstone.** Nice view of the waterfront. Seafood specialties, also steaks. Lounge with entertainment.

LEAVENWORTH. *Moderate:* **Eidelweis Bavarian Restaurant.** In this "Alpine" village one cannot find any better German food than here, especially the apple strudel. Lounge and entertainment.

OLYMPIA. *Moderate–Expensive:* **Craig's Olympia Oyster House.** Variety, but famous for its pan-fried oysters.

PORT ANGELES. *Moderate–Expensive:* **Birney's.** Variety.

Harrington's Restaurant. Midtown. Variety.

PORT TOWNSEND. *Moderate:* **Olympic Inn.** Seafood, Sunday brunch.

SPOKANE. *Moderate–Expensive:* **Chapter 11.** Varies menu (à la carte), soup and salad bar.

Gasthaus Krone. Authentic German food served in a Bavarian atmosphere. Large lounge with entertainment and dancing.

Moderate: **Black Angus.** View of Spokane Falls. Wide choice of steak cuts. Children's menu. Lounge with entertainment and dancing.

Pieroni's. Very popular Italian restaurant. American dishes available. Wines and cocktails.

Inexpensive: **Cyrus O'Leary's.** Over 100 items on menu.

The Old Spaghetti Factory. Choice of several excellent and original sauces, plus sourdough bread, salad and spumoni ice cream. Delightful antique décor.

TACOMA. *Expensive:* **Cliff House.** Excellent spot for steak and lobster while enjoying the view of Mt. Rainier and the Tacoma harbor. Lounge, entertainment.

Moderate–Expensive: **Johnny's Dock.** One of Tacoma's fine seafood restaurants. On the waterfront. Steak, seafoods, own baked goods.

Moderate: **Old City Jail.** (It actually was!) In the basement of the Old City Hall. A fun place in the restored 1890s building. Steaks, seafood, Italian dishes.

Royal Fork. A good place to take a hungry family. A buffet with many choices of salads and entrées. All you can eat. One price for adults, children less.

HAWAII

Honolulu and Six Beautiful Islands

Headquarters for your Honolulu sightseeing is probably a poolside chair or a mat on Waikiki Beach, and you may be tempted to do all your sightseeing from here in a supine position. There is much to be said for this method. It will leave an indelible impression of three things Hawaii is famous for: sun, surf, and girls. However, the inherent problem in this method is that you miss the thousand other things that make Hawaii Hawaii. So, do yourself a favor; roll over, stand up, and see what there is to see.

Walking in Waikiki

Though most Honolulans ride—via bus or car—there is no law against walking. In fact, pedestrians in Honolulu have a sort of favored status. And, should you decide to hoof it, there are a number of places in Honolulu where you can stroll and enjoy the local scenery.

The first of these places is Waikiki, which, despite its many new hotels, smart shops, and crowds, remains in essence a kind of provincial village. The veneer of sophistication is pretty thin here, and you will probably enjoy the International Market Place and other new shopping malls as well as the rest of the passing show on Kalakaua Avenue. But beware, there's plenty of hustle on Kalakaua these days.

Chinatown

The area between Nuuanu Avenue and River Street is where many of the respected Chinese merchants have their stores and restaurants.

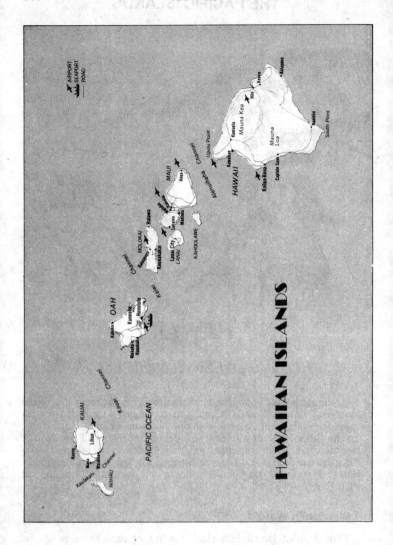

There are herb shops, Oriental dry goods shops, and fascinating Chinese food shops. Don't hesitate to sample the little Chinese restaurants in this neighborhood—you'll go a long way before you find better soup and noodles.

One block beyond Maunakea Street is River Street, which flanks the Nuuanu Stream as it winds its way into Honolulu Harbor. Once the scene of legalized houses of prostitution, River Street has now blossomed with the completion of the River Street Mall, a promenade walk along the stream, that features the Chinese Cultural Plaza. But be warned that much of Hotel Street in their area consists of porno shops and peep shows. It's a bit of a "combat" zone late at night.

Downtown Honolulu

Compared to the aimless wanderings through Waikiki and China-town, the purposeful sauntering along the Fort Street Mall, the down-town shopping center, is an absolute bustle. The Mall, completed in 1969, stretches five blocks from Queen to Beretania Street and a num-ber of interesting restaurants, many atmospheric in renovated old buildings, add to the delight of the "new" downtown. At night the area is less rewarding because of a recent influx of street people.

For a look at the historical side of downtown, the Historical Build-ings Task Force has identified certain interesting structures, many of them in the Merchant Street area.

On Merchant, the Wall Street of Honolulu, is the Kamehameha V Post Office of 1871 at Merchant and Bethel Streets; Royal Hotel Build-ing of 1890 at 14 Merchant; Yokohama Specie Bank of 1910 at 36 Merchant; Bishop Bank of 1877 at 63 Merchant; Bishop Estate Build-ing of 1896 at 71 Merchant; Melchers Building of 1854 at 51 Merchant; and the Stangenwald Building of 1901 at 119 Merchant.

Nearby are the O R & L Terminal of 1925 at 325 North King; Aloha Tower of 1921; Dillingham Transportation Building of 1929 at 735 Bishop; Alexander and Baldwin Building of 1929 at 822 Bishop; McCandless Building of 1906 at 925 Bethel; Friend Building of 1887 at 926 Bethel; C. Brewer and Company of 1930 at 827 Fort; Perry Building of 1888 at Nuuanu and Hotel; and the oldest in the area, Our Lady of Peace Cathedral at 1184 Fort built in 1843.

PRACTICAL INFORMATION FOR HONOLULU

TRANSPORTATION. *Air:* Many major airlines around the world serve the Hawaiian Islands. For inter-island travel there are three major airlines: *Hawaiian, Aloha* and *Mid-Pacific.*

Bus: Public transportation in the capital is by modern Mass Transit Lines buses. There are 30 different lines crisscrossing the city, cutting into the residen-tial valleys and climbing to the heights which separate them. All buses carry signs showing their route number and destination, and the driver will issue a free transfer for another route if you must change. For information call TheBus, 531–1161.

Cabs: Taxi cabs are plentiful, driven by qualified drivers, and metered at 20 cents every sixth of a mile. Waikiki to downtown runs a little more than $5. Since random cruising is not allowed, don't stand on a street corner, pick up a phone instead.

U-Drive Cars: You can hardly take two steps on Kalakaua Avenue, the main drag of Waikiki, without stumbling over a drive-yourself car for rent. The range of cars for hire runs just about the whole gamut of the automotive industry, both domestic and foreign. *Avis* will rent to anyone under 21, if they have a driver's license and a major credit card. *Robert's Hawaii Rent-A-Car* will rent to 18-year-olds if they're married. The major firms in Honolulu are: *Avis,* 148 Kaiulani Ave., in the Outrigger East Hotel; *Budget Rent-A-Car,* 2379 Kuhio Ave. and other Waikiki locations as well as all major airports; *Hertz,* Honolulu Interna-tional Airport, Hilton Hawaiian Village and 6 other major hotels, and *National Car Rental,* 2160 Kalakaua Ave.

GUIDED TOURS. A number of tour and travel services are engaged in conducting tours of the city by bus. Limousines are also available. Some of the major companies are: *Robert's, Gray Line, Hawaiian Discovery Tours,* and *Trade Wind.*

ENTERTAINMENT. The entertainment scene stretches all over Waikiki and includes Danny Kaleikini's slick Polynesian show at the *Kahala Hilton*. All major hotels have some type of show, frequently featuring big-name stars, with dinner and dancing. In addition, the 8,400-seat *Neal S. Blaisdell Arena* and the *Waikiki Shell* put on top-flight shows.

MUSIC. The *Honolulu Symphony Orchestra* plays at the magnificent Honolulu Concert Hall. Donald Johanos, once associated with the Pittsburgh Symphony, is the music director. *Chamber Music Hawaii* sponsors a dozen concerts a year, usually at the Orvis Auditorium at the University, the Honolulu Academy of Arts, or the Lutheran Church near Punahou School, with programs ranging from Bach cantatas to the Budapest String Quartet.

SPORTS. *Golf:* There are 28 good courses on Oahu, counting military and par 3s. The Waialae Country Club in Honolulu is one of the outstanding, lengthy oceanside courses in the world and the scene of a TPA tournament, though it is not open to public play. *Tennis:* There are 108 public tennis courts on the island. Visitors are welcome to play any of them. There are 10 courts at Ala Moana Park, 8 at Keehi Lagoon, 7 at the Diamond Head Tennis Center, 6 at Koko Head, another 4 in Kapiolani Park. Thirty-seven courts are lighted for night play. Other courts are located at Punahou School, and Kailua Racquet Club.

Deep-Sea Fishing: Best waters are off the Waianae Coast, off Koko Head, off Kaneohe Bay, and along the Penguin Banks southwest of Molokai across the Molokai Channel from Oahu. Charter boats available at Kewalo Basin. *Sailing:* The *Waikiki Yacht Club* and *Hawaii Yacht Club* (both at Ala Wai Harbor, Honolulu) welcome members of mainland clubs and extend guest privileges. So does the *Kaneohe Yacht Club* in Kaneohe Bay, windward Oahu. The Navy and Air Force have clubs. If you don't know how to sail, *Hawaiiana Yacht Charters* at 1125 Ala Moana Boulevard will show you. For a twilight dinner sail on the *Hilton Rainbow I,* one of the world's largest catamarans, call 955–3348. For other catamaran cruises the place to go is Kewalo Basin.

Hiking: There are about two dozen trails on Oahu maintained by the *State Forestry Division* at 1151 Punchbowl Street, Honolulu. Maps showing the trails may be obtained both from the state and City Hall. There are hikes scheduled nearly every Sunday by the *Hawaiian Trail and Mountain Club* call 734–5515, from the Iolani Palace grounds at 8 Sunday morning. In recent years, the *Sierra Club* has been offering alternate hikes. They meet at 8 Sunday morning at the Church of the Crossroads on University Avenue.

Skindiving: Call 538–3854. Ken Taylor, *South Seas Aquatics,* 1050 Ala Moana Blvd.

If you just want to look at the fish wiggle by under your toes, take the glassbottom boat that tours off Waikiki 5 times a day. It leaves from Fisherman's Wharf at Kewalo Basin.

Hunting: Oahu quarry includes wild pigs and goats in the Waianae and Koolau Mountains. There are also a few deer, but these are not to be hunted. The *State Fish and Game Division* at 1151 Punchbowl St. can provide you with complete information on hunting in Oahu.

Camping: There are 16 parks on Oahu for those with motor homes. Beach Boy Campers rents Toyota vans. Permits for a week are required and renewable. Telephone the Parks Department at 523–4525.

The *Hawaii Audubon Society,* P.O. Box 5032, Honolulu, is headquarters for bird watchers. They have Sunday morning bird hikes every month, leaving from The Library of Hawaii. Visitors welcome.

HOTELS. Rates are for single rooms—for doubles add 15–25%. Categories are as follows: *Super Deluxe:* $133 and up; *Deluxe:* $60–92; *Expensive:* $40–59; *Moderate:* $30–39; *Inexpensive:* $20–29; *Rock Bottom:* under $20.

Super deluxe: **Halekulani,** 2199 Kalia Rd. The old bungalows of the past have made way for a new opulence.

Kahala Hilton. 5000 Kahala Ave., not far from Waikiki. Fabulous ambience, furnishings, and services.

Deluxe: **Ala Moana Americana.** 410 Atkinson Dr. near Waikiki. All amenities twice over. Huge.

Hawaiian Regent. 2552 Kalakaua Ave., Waikiki. Has class, large, excellent views.

Hilton Hawaiian Village. 2005 Kalia Rd., Waikiki. Fabulous 20-acre complex.

Holiday Inn-Waikiki Beach. 2570 Kalakaua Ave., across the street from Kuhio Beach.

Hyatt Regency. Newest in Waikiki. 2424 Kalakaua Ave. One of the Big Four in Honolulu, with 1260 rooms, pools, restaurants, shops, the works. Opp. Moana.

Outrigger Waikiki. On beach at 2335 Kalakaua Ave., Waikiki, right in the middle of things.

Royal Hawaiian. 2259 Kalakaua Ave., Waikiki. One of the most famous hotels in the world.

Sheraton-Waikiki. Waikiki. 2255 Kalakaua Ave. With 1,846 rooms one of the 10 largest hotels in the world.

Waikiki Beachcomber. 2300 Kalakaua Ave. Swimming pool, shops, restaurant, 400-seat entertainment room.

Westin Ilikai. At gateway to Waikiki. 1777 Ala Moana Blvd. Beautiful, unlimited recreation, spacious.

Expensive: **The Breakers.** 250 Beach Walk, Waikiki. A pace-setter for small hotels.

Hawaiiana. 260 Beach Walk, Waikiki. All rooms with kitchenettes.

Holiday Isle. 270 Lewers St., Waikiki. Near beach. Atmospheric cocktail lounge and restaurant.

Moana. 2365 Kalakaua Ave., on the beach. The old lady of Waikiki, built in 1901.

New Otani Kaimana Beach. 2863 Kalakaua Ave. at Sans Souci is near Waikiki and across from a park.

Princess Kaiulani. 120 Kaiulani Ave. Is close to beach and all the action.

Queen Kapiolani. 150 Kapahulu St., Waikiki. Near beach and zoo. Polynesian motif.

The Reef. 2169 Kalia Rd., Waikiki. Excellent beach. All amenities and more.

Moderate: **Hawaiian King.** 417 Nohonani, Waikiki. Attractive suites with lanai, sitting room, and kitchen.

Ilima. 445 Nohonani St., Waikiki. All units with kitchens.

Outrigger East. 150 Kaiulani Ave., Waikiki. Swimming pool, restaurant, bar, shops.

Waikiki Grand. 134 Kapahulu Ave., Waikiki. Good location, across from the zoo.

Inexpensive: **Nakamura.** 1140 South King St., Honolulu. Midway between downtown and Waikiki.

Reef Lanais. 225 Saratoga Road, Waikiki. Restaurant, pool, cocktail lounge.

Royal Grove. 151 Uluniu Ave., Waikiki. Small, with pool and patio.

Waikiki Circle. 2464 Kalakaua Avenue, Waikiki. Good locale, wide-range views from rooms.

Waikiki Surf. 2200 Kuhio St., Waikiki. Restaurant, pool, bar.

Waikiki Surf West. 412 Lewers St., Waikiki. Attractive units with kitchenettes and private lanais.

Rock Bottom: **Waikiki Terrace.** 339 Royal Hawaiian Ave. In the heart of Waikiki.

OAHU HOTELS OUTSIDE HONOLULU. *Deluxe:* **Sheraton Makaha Resort and Country Club.** In Makaha Valley, surrounded by two golf courses and not far from famed beach.

Turtle Bay Hilton and Country Club. As far from Waikiki as possible, on Kuilima Point. Has it all. Recently remodeled.

OTHERS. Near the airport is the **Holiday Inn-Airport** and **Plaza Hotel,** both on Nimitz Highway. Rates are *moderate.*

Laniloa Lodge Hotel. 55–109 Laniloa St., Laie. Private beach across the road.

Your travel agent also can line you up with a new condominium at reasonable rates. And Earl Thacker Realty, 923–7666, has beach homes for rent.

DINING OUT. The cuisine of contemporary Hawaii is basically American, spiced with the adopted dishes of the many nations which have amalgamated in Hawaii. However, foreign restaurants flourish, and Japanese, Korean and Chinese eateries naturally abound. Dinner in a *Deluxe* restaurant will run approximately $20 or higher; in an *Expensive* restaurant from $15–20; in a *Moderate* restaurant from $8–15, in an *Inexpensive* restaurant from $4–7. Prices are for a complete dinner but do not include drinks, tax or tip.

Our list of the best restaurants in Honolulu follows, and, while the list is completely our own, it at least starts out in agreement with the general consensus.

Deluxe: **Michel's.** In the Colony Surf Hotel. Is the only equal to The Third Floor.

The Third Floor. 2552 Kalakaua Ave. in Hawaiian Regent Hotel. Though costly, it has everything.

Expensive: **Bistro.** 3058 Monsarrat Ave. Very French.

Canlis. 2100 Kalakaua. Interesting architecture and longest at same site.

Cavalier. 1600 Kapiolani. Plush and pleasant.

Chez Michel. At Eaton Square, Hobron Lane. Where Michel himself holds forth.

Maile. Kahala Hilton. International with class, class, class.

Nick's Fish Market. Waikiki Gateway Hotel. Best for seafood, particularly fresh local products.

Peacock Room. Queen Kapiolani Hotel on Kapahulu. Elegant.

The Pottery Steak and Seafood Restaurant. 3574 Waialae in Kaimuki. A steakhouse with a potter's wheel.

Ranch House. 5156 Kalanianaole Highway. A family retreat with animals on the walls.

Victoria Station. 1599 Kapiolani Blvd. London phone booth outside and a little bit of London inside.

Yacht Harbor. Yacht Harbor Towers. French, continental, with piano.

Moderate: **Café Colonnade.** Princess Kaiulani Hotel. Mediterranean décor.

Columbia Inn. 645 Kapiolani, at the Top of the Boulevard, and 98–1226 Kaahumanu St. in Waimalu. Likes newsmen and athletes.

Flamingo Chuckwagon. 1015 Kapiolani. Eat all you want, with prime rib the feature.

La Ronde. In the Ala Moana Buliding. 23 floors up and revolves.

M's Coffee Tavern. 124 Queen St. Downtown financial district. Tops for lunch.

Summit. Ala Moana Americana Hotel. Even higher than La Ronde.

Top of Waikiki. Above the Waikiki Financial Plaza.

Specialty Houses. Chinese. **Golden Dragon.** Hilton Hawaiian Village. May be the nicest Chinese restaurant in Waikiki.

King Tsin. 1486 S. King St. Features Mandarin cooking in intimate setting.

Wo Fat. 115 N. Hotel St. Downtown, elegant, serving authentic Cantonese cuisine. Of the three, this is the least expensive.

Greek. Inexpensive: **It's Greek to Me.** In Royal Hawaiian Center, 2201 Kalakaua Ave. Baklava.

Hawaiian. Inexpensive: **Ono Hawaiian Foods.** 726 Kapahulu Ave. Locals crowd in for local kaukau.

Italian. Moderate: **Matteo's.** 364 Seaside in the Marine Surf Hotel and downtown. Another fine Italian spot.

Trattoria. Cinerama Edgewater. Fine Italian food.

Japanese. Inexpensive: **Kanraku Tea House.** 750 Kohou St. in Kalihi. Sit on the floor as the locals do.

Suehiro's. 1824 S. King St. Again, popular with the locals.

To spend more and see different types of Japanese cooking—at some places, the cook puts on a show at your table—consider *Furusato* in the Waikiki Grand, *Maiko* in the Westin Ilikai, *Benihana of Tokyo* in the Hilton Hawaiian Village, *Chaco's* at 2888 Waialae and other hotels.

Jewish. Inexpensive: **Lyn's Kosher-Style Delicatessen.** Ala Moana Center. Good pastrami.

Korean. Inexpensive: **Kim Chee No. 3.** 1040 S. King St., and four other locations.

Moderate: **Camellia.** 2460 Koa Ave.

...nai is different is that there is only one small hotel, and most ...efer jeeps for transportation. But the drive up over Lanaihale, ... this little gem of an island, is worth making the visit.

...TICAL INFORMATION FOR THE ISLANDS

...information for Oahu is included in the Honolulu section, earlier.)

THE ISLAND OF HAWAII

...O GET THERE. There are more than a dozen flights daily from ...o the Big Island plus a number of special weekend flights. *United* flies ... the West Coast.

...O GET ABOUT. Cheapest way to travel on the Big Island is by bus. ...ome Hilo-based buses that make regularly scheduled round trips to ..., Honokaa, Akaka Falls, Kohala. The bus terminal is at Mooheau ...amehameha Avenue.

There are a dozen or more of these in both the Kailua-Kona and ...you'll see their agents at counters the moment you arrive at Hilo ...veral of the most popular are: *Dollar Rent-A-Car, Budget Rent-A- ...U-Drive* and *Phillips' U-Drive.*

BIG ISLAND TOURS. There are a number of these, all originating either in Hilo or Kailua-Kona. The *Gray Line* conducts four different tours with limousines or custombuilt Grayliners. The U-Drive firms also have ...s.

...Cook Cruises leave the Kailua-Kona wharf every morning and cover ...points of Kealakekua Bay.

...nt to see what's under the surface of Kailua Bay take the *Captain ...lass-bottom boat.

...nt to feel what's under the surface of Kailua Bay, check out scuba ...orkel information with the Kona Activities Center, telephone 329–

SPORTS. *Deep Sea Fishing at Kona:* The waters off the Kona Coast teem with fighting game fish, and everything is available here for the fisherman's pleasure. *Hunting:* If you want to arrange a hunting expedition ...ep, boar, or game birds, get in touch with Hawaii Hunting Tours, ...6, or McCandless Ranch, tel. 328–9313. *Horseback Riding:* There ...r rent at Waikoloa Countryside Stables, Scheherazade Stables near ...ronwood Outfitters on the Kohala Mountain Road. *Hiking and* ...he Elysian fields for these activities are in the Volcano district, and ...il information and permission to camp and hike is the *National Park* ...s opposite the Volcano House.

...e range of camping gear, check *Travel/Camp Inc.* in Hilo. Informa- ...ounty and state parks is available from the *Department of Parks and* ...n Hilo and the *Division of Parks.* Department of Land and Natural ....O. Box 936, Hilo 96720. *Golf.* Two miles from Volcano House is ...se. In Hilo there is the Municipal Golf Course. At Kona is the ...na Golf Club. Best of all are the three courses on the Gold Coast ...ala: Mauna Kea, Waikoloa Beach, and Mauna Lani. Also excellent ...ain near the southern tip of the island. *Tennis:* There are dozens of ...s in the county—18 in Hilo and many more at the hotels, including ...he Kailua-Kona area.

Mexican. **Jose's.** 1134 Koko Head Ave. in Kaimuki. Another good, hot spot. **La Paloma.** Pensacola and Kapiolani. Ditto. **Mama's Mexican Kitchen.** 378 North School St. Most popular Mexican place in city. Bring your own beer.

Thai. Moderate: **Mekong I.** 1295 S. Beretania St. and **Mekong II.** 1726 S. King St. Spicy, hot.

EXPLORING HAWAII ISLAND

Kailua-Kona is the oldest and most developed of the Big Island's resort areas though there is little beach anywhere on this volcanically active island. Resting on a blue bay at the foot of 8,000-foot Mount Haulalai, its single winding street is lined with hotels, small shops, and old churches. Allow yourself time here. Its climate is warm, its pace languid, and historical remnants can be seen in the old stone walls, the petroglyphs, the paved "highway" across the lava, the holua sled runs for the dangerous sledding contests, and the crumbling platforms of Hawaiian temples, called heiaus.

Special stops in Kona: The Mokuaikaua Church, built by young missionaries in 1819, and the Hulihee Palace, across the street from Mokuaikaua. Once the summer palace of Hawaiian kings, it is now a museum displaying artifacts of the Victorian-influenced Hawaiian court.

About 100 miles from Kona is a cool tropical highland called The Volcano. It can be reached by well-paved roads that take you through very interesting country. An area, in fact, that many discerning travelers consider the most fascinating in the Pacific.

Hilo, the only standard-looking city on the island, has a population of 35,303. It is the business, banking and shipping center of the island, as well as the seat of the county government, the law courts and branches of the state government. In addition, it is a seaport and has an international airport.

For the tourist there is a variety of things to see and do: Rainbow Falls, the Lyman House Museum (built in 1839), the sampan fishing fleet, the early morning fish auctions. But the favorite diversion in Hilo is visiting the orchid and anthurium nurseries. About 200,000 packages of orchids, anthuriums and other exotic blooms are air-mailed out each year.

Another tourist favorite is taking the volcano road to the National Park. There are many sights, fragrant ginger, tree ferns, sugar cane, gardenias, slender blossoming palms, and red lehua flowers growing along the road. (In January 1983 the Kilauea volcano exploded into activity and remained hot, bubbly and flowing well into 1985.)

Off the highway, close to Hilo, is an interesting macadamia nut orchard, which welcomes visitors, and there is another at Honokaa on the Hamakua Coast near Waipio, a deep verdant valley.

Worth investigating also is the open ranchland country at Waimea, headquarters of the Parker Ranch. This little bit of Montana includes a lovely tree-covered cool road over Kohala Mountain to Hawi.

EXPLORING MAUI

Best bases for touring the Valley Isle are Kahului, the principal sea and airport, and Wailuku, the county seat three miles away.

Wailuku, nestling at the base of the West Maui Mountains, is a charming provincial town. Its white-steepled church is a bit of New England transplanted by the missionaries in 1837. Hale Hoikeike, the historical museum, was built in 1841, and stands on Iao Road at the mouth of Iao Valley, a beautiful gorge known as the Little Yosemite of Hawaii. The road runs inland to Iao Valley Park and Iao Needle, a volcanic monolith rising in green splendor 2,250 feet straight up from the valley floor.

The most celebrated of Maui's tourist attractions lies 41 miles southeast of Wailuku and 10,000 feet above it. It is Haleakala, House of the Sun. Haleakala's last volcanic outburst occurred two centuries ago. All of Manhattan Island could be deposited within the crater's twenty-one-mile circumference, and the tallest of skyscrapers would not rise above its rim.

Lahaina is no longer the "plantation town" it once was, picturesquely huddled between the sea and 5,800-foot Puu Kukui. Lahaina is actually the Williamsburg of Hawaii.

For a quarter of a century, 1840–1865, it was the center of the whaling industry, and many a whaler found temporary housing in Hale Paahao, the old prison whose massive coral walls have been standing since 1851. The *Carthaginian II,* an old German cargo ship, now a museum.

In addition, you will want to visit the coral stone courthouse, built in 1857, behind which stands the largest banyan tree in the islands, planted in 1873. Nearby is the Old Baldwin House, built by the missionaries early in the 19th century. The house is now a museum.

Even more interesting as a relic of missionary days is Lahainaluna High School, the oldest school west of the Rockies, founded in 1831.

First of the tourist developments on Maui is the elegant tourist hotel complex built around the famed Kaanapali golf courses. Included in the complex is Whaler's Village, the world's only shopping center with a thirty-six-foot whale skeleton hanging over a reflecting pool. Competing for additional resort grandeur in the sun is the Kapalua complex several miles beyond Kaanapali on the north end of West Maui with two golf courses designed by Arnold Palmer, one of which now hosts a major pro tournament, and the Wailea development on the sunny Kihei Coast.

EXPLORING KAUAI

Lihue, your basis for exploring the Garden Island of Kauai, is the county seat, and one of the oldest plantation towns in the islands (founded in 1849).

Wailua River

A trip on the Wailua River is something you should not miss. The place is redolent of history and romance as well as a tropical daydream. You are standing on the spot where the first Polynesians may have landed in Hawaii 1,000 years ago. You are also standing in the middle of Kauai's fastest-growing tourist resort. Near here is Heiau Holo-Holo-Ku, one of the most ancient and impressive temples in Hawaii.

Waimea Canyon

The town of Waimea was a focal point in h[...]
Captain Cook first set foot on Hawaiian soil 2[...]
the first missionaries settled on Kauai, here th[...]
fort and tried to take over, and here that the s[...]
ished. Today, Waimea is a busy plantation tow[...]
nificent Waimea Canyon.

The two roads up to the Canyon one from W[...]
ha wind through forests of koa, silver oak, euca[...]
On your left you will have views of the sea and[...]
are glimpses of the canyon and finally numero[...]

Beyond Puu Ka Pele, whose summit is 3,68[...]
Kauai's wonderful gorge which, at this point, i[...]
deep and a mile wide. Its length is ten miles. [...]

For another striking vista into the gorge and[...]
Swamp, stop at Kaana Ridge. At this point, yo[...]
Kauai's wonderful Kokee district, a tropical r[...]
region is a state forest reserve, and it has an inte[...]
Museum with exhibits of local plants, wildlife, [...]

From here, it is a three-mile drive through a [...]
the end of the road and two lookouts for the view[...]
Four thousand feet below you, a ribbon of san[...]
floor of Kalalau Valley from the sea. Do no[...]
spectacle.

EXPLORING MOLOK[...]

Kaunakakai, famous for its legendary "Coc[...]
capital of Molokai, and is the center of things on [...]
little port town, with its bustling wharf, really c[...]
days. Most of Molokai's 5,905 people come to [...]

Colony at Kalaupapa

Even if you are just stopping over for a few hou[...]
the Friendly Isle, you will probably want to hav[...]
glimpse of the world-famous Hansen's disease se[...]
pa.

It is a far cry from the unaccommodating wild[...]
first people suffering from leprosy were dumped t[...]
Some 111 patients and release patients now live i[...]
therapeutic institutions, and in a few decades, th[...]
will be no more than a legend.

EXPLORING LANAI

The "pineapple" island has several things goi[...]
elsewhere in the archipelago. More pineapples f[...]
there is Shipwreck Beach, a forelorn, lonely plac[...]
And very accessible petroglyphs near the beach. [...]
rarity, cool, protected by Norfolk pine, and with[...]

reason L[...]
visitors [...]
the top [...]

PRA

(Practic[...]

HOW
Honolu[...]
direct fr[...]

HOW
There a[...]
the Vol[...]
Park or[...]
U-Dr[...]
Hilo ar[...]
Airport[...]
Car, Ja[...]

guided [...]
Cap[...]
all hist[...]
If y[...]
Cook[...]
If y[...]
tanks [...]
3171.

for w[...]
tel. 7[...]
are he[...]
Hilo, [...]
Cam[...]
sourc[...]
Hea[...]
Fo[...]
tion [...]
Recr[...]
Reso[...]
a go[...]
Kea[...]
of S[...]
is Se[...]
publ[...]
abo[...]

HAWAII HOTELS. Rates are for single rooms—for doubles add 15–25%. Categories are as follows: *Super Deluxe:* $165 and up; *Deluxe:* $60–125; *First Class:* $40–60; *Moderate:* $25–40; *Inexpensive:* $20–25; *Rock-Bottom:* around $15.

Super Deluxe: **Mauna Kea Beach.** Near Kawaihae. Gorgeous inside and out. All aquatic and outdoor activities.

Kona Village. Isolated spot eight miles from Kailua-Kona. On beach.

Mauna Lani. A splendid arrowhead pointed toward the beach in South Kohala.

Sheraton Royal Waikoloa. On a lava flow in South Kohala.

First class: **Hotel King Kamehameha.** 75–5660 Palani Rd. Short walk to main drag, the waterfront.

Kona Hilton. On Alii Dr., not far from town toward Kealakekua Bay.

Kona Surf. Major attraction at Keauhou. On rugged coast and golf course.

Naniloa Surf. Hilo. Superb views of majestic Mauna Kea.

Volcano House. On the brink of Kilauea Crater. Rustic, unique.

Moderate: **Hilo Pacific Isle TraveLodge.** Hilo. Overlooking Hilo Bay and Mauna Kea. Restaurant, cocktail lounge, and pool.

Inexpensive: **Dolphin Bay.** Hilo. In heart of Hilo's Puueo district.

Hilo Hukilau. Hilo. U-drive and breakfast tie-ins.

Rock Bottom: **Manago.** In the coffee country.

 HAWAII DINING OUT. The hotel dining rooms maintain an excellent standard but can be expensive. For more inexpensive dining, you might try the following restaurants.

Fine Chinese restaurants in Hilo are *Sun Sun Lau* and *Canton Garden.* For Japanese fare in Hilo try *K. K. Tei,* on the Kona side. *Teshima's* restaurant, up the hill at Honalo, has great shrimp. The greatest lunch on the island is at the *Mauna Kea Beach Hotel.*

THE ISLAND OF MAUI

HOW TO GET THERE. Maui is served by 49 flights a day and eight airlines, including the air taxis. *United* has direct service from the West Coast. *U-Drives:* At Kahului Airport many firms will provide you with a late model vehicle. Reservations in advance will help because sometimes they are out.

 TOURS. *Gray Line* has a tour of Iao Valley and Haleakala; *Holo Holo* has a tour to Hana. All tour information is available at the hotels and through the *Hawaii Visitors Bureau* in Wailuku. In Lanaina the *Lahaina Restoration Foundation* has a tour.

 SPORTS. *Horseback Riding:* In the Hana district, guests at the Hotel Hana-Maui use the facilities of the Hana-Maui stable; non-guests can rent from *James Aki, Jr.* nearby. And there are horses at *Thompson's Ranch* in Kula, and Rainbow Ranch at Kapalua. *Fishing:* There are charter boats at Kahului, Lahaina, and Maalaea. The *Hawaii Visitors Bureau* can help you make charter arrangements. *Skindiving:* Maui Divers in Lahaina have skindiving equipment and boats for rent, and offer lessons for divers. *Hunting:* Kula Game Management Area is open on weekends and holidays, and you can take pheasants, quail, and doves during the season. Wild pigs and goats may be hunted all year around. *Golf:* There are 10 golf courses for public play: the seaside course at Waiehu; the two courses at the Kaanapali development; the two new ones at Kapalua; two at Wailea in the Kihei development, at Makena Beach and the Maui Country Club at Sprecklesville, and one at Pukalani. *Tennis:* There are nine lighted county public courts and eleven at the hotels, with the six at the Royal Lahaina Hotel open to the public.

HOTELS AND RESTAURANTS ON MAUI. (Restaurants are within the hotels.) Rates are for single rooms. Add 15–25% for doubles. Categories are as follows: *Super Deluxe:* $125 and up; *Deluxe:* $60–125; *Expensive:* $40–60; *Moderate:* $25–40; *Inexpensive:* under $25.

Super Deluxe: **Hana Maui.** Isolated, one of a kind. Set in a lovely valley on 7,000-acre ranch. The hotel provides all activities and excellent meals.

Deluxe: **Maui Inter-Continental Wailea** is the king of the Wailea development, a class low rise with beach and two golf courses.

Kaanapali Plantation. Apartment hotel a mile from the beach.

Maalaea Surf. On Maalaea Bay. Tennis and swimming pools. Four-day minimum.

Maui Eldorado Resort. Along Kaanapali golf course. Three pools.

Maui Surf. On Kaanapali beach. Three restaurants, a show bar, tennis courts, shops, and a pool.

Nohonani Resort. On beach at Honokowai. Three-day minimum.

Expensive: **Hale Kai.** Located in a very peaceful setting. Seven-day minimum.

Kihei Beach Resort. On beach at Kihei. Three-day minimum.

Maui Lu Resort. 575 S. Kihei Rd. Across from the beach.

Napili Surf Beach Resort. Apartments with kitchens on Napili Bay. Two swimming pools, shuffleboard.

Royal Lahaina Resort. Overlooks the fairways of the golf club as well as the ocean. South Seas elegance.

Sheraton-Maui. Built against the lava outcroppings of Black Rock on Kaanapali Beach. The lobby is at bottom of the cliff, with cottages around it. Excellent cuisine.

Moderate: **Maui Beach.** Maui's newest. Dining room, pool.

Maui Palms Resort. Built around a fresh-water pool. Guest rooms are spacious and well-appointed.

Pioneer Inn. A delightful hotel with high-ceilinged and spacious rooms.

HAWAII DINING OUT. Many outstanding dining rooms are in the large hotels, such as *Raffles* in the Westin Wailea, *Sunset Terrace* at the Hyatt Regency, *LaPerouse* at the **Maui Inter-Continental Wailea.** *Chez Paul* at Olowalu, an unlikely place for a top French restaurant, sets the pace away from the hotels. Less expensive are *Gaspare's Place* in Kihei and Naokee's Too in Lahaina. Downtown Lahaina is full of eating places.

THE ISLAND OF KAUAI

HOW TO GET THERE. *Aloha Airlines, Hawaiian Air* and *Mid-Pacific* have many flights a day from Honolulu, and there are air taxis. *U-Drives:* All companies have stands at the Lihue Airport: *Hertz, Islander U-Drive, Avis* and *Robert's U-Drive & Tours.*

TOURS. *Robert's* and *Grayline* have guided tours of Kauai. *Papillon Helicopters* and others will fly you to places of interest. There are boat trips on the Wailua River, day and night. *Paradise Pacifica,* located on the south side of the Wailua River is a coconut plantation turned into a village of Rolynesian huts and many exotic trees and flowers.

SPORTS. *Horseback Riding:* Horses can be rented at *Highgates Ranch* and *Pooku Stables. Fishing:* Rainbow trout season opens on the first Saturday of August and remains open for 16 days. After that, fishing is permitted only on weekends and holidays through the end of September. Other fish, such as bluegill, are open daily, year-round. *Hunting:* There are four hunting areas: Wailua, Puu Ka Pele, Kakaha, and Kalepa. For all information call the Lihue offices of the *Division of Fish and Game,* phone 245–4444.

Mammal hunting seasons are set by the *State Board of Land and Natural Resources.* Visitors should inquire at the *Lihue Fish and Game* office for current seasons. *Golf:* Two of the five best courses in the state are on Kauai. The king is the 27-hole championship challenge at the Princeville resort near Hanalei.

Best county course is the Wailua course. Kauai Surf Golf Course is located near that hotel, the Kiahuna course is in the Poipu district, and near Kalaheo is the Kukuiolono Course. *Tennis:* There are 20 lighted public courts and 59 at the hotels.

MUSEUM. At Lihue, the *Kauai Museum* has a collection of rare Hawaiian artifacts. Smaller ones are located at Kokee, Hanalei, and Hanamaulu.

HOTELS AND RESTAURANTS IN KAUAI. (Restaurants within the hotels.) Rates are for single rooms. Add 15–25% for doubles. Categories are as follows: *Deluxe:* $60–125; *Expensive:* $40–60; *Moderate:* $25–40; *Inexpensive:* under $25.

Deluxe: **Kiahuna.** Cluster of small beach houses.

Princeville. Luxury houses on the golf course and near Hanalei Valley.

Coco Palms. In a 32-acre coconut palm grove. A wonderful and unique 20th-century inn.

Kauai Surf. A 200-acre resort with all amenities and recreational facilities.

Sheraton-Kauai. 12 acres at Poipu Beach, combining Polynesian and modern architecture.

Expensive: **Kauai Resort.** Three buildings, 13 deluxe cabanas, restaurant, and pool. Near beach.

Kauai Sands. New Hotel with restaurant, pool, and shops.

Poipu Shores. Secluded, surrounded by lava rock.

Inexpensive: **Kokee Lodge.** Twelve cabins in Kokee State Park. For those who love to rough it. Restaurant for lunch only.

Rock Bottom: **Tip Top Motel.** A mile from the airport.

Hale Pumehana. Across from Lihue Shopping Center.

THE ISLAND OF MOLOKAI

HOW TO GET THERE: *Hawaiian Air* and *Aloha Airlines* each connect Honolulu to Molokai. Air taxis such as *Royal Hawaiian* have daily trips. There is air taxi service regularly into Kalaupapa, the Hansen's disease colony. *Damien Tours* will take you all over the peninsula.

HOW TO GET AROUND. U-drives are available, Toyotas to jeeps.

SPORTS. There is the new Kalua Koi golf course next to the Sheraton-Molokai and a nine-holer at Ironwood Hills. Four of the six public *tennis* courts are lighted and other courts are located at the hotels. For *deep sea fishing* check with Hal Newsome at the Hotel Molokai.

HOTELS AND RESTAURANTS IN MOLOKAI. (Restaurants within the hotels.) There are seven hotels on Molokai.

Molokai. *Expensive:* has 56 units, a restaurant, cocktail lounge, and pool. Write Box 546, Kaunakaki, Molokai, Hawaii 96748 for reservations.

Pau Hana Inn. *Inexpensive:* In Kaunakaki, has 39 rooms, a swimming pool, restaurant, and a delightful bar. You can write to Box 860, Kaunakaki, Molokai, Hawaii 96748 for reservations.

Sheraton-Molokai. *Deluxe:* 292 rooms on Kepuhi Beach. Restaurants, golf, tennis, shops. Wildlife park nearby.

Wavecrest has a 90 unit condominium on the beach at Manawai. *Moderate.* The same is true of the **Molokai Shores** at Kaunakaki.

THE ISLAND OF LANAI

HOW TO GET THERE. *Royal Hawaiian* has most of the service to Lanai City. There is also a tour available.

HOW TO GET AROUND. Rent a jeep. Some of the roads are rugged.

SPORTS. Except for *swimming* at Manele Bay there is the Cavendish *golf* course, very inexpensive.

HOTELS. Only one, the *Hotel Lanai.* Ten rooms and a dining room. Sitting on the hotel veranda at sunset is the biggest thing going on this island. Definitely not for someone seeking comforts, action or crowds. *Expensive.*

INDEX

Facts at Your Fingertips

Air travel
  from abroad, 38–9
  within U.S., 22–3
Architecture, 113
Art colonies, 115
Auto travel
  entering U.S., 39
  traffic signs & road markings, 20–1
  within U.S., 18–20
Banking hours, 15–16
Beach vacations, 107
Bird watching, 105–6
Bus travel
  from Canada & Mexico, 39
  within U.S., 24–5
Camping, 30–1
Children, 25–6
Churches & other places of worship, 35
Cities, 107–8
Climate, 8–13
Clothing, 17–18
Clothing sizes, 49
Concerts & festivals, 114–15
Cosmetics, 50
Costs, 3–6
Cowboys, 110
Credit cards, 7–8, 46
Currency & exchange, 45–6
Customs, 41–2
Drinking laws, 33
Dude ranches & guest farms, 110–11
Electricity, 47
Embassies & consulates, 53–4
Fine arts, 63–7
Food & drink, 76–84
Fly/drive vacations, 21–2
Gardens, 104–5
Handicapped travelers, 26–7
Health requirements, 41
Historic trails, 116
Holidays, 15–16
Hotels & motels, 27–30
Hours of business, 46–7
Immigration & customs, 40–2
Indians, 108–9
Industrial sightseeing, 111–12
Insurance, 18
Interpreter services, 44–5
Lakeside vacations, 106–7

Legal aid, 53
Letters of credit, 45–6
Mail, 35
Measurements, 46
Medical care, 51
Movies, 57–60
Museums, 63–7, 112–13
Music & dance, 60–3, 70–5, 114–15
National Parks, 36–7, 85–100
Newspapers & magazines, 50–1
Nightlife, 33
Packing & luggage, 17–18
Pets, 42
Physical features, 40
Postage, 36
Radio & television, 51
Rail travel
  from Canada & Mexico, 39
  within U.S., 23–4
Reconstructed villages & ghost towns, 116–17
Religious settlements, 111
Restaurants, 31–3
Rodeos, 119–20
Scenic wonders, 100–3
Sea travel, 38–9
Seasonal events, 8–13, 13–15
Shopping, 47–9
Space projects, 117–18
Special fares
  domestic, 5–6
  international, 43–4
Spelunking, 106
Sports, 33–5, 119–22
Telephones & telegraph, 36, 50
Theater, 67–70, 113–14
Theme parks, 118–19
Time zones, 13
Tipping, 6–7
Tobacco, 49–50
Travel agents, 16–17
Traveler's checks, 45
Trip planning, 16
Universities & colleges, 115–16
Vaccinations, 41
Visas, 40–1
White-water adventures, 104
Wilderness vacations, 103–4
Wildlife sanctuaries, 105

Geographical

(The letters H and R indicate hotel and restaurant listings)

ALABAMA
Practical Information
Children's entertainment, 373
Drinking laws, 373
Historic sites, 373
Hotels & motels, 373–4
Information sources, 373
Map, 370
Museums & galleries, 373
Restaurants, 375
Sports, 373
Tours, 373
Transportation, 372
Youth hostels, 375

Geographical
Alexander City, H374
Athens, 371
Bellingrath Gardens, 372
Birmingham, 369, H374, R375
Dauphin Island, 372
De Soto St. Pk., 371
Decatur, 371, H374, R375
Florence, 371, H374, R375
Gadsden, 371, H374, R375
Gulf Shores, H374, R375
Guntersville, 371, H374, R375
Huntsville, 371, H374, R375
Little River Canyon, 371

FODOR'S TRAVEL GUIDES

U.S. Guides

Alaska
Arizona
Boston
California
Cape Cod
The Carolinas & the
  Georgia Coast
The Chesapeake
  Region
Chicago
Colorado
Disney World & the
  Orlando Area
Florida
Hawaii
Las Vegas
Los Angeles

Maui
Miami & the
  Keys
New England
New Mexico
New Orleans
New York City
New York City
  (Pocket Guide)
Pacific North Coast
Philadelphia & the
  Pennsylvania
  Dutch Country
Puerto Rico
  (Pocket Guide)
The Rockies
San Diego

San Francisco
San Francisco
  (Pocket Guide)
The South
Texas
USA
The Upper Great
  Lakes Region
Vacations in
  New York State
Vacations on the
  Jersey Shore
Virgin Islands
Virginia & Maryland
Waikiki
Washington, D.C.

Foreign Guides

Acapulco
Amsterdam
Australia
Austria
The Bahamas
The Bahamas
  (Pocket Guide)
Baja & the Pacific
  Coast Resorts
Barbados
Belgium &
  Luxembourg
Bermuda
Brazil
Budget Europe
Canada
Canada's Atlantic
  Provinces
Cancun, Cozumel,
  Yucatan Peninsula
Caribbean
Central America
China
Eastern Europe
Egypt
Europe
Europe's Great
  Cities
France

Germany
Great Britain
Greece
The Himalayan
  Countries
Holland
Hong Kong
India
Ireland
Israel
Italy
Italy 's Great Cities
Jamaica
Japan
Kenya, Tanzania,
  Seychelles
Korea
Lisbon
London
London Companion
London
  (Pocket Guide)
Madrid & Barcelona
Mexico
Mexico City
Montreal &
  Quebec City
Morocco
Munich

New Zealand
Paris
Paris
  (Pocket Guide)
Portugal
Rio de Janeiro
Rome
Saint Martin/
  Sint Maarten
Scandinavia
Scandinavian
  Cities
Scotland
Singapore
South America
South Pacific
Southeast Asia
Soviet Union
Spain
Sweden
Switzerland
Sydney
Thailand
Tokyo
Toronto
Turkey
Vienna & the
  Danube Valley
Yugoslavia

Wall Street Journal Guides to Business Travel

Europe
International Cities

The Pacific Rim
USA & Canada

Special-Interest Guides

Cruises and Ports
  of Call
Healthy Escapes
Fodor's Flashmaps
  New York

Fodor's Flashmaps
  Washington, D.C.
Shopping in Europe
Skiing in North
  America

Smart Shopper's
  Guide to London
Sunday in
  New York
Touring Europe